December 10–13, 2012
Nice, France

I0028941

**Association for
Computing Machinery**

Advancing Computing as a Science & Profession

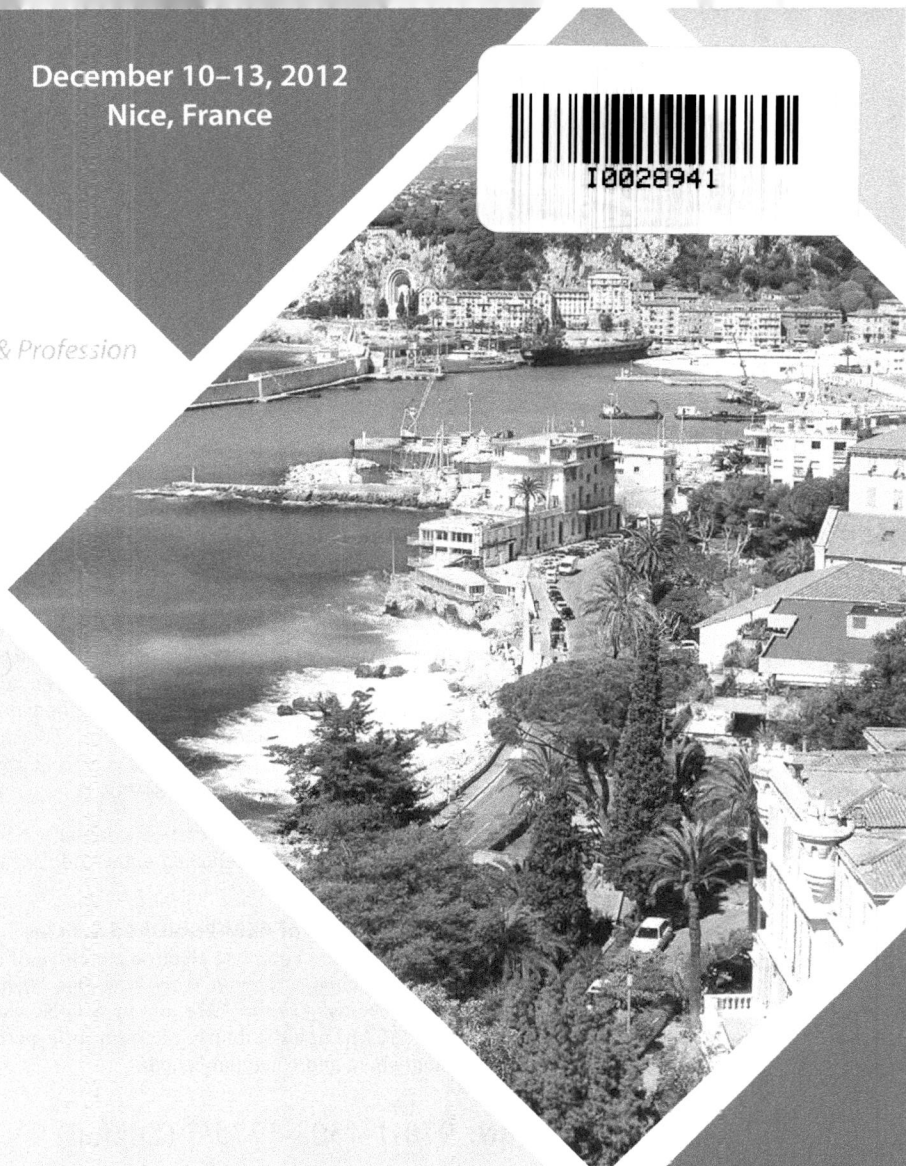

CoNEXT'12

Proceedings of the 2012 ACM

Conference on emerging Networking Experiments and Technologies

Sponsored by:
ACM SIGCOMM

Supported by:
**Cisco, NSF, Symantec, Technicolor, Telefonica, AT&T,
IBM Research, Internet Initiative Japan, Alcatel-Lucent,
Microsoft Research, Internet-Science.EU, Inria, & i3S**

Association for Computing Machinery

Advancing Computing as a Science & Profession

The Association for Computing Machinery
2 Penn Plaza, Suite 701
New York, New York 10121-0701

Notice to Past Authors of ACM-Published Articles
ACM intends to create a complete electronic archive of all articles and/or other material previously published by ACM. If you have written a work that has been previously published by ACM in any journal or conference proceedings prior to 1978, or any SIG Newsletter at any time, and you do NOT want this work to appear in the ACM Digital Library, please inform permissions@acm.org, stating the title of the work, the author(s), and where and when published.

ISBN: 978-1-4503-1775-7 (Digital)

ISBN: 978-1-4503-1934-8 (Print)

Additional copies may be ordered prepaid from:

ACM Order Department
PO Box 30777
New York, NY 10087-0777, USA

Phone: 1-800-342-6626 (USA and Canada)
+1-212-626-0500 (Global)
Fax: +1-212-944-1318
E-mail: acmhelp@acm.org
Hours of Operation: 8:30 am – 4:30 pm ET

Printed in the USA

ACM CoNEXT 2012 General Chairs' Message

On behalf of the organizing committee, we are delighted to welcome you to the Eighth ACM International Conference on emerging Networking EXperiments and Technologies (CoNEXT) in Nice Côte d'Azur, the capital of the French Riviera. Year after year, CoNEXT confirms its leading position as a major forum for technical discussions on networking. We are happy to organize the first CoNEXT with three full days of program, rather than two and half days as in previous editions. You will discover an excellent technical program and enjoy many opportunities to exchange ideas with colleagues from both academia and industry. The main conference is preceded by one day with two topical workshops—Capacity Sharing Workshop (CSWS) and UrbaNe Workshop on Urban Networks—as well as the traditional CoNEXT Student Workshop. The student workshop is a forum that allows students to present their work, and also gives them the opportunity to interact directly with more senior researchers through both panels and poster sessions.

CoNEXT 2012 wouldn't be the same without the help of our sponsor and supporters. Their generousity allowed us to keep registration rates reasonable, despite the costs of organizing a conference at the French Rivera, and to finance 28 travel grants for students from all over the world to attend both the main conference and the student workshop. We consider ourselves lucky with the level of support we obtained and we deeply thank our sponsors ACM and SIGCOMM, and all our supporters. We are grateful to our Platinum supporters: Cisco and the National Science Foundation; our Gold supporter: Symantec; our Silver supporters: Technicolor, Telefonica, and AT&T; our Bronze supporters: IBM Research, the Internet Initiative Japan, Alcatel-Lucent, Microsoft Research, and the European Network of Excellent in Internet Science; and our patrons: Inria and I3S. We also would like to thank SIGCOMM for providing student travel support.

The success of a conference requires a lot of effort and a dedicated organizing committee. We thank everyone who helped us in the organization of this year's CoNEXT for all for their energy and the fruitful interactions. Thanks to K. K. Ramakrishnan and Patrick Thiran for supervising the selection of a high-quality program. Warm thanks to Guillaume Urvoy-Keller for taking care of local arrangements; to Christophe Diot, the treasurer and the social program chair, who also provided us with invaluable advice and mentoring; to the workshop chair, Augustin Chaintreau, as well as the chairs of each of the individual workshops; to our web master, Fabian Schneider, for his excellent job in managing the conference website; to Matteo Varvello, our publications chair; to Christian Kreibich and Steve Uhlig for all their work to apply for funds for student travel grants, allocate the travel grants, and handle student reimbursement; to Jim Kurose for helping pick the social program; to Richard Gass for managing the Internet connectivity during the conference; and to Agnes Cortell from Inria for her assistance through the entire process. We also want to thank our group of student volunteers for their help before and during the conference. Finally, we thank the CoNEXT steering committee for their advice, the ACM staff for their help in the financial and administrative aspects of the conference, and the ACM SIGCOMM executive committee for their strong support of CoNEXT.

We are looking forward to welcoming you to Nice and we count on you all to make this edition of CoNEXT a successful event.

Chadi Barakat
Inria Sophia Antipolis – Méditerranée

Renata Teixeira
CNRS and UPMC Sorbonne Universités

ACM CoNEXT 2012 General Co-Chairs

Foreword from the TPC Chairs

It is our great pleasure to welcome you to the *8th International Conference on emerging Networking EXperiments and Technologies (CoNEXT'12)*. CoNEXT started in 2005 and has now grown into one the premier venues, sponsored by ACM SIGCOMM, for the dissemination of cutting-edge research in all areas of networking. We are both thankful for the opportunity to Chair the Technical Program Committee for the conference.

Here are a few facts and figures for this year's CoNEXT program. We received a record submission of 176 papers, representing an increase of 10% over 2011. For the first time, CoNEXT will have a full 3-day program: these encouraging signs reflect the vibrant activity in our community. A highly skilled and dedicated technical program committee (TPC) of 53 researchers from academia and industry selected the papers to be included in the technical program, after a thorough reviewing process. Five papers were early rejected, because they were out of scope or did not conform to the submission guidelines. During the first round of the review process, each of the 171 papers received three reviews. The resulting 99 most competitive submissions received two additional reviews during a second round (some papers received additional reviews when the consensus among the five reviewers indicated the need for additional input). This second round was followed by an extensive on-line discussion phase over a couple of weeks, after which 59 papers were chosen to be discussed for inclusion in the final program at the TPC meeting, held at the Shannon Laboratory at AT&T Labs-Research in Florham Park, NJ on September 15, 2012. This 9-hour meeting was attended in person by 34 TPC members (other TPC members participated by phone) and resulted in 31 accepted papers that will be presented as part of this year's three-day conference in Nice. Paper notifications and reviews were emailed within hours of the end of the TPC meeting. Every paper was shepherded by a TPC member, to help authors improve the paper and incorporate the useful suggestions for improvement from the TPC.

We wish to thank the many people who have contributed their time, energy, and creativity to support this year's CoNEXT program. Our thanks go first to the hundreds of authors who chose to submit their latest research to CoNext'12 and, by doing so, ensure the vitality and continued growth of the CoNEXT community. Next, we would like to warmly thank the TPC members who all devoted much of their time to review submissions, write comprehensive and constructive reviews, engage in fruitful discussions, and travel to the TPC meeting during a busy period of the year for many of them. Thanks also to Eddie Kohler, the author of the reviewing software HotCRP that greatly simplified our tasks as TPC chairs and to Christoph Dwertmann and Max Ott, who installed and maintained HotCRP on one of their servers at NICTA, Australia. Finally, we also thank the CoNEXT steering committee members and the general chairs for their trust and support.

We hope that you will find this year's program exciting and that the conference provides you with a rewarding forum for fruitful discussions with colleagues from around the world. Welcome to Nice, and enjoy the program and the conference!

K. K. Ramakrishnan
CoNEXT'12 TPC Chair
AT&T Labs-Research, USA

Patrick Thiran
CoNEXT'12 TPC Chair
EPFL, Switzerland

Table of Contents

Session 10: Online Social Networks and Privacy

Session 11: Security

ACM CoNEXT 2012 Committee

General Chairs: Chadi Barakat *(INRIA, Sophia Antipolis, France)*
Renata Teixeira *(UPMC Sorbonne Universités and CNRS, Paris, France)*

Technical Program Chairs: K. K. Ramakrishnan *(AT&T Labs Research, Florham Park, NJ, USA)*
Patrick Thiran *(EPFL, Lausanne, Swizerland)*

Local Arrangements Chair: Guillaume Uvroy-Keller *(Université de Nice, Nice, France)*

Treasurer: Christophe Diot *(Technicolor, Paris, France)*

Social Program Chairs: Christophe Diot *(Technicolor, Paris, France)*
Jim Kurose *(University of Massachusetts, Amherst, MA, USA)*

Workshop Chair: Augustin Chaintreau *(Columbia University, New York, USA)*

Travel Grant Chairs: Christian Kreibich *(ICSI, Berkeley, USA)*
Steve Uhlig *(Queen Mary University of London, UK)*

Publication Chair: Matteo Varvello *(Bell Labs, New Jersey, USA)*

Internet Connectivity Chair: Richard Gass *(Telefónica I&D, Barcelona, Spain)*

Web Chair: Fabian Schneider *(NEC Laboratories Europe, Heidelberg, Germany)*

Steering Committee: Roch Guerin *(University of Pennsylvania, Philadelphia, PA, USA)*
Mostafa Ammar *(Georgia Tech, Atlanta, GA, USA)*
Olivier Bonaventure *(Université catholique de Louvain, Louvain-la-Neuve, Belgium)*
Kenjiro Cho *(IIJ Research Laboratory, Tokyo, Japan)*
Ernst Biersack *(Eurecom, Sophia-Antipolis, France)*
Max Ott *(NICTA, Melbourne, Australia)*
Bruce Davie *(CISCO Systems, USA)*

Program Committee: Aditya Akella *(University of Wisconsin, USA)*
Kevin Almeroth *(University of California Santa Barbara, USA)*
Lachlan Andrew *(Swinburne University of Technology, Australia)*
Yigal Bejarano *(Bell Labs-Lucent, USA)*
Giuseppe Bianchi *(University of Rome "Tor Vergata", Italy)*
Ernst Biersack *(Eurecom, France)*
Sem Borst *(TU Eindhoven and Bell Labs-Lucent, USA and Netherlands)*
Ken Calvert *(University of Kentucky, USA)*
Srjan Capkun *(ETHZ, Switzerland)*
Ranveer Chandra *(Microsoft Research, USA)*

Program Committee (continued):

Augustin Chaintreau *(Columbia University, USA)*
Patrick Crowley *(Washington University, USA)*
Olivier Dousse *(Nokia NRC, Switzerland)*
Ken Duffy *(Hamilton Institute, Ireland)*
Sonia Fahmy *(Purdue University, USA)*
Christos Gkantsidis *(Microsoft Research Cambridge, UK)*
Tim Griffin *(University of Cambridge, UK)*
Carmen Guerrero *(Universidad Carlos III de Madrid, Spain)*
Chuanxiong Guo *(Microsoft Research Asia, China)*
Charlie Hu *(Purdue University, USA)*
Rittwik Jana *(AT&T Labs - Research, USA)*
Gunnar Karlsson *(KTH Stockholm, Sweden)*
Can Emre Koksal *(Ohio State University, USA)*
Dejan Kostic *(IMDEA Networks, Spain)*
Christian Kreibich *(ICSI, USA)*
Arvind Krishnamurthy *(University of Washington, USA)*
Srikanth Krishnamurthy *(University of California, Riverside, USA)*
Renato Lo Cigno *(University of Trento, Italy)*
Peter Marbach *(University of Toronto, Canada)*
Athina Markopolou *(University of California, Irvine, USA)*
Laurent Mathy *(University of Liège, Belgium)*
Ruben Merz *(Deutsche Telekom Laboratories, Germany)*
Vishal Misra *(Columbia University, USA)*
Andrew Moore *(University of Cambridge, UK)*
Cristina Nita-Rotaru *(Purdue University, USA)*
Dina Papagiannaki *(Telefonica Research, Spain)*
Vern Paxson *(University of California, Berkeley, USA)*
Alexandre Proutière *(KTH Stockholm, Sweden)*
Bozidar Radunovic *(Microsoft Research Cambridge, UK)*
Bhaskaran Raman *(IIT Bombay, India)*
Jim Roberts *(INRIA, France)*
Vyas Sekar *(Stony Brook University, USA)*
Ashutosh Sabharwal *(Rice University, USA)*
Prashant Shenoy *(University of Massachusetts, Amherst, USA)*
Oliver Spatscheck *(AT&T Labs - Research, USA)*
Don Towsley *(University of Massachusetts, Amherst, USA)*
Steve Uhlig *(Queen Mary University of London, UK)*
Geoff Voelker *(University of California, San Diego, USA)*
Walter Willinger *(AT&T Labs - Research, USA)*
Ruixi Yuan *(Tsinghua University, China)*
Yin Zhang *(University of Texas at Austin, USA)*

CoNEXT 2012 Sponsor & Supporters

Sponsor: **acm sigcomm**

Platinum Supporters: CISCO

NSF

Gold Supporter: Symantec.

Silver Supporters: technicolor

Telefónica
Telefónica
Investigación y Desarrollo

at&t

Bronze Supporters: **IBM Research**

IIJ
Internet Initiative Japan

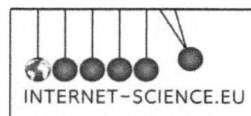

Alcatel·Lucent

Microsoft
Research

INTERNET-SCIENCE.EU

Patrons: *Inria* informatics mathematics

i3s
sophia antipolis

MPTCP is not Pareto-Optimal: Performance Issues and a Possible Solution*

Ramin Khalili[†], Nicolas Gast, Miroslav Popovic, Utkarsh Upadhyay, Jean-Yves Le Boudec
EPFL, IC-LCA2, Switzerland
firstname.lastname@epfl.ch

ABSTRACT

MPTCP has been proposed recently as a mechanism for supporting transparently multiple connections to the application layer. It is under discussion at the IETF. We show, however, that the current MPTCP suffers from two problems: (P1) Upgrading some TCP users to MPTCP can reduce the throughput of others without any benefit to the upgraded users, which is a symptom of not being Pareto-optimal; and (P2) MPTCP users could be excessively aggressive towards TCP users. We attribute these problems to the linked-increases algorithm (LIA) of MPTCP and, more specifically, to an excessive amount of traffic transmitted over congested paths.

The design of LIA forces a tradeoff between optimal resource pooling and responsiveness. We revisit the problem and show that it is possible to provide these two properties simultaneously. We implement the resulting algorithm, called opportunistic linked increases algorithm (OLIA), in the Linux kernel, and we study its performance over our testbed, by simulations and by theoretical analysis. We prove that OLIA is Pareto-optimal and satisfies the design goals of MPTCP. Hence it can avoid the problems P1 and P2. Our measurements and simulations indicate that MPTCP with OLIA is as responsive and non-flappy as MPTCP with LIA, and that it solves problems P1 and P2.

Categories and Subject Descriptors

C.2 [**Computer-communication Networks**]: Network Protocols.; C.4 [**Performance of Systems**]: Design studies, Modeling techniques.

Keywords

Multipath TCP, Congestion control algorithm, Protocol design, Performance evaluation.

*This research has received funding from the EU 7th Framework Programme (FP7/2007-2013) under grant agreement n. 257740 (Network of Excellence "TREND").

†Ramin Khalili is currently affiliated with T-Labs/TU Berlin, ramin@net.t-labs.tu-berlin.de.

1. INTRODUCTION

The regular TCP uses a window-based congestion-control mechanism to adjust the transmission rate of users [1]. It always provides a Pareto-optimal allocation of resources: it is impossible to increase the throughput of one user without decreasing the throughput of another or without increasing the congestion cost [2]. It also guarantees a fair allocation of bandwidth among the users, but favors the connections with lower RTT [3].

Various mechanisms were used to build a multipath transport protocol compatible with the regular TCP. Authors of [4–6] propose a family of algorithms inspired by utility maximization frameworks. These algorithms tend to use only the best paths available to users and are optimal in static settings where paths have similar RTTs. In practice, however, they suffer from several problems [7–9]. First, they sometimes fail to quickly detect free capacity as they do not probe paths with high loss probabilities sufficiently. Second, they exhibit flappiness: When there are multiple good paths available to a user, the user will randomly flip its traffic between these paths. This is not desirable, specifically, when the achieved rate depends on RTTs, as with TCP.

MultiPath TCP (MPTCP) is a concrete proposal for multipath transport; it is under discussion at the IETF [10]. Because of the issues aforementioned, its congestion control part does not follow the algorithms in [4–6]. Instead, it follows an ad-hoc design based on the following goals [10]: (1) Improve throughput: a multipath TCP user should perform at least as well as a TCP user that uses the best path available to it. (2) Do no harm: a multipath TCP user should never take up more capacity from any of its paths than a regular TCP user. And (3) balance congestion: a multipath TCP algorithm should balance congestion in the network, subject to meeting the first two goals.

MPTCP compensates for different RTTs and solves many problems of multipath transport [7, 9]: It can effectively use the available bandwidth; compared to independent TCP flows, it improves throughput and fairness in many scenarios; and it solves the flappiness problem. Through analysis and by using measurements over a testbed, we show, however, that MPTCP still suffers from the following problems:

(P1) Upgrading some regular TCP users to MPTCP can reduce the throughput of other users without any benefit to the upgraded users. This is a symptom of non-Pareto optimality,

(P2) MPTCP users can be excessively aggressive towards TCP users.

We attribute these problems to the "linked increases" algorithm (LIA) of MPTCP [10] and specifically to an excessive amount of traffic transmitted over congested paths. These problems indicate that MPTCP fails to fully satisfy its design goals, especially goal 3.

The design of LIA forces a tradeoff between optimal resource pooling and responsiveness, it cannot provide both at the same time. Hence, to provide good responsiveness, LIA's current implementation must depart from Pareto-optimality, which leads to problems P1 and P2. We revisit the design and show that it is possible to simultaneously provide both properties. We introduce OLIA, the "opportunistic linked increases algorithm", as an alternative to LIA. Based on utility maximization frameworks, we prove that OLIA is Pareto-optimal. Hence it can avoid the problems P1 and P2. Furthermore, its construction makes it as responsive and non-flappy as LIA.

OLIA is a window-based congestion-control mechanism. Similarly to LIA, it couples the additive increases and uses unmodified TCP behavior in the case of a loss. OLIA's increase part, Equation (5), has two terms:

- The first term is an adaptation of the increase term of Kelly and Voice's algorithm [4]. This term is essential to provide Pareto-optimality.

- The second term guarantees responsiveness and non-flappiness of OLIA. By measuring the number of transmitted bits since the last loss, it reacts to events within the current window and adapts to changes faster than the first term.

By adapting the window increases as a function of RTTs, OLIA also compensates for different RTTs.

We implement OLIA in the Linux kernel and study its performance over our testbed, by simulations and by theoretical analysis. Using a fluid model of OLIA based on differential inclusion, we prove that OLIA is Pareto-optimal (Theorem 3) and that it satisfies the design goals of MPTCP (Corollary 2). Our measurements and simulations indicate that MPTCP with OLIA is as responsive and non-flappy as MPTCP with LIA. Moreover, it solves problems P1 and P2. Hence, we believe that IETF should revisit the congestion control part of MPTCP and that an alternative algorithm, such as OLIA, should be considered.

In the next section, we briefly introduce MPTCP and related work. In Section 3, we provide a number of examples and scenarios in which MPTCP with LIA exhibits problems P1 and P2. In Section 4, we introduce OLIA and detail its Linux implementation. In Section 5, we prove that OLIA is Pareto-optimal and satisfies MPTCP's design goals. In Section 6, we study the performance of OLIA through measurements and by simulations.

2. MPTCP AND RELATED WORK

Multipath TCP (MPTCP) is a set of extensions to the regular TCP, which allows users to spread their traffic across potentially disjoint paths [10]. MPTCP discovers the number of paths available to a user, establishes the paths, and distributes traffic across these paths through creation of separate subflows [11, 12].

MPTCP's congestion control algorithm forces a tradeoff between optimal resource pooling and responsiveness [8]. The idea behind the algorithm is to transmit over a path r at a rate proportional to $p_r^{-1/\varepsilon}$, where p_r is the loss probability

over this link and $\varepsilon \in [0, 2]$ is a design parameter. The choice $\varepsilon = 0$ corresponds to the fully coupled algorithm of [4–6]: the traffic is sent only over the best paths, it is Pareto-optimal but is flappy. The choice $\varepsilon = 2$ corresponds to using uncoupled TCP flows on each path: it is very responsive and non-flappy, but does not balance congestion. MPTCP's implementation uses $\varepsilon = 1$ to provide a compromise between optimal resource pooling and responsiveness. This algorithm is called "linked increases" algorithm (LIA) [10].

Let w_r and rtt_r be the window size and the estimated round-trip time on path $r \in \mathcal{R}_u$. $\mathcal{R}_u$ is the set of all paths available to user u. LIA works as follows:

- For each ACK on subflow r, increase w_r by

$$\min\left(\frac{\max_{i \in \mathcal{R}_u} w_i/\mathrm{rtt}_i^2}{(\sum_{i \in \mathcal{R}_u} w_i/\mathrm{rtt}_i)^2}, \frac{1}{w_r} \right). \quad (1)$$

- For each loss on subflow r, decrease w_r by $w_r/2$.

LIA increases by at most $1/w_r$ to be at most as aggressive as regular TCP on any of its paths. When the RTTs are similar, this minimum can be neglected as the first term $(\max_i w_i/\mathrm{rtt}_i^2)/(\sum_i w_i/\mathrm{rtt}_i)^2$ would always be less than $1/w_r$. In this case, a fixed point analysis provides a simple loss-throughput formula for LIA [9]: LIA allocates to a path r a window w_r proportional to the inverse of the loss probability $1/p_r$ and such that the total rate $\sum_{p \in \mathcal{R}_u} w_p/\mathrm{rtt}_p$ equals the rate that a regular TCP user would get on the best path, i.e. $\max_{p \in \mathcal{R}_u} \sqrt{2/p_p}/\mathrm{rtt}_p$. Thus, the window size for the flow on a path r is given by

$$w_r = \frac{1}{p_r} \cdot \frac{\max_{p \in \mathcal{R}_u} \sqrt{2/p_p}/\mathrm{rtt}_p}{\sum_{p \in \mathcal{R}_u} 1/(\mathrm{rtt}_p p_p)}. \quad (2)$$

Besides MPTCP and algorithms in [4–6], a few other algorithms have been proposed to implement multipath protocols. In [13], an opportunistic multipath scheduler measures the path conditions on time scales up to several seconds. [14] uses a mechanism to detect shared bottlenecks and to avoid the use of multiple subflows on the same bottleneck. [15] proposes to use uncoupled TCP flows with a weight depending on the congestion level. These mechanisms are complex, their robustness is not clear, and they need explicit information about congestion in the network. Our proposed algorithm, OLIA, differs from these works as it is implemented, proven to be Pareto optimal, and relies only on information that is available to regular TCP. It also differs from [4–6] as it is not flappy and has a better responsiveness.

3. PERFORMANCE PROBLEMS OF MPTCP

In this section, we investigate the behavior of MPTCP with LIA in three different scenarios: scenarios A, B, and C. Using scenarios A and B, we show that upgrading some regular TCP users to MPTCP could reduce the throughput of other users in the network without any benefit to the upgraded users (problem P1). In Scenario C, we discuss the aggressiveness of MPTCP users that compete with regular TCP users (problem P2). Our conclusions are based on analytical results and measurements over a testbed.

3.1 Testbed Setup

To investigate the behavior of the algorithms, we create three testbed topologies that represent our scenarios.

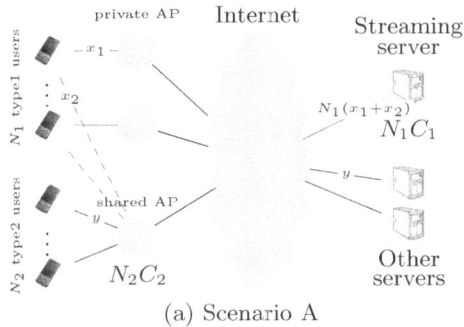

(a) Scenario A

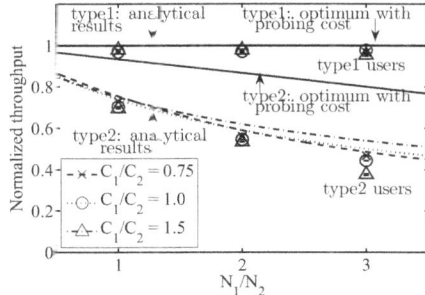

(b) Normalized throughput of users: $(x_1 + x_2)/C_1$ and y/C_2.

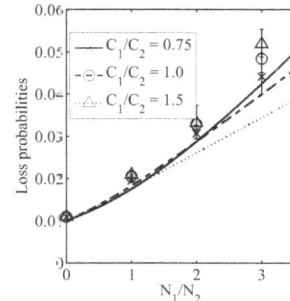

(c) Loss prob. p_2 at the shared AP.

Figure 1: Scenario A: type1 users are all downloading through the same streaming server and have access to both a private high speed access point and a shared access point. Type2 users have access only to the shared access point. The performance of MPTCP with LIA obtained by measurement (points) or numerical analysis (lines) is shown on figures (b) and (c). We observe that it is not Pareto-optimal, penalizes type2 users, and its performance is far from the theoretical optimum with probing cost. It also fails to balance the congestion.

Server-client PCs run MPTCP (with LIA or OLIA) enabled Linux kernels. In all scenarios laptop PCs are used as routers. We install "Click Modular Router" software [16] to emulate topologies with different characteristics. We emulate links with configurable bandwidth and delay with RED queuing (drop-tail queuing is also studied in htsim simulation, see Section 6.2). Figure 2 represents the testbed configuration of the scenario described in Figure 1(a).

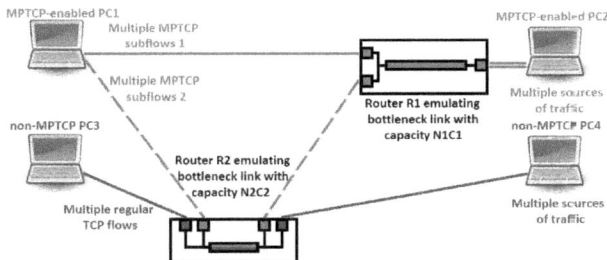

Figure 2: Testbed implementation of scenario A: router R_1 emulates the bottleneck at the server side and router R_2 the shared AP bottleneck. Iperf is used to emulate multiple connections. The red PCs use MPTCP and the blue PCs use regular TCP.

3.2 Scenario A: MPTCP is not Pareto-optimal and penalizes regular TCP users

Consider a network with two types of users as shown in Figure 1(a). There are N_1 users of type1, each with a high-speed private connection, accessing different files on a media streaming server. The server has a network connection with capacity limit of $N_1 C_1$ Mbps. These users can activate a second connection through a shared access point (AP) by using MPTCP. There are also N_2 type2 users that have connections only through the shared AP. They download their contents from the Internet. The shared AP has a capacity of $N_2 C_2$ Mbps.

Let x_1 be the rate that a type1 user receives over its private connection (by symmetry, every user of type1 will receive the same rate x_1). Similarly, let x_2 (resp. y) be the rate that a type1 (resp. type2) user receives over the shared connection. We denote by p_1 and p_2 the loss probability at

the link connected to the streaming server and the shared AP, respectively (the loss probabilities at the Internet backbone and the private APs are negligible).

When type1 users use only their own private AP, we have $x_1 = C_1$, $x_2 = 0$, and $y = C_2$. In this case the normalized throughput for both type1 and type2 users is 1. In the other case, assuming that all paths have RTT rtt, when all type1 users activate their public connections and use MPTCP with LIA to balance load between their connections, we have

$$
\begin{array}{lll}
(a) & N_1(x_1 + x_2) = N_1 C_1 & N_1 x_2 + N_2 y = N_2 C_2 \\[4pt]
(b) & x_1 + x_2 = \frac{1}{\text{rtt}} \sqrt{\frac{2}{p_1}} & x_2 = \frac{1}{2 + p_2/p_1} \frac{1}{\text{rtt}} \sqrt{\frac{2}{p_1}} \\[4pt]
(c) & y = \frac{1}{\text{rtt}} \sqrt{2/p_2} &
\end{array}
$$

where (a) are the capacity constraints at the two bottlenecks, (b) comes from the loss-throughput formula for LIA (Eq.(2)), and (c) follows the TCP loss-throughput formula [17]. This system has a unique solution (see [18], Appendix A). Figure 1(b) depicts the normalized throughput of type1 and type2 users, i.e. $(x_1 + x_2)/C_1$ and y/C_2. As shown in [18], Appendix A, these values depend only on the ratios C_1/C_2 and N_1/N_2.

A theoretically optimal algorithm (as discussed in [4, 5]) will allocate a normalized throughput of 1 to both type1 and type2 users. In practice, however, the value of the congestion windows are bounded below by 1 MSS. Hence, with a window-based congestion-control algorithm, a minimum probing traffic of 1 MSS per RTT will be sent over a path. In this paper, we introduce a theoretical baseline for window-based congestion-control algorithms, called *theoretical optimum with probing cost*; it provides optimal resource pooling in the network, given that a minimum probing traffic of 1 MSS per RTT is sent over each path. It serves as a reference to see how far from the optimum LIA is.

We measure the performance of LIA in Scenario A, by using the testbed, as shown in Figure 2. The measurements are taken for $N_2 = 10$ and three values of $N_1 = 10, 20, 30$. The capacities of R1 and R2 are $N_1 C_1$ and $N_2 C_2$ Mbps, where we set $C_2 = 1$Mbps and $C_1 = 0.75, 1, 1.5$ Mbps. All paths have similar RTTs (link delay plus queuing delay is around 150 ms over all paths). For each case, we took 5 measurements. The results are reported in Figure 1(b). Note that in all cases we present confidence intervals, but

3

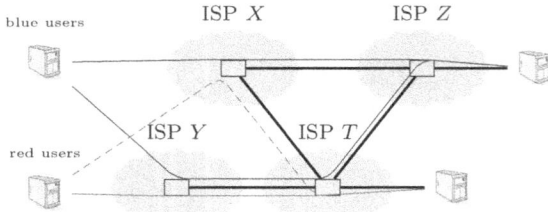

Figure 3: Scenario B. Thick lines represent peering agreements. Blue users are downloading from servers in ISP Z and Red users from servers in ISP T. Blue users use multi-homing and have access to ISPs X and Y. Initially, Red users have access only to ISP Y but upgrade to MPTCP and connect to both X and Y (by activating the dashed connection).

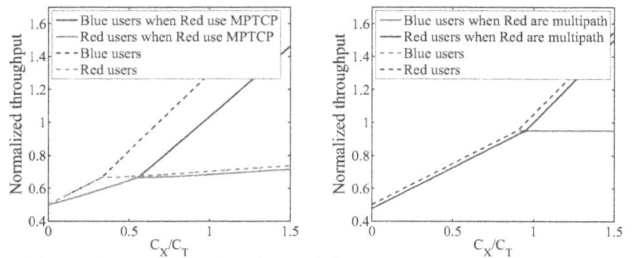

(a) Performance of LIA. (b) Optimum w. probing cost

Figure 4: Scenario B: analytical results for 15 Blue, 15 Red users and C_T=36 Mbps where $C_Y = C_Z = 100$ Mbps. We show the normalized throughput ($15(x_1 + x_2)/C_T$ and $15(y_1 + y_2)/C_T$) as a function of C_X/C_T. Dashed curves: normalized throughput when Red users connect only to ISP Y. Solid curves: the case when Red users upgrade to multipath. For all values of C_X/C_T, the throughput of all users decreases when Red users upgrade to MPTCP.

in many cases they are too small to be visible. The loss probability p_1 depends only on C_1 and is 0.02, 0.009, 0.004 for $C_1 = 0.75, 1, 1.5$ Mbps. We also show our analytical analysis of LIA, as well as the theoretical optimum with probing cost as defined above.

These figures have multiple implications. First, they show that MPTCP with LIA exhibits problem (P1) from the introduction: upgrading type1 users to MPTCP penalizes type2 users without any gain for type1. As the number of type1 users increases, the throughput of type2 users decreases, but the throughput of type1 users does not change as it is limited by the capacity C_1 of the streaming server. For $N_1=N_2$, type2 users see a decrease of about 30%. When $N_1=3N_2$, this decrease is between 50% to 60%. This is explained by the fact that LIA does not fully balance congestion, as shown in Figure 1(c). It excessively increases congestion on the shared AP (not in compliance with goal 3). We observe that LIA performs far from how an optimal algorithm with probing cost would perform. Furthermore, these figures show that the fixed point analysis predicts accurately the behavior of the algorithm: the two curves (theoretical and experimental) exhibit the same trend. As a summary for this section, we conclude that MPTCP with LIA is not Pareto-optimal and can penalize TCP users without any benefit for anybody.

3.3 Scenario B: MPTCP is not Pareto-optimal and can penalize other MPTCP users.

Consider the multi-homing scenario depicted in Figure 3. We have four Internet Service Providers, ISPs, X, Y, Z, and T. Y is a local ISP in a small city, which connects to the Internet through Z. X, Z, and T are nation-wide service providers and are connected to each other through high speed links. X provides Internet services to users in the city and is a competitor of Y. They have access capacity limits of C_X, C_Y, C_Z, and C_T.

Z and T host different video streaming servers. There are two types of users: N_B Blue users download contents from a server in Z, and N_R Red users download from a server in ISP T. Blue users use multi-homing and are connected to both ISPs X and Y to increase their reliability. Red users can connect either only to Y or to both X and Y. We assume that only ISPs X and T are bottlenecks and denote by p_X and p_T the loss probabilities. We assume that all paths have similar RTTs.

We first present a theoretical analysis of the rate that each user would achieve (to simplify the analysis, we assume similar numbers of Blue and Red users). There are two possible cases. When Red users connect only to Y, the analysis is the same as the one of scenario C, given in Section 3.4. Here, we analyze the case when Red users upgrade to MPTCP. The loss throughput formula (Equation (2)) shows that the throughput of the different connections are:

$$\begin{cases} y_1 = \dfrac{1/\text{rtt}}{2 + \frac{p_X}{p_T}} \sqrt{\dfrac{2}{p_T}} \\ y_2 = \dfrac{p_X}{p_T} y_1 \end{cases}, \quad \begin{cases} x_1 = \dfrac{1/\text{rtt}}{1 + p_X/p_T} \sqrt{\max \dfrac{2}{p_X}, \dfrac{2}{p_T}} \\ x_2 = \dfrac{1/\text{rtt}}{1 + p_T/p_X} \sqrt{\max \dfrac{2}{p_X}, \dfrac{2}{p_T}} \end{cases}$$

As shown in [18], Appendix B, this set of equations has a unique positive solution. A numerical evaluation of these formulas is depicted in Figure 4(a). Figure 4(b) depicts the performance of a theoretical optimum with probing cost (see [18], Appendix B). The results are presented for RTT=150 ms, $C_Y = C_Z = 100$ Mbps, and $C_T = 36$ Mbps. We consider 15 Blue and 15 Red users in the network. We depict the normalized throughput ($15(x_1 + x_2)/C_T$ and $15(y_1 + y_2)/C_T$) as a function of C_X/C_T. The results show that upgrading Red users to MPTCP with LIA decreases the performance for everyone. As an example, when $C_X/C_T \approx 0.75$, by upgrading the Red users we reduce the throughput of the Blue users by up to 21%. This decrease is about 3% when we use an optimal algorithm with probing cost (Fig. 4(b)).

We emulate this scenario in our testbed in a similar manner as for Scenario A. The measurement results are reported in Table 1 for a similar setting with $C_X = 27$ Mbps. We observe that when Red users only connect to ISP Y, the aggregate throughput of users is close to the cut-set bound, 63 Mbps. However, Blue users get a higher share of the network bandwidth. Now consider that Red users upgrade to MPTCP by establishing a second connection through X (shown by dashed line in Figure 3). Our results in Table 1 show that Red users do not receive any higher throughput. However, the average rate of Blue users drops by 20%, which results in a drop of 13% in aggregate throughput. This confirms our analytical observation and shows that MPTCP

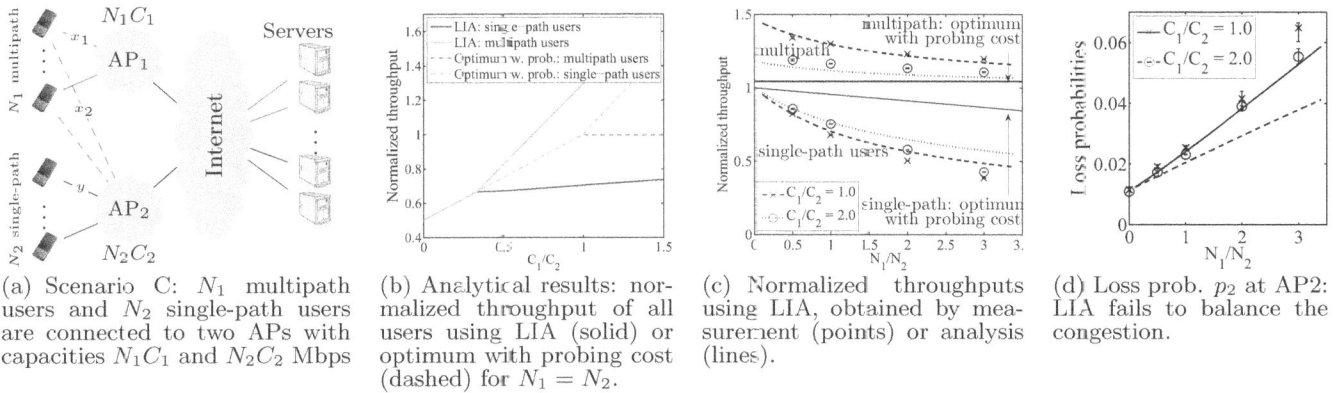

(a) Scenario C: N_1 multipath users and N_2 single-path users are connected to two APs with capacities $N_1 C_1$ and $N_2 C_2$ Mbps

(b) Analytical results: normalized throughput of all users using LIA (solid) or optimum with probing cost (dashed) for $N_1 = N_2$.

(c) Normalized throughputs using LIA, obtained by measurement (points) or analysis (lines).

(d) Loss prob. p_2 at AP2: LIA fails to balance the congestion.

Figure 5: Scenario C: MPTCP with LIA excessively penalizes TCP users (when $C_1/C_2 \geq 1$, for any fairness criterion, MPTCP users should not impact TCP users). We show the normalized throughputs ($(x_1+x_2)/C_1$ and y/C_2) received by the users, as well as p_2. The performance of LIA is far from the theoretical optimum with probing cost.

Red users	Rate/user		Aggregate
	Blue users	Red users	
Single-path	2.5	1.5	59.8
Multipath	2.0	1.4	52.0

Table 1: Measurement results for scenario B, showing the effect of upgrading the Red users from regular TCP to MPTCP with LIA. The number of Red and Blue users is 15 and all values are recorded in Mbps. By upgrading Red users to MPTCP, the throughput drops for all users and the aggregate throughput falls by 13%.

with LIA is not Pareto-optimal and could penalize other MPTCP users without any benefit for anybody.

3.4 Scenario C: MPTCP users could be excessively aggressive towards TCP users.

We consider a scenario with N_1 multipath users, N_2 single-path users, and two APs with capacities $N_1 C_1$ and $N_2 C_2$ Mbps (see Figure 5). Multipath users connect to both APs and they share AP2 with single-path users.

If the allocation of rates is proportionally fair, multipath users will use AP2 only if $C_1 < C_2$ and all users will receive $(N_1 C_1 + N_2 C_2)/(N_1 + N_2)$. When $C_1 > C_2$, a fair multipath user will not transmit over AP2. This fair allocation is represented by dashed lines in Figure 5(b) when we take into account the minimum probing cost. However, using MPTCP with LIA, multipath users get a larger share of bandwidth as soon as $C_1 \geq C_2/(2+N_1/N_2)$. We show this analytically. Let p_1 and p_2 be the loss probabilities at APs x_1 and x_2 be rates that a multipath user receives over its paths, and y be the rate of a single-path user. Assume all RTTs are same. When $C_1/C_2 < 1/(2+N_1/N_2)$, we have $p_1 > p_2$ and all users receive the same rate: $x_1 + x_2 = y = (C_1 + C_2)/2$. When $C_1/C_2 > 1/(2+N_1/N_2)$, we have $p_1 < p_2$ and the fixed point formula of LIA gives:

$$x_1 = \frac{p_2}{p_1 + p_2} \frac{1}{\text{rtt}} \sqrt{\frac{2}{p_1}} \quad \text{and} \quad x_2 = \frac{p_1}{p_1 + p_2} \frac{1}{\text{rtt}} \sqrt{\frac{2}{p_1}}.$$

Moreover, both the APs are bottlenecks and we have $x_1 =$

C_1 and $x_2 + y = C_2$. As shown in [18], Appendix C, this set of equations has a unique positive solution that only depends on the ratio N_1/N_2 and C_1/C_2. Figure 5(b) reports a numerical evaluation of these fixed point equations for the case $N_1 = N_2$. We show the normalized throughputs ($(x_1+x_2)/C_1$ and y/C_2) received by the users, as well as p_2. We observe that LIA is fair with regular TCP users, as long as $C_1 < C_2/3$. However, as C_1 exceeds $C_2/3$, it takes most of the capacity of AP2 for itself.

We emulate the scenario in our testbed and measure the performance of MPTCP with LIA. The results are reported in Figures 5(c) and 5(d) for $C_2=1$ Mbps and $C_1=1$, 2Mbps, with $N_2=10$ and $N_1=5$, 10, 20, 30. As in scenario A, we also present the theoretical optimum with probing cost in Figure 5(c).

When $C_1/C_2 \geq 1$, multipath users should not use AP2 at all. However, our results show that, MPTCP users are disproportionately aggressive and exhibit problem (P2). Figure 5(d) shows the loss probability at AP2. We observe that LIA excessively increases congestion on AP2 and is unable to fully balance congestion in the network. Also, we have $p_1=0.01$ and 0.003 for $C_1=1$ and 2Mbps, respectively. These results confirm our analytical observation and show that LIA is overly aggressive towards TCP users.

4. OLIA: THE OPPORTUNISTIC LINKED INCREASES ALGORITHM

In this section, we introduce OLIA as an alternative for MPTCP's LIA. OLIA is a window-based congestion-control algorithm that couples the increase of congestion windows and uses unmodified TCP behavior in the case of a loss. The increase part of OLIA has two terms. The first term is an adaptation of Kelly and Voice's increase term and provides the Pareto-optimality (Kelly and Voice's algorithm is based on scalable TCP; the first term is a TCP compatible version of their algorithm that compensates also for different RTTs). The second term, with α, guarantees responsiveness and non-flappiness. We first present the algorithm and its Linux implementation. Then, we illustrate with an example its operation and its difference with LIA.

4.1 Detailed Description of OLIA

Let $\mathcal{R}_u$ be the set of paths available to user u and let $r \in \mathcal{R}_u$ be a path. We denote by $\ell_{1r}(t)$ the number of bits that were successfully transmitted by u over path r between the last two losses seen on r, and by $\ell_{2r}(t)$ the number of bits that are successfully transmitted over r after the last loss. If no losses have been observed on r up to time t, then $\ell_{1r}(t) = 0$ and $\ell_{2r}(t)$ is the total number of bits transmitted on r. Also, let $\ell_r(t) = \max\{\ell_{1r}(t), \ell_{2r}(t)\}$ and let $\mathrm{rtt}_r(t)$ and $w_r(t)$ be respectively RTT and the window on r at time t. We define

$$\mathcal{M}(t) = \left\{ i(t) \mid i(t) = \arg\max_{p \in \mathcal{R}_u} w_p(t) \right\} \qquad (3)$$

$$\mathcal{B}(t) = \left\{ j(t) \mid j(t) = \arg\max_{p \in \mathcal{R}_u} \frac{\ell_p(t)}{\mathrm{rtt}_p(t)^2} \right\} \qquad (4)$$

$\mathcal{M}(t)$ is the set of the paths of u with the largest window sizes at time t. $\mathcal{B}(t)$ is the set of the paths at time t that are presumably the best paths for u, as $1/\ell_r(t)$ can be considered as an estimate of packet loss probability on path r at time t, and the rate that path r can provide to a TCP user can be estimated by $\sqrt{2\ell_r(t)}/\mathrm{rtt}_r$ [17].

Our algorithm is as follows (to simplify notation, we drop the time argument t; however, note that w_r, rtt_r, ℓ_r, $\mathcal{M}$, and $\mathcal{B}$ are all functions of time):

- For each ACK on path r, **increase** w_r by:

$$\frac{w_r/\mathrm{rtt}_r^2}{\left(\sum_{p \in \mathcal{R}_u} w_p/\mathrm{rtt}_p\right)^2} + \frac{\alpha_r}{w_r}, \qquad (5)$$

where α_r is calculated as follows:

$$\alpha_r = \begin{cases} \dfrac{1/|\mathcal{R}_u|}{|\mathcal{B} \setminus \mathcal{M}|} & \text{if } r \in \mathcal{B} \setminus \mathcal{M} \neq \emptyset \\[2mm] -\dfrac{1/|\mathcal{R}_u|}{|\mathcal{M}|} & \text{if } r \in \mathcal{M} \text{ and } \mathcal{B} \setminus \mathcal{M} \neq \emptyset \\[2mm] 0 & \text{otherwise.} \end{cases} \qquad (6)$$

$\mathcal{B} \setminus \mathcal{M}$ is the set of elements in $\mathcal{B}$ but not in $\mathcal{M}$, $\emptyset$ is the empty set, and $|\mathcal{R}_u|$ is the number of paths available to u at the time. Note that $\sum_{r \in \mathcal{R}_u} \alpha_r = 0$.

- For each loss on path r, **decrease** w_r by $\frac{w_r}{2}$.

We can see from (3), (4), and (6) that if the best paths have the maximum window size, then $\alpha_r = 0$ for any $r \in \mathcal{R}_u$. However, if there is any best path with a small window size, *i.e.* if $\mathcal{B} \setminus \mathcal{M} \neq \emptyset$, then α_r would be positive if $r \in \mathcal{B} \setminus \mathcal{M}$, negative if $r \in \mathcal{M}$, and zero otherwise. Hence, OLIA increases windows faster on the paths that are the best but that have small windows. The increase is slower on the paths with maximum windows.

4.2 Linux Implementation of OLIA

We implemented OLIA in the MPTCP release supported on the Linux kernel 3.0.0 [19]. Similarly to LIA, our algorithm only applies to the increase part of the congestion avoidance phase. The fast retransmit and fast recovery algorithms, as well as the multiplicative decrease of the congestion avoidance phase, are the same as in TCP [1]. We also use a similar slow start algorithm as in TCP, with the modification that we set the ssthresh (slow start threshold) to be 1 MSS if multiple paths are established. In the case of a single path flow, we use similar minimum ssthresh as in TCP (2 MSS). The purpose of this modification is to avoid

transmitting unnecessary traffic over congested paths when multiple paths are available to a user. The minimum congestion windows size is 1 MSS as in TCP. Our implementation is available online [18].

One important part of our implementation is the measurement of ℓ_r on a path r. This can be done easily by using information that is already available to a regular TCP user. Our algorithm for computing ℓ_r is as follows:

- For each ACK on r: $\ell_{2,r} \leftarrow \ell_{2,r} +$ (number of bits that are acknowledged by ACK)

- For each loss on r: $\ell_{1,r} \leftarrow \ell_{2,r}$ and $\ell_{2r} \leftarrow 0$

where $\ell_r = \max\{\ell_{1,r}, \ell_{2,r}\}$. $\ell_{1,r}$ and $\ell_{2,r}$ are initially set to zero when the connection is established. To compute a smoothed estimate of rtt_r, we use the algorithm, proposed in [20] and implemented in the Linux kernel.

4.3 Illustrative Example of OLIA's Behavior

To give more insight into how OLIA performs, we show the evolution of window sizes and α values for a two-path flow in Figure 6. The measurement results on our testbed are reported in Figures 7 and 8.

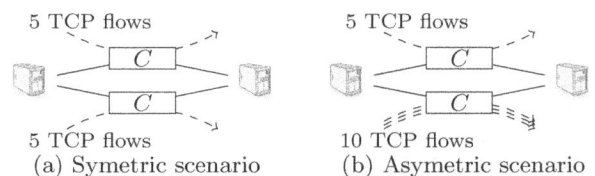

Figure 6: A multipath user sharing two bottlenecks of the same capacity C with single-path users.

We first consider a symmetric case, depicted in Figure 6(a). As both of the paths are equally good, a multipath user will benefit from using both of them. Figure 7(a) shows the evolution of w_r and α_r as a function of time. We observe that OLIA simultaneously uses both of the paths, similarly to LIA (Figure 7(b)), which is the desired behavior. There is no sign of flappiness as α_1 and α_2 react quickly and adjust w_1 and w_2 accordingly.

We now study the asymmetric scenario of Figure 6(b). In this case, the second path is shared with 10 TCP flows and it will be beneficial if multipath users use only the first path. This is what we observe in Figure 8(a). The window on the congested path is 1, most of the time (because of the first increase term). However, due to α, the window increases from time to time over the congested path whenever the path has the largest inter-loss distance ℓ_r. This increase is brief as losses occur more frequently on this path. LIA, however, transmits significant traffic over the congested paths and lower traffic, compared to OLIA, over the good path as depicted in Figure 8(b).

5. PARETO-OPTIMALITY OF OLIA

In this section, we build a fluid model of OLIA by using differential inclusions. We show that this model provides a Pareto-optimal allocation (Theorem 3) that satisfies the three design goals of MPTCP [10] (Corollary 2). Also, we prove that MPTCP with OLIA is fair with TCP: If all routes of a user have the same RTT, then OLIA maximizes the same fairness criteria as the regular TCP (Theorem 4).

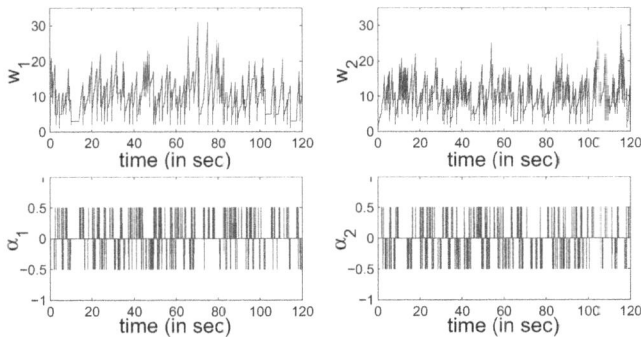

(a) MPTCP - OLIA: window size and α_r as a function of time.

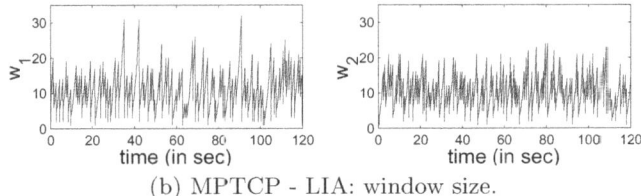

(b) MPTCP - LIA: window size.

Figure 7: Evolution of w and α values for a two-path flow. Each path is shared with 5 regular TCP users. OLIA uses both of the paths, similarly to LIA, and there is no sign of flappiness.

5.1 Fluid Model of OLIA

We consider a network model similar to [3]. The network is static and composed of a set $\mathcal{L}$ of links (or resources). We denote by $\mathcal{R}_u$ the set of paths available to a user u, each path being a set of links. If the route r is available to user u, we write $r \in R_u$. If a route r uses a resource ℓ, we write $\ell \in r$. Similarly, we refer to all routes that cross ℓ as $r \ni \ell$.

Let $x_r(t) \geq 0$ be the rate of traffic transmitted by the user u on a path $r \in \mathcal{R}_u$. We assume that the RTT of a route r is fixed in time and we denote it by rtt_r. In the fluid model, the rate x_r is an approximation of the window size divided by the RTT, i.e. $x_r = w_r/\mathrm{rtt}_r$.

Let $p_\ell(\sum_{\ell \in r} x_r)$ be the loss rate at link ℓ. p_ℓ depends on the capacity of the link, C_ℓ, and the total amount of traffic sent through the link, $\sum_{\ell \in r} x_r$. We assume that p_ℓ is an increasing function of the total traffic. To simplify the notation, we omit the dependence on x and write only p_ℓ. However, note that if x varies with time, p_ℓ will also vary. We assume that the loss probabilities of links are independent and small; hence, the loss probability on a route r is $p_r = 1 - \prod_{\ell \in r}(1 - p_\ell) \approx \sum_{\ell \in r} p_\ell$.

When p_r is small, a user $r \in \mathcal{R}_u$ receives acknowledgments on a route $r \in \mathcal{R}_u$ at rate x_r and increases the window w_r as Equation (5). Losses occur at rate $p_r x_r$ on r, and the user decreases w_r by half whenever it detects a loss. We consider a fluid approximation of OLIA in which we replace the stochastic variations of rates by their expectation. This leads to the differential equation:

$$\frac{dx_r}{dt} = x_r^2 \left(\frac{1/\mathrm{rtt}_r^2}{(\sum_{p \in \mathcal{R}_u} x_p)^2} - \frac{p_r}{2} \right) + \frac{\alpha_r}{\mathrm{rtt}_r^2}, \qquad (7)$$

α_r depends on the values p_p and w_p for all paths $p \in \mathcal{R}_u$ of users u. It is defined by Equation (6). To compute α_r, we approximate ℓ_r by its average: $l_r = 1/p_r$.

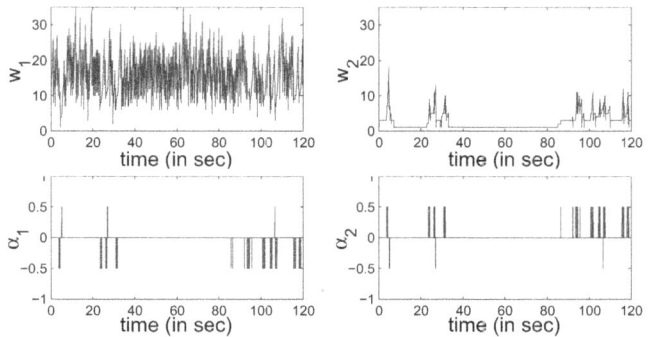

(a) MPTCP - OLIA: window size and α_r as a function of time.

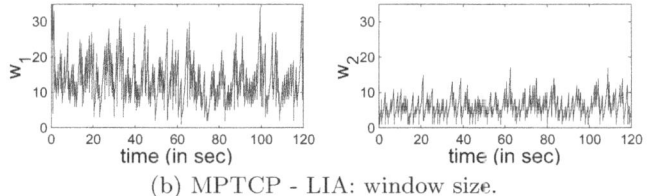

(b) MPTCP - LIA: window size.

Figure 8: Evolution of w and α for a two paths flow. The first path is shared with 5 TCP flows and the second with 10. OLIA uses only the good path. LIA transmits significant traffic over the congested path and less than OLIA over the good path.

For a user u, the set of best paths $\mathcal{B}_u$ and the set of paths with maximum window size $\mathcal{M}_u$ depend non-continuously on the probability of loss on each route, as well as on the various window sizes of the routes of this user. This implies that the right-hand side of Equation (7) is not a continuous function of x_r. Therefore, this differential equation is not well defined and can have no solutions. A natural way to deal with a differential equation with a discontinuous right-hand size is to replace the differential equation (7) by a differential inclusion $dx/dt \in F(x)$ where the discontinuous α_r of (7) is replaced by the convex closure of the possible values of α in a small neighborhood of x [21, 22].

We show in [18], Appendix D, that the differential inclusion corresponding to the Equation (7) is

$$\frac{dx_r}{dt} = x_r^2 \left(\frac{1/\mathrm{rtt}_r^2}{(\sum_{p \in \mathcal{R}_u} x_p)^2} - \frac{p_r}{2} \right) + \frac{\bar{\alpha}_r}{\mathrm{rtt}_r^2}, \qquad (8)$$

where $\bar{\alpha} = (\bar{\alpha}_1 \ldots \bar{\alpha}_{|\mathcal{R}_u|})$ is such that

$$(\bar{\alpha}_r \cdot |\mathcal{R}_u|) \in \begin{cases} [\mathbf{1}_{|\mathcal{B}_u|=1}, 1] & \text{if } r \in \mathcal{B}_u \setminus \mathcal{M}_u \\ [-1, -\mathbf{1}_{|\mathcal{M}_u|=1}] & \text{if } r \in \mathcal{M}_u \setminus \mathcal{B}_u \\ [-\mathbf{1}_{|\mathcal{B}_u|\geq 2}, \mathbf{1}_{|\mathcal{M}_u|\geq 2}] & \text{if } r \in \mathcal{M}_u \cap \mathcal{B}_u \\ \{0\} & \text{if } r \notin \mathcal{M}_u \cup \mathcal{B}_u \end{cases} \qquad (9)$$

with $\sum_{r \in \mathcal{R}_u} \bar{\alpha}_r = 0$ and $\sum_{r \in \mathcal{B}_u} \bar{\alpha}_r = 1/|\mathcal{R}_u|$ if $\mathcal{B}_u \cap \mathcal{M}_u = \emptyset$. The notation $\mathbf{1}_{|\mathcal{B}_u|=1}$ means that this term is equal to 1 if $|\mathcal{B}_u| = 1$ and 0 otherwise. For example, when there is only one best path (i.e. $|\mathcal{B}| = 1$), $\alpha_r = 1/|\mathcal{R}_u|$ for $r \in \mathcal{B}_u \setminus \mathcal{M}_u$. If there are two or more best paths (i.e. $|\mathcal{B}| \neq 1$), then $\alpha_r \in [0, 1/|\mathcal{R}_u|]$ for $r \in \mathcal{B}_u \setminus \mathcal{M}_u$.

Note that there are multiple $\bar{\alpha}$ that correspond to definition (9). The differential inclusion might have multiple solutions, but this does not affect our analysis [18].

5.2 Pareto Optimality of OLIA

A fixed point of the congestion control algorithm (8) is a vector of rates $x = (x_1 \ldots x_{|\mathcal{R}|})$ such that there exists $\bar{\alpha}$ satisfying (9) and such that, Equation (8) is equal to zero for any route r. We say that x is a non-degenerate allocation of rates if each user transmits with a non-zero rate on at least one of its paths. In practice, due to re-establishment routines in traditional TCP, the allocation of rates will not be degenerate. Hence, in our analysis, we consider only the non-degenerate fixed points and analyze their properties.

THEOREM 1. *Any non-degenerate fixed point x of OLIA congestion control algorithm, given by Equation (8), has the following properties:*

(i) *Only the best paths will be used, i.e. paths r with maximum $\sqrt{2/p_r}/\mathrm{rtt}_r$.*

(ii) *The total rate obtained by a user u is equal to the rate that a regular TCP user would receive on the best path available to u:*

$$\sum_{r \in \mathcal{R}_u} x_r = \max_{r \in \mathcal{R}_u} \frac{1}{\mathrm{rtt}_r} \sqrt{\frac{2}{p_r}}.$$

PROOF. The proof is given in Appendix A. □

This theorem implies the following corollary:

COROLLARY 2. *OLIA satisfies the three design goals suggested by the RFC [10].*

PROOF. The proof is given in Appendix B. □

The following theorem gives a global optimality property of OLIA. For a rate allocation x, we define the total congestion cost by $C(x) = \sum_\ell \int_0^{\sum_{r \ni \ell} x_r} p_\ell(y) dy$.

THEOREM 3. *Any non-degenerate fixed point x of our congestion control algorithm (8) is Pareto optimal, i.e.:*

- *It is impossible to increase the quantity $\sum_{r \in \mathcal{R}_u} x_r/\mathrm{rtt}_r^2$ for some users without decreasing it for others or increasing the congestion cost $C(x)$.*

PROOF. The proof is given in Appendix C. □

Remark 1. If the probability p_ℓ is sharp around C_ℓ, i.e. if $p_\ell(y) \approx 0$ when $y < C_\ell$ and p_ℓ grows rapidly when y exceeds C_ℓ, then the cost C is a binary function: it is very small if the capacity constraints $\sum_{r \in \ell} x_r \leq C_\ell$ are respected and grows rapidly otherwise. In this case, Theorem 3 shows that if x is a fixed point of our algorithm, it is impossible to increase the quantity $\sum_{r \in \mathcal{R}_u} x_r/\mathrm{rtt}_r^2$ for some users without decreasing it for others while respecting the capacity constraints.

Remark 2. As pointed out by Kelly [2], as $C(x)$ is an increasing function of rates, single-path congestion control mechanisms are always Pareto optimal and the choice of an allocation of rates is only a matter of fairness. However, if we have multiple paths, it is likely that an algorithm will lead to a non-Pareto optimal allocation [2]. Theorem 3 guarantees that this cannot happen with OLIA. As a consequence, our algorithm will not exhibit either problem P1 nor P2.

Remark 3. Although the utility function of each user $\sum_{r \in \mathcal{R}_u} x_r/\mathrm{rtt}_r^2$ could appear to be an ad-hoc utility function, it reflects the fact that like TCP, OLIA favors paths with low rtt. When all paths belonging to a user have the

same RTT, this theorem implies that the rate allocation of OLIA is such that one user cannot increase its rate without decreasing the rate of some other users. Hence, OLIA can successfully avoid problems P1 and P2. When RTTs over paths available to a user are different, satisfying goals 1 and 2 of the RFC [10] can lead to sending traffic on paths that are not the least congested but have a small round trip times. Therefore, using a TCP-compatible algorithm, it is not possible to avoid problems P1 and P2 in all possible settings. However, we can see from Theorem 1 that by using OLIA, only the best paths available to a user would be used. This indicates that OLIA provides an allocation as close as or closer to the optimal than any TCP-compatible algorithm. To completely avoid problems P1 and P2, it is necessary to depart from the compatibility with regular TCP by using congestion mechanisms that are less sensitive to round trip times, such as CUBIC [23] or STCP [24].

5.3 TCP Compatibility

As we show in Appendix C, OLIA maximizes the utility function $V^*(x)$ given by Equation (11). We now show that our algorithm is fair with the regular TCP under the assumption (A): all the paths belonging to a user u have the same RTT rtt_u. Under this assumption, $V^*(x)$ simplifies as follows:

$$V(x) = \sum_{u \in \mathcal{U}} -\frac{1}{\mathrm{rtt}_u^2 \sum_{r \in \mathcal{R}_u} x_r} - \frac{1}{2} \sum_{l \in \mathcal{L}} \int_0^{\sum_{r \ni l} x_r} p_\ell(x) dx,$$

where x is the set of all the rates of the users.

THEOREM 4. *Under the assumption (A), the congestion control algorithm defined by Equation (8) converges to a maximum of the utility function V:*

$$\lim_{t \to \infty} V(x(t)) = \max_{x \geq 0} V(x).$$

PROOF. The proof is given in Appendix D. □

This implies that OLIA maximizes the same utility function as the regular TCP of [25] where we replace the rate of a connection by the total rate that a user achieves on all its paths. If the probabilities of loss p_ℓ are sharp around C_ℓ, then our algorithm converges to an optimum of the following global maximization problem:

$$\max \sum_{u \in \mathcal{U}} -\frac{1}{\mathrm{rtt}_u^2 \sum_{r \in \mathcal{R}_u} x_r} \quad \text{subject to} \quad \begin{cases} \sum_{r \ni \ell} x_r \leq C_\ell \\ x_r \geq 0. \end{cases}$$

This is analog to the TCP maximization problem.

6. OLIA EVALUATION: MEASUREMENTS AND SIMULATIONS

In this section, we study the performance of MPTCP with OLIA, through measurements and by simulations. We first perform measurements on our testbed to show that OLIA outperforms LIA in all the scenarios from Section 3, as evidence that OLIA solves problems P1 and P2. Results from this section are in line with our theoretical analysis from Section 5. We then study the performance of OLIA in a data center by using htsim simulator [7].

6.1 Performance of OLIA in Scenarios A,B, C

In this section, we study the performance of MPTCP with OLIA, in the scenarios A,B and C described in Sections 3.2

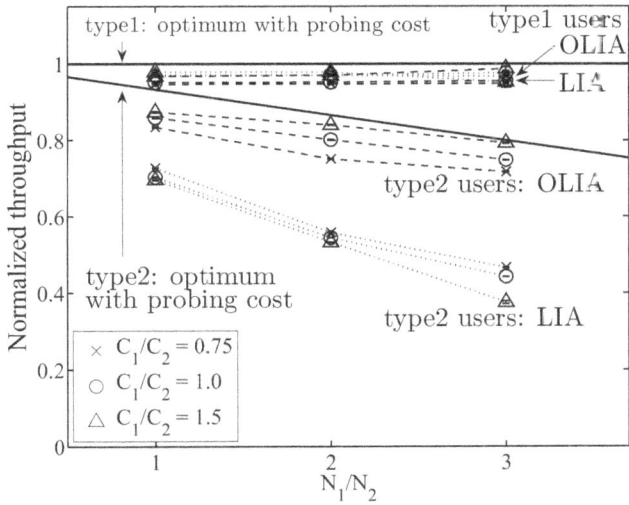

Figure 9: Scenario A - Normalized throughput of type1 and type2 users: we compare performance of LIA and OLIA. By using OLIA, type2 users achieve up to 2 times higher rates. OLIA performs close to the theoretical optimum with probing cost.

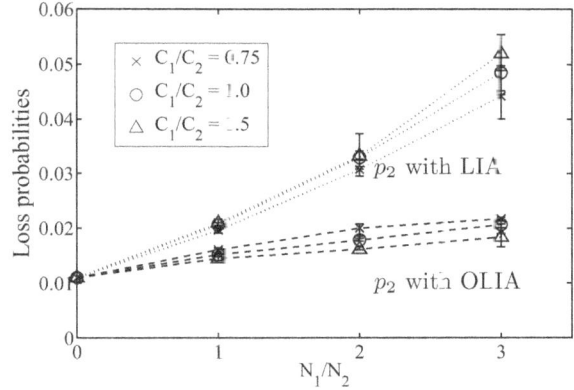

Figure 10: Scenario A - Loss probability p_2 at shared AP: we observe that OLIA significantly reduces the congestion level at this bottleneck and improves the congestion balancing.

to 3.4. We show that in practice, OLIA is very close to the theoretical optimum with probing cost. These results are obtained through measurements over our testbed, by using our Linux implementation of OLIA.

6.1.1 Scenario A

We have shown in Section 3.2 that when the addition of an extra link does not help (like in Scenario A) using MPTCP with LIA can reduce the throughput of competing TCP users. In this section, we show by measurements that MPTCP with OLIA significantly outperforms MPTCP with LIA and comes close to the theoretical optimum with probing cost.

Figures 9 and 10 report measurements obtained on the testbed shown in Figure 2. Figure 9 depicts the normalized throughput of type1 and type2 users that use LIA or OLIA. The results show that OLIA performs close to an optimal multipath algorithm that transmits the minimum traffic over congested paths (theoretical optimum with probing cost). OLIA significantly outperforms LIA: by using OLIA, type2 users achieve rates up to two times higher than with LIA, with no reduction for type1 users.

Figure 10 depicts the measured loss probability p_2 on the shared access point. We observe that OLIA balances congestion much better than LIA. When we use OLIA, p_2 increases only by a factor of 1.3 in the worst case, whereas with LIA, p_2 increases by a factor of 5. p_1 is almost the same when using LIA or OLIA.

6.1.2 Scenario B

We now show the performance of OLIA in the scenario B described in Section 3.3. As we have shown, OLIA is Pareto optimal. Hence, taking into account the minimum probing cost, we expect only 3% reduction in the Blue users' rates and in the aggregate throughput when we upgrade Red users to OLIA (see Figure 4(b)).

Table 2 presents the measurements for the scenario de-

scribed in Section 3.3 using OLIA. We set $C_X=27$, $C_T=36$, $C_Z=100$, all in Mbps. We have 15 Red and 15 Blue users. We set RTTs to 150 ms over all paths. Our results show that there is a 3.5% decrement in aggregate throughput when we update Red users to OLIA, which is much smaller than the 13% reduction we observed when we used LIA (see Table 1). This 3.5% reduction in the aggregate throughput is due to the minimum traffic transmitted by users over congested paths and cannot be reduced as it is bounded below by $1/rtt$ packets/sec.

6.1.3 Scenario C

Finally, we study the performance of MPTCP with OLIA in scenario C described in Section 3.4. Theorems 1 and 4 imply that by using our algorithm, multipath users do not send any traffic on their path crossing AP2. Hence, in theory, OLIA provides a fair allocation among users and performs as an optimal algorithm (Figure 5(b), dashed lines). Next, we show by measurements that OLIA is also fair in practice.

Figure 11 depicts the normalized throughput of single-path and multipath users, as a function of N_1/N_2 and for $C_1/C_2=1$, 2. We show the results for LIA and OLIA, as well as for an optimal algorithm with minimum probing cost. This figure shows that with OLIA multipath users transmit only one packet per RTT over AP2. Compared to LIA, type2 users receive up to 2 times higher throughput. Hence, OLIA is less aggressive than LIA towards regular TCP users.

Red users	Rate/user		Aggregate
	Blue users	Red users	
Single-path	2.2	1.8	59.3
Multipath	2.2	1.7	57.8

Table 2: Measurement results for scenario B showing the effect of upgrading the Red users from regular TCP to MPTCP with OLIA. We observe a small drop of 3.5% in the aggregate throughput, which is due to the overhead of minimum traffic ($1/rtt$) over the congested path. Compared to LIA (see Table 1), we see significant improvement.

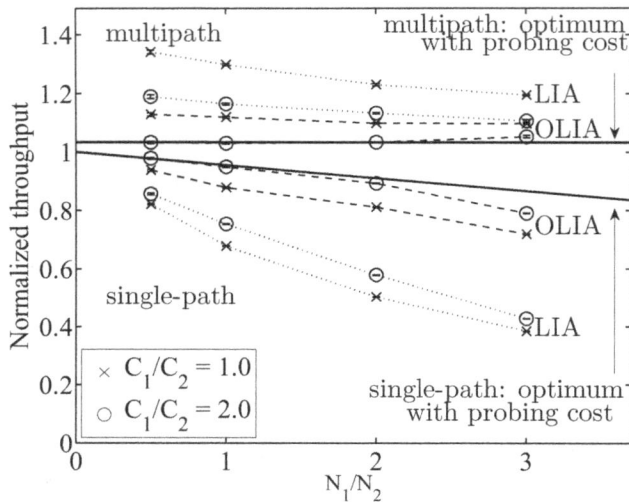

Figure 11: Scenario C - Normalized throughput of single-path and multipath users: we compare the performance of LIA and OLIA. We observe that by using OLIA, type2 users achieve up to 2 times higher rates. OLIA performs close to the theoretical optimum with probing cost.

Figure 12, shows the measured loss probability p_2. The results show again that OLIA balances congestion in the network and reduces the loss probability in bottlenecks much better than LIA. In particular, we observe that by increasing N_1 from 0 to $3N_2$, p_2 increases by a factor of 2 using OLIA, whereas the increase is in the order of 4 to 6 times when using LIA. p_1 is almost the same when using OLIA or LIA.

6.2 Performance of OLIA in Data Center and Dynamic Scenarios

The three preceding examples show that by providing a better congestion balance, MPTCP with OLIA outperforms MPTCP with LIA in Scenarios A, B, and C. In this section, we show that, by being non-flappy and as responsive as LIA, OLIA can fully use the multiple paths available in a data center. Our study is based on a series of scenarios in which MPTCP with LIA is studied in [7]. Because of space constraints, we present the results for only two of the cases where LIA was shown to be very efficient. We observe that OLIA performs as well or better than LIA in these two scenarios. This indicates that it is not flappy and has a very good responsiveness. These results are obtained using `htsim` simulator used in [7], provided by Raiciu et al. We implemented OLIA in the simulator and use the same scenarios as [7].

6.2.1 Static FatTree Topology

We first study exactly the same scenario as in [7], Section 4.2-Throughput: the network is a FatTree with 128 hosts, 80 eight-port switches, 100Mb/s links. Each host sends a long-lived flow to another host chosen at random. Figure 13(a) shows the aggregate throughput achieved by long-lived TCP and MPTCP (LIA and OLIA) flows. We show the results for different numbers of subflows used. Our results show that OLIA can successfully exploit the multiple paths that exist in the network and can use the available capacity.

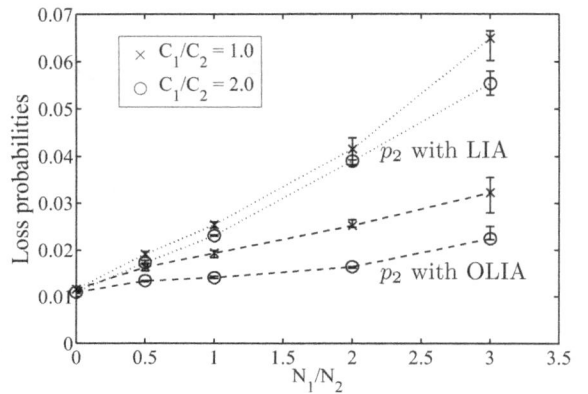

Figure 12: Scenario C - Loss probability p_2 at shared AP: we observe that OLIA significantly reduces the congestion level at this bottleneck (4 to 6 times lower compared tp LIA).

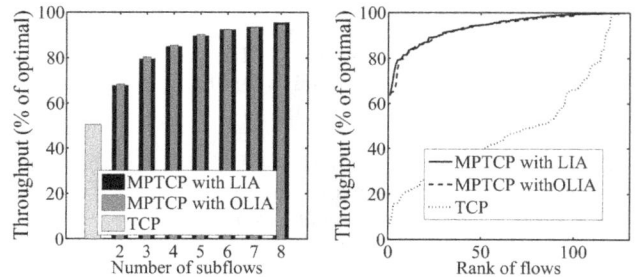

(a) Aggregated throughput.   (b) Throughput of users.

Figure 13: Performance of OLIA in a FatTree with many possible parallel paths between users. It successfully explores the path diversity that exists in the network and uses the available capacity (a sign of non-flappiness). LIA performs similarly as, in this scenario, it can successfully balance the congestion.

This is a sign that it is not flappy. Regular TCP shows a poor performance. Figure 13(b) shows the throughput of individual users ranked in order of achieved throughputs, for LIA and OLIA with 8 subflows per user and with TCP; LIA and OLIA provide similar fairness among users and are more fair than TCP. We observe that, in this scenario, LIA performs close to an optimal algorithm and exhibits a similar performance to OLIA. The reason is that the users have multiple equally good paths. Hence, LIA also successfully balances the congestions in the network, similarly to OLIA, and performs optimally. We measured the loss probabilities of links available to users and results confirm our reasoning.

6.2.2 Dynamic Setting with Short Flows

We study the same scenario as the one described in Section 4.3.4-ShowFlows of [7]. The scenario is a 4:1 oversubscribed FatTree where each host sends to one other host. One-third of the hosts send a continuous flow by using either TCP, MPTCP with LIA (8 subflows) or with OLIA (8 subflows). The remaining hosts send short flows of size 70Kbyte every 200ms on average (they generate these flows according to a Poisson process). They use regular TCP. This is a highly

algorithm	Short flow finish time (mean/stdev)	Network core utilization
MPTCP - LIA	98 ± 57 ms	63.2%
MPTCP - OLIA	90 ± 42 ms	63%
Regular TCP	73 ± 57 ms	39.3%

Table 3: Performance of OLIA in a highly dynamic setting. It uses the available capacity as efficient as LIA, but decreases the average completion time of short flows by 10%.

dynamic setting in which changes occur in the order of milliseconds. Table 3 shows the average completion time for short flows and the network core usage. Figure 14 shows the distribution of completion times of short flows. Our results show that although OLIA uses the available capacity as efficiently as LIA, the average completion time of short flows decreases by 10% using OLIA. Moreover, we observe in Figure 14 that OLIA decreases the completion time of both fast and slow short flows. For slow flows, the decrease is more than 25%. This shows that OLIA has a better responsiveness than LIA, is more fair to TCP users, and uses capacity quickly when it is available. With TCP, we have a lower average completion time for short flows, but very low network utilization.

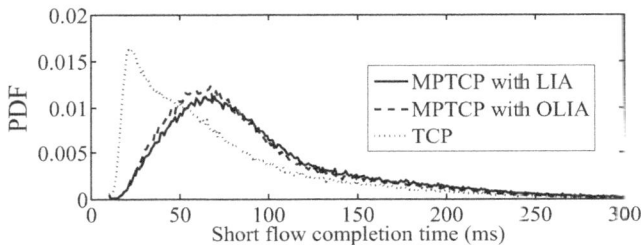

Figure 14: Completion time of short flows competing with long-lived TCP, MPTCP with LIA, or MPTCP with OLIA flows in a highly dynamic setting. OLIA reacts faster to the changes in the network and is fairer toward short flows.

7. CONCLUSION

We have shown that MPTCP with LIA suffers from important performance issues. Moreover, it is possible to build an alternative to LIA, which performs close to an optimal algorithm with probing cost while being as responsive and non-flappy as LIA. Our theoretical results show that our proposed algorithm, OLIA, is Pareto-optimal and satisfies the three design goals of MPTCP [10]. Moreover, we have shown through measurements and by simulation that OLIA is as responsive and non-flappy as LIA, and that it solves identified problems with LIA.

Multiple directions could be explored to go further. A first one would be to act on the minimum probing traffic rate by an adjustment of the retransmit timer – in our current implementation, the minimum window size is 1 and the minimum probing rate is $1/rtt_r$. Another direction comes from the fixed point analysis of Theorem 3. The stability and convergence of OLIA is another important question that will be studied in future work.

8. REFERENCES

[1] M. Allman, V. Paxon, and E. Blanton. Tcp congestion control. In *RFC 5681*, September 2009.

[2] F.P. Kelly. Mathematical modelling of the internet. *Mathematics unlimited-2001 and beyond.*

[3] F.P. Kelly, A.K. Maulloo, and D.K.H. Tan. Rate control for communication networks: shadow prices, proportional fairness and stability. *Journal of the Operational Research Society*, 49, 1998.

[4] F. Kelly and T. Voice. Stability of end-to-end algorithms for joint routing and rate control. *ACM SIGCOMM CCR*, 35, 2005.

[5] H. Han, S. Shakkottai, CV Hollot, R. Srikant, and D. Towsley. Multi-path tcp: a joint congestion control and routing scheme to exploit path diversity in the internet. *ToN*, 14, 2006.

[6] W.H. Wang, M. Palaniswami, and S.H. Low. Optimal flow control and routing in multi-path networks. *Performance Evaluation*, 52, 2003.

[7] C. Raiciu, S. Barre, C. Pluntke, A. Greenhalgh, D. Wischik, and M. Handly. Improving datacenter performance and robustness with multipath tcp. *ACM Sigcomm*, 2011.

[8] D. Wischik, M. Handly, and C. Raiciu. Control of multipath tcp and optimization of multipath routing in the internet. *NetCOOP*, 2009.

[9] D. Wischik, C. Raiciu, A. Greenhalgh, and M. Handly. Design, implementation and evaluation of congestion control for multipath tcp. *Usenix NSDI*, 2011.

[10] C. Raiciu, M. Handly, and D. Wischik. Coupled congestion control for multipath transport protocols. *RFC 6356 (Experimental)*, 2011.

[11] A. Ford, C. Raiciu, M. Handley, S. Barre, and J.Iyengar. Architectural guidelines for multipath tcp development. *RFC 6182 (informational)*, 2011.

[12] A. Ford, C. Raiciu, M. Handley, and O. Bonaventure. Tcp extensions for multipath operation with multiple addresses. *IETF Internet Draft*, 2011.

[13] C. Cetinkaya and E.W. Knightly. Opportunistic traffic scheduling over multiple network paths. In *INFOCOM*, 2004.

[14] M. Zhang, J. Lai, A. Krishnamurthy, L. Peterson, and R. Wang. A transport layer approach for improving end-to-end performance and robustness using redundant paths. In *USENIX*, 2004.

[15] M. Honda, Y. Nishida, L. Eggert, P. Sarolahti, and H. Tokuda. Multipath congestion control for shared bottleneck. In *PFLDNeT workshop*, 2009.

[16] E. Kohler, R. Morris, B. Chen, J. Jannotti, and M. F. Kaashoek. The click modular router. *ACM Trans. Comput. Syst.*, 18, 2000.

[17] V. Misra, W.-B. Gong, and D. Towsley. Fluid-based analysis of a network of AQM routers supporting TCP flows with an application to RED. In *SIGCOMM*, 2000.

[18] R. Khalili, N. Gast, M. Popovic, U. Upadhyay, and J.-Y. Le Boudec. Non pareto-optimality of mptcp: Performance issues and a possible solution. *EPFL Technical report. Available at http://infoscience.epfl.ch/record/177901*, 2012.

[19] http://mptcp.info.ucl.ac.be/.

[20] V. Jacobson. Congestion avoidance and control. In *ACM SIGCOMM CCR*, volume 18, 1988.

[21] N. Gast and B. Gaujal. Mean field limit of non-smooth systems and differential inclusions. *ACM SIGMETRICS Performance Evaluation Review*, 38(2):30–32, 2010.

[22] N. Gast and B. Gaujal. Markov chains with discontinuous drifts have differential inclusion limits. *Performance Evaluation*, 2012.

[23] S. Ha, I. Rhee, and L. Xu. Cubic: A new tcp-friendly high-speed tcp variant. *ACM SIGOPS Operating Systems Review*, 42, 2008.

[24] T. Kelly. Scalable tcp: Improving performance in highspeed wide area networks. *ACM SIGCOMM CCR*, 33, 2003.

[25] S. Kunniyur and R. Srikant. End-to-end congestion control schemes: Utility functions, random losses and ecn marks. *ToN*, 11, 2003.

APPENDIX

We provide sketches of proofs for the results in Section 5. Detailed proofs are available in [18], Appendices E to H.

A. SKETCH OF PROOF (THEOREM 1)

Proof of (i). Let x be a non-degenerate fixed point of OLIA. For any path $p \in \mathcal{R}_u$, the equation dx_p/dt contains two terms, denoted term A and term B in the next equation:

$$0 = \frac{dx_p}{dt} = x_p^2 \underbrace{\left(\frac{1/\text{rtt}_p^2}{(\sum_{s \in \mathcal{R}_u} x_s)^2} - \frac{p_p}{2} \right)}_{\text{term } A} + \underbrace{\bar{\alpha}_p}_{\text{term } B} . \quad (10)$$

Assume that there exists a non-best path $r \notin \mathcal{B}_u$ such that $x_r > 0$. We show that this leads to a contradiction.

Equation (10) shows that the term A is positive for r and hence is strictly positive for any best paths (by definition of best path). If $\mathcal{B}_u \cap \mathcal{M}_u \neq \emptyset$, there exists a best path p with maximum window size. Thus, we have $x_p \neq 0$, which implies that $dx_p/dt > 0$ as α_p is non-negative. If $\mathcal{B}_u \cap \mathcal{M}_u = \emptyset$, then there exists $p \in \mathcal{B}_u$ such that $\alpha_p > 0$, which implies that $\alpha_p > 0$ and thus $dx_p/dt > 0$. In both cases, we have $dx_p/dt > 0$ which contradicts that $dx_p/dt = 0$.

This shows that for any non-best path $r \notin \mathcal{B}_u$, we must have $x_r = 0$.

Proof of (ii). Because of (i), we have $\bar{\alpha}_r = 0$ for all routes $r \notin \mathcal{B}_u$. Thus, we can show that $\bar{\alpha}_r = 0$ for all paths $r \in \mathcal{R}_u$. Therefore, any fixed point x satisfies $x_r = 0$ or $\sum_{p \in \mathcal{R}_u} x_p = 1/\text{rtt}_r \sqrt{2/p_r}$. By assumption, x is non-degenerate, which means that there exists a route $r \in \mathcal{R}_u$ such that $x_r \neq 0$. This concludes the proof of (ii). □

B. SKETCH OF PROOF (COROLLARY 2)

Point (ii) of Theorem 1 implies that OLIA satisfies goal 1: the total rate that OLIA gets ($\sum_{r \in \mathcal{R}_u} x_r$) is the same as the rate that a regular TCP would get on its best link ($\max_{r \in \mathcal{R}_u} \sqrt{2/p_r}/\text{rtt}_r$). Moreover, as OLIA only uses its best paths, it does not transmit more than a regular TCP does on any of its paths and satisfies goal 2. Finally, as OLIA only uses its best path, it perfectly balances congestion and satisfies goal 3. □

C. SKETCH OF PROOF (THEOREM 3)

Let x^* be a fixed point of the algorithm and define the utility function $V^*(x)$ as

$$\sum_{u \in \text{users}} -\frac{1}{\tau_u^2 \sum_{r \in \mathcal{R}_u} \frac{x_r}{\text{rtt}_r^2}} - \frac{1}{2} \sum_{\ell \in \text{links}} \int_0^{\sum_{r \in \ell} x_r} p_\ell(x)dx, \quad (11)$$

where τ_u is defined by: $\tau_u = (\sum_{r \in \mathcal{R}_u} x_r^*)/(\sum_{r \in \mathcal{R}_u} x_r^*/\text{rtt}_r^2)$.

The function V^* is a non-positive function that goes to $-\infty$ when $x \to \infty$. Therefore, it has a maximum, attained for a finite x. By concavity of V^*, a necessary and sufficient condition for a point x to be a maximizer of $\mathcal{U}$ is that for every route r, we have

$$\frac{\partial V^*}{\partial x_r}(x) \leq 0 \quad \text{and} \quad \frac{\partial V^*}{\partial x_r}(x) = 0 \text{ or } x_r = 0.$$

By the definition of V^* and Theorem 1, the fixed point x^* is a maximum of V^*. Since V^* is an increasing function of $\sum_{r \in \mathcal{R}_u} x_r/\text{rtt}_r^2$ and a decreasing function of the congestion cost, it is impossible to increase $\sum_{r \in \mathcal{R}_u} x_r/\text{rtt}_r^2$ for some users without decreasing it for others or increasing the congestion cost. □

D. SKETCH OF PROOF (THEOREM 4)

Theorem 4 assumes that all the paths belonging to user u have the same round trip time rtt_u. In that case, the function V is the same as V^* of Equation 11 with $\tau_u = \text{rtt}^2$.

Let x be one of the solutions of the differential inclusion given by Equation (8). Then, there exists a function $\bar{\alpha}(t)$ satisfying Equation (9) for all t and such that dx_r/dt satisfies Equation (8).

When running the algorithm, the derivative of $V(x(t))$ w.r.t. time satisfies $dV/dt = \sum_{u,r}(\partial V/\partial x_r)(dx_r/dt)$. Thus:

$$\frac{d}{dt} V(x(t)) = \sum_{u \in \mathcal{U}} \sum_{r \in \mathcal{R}_u} \frac{\partial V}{\partial x_r} \frac{dx_r}{dt}$$

$$= \sum_r \left(\frac{1}{\text{rtt}_u^2 (\sum_{r \in \mathcal{R}_u} \frac{w_r}{\text{rtt}_u})^2} - \frac{p_r}{2} \right)$$

$$\cdot \left(\frac{w_r^2}{\text{rtt}_u} \left(\frac{1}{(\sum_{p \in \mathcal{R}_u} w_p)^2} - \frac{p_r}{2} \right) + \frac{\alpha_r}{\text{rtt}_u} \right)$$

$$= \sum_{u \in \mathcal{U}} \sum_{r \in \mathcal{R}_u} x_r^2 \left(\frac{1}{\text{rtt}_u^2 (\sum_{p \in \mathcal{R}_u} x_p)^2} - \frac{p_r}{2} \right)^2 \quad (12)$$

$$+ \sum_{u \in \mathcal{U}} \sum_{r \in \mathcal{R}_u} \left(\frac{1}{\text{rtt}_u^2 (\sum_{p \in u} x_p)^2} - \frac{p_r}{2} \right) \frac{\bar{\alpha}_r}{\text{rtt}_u^2} \quad (13)$$

By definition of $\bar{\alpha}$, we have $\sum_{r \in \mathcal{R}_u} \alpha_r = 0$. Moreover, when all rtt are equal, the best paths are the paths with minimal probability loss and $\alpha_r \leq 0$ for such paths. Thus:

$$\sum_{r \in \mathcal{R}_u} \alpha_r p_r = \sum_{r \in \mathcal{B}_u} \alpha_r p_r + \sum_{r \notin \mathcal{B}_u} \alpha_r p_r \leq \sum_r \alpha_r p_{\min} = 0.$$

These two properties together show that the term (13) is non-negative. Since (12) is also non-negative, this shows that $dV(x(t))/dt \geq 0$ for all t. Thus, the function V is non decreasing. Since V is non-positive, this shows that $\lim_{t \to \infty} dV(x(t))/dt = 0$.

Let x^* be a limit point of $x(t)$. We show in [18], Appendix H, that x^* is a fixed point of the algorithm. Thus, by Theorem 3, it is a maximizer of V. □

Architecting for Edge Diversity:
Supporting Rich Services Over an Unbundled Transport

Fahad R. Dogar
Microsoft Research, Cambridge

Peter Steenkiste
Carnegie Mellon University

ABSTRACT

The end-to-end nature of today's transport protocols is increasingly being questioned by the growing heterogeneity of networks and devices, and the need to support in-network services. To address these challenges, we present Tapa, a transport architecture that systematically combines two concepts. First, it unbundles today's transport such that network specific functions (e.g., congestion control) are implemented on a *per-segment* basis, where a segment spans a part of the end-to-end path that is homogeneous (e.g., wired Internet or an access network) while functions that relate to application semantics (e.g., data ordering) are still implemented end-to-end. Second, it has an explicit notion of in-network services (e.g., caching, opportunistic content retrieval, etc) that can be supported while maintaining precise end-to-end application semantics. In this paper, we present the basic design, implementation and evaluation of Tapa. We also present diverse case studies that show how Tapa can easily support opportunistic content retrieval in online social networks, various mobile and wireless optimizations, and an in-network energy saving service that improves battery life of mobile devices.

Categories and Subject Descriptors

C.2.1 [**Computer-Communication Networks**]: Network Architecture and Design

Keywords

architecture, transport, services, middleboxes

1. INTRODUCTION

Today's Internet is much different from the original Internet of the 1970s. Many of these changes have occurred at the network *edge*, in the form of diverse Internet access technologies (e.g., blue-tooth, ultra-wide-band), edge devices (e.g., cell-phone, PDAs, sensors), applications (e.g., content sharing, gaming, sensing apps), services supported by the network (e.g., caching, mobile users), and the nature of network deployments (e.g., unmanaged residential wireless networks [5], data center networks [6]). Supporting this diversity often requires help from the network, which is hard given the "intelligent end-points, dumb network" principle underlying the Internet architecture. As a result, ad-hoc solutions, such as transparent proxies/middleboxes [9, 11], or CDNs are used; these solutions are complex to manage, fragile, and often violate one or more architectural principles of the Internet [24, 15].

As diversity at the edges is only going to increase in the future, it is critical that we develop architectural mechanisms – rather than point solutions – to accommodate it in the Internet architecture. To this end, we introduce Tapa, a transport architecture that systematically supports rich in-network services on top of an unbundled transport.

The unbundling process moves several functions out of today's end-to-end transport into *segments*. Segments span a portion of the end-to-end path that can be considered homogeneous. Some possible segments include: the "wired Internet", a private network owned by an enterprise, or a wireless mesh network. Each segment provides *best effort data delivery service* to the upper layer – functions that may be required to provide this service (e.g., routing, error control, congestion control, etc) are internal to the segment and hidden from higher layers.

On top of segments is the *transfer* layer, which supports end-to-end data transfers overs multiple segments, similar to how IP supports connectivity in today's Internet. The transfer service runs on both the end-points and network elements, called Transfer Access Points (TAPs), that interconnect segments. In Tapa, the transfer and higher layers work at the granularity of ADUs [13] rather than byte streams or packets. The use of ADUs simplifies the deployment of in-network services, making it easy to leverage advances in technology (e.g., cheap in-network storage).

Finally, the *session* layer implements specific end-to-end application semantics over the transfer layer. The presence of the segment layer makes the session layer lightweight, isolating it from the details of specific network technologies thus making it easier to support heterogeneity in the system. The introduction of segments, combined with the use of ADUs, means that it is easier to implement end-to-end protocols with diverse semantics required by different types of applications (e.g., fully reliable, streaming applications, etc.) It also becomes easier to insert services into the end-to-end path, while maintaining specific semantics between the end-points and the (possibly third party) network service.

Like most architectural proposals, several building blocks used in Tapa are inspired by prior work, including DTNs [23], middleboxes [38], proxies for wireless and mobile users [9], and data/content oriented networking [37] to name a few (See §6 for a detailed discussion on related work). Our core contribution lies in reusing their well understood benefits, modifying them to match our needs, and most importantly, *synthesizing* them in a new architecture.

Another important contribution of this paper is to demonstrate the flexibility of Tapa using three case studies (§4). In Vigilante, we show how Tapa can be used to efficiently disseminate content in online social networks, resulting in improved performance for end users and lower cost for the provider. In Swift, we leverage Tapa to provide various optimizations for mobile and wireless users, such as multiplexing multiple interfaces or optimizing data transfer in a mobile scenario. Finally, Catnap is an in-network traffic shaping service that leverages Tapa to provide significant energy savings to mobile devices.

Finally, as Tapa makes in-network services visible to endpoints, legacy applications need to be rewritten if they want to make full use of Tapa functionality. While this may prove to be a stumbling block towards the adoption of Tapa, we show that this modification effort is manageable. Moreover, our experiences also show that new segments and services can easily be deployed inside Tapa. We discuss these experiences in §5.

2. REQUIREMENTS AND CONCEPTS

We first discuss two key requirements that are important for a new transport architecture.

1. Accommodating Diverse Networks and Devices
The original ARPANET was designed to inter-connect heterogeneous networks and hosts. However, by today's standards, they were in fact fairly homogeneous. For example, it was assumed that links would provide "reasonable" reliability (< 1% loss rate) [12] and that all end-hosts would be powerful enough to support the full TCP/IP stack. The networks that make up the Internet now are very diverse, ranging from very high speed optical backbones, to low speed, unreliable wireless networks that have very different properties from wired links (e.g., higher error rates, variable bandwidth and delay), causing problems for end-to-end protocols such as TCP [9, 22]. Similarly, devices, such as sensors and mobile nodes, are highly resource constrained, compared with traditional endpoints. Dealing with the heterogeneity of devices and networks affects how we distribute functions across devices. For example, when applying the end-to-end argument [35], we can no longer view the communication subsystem as a *single homogeneous module*.

2. Accommodating network services Most applications in today's Internet benefit from diverse network services, e.g., web caching, video transcoding, various services provided by load-balancers inside data center networks, services for mobile and wireless users, etc [21, 34]. Unfortunately, inserting services in an end-to-end path is hard in today's Internet for two reasons. First, the data plane of existing protocols (IP and TCP) works with packets and byte streams, requiring tight coordination between applications and services on how to interpret the data (e.g., object size, naming). Second, and more importantly, TCP's end-to-end semantics are very rigid – they do not allow a role for an intermediary or accommodate different delivery semantics.

Limitations of existing solutions. Today, the above two requirements are addressed in an ad-hoc manner, bringing more complexity and rigidity into the architecture. For example, a common way to deal with network heterogeneity is to use the transparent split proxy approach, with different transport regimes/protocols on either side of the proxy (e.g., I-TCP [9], PEP [11]). Similarly, network services are typically hidden from the end-points (e.g., transparent web proxies) or deployed as overlays. This is not ideal, since there can be poor interactions with other services, like firewalls, and sharing services between applications, users and providers is hard. These hidden, stateful middleboxes also create new failure modes and make it difficult to support mobility (e.g., migrating VMs in a data center or clients in a mobile environment).

On the other hand, a clean solution that accommodates diverse networks and devices, in addition to supporting in-network services, can potentially provide substantial benefits to users, application providers, and network service providers. As we show in this paper, end users and application providers can get improved performance with robust communication semantics. Having visible in-network services can simplify the job of the ISPs, making it easier to deploy new services, including having an explicit role as an advertiser. Moreover, they can also reduce their costs with the use of content centric features supported by Tapa.

2.1 Key Concepts

We now present the two key concepts that form the basis of the Tapa architecture and help in meeting the above requirements.

We unbundle today's transport to better accommodate the needs of heterogeneous networks and in-network services. The unbundling process has both vertical (across layers) and horizontal (across the network topology) dimensions. As a first step, we propose *decoupling network regions with very different properties*, such that the properties of one region do not affect the other. For example, adequate in-network buffering can hide the losses that may be experienced in one region from the other region. Decoupling facilitates the deployment of customized solutions for each region as solutions designed for one region need not worry about the properties of other regions. Decoupling affects modularity of the system in the horizontal direction as it requires the network to support some functions (e.g., buffering). Moreover, nodes that implement decoupling can be used to insert additional functions (e.g., data oriented and higher level services) inside the network.

As a second step, we propose to *raise the level of abstraction that the network provides to the end-to-end layer that implements specific application semantics (e.g., TCP)* as this may make it easier to "hide" diversity at the lower layers. So other than the functions that must be implemented with the help of end-points [35] (i.e., specific application semantics) all other functions are pushed down, affecting modularity of the system in the vertical direction. This allows separation of concerns: the lower half of transport can focus on network specific challenges (with the help of the network) while the upper half of transport can focus on the semantics of applications and higher level services.

The first concept, specifically the notion of decoupling, leads to our second concept: *rich, visible in-network services*. We propose that these services operate at the granularity of

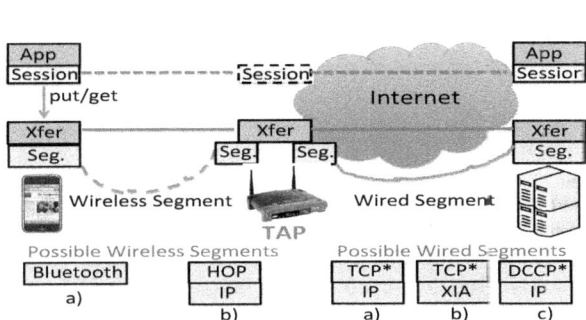

Figure 1: Tapa Overview.

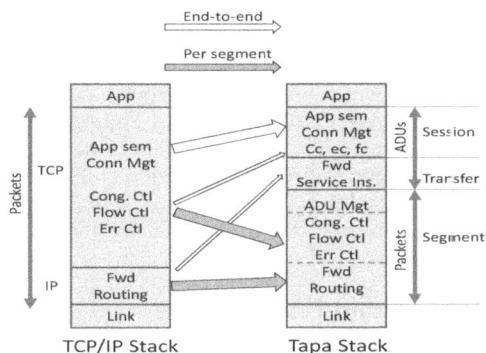

Figure 2: Comparison of protocol stacks.

ADUs, which can be defined by applications to meet their needs. For example, an ADU can correspond to a file (e.g., Catnap[20]), a chunk within a file (e.g., DOT[37]), or an MPEG frame in a video transfer. ADUs can be identified using self-certifying labels i.e., the ADU identifier is a hash of the content [37]. This enables several data-oriented optimizations, such as opportunistically fetching content from arbitrary sources. In addition to the identifier, we also associate *hints* with an ADU, such as possible sources from which the ADU can be retrieved etc. As our case studies show, ADU based services play a central role in enabling applications to benefit from content centric functionality inside the network.

3. TAPA

We introduce Tapa, or TAP-based Architecture, which synthesizes the above two concepts into a coherent architecture. As a result of unbundling, most of the traditional transport functions are put inside the *segment* abstraction. As segments provide a best effort service to the higher layers (i.e., they deliver data with high probability, but delivery is not guaranteed), they appear as Internet-style "links" to the higher layers.

Figure 1 illustrates a typical end-to-end data transfer in Tapa consisting of two segments (wired and wireless). Similar to how IP supports connectivity in today's Internet, Tapa's *transfer* layer supports end-to-end transfer of application data units (ADUs) [13] over multiple segments. It supports two modes of ADU transfers: a push mode, which is useful for interactive applications (e.g., gaming, video conferencing, etc) and a pull mode, which is useful for data oriented applications as it allows an ADU to be retrieved from potentially any source based on the ADU identifier. Finally, a light weight *session* layer implements specific application semantics related to four functions: reliability, data ordering, confidentiality, and data integrity. It can support traditional semantics (e.g., end-to-end reliability, data ordering, etc) or richer semantics involving intermediate services (e.g., delegation).

Figure 2 shows how the transport functions that are currently bundled in TCP are distributed across the Tapa layers. The end-to-end application semantics and connection management function are placed in the session layer. Some connection management is also needed as part of the segment layer. The flow, error, and congestion control functions are distributed over the segment and the session layers. In the session layer, these functions are lightweight because they only have to operate over a limited number of segments/hops.

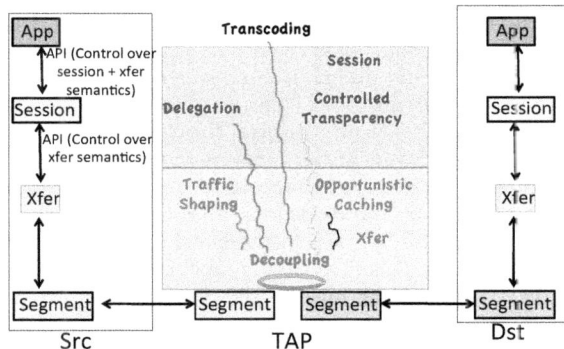

Figure 3: Different types of services in Tapa.

In the segment layer, the functions can be very lightweight (e.g., a point-point wireless link), or complex (i.e. an Internet segment). For Internet segments, this means that we can view Tapa as an overlay, as the segment layer can be broken up into an ADU management layer on top of a TCP (or TCP-like) and IP layers, as suggested by the dashed lines. For single-link segments, Tapa can be viewed as running native, as IP or transport functions are not required.

We now elaborate on the role of services, followed by a discussion on routing and addressing. Finally we describe each of the three layers of Tapa in detail. To illustrate the key functionality, we make use of a running example where a mobile and wireless user, Alice, uses Tapa to communicate with a fixed host over the Internet (similar to Figure 1).

3.1 Services

As shown in Figure 3, Tapa can support various types of services at the transfer and higher levels of the system. Transfer services enhance the data transfer function without affecting the typical end-to-end application semantics. The most basic example is a *decoupling* service that isolates one segment from the other by providing adequate buffering at the TAP. We can also deploy various data oriented services such as application independent caching at TAPs, which can help mask disruptions for mobile users (Swift, §4.2) or by acting as a storage service for content distribution (Vigilante, §4.1). Similarly, we can also have a traffic shaping service that can allow end-devices to sleep by temporarily buffering data (Catnap, §4.3).

Session-level services support end-to-end communication semantics that may be requested by the application. Examples include helping with error recovery for reliable data transfer semantics (i.e., delegation), or an in-network service inspecting encrypted data for performance or policy reasons (i.e., a form of controlled transparency [14]). We provide examples of several such services in §3.5. Finally, application-level services can provide application specific functionality, such as transcoding.

3.2 Routing and Addressing

Today's transport protocols (e.g., TCP) use IP addresses to identify communicating end-points and it is the responsibility of the underlying network layer (i.e., IP) to provide reachability to these identifiers. As IP identifiers are tied to a specific location/address, their use as identifiers makes it difficult for transport protocols to deal with mobility.

For Tapa, mobility is a common use-case, so instead of relying on ad-hoc solutions, the architecture should handle mobility in a graceful fasion. Consequently, similar to many other achitectural proposals [36, 38], Tapa requires that identifiers should be separate from locators, so even if an end-point moves, its identifier remains the same.

Similar to several recent proposals [8, 26], Tapa uses self-certifying flat labels as identifiers, although other options that also distinguish between locators and identifers can also be considered [27]. A self-certifying label corresponding to a host corresponds to the hash of the public key of the host. We can also have similar certifying labels to identify services and content [26]. The use of self-certifying identifers provides several desirable security properties, such as host/service authentication and data integrity verification [8, 26].

Host/Content identifiers are provided by the application and passed down to the segment protocol which is responsible for routing on these identifers. While routing on flat-labels is still a challenging problem, we rely on prior and ongoing work that aims to provide practical solutions to this problem [8, 26]. For example, XIA adds a topological identifier (i.e., identifer of the autonomous domain) to the host identifier to form the host address.

A related question is the role of TAPs in routing. We note that TAPs are not required for end-to-end reachability – even without TAPs, applications can still communicate directly by establishing a direct segment between end-points. However, we still need a TAP discovery mechanism if we want to make use of TAPs and the services they offer. While we leave the design of a generic TAP and service discovery protocol for future work, we do discuss some point solutions that we have built as part of the case-studies, and also point out relevant solutions from prior work. This includes TAP discovery that uses help from lower layers (e.g., similar to AP discovery in WiFi) as is the case in Swift (§4.2), making use of social network information (Vigilante - §4.1), via service discovery protocols [3], resolution services [38], or the application providing this information (e.g., as part of the end-point address, similar to a DAG-based address in XIA [26]).

3.3 Segment Layer

The segment layer is responsible for transferring ADUs across a segment, e.g., client - TAP or TAP - server. Segments can choose the data granularity they use internally (e.g., frames, bytes, etc.) allowing them to optimize communication as appropriate. Segment endpoints do not move, so they *can* use network-specific locators as addresses. For example, in the wired Internet IP addresses based on CIDR may provide the necessary scalability, while MAC addresses may be more appropriate in wireless networks.

The segment layer must be able to translate the identifiers corresponding to the TAPs and end-points into "locators" that can be used to establish the segments; locators may only have meaning locally within a network, i.e. they do not have to be globally unique. Higher layers of Tapa use identifiers and it is the responsibility of the segment layer to resolve them internally to locators. This can be done using either a name service (e.g., DNS for wired Internet segments), or a locally maintained mapping (e.g., MAC addresses for a bluetooth based segment).

3.3.1 Basic Operations and API

As shown in Table 1, the segment API allows higher layers to transfer ADUs across a segment. Similar to today's Internet, the segment layer supports a push model. Senders use a **send** call while receivers **register** a callback to receive incoming ADUs.

Recall that the basic motivation behind segments is to decouple different types of networks in an end-to-end path and to make them fairly homogeneous, so that higher layers need not worry about network specific functions. To achieve this, segments must implement error, flow, and congestion control as needed. Tapa's transfer service expects segments to be *reasonably* reliable, but segments can use very different ways for achieving that, e.g. TCP style retransmissions and ACKs over wired segments versus in-network coding or opportunistic forwarding and block acknowledgments on a wireless segment [30, 10]. Segments reassemble ADUs and deliver them to the transfer layer. In some scenarios, applications may want to send or receive ADUs piecewise for performance reasons; we give an example in §4.3.

The benefit of tailoring the congestion control algorithm to the type of network has similarly been recognized [9, 30]. Some segments may need specialized routing protocols for delivering data over multiple hops within a segment (e.g., wired Internet or mesh network). Some segments (single hop, point-to-point) may not require routing or congestion control. The important point to note is that all these mechanisms are hidden from the transfer and session layers, which focus on application oriented functions.

Figure 1 shows some possible ways to implement these functions for wired and wireless segments. On the wired side, we can use variants of existing transport protocols (e.g., TCP, DCCP) over different network layers (IP, XIA [26]), while on the wireless side we can use completely different protocols. In §5.2, we describe various segment protocols that we use in the Tapa prototype.

Alice and the segment layer: Alice can use various segment protocols on the wireless side. If she is connected to a wireless mesh network, she can use a segment protocol like HOP [30], which relies on per-hop mechanisms for reliability and rate control. She can also bypass IP and traditional link layers, using options as diverse as blue-tooth or wireless USB. This is a direct benefit of raising the level of abstraction – not all networks and devices need to implement heavy-weight functions of TCP/IP (e.g., congestion control) in order to be part of the Internet.

Function	Description
Session Layer Interface for Applications	
get(ADU-id, hint, src, session + xfer options)	Call used to pull an ADU.
put(ADU, dest, session + xfer options)	Call used to push/publish an ADU.
Transfer Layer Interface for Session/Higher Layers	
get(ADU-id, hint, src, xfer options)	Call used to pull an ADU.
put(ADU, dest, xfer options)	Call used to push/publish an ADU.
register(ID, handler)	services/apps registering with the xfer layer to receive ADUs destined to them.
Segment Layer Interface for Higher Layers	
send(ADU)	Call used to send the ADU across a segment
register(ID, handler)	registering to receive incoming ADUs

Table 1: Interfaces used at different levels of the Tapa system. Identifiers (e.g., src, dst, ADU id, etc,) are self-certifying labels. Session and xfer options are a list of (type, value) pairs.

3.4 Transfer Layer

The transfer layer is the "inter-segment" layer of Tapa and its role is somewhat similar to that of IP in today's Internet: providing a best effort data delivery service over multi-hop paths. There are however some differences in both the control and data plane. For example, Internet routing needs to establish routes in large scale but fairly stable networks; in contrast, the Tapa transfer layer establishes short (e.g., two-segment) paths but paths can be very volatile due to the dynamics of the edge network (e.g., mobility and wireless dynamics, volatility in data center networks). The introduction of a transfer layer allows for a separation of concerns. The segment layer can focus on the challenges associated with specific networks (e.g., scalability within core Internet) while the transfer layer can focus on dealing with higher level challenges (e.g. selection of segments based on content or service availability, or mobility).

3.4.1 Basic Operations and API

The service supported by the transfer layer is the transfer of ADUs based on a push/pull model as described below. The push and pull modes of the transfer layer are used by the higher layers through the put and get interfaces respectively. The same API is used by both the end-points as well as by services running at the TAPs. As shown in Table 1, the API takes in an ADU, which is mandatory, hint, src/dst, and *xfer options*, which is an *optional* list of (type, value) pairs that are used to provide more control to higher layers so that they can choose different transfer semantics, if they desire so. The semantics are optional – if they are not specified, default transfer semantics are used. We first describe the working of the two calls with default semantics and then elaborate on optional semantics.

Pull Mode: The get interface allows higher layers to retrieve an ADU based on its identifier, irrespective of which source or transfer mechanism (e.g., choice of segment or interface) is used to retrieve it. The flexibility means that the lower layers are free to choose any source, including local storage,

Applications can aid this decision by providing hints regarding hosts who *may* have the data (e.g., friends in a social network - see Vigilante (§4.1), or a previously used TAP in case of a mobile user – see Swift (§4.2)). We do require the higher layer to specify a source (src) that is *guaranteed* to have the ADU (e.g., a server), so hints are completely optional and are just intended as an optimization. The com-

bined use of a hint and src is somewhat similar to XIA's use of intent and fallback [26]: hints serve as optimization, but if they don't work (or are not provided) then the source is used to retrieve data. This ensures that data is retrieved even if the network cannot "route" on the ADU identifiers or the hints fail. Having the src information, in addition to the content indentifer, is a pragmatic decision given that scalable Internet-scale routing on flat content identifiers is still an open problem.

To inititate an ADU transfer, the transfer layer establishes an end-to-end path between the client and the server passing through the TAP(s). The underlying segment protocol can create a new segment or reuse an existing one, if one already exists. The ADU request is sent to the other end-point and data is returned as a result. In the typical scenario, the data plane of the transfer layer is relatively straightforward: TAPs read data from one-segment and write to the other, ensuring that adequate buffering is provided.

We can also have scenarios where segments may have high volatility or TAPs use more sophisticated services that change the typical behavior of the data plane (e.g., Catnap - §4.3). In such scenarios, suitable buffering at the TAP becomes critical for end-to-end performance. Our experience so far has been limited to various kinds of wireless segments and the challenges they pose for provisioning buffer space at the TAPs. In our case studies, we discuss how additional buffering at the TAP is used in various scenarios.

Finally, the get call returns the actual ADU or a failure notification if the ADU cannot be retrieved. Note that because the higher layers are letting the transfer layer make several transfer decisions, they are likely to observe fewer failures compared to using today's socket API because the transfer layer has more options for failure recovery.

Push Mode: The put interface is used to publish an ADU to a specific destination (dest), which could be a storage service (local or remote) or any other service running on a host. Applications can use this API to publish their data *once* and a generic storage/transfer service can later take care of serving it to future client requests (similar to DOT [37]). This enables temporal decoupling between the publisher and the consumer, so both of them need not be present at the same time. The push mode sends an ADU to a given destination, similar to how IP datagrams are pushed from a source to a destination. Its overhead is also comparable to that of sending UDP datagrams in today's Internet (see Figure 5.3).

A key reason for supporting a push mode is to facilitate real-time applications that cannot benefit from data oriented optimizations. Unlike the pull mode, which requires an extra round trip time for the ADU request, the push mode directly sends an ADU to the intended recipient. Even though Tapa's data oriented optimizations are not applicable in this mode, there are still benefits to using this mode compared to using today's protocols. For example, using appropriate segment protocols, instead of a single end-to-end transport, can provide better performance for real-time applications. We expect the push mode to be used in scenarios where the pull mode is not applicable, such as transferring dynamic data, publishing content or exchanging control messages. The protocol followed in the push mode works similar to the pull mode except that no ADU request precedes the data ADU.

Different Semantics: Higher layers can choose different transfer semantics by extending the basic get and put calls with (type, value) options. Some types that are relevant for the transfer layer include: TAP, service, and segment. Higher layer could use a specific TAP for its communication (e.g., an enterprise TAP for policy reasons) or it can specify a specific type of segment that should be used. For example, a "slow" segment could be used for background transfer of data that is not immediately required, thereby reducing the load on the server.

Alice and the transfer layer: Tapa's transfer layer can help a mobile user like Alice in several ways. First, it can improve performance of data transfers through caching and intelligent use of segments. Consider an example where Alice is downloading a large file from a slow server. Initially she is using her home TAP but in the middle of the download she moves to Starbucks. Her home TAP will continue to download ADUs from the server and cache them in its storage; after she moves to Starbucks, the transfer layer will re-establish a segment to her home TAP via the Starbucks TAP and retrieve the missing ADU (by re-issuing requests for the missing ADU ids). This will be a much faster option compared to going all the way to the slow server to retrieve the missing ADUs. Note that the get call is used for this purpose and the Starbucks TAP information is provided as a hint.

Second, ADUs and segments simplify the use of wireless optimizations that allow multiplexing of multiple interfaces or access points (TAPs in this case). Such optimizations are not only difficult to implement in today's Internet, but are also tied to a specific transport protocol (e.g., TCP) or specific underlying technology (e.g., WiFi) [28]. In Tapa, multiplexing of segments is naturally supported: the transfer layer decides an appropriate segment for each ADU, so for the same application, it can fetch some ADUs using one particular segment while other ADUs can be retrieved using a different segment.

Third, TAPs can pre-establish long-lived segments with popular websites or frequently accessed WAN locations, providing Alice low latency access for interactive communication. Alice will only establish a segment with her local TAP, which will be close-by in most cases, and the TAP will use a pre-existing segment to communicate with the other end-point, gaining vital latency savings on the long RTT part of the end-to-end path. Such techniques are already used by CDN providers to accelerate dynamic website access [2]; with Tapa, such techniques can be used at users' TAPs.

3.4.2 Resource Management

Although congestion control is implemented inside segments, the transfer layer also needs to ensure that TAP buffers do not overflow. We include this broadly under *resource management*, which includes congestion control across a multi-segment path as well as protection against malicious sources (e.g., DoS attacks)

Several Tapa features support a holistic approach towards resource management, enabling TAPs to consider a variety of techniques for congestion prevention, avoidance, and control. For example, Tapa's use of ADU hints, which include the length of the ADU, provides information to the TAPs about future traffic load, which can be used to do admission control. TAPs strategic location at network edges means that they can also coordinate with end-points to install filters against potential DDoS attacks, thereby acting as a first line of defense [31]. The limited number of segments in an end-to-end path means that it is easier for TAPs to coordinate amongst each other in order to avoid congested segments. For example, many techniques that are difficult to use in Internet settings, such as hop-by-hop flow control based on back-pressure (implemented in our prototype) or end-to-end congestion control based on feedback from the network, become feasible in Tapa.

3.5 Session Layer

Similar to IP in today's Internet, the segment and transfer layers offer a best effort service to the transfer and session layer, respectively. This means that they deliver data with high probability, but delivery is not guaranteed. The motivation for the best effort nature of the segment and transfer layers is the same as for IP [35], i.e., full network-level reliability is expensive and not always needed. So the reliability provided by the segment layer is purely a performance enchancement, similar to how, in today's Internet, we have reliability at the link layer (e.g., 802.11) despite having TCP's end-to-end reliability. This follows the end-to-end arguments [35], as lower layers of the system *may* have reliability for performance reasons, but we still need end-to-end reliability for correctness/robustness reasons.

Tapa's session layer provides reliability and other application semantics (e.g., ordering, confidentiality, data integrity, etc) to the end-points, albeit over a very short path consisting of a small number of segments. An important thing to note is that we can easily implement support for different semantics (e.g., partial reliability or out-of-order delivery) as the session layer need not re-implement network specific functions, like congestion control, which are coupled with application semantics in TCP. Another important consideration is that TAPs are visible to the end-points, opening the door for richer semantics that explicitly capture the role of services running on the TAP.

3.5.1 Basic Operations and API

The session API is similar to the transfer API; the only difference is that it takes additional options that are relevant to the session layer semantics. In our design, this includes semantics associated with the four functions discussed earlier: reliability, confidentiality, ordering, and data integrity. If applications do not specify any additional option then the default semantics associated with these functions are chosen. We now describe a specific session protocol that supports semantics associated with these four functions. We briefly present the traditional semantics as well as the new semantics that emerge with the use of in-network services.

Reliability: Applications can choose a fully reliable data delivery (default) or a best effort delivery service. We focus on the reliable delivery case because it is by far the most common use case. For a reliable service, the session layer holds on to the ADU until it is acknowledged by the other end-point. If required, the session layer has to undertake recovery in the face of different kinds of failures (e.g., TAP failure). These are the traditional end-to-end reliability semantics that are offered in today's Internet as well. However, because we also have reliability within segments, Tapa's session layer is likely to experience fewer failures compared to today's transport (TCP) and such instances are mostly limited to TAP failures. In §5.3.2 we quantify the overhead of such end-to-end recovery, showing that we can efficiently recover from TAP failures.

Tapa can also accommodate different reliability semantics where an end-point can *delegate* data transfer responsibility to an intermediate storage service. So even if the sender disconnects after completing the transfer to the intermediary, the transfer is not affected. In such scenarios, applications may be interested in differentiating between when the data is received by the TAP compared to when it is received by the end-points. Of course, this information can be used by the user or application in a number of ways. For example, the application may discard the data if it is received by the server but may like to hold on to the data if it is only received by the intermediary. Our implementation provides allows applications to choose the desired semantics from these different options.

Confidentiality: Tapa can make use of existing security protocols (e.g., SSL/TLS) to provide end-to-end confidentiality and data integrity. Moreover, it opens up new semantics that are not supported in today's Internet. For example, Tapa's use of ADUs allows applications more flexibility in implementing their confidentiality requirements as they can make fine-grained decisions on whether some data needs to be encrypted or not. The main benefit of Tapa, however, comes with the use of in-network services combined with the confidentiality semantics, allowing them to selectively look at certain data with the explicit permission of the application. This is important for both policy and performance reasons. For example, some intermediaries, like an enterprise or government, may require looking at certain types of data. We allow applications to explicitly state whether certain ADUs can be seen by intermediaries or not providing a form of "controlled transparency" [14]. So applications can hide ADUs that contain sensitive information, like credit card number or social security number, while allowing the company TAP to look at other data ADUs.

Similarly, the use of an intermediary with the confidentiality semantics can also result in performance benefits. One advantage is that it can reduce the burden of maintaining SSL connections for servers by shifting it to third party services running at TAPs. Specifically, the intermediary can maintain a *single* encrypted connection with the server and multiple clients can have their individual encrypted connections with the intermediary. Note that as the intermediary service could be provided by a third-party (e.g., an ISP), the semantics of this communication are very different from those of end-to-end encryption as the application/user is also trusting a third party and explicitly involving it in the confidentiality semantics.

Another advantage is that it can improve the effectiveness of redundancy elimination techniques, which are ineffective if the traffic is encrypted [7]. Specifically, applications/user can explicitly involve a trusted intermediary (i.e., ISP) in implementing confidentiality, such that the intermediary can decrypt the data as it enters its network, use RE techniques inside its network, and then encrypt the data again before sending it to the destination/next ISP. Of course, users will only choose weaker confidentiality if ISPs give them additional incentives to do so.

Data Integrity: In addition to verifying end-to-end data integrity, we also allow intermediaries to be involved in these semantics as there are scenarios where there could be legitimate reasons why an intermediary may change the bit-stream (e.g., transcoding, virus scanning proxies, etc). By explicitly involving the intermediary, applications can verify that the data was changed *only* by a legitimate party (i.e., the intermediary) and not by someone else. Data integrity is also closely tied to confidentiality as an application may allow intermediaries to look at the encrypted data but not to modify it (e.g., government or an ISP). With flexible data integrity and confidentiality semantics, applications can choose how an intermediary can read or modify the data.

Ordering: Tapa's use of ADUs helps the session layer in supporting different ordering semantics; these semantics determine whether the session layer presents these ADUs to the application in the same order in which they were generated by the other application end-point, or presented in the order in which they are delivered by the network. Of course, this is based on the assumption that the network does not provide any guarantee with respect to the ordering of ADUs. In fact, the use of Tapa may cause greater reordering compared to today's Internet because of Tapa's use of multiple segments for transferring ADUs.

Alice and the session layer: While Alice can benefit from all the rich semantics offered by Tapa's session layer, the one feature that is specifically useful for mobile users is *delegation*. Alice can benefit from delegation in the following way. Suppose Alice is chatting with her friend, with both users on the road, in a highly mobile setting. With end-to-end TCP, they can only communicate when both of them are simultaneously connected. Using Tapa's delegation semantics, the chat application can delegate the transfer responsibility to the TAP; in this case, both Alice and her friend would be interested in differentiating between whether their messages are actually received by the other end-point or just the TAP. Similar functionality is already offered by a popular messaging application, WhatsApp[1], which lets mobile users know whether their message was received by the intermediate server or the other end-device. With Tapa, any application can make use of this generic delegation service while maintaining correct semantics.

4. CASE STUDIES

We now present three case studies on how Tapa can be used to support diverse services. To support these services, we designed and implemented a proof-of-concept prototype of Tapa that focuses on the data plane of Tapa and a control plane that deals with two-segment paths: a wireless

---

[1]www.whatsapp.com

Vigilante
• put(ADU, serverAdd, reliability = "delegation", (first)segment = "fast", (second)segment = "slow")
• get(ADU-id, hint (friends), serverAdd)
Swift
• get(ADU-id, hint (previous TAP), serverAdd)
Catnap
• get(ADU-id, hint (ADU-length), serverAdd)

Table 2: Some sample API calls used in different case studies.

segment between the client and TAP and a wired segment between the TAP and server. We present the prototype evaluation in §5 while more details of the prototype design and implementation are available elsewhere [19, 17].

4.1 Content Distribution in OSNs

Online Social Networks (OSN) have massive popularity. Facebook (FB) alone has more than 500 million users spread all over the world. Supporting this huge scale is a major challenge for the OSN provider. Despite significant investments in network and data center infrastructure, ensuring a high quality user experience still remains challenging. In order to address the problem of scaling OSNs to billions of users, we have designed and prototyped Vigilante, a system that uses TAPs (e.g., home AP, media center, etc) for storing and distributing online social networking content.

Leveraging Tapa: Tapa facilitates the use of TAPs for storing and distributing OSN content. It provides support for *publishing*, *retrieving*, and *caching* content in an application independent manner. Social networking applications can *aid* these content centric functions of Tapa by providing *hints* or by pushing content in advance to suitable TAPs for performance or availability reasons.

Hints provide information to the TAP on the likely nodes that may have the required ADU in their cache. Hints can be generated and managed in a variety of ways. The simplest solution is to have application generated hints stored on a centralized server. For example, when Bob uploads content, it can include a hint that he is keeping a copy on his TAP. Similarly, after downloading Bob's photos, Lisa can store a copy on her TAP and notify the server. Alternatively, hints can also be managed in an application independent manner by Tapa, for example by having TAPs exchange information about the content (i.e., the self-certifying ADU identifiers) they are caching.

Tapa can also easily support a variety of roles for the TAP in the context of OSNs. In the simplest case, the TAP just maintains a cache of content stored at the server, as described above. However, it is possible to make the TAP the primary source of content, with the server simply keeping a backup copy. It is also possible to control when data is uploaded to the server, for example to reduce server peak loads. The precise role of the TAP can be controlled by the application by associating specific semantics with the transfer, using Tapa's API.

Photo Distribution in OSNs: As part of Vigilante, we have built a photo distribution application that allows users to publish and retrieve photos within a social circle. The working of the system is best illustrated through an example where Lisa wants to share her photos with her friends and

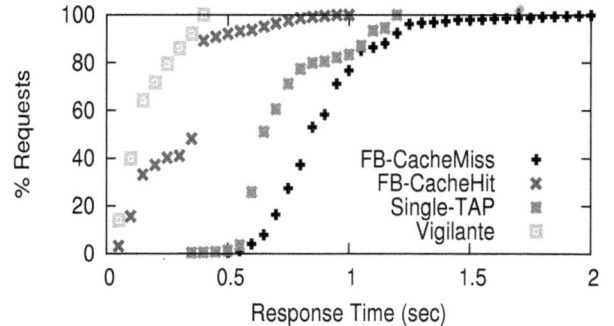

Figure 4: Performance comparison of various schemes for downloading photos.

family. Her social networking application uses Tapa's **put** API to publish the content to both the server and her home TAP. Data transfer from her device to the TAP is done using a normal/fast segment, while the data transfer from the TAP to the server is over a "slow" segment because the server only stores the data for backup purposes. All this is managed through a single put call by controlling the appropriate session and transfer semantics (see Table 2).

The application also sends the meta-data associated with the photo to the server. In addition to other things specific to the photo, the meta-data also includes the ADU identifier corresponding to the photo and information that it is cached at Lisa's TAP. When Bob later contacts the server to get his latest news-feeds, the meta-data corresponding to Lisa's photo is sent to his social networking application. As shown in Table 2, his application uses Tapa's **get** API, specifying the ADU identifier as well as a *hint* that it is likely to be available at Lisa's TAP. Bob's TAP will retrieve the ADU from Lisa's TAP, cache it and serve it to Bob's application. A notification is also sent to the server so that it can update the hints i.e., that Bob's TAP also has a copy of the photo. Later, when Julie wants to retrieve the photo, the hints contain information about TAPs of both Lisa and Bob, so Julie's TAP can choose the one that can provide the better service (we base this decision on the RTT between the nodes). As more users access the photos, more copies are created, helping load balance future requests and also improving the fault-tolerance of the system. A final point is that when Lisa first published the photo, it was also possible to pre-load some other TAPs using the same put API; this further improves the performance and fault-tolerance of the system.

Evaluation: We have conducted an evaluation of Vigilante on the PlanetLab testbed, using more than 150 nodes spread all over the world. We compare the performance of Vigilante with a more centralized design, such as the content distribution infrastructure used by Facebook. Note that Vigilante's performance is comparable to what we might get with a customized P2P based solution, so the key point of this case study is to highlight the flexibility of Tapa in supporting a diverse content distribution model without requiring any changes to the underlying mechanisms.

We run the client application as well as the TAP on the same node. We focus on the performance of photo downloads and consider four schemes/scenarios in this regard:

1. Vigilante: This refers to the implementation described in the previous section but without any pre-loading.

2. Single-TAP: Only the publisher's TAP, which is located in the US, serves the content. We test this scenario by disabling updating of hints.

3. FB-CacheMiss: This refers to downloading the photo from the root photo server of FB. This is the worst case performance with using FB.

4. FB-CacheHit: This refers to the case when the photo is served from the nearest Akamai CDN. This corresponds to the best case for downloading a photo from FB.

We present the results of an experiment under a non-bursty traffic load scenario. We generate a schedule where the consumers make requests to download a 80kB image in a sequential order at roughly 1 photo request per second. This schedule is repeated 10 times and the same process is followed for all four schemes. We present the results for clients who are located outside USA: they have a latency of at least 100ms with the publisher. On the y-axis, we have the CDF of client requests and on the x-axis we have the response times.

As shown in Figure 4, performance is poor for both Single-TAP and FB-CacheMiss as the consumer has to retrieve the content all the way from US, which adds considerable latency. On the other hand, both Vigilante and FB-CacheHit are able to find a nearby cached copy. However, we observed that non-US sites, in general, had a higher latency to the nearest Akamai/Facebook CDN compared to US sites and therefore Vigilante provides greater benefits for such consumers.

4.2 Mobile and Wireless Optimizations

Through Alice's example in the previous section, we have already explained how Tapa can help a mobile and wireless user. We have implemented Swift, a system that implements these various optimizations. Here, we present a proof-of-concept evaluation of Swift that focuses on the optimization of using multiple segments, as this single optimization shows the underlying flexibility that Swift offers. For example, the multiplexed segments could correspond to different protocols (e.g., one segment uses HOP while the other uses TCP), different underlying technologies (e.g., one bluetooth based segment and another 802.11 based segment), and different ISPs/service providers. We have used multiplexing of segments in the following ways: to aggregate AP uplink bandwidth, to aggregate throughput of multiple interfaces, for efficient hand-offs and to to mask failures in highly volatile scenarios (see [19, 17] for detailed experiments and results). As a proof-of-concept, we present results corresponding to the last use-case.

We consider communication between a vehicle and multiple TAPs and how use of multiple segments can mask short disruptions that are difficult to handle if we use a single segment for end-to-end communication. We use link level traces from a real world testbed at Microsoft's campus in Redmond [4]. We pick the two APs in the MS testbed with the best connectivity with the van and emulate their wireless channels. For the experiments, we use an Emulab style testbed that also offers a wireless emulator [1]. The van downloads a 10MB file from a server located over the Internet and having a 60ms RTT with the APs. We compare the performance of Swift with multiple segments (Swift-mult) with the scenario where only a single segment is used (Swift-single). We make 20 requests for each scenario and start times for the requests are randomly selected.

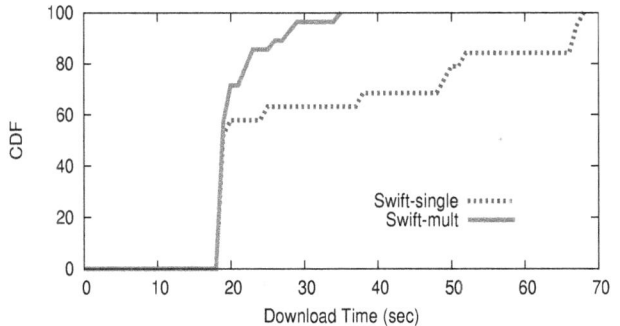

Figure 5: File Download Times in a Vehicular Communication Scenario. Use of multiple segments can mask disruptions that are common in such environments.

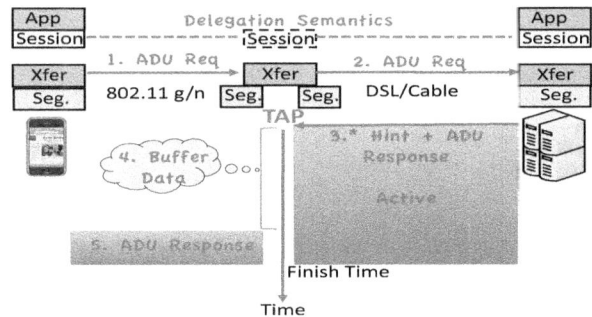

Figure 6: Overview of Catnap.

Figure 5 shows the cdf of the download times achieved in the two scenarios. Around 50% of the transfers do not experience any difference: these transfers are made during periods of good connectivity where there is no need to switch to the alternate segment. However, transfers that occur during bad periods experience severe performance degradation in the case of Swift-single whereas with Swift-mult switching to the alternate segment (if it is available at that time) significantly mitigates the performance degradation.

4.3 Energy Savings through Catnap

Catnap allows a mobile client to sleep *during* ADU transfers by intelligently shaping data before sending it over the wireless segment. Catnap targets settings where the wireless segment is much faster compared to the wired segment; in such scenarios, Catnap allows the wireless segment to remain inactive most of the time while still ensuring that the transfer finishes on time (Figure 6). During the time the wireless segment is inactive, the mobile device can enter into various sleep modes (e.g., 802.11 Power Save Mode, Suspend-to-RAM mode, etc), thereby providing significant energy savings to the mobile client. Catnap can provide up to 2-5x battery life improvement for real mobile devices under certain conditions [20].

Catnap can be viewed as a transfer service that leverages the key concepts of Tapa in the following ways. First, decoupling of segments, through use of different segment protocols and buffering at the TAPs, allows the wireless segment to remain inactive even though data continue to flow on the wired segment. This is not possible with end-to-end TCP as it relies on strict synchronization between end-points through the use of end-to-end acknowledgments. Second, the concept of ADU and associated hints (i.e., length in this case) allows the TAP to know when data will be *consumed* by the client application, so the initial packets of an ADU can be delayed as long as the finish time of the ADU remains the same.

If we consider Catnap in the opposite direction i.e., to upload data from the client to server, then we can see how richer reliability semantics at the session layer can be used to *delegate* transfer responsibility to the TAP. For example, in order to upload a large file to a server, the mobile client can burst the data to the TAP using the fast wireless segment, go offline, and the TAP can take over the responsibility of sending data to the server over the slow wired link.

5. PROTOTYPE EVALUATION

In this section, we present our experience of using various segment protocols and legacy applications with Tapa. We also present micro-benchmarks to quantify the overhead of using Tapa in various scenarios.

5.1 Supporting Legacy Applications

It is important to consider the effort required in developing applications that can leverage Tapa. We focus on modifying *existing applications* – which were not developed with Tapa in mind – as they represent the hard case. We modified the open source `Mozilla Firefox` browser to make use of Tapa API instead of sockets. Specifically, we created a Tapa stub that provided a socket-like interface to the applications and was used by the browser. This greatly simplified the browser modification process once the code was *separated* from sockets. Although there was a general separation of socket communication code and application logic, some of the browser optimizations violated this separation and made the modification process non-trivial. However, the modification effort required is still manageable. Our experiences, as well as earlier similar efforts [37], suggest that typically it is in the order of *1-2 weeks* for reasonably sized applications. Overall, despite the huge code base of the browser the changes made to the browser code were small and required approximately 200 lines of code (LOC)).

5.2 Supporting Diverse Segment Protocols

We now discuss our experience in adding different segment protocols to Tapa – as we expect customized segment protocols for different types of networks, it should be easy to implement and use these protocols within Tapa. In addition to TCP/IP, our prototype supports the following segment protocols:

HOP: HOP is a possible replacement for TCP in multi-hop mesh networks and environments involving mobility and disruption [30]. It runs between a client and a mesh gateway and expects some kind of decoupling at the gateway, so that a TCP-like protocol can work on the wired side for end-to-end transfers. We added a light weight stub (*50 LOC*) that removed the differences between the HOP API and the interface that Tapa expects segment layers to implement. Overall, it took roughly *20 man hours* to fully add support for HOP as a segment layer for Tapa.

Blast: We have specifically designed a protocol for 802.11 based single-hop wireless networks where TCP features, like congestion control and ACK based reliability, are often an over-kill. Blast is built on top of UDP – it offers no congestion

control, but provides light-weight reliability (in the form of NACKs) and flow control. The protocol was developed independently and later integrated with Tapa as a segment protocol, requiring approximately *10 man hours* for the integration effort.

Bluetooth: We also added support for Bluetooth RF-COMM transfer mode as a Tapa segment protocol. As this mode bypasses IP, it is an attractive option for small devices with limited capabilities who want to communicate over the Internet (through a TAP). The API exposed by the bluetooth library uses the socket API (unlike HOP). As a result it was straightforward to incorporate bluetooth as a segment protocol in Tapa, requiring approximately *5 man hours* and *20 LOC* for this task.

Performance: Table 3 shows performance of these different segment layers (with tcp on the wired side) in an end-to-end transfer. TCP, HOP, and Blast used WiFi on the Emulab testbed while the bluetooth (BT) experiment was on the emulator. The results show expected performance under the given conditions.

	TCP	HOP	Blast	BT
Xput	5.95Mbps	6.4Mbps	6.6Mbps	600kbps

Table 3: Download of a 10MB file with different segment protocols. End-to-end TCP throughput i.e., without Tapa, is roughly 5.9Mbps.

5.3 Overheads: Micro-benchmarks

Tapa offers several optimization but not every application can benefit from them, so it is important to consider scenarios where it may hurt to use Tapa. We therefore conduct micro evaluation to evaluate the overhead of using Tapa under a scenario where no optimization is used.

5.3.1 Performance Overhead

We consider a simple scenario involving a wireless client, TAP, and server. TAP and server are connected via a wired network – either LAN or WAN. We use TCP on both the wireless and wired segment. Also, even though Tapa allows reuse of segments which can eliminate connection set up delay, we disable this option for these experiments. This ensures a fair comparison with standard end-to-end tcp.

We compare the time required to complete a short request-response exchange in four different scenarios: `Tapa-ir` which refers to the mode where we push ADUs, `Tapa-pull` where we pull an ADU by first retrieving its id and then retrieving the data, `tcp` and `udp`. Figure 7(a) shows the results in a WAN setting with 80 ms RTT. `tcp` and `Tapa-ir` perform the same whereas `Tapa-pull` requires more time because of the extra RTT involved in making a request for individual ADUs. Figure 7(b) shows that even in a LAN setting Tapa does not introduce any noticeable overhead and performs similar to the underlying segment protocols that it uses (TCP).

The above results for messages as small as 70 bytes show that the extra overhead introduced by Tapa in the form of ADUs and TAP is negligible. It also shows that `Tapa-ir` is a useful mode that can be used by interactive applications with short messages. This analysis suggests that over stable wireless links, Tapa will perform as well as today's protocol stack for a wide range of applications.

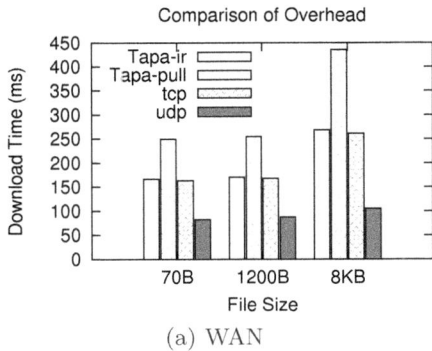

(a) WAN

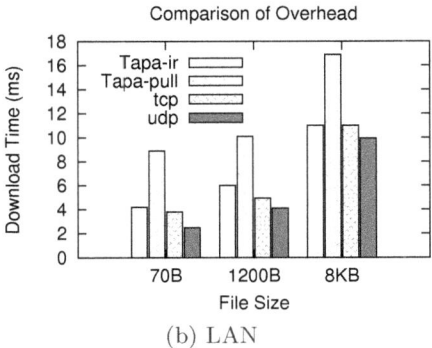

(b) LAN

Figure 7: Tapa adds negligible overhead in both LAN and WAN scenarios. For transfers larger than 1MB (not shown) all scenarios have similar performance.

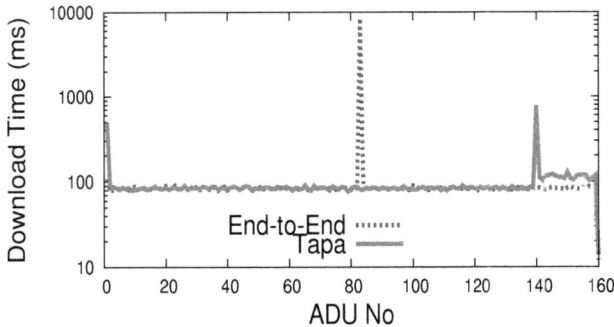

Figure 8: Case of TAP failure. Tapa recovers efficiently from TAP failures. Note log scale.

5.3.2 Reliability

As Tapa has to deal with ADU recovery in case of a TAP failure, we want to measure the overhead of this process. We use the LAN topology with tcp on both segments, and consider a scenario where the TAP fails after 15 sec and loses all its state. It comes up and starts serving the clients again after 5 seconds. This pattern is repeated and clients continue to make requests at random times for a 10MB file. We compare end-to-end tcp which naturally recovers from such AP failures with Tapa, where a TAP failure requires recovering the ADU that was being transmitted and all the ADUs that were yet to be transferred.

Figure 8 shows the download time for each of the 160 ADUs present in the file (note log scale). The spikes show the increased time that is required to download the affected ADU – during whose transfer the TAP failed. Note that as requests are made at random time we pick two typical runs (one each for Tapa and end-to-end tcp) that depicts how the recovery process works in both scenarios. In Tapa, the client discovers that the TAP is down (using absence of hello messages) and establishes another segment with an alternate TAP or waits for the old TAP to appear again. As the transfer service knows the ids of the missing ADU, it sends a new request to the server using the new TAP. As the graph shows, Tapa can recover efficiently from TAP failures.

6. RELATED WORK

Tapa's design is inspired by a large body of work, including the design of the original Internet, wireless and mobility related proposals, overlay networks, and proposals that deal with making middleboxes first-class citizens [12, 35, 9, 36, 18, 16]. We give a brief overview of the most relevant proposals, focusing on the key differences with Tapa.

Visible Middleboxes: Tapa shares the concern of earlier work that hidden middleboxes can be a source of problems, although we focus on "flow middleboxes" that carry transport state (e.g., proxies or other middleboxes that use different transport regimes for an end-to-end connection). This is different from proposals like NUTSS[25] and DOA[38] that deal with network level middleboxes, i.e., ensuring that middleboxes become part of routing and addressing and can therefore process packets (e.g., NATs, firewalls, etc).

The work that is most relevant is the proposal by Ford and Iyengar [24] who break-up the transport layer to accommodate flow middleboxes in the end-to-end path. Tapa provides a more general form of decoupling of segments, allowing use of non-IP protocols within a segment (e.g., XIP [26]). Another key difference is that Tapa uses ADUs and supports various ADU based services (e.g., pull mode of data retrieval).

Delay Tolerant Networks[23] provide a similar level of decoupling as Tapa, but their focus on arbitrary disruptions results in fundamental differences with Tapa. First, Tapa supports reasonably reliable, homogeneous segments whereas DTN regions provide either full reliability or no reliability. Second, DTNs only support push mode of transfers whereas the pull mode is an important mechanism in Tapa. Finally, DTNs do not have a notion of visible services that support new end-to-end semantics.

Overlays: Tapa is designed to be complementary to the Internet as it focuses on application/session semantics while Internet deals with network issues (reachability, forwarding, etc). As a result Tapa has very unique characteristics compared to traditional overlays. For example, Tapa's topology is highly constrained, so we do not need a complex routing protocol. Edge segments can be short-lived, which can result in very dynamic topology. Segments in Tapa mostly line up with network boundaries and as a result, Tapa segments may use very different technologies, e.g., IP on the wired segment and custom protocols on the wireless/data-center segment. Finally, the role of the two end-points (e.g., client and a server) is very asymmetric. All the differences require new mechanisms not found in other overlays.

Transfer Services and Data Oriented Proposals: Tapa's transfer service leverages several concepts used in DOT [37]. However, Tapa focuses on transfer services within

23

the network (TAPs) as well as end-points. Also, in order to provide rich end-to-end semantics, our transfer service is implemented *below* an end-to-end session whereas DOT works on top of existing transport layer protocols.

Recently, Popa et al [33] propose the use of HTTP as the narrow waist of the Internet, so it can be viewed as a transfer service. While the use of HTTP is certainly easier to use in the short-term, it is difficult to exploit many content centric and multi-path optimizations due to the inherent limitations of HTTP (i.e., naming, rigid semantics, etc), Moreover, we also define the roles of layers below and above the transfer service i.e., segment and session layers, which play a key role in the Tapa architecture.

Future Internet Architectures: Tapa's pull mode is inspired by data oriented architectures (e.g., CCN [27]), but there are important differences as we discuss below. First, unlike CCN, Tapa is not a "pure" content-centric architecture, so host and destination identifers are present in the packets even if we are retrieving an ADU based on its identifer. This results in different per-hop router operations as well as different failure modes in Tapa compared to CCN. Second, CCN operates at a per-packet granularity while Tapa uses ADUs. This difference mandates the need for different mechanisms to support traditional transport functions like congestion control, reliability, and data reassembly.

A better positioning of Tapa compared to CCN and other new network architectures is to view it as a transport architecture that can leverage these proposals as part of its segment protocol. For example, if Tapa is implemented over content centric network architectures [27, 26, 29], or service centric architectures [32, 26] then Tapa's transfer service can leverage the inherent features provided by these architectures for content/service routing. This will simplify Tapa's transfer layer and can also potentially improve performance due to late binding, native support for content/service discovery, and intrinsic security [26].

7. FINAL THOUGHTS

We presented the design, implementation, and evaluation of Tapa, a transport architecture that accommodates network heterogeneity and rich in-network services. Tapa unbundles today's transport and makes explicit use of in-network services that operate on ADUs. Our practical experience, as well as the case studies in this paper, confirms that Tapa offers great flexibility at multiple levels: customized solutions as segment protocols; diverse data oriented optimizations at the transfer level; and services with new semantics at the session level.

8. ACKNOWLEDGMENTS

We thank the anonymous reviewers, XIA team members, Ratul Mahajan, Ihsan Qazi, and Dina Papagiannaki for providing useful feedback on this work. This research was funded in part by NSF under award number CNS-1040801.

9. REFERENCES

[1] CMU Wireless Emulator. www.cs.cmu.edu/ emulator/.
[2] Dynamic site acceleration. http://www.akamai.com/html/solutions/dsa_curriculum.html.
[3] Service Location Protocol. RFC 2608.
[4] Vanlan. research.microsoft.com/en-us/projects/vanlan/.
[5] A. Akella, et al. Self-management in chaotic wireless deployments. In *MobiCom '05*, pp. 185–199. 2005.
[6] M. Alizadeh, et al. Data center tcp (dctcp). In *Proceedings of the ACM SIGCOMM 2010*, pp. 63–74. 2010. ISBN 978-1-4503-0201-2.
[7] A. Anand, et al. Redundancy in network traffic: findings and implications. In *Proc. of SIGMETRICS*, pp. 37–48. 2009.
[8] D. G. Andersen, et al. Accountable Internet Protocol (AIP). In *SIGCOMM*. 2008.
[9] A. V. Bakre, B. Badrinath. Implementation and performance evaluation of indirect tcp. *IEEE Transactions on Computers*, 46(3):260–278, 1997.
[10] S. Biswas, R. Morris. Exor: opportunistic multi-hop routing for wireless networks. *SIGCOMM CCR*, 35(4):133–144, 2005.
[11] J. Border, et al. Performance enhancing proxies intended to mitigate link-related degradations, 2001.
[12] D. Clark. The design philosophy of the darpa internet protocols. In *SIGCOMM '88*, pp. 106–114. 1988. ISBN 0-89791-279-9.
[13] D. D. Clark, D. L. Tennenhouse. Architectural considerations for a new generation of protocols. In *SIGCOMM*. 1990.
[14] D. D. Clark, et al. Addressing reality: an architectural response to real-world demands on the evolving internet. *SIGCOMM Comput. Commun. Rev.*, 33(4):247–257, 2003.
[15] D. D. Clark, et al. Making the world (of communications) a different place. *SIGCOMM CCR.*, 35(3):91–96, 2005.
[16] J. Crowcroft, et al. Plutarch: an argument for network pluralism. *SIGCOMM Comput. Commun. Rev.*, 33:258–266, August 2003. ISSN 0146-4833.
[17] F. R. Dogar. Architecting for diversity at the edge: Supporting rich network services over an unbundled transport. PhD thesis. 2012.
[18] F. R. Dogar, P. Steenkiste. M2: Using Visible Middleboxes to Serve Pro-active Mobile-Hosts. In *ACM SIGCOMM MobiArch '08*, pp. 85–90. 2008.
[19] F. R. Dogar, P. Steenkiste. Segment based internetworking to accommodate diversity at the edge. *Technical Report - CMU-CS-10-104*, 2010.
[20] F. R. Dogar, P. Steenkiste, K. Papagiannaki. Catnap: Exploiting high bandwidth wireless interfaces to save energy for mobile devices. In *ACM MobiSys*, pp. 107–122. 2010.
[21] F. R. Dogar, et al. Ditto: a system for opportunistic caching in multi-hop wireless networks. In *ACM MobiCom*. 2008.
[22] J. Eriksson, H. Balakrishnan, S. Madden. Cabernet: vehicular content delivery using wifi. In *MobiCom '08*, pp. 199–210. 2008.
[23] K. Fall. A delay-tolerant network architecture for challenged internets. In *SIGCOMM '03*, pp. 27–34. 2003.
[24] B. Ford, J. Iyengar. Breaking up the transport logjam. In *ACM Hotnets*. 2008.
[25] S. Guha, P. Francis. An end-middle-end approach to connection establishment. In *SIGCOMM*. 2007.
[26] D. Han, et al. XIA: Efficient support for evolvable internetworking. In *Proc. 9th USENIX NSDI*. Apr. 2012.
[27] V. Jacobson, et al. Networking named content. In *CoNEXT '09*, pp. 1–12. 2009.
[28] S. Kandula, et al. FatVAP: Aggregating AP Backhaul Capacity to Maximize Throughput. In *NSDI*. April 2008.
[29] T. Koponen, et al. A data-oriented (and beyond) network architecture. In *SIGCOMM '07*, pp. 181–192. 2007.
[30] M. Li, et al. Block-switched networks: a new paradigm for wireless transport. In *NSDI'09*, pp. 423–436. 2009.
[31] X. Liu, X. Yang, Y. Xia. Netfence: preventing internet denial of service from inside out. In *ACM SIGCOMM 2010*.
[32] E. Nordstrom, et al. Serval: An end-host stack for service-centric networking. In *Proc. 9th USENIX NSDI*. April 2012.
[33] L. Popa, A. Ghodsi, I. Stoica. HTTP as the narrow waist of the future Internet. In *Hotnets 2010*.
[34] S. Roy, et al. Application level hand-off support for mobile media transcoding sessions. In *NOSSDAV '02*, pp. 95–104. 2002.
[35] J. H. Saltzer, D. P. Reed, D. D. Clark. End-to-end arguments in system design. *ACM Trans. Comput. Syst.*, 1984.
[36] I. Stoica, et al. Internet indirection infrastructure. *SIGCOMM Comput. Commun. Rev.*, 32(4):73–86, 2002.
[37] N. Tolia, et al. An architecture for internet data transfer. In *NSDI '06*.
[38] M. Walfish, et al. Middleboxes no longer considered harmful. *OSDI*, pp. 215–230, 2004.

Tuning ECN for Data Center Networks

Haitao Wu, Jiabo Ju[*], Guohan Lu, Chuanxiong Guo, Yongqiang Xiong, Yongguang Zhang
Microsoft Research Asia
Beijing, China
hwu@microsoft.com, v-jiju@microsoft.com, lguohan@microsoft.com, chguo@microsoft.com, yqx@microsoft.com, ygz@microsoft.com

ABSTRACT

There have been some serious concerns about the TCP performance in data center networks, including the long completion time of short TCP flows in competition with long TCP flows, and the congestion due to TCP incast. In this paper, we show that a properly tuned instant queue length based Explicit Congestion Notification (ECN) at the intermediate switches can alleviate both problems. Compared with previous work, our approach is appealing as it can be supported on current commodity switches with a simple parameter setting and it does not need any modification on ECN protocol at the end servers. Furthermore, we have observed a dilemma in which a higher ECN threshold leads to higher throughput for long flows whereas a lower threshold leads to more senders on incast under buffer pressure. We address this problem with a switch modification only scheme - dequeue marking, for further tuning the instant queue length based ECN to achieve optimal incast performance and long flow throughput with a single threshold value. Our experimental study demonstrates that dequeue marking is effective for increasing the maximum incast senders close to the performance limit of ECN, achieving a gain anywhere from 15% to 140%.

Categories and Subject Descriptors

C.2.1 [**Network Architecture and Design**]: Network topology, Packet-switching networks

General Terms

Algorithms, Design

Keywords

TCP, ECN, Incast congestion, RED, Data center networks

---

[*]This work was performed when Jiabo Ju was an intern at Microsoft Research Asia.

1. INTRODUCTION

Data center networks are designed to support various applications [11, 8] and diverse traffic patterns [14]. Advanced topologies and structures [1, 13, 12] have been proposed to achieve higher bandwidth in data center networks. However, there have been some serious concerns about the TCP performance in data centers. For example, TCP incast congestion has become a practical issue in data center networks [22]. TCP incast occurs when many-to-one short flows are barrier synchronized by the applications. A recent study [22] shows that extreme high bandwidth and low latency, true of most data center networks, are preconditions for incast congestion. Moreover, without well-recognized service differentiation support, short-duration TCP flows will further suffer in the interaction with long-duration TCP flows [2]. Short flows require low queue occupancy for smaller task completion time while a large queue has been built up by long flows. A recent study [2] proposes a solution called DCTCP that requires both changing the switch ECN settings and modifying end server ECN in TCP stacks.

In this paper, we propose a further look at ECN implementation at the switches, and see if there is a way to address the above two TCP performance issues with a simple ECN tuning at the switch-side only. First, we have observed that the network latencies across data center networks are extremely low (under a millisecond). This has inspired us to study the use of instant queue length instead of average queue length in ECN. We hypothesize that, if instant queue length is used to trigger ECN, and if the threshold is properly tuned, ECN may actually alleviate the TCP performance impact without requiring end-host modifications. We use ECN* in this paper to denote such a scheme in which instant queue length based ECN is used at the switches and standard ECN congestion control is used at the end hosts.

The notion of using instant queue length to trigger ECN is not new. It has been proposed in previous literature, most recently in DCTCP to obtain the ratio of marked packets in [2], and to some extent to decouple ECN from Active Queue Management (AQM) in [15]. However, DCTCP requires modifying the end-point ECN implementation to make use of the new information, and it remains an open question on how to tune the ECN threshold for instant queue length to achieve a general buffer management scheme on commodity switches for TCP performance gains.

Through a brief analysis of TCP throughput, we discovered that the lower bound of the ECN* threshold is determined by the Bandwidth Delay Product (BDP). Our measurement in a real data center with 40,000 servers revealed that the TCP Round Trip Time (RTT) is hundreds of microseconds, which means the BDP can be as low as tens of kilobytes for Gigabit Ethernet. Furthermore, an ECN threshold based on a small BDP is already effectively supported by existing commodity switches. The preconditions for using ECN* are thus satisfied in data center networks.

Our experimental results show that ECN* achieves a similar performance to DCTCP on low latency networks when the ECN threshold is set by BDP. We believe that this clearly demonstrates the effectiveness of instant queue length based ECN, as ECN* only uses standard ECN[20] at the end servers. However, the results also reveal that there is a dilemma with the ECN threshold setting for both DCTCP and ECN*: a higher threshold leads to a high throughput for TCP long flows while a lower threshold is better for controlling TCP short flows on incast. We therefore designed a switch modification only approach to achieve the optimal performance of both long flows and incast using one threshold: ECN with dequeue marking. By checking whether instant queue length is over the ECN threshold when packets are dequeued, the marking of dequeued packets at the head of queue accelerates the congestion information delivery to the end system.

This paper has two key technical contributions. First, we give the threshold lower/upper bounds for ECN* and show a valid setting on commodity switches. Through our analysis, comprising latency measurements in a real data center and experiments in our tesbed, we have shown that ECN* achieves a similar performance to DCTCP for both short flows competing with long flows as well as incast in low latency data center networks. Second, we have solved the dilemma of setting the ECN threshold for instant queue length schemes, including DCTCP and ECN*. We have proposed, developed, and evaluated a switch modification only approach, namely dequeue marking, that achieves close to optimal incast performance for ECN using the threshold that leads to the high throughput of long flows.

The rest of the paper is organized as follows. Section 2 discusses research background. Section 3 describes ECN*. Section 4 presents dequeue marking. Section 5 presents experimental results. Section 6 discusses issues related to ECN. Section 7 presents related work. Finally, Section 8 concludes the paper.

2. RESEARCH BACKGROUND

2.1 TCP incast

TCP incast has been identified and described by Nagle et al. [18] in distributed storage clusters. In distributed file systems, the files are deliberately stored in multiple servers. When multiple blocks of a file are fetched from multiple servers at the same time, TCP congestion can occur at or near the receiver. This is called TCP incast. Several application specific solutions have been proposed in the context of parallel file systems. In data center networks, there can be many applications and TCP incast problem has become a practical issue [22, 2].

Figure 1 shows the incast goodput achieved on multiple connections versus the number of concurrent senders. Note that this paper uses the term goodput and throughput interchangeably to denote effective throughput obtained at the applications. The results are measured in a testbed as detailed in Section 5. The multiple TCP connections are bar-

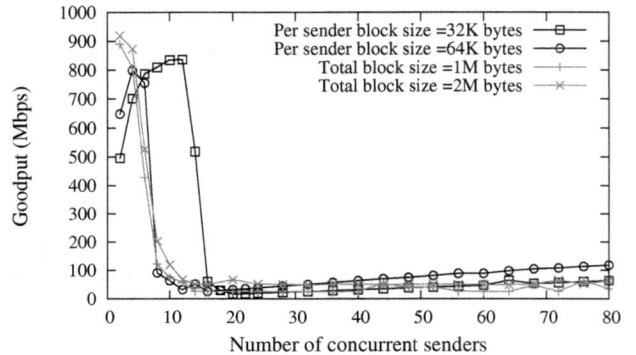

Figure 1: The incast goodput of multiple barrier synchronized TCP connections versus the number of senders.

rier synchronized in our experiments as follows. We first establish multiple TCP connections between all senders and the receiver respectively. Then the receiver sends out multiple small request packets (one per sender) to request each sender to transmit data. TCP connections are issued round by round, and one round ends when all connections in that round have finished their data transfer to the receiver. We present two setups for incast: 1) each connection has a fixed traffic amount with the number of senders increasing, as in [19]; 2) the total traffic amount of all connections is a fixed one, as in [22].

2.2 ECN

As an explicit congestion notification protocol, DECbit [21] is proposed to detect possible congestion at routers. A bit at data packet header is set by intermediate nodes to notify the congestion. When the receiver gets the marked packets, it echoes the information to the sender by marking another bit at the ACK. The sender then decides whether the congestion window should be cut by the ratio of marked ACKs.

Recent switches/routers follow the standard set by RFC [20] in implementing ECN for TCP, which is closely related to Random Early Detection (RED) [10]. RED addresses the global synchronization issue of multiple TCP connections sharing the same bottleneck link, which is caused by a large number of packet losses occurring when the drop tail buffer overflows. For ECN/RED, an average queue length is maintained at the switch, and two (low and high) thresholds for the average queue length are used. In RED, when the average queue length is between the two thresholds, the incoming packet is dropped with a probability capped by a parameter, namely the max drop probability. When the average queue length is over the high threshold, all incoming packets are dropped.

In ECN, the incoming packets will be marked on Congestion Experienced (CE) bits instead of being dropped. In contrast to RED, which works without changing TCP end points, ECN requires a TCP receiver to continuously pass the CE bits as ECE (ECN echo) bits to the TCP sender. The TCP sender then cuts the congestion window in half and marks the first new data with a CWR (congestion window reduced) bit to suppress the ECE bit from the receiver.

A TCP sender responds to the ECE bit only once for a window of data. Later studies have shown that RED/ECN may improve the performance of TCP if the parameters are properly set. However, the setting of the parameters are for the most part very subtle [9].

2.3 DCTCP

DCTCP[2] proposes changes to ECN to address the interaction of short and long TCP flows as well as TCP incast. DCTCP introduces two distinct features that differ from the ECN standard. First, DCTCP uses instant queue length at the switch instead of average queue length to trigger CE marking. Second, DCTCP cuts the congestion window at the sender in proportion to the ratio of CE marking. It does so by requiring the TCP receiver to echo the ECE for every packet (instead of per window of packets). If all ACKs are marked with ECE for a window of data, DCTCP cuts the congestion window size in half. To smooth the reduction of the congestion window, an exponential filter is introduced for the ratio of marked packets at the DCTCP sender.

The use of instant queue length combined with the use of only one threshold can greatly simplify the ECN setup on switches. The idea of using the ratio of marked packets (obtained by one-to-one mapping of ECE on ACKs) changes the binary feedback in ECN into multiple levels. In contrast to DECbit, which reduces the window when the ratio of marked packets is over a certain parameter, DCTCP cuts the congestion window using the value of half of the marked packets ratio. With these two changes, DCTCP can greatly improve the TCP performance with ECN enabled.

3. INSTANT QUEUE LENGTH BASED ECN

In this section, we present a generalized strategy for using instant queue length and a single threshold in ECN at intermediate switches. The scheme using instant queue length ECN with standard ECN [20] at the end servers is denoted as ECN*. We provide an analysis for the threshold setting and present the measurement results to show that existing data center networks are well within the operational region. As an example, we show that this strategy can be easily implemented in existing ECN-capable switches and it achieves similar results with DCTCP (but without end-system modifications).

3.1 ECN*

As already mentioned, instant queue length based ECN has been proposed in previous research to decouple ECN from AQM [15] and for frequent marking of the congestion state [2]. Here, we look at the instant queue length from a more generalized angle. Instant queue length represents the congestion window of all TCP connections sharing the same bottleneck. If the focus is to deal with temporal congestion caused by traffic burstiness, e.g,. incast congestion, a congestion control scheme like ECN can use instant queue length directly. Therefore, as long as the ECN threshold is set according to the window reduction taken by TCP, the TCP throughput performance will not be degraded.

Our generalized ECN strategy works as follows. At the intermediate switch/router, the instant queue length value is compared with a pre-configured threshold value whenever a packet is processed. If the instant queue length is greater than or equal to the threshold, the packet is marked with a CE bit at the IP header. The only configurable parameter that can tune the behavior of this scheme is the ECN threshold.

Our generalized ECN strategy does not make any assumption on the congestion control scheme used by the TCP sender and receiver to handle the marked packets, but we believe different schemes should achieve similar performance and have a similar tradeoff on parameter settings. The congestion control schemes include DCTCP [2], standard ECN as defined in RFC3168 [20], and DECbit.

We designate ECN* as the scheme that uses instant queue length and a single threshold at the switches and uses standard ECN[20] at the TCP sender/receiver.

ECN* is very well supported by today's commodity ECN-capable switches. First, ECN switches allow a weight parameter to adjust the exponential factor for updating the average queue length. By setting this weight to 1, the average queue length is effectively the same as the instant queue length because the values in the history are ignored. Second, ECN switches accept two threshold parameters, the low and high thresholds. By setting the two thresholds to the same value, they become one single threshold and the region in between the low and high thresholds is no longer in effect.

The support of ECN* at end-servers follows the ECN standard[20]. We assume that all packets are ECN-capable in data center networks and will discuss issues of non-ECN-capable packets suggested by the ECN standard [20] in Section 6.

3.2 Analysis of ECN*

We will now analyze the performance of ECN* when congestion occurs. We are interested in the parameter setting of the ECN* threshold, and seek to generalize it for future congestion control strategies deployed by the TCP sender/receiver. As standard ECN cuts the congestion window in half for a marked packet, we believe that the ECN* threshold serves as the upper bound for other schemes like DCTCP that decreases the congestion window more conservatively.

3.2.1 Lower bound of ECN* threshold

We analyze the lower bound for the ECN* threshold at which the TCP throughput performance won't be affected after the congestion window reduction by ECN. To simplify the analysis, we assume that the switch buffer size is large enough so that no packet is dropped due to buffer overflow. Additionally, we start with a case where there is only one TCP connection at the bottleneck link.

We assume that the connection is in a steady state, i.e., in congestion avoidance mode when an ACK with an ECE is received. The TCP sender then cuts its congestion window in half, which leads to buffer draining at the bottleneck link. To ensure that the throughput of this TCP connection does not degrade, the queue length at the bottleneck link should never drain to zero. Therefore, the TCP window saw-tooth phenomena is similar to the case described and analyzed carefully in [4] for switch buffer sizing. The difference is that in our case packets are not dropped after ECN threshold is reached. Instead, the packets are marked and delivered to the receiver. The marked ECE on return ACKs results in congestion window reduction, which is actually the same assumption made in [4]. Note that [4] does not consider a timeout caused by lost packets to simplify the analysis.

For ECN*, there is no timeout and no packet loss, which means that our case closely follows the previous simplified analysis for a drop tail queue with a buffer size the same as the ECN* threshold. Therefore, the ECN threshold h that won't affect TCP throughput is similarly obtained as that by the well-known rule-of-thumb for drop tail buffer size, i.e., the BDP.

$$h \geq T \times C \qquad (1)$$

where T is the averaged Round Trip Time (RTT) for TCP connections in the network, and C is the bottleneck link capacity. For an advanced congestion control scheme like DCTCP, the lower bound of the threshold has been shown to be $O(\sqrt{T \times C})$ in [2, 3]. However, as we will show later in this section, the absolute value of the difference between the lower bounds of DCTCP and ECN* is actually very small for data center networks, which allows ECN* to perform similarly to DCTCP.

The case of multiple TCP connections on the same bottleneck link can be similarly obtained as $h \geq T \times C/\sqrt{N}$, where N is the number of long TCP flows on the bottleneck link. However, as shown in a measurement study of DCTCP by [2], the number of concurrent long TCP connections to a server is generally 2 or 3. For shallow-buffered Top of Rack (ToR) switches that connect servers, synchronization of a small number of TCP connections still takes effect so that the lower bound stays close to BDP in practice.

3.2.2 Upper bound of ECN* threshold

We analyzed the upper bound for the ECN* threshold at which the congestion windows of the TCP connections sharing the bottleneck link are effectively controlled to avoid buffer overflow. In other words, when the ECN* threshold is lower than the upper bound, there is no TCP packet loss.

To obtain the upper bound, we begin with a simplified case where there is only one TCP connection and it has a slow start. We denote its congestion window size as w_e when the ECN threshold is reached at the intermediate switch. To simplify our analysis, we assume that the TCP sender only generates full-sized data packets, and the transmission time is δ for a Maximum Transmission Unit (MTU) on the bottleneck link. TCP aggressively increases the congestion window by the same amount of data acknowledged by the receiver during a slow start, so the largest queue length at this phase is our focus.

To illustrate the evolution of the TCP congestion window and the resulting queue length at the bottleneck link, we present the details of a TCP connection on a slow start in Table 1. A similar method was used in [17] to illustrate the advantage of TCP-Reno over TCP-Tahoe in a steady state. In contrast to previous scenarios, data center networks feature high-bandwidth and low-latency, which results in a small BDP compared to the switch buffer size. We discuss the measurement of latency in datacenter networks in Section 3.3.

In Table 1, the TCP initially starts with the congestion window as 2 packets, which directly results in the switch queue length also having 2 packets. An RTT (T) later the ACK for the first data packet arrives at the sender, which causes the window to increase from 2 to 3 and the packets with sequence 3 and 4 are sent. Since the buffer has drained to empty, the newly arrived packets 3 and 4 cause the queue length to reach 2 again. This phenomena continues, result-

Time	Packets Acked	Window size	Packets sent	Queue length
0		2	1,2	2
T	1	3	3,4	2
$T + \delta$	2	4	5,6	3=2-1+2
$2T$	3	5	7,8	2
$2T + \delta$	4	6	9,10	3=2-1+2
$2T + 2\delta$	5	7	11,12	4
$2T + 3\delta$	6	8	13,14	5
$3T$	7	9	15,16	2
$3T + \delta$	8	10	17,18	3=2-1+2
$3T + 2\delta$	9	11	19,20	4=3-1+2
$3T + 3\delta$	10	12	21,22	5=4-1+2
$3T + 4\delta$	11	13	23,24	6
$3T + 5\delta$	12	14	25,26	7
$3T + 6\delta$	13	15	27,28	8
$3T + 7\delta$	14	16	29,30	9
	...			
		w_e		h
		$w_e + 1$		$h + 1$
		...		
		$2w_e = w_e + w_e$		$h + w_e$

Table 1: Evolution during a slow start phase.

ing in regular mini-cycled initial queue length at the switch with a mini-cycle length of T.

There are two conditions for changing the mini-cycled switch queue length. First, the BDP in the data center must be small, e.g., around 30 packets from our measurement study in Section 3.3. The small BDP leads to insufficient time to completely drain the queue in a mini-cycle before the next mini-cycle starts. That is to say, the queue length increases continuously after the network pipe becomes full. Second, if the switch queue length reaches the ECN* threshold, then the switch starts to mark incoming packets with a CE bit. When the ACKs of those marked packets arrive at the sender, the sender decreases the congestion window. The half-reduced congestion window throttles the outgoing traffic and thus causes the draining of the switch queue.

When the switch queue length reaches threshold h, the congestion window size is w_e. This means that there are w_e packets on the flight (either data packets in the forward direction or the ACKs in the backward direction). Before the congestion information generated by the ECN reaches the sender, the congestion window continues to increase. As the TCP connection is still in the slow start phase, the congestion window will at most become $2w_e$. Considering equation 1 has to be satisfied to maintain TCP performance on throughput, the first condition will always be satisfied when the second condition is reached. Therefore, the queue does not drain and thus the queue length keeps increasing from h to $h + w_e$.

The value of window size w_e is bounded by queue threshold h and the BDP, as the network may hold the packets either in the switch queue or in the network pipe. Therefore, we have

$$w_e \leq h + T \times C. \qquad (2)$$

Note that whether the bound in equation 2 is tight is determined by the value of h and the the BDP. For example, assume the BDP is 30 packets while h is set to 6 packets. From Table 1 we determine that w_e is actually 13 packets when ECN is triggered, and the value 13 is much less than

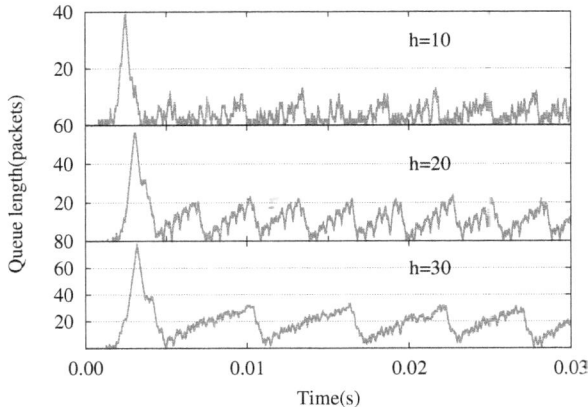

Figure 2: The instant queue length versus time with different ECN* threshold.

$6 + 30$. However, when h is set according to equation 1, the value of w_e is very close to the bound, as the network pipe is close to full. To ensure there is no packet loss, the switch buffer size B should be larger than the maximal value of queue length, i.e.,

$$h + w_e \leq B. \tag{3}$$

From equations 2 and 3, the upper bound for the ECN* threshold to avoid packet loss is

$$h \leq \frac{1}{2}(B - T \times C). \tag{4}$$

As the threshold h also has a lower bound in equation 1, equation 4 also gives the minimal switch buffer size to avoid buffer overflow as

$$B \geq 2h + T \times C \geq 3T \times C. \tag{5}$$

This condition holds for multiple synchronized TCP connections as long as the total congestion window of those connections can be successfully reduced[1].

3.2.3 *Validation in Experimental testbed*

We use experimental results to show that both the lower and upper bound obtained in equations 1 and 4 are valid. The details of our testbed are presented in Section 5. We used a Broadcom Pronto 3290 48-port GbE switch and developed software to log the instant queue length when an incoming packet arrives at the output port. We set up two TCP connections to the same receiver, and we changed the threshold h on the output port to the receiver and logged the queue length of the output port.

We ran the experiments 5 times and the queue length versus time with maximal the peak can be seen in Figure 2. The results show that the queue always jumps to the peak because of the slow start of the TCP connections, and then goes into cycled saw-tooth caused by congestion avoidance of the TCP connections. We observed that when threshold h is set to 20, the queue does not drain to empty and thus

---

[1]For incast, the total minimal congestion windows used in multiple TCP connections may cause switch buffer overflow, which is unavoidable even if DCTCP/ECN* is used in the switch.

maintains the throughput. This phenomena echoes the condition of equation 1 as the BDP in our testbed is close to 20 packets. If we count the BDP, i.e., $T \times C$ as 20 packets, then the peak buffer occupation during the slow start phase clearly echoes the conditions of buffer size requirement as $2h + 20$ in equation 5.

3.3 RTT in data center networks

The threshold for ECN* should be $T \times C$, and the buffer size should be three times larger than the threshold. This requirement translates into a very large buffer requirement for Internet cases [4]. However, we will show that this requirement makes sense for data center networks and most commodity switches have the capacity to support it.

Our interest is to understand the value of $T \times C$. Most data center networks use Gigabit Ethernet Interface, so for the Top of Rack (ToR) switch, the link capacity to servers is one Gigabit. We start with the case of the ToR switch to check whether such a buffer and the ECN threshold requirements can be supported. Upper layers may have 10G or even 40G links, but certainly the buffer size on high profile switches/routers are much larger. We believe our evaluation of ECN* like protocols may provide more information on the buffer size ECN needs for switches in data center networks.

Another key element for BDP is the RTT in data center networks. Paper [2] showed that in the absence of queueing, the RTT is under 250us for inter-rack, and approximately 100us for inner-rack. What we are interested in is the RTT, including queueing latency, in a real data center, so that we can set and tune the ECN threshold and also set the buffer size.

To achieve this goal, we used software to setup TCP connections between different server pairs in a production data center with over 40,000 servers. The connections pattern was like a mesh for the whole data center at the rack level. We purposefully turned off our inner-rack connections to reduce traffic. All servers logged the RTTs for connection establishment then tore down the connections, so that no additional traffic was generated into the data center. We collected the RTT for those TCP connections as samples for RTT in the whole data center. Note that this data center was busy as it serves many customers using diverse products. Actually, we use the same data center to store and process our RTT logs.

Figure 3 shows the inter-rack latency distribution we obtained for one day in December 2011. We actually collected results for several months and found the patterns to be similar. The results show that over 23% of connections have an RTT of less than 200us, and over 74% of connections have an RTT of less than 300us. The connections have an RTT of less than 600us with a probability of 95%. As most of the RTT we observed was less than 400us (90% percentile), we estimate the BDP in data centers for ECN* threshold setting as follows:

$$BDP = T \times C = 1G * 400us = 50KB$$

The default MTU on the Ethernet is 1.5KB, so 50KB means 33 full sized packets.

We suggest using 20 to 30 packets as the ECN* threshold (h) at the switches, as determined by the RTT values in network. In addition, a buffer size in the same amount as the threshold should be reserved for each port on the switches. For a 48 port Gigabit Ethernet switch, the total reserved

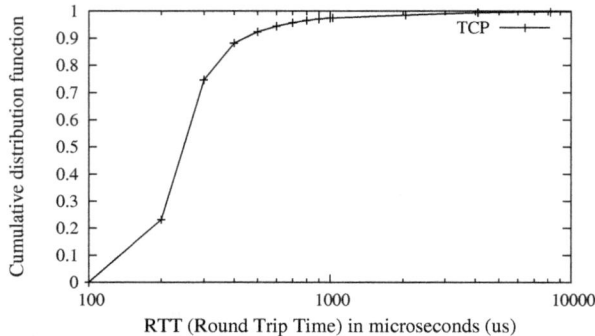

Figure 3: The inter-rack TCP RTT in a production data center with over 40,000 servers.

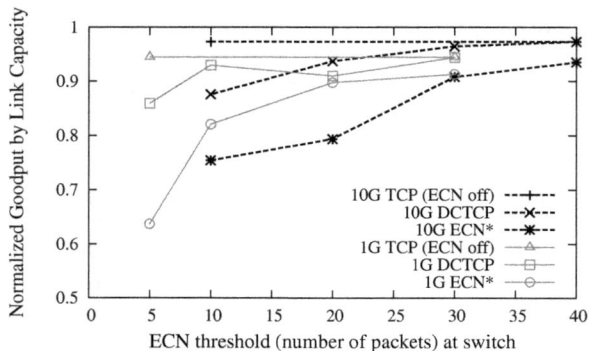

Figure 4: The goodput of two long flows to the same destination server on 1GbE and 10GbE networks.

buffer size is about 2MB(30*1.5K*48). Taking our shallow buffered broadcom switch as an example, it has 4MB shared buffer in total. DCTCP [2] also shows two other shallow buffered commodity ToR switches with a 4MB buffer, a Triumph 48-port, and a Scorpion 24-port. Thus, the ECN* threshold setting is valid for existing shallow buffered ToR switches. Note that ECN* also requires that the actual buffer size should be as large as $3TC$ to handle traffic peak. We consider that the buffer size over the reserved size (TC to $3TC$) can be allocated from the rest of the buffer in a shared way, instead of allocating to ports in a dedicated way. Such configurations for partial dedicated buffers per port and the rest buffers for limited sharing among all ports are actually supported in commodity switches [7].

3.4 Performance of DCTCP and ECN*

Next, we will briefly evaluate the performance of DCTCP and ECN* in our testbed. The setup of our testbed is described in Section 2.1. Both DCTCP and ECN* are designed to handle short flows, especially for incast. Ideally, we expect them to achieve similar performance on long flows and much better performance on incast.

We started by testing their performance on long flows. Figure 4 shows the throughput performance of two long TCP flows to the same destination server. The two flows contend the bandwidth at the switch output port to the server, and the total goodput is normalized by the link capacity. We chose two flows because paper [2] showed that the number of concurrent long flows is around 2 to 3, and 2 is the lowest number to cause contention. Additionally, as we discussed in Section 3.2, a larger number of TCP flows

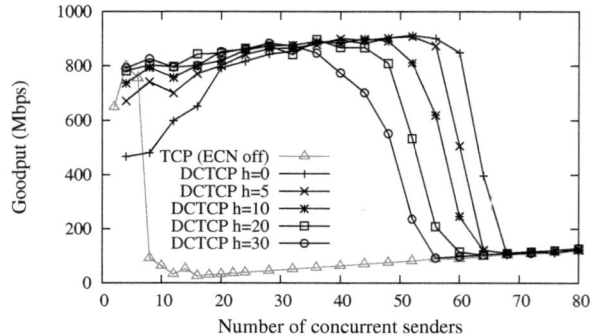

Figure 5: Incast Goodput of TCP (ECN off) and DCTCP with varied ECN thresholds(h).

requires a smaller threshold to maintain throughput. We also present the throughput achieved by TCP (ECN off) as the target throughput for DCTCP/ECN*. For both 1G and 10G link cases, the buffer size is set at 100 MTUs. We used 1500bytes MTU for 1GbE and 9000bytes jumbo frame MTU for 10GbE.

For both DCTCP and ECN*, the achieved throughput increases with the threshold and converges at TCP (ECN off). DCTCP [2] recommends using 20 packets as the threshold for a Gigabit Ethernet. ECN* can follow the same setup and achieve a similar performance. For 10GbE, we found the threshold should be set to 30+ packets, which is reasonable considering the ratio of link capacity to packet sizes. The figure also shows the slight throughput advantage of DCTCP on the smaller threshold requirements of 10GbE. The threshold requirements for DCTCP and ECN* to achieve high throughput on long flows are actually both well supported by existing commodity switches.

Next we evaluate the incast performance of TCP (ECN off), DCTCP, and ECN* respectively. One problem with incast is the question of how to set the threshold. As we discussed in Section 3.3, the ECN threshold used for ECN* should be around 30 packets considering the typical RTT in data center networks. To understand the impact of the ECN threshold on incast performance, we present the incast throughput of DCTCP and ECN* with different thresholds in Figure 5 and 6, respectively. The transmission block size for each sender is fixed at 64KB. Similar performance gaps are also observed for other incast setups, e.g., the total fixed block size as 1MB or 2MB.

Figures 5 and 6 show that the incast performance of DCTCP and ECN* is significantly affected by the ECN threshold. Larger thresholds lead to a smaller number of concurrent incast senders being supported. In the two figures, the curves of the threshold at 0 are just shown for the incast performance limit, i.e., the maximal number of parallel senders that can be supported on incast. When threshold is set to 0, all the incoming packets will be marked by CE unconditionally, so that the congestion window at the senders will never be increased. Note that such an unconditional marking strategy or a small threshold actually degrades the performance when the number of senders is small. The idea case for incast performance is non-degraded throughput until the largest number of incast senders is reached.

We have observed the tradeoff with the ECN threshold

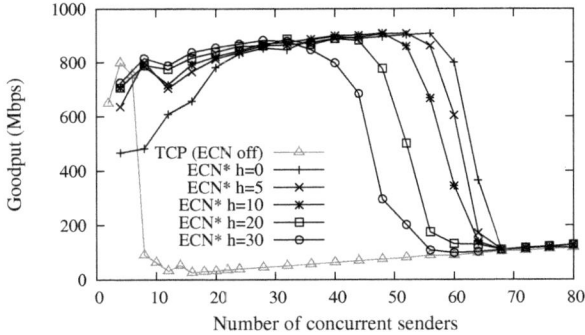

Figure 6: Incast Goodput of TCP (ECN off) and ECN* with varied ECN thresholds(h).

setting: a larger threshold leads to a higher long flow through-put but a smaller number of concurrent senders on incast, and a smaller threshold greatly improves incast performance but degrades the throughput of long flows. As we observe this same tradeoff for both DCTCP and ECN*, we believe this is a fundamental tradeoff for all congestion control schemes using instant queue based ECN.

Since the total number of supported incast senders is close to the number of the switch port at 48, why should we care about the performance difference. As we will show in Section 5, the maximum number of concurrent senders is actually determined by the switch buffer size. And as we have discussed in Section 3.3, for shallow buffered ToR switches, the buffer is actually shared among ports [7]. Therefore, with a smaller effective buffer size, e.g., due to high buffer pressures caused by buffer occupation on other ports, or with multiple incast applications occurring at the same time, the worst situation can be amplified.

4. DEQUEUE MARKING

4.1 Problem statement

To understand the impact of the ECN threshold setting on performance, we categorize the traffic in data center networks into three categories as follows.

First, all competing TCP flows are long flows. In this case, the performance is mainly determined by the throughput of the long flows. A recent study in [2] showed that there are usually 2 or 3 competing long flows. Second, a few short flows are trying to deliver a small volume of data as fast as possible, while there are other background long flows competing for bandwidth. In this case, the completion time of those short flows is the focus of performance. Third, during TCP incast, a large number of short flows are competing for a specific network port in a very short time. TCP incast happens whether or not there are ongoing background long flows. The performance of TCP incast is determined by the completion time of the last finished short flow.

As shown in Section 3.4, TCP (ECN off) actually works well for the first category. However, the large buffer occupation of TCP (ECN off) makes it work poorly for the second and third cases. ECN* and DCTCP use congestion control based on instant queue length. Thus, compared with TCP, both methods achieve similar performance for the first category and much better performance for the second and third

categories. Considering the throughput of TCP connections is still fundamental to performance, we need a scheme that improves the performance of both DCTCP and ECN* during the last two categories by assuming the threshold is set for the first category.

In Section 3.2, we present the relationship of throughput and the threshold setting of ECN*. For DCTCP, the relationship has also been analyzed previously in [3]. Given that the ECN threshold has been set, we must next address how to make the instant queue length represent the traffic and thus trigger the threshold faster. Note that we don't wish to change the ECN threshold dynamically according to the traffic categories as we believe that such a solution is hard to implement due to the traffic dynamics in a data center.

4.2 Dequeue marking scheme

We have proposed, implemented, and evaluated a pure switch based solution - dequeue marking. The purpose of dequeue marking is not only to provide a complete switch only solution for ECN*, but also to understand the performance limit of instant queue length based ECN (both ECN* and DCTCP). Customers that have concerns with TCP stack modifications at the end server, e.g., DCTCP, can use dequeue marking and ECN*.

At the concept level, dequeue marking seems similar to the well-known drop-from-front method [16], which was proposed for TCP over ATM. A previous study in [16] shows that drop-from-front greatly improves performance over tail-drop, but for RED, front-drop and tail-drop are similar. In existing commodity switches, ECN follows the implementation of RED. As the switch buffer uses a First Come First Service (FIFO) rule, RED checks whether a packet should be dropped (or marked if ECN is enabled) when an incoming packet is queued at the switch output port. Such a dropping/marking policy for original RED/ECN works well as the rule is performed by an exponential filter based on the average queue length.

In this paper, we argue that for instant queue length based ECN, the marking policy performed when packets are queued is not longer efficient. For instant queue length based ECN, e.g., ECN* as analyzed in Section 3.2, the performance has been analyzed by assuming that congestion information is generated when the instant queue length is over the threshold. However, in existing ECN implementation, such congestion information (marked CE bit on packets just queued) must wait until the marked packet moves to the head of the queue. If the ECN threshold is set to a large value to accommodate TCP throughput of long flows, we believe that setting ECN mark when packets are queued severely delays the delivery of congestion information.

In this paper, we propose the use of dequeue marking for instant queue length based ECN at switches. When an ECN-capable packet is about to be dequeued, we check the instant queue length and the ECN threshold. If the instant queue length is larger or equal to the ECN threshold, then the packet is marked with a CE bit.

There are two benefits to dequeue marking. First, the latency to deliver the congestion information is reduced, so a better incast performance is expected. Second, our analysis and experimental results (skipped due to space limitation) for dequeue marking show a minimal buffer size (threshold upper bound) of ECN* as $B \geq h+T \times C \geq 2T \times C$, compared with equation 5 for the original enqueue marking.

Dequeue marking decides whether a packet should be marked when a packet is about to transmit, which is different from a straightforward extension of drop-from-front strategy of RED [16] to a mark-from-front strategy of ECN. This is because for both RED and ECN, the dropping/marking decision is made when a packet is enqueued. Considering that the traffic is highly bursty during TCP incast and multiple packets are enqueued at the same time, the front-mark of ECN may only mark the packets waiting for transmission when other packets are enqueued, while dequeue marking continuously marks all outgoing packets until the queue length is less than the threshold. To this end, front-mark may leave some "holes" (unmarked packets) and thus we believe dequeue marking is more suitable for instant queue based ECN.

4.3 Implementation on commodity switches

Dequeue marking does not require any change of the ECN protocol, as it changes the start time of when the packets are marked.

Readers may have concerns of whether this method will introduce large process latency for the outgoing packets if we modify the CE bits when the packet is about to dequeue. From our experience, changing bits on the packet header during dequeue is well supported on commodity switches. However, the switch does not provide a hardware solution to check the current buffer length when a packet is about to dequeue. To solve this problem, we developed a software solution using the broadcom switch SDK and started a dedicated thread to check queue length continuously. Our measurement results show that queue length reading costs about 6 us (microseconds). That is to say, the first packet to get a CE mark is 6us behind the time when the queue length is over the ECN threshold. Note that the delay is not the process latency introduced per packet. Since the hardware on the broadcom switch also requires a 4us interval for the queue length update during normal ECN marking (when packets are queued), we think that our software solution for dequeue marking at 6us is acceptable.

Similar operations can be made for other types of switches and we believe there is no other barrier to implementing dequeue marking on chips.

5. EXPERIMENTAL RESULTS

We deployed a testbed with 50+ servers and one Broadcom Pronto 3290 48-port Gigabit Ethernet switch. This switch supports ECN, and has 48 1GbE ports and 4 10GbE ports. The topology of our testbed is such that 47 servers connect to the GbE ports, and the other 4 servers connect to the 10GbE ports. Each server has two 2.2G Intel Xeon CPUs E5520 (four cores in total), 32G RAM, and a 1T hard disk. We use 47 Intel PRO/1000 PT Dual Port GbE Adapters and four Mellanox ConnectX 10GbE Adapters. The OS of each server is Windows Server 2008 R2 Enterprise 64-bit version. The CPU, memory, or hard disk was never a bottleneck in any of our experiments. We modified the iperf to create an incast scenario in which multiple sending servers generate TCP traffic to a receiving server under the same switch.

The implementation of DCTCP followed the description in paper [2]. For ECN*, we used existing Windows 2008r2 TCP/IP stack with no modification, which was New-Reno like. We didn't use SACK (Selective Acknowledgment) in our experiments as a previous study [19] shows that it does

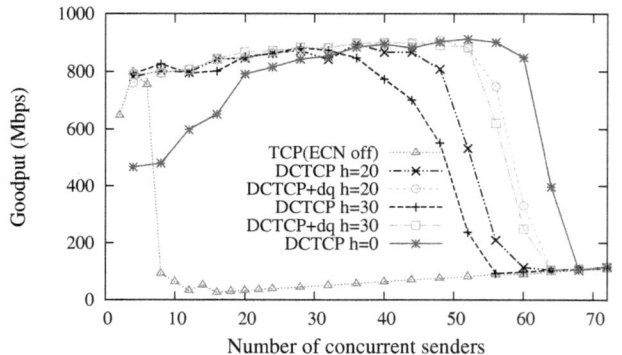

Figure 7: Incast performance of TCP and DCTCP with and without dequeue marking. ECN Threshold is set at 20 and 30 packets.

not help much with incast congestion. We turned on ECN support at both the sender and receiver servers. All other settings followed those in the data center network we accessed. The default timeout of TCP on Windows server is 300 milliseconds (ms).

We use "**dq**" to denote the results which featured dequeue marking for DCTCP/ECN*. We evaluated instant queue based ECN and found improvements according to the traffic categories described in Section 4.1. Our experiments started with incast as our schemes are motivated by degraded incast performance on a large ECN threshold. Then we evaluated the interaction between short and long flows and finally the case of long flows only.

5.1 Incast

In our incast congestion experiments, we evaluated two cases as described in Section 2.1: fixed per sender block size and fixed total block size. The trends and improvement obtained were similar, so due to space limitation we only present the results for when the amount of data transmitted by each connection is fixed at 64kbytes. When the number of concurrent senders is less than 44, each server generates at most one connection. To evaluate a situation with more senders (over 44), each server may generate at most two connections. *The incast performance of DCTCP and ECN* with the same ECN threshold is fairly similar*, so we present two cases for DCTCP and ECN* with the threshold set at 20 and 30 packets respectively.

In Figures 7 and 8, we show the incast performance of DCTCP and ECN* versus TCP, respectively. TCP (ECN off), DCTCP, and ECN* with the ECN threshold set at 0 ($h=0$) are the same as those in Figures 5 and 6. The curves with $h=0$ show the maximum number of servers that can be supported by using instant queue length based ECN in practice.

Dequeue marking does not degrade performance when the number of senders is small, compare with the results achieved by setting $h=0$. In addition, we have observed that with dequeue marking enabled, both DCTCP and ECN* achieve incast performance close to the limit of ECN protocol by marking packets unconditionally ($h=0$), but without sacrificing throughput when the number of senders is small. Dequeue marking effectively mitigates the performance dif-

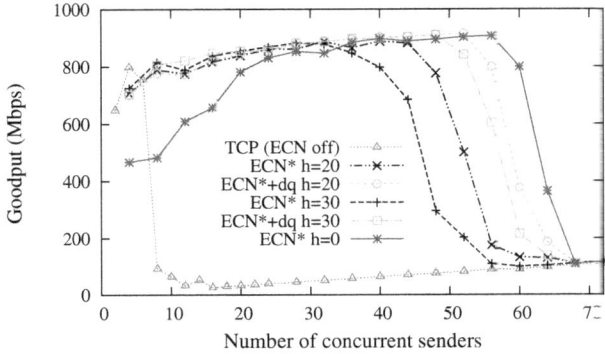

Figure 8: Incast performance of TCP and ECN* with and without dequeue marking. ECN Threshold is set at 20 and 30 packets.

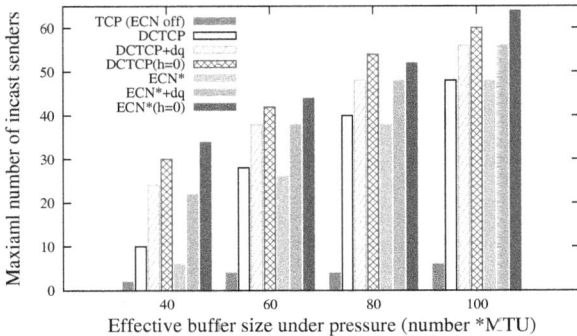

Figure 9: Incast performance of TCP, DCTCP, and ECN* with and without dequeue marking versus varied switch buffer size caused by buffer pressure. The ECN threshold at the switch is set at 20 packets.

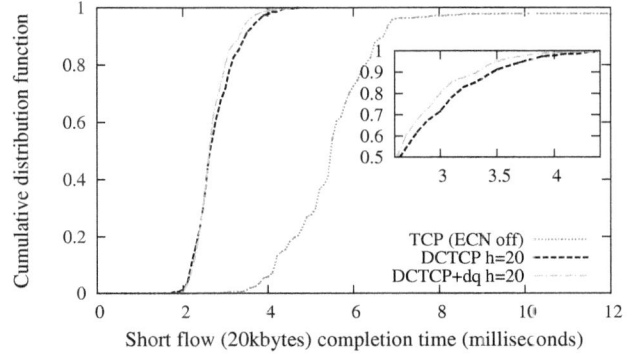

Figure 10: Short flow (20k bytes) completion time of TCP and DCTCP, with two background long TCP/DCTCP flows respectively. The ECN threshold (h) at switch was set at 20 packets.

ference of DCTCP and ECN* when using different thresholds.

Dequeue marking supports more senders during incast. To evaluate the performance when the buffer size on the switches is constrained, e.g., the shared buffer is occupied by flows on other ports, we designed an experiment for buffer pressure as follows. The ECN threshold at the switch was kept at 20 packets, and we varied the buffer size from 40 to 100 link MTU and compared the incast performance of TCP, DCTCP, and ECN*. For DCTCP/ECN*, we turned on dequeue marking and compared the performance with the ECN limit ($h = 0$), so that in total we have seven candidates in Figure 9.

The performance was judged by the maximum number of concurrent senders without obtaining goodput below 600Mbps. We observed that when the buffer pressure is high, caused by either a constrained buffer size per port or sharing the buffer occupied by other ports in practice, the relative gain obtained by dequeue marking was also higher. For example, when the buffer size was equal to 40(100) link MTU, dequeue marking increased the maximum number of DCTCP senders from 10 to 24 (48 to 56), achieving a gain of 140% (16%). The larger buffer size supports more concurrent in-

cast senders and the performance of DCTCP and ECN* were almost the same for the buffer size satisfying equation 5.

We tried other incast setups and obtained larger improvement when the threshold was larger. We have observed that: *first, with dequeue marking enabled, the maximum number of incast senders of DCTCP and ECN* with a large threshold are fairly close to the performance limit of ECN (h=0).* Second, given a threshold and the varied buffer size caused by buffer sharing, the improved ratio of dequeue marking increases with smaller buffer size.

5.2 Interaction of long flows and short flows

Dequeue marking is proposed to address the ECN threshold setting problem for incast. Readers may have concerns over whether such modifications will make short flows unnecessarily conservative when competing with long flows that have a larger congestion window and queue occupation at the switches.

To evaluate the interaction between long and short flows, we first established two long connections to the same receiver that occupy the buffer on the bottleneck link. Then we continuously established and tore down a new TCP connection to transmit 20kbytes data to the same destination server of the two long flows. The duration of the long connections was just long enough to cover the transmission of all the 20kbytes short connections. Both long and short TCP connections were started using iperf. All the servers were under the same GbE switch. We selected 20kbytes as it has been used in related research [2].

We evaluated the performance according to two aspects of the interaction: the completion time observed by short flows and the throughput obtained by long flows.

In Figure 10 and Figure 11, we show the distribution of completion time of short flows. Note that the completion time of TCP (ECN off) was actually worse and had over a 2% probability of encountering a timeout (over 300ms and not shown in the two figures). As the completion time distributions of dequeue marking for both enabled and not enabled are fairly close, we provide a zoomed in look. We have observed that dequeue marking always slightly decreases the completion time for short flows. Moreover, the completion time of short flows was similar for DCTCP and ECN*, which

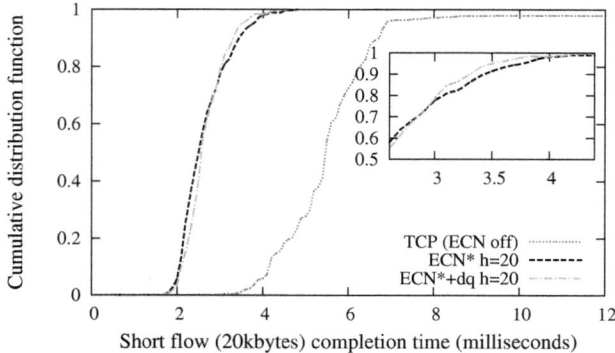

Figure 11: Short flow (20k bytes) completion time of TCP and ECN*, with two background long TCP/ECN* flows respectively. The ECN threshold (h) at switch was set at 20 packets.

Stacks	Original	Dequeue marking
TCP (ECN off)	944.85	-
DCTCP	918.7	903.87
ECN*	895.2	897.75

Table 2: Comparison of total achieved throughput (Mbps) of two long flows when there is a short flow continuously downloading 20kbytes traversing the same bottleneck link.

indicates that the queue occupancy caused by the two long TCP connections was similar for the two schemes.

In Table 2, we present the throughput of long flows when there are short flows continuously traversed. TCP (ECN off) achieves the largest throughput of long flows, with the worst completion time on short flows. The throughput of long flows under both DCTCP and ECN* are very close, especially when dequeue marking is enabled.

To this end, we found a slightly better large percentile completion time for short flows when dequeue marking was enabled. Meanwhile, the throughput of long flows on DCTCP and ECN* was close.

5.3 Long flows with large latency

We evaluated an extreme latency case for instant queue length based schemes, including both DCTCP and ECN*. In Figure 3 we have shown that the latency in data center network is less than 1ms with a probability around 98%. We are interested in the performance degradation in the remaining 2% of cases. The worst case occurs when two long flows are competing on the same bottleneck. We introduced extra latency by adding a fixed 1 millisecond delay using software for each outgoing packet at the two sender servers in our testbed. We measured the throughput achieved with these two long flows and the results are shown in Figure 12.

We observed that DCTCP achieves much higher throughput compared with ECN*, when the network latency was over 1ms but the threshold was set to a low value according to 90 percentile latency. For example, for ECN threshold $h=30$, DCTCP was 929.8Mbps while ECN* was 736.7Mbps (79%). Note that ECN* quickly gained more throughput if there were more connections, e.g., 3, and thus it's still as competitive as DCTCP in data center networks. An-

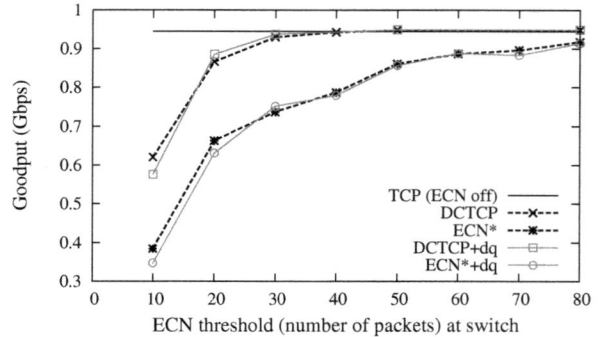

Figure 12: The goodput of two long flows to the same destination server on 1GbE. There is an additional 1ms latency at the sender servers.

other observation is that dequeue marking slightly degraded throughput if the ECN threshold was set too low, e.g., lower than the recommended $h=30$ determined by the normal latency in data center networks.

6. DISCUSSIONS

The ECN standard defines ECN-capable (ECT) bits at the IP header to indicate switches that mark the packet in order to make the connection respond in the same manner as dropping. However, the behavior of switches handling non-ECT packets when ECN is triggered is not specified. By ECN triggering we mean the instant queue length is over the ECN threshold in our setting. We observe that the broadcom switch simply drops the packets that are not ECN-capable when ECN is triggered. This behavior gives the ECN-capable packets preference as the ECT packets just get marked.

The ECN standard states that TCP retransmitted packets and SYN packets must not be marked as ECT at the IP header. The concerns behind the statements are mainly rooted in security and the desires to make ECN more robust. The queue size in Figure 2 shows that the queue length is periodically over the ECN threshold. Therefore, if SYN packets for new connections or retransmitted packets meet the conditions during congestion, these packets may get dropped and the performance degraded. In this paper, we suggest that all such packets can be marked as ECT in data center networks.

7. RELATED WORK

Paper [15] describes instant queue length based ECN, and DCTCP uses the ratio of marked packets in its congestion control algorithm. In this paper, we analyze the ECN threshold setting. Our analysis and measurements of use in a data center show that ECN*, which uses instant queue at the switch and standard stack at the end system, can perform as well as DCTCP in three traffic categories.

Besides DCTCP, there are other schemes proposed for mitigating the impact of incast congestion. Paper [22] uses a smaller retransmission timeout for incast. We consider an instant queue length based ECN approach is complementary to smaller timeouts. Meanwhile, avoiding a timeout is more appealing than a fast recovery after packet loss. ICTCP [23] is proposed to mitigate incast by overloading the TCP receive window for congestion control. ICTCP also targets the avoidance of packet loss caused by buffer overflow. We believe ECN* has several benefits compared to ICTCP: 1) ECN is more general and can be used for all bottlenecks in the network while ICTCP only works for the last hop congestion; 2) In addition to incast, ECN* also reduces the completion time of short flows by controlling queue occupation and mitigates the interaction of short and long TCP flows.

Previously, there have been some approaches for dynamic tuning RED thresholds, e.g., [9], but they are only designed for average queue length. Control theoretic analysis of RED and improved designs are proposed in [5, 6], namely the Proportional and the Proportional-Integral (PI) controller. The proportional controller also uses the instant queue length instead of the average queue length. However, the identified stability conditions for Proportional controllers can't be applied to ECN*. This is because ECN* sets the two (low and high) thresholds for ECN at the same value, which essentially is a bang-bang control (on-off control). Therefore, ECN* only uses the ECN implementations on commodity switches, but has different properties when compared with ECN.

Actually, both DCTCP and ECN* share the same difference. The stability of DCTCP is analyzed in [3]. This paper proposes a simple model to analyze the queue occupancy properties following the methods in [15] and [17]. Our analyzed bounds for ECN* thresholds are briefly validated using experiments, and we show that the setup for the threshold determines TCP performance, especially for incast.

Commodity switches use tail-drop when buffer overflows. In drop-from-front [16], when a cell arrives at a full buffer or meeting, the cell closet to being transmitted is dropped instead of the tail. With partial frame drop, drop-from-front achieves similar performance to RED. A previous study in [16] shows tail-drop and front-drop are equally good when either is applied to RED. Compared with the marking approach when the packet is queued, the idea of dequeue marking greatly speeds up congestion information delivery for instant queue length based ECN.

This paper uses instant queue length and demonstrates the feasibility of dequeue marking on commodity Broadcom switches. We believe that the final deployment of dequeue marking in switch chips has no fundamental technical barriers.

8. CONCLUSIONS

In this paper, we demonstrate that instant queue length based ECN* achieves a similar performance when compared with DCTCP in high-bandwidth low-latency networks. ECN* does not need to modify ECN protocols at end servers. We observed that both DCTCP and ECN* have a dilemma with the ECN threshold: a larger ECN threshold to achieve high throughput for long flows may have worse performance during incast. To achieve both high throughput and optimal incast performance with a single ECN threshold, we propose dequeue marking for DCTCP and ECN*. Dequeue marking checks the queue length when packets are dequeued and speeds up the delivery of the congestion signal by the packets at the queue head instead of the queue tail.

We have developed dequeue marking ECN on Broadcom switch Pronto 3290. We built a testbed with 50+ servers and a 48-port Ethernet Gigabit switch. Our experimental results

demonstrate that dequeue marking is effective for enlarging the maximum incast senders of DCTCP and ECN* fairly close to the performance limit of ECN using unconditional marking. Depending on the buffer size and ECN threshold, the gain obtained by dequeue marking varies from 16% to 140%.

9. REFERENCES

[1] M. Al-Fares, A. Loukissas, and A. Vahdat. A Scalable, Commodity Data Center Network Architecture. In *Proc. SIGCOMM*, 2008.

[2] M. Alizadeh, A. Greenberg, D. Maltz, J. Padhye, P. Patel, B. Prabhakar, S. Sengupta, and M. Sridharan. DCTCP: Efficient Packet Transport for the Commoditized Data Center. In *Proc. SIGCOMM*, 2010.

[3] M. Alizadeh, A. Javanmard, and B. Prabhakar. Analysis of DCTCP: Stability, Convergence, and Fairness. In *Proc. SIGMETRICS*, 2011.

[4] G. Appenzeller, I. Keslassy, and N. McKeown. Sizing Router Buffers. In *Proc. SIGCOMM*, 2004.

[5] C.V.Hollot, V.Misra, D.Towsley, and W.Gong. A Control Theoretic Analysis of RED. In *Proc. INFOCOM*, 2001.

[6] C.V.Hollot, V.Misra, D.Towsley, and W.Gong. On Designing Improved Controllers for AQM Routers Supporting TCP Flows. In *Proc. INFOCOM*, 2001.

[7] S. Das and R. Sankar. Broadcom Smart-Buffer Technology in Data Center Switches for Cost-Effective Performance Scaling of Cloud Applications. http://www.broadcom.com/collateral/etp/SBT-ETP100.pdf.

[8] J. Dean and S. Ghemawat. MapReduce: Simplified Data Processing on Large Clusters. In *OSDI'04*, 2004.

[9] S. Floyd, R. Gummadi, and S. Shenker. Adaptive RED: An Algorithm for Increasing the Robustness of RED's Active Queue Management, 2001. http://www.icir.org/floyd/papers/adaptiveRed.pdf.

[10] S. Floyd and V. Jacobson. Random Early Detection gateways for Congestion Avoidance. *IEEE/ACM Transactions on Networking*, Aug. 1993.

[11] S. Ghemawat, H. Gobioff, and S. Leung. The Google File System. In *ACM SOSP'03*, 2003.

[12] C. Guo, G. Lu, D. Li, H. Wu, X. Zhang, Y. Shi, C. Tian, Y. Zhang, and S. Lu. BCube: A High Performance, Server-centric Network Architecture for Modular Data Centers. In *Proc. SIGCOMM*, 2009.

[13] C. Guo, H. Wu, K. Tan, L. Shi, Y. Zhang, and S. Lu. DCell: A Scalable and Fault Tolerant Network Structure for Data Centers. In *Proc. SIGCOMM*, 2008.

[14] S. Kandula, S. Sengupta, A. Greenberg, P. Patel, and R. Chaiken. The Nature of Datacenter Traffic: Measurements & Analysis. In *Proc. IMC*, 2009.

[15] A. Kuzmanovic. The Power of Explicit Congestion Notification. In *Proc. SIGCOMM*, 2005.

[16] T. V. Lakshman, A. Neidhardt, and T. J. Ott. The Drop from Front Strategy in TCP and in TCP over ATM. In *INFOCOM*, pages 1242–1250, 1996.

[17] T.V. Lakshman and U. Madhow. The Performance of TCP/IP for Networks with High Bandwidth-Delay Products and Random Loss. *IEEE/ACM Transactions on Networking*, Jun. 1997.

[18] D. Nagle, D. Serenyi, and A. Matthews. The Panasas ActiveScale Storage Cluster: Delivering scalable high bandwidth storage. In *Proc. SC*, 2004.

[19] A. Phanishayee, E. Krevat, V. Vasudevan, D. Andersen, G. Ganger, G. Gibson, and S. Seshan. Measurement and Analysis of TCP Throughput Collapse in Cluster-based Storage Systems. In *Proc. USENIX FAST*, 2008.

[20] K. Ramakrishnan, S. Floyd, and D. Black. The Addition of Explicit Congestion Notification (ECN) to IP. *RFC3168*, Sept. 2001.

[21] K. Ramakrishnan and R. Jain. A Binary Feedback Scheme for Congestion Avoidance in Computer Networks. *Digital Equipment*, 1990.

[22] V. Vasudevan, A. Phanishayee, H. Shah, E. Krevat, D. Andersen, G. Ganger, G. Gibson, and B. Mueller. Safe and Effective Fine-grained TCP Retransmissions for Datacenter Communication. In *Proc. SIGCOMM*, 2009.

[23] H. Wu, Z. Feng, C. Guo, and Y. Zhang. ICTCP: Incast Congestion Control for TCP in Data Center Networks. In *Proc. Conext*, 2010.

Datacast: A Scalable and Efficient Reliable Group Data Delivery Service for Data Centers

Jiaxin Cao[1*], Chuanxiong Guo[2], Guohan Lu[2], Yongqiang Xiong[2], Yixin Zheng[3*],
Yongguang Zhang[2], Yibo Zhu[4*], Chen Chen[5]

University of Science and Technology of China[1],   Microsoft Research Asia[2],
Tsinghua University[3],   University of California, Santa Barbara[4],   University of Pennsylvania[5]
caojx@mail.ustc.edu.cn[1],   {chguo, lguohan, yqx, yqz}@microsoft.com[2]
zhengyx12@mails.tsinghua.edu.cn[3],   yibo@cs.ucsb.edu[4],   chenche@seas.upenn.edu[5]

ABSTRACT

Reliable Group Data Delivery (RGDD) is a pervasive traffic pattern in data centers. In an RGDD group, a sender needs to reliably deliver a copy of data to all the receivers. Existing solutions either do not scale due to the large number of RGDD groups (e.g., IP multicast) or cannot efficiently use network bandwidth (e.g., end-host overlays).

Motivated by recent advances on data center network topology designs (multiple edge-disjoint Steiner trees for RGDD) and innovations on network devices (practical in-network packet caching), we propose *Datacast* for RGDD. Datacast explores two design spaces: 1) Datacast uses multiple edge-disjoint Steiner trees for data delivery acceleration. 2) Datacast leverages in-network packet caching and introduces a simple soft-state based congestion control algorithm to address the scalability and efficiency issues of RGDD.

Our analysis reveals that Datacast congestion control works well with small cache sizes (e.g., 125KB) and causes few duplicate data transmissions (e.g., 1.19%). Both simulations and experiments confirm our theoretical analysis. We also use experiments to compare the performance of Datacast and BitTorrent. In a BCube(4, 1) with 1Gbps links, we use both Datacast and BitTorrent to transmit 4GB data. The link stress of Datacast is 1.01, while it is 1.39 for BitTorrent. By using two Steiner trees, Datacast finishes the transmission in 16.9s, while BitTorrent uses 52s.

Categories and Subject Descriptors

C.2.2 [**Computer-Communication Networks**]: Network Protocols—*Applications*; C.2.4 [**Computer-Communication Networks**]: Distributed Systems—*Distributed applications*

---

*The work was performed while Jiaxin Cao, Yixin Zheng, Yibo Zhu and Chen Chen were research interns at Microsoft Research Asia.

General Terms

Algorithms, Performance, Theory

Keywords

Multicast, congestion control, content distribution

1. INTRODUCTION

Reliable Group Data Delivery (RGDD) is widely used in cloud services (e.g., GFS [15] and MapReduce [5]) and applications (e.g., social networking, Search, scientific computing). In RGDD, we have a group which contains one data source and a set of receivers. We need to reliably deliver the same copy of bulk data from the source to all the receivers.

Existing solutions for RGDD can be classified into two categories: 1) Reliable IP multicast. IP multicast suffers from scalability issues, since it is hard to manage a large number of group states in the network. Adding reliability is also challenging, due to the ACK implosion problem [13]. 2) End-host based overlays. Overlays are scalable since devices in the network do not maintain group states. Reliability is easily achieved by using TCP in overlays. However, overlays do not use network bandwidth efficiently. The same copy of data may traverse the same link several times, resulting high link stress. For example, ESM [18] reported that the average and worst-case link stresses are 1.9 and 9, respectively.

Motivated by the recent progresses on data center network (DCN) topologies and network devices, we explore new opportunities in supporting RGDD for DCN: 1) Recently proposed DCN topologies have multiple edge-disjoint Steiner trees, which has not been well studied before. These multiple Steiner trees may enable full utilization of DCN bandwidth. 2) There is a clear technical trend that network devices are providing powerful packet processing abilities by integrating CPUs and large memory. This makes in-network packet caching practical. By leveraging in-network packet caching, we can address the scalability and bandwidth efficiency issues of RGDD.

However, it is challenging to take advantage of these opportunities. It has been proved that even calculating a single Steiner tree is NP-hard [16]. In RGDD, we have to calculate multiple Steiner trees within a short time, which makes the problem even harder. Although network devices are becoming capable of in-network packet caching, the resource is not unlimited. We need to use as small caches as possible for each group to maximize the number of simultaneously supported groups. At the same time, we need to increase bandwidth efficiency by reducing duplicate packets transmitted in the network.

In this paper, we design *Datacast* to address the above challenges. Leveraging the properties of the DCN topologies, Datacast introduces an efficient algorithm to calculate multiple edge-disjoint Steiner trees, and then distributes data among them. In each Steiner tree, Datacast leverages the concept of CCN [14]. To help Datacast achieve high bandwidth efficiency with small cache size in intermediate nodes, we design a rate-based congestion control algorithm, which follows the classical Additive Increase and Multiplicative Decrease (AIMD) approach. Datacast congestion control leverages a key observation: the receiving of a duplicate packet request at the source can be interpreted as a congestion signal. Different from previous work (e.g., TFMCC [26] and pgmcc [21]), which uses explicit information exchanges between the source and receivers, Datacast is much simpler. To understand the performance of Datacast, we build a fluid model. By analyzing the model, we prove that Datacast works at the full rate when the cache size is greater than a small threshold (e.g., 125KB), and also derive the ratio of duplicate data sent by the data source (e.g., 1.19%). We have built Datacast in NS3, and also have implemented it with the ServerSwitch [8] platform. Simulations and experiments verify our theoretical results, which suggest that Datacast achieves both scalability and high bandwidth efficiency.

This paper makes the following contributions:

- We design a simple and efficient multicast congestion control algorithm, and build a fluid model to understand its properties.

- We propose a low time-complexity algorithm for multiple edge-disjoint Steiner trees calculation.

- We implement Datacast with the ServerSwitch platform, and validate its performance.

The rest of this paper is organized as follows. In Section 2, we introduce the background. We briefly overview Datacast design in Section 3. We design the Steiner trees algorithm in Section 4, and build the Datacast transport protocol in Section 5. We present simulation results in Section 6, implementation and experiments in Section 7. Finally, we discuss the related work and conclude the paper in Section 8 and 9, respectively.

2. BACKGROUND

2.1 Reliable group data delivery

In data center applications and services, Reliable Group Data Delivery (RGDD) is a pervasive traffic pattern. The problem of RGDD is, *given a data source, Src, and a set of receivers, $R_1, R_2, \cdots, R_n$, how to reliably transmit bulk data from Src to all the receivers*. A good RGDD design should be scalable and achieve high bandwidth efficiency. The following cases are typical RGDD scenarios.

Case 1: In data centers, servers are typically organized as physical clusters. During bootstrapping or OS upgrading, the same copy of the OS image needs to be transferred to

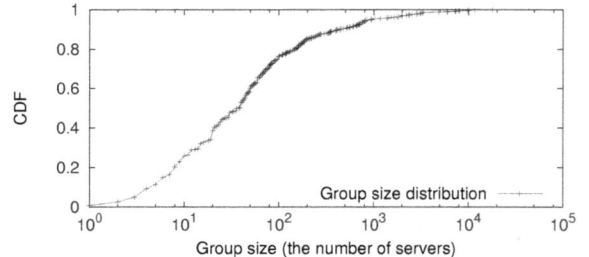

(a) The group size distribution in a large data center.

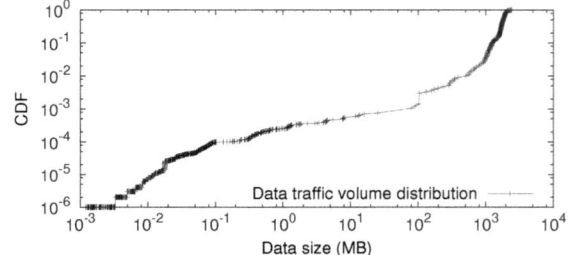

(b) The traffic volume distribution for a large distributed execution engine.

Figure 1: RGDD groups and traffics in data centers.

all the servers in the same cluster. A physical cluster is further divided into sub-clusters of different sizes. A sub-cluster is assigned to a service. All the servers in the same sub-cluster may need to run the same set of applications. We need to distribute the same set of program binaries and configuration data to all the servers in the sub-cluster.

Case 2: In distributed file systems, e.g., GFS [15], a chunk of data is replicated to several (typically three) servers to improve reliability. The sender and receivers form a small replication group. A distributed file system may contain tens of Peta bytes using tens of thousands machines. Hence the number of replication groups is huge. In distributed execution engine, e.g., Dryad [19], a copy of data may need to be distributed to many servers for JOIN operations.

Case 3: In Amazon EC2 or Windows AZure, a tenant may create a set of virtual machines. These virtual machines form an isolated computing environment dedicated to that tenant. When setting up the virtual machines, customized virtual machine OSes and application images need be delivered to all the physical servers that host these virtual machines.

Figure 1(a) and 1(b) show the group size and traffic volume distributions for a RGDD service in a large production data center. We use these two figures to illustrate the challenges in supporting RGDD.

The system should be scalable. As we have mentioned in the above scenarios, we need to support a large number of RGDD groups in large data centers. Figure 1(a) further shows that the group size varies from several servers to thousands of servers and even more. The large number of groups and the varying group sizes pose scalability challenges, since maintaining a large number of group states in the network is hard (as demonstrated by IP multicast).

Bandwidth should be efficiently and fully used. Figure 1(b) shows the traffic volume distribution for group communications. It shows that the groups transmitting more than 550MB data contribute 99% RGDD data traffic volume. Due to the large number of groups and the large data sizes, RGDD contributes a significant amount of traffic. This requires that RGDD uses network bandwidth efficiently. On the other hand, the new DCN topologies (e.g., BCube [7] and CamCube [9]) provide high network capacity with multiple data delivery trees. An RGDD design should take full advantage of these new network topologies to speedup data delivery.

In what follows, we introduce recent technology progresses on DCN topologies and network devices, which we leverage to address the above challenges.

2.2 New opportunities

Multiple edge-disjoint Steiner trees. Different from the Internet, DCNs are owned and operated by a single organization. As a result, DCN topologies are known in advance, and we can assume that there is a centralized controller to manage and monitor the whole DCN. Leveraging such information, we can improve RGDD efficiency by building efficient data delivery trees. Furthermore, several recently proposed DCNs (e.g., BCube [7] and CamCube [9]) have multiple edge-disjoint Steiner trees which can be used to further accelerate RGDD.

In-network packet caching becomes practical. Recently, we observe a clear technical trend for network devices (switches and routers). First, powerful CPUs and large memory are being included in network devices. The new generation of devices are equipped with multi-core X64 CPUs and several GB memory, e.g., Arista 7504 has 2 AMD Athlon X64 Dual-Core CPUs and 4GB DRAM. Second, the merchant switching ASIC, CPU and DRAM can be connected together by using the state-of-the-art PCI-E interface, as demonstrated by research prototype (e.g., ServerSwitch [8]) and products (e.g., Force10 S7000 [20]). With the new abilities of network devices, many in-network packet processing operations (e.g., in-network packet caching) become practical. In this paper, we explore in-network packet caching. By turning hard-states for group managements in intermediate network devices into soft-states based packet caching, we address the scalability and efficiency issues of RGDD.

However, technical challenges exist to take advantage of these opportunities. First, given the network topology, calculating one single Steiner tree with minimal cost is NP-hard [16]. What is more challenging is that we have to calculate multiple Steiner trees, and the calculation has to be fast enough (otherwise it may be more time consuming than data dissemination). Second, we have a large number of RGDD groups to support and have limited resources in intermediate network devices. How to use as few resources as possible to support more RGDD groups is a challenge.

We design Datacast to explore the new design spaces provided by the new opportunities. The design goal of Datacast is *to achieve scalability and also high bandwidth efficiency*. In what follows, we first introduce the architecture of Datacast, then describe how Datacast addresses the above technical challenges.

3. DATACAST OVERVIEW

Figure 2 shows the architecture of Datacast. There are five components in Datacast: Fabric Manager, Master, data source, receivers, and intermediate devices (IMD). Fabric Manager is a centralized controller, which maintains a glob-

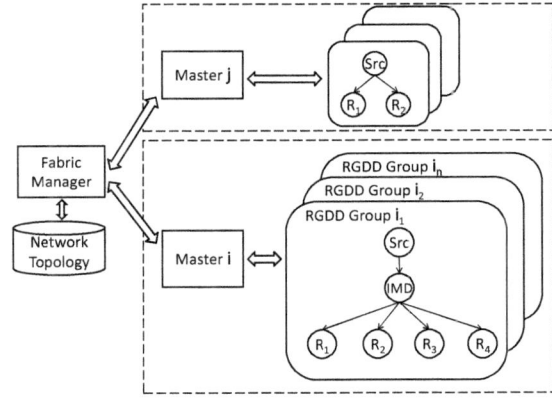

Figure 2: The architecture of Datacast. There are five major components in Datacast, Fabric Manager, Master, data source (Src), receivers (R_i), and intermediate devices (IMD).

al view of the network topology. When we need to start an RGDD group, we first start a Master. The Master will get topology information from Fabric Manager and then calculate multiple edge-disjoint Steiner trees. After that, the Master will send the tree information and other signalling messages (e.g., which file to fetch) to receivers via a signalling protocol. Then data transmission begins. When transmitting data, the data source will run our congestion control algorithm. During the whole process, intermediate devices do not interact with Fabric Manager, Master, the source or any receivers. These devices just cache and service data based on their local decisions.

To deliver signalling messages efficiently, we have built a signalling protocol, which uses a hierarchical transmission tree structure (generated by the Breadth First Search algorithm) to transmit signalling messages. It encodes the transmission tree into the message. Each node in the transmission tree decodes the signalling message, splits the tree into subtrees and forwards each subtree to its corresponding children. When the signalling messages reach the leaves, ACKs are generated and aggregated along the paths from leaves to the root. Using the message split and aggregation, signalling messages can be reliably and efficiently delivered.

In large data centers, failures are inevitable. Different from BitTorrent [4], which achieves fault tolerant in a distributed way, Datacast handles network failures in a centralized manner. In Datacast, Fabric Manager monitors the network status in real time. When network failures happen, Fabric Manager will send the new topology information to all the Masters, and each Master will recalculate the Steiner trees and notify the affected receivers accordingly. Due to space limitation, we omit the details of the signalling protocol and the failure handling details, but we do use real implementation and experiment to evaluate their performance in Section 7.2.3.

In the following sections, we will present two key designs of Datacast: the fast calculation of multiple edge-disjoint Steiner trees, and the Datacast congestion control protocol which helps Datacast achieve scalability and high bandwidth efficiency.

4. MULTIPLE EDGE-DISJOINT STEINER TREES IN DCN

In this section, we first present the algorithm on multiple Steiner trees calculation, then discuss how to use these multiple Steiner trees for data delivery.

4.1 Calculation of multiple Steiner trees

It has been known that using multiple Steiner trees can improve the transmission efficiency [3]. However, constructing multiple edge-disjoint Steiner trees in a given (data center) topology has not been investigated before. The problem is, *for a given network $G(V, E)$, where V is the set of nodes and E is the set of edges, and a group D containing one source and a set of receivers, how to calculate the maximum number of edge-disjoint Steiner trees.* This is the well known multiple edge-disjoint Steiner trees problem, which has been studied for decades. Unfortunately, calculating Steiner trees is NP-hard [16].

We therefore turn our attention to heuristic algorithms. One reasonable approach is as follows. There are algorithms for calculating multiple edge-disjoint spanning trees (e.g., [6]). We can first find the multiple edge-disjoint spanning trees, and then prune the unneeded edges and nodes to get the Steiner trees.

However, the generic multiple spanning trees algorithms do not work well for our case. First, the time complexity of calculating the spanning trees is high. The best algorithm we know is Po's algorithm [24]. Its time complexity is $O((k')^2|V||E|)$, which is too high for RGDD (we will see that in Section 6.1.1). Second, the depths of the spanning trees generated by the generic algorithm can be very large. For example, in the previous example for BCube, the average and worst-case depths of the trees can be 1000+ and 2000+ hops, whereas the network diameter is only 8.

Fortunately, we observe that DCNs, e.g., Fattree, BCube and multi-dimensional Torus, are well structured topologies. These topologies are also well studied. Multiple spanning trees construction algorithms for these topologies are already known (e.g., [7, 22]), and these spanning trees have good qualities, e.g., small tree depths. However, network failures (e.g., link failures) are common in real networks. Without reorganizing the spanning trees, network failures could possibly break all the trees generated by these algorithms. In order to solve the problem, we propose a multiple edge-disjoint Steiner trees algorithm, which is shown in Figure 3. The algorithm contains three parts.

The first part of this algorithm uses specific algorithms to construct spanning trees for specific DCN topologies (without considering network failures). For example, in Fattree [1], Breadth First Search (BFS) can generate a spanning tree, and the spanning trees algorithms for BCube and Torus are proposed in [7] and [22]. The time complexity of these algorithms are $O(k|V|)$, where k is the number of edge disjoint Spanning trees. Please see [10] for the algorithm details.

The second part prunes the links that are not used in data transmissions. To prune the spanning tree, we calculate the paths from the receivers to the source in the spanning tree. Then the set of links involved in the paths form a Steiner tree. The time complexity of pruning all the spanning trees is $O(|E|)$, since each link will only be traversed once.

The third part tries to repair the broken trees affected by link failures. The core idea of repairing a Steiner tree is: *we first release the broken tree, and then try to use BFS to*

```
// G is the DCN network, D is the Datacast group.
CalcSteinerTrees(G, D):
  // 1) construct multiple spanning trees
  SPTSet = G.CalcSpanningTrees(D.src);

  // 2) prune each spanning trees
  foreach (SPT in SPTSet)
    SteinerTree = Prune(SPT, D);
    SteinerTreeSet.add(SteinerTree);

  // 3) repair Steiner trees if they are broken
  foreach (SteinerTree in SteinerTreeSet)
    if (SteinerTree has broken links)
      if (RepairSteinerTree(SteinerTree, G) == false)
        Release(SteinerTree);
        SteinerTreeSet.remove(SteinerTree);
  return SteinerTreeSet;
```

Figure 3: The algorithm for multiple edge-disjoint Steiner trees calculation.

traverse the free and active links to construct a new Steiner tree. The repairing algorithm applies this idea to the broken trees one by one as shown in Figure 3. Although this idea is simple, it has the following benefits: 1) It guarantees at least one Steiner tree if all the receivers are connected. 2) The depth of the tree is locally minimized due to the use of BFS. The time complexity of repairing all the trees is $O(k'|E|)$, where k' is the number of Steiner trees to be repaired.

Our multiple Steiner trees calculation algorithm is fast. The time complexity of the algorithm is $O(k|V|) + O(|E|) + O(k'|E|)$, which contains the construction and pruning of spanning trees and the repairing of Steiner trees.

Our algorithm has good performance (in terms of the number of Steiner trees) and is fault tolerant. Even if there are network failures, we can still create a number of Steiner trees. We have derived an upper bound of the number of Steiner trees, and found that the number of Steiner trees generated by our algorithm is very close to the upper bound (details will be shown in Section 6.1.2). For Fattree, although it has only one Steiner tree, our algorithm guarantees that it always generates a Steiner tree as long as the network is connected.

In this paper, we evaluate our algorithm on Fattree, BCube and Torus. However, our algorithm is not constrained to these topologies. To use our algorithm for other topology, we only need to change the spanning trees construction part. Since data center networks are well structured and have been studied extensively, the spanning tree algorithms have already been proposed (e.g., HyperCube [27]), it is easy to adapt our algorithm for these topologies.

4.2 Data distribution among multiple Steiner trees

To use multiple Steiner trees for data delivery, we first split the data into blocks, and then feed each tree with a block. When a Steiner tree finishes transmitting the last data packet of the current block, we know that the transmission of the current block is finished. Then the data source will use our signalling protocol to deliver the information of the next block to be transferred, e.g., the name of the block, to the receivers. After that the Steiner tree will start to transmit the next block. This process repeats until all the blocks are successfully delivered.

5. DATACAST TRANSPORT PROTOCOL

In this section, we introduce in-network packet caching in Datacast, present the Datacast congestion control algorithm and discuss the cache management mechanism. By building a fluid model for the congestion control, we also derive the condition under which Datacast operates at the full rate, and its efficiency.

5.1 Data transmission with in-network caching

In-network packet caching has been used in many previous works, including Active Networking [23], RE (redundancy elimination) [2], and CCN [14]. Datacast is built on top of CCN. In CCN, every single packet is assigned a unique, hierarchical name. A user needs to explicitly send an interest packet to ask for the data packet. Any intermediate device that has the requested data along the routing path can respond with the data packet. The network devices along the reverse routing path then cache the data packet in their content stores for later uses. CCN therefore turns group communication into in-network packet caching.

Datacast improves CCN as follows: 1) Datacast introduces a congestion control algorithm to achieve stability and high bandwidth efficiency. 2) Datacast only caches data packets at branching nodes, which helps the whole system save memory. 3) Datacast uses source routing to enforce routing paths, so no Forwarding Information Base (FIB) management is needed at the intermediate devices.

Figure 4 shows an example of data delivery with in-network caching supports. The green node, 00, is the data source. The blue nodes, 12, 13, 21 and 33, are the receivers. The two Steiner trees calculated by the algorithm proposed in Section 4 are shown in solid lines and dashed lines separately. The transmission in Steiner tree A could take the following steps: 1) Node 21 sends an interest packet to node 00 through the path {21, 11, 01, 00}. Node 00 sends the requested data back along the reverse path. Then the data packet is cached at the branch node 01. 2) Node 12 sends an interest packet along the path {12, 02, 01, 00} asking for the same data. When the interest arrives at node 01, node 01 finds that it has already cached the data packet, so it terminates the interest and sends back the data packet. Then the data are cached at node 02 and 12. 3) Node 13 sends its interest along the path {13, 12, 02, 01, 00}. Then the data is replied by node 12, since it has cached the data. 4) Node 33 sends its interest along the path {33, 32, 02, 01, 00}, and node 02 returns the data packet.

Note that the execution order of the four steps in the example is not important. They can be executed in an arbitrary order, and still achieves the same result. The reason is that, in the end, all the steps together cover the same Steiner tree by traversing every link of the tree exactly once.

The benefits of in-network caching are two-fold: 1) By leveraging in-network caching, the network devices do not need to maintain hard group states. The intermediate devices do not even know that they are part of a group communication session. Hence Datacast is inherently scalable. 2) In-network caching makes reliable transmission easier to achieve. When a packet is dropped, the receiver will resend an interest packet requesting the same data packet (after timeout). This interest packet could be served by the nearest node that caches the requested data packet. The sender does not even necessarily know that there are packet losses

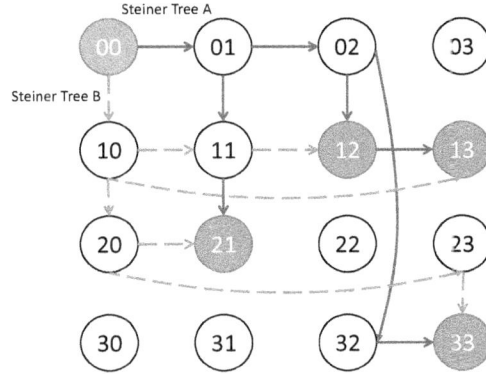

Figure 4: An illustration of in-network caching. The green node, 00, is the data source, while the blue ones, 12, 13, 21 and 33, are the receivers. Two Steiner trees are calculated, shown in the solid and dashed lines, respectively.

in the network, so the ACK/NAK implosion problem does not occur.

5.2 Datacast congestion control algorithm

Datacast congestion control algorithm works for a single Steiner tree. It is one of the most important part of Datacast to realize its design goal, i.e., to achieve scalability and high bandwidth efficiency. Since Datacast turns hard group states into soft-state based packet caching, it is natural to require that the cache size in intermediate devices for each group is as small as possible (so as to support more groups), and the rates of receivers are synchronized (so as to improve bandwidth efficiency). If the rates of receivers are synchronized, only one copy of each packet is delivered in a Steiner tree. When receivers have different receiving bandwidths, we expect all the rates of receivers are synchronized to the receiving rate of the slowest receiver.

A synchronized scheme may suffer from significant throughput degradation if a receiver in the group has a small receiving rate. In this case, we may either kick out the very slow receivers, or split the data delivery group into multiple ones. These topics are our future work.

Datacast uses the classical AIMD for congestion control. This is not new. What is new in Datacast is how congestion is detected. Datacast uses *duplicate interests* as congestion signals. A duplicate interest is an interest requiring the same data which has been asked before. The source receives a duplicate interest under the following two cases: 1) The network is congested, so some packets are dropped. Then the receiver will retransmit the interest, which serves as a duplicate interest. 2) Receivers are out of sync. When slow receivers cannot keep up with the fast ones, their interests will not be served by the cache of the intermediate devices. The interests will finally be sent to the data source, which serves as duplicate interests. In these cases, the source needs to slow down its sending rate. On the other hand, if there is no congestion and the rates of receivers are well synchronized, there will be no duplicate interests, and the source should increase its sending rate.

After congestion is detected, the rate adjustment becomes easy: when the source receives a duplicate interest, it decreases its sending rate by half; when no duplicate interest is received in a time interval T, the source increases the sending rate by δ. Datacast congestion control is therefore rate-based. The source maintains and controls a sending rate r[1]. Note that the sending rate of the duplicate data packet is not constrained by the congestion control, since the corresponding duplicate interest packets are from the slowest receiver, and the receiving rate of the slowest receiver should not be further reduced.

At the receivers' side, each receiver is given a fixed number of credit, w, which means that one receiver can send at most w interests into the network. When a receiver sends out an interest, the credit is decremented by one. When it receives a data packet, its credit is incremented by one. In Datacast, the guideline for setting w is to saturate the pipe. In a DCN with 1Gbps link, when the RTT is 200us (which is a typical network latency in a data center environment), $w = 16$ can saturate the link. To achieve reliability, the receiver retransmits an interest if the corresponding data packet does not come back after a timeout. The timeout is calculated in the same way as TCP.

To summarize, Datacast congest control algorithm works as follows.

$$r = \left\{ \begin{array}{ll} \frac{r}{2} & \text{when a duplicate interest is received.} \\ r + \delta & \text{when there is no duplicate interest in T.} \end{array} \right.$$

As we can see, the Datacast congestion control algorithm is simple. The source does not need to know which receiver is the slowest one, and what is the available bandwidth of that slowest receiver. In Section 5.4, we will show analytically that Datacast uses small caches size and results in few duplicate data transmissions.

5.3 Cache management

To prevent cache interferences among different transmission trees, we use a *per-tree based* cache replacement algorithm. Each device uses a per Datacast tree based cache with size C. This is possible due to the following reasons: 1) A Datacast tree can be uniquely identified by a global unique tree transmission id (assigned by Master). 2) The cache size needed by each tree is small (as we will show in the next subsection).

In each tree, we find that the most popular data packets are the new ones, since new data packets will always be accessed by other receivers in the future. To keep new data packets in caches and erase old data packets, Datacast chooses First In First Out (FIFO) as its per-tree cache replacement policy. To prevent unpopular data packets from being put into caches, Datacast does not cache duplicate data packets.

Note that although this is a per-tree strategy, it is a scalable solution. The reasons are: 1) Compared with IP multicast, we do not need any protocol (e.g., IGMP) to maintain Datacast's per-tree states. Switches just use local decisions to manage its cache. 2) Datacast can work efficiently with small caches, e.g., 125KB, and large memory is expected for future network devices, e.g., 16GB memory for a switch. If it uses 4GB as Datacast cache, a network device can support up to 32k ($\approx \frac{4GB}{125KB}$) simultaneous trees.

---

[1]To be exact, this is the rate of the source's token bucket. The source cannot achieve this rate if there are not enough interests from the receivers.

5.4 Properties of Datacast congestion control algorithm

In this subsection, we study the following questions: 1) What is the condition for Datacast to work at the full rate (i.e., the receiving rate of the slowest receiver)? 2) When Datacast works at the full rate, how much duplicate data will be sent from the data source? We define the *duplicate data ratio* as the ratio of the duplicate data sent by the source to all the new data sent. To answer these questions, we have built a fluid model and derived the following theorems. (Details are presented in Appendix.)

THEOREM 1. *Datacast works at the full rate, i.e., the rate of the slowest receiver, R, if the cache size, C, satisfies*

$$C > \frac{R^2 T}{2\delta}$$

THEOREM 2. *When Datacast works at the full rate, the duplicate data ratio of Datacast is*

$$\frac{\frac{\delta}{T}}{\frac{\delta}{T} + \frac{R^2}{2MTU}}$$

Theorem 1 tells us Datacast works at the full rate when the cache size is greater than $\frac{R^2 T}{2\delta}$. For example, when $\delta = 5$Mbps, $T = 1$ms, and $R = 100$Mbps, Datacast works at the full rate when the cache size C is larger than 125KB. Theorem 2 reveals the bandwidth efficiency of Datacast. In the above example, the duplicate data ratio is 1.19%. Theorem 1 and 2 tell us that Datacast can achieve the goal of high bandwidth efficiency, and at the same time it also meets the requirement of using small cache size in the intermediate devices.

6. SIMULATION

In this section, we use simulations to study Datacast. First, we evaluate our multiple Steiner trees algorithm. Second, we design micro benchmarks to study Datacast congestion control algorithm. Third, we compare the performance of Datacast with the most widely used P2P overlay, BitTorrent.

6.1 Evaluation of the multiple Steiner trees algorithm

To study the performance of the multiple Steiner trees algorithm, we use a Dell PowerEdge R610 server, which has two E5520 Intel Xeon 2.26GHz CPU and 32GB RAM. We study our algorithm under three topologies, Fattree(24, 3), BCube(8, 3) and Torus(16, 3). The BCube and Torus contain 4096 servers, while the Fattree contains 3456 servers. For each simulation, we randomly generate link failures. The link failure rates (LFR) include 1%, 3% and 5%. We ignore the cases when the network is not connected.

6.1.1 Running time

Figure 5 shows the running times of our algorithm. From the results, we can see that our algorithm can finish all of the tree calculations within 10ms.

We compared our algorithm with the generic algorithm which first calculates the spanning trees using Po's algorithm [24], then prunes them to get Steiner trees. The time complexity of the generic algorithm is dominated by

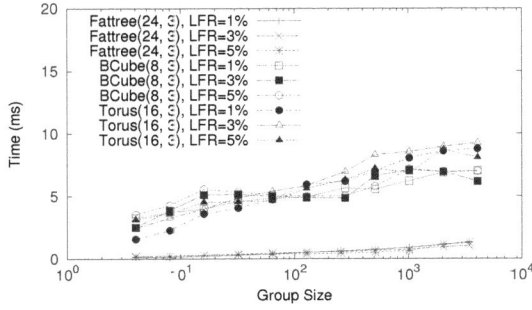

Figure 5: Running times of our Steiner tree algorithm.

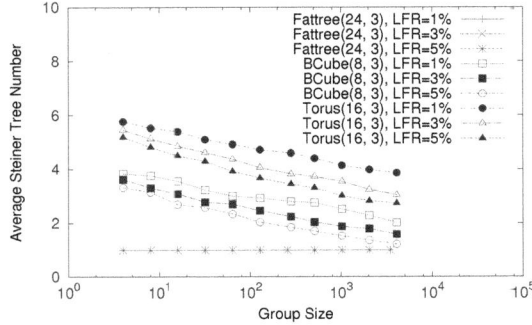

Figure 6: The numbers of Steiner trees with different failure rates and group sizes.

the spanning tree calculation. The times needed for calculating spanning trees for Fattree(24, 3), BCube(8, 3) and Torus(16, 3) are 1, 39 and 42 seconds respectively. This algorithm therefore cannot be used in Datacast.

6.1.2 Steiner tree number

Figure 6 shows the numbers of Steiner trees constructed by our algorithm. For BCube and Torus, the numbers of Steiner trees decrease as the group size and the link failure rate increase. This is expected, since a large group would experience more link failures, and more link failures will break more trees. Though Fattree has only one Steiner tree, our algorithm helps on failure recovery when the original tree is broken by link failures.

To check whether our algorithm can create enough Steiner trees, we have derived a bound of the Steiner tree number, which is the minimum value of the out-degree of the source and the in-degrees of all the receivers. The Steiner tree numbers produced by our algorithm are only 0.3% less than the bounds on average.

6.1.3 Steiner tree depths

Our algorithm also guarantees small tree depths. For example, when the link failure rate is 1%, the average Steiner tree depths for BCube, Torus and Fattree, are 9.99, 24.31 and 6.00, respectively.

6.2 Micro benchmarks for Datacast congestion control algorithm

We have built Datacast in NS3. In this subsection, we use micro benchmarks to study Datacast congestion control

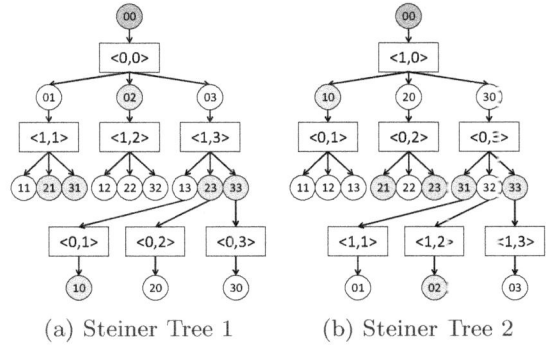

(a) Steiner Tree 1   (b) Steiner Tree 2

Figure 7: The simulation and experiment setup. The green node, 00, is the source, while the blue ones, 02, 10, 21, 23, 31 and 33, are the receivers.

Cache Size (KB)	Throughput (Mbps)	Duplicate Data Ratio (%)
8	91.380	1.15
32	95.076	1.14
128	98.799	1.11
512	98.799	1.10
2048	98.799	1.12

Table 1: Datacast's performance under different cache sizes.

algorithm in a BCube(4, 1). We use a single multicast tree shown in Figure 7(a). The green node, 00, is the source, while the blue ones, 02, 10, 21, 23, 31 and 33, are the receivers. $\delta = 5$Mbps, $T = 1$ms and MTU = 1.5KB. The link rates are 1Gbps, and the propagation delays are 5us. We slow down the link from switch <0,0> to node 02 to 100Mbps to make node 02 the slowest receiver. The queue size for each link is 100 packets. The headers of the interest and data packets are both 16 bytes. The initial rate of the source is 500Mbps.

6.2.1 Efficiency study

We first verify Theorem 1. We vary the cache sizes from 8KB to 2048KB. Based on Theorem 1, Datacast works at the full rate when the cache size is larger than 125KB. The simulation results are shown in Table 1. From the results, we can see that Datacast works at the full rate when the cache size is larger than 125KB. Its throughput, 98.799Mbps, is very close to the optimal results, which is 98.933Mbps (= 100Mbps $\times \frac{1500-16}{1500}$). The table also shows that the throughput of Datacast degrades gracefully when the cache size is smaller than 125KB.

The table shows that the duplicate data ratio is about 1.12%. This is close to the result produced by Theorem 2, 1.19%. It also shows that the duplicate data ratio does not depend on the cache size once Datacast works at the full rate. To examine the accuracy of Theorem 2, we also vary the rate increase, δ, from 0.10Mbps to 102.40Mbps. From the results shown in Figure 8, we can see that the duplicate data ratio derived from our model is consistent with the simulation results.

6.2.2 Performance under packet losses

To see whether Datacast is resilient to packet losses, we randomly drop data packets at the link from switch <0,0>

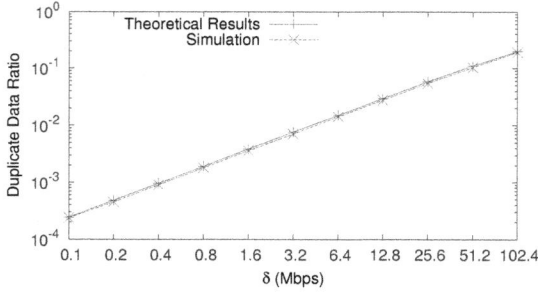

Figure 8: Duplicate data ratio vs. δ.

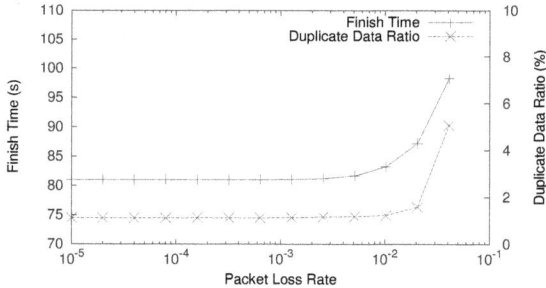

Figure 9: Datacast's performance under different packet loss rates.

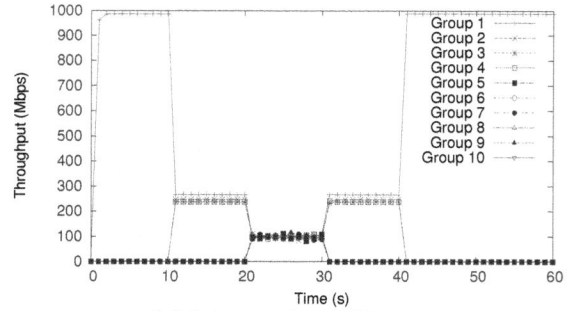

(a) Intra-protocol fairness.

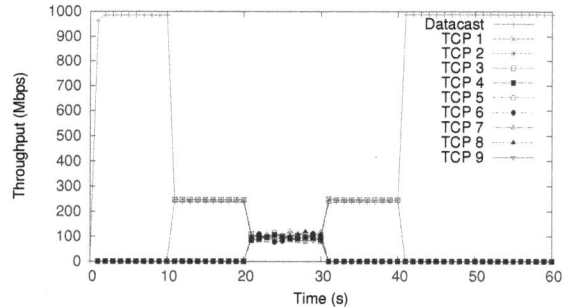

(b) Inter-protocol fairness with TCP.

Figure 10: Intra-protocol and inter-protocol fairness.

to node 02. The packet drop rate ranges from 0.001% to 4.096%. The cache sizes are set to 128KB. The results in Figure 9 shows that Datacast is quite resilient to packet losses. Even when the packet loss rate is 1.02%, the finish time only increases by 2.76% and the duplicate ratio is 1.23%.

6.2.3 Fairness

In this simulation, we set all the links back to 1Gbps. To study intra-protocol fairness, we set up multiple Datacast groups. The first group, which is shown in Figure 7(a), starts at time 0s. At time 10s, we start three new groups, whose source is node 00 and receivers are node 12, 22, 32. These three groups stop at time 40s. At time 20s, we start another six groups, whose source is node 00 and receivers are node 11 and 21. These groups end at time 30s. The ten groups share a congestion point at the link from node 00 to switch <0,0>. From the results shown in Figure 10(a), we can see that the first four groups equally get about 250Mbps throughput after time 10s, and the ten groups equally get about 100Mbps after time 20s. This means that Datacast congestion control algorithm achieves good intra-protocol fairness.

We also investigate whether Datacast congestion control algorithm is friendly to TCP. Similarly, we set up a Datacast group shown in Figure 7(a), which starts at time 0s. At time 10s, three TCP connections from node 00 to node 02 start. The three connections end at time 40s. At time 20s, six TCP connections from node 00 to node 01 start, which end at time 30s. The Datacast and TCP connections congest at the link from node 00 to switch <0,0>. The results are shown in Figure 10(b), which suggest that Datacast congestion control algorithm has good inter-protocol fairness with TCP.

Datacast achieves good inter-protocol fairness with TCP, since their additive increase parts are at the same magnitude. In this simulation, we measure that the RTT of TCP is about 1ms when there are nine TCP flows and one Datacast group. TCP increases its rate at the speed of 12Mbps ($= \frac{MTU}{RTT}$) per RTT (1ms), while Datacast increases its rate at the speed of 5Mbps per millisecond. Therefore, Datacast and TCP achieve good inter-protocol fairness.

6.2.4 Cache replacement algorithms

We study the performance of Datacast when different cache management policies are used. We find that the cache management algorithms affect the duplicate data ratio. We evaluate three representative cache management algorithms, Least Recently Used (LRU), Least Frequently Used (LFU) and First In First Out (FIFO). The three algorithms differ in the replacement of cache items. When we need to replace an old item with a new one, LRU replaces the one that has been least used recently, LFU replaces the one that has the lowest used frequency, and FIFO replaces the one that first enters the cache.

The cache miss ratios for LRU, LRU and FIFO are 3.90%, 1.63% and 1.12%, respectively. LRU and LFU cause larger duplicate data ratios due to the following reason. When the slowest receiver cannot keep up with the fast ones, its interests will be sent to the data source as duplicate interests, and then the source slows down its sending rate. During the process that the slowest receiver is catching up with the fast ones, it accesses the old data packets in the caches and makes its next data packet as the least recently (or frequently) used when LRU (or LFU) is used. So if the source sends out a new packet for the fast receivers, it will erase the next data packet for the slowest receiver in intermediate devices' caches, resulting in more cache misses and duplicate data.

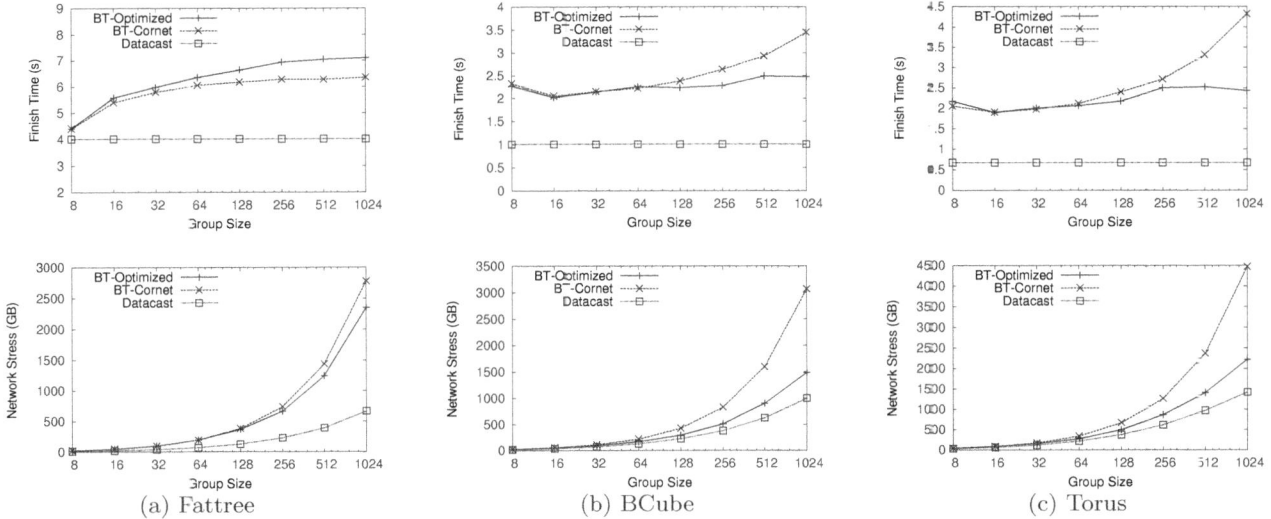

Figure 11: Performance comparison of Datacast and BitTorrent.

6.3 Performance comparison

BitTorrent was originally designed for P2P file sharing in the Internet. Since a data center is a collaborative environment and the network topology can be known in advance, we use techniques similar to Cornet [11] to improve the original BitTorrent. Cornet improvements include: a server does not immediately leave the system after it receives all the content; no SHA1 calculation per block; use large block size (4MB). Cornet suggests using large block size (4MB). Our simulations demonstrate that smaller block size results in better performance. We choose 108KB as the block size in the simulations. We call the Cornet optimized version BT-Cornet. Similar to Cornet, we also consider the topology awareness. Since the topologies we use have rich topological information, we design the following neighbor selection algorithm: a server selects 10 peers (when the group size is less than 10, all the members are peers). It sorts the group members via the distance. It prefers peers with a small distance, but guarantees that at least one member (if it exists) is selected as its peer at each distance range. Similar to Cornet, tit-for-tat and choke-unchoke are disabled. We call the optimized version BT-Optimized.

We use two metrics for the comparison. The first metric is the network stress, which is the sum of all the bytes transmitted on all the links. The second is the finish time.

In all the simulations, the source sends 500MB data. Figure 11 shows the performances of Datacast, BT-Cornet, BT-Optimized under different group sizes for three different topologies, Fattree(24, 3), BCube(8, 3) and Torus(16, 3). The group size varies from 8 to 1024. Our results clearly demonstrate that Datacast is better than BT-Cornet and BT-Optimized in terms of the network stress of the finish time. On BCube and Torus, Datacast is much faster since each server has multiple 1GbE ports. In all the simulations, the network stresses of BT-Optimized are 1.2-3.5X than Datacast, and Datacast is 1.1-3.7X faster than BT-Optimized.

We also note that in our simulations, when the topology is Fattree, the finish time with BT-Cornet is smaller than with BT-Optimized. This is because with BT-Optimized, we

prefer peers that are close with each other. This preference may result in small cliques which may not be fully connected. BCube does not have such an issue because its structure does not have hierarchy.

In the experiments, Datacast's finish times are quite close to the ideal cases. There is one Steiner tree in Fattree(24, 3), and there are four Steiner trees in BCube(8, 3), and six in Torus(16, 3). Therefore the ideal finish times are 4s, 1s and 0.67s for Fattree(24, 3), BCube(8, 3) and Torus(16, 3), respectively. The finish times of Datacast are 0.67% larger than the ideal cases on average. Datacast is also efficient. The average link stress of Datacast is only 1.002, which means that each packet only traverse each Steiner tree link 1.002 times on average.

7. IMPLEMENTATION

7.1 ServerSwitch based implementation

We have implemented Datacast using the design shown in Figure 2. Fabric Manager, Master, data source and receivers are all implemented as user-mode applications. Each node in the data center runs a Datacast daemon, which is responsible for forwarding and receiving signalling messages. When Datacast is trying to start a group for data transmission, it first starts a Master process. The Master process calculates multiple Steiner trees, and then sends signalling messages to the group members. The daemons on these nodes will start the data source process and the receiver processes. Then the transmission starts.

To cache data packets in intermediate nodes, we use the ServerSwitch platform [8]. ServerSwitch is composed of an ASIC switching chip and a commodity server. The switching chip is connected to the server CPU and memory using PCI-E. ServerSwitch's switching chip is programmable. It uses a TCAM table to define operations for specific types of packets. To implement data packet caching in switches, we use User Defined Lookup Keys (UDLK) to forward data packets to the Datacast kernel mode driver at branch nodes. The driver is used to do the in-network data packet caching. At non-branch nodes, the data packets are directly forwarded by hardware.

7.2 Evaluation

In this subsection, we use our real testbed implementation to evaluate Datacast. We use a BCube(4, 1) with 1Gbps links for our study. 8KB jumbo frame is used in the experiment.

7.2.1 Efficiency study

We study Datacast's performance when different cache sizes are set for branching nodes. We use a single Steiner tree shown in Figure 7(a) and slow down the link from switch <1,3> to node 23 to 100Mbps. We let $\delta = 5$Mbps and $T = 2$ms. Based on Theorem 1, Datacast works at the full rate when the cache size is larger than 256KB. When we use 64KB cache, the average throughput is 91.998Mbps, which is still acceptable due to the graceful throughput degradation of Datacast. When the cache size is 256KB, the average throughput is 99.595Mbps, and the duplicate data ratio is 3.48%, which is close to the theoretical result of Theorem 2, 3.10%.

7.2.2 Performance comparison

We compare the performance of Datacast with BitTorrent (we use μtorrent). In this experiment, we use both Datacast and BitTorrent to transfer 4GB data. The cache size on each branch node is 512KB. For Datacast, $\delta = 125$Mbps and $T = 1$ms.

Datacast finishes the transmission within 16.9s. The source achieves 1.89Gbps throughput on average, which is close to the 2Gbps capacity of the two 1GbE Steiner trees. The link stress of Datacast is 1.01. This means that Datacast achieves high bandwidth efficiency, since each packet only traverses each Steiner tree link 1.01 times on average. We compare Datacast with BitTorrent. Using BitTorrent, the receivers finish the downloading in 41-52s, and the link stress is 1.39. So BitTorrent is 2.75 times slower than Datacast on average, while its link stress is 1.38 times larger.

7.2.3 Failure handling

To study the failure handling of Datacast, we manually tear down the slow link. Our Fabric Manager detects the link failure in 483ms, and then notifies all the Masters. The Master uses the signalling protocol proposed in Section 3 to deliver the signalling messages to all the receivers in 2.592ms. (As a comparison, using TCP to send the signalling messages to receivers in parallel takes 20.122ms.) Then the transmission continues.

8. RELATED WORK

RGDD is an important traffic pattern, which has been studied for decades. Existing solutions can be classified into two categories.

Reliable IP multicast. The design space of reliable IP multicast has been nicely described in [12]. IP multicast has scalability issues for maintaining a large number of group states in the network. Adding reliability to IP multicast is also hard due to the ACK implosion problem [13].

We compare Datacast with two representative reliable multicast systems: pgm congestion control (pgmcc) [21] and Active Reliable Multicast (ARM) [25]. Pgmcc needs to explicitly track the slowest receiver for congestion control, and

the congestion control protocol needs to be run between the sender and the slowest receiver. Datacast does not need to track which receiver is the slowest. This is because Datacast uses the duplicate interest packets as congestion signals, hence congestion control becomes the local action of the sender. ARM uses the active network concept and network devices also cache packet, but the cached packets are used only for re-transmission. Hence most likely the cached packets will not be used even once. Furthermore, re-transmitted packets are broadcasted along the whole sub-tree in ARM, whereas they are delivered only to the needed receivers in Datacast.

End-host based overlay system. End-host based overlay system overcomes the scalability issue by transmitting data among peers. No group states are needed in network devices, and reliability is easily achieved by directly using TCP. It is widely used in the Internet. However, end-host based overlay systems suffer from low bandwidth efficiency. For example, the worst-case link stress of SplitStream can be tens [3], and the average and worst-case link stresses of End System Multicast (ESM) [18] are 1.9 and 9, respectively.

Recently, in the work of Orchestra [11], Cornet is proposed, which is an optimized version of BitTorrent for DCNs. Different from the distributed manner of Cornet, Datacast is a centralized approach. Due to the fact that a data center network is built and managed by a single organization, centralized designs become possible (e.g., software-defined networking [17]). Due to its centralized nature, Datacast is able to utilize multiple Steiner trees for data delivery, and achieve minimum finish time. Since the routing path from a receiver to data source is predetermined, high cache utilization is achieved. Furthermore, as we have demonstrated in the paper, the intermediate device only needs to maintain small cache per Steiner tree. All these benefits are hard, if not totally impossible, to be achieved by distributed approaches like Cornet.

9. CONCLUSION

In this paper, we have presented the design, analysis, implementation and evaluation of Datacast for RGDD in data centers. Datacast first calculates multiple edge-disjoint Steiner trees with low time complexity, and then distributes data among them. In each Steiner tree, by leveraging in-network packet caching, Datacast uses a simple, but effective congestion control algorithm to achieve scalability and high bandwidth efficiency.

By building a fluid model, we show analytically that the congestion control algorithm uses small cache size for each group (e.g., 125KB), and results in few duplicate data transmissions (e.g., 1.19%). Our analytical results are verified by both simulations and experiments. We have implemented Datacast using the ServerSwitch platform. When we use Datacast to transmit 4GB data in our 1GbE BCube(4, 1) testbed with two edge-disjoint Steiner trees, the link stress is only 1.01 and the finish time is 16.9s, which is close to the 16s lower bound.

10. ACKNOWLEDGEMENT

We thank Zhenyu Guo, Wei Lin, Zhengping Qian, Ming Wu for helping us understand more about RGDD, and Xin Liu for suggestions on the model improvements. We thank our shepherd Prof. Vishal Misra and the anonymous reviewers for their valuable suggestions that improve the presentation of the paper.

11. REFERENCES

[1] M. Al-Fares, A. Loukissas, and A. Vahdat. A Scalable, Commodity Data Center Network Architecture. In *SIGCOMM*, 2008.

[2] Ashok Anand, Archit Gupta, Aditya Akella, Srinivasan Seshan, and Scott Shenker. Packet Caches on Routers: The Implications of Universal Redundant Traffic Elimination. In *SIGCOMM*, 2008.

[3] Miguel Castro, Peter Druschel, Anne-Marie Kermarrec, Animesh Nandi, Antony Rowstron, and Atul Singh. SplitStream: High-Bandwidth Multicast in Cooperative Environments. In *SOSP*, 2003.

[4] Bram Cohen. Incentives Build Robustness in BitTorrent. In *Workshop on Economics of Peer-to-Peer Systems*, 2003.

[5] J. Dean and S. Ghemawat. MapReduce: Simplified Data Processing on Large Clusters. In *OSDI*, 2004.

[6] J. Edmonds. Edge-disjoint branchings. In R. Rustin, editor, *Combinatorial Algorithms*, pages 91–96. Algorithmics Press, New York, 1972.

[7] C. Guo et al. BCube: A High Performance, Server-centric Network Architecture for Modular Data Centers. In *SIGCOMM*, 2009.

[8] Guohan Lu et al. ServerSwitch: A Programmable and High Performance Platform for Data Center Networks. In *NSDI*, 2011.

[9] Hussam Abu-Libdeh et al. Symbiotic Routing in Future Data Centers. In *SIGCOMM*, 2010.

[10] J. Cao et al. Datacast: A Scalable and Efficient Group Data Delivery Service for Data Centers. Technical Report MSR-TR-2012-57, MSR, 2012. http://research.microsoft.com/apps/pubs/?id=166825.

[11] M. Chowdhury et al. Managing Data Transfers in Computer Clusters with Orchestra. In *SIGCOMM*, 2011.

[12] M. Handley et al. The Reliable Multicast Design Space for Bulk Data Transfer, Aug 2000. RFC2887.

[13] Sally Floyd et al. A Reliable Multicast Framework for Light-weight Sessions and Application Level Framing. *IEEE trans. Networking*, Dec 1997.

[14] Van Jacobson et al. Networking Named Content. In *CoNEXT*, 2009.

[15] S. Ghemawat, H. Gobioff, and S. Leung. The Google File System. In *SOSP*, 2003.

[16] R. L. Graham and L. R. Foulds. Unlikelihood That Minimal Phylogenies for a Realistic Biological Study Can Be Constructed in Reasonable Computational Time. *Mathematical Bioscience*, 1982.

[17] K. Greene. Special reports 10 emerging technologies 2009. MIT Technology Review, 2009. http://www.technologyreview.com/biotech/22120/.

[18] Yang hua Chu, Sanjay G. Rao, Srinivasan Seshan, and Hui Zhang. A Case for End System Multicast. *IEEE JSAC*, Oct 2002.

[19] M. Isard, M. Budiu, and Y. Yu. Dryad: Distributed Data-Parallel Programs from Sequential Building Blocks. In *EuroSys*, 2007.

[20] Force10 networks. Force10 s7000. www.force10networks.com.

[21] Luigi Rizzo. pgmcc: a TCP-friendly Single Rate Multicast Congestion Control Scheme. In *SIGCOMM*, 2000.

[22] Shyue-Ming Tang, Jinn-Shyong Yang, Yue-Li Wang, and Jou-Ming Chang. Independent Spanning Trees on Multidimensional Torus Networks. *IEEE Trans. Computers*, Jan 2010.

[23] David L. Tennenhouse and David J. Wetherall. Towards an Active Network Architecture. *SIGCOMM CCR*, Apr 1996

[24] Po Tong and E. L. Lawler. A Fast Algorithm for Finding Edge-disjoint Branchings. *Information Processing Letters*, Aug 1983.

[25] Li wei H. Lehman, Stephen J. Garland, and David L. Tennenhouse. Active Reliable Multicast. In *INFOCOM*, 1998.

[26] J. Widmer and M. Handley. TCP-Friendly Multicast Congestion Control (TFMCC): Protocol Specification, Auguest 2006. RFC 4654.

[27] J.S. Yang, S.M. Tang, J.M. Chang, and Y.L. Wang. Parallel Construction of Optimal Independent Spanning Trees on Hypercubes. *Parallel Computing*, 33, 2007.

Notation	Meaning
t	The current time.
$x_s(t)$	The data sequence position of the data source.
$x_r(t)$	The data sequence position of the slowest receiver.
R	The rate of the slowest receivers.
C	The size of the cache (the content store).
MTU	The size of a full Datacast data packet.
δ, T	The two parameters of Datacast congestion control, which are proposed in Section 5.2.
t_a	The start time of state 0.
t_b	The end time of state 0, and the start time of state 1.
t_c	The end time of state 1.
$\Delta x(t)$	$x_s(t) - x_r(t)$

Table 2: Notations used in the fluid model.

APPENDIX

A. PROOF OF THE DATACAST THEOREMS

We build a fluid model to analyze the performance of Datacast. We make the following assumptions: 1) The (desired[2]) rate of the slowest receiver, R, does not change over time. 2) Network latencies and queueing delays are negligible. In data center environment, network latency is small and around several hundreds of microseconds. 3) The credit number w is large enough to saturate the pipe. Table 2 shows the notations that are used in the analysis. Our fluid model can be described by the following equations:

$$x_s''(t) = (1 - p(t))\frac{\delta}{T} - p(t)\frac{x_s'(t)}{2}\frac{x_r'(t)}{MTU} \quad (1)$$

$$x_r'(t) = \begin{cases} R & \text{if } x_r(t) < x_s(t) \\ \max\{R, \ x_s'(t)\} & \text{if } x_r(t) = x_s(t) \end{cases} \quad (2)$$

$$p(t) = \mathbb{1}_{\{x_s(t) - x_r(t) > C\}} \quad (3)$$

In this model, Equation (2) captures the slowest receiver's (actual) rate. When the source is ahead of the slowest receiver, the slowest receiver's rate is R. When the slowest receiver catches up with the source, its rate is constrained by both the source's rate and R. Equation (3) is an indicator function. $p(t) = 1$ when the data source receives a duplicate interest, otherwise $p(t) = 0$. Equation (1) models the rate control at the data source. $\frac{\delta}{T}$ captures a constant rate increase δ in every time period T if there is no duplicate interest. The second term is the rate decrease when duplicate interests are received (i.e., $p(t) = 1$). When $p(t) = 1$, the data source receives one duplicate interest from the slowest receiver in every time period $\frac{MTU}{x_r'(t)}$, and decreases its sending rate by half. The decreasing rate therefore is $\frac{x_s'(t)}{2} / \frac{MTU}{x_r'(t)} = \frac{x_s'(t)}{2}\frac{x_r'(t)}{MTU}$.

We say the system is in **state 0** when $p(t) = 0$, in **state 1** when $p(t) = 1$. It is easy to see that the system will oscillate between the two states, since $x_s''(t) > 0$ in state 0, and

---

[2]Here "desired" means that the rate of the slowest receiver is not constrained by the sending rate of the data source.

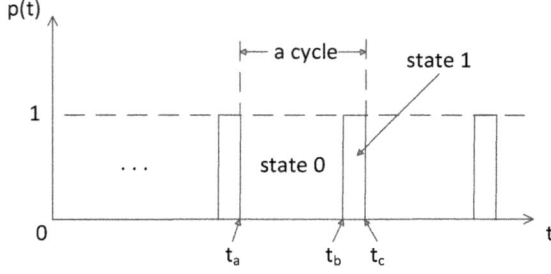

Figure 12: An illustration of the state changes in Datacast.

$x''_s(t) < 0$ in state 1. We call it a **cycle** from the start of state 0 to the end of state 1. Figure 12 gives us an illustration of how state changes in Datacast.

Proof of Theorem 1:

PROOF. We first prove that if $C > \frac{R^2 T}{2\delta}$, the rate of the slowest receiver is R, i.e., $x'_r(t) = R$. To prove that, we first prove $\Delta x(t) > 0$. It is easy to see it holds in state 1, since it is $\Delta x(t) > C$ in state 1. In state 0, we have $x''_s(t) = \frac{\delta}{T}$, and we can calculate

$$x'_s(t) = x'_s(t_a) + \frac{\delta}{T}(t - t_a)$$

From Equation (2), we have $x'_r(t) \leq R$. Then we can derive

$$\Delta x'(t) \geq x'_s(t_a) + \frac{\delta}{T}(t - t_a) - R \qquad (4)$$

Based on Inequality (4) and $\Delta x(t_a) = C$, we can derive

$$\Delta x(t) \geq \frac{\delta}{2T}(t - t_a)^2 + (x'_s(t_a) - R)(t - t_a) + C \qquad (5)$$

The right side of Inequality (5) achieves its minimum value when $t = t_a + \frac{T}{\delta}(R - x'_s(t_a))$, and $t_a + \frac{T}{\delta}(R - x'_s(t_a))$ is in the region of (t_a, t_b). It is greater than t_a, since $x'_s(t_a) < R$. It is lower than t_b, since $t_b = t_a + \frac{T}{\delta}(x'_s(t_b) - x'_s(t_a))$ and $x'_s(t_b) > R$. Put it into Inequality (5), we get

$$\Delta x(t) \geq \frac{\delta}{2T}(\frac{T}{\delta})^2(R - x'_s(t_a))^2 - \frac{T}{\delta}(R - x'_s(t_a))^2 + C$$
$$= C - \frac{T}{2\delta}(R - x'_s(t_a))^2$$
$$\geq C - \frac{R^2 T}{2\delta}$$

Since $C > \frac{R^2 T}{2\delta}$, we have $\Delta x(t) > 0$ in state 0. $\Delta x(t)$ is therefore always greater than 0 in both states.

Putting $\Delta x(t) > 0$ into (2), we get $x'_r(t) = R$, which means that the slowest receiver's rate is not slowed down. We can further prove that the average sending rate of the data source will converge to R (which is omitted due to the space limitation), i.e., Datacast works at the full rate when $C > \frac{R^2 T}{2\delta}$. □

Theorem 1 provides a sufficient condition to guarantee $x'_r(t) = R$. When C is not large enough, $x'_r(t)$ can be constrained by $x'_s(t)$ in state 0. However, $x'_s(t)$ will grow at a constant speed, $\frac{\delta}{T}$. $x_s(t)$ will soon be greater than $x_r(t)$, which means that the slowest receiver's rate is back to R. Even when C is not large enough, the system will experience

graceful performance degradation instead of abrupt performance changes, as we have observed in the simulations and experiments.

Proof of Theorem 2:

PROOF. The duplicate ratio can be calculated as

$$\frac{(t_c - t_b)R}{x_s(t_c) - x_s(t_a)}$$

when Datacast works at full rate, i.e., $x'_r(t) = R$. $(t_c - t_b)R$ is the amount of duplicate data that the slowest receiver requested in state 1, while $x_s(t_c) - x_s(t_a)$ is the amount of new data sent from the source in the whole cycle. Noticing that $\Delta x(t_a) = \Delta x(t_c) = C$, we have $x_s(t_c) - x_s(t_a) = x_r(t_c) - x_r(t_a)$. Since $x'_r(t) = R$, $x_r(t_c) - x_r(t_a) = (t_c - t_a)R$. The duplicate data ratio can be calculated as

$$\frac{t_c - t_b}{t_c - t_a} \qquad (6)$$

To calculate (6), we first derive the durations of two states. In state 0, $x''_s(t) = \frac{\delta}{T}$ and $x'_r(t) = R$, based on which we get

$$\Delta x(t) = \frac{\delta}{2T}(t - t_a)^2 + (x'_s(t_a) - R)(t - t_a) + C \qquad (7)$$

In state 0, since $x'_s(t)$ increases linearly, we have

$$x'_s(t_b) = x'_s(t_a) + \frac{\delta}{T}(t_b - t_a) \qquad (8)$$

Combining $\Delta x(t_b) = C$ and Equation (7) and (8), we get

$$x'_s(t_b) = 2R - x'_s(t_a) \qquad (9)$$

Putting Equation (9) back into Equation (8), we have

$$t_b - t_a = \frac{2(R - x'_s(t_a))}{\frac{\delta}{T}} \qquad (10)$$

In state 1, $x''_s(t) = -\frac{x'_s(t)}{2}\frac{x'_r(t)}{MTU}$ and $x'_r(t) = R$, based on which we can derive

$$\Delta x(t) = \frac{2MTU}{R}x'_s(t_b)(1 - e^{-\frac{R}{2MTU}(t - t_b)}) - (t - t_b)R + C \qquad (11)$$

In state 1, since $x'_s(t)$ decreases exponentially, we have

$$x'_s(t_c) = x'_s(t_b)e^{-\frac{R}{2MTU}(t_c - t_b)} \qquad (12)$$

Combining Equation (9), (11) and (12), we derive

$$t_c - t_b = \frac{2R - x'_s(t_a) - x'_s(t_c)}{\frac{R^2}{2MTU}}$$

The end of state 1 is also the start of state 0 in the next cycle. In stable state, $x'_s(t_c)$ and $x'_s(t_a)$ are the same, we thus have

$$t_c - t_b = \frac{2(R - x'_s(t_a))}{\frac{R^2}{2MTU}} \qquad (13)$$

Combining (6) with the durations of the two states, (10) and (13), the duplicate ratio is

$$\frac{t_c - t_b}{t_c - t_a} = \frac{\frac{2(R - x'_s(t_a))}{\frac{R^2}{2MTU}}}{\frac{2(R - x'_s(t_a))}{\frac{R^2}{2MTU}} + \frac{2(R - x'_s(t_a))}{\frac{\delta}{T}}} = \frac{\frac{\delta}{T}}{\frac{\delta}{T} + \frac{R^2}{2MTU}}$$

□

PAST: Scalable Ethernet for Data Centers

Brent Stephens   Alan Cox
Rice University
Houston, TX
brents,alc@rice.edu

Wes Felter   Colin Dixon   John Carter
IBM Research
Austin, TX
wmf,ckd,retrac@us.ibm.com

ABSTRACT

We present PAST, a novel network architecture for data center Ethernet networks that implements a *Per-Address Spanning Tree* routing algorithm. PAST preserves Ethernet's self-configuration and mobility support while increasing its scalability and usable bandwidth. PAST is explicitly designed to accommodate unmodified commodity hosts and Ethernet switch chips. Surprisingly, we find that PAST can achieve performance comparable to or greater than Equal-Cost Multipath (ECMP) forwarding, which is currently limited to layer-3 IP networks, without *any* multipath hardware support. In other words, the hardware and firmware changes proposed by emerging standards like TRILL are not required for high-performance, scalable Ethernet networks. We evaluate PAST on Fat Tree, HyperX, and Jellyfish topologies, and show that it is able to capitalize on the advantages each offers. We also describe an OpenFlow-based implementation of PAST in detail.

Categories and Subject Descriptors

C.2 [**Internetworking**]: Network Architecture and Design

General Terms

Algorithms, Design, Management, Performance

Keywords

Software Defined Networking, OpenFlow, Data Center

1. INTRODUCTION

The network requirements of modern data centers differ significantly from traditional networks, so traditional network designs often struggle to meet them. For example, layer-2 Ethernet networks provide the flexibility and ease of configuration that network operators want, but they scale poorly and make poor use of available bandwidth. Layer-3 IP networks can provide better scalability and bandwidth, but are less flexible and are more difficult to configure and manage. Network operators want the benefits of both designs, while at the same time preferring commodity hardware over expensive custom solutions to reduce costs. Thus, our challenge is

to provide the ease of use and flexibility of Ethernet and the scalability and performance of IP using only inexpensive commodity hardware.

More precisely, a modern data center network should meet the following four functional requirements [12, 23, 33, 37].

1. **Host mobility:** Hosts—especially virtual hosts—must be movable without interrupting existing connections or requiring address changes. *Live migration is needed to tolerate faults and achieve high host utilization.*

2. **Effective use of available bandwidth:** A workload should not be limited by network bandwidth while usable bandwidth exists along alternate paths. *Path selection that prevents using available bandwidth reduces cost-effectiveness.*

3. **Self-configuration:** Network elements, e.g., routers or (v-)switches, must be able to forward traffic without manual configuration of forwarding tables. *At scale, manual configuration makes management untenable.*

4. **Scalability:** The network should scale to accommodate the needs of modern data centers without violating the preceding requirements. *Scaling by hierarchically grouping smaller networks, e.g., grouping Ethernet LANs via IP, may not satisfy our requirements.*

In addition to these functional requirements, we limit our design space to architectures that can be implemented and managed efficiently with commodity hardware and software, which leads to three additional design requirements:

1. **No hardware changes:** The architecture must work with commodity networking hardware. *Architectures that require proprietary hardware are harder to deploy and lose the advantages offered by economies of scale.*

2. **Respects layering:** The architecture must work with unmodified software stacks, e.g., operating systems and hypervisors, and higher layers must not need to understand details of the architecture's implementation. *Customers have made large investments in their current software stacks and will resist adopting a network architecture that breaks them.*

3. **Topology independent:** The architecture must work with arbitrary topologies, e.g., Fat Tree, HyperX, or Jellyfish. *Restricting the network to a particular topology, e.g., Fat Tree, prevents network operators from considering alternate topologies that may offer better performance, lower cost, or both.*

Table 1 compares existing data center network architectures and recent academic work against the above requirements. We can see that no existing architecture meets all of them. One reason is that the requirements often conflict with one another.

Architecture	Functional Requirements				Design Requirements		
	Mobility	High BW	Self Config	Scales	No H/W Changes	Respect Layers	Topo Ind
Ethernet with STP	✓	X	✓	X	✓	✓	✓
IP (e.g. OSPF)	X	✓	X	✓	✓	✓	✓
MLAG [29]	✓	✓	✓	X	✓	✓	✓
SPAIN [30]	✓	✓	✓	X	✓	X	✓
PortLand [33]	✓	✓	✓	✓	✓	✓	X
VL2 [14]	X	✓	X	✓	✓	X	X
SEATTLE [23]	✓	X	✓	✓	✓	✓	✓
TRILL [36]	✓	✓	✓	X	X	✓	✓
EthAir [37], VIRO [21]	✓	X	✓	✓	✓	✓	✓
PAST	✓	✓	✓	✓	✓	✓	✓

Table 1: Comparison of data center network architectures.

For example, Ethernet's distributed control protocol provides host mobility with little or no configuration. However, it does not scale well beyond roughly one-thousand hosts due to its use of broadcast for name resolution. Further, it makes poor use of available bandwidth because it uses a single spanning tree for packet forwarding—a limitation imposed to avoid forwarding loops.

To address these problems, current large data center networks connect multiple Ethernet LANs using IP routers [13] and run scalable routing algorithms over a smaller number of IP routers. These layer-3 routing algorithms allow for shortest path and Equal-Cost Multipath (ECMP) routing, which provide much more usable bandwidth than Ethernet's spanning tree. However, the mixed layer-2/layer-3 solution requires significant manual configuration and (typically) limits host mobility to be within a single LAN.

The trend in recent work to address these problems is to introduce special hardware and topologies. For example, Port-Land [33] is only implementable on Fat Tree topologies and requires ECMP hardware, which is not available on every Ethernet switch. TRILL [36] introduces a new packet header format and thus requires new hardware and/or firmware features.

We pose the following question: Are special hardware or topologies necessary to implement a data center network that meets our requirements, or can we build such a data center network with only commodity Ethernet hardware?

Surprisingly, we find that we *can* build a data center network that meets all of the requirements using only the most basic Ethernet switch functionality. Contrary to the suggestions of recent work, special hardware and restricted topologies are *not* necessary.

To prove this point, we present PAST, a flat layer-2 data center network architecture that supports full host mobility, high end-to-end bandwidth, autonomous route construction, and tens of thousands of hosts on top of common commodity Ethernet switches. PAST satisfies our functional and design requirements as follows. When a host joins the network or migrates, a new spanning tree is installed to carry traffic destined for that host. This spanning tree is implemented using only entries in the large Ethernet (exact match) forwarding table present in commodity switch chips, which allows PAST to support as many hosts as there are entries in that table. In aggregate, the trees spread traffic across all links in the network, so PAST provides aggregate bandwidth equal to or greater than layer-3 ECMP routing. PAST provides Ethernet semantics and runs on unmodified switches and hosts without appropriating the VLAN ID or other header fields. Finally, PAST works on arbitrary network topologies, including HyperX [2] and Jellyfish [38], which can perform as well as or better than Fat Tree [33] topologies at a fraction of the cost.

PAST can be implemented in either a centralized or distributed fashion. We prefer a centralized software-defined network (SDN) architecture that computes the trees on a high-end server processor rather than using the underpowered control plane processors present in commodity Ethernet switches. Our OpenFlow-based PAST implementation was crafted carefully to utilize the kinds of match-action rules present in commodity switch hardware, the number of rules per table, and the speed with which rules can be installed. By restricting PAST to route solely using destination MAC addresses and VLAN tags, we can use the large layer-2 forwarding table, rather than relying on the more general, but much smaller, TCAM forwarding table, as is done in previous OpenFlow architectures.

The main contributions of this paper are as follows:

1. We present PAST, a novel network architecture that meets all of the requirements described above using a per-address spanning tree routing algorithm.

2. We present an implementation that makes efficient use of the capabilities of commodity switch hardware.

3. We evaluate PAST on Fat Tree, HyperX and Jellyfish topologies and show that it can make full use of the advantages that each offers. We also offer the first comparison of the HyperX and Jellyfish topologies.

The remainder of the paper is organized as follows. In Section 2 we present background information on switch hardware and routing. We describe the design of the PAST routing algorithm in Section 3 and its implementation in Section 4. In Section 5 we present the experimental methodology that we use to evaluate PAST, describe the topologies and workloads that we use in our evaluation, and present the results of our evaluation. We describe the previous work that most influenced PAST in Section 6. Finally, in Section 7 we draw conclusions and present ideas for future work.

2. BACKGROUND

This section describes how current commodity Ethernet forwarding hardware works and discusses the state-of-the-art in data center network routing.

2.1 Switch Hardware Overview

While many vendors produce Ethernet forwarding hardware, the hardware tends to exhibit many similarities due in part to the trend of using "commodity" switch chips from vendors such as Broadcom and Intel at the core of each switch. In the following discussion, we focus on one such switch chip, the Broadcom StrataXGS

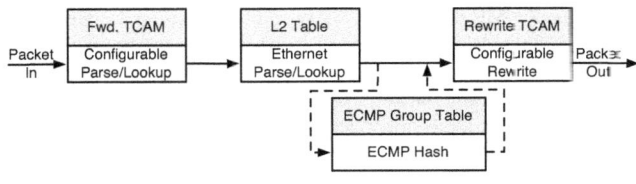

Figure 1: Partial Broadcom Switch Pipeline

Table	Broadcom Trident	HP ProVision	Intel FM6000	Mellarox SwitchX
TCAM	~2K + 2K	1,500	24K	0?
L2/Eth	~100K	~64K	64K	48K
ECMP	~1K	unknown	0	unknown

Table 2: 10 Gbps Ethernet Switch Table Sizes (number of entries)

BCM56846 [6] ("Trident"), and the IBM RackSwitch G8264 top-of-rack switch [17] that uses the Trident chip at its core. We believe this design is representative of 10 Gigabit Ethernet switches with the best price/performance currently available on the market. While our discussion focuses on a particular switch and switch chip, our work exploits chip features and design tradeoffs that are common in modern switches. Our choice of Trident and G8264 was driven by what we have available and the fact that the G8264 firmware exposes the ability for OpenFlow to install rules in the L2 table.

The rise of commodity switch chips is well-known in the networking community [25], but chip vendors typically provide only short data sheets with few details to the public; the specific details of the switch firmware are proprietary. This lack of information about switch internals makes it difficult for networking researchers to consider the constraints of real hardware. If a new switch capability is needed to enable a research idea, it is difficult to estimate whether it is available in current firmware, can be added with just firmware changes, or requires hardware changes. Similarly, designing forwarding mechanisms without understanding the size, cost, and functionality of the switch forwarding tables can lead to inefficient or non-scalable designs.

2.1.1 The Trident Switch Chip

Figure 1 presents a high-level overview of the relevant portion of the Trident packet processing pipeline. Each box represents a table that maps packets with certain header fields to an action. Each table differs in which header fields can be matched, how many entries it holds, and what kinds of actions it allows, but all tables are capable of forwarding packets at line-rate. Typical actions include sending a packet out a specific port or forwarding it to an entry in another table. The order in which tables can be traversed is constrained; the allowed interactions are shown with directed arrows. Table 2 presents the approximate size of each of these tables for several commodity Ethernet switch chips. The Trident pipeline contains dozens of other configurable tables to support features such as IP routing, DCB, MPLS, and multicast, but we do not discuss those tables further.

The L2 (or Ethernet) table performs an exact match lookup on two fields: VLAN ID and destination MAC address. It is by far the largest table, having tens of thousands of entries, because it can

be implemented with SRAM. The output of the L2 table is either an output port or a *group*, which can be thought of as a virtual port used to support multipathing or multicast. If the action for a packet is to output it to an ECMP group, the switch hashes configurable header fields (usually source and destination IP address and port number) to select a port through which the packet should be forwarded. ECMP allows traffic to be load balanced across multiple paths between hosts. Traditionally, ECMP uses minimum hop count paths, but the hardware does not enforce this. Trident can be configured to support one thousand ECMP groups, each with four ports.

The rewrite and forwarding TCAMs (Ternary Content Addressable Memories) are tables that can wildcard match on most packet header fields, including per-bit wildcards. The rewrite TCAM supports output actions that modify packet headers, while the forwarding TCAM is used to more flexibly choose an output port or group. The greater flexibility of TCAMs comes at a cost. They consume much higher area and power per entry than SRAM. Therefore on-chip TCAM sizes are typically limited to a few thousand entries.

2.1.2 Switch Control Plane

The switch chip is not a general purpose processor, so switches typically also contain a control plane processor that is responsible for programming the switch chip, providing the switch management interface, and participating in control plane protocols such as spanning tree or OSPF. In a software-defined network, the control processor also translates controller commands into switch chip state.

Unique among current switches, the G8264's OpenFlow 1.0 implementation allows OpenFlow rules to be installed in the L2 table. Specifically, if it receives a rule that exact matches on (only) the Destination MAC address and VLAN ID, it installs the rule in the L2 table. Otherwise it installs the rule in the appropriate TCAM, as is typical of OpenFlow implementations.

In traditional Ethernet, much of the forwarding state is learned automatically by the switch chip based on observed packets. A software defined approach shifts some of this burden to the control plane processor and controller, adding latency and potential bottlenecks.

To provide an OpenFlow control plane performance baseline, we characterize the G8264's performance with custom microbenchmarks using the OFlops [34] framework. The G8264 can install 700-1600 new rules per second, and each rule installation takes 2-12ms, depending on how many rules are batched in each request. Also, each time the switch receives a packet for which no forwarding rule exists, the switch must generate a message to the controller. If the switch receives more than 200 packets per second for which no route exists, the control plane becomes saturated, which can result in message latency on the order of seconds and message losses. This is problematic, since data centers often operate under tight SLAs on the order of 10-100ms [5], and violating these SLAs can have serious consequences, such as decreasing the quality of results in the case of Google [5] and reducing sales in the case of Amazon [15].

These measurements convince us that reactive forwarding rule installation will not provide acceptable performance, at least with the G8264's current control plane processor. Thus, we adopt the approach of DevoFlow [7] whereby routes are eagerly computed and installed before their first use. It is worth nothing that eager routing does not prevent hosts, switches, or links from dynamically being added and removed from the network. Rather, eager routing means that corresponding routes are updated eagerly when any such network events occur.

Algorithm 1 – Per-Address Spanning Tree (PAST)

Input: network topology $G = (V, E)$ and sets $H, S \subseteq V$, where H is the set of hosts and S is the set of switches
Output: a forwarding table T_s for each switch $s \in S$
  begin
    Initialize: $\forall s \in S, T_s = \{\}$
    Define: $BFS\_ST(h, G)$ returns a shortest path spanning tree of G, rooted at h
    Define: $v.parent\_edge(Tree)$ returns the edge in the tree $Tree$ that connects v to its parent
    for all $h \in H$ **do**
      $G_{st} = BFS\_ST(h, G)$
      for all $s \in S$ **do**
        $T_s[h] = s.parent\_edge(G_{st})$
      end for
    end for

2.2 Routing Design Space

Generally speaking, there are two approaches to scalable routing. The first entails making addresses topologically significant so routes can be aggregated in routing tables. The second is simply to have enough space in routing tables to allow for all routable addresses to have at least one entry.

As described above, the two forwarding tables (Ethernet and TCAM) differ in size by roughly two orders of magnitude. Given its small size, any routing mechanism that requires the flexibility of a TCAM for matching must aggregate routes, otherwise the few thousand TCAM entries per switch will be quickly exhausted. The larger size of the Ethernet forwarding table means that any forwarding mechanism that matches only on Destination MAC and VLAN ID can fit one entry per routable address per switch, even for large networks. Note that aggregation cannot be used with the Ethernet forwarding table as it allows for exact matching only.

Previous SDN proposals employ TCAM rules, so they have been forced to use aggregate routes [3, 33]. Aggregating routable addresses means that either the topology must be constrained or a virtual topology must be created on top of the physical one, which introduces inefficiencies. For example, PortLand [33] constrains the topology to a Fat Tree and assigns addresses based on each node's position in the tree, allowing for aggregation at each level. Virtual ID Routing [26] and Ethernet on Air [37] both build a tree and hierarchically assign addresses within the tree. While this approach works on arbitrary topologies, it does so by disabling some links and introducing paths that are up to a factor of two longer than necessary.

In contrast, the traditional Ethernet spanning tree protocol (STP), its would-be successor TRILL [36], and PAST place rules in the Ethernet forwarding table and exploit its larger size to have one entry per routable address in each switch. As a result, these routing algorithms work on arbitrary topologies, including ones that offer better price-performance than Fat Tree, like Jellyfish and HyperX. However, STP does not exploit the potential advantages of such topologies because, to avoid routing loops, it forwards all traffic along a single tree. Extensions to STP that allow one spanning tree per VLAN (as in SPAIN [30]) and vendor-specific techniques like multi-chassis link aggregation (MLAG) [29], which creates a logical tree on top of a physical mesh, can mitigate some, but not all, of STP's routing inefficiency. In an enterprise or cloud environment, VLAN IDs are needed to support security and traffic isolation, and thus should not be used for normal routing. TRILL generalizes these approaches by running IS-IS to build shortest path routes between switches. All of these approaches, except PAST, use broadcast for address resolution, limiting their scalability.

Two orthogonal extensions to routing are commonly used to fully exploit available bandwidth: *multipath routing* and *Valiant load balancing*. ECMP allows traffic between two hosts to use any minimal path, increasing path diversity and decreasing the likelihood of artificial 'hot spots' in the network where two flows collide even though non-colliding paths exist. Because ECMP requires there to be multiple paths, it has only been possible on architectures that can find all shortest paths, such as IP routing and TRILL. Valiant load balancing increases path diversity by using non-minimal paths. In Valiant routing, traffic is first forwarded minimally to a random switch and then follows the minimal path to its destination. This design also helps avoid artificial hot spots.

3. PAST DESIGN

As Table 1 shows, no existing architecture meets the requirements laid out in Section 1. PAST fills this gap by providing traditional Ethernet benefits of self-configuration and host mobility while using all available bandwidth in arbitrary topologies, scaling to tens of thousands of hosts, and running on current commodity hardware. PAST does so by installing routes in the Ethernet table without the constraints of STP. PAST is a previously unexplored point in the design space.

3.1 PAST Routing

PAST's design is guided by the structure of commodity switches' Ethernet forwarding tables. Any routing algorithm that can express its forwarding rules as a mapping from a <Destination MAC addr, VLAN ID> pair to an output port can be implemented using the large Ethernet forwarding table. By design, it is possible to represent an arbitrary spanning tree using rules of this form. The Ethernet table was designed to support the traditional spanning tree protocol (STP), but we observe that it can also implement a separate spanning tree per destination host, which results in PAST. It is possible to construct a spanning tree for any connected topology, so PAST is topology-independent.

The topologies we consider have high path diversity, so many possible spanning trees can be built for an address. Each individual tree uses only a fraction of the links in the network, so it is beneficial to make the different trees as disjoint as possible to improve aggregate network utilization. The literature is rife with spanning tree algorithms—in this paper we explore several alternatives and we plan to explore more in the future.

3.1.1 Baseline PAST

For our baseline PAST design, we build destination-rooted shortest-path spanning trees. The intuition behind this design is that shortest-path trees reduce latency and minimize load on the network. We employ a breadth-first search (BFS) algorithm to construct the shortest-path spanning trees, as shown in Algorithm 1. A BFS spanning tree is built for every address in the network. This spanning tree, rooted at the destination, provides a minimum-hop-count path from any point in the network to that destination. Any given switch only uses a single path for forwarding traffic to the host, and the paths are guaranteed to be loop-free because they form a tree. No links are ever disabled. Because a different spanning tree is used for each destination, the forward and reverse paths between two hosts in a PAST network are not necessarily symmetric.

When building each spanning tree, we often have multiple options for the next-hop link. The way that the next-hop link is selected may impact path diversity, load balance, and performance. We evaluated two options, one that simply picks a uniformly random next-hop and one that employs weighted randomization. We refer to these two baseline designs as PAST-R (random) and

PAST-W (weighted), respectively. PAST-R performs breadth-first search with random tie-breaking. Intuitively, this causes the spanning trees to be uniformly distributed across the available links. However, not all links in a spanning tree are the same—links closer to the root are likely to carry more traffic than links lower in the tree. Thus PAST-W weights its random selection by considering how many hosts (leaves) each next-hop switch has as children, summed across all spanning trees built so far.

PAST does not care whether an address (MAC address-VLAN pair) represents a VM, a physical host, or a switch. This is the choice of the network operator. Since PAST can support tens of thousands of addresses on commodity hardware, there is no need to share, rewrite, or virtualize addresses in a network. Likewise, a host may use any number of addresses if it wishes to increase path diversity at the cost of forwarding state.

PAST has similarities to ECMP. ECMP enables load-balancing across minimum-hop paths at per-flow granularity. PAST enables load-balancing across minimum-hop paths at per-destination granularity. As the number of destinations per switch increases relative to the number of minimum-cost paths, we expect the performance of PAST to approach that of ECMP. We show this is the case in practice in Section 5.

3.1.2 Non-minimal PAST

As noted in Section 2.2, some topologies, e.g., HyperX, require non-minimal routing algorithms like Valiant routing to achieve high performance under adversarial workloads. To support these topologies, we implemented a variant of the baseline PAST algorithm that selects a random intermediate switch i as the root for the BFS spanning tree for each host h. The switches along the path in the tree from i to h are then updated to route towards h, not i, so that h is the sink of the tree. We refer to this approach as NM-PAST (non-minimal PAST). As with the baseline algorithm, we implemented both random (NM-PAST-R) and weighted random (NM-PAST-W) variants.

NM-PAST is inspired by Valiant load balancing. In Valiant load balancing, all traffic is first sent through randomly chosen intermediate switches. Similarly, most traffic in NM-PAST sent to h will first be sent through the randomly chosen switch i. Only the hosts along and below the path in the tree from i to h do not forward traffic through i.

3.2 Discussion

Broadcast/Multicast: PAST is currently intended only for unicast traffic. We treat unicast and multicast routing as orthogonal features; it is possible to simultaneously use PAST for unicast and some other system such as STP for multicast. Both traditional solutions, such as STP, and novel solutions, such as building multicast and broadcast groups with SDN, are compatible with PAST. We believe it is possible to optimize multicast traffic by building a separate multicast distribution tree for each multicast address, but we do not explore this possibility. Additionally, if performance isolation of unicast from broadcast and multicast traffic is desired, the network can ensure that the unicast spanning trees do not use any of the links used for broadcast and multicast.

Security: PAST does not reuse or rewrite the Ethernet VLAN header, so VLANs can be employed for security and traffic isolation, as in traditional Ethernet.

Flow Splitting: In order to benefit from flow splitting, such as MPTCP [39], the network is required to offer multiple paths to a destination. This is possible with PAST because the Ethernet forwarding table matches on the <Destination MAC addr, VLAN ID> pair. If hosts are configured as members of multiple VLANs,

then MPTCP can perform flow splitting across VLANs. In fact, the probability of benefiting from flow splitting is greater in PAST than in ECMP because it is possible to actively try to build edge disjoint spanning trees for each VLAN of an address, whereas hash collisions are possible in ECMP.

Virtualization: As stated earlier, PAST provides standard Ethernet semantics with no need for hosts to understand any of PAST's implementation details. As a consequence, any higher layer, including network virtualization overlays like NetLord [32], SecondNet [16], MOOSE [28], and VXLAN [27], can operate seamlessly atop PAST.

Live VM migration is an expected feature in virtualized clusters, and PAST must be able to update the tree for the migrating host quickly to avoid delaying the migration. Both Xen and VMware send a gratuitous ARP from the VM's new location during migration, effectively notifying the controller that the it should reroute traffic for that VM. As we discuss in Section 4, updating a single tree in PAST is expected to take less than 20ms, which is comparable to the existing pause time involved in VM migration.

4. PAST IMPLEMENTATION (SDN)

A network architecture requires more than a routing algorithm to meet the requirements laid out earlier. In this section we describe other aspects of PAST, including address detection, address resolution, broadcast/multicast, topology discovery, route computation, route installation, and failure recovery.

We implemented the PAST architecture as an extension to the Floodlight [11] OpenFlow controller and a collection of IBM RackSwitch G8264 switches. While PAST should work with any OpenFlow 1.0 compliant switch, to the best of our knowledge the G8264 is the only switch that currently supports installing OpenFlow rules in the Ethernet forwarding table. Our implementation falls back to putting entries into the (much smaller) TCAM table if there is no way to access the larger Ethernet forwarding table, but this limits the scalability of the implementation. By using only the Ethernet forwarding table, the TCAM table(s) can be used for other purposes such as ACLs and traffic engineering.

Address detection: Our controller configures each switch to snoop all ARP traffic and forward it to the controller. The gratuitous ARPs that are generated on host boot and migration provide timely notification of new or changed locations and trigger (re)computation of the spanning tree for the given address. The controller also tracks the IP addresses associated with each address so that it can respond to ARP requests.

Address resolution: Our implementation eliminates the scaling problems of flooding for address resolution by using the controller for address resolution, specifically ARP. Broadcast ARP packets are encapsulated in `packet_in` messages and sent to the controller, which responds to the request. Additional protocols that require broadcast to operate, such as DHCP, IPv6 Neighbor Discovery, and Router Solicitation, can also be intercepted and handled by the network controller, although we did not need these protocols in our current implementation. This kind of interposition is technically a layering violation since Ethernet is normally oblivious to higher-layer protocols, but it increases scalability for large networks. However, we note that this interception is an optimization that is not required for correctness and a network operator could forgo it at the cost of scalability.

Broadcast/Multicast Our current prototype focuses on unicast and thus we have not implemented optimized versions of broadcast and multicast. We currently fall back to the Floodlight implementation of multicast and broadcast which treats both as broadcast and forwards them using a single spanning tree for the entire network.

In the future we intend to support multiple spanning trees to handle broadcast and multicast traffic extending PAST's benefits to them as well.

Topology discovery: We use Floodlight's built-in topology discovery mechanism, which sends and receives Link Layer Discovery Protocol (LLDP) messages on each port in the network using OpenFlow `packet_out` and `packet_in` messages. LLDP messages discover whether a link connects to another switch and, if it is a switch, the other switch's ID.

Route computation: Upon discovering a new (or migrated) address, PAST (re)computes the relevant tree. The time for the controller to compute the tree does not bottleneck the system. In our implementation, computing a single tree with a cold cache on topologies with 8,000 and 100,000 hosts takes less than 1ms and 5ms, respectively. If multiple trees are computed and the cache is warm, the time decreases to less than $40\mu s$ and $500\mu s$, respectively, and multiple cores can be used to increase throughput because computation of each tree is independent and thus trivially parallel. For example, on a single core we are able to compute trees for all hosts in the network in approximately 300ms for an 8,000 host network and 40 seconds for a 100,000 host network. Loosely speaking, our computation scales linearly with the number of switch-to-switch links in the network and in the limit can create a tree in one μs per 300 links in the network on a single core of a 2.2 GHz Intel Core i7 processor.

Route installation: Whenever a tree is (re)computed, PAST pipelines the installation of the relevant rules on the switches. Once a switch has received an installation request, installing the rule takes less than 12ms. To ensure a rule is placed in the Ethernet forwarding table, our switches require that the rules specify an exact match on destination MAC address and VLAN (only) and have priority 1000. While in theory it is possible that installing a recomputed tree could create a temporary routing loop, we have yet to observe this in practice. This problem could be prevented at a cost in latency by first removing rules associated with trees being replaced and issuing an OpenFlow barrier to ensure they are purged, before installing new trees.

Failure Recovery Failures are common events in large networks [14] and should be handled efficiently. While it has been sufficient for our current implementation to naively recompute all affected trees when switches and links leave and join the network, more scalable incremental approaches are possible. For example, when a new switch is added to the network, it can be initially added as a leaf node to all existing trees so that only the new switch needs to be updated with the existing hosts. Similarly, only portions of trees will be affected by switch and link failures, and it is possible to patch the trees to restore connectively to the affected hosts without disturbing the unaffected traffic. It is worth noting that new links appearing do not affect any existing trees, but they are of no benefit until they are incorporated into a tree. We rebuild random trees at regular intervals to gradually exploit new links and re-optimize our trees.

The bottleneck in failure recovery is installing flow entries; updating 100K trees would take over a minute. Optimizing flow installation is thus a critical concern in OpenFlow switches.

Other details: Our current PAST implementation consists of approximately 4,000 lines of Java. Most code belongs to a few modules that implement tree computation and address resolution, but we also made modifications to the Floodlight core to install trees instead of simple paths and to place rules in the Ethernet table rather than the TCAM. Our controller connects to all switches using a separate (out-of-band) control network that is isolated from the data network. This isolation allows PAST to bootstrap the network quickly and recover from failures that could partition the data network.

5. EVALUATION

In this section, we describe a set of simulation experiments that we use to compare PAST's performance and scalability against several existing network architectures. We find that it performs equal to or better than existing architectures, including ECMP on Fat Tree (e.g., PortLand) and ECMP on arbitrary topologies (e.g., TRILL). We have a working implementation of PAST, but our testbed only includes 20 servers with a total of 80 NICs, necessitating simulation to evaluate at scale.

We first describe our experimental methodology, including brief descriptions of our simulator, workload data, and topologies. We then provide a short comparison of the three topologies that we evaluated (Fat Tree, HyperX, and Jellyfish), which confirms prior findings that HyperX and Jellyfish topologies can offer better performance than Fat Trees at lower cost. This work also represents the first comparison of the HyperX and Jellyfish topologies. Finally, we evaluate the topology-independent PAST algorithm and its variants. While we do not find a significant difference between the uniform and weighted random PAST variants, our results show that PAST performs as well as ECMP on all topologies under uniform random workloads and NM-PAST performs better than ECMP routing and Valiant load-balancing under adversarial workloads.

5.1 Methodology

We built a working implementation of PAST running on four IBM RackSwitch G8264 10GbE switches to validate the feasibility of our design. Since our testbed only includes 20 servers with a total of 80 NICs, we use simulation to generate the results presented below.

5.1.1 Simulator

To evaluate issues that arise at scale and to explore the scaling limits of various designs, we wrote a custom discrete event network simulator. Our network simulator can replay flow traces in open-loop mode or programmatically generate flows in closed-loop mode. For performance, the simulator models flows instead of individual packets, omitting the details of TCP dynamics and switch buffering. The bandwidth consumption of each flow is simulated by assuming that each TCP flow immediately receives its max-min fair share bandwidth of the most congested link that it traverses. We simulate three data center network topologies on four different workloads to compare the performance of different forwarding algorithms that can be implemented with current Ethernet switch chips.

The simulator uses Algorithm 2 to compute the rate of the TCP flows in the network. This algorithm was first used by Curtis *et al.* in the DevoFlow [7] network simulator. The end result of this algorithm is that each flow receives its fair share of bandwidth of the most congested port it traverses.

5.1.2 Workloads

We use four different workloads in our evaluation.

The first two workloads represent adversarial (*Stride*) and benign (*URand*) communication patterns. On a network with N hosts, the Stride-s workload involves each host with index i sending data to the host with index $(i + s)mod(N)$. In the URand-u workload, each host sends data to u other hosts that are selected with uniform probability.

Algorithm 2 – Flow rate computation – Adapted from DevoFlow [7]

Input: a set of flows F, a set of ports P, and a rate $p.rate()$ for each $p \in P$. Each $p \in P$ is a set of flows such that $f \in p$ iff flow f traverses through port p.
Output: a rate $r(f)$ of each flow $f \in F$

> **begin**
> **Initialize:** $F_a = \emptyset; \forall f, r(f) = 0$
> **Define:** $p.used() = \sum_{f \in F_a \cap p} r(f)$
> **Define:** $p.unassigned\_flows() = p - (p \cap F_a)$
> **Define:** $p.flow\_rate() =$
> $\quad (p.rate() - p.used())/|p.unassigned\_flows()|$
> **while** $P \neq \emptyset$ **do**
> $\quad p = \arg\min_{p \in P} p.flow\_rate()$
> $\quad P = P - p$
> $\quad rate = p.flow\_rate()$
> $\quad$ **for all** $f \in p.unassigned\_flows()$ **do**
> $\quad\quad r(f) = rate$
> $\quad\quad F_a = F_a \cup f$
> $\quad$ **end for**
> **end while**

The next two workloads are representative of data center communication patterns. The first data center workload is a closed-loop data shuffle based on MapReduce/Hadoop communication patterns. Inspired by Hedera [4] and DevoFlow [7], we examine a synthetic workload designed to model the shuffle phase of a map-reduce analytics workload. In this *Shuffle* workload, each host transfers 128 MB to every other host, maintaining k simultaneous connections. In this workload, every host is constantly adding load to the network. For our simulations, we set $k = 10$.

The second data center workload is generated synthetically from statistics published about traffic in a data center at Microsoft Research (MSR) by Kandula *et al.* [22], who instrumented a 1500-server production cluster at MSR for two months and characterized its network traffic. We generated synthetic traces based on these characteristics to create the *MSR* workload. Specifically, we sample from the number of correspondents, flow size, and flow inter-arrival time distributions for intra-rack and entire cluster traffic. Because of the inter-arrival time distribution, it is possible for hosts to be idle during parts of the simulation.

5.1.3 Topologies

We evaluate three different data center topologies: *EGFT* (extended generalized fat trees[35]), *HyperX*, and *Jellyfish*. We also evaluate the *Optimal* topology, an unrealistic topology consisting of a single, large, non-blocking switch. We build all three data center topologies using 64-port switches.

While much of the research literature focuses on full-bisection-bandwidth networks, most large-scale data center networks employ some degree of *oversubscription*. Thus, we consider a range of oversubscribed networks for each topology, ranging from $1:1$, which represents a full-bisection network, to $1:5$, which represents a network with bisection bandwidth one-fifth that of a full-bisection network.

When comparing topologies, we simulate instances with equal bisection bandwidth ratio (often referred to as the *oversubscription ratio*). Informally, the bisection bandwidth ratio of a graph is the ratio of the bandwidth of the links that cross a cut of the network to the bandwidth of the hosts on one side of the cut, for the worst case cut of the network that splits the network in half. Formally, the bisection bandwidth ratio of a network $G = (V, E)$, adapted from the definition given by Dally and Towles [8], is:

$$bisec(G) = \min_{S \subseteq V} \frac{\sum_{e \in \delta(S)} w(e)}{\min\{\sum_{v \in S} r(v), \sum_{v \in \bar{S}} r(v)\}}$$

where $\delta(S)$ is the set of edges with one endpoint in S and another in $\bar{S}$, $r(v)$ is the total bandwidth that vertex v can initiate or receive, $w(e)$ is the bandwidth of edge e, and $|\bar{S}| \leq |S| \leq |\bar{S}| + 1$. The bisection bandwidth ratio is a useful metric for comparing topologies because it bounds performance if routing is optimal [8]. Different topologies typically require different numbers of switches and inter-switch links to achieve a particular bisection bandwidth, but the bisection bandwidth for all of the topologies we evaluate can be calculated directly from the properties of the topology. We refer the reader to the references for the specific equations for each topology.

EGFT: Simple fat tree and extended generalized fat tree (EGFT[35]) topologies have long been used in supercomputer interconnects. In recent years they have been proposed for use in Ethernet-based commercial data center networks [3, 9, 33]. One compelling property of EGFT topologies is that they have similar performance on all traffic patterns.

HyperX: The HyperX topology [2] and its less general form, the Flattened Butterfly topology, have also made the transition from supercomputing to Ethernet in recent papers [1]. HyperX topologies are known to make better use of available bisection bandwidth than Fat Trees, and thus can support certain traffic patterns at a lower cost than EGFT. For example, a $1:2$ oversubscribed HyperX can forward uniformly distributed traffic from every host at full line-rate, whereas a $1:2$ oversubscribed EGFT can only forward traffic from every host at half line-rate [24].

Jellyfish: The recently-proposed Jellyfish topology [38] connects switches using a regular random graph. The properties of such graphs have been extensively studied and are well understood. Like HyperX, it can efficiently exploit available bandwidth.

A unique strength of the Jellyfish topology is its flexibility. A Jellyfish network can be upgraded by simply adding switches and performing localized rewiring. On a Jellyfish topology, adding a switch with k inter-switch links only requires moving k other links in the network. In contrast, upgrades to EGFT and HyperX networks tend to be disruptive and/or only efficient for certain network sizes. Additionally, switches in a Jellyfish network do not need to have the same radix, which allows multiple switch generations to coexist in a single data center. Both upgrades and equipment failures preserve the Jellyfish's lack of structure, and the Jellyfish is very cost-effective since all switch ports are utilized, which maximizes use of expensive hardware.

Optimal: The optimal topology is a fictitious network modeled by attaching all hosts to one large, non-blocking switch. In this topology, the throughput of each host is only limited by the capacity of the link that connects it to the switch. Building the optimal topology is not possible in practice, but it provides a useful benchmark against which to compare. Because we assume that all switches are non-blocking, it is not possible to oversubscribe the optimal topology.

5.2 Topology Comparison

The primary focus of this paper is not to compare data center topologies, but since one of PAST's strengths is that can be implemented efficiently on arbitrary topologies, we compared topologies as a matter of course. This section presents the results of that comparison, after which we present a more in-depth evaluation of our

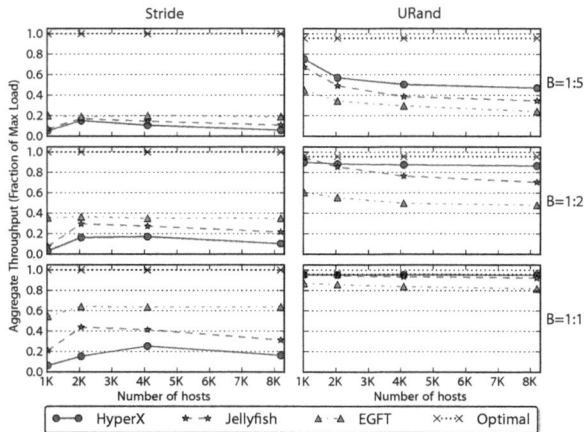

Figure 2: Throughput Comparison of Equal Bisection Bandwidth HyperX, Jellyfish, and EGFT Topologies for Both the Stride-64 and URand-8 Workloads

		Topology		
Ratio	Hosts	EGFT	HyperX	JFish
1 : 1	1K	48	64	57
	2K	96	162	114
	4K	320	338	228
	8K	640	676	456
1 : 2	1K	36	32	38
	2K	70	92	76
	4K	205	210	152
	8K	410	420	304
1 : 5	1K	24	27	26
	2K	50	57	52
	4K	125	119	103
	8K	243	238	206

Table 3: Number of 64-port switches needed to implement each topology.

PAST variants and how they compare to existing data center architectures.

Current best practices for data center networking recommend a Fat Tree or a variant thereof, e.g., EGFT. PortLand [33] describes a routing algorithm for EGFT topologies that scales to arbitrary network sizes and achieves near-optimal performance. If the EGFT topology dominated alternate topologies, there would be little need for better architectures. However, prior work [2, 31, 38] has shown that other topologies can offer equivalent or better performance than EGFTs at lower cost for many workloads. We confirm those observations here showing that Jellyfish [38] and HyperX [2] do provide higher performance at the same cost. We also present the first comparison of the Jellyfish and HyperX topologies, finding that neither dominates the other.

5.2.1 Performance

We compare all four topologies assuming ECMP routing because it is the current best practice to make effective use of all available bandwidth and it is the only per-flow multipath mechanism implemented in commodity Ethernet switch hardware. We simulated each of the four topologies for the Stride-64 and URand-8 workloads to compute their aggregate network throughput with ECMP enabled. Figure 2 presents the results of these experiments at three different bisection bandwidth ratios, 1 : 5, 1 : 2, and 1 : 1. Aggregate throughput is normalized to the maximum network load, i.e., when every server transmits and receives at full line-rate. Results for other Stride and URand workloads are omitted for space due to their similarity.

For both workloads, the Jellyfish topology performs somewhere between the HyperX and EGFT topologies. Intuitively, this occurs because the Jellyfish is not optimized for either adversarial, e.g., Stride, or benign, e.g., uniform, traffic, while EGFT is optimized for arbitrary workloads and HyperX is optimized for uniform traffic. This intuition also explains why HyperX performs worst under the adversarial Stride workload. Jellyfish performs better because it is expected to have more minimal paths to nearby hosts than HyperX, and EGFT performs best because minimal routing is optimal on an EGFT.

Under the URand workload, the Jellyfish throughput matches that of the HyperX at low network sizes and gradually decreases

as the network size increases. This performance difference is because Jellyfish uses fewer switches and links than a similar size HyperX topology. EGFT underperforms on this workload because it is the most adversely affected by ECMP hash collisions.

5.2.2 Cost

The previous section compared equal bisection bandwidth topologies, but the different topologies require different numbers of switches to achieve the same bisection bandwidth, and thus have different costs. To account for this, we compare the topologies using a switch-based cost model. While simply counting the number of switches required to implement a given topology does not fully account for cost, it provides a reasonable proxy to compare topologies.

For a fair cost comparison, we implement each topology with the fewest number of switches that provides the necessary bisection bandwidth, subject to host count and switch radix (64-port) constraints. We generated the EGFT and HyperX topologies by searching the space of possible topologies to find the smallest switch count that satisfies the constraints. No search was needed for Jellyfish, because the number of switches in a Jellyfish topology is a function of the network size, bisection bandwidth, and switch radix.

Table 3 shows the number of switches needed for the different topologies. As the network size increases, the number of switches needed for equal bisection bandwidth EGFT and HyperX topologies approach one another. The number of switches needed for the Jellyfish topology remains lower than a comparable size EGFT or HyperX network.

The results in Section 5.2.1 combined with Table 3 show that the performance-to-cost ratio of EGFT is half that of HyperX and Jellyfish for uniform random workloads. Comparing HyperX and Jellyfish is more nuanced. While the performance of the Jellyfish decreases relative to the performance of the HyperX, so does the number of switches used. Also, Jellyfish's flexibility allows a network operator to reverse this trend by adding additional "interior" switches to increase bisection bandwidth. When the performance-per-cost ratios are compared, the results are similar.

5.3 PAST Variants Comparison

In Section 3, we presented two basic PAST routing algorithms, a min-hop destination-rooted variant (PAST) and a non-min-hop one that first routed to an intermediate switch before being forwarded to the final destination (NM-PAST). We also described two ways to

56

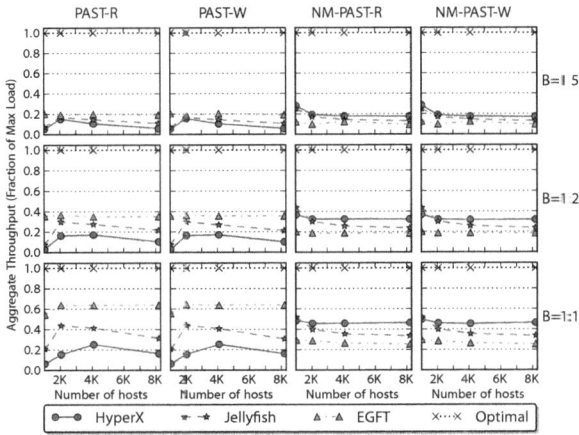

Figure 3: Throughput Comparison of PAST Variants for the Stride-64 Workload

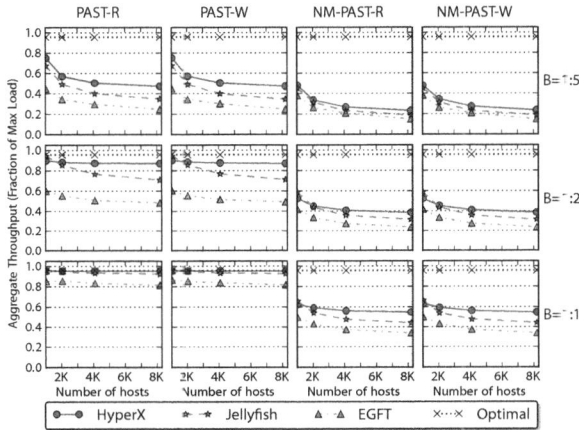

Figure 4: Throughput Comparison of PAST Variants for the URand-8 Workload

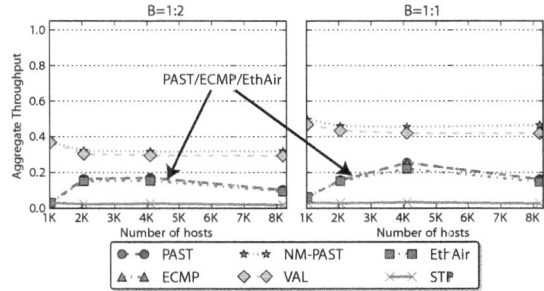

Figure 5: Throughput Comparison of Routing Algorithms for the Stride-64 Workload and HyperX Topology

build each spanning tree, one that simply chose any random next-hop link (Random) and one that employed a weighted randomization factor to account for non-uniformity in load (Weighted) In total this results in four PAST forwarding mechanisms: *PAST-R*, *PAST-W*, *NM-PAST-R*, and *NM-PAST-W*. We simulated each variant to determine their aggregate throughput at several levels of over-subscription (1 : 1, 1 : 2, and 1 : 5). The results of these experiments are presented in Figure 3 and Figure 4 for the Stride and URand workloads, respectively.

These results show that both the random and weighted spanning tree algorithms perform identically. Although we omit the results, the different spanning tree algorithms also perform identically on the Shuffle and MSR workloads. One possible explanation for this result is that the regularity of the topologies that we evaluated leads to there being little difference between the spanning trees built by each algorithm. This explanation is corroborated by simulations not presented here on HyperX topologies where different dimensions have significantly different bisection bandwidths In these simulations, the weighted spanning tree algorithm achieved

roughly 10% higher throughput than the uniform random algorithm.

The results for the Stride workload shown in Figure 3 indicate that the NM-PAST algorithm performs better than the PAST algorithm on HyperX topologies. This result is expected because minimally routing the Stride workload on a HyperX causes all flows for a switch to traverse the same small number of links, while Valiant routing takes advantage of the high uniform throughput of a HyperX. In contrast, the PAST algorithm performs better than the NM-PAST algorithm on an EGFT topology. This result is expected because minimal routing on an EGFT already implements Valiant routing, so forwarding to an additional intermediate switch in Valiant routing simply wastes bandwidth.

Surprisingly, under the stride workload, the PAST and NM-PAST algorithms perform almost identically on Jellyfish topologies, even though the routes in NM-PAST are roughly twice the length of routes in PAST. This result arises because there are two competing factors that affect throughput: path diversity and path length. The NM-PAST algorithm increases path diversity at the cost of increasing path length. Increasing path length causes added contention in the network interior, which reduces available bisection bandwidth. These results show that, for the Stride workload, the performance benefit of the improved path diversity of NM-PAST is cancelled out by the increased path length that it requires.

The results for the URand workload (Figure 4) show that the NM-PAST algorithm achieves half of the throughput of the PAST algorithm. This is because NM-PAST does not increase path diversity on the URand workload, yet effectively doubles the load on the network by increasing the average path length by a factor of 2.

5.4 Routing Comparison

The previous section compared the PAST variants against one another. In this section, we compare the best PAST variants against other scalable routing algorithms. Specifically, we compare weighted PAST and NM-PAST against ECMP, Valiant (*Val*), Ethernet on AIR (*EthAir*), and STP routing algorithms. The Valiant routing algorithm is considered, despite not being a scalable routing algorithm, because it provides a useful comparison for NM-PAST. We assume that ECMP is used in *EthAir*. The STP algorithm is used to show the performance of traditional Ethernet.

Figure 5, Figure 6, and Figure 7 present the throughput of each of the routing algorithms on the Stride, URand, and Shuffle workloads, respectively. Results from the MSR workload are omitted for space reasons because the relatively light load offered from the MSR workload does not induce significant performance differences between most of the routing algorithms. The figures only show re-

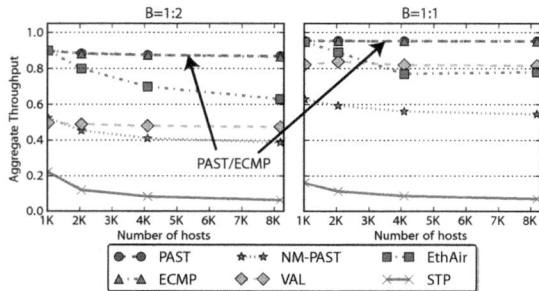

Figure 6: Throughput Comparison of Routing Algorithms Variants for the URand-8 Workload and HyperX Topology

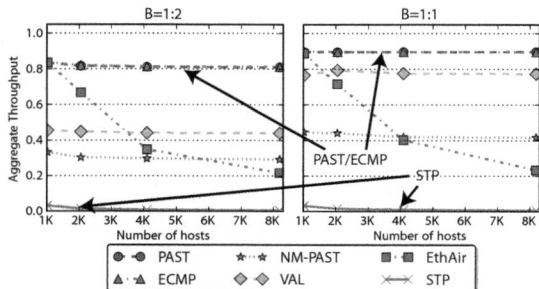

Figure 7: Throughput Comparison of Routing Algorithms Variants for the Shuffle Workload and HyperX topology

Wildcard ECMP	PAST	STP	TRILL ECMP
∞	~100K	~100K	~12K-55K

Table 4: Maximum Number of Physical Hosts for Different Eager Routing Algorithms Implemented with Broadcom Trident Chip

sults for the HyperX topology and 1:2 and 1:1 oversubscription ratio to save space—the other topologies had similar trends.

Our first observation is that the PAST and ECMP routing algorithms perform identically under all workloads. Also, both algorithms perform within 10% of optimal throughput on the 1:2 oversubscription ratio topologies for the URand and Shuffle workloads.

NM-PAST uses some minimal paths and does not choose a new random intermediate switch for each flow, so we expect the performance of VAL to be greater than that of NM-PAST. This is the case for the URand and shuffle workloads, but as seen in Figure 5, the NM-PAST and VAL routing algorithms perform similarly on the Stride workload. They are the best performing algorithms, even though the throughput of VAL is far from the optimal throughput, which is equal to the oversubscription ratio [24]. The Stride workload only has a single flow per host, which can cause hash collisions. As the number of flows increase, we anticipate that the throughput of both NM-PAST and VAL will increase.

Overall, the performance of EthAIR is poor. Figure 6 shows that, under the URand workload, the performance of EthAIR is 17%-48% worse than ECMP and PAST. Similarly, under the more demanding shuffle workload shown in Figure 7, EthAIR performs 71%-92% worse than ECMP and PAST at the largest topology size.

The STP algorithm is presented as a strawman to show the baseline performance of traditional Ethernet, even if all broadcasts are disallowed. STP performs significantly worse than all of the other routing algorithms on every topology and bisection bandwidth. This is expected because restricting forwarding to a single tree forces flows to collide.

Table 4 shows the scalability in terms of the number of physical hosts for each of the routing algorithms described earlier, if the routing algorithm were implemented using a network of Trident-based switches. The wildcard ECMP algorithm includes both wildcard ECMP routing on an EGFT topology as well as using EthAir to perform wildcard ECMP on arbitrary topologies. Although both algorithms scale to arbitrary network sizes, the EthAir algorithm restricts the set of usable paths in the network, which reduces performance. Both PAST and STP only require one Ethernet table entry per routable address, so the scalability of both PAST and STP is only limited to the size of the Ethernet table. TRILL ECMP does not scale to networks as large as can be supported by PAST and STP because TRILL ECMP requires ECMP table state, which is exhausted. The scalability of TRILL ECMP is a range because the required number of ECMP table entries varies across topologies and bisection bandwidths.

6. RELATED WORK

In this section, we discuss the design of PAST in the context of related network architectures. To save space, we omit architectures that have already been discussed, including PortLand, SEATTLE, and Ethernet on AIR. For the sake of discussion, we group related architectures together by the following properties: spanning tree algorithms, link-state routing protocols, and SDN architectures.

MSTP [18], SPAIN [30], and GOE [19] are all architectures that build a spanning tree per VLAN. None of them meet our requirements. MSTP does not achieve high performance because all traffic for a given VLAN is still restricted to a single spanning tree. SPAIN solves this problem by modifying hosts to load balance across VLANs, but SPAIN violates layering and does not scale because each host requires an Ethernet table entry per VLAN. GOE assigns each switch a VLAN and uses MSTP to build a unique spanning tree for each switch. This design limits the total network size to roughly 2K switches and decreases available path diversity and performance compared to PAST. Additionally, all of these architectures limit performance and scalability by requiring broadcast for address learning.

TRILL [20, 36] and Shortest-Path Bridging (SPB) [10] both use IS-IS link-state routing instead of the traditional spanning tree protocol. IS-IS may either use single path or multipath routing. Single path routing limits TRILL to forwarding on switch addresses instead of host addresses, and in SPB it restricts the number of forwarding trees. Using ECMP for multipath routing improves the performance of both architectures, but limits their scalability to the size of the ECMP table. As a result, PAST is more scalable. TRILL and SPB both require specific hardware support that is present in some but not all commodity switch chips, while PAST is designed to use the same hardware as classic Ethernet.

Hedera [4] and DevoFlow [7] are SDN architectures that provide additional functionality compared to PAST. Hedera, DevoFlow, and PAST all eliminate broadcasts and eagerly install routes, but Hedera and DevoFlow both improve performance by explicitly scheduling large flows onto better paths. PAST can complement these traffic engineering mechanisms by efficiently routing flows that are too small to merit explicit scheduling (non-elephant flows). We plan to explore traffic engineering in conjunction with PAST, which will benefit from the fact that PAST does not use the TCAM, so all TCAM entries can be used for traffic engineering.

7. CONCLUSIONS AND FUTURE WORK

Data center network designs are migrating from low-bisection-bandwidth single-rooted trees with hybrid Ethernet/IP forwarding to more sophisticated topologies that provide substantial performance benefits through multipathing. Unfortunately, existing Ethernet switches cannot efficiently route on multipathed networks, so many researchers have proposed using programmable switches (e.g., with OpenFlow) to implement high-performance routing and forwarding. Unfortunately, most OpenFlow firmware implementations and other architectures do not exploit the full capabilities of modern Ethernet switch chips.

In this paper, we presented PAST, a flat layer-2 data center network architecture that supports full host mobility, high end-to-end bandwidth, self-configuration, and tens of thousands of hosts using Ethernet switches built from commodity switch chips. We demonstrate that by designing a network architecture with explicit consideration for switch functionality—in particular the exact-match Ethernet table—it is possible to support heavily multipathed topologies that allow cost and performance tradeoffs. We show that PAST is able to provide near-optimal throughput without using a Fat Tree network. We further show that it is possible to perform efficient multipath routing without using ECMP or similar hashing hardware, which simplifies route computation and installation and could reduce hardware complexity because using ECMP is guaranteed to require more hardware than PAST. Finally, we show that PAST can be easily extended to provide non-shortest-path routing, which benefits adversarial workloads. In the worst case, PAST performs the same as ECMP, while in the best case PAST more than doubles the performance of ECMP.

PAST has implications for the design of future Ethernet switch chips, since our results indicate that layer-2 ECMP is not as useful (or necessary) as previously assumed. We believe PAST will scale well with future networks because the SRAM-based Ethernet table is area-efficient and can easily be increased in size, while it is costly to increase TCAM table size.

Although much has been written about network topologies, we have presented the first three-way comparison between EGFT, HyperX, and Jellyfish. We have also evaluated oversubscribed networks, revealing that in some cases they provide very similar performance to full-bisection-bandwidth topologies but at lower cost. In general, we agree with previous work that Fat Trees are not ideal for any use case. Our work does not provide insight regarding whether HyperX or Jellyfish is the better topology; the outcome is likely to depend on practical considerations, such as ease of cabling, and thus may vary between data centers.

We are excited by the potential of PAST for supporting large enterprise and cloud data centers. We plan to extend it in a number of ways. For example, we are working on an online variant of the per-address spanning tree algorithm that attempts to minimize the amount of new state that needs to be computed and installed when the physical topology or set of addressable hosts changes. We also plan to develop a more detailed cost model for comparing equal-performance HyperX and Jellyfish topologies. Finally, we are exploring ways to integrate traffic engineering, traffic steering, converged storage, high availability, and other advanced networking features into our PAST architecture.

8. ACKNOWLEDGEMENTS

We thank our shepherds, Andrew Moore and Chuanxiong Guo, and the anonymous reviewers for their comments. We also thank Joe Tardo and Rochan Sankar from Broadcom for providing detailed information about the Trident architecture and permission to publish some details here.

References

[1] D. Abts and J. Kim. *High Performance Datacenter Networks: Architectures, Algorithms, and Opportunities.* Morgan and Claypool, 2011.

[2] J. H. Ahn, N. Binkert, A. Davis, M. McLaren, and R. S. Schreiber. Hyperx: topology, routing, and packaging of efficient large-scale networks. *SC Conference*, 2009.

[3] M. Al-Fares, A. Loukissas, and A. Vahdat. A scalable, commodity data center network architecture. In *SIGCOMM*, 2008.

[4] M. Al-fares, S. Radhakrishnan, B. Raghavan, N. Huang, and A. Vahdat. Hedera: Dynamic flow scheduling for data center networks. In *NSDI*, 2010.

[5] M. Alizadeh, A. Greenberg, D. A. Maltz, J. Padhye, P. Patel, B. Prabhakar, S. Sengupta, and M. Sridharan. Data center TCP (DCTCP). In *SIGCOMM*, 2010.

[6] Broadcom BCM56846 StrataXGS 10/40 GbE Switch. http://www.broadcom.com/products/features/BCM56846.php.

[7] A. R. Curtis, J. C. Mogul, J. Tourrilhes, and P. Yalagandula. DevoFlow: Scaling flow management for high-performance networks. In *SIGCOMM*, 2011.

[8] W. Dally and B. Towles. *Principles and Practices of Interconnection Networks.* Morgan Kaufmann Publishers Inc., San Francisco, CA, USA, 2003.

[9] N. Farrington, E. Rubow, and A. Vahdat. Data center switch architecture in the age of merchant silicon. In *Hot Interconnects*, 2009.

[10] D. Fedyk, P. Ashwood-Smith, D. Allan, A. Bragg, and P. Unbehagen. IS-IS Extensions Supporting IEEE 802.1aq Shortest Path Bridging. RFC 6329, Apr 2012.

[11] Floodlight openflow controller. http://floodlight.openflowhub.org/.

[12] I. Gashinsky. SDN in warehouse scale datacenter v2.0. In *Open Networking Summit*, 2012.

[13] A. Greenberg, J. Hamilton, D. A. Maltz, and P. Patel. The cost of a cloud: Research problems in data center networks. In *ACM CCR*, January 2009.

[14] A. Greenberg, J. R. Hamilton, N. Jain, S. Kandula, C. Kim, P. Lahiri, D. A. Maltz, P. Patel, and S. Sengupta. VL2: A scalable and flexible data center network. In *SIGCOMM*, 2009.

[15] Greg Linden. Make data useful. http://www.scribd.com/doc/4970486/Make-Data-Useful-by-Greg-Linden-Amazoncom, 2006.

[16] C. Guo, G. Lu, H. J. Wang, S. Yang, C. Kong, P. Sun, W. Wu, and Y. Zhang. SecondNet: A data center network virtualization architecture with bandwidth guarantees. In *Co-NEXT*, 2010.

[17] IBM BNT RackSwitch G8264. http://www.redbooks.ibm.com/abstracts/tips0815.html.

[18] IEEE. *Std 802.1s Multiple Spanning Trees.* 2002.

[19] A. Iwata, Y. Hidaka, M. Umayabashi, N. Enomoto, and A. Arutaki. Global Open Ethernet (GOE) system and its performance evaluation. *Selected Areas in Communications, IEEE Journal on*, 2004.

[20] J. Touch and R. Perlman. Transparent Interconnection of Lots of Links (TRILL): Problem and Applicability Statement. RFC 5556, May 2009.

[21] S. Jain, Y. Chen, Z.-L. Zhang, and S. Jain. Viro: A scalable, robust and namespace independent virtual id routing for future networks. In *INFOCOMM*, 2011.

[22] S. Kandula, S. Sengupta, A. Greenberg, and P. Patel. The nature of datacenter traffic: Measurements and analysis. In *IMC*, 2009.

[23] C. Kim, M. Caesar, and J. Rexford. Floodless in SEATTLE: A scalable Ethernet architecture for large enterprises. In *Proceedings of ACM SIGCOMM*, 2008.

[24] J. Kim and W. J. Dally. Flattened butterfly: A cost-efficient topology for high-radix networks. In *ISCA*, 2007.

[25] G. Lu, C. Guo, Y. Li, Z. Zhou, T. Yuan, H. Wu, Y. Xiong, R. Gao, and Y. Zhang. ServerSwitch: A programmable and high performance platform for data center networks. In *NSDI*, 2011.

[26] G.-H. Lu, S. Jain, S. Chen, and Z.-L. Zhang. Virtual id routing: A scalable routing framework with support for mobility and routing efficiency. In *MobiArch*, 2008.

[27] M. Mahalingam, D. Dutt, K. Duda, P. Agarwal, L. Kreeger, T. Sridhar, M. Bursell, and C. Wright. VXLAN: A Framework for Overlaying Virtualized Layer 2 Networks over Layer 3 Networks. Internet-Draft draft-mahalingam-dutt-dcops-vxlan-00.txt, IETF Secretariat, Jan. 2012.

[28] A. M. Malcolm Scott and J. Crowcroft. Addressing the scalability of Ethernet with MOOSE. In *DC-CAVES*, 2009.

[29] MC-LAG. http://en.wikipedia.org/wiki/MC_LAG.

[30] J. Mudigonda, P. Yalagandula, M. Al-Fares, and J. C. Mogul. SPAIN: COTS data-center Ethernet for multipathing over arbitrary topologies. In *NSDI*, 2010.

[31] J. Mudigonda, P. Yalagandula, and J. C. Mogul. Taming the flying cable monster: a topology design and optimization framework for data-center networks. In *USENIXATC*, 2011.

[32] J. Mudigonda, P. Yalagandula, J. C. Mogul, B. Stiekes, and Y. Pouffary. NetLord: a scalable multi-tenant network architecture for virtualized datacenters. In *SIGCOMM*, pages 62–73, 2011.

[33] R. N. Mysore, A. Pamboris, N. Farrington, N. Huang, P. Miri, S. Radhakrishnan, V. Subramanya, and A. Vahdat. PortLand: A scalable fault-tolerant layer 2 data center network fabric. In *SIGCOMM*, 2009.

[34] OFlops. http://www.openflow.org/wk/index.php/Oflops.

[35] S. Ohring, M. Ibel, S. Das, and M. Kumar. On generalized fat trees. *Parallel Processing Symposium, International*, 0:37, 1995.

[36] R. Perlman. Rbridges: Transparent routing. In *INFOCOMM*, 2004.

[37] D. Sampath, S. Agarwal, and J. Gacia-Luna-Aceves. 'ethernet on air' : Scalable routing in very large ethernet-based networks. In *ICDCS*, 2010.

[38] A. Singla, C.-Y. Hong, L. Popa, and P. B. Godfrey. Jellyfish: Networking data centers randomly. In *NSDI*, April 2012.

[39] D. Wischik, C. Raiciu, A. Greenhalgh, and M. Handley. Design, implementation and evaluation of congestion control for multipath TCP. In *NSDI*, 2011.

VALE, a Switched Ethernet for Virtual Machines

Luigi Rizzo
Dip. di Ingegneria dell'Informazione
Università di Pisa, Italy
rizzo@iet.unipi.it

Giuseppe Lettieri
Dip. di Ingegneria dell'Informazione
Università di Pisa, Italy
g.lettieri@iet.unipi.it

ABSTRACT

The growing popularity of virtual machines is pushing the demand for high performance communication between them. Past solutions have seen the use of hardware assistance in the form of "PCI passthrough" (dedicating parts of physical NICs to each virtual machine) and even bouncing traffic through physical switches to handle data forwarding and replication.

In this paper we show that, with a proper design, very high speed communication between virtual machines can be achieved completely in software. Our architecture, called VALE, implements a Virtual Local Ethernet that can be used by virtual machines, such as QEMU, KVM and others, as well as by regular processes. VALE achieves a throughput of over 17 million packets per second (Mpps) between host processes, and over 2 Mpps between QEMU instances, without any hardware assistance.

VALE is available for both FreeBSD and Linux hosts, and is implemented as a kernel module that extends our recently proposed netmap framework, and uses similar techniques to achieve high packet rates.

Categories and Subject Descriptors

D.4.4 [**Operating Systems**]: Communications Management; D.4.7 [**Operating Systems**]: Organization and Design

General Terms

Design, Experimentation, Performance

Keywords

Virtual Machines, Software switches, netmap

1. INTRODUCTION

A large amount of computing services nowadays are migrating to virtualized environments, which offer significant advantages in terms of resource sharing and cost reduction. Virtual machines need to communicate and access peripherals, which for systems used as servers mostly means disks and network interfaces. The latter are extremely challenging to deal with even in non-virtualized environments, due to the high data and packet rates involved, and the fact that, unlike disks, traffic generation is initiated by external entities on which the receiver has no control. It is then not a surprise that virtual machines may have a tough time in operating network interfaces at wire speed in all possible conditions.

As it is often the case, hardware assistance comes handy to improve performance. As shown in Section 2.2, some proposals rely on multiqueue network cards exporting resources to virtual machines through PCI passthrough, and/or on external switches to copy data between interfaces. However this solution is expensive and not necessarily scalable. On the other hand, software-only solutions proposed to date tend to have relatively low performance, especially for small packet sizes.

We then wondered if there was an inherent performance problem in doing network switching in software. The result we found is that high speed forwarding between virtual machines is achievable even without hardware support, and at a rate that exceeds that of physical 10 Gbit/s interfaces, even with minimum-size packets.

Our contribution: The main result we present in this paper is a system called VALE, which implements a Virtual Local Ethernet that can be used to interconnect virtual machines, or as a generic high speed bus for communicating processes. VALE is accessed through the netmap API, an extremely efficient communication mechanism that we recently introduced [17]. The same API can be trivially used to connect VALE to hardware devices, thus also providing communications with external systems at line rate [16].

VALE is 10..20 times faster than other software solutions based on general purpose OSes (such as in-kernel bridging using TAP devices or various kinds of sockets). It also outperforms NIC-assisted bridging, being capable to deliver well over 17 Mpps with short frames, and over 6 Mpps with 1514-byte frames (corresponding to more than 70 Gbit/s).

The use of the netmap API is an enabling factor for such performance, but the packet rates reported in this paper could have not been achieved without engineering the forwarding code in a way that exploits batched processing. Section 3.3 discussed the solutions we use.

To prove that VALE's performance can be exploited by virtual machines, we then added VALE support to

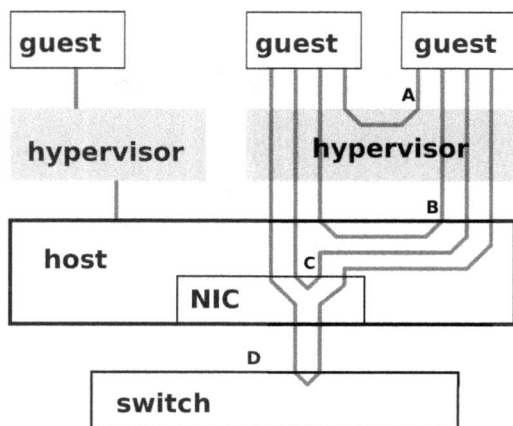

Figure 1: Possible paths in the communication between guests: A) through the hypervisor; B) through the host, e.g. via native bridging; C) through virtual queues the NIC; D) through an external network switch.

QEMU [4] and KVM [9], and measured speedups between 2 and 6 times for applications running on the guest OS[1], reaching over 2.5 Mpps with short frames, and about 2 Mpps with 1514-byte frames, corresponding to 25 Gbit/s. We are confident that we will be able to reach this level of performance also with other hypervisors and guest NIC drivers.

The paper is structured as follows. In Section 2 we define the problem we are addressing in this paper, and present some related work that is also relevant to describe the solutions we adopted. Section 3 details the architecture of our Virtual Local Ethernet, discussing and motivating our design choices. Section 4 comments on some implementation details, including the hypervisor modifications needed to make use of the VALE infrastructure, and device emulation issues. We then move to a detailed performance measurement of our system, comparing it with alternatives proposed in the literature or implemented in other products. We first look at the raw switch performance in Section 5, and then study the interaction with hypervisors and guest in Section 6. Finally, Section 7 discusses how our work can be used by virtualization solutions to achieve large speedups in the communication between virtual machines, and indicates some directions for future work.

2. PROBLEM DEFINITION

The problem we address in this paper is how to implement a high speed Virtual Local Ethernet that can be used as a generic communication mechanism between virtual machines, OS processes, and physical network interfaces.

Solutions to this problem may involve several components. Virtual machine instances in fact use the services supplied by a *hypervisor* (also called Virtual Machine Monitor, VMM) to access any system resource (from CPU to memory to communication devices), and consequently to communicate with each other. Depending on the architecture of the system, resource access from the guest can be mediated by the hypervisor, or physical resources may be partially or com-

---
[1]especially when we can overcome the limitations of the emulated device driver, see Section 6

pletely allocated to the guest, which then uses them with no interference from the hypervisor (except when triggering protection mechanisms).

Figure 1 illustrates implementations of the above concepts in the case of network communication between virtual machines. In case A, the hypervisor does a full emulation of the network interfaces (NICs), and intercepts outgoing traffic so that any communication between the virtual machine instances goes through it; in QEMU, this is implemented with the -net user option. In case B, the hypervisor still does NIC emulation, but traffic forwarding is implemented by the host, e.g. through an in-kernel bridge (-net-tap) or a module such as the one we present in this paper.

Other solutions give the virtual machine direct access to the NIC (or some of its queues). In this case, the NIC itself can implement packet forwarding between different guests (see the path labeled C), or traffic is forwarded to an external switch which in turn can bounce it back to the appropriate destination (path D).

NIC emulation, as used in A and B, gives the hypervisor a lot of control on the operations done by the guest, and works as a nice adaptation layer to run the guest on top of hardware that the guest OS would not know how to control.

Common wisdom suggests that NIC emulation is slow, and direct NIC access (as in C and D) is generally necessary for good virtual network performance, even though it requires some form of hardware support to make sure that the guest does not interfere with other critical system resources.

However, the belief that NIC emulation is inherently slow is wrong, and mostly the result of errors in the emulation code [15] or missing emulation of features (such as interrupt moderation, see [14]) that are fundamental for high rate packet processing. While direct hardware access may help in communication between the guest and external nodes, virtio [20], proprietary virtual device emulators [22,23], and as we show in this paper, even e1000 emulation, done properly, provide excellent performance, comparable or even exceeding that of real hardware in VM-to-VM communication.

2.1 Organization of the work

In summary, the overall network performance in a virtual machine depends on three components:

- the guest/hypervisor communication mechanism;
- the hypervisor/host communication mechanism;
- the host infrastructure that exposes multiple physical or virtual NIC ports to its clients.

In this paper we first present an efficient architecture for the last component, showing how to design and implement an extremely fast Virtual Local Ethernet (VALE) that can be used by the hypervisors (and possibly exported to the guest OS), or even used directly by regular host processes. We then extend some popular hypervisors so that their communication with the host can be made efficient and exploit the speed of VALE. Finally, we discuss mechanisms that we implemented in previous work and that can be extremely effective to improve performance in a virtualized OS.

2.2 Related work

There are three main approaches to virtualized I/O, which rely on different choices in the communication between guest and hypervisor, and between hypervisor and the host/bridging infrastructure. We examine them in turn.

2.2.1 Full virtualization

The simplest approach (in terms of requirements for the guest) is to expose a virtual interface of the type known to the guest operating system. This typically involves intercepting all accesses to critical resources (NIC registers, sometimes memory regions) and use them to update a state machine in the hypervisor that replicates the behaviour of the hardware. Historically, this is the first solution used by most emulators, starting from VMware to QEMU [4] and other recent systems.

With this solution the hypervisor can be a simple process that accesses the network using standard facilities offered by the host: TCP/UDP sockets (usually to build tunnels or emulate ethernet segments), or BPF/libpcap [10] or virtual interfaces (TAP) to inject raw packets into the network.

TAP is a software device with two endpoints: one is managed as a network interface (NIC) by the operating system, the other one is a file descriptor (FD) driven by a user process. Data blocks sent to the FD endpoint appear as ethernet packets on the NIC endpoint. Conversely, ethernet packets that the operating system sends to the NIC endpoint can be read by the user process from the FD endpoint. A hypervisor can then pass the guest's traffic to the FD endpoint of a TAP device, whose NIC endpoint can be connected to other NICs (TAPs or physical devices) using the software bridges available in the Linux and FreeBSD kernels, or other software bridges such as Open vSwitch [12].

There also exist solutions that run entirely in user space, such as VDE [8], providing configurable tunnels between virtual machines. In general, this kind of solution offers the greatest ease of use, at the expense of performance. Another possibility is offered by MACVTAPs [1], which are a special kind of TAP devices that can be put in a "bridge" mode, so that they can send packets to each other. Their main purpose is to simplify networking setup, by removing the need to configure a separate bridge.

2.2.2 Paravirtualization

The second approach goes under the name of paravirtualization [3] and requires modifications in the guest. The guest becomes aware of the presence of the hypervisor and cooperates with it, instead of being intercepted by it. As far as I/O is concerned, the modifications in the guest generally come in the form of new drivers for special, "paravirtual" devices. VMware has always offered the possibility to install the VMware Tools in the guest to improve interoperability with the host and boost I/O performance. Their vSphere virtualization infrastructure also offers high performance vSwitches to interconnect virtual machines [22].

Xen offers paravirtualized I/O in the form a special *driver domain* and pairs of backend-frontend drivers. Frontend drivers run in the guests and exchange data with the backend drivers running in the driver domain, where a standard Linux kernel finally completes the I/O operations. This architecture achieves fault isolation and driver reuse, but performance suffers [11]. Bridging among the guests is performed by a software bridge that connects the driver backends in the guest domain.

XenLoop [24] is a solution that improves throughput and latency among Xen guests running on the same host. It uses FIFO message queues in shared memory to bypass the driver domain. XenLoop is tightly integrated with the hypervisor, and in fact, its exclusive focus seems to provide a fast network channels to hypervisors. For this reason is not completely comparable with the VALE switch presented in this work, which also aims to implement be a generic communication mechanism useful also outside the virtualization world. In terms of performance, XenLoop seems to peak at around 200 Kpps (on 2008 hardware), which is significantly below the performance of VALE.

The KVM [26] hypervisor and the Linux kernel (both as a guest and a host) offer support for virtio [20] paravirtualization. Virtio is an I/O mechanism (including virtio-net for network and virtio-disk for disk support) based on queues of scatter-gather buffers. The guest and the hypervisor export shared buffers to the queues and notify each other when batches of buffers are consumed. Since notifications are expensive, each endpoint can disable them when they are not needed. The main idea is to reduce the number of context switches between the guest and the hypervisor.

Vhost-net [2] is an in-kernel data-path for virtio-net. Vhost-net is used by KVM, but it is not specifically tied to it. In KVM, virtio-net *notify* operations cause a hardware-assisted VM-exit to the KVM kernel module. Without vhost-net, the KVM kernel module then yields control to the KVM process in user space, which then accesses the virtio buffers of the guest, and writes packets to a TAP device using normal system calls. A similar, reversed path is followed for receive operations.

With vhost-net enabled, instead, the KVM kernel module completely bypasses the KVM process and triggers a kernel thread which directly writes the virtio buffers to the TAP device. The bridging solutions for this technique are the same as those for full virtualization using TAP devices, and the latter typically become the performance bottleneck.

2.2.3 Direct I/O access

The third approach is to avoid guest/hypervisor communication altogether and allow the guest to directly access the hardware [25]. In the simplest scenario a NIC is dedicated to a guest which gains exclusive access to it, e.g., by PCI passthrough. This generally requires hardware support to be implemented safely. Moreover, DMA transfers between the guest physical memory and the peripheral benefit from the presence of an IOMMU [7]. More complex scenarios make use of multi-queue NICs to assign a separate queue to each guest [21], or of programmable network devices to implement device virtualization in the device itself [13]. These solutions are generally able to achieve near native performance in the guest, but at the cost of requiring specialized hardware. Bridging can be performed either in the NIC itself, as in [21], or by connecting real external switches.

3. VALE, A VIRTUAL LOCAL ETHERNET

The first goal of this work is to show how we built a software, high performance Virtual Local Ethernet (which we call VALE), that can provide access ports to multiple clients, be them hypervisors or generic host processes, as shown in Figure 2. The target throughput we are looking for is in the millions of packets per second (Mpps) range, comparable or exceeding that of 10 Gbit/s interfaces. Given that the hypervisor might be running the guest as a userspace process, it is fundamental that the virtual ethernet is accessible from user space with low overhead.

As mentioned, network I/O is challenging even for systems running on real hardware, for the reasons described in [17]:

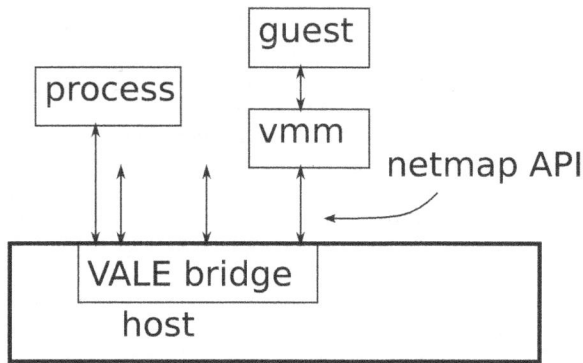

Figure 2: A VALE local ethernet exposes multiple independent ports to hypervisors and processes, using the netmap API as a communication mechanism.

expensive system calls and memory allocations are incurred on each packet, while packet rates of millions of packets per second exceed the speed at which system calls can be issued.

In netmap [16] we solved these challenges through a series of simple but very effective design choices, aimed at amortizing or removing certain costly operations from the critical execution paths. Given the similarity to the problem we are addressing in VALE, we use the netmap API as the communication mechanism between the host and the hypervisor. A brief description of the netmap API follows.

3.1 The netmap API

The netmap framework was designed to implement a high performance communication channel between network hardware and applications in need of performing raw packet I/O. The core of the framework is based on a shared memory region (Figure 3), which hosts packet buffers and their descriptors, and is accessible by the kernel and by userspace processes. A process can gain access to a NIC, and tell the OS to operate it in netmap mode, by opening the special file /dev/netmap. An ioctl() is then used to select a specific device, followed by an mmap() to make the netmap data structures accessible.

The content of the memory mapped region is shown in Figure 3. For each NIC, it contains preallocated buffers for transmit and receive packets, and one or more[2] pairs of circular arrays (*netmap rings*) that store metadata for the transmit and receive buffers. Besides the OS, buffers are also accessible to the NIC through its own *NIC rings* – circular arrays of buffer descriptors used by the NIC's hardware to store incoming packets or read outgoing ones.

Using a single ioctl() or poll() system call, a process can notify the kernel to send multiple packets at once (as many as they fit in the ring). Similarly, receive notifications for an entire batch of packets are reported with a single system call. This way, the cost of system calls (up to 1 μs or more even on modern hardware) is amortized and their impact on individual packets can become negligible.

The other expensive operations – buffer allocations and data copying – are removed because buffers are preallocated and shared between the user process and (ultimately) the NIC itself. The role of the system calls, besides notifications, is to validate and convert metadata between the netmap and

---

[2]for NICs with multiple transmit and receive queues

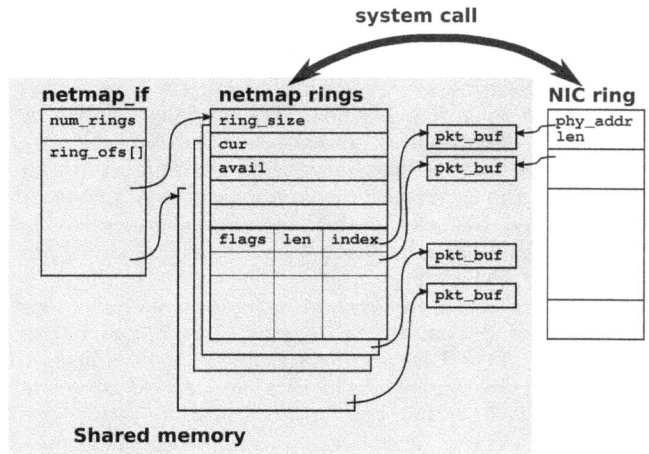

Figure 3: The memory areas shared between the operating system and processes, and manipulated using the netmap API.

the NIC ring, and to perform safety-critical operations such as writing to the NIC's register. The implicit synchronization provided by the system call makes access to the netmap ring safe without the need of additional locking between the kernel and the user process.

Netmap is a kernel module made of two parts. Device-independent code implements the basic functions (open(), close(), ioctl(), poll()/select()), while device-specific *netmap-backends* extend device drivers and are in charge of transferring metadata between the netmap ring and the NIC ring (see Figure 3). The backends are very compact and fast, allowing netmap to send or receive packets at line rate even with the smallest packets (14.88 Mpps on a 10 Gbit/s interface) and with a single core running at less than 900 MHz. True zero-copy between interfaces is also supported, achieving line-rate switching with minimum-sized packets at a fraction of the maximum CPU speed.

3.2 A netmap-based Virtual Local Ethernet

From a user's perspective, our virtual switch shown in Figure 2 offers each user an independent, virtual NICs connected to a switch and accessible with the netmap API. NIC names start with the prefix vale (to differentiate them from physical NICs); both virtual NICs and switches are created dynamically as users access them.

When the netmap API requests to access a NIC named valeX:Y (where X and Y are arbitrary strings), the system creates a new VALE switch instance called X (if not existing), and attaches to it a port named Y.

Within each switch instance, packets are transferred between ports as in a learning ethernet bridge: the source MAC address of each incoming packet is used to learn on which port the source is located, then the packet is forwarded to zero or more outputs depending on the type of destination address (unicast, multicast, broadcast) and whether the destination is known or not. The following pseudocode describes the forwarding algorithm. The set of destinations is represented by a bitmap, so up to 64 output ports can be easily supported. A packet is forwarded to port j if dst & (1<<j) is non zero.

```
void tx_handler(ring, src_if) {
    cur = ring->cur; avail = ring->avail;
    while (avail-- > 0) {
        pkt = ring->slot[cur].ptr;
        // learn and store the source MAC
        s = mac_hash(pkt->src_mac);
        table[s] = {pkt->src_mac, src_if};
        // locate the destination port(s)
        d = mac_hash(pkt->dst_mac);
        if (table[d].mac == pkt->dst_mac)
            dst = table[d].src;
        else
            dst = ALL_PORTS;
        dst &= ~(1<<src_if); // avoid src_if
        // forward as needed
        for (j = 0; j < max_ports; j++) {
            if (dst & (1<<j)) {
                lock_queue(j);
                pkt_forward(pkt, ring->slot[cur].len, j);
                unlock_queue(j);
            }
        }
        cur = NEXT(cur);
    }
    ring->cur = cur; ring->avail = avail;
}
```

This code, operating on one packet at a time, is very similar to the implementation of most software switches found in common OSes. However its performance is poor (relatively speaking; we measured almost 5 Mpps as shown in Figure 8, which is still 5 times faster than existing in-kernel bridging code), for two main reasons: locking and data access latency.

The incoming queue on the destination port, in fact, must be protected against concurrent accesses, and in the above code the cost of locking (or equivalent mechanism) is paid on each packet, possibly exceeding the packet processing costs related to bridging. Secondly, the memory accesses to read the metadata and headers of each packet may have a significant latency if these data are not in cache.

3.3 Performance enhancements

To address these performance issues, we use a different sequence of operations, which permits processing packets in batches and supports data prefetching.

Batching is a well know technique to amortize the cost of some expensive operations over a large set of objects. The downside of batching is that, depending on how it is implemented, it can increase the latency of a system. Given that the netmap API used by VALE supports the transmission of potentially large sets of packets on each system call, we want to provide the system administrator with mechanisms to enforce the desired tradeoffs between performance and latency.

The key idea is to implement forwarding in multiple stages. In a first stage we collect a batch of packets of *bounded maximum batch size* from the input set of packets; a short batch is created if there are fewer packets available than the batch size. In this stage we copy metadata (packet sizes and indexes/buffer pointers), and also issue prefetch instructions for the payload of the packets in the batch, so that the CPU can start moving data towards caches before using them. Figure 4 shows how packets from the netmap ring are copied into a working array (**pool**) which also has room to store the set of destinations for each packet (these fields will be filled in the next stage). The pseudocode for this stage is the following:

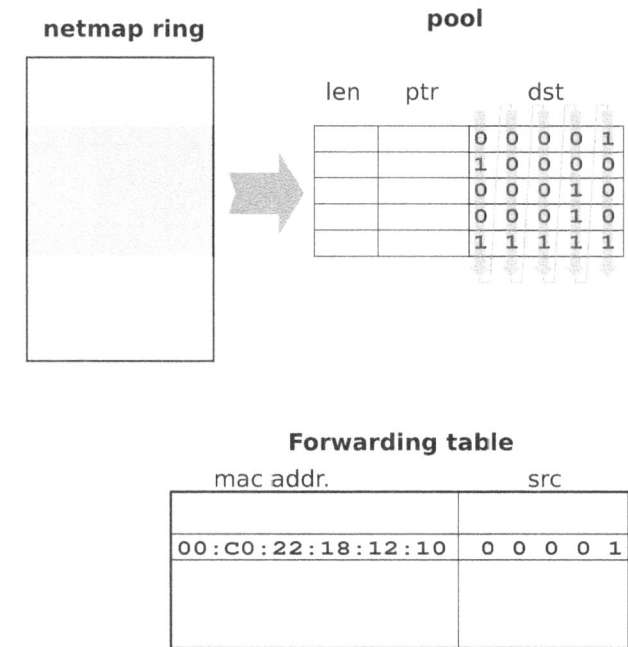

netmap ring		pool						
	len	ptr		dst				
			0	0	0	0	1	
			1	0	0	0	0	
			0	0	0	1	0	
			0	0	0	1	0	
			1	1	1	1	1	

Figure 4: **The data structures used in VALE to support prefetching and reduce the locking overhead. Chunks of metadata from the netmap ring are copied to a temporary array, while at the same time prefetching packets' payloads. A second pass then runs a destination lookup in the forwarding table, and finally the temporary array is scanned in column order to serve each interface in a single critical section.**

Forwarding table

mac addr.	src				
00:C0:22:18:12:10	0	0	0	0	1

```
void tx_handler(ring, src_if) {
    // stage 1, build batches and prefetch
    i = 0; cur = ring->cur; avail = ring->avail;
    for (; avail-- > 0; cur = NEXT(cur)) {
        slot = &ring->slot[cur];
        prefetch(slot->ptr);
        pool[i++] = {slot->ptr, slot->len, 0};
        if (i == netmap_batch_size) {
            process_batch(pool, i, src_if);
            i = 0;
        }
    }
    if (i > 0)
        process_batch(pool, i, src_if);
}
```

3.3.1 Processing a batch

The next processing stage involves updating the forwarding table, and computing the destination port(s) for each packet. The fact that the packet's payload has been brought into caches by the previous prefetch instructions should reduce the latency in accessing data. Furthermore, repeated source/destination addresses within a batch should improve locality in accessing the forwarding table.

Once destinations have been computed, the final stage can forward traffic iterating on output ports, which satisfies our requirement of paying the cost of locking/unlocking a port only once per batch. The following pseudocode shows a simplified version of the forwarding logic.

```
void process_batch(pool, n, src_if) {
    // stage 2, compute destinations
    for (i = 0; i < n; i++) {
        pkt = pool[i].ptr;
        s = mac_hash(pkt->src_mac);
        table[s] = {pkt->src_mac, src_if};
        d = mac_hash(pkt->dst_mac);
        if (table[d].mac == pkt->dst_mac)
            pool[i].dst = table[d].src;
        else
            pool[i].dst = ALL_PORTS;
    }
    // stage 3, forward, looping on ports
    for (j = 0; j < max_ports; j++) {
        if (j == src_if)
            continue; // skip src_if
        lock_queue(j);
        for (i = 0; i < n; i++) {
            if (pool[i].dst & (1<<j))
                pkt_forward(pool[i].pkt, pool[i].len, j);
        }
        unlock_queue(j);
    }
}
```

In the actual implementation, the final stage is further optimized to reduce the cost of the inner loop. As an example, the code skips ports for which there is no traffic, and delays the acquisition of the lock until the first packet for a destination is found, to shorten of critical sections[3].

3.3.2 Avoiding multicast

Forwarding to multiple destinations is a significant complication in the system, both in terms of space and runtime. The worst case complexity of stage 3, even for unicast traffic, is still $O(N)$ per packet, where N is the number of ports in the bridge. If a bridge is expected to have a very large number of ports (e.g. connected to virtual machines), it may make sense to remove support for multicast/broadcast forwarding[4].

To achieve this, the field used to store bitmap addresses can be recycled to build lists of packets for a given destination, thus avoiding an expensive worst case behaviour. Traffic originally directed to multiple ports (unknown destinations, or ARP requests/advertisements, BOOTP/DHCP requests, etc.) can be directed to a default port where a user-level process will respond appropriately, e.g. serving ARP and DHCP requests (a similar strategy is normally used in access nodes – DSLAM/BRAS – that terminate DSL lines).

3.3.3 Alternative forwarding functions

We should note that stage 2 is the only place where the forwarding function is invoked. It is then relatively simple, and it will be the subject of future work, to replace it with alternative algorithms such as an implementation of a OpenFlow dataplane.

3.4 Copying data

The final processing stage calls function `pkt_forward()`, which is in charge of queueing the packet on one of the destination ports. The simplest way to do this, and the one

---

[3]Computing the first and last packet for each destination is a lot more expensive in the generic case, as it requires iterating on the bitmap containing destinations. Even more expensive, from a storage point of view, is tracking the exact set of packets for a given destination.

[4]This feature will be implemented in future releases.

we use in VALE, is to copy the payload from the source to the destination buffer. Copying is especially convenient because it supports the case where the source and destination ports have buffers mapped in mutually-inaccessible address spaces. This is exactly one of the key requirements in VALE, where clients attached to the ports are typically virtual machines, or other untrusted entities, that should not interact in other ways than through the packets sent to them.

Ideally, if a packet has only a single destination, we could simply swap buffers between the transmit and the receive queue. However this method requires that buffers be accessible in both the sender and the receiver's address spaces and is not compatible with the need to isolate virtual machines.

While data copies may seem expensive, on modern systems the memory bandwidth is extremely high so we can achieve good performance as long as we make sure to avoid cache misses. We use an optimized copy function which is extremely fast: if the data is already in cache (which is likely, due to the `prefetch()` and the previous access to the MAC header), it takes less than 15 ns to copy a 60-bytes packet, and 150 ns for a 1514-bytes packet.

4. IMPLEMENTATION DETAILS

VALE is implemented as a kernel module, and is available from [19] for both FreeBSD and Linux as an extension of the netmap module. Thanks to the modular architecture of the netmap software, the additional features to implement VALE required less than 1000 additional lines of code, and the system was running on both FreeBSD and Linux from the very first version. The current prototype supports up to 8 switches per host (the number is configurable at compile time), with up to 64 ports each.

4.1 External communication

As presented, VALE implements only a local ethernet switch, whose use is restricted to processes and hypervisors running on the same host. The connection with external networks is however trivially achieved with one of the tools that are part of our netmap framework, which can bridge two arbitrary netmap interfaces at line rate, using an arrangement similar to that in Figure 5. We can use one netmap-bridge to connect to the host stack, and one or more to connect to physical interfaces.

Because the relevant code is already existing and operational with the desired performance, we will not discuss it in

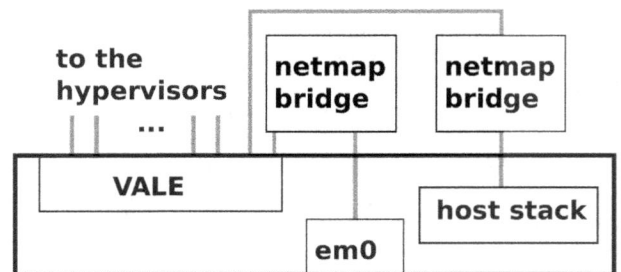

Figure 5: The connection between VALE, physical network interfaces and the host stack can be built with existing components (netmap bridge) which implement zero-copy high speed transfer between netmap-compatible ports.

the experimental section. As part of future work, we plan to implement a (trivial) extension of VALE to directly access the host stack and network interfaces without the help of external processes.

4.2 Hypervisor changes

In order to make use of the VALE network, hypervisors must be extended to access the new network backend. For simplicity, we have made modifications only to two popular hypervisors, QEMU [4] and KVM [9], but our changes apply in a similar way to VirtualBox and other systems using host-based access to network interfaces. We do not foresee much more complexity in making VALE ports accessible to Xen DomU domains.

The QEMU/KVM backend is about 400 lines of code and it implements the open and close routines, and the read and write handlers called on the VALE file descriptor when there is traffic to transfer.

Both QEMU and KVM access the network backend by poll()'ing on a file descriptor, and invoking read/write handlers when ready. For VALE, the handlers do not need to issue system calls to read or write the packets: the payload and metadata are already available in shared memory, and information on new packets to send or receive are passed to the kernel the next time the hypervisor calls poll(). This enables the hypervisor to exploit the batching, in turn contributing to reduce the I/O overhead.

As we will see in the performance evaluation, VALE is much faster than other software solutions used to implement the network backend. This extra speed may stress the hypervisor in unusual ways, possibly emphasizing some pre-existing performance issue or bugs. We experienced similar problems when modifying Open vSwitch to use netmap [18], and we found similar issues in this work.

Specifically, we encountered two performance-related bugs in the NIC emulation code in QEMU.

First of all, after some asymmetric tx versus rx performance results [15], we discovered that the code involved in the guest-side emulation of most network cards was missing a notification to the backend when the receive queue changed status from full to not-full. This made the input processing timeout-based rather than traffic based, effectively limiting the maximum receive packet rate to 100-200 Kpps. The fix, which we pushed to the QEMU developers, was literally one line of code and gave us a speedup of almost 10 times, letting us reach 1-2 Mpps range depending on the hypervisor.

The second problem involves the emulation of interrupt moderation, a feature that is fundamental to achieve high packet rates even on real hardware. Moderation is even more important in virtual machines where the handling of interrupts (which involves numerous accesses to I/O ports) is exceptionally expensive. We found that the e1000 emulation code implements the registers related to moderation, but then makes no use of them, causing interrupts to be generated immediately on every packet transmission or reception. We developed a partial fix [14] which improved the transmit performance by 7-8 times with this change alone.

We note that problems of this kind are extremely hard to identify (it takes a very fast backend to generate this much traffic, and a fast guest to consume it) and easy to misattribute. As an example, the complexity of device emulation is usually indicated as the main reason for poor I/O performance, calling for alternative solutions such as virtio [20] or other proprietary APIs [23].

4.3 Guest issues

A fast network backend and a fast hypervisor do not imply that the guest machines can communicate at high speed. Several papers in the literature show that even on real hardware, packet I/O rates on commodity operating systems are limited to approximately 1 Mpps per core. High speed communication (1..10 Gbit/s) is normally achieved thanks to a number of performance-enhancing techniques such as the use of jumbo buffers and hardware offloading of certain functions (checksum, segmentation, reassembly).

As we recently demonstrated [16], this low speed is not an inherent limitation in the hardware, but rather the result of exceeding complexity in the operating system, and we have shown how to achieve much higher packet rates using netmap as the mechanism to access the network card.

As a consequence, for some of our high speed tests we will use the network device in netmap mode *also within the guest*. The same reasons that make netmap very fast on real hardware, also help when running on emulated hardware: on both the transmit and the receive side, operations that need to be run in interpreted mode, or to trap outside the emulator, are executed once per each large batch of packets, thus contributing to improving performance.

5. PERFORMANCE EVALUATION

We have measured the performance of VALE on a few different multicore systems, running both FreeBSD and Linux as the host operating systems, and QEMU and KVM as hypervisors. In general, these experiments are extremely sensitive to CPU and memory speeds, as well as to data layout and compiler optimizations that may affect the timing of critical inner loops of the code. As a consequence for some of the (many) tests we have run there are large variations (10-20%) of the experimental results, also due to slightly different versions of the code or to the synchronization of the processes involved. We also noted a steady and measurable decline in QEMU/KVM network throughput (about 15% on the same hardware) between versions 0.9, 1.0 and 1.1.

This said, the difference in performance between VALE and competing solutions is much larger (4..10 times) than the variance on the experimental data, so we can draw correct conclusions even in presence of noisy data.

For the various tests, we have used a combination of the following components:

- **Hardware and host operating systems:**
  i7-2600K (4 core, 3.2 GHz) + FreeBSD-9;
  i7-870 (4 core, 2.93 GHz) + FreeBSD-10;
  i5-750 (4 core, 2.66 GHz) + Linux 3.2.12.
  i7-3930K (6 core/12 threads, 3.2 GHz) + Linux 3.2.0.
  In all cases RAM is DDR3-1.33 GHz and the OS is running in 64-bit mode.

- **Hypervisors:** QEMU 1.0.1 (both FreeBSD and Linux); KVM 1.0.1/1.1.0 (Linux).

- **Network backends:** TAP with/without vhost-net (Linux); VALE (Linux and FreeBSD).

- **Guest network interface/OS:** plain e1000, e1000-netmap (Linux and FreeBSD); virtio (only Linux).

Not all combinations have been tested due to lack of significance, unavailability, or bugs which prevented certain configurations from working. We should also mention that, especially for the data reporting peak performance, the numbers we report here are conservative. During the development of this work we have implemented some optimizations that shave a few nanoseconds from each packet's processing time, resulting in data rates in excess of 20 Mpps at minimum packet sizes.

Following the same approach as in the description of the system, we first benchmark the performance of the virtual local ethernet, be it our VALE system or equivalent ones. This is important because in many cases the clients are much slower, and their presence would lead to an underestimate of the performance of the virtual switch.

5.1 Bridging performance

The first set of tests analyzes the performance of various software bridging solutions. The main performance metric for packet forwarding is the throughput, measured in *packets per second* (pps) and *bits per second* (bps).

pps is normally the most important metric for routers, where the largest cost factors (source and destination lookup, queueing) are incurred on each packet and are relatively independent of packet size. Bridges and switches, however, need *also* (but not *only*) a characterization in bps, because they operate at very high rates and often hit other bottlenecks such as memory or bus bandwidth. We will then run our experiments with both minimum and maximum ethernet-size packets (60 and 1514 bytes).

Note that many *bps* figures reported in the literature are actually measured using jumbograms (8-9 Kbytes). The corresponding *pps* rates are between $1/6$ and $1/150$ of those shown here.

The traffic received by a bridge should normally go to a single destination, but there are cases (multicast or unknown destinations) where the bridge needs to replicate packets to multiple ports. Hence the number of active ports impacts the throughput of the system.

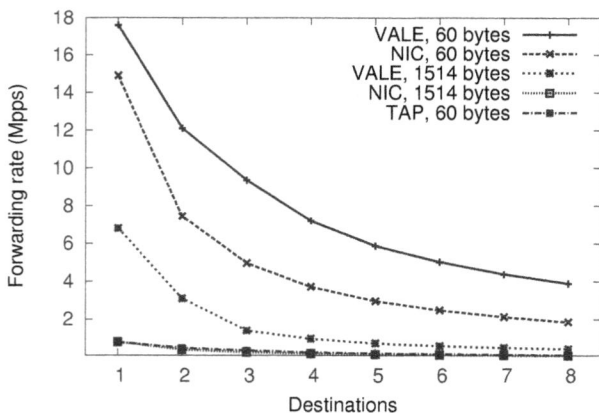

Figure 6: Forwarding rate versus number of destinations. VALE beats even NIC-based bridging, with over 17 Mpps (vs. 14.88) for 60-byte packets, and over 6 Mpps (vs. 0.82) for 1514-byte packets. TAP is at the bottom, peaking at about 0.8 Mpps in the best case.

In Figure 6 we compare the forwarding throughput when using 60 and 1514 byte packets, for three technologies: TAP plus native Linux bridging[5], our VALE bridge, and NIC/switch-supported bridging (in this case we report the theoretical maximum throughput on a 10 Gbit/s link).

Since the traffic directed to a bridge can be forwarded[6] to a single output port (when the destination is known), or to multiple ports (for multicast/broadcast traffic, or for unknown destinations), we expect a decrease in the forwarding rate as the number of active ports grows.

Indeed, all the three solutions (VALE, NIC, TAP) expose a $1/N$ behaviour. For VALE and TAP this is because the forwarding is done by a single core while the work is proportional to the number of ports. For switch-based bridging, the bottleneck is instead determined by the bandwidth available on the link from the switch, which has to carry all the replicas of the packet for the various destinations. A similar phenomenon occurs for NIC-based bridging, this time the bottleneck being the PCI-e bus.

In absolute terms, for traffic delivered to a single destination and 60-byte packets, the best options available for Linux bridging achieve a peak rate of about 0.80 Mpps. Next comes NIC-based forwarding, which is limited by the bandwidth on the PCI-e interconnection between the NIC and the system. Most 10 Gbit/cards on the market use 4-lane PCI-e slots per port, featuring a raw speed of 16 Gbit/s per port per direction. Considering the overhead for the transfer of descriptors, each port has barely enough bandwidth to sustain line rate. In fact, as we measured in [16], packet sizes that are not multiple of a cache line size cannot even achieve line rate due to extra traffic generated to read and write entire cache lines.

The curves for VALE are still above, peaking at 17.6 Mpps for a single destination and 60-byte packets, again decreasing as the number of receivers grows. Here the bottleneck is given by the combination of CPU cycles (needed to do the packet copies) and memory bandwidth.

The numbers for 1514-byte packets are even more impressive. Linux bridging is relatively stable at a low value (packet size is not a major cost item). NIC based forwarding is still limited to line rate, approximately 820 Kpps, whereas VALE reaches over 6 Mpps, or 72 Gbit/s.

5.1.1 Per packet time

Using the same data as in Figure 6, Figure 7 shows the per-packet processing time used by VALE depending on the number of destinations. This representation gives a better idea of the time budget involved with the various operations (hashing, address lookups, data copies, loop and locking overheads). Among other things, these figures can be used to determine a suitable batch size so that the total processing time matches the constraint of latency-sensitive applications.

The figure shows that for one port and small packets the processing time is 50-60 ns per packet when using large batches (128 and above). With separate measurements we estimated that about 15 ns are spent in computing the Jenk-

---

[5]we also tested the in-kernel Open vSwitch module, but it was always slightly slower than native bridging.

[6]In principle we should also consider the case of traffic being dropped by the bridge, but this is always much faster than the other cases (as an example, VALE can drop packets at almost 100 Mpps), so we do not need to worry about it.

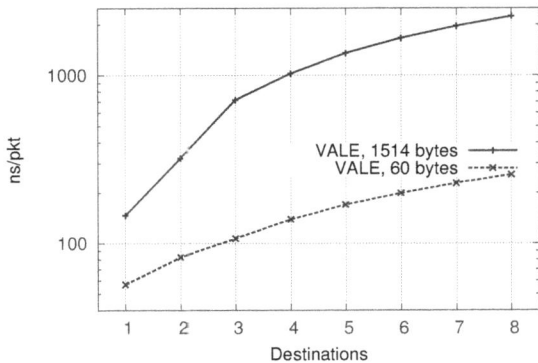

Figure 7: Per-packet time versus number of destinations for VALE. See text in Section 5.1.1 for details.

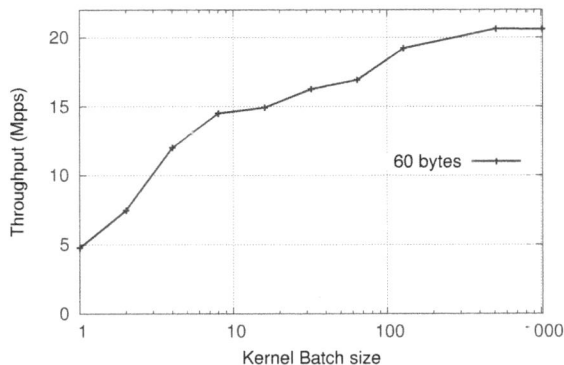

Figure 9: Throughput versus receive batch size. Kernel and sender use batch=1024.

ins hash function, taken from the FreeBSD bridging code, and approximately 15 ns are also necessary to perform a copy of a 60-byte packet (with data in cache). The cost of copying a 1514 byte packet is estimated at about 150 ns.

As mentioned in Section 3.4, VALE uses data copies in all cases. In the case of multicast/broadcast traffic, the only alternative to copying data would be to implement shared readonly buffers and a reference-counted mechanism to track when the buffer can be freed. Apart from the complications of the mechanism, the cost in accessing the reference count from different CPU cores is likely comparable or greater than the data copy costs, even for 1514-byte packets.

5.2 Effectiveness of batching

The huge difference in throughput between VALE and other solutions depends on both the use of the netmap API, which amortizes the system call costs, and also on the processing of packets in batches in the forwarding loop. Figure 6 has been computed for a batch size of 1024 packets but as we will show, even smaller batch sizes are very effective.

There are in fact three places where batching takes place: on the TX and RX sides, where its main goal is to amortize the cost of the system call to exchange packets with the kernel; and within the kernel, as discussed in Section 3.3, where the goal is to reduce locking contention.

The following experiments show the effect of various com-

binations of these three batching parameters. Experiments have been run on a fast i7-3930K using Linux 3.2, and unicast traffic between one sender and one receiver; the CPU has multiple cores so we expect sender and receiver to run in parallel on different cores.

Figure 8 shows the throughput versus kernel batch size, when both sender and receiver use a large value (1024) to amortize the system call cost as much as possible. Starting at about 5 Mpps with a batch of 1, we achieve dramatic increase even with relatively small kernel batches (e.g. 8 packets), and there is a diminishing return as we move above 128 packets. Here we have the following dynamics: the kernel, with its small batch size, acts as the bottleneck in the chain, waking up the receiver frequently with small amounts of packets. Because it uses a large batch size, the receiver cannot become the bottleneck: if during one iteration it is too slow in processing packets, in the next round it will be able to catch up draining a larger set of packets.

Figure 9 shows the behaviour of the system with different receiver batch sizes, and kernel and sender using a batch of 1024. In this experiment the receiver is the bottleneck, and the main cost component here is the system call, which however always finds data available so it never needs to sleep (a particularly costly operation). As a consequence, a small batching factor suffices to reach the peak performance.

Finally, Figure 10 shows the effect of different transmit

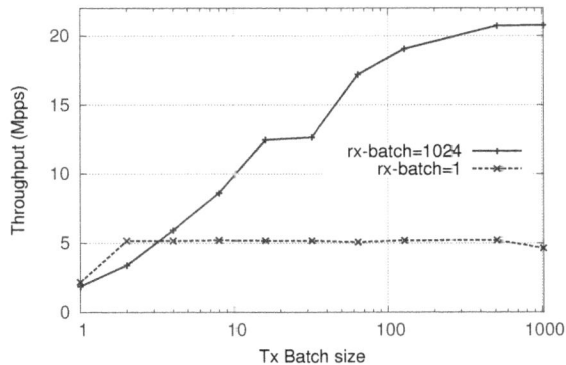

Figure 8: Throughput versus kernel batch size. Sender and receiver use batch=1024.

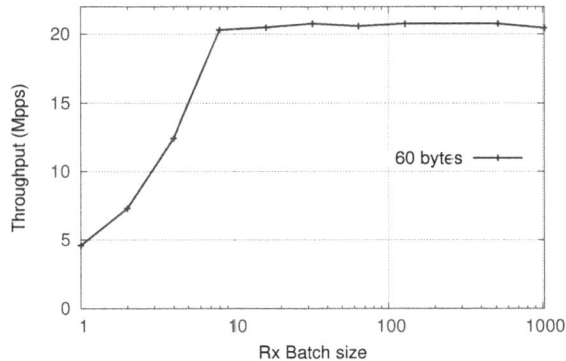

Figure 10: Throughput versus transmit batch size. Kernel uses batch=1024.

batch sizes. The kernel is always using a batch of 1024. The top curve, with a receive batch of 1024, resembles the behaviour of Figure 8. The kernel (and the receiver) indeed behave in a similar way in the two cases, because the sender in the first place is feeding the bridge with only a few packets at a time. The initial region, however, shows lower absolute values because the interval between subsequent invocations of `process_batch()` now includes a complete system call, as opposed to a simple iteration in `tx_handler()`.

The bottom curve, computed with a receive batch of 1 packet, gives a better idea of where the bottleneck lies depending on the tx and rx batch sizes. A small batching factor on the receiver will definitely limit throughput no matter how the other components work, but the really poor operating point – about 2 Mpps in these experiments – is *when the entire chain processes one packet at a time*. It is unfortunate that this is exactly what happens in practice with most network APIs.

5.3   Processing time versus packet size

Coming back to the comparative analysis of different bridging solutions, we now move to the evaluation of the effect of packet size on throughput. Same as in Section 5.2, we run the test between one sender and one receiver connected through a bridge (VALE or native linux bridging), and for variable packet sizes. The measurement is done in the best possible conditions (which, for VALE, means large batches). Also, it is useful to study the effect of packet sizes by looking at the time per packet, rather than absolute throughput.

Figure 11, presents the packet processing time versus the packet size. At these timescales the most evident phenomenon is the cost of data copies. VALE and TAP operate at the speed of the memory bus. This is confirmed by the experimental data, as the two curves have a similar slope. TAP of course has a much higher base value, which is the root cause of its overall poor performance. The curve for NIC-based bridging, instead, is much steeper. This is also

expected, because the bottleneck bandwidth (PCI-e or link speed) is several times smaller than that of the memory bus.

The curve for TAP presents a small dip between 60 and 128 bytes, which has been confirmed by a large number of tests. While we have not investigated the phenomenon, it is not unlikely that the code tries (and fails) to optimize the processing of small packets.

5.4   Latency

We conclude our performance analysis with an investigation on the communication latency. This test is mostly pointing out the poor performance of the operating system's primitives involved, rather than the qualities of the bridging code. Nevertheless it is important to know what kind of latency we can expect at best between communicating processes on the same system.

Figure 12 shows the round trip time between two processes talking through VALE (bottom curve) or a TAP bridge (top curve). In this experiment a "client" transmits a single packet and then blocks until a reply is received. The "server" instead issues a first system call to receive the request, and a second one to send the response. The actual amount of processing involved in the process (in the sender, receiver and forwarding code) is negligible, well below 1 μs, which means that the cycle is dominated by the system calls and the interactions with the scheduler (both client and server block waiting for the incoming packet).

As expected, VALE is almost unaffected by the message size (in the range of interest), as there is only a single, and very fast, copy in each direction. TAP instead uses at least two (and possibly three) copies on each direction, hence the different slope.

Care should be taken in comparing these numbers with other RPC mechanisms (e.g. InfiniBand, RDMA, etc.) designed to achieve extremely low latency. These system in fact exploit a number of latency-removal techniques that often require direct hardware access (such as exposing device registers to userspace to save the cost of system calls), are not efficient (such as running a busy-wait loop on the client to remove the scheduler cost), and rely on hardware sup-

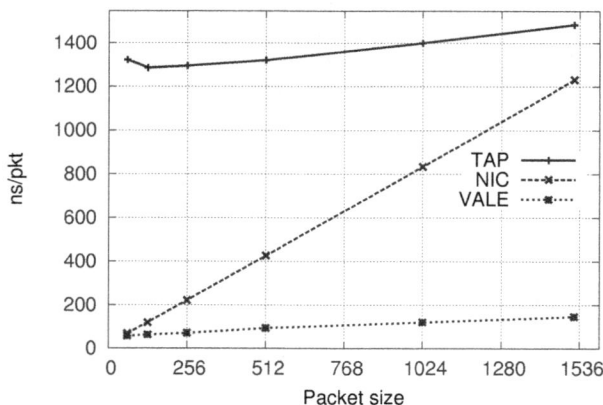

Figure 11: Per-packet time versus packet size. This experiments shows the impact of data copies. VALE and TAP have a similar slope, as they operate at memory bus speed. NIC-based bridging operates at a much lower (PCI-e or link) speed, hence producing a steeper curve.

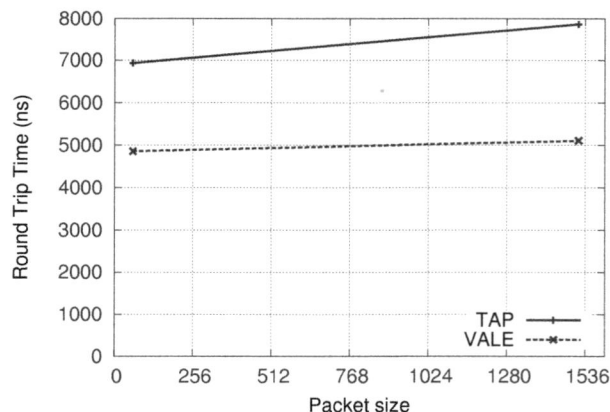

Figure 12: Round trip time in the communication between two processes connected through a linux native bridge (top) or VALE (bottom). In both cases, the times are dominated by the cost of the `poll()` system call on the sender and the receiver.

| Configuration | Speed, Mpps | | | | Notes |
| | TAP | | VALE | | |
	tx	rx	tx	rx	
Raw bridge speed	.90	.90	19.7	19.7	
e1000 QEMU	.018	.014	.023	.023	
e1000 KVM	.020	.020	.024	.024	
netperf virtio QEMU	.012	.010	.023	.012	
virtio KVM	.400	.300	.480	.470	kvm 1.0.1
virtio KVM	.370	.300	1.200	–	kvm 1.1.1
virtio KVM vhost	.600	.580			
pkt-gen e1000 QEMU	.490	.490	2.400	1.850	
pkt-gen e1000 KVM	.550	.550	3.470	2.550	
pkt-gen e1000 KVM	.500	.490	2.300	2.000	1514 b
vmxnet3 ESX	.800	.800	-	-	see [22]
vmxnet3 vSphere	.800	.800	-	-	see [23]

Table 1: Communication speed between virtual machine instances for different combinations of source/sink (netperf if not specified), emulated device, and hypervisor. Some combinations were not tested due to software incompatibilities. The numbers for VMWare are extracted from [23] and [22] and refer to their own software switch.

port (e.g. in RDMA the the server side is completely done in hardware, thus cutting almost half of the processing cost).

Some improvements could be achieved also in our case, e.g. spinning on a shared memory location to wait for data, but our goal is mostly to show what level of performance can be achieved with safe and energy-efficient techniques without hardware assist.

6. RUNNING A HYPERVISOR ON A FAST BRIDGE

The final part of this paper measures how the hypervisor and the guest OS can make use of the fast interconnection provided by VALE. All tests involve:

- a traffic source and sink, running in the guest. We use netperf, a popular test tool which can source or sink TCP or UDP traffic, and pkt-gen, a netmap-based traffic source/sink which generates UDP traffic;

- an emulated network device. We use e1000 (emulating a 1 Gbit/s device) and virtio, which provides a fast I/O interface that can talk efficiently to the hypervisor;

- a hypervisor. We run our tests with QEMU and KVM;

- a virtual bridge. We use native linux bridging accessed with TAP+vhost, and VALE.

The performance of some of the most significant combinations is shown in Table 1. In some cases we were unable to complete the tests due to incompatibilities between the various options.

All tests were run on an i7-3930K CPU running Linux 3.2 in the host, and with Linux guests.

In the table, the top row reports the raw speed of the bridge for both TAP and VALE. This serves as a baseline to evaluate the virtualized versus native throughput.

The next two rows report standard configurations with netperf and e1000 driver, running on QEMU or KVM. In both cases the packet rate is extremely low, between 14 and 24 Kpps. The interrupt moderation patches [14] bring the transmit rate to 56 and 140 Kpps, respectively, though we are still far from the the throughput that can be achieved

on real hardware (about 1.3 Mpps in this configuration). Measurements on QEMU show that, on each packet transmission, the bottom part of the device driver emulation consumes almost 50 μs, a big part of which is spent for handling interrupts.

The virtio driver improves the situation at least when running on top of KVM. Here the use of VALE as a backend gives some improvements[7], although limited by the fact that both source and sink process only one packet at a time.

With such a high per-packet overhead, replacing the TAP bridge with the (much faster) VALE switch can only have a very limited effect on performance. The recipe for improving performance is thus to make better use of the (emulated) network device. The netmap API comes to our help in this case, and the numbers using pkt-gen prove that.

When running pkt-gen on top of e1000+QEMU (or KVM), the throughput increases by a large factor, even with the TAP bridge (from 20 to $\approx$500 Kpps). The main reasons are that pkt-gen accesses the NIC's registers very sparingly, typically once or twice per group of packets, thus making the emulation a lot less expensive. The improvement is even more visible when running on top of the VALE, which can make use of the aggregation in the guest, and issue a reduced number of system calls to transfer packets from/to the host.

This experiment shows that even without virtio is in principle possible to transfer minimum-size packets at rates that exceed the speed of a 1 Gbit/s interface, and for 1514-byte packets we reach 20 Gbit/s even without virtio.

A lot of these performance improvements come from the use of larger batch sizes when talking to the backend. We are investigating solutions to exploit this operating regime, both with the help of modified device drivers in the host, and implementing mechanisms similar to interrupt moderation within the VALE switch.

6.1 Comparison with other solutions

QEMU and KVM are neither the only nor the fastest hypervisors on the market. Commercial solutions go to great lengths to increase the speed of virtualized I/O devices. To the best of our knowledge, solutions such as vSphere [23] and ESX [22] are among the best performer on the market[8], claiming a speed of about 800 Kpps between two virtual machines (which translates to slightly less than 10 Gbit/s with 1514-byte packets). The vendor's documentation [23] reports up to 27 Gbit/s TCP throughput with jumbo frames (9000 bytes) which should correspond to packet rates in the 4-500 Kpps range.

These numbers cannot be directly compared with the ones we achieved on top of VALE. Even though we get higher packet rates, we are not running through a full TCP stack on the guest; on the other hand we have a much worse virtualization engine and device driver to deal with. What we can still claim, however, is that we are able to achieve the same level of performance of high-end commercial solutions.

7. CONCLUDING REMARKS

We have presented the architecture of VALE, a high speed Virtual Local Ethernet freely available for FreeBSD and Linux, and given a detailed performance evaluation compar-

---

[7] the low number for KVM+VALE on the receive side seems due to a livelock in KVM 1.1.1 which we are investigating
[8] possibly not the only ones to provide such speeds.

ing VALE with NIC-based bridging and with various existing options based on linux bridging. Additionally, we have developed QEMU and KVM modifications that show how these hypervisors, with proper traffic sources and sinks, can make use of the fast interconnect and achieve very significant speedups.

We should note that VALE is neither limited to use with virtual machines, nor to pure ethernet bridging.

Indeed, the fact that VALE ports use the netmap API, and the availability of `libpcap` emulation library for netmap, means that a VALE switch can be used to interconnect various packet processing tools (traffic generators, monitors, firewalls etc.), and this permits performance testing at high data rates without the need of expensive hardware.

As an example, we recently used VALE switches to test a high speed version of the ipfw and dummynet traffic shaper [5], including the QFQ packet scheduler [6]. In this environment we were able to validate operation at rates exceeding 6 Mpps, well beyond the ability of regular OSes to source or sink traffic, let alone pass it to applications.

Also, the code that implements the forwarding decision (which in VALE is simply a lookup of the destination MAC address) can be trivially replaced with more complex actions, such as a software implementation of an OpenFlow switch. The main contribution of VALE, in fact, is in the framework to move traffic efficiently between ports and the module implementing forwarding decisions.

We are confident that, as part of future work, we will be able to make VALE compatible with better hypervisors and emulated device drivers (virtio and similar ones), and make its speed exploitable also by the network stack in the guest. At the high pps rates supported by VALE, certain operating systems functions (schedulers, synchronizing system calls) and emulator-friendliness need to be studied in some detail to identify possible performance bottlenecks.

The simplicity of our system and its availability should help the identification and removal of performance problems related to virtualization in hypervisors, device drivers and operating systems.

Acknowledgements

This work was funded by the EU FP7 projects CHANGE (257422) and OPENLAB (287581).

8. REFERENCES

[1] http://virt.kernelnewbies.org/MacVTap.
[2] http://www.linux-kvm.org/page/VhostNet.
[3] P. Barham, B. Dragovic, K. Fraser, S. Hand, T. Harris, A. Ho, R. Neugebauer, I. Pratt, and A. Warfield. Xen and the art of virtualization. In *SOSP'03*, Bolton Landing, NY, USA, pages 164–177. ACM, 2003.
[4] F. Bellard. Qemu, a fast and portable dynamic translator. In *USENIX Annual Technical Conference ATC'05*, Anaheim, CA. USENIX Association, 2005.
[5] M. Carbone and L. Rizzo. An emulation tool for planetlab. *Computer Communications*, 34:1980–1990.
[6] F. Checconi, P. Valente, and L. Rizzo. QFQ: Efficient Packet Scheduling with Tight Guarantees. *IEEE/ACM Transactions on Networking*, (to appear, doi:10.1109/TNET.2012.2215881), 2012.
[7] Y. Dong, J. Dai, Z. Huang, H. Guan, K. Tian, and Y. Jiang. Towards high-quality I/O virtualization. In *SYSTOR 2009: The Israeli Experimental Systems Conference*, pages 12:1–12:8. ACM, 2009.
[8] M. Goldweber and R. Davoli. VDE: an emulation environment for supporting computer networking courses. *SIGCSE Bull.*, 40(3):138–142, June 2008.
[9] R. A. Harper, M. D. Day, and A. N. Liguori. Using KVM to run Xen guests without Xen. In *2007 Linux Symposium*.
[10] J. R. Lange and P. A. Dinda. Transparent network services via a virtual traffic layer for virtual machines. In *16th Int. Symposium on High Performance Distributed Computing*, HPDC'07, pages 23–32, Monterey, California, USA, 2007. ACM.
[11] A. Menon, A. L. Cox, and W. Zwaenepoel. Optimizing network virtualization in xen. In *USENIX Annual Technical Conference ATC'06*, Boston, MA. USENIX Association, 2006.
[12] B. Pfaff, J. Pettit, T. Koponen, K. Amidon, M. Casado, and S. Shenker. Extending networking into the virtualization layer. In *Proc. of workshop on Hot Topics in Networks (HotNets-VIII)*, 2009.
[13] H. Raj and K. Schwan. High Performance and Scalable I/O Virtualization via Self-Virtualized Devices. In *Proc. of HPDC'07*, pages 179–188, 2007.
[14] L. Rizzo. Email to qemu-devel mailing list re. interrupt mitigation for hw/e1000.c, 24 july 2012. https://lists.gnu.org/archive/html/qemu-devel/2012-07/msg03195.html.
[15] L. Rizzo. Email to qemu-devel mailing list re. speedup for hw/e1000.c, 30 may 2012. https://lists.gnu.org/archive/html/qemu-devel/2012-05/msg04380.html.
[16] L. Rizzo. netmap: A Novel Framework for Fast Packet I/O. In *USENIX Annual Technical Conference ATC'12*, Boston, MA. USENIX Association, 2012.
[17] L. Rizzo. Revisiting network I/O APIs: the netmap framework. *Communications of the ACM*, 55(3):45–51, 2012.
[18] L. Rizzo, M. Carbone, and G. Catalli. Transparent acceleration of software packet forwarding using netmap. In *Infocom 2012*. IEEE, 2012.
[19] L. Rizzo and G. Lettieri. The VALE Virtual Local Ethernet home page. http://info.iet.unipi.it/~luigi/vale/.
[20] R. Russell. virtio: towards a de-facto standard for virtual I/O devices. *Operating Systems Review*, 42(5):95–103, 2008.
[21] S. Tripathi, N. Droux, T. Srinivasan, and K. Belgaied. Crossbow: from hardware virtualized nics to virtualized networks. In *1st ACM workshop on Virtualized infrastructure systems and architectures*, VISA '09, pages 53–62, Barcelona, Spain, 2009. ACM.
[22] VMWare. Esx networking performance. http://www.vmware.com/files/pdf/ESX_networking_performance.pdf.
[23] VMWare. vSphere 4.1 Networking performance. http://www.vmware.com/files/pdf/techpaper/PerformanceNetworkingvSphere4-1-WP.pdf.
[24] J. Wang, K.-L. Wright, and K. Gopalan. Xenloop: a transparent high performance inter-vm network loopback. In *Proceedings of the 17th international symposium on High performance distributed computing*, HPDC '08, pages 109–118, New York, NY, USA, 2008. ACM.
[25] P. Willmann, S. Rixner, and A. L. Cox. Protection strategies for direct access to virtualized i/o devices. In *USENIX 2008 Annual Technical Conference, ACT'08*, pages 15–28, Boston, Massachusetts, 2008. USENIX Association.
[26] B. Zhang, X. Wang, R. Lai, L. Yang, Z. Wang, Y. Luo, and X. Li. Evaluating and optimizing i/o virtualization in kernel-based virtual machine (kvm). In *NPC'10*, pages 220–231, 2010.

Towards TCAM-based Scalable Virtual Routers

Layong Luo*†, Gaogang Xie*, Steve Uhlig‡,
Laurent Mathy§, Kavé Salamatian¶, and Yingke Xie*

*Institute of Computing Technology, Chinese Academy of Sciences (CAS), China
†University of CAS China, ‡Queen Mary, University of London, UK
§University of Liège, Belgium, ¶University of Savoie, France
{luolayong, xie, ykxie}@ict.ac.cn, steve@eecs.qmul.ac.uk,
laurent.mathy@ulg.ac.be, kave.salamatian@univ-savoie.fr

ABSTRACT

As the key building block for enabling network virtualization, virtual routers have attracted much attention recently. In a virtual router platform, multiple virtual router instances coexist, each with its own FIB (Forwarding Information Base). The small amount of high-speed memory in a physical router platform severely limits the number of FIBs supported, which leads to a scalability challenge. In this paper, we present a method towards TCAM (Ternary Content Addressable Memory) based scalable virtual routers, through a merged data structure that enables the sharing of prefixes from several FIBs in TCAMs. Based on this data structure, we propose two approaches to merge multiple FIBs in TCAMs, paving the way for scalable virtual routers. Experimental results show that, by using the two approaches for storing 14 full IPv4 FIBs, the TCAM memory requirement can be reduced by about 92% and 82% respectively, compared with the conventional approach of treating FIBs as independent entities.

Categories and Subject Descriptors

C.2.6 [**Internetworking**]: Routers

General Terms

Algorithms, Design, Experimentation, Performance

Keywords

Virtual routers, TCAM, FIB completion, FIB splitting

1. INTRODUCTION

Network virtualization [5] is a promising way to achieve cost-efficient utilization of networking resources, to support customized routing, e.g., for application-specific forwarding, customer-based routing, and to enable experimentation and deployment of new network protocols, e.g., CCN, without

interrupting normal network operations. Indeed, network virtualization allows multiple virtual networks to coexist on an underlying shared substrate, in isolation from each other.

As the key building block for enabling network virtualization, virtual routers have attracted much attention in recent years [4,6–10,18,19,22]. When multiple virtual router instances are supported on the same physical equipment, we will use the term *virtual router platform*. In a virtual router platform, multiple virtual router instances coexist and each has its own FIB (Forwarding Information Base). To achieve high forwarding performance, these FIBs are preferably stored in high-speed memory, such as TCAMs (Ternary Content Addressable Memory) or SRAMs (Static Random Access Memory). However, due to physical limitations (e.g., cost, power, and board space), high-speed memory turns out to be a scarce resource, and its size is limited.

On the other hand, with the growing demand for virtual routers, the number of virtual router instances supported in a virtual router platform is expected to keep increasing, with the size of each FIB also expected to grow. This creates a high requirement for large high-speed memory. The gap between the high demand and the limited memory size will create a scalability issue on the virtual router platform. That is, the small amount of high-speed memory severely limits the number of virtual router instances supported. For example, a very large TCAM on today's market has up to 1M entries [2], while a full IPv4 FIB contains about 400K prefixes currently [1], which means that only two FIBs can be stored in such a device.

Efforts in two areas can be made to improve the scalability of a virtual router platform. First, the size of the high-speed memory can be increased to support as many virtual router instances as possible. However, this effort usually results in high power consumption and high cost, which makes it unsustainable in the long term. Second, the amount of memory required for storing multiple FIBs can be reduced by merging and compressing FIBs, so that more FIBs can fit in a given memory size, without the needs to increase system power and cost. We believe this latter approach to be more viable.

In the last few years, the scalability challenge brought by virtual routers has created interest from the research community, and previous work [7–10,18] mainly focused on SRAM-based scalable virtual routers. Tree-based (e.g., trie or 2-3 tree) algorithms have been proposed to merge multiple FIBs into a single tree, and thereby many FIBs can be efficiently stored in the SRAMs. However, none of the previous work was targeted towards using TCAMs to build scalable virtual routers.

TCAMs are popular and promising devices to build IP lookup engines, thanks to their deterministic high performance and simplicity [12, 25]. TCAMs always guarantee a deterministic high lookup throughput of one lookup per clock cycle. Although an SRAM may run at a higher clock frequency than a TCAM (thus requiring less time for each memory access), SRAM-based solutions usually have variable lookup performance, and require multiple memory accesses for one lookup in the worst case [16]. TCAMs have traditionally exhibited higher power consumption and lower densities than SRAMs, although as semiconductor technology improves and demand increases, high-capacity, very high-speed TCAMs have become available. For example, the NL9000 family TCAMs [2] from NetLogic Microsystems, which contain up to 1 million 40-bit entries, can perform up to 1200 million decisions per second. All this suggests that TCAMs should also be a viable option to build virtual routers.

In this paper, we propose a merged data structure to share prefixes from individual FIBs in TCAMs. We propose two approaches based on this data structure to build TCAM-based scalable virtual routers. The first approach called FIB completion, merges the prefixes from all the FIBs into one TCAM. This approach exhibits the best scalability, but a large worst-case update overhead. The second approach, called FIB splitting, mixes the advantages of merged and non-shared data structures by splitting the prefixes into two prefix sets. This approach also yields very good scalability, with a much more reasonable worst-case update overhead. We provide experimental results showing that, for 14 full IPv4 FIBs, the proposed approaches can achieve a TCAM memory reduction of 92% and 82%, respectively, compared with a non-shared approach. This suggests that VPNs (Virtual Private Network) and experimental network testbeds can also benefit from our approaches.

The rest of the paper is organized as follows. In Section 2, we discuss the background on TCAM-based lookup engines and describe the non-shared approach for TCAM-based virtual routers. In Section 3, we describe the merged data structure that is the basis of this work. In Sections 4 and 5, we present two approaches based on the merged data structure. We evaluate the two approaches and compare them with the non-shared approach in Section 6. We discuss the related work in Section 7 and conclude in Section 8.

2. BACKGROUND

A TCAM is a fully associative memory, in which each bit of an entry can be specified in one of three states: '0', '1' and 'X' meaning "do not care", also called wildcard bits. Thanks to the wildcard bits, the TCAM is very suited for storing IP prefixes in IP lookup engines. Given a destination IP address, all the prefixes stored in the TCAM can be compared with the IP address simultaneously. Indeed, multiple prefixes may match the IP address, and the matched prefix at the lowest address will be selected as the only matching result, as the TCAM entries have an intrinsic priority, *i.e.*, an entry at a lower address has a higher priority. Although some TCAMs may have different priority logics, we assume in this paper that the TCAMs we use hereafter implement the above priority. After the matching result is determined, the TCAM returns the address of the matched prefix. The

Figure 1: Two sample FIBs

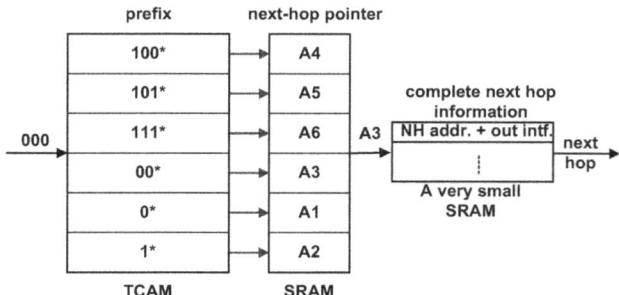

Figure 2: A TCAM-based IP lookup engine

TCAM usually completes an IP lookup every clock cycle, resulting in consistent very high lookup speed.

2.1 Traditional TCAM-based IP Lookup

To fix ideas, let us start by considering a traditional router, which is a platform hosting a single router instance, with only one FIB. Each entry in the FIB is comprised of an IP prefix and its corresponding next hop (NH). Figure 1(a) shows a sample FIB.

In a typical TCAM-based IP lookup engine, the IP prefixes are stored in the TCAM in decreasing prefix-length order for correct longest prefix matching (LPM) [17]. The NH pointers are stored in an associated SRAM, and the complete NH information is stored in another very small SRAM. Figure 2 shows a TCAM-based IP lookup engine containing the FIB shown in Figure 1(a). Generally, a complete NH consists of the IP address of the NH and the output interface, consuming about 5 bytes per NH. The number of unique NHs is small due to the limited number of interfaces in a router. One can assume that this number is less than 256 [7], so that a 1-byte NH pointer can represent the NH. Therefore, storing the NH pointers in the associated SRAM instead of the complete NHs consumes much less memory. The complete NHs can be stored in another very small SRAM, and the NH pointers are used to locate the final complete NHs (see Figure 2). The total size of the complete NHs is the same for all approaches, and is so small that we will ignore it in the remainder of the paper. Hereafter, for simplicity, we will use the term "NH" to mean "NH pointer", and focus our attention only on the TCAM and its associated SRAM storing NH pointers in the TCAM-based IP lookup engine.

In the TCAM-based IP lookup engine shown in Figure 2, given destination IP address 000 to lookup, the two prefixes 00* and 0* are matches, and the address of prefix 00*

prefix	next hop
0100*	A4
0101*	A5
0111*	A6
000*	A3
00*	A1
01*	A2
1100*	B4
1101*	B5
1111*	B6
111*	B3
10*	B1
11*	B2
TCAM	**SRAM**

Figure 3: A non-shared approach for virtual routers

will be returned by the TCAM, because it is stored at a lower TCAM address (*i.e.*, a higher priority). Then, this address is used to find the corresponding NH pointer A3 in the associated SRAM. Finally, the complete NH is obtained in another SRAM through pointer A3, and the packet is forwarded towards this NH.

2.2 Naive Approach for Virtual Routers

In the context of virtual routers, multiple FIBs are hosted in a physical platform. One way to arrange prefix sets from several FIBs in one TCAM is to put each prefix set in a separate region. We will call this approach the "non-shared approach", as identical prefixes from different FIBs are not shared. We use the two FIBs shown in Figure 1 to illustrate this non-shared approach for TCAM-based virtual routers.

In a virtual router platform, a Virtual router ID (VID) identifies each router and its FIB. Assume that VID 0 is assigned to FIB 0 and VID 1 is assigned to FIB 1 in Figure 1. Before storing the two FIBs in the TCAM, the VID is prepended to each prefix to form a virtual prefix. For example, the virtual prefix for prefix 0* in FIB 0 is 00*, while the corresponding virtual prefix is 10* for the same prefix in FIB 1. After virtual prefixes are formed, the virtual prefix sets from different FIBs can be directly stored in a TCAM without interfering with each other, as the VID for each FIB is unique. Then, their corresponding NHs are stored in an associated SRAM. Figure 3 illustrates one way of storing FIB 0 and FIB 1 using this approach.

In the non-shared approach, the IP lookup process is as follows. For an incoming packet, the destination IP is extracted from the packet header and the VID is determined from contextual information (*e.g.*, packet header, virtual interface). A Virtual IP address (VIP) is formed by prepending the VID to the destination IP address. Then, the VIP is sent to the TCAM for lookup. For example, given destination IP 000 and VID 1, VIP 1000 is looked up in the TCAM shown in Figure 3, and the virtual prefix 10* is matched. Then, the corresponding NH B1 is found in the associated SRAM. Note that the lookup process in the non-shared approach is similar to that in traditional routers, except for the use of the VIP for TCAM search.

The main issue with the non-shared approach is the TCAM memory requirement, which increases significantly as the number of FIBs increases. For example, in Figure 1, there are 6 entries in each of the two FIBs, and the total number of TCAM entries in the non-shared approach (see Figure 3) is 12, which is the sum of the number of entries in the individual FIBs.

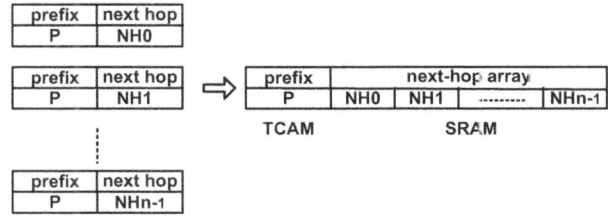

prefix	next hop
P	NH0

prefix	next hop
P	NH1

$\Rightarrow$

prefix	next-hop array			
P	NH0	NH1	....	NHn-1

TCAM   **SRAM**

prefix	next hop
P	NHn-1

Figure 4: The merged data structure

prefix	next hop	
100*	A4	B4
101*	A5	B5
111*	A6	B6
00*	A3	0
11*	0	B3
0*	A1	B1
1*	A2	B2
TCAM	**SRAM**	
(a)		

prefix	next hop	
100*	A4	B4
101*	A5	B5
111*	A6	B6
00*	A3	B1
11*	A2	B3
0*	A1	B1
1*	A2	B2
TCAM	**SRAM**	
(b)		

Figure 5: (a) The basic merged FIB, and (b) its completed version

3. MERGED DATA STRUCTURE

In the non-shared approach, the total memory space required in the TCAM increases significantly as the number of FIBs increases, and thus the number of virtual router instances supported cannot scale well.

We argue that the prefix similarity among different FIBs can be exploited to significantly reduce the TCAM memory requirement. A key observation is that, if two entries from different FIBs share the same prefix, they can be merged into a single entry in the TCAM-based lookup engines. For example, an entry <P, NH0> in FIB 0 and an entry <P, NH1> in FIB 1 can be merged into a single entry <P, [NH0, NH1]>. The prefix P is stored in the TCAM, and its corresponding NH array [NH0, NH1] is stored in the associated SRAM.

Figure 4 shows the merged data structure for n FIBs in TCAM-based lookup engines. If there is a common prefix P in n FIBs, these n entries can be merged into a single entry, with prefix P associated with a NH array containing n NHs. In the NH array, the ith next hop (NHi) is the one associated with prefix P in the ith FIB.

Based on the merged data structure, the two FIBs shown in Figure 1 can be represented by the merged FIB in Figure 5(a). The prefix set in the merged FIB consists of the union of the prefixes in the individual FIBs, and is henceforth called the Union Prefix Set (UPS). To get the UPS from multiple FIBs, we adopt the trie merging approach proposed in [7].

Initially, an auxiliary 1-bit trie is built from each individual FIB. Figure 6 shows two 1-bit tries, which are built from the two sample FIBs in Figure 1, respectively. In these tries (we will use the terms "1-bit trie" and "trie" interchangeably hereafter), a prefix which does not correspond to any NH in the FIB is associated with an invalid NH (represented as 0). After all the tries are built, they are merged into a merged trie using the strawman approach in [7]. The nodes corresponding to a same prefix in different tries can be merged,

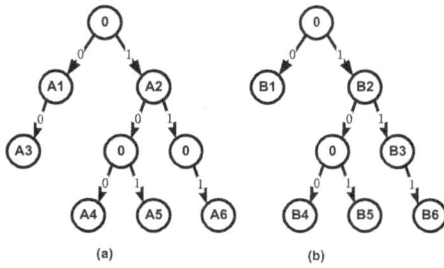

Figure 6: Auxiliary tries for the two FIBs in Figure 1

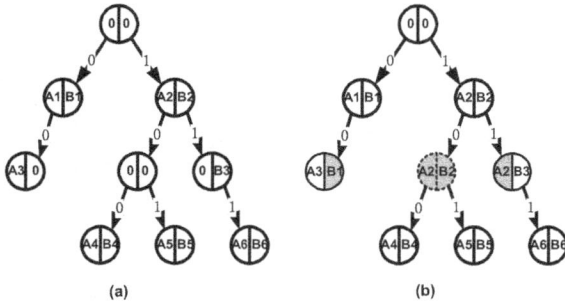

Figure 7: (a) The merged trie, and (b) its completed version

and the NHs for all virtual routers are stored in the merged node. Using this approach, the two tries shown in Figure 6 can be merged into the merged trie depicted in Figure 7(a).

The prefix set represented by the merged trie is the UPS. Note, however, that prefixes represented by merged trie nodes that contain only invalid NHs are not in the UPS, as they do not appear in any of the merged FIBs (*e.g.*, this is the case for prefix 10* in the merged trie in Figure 7(a)).

To clearly show the difference between the merged FIB and the non-shared FIB, we take prefix 100* as an example. We have an entry <100*, A4> in FIB 0 and an entry <100*, B4> in FIB 1. In the non-shared approach (see Figure 3), two separate entries are needed. In the merged FIB, we have a single entry <100*, [A4, B4]>, which denotes that prefix 100* is a prefix in both FIBs, with a corresponding NH A4 for FIB 0, and B4 for FIB 1.

However, a prefix in the UPS does not always exist in all FIBs. For example, prefix 00* exists in FIB 0 but not in FIB 1. In this case, we introduce an invalid NH 0 (null NH). A NH is null when the prefix does not exist in the corresponding individual FIB. For example, prefix 00* does not exist in FIB 1, and therefore the second NH associated with prefix 00* in the merged FIB is denoted as 0 in Figure 5(a).

Using the merged data structure, the number of entries in the merged FIB is significantly lower than the sum of the number of entries in the individual FIBs, which dramatically reduces the TCAM memory requirement. In our example, the number of TCAM entries needed to store the prefixes in the merged FIB (*i.e.*, the UPS) in Figure 5(a) is 7, down from 12 in the non-shared approach shown in Figure 3.

The IP lookup process based on this merged data structure works as follows. The destination IP address is used as the key to be searched in the TCAM. After the search terminates, the address of the matched prefix is used to locate the NH array containing the corresponding n NHs in

the associated SRAM. Then, the VID is used as an offset to find the corresponding NH in the NH array. For example, in Figure 5(a), given IP address 100 and VID 1, the first entry in the TCAM will match the IP address, and [A4, B4] is the corresponding NH array. VID 1 is then used as the offset to yield NH B4.

In essence, the proposed method looks up an IP address in all the FIBs simultaneously, and the VID is used to select the relevant NH. While this approach is, at first glance, straightforward, it does introduce inconsistencies and results in incorrect lookups in some cases. For example, given IP address 000 and VID 1, the correct NH should be B1 (see Figure 1(b)). However, if this lookup is performed in the merged FIB shown in Figure 5(a), the NH is 0, which indicates an invalid NH. The reason for this is that the TCAM always returns the first matching result (*i.e.*, the address of the longest matching prefix), while the matched prefix 00* does not exist in FIB 1.

The fundamental issue is that the merged data structure yields a merged FIB that contains all the prefixes appearing in at least one of the individual FIBs (*i.e.*, prefixes from the UPS). This can result in the "artificial" insertion of prefixes in individual FIBs (*e.g.*, insertion of prefix 00* with NH 0 in FIB 1 in Figure 5(a)), while those "added" prefixes can in turn "mask" correct, but shorter-length entries during the matching process (*e.g.*, given IP address 000 and VID 1, the "added" prefix 00* masks the valid prefix 0* in FIB 1 in Figure 5(a)). Note that this issue is specific to FIB merging in a TCAM environment, because of the intrinsic priority matching service provided by such components.

To ensure correct prefix matching, TCAM-based virtual router FIB management methods must *avoid incorrect matching, resulting from the masking of a shorter prefix in an individual FIB by a longer prefix in the merged FIB.*

In the following sections, we present two TCAM FIB merging approaches that avoid the prefix masking issue.

4. FIB COMPLETION

4.1 Completion Approach

Our first TCAM FIB merging approach, called *FIB completion*, addresses the prefix masking issue described in the previous section in a direct way: whenever a prefix from the UPS does not appear in a given individual FIB, we simply associate it with a valid NH in this FIB. The valid NH is the one associated with the longest ancestor prefix in the same FIB. In other words, each null NH entry described in Section 3 is replaced by the first valid NH entry encountered when going up the corresponding trie branch towards the root.

Figure 7(b) shows the merged trie in FIB completion version, which corresponds to the original merged trie shown in Figure 7(a). For example, in Figure 7(a), prefix 11* from the UPS does not appear in FIB 0. In this case, we associate prefix 11* with NH A2, copied from the NH associated with its longest ancestor prefix in the same FIB (*i.e.*, prefix 1* in FIB 0). Therefore, entry <11*, [0, B3]> is replaced by <11*, [A2, B3]>, as A2 is the correct NH according to the LPM rule. Note that this copied NH A2 is drawn in gray in Figure 7(b), which denotes that it is a completed NH, as opposed to a NH originally associated with the corresponding prefix (which we call original NH). Likewise, <00*, [A3, B1]> results from the completion process, so that the longer prefix 00*, not present in FIB 1 and masking the valid prefix 0*, yields the expected NH B1. Note that as prefix 10* does not appear in any of the original individual FIBs (*i.e.*, prefix 10* does not exist in the UPS), this prefix will not be included in the TCAM. We dash the nodes corresponding to prefixes not in the UPS in Figure 7(c). For those prefixes not in the UPS, completion is also performed (*e.g.*, see <10*, [A2. B2]> in Figure 7(b)) to simplify the update process.

Using the FIB completion approach, the merged FIB shown in Figure 5(a) is transformed into the one shown in Figure 5(b). The TCAM-based lookup engine with FIB completion is the same as that described in Section 3. When compared with the merged FIB shown in Figure 5(a), the only difference is that the null NHs in the associated SRAM are replaced by entries yielding correct lookup results.

4.2 Lookup and Update Process

The IP lookup process in the FIB completion approach is exactly the same as the one described in Section 3. However, the update process is different.

For merged trie maintenance purposes, the FIB completion algorithm must keep track of which NH entry exists in the corresponding individual FIB (*i.e.*, original NH), and which NH is an entry resulting from masking (*i.e.*, completed NH).

When an update occurs in a node of the trie, some completed NHs in the sub-trie rooted at that node will have to be updated to reflect correct matching. This downward propagation in the trie, which we call "masking prefix correction", stops as soon as nodes containing original NH entries are encountered. This process ensures that all the masking prefixes (*i.e.*, prefixes that are not present in the individual FIB but are present in the merged FIB) that are direct descendants of a masked prefix (*i.e.*, a prefix present in the individual FIB), all yield the same NH as the masked prefix. This ensures the correct lookup result.

In the following, we show the update process in detail and illustrate the typical update scenarios in Figure 8. Note that we will use NH Ai in FIB 0, and NH Bi in FIB 1, and that the background colour of the NH denotes the entry type, with white for original NHs, and gray for completed NHs. The original merged trie shown in Figure 8(a) is used as the starting point for each update scenario.

When a new prefix is inserted in an individual FIB, three cases are possible, see Figure 8(b). First, when the prefix already exists in the UPS, the corresponding NH is updated and this NH is flagged as original and the masking prefix correction process is applied from the children of the modified node. For example, if <11*, A8> is inserted into the original merged trie, the corresponding entry becomes <11*, [A8, B3]>, and the masking prefix correction is performed on the sub-trie rooted at <11*, [A8, B3]>. Second, when the prefix (*e.g.*, prefix 010*) corresponds to a new leaf node of the merged trie, the corresponding branch of the trie is extended as required by duplicating the closest ancestor node (*e.g.*, the node <0*, [A1, B1]>) as many times as necessary, but with all entries in the NH array flagged as completed, as those trie nodes correspond to prefixes that are not in the UPS. For example, all NHs in node <01*, [A1, B1]> are flagged as completed. The NH array in the new leaf is identical to that in the nearest ancestor node but for the inserted NH flagged as original in the appropriate FIB (the new leaf is thus added to the UPS). Third, when the prefix

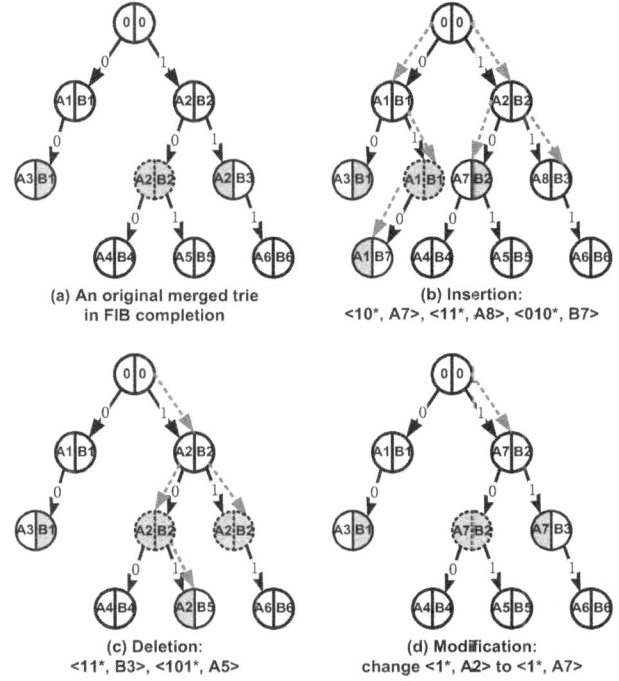

(a) An original merged trie in FIB completion

(b) Insertion: <10*, A7>, <11*, A8>, <010*, B7>

(c) Deletion: <11*, B3>, <101*, A5>

(d) Modification: change <1*, A2> to <1*, A7>

Figure 8: Update scenarios in FIB completion

corresponds to a non-leaf node and this prefix is not in the UPS (*e.g.*, prefix 10*), this prefix is added in the UPS, and the corresponding NH is updated and flagged as original (*e.g.*, <10*, A7>). Besides, the masking prefix correction process is applied on the sub-trie rooted at this node.

When a prefix is deleted from a FIB (*e.g.*, see the deletion of <101*, A5> in Figure 8(c)), the corresponding entry in the NH array in the node where the update occurs is flagged as completed. The NH of this node's closest ancestor (*e.g.*, <10*, A2>) is then determined, and used in the masking prefix correction process applied from the modified node. Note that if the deleted prefix corresponds to the last original entry in the NH array of the node, the prefix will be removed from the UPS. For example, following the deletion of <11*, B3>, prefix 11* will be removed from the UPS, as B3 is the last original NH in the corresponding NH array.

When the NH for an existing prefix is modified, the corresponding NH entry in the appropriate node of the merged trie is also modified, and the masking prefix correction process is applied from the children of the modified node. For example, if we modify <1*, A2> into <1*, A7>, the corresponding NH A2 is replaced by A7. Besides the completed NHs in the sub-trie rooted at node <1*, [A7, B2]> are updated (*e.g.*, see the NHs in gray associated with prefix 10* and prefix 11* in Figure 8(d)).

Once these update procedures have been applied to the merged trie, all modifications to nodes representing prefixes in the UPS must then be reflected in the TCAM-based lookup engine.

The masking prefix correction process only changes the NHs, not the prefixes, so that for one FIB update, at most one TCAM update should be affected. In the worst case, for one FIB update, the masking prefix correction may traverse the whole trie, and modify a NH in each node. Therefore,

$2^{W+1} - 1$ NHs should be modified in the associated SRAM for one update in the worst case, where W is the length of the IP address. We expect the worst case to be unlikely to happen in practice and the average update overhead to be much less costly, as shown in Section 6.

5. FIB SPLITTING

The main drawback of FIB completion is the high worst-case update overhead, which is caused by the masking prefix correction process. Masking prefix correction is required in FIB completion as masking prefixes and their corresponding masked prefix coexist in the same TCAM. A key observation is that, if only disjoint prefixes are merged in the TCAM, the prefix masking issue does not exist any longer, as at most one prefix in a disjoint prefix set can match a given IP address. Previous work [13] has shown that about 90% of prefixes in the tries built from real FIBs are leaf prefixes, which are, by definition, naturally disjoint. This property will also be true for the merged trie built from such FIBs. Based on the above observations, we propose the following approach, which we call *FIB splitting*.

1. The disjoint leaf prefixes in the merged trie are stored in one TCAM based on the basic merged data structure described in Section 3.

2. The remaining prefixes in the merged trie are stored in another TCAM using the non-shared approach.

As disjoint prefixes are merged in their own TCAM, masking prefix correction can be totally avoided. The remaining overlapping prefixes (*i.e.*, they are not necessarily disjoint with each other[1]) [13] are stored in another TCAM, where the prefix masking issue still exists if TCAM FIB merging is performed. However, experiments show that the number of remaining prefixes is very small. Therefore, the non-shared approach is used to manage the remaining prefixes in this second TCAM. By giving priority to matches from the TCAM storing the disjoint leaf prefix set (which necessarily are LPMs), this yields correct lookup results, while keeping good memory scalability as most of prefixes are merged. Additionally, this approach has a more reasonable upper bound on the worst-case update overhead, as masking prefix correction is totally avoided.

5.1 Splitting Approach

In FIB splitting, the first step is to split the prefix set into two sets: a disjoint leaf prefix set and the remaining set (*i.e.*, an overlapping prefix set).

All the FIBs should first be merged, and then the merged prefix set is partitioned. We use the same approach as described in Section 3 for trie merging. Then, the merged trie is split as follows. For a given merged trie, its root node is first checked. If it is a non-leaf node and its corresponding prefix is a valid prefix, this prefix belongs to the overlapping prefix set; if it is a leaf node, its corresponding prefix must be a valid prefix, which belongs to the disjoint leaf prefix set. Then, the left child and right child of the current node are checked recursively.

For example, if the merged trie shown in Figure 7(a) is partitioned, the disjoint leaf prefix set is shown in Figure 9(a). Note that prefixes in this part are merged in one

---

[1]Prefix overlapping may exist in the remaining set.

prefix	next hop	
00*	A3	0
100*	A4	B4
101*	A5	B5
111*	A6	B6

(a)

prefix	next hop
00*	A1
01*	A2
111*	B3
10*	B1
11*	B2

(b)

Figure 9: (a) The merged disjoint prefix set, and (b) the non-shared overlapping prefix set

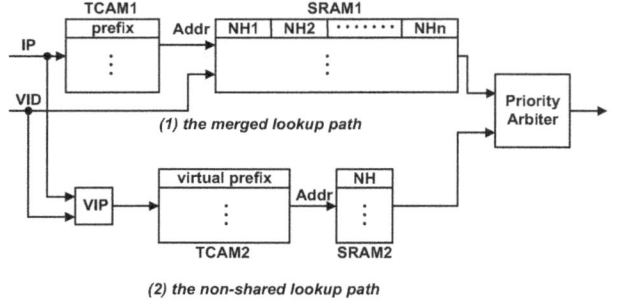

(1) the merged lookup path

(2) the non-shared lookup path

Figure 10: The lookup engine architecture in FIB splitting

TCAM based on the merged data structure shown in Figure 4. The remaining prefixes are overlapping, and we use the non-shared approach to manage them. As in the non-shared approach only prefixes associated with valid NH entries need to be considered, the issue of masking prefixes is avoided altogether in this set, see Figure 9(b).

5.2 Lookup Engine Architecture

The lookup engine architecture is depicted in Figure 10. It consists of two TCAM-based IP lookup paths. The first lookup path (TCAM1/SRAM1) stores the disjoint leaf prefix set (*e.g.*, see Figure 9(a)) as a merged data structure. Note that this disjoint prefix set can be stored in the TCAM without any order constraint. The NH arrays are stored in the associated SRAM. This lookup engine path will be referred to as "*the merged lookup path*".

The second lookup path (TCAM2/SRAM2) stores the overlapping prefix set (*e.g.*, see Figure 9(b)) using the non-shared approach. The virtual overlapping prefix set, which is formed by prepending VIDs to prefixes in the overlapping prefix set, is stored in the TCAM in decreasing prefix-length order. More precisely, only the prefixes with the same VID should be stored in order of relative decreasing prefix lengths. For each entry of the virtual prefix, its associated NH is stored in the SRAM. This lookup engine path will be referred to as "*the non-shared lookup path*".

For an incoming packet, the IP address and the VID are sent to both lookup paths to search in parallel. After both lookups complete, at most two valid NHs are obtained. The priority arbiter module chooses the final NH, based on the observation that if both NHs are valid, the one generated by the merged lookup path always has a higher priority, since the length of the matched prefix in the disjoint prefix set is by design longer than that in the overlapping prefix set.

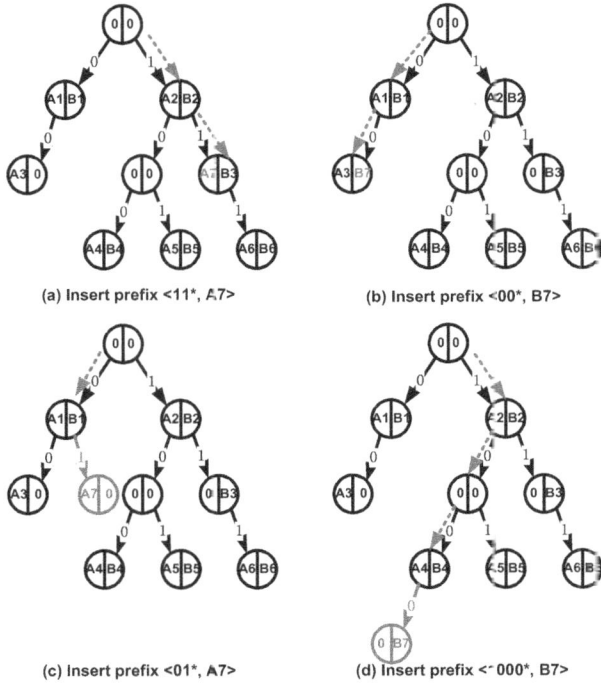

Figure 11: Some insertion scenarios in FIB splitting

5.3 Update Process

One route update involves two phases. First, the update is performed in the auxiliary merged trie in software, and changes in both prefix sets are found; second, according to these changes, update operations are effected in each individual lookup path.

A route update falls into three categories: insertion of a new prefix, deletion of an existing prefix, and modification of an existing prefix. Due to limited space, we only show four typical insertion scenarios in detail. All the other kinds of updates are performed in a similar way. Note, in Figure 11, we will only use NH Ai in FIB 0, and NH Bi in FIB 1, and use the original merged trie shown in Figure 7(a) as the basis from which the updates occur.

Figure 11(a) shows the insertion of a non-leaf prefix 11* with NH A7. This insertion causes the addition of the prefix into the overlapping prefix set for FIB 0. Therefore, virtual prefix 011* and its NH A7 (i.e., entry <011*, A7>) should be inserted in the non-shared lookup path.

Figure 11(b) depicts the insertion of a leaf prefix 00* with NH B7. Prefix 00* already exists in the disjoint prefix set, and thus this insertion only leads to a modification of the corresponding NH array in the SRAM of the merged lookup path. That is, the NH array corresponding to prefix 00* is changed from [A3, 0] to [A3, B7].

Figure 11(c) gives an example of inserting a leaf prefix 01* with NH A7. Since prefix 01* does not already exist in the disjoint prefix set, a new entry <01*, [A7, 0]> should be inserted in the merged lookup path.

Figure 11(d) shows the scenario of inserting a leaf prefix 1000* with NH B7. This insertion turns the prefix 100* from a leaf prefix into a non-leaf prefix, as the prefix 1000* gets inserted as a leaf. As a result, the insertion in this case leads to three changes: (1) entry <1000*, [0, B7]> must be inserted

in the merged lookup path; (2) entry <100*, [A4, B4]> should be deleted from the merged lookup path; and (3) entry <0100*, A4> and <1100*, B4> (note that 0100* and 1100* are virtual prefixes) must be inserted in the non-shared lookup path. Changes (1) and (2) can be merged into one write operation by just overwriting entry <100*, [A4, B4]> with entry <1000*, [0, B7]>.

Note that, in software, we do not need to partition the merged trie each time a new route update occurs to find the changes in both prefix sets. Instead, we can find the changes by just performing the update in the merged trie as shown in Figure 11, with time complexity of O(l), where l is the length of the prefix to be updated.

After changes are found in software, update operations must be performed in the lookup paths. We have shown in our previous work [13] that, one route update in the trie always affects at most one leaf prefix and one non-leaf prefix. However, there are some subtle differences in FIB splitting due to the simultaneous existance of multiple FIBs. Changing one leaf prefix leads to at most one write operation in the TCAM of the merged lookup path. Additionally, all the individual NHs associated with this prefix should be written into the associated SRAM. On the other hand, changing one non-leaf prefix triggers the update of at most N virtual prefixes (where N is the number of FIBs) in the TCAM of the non-shared lookup path (e.g., see prefix 100* in Figure 11(d)), as well as N NHs in the associated SRAM.

6. PERFORMANCE EVALUATION

In this section, we evaluate and compare the non-shared approach, FIB completion, and FIB splitting in terms of TCAM size, SRAM size, total cost of the system, and lookup and update performance.

To perform the evaluation, we rely on publicly available BGP routing tables. While these may not be representative of the future routing tables of virtual routers, they provide a reasonable reference point for future research in the area. We collected the 14 full BGP routing tables from the RIPE RIS Project [3], on September 29, 2011. These routing tables were collected from a wide range of locations around the world. In Table 1, we provide the RIPE collector from which each routing table was obtained, the location of the collector, as well as the number of unique IPv4 and IPv6 prefixes in each routing table. The unique prefixes in each routing table are extracted as the prefixes of the corresponding FIB. Note that there are 14 IPv4 FIBs and 13 IPv6 FIBs. In our performance evaluation, we assume that a virtual router platform will host a given number of these FIBs.

6.1 TCAM Size

The TCAM size is determined by the TCAM entry size and the number of entries.

For IPv4 FIBs, the largest prefix length is 32 bits. As we can only get a maximum of 14 IPv4 FIBs for the evaluation, a 4-bit VID is enough to identify them. Therefore, the largest length of a virtual prefix, which is used in the non-shared approach, is 36 bits. Both the lengths of prefix and virtual prefix are under 40 bits, and thus they all fit in TCAMs with 40-bit entry size [2]. As a result, the number of TCAM entries can be used as the only metric to compare TCAM memory requirements in the three approaches.

Figure 12 shows the comparison results of TCAM entry requirements for IPv4 FIBs. In the non-shared approach,

Table 1: Routing tables (2011.09.29, 08:00)

Routing Tables	Location	# of IPv4 prefixes	# of IPv6 Prefixes
rrc00	Amsterdam	399,439	7,218
rrc01	London	375,751	7,294
rrc03	Amsterdam	373,306	7,225
rrc04	Geneva	382,122	5,541
rrc05	Vienna	375,196	7,186
rrc06	Otemachi	367,984	0
rrc07	Stockholm	379,788	7,098
rrc10	Milan	373,024	7,185
rrc11	New York	379,166	7,208
rrc12	Frankfurt	386,924	7,469
rrc13	Moscow	381,561	7,352
rrc14	Palo Alto	380,048	7,280
rrc15	Sao Paulo	392,537	7,137
rrc16	Miami	382,552	6,968

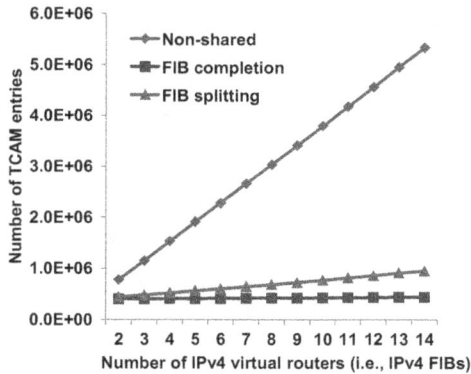

Figure 12: Comparison of TCAM size for IPv4 FIBs

the total number of TCAM entries is the sum of the number of entries in each FIB. Therefore, the TCAM entry requirement increases linearly with the number of virtual routers. When 14 FIBs are stored, 5,329,398 TCAM entries are required in the non-shared approach. In FIB completion, the total number of TCAM entries is equal to the total number of unique prefixes across all FIBs. As the similarity of FIBs is fully exploited (*i.e.*, all the common prefixes are merged in the TCAM), this approach shows the best TCAM memory scalability. With 14 IPv4 FIBs, about 439,467 TCAM entries are required, corresponding to a significant memory reduction of 92% when compared to the non-shared approach. In FIB splitting, most of the prefixes are also merged in the TCAM, and thus good memory scalability is also achieved. For 14 IPv4 FIBs, about 950,722 TCAM entries are required, which corresponds to a memory reduction of 82% when compared to the non-shared approach.

For IPv6 FIBs, the longest prefix is 128 bits. Given a 4-bit VID, the longest virtual prefix is 132 bits. Therefore, the TCAM should be configured to hold 160-bit entries [2] to store the prefixes or virtual prefixes. Again, all prefixes fit in the same TCAM entry size and the number of TCAM entries can be used as the comparison metric. With 13 IPv6 FIBs, the non-shared approach requires 92,161 TCAM entries, while only 7,880 TCAM entries are needed in FIB completion, and 15,783 TCAM entries are needed in FIB

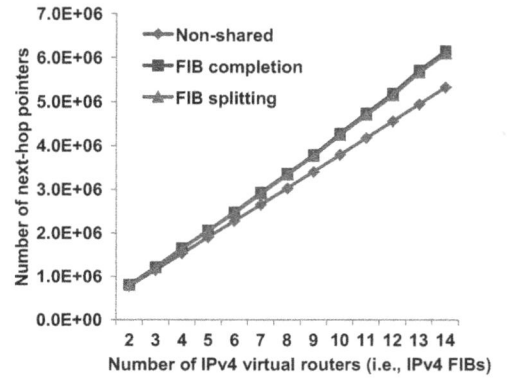

Figure 13: Comparison of SRAM size for IPv4 FIBs

splitting, which corresponds to a memory reduction of 91% and 83%, respectively. The growth trends for IPv6 FIBs are similar to those shown in Figure 12, and the proposed two approaches are also more scalable than the non-shared approach in the case of IPv6.

6.2 SRAM Size

Storing NH pointers instead of the complete NHs in the associated SRAM saves memory. Therefore, the number of NH pointers can be used as the metric to evaluate SRAM footprint. In the non-shared approach, the number of NH pointers is equal to the number of TCAM entries. In FIB completion, each prefix is associated with a NH array, which contains N (*i.e.*, the number of FIBs) NH pointers. Therefore, the total number of NH pointers is N times the number of TCAM entries. In FIB splitting, the number of NH pointers in the non-shared lookup path is equal to the number of TCAM entries, and the number of NH pointers in the merged lookup path is N times the number of TCAM entries.

Obviously, as a NH array must be associated with each prefix in the merged FIB, the SRAM usage for FIB completion and FIB splitting are expected greater than that for non-shared approach. This is confirmed in Figure 13, for IPv4 FIBs. When the number of IPv4 FIBs is 14, the non-shared approach only needs to store 5,329,398 NH pointers, against 6,152,538 NH pointers for FIB completion, and 6,103,129 NH pointers for FIB splitting. This inflation of roughly 15% in SRAM footprint is in stark contrast with the reduction of over 80% in TCAM footprint, given the much cheaper cost per MB for SRAMs.

To estimate the corresponding SRAM size, we assume that the NH pointer is 8-bit long, as mentioned in Section 2.1. For 14 IPv4 FIBs, the resulting SRAM size would be 40.7Mb in the non-shared approach, 46.9Mb in FIB completion, and 46.6Mb in FIB splitting. The proposed two approaches thus lead to reasonable SRAM requirements, well below what is available on current line cards. Indeed, the size of a large SRAM on a modern line card is around 72Mb and can go up to 144Mb.

For 13 IPv6 FIBs, the non-shared approach requires 92,161 NH pointers, against 102,440 NH pointers for FIB completion, and 101,991 NH pointers for FIB splitting (about 11% increase). As a result, the SRAM size is 720.0Kb in the non-shared approach, 800.3Kb in FIB completion, and 796.8Kb in FIB splitting.

Table 2: Reference prices of TCAMs and SRAMs

Memory	Part No.	Capacity	Speed	Price
TCAM	NL9512	512K×40bit	250MHz	$387.2
SRAM	CY7C1525	8M×9bit	250MHz	$89.7

Table 3: Cost of the three approaches for IPv4 FIBs

	# of TCAMs	# of SRAMs	Total Cost
Non-shared	11	1	$4348.9
FIB completion	1	1	$476.9
FIB splitting	3	2	$1341

6.3 Total Cost of the System

We now quantify the cost-effectiveness of the trade-off between the reduction in TCAM and the increase in SRAM footprints, as achieved by our proposed FIB merging methods.

To evaluate the cost of the system, we rely on reference prices at the time of writing, see Table 2. The TCAM NL9512 from NetLogic Microsystems contains 512K 40-bit entries, and costs about 390 dollars per chip. The SRAM CY7C1525 from Cypress Semiconductor contains 8M 9-bit entries, and the quoted price is about 90 dollars per chip. Although the actual prices may vary depending on the quantity ordered, the prices shown in Table 2 are representative of the magnitude of the cost.

In our IPv4 scenario, when the number of FIBs is 14, the non-shared approach needs to store 5,329,398 prefixes and 5,329,398 NH pointers, requiring 11 TCAM chips and 1 SRAM chip, for a total cost of about 4350 dollars. In FIB completion, there are 439,467 prefixes and 6,152,538 NH pointers, requiring 1 TCAM and 1 SRAM, for a total cost of about 480 dollars. In FIB splitting, there are two TCAM-based lookup paths. In the merged lookup path, there are 396,339 prefixes and 5,548,746 NH pointers, requiring 1 TCAM and 1 SRAM. In the non-shared lookup path, there are 554,383 prefixes and 554,383 NH pointers, requiring 2 TCAMs and 1 SRAM. Therefore, 3 TCAMs and 2 SRAMs are needed, and the total cost is about 1340 dollars.

Table 3 summarizes the cost of the system for IPv4 FIBs. When compared to the non-shared approach, the total cost can be reduced by 89% in FIB completion, and by 69% in FIB splitting. This result shows that our proposed approaches are cost-effective.

We repeat our cost calculation for the IPv6 scenario. However, the TCAM entry size should be changed to 160 bits for IPv6 prefixes and virtual prefixes. Therefore, the TCAM shown in Table 2 should be configured into the following organization: 128K×160 bit, which is supported by the NL9512 TCAM [2]. Table 4 summarizes the cost of the system for the 13 IPv6 FIBs shown in Table 1.

In the non-shared approach, there are 92,161 prefixes and 92,161 NH pointers, which requires 1 TCAM and 1 SRAM. Therefore, the total cost is about 480 dollars. In FIB completion, there are 7,380 prefixes and 102,440 NH pointers, which requires 1 TCAM and 1 SRAM, for a total cost of

---

[2]This cost is calculated when using a small TCAM 75P42100.

Table 4: Cost of the three approaches for IPv6 FIBs

	# of TCAMs	# of SRAMs	Total Cost
Non-shared	1	1	$476.9
FIB completion	1	1	$476.9 $189.0[2]
FIB splitting	2	2	$953.8 $378.0[2]

Table 5: Theoretical worst-case lookup performance and update overhead

	Lookup	Update
Non-shared	$O(1)$	$W/2$
FIB completion	$O(1)$	$2^{W+1} - 1$
FIB splitting	$O(1)$	$NW/2$

about 480 dollars. In FIB splitting, there are 7,184 prefixes and 93,392 NH pointers in the merged lookup path, and 8,599 prefixes and 8,599 NH pointers in the non-shared lookup path. Therefore, 2 TCAMs and 2 SRAMs are needed in FIB splitting, and the total cost is about 950 dollars. FIB splitting costs more than the other two approaches, as it contains two lookup paths, consisting of at least 2 TCAMs and 2 SRAMs irrespective of the size of the prefix sets.

However, it is very important to note that, the TCAM shown in Table 2 is too large for the IPv6 prefix sets in FIB completion and FIB splitting, as the utilization of each TCAM is below 7%. Obviously, smaller and cheaper TCAMs could be used in such a case. For example, the smaller TCAM 75P42100 from NetLogic with 16K 144-bit entries could be used instead. This small TCAM costs only 99.3 dollars per chip. If using this TCAM for the 13 IPv6 FIBs, the cost of FIB completion is about 190 dollars and the cost of FIB splitting is about 380 dollars, both of which are much lower than the cost of the non-shared approach.

6.4 Lookup and Update Performance

We now turn to the lookup and update performance of the three approaches, in terms of theoretical analysis and experimental evaluation.

Table 5 summarizes the theoretical worst-case lookup and update performance. The lookup performance of the three approaches is the same, with $O(1)$ time complexity even in the worst case, thanks to the ability of TCAMs to deliver a deterministic high throughput of one lookup per clock cycle. When using the TCAM and the SRAM shown in Table 2, the lookup throughput can be up to 250 million lookups per second. Considering 64-byte minimum size packets, this lookup rate would sustain well in excess of 100Gbps.

For update performance, we consider the update overhead in the data plane (i.e., in the TCAM-based lookup engines), as updates in the data plane actually affect the packet forwarding process and are therefore critical. Generally, in TCAM-based lookup engines, both the TCAM and its associated SRAM can be updated simultaneously. We assume that, in a TCAM-based lookup engine, a TCAM write operation and an SRAM write operation take the same amount of time, as the TCAM and its associated SRAM are usually driven by the same clock, and both of them usually take just one clock cycle to complete a write operation. In this case, the larger number of memory write accesses in either part can be used as the metric to evaluate the update overhead. Additionally, in the following update evaluation, we refer to the PLO_OPT approach [17] to manage prefixes in the TCAM. That is, when needed, all the prefixes are stored in the TCAM in order of decreasing prefix lengths, and free TCAM space is reserved in the middle of the TCAM.

In the non-shared approach, PLO_OPT requires at most $W/2$ TCAM memory accesses per route update, where W is the length of the IP address. Therefore, the number of write operations per update is upper bounded by $W/2$ in the worst case.

In FIB completion, the number of write operations per update is upper bounded by $2^{W+1} - 1$ in the worst case, as one route update may cause at most $2^{W+1} - 1$ NH pointers to be modified in the associated SRAM, due to the masking prefix correction process.

In FIB splitting, one prefix change in the disjoint prefix set requires at most one write operation in the merged lookup path, as it only contains disjoint prefixes and prefix order constraint can be avoided [13]. However, one prefix change in the overlapping prefix set leads to at most N virtual prefix changes in the TCAM of the non-shared lookup path, which causes $NW/2$ write operations in the worst case when using PLO_OPT [17].

As mentioned before, we expect the worst-case update overhead in our approaches is unlikely to happen in practice. In order to evaluate the actual update overhead, we collected 12 hours' worth of route updates that happened on the 14 IPv4 routing tables shown in Table 1 from the RIPE RIS Project [3]. These update traces contain a total of 22,765,563 prefix announcements and 3,694,904 prefix withdrawals. We replayed these updates in the order of their timestamp, and evaluated the actual update overhead in FIB completion and FIB splitting.

We present in Figure 14, the complementary cumulative distribution of the update overhead over the 12 hours, in FIB completion (Figure 14(a)) and FIB splitting (Figure 14(b)). We observe that in both FIB completion and FIB splitting, most of route updates cost only 1 write access per update, and route updates rarely lead to large number of write accesses in the TCAM-based lookup engines. For example, the percentage of updates costing more than 100 write accesses per update (we call these updates the big updates) is only 0.004% in FIB completion, and only 0.003% in FIB splitting. To fix ideas, we take an approximate calculation: one big update happens roughly every 40s on average (0.004% of updates over 12 hours). If we assume only big updates cause significant packet drop, and every big update needs 100 write accesses (i.e., 400ns total for the chips we consider), the total amount of dropped data is about 5KB, out of a possible 500GB per 40s in a 100Gbps network. The disruption caused by big updates is thus negligible.

Table 6 summarizes the actual update overhead. In FIB completion, the average update overhead in practice is only 1.22 write accesses per update, which is very small and close to the minimum update overhead. This is expected, as we find by experiment, that most updates don't cause any prefix changes in the UPS, and the masking prefix correction often stops quickly in practice. The worst-case update overhead in FIB completion is 2,206 write accesses per update, which is much smaller than what is predicted by the theoretical worst case. In FIB splitting, the average update overhead is

Table 6: Update overhead in practice

	Maximum	Average	Minimum
FIB completion	2206	1.22	1
FIB splitting	112	1.05	1

only 1.05 write access per update, and the worst-case update overhead is 112 write accesses per update.

We also evaluate the pre-processing overhead of the updates in software, that does not affect the packet forwarding process. We find by experiment that the average number of trie node accesses per update is about 23 in FIB completion, and about 22 in FIB splitting. We assume that one node access requires one memory reference, which takes 60ns with a cache miss. In this case, we can pre-process over 700K updates per second in software, which exceeds largely the peak update frequency of modern routers [1].

7. RELATED WORK

The use of TCAMs to build high-speed lookup engines has been investigated in the past. Previous work mainly focused on addressing the challenges of memory consumption [11, 14, 15], power dissipation [23], and update overhead [17, 21], in the context of traditional routers, not virtual routers.

In the context of virtual routers, memory scalability is one of the major challenges. Previous work mainly focused on the scalability of SRAM-based virtual routers. Fu et al. [7] propose a small, shared data structure to merge multiple tries built from FIBs of virtual routers. The similarity between multiple tries is exploited and many trie nodes are shared during merging, leading to a significantly smaller trie. However, this scheme works well only when the original tries are similar. To address this issue, Song et al. [18] propose trie braiding, which enables each trie node to swap its left and right sub-tries freely. Hence, the shape of dissimilar tries can be adjusted and these tries can become as similar as possible. Ganegedara et al. [8] argue that, for provider edge router virtualization, even the trie braiding approach is not sufficient since prefix sets belonging to different provider edge routers have different common portions. Therefore, they propose to merge the tries of different provider virtual routers at the split nodes instead of the root nodes. Le et al. [10] propose a 2-3 tree-based approach to merge multiple FIBs. A unique virtual ID is attached in front of every prefix in the individual FIB, so that all the FIBs can be merged into a single one directly. Then, a trie is built from the merged FIB, and two disjoint prefix sets are generated by partitioning the trie. Finally, two 2-3 tree-based pipelines are built for the two disjoint prefix sets.

Another related area to ours is FIB aggregation [20, 24], which aims to reduce the size of the FIB. In the context of virtual routers, this approach can be used to compress each FIB separately, and then the compressed FIBs can be put together using the non-shared approach.

8. CONCLUSION

In a virtual router platform, our solutions work best when the prefix sets of different FIBs are similar (i.e., they have a substantial share of common prefixes). Nowadays, private IP addresses are widely used in campus and enterprise networks. It is therefore reasonable to expect virtual routers

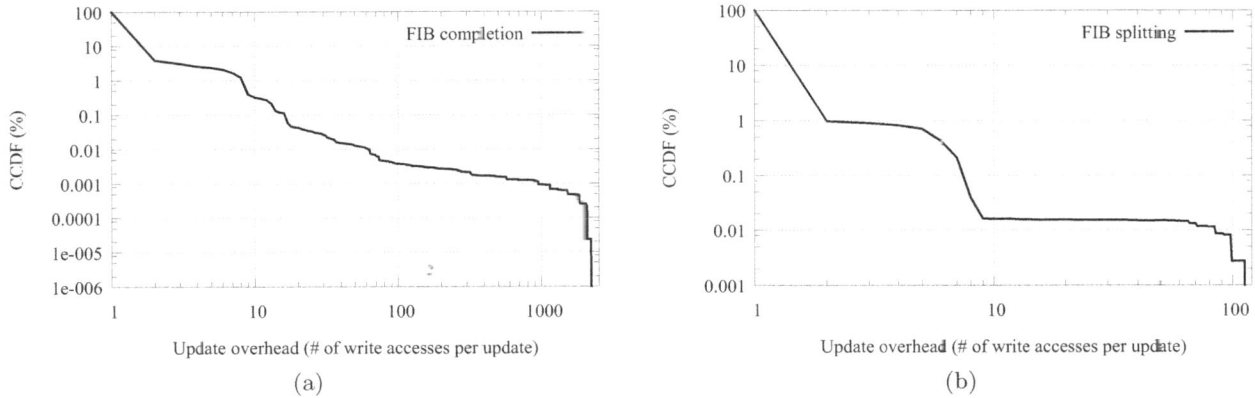

Figure 14: Complementary cumulative distribution function of update overhead in (a) FIB completion and (b) FIB splitting

will likely contain many private addresses in their FIBs, which will have a lot of addresses in common, as the address range of private IP addresses is very limited. In that case, our approaches will be useful.

However, if future virtual routers contain very dissimilar FIBs, merging them directly based on our approaches is not a good idea. For very different FIBs, there will be two possible directions for future work.

First, if dissimilar prefix sets of different FIBs can be transformed into similar ones, our solutions will be useful after the transformation. However, transforming very different prefix sets into similar ones is a major challenge for TCAM-based scalable virtual routers, as it depends largely on the still unknown properties of future FIBs in virtual routers.

Second, if portions of prefix sets are similar, we can merge these portions in TCAMs. If different FIBs do not have a substantial share of common prefixes, but there is similarity among different portions of prefix sets, some solutions, such as multiroot [8], can be adopted in our approaches to merge VPN FIBs in TCAMs. Indeed, multiroot has been proposed to address the dissimilarity problem for VPN FIBs.

However, if the forwarding entries of FIBs are totally different (*e.g.*, name strings for CCN, and IP addresses for IPv4), it is not a good idea to merge these FIBs together using our approaches. as there is little similarity to exploit. A more viable way is to partition all these FIBs into several groups, each group containing the same kind of forwarding entries. For example, one group is for IPv4 FIBs, one group is for IPv6 FIBs, and another group is for CCN FIBs. Then, similarity can be exploited, and merging is performed in each individual group, respectively.

Nevertheless, our proposed approaches have been shown to be very effective when the various FIBs exhibit enough similarity:

1. For large or densely populated FIBs, such as in the case of IPv4, the proposed two approaches exhibit very good scalability. Indeed, the TCAM size requirements are much lower, at the cost of marginally larger SRAM requirements, which is very cost-effective.

2. For small or sparsely populated FIBs, as currently in IPv6, our approaches also exhibit very good scalability. However, if FIB size is not so important, the non-shared approach might be a good choice as it guarantees a low upper bound on the update overhead.

3. Both FIB completion and FIB splitting perform well in terms of lookup and update performance. The lookup performance is up to 1 lookup per clock cycle, and the average update overhead is as low as around 1 write access per update. Although the theoretical worst-case update overhead is high, it is a loose bound unlikely to happen in practice.

In many practical settings, our proposed merged data structure is therefore effective at reducing TCAM footprint in virtual routers, and our proposed algorithms are efficient, at resolving the prefix masking issue encountered in TCAM FIB merging.

As far as we know, our work is the first to exploit the possibility of using TCAMs to build scalable virtual routers. In future work, we will implement our approaches on our PEARL platform [22], and address the remaining challenges, such as power consumption and dissimilar FIBs.

9. ACKNOWLEDGMENTS

We thank our shepherd Patrick Crowley and the anonymous reviewers for their valuable comments on the paper.

This work was supported in part by National Basic Research Program of China with Grant 2012CB315801, National Natural Science Foundation of China (NSFC) with Grants 61133015 and 61061130562, Strategic Priority Research Program of the Chinese Academy of Sciences with Grant XDA06010303, and National Science and Technology Major Project of Ministry of Science and Technology of China with Grant 2011ZX03002-005-02.

10. REFERENCES

[1] BGP Reports. http://bgp.potaroo.net/.
[2] NetLogic NL9000 Family. http://www.netlogicmicro.com/Products/Layer4/index.asp.
[3] RIPE RIS Raw Data. http://www.ripe.net/data-tools/stats/ris/ris-raw-data.
[4] M. B. Anwer, M. Motiwala, M. b. Tariq, and N. Feamster. Switchblade: a platform for rapid

deployment of network protocols on programmable hardware. In *Proc. ACM SIGCOMM*, pages 183–194, 2010.

[5] N. M. M. K. Chowdhury and R. Boutaba. A survey of network virtualization. *Computer Networks*, 54(5):862–876, 2010.

[6] N. Egi, A. Greenhalgh, M. Handley, M. Hoerdt, F. Huici, and L. Mathy. Towards high performance virtual routers on commodity hardware. In *Proc. ACM CoNEXT*, pages 1–12, 2008.

[7] J. Fu and J. Rexford. Efficient IP-address lookup with a shared forwarding table for multiple virtual routers. In *Proc. ACM CoNEXT*, pages 1–12, 2008.

[8] T. Ganegedara, W. Jiang, and V. Prasanna. Multiroot: Towards memory-efficient router virtualization. In *Proc. IEEE ICC*, pages 1–5, 2011.

[9] T. Ganegedara, H. Le, and V. K. Prasanna. Towards on-the-fly incremental updates for virtualized routers on FPGA. In *Proc. International Conference on Field Programmable Logic and Applications (FPL)*, pages 213–218, 2011.

[10] H. Le, T. Ganegedara, and V. K. Prasanna. Memory-efficient and scalable virtual routers using FPGA. In *Proc. ACM/SIGDA FPGA*, pages 257–266, 2011.

[11] H. Liu. Routing table compaction in ternary CAM. *IEEE Micro*, 22(1):58–64, 2002.

[12] W. Lu and S. Sahni. Low-power TCAMs for very large forwarding tables. *IEEE/ACM Transactions on Networking*, 18(3):948–959, 2010.

[13] L. Luo, G. Xie, Y. Xie, L. Mathy, and K. Salamatian. A hybrid IP lookup architecture with fast updates. In *Proc. IEEE INFOCOM*, pages 2435–2443, 2012.

[14] V. Ravikumar and R. N. Mahapatra. TCAM architecture for IP lookup using prefix properties. *IEEE Micro*, 24(2):60–69, 2004.

[15] V. Ravikumar, R. N. Mahapatra, and L. N. Bhuyan. EaseCAM: an energy and storage efficient TCAM-based router architecture for IP lookup. *IEEE Transactions on Computers*, 54(5):521–533, 2005.

[16] M. A. Ruiz-Sanchez, E. W. Biersack, and W. Dabbous. Survey and taxonomy of IP address lookup algorithms. *IEEE Network*, 15(2):8–23, 2001.

[17] D. Shah and P. Gupta. Fast updating algorithms for TCAMs. *IEEE Micro*, 21(1):36–47, 2001.

[18] H. Song, M. Kodialam, F. Hao, and T. Lakshman. Building scalable virtual routers with trie braiding. In *Proc. IEEE INFOCOM*, pages 1–9, 2010.

[19] J. S. Turner, P. Crowley, J. DeHart, A. Freestone, B. Heller, F. Kuhns, S. Kumar, J. Lockwood, J. Lu, M. Wilson, C. Wiseman, and D. Zar. Supercharging planetlab: a high performance, multi-application, overlay network platform. In *Proc. ACM SIGCOMM*, pages 85–96, 2007.

[20] Z. A. Uzmi, M. Nebel, A. Tariq, S. Jawad, R. Chen, A. Shaikh, J. Wang, and P. Francis. SMALTA: practical and near-optimal FIB aggregation. In *Proc. ACM CoNEXT*, pages 1–12, 2011.

[21] B. Vamanan and T. N. Vijaykumar. TreeCAM: decoupling updates and lookups in packet classification. In *Proc. ACM CoNEXT*, pages 1–12, 2011.

[22] G. Xie, P. He, H. Guan, Z. Li, Y. Xie, L. Luo, J. Zhang, Y. Wang, and K. Salamatian. PEARL: a programmable virtual router platform. *IEEE Communications Magazine*, 49(7):71–77, 2011.

[23] F. Zane, G. Narlikar, and A. Basu. CoolCAMs: power-efficient TCAMs for forwarding engines. In *Proc. IEEE INFOCOM*, pages 42–52 vol.1, 2003.

[24] X. Zhao, Y. Liu, L. Wang, and B. Zhang. On the aggregatability of router forwarding tables. In *Proc. IEEE INFOCOM*, 2010.

[25] K. Zheng, C. Hu, H. Lu, and B. Liu. A TCAM-based distributed parallel IP lookup scheme and performance analysis. *IEEE/ACM Transactions on Networking*, 14(4):863–875, 2006.

Modeling Complexity of Enterprise Routing Design

Xin Sun
School of Computing and
Information Sciences
Florida International University
xinsun@cs.fiu.edu

Sanjay G. Rao
School of Electrical and
Computer Engineering
Purdue University
sanjay@purdue.edu

Geoffrey G. Xie
Department of Computer
Science
Naval Postgraduate School
xie@nps.edu

ABSTRACT

Enterprise networks often have complex routing designs given the need to meet a wide set of resiliency, security and routing policies. In this paper, we take the position that minimizing design complexity must be an explicit objective of routing design. We take a first step to this end by presenting a systematic approach for modeling and reasoning about complexity in enterprise routing design. We make three contributions. First, we present a framework for precisely defining objectives of routing design, and for reasoning about how a combination of routing design primitives (e.g. routing instances, static routes, and route filters etc.) will meet the objectives. Second, we show that it is feasible to quantitatively measure the complexity of a routing design by modeling individual routing design primitives, and leveraging configuration complexity metrics [5]. Our approach helps understand how individual design choices made by operators impact configuration complexity, and can enable quantifying design complexity in the absence of configuration files. Third, we validate our model and demonstrate its utility through a longitudinal analysis of the evolution of the routing design of a large campus network over the last three years. We show how our models can enable comparison of the complexity of multiple routing designs that meet the same objective, guide operators in making design choices that can lower complexity, and enable what-if analysis to assess the potential impact of a configuration change on routing design complexity.

Categories and Subject Descriptors

C.2.3 [**Computer-Communication Networks**]: Network Operations—*Network management*

Keywords

Network complexity, Routing design, Top-down modeling

1 Introduction

Recent studies [16, 20] show that routing designs of many enterprise networks are much more complicated than the simple models presented in text books and router vendor documents. Part of the complexity is inherent, given the wide range of operational objectives that these networks must support, to include security (e.g., implementing a subnet level reachability matrix) resiliency (e.g., tolerating up to two component failures), safety (e.g., free of forwarding loops), performance, and manageability. There is also evidence, however, to suggest that some of the network design complexity may have resulted from a semantic gap between the high level design objectives and the diverse set of routing protocols and low level router primitives for the operators to choose from [24]. Often, multiple designs exist to meet the same operational objectives, and some are significantly easier to implement and manage than others for a target network. For example in some cases, route redistribution may be a simpler alternative to BGP for connecting multiple routing domains [16]. Lacking an analytical model to guide the operators, the current routing design process is mostly ad hoc, prone to creating designs more complex than necessary.

In this paper, we seek to quantitatively model the complexity associated with a routing design, with a view to developing alternate routing designs that are less complex but meet the same set of operational objectives. Quantitative complexity models could enable systematic abstraction-driven top-down design approaches [24], and inform the development of clean slate network architectures [9,13], which seeks to simplify the current IP network control and management planes.

The earliest and most notable work on quantifying complexity of network management was presented by Benson et al. [5]. This work introduced a family of complexity metrics that could be derived from router configuration files such as dependencies in the defintion of routing configuration components. The work also showed that networks with higher scores on these metrics are harder for operators to manage, change or reason correctly about.

While [5] is an important first step, it takes a bottom-up approach in that it derives complexity metrics from router configuration files. This approach does not shed direct light on the intricate top-down choices faced by the operators while designing a network. Conceivably, an operator could enumerate all possible designs, translate each into configurations, and finally quantify the design complexity from the configurations. However, such a brute-force approach may only work for small networks where the design space is relatively small. Additionally, this approach still requires a model to determine which designs actually are correct, i.e., meeting the design objectives.

In this paper, we present a top-down approach to characterizing the complexity of enterprise routing design given only key high-level design parameters, and in the absence of actual configuration files. Our model takes as input abstractions of high-level design objectives such as network topology, reachability matrix (which pairs of subnets can communicate), and design parameters such as the routing instances [20] (see Section 2 for formal definition), and choice of connection primitive (e.g., static routes, redistribution etc). Our overall modeling approach is to (i) formally abstract the operational objectives related to the routing design which can help reason about whether and how a combination of design primitives will meet the objectives; and (ii) decompose routing design into its constituent primitives, and quantify the configuration complexity of individual design primitives using the existing bottom-up complexity metrics [5].

A top-down approach such as ours has several advantages. By working with design primitives directly (independent of router configuration files), the model is useful not only for analyzing an existing network, but also for "what if" analysis capable of optimizing the design of a new network and similarly, a network migration [25], or evaluating the potential impact of a change to network design. Further, our models help provide a conceptual framework to understand the underlying factors that contribute to configuration complexity. For example, reachability restrictions between subnet pairs may require route filters or static routes, which in turn manifest as dependencies in network configuration files.

We demonstrate the feasibility and utility of our top-down complexity modeling approach using longitudinal configuration data of a large-scale campus network. Our evaluations show that our model can accurately estimate configuration complexity metrics given only high-level design parameters. Discrepancies when present were mainly due to redundant configuration lines introduced by network operators. Our models provided important insights when applied to analyzing a major routing design change made by the operators undertaken with an explicit goal to lower design complexity. Our model indicated that while some of the design changes were useful in lowering complexity, others in fact were counterproductive and increased complexity. Further, our models helped point out alternate designs that could further lower complexity.

2 Dimensions of Routing Design

According to most computer networking textbooks, routing design is nothing more than selecting and configuring a single interior gateway protocol (IGP) such as OSPF on all routers and setting up one or more BGP routers to connect to the Internet. In reality, as one would quickly discover from meetings and online discussion forums of the operational community, network operators consistently rate routing design as one of the most challenging tasks.

In this section, using a toy example, we briefly break down the challenges of routing design along two structural dimensions, each made of a distinct logical building block. The goal is to identify the general sources of its complexity by exposing the major design choices that operators must make.

Consider Fig. 1, which illustrates a hypothetical company network that spans two office buildings. Assume that the physical topology has been constructed, including three subnets (Sales, Support and Data Center) in the main building and two additional subnets in building 2.

2.1 Policy groups

An integral part of almost every enterprise's security policy is to compartmentalize the flow of corporate information in its network. For the example network, there are two categories of users: Sales and Support. Suppose the Data Center subnet contains accounting servers that should be accessible only by the Sales personnel. A corresponding requirement of routing design would be to ensure that only the Sales subnets have good routes to reach the Data Center subnet.

We refer to the set of subnets belonging to one user category and have similar reachability requirements as *policy group*. We note

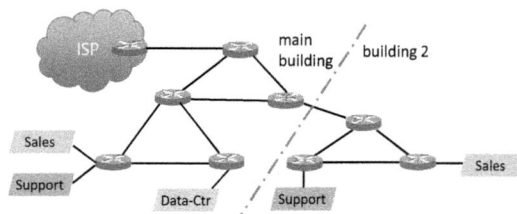

Figure 1: Example enterprise network spanning two offices

that policy groups are similar to policy units introduced in [6], though there are some differences (see Sec. 9). A primary source of complexity for routing design is to support the fine grained reachability requirements of policy groups. This is particularly challenging since business stipulations often imply that subnets of a policy group may need to be distributed across multiple buildings, multiple enterprise branches, or even multiple continents.

The operator faces several choices in designing networks to meet these reachability requirements. The operator may choose to deploy a single IGP over the entire network to allow full reachability and then place packet filters on selected router interfaces to implement the required reachability policy. This is a viable solution for small networks. However, for medium to large networks, a large number of filtering rules need to be configured, and on many router interfaces. Doing so will likely introduce performance problems because packet filters incur per packet processing. In addition, according to a recent study [24], proper placement of packet filters in itself is a complex task, particularly when the solution must be resilient against link failures and other changes in the network topology.

Alternatively, the operator may choose to deploy a separate routing protocol instance to connect the subnets of each policy group. For the example network, two independent OSPF instances (OSPF 10 and OSPF 20) may be used to join the subnets of Sales and Support, respectively. Such a design is not straightforward either. First, the operator must decide which routers to include in each routing instance, subject to additional requirements such as resiliency. Second, the operator must select a small number of routers as border routers and configure connecting primitives [16, 19] to "glue" the different routing protocol instances together. (The next section has a detailed description of the tradeoffs involved in this step.) Last but not the least, the operator may need to configure route filters at the border routers to implement the required reachability policy. For the example network, route filters should be configured to prevent routes to Data Center subnets from leaking into Support.

2.2 Routing instances

In several recent papers [4, 16, 20], researchers have revealed the common use of multiple routing protocol instances in one enterprise network. This is not surprising as the evolution of an enterprise's computer network parallels that of its business. Networks of different routing designs are fused at times of company mergers and acquisitions. Also, large enterprises and universities are usually made of a group of autonomous business units with quasi-independent IT staff; each unit often has a large degree of freedom in managing its part of the enterprise network, including the choice of which routing protocol to use.

We adopt from these prior works the definition of a routing protocol instance, or simply *routing instance*, to refer to a connected component of the network where all member routers run the same routing protocol, use matching protocol parameters, and are configured to exchange routes with each other. When dealing with a

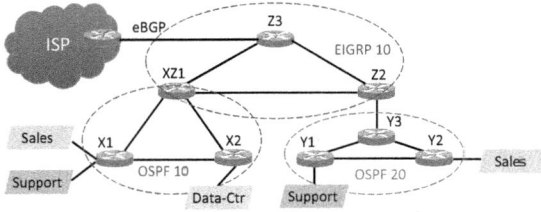

Figure 2: A design with multiple IGP instances

S_i	subnet i	R_i	router i
I_i	routing instance i	Z_i	policy group i
$\mathbf{M_C}$	connecting primitive matrix	$\mathbf{M_R}$	reachability matrix
$\mathbf{M_B}$	border-router matrix	$\mathbf{M_X}$	route-exchange matrix
$\mathbf{M_A}$	arc matrix	T_i	the internal routes that I_i has
W_i	the entire set of routes that I_i has	K_{rr}	complexity of configuring one-way route redistribution
K_{sr}	complexity of configuring one static route	K_{dr}	complexity of configuring one default route
K_{bgp}	complexity of configuring a BGP session on a border router	K_{obj}	complexity of installing object tracking to one static route
$h(i,j)$	a binary function denoting whether filtering is needed	$f(x)$	complexity of configuring a route filter to allow a set of routes x
$|x|$	the size of the set x		

Table 1: Notation table

routing design with multiple routing instances, the operator must weigh different options of joining the different routing instances together while implementing the company's security policy.

To illustrate, suppose the operator of the example network of Fig. 1 has created a routing design with three routing instances, as shown in Fig. 2. Each office building has its own routing instance (OSPF 10 or OSPF 20) while the EIGRP 10 instance serves as the backbone of the network.

The operator has chosen to use BGP to connect to the Internet. It is straightforward to configure an external BGP (eBGP) peering session and mutual route redistribution (RR) between the EIGRP and BGP instances to allow routes to be exchanged between the enterprise network and its ISP. The complexity increases significantly, however, if the operator needs to configure route filters to reject certain incoming and outgoing routes. The problem would be compounded for multi-homed enterprise networks because of additional policy requirements such as the designation of primary and backup or load balancing.

For connecting the routing instances of OSPF 10 and the backbone, the operator has chosen to use a single border router (i.e., XZ1) that participates in both routing instances. (For brevity, we do not consider the resiliency requirement in this example.) This removes the need for BGP peering to advertise routes across the boundaries of the instances. However, the operator must still configure route redistribution and possibly route filters to allow the injection of routes between the two instances. Another complication is that multiple routing instances may simultaneously offer routes to the same destination at a border router. The operator must implement the correct order of preference between the instances, sometimes requiring an override of some protocols' default Administrative Distance (AD) [4, 18] values on a per border router basis.

For connecting the routing instances of OSPF 20 and the backbone, the operator has adopted a different approach. Two border routers (i.e., Y3 and Z2) are used as in the case of the ISP connection. However, instead of using a dynamic protocol, the operator has configured two sets of static routes, on the two border routers respectively, to achieve reachability across routing instances. This design incurs considerable amount of manual configuration on a per destination prefix basis. For example, on Y3, static routes are required for destination prefixes not only within EIGRP 10 but also within OSPF 10. Clearly, due to its static nature, the design may not bode well when the subnet prefixes frequently change or dynamic re-routing is required. However, it has one advantage over dynamic mechanisms like BGP or co-location of routing processes in one border router: the packet forwarding paths across routing instances are much easier to predict when hardcoded. In contrast, both BGP and RR can result in routing anomalies in ways that are difficult to identify from their configurations [18].

3 Abstractions for Modeling Routing Design

This section first presents a set of formal abstractions that capture the routing design primitives, and design objectives and constraints.

These abstractions form the foundation for modeling design complexity. We then describe the metrics we used for quantifying the complexity of a given design instance that makes use of a specific set of design primitives and targets a specific network topology. Table 1 summarizes the notations used in this and the following sections.

3.1 Abstracting essential elements of routing design

We use $S_1, S_2, ...$ to denote the host subnets in the network. Each subnet is assigned a unique IP prefix address (e.g., "192.168.1.0/24"). We use $R_1, R_2, ...$ to denote the routers in the network. Each subnet connects to a router and uses that router as its gateway (i.e. the router routes all the packets generated by the subnet). A "route" is considered as an IP prefix address, plus additional attributes (e.g., weight) that may be used for calculation of a next-hop for the route. A router always has routes to all the connected subnets for which it is the gateway. In addition, routes may be manually injected into a router via configuration of static routes (Sec. 5.3). Routers may exchange routes by running one or more dynamic routing protocols. To participate in each routing protocol, a router must run a separate routing process. Each routing process maintains a separate Routing Information Base, or RIB. The RIB contains all the routes known to the routing process, each associated with one or more next-hops. A router maintains a global RIB (also referred to as the forwarding information base, or FIB, in the literature), and uses selection logic to select routes from its routing process RIBs, as well as routes to connected subnets and statically configured routes, to enter the global RIB. A router uses the global RIB to make forwarding decisions. (Readers are referred to [20] for a more detailed description.)

We say that "a router R_i has a route to a subnet S_j", if the prefix address of S_j matches a route in the global RIB of R_i. Furthermore, we say that "a subnet S_i is routable from another subnet S_j", if the gateway router for S_j has a route to S_i. Finally, since this paper concerns only the routing design and uses routing as the only mechanism to implement reachability, we use the terms "reachable" and "routable" inter-changeably.

Let $\mathcal{I} = \{I_1, I_2, ...\}$ denote the set of routing instances (Sec. 2.2), an essential routing design component that abstracts route propagation in the network. As described in Sec. 2.2, routing processes in the same routing instance exchange all their routes freely. As a result, all the routing processes share the same set of routes. To change this behavior, route filters are typically used to filter route updates between routing processes (Sec. 4). On the other hand, routing processes in different routing instances do not exchange any route. To change this behavior, *connecting primitives* must be used (e.g., static routes, route redistribution and BGP). The routers where connecting primitives are implemented are termed *border routers*.

We assume that we are given the set of routing instances $\mathcal{I}$ and

```
Router 1
1.    interface GigabitEthernet 1/1
2.        ip address 10.1.0.1 255.255.255.252
3.    !
4.    router eigrp 10
5.        distribute-list prefix TO-SAT out GigabitEthernet1/1
6.    !
7.    ip prefix-list TO-SAT seq 5 permit 192.168.1.0/24
8.    ip prefix-list TO-SAT seq 10 premit 192.168.5.0/24

Router 2
9.    interface FastEthernet1/1
10.       ip address 192.168.1.1 255.255.255.0
11.   !
12.   interface FastEthernet2/1
13.       ip address 192.168.5.1 255.255.255.0
14.   !
```

Figure 3: Configuration snippets of two routers.

their member routers and routing processes. We are also given the connecting primitive matrix $\mathbf{M_C}$. Each cell $\mathbf{M_C}(i, j)$ specifies the connecting primitive used by I_i and I_j, to allow routes to be sent from I_i to I_j.

In this paper, we focus on the primary use of routing design: implementing reachability policies. The primary layer-three mechanisms to implement reachability are the connecting primitives and route filters. We do not model the selection logic, which is used to prefer one routing path over another, as this is typically used for traffic engineering purposes, rather than implementing reachability.

3.2 Abstracting design objectives and constraints

The design objectives and constraints considered in this paper include reachability and resiliency, as well as routing path policies. First, to capture the reachability requirements, it is assumed that we are given the reachability matrix $\mathbf{M_R}$. Each cell $\mathbf{M_R}(i, j)$ denotes whether the subnet S_i can reach the subnet S_j. Note that in the routing design we only consider reachability at the subnet level. We do not consider host-level reachability as it is typically implemented by data plane mechanisms such as packet filters.

To capture the resiliency requirement, we assume that we are given the border-router matrix $\mathbf{M_B}$. Each cell $\mathbf{M_B}(i, j)$ specifies the set of I_i's border routers that enable I_i to advertise routes to I_j. Note that a routing instance may use different border routers to communicate with different neighboring instances.

To capture the path policies, it is assumed that we are given the route-exchange matrix $\mathbf{M_X}$. Each cell $\mathbf{M_X}(i, j)$ specifies the set of routes that I_i should advertise to I_j to meet the reachability requirement. We assume that the routes in the matrix is in the most aggregated form. Clearly the set of *external* routes that I_i has may be calculated as $\bigcup_j \mathbf{M_X}(j, i)$. Let T_i denote the set of *internal* routes that I_i has (i.e., routes originated by subnets inside I_i). Let W_i denote the entire set of routes that I_i has, which may be calculated as follows:

$$W_i = (\bigcup_j \mathbf{M_X}(j, i)) \bigcup T_i \qquad (1)$$

3.3 Measuring complexity

Using these abstractions, we are able to precisely define the objectives, or the correctness criteria, of a routing design, and reason about how a combination of routing primitives (e.g., routing instances, static routes, route filters, etc.) will meet the objectives. We then leverage metrics developed by previous work to measure how the choice of different routing primitives may impact the complexity of the resulting network.

The particular metric that we use is proposed by [5], which captures the complexity in configuring a network by counting the number of *referential links* in the device configuration files. Basically a referential link is created when a network object (e.g., a route filter,

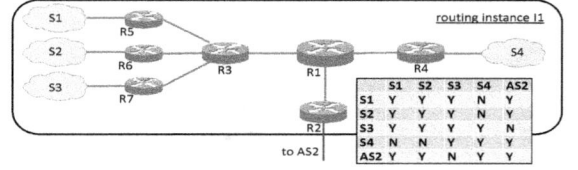

(a) An example network and reachability policy. The matrix has one row (column) per subnet. Y (N) indicates the subnets can (cannot) reach each other.

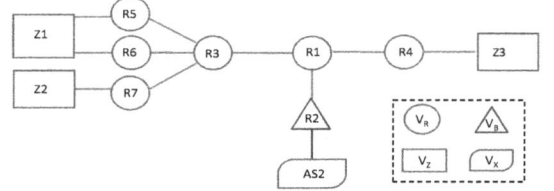

(b) The per-instance routing graph of routing instance I1

Figure 4: Illustrating need for route filters.

a subnet) is defined in one configuration block, and is subsequently referred to in another configuration block, in either the same configuration file or a different file. As an example, consider Fig. 3 that shows configuration snippets from two routers. The referential links are shown in italics. In line 5 in Router 1's configuration, a route filter named TO-SAT is applied to the interface GigabitEthernet1/1 to filter two routes in the outgoing direction. This line introduces two referential links: one to the name of the filter (defined in lines 7-8), and the other to the name of the interface (defined in line 1). Moreover, the definition of the route filter (lines 7-8) introduces two referential links to the two subnet prefixes, which are defined in Router 2's configuration file (line 10 and 13). Clearly, the existence of referential links increases the configuration complexity as it introduces dependencies between configuration blocks either in the same configuration file or in different configuration files.

We choose to use this metric because it has been extensively validated in [5] through operator interviews. Our own interaction with operators also suggests that the metric reflects operator perceived complexity reasonably well. We note that other complexity metrics have been proposed in [5] such as the number of routing instances, and the number of distinct router roles. Many of these other metrics are relatively straight-forward to estimate from the design. For example, the number of distinct router roles could be estimated based on the insight that border and non-border routers play different roles. Further, we have observed in our evaluation settings that the referential link metric shows the most variation across designs, making it particularly useful in facilitating comparisons.

4 Modeling Intra-Instance Complexity

This section presents a framework for estimating complexity existing *within* a routing instance. We first show that such complexity results from the need to install route filters inside the routing instance, in order to implement the different reachability requirements of different subnets. We then present models to quantify the complexity associated with such route filters. In doing so, our models determine the route filter placement and the filter rules.

4.1 Source of intra-instance complexity

The complexity within a routing instance primarily comes from the route filters installed inside the instance. By definition, all routing processes of the same routing instance have the same routing tables. This means that all the subnets connecting to those routing processes will have the same reachability toward other subnets. If this is not desired, route filters must be used to implement reachability policies inside a routing instance.

As an example, consider the network shown in Fig. 4a. Routers R1-R7 and subnets S1-S4 are placed in routing instance I1. Border router R2 runs eBGP with another autonomous system AS2 and injects eBGP learned routes to I1. The figure also shows the desired reachability matrix. To implement the reachability matrix, route filters must be carefully placed. For example, to prevent S1 and S2 from reaching S4, while permitting S3 to reach S4, route filters must be installed between R3 and R5, and between R3 and R6. Similarly, a route filter must be installed between R1 and R4 to prevent S4 from reaching S1 and S2. In addition, another route filter must be installed between R3 and R7, to prevent S3 from reaching the external routes of I2.

In general, the degree of diversity in terms of reachability among subnets of the same routing instance directly impacts the amount of filtering required, which in turn determines the complexity inside that routing instance. To capture this degree of diversity, we leverage the notion of *policy groups* discussed in Sec 2.1

Policy groups: Formally, let $\mathcal{Z} = \{Z_1, Z_2, ...\}$ denote the set of policy groups in a network. A policy group $Z_i \in \mathcal{Z}$ is a set of subnets that (i) can reach each other, and (ii) are subject to the same reachability treatment *toward* other subnets (e.g., if a subnet $S_a \in Z_i$ can reach another subnet $S_b \in Z_j$, then all subnets in Z_i must be able to reach S_b as well). Clearly, policy groups divide the set of all subnets, and each subnet belongs to one and only one policy group. The set of policy groups of a given network can be easily derived from the reachability matrix $\mathbf{M_R}$. In the example in Fig. 4a, S1 and S2 form a policy group, while S3 and S4 each constitute a separate policy group.

By definition, there is no need for filtering within a policy group. Thus if a routing instance contains only a single policy group, the intra-instance complexity is zero. On the other hand, if a routing instance contains subnets of multiple policy groups, route filters must be installed among them to implement their different reachability constraints, and thus incur complexity.

4.2 Modeling the complexity

Intuitively, the degree of complexity of a given routing instance I_a depends on two factors:

- The number of route filters installed inside I_a, as each installation of a filter creates a referential link to the name of that filter (e.g., line 5 of router 1 in Fig 3).
- The complexity associated with each filter, which is measured by the number of rules in each filter, as each rule creates a referential link to a prefix address (e.g., lines 7-8 of router 1 in Fig 3).

Below we model the two factors separately.

4.2.1 Estimating number of filters

In order to estimate the number of route filters needed to be installed inside a given routing instance I_a, we first introduce an undirected graph $G_a(V_R, V_Z, V_X, V_B, E)$, called the *per-instance routing graph* of I_a. We then show how we use this graph to do the estimation for different network topologies.

Per-instance routing graph: The purpose of the per-instance routing graph is to model how policy groups are inter-connected. There are four types of nodes in the graph for a given routing design V_R, V_Z, V_X and V_B. V_R denotes the set of routers that participate in this routing instance. V_Z denotes the set of policy groups that are placed inside this routing instance. V_X denotes networks external to this routing instance (i.e., other routing instances in the same AS

and external ASes as well), whose routes are injected into this routing instance by one or more border routers. Finally, V_B denotes the set of border routers of this routing instance.

E denotes the set of edges. First, there is an edge between two nodes $v_i, v_j \in V_R$ if the two routers are physically connected, and the corresponding routing processes running on them are *adjacent*, i.e., can exchange routing updates [20]. Second, there is an edge between $v_i \in V_Z$ and $v_j \in V_R$ if one or more subnets in policy group v_i connect to the routing process running on v_j. Finally, there is an edge between $v_i \in V_X$ and $v_j \in V_B$, if the border router v_j injects the routes of the external network v_i.

For example, the per-instance routing graph of I1 in Fig. 4a is shown in Fig. 4b.

Determine filters needed for one policy group: Using the per-instance routing graph, we determine the route filters needed for implementing the reachability of a policy group $v_i \in V_Z$ *toward* other subnets. First, consider every policy group $v_j \in V_Z$. If v_j contains one or more subnets that v_i can not reach, then a route filter must be placed on every possible path between v_i and v_j on the per-instance routing graph, to filter out routing updates corresponding to those subnets before they reach any gateway router of v_i. Similarly, consider every external network $v_k \in V_X$. If there exist one or more subnets in v_k that v_i cannot reach, a route filter must be placed on every possible path between v_i and v_k to filter routing updates corresponding to those subnets as well.

Upper and lower bounds on the number of filters: In both cases described above, the *upper bound* on the number of route filters needed for policy group v_i is the total number of paths between v_i and v_j (v_k), summed over all v_j and v_k for which filtering is needed. The upper bound can always be achieved by placing the filters on the on gateway routers of v_i. The *lower bound* is the number of links in the smallest edge-cut set between v_i and v_j (v_k), summed over all v_j and v_k for which filtering is needed. However, the lower bound may not always be achievable, as some links may be included in the smallest edge-cut sets between multiple pairs of policy groups. For example, in Fig. 4b routing updates of Z3 must be filtered before they reach Z1, as Z1 is not allowed to reach Z3. While one smallest edge-cut set between Z1 and Z3 is the link R1-R3, we cannot place the filter on that link, as doing so would wrongfully prevent Z2 from getting those routing updates.

The lower bound can be achieved for a special type of star topology, which we believe is typical in many enterprise networks. In this type of topology, any path between a pair of policy groups, or between a policy group and an external network, always goes through the core router tier. This ensures that the paths between the core tier and different policy groups do not share any common router. Given this special topology, it may be shown that (i) the core tier will have the complete set of routes, and (ii) it is sufficient to place the route filters between the core tier and each policy group. Hence it is now feasible to place the filters on the smallest edge-cut set between the core tier and each policy group.

4.2.2 Estimating number of rules in each filter

Consider using a route filter to implement a policy group Z_j's reachability constraint toward another policy group Z_i. The number of rules in this filter depends on the number of routes to be blocked from Z_i to Z_j, as one route translates to one filter rule (see Fig. 3 for an illustration).

For example, as we have discussed above, a route filter must be installed between Z1 and Z3 in the toy network (Fig. 4b), to prevent the routes of S1 and S2 from being advertised to S4. The number of rules in this filter will be two, as there are two prefixes to be blocked. (Note that the number of rules may be reduced, if several

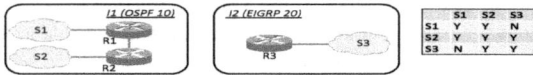

Figure 5: A toy network with two routing instances.

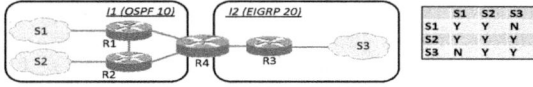

(a) The network design using route redistribution.

```
Router 4
1.     router ospf 10
2.       redistribute eigrp 20
3.     !
4.     router eigrp 20
5.       redistribute ospf 10 route-map OSPF-TO-EIGRP
6.     !
7.     route-map OSPF-TO-EIGRP permit 10
8.       match ip address 1
9.     !
10.    access-list 1 permit S2
```

(b) Configuration snippet of the border router R4

Figure 6: Design using route redistribution for the network shown in Fig. 5.

prefixes can be aggregated into a larger prefix. For simplicity we do not consider such route aggregation in this work.)

5 Modeling Inter-Instance Complexity

This section presents a framework for estimating the inter-instance complexity. We show that this complexity results from the use of connecting primitives. We then present models for estimating the complexity of the three typical connecting primitives described in Sec. 2.2: route redistribution, static and default routes, and BGP.

5.1 Source of inter-instance complexity

The inter-instance complexity comes from the need for connecting primitives to connect multiple routing instances. Consider the toy network shown in Fig. 5 as an example. There are two routing instances: I1 running OSPF with process ID 10, and I2 running EIGRP with process ID 20. I1 contains subnets S1 and S2, and I2 contains S3. The reachability policy specifies that S1 and S2 can reach each other and so do S2 and S3, but S1 and S3 can not. Given the network as such, I1 and I2 cannot exchange any route, and thus cannot communicate at all. To implement the reachability between I1 and I2, one or more border routers must be deployed to physically connect the two routing instances, and in addition, a connecting primitive must be configured on the border routers to enable route exchange.

An important factor that impacts the degree of inter-instance complexity is the resiliency requirement (Sec. 3.1), which specifies the number of border routers each routing instance should have. While having more border routers improves resiliency, it also introduces potential anomalies (e.g., routing loops) and complicates the configuration, as we will show in the next section.

In this section we focus on the most basic scenario where each routing instance uses a single border router (i.e., minimum resiliency). We discuss the case with multiple border routers in the next section.

5.2 Route redistribution

The first connecting primitive we consider is route redistribution, which dynamically sends routes from one routing instance to another. Using route redistribution to connect two routing instances requires having a common border router that runs routing processes in both routing instances. The border router then may be configured to redistribute routes from one routing instance to the other, and vice versa. (Note that route redistribution must be separately configured for each direction.) For example, Fig. 6a illustrates the design using route redistribution for the network shown in Fig. 5. Router R4 is the border router and is configured to redistribute routes between I1 and I2.

Fig. 6b shows the relevant configuration snippet of R4 in Cisco IOS syntax, with referential links highlighted in italics. Line 1 and 4 create two routing processes, one participating in each routing instance. Line 2 and 5 redistribute routes from I2 to I1 and from I1 to I2 respectively.

We note that by default, route redistribution will redistribute *all* the active routes [17]. For example, R4 in Fig. 6a will redistribute routes of both S1 and S2 to I2. This enables S3 to reach both S1 and S2, which does not conform to the reachability policy as shown. To change the default behavior, a route filter (in the form of route-map) must be used in conjunction with route redistribution, as shown in line 5 in Fig. 6b. The route filter permits a subset of routes to be redistributed as specified by the filtering rules (line 7 and 8), and blocks the rest routes.

Modeling complexity: Consider route redistribution from I_i to I_j. Route redistribution in the other direction may be modeled similarly and separately. As shown above, the configuration may include two components: (i) configuration of the route redistribution itself, which has a constant complexity; and (ii) configuration of a route filter, which is needed if only a subset of I_i's routes should be redistributed to I_j. Let K_{rr} denote the complexity of configuring the route redistribution itself. Let the function $f(x)$ denote the complexity of configuring and installing a route filter with x rules (i.e., the filter permits x routes). We note that $f(x)$ includes: (i) the complexity of defining the route filter, which is linear to the number of rules to be defined, and (ii) the complexity of installing the filter by referring to its name, which is a constant factor. In addition, we let $h(i,j)$ be the following binary function that denotes whether a filter is needed: (Recall that a filter is not needed if all the routes I_i has, i.e. W_i, can be redistributed into I_j.)

$$h(i,j) = 0, \text{ if } \mathbf{M_X}(i,j) = W_i; \tag{2}$$

$$h(i,j) = 1, \text{ otherwise.} \tag{3}$$

The overall complexity denoted by $C_{rr}(i,j)$ can be calculated as follows:

$$C_{rr}(i,j) = K_{rr} + f(\mathbf{M_X}(i,j)) * h(i,j) \tag{4}$$

5.3 Static routes

Another way to connect two routing instances is to use static routes, which can be viewed as manually entered routing table entries. A design using static routes for the network in Fig. 5 is shown in Fig. 7a. In such designs, each routing instance must have its own border router that participates in only that routing instance. Static routes are configured on the border routers to point to destination subnets in the other routing instance. One static route is needed for every destination subnet. Further, the static routes are redistributed into the respective routing instance so that internal routers in the routing instance also have those routes.

Fig. 7b shows the relevant configuration snippets of the two border routers R4 and R5, with referential links highlighted in italics. On R4, a static route is configured in line 4. The static route points to S3 as the destination, and specifies R5 as the next-hop to reach the destination. This static route enables R4 to have a route to S3. Further, line 2 redistributes the static route into I1, so that other routers of I1 (i.e., R1 and R2) also have a route to reach S3. Sim-

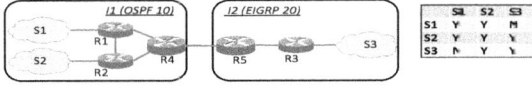

(a) The network design using either static routes or BGP.

```
Router 4
1.    router ospf 10
2.       redistribute static
3.    !
4.    ip route S3 R5

Router 5
5.    router eigrp 20
6.       redistribute static
7.    !
8.    ip route S2 R4
```

(b) Configuration snippets of the border routers using static routes.

Figure 7: Design using static routes for the network shown in Fig. 5.

```
Router 4
1.    router ospf 10
2.       redistribute bgp 64501
3.    !
4.    router bgp 64501
5.       neighbor R5 remote-as 64502
6.       neighbor R5 distribute-list 1 out
7.       redistribute ospf 10
8.    !
9.    access-list 1 permit S2

Router 5
10.   router eigrp 20
11.      redistribute bgp 64502
12.   !
13.   router bgp 64502
14.      neighbor R4 remote-as 64501
15.      redistribute eigrp 20
16.   !
```

Figure 8: Configuration snippets of the border routers using BGP, for the network shown in Fig. 7a

ilarly, a static route to S2 is configured on R5 (line 8) and redistributed to I2 (line 6).

Modeling complexity: Consider using static routes to allow I_i to reach a set of subnets in I_i as specified by $\mathbf{M_X}(i, j)$. Let $|\mathbf{M_X}(i, j)|$ denote the size of $\mathbf{M_X}(i, j)$. Since one static route is needed for each subnet in $\mathbf{M_X}(i, j)$, there will be $|\mathbf{M_X}(i, j)|$ static routes to configure. Let K_{sr} denote the complexity of configuring one static route, which is a constant factor. The total complexity denoted by $C_{sr}(i, j)$ can be calculated as follows:

$$C_{sr}(i, j) = |\mathbf{M_X}(i, j)| * K_{sr} \qquad (5)$$

Finally, we note that a *default route* is a special case of static routes, which injects a default gateway to the router. A default route has a constant complexity denoted by K_{dr}. We refer readers to the extended technical report [23] for more details on modeling default routes.

5.4 BGP

A third connecting primitive is BGP, which is a dynamic routing protocol that enables routes to be exchanged among routing instances. BGP typically requires each routing instance to have its own border router(s). The design using BGP for the same example network is shown in Fig. 7a. Again R4 and R5 are the border routers for I1 and I2 respectively. In addition to running the respective IGP routing process, R4 and R5 each also runs a separate BGP

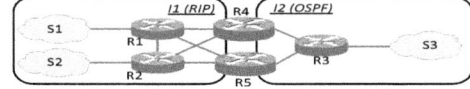

Figure 9: Both border routers R4 and R5 are performing mutual route redistribution between I1 and I2. Assume full reachability among all subnets.

routing process. A BGP peering relationship is established between R4 and R5, so that R4 can advertise S2 to R5, and R5 can advertise S3 to R4. R4 and R5 also redistribute the BGP-learned routes to their respective routing instance, so that other routers in the routing instance have those routes too.

Fig. 8 shows the relevant configuration snippets of R4 and R5. Configuring R4 involves: (i) starting a BGP routing process (line 4); (ii) redistributing routes from the IGP into the BGP process (line 7); (iii) establishing a BGP peering session with the neighboring border router R5 and exchanging routes with it (line 5); (iv) installing an optional route filter to restrict the routes to be advertised (line 6); and (v) redistributing the BGP-learned routes into IGP (line 2). Similar configuration is done on R5 too. We wish to note two things here. First, the BGP process does not have any route by default, and hence routes must be explicitly redistributed from the IGP to the BGP, i.e., the step (ii) above. Second, BGP advertises all its routes to neighbors by default. If this is not desired, a route filter must be used to restrict routes to be advertised, i.e. the step (iv) above.

Modeling complexity: Consider that I_i advertises a set of routes to I_j using BGP. The complexity of configuring BGP on I_i's border router consists of three components: (i) the complexity of configuring the BGP session itself, including configuring the BGP process and the peering relationship with the neighbor; (ii) the complexity of configuring mutual route redistribution between the IGP and the BGP processes; and (iii) the complexity of configuring a route filter, if it is needed (i.e., if only a subset of I_i's routes can be advertised to I_j). Let K_{bgp} denote the complexity of configuring the BGP session itself, which is a constant factor. Let $f(x)$ and $h(i, j)$ be the same functions as defined in Sec. 5.2. The total complexity denoted by $C_{bgp}(i, j)$ can be calculated as follows:

$$C_{bgp}(i, j) = K_{bgp} + 2 * K_{rr} + f(\mathbf{M_X}(i, j)) * h(i, j) \qquad (6)$$

6 Complexity With Multiple Border Routers

We now consider designs where a routing instance uses multiple border routers to connect to another routing instance. An example of such a design is shown in Fig. 9, where both border routers R4 and R5 are configured to perform mutual route redistribution between I1 and I2. The main benefit of using multiple border routers is increased resiliency. For example, even if one border router in Fig. 9 fails, I1 and I2 can still communicate through the other one. On the other hand, using multiple border routers can cause several routing anomalies. To prevent the anomalies, additional configuration is needed, which may increase the complexity of the design.

In this section, we model the additional complexity resulting from ensuring both *safety* and *resiliency* of designs with multiple border routers:
- **Safety**: the routing must function correctly when all the border routers are alive and running, e.g., no routing loop will occur;
- **Resiliency**: when one or more border routers and/or links are down, the routing must be able to adapt and re-route traffic though live routers and/or links.

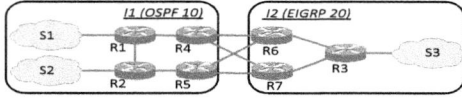

Figure 10: Static routes are configured on all border routers R4 - R7. Assuming full reachability among all subnets.

We examined all three connecting primitives and found that (i) for route redistribution, additional mechanisms are required to ensure safety; (ii) for static routes, additional mechanisms are required to ensure resiliency; and (iii) for BGP, no additional mechanism is needed. Below we focus on modeling the additional complexity resulting from route redistribution and static routes. For the case of BGP we refer readers to the extended technical report [23].

6.1 Ensuring safety with route redistribution

Consider a design scenario where route redistribution is configured on multiple border routers to redistribute routes from I_i to I_j. The complexity of this design depends on what connecting primitive is used to send routes in the reverse direction (i.e., from I_j to I_i), as we discuss below.

On the one hand, if no connecting primitive or a different connecting primitive than route redistribution is used in the reverse direction, the complexity C_{rr} is simply the single-border-router complexity (Sec. 5.2) multiplied by the number of border routers, i.e.,

$$C_{rr}(i,j) = (K_{rr} + f(\mathbf{M_x}(i,j)) * h(i,j)) * |\mathbf{M_B}(i,j)| \quad (7)$$

Recall that $\mathbf{M_B}(i,j)$ denotes the set of border routers that I_i uses to reach I_j, which is an input to our framework (Sec. 3.2). $|\mathbf{M_B}(i,j)|$ denotes the size of this set, i.e., the number of border routers.

On the other hand, if route redistribution is also used in the reverse direction, then a potential anomaly called *route feedback* may occur. Route feedback happens when a route is first redistributed from I_i to I_j by one border router, but then is redistributed back from I_j to I_i by another border router. For example, in the network in Fig. 9, S1 may be first redistributed from I1 (RIP) to I2 (OSPF) by router R4. So router R5 may learn S1 from both RIP and OSPF. If R5 prefers the OSPF-learned route, it will redistribute the route back to RIP. Route feedback *can* lead to several problems such as routing loops and route oscillations [17]. Clearly route feedback can happen only when mutual route redistribution is conducted by multiple border routers between two routing instances.

As a common conservative solution to this issue, a route filter is used in conjunction with route redistribution to prevent any route from re-entering a routing instance that it's originally from. In the above example, a route filter should be installed on R4 and R5 to allow only the route S3 to enter I1, and prevent the routes S1 and S2 from re-entering I1. Note that such a filter may be already in place to implement reachability as described in Sec. 5.2 (i.e., to permit only a subset of I_j's routes to be redistributed to I_i, and block all other routes). In such case, there is no additional complexity introduced. Only in the case where the filter is not needed otherwise (i.e. $\mathbf{M_x}(j,i) = W_j$), a route filter needs to be configured for the sole purpose of preventing route feedback. To summarize, in the mutual route redistribution case, the total inter-instance complexity of using route redistribution to advertise routes from I_i to I_j is:

$$C_{rr}(i,j) = (K_{rr} + f(\mathbf{M_x}(i,j))) * |\mathbf{M_B}(i,j)| \quad (8)$$

The complexity on the reverse direction can be similarly modeled.

6.2 Ensuring resiliency with static routes

Consider that a routing instance I_j uses static routes to reach a set of subnets in I_i, as is the case with routing instances I1 and I2 in the example network in Fig. 10. On each border router of I_j (e.g., R6 in Fig. 10), and for each destination subnet in I_i (e.g., S2), multiple static routes may be configured, each using a different border router of I_i as the next-hop. For example, two static routes may be configured on R6 to reach S2, one using R4 as the next-hop, and the other using R5. We assume that we are also given as input an *arc matrix* $\mathbf{M_A}$, where each cell $\mathbf{M_A}(i,j)$ specifies the set of arcs from the set of border routers in I_j to the set of border routers in I_i. An "arc" is said to exist from one border router $R_b \in \mathbf{M_B}(j,i)$ to another border router $R_a \in \mathbf{M_B}(i,j)$, if there exists a static route on R_b that uses R_a as the next hop.

One limitation with static routes is that they may not be able to automatically detect the failure of the next-hop router or the link in between, and will continue to try to route traffic to the bad path, even when other valid paths exist. This will result in packets being dropped. For example, in Fig. 10, when there is no failure, R6 will load balance the two static routes and use both R4 and R5 to route traffic to I1. R7 will do the same thing. However, if R4 fails, R6 and R7 will not be able to detect the failure or remove the corresponding static route that uses R4 as the next-hop. Instead, they will continue to try to route half of the traffic to R4, resulting in those packets being dropped.

A common solution to this problem is using *object tracking* [10] along with each static route. In doing so, each static route involves referring to an object tracking module. At a high level, object tracking will periodically ping the destination subnet of the static route, using the same next-hop router as specified in the static route. When a failure occurs and the destination is no longer reachable via the particular next-hop, the static route will be removed from the RIB at that point.

Let K_{obj} denote the complexity of installing object tracking to one static route. The total complexity of using static routes to enable I_j to reach I_i can be modeled as follows, assuming each arc contains static routes to reach all subnets in $\mathbf{M_x}(i,j)$:

$$C_{sr}(i,j) = |\mathbf{M_A}(i,j)| * |\mathbf{M_x}(i,j)| * (K_{sr} + K_{obj}) \quad (9)$$

That is, the total complexity is the single-arc complexity (which includes both the complexity of configuring the set of static routes, and the complexity of installing object tracking to each static route), multiplied by the total number of arcs from I_j to I_i (denoted by $|\mathbf{M_A}(i,j)|$).

7 Evaluation

In this section, we evaluate our framework using configuration files obtained from the campus network of a large U.S. university with tens of thousands of users. Our data-set includes multiple snapshots of the configuration files of all switches and routers from 2009 to 2011. It also includes snapshots of the complete layer-two topology data, collected using Cisco CDP at the same time each configuration snapshot was collected. The network has more than 100 routers and more than 1000 switches, all of which are Cisco devices. It also has tens of thousands of user hosts, and around 700 subnets, most of which are /24.

7.1 Framework validation

We first evaluate the accuracy of our framework in estimating complexity. In doing so, we run the framework on one of the configuration snapshots, and compare the predicted complexity numbers with the actual numbers obtained from measuring the configuration files directly.

K_{rr}	K_{sr}	K_{dr}	K_{bgp}	K_{obj}	$f(x)$
1	2	1	2	1	$|x|+2$

Table 2: Realizing framework parameters

	DATA	RSRCH	GRID	INT
DATA	-	H-1	×	✓
RSRCH	✓	-	✓	✓
GRID	×	H-1-1	-	×
INT	D-1	H-1-1	×	-

Table 3: Each cell (*row, column*) shows whether the policy group *column* can be reached by the policy group *row*. ✓/× means full/no reachability. *D-1*, *H-1* and *H-1-1* each denotes a subset of the subnets in *DATA* and *RSRCH*, which can be reached by the corresponding *row*. *H-1-1* is in turn a subset of *H-1*.

7.1.1 Inferring model parameters and framework inputs

We only need to calculating the model parameters for the Cisco IOS platform, as this platform is exclusively used by the campus network. Obtaining these parameters is straightforward, as we just need to run the heuristics proposed in [5] on corresponding configuration blocks that relate to each parameter, and count the number of referential links introduced. The results are shown in Table 2.

To infer the inputs as described in Sec. 3.2, we used a methodology that combines reverse-engineering the configuration files and discussions with operators. We were able to identify the inputs as follows. Table 3 shows the policy groups and the reachability policies among them. Fig. 11a shows the topology and what policy groups each routing instance contains. In particular the campus network has two routing instances denoted as EIGRP and OSPF. There are two policy groups in the network denoted as *DATA* and *RSRCH*. In addition, two external AS-es (denoted as GRID and INT) peer with this campus network. Each external AS can be viewed both as a single policy group and as a single routing instance. Finally, the $\mathbf{M_x}$ matrix, i.e., the set of routes exchanged between every pair of routing instances, is shown in Table 4.

7.1.2 Estimating intra-instance complexity

First, according to our framework, only the EIGRP instance will incur intra-instance route filters as it is the only instance that contains multiple policy groups.

Second, the EIGRP instance employs the typical star topology (Sec. 4.2.1), as shown in Fig. 11b. The border router R_1 also serves as the core router and connects the two policy groups: *DATA* and *RSRCH*. R_1 also directly connects to the other borders R_2, R_3 and R_4. Note that there is no direct link between the two policy groups, or between either policy group and $R_2/R_3/R_4$.

From the reachability matrix (Table 3), it is easy to see that intra-instance filtering is needed between the core router R_1 and the *DATA* policy group as only a subset of routes from R_1 can be sent to *DATA*. More specifically, the routes learned from *GRID* cannot be exposed to *DATA*. Using the model presented in Sec. 4 the route filter placement is determined and shown in Fig. 11b. Route filtering is not needed between R_1 and *RSRCH*, as *RSRCH* has full reachability to all other policy groups. The predicted complexity is shown by the diagonal cells in Table 5.

Comparing with the actual configuration: We measured the actual configuration complexity in the configuration files. The result is shown in the diagonal cells in Table 6. As predicted, only the EIGRP routing instance incurs intra-instance route filters, and the filter placement is exactly as predicted. Furthermore, the measured complexity numbers also match the estimated value well.

	EIGRP	OSPF	GRID	INT
EIGRP	-	all	H-1-1	D-1, H-1-1
OSPF	all	-	-	-
GRID	all	-	-	-
INT	all	-	-	-

Table 4: Each cell (*row, column*) shows the set of routes that routing instance *row* should advertise to routing instance *column*. "All" means that *row* should advertise all its routes (both internal and external ones) to *column*.

	EIGRP	OSPF	GRID	INT
EIGRP	7	1	6	30
OSPF	1	0	-	-
GRID	1	0	-	-
INT	2	-	-	-

Table 5: Estimated complexity for the original design. Each non-diagonal cell (*row, column*) shows the inter-instance complexity of advertising routes from *row* to *column*. The cells on the diagonal show the intra-instance complexity. "-" indicates that the two instances are not directly connected.

7.1.3 Estimating inter-instance complexity

Using the models presented in Sec. 5, we estimate the inter-instance complexity, and the result is shown in Table 5.

Comparing with the actual configuration: We compare the predicted inter-instance complexity with the complexity measured in the configuration files. The differences are shown in Table 6. We see that the majority of the predicted numbers match the actual configuration well. There is a mismatch in the case of filtering routes between GRID and EIGRP. The measured value is greater than the prediction, which makes sense as the prediction is the minimum necessary complexity. The actual configuration may incur higher complexity, for example, due to redundant configurations or sub-optimal configurations.

In particular, the outgoing routes from EIGRP to GRID are subject to filtering as only a subset of EIGRP routes can be sent to GRID. We note that the filtering may be configured either at the re-distribution point (i.e. permitting only the subset of routes to enter BGP), or within the BGP session (i.e. permitting only the subset of routes to be advertised to GRID). However, in the actual configuration, the exact same filtering is implemented at *both* places. This is redundant configuration, and results in unnecessary increase in the complexity. Further, GRID can advertise all its routes to EIGRP, so there is no route filter needed in that direction. However, in the actual configuration, an unnecessary filter is configured which simply allows all routes to pass. As a result, several referential links were created.

Overall, these results confirm that our framework can accurately estimate the complexity of a given routing design.

7.2 Case study of a routing design change

The campus network experienced a major design change recently. The change was primarily motivated by the need to increase the resiliency of the original design. Thus as the second part of the evaluation, we apply our framework to compare the new routing design with the original one. We first use our framework to analyze the change in complexity due to the redesign. We then consider whether alternative designs could have met the same resiliency objectives but with lower complexity.

7.2.1 Impact of redesign on complexity

Fig. 11c illustrates the new instance-level graph after the network redesign was completed. The primary purpose of the redesign was

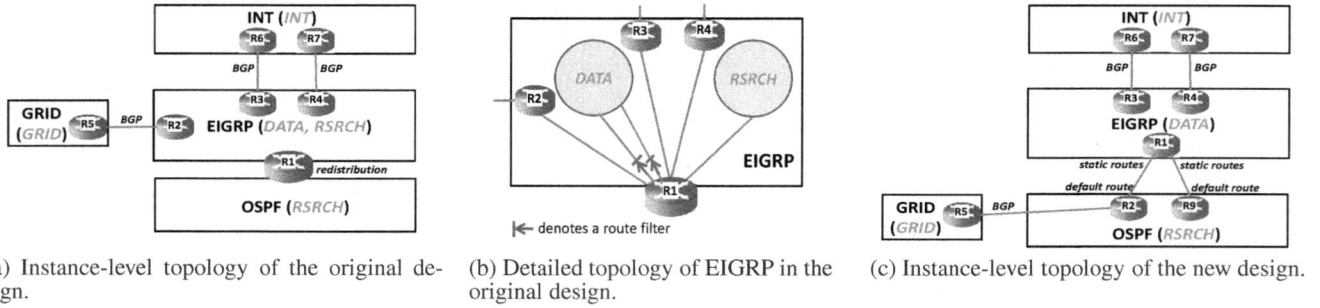

(a) Instance-level topology of the original design.

(b) Detailed topology of EIGRP in the original design.

(c) Instance-level topology of the new design.

Figure 11: The original and new routing designs.

	EIGRP	OSPF	GRID	INT
EIGRP	$\epsilon = 0$	$\epsilon = 0$	$\epsilon = -6$	$\epsilon = 0$
OSPF	$\epsilon = 0$	$\epsilon = 0$	-	-
GRID	$\epsilon = -3$	$\epsilon = 0$	-	-
INT	$\epsilon = 0$	-	-	-

Table 6: Difference between complexity estimated using our models and the actual complexity measured from the configuration files for the original design.

	EIGRP	OSPF	GRID	INT
EIGRP	$\delta = -7$	$\delta = 7$	$\delta = -6$	$\delta = 0$
OSPF	$\delta = 29$	$\delta = 0$	$\delta = 6$	-
GRID	$\delta = -1$	$\delta = 1$	-	-
INT	$\delta = 0$	-	-	-

Table 7: Increase in the intra- and inter-instance complexity after the redesign.

to increase resiliency. In particular, the number of border routers connecting the OSPF instance to EIGRP was increased to two. In addition, two other changes were made: (i) the connecting primitive between EIGRP and OSPF was changed from route redistribution to static routes (configured on the EIGRP side) and default routes (configured on the OSPF side); and (ii) the subnets of the policy group *RSRCH* that were in the EIGRP instance were moved to OSPF. As a result, in the new design, EIGRP only contains subnets of the policy group *DATA*, while OSPF contains all subnets of the policy group *RSRCH*. Finally, we note that the policy groups and the reachability matrix were unchanged after the redesign.

Table 7 presents the change in complexity estimated by our framework. Overall, the total complexity in the new design increased. This is in part due to the fact that the resilience of the new design also increased, i.e., it used two border routers for the OSPF routing instance, compared to one in the old design. We note that the new design eliminated the intra-instance complexity in the EIGRP routing instance, as now EIGRP only contained a single policy group. On the other hand, the inter-instance complexity between EIGRP and OSPF increased in the new design, caused by the need to implement the different reachability requirements for the two policy groups *RSRCH* and *DATA*.

7.2.2 Could alternative designs lower complexity?

In the previous section, we noted that while the primary goal of the redesign was to improve resiliency, operators made two additional changes that were not strictly necessary to achieve this goal: (i) changing the connecting primitive between OSPF and EIGRP from route redistribution to static/default routes; and (ii) moving all *RSRCH* subnets to OSPF. We hypothesized these changes may have been made to lower complexity. To isolate the impact of each

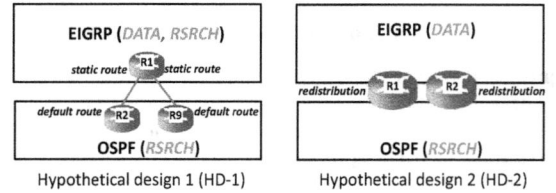

Figure 12: The two hypothetical designs.

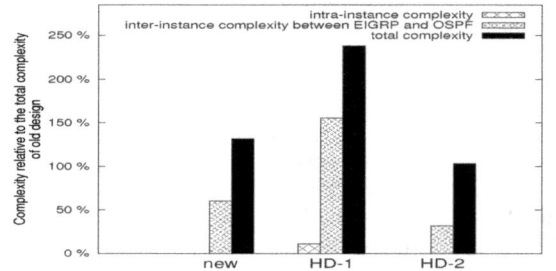

Figure 13: Comparison of complexity of different designs.

of these changes, we considered two hypothetical designs termed *HD-1* and *HD-2*, as shown in Fig. 12. Both designs use two border routers for OSPF, to achieve the same resiliency requirement as the new design. *HD-1* uses static and default routes to connect EIGRP and OSPF, and represents a design where only the first of the two additional changes above were made. *HD-2* involves a rearrangement of policy groups and represents a design where only the second of the two additional changes above were made. Route redistribution is used to connect the instances.

We apply our framework to estimate the complexity for both hypothetical designs. The results are shown in Fig 13. For ease of comparison, we normalized all bars to the total complexity of the original campus design. We see that while *HD-1* is a worse alternative design as its total complexity (third bar) increases compared to the actual new design, *HD-2* is a better alternative as its total complexity decreases compared to the actual new design.

We next seek to better understand why *HD-1* has higher complexity than the actual new design. The main difference between the two designs is whether the policy group *RSRCH* is placed entirely in the OSPF routing instance (actual new design), or split across both OSPF and EIGRP (*HD-1*). We observe that by placing *RSRCH* entirely in OSPF, the address space of OSPF is more unified, which allows better aggregation of its routes. This results in a reduction of the size of $\mathbf{M_x}(OSPF, EIGRP)$ from 9 to 3, which translates to fewer static routes needed, and thus results in less

	static route	redistribution	BGP
default route	38	20	25
redistribution	38	20	25
BGP	43	25	26

Table 8: Complexity associated with different choices of connecting primitive between EIGRP and OSPF. Each cell (*row, column*) shows the complexity of the design that uses the *row* (*column*) connecting primitive on the OSPF (EIGRP) side.

inter-instance complexity (second bar in Fig. 13). In addition, *HD-1* incurs significant intra-EIGRP complexity (first bar), while the actual new design eliminates that complexity.

Next, we compare the actual new design and *HD-2*. The main difference between the two is the connecting primitive used to connect OSPF and EIGRP. We found that using route redistribution (*HD-2*) lowers the complexity compared to using static routes (actual new design). This indicates that by changing the connecting primitive from redistribution to static/default routes during the re-design process, the operators introduced unnecessary design complexity.

Given these insights, we next want to find out whether mutual route redistribution is the best connecting primitive to use to connect EIGRP and OSPF, and if alternative primitives could further lower complexity. For this purpose, we enumerate all possible connecting primitives, and apply our framework to estimate the complexity associated with each alternative design choice. The results are shown in Table 8. Note that it is not feasible to use static routes (default routes) on the OSPF (EIGRP) side, so the corresponding column and row are omitted. The table shows that mutual route redistribution indeed achieves the minimum complexity. A similar complexity could have also been obtained through a design that uses a combination of default routes and route redistribution. We also see that different choices of connecting primitive may lead to significant difference in resulting complexity.

In summary, these results show that (i) the design change of moving subnets of the policy group *RSRCH* from EIGRP to OSPF greatly reduced both intra- and inter-instance complexity; and (ii) the change of connecting primitive actually made the network more complex and thus should have been avoided; and (iii) different design choices may result in significantly different complexity. Overall, this case study highlights the power of our framework in systematically comparing multiple design alternatives and in guiding operators towards approaches that lower complexity while meeting the same design objectives.

7.3 Operator interview

We discussed the above results with the operators of the campus network, and they were able to confirm many of our observations. In particular, they confirmed that moving the *RSRCH* subnets from EIGRP to OSPF significantly reduced the management complexity. In fact, the motivation of that change was to make the *RSRCH* network more unified and simplify the network design. In addition, the operators also acknowledged that our hypothetical design 2 (*HD-2* in Fig. 12) that uses route redistribution instead of static routes could indeed be a less complex design. The primary reason they decided to use static routes in the new design was because this particular operator team consisted of people with varying expertise and skill levels (including senior operators, part-time student workers, and new hires), all of whom could potentially alter configuration files. While configuring static routes did not require extensive prior knowledge, configuring route redistribution required greater knowledge and expertise, particularly given the potential for routing loops. The operators indicated however that they would prefer

route redistribution if only a small number of senior operators managed the network. Overall, these results confirm that our framework provides useful guidance to operators. An open question for future work is whether current complexity metrics must be refined to take operator skill levels into account.

8 Discussion and Open Issues

Incorporating other design objectives and constraints: In putting together a routing design, operators must reconcile a variety of objectives and constraints such as performance, complexity, hardware constraints etc. This paper focuses on the design complexity, given that it is very important, is difficult to quantify, and has received limited attention from the community. In future, it would be interesting to also factor in other important requirements. For example, hardware constraint may restrict the number of route filters that a router can support. Such restriction may in turn impact both intra- and inter-instance route filter placements. We believe our framework can be easily enhanced to systematically determine the best filter placements, so that the hardware constraint is honored, while the total design complexity is minimized. In addition, it may be interesting to consider other design objectives such as performance (e.g., measured as average hop counts between any two subnets), and costs (restricting the number and hardware capacity of devices that can be used). While some of these objectives and constraints may not be critical in a typical over-provisioned enterprise environment, they are nevertheless worthwhile to consider.

Joint optimization of multiple design tasks: This work builds upon a "divide and conquer" network design strategy that is commonly practiced by the operational community [24]. In particular, such a design process consists of four distinct stages: (i) wiring and physical topology design; (ii) VLAN design and IP address allocation; (iii) routing design; and (iv) deployment of services such as VoIP and IPsec. We further break down the task of routing design into two sequential steps: (1) creating routing instances and determining the set of routes to be exchanged between each pair of these instances, and then (2) configuring policy groups and the necessary glue logic. Step (1) is relatively straightforward, typically influenced by factors such as the proximity of routers (e.g., in the same building, city, etc.), administrative boundaries (e.g., different network segments are managed by different operators), and equipment considerations (e.g., EIGRP is available only on Cisco routers). Therefore, this work focuses on the second step while assuming that the first step has been accomplished. In future, it should be beneficial to consider multiple design stages and steps in one framework and explore ways to improve routing design further through joint optimization of all pertinent design choices.

Complexity-aware top-down design: The complexity models presented in this paper pave the way for complexity-aware top-down routing design. Such top-down design takes as input the high-level design objectives and constraints, and seeks to minimize design complexity while meeting other design requirements. In doing so, our complexity models can be used to guide the search of the design space to systematically determine (i) how policy groups should be grouped into routing instances; (ii) optimum placement of route filters; and (iii) what primitives should be used to connect each pair of routing instances. We defer the development of such a top-down design framework to future work.

Emerging architectures and configuration languages: In recent years, researchers have started investigating new network architectures based on logically centralized controllers (e.g., software defined networking [2]), and declarative configuration languages (e.g., Frenetic [11]). These approaches have the potential to simplify network management by shifting complexity away from the configuration of individual devices to programming of the centralized controllers. While these approaches have much potential, hard problems remain such as the need to update network devices in a consistent fashion [22], and building appropriate coordination mechanisms across multiple controllers. Further exploration of the opportunities and challenges of utilizing these new architectures to simplify network design complexity is an important area of future work.

9 Related Work

In recent years, there has been much interest in both industry [1], and academia [5] in developing formal metrics to capture network configuration complexity. We have discussed in detail how our work differs from [5] in Sec. 1. Similarly, our work also differs from other research [7, 15] that measures the configuration complexity in longitudinal configuration data-sets in a bottom-up fashion. There is a considerable amount of prior work on modeling individual routing protocols, particularly BGP [3, 8, 12, 14], and also OSPF [21], to ensure correct, safe, and efficient behaviors from these protocols. There is also recent progress on safe migration of IGP protocols [25] and on modeling the interaction between multiple routing algorithms deployed in the same network [4]. In contrast, our work analyzes how specific routing protocols and primitives should be combined to meet a given set of design objectives, and the focus is on minimizing the complexity of the resulting design. Our notion of policy groups is similar to policy units introduced in [6], but has some differences in that (i) we require subnets within the same policy group to be full reachable to each other; and (ii) we restrict our definition to reachability restrictions on the routing plane since our focus is on routing design, (i.e., we do not consider data-plane mechanisms like packet filters, firewalls, etc.). Algorithms to extract policy units from low-level configuation files were introduced in [6]. In contrast, our focus is on estimating the number of route filters and filter rules, and consequently the resulting configuration complexity, when multiple policy groups are present in a routing instance.

10 Conclusion and Future Work

In this paper, we present a top-down approach to characterizing the complexity of enterprise routing design given only key high-level design parameters, and in the absence of actual configuration files. Our overall modeling approach is to (i) formally abstract the routing specific operational objectives which can help reason about whether and how a combination of design primitives will meet the objectives; and (ii) decompose routing design into its constituent primitives, and quantify the configuration complexity of individual design primitives using bottom-up complexity metrics [5]. We have validated and demonstrated the utility of our approach using longitudinal configuration data of a large-scale campus network. Estimates produced by our model accurately match empirically measured configuration complexity metrics. Discrepancies when present were mainly due to redundant configuration lines introduced by network operators. Our models enable what-if analysis to help evaluate if alternate routing design choices could lower complexity while achieving the same objectives. Analysis of a major routing design change made by the operators indicates that while some of their design changes were useful in lowering complexity, others in fact were counter-productive and increased complexity. Further, our models helped point out alternate designs that could further lower complexity.

Overall, we have taken an important first step towards enabling systematic top-down routing design with minimizing design complexity being an explicit objective. Future work includes modeling

a wider range of routing design objectives and primitives (such as selection logic), developing algorithms for automatically producing complexity-optimized routing designs in a top-down fashion, and using similar models to capturing complexity of other enteprise design tasks.

11 Acknowledgments

This material is based upon work supported by the National Science Foundation (NSF) Career Award No. 0953622, NSF Grant CNS-0721574, and Cisco. Any opinions, findings, and conclusions or recommendations expressed in this material are those of the author(s) and do not necessarily reflect the views of NSF or Cisco. We thank Brad Devine for his insights on Purdue's network design. We thank Michael Behringer, Alexander Clemm, Ralph Droms and our shepherd Vyas Sekar for feedback that greatly helped improve the presentation of this paper.

12 References

[1] IRTF Network Complexity Research Group. http://irtf.org/ncrg.

[2] Open Networking Foundation. http://www.opennetworking.org.

[3] C. Alaettinoglu, C. Villamizar, E. Gerich, D. Kessensand, D. Meyer, T. Bates, D. Karrenberg, and M. Terpstra. *Routing Policy Specification Language (RPSL)*. Internet Engineering Task Force, 1999. RFC 2622.

[4] M. A. Alim and T. G. Griffin. On the interaction of multiple routing algorithms. In *Proc. ACM CoNEXT*, 2011.

[5] T. Benson, A. Akella, and D. Maltz. Unraveling the complexity of network management. In *Proc. of USENIX NSDI*, 2009.

[6] T. Benson, A. Akella, and D. A. Maltz. Mining policies from enterprise network configuration. In *Proceedings of the 9th ACM SIGCOMM conference on Internet measurement conference*, pages 136–142, 2009.

[7] T. Benson, A. Akella, and A. Shaikh. Demystifying configuration challenges and trade-offs in network-based isp services. In *Proc. of ACM SIGCOMM*, 2011.

[8] H. Boehm, A. Feldmann, O. Maennel, C. Reiser, and R. Volk. Network-wide inter-domain routing policies: Design and realization. Apr. 2005. Draft.

[9] M. Casado, M. J. Freedman, J. Pettit, J. Luo, N. McKeown, and S. Shenker. Ethane: Take control of the enterprise. In *Proc. ACM SIGCOMM*, 2007.

[10] Cisco Systems Inc. Reliable static routing backup using object tracking. http://www.cisco.com/en/US/docs/ios/12_3/12_3x/12_3xe/feature/guide/dbackupx.html.

[11] N. Foster, R. Harrison, M. J. Freedman, C. Monsanto, J. Rexford, A. Story, and D. Walker. Frenetic: a network programming language. In *Proceedings of the 16th ACM SIGPLAN international conference on Functional programming*, pages 279–291, 2011.

[12] J. Gottlieb, A. Greenberg, J. Rexford, and J. Wang. Automated provisioning of BGP customers. In *IEEE Network Magazine*, Dec. 2003.

[13] A. Greenberg, G. Hjalmtysson, D. A. Maltz, A. Myers, J. Rexford, G. Xie, H. Yan, J. Zhan, and H. Zhang. A clean slate 4D approach to network control and management. *ACM Computer Communication Review*, October 2005.

[14] T. G. Griffin and J. L. Sobrinho. Metarouting. In *Proc. ACM SIGCOMM*, 2005.

[15] H. Kim, T. Benson, A. Akella, and N. Feamster. The evolution of network configuration: A tale of two campuses. In *Proc. of ACM IMC*, 2011.

[16] F. Le, G. G. Xie, D. Pei, J. Wang, and H. Zhang. Shedding light on the glue logic of the Internet routing architecture. In *Proc. ACM SIGCOMM*, 2008.

[17] F. Le, G. G. Xie, and H. Zhang. Understanding route redistribution. In *Proc. International Conference on Network Protocols*, 2007.

[18] F. Le, G. G. Xie, and H. Zhang. Instability free routing: Beyond one protocol instance. In *Proc. ACM CoNEXT*, 2008.

[19] F. Le, G. G. Xie, and H. Zhang. Theory and new primitives for safely connecting routing instances. In *Proc. ACM SIGCOMM*, 2010.

[20] D. Maltz, G. Xie, J. Zhan, H. Zhang, G. Hjalmtysson, and A. Greenberg. Routing design in operational networks: A look from the inside. In *Proc. ACM SIGCOMM*, 2004.

[21] R. Rastogi, Y. Breitbart, M. Garofalakis, and A. Kumar. Optimal configuration of ospf aggregates. *IEEE/ACM Transaction on Networking*, 2003.

[22] M. Reitblatt, N. Foster, J. Rexford, C. Schlesinger, and D. Walker. Abstractions for network update. In *Proceedings of the ACM SIGCOMM*, 2012.

[23] X. Sun, S. Rao, and G. Xie. Modeling complexity of enterprise routing design. Technical Report TR-ECE-12-10, School of ECE, Purdue University, 2012.

[24] E. Sung, X. Sun, S. Rao, G. G. Xie, and D. Maltz. Towards systematic design of enterprise networks. *IEEE/ACM Trans. Networking*, 19(3):695–708, June 2011.

[25] L. Vanbever, S. Vissicchio, C. Pelsser, P. Francois, and O. Bonaventure. Seamless network-wide IGP migrations. In *Proc. ACM SIGCOMM*, 2011.

Improving Fairness, Efficiency, and Stability in HTTP-based Adaptive Video Streaming with FESTIVE

Junchen Jiang
Carnegie Mellon University
junchenj@cs.cmu.edu

Vyas Sekar
Stony Brook University
vyas@cs.stonybrook.edu

Hui Zhang
Carnegie Mellon
University/Conviva Inc.
hzhang@cs.cmu.edu

ABSTRACT

Many commercial video players rely on bitrate adaptation logic to adapt the bitrate in response to changing network conditions. Past measurement studies have identified issues with today's commercial players with respect to three key metrics—efficiency, fairness, and stability—when multiple bitrate-adaptive players share a bottleneck link. Unfortunately, our current understanding of why these effects occur and how they can be mitigated is quite limited.

In this paper, we present a principled understanding of bitrate adaptation and analyze several commercial players through the lens of an abstract player model. Through this framework, we identify the root causes of several undesirable interactions that arise as a consequence of overlaying the video bitrate adaptation over HTTP. Building on these insights, we develop a suite of techniques that can systematically guide the tradeoffs between stability, fairness and efficiency and thus lead to a general framework for robust video adaptation. We pick one concrete instance from this design space and show that it significantly outperforms today's commercial players on all three key metrics across a range of experimental scenarios.

Categories and Subject Descriptors

C.2.4 [**Computer-Communication Networks**]: Distributed systems—*Distributed applications* ; C.4 [**Performance of Systems**]: [measurement techniques]

General Terms

Design, Performance, Measurement

Keywords

Video, HTTP, DASH, Adaptation

1. INTRODUCTION

Video traffic is becoming the dominant share of Internet traffic today [5]. This growth in video is accompanied, and in large part driven, by a key technology trend: the shift from customized connection-oriented video transport protocols (e.g., RTMP [10]) to HTTP-based adaptive streaming protocols (e.g., [1, 11, 13, 4]).

With an HTTP-based adaptive streaming protocol, a video player can dynamically (at the granularity of seconds) adjust the video bitrate based on the available network bandwidth. As video traffic is expected to dominate Internet traffic [5], the design of robust adaptive HTTP streaming algorithms is important not only for the performance of video applications, but also the performance of the Internet as a whole. Drawing an analogy to the early days of the Internet, a robust TCP was critical to prevent "congestion collapse" [29]; we are potentially at a similar juncture today with respect to HTTP streaming protocols.

Building on this high-level analogy, it is evident that the design of a robust adaptive video algorithm must look beyond a single-player view to account for the interactions across *multiple* adaptive streaming players [14, 15, 22] that compete at bottleneck links. In this respect, there are three (potentially conflicting) goals that a robust adaptive video algorithm must strive to achieve:

- *Fairness:* Multiple competing players sharing a bottleneck link should be able to converge to an equitable allocation of the network resources.
- *Efficiency:* A group of players must choose the highest feasible set of bitrates to maximize the user experience.
- *Stability:* A player should avoid needless bitrate switches as this can adversely affect the user experience.

Recent measurements show that two widely used commercial solutions fail to achieve one or more of these properties when two players compete at a bottleneck link [14, 27]. We extend these experiments (Section 2) and confirm that the problems manifest across many state-of-art HTTP adaptive streaming protocols: Smooth-Streaming [12], Netflix [8], Adobe OSMF [2], and Akamai HD [3]. Furthermore, these problems worsen as the number of competing players increases.

While such measurements are valuable in identifying the shortcomings of today's players, our understanding of the root causes of these problems is limited. To this end, we systematically study these problems through the lens of an abstract video player that needs to implement three key components (see Section 2): (1) scheduling a specific video "chunk" to be downloaded, (2) selecting the bitrate for each chunk, and (3) estimating the bandwidth. At a high-level, the aforementioned problems arise as a result of *overlaying* the adaptation logic on top of several layers that may hide the true network state. Consequently, the feedback signal that the player receives from the network is not a true reflection of the network state. Furthermore, this feedback can also be biased by the decisions the player makes as well. Specifically, we observe that periodic chunk scheduling used in conjunction with stateless bitrate selection used by players today can lead to undesirable feedback loops with bandwidth estimation and cause unnecessary bitrate switches and unfairness in the choice of bitrates.

We leverage measurement-driven insights to design robust mechanisms for the three player components to overcome these biases. Our specific recommendations are (Section 3): (1) *randomized chunk scheduling* to avoid synchronization biases in sampling the network state, (2) a *stateful bitrate selection* that compensates for the biased interaction between bitrate and estimated bandwidth, (3) a *delayed update* approach to tradeoff stability and efficiency, and (4) a bandwidth estimator that uses the *harmonic mean* of download speed over recent chunks to be robust to outliers. Taken together, these approaches define a family of adaptation algorithms that vary in the tradeoff across fairness, efficiency, and stability. For example, we can consider player designs that choose the randomized scheduling with the stateful bitrate selection, without implementing the delayed update or the new bandwidth estimator.

As a concrete instance, we also show how to pick a sweet spot in this tradeoff space called the FESTIVE algorithm.[1] We implement FESTIVE using the Open Source Media Framework and show that our proposed logic is easy to implement and incurs low overhead. We evaluate FESTIVE against several real and emulated commercial players across a range of scenarios that vary the overall bandwidth and number of users. Compared to the closest alternative, FESTIVE improves fairness by 40%, stability by 50% and efficiency by at least 10%. Furthermore, FESTIVE is robust to the number of players sharing a bottleneck, increase in bandwidth variability, and the available set of bitrates.

In summary, this paper makes the following contributions:

- We systematically explore the design space of adaptive video algorithms with the goals of fairness, stability, and efficiency.
- We identify the main factors in bitrate selection and chunk scheduling employed in state-of-art players today that lead to undesirable feedback loops and instability.
- We design robust mechanisms for chunk scheduling, bandwidth estimation, and bitrate selection that inform the design of a suite of adaptation algorithms that vary in the tradeoff between stability, fairness and efficiency.
- We identify one concrete design from this family of algorithms as a reasonable point in this tradeoff space and show that it outperforms state-of-art players under most of the considered scenarios.

2. BACKGROUND AND MOTIVATION

We begin with a high-level overview of how HTTP-based adaptive video streaming works and point out key differences w.r.t TCP-level control logic. Then, we formally define metrics to capture the three key requirements of fairness, efficiency, and stability, and evaluate how well today's state-of-art video players perform.

2.1 HTTP Adaptive Video Streaming

Early Internet video technologies (e.g., Apple QuickTime [4], Adobe Flash RTMP [10]) were based on connection-oriented video transport protocols. As shown in Figure 1(a), these protocols have a session abstraction between the client and the server, that both maintain per-session state and use a (proprietary) stateful control protocol to manage the data delivery. The new generation of Internet video technologies such as Microsoft SmoothStreaming [12], Apple's HLS [41], and Adobe's HDS [1], however, are HTTP-based adaptive streaming protocols.

In HTTP adaptive streaming, a video is encoded at multiple *discrete* bitrates. Each bitrate stream is broken into multiple 2-10 seconds segments or "chunks". The ith chunk from one bitrate

---

[1]The name FESTIVE refers to a **F**air, **E**fficient, and **S**table adap**TIVE** algorithm.

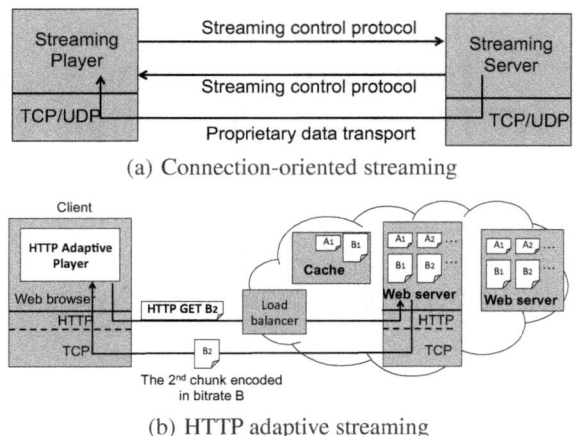

(a) Connection-oriented streaming

(b) HTTP adaptive streaming

Figure 1: Difference between connection-oriented and HTTP adaptive streaming protocol.

stream is aligned in the video time line to the ith chunk from another bitrate stream so that a video player can smoothly switch to a different bitrate at each chunk boundary. As shown in Figure 1(b), HTTP-based adaptive streaming protocols differ from the traditional connection-oriented video transport protocols in several important aspects. First, clients use the standard HTTP protocol which provides more ubiquitous reach as this traffic can traverse NATs and firewalls [42]. Second, the servers are commodity Web servers or caches; this use of existing CDN and server technology has been a key driver for rapid growth and low costs. Third, the use of HTTP implies caches deployed by enterprise and service providers automatically improve the performance and reduce network load. Finally, a client fetches each chunk *independently* and maintains the playback session state while servers do not need to keep any state. This makes it possible for the client to receive chunks from multiple servers: enabling load-balancing and fault tolerance on both CDN side (across multiple servers) and client side (across multiple CDNs) [35, 36].

The client-side video player usually implements the adaptive logic in a constrained sandbox environment such as Flash or Silverlight. The adaptive part arises because the player uses the throughput observed for each chunk and the chunk size to estimate the available network bandwidth. These estimates are used to choose a suitable bitrate for the next chunk to be downloaded. The player tries to maintain an adequate video playback buffer to minimize rebuffering which can adversely impact user engagement [21].

2.2 Desired properties

We are specifically interested in a multi-player setting when multiple video players share a bottleneck link [14,15,27]. To formally define the metrics, we consider a setting with N players sharing a bottleneck link with bandwidth W, with each player x playing bitrate $b_{x,t}$ at time t.

- *Inefficiency:* The inefficiency at time t is $\frac{|\sum_x b_{x,t} - W|}{W}$. A value close to zero implies that the players in aggregate are using as high an average bitrate as possible to improve user experience [21].
- *Unfairness:* Now, some players could see a low bitrate while other players may see high quality. Akhshabi et al., use the difference between bitrates in a two-player setting to compute the unfairness [14]. We generalize this to multiple players as $\sqrt{1 - JainFair}$, where $JainFair$ is the Jain fairness index [43] of $b_{x,t}$ over all player x, because we want to quantify unfairness. A lower value of the metric implies a more fair allocation.

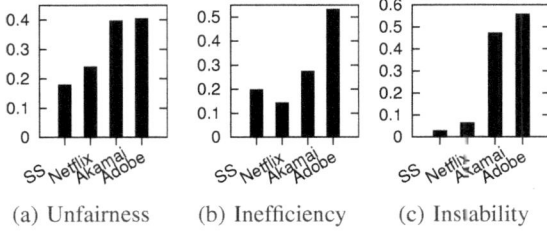

(a) Unfairness (b) Inefficiency (c) Instability

Figure 2: Performance of today's commercial players (SS stands for SmoothStreaming).

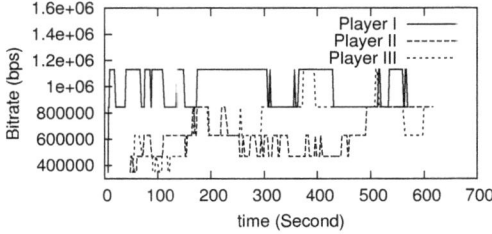

Figure 3: Visualizing unfairness and instability in Smooth-Streaming

- *Instability:* Studies suggest users are likely to be sensitive to frequent and significant bitrate switches [18, 39]. We define the instability metric as $\frac{\sum_{d=0}^{k-1} |b_{x,t-d} - b_{x,t-d-1}| \cdot u(d)}{\sum_{d=1}^{k} b_{x,t-d} \cdot w(d)}$, which is the weighted sum of all switch steps observed within the last $k = 20$ seconds divided by the weighted sum of bitrates in the last $k = 20$ seconds. We use the weight function $w(d) = k - d$ to add linear penalty to more recent bitrate switch.

At first glance, these requirements for video adaptation seem analogous to traditional TCP. There are, however, key architectural differences between HTTP video adaptive streaming and TCP. First, the two control algorithms operate at different levels in the protocol stack. For example, video players can only access coarse information as they run in an application-level sandbox. Second, TCP is a connection-oriented protocol with control logic implemented at the sender-side while video adaptation is a connectionless protocol with receiver-side control. Third, the granularity of data and time are very different. TCP operates at the packet level (~1KB), has multiple packets in transit, and the control loop acts on the timescale of milliseconds. Video adaptation operates at the chunk level (~ hundreds of kilobytes), has only one chunk in transit, and the control loop runs at the timescale of seconds (i.e., chunk fetch delay). Last, due to the video-specific requirement that the buffer cannot be empty, the control actions are very different: a TCP sender delays packet transmission under congestion whereas the receiver in a video adaptation algorithm requests a lower bitrate chunk. Taken together, these factors mean that the rich literature and experience in designing TCP is not directly applicable here.

2.3 Performance of today's solutions

Given these formal metrics, we analyze the performance of existing commercial solutions—SmoothStreaming [11], Akamai HD [3], Netflix [8], and Adobe OSMF [2]. In doing so, we generalize the measurements from previous work that study 1 or 2 of these players in isolation and demonstrate that these problems are more widespread.

We consider a setup with three players sharing a bottleneck link with a stable bandwidth of 3 Mbps with default player settings. Each player runs in a separate Windows machine running on a

# players	BW (bps)	Unfairness	Inefficiency	Instability
5	5M	0.140	0.184	0.0537
11	11M	0.180	0.230	0.0648
19	19M	0.235	0.343	0.0909

Table 1: The performance of SmoothStreaming worsens as the number of players increases. We see similar trends with other players too (not shown for brevity).

2.8 Ghz desktop and accesses the respective demo website. Figure 2 shows the unfairness, inefficiency, and instability. We see that the Akamai and Adobe players are very unstable, while all of them are quite unfair. To give some context for what this unfairness index means, Figure 3 shows a time series of the bitrates of the three SmoothStreaming players which visually confirms that the allocation is quite unfair even for the best player in the above result. (In this case, the optimal allocation would be for all players to pick the same bitrate at all times.) Furthermore, Table 1 shows that the problems become worse as the number of players competing for the bottleneck link increases. Here, with a N player setup, we assume a stable bottleneck of $N \times 1$ Mbps. For brevity, we only show the result SmoothStreaming because this was the best overall player across all three metrics in our earlier experiment.

2.4 Design Space

Next, we describe the broader design space of how we can potentially address the above problems along three key dimensions:

- *What level in the protocol stack?*
  Video players can only access coarse information as they run in an application-level sandbox. To address this concern, we can re-architect the transport layer for video players; e.g., a new TCP variant or running it atop UDP and avoiding unnecessary interactions with the lower layer control loop. Alternatively, we can consider joint design of the video and transport layers. While this might be a better clean-slate solution, it does face deployment concerns—it may not be possible to upgrade the users' OS and new transport mechanisms may not work with middleboxes such as NATs and firewalls.

- *Where in the network?*
  There are three natural options: client-side, server-side, and in-network. For instance, TCP relies largely on sender-side control while video adaptation is a connectionless protocol with receiver-side control. Server-side solutions increase the requirements of CDN deployments beyond today's commodity web server designs. In-network solutions such as fair queuing or rate limiting in routers may offer more optimal solutions, but require a significant overhaul of the network infrastructure. Ultimately, the receiver is in the best situation to infer network bottlenecks and also take into account other user-side considerations (e.g., CPU load, bandwidth quotas) and thus we believe this is a pragmatic choice going forward.

- *Coordinated vs. Decentralized?*
  At one extreme, we can envision a logically centralized video controller that can have a global view of network conditions to assign bitrates to each user [36]. At the other extreme, we have purely decentralized solutions where the adaptation is purely receiver-driven. While this controller may be effective for coarse-grained decisions (e.g., choosing the CDN and bitrate at the start of a session), there are obvious challenges with respect to scale, visibility into client-side effects, and responsiveness for realizing such a controller in practice.

In this paper, we focus on a specific point in this design space—application-layer, receiver-driven, and decentralized adaptation. We cannot claim that this is the only or the ideal point in this space.

Rather, we pick this point as a pragmatic choice with a view toward a solution that is immediately deployable and that is backwards-compatible with today's video delivery ecosystem.

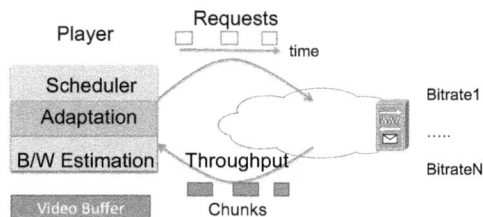

Figure 4: General framework of HTTP adaptive video streaming. The server supports multiple bitrate encodings, each a separate logically chunked file. The player issues GET requests for each chunk at a specific bitrate and adapts the bitrate based on the observed throughput.

3. DESIGN

As the previous section showed, today's state-of-art players do not satisfy the goals of fairness, efficiency, and stability. In this section, we describe how we design a adaptive streaming player that satisfies these properties. As the high-level model from Figure 4 shows, an adaptive streaming player involves three components:

1. Schedule when the next chunk will be downloaded.
2. Select a suitable bitrate for the next chunk.
3. Estimate the network bandwidth.

In designing each component, we make a conscious decision to be compatible with today's deployments and end-host stacks and do not require modifications to end-hosts' operating system stacks or CDN servers. For each component, we use measurement-driven insights to analyze problems with today's players to arrive at a suitable design. We validate each component in Section 6.2 and their interaction in Section 6.3.

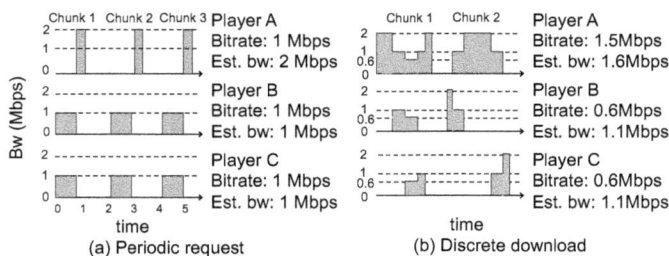

Figure 5: Two sources of bias with today's players: periodic request intervals lead to start-time biases and higher bitrates can cause players to estimate higher bandwidths.

3.1 Chunk Scheduling

The feedback that a player gets from the network is the observed throughput for each chunk. However, the discrete nature of the chunk download implies that the throughput a player observes is coupled to the time when the player "occupies" the link. This is in contrast to a long-running TCP flow that will observe its true share. Thus, we need a careful chunk scheduling approach to avoid biases in observing the network state.

We begin by considering two strawman options: (1) download the next chunk *immediately* after the previous chunk has been downloaded and (2) download chunks *periodically* so that the player

buffer is sufficiently full. For example, SmoothStreaming uses the periodic strategy [14]. However, there are subtle issues with both approaches that we highlight next.

Immediate download: This greedily builds up the player buffer to avoid future buffering events. This approach, however, can be suboptimal for the following reasons. First, greedily downloading at the highest bitrate may needlessly increase the server's bandwidth costs, especially if users leave prematurely [23]. Second, greedily downloading low bitrate chunks may preclude the option of switching to a higher quality in case the network conditions improve. Furthermore, in the case of live content, future chunks may not even be available and thus this is not a viable option. While this greedy download option might be useful in the initial ramp-up phase for a player, the above reasons make it unsuitable in the steady state.

Periodic download: The periodic request strategy tries to maintain a *constant* playback buffer to minimize rebuffering [14]. This target buffer size is usually a fixed number of chunks; e.g., Smooth-Streaming uses a 2-second chunk and a target playback buffer of 30 seconds (i.e., 15 chunks) [15]. This approach works as follows. Let t_i^{start} be the time when the ith chunk is requested, t_i^{end} be the time that it is downloaded, and Δ denote the length of each chunk (in seconds). Suppose $buffer_i$ is length of the playback buffer (in seconds) at t_i^{end} and $targetbuf$ is the target buffer size (e.g., 30s). Then, the time to request the next chunk t_{i+1}^{start} can be written as:[2]

$$t_{i+1}^{start} = \begin{cases} t_i^{end}, \text{if } buffer_i < targetbuf \\ t_i^{end} + buffer_i - targetbuf, \text{otherwise.} \end{cases} \quad (1)$$

While this avoids wasting network bandwidth and prematurely committing to low quality, it suffers a different issue – players may see a biased view of the network state. Specifically, with the periodic download, the players' initial conditions may cause it to get stuck in suboptimal allocations. Figure 5(a) illustrates this problem. Suppose the players use a fixed request period of 2 seconds and the total bandwidth is 2 Mbps. Players A and B always request the next chunk at even seconds (i.e., 0,2,4,...), while player C requests it at odd seconds (i.e., 1,3,5,...). The throughput observed by A and B will be 1 Mbps (half the bandwidth) whereas C estimates it to be 2 Mbps (whole bandwidth). In other words, the initial conditions can lead to unfairness in bandwidth allocation.

Randomized scheduling: In order to avoid this bias induced by the initial conditions, we introduce a *randomized* scheduler that extends the periodic strategy. As before, we want to maintain a reasonable playback buffer. Instead of requiring a constant $targetbuf$, however, we treat it as an *expected* value. Specifically, for each chunk i we choose a target buffer size $randbuf_i$ uniformly at random from the range $(targetbuf - \delta, targetbuf + \delta)$. Specifically, we choose $\delta = \Delta$ which is driven by the analysis from Section 4. Then, the time to request the next chunk is:

$$t_{i+1}^{start} = \begin{cases} t_i^{end}, \text{if } buffer_i < randbuf_i \\ t_i^{end} + buffer_i - randbuf_i, \text{otherwise.} \end{cases} \quad (2)$$

At steady state, the chunks will be downloaded roughly periodically, but with some jitter as we randomize the target buffer size. We show via analysis in Section 4 and measurements in Section 6, that this strategy ensures that the time to request each chunk, and consequently the estimated bandwidth, is independent of the time at which a player arrives.

---

[2]We can prove that this downloads one chunk every Δ seconds at steady state; we do not show this for brevity.

3.2 Bitrate Selection

Having chosen a chunk scheduling strategy that ensures that each player is not biased by its start time, we move to bitrate selection. Our high-level goal here is to ensure that the players will eventually *converge* to a fair allocation irrespective of their current bitrates.

Bias with stateless selection: A natural strategy is to choose the highest available bitrate lower than the estimated bandwidth. We refer to this as *stateless* approaches as it only considers the estimated bandwidth without considering the current bitrate or whether it is ramping up or ramping down its bitrate. For example, if the available bitrates are 400, 600, and 800 Kbps and the estimated bandwidth is 750 Kbps, the player chooses 600 Kbps.

While this stateless approach seems appealing, it can result in an unfair allocation of a bottleneck link. To understand why this happens, let us look at an example in Figure 5(b) with three players A, B and C sharing a bottleneck link with an available bandwidth of 2Mbps, using the randomized scheduler. There are three bitrates available: 600, 1200, and 1500Kbps. Suppose Player A is currently using a bitrate of 1500 Kbps and Player B and C are currently using bitrate 600 Kbps. As shown in Figure 5(b), because Player A uses a higher bitrate, its "wire occupancy" is higher than Player B and C. This implies that there are points in time where Player A is occupying the bottleneck link alone and thus Player A's estimated bandwidth will be higher than Player B and C. In other words, the process of discretely downloading individual chunks naturally introduces a bias: *players currently using a higher bitrate observe a higher bandwidth*. We formally derive the relationship between estimated bandwidth and bitrates in Section 4.

Round	Bitrates (Kbps)	→	Estimated bw. (Kbps) (network feedbacks)
1	[350,350,1520]	→	[730,730,1356]
2	[470,470,1130]	→	[717,717,1146]
3	[470,470,1130]	→	[717,717,1146]
...	...	...	...

Table 2: Example of unfairness with stateless bitrate selection. The bitrate levels are {350,470,730,845,1130,1520}Kbps and the total bandwidth is 2Mbps.

Because there are only a discrete set of available bitrates (e.g., 4-5 encodings), players sharing a bottleneck link can often converge to an equilibrium state that is inherently unfair; e.g., in Figure 5(b), Player B and C will never increase their bitrate. This scenario is not merely hypothetical. For example, Table 2 shows an actual run using our setup (described in detail in Section 6), where the players converge to an equilibrium state that is inherently unfair.

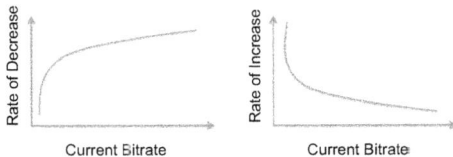

Figure 6: Intuition behind stateful selection: we want players with lower bitrate to ramp up aggressively or players with higher bitrate to ramp down aggressively.

Our approach: At a high-level, we need to compensate for the above bias so that the players can converge to a fair allocation irrespective of their current bitrates. We can achieve this in one of two ways as shown in Figure 6: (1) the rate of decrease is a monotonically increasing function of the bitrate or (2) the rate of increase is a monotonically decreasing function of the bitrate. Intuitively, we are making the player *stateful* by accounting for its current bi-

trate.[3] Our current design chooses option (2) and we simply keep the rate of decrease a constant function. In the example in Table 2, this approach causes the players starting at 350 Kbps to ramp up their bitrates more aggressively so that they will observe the true network state after 2-3 switches.

This stateful strategy can be realized either by allowing *multi-level* bitrate switches (e.g., from 350 to 1130 and skipping intermediate levels) or by altering the *rate* of switching the bitrates (e.g., once per chunk at 350 but once every 5 chunks at 1130). While we do not conclusively know if users are more sensitive to multi-level switches or the number of switches [18], recent work suggests that changing quality levels gradually is preferable [39]. Thus, we choose a *gradual* switching strategy where the player only switches to the next highest level and uses a lower rate of upward switches at higher bitrates. We discuss our specific approach in Section 3.5. We do note that the property achieved by a stateful approach is agnostic to how specific players implement the mechanism from Figure 6.

3.3 Delayed Update

While the previous discussion provides guidelines for choosing the bitrate to converge to a fair allocation, it does not consider the issue of *stability*—switching too frequently is likely to annoy users (e.g., [18]) and thus in this section, we focus on balancing these two potentially conflicting goals: efficiency and fairness on one hand vs. stability on the other.

To this end, we introduce a notion of *delayed update*. We treat the bitrate from the previous section only as a *reference* bitrate and defer the actual switch based on a measured tradeoff between efficiency/fairness and stability. Specifically, we compute how close to the efficient or stable allocation the current (b_{cur}) and the reference bitrate computed from the previous discussion (b_{ref}) are.

The *efficiency cost* for bitrate b is:

$$score_{efficiency}(b) = \left| \frac{b}{\min(w, b_{ref})} - 1 \right|$$

Here, w is the estimated bandwidth and b_{ref} is the reference bitrate from the previous section. Intuitively, the score is the best and equal to zero when $b = b_{ref}$. (The "min" in the denominator corrects for the fact that the reference bitrate may be underutilizing or overutilizing the bottleneck link.)

The *stability cost* for a given bitrate b is a function of the number of bitrate switches the player has undergone recently. Let n denote the number of bitrate switches in the last $k = 20$ seconds. Then the stability metric is,

$$score_{stability}(b) = \begin{cases} 2^n + 1 & \text{if } b = b_{ref} \\ 2^n & \text{if } b = b_{cur} \end{cases}$$

The reason to model the stability score using an exponential function of n is that $score_{stability}(b_{ref}) - score_{stability}(b_{cur})$ is monotonically increasing with n, which adds more penalty of adding a new switch if there have already been many switches in recent history.[4]

The combined score is simply the weighted average:

$$score_{stability}(b) + \alpha \times score_{efficiency}(b)$$

The player computes this combined score for both the current and reference bitrates, and picks the bitrate with the lower combined score. The factor α here provides a tunable knob to control

---

[3]We can show that this approach is sufficient; we do not claim that this is necessary.

[4]It is not necessary to model the stability score via an exponential function; this scheme has proven sufficient in our experiments.

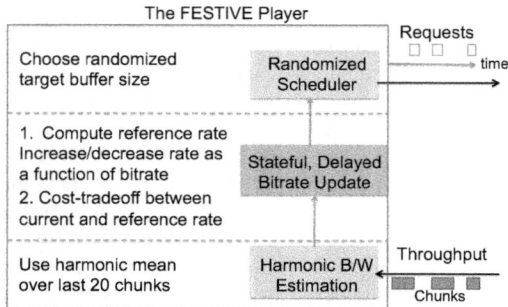

Figure 7: Overview of the FESTIVE adaptive video player.

the tradeoff between efficiency and fairness on one hand and stability on the other. We provide empirical guidelines on selecting a suitable value for α in Section 6.2.

3.4 Bandwidth Estimation

As we saw in the previous discussion, the throughput observed by a player for each chunk is not a reliable estimate of the available capacity. We suggest two guidelines to build a more robust bandwidth estimator. First, instead of using the instantaneous throughput, we use a *smoothed* value computed over the last several chunks. In our current prototype, we use the last 20 samples.[5] Second, we want this smoothing to be *robust* to outliers. For example, using the arithmetic *mean* is biased by outliers if one chunk sees a very high or low throughput. To this end, we use the *harmonic mean* over the last 20 samples. The reason for using this approach is twofold. First, the harmonic mean is more appropriate when we want to compute the average of rates which is the case with throughput estimation. Second, it is also more robust to larger outliers [7]. This is especially relevant in the context of our randomized scheduler. With a randomized scheduler, if there are fewer competitors for a certain chunk, the estimated throughput will be larger. In such cases, the harmonic mean minimizes the impact of outliers. (If there are more competitors, then each player is more likely to observe a bandwidth close to its fair share.)

3.5 The FESTIVE algorithm

We now proceed to put the different design components together to describe the FESTIVE (Fair, Efficient, Stable, adaptIVE) algorithm. Figure 7 shows a high-level overview of FESTIVE. FESTIVE retains the same external-facing interface as today's HTTP video streaming players. That is, FESTIVE selects the bitrate for each chunk and decides when to schedule the request and the input to FESTIVE is the throughput observed per-chunk.

In describing FESTIVE, we focus on the steady-state behavior. The ramp up behavior of FESTIVE can be identical to today's players; e.g., aggressively download chunks (potentially at a low bitrate) to start playing the video as soon as possible. As discussed in the previous sections, FESTIVE has three key components:

1. The *harmonic bandwidth estimator* computes the harmonic mean of the last $k = 20$ throughput estimates. This provides *reliable* bandwidth estimates on which future bitrate update decisions can be made. In the initial phase before we have a sufficient number of samples, FESTIVE does not employ any rate switches because its bandwidth estimate will be unreliable.
2. The *stateful and delayed bitrate update* module receives throughput estimates from the bandwidth estimator and computes a reference bitrate. As a specific implementation of Figure 6, we use

---

[5] We do not claim this is new; commercial players likely already implement some smoothing.

a gradual switching strategy; i.e., each switch is only to the next higher/lower level. Here, we increase the reference bitrate at bitrate level k only after k chunks, but decrease the bitrate level after every chunk if a decrease is necessary. This ensures that the bitrates eventually *converge* to a fair allocation despite the biased bitrate-to-bandwidth relationship. To decide if we need to decrease, we compare the current bitrate with $p = 0.85 \times$ the estimated bandwidth. The parameter p helps tolerate the buffer fluctuation caused by variability in chunk sizes [15]. For the delayed update, we use a value of the tradeoff factor $\alpha = 12$ (see Section 6.2).

3. The *randomized scheduler* works as shown in Eq (2). It schedules the next chunk to be downloaded immediately if its playback buffer is less than the target buffer size. Otherwise, the next chunk is scheduled with a random delay by selecting a randomized target buffer size. This ensures there are no *start time biases*.

4. ANALYSIS OF FESTIVE

In this section, we show that:

- The randomized scheduler ensures that the request time of a player is independent of its start time.
- The stateful bitrate selection ensures that bitrates will eventually converge to a fair allocation.

Together, these ensure that the network state observed by competing players will not be biased by their arrival time or by the initial bitrates of other players.

Notation: We use i, k to denote chunk indices, j for a specific epoch, and x, y, z to denote players. Let n be the number of players and m be the number of chunks and let the bottleneck bandwidth be W. We use Δ to denote the length (in time) of each chunk.

Model: Our focus here is on the steady state behavior and not the initial ramp up phase. To make the analysis tractable, we make four simplifying assumptions. First, we assume the bottleneck bandwidth is stable. Second, this bandwidth is not saturated by the summation of bitrate, and each player's bitrate is less than its allocated bandwidth. As a result, for each chunk, a player will complete the download before the deadline, so the $buffer_i > randbuf_i$ will hold for most chunks. Third, if n players are simultaneously downloading over a bottleneck of bandwidth W, we assume that each player will get a bandwidth share of $\frac{W}{n}$. Last, we consider an *epoch-based* model, where players synchronously choose a new bitrate at the start of each epoch and estimate the bandwidth at the end of each epoch.[6]

4.1 Randomized scheduler

The goal of the randomized scheduler is to ensure the request time is independent of a player's start time. Formally, we want to show that:

Theorem 1. *If a player uses* $randbuf_i$ *drawn uniformly at random between* $(targetbuf - \Delta, targetbuf + \Delta]$ *and* $buffer_i > randbuf_i$ *for each chunk* i $(i = 1, \ldots, m)$, *then the probability distribution of chunk request times does not depend on the start time* t_0^{start}.

PROOF. The buffer length at time t_i^{end}, when chunk $i - 1$ has been downloaded is $buffer_{i-1} = (i-1)\Delta - (t_{i-1}^{end} - t_0^{start})$ where $(i-1)\Delta$ is the length of content downloaded so far and $t_{i-1}^{end} - t_0^{start}$ is the amount of video played. If $buffer_{i-1} > randbuf_{i-1}$, then by Eq (2), the time to request the next chunk:

---

[6] Each epoch can consist of multiple chunks.

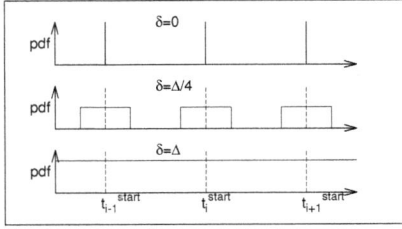

Figure 8: Intuition for Theorem 1.

$$t_i^{start} = t_{i-1}^{end} + buffer_{i-1} - randbuf_{i-1} =$$
$$t_{i-1}^{end} + (i-1)\Delta - (t_{i-1}^{end} - t_0^{start}) - randbuf_{i-1}$$
$$= t_0^{start} + (i-1)\Delta - randbuf_{i-1}$$

Because each $randbuf_{i-1}$ is a uniform random variable in the range $(targetbuf - \Delta, targetbuf + \Delta]$, this means that for a given i, t_i^{start} is a uniform random variable in the range $(t_0^{start} + (i-1)\Delta - targetbuf - \Delta, t_0^{start} + (i-1)\Delta - targetbuf + \Delta]$. Let T denote a random variable representing the request time. Then $T = t$ can occur for exactly two intervals i^* and $i^* + 1$, with $i^* = \frac{1}{\Delta}(t + targetbuf - t_0^{start})$ as shown in Figure 8. Thus, $f(T = t) = f(t_{i^*}^{start} = t$ or $t_{i^*+1}^{start} = t) = 2 * \frac{1}{2\Delta} = \frac{1}{\Delta}$ which is independent of t_0^{start}. $\square$

Notice that for other $\delta \neq \Delta$, if $randbuf_i$ is at random in range $(targetbuf - \delta, targetbuf + \delta]$, then the same argument of Theorem 1 does not hold. For example, if $\delta = \frac{1}{r}\Delta$ where $r > 2$, then the ranges of t_i^{start} for different i will not overlap (see Figure 8). Consequently, for any t, there will be at most one t_i^{start} whose range covers t. That is, $f(T = t)$ will be $\frac{1}{2\delta}$ for exactly one k such that $t_0^{start} + k\Delta - targetbuf - \delta < t \leq t_0^{start} + k\Delta - targetbuf + \delta$ and 0 otherwise. In other words, the request time distribution depends on the start time t_0^{start}. The periodic scheduler is an extreme case with $r \to \infty$.

4.2 Stateful bitrate selection

We begin by deriving the relationship between estimated bandwidth and bitrate in Lemma 1 which shows that a player with higher bitrate will see relatively higher bandwidth.

Lemma 1. *For two players, x and y, let w_x and w_y be the harmonic mean of the throughput seen by them and b_x, b_y be their bitrates. Then, $\frac{w_x}{w_y} = \frac{t_x + W}{t_y + W}$.*

PROOF. Since we are using the randomized scheduler, each player will join the link randomly. Let n_{ix} be the number of competitors when player x downloads chunk i, then the bandwidth allocation of chunk i is $\frac{W}{n_{ix}+1}$. Thus, the download time for chunk i is $d_{ix} = \frac{b_x\Delta(n_{ix}+1)}{W}$ where $b_x\Delta$ is the chunk size. The total download time is $\sum_{i=1}^m d_{ix}$, and the fraction of time when player x is downloading is:

$$q_x = \frac{1}{m\Delta}\sum_{i=1}^n d_{ix} = \frac{1}{m\Delta}\sum_{i=1}^m \frac{b_x\Delta(n_{ix}+1)}{W}$$
$$= \frac{b_x}{W}\sum_{i=1}^m \frac{(1+n_{ix})}{m} = \frac{b_x}{W}N_x$$

where $N_x = 1 + E(n_{ix})$ is the expected number of competitors for x. When each chunk length is small, the probability that player i is competing for the bandwidth is simply the fraction of time spent downloading $= q_x$. Thus, we have $N_x = 1 + E(n_{ix}) = 1 +$

$\sum_{z \neq x} q_z$.[7] Thus, we have

$$\frac{q_x W}{b_x} + q_x = 1 + \sum_z q_z = \frac{q_y W}{b_y} + q_y \Rightarrow \frac{b_x + W}{b_y + W} = \frac{\frac{b_x}{q_x}}{\frac{b_y}{q_y}}$$

Now, the harmonic mean of bandwidth is simply:

$$w_x = \frac{m}{\sum_{i=1}^m \frac{1}{w_{ix}}} = \frac{W}{\frac{1}{m}\sum_{i=1}^m (1+n_{ix})} = \frac{W}{N_x} = \frac{b_x}{q_x}$$

Thus, we have $\frac{b_x + W}{b_y + W} = \frac{w_x}{w_y}$. $\square$

Notice that w_x is a harmonic mean, rather than expectation, of the bandwidth the player sees, which is consistent with how bandwidth is estimated in FESTIVE.

Based on this, we have the following theorem which proves bitrate convergence. Recall from Section 3.5 that if bitrate $b_x > pw_x$ where w_x is the harmonic mean of bandwidth of the epoch and p is a real value parameter, then the player x will decrease bitrate in the next epoch (i.e., stateless decrease). Otherwise, it will increase in a rate which depends on the bitrate level (i.e., stateful increase).

Theorem 2. *Let l_x^j and l_y^j be the bitrate levels of players x and y in j^{th} epoch with $l_y^j - l_x^j \geq 2$. Then the gap will eventually converge to be at most one level, i.e., $\exists j' > j$, where $|l_x^{j'} - l_y^{j'}| \leq 1$.*

PROOF. Given $l_y^j - l_x^j \geq 2$, we show that $l_y^j - l_x^j$ monotonically decreases as a function of j until $|l_y^j - l_x^j| = 1$. Let b_x^j, b_y^j denote the bitrates and w_x^j, w_y^j be the bandwidth in epoch j. By Lemma 1, there is no p for which $pw_x < b_x^j$ and $b_y^j < pw_y$. (Otherwise, $\frac{w_x^j}{w_y^j} < \frac{b_x^j}{b_y^j} < \frac{b_x^j + W}{b_y^j + W}$, which contradicts Lemma 1.) Therefore, there are only three cases for the estimated bandwidths w_x^j, w_y^j, (i) $pw_x^j > b_x^j, pw_y^j < b_y^j$, (ii) $pw_x^j < b_x^j, pw_y^j < b_y^j$, and (iii) $pw_x^j > b_x^j, pw_y^j > b_y^j$. For (i), b_y^j will decrease, and b_x^j will not decrease, therefore, $l_y^{j+1} - l_x^{j+1} \leq l_y^j - l_x^j - 1$. For (iii), before switching to (i) or (ii), x will increase earlier than y according to the stateful bitrate update (Figure 6), so $l_y^j - l_x^j$ will decrease. For (ii), since the two players cannot always decrease bitrate in (ii), so eventually, they will enter (iii) or (i). As a result, in each epoch, $l_x^j - l_y^j$ cannot increase and it will not always remain constant. $\square$

5. OSMF-BASED IMPLEMENTATION

We have implemented our FESTIVE algorithm in an open source Flash video player. The implementation builds on the Open Source Media Framework (OSMF codebase (v2.0) and is written in ActionScript [9]. OSMF is an open-source framework developed by Adobe which provides most of the basic functionalities of a commercial video player.

OSMF provides a well-defined API for different player functions. There are two specific "hooks" that we leverage to implement the FESTIVE logic: (1) the function `play2(streamName)` that can be used to specify a target bitrate (via its URL prefix `streamName`), and (2) the function `bufferTime(t)` that can be used to specify target buffer length of `t`. One challenge, however, is that the function `play2` as currently implemented may not always change bitrate for downloading the next chunk. Thus, we extended `play2` by adding check points at the boundary of each chunk. At these points, our additional code receives the throughput of last chunk, and decides the target buffer length and the bitrate of the next chunk. We implement the specific FESTIVE logic in a separate class and set the bitrate (via extended `play2`) and target buffer length (via `bufferTime`). The additional code is ≈ 500

---

[7] This is by linearity of expectation.

103

lines, a small fraction compared to the full OSMF codebase (125K lines of code). We have run several microbenchmarks over a range of bitrates and confirmed that our FESTIVE code adds little or no CPU overhead to the existing player logic for downloading, buffering, decoding, and rendering (not shown for brevity).

6. EVALUATION

We divide our evaluation into four high-level sections:

1. We compare the performance of FESTIVE against (emulated) commercial players (Section 6.1).
2. We validate each component—randomized chunk scheduling, stateful and delayed bitrate selection, and harmonic bandwidth estimation (Section 6.2).
3. We evaluate how critical each component is to the overall performance of FESTIVE (Section 6.3).
4. Finally, we evaluate the robustness of FESTIVE as a function of bandwidth variability, number of players, and the set of available bitrates (Section 6.4).

Evaluation setup: We use our OSMF-based implementation and real commercial players wherever possible. However, it is difficult to run controlled experiments with the real commercial players due to the lack of access to their code and the difficulty in automating experiments with multiple players on different machines. Our goal is to evaluate the underlying *adaptation logic* of different adaptive players. However, the proprietary nature of the client/server code for these players makes it difficult to do a head-to-head comparison. Specifically, using the commercial players conflates external effects: network (e.g., wide-area bottlenecks) and server-side (e.g., CDN load) effects, issues w.r.t video encoding/decoding, and player plug-in performance.

Thus, in order to do a fair comparison, we augment these real player experiments with a custom emulation framework. Here, we heuristically create *emulated* clones that closely mimic each commercial player. In each case, we verified over a range of settings that our emulated clone is a *conservative* approximation of the commercial player; i.e., the unfairness, inefficiency, and instability with the emulated clone are *lower bounds* for the actual player. Our heuristic approach works as follows. We start with a basic algorithm that uses the periodic scheduler and the harmonic bandwidth estimation algorithms. Based on trace-driven analysis, we observed that most commercial players appear to employ a *stateless* bitrate selection algorithm that can be modeled as a linear function of the throughput estimated for the previous chunk(s). We use linear regression to find the best fit for each commercial player separately. For example, the SmoothStreaming player appears to pick the highest available bitrate below $0.85\times$ the estimated bandwidth [8]. We do not claim that these are the exact algorithms; our goal is to use these as conservative approximations of the players to do a fair comparison with FESTIVE.

We implemented a flexible framework that allows us to evaluate different algorithms for chunk scheduling, bitrate selection, and bandwidth estimation. Our setup consists of client players, video servers, and a bottleneck link. Both client and server side mechanisms are implemented as Java modules (about 1000 lines each) that run on different machines within a local network. The client player decides the bitrate for the next chunk and when to issue the request. Once the video server receives the request which explicitly encodes the bitrate, it generates a file with size dependent on the bitrate. The client downloads this chunk over a regular TCP

---

[8]Based on linear regression between selected bitrate and bandwidth estimated by update function $bw_{next} = 0.9bw_{prev} + 0.1bw_{cur}$

socket. All traffic between clients and servers goes through the bottleneck which uses Dummynet [46] to control the total bandwidth and delay. Unless specified otherwise, we emulate a ten-minute long video with eight bitrate levels from 350Kbps to 2750Kbps and using 2 second chunks. (This is based on the parameters we observe in the demo website [11]). We use chunk sizes of an encoded video for each bitrate by analyzing real traces of commercial players from [11].

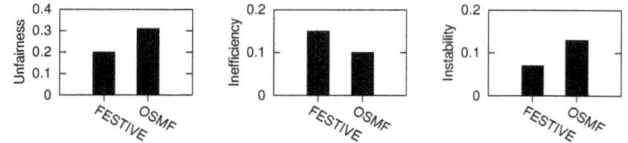

Figure 9: Comparison between real OSMF player and OSMF player using FESTIVE.

6.1 Comparison with Commercial Players

OSMF implementation: First, we use our real implementation atop the OSMF framework and compare it to the current OSMF adaptation logic using the video at [6]. Here, we consider a setup with three players that share a bottleneck link of 3 Mbps. Figure 9 shows the unfairness, inefficiency, and instability of FESTIVE vs. the OSMF logic. We observe that our implementation outperforms OSMF on two of three metrics. Our inefficiency, however, is slightly higher. We speculate that this is because our FESTIVE parameters are customized for the chunk sizes and bitrate levels seen in the SmoothStreaming demo as we discussed in Section 5.

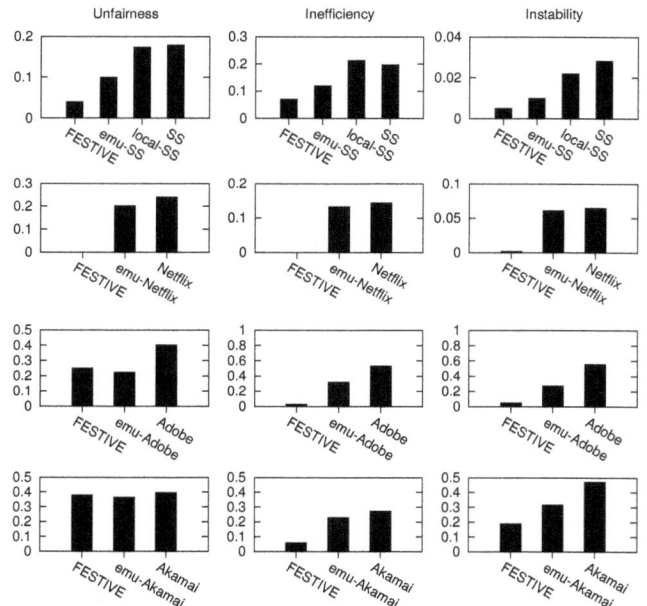

Figure 10: Comparison between FESTIVE, emulated commercial players, and the actual commercial players with 3 players sharing a bottleneck link of 3 Mbps. Here, SS stands for SmoothStreaming; "emu-X" stands for our conservative emulation of the "X" commercial player; and local-SS is running a local SmoothStreaming server.

Other players: As we discussed, the chunk lengths and bitrate levels vary across commercial players. Thus, in each result we use the corresponding bitrate levels and chunk lengths observed in the players' (demo) websites to compare FESTIVE, the emulated player, and real player. Our goal here is to compare FESTIVE to each commercial player independently; it is not meaning-

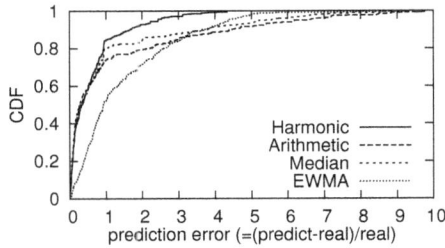

Figure 11: Prediction error in bandwidth estimation.

ful to draw any conclusions across players (e.g., is SmoothStreaming better than Netflix?) since the parameters such as chunk sizes and bitrate levels across the demo sites vary significantly. Figure 10 compares the performance of FESTIVE to the emulated commercial players, with the median value over 15 runs. In each case, a lower value of the performance metric is better. For reference, we also show the performance of the commercial players with an equivalent three player setup (using respective demo sites). For Smooth-Streaming, we also have access to the server implementation. Thus, we also evaluate a local setup with the real players and server. For each commercial player, we confirm that the emulated version is a conservative approximation. We see that FESTIVE outperforms the next best solution, SmoothStreaming, by at least 2× in all three metrics. We also observed that FESTIVE provides higher benefits as we increase the number of players (not shown). For example, our stability of 19 players (with 19Mbps bottleneck bandwidth) is still about 2× higher than SmoothStreaming, but the gap between SmoothStreaming and us is 4× larger than that of 3 players.

6.2 Component-wise Validation

Next, we examine whether each component achieves the properties outlined in Section 3. As a baseline point of reference, we use the emulated SmoothStreaming player and evaluate the effect of incrementally adding each component.

Bandwidth estimator: We begin by comparing the accuracy of four bandwidth estimation strategies: arithmetic mean, median, EWMA,[9] and harmonic mean. Each method computes the estimated bandwidth using the observed throughput of the $k = 20$ previous chunks. For this analysis, we extract the observed chunk throughputs from the real SmoothStreaming setup from Section 2 with 19 competing players and emulate each estimation algorithm. We report the CDF of the prediction error $\frac{|Predicted BW - Actual BW|}{Actual BW}$ in Figure 11. The result shows that the harmonic mean outperforms the other methods. (The large prediction errors in the tail appear because the observed bandwidth for each chunk depends on the number of competing players that chunk sees which is highly variable.) We also manually confirmed that the harmonic mean is effective when a new observed throughput is an outlier. Thus, for the rest of this section, we consider the baseline algorithm with a harmonic bandwidth estimator.

Chunk scheduling: Here, the baseline player uses stateless bitrate selection, instant update, harmonic bandwidth estimation, and the periodic chunk scheduling discussed in Section 3. We consider a modified baseline that uses the randomized scheduling instead but retains the other components. Figure 12 shows the perceived bandwidth for the three players over time for one run. (The results are consistent across runs, we do not show them for brevity.) We can visually confirm that the periodic scheduler leads to large bias in the estimated bandwidth, while the randomized scheduler ensures a more equitable bandwidth share. The result also shows the differ-

---

[9]Using the update function $bw_{next} = 0.9 bw_{prev} + 0.1 bw_{cur}$

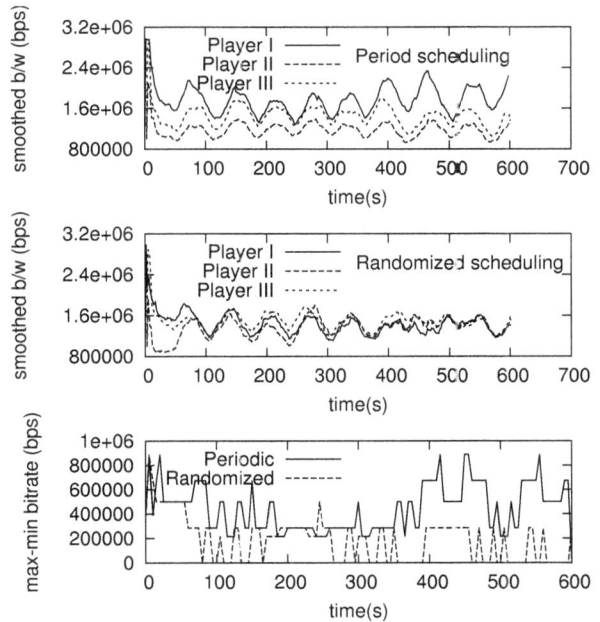

Figure 12: Randomized scheduling avoids start-time biases and ensures a fair allocation of bandwidth

ence between maximum and minimum bitrate to confirm that this bias in observed bandwidth also translates into unfairness in bitrate selection.

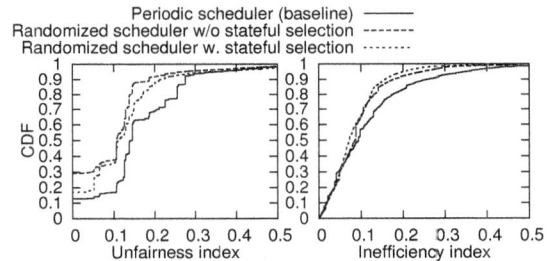

Figure 13: Stateful bitrate selection improves fairness with minimal impact on efficiency.

Stateful bitrate selection: The goal of the stateful bitrate selection approach is to ensure that different players will eventually converge to a fair allocation. To validate this, we consider ten players sharing a bottleneck link of 10 Mbps. Each player picks a start time uniformly at random in the interval of $[0, 30]$ seconds.

Figure 13 compares the efficiency and fairness achieved by three player settings: (1) fixed scheduler with stateless selection (baseline), (2) randomized scheduler with stateless selection, and (3) randomized scheduler with stateful selection. (We disable delayed update and use harmonic mean estimator for all three.) We see that stateful selection works well in conjunction with randomized scheduling and further improves the fairness. One concern with stateful bitrate selection is that players may increase/decrease bitrate synchronously and lead to over/under utilization (low efficiency). The result also shows that the efficiency is almost unaffected and may even be better than the stateless approach. The reason is that once the players converge to a fair allocation, all subsequent switches are only between two consecutive levels, which keeps the inefficiency small.

Delayed Update: The parameter α provides a way to tune the tradeoff between efficiency and stability. We examine this tradeoff with different number of players and bandwidth variability in Figure 14. (We discuss the exact variability model in Section 6.4).

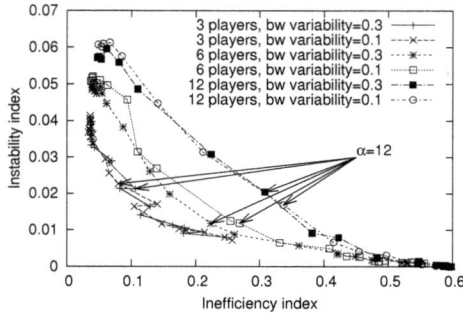

Figure 14: Tradeoff of delayed update between efficiency and stability: 'knee' points using $\alpha = 12$.

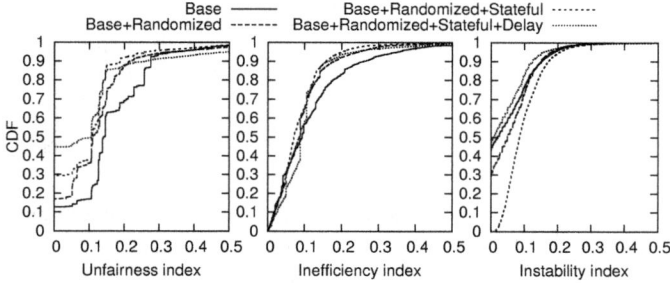

Figure 15: Break-down evaluation of FESTIVE.

From the bottom-right to top-left, α increases from 5 to 30; larger α provides higher efficiency at the cost of stability (Section 3). We suggest a guideline of picking the α that is close to the "knee" of the curve or the point closest to the origin. Across most scenarios, we find this roughly corresponds to $\alpha = 12$; we use this value for FESTIVE.

6.3 How critical is each component?

To see the effect of each component in FESTIVE, Figure 15 shows the effect of incrementally adding the randomized scheduler, stateful bitrate selection, delayed update to the baseline. For this result, we consider the scenario with 10 players competing for a 10 Mbps bottleneck link. First, we see that the randomized scheduler improves the fairness and efficiency over the baseline (by avoiding bias of starting time), and stateful bitrate selection further improves these (by avoiding bias of initial bitrates). However, these components are likely to increase the instability relative to the baseline. The delayed update then helps control this tradeoff between efficiency and stability; it reduces the efficiency slightly but improves stability significantly.

6.4 Robustness

Last, we investigate FESTIVE's performance in the presence of varying number of concurrent players, bandwidth variability and available bitrate sets.

Number of concurrent players: We fix the total bandwidth at 10Mbps and vary the number of concurrent players from 2 to 30. In each run, the players arrive randomly within the first 30 seconds after the first player starts. For each setting, we report the median and error bars over 15 runs for both baseline and FESTIVE in Figure 16. First, we see that FESTIVE outperforms the baseline across all settings and that the performance variability of FESTIVE is much smaller. Second, we see that unfairness and instability issues are lower when there are too few or too many players. In the former case, all player can sustain the highest bitrate and in the latter case

the only feasible solution is for all players to choose the lowest bitrate (350 Kbps). Finally, we see an interesting effect where the metrics are not monotone in the number of players. Specifically, the case of 12 and 20 players are much better than their nearby points. This is essentially an effect of the discreteness of the bitrate levels. For example, when 12 players share a 10Mbps bottleneck, each player is very likely to stay at 845Kbps and saturate the link. However, at 10 players or 14 players, the player will try lower or higher bitrate because there is no optimal saturation bitrate.

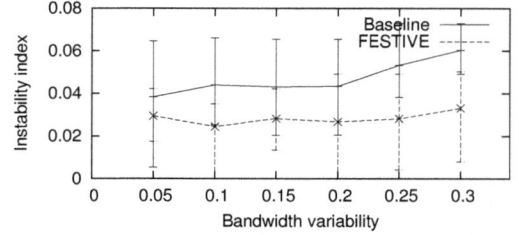

Figure 17: Instability vs. bandwidth variability when 10 players compete for a 10Mbps (expected) link

Bandwidth variability: We focus on the 10 player scenario with an *expected* bottleneck bandwidth of 10 Mbps. All players arrive within the first 30 seconds and we report the results from 15 runs per parameter. This bottleneck bandwidth is an expected value, because we vary the bandwidth every 20 second by picking a value uniformly at random $[BW \times (1 - \epsilon), BW \times (1 + \epsilon)]$. Figure 17 plots the performance of baseline and FESTIVE as a function of this parameter ϵ. We see that FESTIVE is more robust to the bandwidth variability (from $\epsilon = 0.05$ to $\epsilon = 0.3$) and in fact the improvement with FESTIVE increases with higher variability.

	Unfairness		Instability		Inefficiency	
g	Base.	FESTIVE	Base.	FESTIVE	Base.	FESTIVE
1.2	0.128	0.071	0.052	0.039	0.111	0.126
1.4	0.154	0.061	0.049	0.005	0.125	0.095
1.6	0.172	0.076	0.002	0.0	0.104	0.117
1.8	0.184	0.051	0.040	0.0	0.133	0.121

Table 3: Performance metrics vs. bitrate gaps when 10 players compete a bottleneck of 10Mbps

Available bitrates: Last, we test robustness to the set of available bitrate levels. We create a set of 10 available bitrate levels by $\{b_i = g^i \cdot 350Kbps\}_{i=0,...9}$, where g controls the gap between the bitrates, i.e., how discrete the bitrate levels are. A value of g close to 1 means that the gaps between consecutive levels are small and vice versa for larger g. Table 3 compares the performance of baseline and FESTIVE under g. FESTIVE consistently outperforms the baseline. The baseline becomes more unfair as g increases while FESTIVE works robust against higher g.

6.5 Summary of main results

In summary, our evaluation shows

- FESTIVE outperforms existing solutions in terms of fairness by $\geq 40\%$, stability by $\geq 50\%$, and efficiency by $\geq 10\%$.
- Each component of FESTIVE works as predicted by our analysis and is necessary as they complement each other.
- FESTIVE is robust against various number of players, bandwidth variability, and different available bitrate set.

7. DISCUSSION

We discuss three outstanding issues w.r.t the design of adaptive video players.

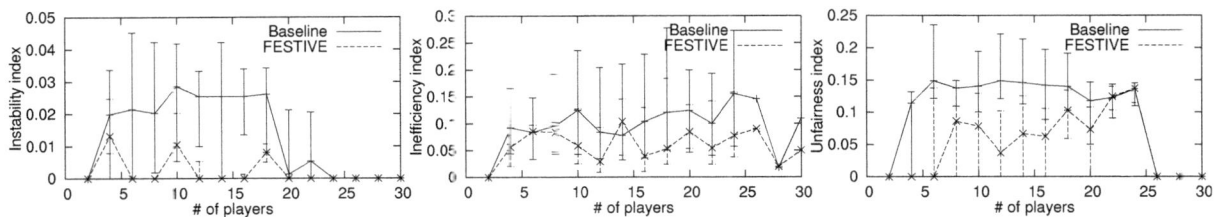

Figure 16: Performance of FESTIVE **and the baseline player as a function of the number of concurrent players. Here, we assume the players are sharing a 10 Mbps bottleneck link.**

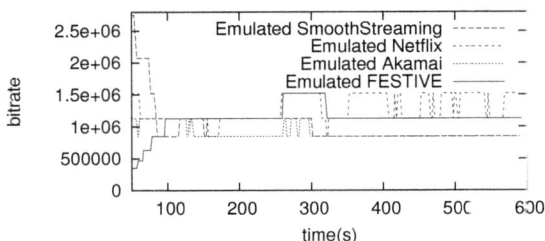

Figure 18: 8 emulated players including FESTIVE, **Smooth-Streaming, Netflix and Akamai HD with random start time share a bottleneck of 8Mbps, and 4 of them are presented.** FESTIVE **appears to be more stable and stays on an efficient bitrate.**

Heterogeneous algorithms: With the diversity of video content providers, we expect that there will be heterogeneity in player designs. So far, we have considered a homogeneous settings where all players run FESTIVE or existing commercial algorithms. One natural concern here is the interaction between different players. As a preliminary result, we consider a mixed workload with 8 emulated players, 2 players each for FESTIVE, SmoothStreaming, Netflix and Akamai HD, sharing a 8Mbps bottleneck link. For a fair comparison, we use emulated players and let them use the same set of bitrates found on respective demo sites. Each player arrives at random in the first 20 seconds. We pick one player instance for each algorithm and show the time series of bitrate in Figure 18. We see that FESTIVE is more stable than the other players, and spends most of the time at an efficient bitrate (1130kbps). There are many other questions with heterogeneous players; e.g., Are there specific cases of unfairness or starvation when a particular combination of players compete? Can we incentivize players to be "good citizens" and avoid being greedy? Is there an analog to TCP-friendliness? Studying the interaction between multiple heterogeneous players is an interesting and rich direction of future work.

Interaction with non-video traffic: Another natural question is how video adaptation logic interacts with non-video traffic (e.g., short Web transfers) [32]. Because FESTIVE retains the single-connection HTTP-based interface, it retains TCP-level friendliness *per chunk*. We use an example scenario of Figure 19 to confirm the intuition. Here, 3 FESTIVE players share a bottleneck with available bandwidth of 3Mbps, and one short TCP session joins at the 30th second and two short TCP sessions join at the 150th second. The gray line gives the bitrate selected by one FESTIVE instance. The figure shows that when TCP sessions join, FESTIVE will still achieve a fair share of the bandwidth when downloading a chunk; FESTIVE trades efficiency for stability, so bitrate almost does not vary with the interference of short TCP sessions. At the same time, the TCP sessions are able to get a throughput that is not too much less than the fair share. This is only a preliminary result and we need to more systematically explore these effects.

Wide-area effects: Another interesting direction of future work is to see if and how the efficiency, fairness, and stability issues man-

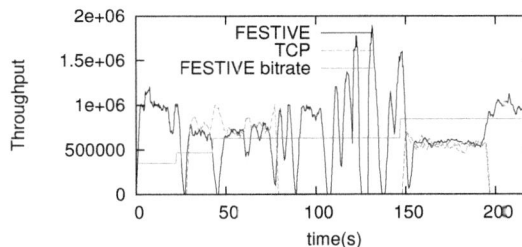

Figure 19: FESTIVE **vs. short TCP sessions: short TCP sessions do not impact** FESTIVE **and vice versa.**

ifest in the wide area. For instance, wide area effects imply more background traffic, less synchronization but many more players, multiple bottlenecks, interaction with router buffer sizing, among a host of other factors.

8. RELATED WORK

Measurements of commercial players: Early studies focused on the bitrate switching behavior of a single player in response to bandwidth variation (e.g., [15, 19, 40, 44]). More recent work analyzes fairness, efficiency, and stability when two players share a bottleneck link [14, 27]. These have identified the periodic behavior as a potential problem similar to Section 3. Recent work has also identified some of the biased feedback loop effects we observe [28]. We confirm these problems on a broader set of commercial players and extend these beyond the two-player setting. More importantly, we provide a detailed understanding of the causes and present a concrete design to address these shortcomings.

Quality metrics: A key aspect in video delivery is the need to optimize user-perceived quality of experience. There is evidence that users are sensitive to frequent switches (e.g., [18]), sudden changes in bitrate (e.g., [39]), and buffering (e.g., [21]). The design of a good QoE metric (e.g., [47] [16]) is still an active area of research. As our understanding of video QoE matures, we can extend FESTIVE to be QoE-aware.

Player optimizations: The use of multiple connections or multipath solutions can improve throughput and reduce the bandwidth variability (e.g., [25, 26, 31, 33]). However, these require changes to the application stack and/or server-side support. Furthermore, they may not be friendly to background traffic. In contrast, FESTIVE retains the same single TCP connection interface and requires no modifications to the server infrastructure or the end-host stack. Other approaches use better bandwidth prediction and stability techniques (e.g., [34, 38, 40]). These proposals are largely complementary to the design of FESTIVE.

Server and network-level solutions: This includes the use of server-side bitrate switching (e.g., [32]), TCP changes to avoid bursts (e.g., [24]), and in-network bandwidth management and caching (e.g., [27, 40, 45]). Our focus is on client-side mechanisms without requiring changes to the network or servers. While these approaches will further improve the performance, we believe that a client-side solution is fundamentally necessary for two reasons. First, the client is in the best position to detect and respond to dynamics. Second, recent work suggests the need for cross-CDN optimizations that implies the need for keeping minimal state in the network or servers [35, 36].

Video Coding: Layered or multiple description coding offers more graceful degradation of video quality (e.g., [17]). However, they impose higher overhead on content providers and the delivery infrastructure and thus we do not consider this class of solutions.

9. CONCLUSIONS

With the growth of video traffic, we are revisiting classical networking problems w.r.t resource sharing and adaptation. These problems have a rich literature with solutions at the network (e.g., [20]), transport (e.g., [29]), and application layers (e.g., [17, 37]). However, there are several factors that make the problem unique and challenging in today's HTTP-based video delivery: the granularity of the control decisions, the timescales of adaptation, the nature of feedback from the network, and the interactions with other (indepedent) control loops in lower layers of the networking stack.

In this work, we have taken a pragmatic stance to work within the constraints that have spurred the growth of video traffic—using HTTP, no modifications to end-host stacks, and imposing no modification to the network and CDN server infrastructure. Within this context, we provide a principled understanding of problems that lead to inefficiency, unfairness, and instability when multiple players compete for a bottleneck link. Building on these insights, we provide guidelines on designing better scheduling and bitrate selection techniques to overcome these problems.

There are several open questions with respect to co-existence of video and non-video traffic, competition among heterogeneous players (e.g., FESTIVE vs. legacy players?), the interaction with management optimizations in other aspects of the video delivery system [36], and exploring "clean-slate" solutions that can redesign network and transport layers to support video traffic [30]. We hope that our work acts as a fillip to address these broad spectrum of issues as new standards for video transport emerge [13].

10. ACKNOWLEDGEMENTS

We are grateful to our shepherd Rittwik Jana and anonymous reviewers for their feedback. This research was supported in part by the National Science Foundation under awards CNS-1040757, CNS-1040800, and CNS-1040801.

11. REFERENCES

[1] Adobe http dynamic streaming.
www.adobe.com/products/hds-dynamic-streaming.html.

[2] Adobe osmf player. http://www.osmf.org.

[3] Akamai hd adaptive streaming.
http://wwwns.akamai.com/hdnetwork/demo/index.html.

[4] Apple quicktime. www.apple.com/quicktime/download/.

[5] Cisco forecast. http://goo.gl/hHzW4.

[6] Crystal-clear hd with adobe http dynamic streaming. http://zeridemo-f.akamaihd.net/content/adobe/demo/1080p.f4m.

[7] Harmonic mean.
http://en.wikipedia.org/wiki/Harmonic_mean.

[8] Mail service costs Netflix 20 times more than streaming.
http://goo.gl/msuYK.

[9] Osmf 2.0 release code. http://sourceforge.net/projects/osmf.adobe/files/latest/download.

[10] Real-time messaging protocol. www.adobe.com/devnet/rtmp.html.

[11] Smoothstreaming experience.
http://www.iis.net/media/experiencesmoothstreaming.

[12] Smoothstreaming protocol.
http://go.microsoft.com/?linkid=9682896.

[13] I. Sodagar. The MPEG-DASH Standard for Multimedia Streaming Over the Internet. *IEEE Multimedia*, 2011.

[14] S. Akhshabi, L. Anantakrishnan, C. Dovrolis, and A. C. Begen. What Happens when HTTP Adaptive Streaming Players Compete for Bandwidth? In *Proc. NOSSDAV*, 2012.

[15] S. Akhshabi, A. Begen, and C. Dovrolis. An Experimental Evaluation of Rate Adaptation Algorithms in Adaptive Streaming over HTTP. In *Proc. MMSys*, 2011.

[16] A. Balachandran, V. Sekar, A. Akella, S. Stoica, and H. Zhang. A quest for an internet video quality-of-experience metric. 2012.

[17] J. Byers, M. Luby, and M. Mitzenmacher. A digital fountain approach to asynchronous reliable multicast. *IEEE JSAC*, Oct. 2002.

[18] N. Cranley, P. Perry, and L. Murphy. User perception of adapting video quality. *International Journal of Human-Computer Studies*, 2006.

[19] L. De Cicco and S. Mascolo. An experimental investigation of the akamai adaptive video streaming. *HCI in Work and Learning, Life and Leisure*.

[20] A. Demers, S. Keshav, and S. Shenker. Analysis and Simulation of a Fair Queueing Algorithm. In *Proc. SIGCOMM*, 1989.

[21] F. Dobrian, V. Sekar, A. Awan, I. Stoica, D. A. Joseph, A. Ganjam, J. Zhan, and H. Zhang. Understanding the impact of video quality on user engagement. In *Proc. SIGCOMM*, 2011.

[22] J. Esteban, S. Benno, A. Beck, Y. Guo, V. Hilt, and I. Rimac. Interactions Between HTTP Adaptive Streaming and TCP. In *Proc. NOSSDAV*, 2012.

[23] A. Finamore, M. Mellia, M. Munafo, R. Torres, and S. G. Rao. Youtube everywhere: Impact of device and infrastructure synergies on user experience. In *Proc. IMC*, 2011.

[24] M. Ghobadi, Y. Cheng, A. Jain, and M. Mathis. Trickle: Rate Limiting YouTube Video Streaming. In *Proc. USENIX ATC*, 2012.

[25] S. Gouache, G. Bichot, A. Bsila, and C. Howson. Distributed and Adaptive HTTP Streaming. In *Proc. ICME*, 2011.

[26] D. Havey, R. Chertov, and K. Almeroth. Receiver driven rate adaptation for wireless multimedia applications. In *Proc. MMSys*, 2012.

[27] R. Houdaille and S. Gouache. Shaping http adaptive streams for a better user experience. In *Proc. MMSys*, 2012.

[28] T.-Y. Huang, N. Handigol, B. Heller, N. McKeown, and R. Johari. Confused, Timid, and Unstable: Picking a Video Streaming Rate is Hard. In *Proc. IMC*, 2012.

[29] V. Jacobson. Congestion avoidance and control. In *ACM SIGCOMM Computer Communication Review*, volume 18, pages 314–329. ACM, 1988.

[30] V. Jacobson, D. K. Smetters, J. D. Thornton, M. F. Plass, N. H. Briggs, and R. L. Braynard. Networking Named Content. In *Proc. CoNext*, 2009.

[31] R. Kuschnig, I. Kofler, and H. Hellwagner. Evaluation of http-based request-response streams for internet video streaming. *Multimedia Systems*, pages 245–256, 2011.

[32] L. De Cicco, S. Mascolo, and V. Palmisano. Feedback Control for Adaptive Live Video Streaming. In *Proc. of ACM Multimedia Systems Conference*, 2011.

[33] C. Liu, I. Bouazizi, and M. Gabbouj. Parallel Adaptive HTTP Media Streaming. In *Proc. ICCCN*, 2011.

[34] C. Liu, I. Bouazizi, and M. Gabbouj. Rate adaptation for adaptive http streaming. *Proc. ACM MMSys*, 2011.

[35] H. Liu, Y. Wang, Y. R. Yang, A. Tian, and H. Wang. Optimizing Cost and Performance for Content Multihoming. In *Proc. SIGCOMM*, 2012.

[36] X. Liu, F. Dobrian, H. Milner, J. Jiang, V. Sekar, I. Stoica, and H. Zhang. A Case for a Coordinated Internet Video Control Plane. In *SIGCOMM*, 2012.

[37] S. McCanne, M. Vetterli, and V. Jacobson. Low-complexity video coding for receiver-driven layered multicast. *IEEE JSAC*, Aug. 1997.

[38] K. Miller, E. Quacchio, G. Gennari, and A. Wolisz. Adaptation Algorithm for Adaptive Streaming over HTTP. In *Proc. Packet Video Workshop*, 2012.

[39] R. K. P. Mok, E. W. W. Chan, X. Luo, and R. K. C. Chang. Inferring the QoE of HTTP Video Streaming from User-Viewing Activities . In *SIGCOMM W-MUST*, 2011.

[40] R. K. P. Mok, X. Luo, E. W. W. Chan, and R. K. C. Chang. QDASH: A QoE-aware DASH system. In *Proc. MMSys*, 2012.

[41] R. Pantos. Http live streaming. 2011.

[42] L. Popa, A. Ghodsi, and I. Stoica. HTTP as the narrow waist of the future internet. In *Proc. HotNets*, 2010.

[43] R. Jain, D. Chiu, and W. Hawe. A quantitative measure of fairness and discrimination for resource allocation in shared computer system. Technical Report, DEC, 1984.

[44] A. Rao, Y.-S. Lim, C. Barakat, A. Legout, D. Towsley, and W. Dabbous. Network Characteristics of Video Streaming Traffic. In *Proc. CoNext*, 2011.

[45] R. Rejaie and J. Kangasharju. Mocha: A quality adaptive multimedia proxy cache for internet streaming. In *Proc. NOSSDAV*, 2001.

[46] L. Rizzo. Dummynet: a simple approach to the evaluation of network protocols. *ACM SIGCOMM Computer Communication Review*, 27(1):31–41, 1997.

[47] H. H. Song, Z. Ge, A. Mahimkar, J. Wang, J. Yates, Y. Zhang, A. Basso, and M. Chen. Q-score: Proactive Service Quality Assessment in a Large IPTV System. In *Proc. IMC*, 2011.

Towards Agile and Smooth Video Adaptation
in Dynamic HTTP Streaming

Guibin Tian and Yong Liu
Department of Electrical and Computer Engineering
Polytechnic Institute of New York University
Brooklyn, NY, USA 11201
gtian01@students.poly.edu, yongliu@poly.edu

ABSTRACT

Dynamic Adaptive Streaming over HTTP (DASH) is widely deployed on the Internet for live and on-demand video streaming services. Video adaptation algorithms in existing DASH systems are either too sluggish to respond to congestion level shifts or too sensitive to short-term network bandwidth variations. Both degrade user video experience. In this paper, we formally study the responsiveness and smoothness trade-off in DASH through analysis and experiments. We show that client-side buffered video time is a good feedback signal to guide video adaptation. We then propose novel video rate control algorithms that balance the needs for video rate smoothness and high bandwidth utilization. We show that a small video rate margin can lead to much improved smoothness in video rate and buffer size. The proposed DASH designs are also extended to work with multiple CDN servers. We develop a fully-functional DASH system and evaluate its performance through extensive experiments on a network testbed and the Internet. We demonstrate that our DASH designs are highly efficient and robust in realistic network environment.

Categories and Subject Descriptors

H.5.1 [**Information Systems**]: Multimedia Information Systems—*Video(e.g., tape, disk, DVI)*

General Terms

Design

Keywords

Adaptation, DASH, Emulab, Multiple CDN, SVR

1. INTRODUCTION

Video traffic dominates the Internet. The recent trend in online video streaming is *Dynamic Adaptive Streaming over HTTP* (DASH) that provides uninterrupted video streaming service to users with dynamic network conditions and heterogeneous devices. Notably, Netflix's online video streaming service is implemented using DASH [1, 2]. In DASH, a video content is encoded into multiple versions at different rates. Each encoded video is further fragmented into small video chunks, each of which normally contains seconds or tens of seconds worth of video. Video chunks can be served to clients using standard HTTP servers in either live or on-demand fashion. Upon network condition changes, a client can dynamically switch video version for the chunks to be downloaded.

Different from the traditional video streaming algorithms, DASH does not directly control the video transmission rate. Transmission rate of a chunk is totally controlled by the TCP protocol, which reacts to network congestion along the server-client path. Intuitively, if TCP throughput is high, DASH should choose a high video rate to give user better video quality; if TCP throughput is low, DASH should switch to a low video rate to avoid playback freezes. To maximally utilize throughput achieved by TCP and avoid video freezes, DASH video adaptation should be *responsive* to network congestion level shifts. On the other hand, TCP congestion control incurs inherent rate fluctuations; and cross-traffic rate has both long-term and short-term variations. Adapting video rate to short-term TCP throughput fluctuations will significantly degrade user experience. It is therefore desirable to adapt video rate *smoothly*.

In this paper, we propose client-side video adaptation algorithms to strike the balance between the responsiveness and smoothness in DASH. Our algorithms use client-side *buffered video time* as feedback signal. We show that there is a fundamental conflict between buffer size smoothness and video rate smoothness, due to the inherent TCP throughput variations. We propose novel video rate adaptation algorithms that smoothly increase video rate as the available network bandwidth increases, and promptly reduce video rate in response to sudden congestion level shift-ups. We further show that imposing a buffer cap and reserving a small video rate margin can simultaneously decrease buffer size oscillations and video rate fluctuations. Adopting a machine-learning based TCP throughput prediction algorithm, we also extend our DASH designs to work with multiple CDN servers. Our contribution is four-fold.

1. We formally study the responsiveness and smoothness trade-off in DASH through analysis and experiments. We show that buffered video time is a good reference signal to guide video rate adaptation.

2. We propose novel rate adaptation algorithms that balance the needs for video rate smoothness and bandwidth utilization. We show that a small video rate margin can lead to much improved smoothness in video rate and buffer size.

3. We are the first to develop DASH designs that allow a client to work with multiple CDN servers. We show that machine-learning based TCP throughput estimation algorithms can ef-

fectively guide DASH server switching and achieve the multiplexing gain.

4. We implement the proposed algorithms into a fully-functional DASH system, which is evaluated through extensive experiments on network testbed and the Internet. We demonstrate that our DASH designs are highly efficient and robust in realistic network environment.

The rest of the paper is organized as follows. Section 2 describes the related work. DASH designs for single server are developed in Section 3. Extensions to the multiple-server case are presented in Section 4. In Section 5, we report the experimental results for single-server case and multi-server case on both Emulab testbed and the Internet. We conclude the paper with summary and future work in Section 6.

2. RELATED WORK

Although DASH is a relatively new application, due to its popularity, it has generated lots of research interests recently. In [3], Watson systematically introduced the DASH framework of Netflix, which is the largest DASH stream provider in the world. In [4], authors compared rate adaptation of three popular DASH clients: Netflix client, Microsoft Smooth Streaming [5], and Adobe OSM-F [6]. They concluded that none of them is good enough. They are either too aggressive or too conservative. Some clients even just jump between the highest video rate and the lowest video rate. Also, all of them have relatively long response time under network congestion level shift. It was shown in [7] that dramatic video rate changes lead to inferior user quality-of-experience. They further proposed to gradually change video rate based on available bandwidth measurement. In [8], authors proposed a feedback control mechanism to control the sending buffer size on the server side. Our video adaptation is driven by buffered video time on the client-side, which has direct implication on client video playback. Our scheme does not require any change on the server side. There are also papers on DASH in wireless and mobile networks. In [9], several adaptive media players on the market were tested to see how they perform in challenging streaming scenarios in a mobile 3G network. In [10], Mueller et al implemented a DASH system and proved it works in vehicular network environments. In [11], a DASH-like algorithm was proposed for a server to regulate the video uploading from a mobile client. In DASH, it is important to predict TCP throughput and quickly detect congestion level shifts. One way is to monitor the path using network bandwidth measurement tools like pathload [12]. But measuring available bandwidth itself injects probing traffic into the path, and it may take long time to converge to an acceptable result. And the accuracy of such tools is not guaranteed. And in [13] and [14], authors presented history-based and machine-learning-based TCP throughput prediction. In DASH, video chunks are continuously transmitted from the server to the client. In this scenario, TCP throughput data can be collected in realtime. In our experiments, we found that even simple history-based TCP throughput prediction can achieve higher accuracy than those reported in [13] and [14]. For multi-server DASH, a client needs to continuously evaluate the throughput of a DASH server before switching to it. We implement the light-weight machine learning approach proposed in [14] for the TCP throughput predict of candidate DASH servers.

3. DASH WITH SINGLE SERVER

We start with DASH system where a client only downloads video chunks from a single server. We will extend our designs to the multiple server case in Section 4.

3.1 Buffered Video Time

To sustain continuous playback, a video streaming client normally maintains a video buffer to absorb temporary mismatch between video download rate and video playback rate. In conventional single-version video streaming, video buffer is measured by the size of buffered video, which can be easily mapped into buffered video playback time when divided by the average video playback rate. In DASH, different video versions have different video playback rates. Since a video buffer contains chunks from different versions, there is no longer direct mapping between buffered video size and buffered video time. To deal with multiple video versions, we use buffered video time to directly measure the length of video playback buffer.

Buffered video time process, denoted by $q(t)$, can be modeled as a single-server queue with constant service rate of 1, i.e., with continuous playback, in each unit of time, a piece of video with unit playback time is played and dequeued from the buffer. The enqueue process is driven by the video download rate and the downloaded video version. Specifically, for a video content, there are L different versions, with different playback rates $V_1 < V_2 < \cdots < V_L$. All versions of the video are partitioned into chunks, each of which has the same playback time of Δ. A video chunk of version i has a size of $V_i \Delta$. A client downloads video chunks sequentially, and for each chunk, he can choose one out of the L versions. Without loss of generality, a client starts to download chunk k from version i at time instant $t_k^{(s)}$. Then the video rate requested by the client for the k-th chunk is $v(k) = V_i$. Let $t_k^{(e)}$ be the time instant when chunk k is downloaded completely. In a "greedy" download mode, a client downloads chunk k right after chunk $k-1$ is completely downloaded, in other words, $t_{k-1}^{(e)} = t_k^{(s)}$. For the buffered video time evolution, we have:

$$q(t_k^{(e)}) = \Delta + \max\left(q(t_k^{(s)}) - (t_k^{(e)} - t_k^{(s)}), 0\right), \quad (1)$$

where the first term is the added video time upon the completion of the downloading of chunk k, the second term reflects the fact that the buffered video time is consumed linearly at rate 1 during the downloading of chunk k.

Using fluid approximation, we evenly distribute the added video time of Δ over the download interval $(t_k^{(s)}, t_k^{(e)}]$, then

$$\frac{dq(t)}{dt} = \frac{\Delta}{t_k^{(e)} - t_k^{(s)}} - \mathbf{1}(q(t) > 0), \quad (2)$$

$$= \frac{v(k)\Delta}{v(k)(t_k^{(e)} - t_k^{(s)})} - \mathbf{1}(q(t) > 0), \quad (3)$$

$$= \frac{\bar{T}(k)}{v(k)} - \mathbf{1}(q(t) > 0), \quad t \in (t_k^{(s)}, t_k^{(e)}], \quad (4)$$

where $\mathbf{1}(\cdot)$ is the indicator function, and $\bar{T}(k)$ is the average TCP throughput when downloading chunk k. The buffered video time remains constant when the requested video rate $v(k)$ exactly matches $\bar{T}(k)$ which is not practical. In practice, $v(k)$ can only assume one of the L predefined video rates. There will be unavoidable rate mismatches, thus buffer fluctuations.

3.2 Control Buffer Oscillations

From (4), if the requested video rate is higher than the actual TCP throughput, the buffered video time decreases, and video playback freezes whenever $q(t)$ goes down to zero; if the requested video rate is lower than the actual TCP throughput, the buffered video time ramps up, it suggests that user gets stuck at low video rate even though his connection supports higher rate. A responsive video

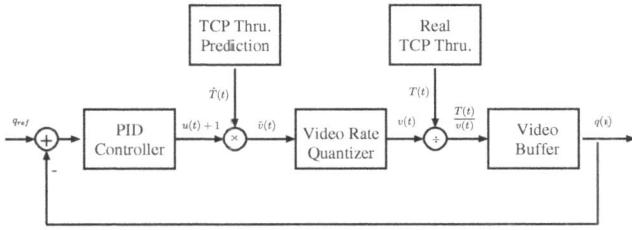

Figure 1: PID control oriented adaptive streaming

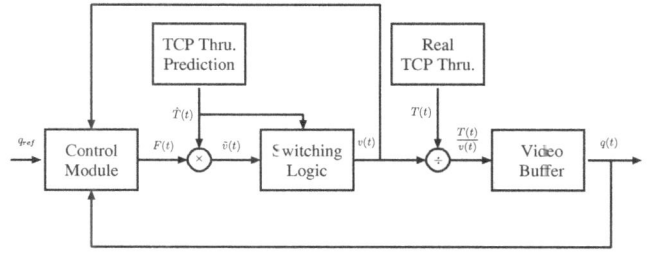

Figure 2: Buffer size oriented adaptive streaming

adaptation scheme should control video rate to closely track TCP throughput so that $q(t)$ stays within a bounded region. As a result, no video freeze happens, and the requested video rate matches the TCP throughput in long-run.

To maintain a stable queue length, one can employ a simple rate adaptation scheme:

$$v(k) = \underset{\{V_i, 1 \leq i \leq L\}}{\mathbf{argmin}} |V_i - \hat{T}(k)|,$$

where $\hat{T}(k)$ is some estimate of TCP throughput before downloading chunk k. In other words, a client always downloads the version with a rate "closest" to the estimated TCP throughput. However, it is well-known that it is hard to accurately estimate TCP throughput. Such an open-loop design is not robust against TCP throughput estimation errors. To address this problem, we investigate a closed-loop feedback control design for video rate adaptation.

Instead of directly matching the requested video rate $v(k)$ with TCP throughput estimate, we use the evolution of buffered video time $q(t)$ as feedback signal to adjust $v(k)$. One straightforward way is to set up a reference queue length q_{ref}, i.e. the target video buffer time, and build a PID controller to regulate the requested video rate.

PID is the most commonly used feedback controller in industrial control systems. A PID controller calculates an "error" value as the difference between a measured process variable and a desired set point. The controller attempts to minimize the error by adjusting the process control inputs. The PID controller calculation (algorithm) involves three separate parameters: the proportional factor, the integral factor and derivative factor, denoted by K_P, K_I, and K_D respectively. Heuristically, these values can be interpreted in terms of time: K_P depends on the present error, K_I on the accumulation of past errors, and K_D is a prediction of future errors, based on current rate of change. The weighted sum of these three actions is used to adjust the process via the output of the controller. In practice, a PID controller doesn't have to set all the three parameters. There are very common usage of variations of PID controller. In our research, because of inherent rate fluctuations of TCP transmission, we use PI controller instead of PID controller because the derivative factor may amplify the impact of TCP fluctuations.

Figure 1 illustrates the diagram of the control system. We adopt a Proportional-Integral (PI) controller, with control output driven by the deviation of buffered video time:

$$u(t) = K_p(q(t) - q_{ref}) + K_I \int_0^t (q(\tau) - q_{ref})d\tau,$$

where K_p and K_I are the P and I control coefficients respectively. The target video rate for chunk k is

$$\tilde{v}(k) = (u(t_k^{(s)}) + 1)\hat{T}(t_k^{(s)}),$$

where $\hat{T}(t_k^{(s)})$ is the TCP throughput estimate right before down-

loading chunk k. Taking into account the finite discrete video rates, the actual requested video rate for chunk k is the highest video rate lower than $\tilde{v}(k)$,

$$v(k) = Q(\tilde{v}(k)) \triangleq \max_{\{V_i : V_i \leq \tilde{v}(k)\}} V_i \qquad (5)$$

where $Q(\cdot)$ is the quantization function. When $q(t)$ oscillates around q_{ref} with small amplitude, the control signal $u(t)$ is small, the requested video rate is set close to the predicted TCP throughput. The throughput estimation error and video rate quantization error will be absorbed by the video buffer and closed-loop control.

3.3 Control Video Rate Fluctuations

To accurately control the buffer size, one has to constantly adapt the requested video rate to realtime TCP throughput. If the achieved TCP throughput is larger than the requested video rate, the buffer size will increase and the feedback control module will increase the video rate, which, according to (4), will slow down buffer increase, and vice versa. Since TCP throughput is by-nature time varying, the requested video rate will also incur constant fluctuations.

From control system point of view, there is a fundamental conflict between maintaining stable video rate and stable buffer size, due to the unavoidable network bandwidth variations. From end user point of view, video rate fluctuations are much more perceivable than buffer size oscillations. Recent study has shown that switching back-and-forth between different video versions will significantly degrade user video experience [7]. Meanwhile, buffer size variations don't have direct impact on video streaming quality as long as the video buffer does not deplete. In this section, we revisit our video rate adaptation design with the following goals:

1. avoid video rate fluctuations triggered by short-term bandwidth variations and TCP throughput estimation errors;

2. increase video rate smoothly when the available network bandwidth is consistently higher than the current video rate;

3. quickly decrease video rate upon the congestion level shift-ups to avoid video playback freezes.

To simultaneously achieve the three goals, one has to strike the right balance between the responsiveness and smoothness of video rate adaptation upon network bandwidth increases and decreases. Classical feedback control, such as those presented in Figure 1, is no longer sufficient. We develop a new rate control system as shown in Figure 2.

3.3.1 Control Module

The control module still uses buffered video time $q(t)$ as feedback signal, since it directly reflects the mismatch between the video rate and realtime TCP throughput. Instead of controlling $q(t)$ to a target level q_{ref}, we only use $q(t)$ to guide the video rate selection. To determine video rate $v(k)$ for chunk k, we need TCP

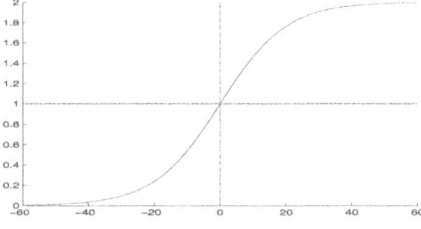

Figure 3: Adjustment Function for Buffer Size Deviation

throughput prediction $\hat{T}(k)$ and an adjustment factor $F(k)$, which is a function of the target buffer size, current buffer size, previous buffer size, and the current video rate:

$$F(k) = F_q(k) * F_t(k) * F_v(k), \qquad (6)$$

with

$$F_q(k) = 2 * \frac{e^{p*(q(t_k^{(s)})-q_{ref})}}{1 + e^{p*(q(t_k^{(s)})-q_{ref})}} \qquad (7)$$

$$F_t(k) = \frac{\Delta}{\Delta - (q(t_k^{(s)}) - q(t_{k-1}^{(s)}))} \qquad (8)$$

$$F_v(k) = \frac{V_L}{v(k-1) + W} + \frac{W}{V_L + W} \qquad (9)$$

In (6), the adjustment factor $F(k)$ is a product of three sub-factors: buffer size adjustment $F_q(k)$, buffer trend adjustment $F_t(k)$, and video chunk size adjustment $F_v(k)$, which we explain one-by-one in the following.

Buffer Size Adjustment $F_q(k)$ is an increasing function of buffer size deviation $q(t_k^{(s)}) - q_{ref}$ from the target buffer size in (7). Larger buffer size suggests one should be more aggressive in choosing higher video rate. As illustrated in Figure 3, when the buffer size matches the target q_{ref}, the adjustment is neutral (with value 1); when the deviation is small, the adjustment is approximately $1 + p(q(t_k^{(s)}) - q_{ref})$, mimicking a simple P-controller, with stationary output of 1 and $K_p = p$; when the deviation is large, the adjustment factor increases/decreases smoothly with upper bound of 2 and lower bound of 0. This is to avoid F_q overpowers the other two factors.

Buffer Trend Adjustment $F_t(k)$ is an increasing function of buffer size growth $q(t_k^{(s)}) - q(t_{k-1}^{(s)})$ since the downloading of the previous video chunk, as calculated in (8), where Δ is the video time contained in one chunk. If there is no buffer size growth, the adjustment is neutral (with value 1). If the buffer size grows fast, it suggests that the previous video rate is too conservative, one should increase the video rate; if the buffer size decreases fast, it suggests that the previous video rate is too aggressive, one should decrease the video rate. From equations (1) to (4), in a greedy download mode with $t_{k-1}^{(e)} = t_k^{(s)}$, it can be shown that with fluid approximation:

$$F_t(k) = \frac{\bar{T}(k-1)}{v(k-1)} = \frac{dq(t)}{dt} + \mathbf{1}(q(t) > 0). \qquad (10)$$

In other words, $F_t(k)$ is the ratio between the actual download throughput and video rate for chunk $k-1$. F_t is essentially a *Derivative D-controller*, that responds fast to increase/decrease trend in buffered video time.

Video Chunk Size Adjustment $F_v(k)$ is a decreasing function of the previous video rate $v(k-1)$, calculated in (9), where W

is a constant. If $v(k-1) = V_L$, the adjustment is neutral; if $v(k-1) < V_L$, $F_v(k) > 1$. This is because HTTP adaptive streaming uses TCP transmission. If a chunk is small, TCP has to go through slow-start process to open up its congestion window, leading to low TCP throughput even if the available bandwidth is much higher. This compensation enables fast rate increase when a DASH session starts or resumes from a low video rate. If the client connects to the server with persistent HTTP connection, there will be no such problem because only the first chunk will experience slow start. In such scenario, we can just set this adjustment factor to constant 1. Notice that, each adjustment factor assumes value of 1 when the system is at the equilibrium point, i.e., $q(t_k^{(s)}) = q_{ref}$, $q(t_k^{(s)}) = q(t_{k-1}^{(s)})$, $v(k-1) = V_L$. When the system operates within the neighborhood of the equilibrium point, each adjustment factor takes small positive or negative deviation from one. The total deviation of their product from one is approximately the summation of the individual deviations, similar to the PI controller in the previous section. Different from the PI controller, the product deviation changes smoothly within a bounded region when the system operates away from the equilibrium point.

3.3.2 Rate Switching Logic

After we get the final adjustment factor $F(k)$, similar to the buffer control case in Section 3.2, we can multiply it with the TCP throughput estimate and set a target video rate $\tilde{v}(k) = F(k)\hat{T}(t_k^{(s)})$, then use the quantization function $Q(\cdot)$ in (5) to convert it to a discrete video rate $v(k)$. If we adjust the video rate directly according to the quantized target video rate, there will be again frequent fluctuations. To resolve this, a rate switching logic module is added after the quantizer as shown in Figure 2. It controls video rate switch according to algorithm 1.

Algorithm 1 Smooth Video Adaptation Algorithm.

1: $\tilde{v}(k) = F(k)\hat{T}(t_k^{(s)})$;
2: **if** $q(t_k^{(s)}) < \frac{q_{ref}}{2}$ **then**
3: $\quad v(k) = Q(\bar{T}(k-1))$;
4: $\quad$ return;
5: **else if** $\tilde{v}(k) > v(k-1)$ **then**
6: $\quad Counter + +$
7: $\quad$ **if** $Counter > m$ **then**
8: $\quad\quad v(k) = Q(\hat{T}(t_k^{(s)}))$;
9: $\quad\quad Counter = 0$;
10: $\quad\quad$ return
11: $\quad$ **end if**
12: **else if** $\tilde{v}(k) < v(k-1)$ **then**
13: $\quad Counter = 0$
14: **end if**
15: $v(k) = v(k-1)$; return;

If the buffer size drops below half of the target size $\frac{q_{ref}}{2}$, it indicates that the current video rate is higher than the TCP throughput, and there is a danger of buffer depletion and playback freeze. We then immediately reduce the video rate to $v(k) = Q(\bar{T}(k-1))$, where $\bar{T}(k-1)$ is the actual TCP throughput of the previous chunk transmission. Due to the quantization, $v(k) < \bar{T}(k-1)$, if TCP throughput in the current round is close to the previous round, the buffer size is expected to increase until it goes back to above $\frac{q_{ref}}{2}$. If the buffer size is larger than $\frac{q_{ref}}{2}$, we consider it safe to keep the current rate or switch up to a higher rate. To avoid small time-scale fluctuations, video rate is switched up only if the target video rate $\tilde{v}(k)$ calculated by the controller is larger than the current rate

$v(k-1)$ for m consecutive chunks. Whenever a switch-up is triggered, the video rate is set to match the TCP throughput estimate $\hat{T}(t_k^{(s)})$. Before the switch-up counter reaches m, if the target video rate calculated for one chunk is smaller than the current video rate, the switch-up counter will be reset and start over.

The parameter m controls the trade-off between the responsiveness and smoothness of rate adaptation. Larger m will definitely make the adaptation smoother, but sluggish. If the video rate is at low levels, the user will have to watch that video rate for a long time even if there is enough bandwidth to switch up. To address this problem, we dynamically adjust m according to the trend of buffer growth. More specifically, for chunk k, we calculate a switch-up threshold as a decreasing function of the recent buffer growth: $m(k) = f_m(q(t_k^{(s)}) - q(t_{k-1}^{(s)}))$, and video rate is switched up if the switch-up counter reaches $(m(k) + m(k-1) + m(k-2))/3$. The intuition behind this design is that fast buffer growth suggests TCP throughput is persistently larger than the current video rate, one should not wait for too long to switch up. Similar to (10), it can be shown that if buffer is non-empty,

$$q(t_k^{(s)}) - q(t_{k-1}^{(s)}) = \Delta \left(1 - \frac{v(k-1)}{\hat{T}(k-1)} \right).$$

One example dynamic-m function we use in our experiments is a piece-wise constant function which we got from empirical study:

$$m(k) = \begin{cases} 1 & \text{if } q(t_k^{(s)}) - q(t_{k-1}^{(s)}) \in [0.4\Delta, \Delta); \\ 5 & \text{if } q(t_k^{(s)}) - q(t_{k-1}^{(s)}) \in [0.2\Delta, 0.4\Delta); \\ 15 & \text{if } q(t_k^{(s)}) - q(t_{k-1}^{(s)}) \in [0, 0.2\Delta); \\ 20 & \text{otherwise.} \end{cases} \quad (11)$$

3.4 Control Buffer Overflow

So far we assume a "greedy" client mode, where a client continuously sends out "GET" requests to fully load TCP and download video chunks at the highest rate possible. In practice, this may not be plausible for the following reasons: 1) A DASH server normally handles a large number of clients. If all clients send out "GET" requests too frequently, the server will soon be overwhelmed; 2) If the requested video rate is consistently lower than TCP throughput, the buffered video time quickly ramps up, leading to *buffer overflow*. In Video-on-Demand (VoD), it means that the client pre-fetches way ahead of the its current playback point, which is normally not allowed by a VoD server. In live video streaming, pre-fetching is simply not possible for content not yet generated. The buffered video time is upper-bounded by the user tolerable video playback lag, which is normally in the order of seconds; 3) Finally, fully stressing TCP and the network without any margin comes with the risk of playback freezes, especially when the client doesn't have large buffer size, like in the live streaming case.

To address these problems, we introduce a *milder* client download scheme. To avoid buffer overflow, we introduced a *buffer cap* q_{max}. Whenever the buffered video time goes over q_{max}, the client keeps idle for a certain timespan before sending out the request for the next chunk. Also, to mitigate the TCP and network stresses, we reserve a *video rate margin* of $0 \leq \rho_v < 1$. For any target video rate $\tilde{v}(k)$ calculated by the controllers in the previous sections, we only request a video rate of $v(k) = Q((1 - \rho_v)\tilde{v}(k))$. With the video rate margin, the buffered video time will probably increase. When $q(t)$ goes over q_{max}, the client simply inserts an idle time of $q(t) - q_{max}$ before sending out the next download request. As will be shown in our experiments, even a small video rate margin can simultaneously reduce the buffer size oscillations and video rate fluctuations a lot.

4. DASH WITH MULTIPLE SERVERS

While most DASH services employ multiple servers hosting the same set of video contents, each client is only assigned to one server [1]. It is obviously more advantageous if a DASH client is allowed to dynamically switch from one server to another, or even better, simultaneously download from multiple servers. Our video adaptation algorithms in Section 3 can be easily extended to the case where a client can download from multiple servers. We consider two cases. In the first case, given n servers, a client always connects to the server which can provide the highest video download rate. In the second case, a client simultaneously connects to s out of n servers, and downloads different chunks from different servers then combine them in the order of the video.

4.1 TCP Throughput Prediction

In single-server study, since we keep downloading video chunks from the same server, we can use simple history-based TCP throughput estimation algorithm [13] to predict the TCP throughput for downloading new chunks. With multiple servers, it is necessary for a client to estimate its TCP throughput to a server even if it has not downloaded any chunk from that server. We adopt a light-weight TCP throughput prediction algorithm proposed in [14]. The authors showed that TCP throughput is mainly determined by packet loss, delay and the size of the file to be downloaded. They propose to use the Support Vector Regress (SVR) algorithm [15] to train a TCP throughput model $\hat{T}(p_l, p_d, f_s)$ out of training data consisting of samples of packet loss rate $p_l^{(i)}$, packet delay $p_d^{(i)}$, file size $f_s^{(i)}$ and the corresponding actual TCP throughput $T^{(i)}$. To predict the current TCP throughput, one just need to plug in the current measured packet loss, delay, and the download file size. For our purpose, we download each chunk as a separate file. Chunks from different video versions have different file sizes. In our SVR TCP model, we use video rate V_i in place of file size f_s.

4.2 Dynamic Server Selection

In the first case, we allow a client to dynamically switch to the server from which it can obtain the highest TCP throughput. While a client downloads from its current DASH server, it constantly monitors its throughput to other candidate servers by using the SVR TCP throughput estimation model. To accommodate the SVR throughput estimation errors, which was reported around 20% in [14], the client switches to a new DASH server only if the estimated throughput to that server is at least 20% higher than the achieved throughput with the current DASH server.

To avoid wrong server switch triggered by SVR estimate errors, we use trial-based transition. When a client decides to switch to a new server, it establishes TCP connections with the new server, and also keeps the connections with the current server. It sends out "GET" requests to both servers. After a few chunk transmissions, the client closes the connections with the server with smaller throughput and uses the one with larger throughput as its current DASH server.

4.3 Concurrent Download

In the second case, a clients is allowed to simultaneously download chunks from s out of n servers. The client-side video buffer is fed by s TCP connections from the chosen servers. The video rate adaptation algorithms in Section 3 work in a similar way, by just replacing TCP throughput estimate from the single server with the aggregate TCP throughput estimate from s servers.

A simple client video chunk download strategy is to direct different chunk download requests to different servers, with the number of chunks assigned to a server proportional to its TCP throughput

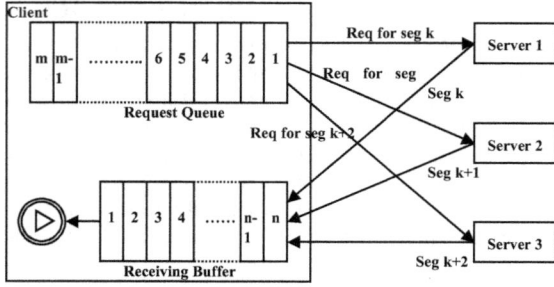

Figure 4: Self-adaptive Concurrent DASH Downloading.

estimate. But such a scheme is not robust against throughput estimation error. If the throughput to a server is overestimated, the server will be overloaded, and the chunks assigned to it cannot be downloaded in time, which will delay the overall video playback. To solve this problem, we introduce self-adaptive chunk assignment and timeout chunk retransmission.

Self-adaptive Chunk Assignment. We assume that all the DASH servers have the same copies of all the chunks of the same video. As illustrated in Figure 4, on the client side, all connections to chosen servers share a common chunk download request queue, which is sequentially injected with download requests for vide chunks at rates specified by the video adaptation algorithm. After a connection finishes downloading a chunk, it takes another chunk download request from the head of the download queue. This way, the distribution of chunks to each connection is automatically regulated by its TCP throughput, instead of the TCP throughput prediction. To avoid video buffer overflow, idle time is inserted to all connections.

Chunk Timeout Retransmission. Even with self-adaptive assignment, if the connection to a server suddenly incurs bandwidth deficiency, the chunk already assigned to that connection still cannot be downloaded in-time, which again will delay the video playback. To avoid this problem, we introduce timeout-based chunk retransmission mechanism. Based on the history-based throughput estimation and the chosen video rate, we can calculate the expected transmission time for each chunk on each connection. Every time a HTTP "GET" request for a chunk is sent to a server, one timer starts for the chunk. The timer will expire in twice of the expected chunk transmission time. If the chunk has not been completely downloaded before the timer expires, a download request for that chunk will be sent to another server.

4.4 Probabilistic Server Switching

If there are a large number of clients using the same DASH service, there is a possibility that many clients simultaneously detect and switch to the same lightly loaded server which will overload that server quickly, the client will then switch back. This will definitely causes oscillations in server selection to the whole system. To resolve this problem, probabilistic switching can be introduced into the system. In this solution, when a client detects that it should switch to a better server, it sorts all the servers that are better than its current server with their predicted throughput, and then switch to different servers with different probability. Assume there are n servers that are better than the current server, and T_i is the predicted throughput of the ith server, T_c is the real-time throughput of the current server, then the probability to switch to the ith server can be calculated as $T_i/(\sum_{k=1}^{n} T_k + T_c)$, also, the probability to stay at the current server is $T_c/(\sum_{k=1}^{n} T_k + T_c)$. This induces that a lighter loaded server has higher probability to be chosen and

probabilistic switching reduces the possibility of synchronization between clients.

In this paper, we didn't implement probabilistic switching in our system because we only focus on single client case. In multiple clients scenarios, this mechanism should be implemented to avoid system oscillations.

5. PERFORMANCE EVALUATION

We implemented our video rate adaptation algorithms into a fully-functional DASH system, and extensively evaluated it using controlled experiments on a network testbed, the Emulab [16], as well as real Internet experiments, with both wireline and wireless clients.

5.1 System Implementation

Our DASH system runs on linux/unix platforms. It consists of a vanilla Apache HTTP server and a customized HTTP client. All the proposed video rate adaptation algorithms are implemented on the client side using C++. For multi-server experiments, we also implemented the SVR-based TCP throughput estimation algorithm proposed in [14]. A light-weight network measurement thread runs on the server and the client to periodically collect packet loss and delay statistics for TCP throughput estimation. To train the SVR TCP throughput model, the client sends HTTP "GET" requests to a server to get video chunk files. Since TCP throughput is affected by file size, the training data need to be collected for different video rates. Since we use a large number of video rates in our experiments, that would make the training process too long and too intrusive to the network. To reduce training experiments, we design a mechanism to collect TCP throughput data for all the video rates in one single HTTP "GET" request. On the server side, the file used for training is larger than the size of a video chunk at the highest video rate. After the client sends out a "GET" request to download the training file, it records the time lags when the total number of the received data bytes reaches the video chunk sizes at all possible video rates. TCP throughput to download a chunk at a video rate is calculated as the video chunk size divided by the recorded time lag for that rate. This way we can get the training data for all the video rates in one transmission. As mentioned above, we use non-persistent HTTP connection in this paper, so a separate HTTP connection is used for downloading each video chunk in the training. For persistent HTTP connection, we should use a persistent HTTP connection for downloading video chunks in training. It is expected that the chunk size has less impact on the obtained TCP throughput in that case.

5.2 Emulab Experiments Setup

Emulab network testbed allows us to conduct controlled and repeatable experiments to compare different designs. The structure of the our Emulab testbed is shown in Figure 5. It consists of five nodes, among which one node acts as the DASH client, the other four nodes are DASH servers. Each node runs the standard FreeBSD of version 8.1. The servers have Apache HTTP server of version 2.4.1 installed. Also, Ipfw and Dummynet are used on the servers to control the bandwidth between nodes.

In all our experiments, the server provides 51 different video rates, ranging from $100Kbps$ to $5.1Mbps$, with rate gap between two adjacent versions $100Kbps$. The link capacity between the client and server is set to be $5Mbps$. In this setting, even if there is no background traffic, the client still cannot sustain the highest video rate. To generate realistic network bandwidth variations with congestion level shift, we inject background TCP traffic between the servers and the client. Twenty TCP connections are established for each server-client pair. We control the rate at which data is

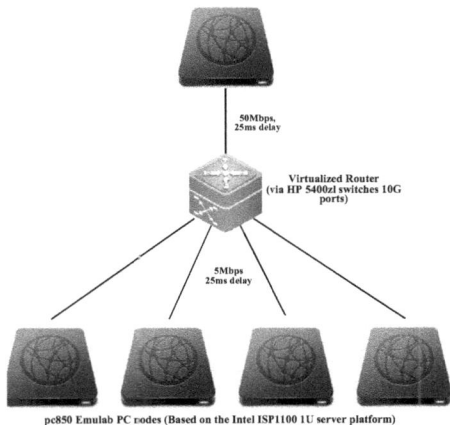

Figure 5: Emulab Testbed

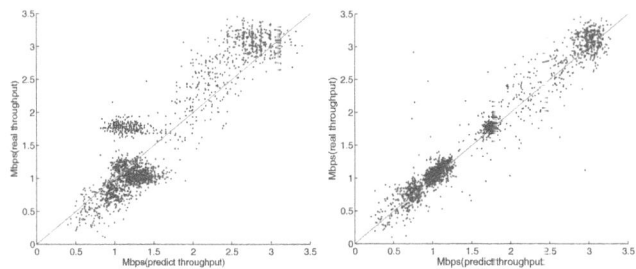

(a) SVR: average error 25.7%   (b) History: average error 9.6%

Figure 7: TCP Throughput Prediction Accuracy.

injected to a background TCP connection to emulate network congestion level shift. The background TCP traffic we use for all single server experiments is shown in Figure 6. The aggregate background traffic rate jumps between three different levels, oscillations within the same level are due to TCP congestion control mechanisms.

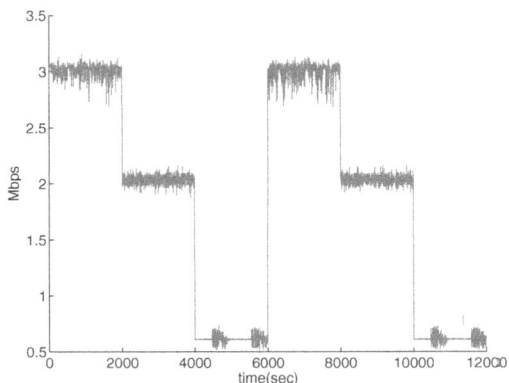

Figure 6: Background Traffic with Level-shift

5.3 TCP Throughput Prediction Accuracy

For DASH from single server, since a client continuously downloads video chunks from the same server which makes realtime TCP throughput data available, we use simple history-based TCP throughput prediction. The client measures the time it takes to download each chunk and calculates the average TCP throughput for each chunk. To predict TCP throughput for the next chunk downloading, it simply takes an average of TCP throughput for the previous W chunks, discarding the largest one and the smallest one. If W is too small, the estimate tends to be noisy, if W is too large, the estimate reacts slowly to sudden congestion level shift. In our experiments, we set $W = 10$. While some other history-based TCP throughput prediction algorithms have been proposed, e.g., [13], we found in our experiments that even the simple one works well in the context of DASH. For DASH with multiple servers, if a client has never downloaded from a server, there is no TCP throughput history to extrapolate on. We instead use SVR TCP throughput prediction [14] with initial offline training and light-weight online measurement. For our controlled experiments, single run of offline

training is good enough. In practice, offline training can be done periodically to make the SVR model up-to-date.

We now compare the accuracy of history-based and SVR TCP throughput prediction in our Emulab experiments. TCP background traffic follows the same trend as in Figure 6. To get more samples, we increase the duration of each congestion level to 160 minutes. During the experiments, the client downloads video chunks at all the 51 video rates. Figure 7 compares the accuracy of SVR prediction with history-based prediction. We can see that our history-based prediction is obviously better than SVR prediction. The average error for history-based prediction is 9.6%, while the error for SVR prediction is about 25.7%, which is consistent with the results reported in [14]. The high accuracy of history-based prediction in DASH is because chunks are downloaded by TCP continuously and TCP throughput for adjacent chunks are highly correlated. On the other hand, SVR prediction is light-weight, its accuracy is already good enough to guide the server selection in multi-server DASH. In our following experiments, the accuracy of history-based prediction is even lower than 5%. This is because the TCP throughput prediction accuracy at low video rates is worse than at high video rates. At low video rates, because the video chunk size is small, very small absolute estimation error can cause large relative error which doesn't happen for high video rates. In this accuracy experiment, we do the transmission for all 51 video rates from $100Kbps$ to $5.1Mbps$ while in real DASH experiments, for most of the time, the video rate is higher than $1Mbps$.

5.4 Single-server DASH Experiments

We present Emulab results for DASH from single-server.

5.4.1 Buffer Size Control

We first evaluate the performance of PID-based buffer control proposed in Section 3.2. We set $K_p = 0.1$, $K_I = 0.01$ and the reference buffered video time is $q_{ref} = 20$ seconds. The duration for each congestion level is scaled down to 500 seconds. In Figure 8(a), we can see that the buffer size can be controlled around 20 very well. In Figure 8(b), the requested video rate tracks the TCP throughput perfectly under all congestion level shifts. But the frequent video rate fluctuations are not acceptable to users. As stated in Section 3.3, instead of accurately controlling buffer size, one should smoothly reach high video rate under the throughput that can be achieved by TCP.

5.4.2 Smooth Video Adaptation

We conduct single-server DASH experiments using the smooth video adaptation algorithm proposed in Section 3.3. Figure 9 shows the results by setting the rate switch-up threshold m to 1, 5, 20, and dynamic value defined in (11) respectively.

(a) m=1　　　　(b) m=5　　　　(c) m=20　　　　(d) dynamic m

(e) m=1　　　　(f) m=5　　　　(g) m=20　　　　(h) dynamic m

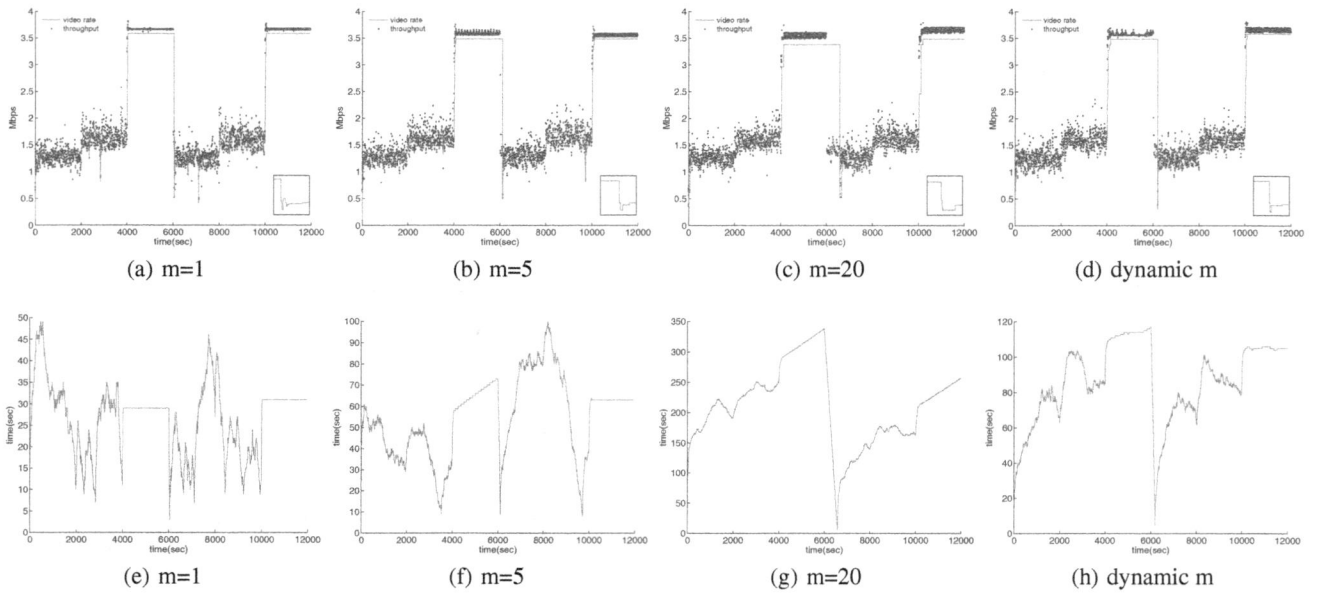

Figure 9: Smooth Video Adaptation: (a)-(d): video rate and throughput; (e)-(h): buffer size evolution

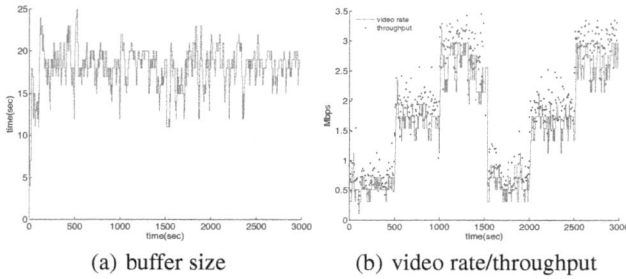

(a) buffer size　　　　(b) video rate/throughput

Figure 8: PID-based Buffer Size Control.

Table 1 shows the average video rate and buffer size.

Table 1: average video rate and buffer size for single server

m	avg. video rate(Mbps)	avg. buffer size(second)
1	2.16	26.75
5	2.15	55.39
20	2.10	209.17
Dyn.	2.13	86.34

Compared with Figure 8(b), the video rate smoothness has significant improvement. Larger m has smoother video rate, but incurs much larger oscillations in buffer size. This again reflects the fundamental design trade-off between video rate smoothness and buffer size smoothness. The average video rate of all the cases are close, with larger m has slightly lower rate. This is because, with larger m, it takes longer to switch-up video rate after TCP throughput increases. The buffered video time keeps increasing, leading to large buffer size overshoot. Since the rate switch-down is triggered only after the buffer size goes down to half of the reference size, large buffer size overshoots with larger m also make it react slowly to the sudden congestion level leaps. In Figure 9(c), the video rate remains at high level way after the actual TCP through-

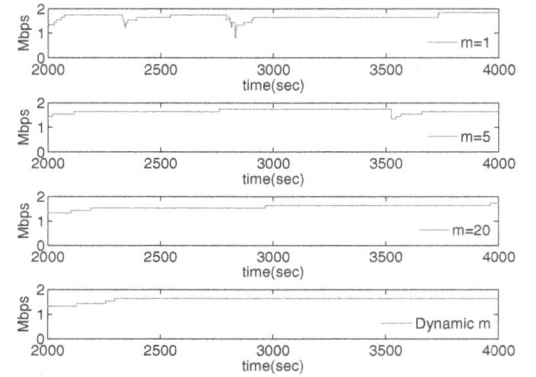

Figure 10: Video Smoothness of different m values

put goes down around $6,000$ second, until the buffer size falls back to 10 seconds. The small windows at bottom-right corner of Figure 9 (a)-(d) are the zoom-in views of video rate within 200 seconds after the big rate switch-down around $6,000$ second. It is obvious that, with a larger m, it takes much longer time to switch up to a higher rate. In Figure 9(d) and Figure 9(h), by dynamically adjusting m based on the queue length increase trend, dynamic-m simultaneously achieves video rate smoothness of large m and switch responsiveness of small m.

Figure 10 further shows the video rate trends between $2,000$ second and $4,000$ second for different m. For non-dynamic m algorithms, larger m leads to smoother video rate, but as shown in Figure 9, larger m results in slower responsiveness. As for dynamic m algorithm, it maintain good smoothness of the video rate trend while achieving fast responsiveness.

5.4.3 Adaptation with Buffer Cap and Rate Margin

As stated in Section 3.4, large buffer size is not possible in live streaming and not plausible in VoD; reserving a bandwidth margin can potentially reduce video rate fluctuations. In the first set

116

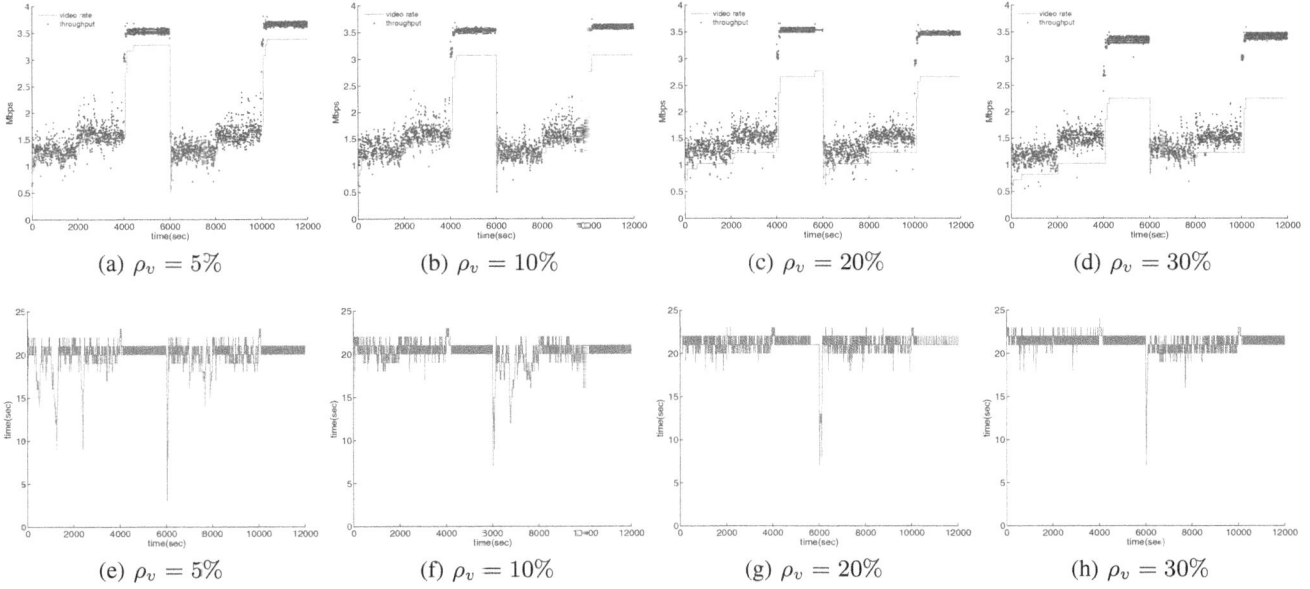

(a) $\rho_v = 5\%$ (b) $\rho_v = 10\%$ (c) $\rho_v = 20\%$ (d) $\rho_v = 30\%$

(e) $\rho_v = 5\%$ (f) $\rho_v = 10\%$ (g) $\rho_v = 20\%$ (h) $\rho_v = 30\%$

Figure 11: Video Adaptation under Buffer Cap of 20 Seconds and Different Video Rate Margins.

of experiments, we set the buffer cap q_{max} to 20 seconds and try different bandwidth margins. Figure 11 shows the results for different margins. Table 2 shows the average video rate, TCP throughput utilization (calculated as average video rate over average TCP throughput), and average buffer size for each case. With bandwidth margin and buffer cap, the buffer size oscillates within a small neighborhood of the buffer cap. Video rate adapts smoothly to congestion level shifts, and the TCP throughput utilization is close to the target value of $1 - \rho_v$.

Table 2: Adaptation with Buffer Cap and Bandwidth Margin

margin ρ_v	average video rate(Mbps)	TCP throughput utilization (%)	average buffer size(second)
5%	1.99	91.98	19.79
10%	1.87	87.32	20.13
20%	1.6	76.43	20.98
30%	1.42	69.57	21.31

In live streaming, buffer cap q_{max} reflects the tolerable user playback lag. By setting q_{max} to a small value, we can simulate a live streaming session. Figure 12 shows the results for buffer cap of 5 seconds and 10 seconds. Table 3 shows the average video rate, utilization ratio and average buffer size. For both cases, the margin is set to 10%. We can see that when $q_{max} = 5$, there can be playback freezes when the background traffic suddenly jumps from $0.6Mbps$ to $3Mbps$ around $6,000$ second. Such a steep jump is a rare event in practice. When $q_{max} = 10$, the buffer never depletes.

Table 3: Live Streaming Simulation

buffer-cap second	avg. video rate(Mbps)	TCP throughput utilization (%)	avg. buffer size(second)
5	1.84	86.92	5.48
10	1.90	85.77	10.79

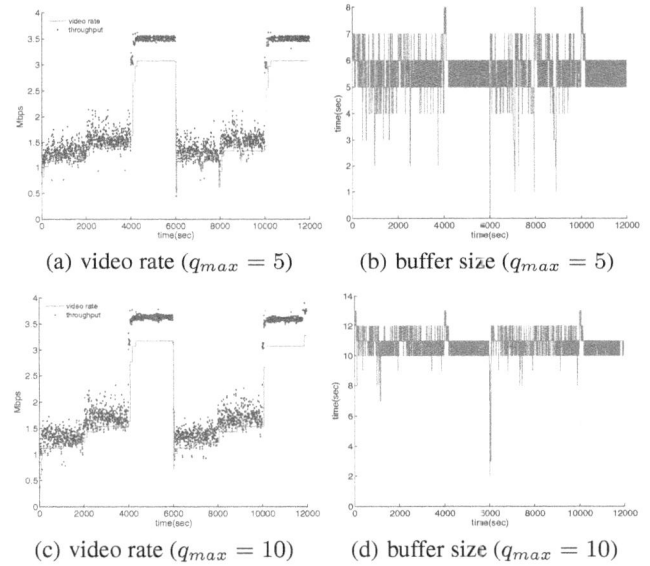

(a) video rate ($q_{max} = 5$)   (b) buffer size ($q_{max} = 5$)

(c) video rate ($q_{max} = 10$)   (d) buffer size ($q_{max} = 10$)

Figure 12: Simulation of live DASH streaming

5.4.4 Side-by-side Comparison

There have already been some client side video adaptation algorithms as introduced in Section 2. As a comparison, we implement the client side adaptation algorithm proposed in [17]. In [17], authors use $\mu = MSD/SFT$ as the transmission metrics to decide whether to switch up or switch down where MSD is the media segment duration and SFT is segment fetch time. If $\mu > 1 + \epsilon$, the chosen video rate will switch up one level, where $\epsilon = \max_i (b_{r_{i+1}} - b_{r_i})/b_{r_i}$ and b_{r_i} is the video rate of representation level i. If $\mu < \gamma_d$ where γ_d denotes switch down threshold, the chosen video rate switches down to the highest video rate level i that satisfies $b_{r_i} < \mu * b_c$ where b_c is the current video rate.

And also, to limit the maximum buffer size, idle time is added

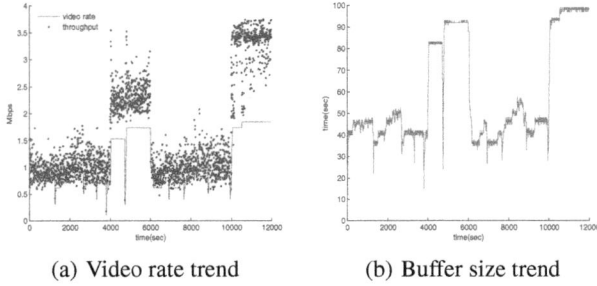

(a) Video rate trend   (b) Buffer size trend

Figure 13: Video rate and buffer size trend for [17]

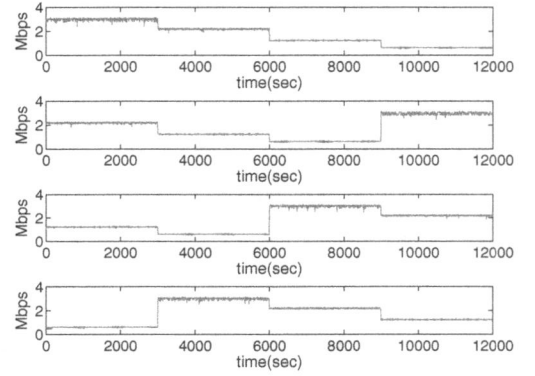

Figure 14: Background Traffic for Multiple Server DASH

between two consecutive chunk fetches. The idle time is calculated according to (12) where t_s, t_m and t_{min} denote the idle time, the buffered media time, the predefined minimum buffered media time respectively, b_c and b_{min} denote the current representation bitrate and the minimum representation bitrate respectively.

$$t_s = t_m - t_{min} - \frac{b_c}{b_{min}} MSD \qquad (12)$$

We implemented the algorithm exactly as proposed in [17]. We did the same experiments as in our algorithm, the same curves are plotted to do side-by-side comparison with our algorithm. During the experiments, all configurations of the network including hardware, operating system and bandwidth settings between nodes are exactly the same as for our algorithm. Also, We added the same background traffic as shown in Figure 6.

The results are presented in Figure 13. By comparing with the results in Figure 9 and Figure 11, we can see that the average video rate in Figure 13 is much lower. This happens because the algorithm is too conservative and can't make full use of the available bandwidth. When the algorithm decides to switch up, it only switches up one level without considering the actual TCP throughput. Also, there are many video rate fluctuations because of the lack of smoothing mechanism in this algorithm. We can see that even one TCP throughput out-lier will cause the video rate to switch up or switch down.

To be more specific, Table 4 shows the detailed comparison of average video rate achieve by both algorithms at different congestion levels. During the whole experiments, background traffic consists of six stages with each stage of 2000 seconds, From Table 4, our algorithms achieve significantly higher video rates in a smoother fashion than the algorithm proposed in [17].

Table 4: Average Video Rates (Mbps) at different congestion levels

Algorithm / Stage	m=1	m=5	m=20	Dyn m	[17]
0 ∼ 2000	1.30	1.28	1.17	1.24	0.75
2000 ∼ 4000	1.66	1.66	1.57	1.24	0.75
4000 ∼ 6000	3.56	3.44	3.32	3.44	1.62
6000 ∼ 8000	1.28	1.31	1.47	1.34	0.70
8000 ∼ 10000	1.64	1.72	1.60	1.61	0.84
10000 ∼ 12000	3.56	3.44	3.41	3.55	1.80

5.5 DASH with Multiple Servers

We set up four Emulab nodes as DASH servers, and conducted two types of multi-server DASH experiments.

5.5.1 Dynamic Server Selection

In the first experiment, we introduce background TCP traffic to each of the four servers. As illustrated in Figure 14, each server rotates between four background traffic levels, each level lasts for 3,000 seconds. The whole experiment lasts for 200 minutes which is generally the length of an epic Hollywood movie. In the experiment, using SVR throughput prediction, the client is able to quickly detect traffic level shifts on all DASH servers, and dynamically switch to the server with the highest TCP throughput. As shown in Figure 15(a), the video rate is always maintained at a high level, independent of traffic level shifts on individual servers. There are several traffic rate dips. When we use a video rate margin of 10%, the rate smoothness is improved, as seen in Figure 15(b).

5.5.2 Concurrent Download

Figure 15(c) and Figure 15(d) show the experimental results when the client concurrently connects to two servers that offer the highest TCP throughput. To make a fair comparison with the single-connection case in the previous section, we reduce the link capacity and background traffic rate on all servers by roughly half. As shown in Figure 15(c), the client dynamically downloads chunks from the top-2 servers to sustain a high video rate throughout the experiments. The aggregate TCP throughput from top-2 servers has smaller variance than in the single dynamic server case, this leads to a much smoother video rate. The video rate can be further smoothed out when a bandwidth margin of 10% is added, as plotted in Figure 15(d). According to our experiment log, in both single connection and multiple connections cases, the switching of servers absolutely follows our prediction. This shows that SVR is accurate enough to monitor major congestion level shift and trigger DASH server switching.

5.6 Internet Experiments

Finally, we test our DASH system on the Internet. We only do experiments for the single-server case.

5.6.1 Client with Wireline Access

We set up a Planetlab node in Shanghai, China ($planetlab - 1.sjtu.edu.cn$) as the DASH server, and an Emulab node located in Utah, USA as the DASH client. We don't inject background traffic between the server and client.

Figure 16 and Table 5 show the results at different rate margins. Since different experiments are conducted sequentially, the TCP throughput patterns are not controllable. In all experiments, we do observed long-term shifts and short-term fluctuations of TCP throughput along the same Internet path. Our video adaptation al-

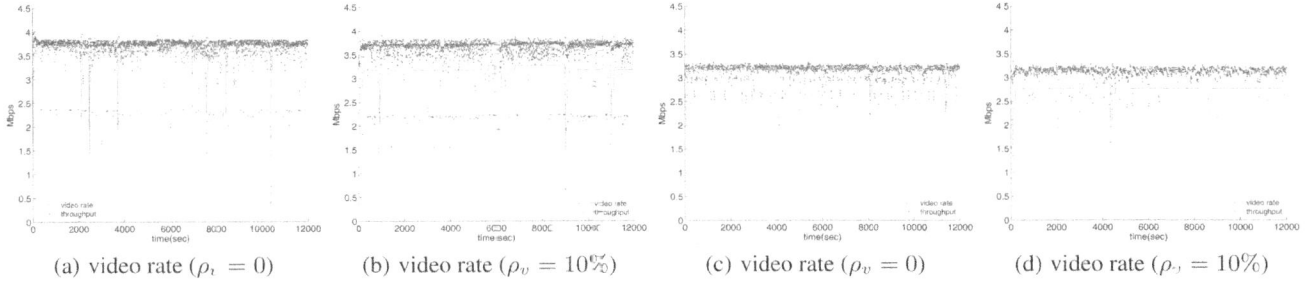

(a) video rate ($\rho_t = 0$) (b) video rate ($\rho_v = 10\%$) (c) video rate ($\rho_v = 0$) (d) video rate ($\rho_v = 10\%$)

Figure 15: Emulab Experiments with Multiple Servers: (a),(b) client only downloads from a single best server; (c),(d): client downloads concurrently from the top-2 servers.

gorithms can adapt well to the network condition changes, which is consistent with our Emulab results. In fact, the video rate is even smoother than our Emulab experiments. This is because the background traffic injected in Emulab experiments is more volatile than the real cross-traffic on the Internet path. Another difference from Emulab experiments is that when the rate margin is large e.g, $\rho_v = 30\%$, the achieved TCP throughput in Figure 16(d) is lower than with no or small margins. This is because in Emulab experiments, we control the total rate of background traffic. But in Internet experiments, background traffic is out of our control. When our DASH system is more conservative, the requested video chunks are smaller, which puts TCP at a disadvantage when competing with other cross-traffic.

Table 5: Wireline Internet Experiments

margin	average video rate(Mbps)	TCP throughput utilization (%)	average buffer size(second)
0%	3.34	97.80	32.99
5%	2.82	91.83	19.95
10%	2.55	86.32	20.50

5.6.2 Client with Wireless Access

We also test our system on wireless clients. The server resides in Emulab, the client is a laptop in a residential network in New York City, which connects to Internet through a Wi-Fi router. we change the distance between the laptop and the router to create dynamic bandwidth while running the DASH client is running. Figure 17 and Table 6 show the results with different rate margins for the wireless client.

Table 6: Internet Experiments with Wireless Client

margin	average video rate(Mbps)	TCP throughput utilization (%)	average buffer size(second)
0%	2.80	97.24	57.83
20%	2.33	81.23	20.40
30%	1.27	63.44	21.11

When we take the laptop far away from the wireless router, the wireless connection is very unstable. TCP throughput varies over a wide range, and it is not repeatable across different experiments. Without a rate margin, the video rate also fluctuates a lot, and there are several video freezes. Increasing rate margin to 20% reduces video rate fluctuation and eliminates freezes. However, for the experiments with 30% margin in Figure 17(e) and Figure 17(f), the

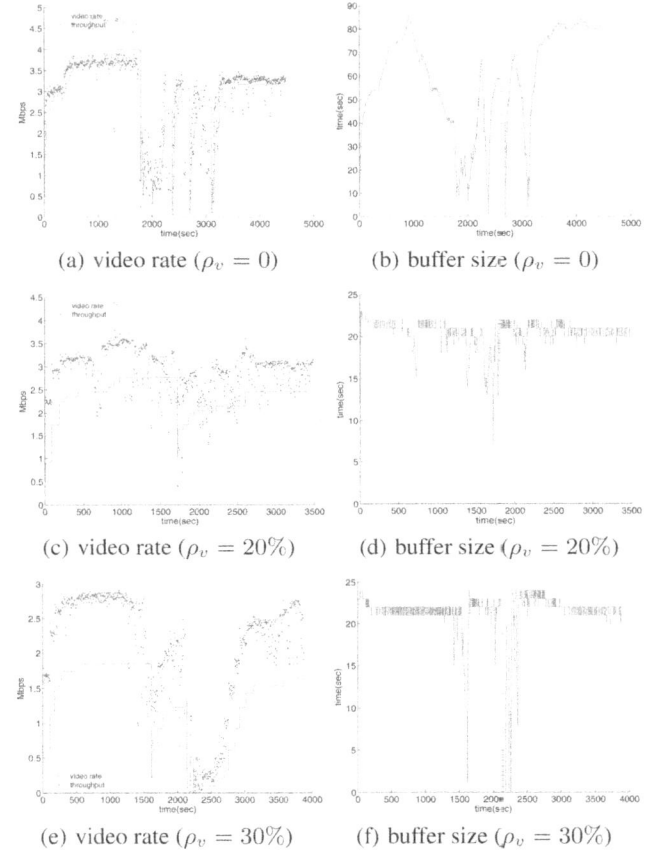

(a) video rate ($\rho_v = 0$) (b) buffer size ($\rho_v = 0$)

(c) video rate ($\rho_v = 20\%$) (d) buffer size ($\rho_v = 20\%$)

(e) video rate ($\rho_v = 30\%$) (f) buffer size ($\rho_v = 30\%$)

Figure 17: Internet Experiments with Wireless Client: comparison of different rate margins

TCP throughput is extremely low from 1600 seconds to 2600 seconds, when the laptop was taken very far away from the router. The video rate is kept at $100Kbps$, and the video buffer depletes for many times. When the laptop is moved back closer to the router, the TCP throughput starts to increase, and the video rate switches up steadily.

6. CONCLUSIONS AND FUTURE WORK

In this paper, we developed video adaptation algorithms for DASH. Our algorithms use client-side buffered video time as feedback signal, and smoothly increase video rate as the available network band-

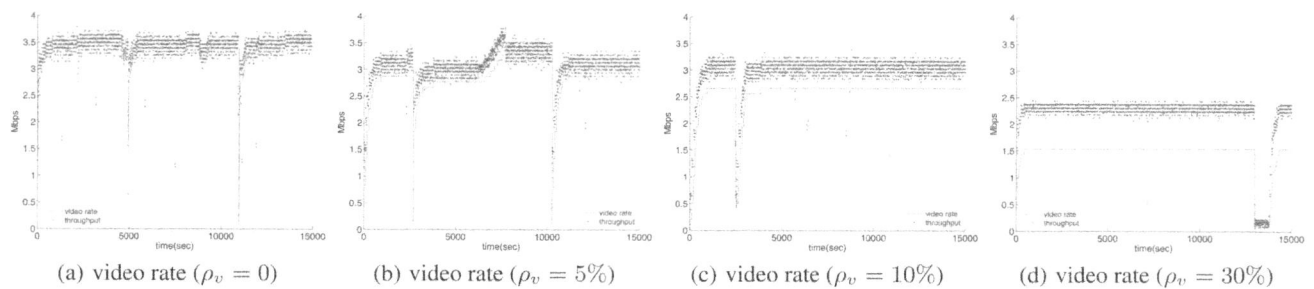

(a) video rate ($\rho_v = 0$) (b) video rate ($\rho_v = 5\%$) (c) video rate ($\rho_v = 10\%$) (d) video rate ($\rho_v = 30\%$)

Figure 16: Internet Experiments with Wireline Client

width increases, and promptly reduce video rate in response to sudden congestion level shift-ups. By introducing buffer cap and small video rate margin, our algorithms simultaneously achieved stable video rate and buffer size. Using machine-learning based TCP throughput prediction, we extended our designs so that a DASH client simultaneously works with multiple servers to achieve the multiplexing gain among them. We conducted extensive controlled experiments on Emulab, as well as Internet experiments with wireline and wireless clients. We demonstrated that the proposed DASH system is highly responsive to congestion level shifts and can maintain stable video rate in face of short-term bandwidth variations.

Our wireless experiments demonstrated the unique challenges of delivering DASH in wireless networks. We are interested in refining our current adaptation algorithms for WiFi and 3G/4G cellular networks. In this paper, we mostly focus on the adaptation of single DASH client. When there are multiple DASH clients in the same service session, they compete with each other through the common TCP protocol at the transport layer and diverse video adaptation protocols at the application layer. We are interested in studying the fairness and stability of user video Quality-of-Experience among multiple competing DASH clients. Server-side DASH algorithms will be investigated to regulate the competition between them. Another direction is to investigate the application of DASH in P2P streaming systems. In P2P DASH, the video adaptation on a peer is not only driven by download throughput from the server, but also by upload/download throughput to/from other peers.

7. ACKNOWLEDGMENT

The authors would like to thank the anonymous reviewers and the Shepherd Dr. Yin Zhang for their valuable feedbacks and suggestions to improve the paper quality. The work is partially supported by USA NSF under contracts CNS-0953682, CNS-0916734, and CNS-1018032.

8. REFERENCES

[1] V. K. Adhikari, Y. Guo, F. Hao, M. Varvello, V. Hilt, M. Steiner, and Z.-L. Zhang, "Unreeling netflix: Understanding and improving multi-cdn movie delivery," in *Proceedings of IEEE INFOCOM*, 2012.

[2] J. F. Kurose and K. Ross, *Computer Networking: A Top-Down Approach Featuring the Internet*, 6th ed. Addison-Wesley, 2012.

[3] M. Watson, "Http adaptive streaming in practice," Netflix, Tech. Rep., 2011.

[4] S. Akhshabi, A. C. Begen, and C. Dovrolis, "An experimental evaluation of rate-adaptation algorithms in adaptive streaming over http," in *ACM Multimedia Systems*, 2011.

[5] Microsoft, "IIS Smooth Streaming," http://www.iis.net/download/SmoothStreaming.

[6] Adobe, "Open Source Media Framework," http://www.osmf.org/.

[7] E. C. R. Mok, X. Luo and R. Chang, "Qdash: A qoe-aware dash system," in *ACM Multimedia Systems*, 2012.

[8] S. M. L. De Cicco and V. Palmisano, "Feedback control for adaptive live video streaming," in *ACM Multimedia Systems*, 2011.

[9] H. S. B. Haakon Riiser and P. Vigmostad, "A comparison of quality scheduling in commercial adaptive http streaming solutions on a 3g network," in *ACM Multimedia Systems*, 2012.

[10] S. L. Christopher Mueller and C. Timmerer, "An evaluation of dynamic adaptive streaming over http in vehicular environments," in *ACM Multimedia Systems*, 2012.

[11] W. C. B. Seo and R. Zimmermann, "Efficient video uploading from mobile devices in support of http streaming," in *ACM Multimedia Systems*, 2012.

[12] C. Dovrolis, M. Jain, and R. Prasad, "Measurement tools for the capacity and load of Internet paths," http://www.cc.gatech.edu/fac/Constantinos.Dovrolis/bw-est/.

[13] Q. He, C. Dovrolis, and M. Ammar, "On the predictability of large transfer tcp throughput," in *Proceedings of ACM SIGCOMM*, 2005.

[14] M. Mirza, J. Sommers, P. Barford, and X. Zhu, "A machine learning approach to tcp throughput prediction," in *ACM SIGMETRICS*, 2007.

[15] A. J. Smola and B. Schölkopf, "A tutorial on support vector regression," *Statistics and Computing*, vol. 14, no. 3, pp. 199–222, Aug. 2004.

[16] Emulab-Team, "Emulab - Network Emulation Testbed Home," http://www.emulab.net/.

[17] C. Liu, I. Bouazizi, and M. Gabbouj, "Rate adaptation for adaptive http streaming," in *ACM Multimedia Systems*, 2011.

QAVA: Quota Aware Video Adaptation

Jiasi Chen, Amitabha Ghosh, Josphat Magutt, and Mung Chiang
Princeton University, Princeton, New Jersey, USA
{jiasic, amitabhg, jmagutt, chiangm}@princeton.edu

ABSTRACT

Two emerging trends of Internet applications, *video traffic becoming dominant* and *usage-based pricing becoming prevalent*, are at odds with each other. Given this conflict, is there a way for users to stay within their monthly data plans (data quotas) without suffering a noticeable degradation in video quality? In this work, we develop an online video adaptation system, called Quota Aware Video Adaptation (QAVA), that manages this tradeoff by leveraging the compressibility of videos and by predicting consumer usage behavior throughout a billing cycle. We propose the QAVA architecture and develop its main modules, including Stream Selection, User Profiling, and Video Profiling. Online algorithms are designed through dynamic programming and evaluated using real video request traces. Empirical results suggest that QAVA can provide an effective solution to the dilemma of usage-based pricing of heavy video traffic.

Categories and Subject Descriptors

C.2.5 [**Local and Wide-Area Networks**]: Internet; H.5.1 [**Multimedia Information Systems**]: Video

Keywords

Video streaming, Video rate adaptation, Data quota.

1. INTRODUCTION

1.1 Motivation for Online Video Adaptation

This paper is motivated by two recent and conflicting trends in Internet applications, which may be summarized by two numbers: 70 and 10.

- 70 is the predicted percentage of mobile traffic from video alone by 2016 [1]. Together with YouTube, Netflix, Hulu, HBO Go, iPad personalized video magazine apps, and news webpages with embedded videos, video traffic is surging on both wireline and wireless Internet.

- 10 is the dollars per gigabyte (GB) charged by the two major US cellular carriers once a baseline data quota is exceeded during a monthly billing cycle. Tiered pricing, or usage-based pricing, is becoming increasingly commonplace in other countries and even for wireline broadband. For example, in May 2011, AT&T wireline U-Verse high-speed Internet began charging $10 per 50 GB beyond a baseline data quota. In Canada, the charges are even steeper, with Rogers charging $2 per GB overage fees on its high-speed Internet service [2]. And in India, Reliance charges 0.02 rupees per 10 kB overage on its 3G mobile data plans [3].

These two trends, *video traffic becoming dominant* and *usage-based pricing plans becoming prevalent*, are at odds with each other. On the one hand, videos, especially on high-resolution devices (e.g., iPhone 5, iPad, Android tablets), consume much more data than other types of traffic; for instance, 15 min of low bitrate YouTube videos per day uses 1 GB a month, and a single standard-definition movie can take up to 2 GB. On the other hand, usage-based pricing threatens the business model of delivering entertainment via the high speed Long Term Evolution (LTE). These factors can result in high overage charges by the service provider, subscription to more expensive data plans, or discontinuation of data service by disgruntled users. Given this conflict, a natural question to ask is: *Can a consumer stay within her monthly data quota without suffering a noticeable drop (distortion) in video quality?*

In today's practice, there are two main approaches to balancing the competing goals of delivering high quality video while consuming less data:

- Consumers may be warned by service providers (or by self-imposed warnings) to stop watching more videos once their usage-based charges become too high. This straight-forward "solution" can be undesirable as it could result in dissatisfied users [4].

- Content providers can take a *"one size fits all"* approach of cutting back bit rates across all video requests, for all users, and at all times. For example, the YouTube mobile app automatically chooses low quality video when the request is made over the cellular data network. Netflix implemented a similar approach in Canada in March 2011, in light of expensive usage-based charges by Canadian Internet Service Providers (ISPs), even for wireline customers.

In contrast, Quota Aware Video Adaptation (QAVA) in this paper exploits the dynamic range of video compressibility and users' temporal data consumption patterns. To the best of our knowledge, video adaptation with respect to each user's data quota in the context of usage-based pricing has not been systematically investigated.

1.2 Trading off Quality vs. Cost vs. Volume

Our premise is the following: *Not every video bit is needed for every consumer*, and the bit rates can be adjusted not only based on screen resolution and channel conditions but also usage patterns. QAVA can be customized to each user's demand and monthly data quota by adaptively choosing an appropriate bit rate for each video request, thereby *shaping the supply* for the user. We will show that by leveraging *video compressibility* and profiling *usage behavior*, QAVA can significantly mitigate the conflict between growing video traffic demand and usage-based pricing.

At the heart of QAVA is a *Stream Selector* (SS), which takes inputs from a *User Profiler* (UP) and a *Video Profiler* (VP), to select a particular bit rate and pre-emptively compress the more compressible videos early in the billing cycle. The VP provides information related to a video, such as its compressibility, which measures the extent to which the size of a video can be reduced without a significant distortion in quality. The UP predicts consumer usage patterns from past history and customizes the system to every user's flavor for watching certain types of videos. The SS then uses the information provided by the VP and UP to optimize QAVA for each user based on her monthly data quota.

The benefits to a QAVA-enabled user include the ability to watch more videos under a given monthly data plan without suffering a noticeable distortion in video quality, as compared to a non-QAVA user. Or, phrased differently, if a user's demand for video traffic remains the same or goes down, QAVA tries to save money for the user with a minimum impact on video quality. This 3-way tradeoff is illustrated in Figure 1. Across the three competing goals of minimizing cost, maximizing the number of videos watched, and minimizing distortion, QAVA strikes a graceful, tunable tradeoff.

1.3 Incentives of Players in QAVA Ecosystem

A natural question to our proposed approach is: *What are the incentives for different players in the ecosystem to use QAVA?* We address this from the perspective of three major players: users, ISPs, and content providers.

Users: A user has the most obvious incentive, because QAVA enables her to stop worrying about her monthly data plan and watch all the videos she wants with minimal distortion.

ISPs: An ISP has two options: it may wish to (a) reduce data traffic to lower network congestion and thereby operational and capital expenditure costs, or (b) preserve traffic to continue receiving overage charges from customers and/or usage fees from content providers. In the first case, QAVA ensures that all customers remain below their quota, which indirectly lowers the traffic rate. In the second case, the ISP can set the user's quota parameter to ensure that the user still consumes the same amount of data as a non-QAVA user, but receives better video quality.

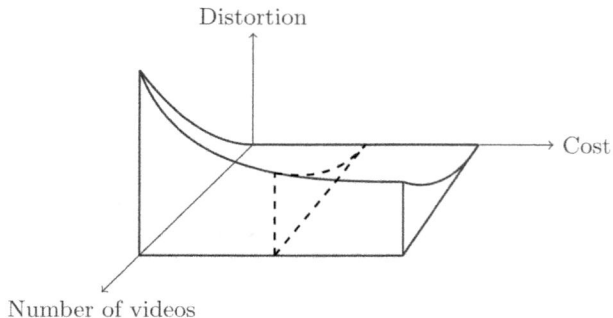

Figure 1: A 3-way tradeoff between distortion, cost, and the number of videos watched. For a fixed cost, QAVA enables a user to watch the desired videos while minimizing distortion.

Content providers: The advantages for the content provider (CP) are three-fold. Firstly, since QAVA allows a user to access more content under the same data plan, the CP achieves greater profit by increasing the content consumption and thereby advertising revenue. Secondly, the CP improves customer satisfaction by removing her worries about exceeding her quota, which can be marketed as a competitive advantage over other CPs. Thirdly, QAVA reduces the potential need for the CP to pay the ISP for the customer's data charges.

QAVA is thus mutually advantageous from the perspectives of all three players. We summarize our contributions along four different dimensions:

- **Architecture:** We design a modular system architecture for QAVA comprising three functional modules: SS, UP, and VP. Our design makes QAVA a deployable system that can be used by real-world consumers.

- **Algorithms:** We design an online bit rate selection algorithm for the SS module based on finite-horizon Markov Decision Process (MDP) [8]. This algorithm runs at the heart of QAVA, enabling it to provide a graceful, tunable control of the quality, cost, and volume tradeoff.

- **Experiments:** We evaluate the performance of QAVA in simulations using real video request traces.

- **Implementation:** We implement QAVA as an Android application and deploy it among several volunteers from the Princeton University community in an ongoing trial. Further trials are being planned with several major carriers and content providers.

The rest of the paper is organized as follows. In Section 2, we describe the QAVA system architecture and discuss design considerations. The individual modules are described in detail in Sections 3 and 4. We provide simulation results in Section 5 and implementation details in Section 6. Lastly, we discuss related works in Section 7, and conclude in Section 8.

2. QAVA SYSTEM ARCHITECTURE

In this section, we describe the architecture of QAVA and the different modules that comprise the system. For each module, we describe its functionality as well as its connection with other modules.

2.1 A Modular Architecture Design

The architecture of QAVA comprises three different modules, each responsible for a specific function. The modules work together to enable QAVA to optimize across the three performance goals shown in Figure 1. We first describe the motivation for each of the modules.

Selecting Right Bit Rates: The basic operation of QAVA is to choose an appropriate bit rate for every video request made by a user. This bit rate selection is based on two factors: (i) the user's data consumption pattern, and (ii) the particular video requested. This job is performed by a *Stream Selector* module running at the heart of QAVA on the content provider's server, as shown in Figure 2. Due to space limitation, we focus on the pre-encoded bit stream scenario, where each video has multiple copies, each copy pre-encoded in a different bit rate and stored on the content provider's server. The number of copies with different bit rates of a video is pre-determined by the content provider.

Profiling Usage Behavior: A user's past data consumption history gives an indication of her future usage pattern. Since the video requests from a user can arrive at different times without any prior knowledge, a prediction of these arrival times is helpful to QAVA so it can choose appropriate bit rates to serve the requests. A simple usage pattern could be watching on average x_d number of videos (or, equivalently, y_d bytes) on day d of a week. When the number x_d (or y_d) remains approximately the same for the same day d across different weeks, we may notice a weekly pattern. More complex usage behavior can lead to small-scale seasonal variations (daily or hourly) as well as *trends*, which are long term variations due to habitual changes that lead to a steady increase or decrease in data usage over months or years.

QAVA employs a *User Profiler* module to find patterns in usage behavior and to predict future video requests. In particular, the UP module estimates the probability of a video request arriving in a given time interval. The length of this interval can be uniform or variable depending on the past data consumption history, and is configured by a system parameter. We design the UP module as an application that can be installed on a user device (client), as shown in Figure 2.

Estimating Video Compressibility: In addition to staying within a monthly data quota, the SS algorithm also aims to minimize video distortion. For this, the algorithm needs to know to what extent the requested video can be compressed and how much distortion it would cause in doing so. Different videos have different levels of compressibility depending on their spatial or temporal activity, as well as on the choice of encoder. For example, a talk show that has very little motion in it can be greatly compressed using an H.264/AVC encoder, whereas a motion-rich sports video may not be compressible to the same extent.

The SS algorithm should be careful in choosing the right bit rate for every video request to avoid the following undesirable situation. Suppose the algorithm chooses a high bit rate for an easily compressible video when the user has

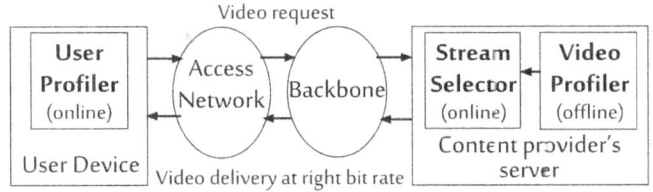

Figure 2: QAVA's modular system architecture: The UP module sits on a user device, whereas the SS and VP modules are located on a content provider's server. A video request originating from a user device travels through the access network and the backbone to the server, which then runs a stream selection algorithm to choose an appropriate bit rate to deliver to the user.

a lot of quota left, possibly in the beginning of a month. Then it might be forced to choose low bit rates for some not-so-easily compressible videos near the end of the billing cycle in order to stay within the monthly budget, thus causing significant distortion. A possible remedy is to choose low bit rates for easily compressible videos *even when* there is sufficient quota left. However, such intelligent online decisions can be made only if the system knows about the distortion vs. bit rate tradeoff for every video and can learn the quota consumption pattern over a billing cycle for each user. An example of this tradeoff is shown in a demo video at http://snipurl.com/23uozdh. QAVA employs an offline *Video Profiler* module to compute this distortion for every bit rate and store it on the content provider's server, as shown in Figure 2.

We now summarize the three modules of QAVA:

- **Stream Selector (SS):** The SS module is at the heart of QAVA and is located on the content provider's server. It is an online module which decides on the right bit rate for every video request.

- **User Profiler (UP):** The UP module predicts the probability of future video requests from past usage history, and also computes a user-specific distribution of video types reflecting the user's taste of watching different types of videos. It is an online module and is located on the user device.

- **Video Profiler (VP):** The VP module is also located on the content provider's server and is an offline entity. It computes the distortion for every bit rate version of all the stored videos. We loosely call this the "*compressibility*" of the videos.

Input-Output Connections Between Modules: Based on the preceding discussion, the relationship between the different modules describing their inputs, outputs, and update frequencies is shown in Table 1. The input to the SS module is the compressibility of the requested video, the user's remaining monthly budget, and the user's profile as output by the UP module. For every request, it runs the stream selection algorithm and outputs the selected bit rate version. The input to the VP module is the set of all videos stored on the content provider's server, and its output is the compressibility for each video. The input to the UP module

Module	Input	Output	Frequency
Stream Selector (SS)	Compressibility of video request, remaining monthly budget, and the user profile.	Selected bit rate version to deliver for the video request.	Every request
User Profiler (UP)	Time stamps and compressibility all past video requests.	Probability of a video request arriving at a time interval, and the video compressibility distribution for all past requests. Together these comprise the user profile.	Every billing cycle
Video Profiler (VP)	All videos stored in the content provider's server.	Compressibility of all videos.	Offline

Table 1: Three key functional modules of QAVA with their inputs, outputs, and update frequency.

are the time stamps for the user's past video requests, as well as the compressibility of those videos. Its output is the predicted video request probability and the video type distribution (i.e., compressibility distribution) specific to that user. These quantities characterize the user's behavior and are fed to the SS module. These predictions can be made at the beginning of the billing cycle, or updated more periodically throughout the billing cycle.

To be concrete, we give an operational example.

1. The content provider computes and stores the compressibility of all the videos on the server.

2. In the beginning of a billing cycle, the UP makes predictions (to be used in the current cycle) of the video request probability and the compressibility distribution based on its log of the past requests of the user.

3. When the user requests a video in the current billing cycle, the request is sent to the SS module, which selects the bit rate to be delivered. The content provider also sends the compressibility of the requested video to the UP. The UP logs this as well as the timestamp of the request.

4. Once the current billing cycle is over, the UP updates its predictions based on the recent request logs. Steps 2–4 repeat for the next billing cycle.

2.2 Design Considerations

There are several alternatives and variants for designing the QAVA architecture. We briefly describe these alternatives, their advantages and disadvantages, and our design decisions.

Availability of Video Versions: In this paper, we assume that the videos are pre-encoded and stored on the content provider's server. An alternative to this is on-the-fly transcoding and adaptation, which requires compressing the video dynamically at the particular bit rate determined by the SS module. This can be a time-consuming operation and has significant implementation challenges; however, it would be capable of adapting video feeds for live events. In contrast, pre-encoded streams can be selected with minimal computation, but cannot handle video streams of live events.

We also assume that the different version of the video from which the SS module chooses are supported by the channel in terms of bandwidth requirement. These sustainable video versions may be pre-selected by the CP based on typical wireless or wireline bandwidth, or chosen on-the-fly based

on bandwidth estimation techniques currently proposed for use in adaptive HTTP video streaming algorithms [9].

Time Scale of Video Adaptation: There are two choices for the time scale of video adapation: (i) inter-video adaptation, and (ii) intra-video adaptation. Inter-video adaptation is choosing a single bit rate stream for entire duration of the requested video, whereas intra-video adaptation involves dividing each video into smaller clips and choosing the correct adaptation operation for each clip.

Inter-video adaptation is suitable for video clips of short duration (e.g., Youtube videos of less than 5 minutes), because the spatial and temporal activity tends to be similar throughout the duration. However, for longer videos such as movies, it is more appropriate to stream different bit rate versions for different parts of the video depending on the spatial and temporal activity. The algorithms developed in this paper apply equally to inter- or intra-video rate switching. QAVA can be used for intra-video adaptation by considering each smaller segment as a separate video request. Such intra-video switching requires synchronous bit stream switching, which can be achieved with the advent of new video streaming protocols such as MPEG-DASH [20]. QAVA can also work with existing channel-based switching algorithms by optimizing and restricting the rates available to the existing algorithm.

Heterogeneous Data Quota: Data usage under a single data plan can be decomposed into three usage layers: (i) multiple users, (ii) muliple devices per user, and (iii) multiple traffic types per device per user. QAVA's control knob is the video traffic per user per device; thus, the "video quota" per device must be set. To accomodate non-video data traffic, the video quota should be set to a percentage of the total data quota, based on historical video data usage. Running QAVA per user is also possible by aggregating video request logs across devices. This results in coarser granularity user profiling, but may also improve performance by decreasing the sensitivity to noise. For the remainder of this work, we focus on the case of a single fixed video quota and a single user with a single device, but QAVA could easily be extended to encompass the other cases as just outlined.

Module Placement: The placement of the UP and VP modules is fairly intuitive: by necessity, the VP module is located on the CP's server, since only the CP provider knows about the video characteristics. Profiling the video on the user device is not feasible due to CPU and battery limitations. The UP module logs user data, so it should be placed on the user device to alleviate user concerns over data collection and privacy.

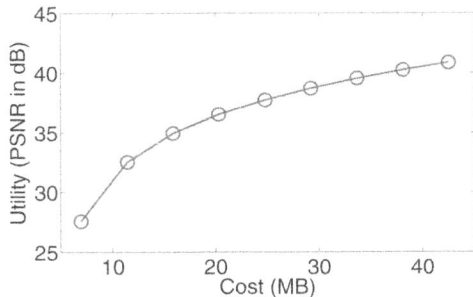

Figure 3: Video utility vs. cost showing diminishing returns for increasing cost. The x-axis represents the size of the video when encoded from 100–900 Kbps in 100 Kbps increments.

Symbol	Meaning
u_{tj}	Utility of bit rate version j for a video request arriving at t.
c_{tj}	Cost of bit rate version j for a video request arriving at t.
x_{tj}	Indicator variable (1 if bit rate j is chosen for video request at t; 0 otherwise).
M	Number of bit rates for each video.
T	Number of time periods in a billing cycle.
$P(\mathbf{u}, \mathbf{c})$	User-specific joint probability distribution of video types based on past history.
p_t	Probability of a video request at t.

Table 2: Table of key notation.

The location of the SS module that runs the bit rate selection algorithm is, however, not so intuitive. For every video request, the SS module requires inputs from both the UP and VP. One possibility is to place the SS module in the access network. Then, in order to satisfy a video request, the SS module first needs the video compressibility to be sent from the CP and the user information from the UP module. After receiving these inputs, the SS module runs the stream selector algorithm to choose the right bit rate. It then sends another request to the server to transmit the actual video in the selected bit rate. Overall, this results in unnecessary messages and potential delay, which is undesirable for delay-sensitive traffic such as video. Placing the SS module on the CP's server is thus more desirable. This also makes QAVA complementary to other video adaptation approaches [24].

Placing the SS and VP modules on the CP's server incurs some monetary cost to the content provider, which must be overcome by the advantages discussed in Section 1.3. We argue that the cost to the content provider is small: it must install the SS module on its server (one-time), and compute the video profiles of all videos (a small amount of text data compared to video data size). And regardless of where the SS module is placed, our algorithms are equally applicable.

Modularization: The QAVA system is separated into three modules: SS, UP, and VP. Each module has a fixed set of input and output and runs some internal algorithms. The advantage of this modularization is that the internal algorithms can be upgraded without changing the architecture of the rest of the system, thus simplifying testing and maintenance.

Other types of module separation and interconnection are also possible. For example, the VP and SS modules can be combined into a single module performing joint optimization. The stream selector requests videos of a certain compressibility, and the video profiler optimizes over various codecs to generate videos with desired characteristics. This would provide a finer decision granularity to the stream selector, but is computationally complex since the video profiler also runs video encoding operations.

3. STREAM SELECTION

In this section, we first describe the video request, utility, and cost model and then formulate the bit rate selection problem. We also introduce the key notation used in the paper, as summarized in Table 2.

3.1 Video Request, Utility, and Cost Model

We divide the length of a billing cycle (e.g. month) into T time intervals, indexed by $t = 1, \ldots, T$, and assume that the user has a total budget B (measured in bytes) in one billing cycle. In each time interval t, a video request arrives with a certain probability, which we denote by p_t. The remaining budget of the user at time t is b_t. The request probability p_t and budget b_t are provided by the UP module for each user.

Each video is encoded into M different bit rates, indexed by $j = 1, \ldots, M$. Associated with each video request arriving at time t is a vector of utilites $\mathbf{u}_t = (u_{t1}, \ldots, u_{tM})$, and a vector of costs $\mathbf{c}_t = (c_{t1}, \ldots, c_{tM})$ for different bit rate versions of the video.[1] When there is no video request arrival at time t, the vectors $\mathbf{u}_t$ and $\mathbf{c}_t$ are null vectors with all components being zero, because then no bit rate is selected. The VP module provides the utility and cost of each video, $\mathbf{u}_t$ and $\mathbf{c}_t$, respectively.

Each user might prefer different types of videos with different compressibilities. For example, she might want to watch news clips that have different compressibilities than sports videos. To capture this effect, we introduce a joint probability distribution $P(\mathbf{u}, \mathbf{c})$, which is user-specific and represents the probability that a user requests videos with certain utility–cost characteristics. The distribution $P(\mathbf{u}, \mathbf{c})$ is provided by the UP module for each user.

In Figure 3, we show a typical utility vs. cost function for a video encoded using the H.264/AVC codec with a resolution of 720×480 pixels. Such utility–cost curves are usually concave with diminishing returns for utility at higher cost (or equivalently, higher bit rate, since bit rate is proportional to data size for a fixed-length video). A video with a flat utility-cost curve is "easily compressible" because lowering the bit rate decreases the utility only slightly. In contrast, a "hard-to-compress" video has a steep curve. We measure the utility u_{tj} of bit rate version j as its *peak signal-to-noise ratio* (PSNR) $\times$ the duration of the video [6]. The cost c_{ij} is the size in bytes. Discussion of the utility and cost metrics is reserved for Section 4.2.

---

[1] We note that these utility and cost vectors are fixed and not time-dependent. The use of the time index t in u_{tj} and c_{tj} is purely for the ease of exposition.

3.2 Stream Selection as Knapsack Problems

We now formulate the problem of choosing the right bit rate by the SS module as different versions of the well-known knapsack problem [7] studied in combinatorial optimization. We first present an offline formulation, which is easy to understand, and then motivate the need for an online stochastic formulation.

3.2.1 Offline Multiple-Choice Knapsack Problem

The goal of the stream selector is to choose the right bit rate for every video request made by the user in a single billing cycle. We aim to maximize the sum of the utilities across all the video requests without exceeding the user's quota. In other words, we maximize the average video utility. An alternative formulation is to maximize the minimum utility across all videos requested during the billing cycle. Since the high-level goal of QAVA is to maximize the overall user satisfaction, we optimize for the average utility over time instead of the worst-case experience, as in the alternative formulation.

For a video request arriving at time t, we define a decision vector $\mathbf{x}_t = (x_{t1}, \ldots, x_{tM})$, where each x_{tj} takes the value 1 if bit rate version j is chosen, and 0 otherwise. Then our problem is:

$$\text{maximize} \quad \sum_{t=1}^{T} \sum_{j=1}^{M} u_{tj} x_{tj}$$

$$\text{subject to} \quad \sum_{t=1}^{T} \sum_{j=1}^{M} c_{tj} x_{tj} \leq B \tag{1}$$

$$\sum_{j=1}^{M} x_{tj} = 1, \ \forall\, t$$

$$\text{variables} \quad x_{tj} \in \{0, 1\}, \ \forall\, t, j,$$

where the first constraint says that the cost of the selected bit rates for all the videos requested in a billing cycle must not exceed the quota B, and the second constraint says that one bit rate version may be selected for each video.

This optimization problem is known as the Multiple-Choice Knapsack Problem (MCKP) [7]. In the regular single-choice knapsack problem, we are given a set of items, each with an associated value and weight. The objective is to pick a subset of the items such that the total value is maximized while not exceeding the knapsack capacity. In our stream selection problem, the items are the individual bit rate versions of the videos, and the multiple choices arise because exactly one version of each video must be selected.

The traditional offline version of the MCKP, where all the input items are known in advance, is well-studied. The problem is NP-hard, but pseudo-polynomial time dynamic programming (DP) solutions exist [7]. Contrary to this offline version, the SS module does not know the video requests in advance, and so needs to make decisions in an online fashion. This requires a modification to the formulation to handle online requests.

3.2.2 Online Stochastic Knapsack Problem

Unlike the traditional offline MCKP, in our scenario, the video requests are revealed one-by-one *online*. Thus, existing DP solutions to the offline knapsack problem cannot be used. Online algorithms handle this situation by making a

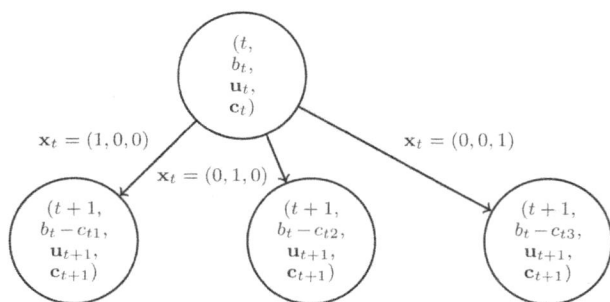

Figure 4: Stream selection modeled as a finite-horizon Markov decision process. A one step state transition is shown with 3 bit rate choices.

decision on-the-fly when a new video request arrives, without any prior knowledge of future requests. However, once a decision is made, it cannot be revoked or changed in the future.

Finite-Horizon Markov Decision Process: Since the data quota resets after the billing cycle is over, there is a time deadline before which all actions must be made. We also note that the bit rate decisions for future intervals should not depend on the decisions taken at previous intervals, given the current remaining budget. This implies the Markov property. The problem can naturally be modeled as a finite-horizon Markov decision process (MDP). A key assumption is that the video requests are independent of time, and therefore the transition probabilities are stationary.

The MDP formulation allows the SS module to make foresighted bit rate selection decisions by taking into account the future impact of its current decisions on the long-term utility. This is better than just an online algorithm which makes myopic decisions at every time step. For example, a greedy solution might choose a bit rate that maximizes the utility of the current request without overshooting the quota.

Figure 4 shows a simple example of choosing between three different bit rates over one time step. The state of the system is defined as the four-tuple $s_t = (t, b_t, \mathbf{u}_t, \mathbf{c}_t)$, comprising the current time interval t, the remaining quota b_t, and the utility and cost vectors $\mathbf{u}_t$ and $\mathbf{c}_t$. There are three possible actions: (i) choose the lowest bit rate, i.e., $\mathbf{x}_t = (1, 0, 0)$; (ii) choose the second bit rate, i.e., $\mathbf{x}_t = (0, 1, 0)$; or (iii) choose the third bit rate, i.e., $\mathbf{x}_t = (0, 0, 1)$. If the lowest bit rate is chosen, the system moves to time $t + 1$ with remaining budget $b_t - c_{t1}$. The algorithm collects utility (reward) u_{t1} and receives the new video request with utility and cost vectors $\mathbf{u}_{t+1}$ and $\mathbf{c}_{t+1}$. If the second bit rate is chosen, the system moves to time $t + 1$, but now subtracts the cost c_{t2} from its remaining budget, leaving it with $b_t - c_{t2}$. It also collects utility u_{t2}. A similar state transition results from choosing the third bit rate.

The set of actions $\{\mathbf{x}_1, \ldots, \mathbf{x}_T\}$ taken by the algorithm at every time step is called a *policy*. A policy that solves the MCKP of (1) is called an optimal policy. If the arriving video requests were known, an optimal policy can be determined using the traditional offline techniques previously mentioned. However, since the video requests are not known *a priori*, the MDP finds a policy that instead maximizes the *expected* sum utility. We develop a solution using DP and online optimization.

3.3 Solving Finite-Horizon MDP

Online Optimization: The optimal policy can be found using standard backward induction techniques for finite-horizon MDPs [8]. We first define $U_t(b_t)$ as the expected utility accumulated from time t until the end of the billing cycle at time T, when the remaining quota is b_t. This expected utility assumes that the optimal action is applied in each state. Then, the optimal action at each time step t is found by solving:

$$
\begin{aligned}
\text{maximize} \quad & u_{tj}x_{tj} + U_{t+1}(b_t - c_{tj}x_{tj}) \\
\text{subject to} \quad & c_{tj}x_{tj} \leq b_t \\
& \sum_{j=1}^{M} x_{tj} = 1 \\
\text{variables} \quad & x_{tj} \in \{0,1\}, \ \forall j,
\end{aligned}
\tag{2}
$$

where the first constraint ensures that the cost of the selected bit rate is less than the remaining quota. The objective function has an intuitive meaning: It maximizes the current utility plus the sum of the expected utilities, subject to the remaining quota. The problem can be solved in $O(M)$ time by discarding the bit rates that violate the constraints, and then picking the bit rate j^* that maximizes the objective function. It is solved every time a video is requested.

DP Computation: Solving (2) requires the computation of $U_t(b_t)$. Since $U(\cdot)$ is an expectation over all future requests, it does not change with every new request, and thus can be pre-computed using DP before running the online algorithm.

Suppose we are at time t with remaining budget b_t, and a new video request arrives. Assuming that the algorithm chooses an optimal bit rate j^* by solving (2), the expected accumulated utility is equal to the utility of the current request, plus the future utility accumulated from time $t + 1$ onward, given that we have already spent c_{tj^*} of our budget. This utility from time $t + 1$ onward is unknown because the future video requests are unknown, and so we must take the expectation. Mathematically, this translates to:

$$
\begin{aligned}
U_t(b_t) = {}& p_t \left(u_{tj^*} + E_{(\mathbf{u},\mathbf{c})}\left[U_{t+1}\left(b_t - c_{tj^*}\right) \right] \right) \\
& + (1 - p_t)U_{t+1}(b_t).
\end{aligned}
\tag{3}
$$

The $(1 - p_t)$ term represents the probability that no video request arrives, and so no bit rate decision is made. The accumulated utility at time t is then equal to the utility at time $t + 1$.

A crucial component of any DP solution is the boundary condition that allows the initial values of $U(\cdot)$ to be calculated. Our boundary condition is that the expected accumulated utility is 0 when the billing cycle is over, or the remaining budget is less than 0. The optimal action at time $T - 1$ is to accept any video that fits in the remaining budget, and thus $U_{T-1}(b_{T-1})$ is known. Then using (3), the remaining entries of $U(\cdot)$ can be calculated. In this work, we choose the budget granularity to be 1, so b_t takes on possible values $1, \ldots, B$. The running time of computing the $U(\cdot)$ matrix is $O(TBM\Gamma)$, where Γ is the cardinality of the set $\{(\mathbf{u},\mathbf{c})\}$ in the video type distribution.

The online and offline components of the MDP stream selection algorithm are summarized in Algorithm 1. In the special case of two bit rates ($M = 2$), our algorithm reduces to that of Papastavrou et al. [10]. With accurate user and video profiling, Algorithm 1 maximizes the sum utility while

---

Algorithm 1 MDP Stream Selection Algorithm

DP Computation of Utility Matrix
Input: Video type distribution $P(\mathbf{u},\mathbf{c})$, quota B, and billing cycle length T.

Output: A matrix $\mathbf{U}$ of size $T \times B$.

1. Compute each entry $U_t(b_t)$ of $\mathbf{U}$, using (3).

Online Bit Rate Selection
Input: Utility and cost vectors $\mathbf{u}_t$ and $\mathbf{c}_t$, remaining capacity b_t, billing cycle length T, and matrix $\mathbf{U}$.

Output: Optimal bit rate j^*.

1. Discard the bit rates with cost greater than b_t.

2. For each of the remaining bit rates, compute j^* that maximizes the objective function of (2).

---

staying under the quota. In the case of inaccurate inputs, however, the algorithm may exceed the quota. In that case, the algorithm should simply choose the lowest bit rate, although this case never occurs in our numerical simulations.

4. USER AND VIDEO PROFILERS

In this section, we detail the functionality of the UP and VP modules. We first describe different patterns in user behavior and tastes, and then propose the user profiler algorithm. The VP module is also briefly explained.

4.1 Profiling User Behavior

The user profiler runs on the client device and characterizes each user through (i) the video request probability at each time interval, and (ii) the distribution of video types preferred by the user.

User Viewing Pattern and Taste: Depending on their lifestyles, different users have different time preferences for watching videos. For example, some users prefer watching videos on weekends rather than on weekdays, while others watch more in the evening after working hours than in the mornings. The taste in content of the users can also be different. For example, some users watch sports videos more often than movie trailers, while some others watch more news clips than music videos. Such preferences in user behavior can lead to well-defined patterns, both in terms of the viewing times and the types of the videos being watched.

The job of the user profiler is to estimate these temporal viewing patterns and video type preferences for each user. The UP module does this based on the user's past video request records, spanning either the previous billing cycle, or the entire history. In this work, we consider requests from the last billing cycle.

Computing Video Request Probability: In each time interval t, there is a certain probability p_t that the user requests a video. This request probability can either vary with each interval or be constant. As a first attempt, we compute the *average* request probability per interval, and set p_t for each interval equal to this average. The average request probability is computed by summing the number of requests in the previous billing cycle and dividing by the number of periods T. The time interval should be set small

Algorithm 2 User Profiling Algorithm

Input: Time stamps and utility–cost vectors $(\mathbf{u}_t, \mathbf{c}_t)$ of each video request in the previous billing cycle.

Output: Video request probability p_t, $\forall t$, and the video type joint probability distribution $P(\mathbf{u}, \mathbf{c})$.

1. Count the number of requests n_r, and the number of time intervals T in the previous billing cycle.

2. Compute average request probability as $\bar{p} = n_r/T$, and set $p_t = \bar{p}$, $\forall\, t$.

3. Count the number of times each $(\mathbf{u}_t, \mathbf{c}_t)$ pair appears in the past; denote this count by $n_{(\mathbf{u}_t, \mathbf{c}_t)}$.

4. Construct the joint probability distribution by computing the individual probabilities as: $p(\mathbf{u}_t, \mathbf{c}_t) = n_{(\mathbf{u}_t, \mathbf{c}_t)} / \sum_{(\mathbf{u}'_t, \mathbf{c}'_t)} n_{(\mathbf{u}'_t, \mathbf{c}'_t)}$

---

enough so that the average request probability is less than 1, but not so small as to inhibit the computation of (3).

There are several alternative approaches, including fitting distributions and prediction-based techniques. The arrival rate of videos might follow a particular known distribution (e.g., Poisson), in which case the probability of an arrival can be computed directly from the distribution itself. Alternatively, one can use more sophisticated time series analysis techniques. For example, at the beginning of the billing cycle, one can predict the sequence of future viewing times in the upcoming billing cycle, then compute the average request probability by adding up the predicted number of requests, and finally dividing that by the number of intervals. One can also design online algorithms, such as predicting the sequence of viewing times for intervals $t+1, t+2, \ldots, T$, while at interval t, and updating the predictions when a new video request arrives. Such alternatives trade off accuracy versus computation need.

We have developed one such online algorithm based on "triple exponential smoothing" [11]. However, here we will employ the simple averaging technique previously mentioned. The resulting computation requires less memory and power, and can be performed easily on a resource-constrained (in terms of battery and memory) client device. Our goal is not necessarily to develop the best user profiler, but to find a method that works well in the system as a whole. To establish this, we run trace-drive simulations in Section 5 to compare the performance of QAVA when the UP module uses the average request probability, to a scenario when the UP module has perfect knowledge of future arrivals. We find that our technique, while simple, achieves close to optimal performance (more than 95% on average).

Computing Video Type Distribution: The joint probability distribution $P(\mathbf{u}, \mathbf{c})$ reflects a user's preference for watching different types of videos. For example, a user who watches a lot of sports videos (which are not-so-compressible) will have a different distribution from a user who watches a lot of talk shows (more compressible). This video type distribution can remain the same over the length of a billing cycle, or can be time-dependent, reflecting, for instance, the fact that a user watches more sports videos at night and more news clips in the morning. As a first-order approxima-

tion, we assume that the distribution does not change with time. The distribution is computed once at the beginning of a billing cycle based on the video requests in the last billing cycle.

Our method is as follows: Each video request arriving at time interval t in the previous billing cycle has a $(\mathbf{u}_t, \mathbf{c}_t)$ pair associated with it. The probability distribution is calculated by counting the frequency of each $(\mathbf{u}_t, \mathbf{c}_t)$ pair from the last billing cycle, and then normalizing appropriately to form a probability distribution. Since the utility and cost are continuous variables, they can be binned for greater computational efficiency; however, in our dataset we find this optimization unnecessary. Through simulation, we show that this estimate performs very well, compared to the ideal scenario when the distribution of the requested videos is perfectly known ahead of time. Our user profiling algorithms are summarized in Algorithm 2.

4.2 Profiling Video Cost and Utility

The purpose of the video profiler running on the VP module is to estimate the utility and cost for all the bit rate versions of all videos stored on the content provider's server. There are many estimation techniques for computing the quality of a video. One standard objective metric is the PSNR, which we employ. The PSNR is a well-known objective metric for measuring video quality. A video typically comprises a sequence of images, and the PSNR for each image is defined as a function of the mean square error (MSE) between the original and compressed image. Mathematically, it is expressed in the logarithmic unit of decibel (dB) as $\text{PSNR} = 10\log_{10}(Q^2/D)$, where D is the pixel-wise MSE between the original and reconstructed image, and Q is the maximum pixel value (usually 255). We compute the video PSNR as the PSNR averaged over all images in the sequence. Typical PSNR values for lossy video compression are between 20 and 30 dB, where higher is better. To account for the duration of the video, we set the utility equal to the PSNR $\times$ the video duration. An example utility-cost curve is shown in Figure 3.

There exist other, potentially more accurate, metrics of video utility (e.g., Mean Opinion Scores [12] or MOS), **as well as means of calculating subjective metrics from objective measurements [13, 23, 26].** However, we choose PSNR as it can be easily computed using a mathematical formula (in contrast to MOS that requires time consuming human experiments) and is very well known to the multimedia community.

Measuring the cost of a video in bytes naturally follows from the fact that the data quota is measured in bytes. The video profiler calculates the utility and the cost in MB for all the videos only once. These utility and cost vectors are stored alongside the videos on the content provider's server.

5. PERFORMANCE EVALUATION

We evaluate the performance of QAVA stream selection by comparing it with three alternatives: (i) a hindsight-based offline, optimal algorithm that knows all the video requests in a billing cycle ahead of time; (ii) a worst-case online algorithm; and (iii) a naïve method (used by, for example, Netflix). We also explore the sensitivity of QAVA to user profiler prediction errors.

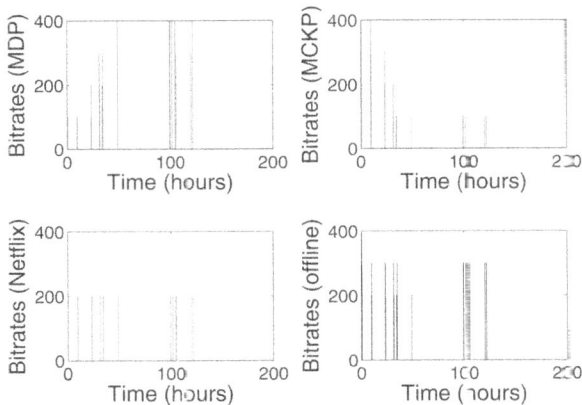

Figure 5: Bit rate selection by different algorithms for a single user. The MDP and MCKP algorithms choose different bit rates over time, while Netflix chooses a constant bit rate and the offline algorithm chooses the optimal bit rates.

5.1 Experimental Setup

Our simulations are based on the public-domain traces of 2 weeks of YouTube video requests from a wireless campus network [14]. The data comprises 16,337 users making a total of 611,968 requests over 14 days. YouTube is the largest source of video traffic, so the dataset captures a major portion of video viewing behavior [25]. The first week of trace data is used to train both video and user profilers. The second week emulates a billing cycle where the stream selector is run for each user's requests.

Each video is encoded in H.264/AVC at 100, 200, 300, 400, and 500 Kbps. The stream selector chooses one bitrate from the first four choices. The 500 Kbps version is treated as a reference for computing the PSNR of the other bit rates. The cost of each video is its size in MB. We set the user's quota at the halfway point between the minimum data usage (always selecting 100 Kbps) and the maximum data usage (always selecting 400 Kbps), and also sweep across quotas when appropriate. The period length is set to 30 minutes, since we experimentally find that varying the period length does not greatly change system performance.

One limitation of this evaluation is that not all videos were available from YouTube at the time of this study. In the training phase, missing videos are not included while generating the video type probability distribution. In the test phase, the utility–cost curves of missing videos are sampled from the video type distribution of the training phase. This gives an advantage to our algorithm, because the probability distribution of the training phase is similar to that of the test phase. We also examine the effect of misestimation of the distribution.

5.2 Comparing Stream Selection Algorithms

We first evaluate the offline algorithm that solves problem (1) with the knowledge of all future video requests. It achieves the best possible performance and is treated as the benchmark against which we compare the performance of the online algorithms. We call this the *hindsight offline optimal* algorithm.

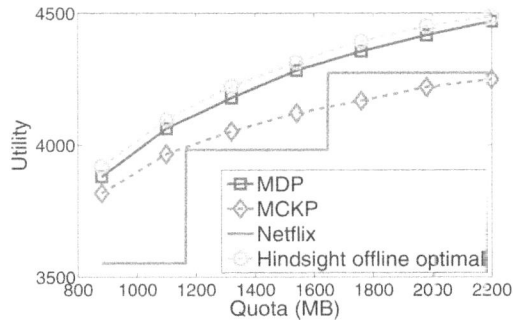

Figure 6: Quality–cost tradeoff for a single user with different quota and fixed video requests. MDP obtains close to optimal utility, while MCKP and Netflix perform sub-optimally.

Zhou *et al.* present an online algorithm to solve (1) with a worst-case performance guarantee regardless of the sequence of video requests [15]. We call this the online *MCKP* algorithm and chose this to compare with our MDP algorithm because it optimizes for the *worst-case* performance, while our algorithm optimizes for *expected* performance. The MCKP algorithm, however, uses less information than our MDP algorithm, needing only the maximum and minimum utility-to-cost ratio across all requested videos, and an estimate of the sum data of the smallest bit rates. The MCKP algorithm does not use prediction or time deadlines, but requires only the quota.

The second online algorithm we compare with is the naïve solution currently used by Netflix. Netflix allows subscribers to select a default streaming bit rate. We assume that a Netflix user chooses one bit rate for the entire billing cycle, and is also intelligent enough to presciently choose the maximum bit rate that fits all videos in the quota. *Clearly, this algorithm is an ideal algorithm and not suitable for practical use, because it assumes advance knowledge of the number of videos to be watched.* Comparison with this Netflix method allows us to evaluate how our MDP algorithm performs against an existing practical solution.

5.3 Single User Examples

To understand the operation of the stream selector, we first run the algorithm for a single user with a target quota of 1426 MB (see Figure 5). The video requests arrive in bursts, and each algorithm selects bit rates. The Netflix method always chooses 200 Kbps. The MDP algorithm has foresight and thus chooses lower bit rates in the beginning of the billing cycle, knowing to save for later. The MCKP algorithm does not use time deadlines, only the remaining quota, and so it chooses high bit rates in the beginning before cutting back as it starts depleting the quota. The offline optimal algorithm chooses a variety of bitrates over time.

We also sweep across different monthly quotas and measure the utility obtained by each algorithm (see Figure 6). The offline algorithm performs the best, with MDP and MCKP close behind. The Netflix method exhibits a staircase-like shape because as the quota increases, the default user-selected bit rate can increase. In all cases, the algorithms use less data than the target quota.

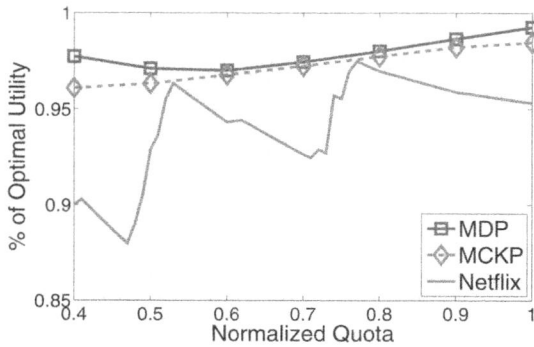

Figure 7: Quality–cost tradeoff averaged and normalized over multiple users. The MDP algorithm achieves nearly optimal performance, with the MCKP algorithm close behind. Both algorithms outperform the naïve Netflix method.

5.4 Multi-User Stream Selection

Average Performance: We now present the evaluation results of the MDP algorithm for multiple users. Each trial takes as input a fixed set of video requests and a quota, and computes the utility obtained by each algorithm. Some input combinations achieve higher utility than others. In order to fairly compare across multiple trials, we normalize the utility across different users by measuring the utility of the online algorithm as a fraction of the offline optimal utility. To normalize the quota, we measure data as a fraction of the total data if the 400 Kbps bit rate were always selected.

Figure 7 shows the average utility across 10 different users. We observe that, on average, the MDP algorithm performs better than the MCKP algorithm. The Netflix method resembles a staircase function as in the single-user case, and obtains especially low utility for low quotas. This is arguably the most important scenario: When the user's quota is small compared to the number of videos she wishes to watch. For these low quotas, the MDP has a definite advantage over MCKP, which in turn outperforms the Netflix method.

Performance Variability: To examine the utility distribution, and not just the average, we plot their cumulative distribution functions (CDFs) in Figure 8(a) across multiple quotas and users. The ideal result is a step function at 1, indicating 100% of the trials result in optimal utility. We see the Netflix method performs the worst, obtaining, for example, less than 95% utility 50% of the time. The MCKP curve is steeper, indicating it has less performance variation, which makes intuitive sense as the algorithm optimizes for the worst-case. The MDP algorithm optimizes for the average-case performance but not the spread, and thus exhibits greater variation, but is closer to the ideal step function.

The MDP and MCKP algorithms are further compared in Figure 8(b), which shows the CDF of their percentage utility difference. If the MDP were always better than the MCKP, we would see a step function at 0. However, we observe that the MCKP sometimes outperforms the MDP algorithm.

On the surface, these simulations seem to suggest the Netflix method performs reasonably well in general. It achieves above 85% of the optimal utility, suggesting that this naïve solution is acceptable for most users. However, the caveat is

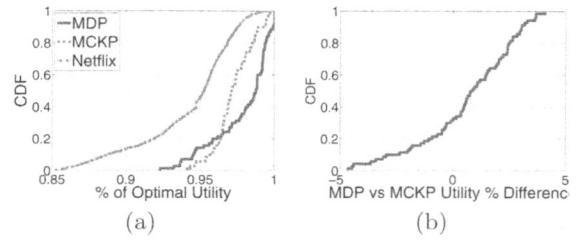

Figure 8: (a) CDF of the utility achieved by MDP, MCKP, and Netflix algorithms. (b) Distribution of MDP performance improvement over MCKP.

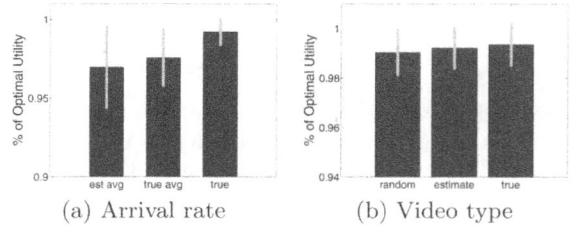

Figure 9: Effect of user profiler prediction error.

that our simulated Netflix method assumes perfect knowledge of the number of video requests in the billing cycle, so that the user knows how to correctly set the default bit rate given the quota. This is represented by the sharp jumps with increasing quota in Figure 6 and 7. If the user sets the default bit rate too high, she will overshoot her quota. If the user sets the default bit rate too low, she will obtain suboptimal utility. A main advantage of QAVA is that it automatically adjusts the bit rate, so the Netflix user does not need to estimate her usage to set her default bit rate, which might result in these over- or under-shooting problems.

5.5 Sensitivity to Prediction Error

It is important to examine how errors from the UP module affect the performance of the stream selection algorithm. There are two possible sources of error: video request probability and video type distribution. To test sensitivity to request probability error, we measure the utility obtained by the MDP algorithm when it uses (1) the estimated average arrival rate trained on historical data, (2) the true average arrival rate of the test data, and (3) the true request times. These results are averaged across multiple users and shown in Figure 9(a), with the error bars indicating standard deviation. We observe that the greater the information accuracy, the greater the average utility. The performance difference is quite small, which suggests that the MDP algorithm performs well independent of arrival probability accuracy. Moreover, the average percentage difference between the true and estimated arrival rate is 8%.

To analyze the sensitivity of the stream selector to video type prediction errors, we perform the following experiment. We calculate the true video type distribution of the test data, and also randomly generate a video type distribution. This random distribution has both random videos (drawn from the pool of requested videos from all users), and random probabilities. The utility obtained by the MDP algorithm using the random, estimated, and true distributions,

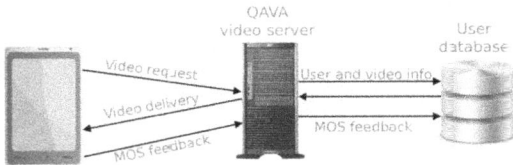

Figure 10: Android implementation of QAVA for running real-world trials within the Princeton University community.

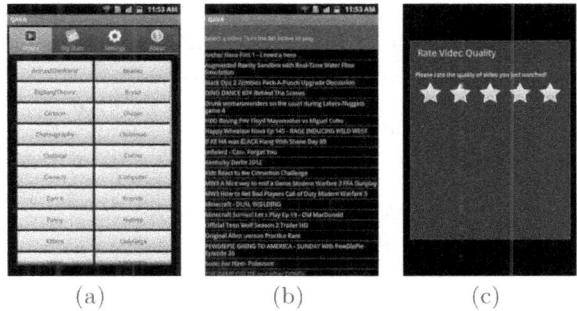

(a)　　　　　　　　(b)　　　　　　　　(c)

Figure 11: Screenshots of QAVA Android app. (a) Different video categories; (b) List of videos within a category; and (c) Feedback screen.

averaged across all users, is shown in Figure 9(b) with the error bars indicating standard deviation. We find that the average utility increases only slightly as more accurate information is known, suggesting robustness of the MDP algorithm to video type distribution errors.

6. DISCUSSION ON IMPLEMENTATION

6.1 Implementation on Android

In addition to evaluating QAVA through simulations with YouTube video request traces, we have implemented QAVA to run on the Android platform. This enables us to evaluate the performance of QAVA on a commercial operating system using real users' video requests. We are currently conducting a trial, starting with 15 community volunteers.

In this section, we briefly summarize the implementation of QAVA, as shown in Figure 10. Approximately 500 videos are stored in our server, each with a resolution of 640×480 pixels and encoded using H.264/AVC in 5 different bitrates: 100, 200, 300, 400, and 500 Kbps. Participants can install the QAVA application on their mobile devices and request any of the stored videos. The videos are streamed from our server at a bit rate determined by the SS module on the server. The server also logs the time stamp, user ID, video name, and video utility and cost in a database. When the user stops watching the video, she is asked to provide a feedback on the video quality by choosing a rating on a scale of 1–5, where 1 indicates "very annoying", and 5 indicates "imperceptible distortion".

Screenshots of the GUI are shown in Figure 11. When the users opens the QAVA application, she is presented with the screen in Figure 11(a), which lists different video categories, such as music, movies, cartoons, etc. Each category contains a list of videos, which is shown on the second screen in Figure 11(b) once the user selects a category. By selecting any of the videos listed under that category, the user can start watching the video. The last screen in Figure 11(c) shows the feedback mechanism, where the user rates the video by selecting one of the 5 stars. A video demonstrating our GUI can be found at http://snipurl.com/23upjft.

To increase the choice of content available to trial participants, we have also used the YouTube API to implement a feature that allows users to access any YouTube video through the QAVA application. We first store a large number of YouTube videos on our server. If the user requests a YouTube video that was already pre-fetched, we run QAVA; otherwise, the video is streamed from YouTube.

6.2 Client-based Architectures

Our trial architecture of Figure 10 is sufficient when the SS module is located on the CP and can choose which bit rate video to stream to the user. In a practical scenario, it may be that the bit rate selected by the SS module cannot be streamed by the CP, either due to unavailability of video versions, or lack of support from the CP. To address this, we are exploring options for a *client-based* implementation architecture for QAVA. There are two possibilities: a transcoding-based system, and a throttling-based system.

In the transcoding-based solution, all traffic from the client is routed through a web proxy. By inspecting the packets, video traffic may be distinguished and transcoded on-the-fly by the proxy server to the correct bit rate. This approach has the advantage of using standard web proxy technology, and can handle all types of videos as long as the transcoder has the appropriate codec. However, there are significant implementation challenges in terms of latency minimization: the proxy and transcoder must perform quickly in order to satisfy the demands of delay-sensitive video traffic. Moreover, implementing a transcoder for HTTP video streams is also difficult.

The throttling-based solution leverages the emerging popularity of adaptive HTTP video streaming [20]. In this technology, the videos automatically adjust their bit rate based on their estimate of TCP throughput. By limiting the bandwidth observed by the rate switching algorithm, QAVA can force the video bit rate to automatically settle to the rate determined by the SS module. This throttling can be performed on the client device or on a web proxy. In terms of implementation, this approach is simpler than the transcoding-based solution, but it suffers from the limitation that only adaptive HTTP video streams can be modified in this way.

7. RELATED WORK

Adapting video quality with respect to resource constraints and user utility has been extensively studied since the 1990s, as surveyed for example by Chang and Vetra [16]. The algorithms and systems to perform such video adaptation have long been studied in the research community [9, 18, 19, 24]. There has also been increasing interest from industry: Apple, Microsoft, and Adobe have developed proprietary HTTP video streaming protocols that perform intra-video bit rate switching to adapt to varying channel conditions.

Recent progress by an industrial consortium has resulted in the MPEG-DASH standard [20], which aims to address the lack of inter-operability between current video streaming protocols by providing an open interface to access the quality levels of a video. However, these lines of work still focus on channel-based video adaptation. To the best of our knowledge, video adaptation with respect to each user's *data quota* in the context of usage-based pricing has not been systematically investigated prior to this work.

Jan *et al.* [21] developed a system for compressing images on webpages under a data quota. Although the motivation is similar, the application to images and webpages is different. It also differs in that the decisions are made with full knowledge of the images to be compressed. Compared to this, QAVA needs to make *online* decisions without the knowledge of future video requests.

Recently, systems like Onavo [22] enable users to save on data plans by forwarding all data through a proxy server and compressing images and text. However, they do not exploit consumer usage patterns or the dynamic range of video compressibility. To this end, QAVA offers substantial data saving opportunities, because video traffic is much more compressible (than images and text), and comprises the bulk of mobile data consumption.

8. CONCLUSIONS

The continuous rise of mobile video traffic and the $10 per GB usage-based pricing are at odds. Managing demand through Smart Data-Pricing (SDP) is a possible solution approach, e.g., time-shifting delay-tolerant traffic [17]. Adapting video quality offers another approach, especially for streaming video traffic. We presented QAVA, a system to mediate the conflicting trends of increased video streaming on mobile devices vs. usage-based pricing by cellular and broadband ISPs. QAVA automatically selects the best bit rate to enable the consumer to stay under her data quota, while suffering minimal distortion. By evaluting the performance on real video traces, we demonstrated that QAVA performed better than existing approaches in literature and practical solutions.

Our major ongoing work is the development and testing of user trials, in collaboration with several carriers and content providers in the US, as well as improvement of the UP and VP algorithms. A future area of exploration is the longer timescale problem of video bit rate selection and placement on limited capacity servers. Another interesting issue is the feedback between user behavior and QAVA bit rate delivery, which we have ignored so far, but merits further study. Other possible extensions include more sophisticated user and video profiler methods; bit rate selection with respect to heterogeneous devices and quota; and integration of the QAVA algorithms with upcoming video streaming standards.

Acknowledgements

This work was supported by AFOSR FA9550-09-1-0643, NSF CNS-1011962, and PECASE N00014-09-1-0449. We would like to thank our colleagues, Sangtae Ha, our shepherd Oliver Spatscheck, and the anonymous reviewers for their valuable comments.

9. REFERENCES

[1] "Cisco Visual Networking Index: Global Mobile Data Traffic Forecast Update", 2011-2016.

[2] "Rogers Hi-speed Internet FAQ", <http://www.keepingpace.ca/faq.html>

[3] "Reliance 3G Plans & Pricing", <http://www.rcom.co.in/Rcom/personal/3G/HTML/PostpaidDataPlans.html>.

[4] *DataWiz*, <http://www.datami.com/>.

[5] Troianovski A, "AT&T May Try Billing App Makers", *Wall Street Journal*, Feb. 28 2012.

[6] Bovik A, *The Essential Guide to Video Processing*, Elsevier 2009.

[7] Kellerer H, Pferschy U, Pisinger D, *Knapsack Problems*, Springer 2004.

[8] Puterman ML, *Markov Decision Processes: Discrete Stochastic Dynamic Programming*, Wiley 2005.

[9] Liu C, Bouazizi I, Gabbouj M, "Rate Adaptation for Adaptive HTTP Streaming", *ACM MMSys*, 2011.

[10] Papastavrou JD, Rajagopalan S, Kleywegt AJ, "The Dynamic and Stochastic Knapsack Problem with Deadlines", *Management Science*, 1996.

[11] Winters PR, "Forecasting Sales by Exponentially Weighted Moving Averages", *Management Science* 6(3):324-42, 1960.

[12] "Recommendation BT.500: Methodology for the subjective assessment of the quality of television pictures", *International Telecommunication Union*, 2012.

[13] Wang Y, Schaar M, Chang S, Loui AC, "Classification-Based Multidimensional Adaptation Prediction for Scalable Video Coding Using Subjective Quality Evaluation", in *IEEE Trans. Circuits Sys. Video Tech.*, 15(10):1270-8, 2005.

[14] Zink M, Suh K, Gu Y, Kurose J, "Watch Global Cache Local: YouTube Network Traces at a Campus Network - Measurements and Implications", *IEEE MMCN*, 2008.

[15] Zhou Y, Chakrabarty D, Lukose R. "Budget Constrained Bidding in Keyword Auctions and Online Knapsack Problems", *WWW*, 2007.

[16] Chang SF, Vetra A, "Video Adaptation: Concepts, Technologies, and Open Issues", in *Proc. IEEE*, 93(1):148-58, 2005.

[17] Ha S, Sen S, Joe-Wong C, Im Y, Chiang M, "TUBE: Time-Dependent Pricing for Mobile Data", *ACM SIGCOMM*, 2012.

[18] Rejaie R, Handley M, Estrin D, "Quality adaptation for congestion controlled video playback over the Internet", *ACM SIGCOMM* 1999.

[19] Liu J, Li B, Zhang Y, "An End-to-End Adaptation Protocol for Layered Video Multicast Using Optimal Rate Allocation", in *IEEE Trans. Mult.*, 6(1):87-102, 2004.

[20] MPEG-DASH, <http://dashpg.com/>.

[21] Jan RH, Lin CP, Chern MS, "An optimization model for Web content adaptation", *Computer Networks* 50(7):953-65, 2006.

[22] Onavo, <http://www.onavo.com/>.

[23] Dobrian F, Sekar V, Awan A, Stoica I, Joseph DA, Ganjam A, Zhan J, Zhang H, "Understanding the Impact of Video Quality on User Engagement", *ACM SIGCOMM*, 2011.

[24] Liu X, Dobrian F, Milner H, Jiang J, Sekar V, Stoica I, Zhang H, "A Case fo a Coordinated Internet Video Control Plane", *ACM SIGCOMM*, 2012.

[25] "Global Interet Phenomena Report", *Sandvine*, 2012.

[26] Chen KT, Huang CY, Huang P, Lei CL, "Quantifying Skype User Satisfaction", *ACM SIGCOMM*, 2006.

Orchestrating Massively Distributed CDNs

Joe Wenjie Jiang*
Princeton University
Princeton, NJ
wenjiej@cs.
princeton.edu

Stratis Ioannidis
Technicolor
Palo Alto, CA
stratis.ioannidis@
technicolor.com

Laurent Massoulié
INRIA
Paris, France
laurent.massoulie@
inria.fr

Fabio Picconi
Technicolor,
Paris, France
fabio.picconi@
technicolor.com

ABSTRACT

We consider a content delivery architecture based on geographically dispersed groups of "last-mile" CDN servers, *e.g.*, set-top boxes located within users' homes. These servers may belong to administratively separate domains, such as multiple ISPs. We propose a set of scalable, adaptive mechanisms to jointly manage content replication and request routing within this architecture. Relying on primal-dual methods and fluid-limit techniques, we formally prove the optimality of our design. We further evaluate its performance on both synthetic and trace-driven simulations, based on real BitTorrent traces, and observe a reduction of network costs by more than 50% over traditional mechanisms such as LRU/LFU with closest request routing.

Categories and Subject Descriptors

C.4 [**Computer-Communication Networks**]: [Distributed Systems]

Keywords

Distributed Content Distribution Networks, Content Placement, Request Routing

1. INTRODUCTION

The total Internet traffic per month was already in excess of 10^{19} Bytes in 2011 [1]. Video-on-demand traffic alone is predicted to grow to three times this amount by 2015. Existing content providers such as Youtube and Netflix, which represent a large fraction of today's Internet video traffic, use content delivery networks (CDNs) to replicate, cache, and stream videos at many servers across the world. Nevertheless, the large volumes of traffic exiting the CDN infrastructure incur significant operational costs for the content providers. This state of affairs prompts a rethinking of the current content delivery architecture.

---

*The author is currently at Google Inc.

A promising evolution from today's approach consists of extending the CDN to the "last mile" of content delivery by incorporating small servers close to the edge of the network. For instance, this approach leverages devices within users' homes, such as set-top boxes or broadband gateways, as advocated by the Nano Datacenter [2] consortium, network attached storage (NAS) such as Boxee [3], or appliances promoted by business initiatives such as AppleTV. Part of or the entire storage and bandwidth capacities of these devices can be leased to a CDN or a content provider. The latter leverage these resources to store content and serve download requests effectively in a managed peer-to-peer fashion.

Such an architecture has considerable advantages for both providers as well as users. First, it harnesses available bandwidth and storage resources of appliances already deployed at users' homes. Second, it enables serving requests locally, *e.g.*, from a device within the same ISP or even within the same neighborhood. In addition to reducing latency, this alleviates CDN server traffic while also reducing cross-traffic among ISPs, thereby significantly decreasing the operational cost of the CDN. In practice, the service operator can make a combined use of the traditional CDN and distributed CDNs to optimize performance and reduce cost simultaneously.

Ideally, one would like to optimize the design of this "diffuse cloud" of nano-servers so that such cross-traffic costs are minimized. There are two degrees of freedom in this design: (a) *content placement*, *i.e.*, identifying what content to cache in each device, and (b) *request routing*, identifying which device is to serve an incoming request for content.

As devices have limited resources, the *storage and bandwidth constraints* of each device need to be taken into account in the above optimization. Also, optimal placement and routing decisions depend on the *demand* for content across users; to reduce traffic costs, it is preferable to cache content closer to where it is most frequently requested.

Nevertheless, this optimization raises several important challenges. First, while traditional CDN design has addressed content caching and request routing separately, a *joint optimization* is required as both decisions impact each other in the case of massively distributed last-mile servers. Second, as the optimization is to be performed over millions of devices, *scalability* is a crucial issue. Third, the system comprises devices dispersed across multiple ISPs and their *heterogeneity*—in terms of bandwidth and storage resources, as well as the relative costs of serving requests—needs to be addressed. In addition, managing many boxes over different ISPs requires a distributed and collaborative solution that does not reveal the internal structure of ISPs. Finally, though optimal placement and routing decisions depend on demand, the latter may be a priori unknown or time-variant. Hence, *adaptive* placement and routing schemes that react to changes in user demand, are preferred.

In this work, we address these challenges by developing a solution for efficient traffic management in next-generation CDNs. We make the following contributions:

- We propose a distributed, adaptive content placement and routing architecture, designed to scale over millions of heterogeneous devices.

- Building upon primal-dual decomposition techniques, we formally establish that our adaptations jointly optimize both content placement and routing, and prove that they minimize CDN traffic costs.

- To establish these results, we characterize the asymptotic loss probability of the *uniform-slot* service assignment policy (determining which device serves a request inside an ISP), a crucial component of our design. We show that although much simpler to implement than prior art, it exhibits the same asymptotic behavior.

- As part of this design, we propose a novel content placement scheme that changes cache contents, and prove that it is order-optimal: it reaches a targeted replication within a constant factor from the optimal number of write operations necessary.

- We conduct simulations driven by BitTorrent traces, with all the associated features of real traffic (burstiness, long-tail distribution), and show that our mechanism reduces network costs by more than half, as compared to traditional solutions based on LRU cache management and nearest-neighbor routing.

The remainder of this paper is organized as follows. We first review related work (Section 2) and describe our problem setup (Section 3). In Section 4 we overview our system architecture. The theoretical guarantees of our adaptation, request routing and content placement algorithms are presented in Sections 5 and 6. Finally, in addition to this theoretical underpinning, our architecture is further validated experimentally in Section 7.

2. RELATED WORK

Peer-assistance of CDNs has been studied from several perspectives. Recent work has shown that it can reduce CDN server traffic [4] and energy consumption [5] by more than 60%. Early research compared the efficiency of prefetching policies for peer-assisted VoD [6], and bandwidth allocation across different P2P swarms [7]. Peer incentivization, *e.g.*, through rebates or service fee reductions, has also been studied [8–10]. Moreover, the use of dedicated home devices as an extension of a CDN's infrastructure has been the model of at least one recent start-up [11] and has been the subject of several recent papers [5,12]. We build and extend upon these works by providing a formal framework for joint placement and routing optimization.

Minimizing cross-traffic is extensively studied in the context of "ISP-friendly" P2P system design and is known to reduce both ISP cross-traffic and download delays [13,14]. Typically, the selection of download sources is biased towards nearby peers; peer proximity can be inferred either

through client-side mechanisms [15] or through a service offered by the ISP [16–18]. In the latter case, the ISP can explicitly recommend which neighbors to download content from by solving an optimization problem that minimizes cross-traffic [18]. In the context of peer-assisted CDNs, an objective that minimizes a weighted sum of cross-traffic and the load on the content server can also be considered [17]. Prior work on ISP-friendliness reduces cross traffic solely by performing *service assignment* to suitable peers. We add a control knob on top of service assignment, namely *content placement*: our optimization selects not only where requests are routed, but also where content is stored.

In the *cooperative caching problem*, clients generate a set of requests for items, that need to be mapped to caches that can serve them; each client/cache pair assignment is associated with an access cost. The goal is to decide how to place items in caches and assign requests to caches that can serve them, so that the total access cost is minimized. The problem is NP-hard, and a 10-approximation algorithm is known [19]. Motivated by CDN topologies, Borst *et al.* [20] obtain lower approximation ratios as well as competitive online algorithms for the case where cache costs are determined by weights in a star graph. A polynomial algorithm is known in the case where caches are organized in a hierarchical topology and the replica accessed is always the nearest replica [21]. We significantly depart from the above studies by explicitly dealing with bandwidth constraints, assuming a stochastic demand for items and proposing an adaptive, distributed algorithm for joint content placement and service assignment among multiple *classes* of identical caches.

Finally, recent work [22–24] has considered cache management specifically in the context of P2P VoD systems, and is in this sense close to our work. However, the heterogeneous (*e.g.*, across multiple ISPs) aspect of our system is not present in any of the above works. As in [24], we capture box service behavior through a loss model; our Thm. 2 extends their analysis, by establishing that a simple service assignment policy (the "uniform slot" policy), has asymptotically the same behavior as the one proposed in [24] (see also Section 6.1).

3. PROBLEM FORMULATION

In the system we consider, a content provider such as YouTube or Netflix delivers content (*e.g.*, videos or music) to home users subscribing to its services. Users access the service through devices installed at their home, such as set-top boxes (providing common Internet connectivity and limited storage) or network-attached storage (NAS) devices. Part of the storage and upload capacities of these boxes is leased to the content provider. The latter uses these resources to serve requests for its content, alleviating the load on its CDN.

Users are geographically dispersed across ISPs. Serving them incurs a cost depending on the cross-traffic they generate. The content provider's goal is to determine (a) where to cache content and (b) how to serve user requests for content, in order to minimize this cost. The remainder of this section formalizes our setup; our key notation is in Table 1.

3.1 Box Classes

We represent the users' home devices by a set $\mathcal{B}$, the set of *boxes*, where $B = |\mathcal{B}|$. We partition $\mathcal{B}$ into D classes $\mathcal{B}^d$, $d \in \mathcal{D} = \{1, \ldots, D\}$, with size $B^d = |\mathcal{B}^d|$. Such partitioning may correspond, *e.g.*, to grouping together boxes managed by the

s	Existing CDN infrastructure.
$\mathcal{B}$	Set of all boxes in the system.
$\mathcal{C}$	Content catalog.
$\mathcal{D}$	Set of all set-of-box classes.
$\mathcal{B}^d$	Boxes in class $d \in \mathcal{D}$.
M^d	Storage capacity of boxes in $\mathcal{B}^d$.
U^d	Upload capacity of boxes in $\mathcal{B}^d$.
$\mathcal{F}_b$	Cache content of box b.
p_c^d	Replication ratio of content c in $\mathcal{B}^d$.
λ_c^d	Request rate for content $c \in \mathcal{C}$ in $\mathcal{B}^d$.
$w^{dd'}$	Cost of a transfer from $d' \in \mathcal{D} \cup \{s\}$ to $d \in \mathcal{D}$.
$r_c^{dd'}$	Rate of requests for c forwarded from $d \in \mathcal{D}$ to $d' \in \mathcal{D} \cup \{s\}$.
r_c^d	Aggregate rate of incoming requests for c to $d \in \mathcal{D}$.
R^d	$R^d = B^d U^d$, the total upload capacity in class d.

Table 1: Summary of key notation

same ISP. Different levels of aggregation or granularity may be used: for example, each class may comprise boxes within the same city or even the same city block. Throughout the text, we use the index d for a class in $\mathcal{D}$ and the index s (as in "server") to indicate the existing CDN infrastructure.

Through the CDN, boxes gain access to the provider's content collection, such as, e.g., movies, clips or shows. We denote this collection by $\mathcal{C}$ and call it the *content catalog*. We assume that items in $\mathcal{C}$ have identical size—if not, the original content can be partitioned into fixed-size chunks, and $\mathcal{C}$ viewed as a collection of chunks. Classes are heterogeneous: storage and bandwidth capacities as well as traffic costs associated with serving requests differ across classes. Nevertheless, as described below, boxes within the same class have the same capacities and incur the same costs.

3.2 Storage and Bandwidth Capacity

Part of the boxes' storage is allocated to and managed by the CDN. Each box in $\mathcal{B}^d$ has M^d storage "slots", used by the CDN to store content items. We call M^d the *storage capacity* of boxes in $\mathcal{B}^d$. For each $b \in \mathcal{B}^d$, we denote the set of items cached in box b by $\mathcal{F}_b \subset \mathcal{C}$, where $|\mathcal{F}_b| = M^d$. Note that $\mathcal{F}_b$ is determined by the CDN, not the user. Users may store (or delete at will) content they retrieve in private storage devices, or even at the spare storage of their box, but such replicas are not managed or shared by the CDN.

Boxes can serve incoming requests for content they store in this designated space. We model this service behavior through a *loss model* [25], rather than a queueing model. A box in $\mathcal{B}^d$ can upload at most U^d content items concurrently, each at a fixed rate. We refer to U^d as the *upload capacity* of boxes in class d. Alternatively, each box has U^d upload "slots": if a box receives a request for a content it stores and has a free upload slot, this slot is used to serve the request and upload the requested content. The service time, i.e., the duration of an upload, is assumed to be exponentially distributed with one-unit mean. Slots remain busy until the upload terminates, at which point they become free again.

The use of a loss model ensures that incoming requests are immediately served by a box at a guaranteed rate and no queuing delays are incurred. Moreover, most of today's content services, such as video streaming, require a constant bit-rate and do not consume additional bandwidth, so partitioning uplink bandwidth into "slots" makes sense.

3.3 Request Load

Users (boxes) generate content requests at varying rates across different classes. We model requests for content c generated by each box $b \in \mathcal{B}^d$ through a Poisson process with rate $\tilde{\lambda}_c^d$. Hence, the aggregate request process for c in class d is also Poisson with rate $\lambda_c^d = \tilde{\lambda}_c^d B^d$, which scales proportionally to the class size. When a box $b \in \mathcal{B}^d$ storing $c \in \mathcal{C}$ (i.e., $c \in \mathcal{F}_b$) generates a request for c, it is served by the local cache—no downloading is necessary. Otherwise, the request must be served by either the CDN's pre-existing infrastructure or some other box in $\mathcal{B}$.

Though our analysis assumes that the request generation process is stationary and Poisson (Thms. 1-3) we relax this assumption in Section 7, evaluating our system over requests of time-varying intensity generated by real-life P2P users.

3.4 Minimizing Traffic Costs

Serving a user request from class d using either the existing CDN infrastructure or another class d' requires transferring content across the class boundaries. In general, cross-traffic costs are dictated by the transit agreements between peering ISPs and may vary from one class to the next. As such, we denote by $w^{dd'}$, $d, d' \in \mathcal{D}$, the traffic cost for serving a request from class d by a box in class d'. Similarly, we denote by w^{ds} as the traffic cost of serving a request from class d by the CDN's existing infrastructure.

The content provider that manages the boxes pays incurred cross-traffic costs to ISPs. Hence, it is in its interest to minimize such costs. In particular, the service provider needs to determine (a) the content $\mathcal{F}_b$ placed in each box b, and (b) where the request generated by each box should be directed to, so that its aggregate traffic costs are minimized.

Solving this problem over millions of devices, while satisfying the constraints imposed by the limited storage and bandwidth capacities at each box, poses a significant scalability challenge. Further, deciding where to place content and how to route requests is, in general, a computationally intractable combinatorial problem [19]. In addition, managing boxes from different ISPs raises the need for a distributed solution that does not require the ISPs to reveal their internal structure to each other. Finally, the optimal placement and routing scheme depends on the demands λ_c^d; these may dynamic and a priori unknown to the CDN. As such, an adaptive scheme, that measures and reacts to user demand, is preferable. We present a system design that addresses these challenges in the next section.

4. SYSTEM ARCHITECTURE

To address the challenges above, we propose a distributed, adaptive scheme for joint placement and routing. Through a combination of asymptotic results, we show our design is optimal, in the sense that it minimizes the CDN's aggregate traffic cost when the number of boxes is large.

4.1 Overview

Rather than centralizing the management of the distributed CDN, our solution delegates management to one device per class, termed the *class tracker*. Class trackers are deployed by the content provider, either as separate servers or as designated boxes within each class. They manage (a) content placement within their classes, (b) the routing of requests either generated or served by boxes in their classes.

Each tracker has a full view of the state of boxes within its class, knowing, *e.g.*, the contents of each box's cache and the number of its free upload slots. Nevertheless, the tracker does not have access to the same information about boxes in other classes. In fact, its knowledge about the state in other classes is limited to lightweight *congestion signals* exchanged periodically between trackers.

Overall, trackers perform the following operations:

Adaptation. For each content $c \in \mathcal{C}$, the tracker maintains the desirable *replication ratio* p_c^d, *i.e.*, the fraction of boxes in the class that store c. In addition, it also maintains the desirable *forwarding rates* $r_c^{dd'}$, $d' \in \mathcal{D} \cup \{s\}$, which correspond to the rate of outgoing requests for c, forwarded to other class trackers as well as the CDN infrastructure (denoted by s). These variables are stored locally by the tracker and updated periodically, at fixed time intervals (*e.g.*, once every day). The updated values are used as inputs to the tracker's placement and routing algorithms within the next adaptation round. Updating these variables allows the trackers to adapt both their placement and routing decisions, in a way that the system reaches a global objective (namely, the minimization of aggregate costs).

Content Placement. At the termination of each adaptation round, after deciding the replication ratios p_c^d of each content item in class d, the tracker allocates the content items to boxes: for each box $b \in \mathcal{B}^d$, it determines $\mathcal{F}_b$ in a manner so that the fraction of boxes storing c is indeed p_c^d.

Request Routing. Trackers are responsible for routing requests either generated or served by boxes in their classes. We separate the routing of requests into two phases: *request forwarding* and *service assignment*. Request forwarding determines to which class a request generated by a local box is forwarded, so that the desirable forwarding rates $r_c^{dd'}$ are maintained. Upon receiving a request, the tracker of the class selects a box within its class to serve the request; we refer to this selection as service assignment.

In the remainder of this section, we formally define the optimization performed by the tracker through adaptation and describe our request routing algorithm in detail. We also outline our distributed adaptation and content placement algorithms; their full specification is in Sec. 5 and 6.

4.2 Tracker Information

As stated above, each class tracker has a complete view of the current state of every box inside its own class. In particular, it knows (a) which content items are stored in each box, and (b) how many free upload slots it has. The trackers also collect traffic statistics: the class d tracker maintains estimates of λ_c^d, $c \in \mathcal{C}$, the rate with which requests for content c are generated within the class. It also maintains estimates of the *incoming* rate of requests for content c in class d. All the above are measured and maintained locally at the tracker; this is possible precisely because it manages both content placement and request routing within its class.

Nevertheless, trackers are *a-priori* unaware the states of boxes in other classes: they learn about congestion in other classes through the exchange of appropriate light-weight congestion signals, at the end of each adaptation round.

4.3 Replication and Forwarding Policies

In addition to the above information pertaining to their classes, trackers maintain $|\mathcal{C}|$ local variables $p_c^d \in [0, 1]$, for

$c \in \mathcal{C}, d \in \mathcal{D}$. We call p_c^d the *replication ratio* of item c in class d, and the vector $\boldsymbol{p}^d = [p_c^d]_{c \in \mathcal{C}}$ the *replication policy* of class d. At any point in time, the replication ratios satisfy:

$$p_c^d = \sum_{b \in \mathcal{B}^d} \mathbb{1}_{c \in \mathcal{F}_b} / B^d, \quad \forall c \in \mathcal{C}, d \in \mathcal{D}, \qquad (1)$$

i.e., the replication ratio p_c^d equals the fraction of boxes in $\mathcal{B}^d$ that store content $c \in \mathcal{C}$. Also, by summing (1) in terms of c, it is easy to see that, when all caches are full,

$$\sum_{c \in \mathcal{C}} p_c^d = M^d, \quad \forall d \in \mathcal{D}. \qquad (2)$$

The replication policy of a tracker serves as an input to its content placement algorithm. That is, the tracker updates it replication policy (or, its desired replication ratios) at the end of every adaptation round. Subsequently, the replication policy is used to determine the placement of content to boxes in $\mathcal{B}^d$, so that (1) is indeed satisfied.

In addition to its replication policy, the tracker maintains $(|\mathcal{D}| + 1) \times |\mathcal{C}|$ additional local variables

$$r_c^{dd'}, \quad d' \in \mathcal{D} \cup \{s\}, c \in \mathcal{C}.$$

We call these the *forwarding rates* of class d, and the vector $\boldsymbol{r}^d = [r_c^{dd'}]_{d' \in \mathcal{D} \cup \{s\}c}$ of these values the *forwarding policy* of d. At any point in time each variable $r_c^{dd'} \in \mathbb{R}_+$, for $d' \in \mathcal{D}$, equals the rate of requests for content c that the tracker forwards from class d to d'. Similarly, each variable $r_c^{ds} \in \mathbb{R}_+$ equals the rate of requests for c forwarded by the tracker directly to the CDN's existing infrastructure. The forwarding policies satisfy the equalities:

$$r_c^{ds} + \sum_{d' \in \mathcal{D}} r_c^{dd'} = \lambda_c^d (1 - p_c^d), \quad \forall c \in \mathcal{C}, d \in \mathcal{D}, \qquad (3)$$

i.e., requests not immediately served by local caches are forwarded to the CDN or a box in another class.

The tracker also updates its forwarding policy at the end of an adaptation round. The updated values are subsequently used as inputs to the tracker's request forwarding algorithm for the next round. In particular, the tracker implements a routing scheme that ensures that the rate of requests for item c forwarded to $d' \in \mathcal{C} \cup \{s\}$ is precisely $r_c^{dd'}$.

4.4 Request Routing and Loss Probabilities

As mentioned above, the routing of requests in our scheme consists of two phases, *request forwarding* and *service assignment*. We describe these in detail below.

Request Forwarding. In the request forwarding phase, a box $b \in \mathcal{B}^d$ generating a request for an item $c \in \mathcal{C}$ first checks if it already stores c, *i.e.*, $c \in F_b$. If so, the request is served immediately and no downloading is necessary. If not, the box contacts the class tracker; the latter determines whether the request should be forwarded to (a) another box within the class, (b) a box in another class, or (c) served directly by the CDN's infrastructure. If the tracker determines that the request is to be forwarded to class d' (case (b)), it routes the request to the tracker managing this class.

To select among these 3 outcomes, the tracker uses $\boldsymbol{r}^d$ as follows: it forwards a request to $d' \in \mathcal{D} \cup \{s\}$ with a probability proportional to $r_c^{dd'}$. As a result, provided that (3) is satisfied, requests forwarded from class d to d' form independent Poisson processes with rates $r_c^{dd'}$.

Service Assignment. In the service assignment phase, the class d tracker assigns a request for a content c to the box in its class that is to serve it. Requests can be local, *i.e.*, generated by a box in $\mathcal{B}^d$ and deemed to be served locally during the forwarding phase, or external, *i.e.*, generated by a box in a different class d' and forwarded to the class d tracker by the tracker of d'. To assign requests to boxes, the tracker follows a *uniform slot* policy. Under this policy, an incoming request for content c is assigned to a box selected among all boxes currently storing c and having an empty upload slot. Each such box is selected with a probability proportional to the number of its empty slots. Equivalently, the request is matched to a slot selected uniformly from all free upload slots of boxes storing c: for X_b the number of free slots of box $b \in \mathcal{B}^d$, an incoming request for content c is mapped to a slot selected uniformly at random among the $\sum_{b \in \mathcal{B}^d : c \in \mathcal{F}_b} X_b$ slots of boxes that can serve this request.

Loss Probabilities. It is possible that no free upload slots in the class exist when the request for c arrives (*i.e.*, $\sum_{b \in \mathcal{B}^d : c \in \mathcal{F}_b} X_b = 0$). In such a case, a request is re-routed to the CDN's infrastructure. Hence, *not all requests for content* c that arrive at class d are served by boxes in $\mathcal{B}_d$.

Let ν_c^d be the *loss probability* of item c in class d, *i.e.*, the probability that a request for c cannot be served and is re-routed to the infrastructure. We say that requests for item c are served *with high probability* (w.h.p.) in class d, if

$$\lim_{B^d \to \infty} \nu_c^d(B^d) = 0, \qquad (4)$$

i.e., as the total number of boxes increases, the probability that a request for content c fails goes to zero. Two necessary constraints (see, *e.g.*, [24]) for (4) to hold in class $d \in \mathcal{D}$ are:

$$\sum_{c \in \mathcal{C}} r_c^{\cdot d} < B^d U^d, \qquad (5)$$

$$r_c^{\cdot d} < B^d U^d p_c^d, \quad \forall c \in \mathcal{C}, \qquad (6)$$

where $r_c^{\cdot d} = \sum_{d' \in \mathcal{D}} r_c^{d'd}$ is the aggregate request rate for content c received by class d. Constraint (5) states that the aggregate traffic load imposed on class d should not exceed the total upload capacity over all boxes; (6) states that the traffic imposed on d by requests for c should not exceed the total capacity of boxes storing c.

4.5 Content Placement

Our content placement algorithm is presented in detail in Section 6. In summary, the algorithm is executed at the end of every adaptation round. It receives as input the replication policy $\boldsymbol{p}^d$ and generates a placement $\{\mathcal{F}_b\}_{b \in \mathcal{B}^d}$ that is consistent with (1).

Implementing the new placement requires copying new contents to box caches; transferring content incurs traffic costs. Our design ensures these costs are small in two ways. First, policy adaptations are *smooth*, *i.e.*, changes in $\boldsymbol{r}^d, \boldsymbol{p}^d$ are gradual. Second, we implement the new placement by performing *as few changes to box contents as possible*.

Crucially, our placement also satisfies the following property: when uniform slot service assignment is used, *all requests are satisfied w.h.p.* In particular, our placement is such that (5) and (6) are not only necessary but also *sufficient* for (4) to hold (*c.f.* Thms. 2 and 3). As such, our content placement ensures that, asymptotically, almost no requests are re-routed to the CDN.

4.6 Global Optimization

Recall that the cost incurred when a request originating from class d is served by $d' \in \mathcal{D} \cup \{s\}$ is $w^{dd'}$. Moreover, the rate of requests for content c forwarded from d to d' is $r_c^{dd'}$.

Hence, the total traffic cost is

$$\sum_{c \in \mathcal{C}} \sum_{d \in \mathcal{D}} [w^{ds} r_c^{ds} + \sum_{d'} \left(w^{dd'} r_c^{dd'} (1 - \nu_c^{d'}) + w^{ds} r_c^{dd'} \nu_c^{d'} \right)].$$

This is because a fraction ν_c^d requests for content c arriving at class d are re-routed to the CDN. In general, this is not a convex function, due to the loss probabilities ν_c^d. However, given that (4) holds, the contribution of these losses becomes negligible for large system sizes. The total system costs can thus be approximated as $\sum_{d \in \mathcal{D}} F^d(\boldsymbol{r}^d)$, where

$$F^d(\boldsymbol{r}^d) = \sum_{c \in \mathcal{C}} \left(w^{ds} r_c^{ds} + \sum_{d' \in \mathcal{D}} w^{cd'} r_c^{dd'} \right) \qquad (7)$$

is the total traffic cost generated by class d. Hence, the operator's minimal cost is a solution to the linear program:

GLOBAL

$$\text{Min. } \sum_{d \in \mathcal{D}} F^d(\boldsymbol{r}^d) \qquad (8a)$$

$$\text{subj. to } \sum_{c \in \mathcal{C}} p_c^d = M^d, \ \forall d \in \mathcal{D} \qquad (8b)$$

$$\sum_{d' \in \mathcal{D}} r_c^{dd'} + r_c^{ds} = \lambda_c^d (1 - p_c^d), \ \forall c \in \mathcal{C}, d \in \mathcal{D} \qquad (8c)$$

$$\sum_{c \in \mathcal{C}} r_c^{\cdot d} < R^d, \ \forall d \in \mathcal{D} \qquad (8d)$$

$$r_c^{\cdot d} < R^d p_c^d, \ \forall c \in \mathcal{C}, d \in \mathcal{D} \qquad (8e)$$

$$r_c^{dd'} \geq 0, r_c^{ds} \geq 0, 1 \geq p_c^d \geq 0, \ \forall c \in \mathcal{C}, d, d' \in \mathcal{D}$$

$$\text{var. } \boldsymbol{r}^d, \boldsymbol{p}^d, \forall d \in \mathcal{D}$$

where $R^d = B^d U^d$ is the total upload capacity in class d. The objective of this optimization problem is to minimize the total cost incurred by content transfers. Constraints (8b) and (8c) correspond to equations (2) and (3); they state that the full storage capacity of each class is used and that all requests are eventually served, respectively. Constraints (8d) and (8e) correspond to (5) and (6), respectively.

GLOBAL is a linear program in $\boldsymbol{r}^d, \boldsymbol{p}^d$, $d \in \mathcal{D}$. Our distributed, adaptive method for updating the routing and placement policies, is presented in detail in Section 5. It is designed in a way so that (a) trackers measure and adapt their policies to user demand, and (b) policy updates are computed in a distributed fashion, thus scaling well as the number of boxes increases. Most importantly, the policies of our design converge to a solution of **GLOBAL** (see Thm. 1), *i.e.*, our design minimizes aggregate traffic costs.

The formal properties of our design are shown in the next two sections. In Section 5, we specify how trackers update their policies so that they converge to a solution of (8). In Section 6, we characterize content placements under which requests assigned by a uniform slot policy are served w.h.p. Moreover, we show that if (8d) and (8e) hold, such a content placement exists, and give an algorithm implementing it.

5. POLICY ADAPTATION

We now present how the trackers solve **GLOBAL** and determine their replication and forwarding policies in a distributed fashion. In short, trackers exchange congestion signals and update $\boldsymbol{p}^d, \boldsymbol{r}^d$ over several rounds. We ensure that both are updated in a smooth fashion, *i.e.*, changes between two rounds are incremental and the system does not oscillate wildly. We proceed by first discussing the challenges in solving (8) in a distributed fashion with classical methods, and then presenting our distributed implementation.

5.1 Standard Dual Decomposition

Consider the partial Lagrangian of (8).

$$\mathcal{L}(\boldsymbol{r}, \boldsymbol{p}; \boldsymbol{\alpha}, \boldsymbol{\beta}) = \sum_d F^d(\boldsymbol{r}^d) + \sum_{d'} \beta^{d'} \left(\sum_{c,d} r_c^{dd'} - R^{d'} \right)$$
$$+ \sum_{d'} \sum_c \alpha_c^{d'} \left(\sum_d r_c^{dd'} - R^{d'} p_c^{d'} \right)$$

where $\alpha_c^{d'}, \beta^d$ are the dual variables (Lagrange multipliers) associated with the constraints (8d) and (8e), respectively. Observe that $\mathcal{L}$ is separable in the primal variables, *i.e.*, it can be written as $\mathcal{L}(\boldsymbol{r}, \boldsymbol{p}, \boldsymbol{\alpha}, \boldsymbol{\beta}) = \sum_d \mathcal{L}^d(\boldsymbol{r}^d, \boldsymbol{p}^d; \boldsymbol{\alpha}, \boldsymbol{\beta})$ where

$$\mathcal{L}^d(\boldsymbol{r}^d, \boldsymbol{p}^d, \boldsymbol{\alpha}, \boldsymbol{\beta}) = F^d(\boldsymbol{r}^d) - \beta^d R^d - \sum_c \alpha_c^d R^d p_c^d$$
$$+ \sum_{d'} \left(\beta^{d'} \sum_c r_c^{dd'} + \sum_c \alpha_c^{d'} r_c^{dd'} \right).$$

This suggests a standard dual decomposition algorithm [26] for solving **GLOBAL**. Recall that a dual decomposition algorithm runs in multiple rounds $t = 0, 1, \ldots$. The class d tracker maintains the primal variables $\boldsymbol{r}^d, \boldsymbol{p}^d$, as well as the dual variables $\boldsymbol{\alpha}^d = [\alpha_c^d]_{c \in \mathcal{C}}$, β^d, associated with the coupling constraints (8d) and (8e). At the end of each round, the tracker updates the dual variables α_c^d, β^d, increasing them when the respective constraints (8d) and (8e) are violated or decreasing them when the constraints are loose. Subsequently, each tracker broadcasts its current dual variables with all other trackers. Having all dual variables $\boldsymbol{\alpha}$, $\boldsymbol{\beta}$ in the system, the trackers adapt their primal variables, reducing traffic forwarded to congested classes and increasing traffic forwarded to non-congested ones. This can be performed by each tracker solving the linear program:

$$(\boldsymbol{r}^d, \boldsymbol{p}^d)(t+1) = \underset{(\boldsymbol{r}^d, \boldsymbol{p}^d) \in \mathcal{I}^d}{\operatorname{argmin}} \mathcal{L}^d(\boldsymbol{r}^d, \boldsymbol{p}^d; \boldsymbol{\alpha}(t), \boldsymbol{\beta}(t)). \quad (9)$$

where $\mathcal{I}^d$ is the set of pairs $(\boldsymbol{r}^d, \boldsymbol{p}^d)$ defined by (8b) and (8c) as well as the non-negativity constraints. Such adaptations are known to converge to a maximizer of the primal problem *when the functions $\mathcal{L}^d$ are strictly convex* (see, *e.g.*, [26] Section 3.4.2, pp. 229-230). Unfortunately, this is not the case in our setup, as $\mathcal{L}^d$ are linear in $\boldsymbol{r}^d, \boldsymbol{p}^d$: convergence to optimal policies does not readily follow. In practice, the lack of strict convexity makes $\boldsymbol{r}^d, \boldsymbol{p}^d$ oscillate wildly with every application of (9). This is disastrous: wide oscillations of $\boldsymbol{p}^d$ imply that a large fraction of boxes in $\mathcal{B}^d$ need to change their content in each round. This is both impractical and costly; ideally, we would like each round to change the contents of each class smoothly, so that the cost of implementing these changes is negligible.

5.2 A Smooth Distributed Implementation

To address these issues, we use an interior point method that deals with the lack of strict convexity called *the method of multipliers* [26]. Applied to **GLOBAL** this implementation yields the algorithm summarized in Fig. 1. The following theorem, proved in App. A, follows from the analysis in [26] and establishes that this algorithm indeed solves (8):

THEOREM 1. *Assume that the tracker in class d correctly estimates $\lambda_c^d, r_c^{\cdot d}$ in each round, and that $\{\theta(t)\}_{t \in \mathbb{N}}$ is a non-decreasing sequence of non-negative numbers. Then, under the adaptation algorithm in Fig. 1, $\boldsymbol{r}^d(t), \boldsymbol{p}^d(t)$ converge to an optimal solution of (8).*

Crucially, the algorithm in Fig. 1 performs smooth adaptations of $\boldsymbol{r}^d, \boldsymbol{p}^d$. Though the theorem assumes that trackers

---

> Tracker d at the end of round t:
>   Obtain estimates of $\lambda_c^d, r_c^{\cdot d}, c \in \mathcal{C}$.
>   // Update dual variables
> $s_{tot}^d \leftarrow \frac{1}{|\mathcal{D}|} \left(\sum_{c \in \mathcal{C}} r_c^{\cdot d} + y^d - R^d \right)$
> $\beta^d \leftarrow \beta_c^d + \theta s_{tot}^d$
>   **for** each content c
> $s_c^d \leftarrow \frac{1}{|\mathcal{D}|} \left(r_c^{\cdot d} + z_c^d - R^d p_c^d \right)$
> $\alpha_c^d \leftarrow \alpha_c^d + \theta s_c^d$
>   **end for**
>   Broadcast $(\boldsymbol{\alpha}^d, \beta^d, \boldsymbol{s}^d, s_{tot}^d)$ to other trackers $d' \in \mathcal{D}$
>   Receive dual variables from all other trackers $d' \in \mathcal{D}$
>   // Update primal variables
> $(\boldsymbol{r}^d, \boldsymbol{p}^d, \boldsymbol{z}^d, y^d) \leftarrow \underset{\mathcal{I}^d}{\operatorname{argmin}} \textbf{LOCAL}^d(\boldsymbol{r}^d, \boldsymbol{p}^d, \boldsymbol{z}^d, y^d, \boldsymbol{\alpha}, \boldsymbol{\beta}, \boldsymbol{s}, s_{tot})$

Figure 1: Decentralized solution to the global problem GLOBAL.

---

correctly estimate the request rates λ_c^d, which are stationary, we relax both assumptions in Section 7, evaluating our adaptive approach under real-life, time-varying traffic.

We describe the operations performed and messages exchanged by each tracker below. The class d tracker maintains $\boldsymbol{r}^d(t), \boldsymbol{p}^d(t), \boldsymbol{\alpha}^d(t), \beta^d(t)$, the primal and dual variables of (8), as well as the *slack variables* $y^d, \boldsymbol{z}^d = [z_c^d]_{c \in \mathcal{C}}$, resulting from converting of (8d) and (8e) to equality constraints:

$$\sum_{c \in \mathcal{C}} r_c^{\cdot d} + y^d = R^d, \qquad \forall d \in \mathcal{D} \quad (10a)$$
$$r_c^{\cdot d} + z_c^d = R^d p_c^d, \qquad \forall c \in \mathcal{C}, d' \in \mathcal{D} \quad (10b)$$
$$y^d \geq 0, z_c^d \geq 0, \qquad \forall c \in \mathcal{C}, d \in \mathcal{D} \quad (10c)$$

In addition, for every $c \in \mathcal{C}$, the tracker maintains an estimate of λ_c^d, *i.e.*, the request rate of c from boxes within its own class, as well as an estimate of $r_c^{\cdot d}, i.e.$, the request rate for content c served by boxes in $\mathcal{B}^d$. These can be estimated through appropriate counters or through more sophisticated moving-average methods (such as, *e.g.*, EWMA).

Using these estimates, the primal and dual variables are updated as follows. At the end of round t, the tracker in class d uses the estimates of $r_c^{\cdot d}$ to see whether constraints (10a) and (10b) are violated or not. In particular, the tracker computes the quantities:

$$s_{tot}^d(t) = \left(\sum_c r_c^{\cdot d}(t) + y^d(t) - R^d \right) / |\mathcal{D}|$$
$$s_c^d(t) = \left(r_c^{\cdot d}(t) + z_c^d(t) - R^d p_c^d(t) \right) / |\mathcal{D}|, \quad \forall c \in \mathcal{C}$$

and updates the dual variables as follows:

$$\beta^d(t) = \beta^d(t-1) + \theta(t) s_{tot}^d(t)$$
$$\alpha_c^d(t) = \alpha_c^d(t-1) + \theta(t) s_c^d(t), \quad \forall c \in \mathcal{C}$$

where $\{\theta(t)\}_{t \in \mathbb{N}}$ are positive and non-decreasing. Subsequently, the tracker broadcasts to *every other tracker in $\mathcal{D}$* its congestion signals $\boldsymbol{\alpha}^d(t), \beta^d(t), \boldsymbol{s}^d(t), s_{tot}^d(t)$. This entails the exchange of $2|\mathcal{D}|(|\mathcal{D}|+1)$ values, in total.

For any $d, d' \in \mathcal{D}$, let $G_{tot}^{dd'}(\boldsymbol{r}^d, y^d) = \sum_c r_c^{dd'} + \mathbb{1}_{d=d'} y^d$, and $G_c^{dd'}(\boldsymbol{r}^d, \boldsymbol{p}^d, \boldsymbol{z}^d) = r_c^{dd'} + \mathbb{1}_{d=d'}(z_c^d - R^d p_c^d)$. Intuitively, these capture the "contribution" of the primal variables of class d to the constraints (10a) and (10b) of class d'. After the tracker in class d has received all the messages sent by other trackers, it solves the following quadratic program:

$$\textbf{LOCAL}^d(\boldsymbol{r}^d(t), \boldsymbol{p}^d(t), \boldsymbol{z}^d(t), \boldsymbol{y}^d(t), \boldsymbol{\alpha}(t), \boldsymbol{\beta}(t), \boldsymbol{s}(t), \boldsymbol{s}_{tot}(t))$$

$$\text{Min. } F^d(\boldsymbol{r}^d) + \sum_{d'} \beta^{d'}(t) G_{tot}^{dd'}(\boldsymbol{r}^d, y^d)$$

$$+ \sum_{d',c} \alpha_c^{d'}(t) G_c^{dd'}(\boldsymbol{r}^d, \boldsymbol{p}^d, \boldsymbol{z}^d)$$

$$+ \frac{\theta(t)}{2} \sum_{d'} \left[\left(G_{tot}^{dd'}(\boldsymbol{r}^d - \boldsymbol{r}^d(t), y^d - y^d(t)) + s_{tot}^{d'}(t) \right)^2 \right.$$

$$\left. + \sum_c \left(G_c^{dd'}(\boldsymbol{r}^d - \boldsymbol{r}^d(t), \boldsymbol{p}^d - \boldsymbol{p}^d(t), \boldsymbol{z}^d - \boldsymbol{z}^d(t)) + s_c^{d'}(t) \right)^2 \right]$$

$$\text{s.t. } (\boldsymbol{r}^d, \boldsymbol{p}^d, \boldsymbol{z}^d, y^d) \in \mathcal{J}^d, \ \forall d \in \mathcal{D}$$

$$\text{var } \boldsymbol{r}^d, \boldsymbol{p}^d, \boldsymbol{z}^d, y^d, \quad d \in \mathcal{D}$$

where $\mathcal{J}^d$ is the set of quadruplets $(\boldsymbol{r}^d, \boldsymbol{p}^d, y^d \ \boldsymbol{z}^d)$ defined by (8b) and (8c) as well as the non-negativity constraints. $\textbf{LOCAL}^d$ thus receives as input *all* the dual variables $\boldsymbol{\alpha}$, $\boldsymbol{\beta}$, the congestion variables $\boldsymbol{s}^d$, $\boldsymbol{s}_{tot}^d$, *as well as* all the local primal variables at round t. The last four are included in the quadratic terms appearing in the objective function, and ensure the smoothness of the changes to the primal variables from one round to the next.

6. CONTENT PLACEMENT

The previous section establishes that, through an appropriate exchange of congestion signals, trackers can solve (8) in a distributed fashion. Nevertheless, the objective (8a) is only an approximation of the actual traffic; this is because requests reaching a class may be "dropped" and redirected to the CDN infrastructure. In this section, we describe our content placement scheme and show that it ensures that all incoming requests are satisfied *w.h.p.*.

6.1 Conditions for Non-Redirection

We begin by establishing the necessary and sufficient conditions for requests to succeed *w.h.p.*, when the trackers implement the uniform slot service assignment.

Consider a collection of contents $\mathcal{F} \subset \mathcal{C}$ such that $|\mathcal{F}| = M^d$. Let $\mathcal{B}_{\mathcal{F}}^d = \{b \in \mathcal{B}^d : \mathcal{F}_b = \mathcal{F}\}$ be the set of boxes in the class that store exactly $\mathcal{F}$. These sets partition $\mathcal{B}^d$ into sub-classes, each comprising boxes that store identical contents. Let the number of boxes $B = |\mathcal{B}|$ go to infinity, while scaling both the request arrival rates r_c^d and the size of the subclasses $B_{\mathcal{F}}^d = |\mathcal{B}_{\mathcal{F}}^d|$ proportionally to B. That is, the quantities r_c^d/B, $B_{\mathcal{F}}^d/B$ are constants that do not depend on B as the latter increases. This scaling is consistent with our design: as B increases, the aggregate content demand and the storage and upload capacities grow proportionally with B. The following theorem, proved in App. B, characterizes the conditions under requests succeed *w.h.p.*

THEOREM 2. *Assume that requests are assigned according to the uniform slot policy. Then, requests for every content $c \in \mathcal{C}$ are served w.h.p. if and only if*

$$\sum_{c \in A} r_c^d < \sum_{\mathcal{F}: \mathcal{F} \cap A \neq \emptyset} B_{\mathcal{F}}^d U^d, \quad \text{for all } A \subseteq \mathcal{C}, \qquad (11)$$

Condition (11) stipulates that for any set of items $A \subseteq \mathcal{C}$ the arrival rate of requests for these items does not exceed the total upload capacity of class d boxes storing these items.

It is relatively straightforward to see that (11) is *necessary* for (4) to hold (see [24]). It has recently shown that it is also *sufficient* when the service assignment policy used is the

so-called *repacking policy* [24]. At the arrival of a request, repacking re-assigns requests already served in boxes in the system in order to accommodate this request. Performing this "repacking" requires finding a maximum matching in a bipartite graph of $2B^d U^d$ nodes. Our uniform slot policy is thus easier to implement than repacking; moreover, Thm. 2 establishes that, despite its simplicity, it exhibits the same asymptotic performance.

The theorem implies that, to serve all requests in a class *w.h.p.*, the content placement should be such that condition (11) is satisfied. Unfortunately, this condition consists of a number of inequalities that is exponential in the catalog size $|\mathcal{C}|$, and is not a priori clear how to construct a content placement scheme. We address this in the next section.

6.2 Placement Algorithm

In this section, we show that if the conditions (8d) and (8e) of $\textbf{GLOBAL}$ hold, there exists a simple content placement scheme that satisfies (11). This has the following immediate implications. First, it simplifies our design, as we only need to ensure that the $O(|\mathcal{D}||\mathcal{C}|)$ constraints (8d) and (8e) hold, rather than the exponentially many constraints in (11); indeed it is only these constraints that our adaptation scheme of Section 5 takes into account. Second, by Thm. 2, implementing the placement in this section along with a uniform slot assignment ensures that all requests are served *w.h.p.*

Below, we first describe this placement scheme, *i.e.* the mapping of contents to boxes caches, that satisfies (11). We then present an algorithm that, at each round, reshuffles cache contents in the class to reach this placement with as few item transfers as possible.

Designated Slot Placement. We now show that if (8d) and (8e) hold, there exists a simple placement scheme—*i.e.*, a set of cache contents $\{F_b\}_{b \in \mathcal{B}^d}$—that satisfies (11).

For every box $b \in \mathcal{B}^d$, we identify a special storage slot which we call the *designated slot*. We denote the content of this slot by D_b and the remaining contents of b by $L_b = \mathcal{F}_b \setminus \{D_b\}$. For all $c \in \mathcal{C}$, let $\mathcal{E}_c^d = \{b \in \mathcal{B}^d : D_b = c\}$ be the set of boxes storing c in their designated slot. The following lemma implies that if a sufficient number boxes store c in their designated slot, then (11) is satisfied.

LEMMA 1. *If $|\mathcal{E}_c^d| > r_c^d/U^d$ then (11) holds.*

PROOF. As $\mathcal{E}_c^d$ are disjoint, we have $\sum_{\mathcal{F}: \mathcal{F} \cap A \neq \emptyset} B_{\mathcal{F}}^d U^d = \sum_{b \in \mathcal{B}^d: \mathcal{F}_b \cap A \neq \emptyset} U^d = \sum_{b \in \mathcal{B}^d: D_b \in A} U^d + \sum_{b \in \mathcal{B}^d: D_b \notin A} U^d \geq \sum_{c \in A} |\mathcal{E}_c^d| U^d > \sum_{c \in A} r_c^d$, for all $A \subseteq \mathcal{C}$. $\square$

Hence, to ensure that (11) is satisfied, it suffices that at least r_c^d/U^d boxes store c in their designated slot. We call such a placement scheme a *designated slot placement*. On the other hand, the fraction of boxes that store c in *any* slot must not exceed p_c^d. The following lemma states that is possible to place contents in each designated slot to ensure that both constraints are satisfied when (8d) and (8e) hold:

LEMMA 2. *Given a class d, consider r_c^d and p_c^d, $c \in \mathcal{C}$, for which (8d) and (8e) hold. There exist $q_c^d \in [0, 1]$, $c \in \mathcal{C}$, such that $\sum_c q_c^d = 1$ and*

$$0 \leq r_c^d/B^d U^d < q_c^d \leq p_c^d \leq 1, \ \forall c \in \mathcal{C}. \qquad (12)$$

Moreover, such q_c^d can be computed in $O(|\mathcal{C}| \log |\mathcal{C}|)$ time.

The proof can be found in App. C. In summary, if (8d) and (8e) hold, ensuring that requests for all contents are served

Input: Initial placement $\{F_b\}_{b\in\mathcal{B}}$ and target ratios q'_c, p'_c
Let $A^+ := \{c \in \mathcal{C} : q_c > q'_c\}$, $A^- := \{c :\in \mathcal{C} : q_c < q'_c\}$;
while there exists $b \in \mathcal{B}$ s.t. $D_b \in A^+$ and $L_b \cap A^- \neq \emptyset$
  Pick $c \in L_b \cap A^-$, and swap it locally with the content of D_b.
  Update $\boldsymbol{q}$, $\boldsymbol{\pi}$, A^+, A^- accordingly
while there exists $b \in \mathcal{B}$ s.t. $D_b \in A^+$ and $L_b \cap A^- = \emptyset$
  Pick $c \in A^-$ and place c in the designated slot D_b;
  Update $\boldsymbol{q}$, $\boldsymbol{\pi}$, A^+, A^- accordingly
Let $C^+ := \{c : \pi_c > \pi'_c\}$; $C^+ := \{c : \pi_c < \pi'_c\}$;
$C^0 := \mathcal{C} \setminus (C^+ \cup C^-)$.
Let $G := \{\ b \in \mathcal{B}$ s.t. $C_+ \cap L_b \neq \emptyset$ and $C_- \setminus (D_b \cup L_b) \neq \emptyset\ \}$;
while $(G \neq \emptyset)$ **or** (there exists $c \in C^-$ s.t. $(\pi_c - \pi'_c)B \geq 2$)
  if $(G \neq \emptyset)$ **then**
    Pick any $b \in G$
    Replace some $c \in C_+ \cap L_b$ with some $c' \in C_- \setminus (D_b \cup L_b)$;
  else
    Pick $c \in C^-$ s.t. $(\pi_c - \pi'_c)B \geq 2$.
    Find a box b that does not store c.
    Pick $c' \in C_0 \cap L_b$ and replace c' with c.
  update G, $\boldsymbol{\pi}$, C^+, C^-, C^0 accordingly.

Figure 2: Placement Algorithm

w.h.p. in class d is achieved constructing a designated slot placement. Such a placement stores content c in the designated slot of at least $q_c^d B^d$ boxes, where $q_c^d B^d$ are determined as in Lemma 2; the remaining slots are used to achieve an overall replication ratio of p_c^d within the class. Below, we describe an algorithm that, given ratios q_c^d and p_c^d, places content in class d in a way that these ratios are satisfied. For simplicity, we drop the superscript d in the remainder of this section, referring to content placement in a single class.

Constructing a Designated Slot Placement. We now describe how to change cache contents at the end of each adaptation round. The tracker is aware of the initial content placement $\{\mathcal{F}_b\}_{b\in\mathcal{B}}$ over B boxes in set $\mathcal{B}$, prior to the adaptation, as well as the target (*i.e.*, adapted) replication ratios p'_c and q'_c, $c \in \mathcal{C}$, satisfying (12); the former are given by the adaptation algorithm, and the latter by Lemma (2). The placement algorithm, outlined in Fig. 2, receives these as inputs and outputs a new content placement $\{\mathcal{F}'_b\}_{b\in\mathcal{B}}$ in which $q'_c B$ boxes store c in their designated slot, while *approximately* $p'_c B$ boxes store c overall. Crucially, the placement requires *as few cache changes as possible.*

We assume that $q'_c B$ and $p'_c B$ are integers—for large B, this is a good approximation. Let q_c, p_c be the corresponding designated slot and overall fractions in the input placement $\{F_b\}_{b\in\mathcal{B}}$. Let $\pi_c = p_c - q_c$, $\pi'_c = p'_c - q'_c$. A lower bound on the cache modification operations needed to attain the target replication ratios q'_c and p'_c is given by $B(\alpha+\beta)/2$, where $\alpha = \sum_c |q_c - q'_c|$, $\beta = \sum_c |\pi_c - \pi'_c|$. We also express the number of operations performed in terms of these quantities. The complexity and correctness of the algorithm are established in the following theorem, whose proof is in App. D:

THEOREM 3. *The content placement algorithm in Fig. 2 leads to a content replication $\{F'_b\}_{b\in\mathcal{B}}$ in which exactly $q'_c B$ boxes store c in their designated slot, and $p''_c B$ boxes store c overall, where $\sum_c |p'_c - p''_c| B < 2M$, and $|p'_c - p''_c| B \leq 1$, for all $c \in \mathcal{C}$. The total number of write operations is at most $B[\alpha + (M-1)(\alpha+\beta)]/2$.*

In summary, our algorithm produces a placement in which at most $2M$ items are either under or over-replicated, each by *only one* replica. Most importantly, the placement is achieved with at most $O(B(\alpha+\beta))$ write operations, which is order-optimal. If replication ratios change gradually (and, thus, α and β are small), as ensured by our policy adaptation, the algorithm does not perform a large number of cache changes. We describe the algorithm in more detail below.

The algorithm proceeds in three phases. In the first phase, the algorithm modifies the designated slots to reach the desired ratios $\boldsymbol{q}'$. To do so, the algorithm picks any over-replicated content c in set $A_+ = \{c : q_c > q'_c\}$. For any user holding c in its designated slot, it checks whether it holds in its normal slots an under-replicated content $c' \in A_- = \{c : q_c < q'_c\}$. If such content exists, it renames the corresponding slot as "designated" and the slot holding c as "normal". This is repeated until an under-replicated content c' cannot be found within the normal cache slots of boxes storing some $c \in A_+$. If there still are over-replicated items in A_+, some $c' \in A_-$ is selected arbitrarily and overwrites c within the designated slot. At the end of this phase, the replication rates within the designated slots have reached their target $B\vec{q'}$, and the resulting caches are free of duplicate copies. Also, after these operations, the intermediate replication rates π''_c within the normal cache slots verify $|B\pi_c - B\pi''_c| \leq |Bq_c - Bq'_c|$.

In the second phase, the algorithm begins transforming these intermediate replication rates π''_c into π'_c. To this end, we distinguish contents c that are over-replicated, under-replicated and perfectly replicated by introducing $C_+ = \{c: \pi_c > \pi'_c\}$, $C_- = \{c: \pi_c < \pi'_c\}$, and $C_0 = \{c: \pi_c = \pi'_c\}$.
$C_+ = \{c : \pi_c > \pi'_c\}, C_- = \{c : \pi_c < \pi'_c\}, C_0 = \{c : \pi_c = \pi'_c\}$.

For any box b, if there exists $c \in C_+ \cap L_b$, and $c' \in C_- \setminus (D_b \cup L_b)$, the algorithm replaces c by c' within L_b. We call the corresponding operation a *greedy reduction*. Greedy reductions are repeated until the algorithm arrives at a configuration where no such changes are possible; this terminates the second phase. At that point, for any box b such that $C_+ \cap L_b$ is not empty, necessarily $C_- \subset (L_b \cup D_b)$. Hence, the size of C_- is at most $M-1$. If any of the elements in C_- is under replicated by at least two replicas, the algorithm enters its third phase. In this phase, the algorithm picks some content c' that is under-replicated by at least 2 replicas, and finds a user b which does not hold c', *i.e.* $c' \in C_- \setminus (D_b \cup L_b)$. It also selects some content c within $C_0 \cap L_b$: such content must exist, since $|C_-| \leq M-1$, and $C_- \cap L_b \subset C_- \setminus \{c'\}$ has size strictly less than $M-1$, the size of L_b; the remaining content c must belong to C_0 since otherwise we could have performed a greedy reduction.

The algorithm then replaces content c by content c'. We call this operation a *switch.* This augments the size of set C_-: indeed content c is now under-replicated (one replica missing). The algorithm then tries to do a greedy reduction, *i.e.*, a replacement of an over-replicated content by c if possible. If not, it performs another switch, *i.e.*, by identifying some content under-replicated by at least 2, and creating a new replica in place of some perfectly replicated item, thereby augmenting the size of C_-. Hence, in at most $M-1$ steps, the algorithm inflates the size of C_- to at least M, at which stage we know that a greedy reduction can be performed. This alteration between greedy reductions and switches is repeated until the size of C_- is at most $M-1$, and each such content is missing *exactly one replica.*

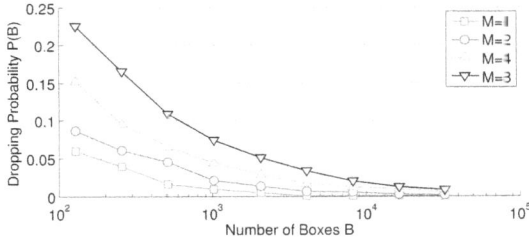

Figure 3: Dropping probability decreases fast with uniform slot strategy. Simulation in a single class with a catalog size of $C = 100$.

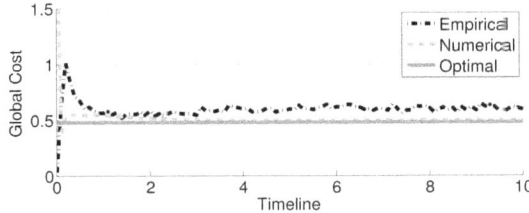

Figure 4: Decentralized optimization, content placement scheme and uniform-slot policy, under parameters $C = 1000$, $D = 10$, $\bar{B} = 1000$, $\bar{U} = 3$, $\bar{M} = 4$.

7. PERFORMANCE EVALUATION

In this section, we evaluate our algorithms under synthesized traces and a real-life BitTorrent traffic trace. We implement an event-driven simulator that captures box-level content placement and service assignment. In particular, we implement the solutions we proposed in Section 5 (decentralized optimization) and Section 6 (Designated Slot Placement). We also implement class trackers that execute the decentralized solution in Fig. 1.

In the rest of this section, all evaluations are performed using a cost matrix with random class-pairwise sampled uniformly from [0, 1]. The download cost from a box in the same class is 0, while the cost of downloading from the infrastructure is set to 3 for all classes.

7.1 Simulation on Synthesized Trace

First, we show that the uniform-slot policy achieves close-to-optimal service assignment, given that content-wise capacity constraints are respected. We focus on a single ISP and assign requests to individual boxes under the uniform-slot policy. Fig. 3 shows the loss probability under various settings of B and M. We utilize a synthesized trace with Poisson arrivals and exponentially distributed service time of mean one. Content popularity follows a Zipf distribution. We scale the total request rate to be proportional to the number of boxes. As predicted by the theory, the dropping probability quickly vanishes as B grows. For the same B, the dropping probability is higher when M is larger. When the storage is rich, our scheme tries to allocate popular content in caches in order to minimize cost. The locally absorbed requests are not counted in calculating the dropping probability. In fact, the effective requests come from unpopular contents, which is expected to generate a higher drop rate.

We next show the optimality of our full solution, again utilizing a synthesized trace generated as above. Content popularities are heterogeneous in different classes. Fig. 4 illustrates the average empirical cost per request, compared to (a) the fluid prediction under distributed optimization, when λ_c^d and $r_c^{dd'}$ are estimated perfectly, and (b) the optimal cost computed offline. Though the number of boxes is finite, and the above quantities are estimated empirically, the distributed algorithm converges close to the global optimum after a handful of rounds.

7.2 Simulation on BitTorrent Trace

We next employ a real-life trace collected from the global Vuze network, one of the most popular BitTorrent clients. Our main motivation for using the BitTorrent trace is to validate our solution under realistic content popularity and access patterns.

Trace Collection and Evaluation Setup. Vuze clients issue a *put* each time they start downloading a file, and route the *put* to the 20 nodes whose IDs are closest to the file identifier. To collect these traces, we ran 1000 DHT nodes with randomly-chosen IDs, and logged all DHT *put* messages routed to our nodes. Therefore, our traces show all downloads for those files whose identifiers are close to the ID of one of our 1000 DHT nodes. Since the Vuze DHT has around 1 million nodes, and each file download is observed by 20 nodes, by running 1000 nodes we observe around $10^6/20/1000$, *i.e.*, 2% of all download requests. During 30 days we traced the downloads of around 2 million unique files by 8 million unique IP addresses. We determined the country of each IP using Maxmind's GeoLite City database [27]. We use the country-level geo-locality of BT users to organize them into classes. We do not model interclass cost, *e.g.*, latency on geo-locality, as measuring and estimating such costs are outside the scope of this paper.

To limit the runtime of our event-driven simulations, we trim the traces by considering only the top 1,000 most popular files, which contribute 52% of the total downloads. Given a fixed number of boxes and cache size, there are very few copies of unpopular contents cached in these boxes. As a result, adding more contents will not significantly change the system configuration and the overall cost.

Fig. 5(a) illustrates the total number of download events and unique IPs, grouped by countries in a decreasing order of total downloads during the 30-day period, and the cumulative counts in Fig. 5(b). We select the top 20 countries as classes in our evaluation, comprising over 80% of all downloads. The trace shows that one user issues, on average, approximately one content request. We use 2 upload slots and 2 storage slots for each user (box) in our simulation.

Previously we have shown the efficiency of our algorithm given fixed request rates. In practice, the content popularity may change over time. The content demand should remain sufficiently stable in order for our algorithm to work well and not oscillate wildly. In our evaluation, we measure content demands based on a 24-hour interval, and simply use the demand from the previous day to *project* the request rates for the next day. This undoubtedly only provides a conservative estimate for our solution, as a more accurate traffic prediction will further improve the performance of our approach. Fig. 5(c) shows the relative difference between the predicted rate and the true rate, grouped by content in decreasing order of popularity. Each data point is averaged over the

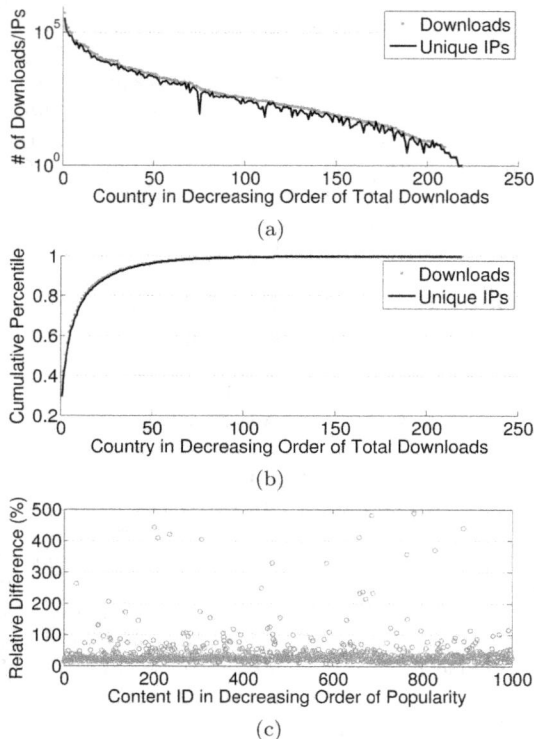

(a)

(b)

(c)

Figure 5: BitTorrent trace statistics. (a) Cumulative counts of downloads/boxes. (b) Per-country counts of downloads/boxes. (c) Predictability of content demand in 1-hour interval over 1 month.

entire 30-day period. The results show that demand is stable over 24 hrs for most content. High variations are due to new contents such as videos that reach a popularity peak during the first few days after their releases.

Evaluation results. We compare our solution to frequently used caching strategies, as well as a request routing heuristic. In particular, we implement Least Recently Used (LRU), and Least Frequently Used (LFU) caching algorithm. Each box implements the cache eviction policy locally. The recency and frequency counts apply to *all* contents, *i.e.*, including both local and remote requests. We also implement a local request routing heuristic, *i.e.*, the "closest" policy. When a download request is issued, all classes are examined in a greedy manner, *e.g.*, starting from its own class, to remote classes in an increasing order of cost. The request is accepted by a class whenever there exists at least one box in this class which stores the desired content and has one or multiple free slots. If no such a class is found, the request is directed to the CDN server. We implement the following solutions: (i) LRU-closest and (ii) LFU-closest, the combinations of caching and request routing heuristics, (iii) Decentralized, the full set of solution proposed in this paper, and (iv) Offline Optimal, which assumes the perfect knowledge of content demands and is the optimal solution to the global problem. The offline optimal provides a lower-bound for download costs, but does not reflect content shuffling costs between different periods.

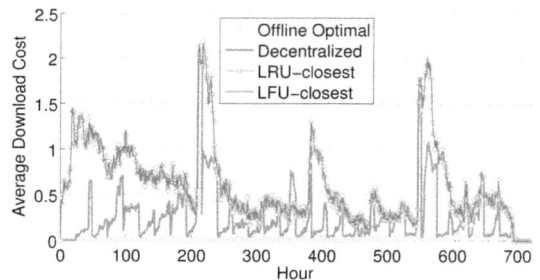

Figure 6: Performance of different algorithms over a real 30-day BitTorrent trace.

We evaluate the same BitTorrent trace under the four solutions. All scenarios begin with the same initial content placement over all boxes. Fig. 6 shows the average download cost (between 0 and 3) every hour for the entire 30-day period. Results demonstrate that our solution significantly reduces cross traffic between classes compared to the two heuristics. This is not surprising because both LRU and LFU are local heuristics that do not consider the global demand and optimize overall costs, and are implemented on top of a greedy local routing policy, which is certainly sub-optimal than a *jointly* optimized scheme. Our results provide an evidence that such an optimal gap can be quite large. The spiked cost is a consequence of content shuffles and temporary request drops when new popular contents are introduced. Our solution is able to quickly adapt to such changes and save a significant amount of costs.

8. SUMMARY

We offer a solution to regulate cross-traffic and minimize content delivery costs in decentralized CDNs. We present an optimal request routing scheme that can nicely accommodate user demands, an effective service mapping algorithm that is easy to implement within each operator, and an adaptive content caching algorithm with low operational costs. Through a live BitTorrent trace-based simulation, we demonstrate that our distributed algorithm is simultaneously scalable, accurate and responsive.

9. REFERENCES

[1] "Cisco visual networking index: Forecast and methodology, 2010-2015."
[2] "Nanodatacenters: http://www.nanodatacenters.eu/."
[3] "Boxee." http://www.boxee.tv/.
[4] C. Huang, A. Wang, J. Li, and K. W. Ross, "Understanding hybrid CDN-P2P: why Limelight needs its own Red Swoosh," in *NOSSDAV*, 2008.
[5] V. Valancius, N. Laoutaris, L. Massoulié, C. Diot, and P. Rodriguez, "Greening the Internet with nano data centers," in *CoNEXT*, 2009.
[6] C. Huang, J. Li, and K. W. Ross, "Peer-assisted VoD: Making Internet video distribution cheap," in *IPTPS*, 2007.
[7] R. S. Peterson and E. G. Sirer, "Antfarm: Efficient content distribution with managed swarms," in *NSDI*, 2009.
[8] Y. Chen, Y. Huang, R. Jana, H. Jiang, M. Rabinovich, B. Wei, and Z. Xiao, "When is P2P technology beneficial for IPTV services?" in *NOSSDAV*, 2007.
[9] Y. F. Chen, Y. Huang, R. Jana, H. Jiang, M. Rabinovich, J. Rahe, B. Wei, and Z. Xiao, "Towards capacity and profit optimization of video-on-demand services in a peer-assisted

IPTV platform," *Multimedia Systems*, vol. 15, no. 1, pp. 19–32, 2009.

[10] V. Misra, S. Ioannidis, A. Chaintreau, and L. Massoulié, "Incentivizing peer-assisted services: A fluid Shapley value approach," in *ACM SIGMETRICS*, 2010.

[11] "People's CDN: http://pcdn.info/.".

[12] D. Han, D. G. Andersen, M. Kaminsky, K. Papagiannaki, and S. Seshan, "Hulu in the neighborhood," in *COMSNET*, 2011.

[13] R. Bindal, P. Cao, W. Chan, J. Medved, G. Suwala, T. Bates, and A. Zhang, "Improving traffic locality in bittorrent via biased neighbor selection," in *ICDCS*, 2006.

[14] R. Cuevas, N. Laoutaris, X. Yang, G. Siganos, and P. Rodriguez, "Deep diving into BitTorrent locality," in *INFOCOM*, 2011.

[15] D. R. Choffnes and F. E. Bustamante, "Taming the torrent: a practical approach to reducing cross-ISP traffic in peer-to-peer systems," in *SIGCOMM*, 2008.

[16] V. Aggarwal, A. Feldmann, and C. Scheideler, "Can ISPs and P2P users cooperate for improved performance?," *ACM SIGCOMM Computer Communication Review*, vol. 37, pp. 29–40, July 2007.

[17] J. Wang, C. Huang, and J. Li, "On ISP-friendly rate allocation for peer-assisted VoD," in *Multimedia*, 2008.

[18] H. Xie, Y. R. Yang, A. Krishnamurthy, Y. Liu, and A. Silberschatz, "P4P: Provider Portal for (P2P) Applications," in *SIGCOMM*, 2008.

[19] I. Baev, R. Rajaraman, and C. Swamy, "Approximation algorithms for data placement in arbitrary networks," *SIAM Journal of Computing*, vol. 38, no. 4, 2008.

[20] S. C. Borst, V. Gupta, and A. Walid, "Distributed caching algorithms for content distribution networks," in *INFOCOM*, 2010

[21] M. R. Korupolu, C. G. Plaxton, and R. Rajaraman, "Placement algorithms for hierarchical cooperative caching," *Journal of Algorithms*, vol. 38, 2001

[22] Y. Zhou, T. Z. J. Fu, and D. M. Chiu, "Modeling and analysis of P2P replication to support VoD service," in *INFOCOM*, 2011.

[23] W. Wu and J. C. S. Lui, "Exploring the optimal replication strategy in P2P-VoD systems: characterization and evaluation," in *INFOCOM*, 2011.

[24] B. R. Tan and L. Massoulié, "Optimal content placement for peer-to-peer video-on-demand systems," in *INFOCOM*, 2011.

[25] K. W. Ross, *Multiservice Loss Networks for Broadband Telecommunications Networks*. Springer-Verlag, 1995.

[26] D. P. Bertsekas and J. N. Tsitsiklis, *Parallel and Distributed Computation: Numerical Methods*. Athena Scientific, 1997.

[27] "http://www.maxmind.com/app/geolitecity.".

[28] L. Massoulié, "Structural properties of proportional fairness," *The Annals of Applied Probability*, vol. 17, no. 3, 2007.

[29] H. Kushner and G. Yin, *Stochastic approximation and recursive algorithms and applications*. Springer, 2003.

[30] M. Benaïm and J.-Y. LeBoudec, "A class of mean field interaction models for computer and communication systems," *Perform. Eval*, pp. 11–12, 2008.

APPENDIX

A. PROOF OF THEOREM 1

After the conversion of (8d) and (8e) to equality constraints through (10), **GLOBAL** has the following properties. First, the objective (8a) is separable in the local variables $(\boldsymbol{r}^d, \boldsymbol{p}^d, y^d, \boldsymbol{z}^d)$, corresponding to each class. Second, the constraints (10a) and (10b) coupling the local variables are linear equalities. Finally, the remaining constraints

(8b) and (8c) as well as the positivity constraints define a bounded convex domain for the local primal variables. These properties imply that the method of multipliers admits the distributed implementation in [26], Example 4.4., pp. 249–251, and the theorem follows. □

B. PROOF OF THEOREM 2

We partition the set of boxes $\mathcal{B}$ according to the contents they store in their cache. In particular, each of the boxes in $\mathcal{B}$ are grouped into L sub-classes $\mathcal{B}_1, \mathcal{B}_2, \ldots, \mathcal{B}_L$, where all boxes in the i-th class $\mathcal{B}_i$, $1 \leq i \leq L$, store the same set of contents $\mathcal{F}_i \subset \mathcal{C}$ such that $|\mathcal{F}_i| = M$. We denote by $\mathcal{L} = \{1, 2, \ldots, L\}$ and by $B_i = |\mathcal{B}_i|$ the number of boxes in the i-th sub-class. For $A \subseteq \mathcal{C}$, let $\mathsf{supp}(A) = \{i \in \mathcal{L} : \mathcal{F}_i \cap A \neq \emptyset\}$ be the set of sub-classes of boxes storing at least one content in A, and $\beta_i = \frac{B_i U}{BU}$, $i \in \mathcal{L}$ and $o_c = \frac{r_c}{BU}$, $c \in \mathcal{C}$. Note that, by our scaling assumption, when $B \to \infty$, the above quantities remain constant, and that (11) can be rewritten as: $\sum_{c \in A} \rho_c < \sum_{j \in \mathsf{supp}(A)} \beta_j$, $\forall A \subseteq \mathcal{C}$.

Let X_i be the number of empty slots in the i-th subclass. Then, under the uniform slot service assignment policy, the stochastic process $\mathbf{X} : \mathbb{R}_+ \to \mathbb{N}^L$ is a Markov process and can be described as follows:

$$X_i(t) = X_i(0) + E_i^+ \left(\int_0^t B_i U - X_i(\tau) d\tau \right) - E_i^- \left(\int_0^t \sum_{c \in \mathcal{F}_i} r_c \frac{X_i(\tau)}{\sum_{j:c \in \mathcal{F}_j} X_j(\tau)} d\tau \right), \quad i \in \mathcal{L}, \quad (13)$$

where E_i^+, E_i^-, $i \in \mathcal{L}$, are independent unit-rate Poisson processes. Assume by convention that for all $i \in \mathcal{L}$ and all $c \in \mathcal{F}_i$, $\frac{X_i(\tau)}{\sum_{j:c \in \mathcal{F}_j} X_j(\tau)} = 0$ whenever $\sum_{j:c \in \mathcal{F}_j} X_j(\tau) = 0$. A mapping $\mathbf{x} : \mathbb{R}_+ \to [0, 1]^L$ is a *fluid trajectory* of the system if it satisfies the following set of equations for all $i \in \mathcal{L}$.

$$x_i(t) = x_i(0) + \beta_i t - \int_0^t x_i(\tau) d\tau - \sum_{c \in \mathcal{F}_i} \rho_c \int_0^t z_{c,i}(\mathbf{x}(\tau)) d\tau, \quad (14)$$

where $z_{c,i}$, $c \in \mathcal{F}_i$, are functions satisfying

$$z_{c,i}(\mathbf{x}) = \frac{x_i}{\sum_{j:c \in \mathcal{F}_j} x_j}, \text{ if } \sum_{j:c \in \mathcal{F}_j} x_j > 0, \text{ and} \quad (15a)$$

$$z_{c,i}(\mathbf{x}) > 0, \quad \sum_{i \in \mathsf{supp}(\{c\})} z_{c,i} \leq 1 \text{ otherwise} \quad (15b)$$

Given a vector $\mathbf{x}_0 \in [0, 1]^L$, we define $S(\mathbf{x}_0)$ to be the set of fluid trajectories defined by integral equation (14) with initial condition $\mathbf{x}(0) = \mathbf{x}_0$.

LEMMA 3. *Consider a sequence of positive numbers $\{B^k\}_{k \in \mathbb{N}}$ such that $\lim_{k \to \infty} B^k = +\infty$, and a sequence of initial conditions $\mathbf{X}^k(0) = [x_i^k]_{1 \leq i \leq L}$ s.t. the limit $\lim_{k \to \infty} \frac{1}{B^k} \mathbf{X}^k(0) = \mathbf{x}_0$ exists. Let $\{\mathbf{X}^k(t)\}_{t \in \mathbb{R}_+}$ denote the Markov process given by (13) given that $B = B_k$, and consider the rescaled process $\mathbf{x}^k(t) = \frac{1}{B_k U} \mathbf{X}^k(t)$, $t \in \mathbb{R}_+$. Then for all $T > 0$ and all $\epsilon > 0$, $\lim_{k \to \infty} \mathbf{P} \left(\inf_{\mathbf{x} \in S(\mathbf{x}_0)} \sup_{t \in [O,T]} |\mathbf{x}^k(t) - \mathbf{x}(t)| \geq \epsilon \right) = 0$.*

PROOF. The proof is identical to the one in [28]. The only steps that we need to verify is that for every i and every $c \in F_i$, $X_i / \sum_{j:c \in \mathcal{F}_j} X_j$ is bounded (by 1), and at its points of discontinuity $\mathbf{x}'$ such that $\sum_{j:c \in F_j} X_j$ is zero, $\limsup_{\mathbf{x} \to \mathbf{x}'} X_i / \sum_{j:c \in \mathcal{F}_j} X_j = 1$. Both are easy to verify. □

Lemma 3 implies that (a) the set of fluid trajectories $S(\mathbf{x})$ is non-empty and (b) the rescaled process $\mathbf{x}^k$ converges on every finite set $[0, T]$ to a fluid trajectory, as $B \to \infty$, in probability. We therefore turn our attention to studying the asymptotic behavior of such fluid trajectories.

Given an $\mathbf{x}_0 \in [0, 1]^L$, consider a fluid trajectory $\mathbf{x} \in S(\mathbf{x}_0)$. Since $z_{i,c}$ are bounded by 1, (14) implies that x is Lipschitz continuous (with parameter $\sum_c \rho_c$). By Rademacher's theorem, $\dot{x}$ exists almost everywhere and is given by

$$\dot{x}_i = \beta_i - x_i - \sum_{c \in F_i} \rho_c z_{c,i}(\mathbf{x}), \quad i \in \mathcal{L}. \qquad (16)$$

Let $J = \lim_{t \to \infty} \bigcup_{\mathbf{y} \in [0,1]^L} \{\mathbf{x}(s), s \geq t : \mathbf{x}(0) = \mathbf{y}\}$ be the *limit set* [29] of ODE (16). Then, Lemma 3 implies (see Thm. 3 in Benaïm and Le Boudec [30]) that, as k tends to infinity, the support of the steady state probability of $\mathbf{X}^k$ converges to a subset of J. Thus, to show that the probability that queries for every content item succeed asymptotically almost surely, it suffices to show that $x_i^* > 0$ for every $\mathbf{x}^* \in J$. Indeed, let $I_0(\mathbf{x}) = \{i : x_i = 0\}$ be the zero-valued coordinates of $\mathbf{x}$ and $C(I) = \{c \in \mathcal{C} : \mathsf{supp}(\{c\}) \subseteq I\}$ denote the set of items stored only by classes in $I \subseteq \mathcal{L}$. Consider the following candidate Lyapunov function: $G(\mathbf{x}) = \sum_{i \in \mathcal{L}} \beta_i \log(x_i) - \sum_{i \in \mathcal{L}} x_i - \sum_{c \in \mathcal{C}} \rho_c \log\left(\sum_{j \in \mathsf{supp}(\{c\})} x_j\right)$, if $\mathbf{x} > 0$ and $G(\mathbf{x}) = -\infty$ otherwise.

LEMMA 4. *Under* (11), G *is continuous in* $[0, 1]^L$.

PROOF. Consider a $\mathbf{x}'$ such that $I \equiv I_0(\mathbf{x}') \neq \emptyset$. Consider a sequence $\mathbf{x}^k \in [0, 1]^L$, $k \in \mathbb{N}$, s.t. $\mathbf{x}^k \to \mathbf{x}$ in the $\|\cdot\|_\infty$ norm (or any equivalent norm in $\mathbb{R}^L$). We need to show that $\lim_{k \to \infty} G(\mathbf{x}^k) = -\infty$. If $I_0(\mathbf{x}^k) \neq \emptyset$ for some k, then $G(\mathbf{x}^k) = -\infty$; hence, w.l.o.g., we can assume that $\mathbf{x}^k \in (0, 1]^L$. Then $G(\mathbf{x}^k) = A^k + B^k$, where $A^k = \sum_{i \in \mathcal{L} \setminus I} \beta_i \log(x_i^k) - \sum_{i \in \mathcal{L}} x_i^k - \sum_{c \in \mathcal{C} \setminus C(I)} \rho_c \log\left(\sum_{j \in \mathsf{supp}(\{c\})} x_j^k\right)$, and $B^k = \sum_{i \in I} \beta_i \log(x_i^k) - \sum_{c \in C(I)} \rho_c \log\left(\sum_{j \in \mathsf{supp}(\{c\})} x_j^k\right)$. The by the continuity of the log function, and the fact that $x_i' > 0$ for all $i \notin I$, it is easy to see that $\lim_{k \to \infty} A^k$ exists and is finite. On the other hand, if $C(I) = \emptyset$, B^k obviously converges to $-\infty$. Assume thus that $C(I)$ is non-empty. Partition I into classes $I_1, \ldots, I_m$ s.t. $x_i^k = y_\ell^k$ for all $i \in I_\ell$ (*i.e.*, all coordinates in a class assume the same value). Then

$$B^k \leq \sum_{i \in I} \beta_i \log(x_i^k) - \sum_{c \in C(I)} \rho_c \log(\max_{j \in \mathsf{supp}(\{c\})} x_j^k)$$

$$= \sum_{\ell=1}^m \log(y_\ell^k) \sum_{i \in I_\ell} \beta_i - \sum_{\ell=1}^m \log(y_\ell^k) \sum_{c \in C(I)} \rho_c \mathbb{1}_{y_\ell^k = \max_{j \in \mathsf{supp}(\{c\})} x_j^k}$$

$$\leq \sum_{\ell=1}^m \log(y_\ell^k)\left(\sum_{i \in I_\ell} \beta_i - \sum_{c \in C(I_\ell)} \rho_c\right)$$

since $\mathbb{1}_{y_\ell^k = \max_{j \in \mathsf{supp}(\{c\})} x_j^k} \leq \mathbb{1}_{\mathsf{supp}(\{c\}) \cap I_\ell = \emptyset}$ and $\log(y_\ell^k) < 0$ for k large enough. Under (11), the above quantity tends to $-\infty$ as $k \to \infty$, and the lemma follows. $\square$

Suppose that $I_0(\mathbf{x}(t)) = \emptyset$, *i.e.*. $\mathbf{x}(t) > 0$. Then (16) gives $\frac{d(\log x_i)}{dt} = \frac{\dot{x}_i}{x_i} = \frac{\beta_i}{x_i} - 1 - \sum_{c \in F_i} \rho_c \frac{1}{\sum_{j : c \in F_j} x_j} = \frac{\partial G}{\partial x_i}$. Hence, $\frac{dG(\vec{x}(t))}{dt} = \sum_i \frac{\partial G}{\partial x_i} \dot{x}_i = \sum_i x_i \left(\frac{\partial G}{\partial x_i}\right)^2 \geq 0$, *i.e.*, when at $\mathbf{x}$, G is increasing as time progresses under the dynamics

(16). This, implies that if $\mathbf{x}(t) > 0$ then the fluid trajectory will stay bounded away from any $\mathbf{x}'$ s.t. $I_0(\mathbf{x}) \neq \emptyset$, as $G(\mathbf{x}') = -\infty$ and by Lemma 4 to reach such an x' the quantity $G(\mathbf{x}(t))$ would have to decrease, a contradiction.

Suppose now that $I = I_0(\mathbf{x}(t)) \neq \emptyset$. We will show that $I_0(\mathbf{x}(t + \delta)) = \emptyset$, for small enough δ. Our previous analysis for the case $I_0(\mathbf{x})$ therefore applies and the theorem, as the limit set L cannot include points $\mathbf{x}^*$ such that $I_0(\mathbf{x}^0) \neq \emptyset$. By (14) and (15), fluid trajectories are Lipschitz continuous; hence, for δ small enough, $x_i(t + \delta) > 0$ for all $i \notin I$. By (16), $\sum_{i \in I} \frac{dx_i}{dt} = \sum_{i \in I} \beta_i - \sum_{\substack{i \in I \\ c \in F_i}} \rho_c z_{c,i}(\mathbf{x}) \overset{(15a)}{=} \sum_{i \in I} \beta_i - \sum_{\substack{i \in I \\ c \in F_i \cap C(I)}} \rho_c z_{c,i}(\mathbf{x}) \overset{(15b)}{\geq} \sum_{i \in I} \beta_i - \sum_{c \in C(I)} \rho_c \overset{(11)}{>} 0$. Hence, for δ small enough, there exists at least one $i \in I$ such that $x_i(t + \delta) > 0$. Given that x_i, $i \notin I$, will stay bounded away from zero within this interval, this implies that within δ time (where δ small enough) all coordinates in I will become positive. Hence, $I_0(\mathbf{x}(t + \delta)) = \emptyset$, for small enough δ. $\square$

C. PROOF OF LEMMA 2

We provide a constructive proof below, calculating q_c^d that satisfy (12). If $M^d = 1$, the lemma trivially holds for $q_c^d = p_c^d$. Now suppose that $M^d \geq 2$. Let $\epsilon = 1 - \sum_{c \in \mathcal{C}} r_c^{\cdot d}/B^d U^d$ and $\epsilon_c = p_c^d - r_c^{\cdot d}/B^d U^d$. From (8d) and (8e), we have that $\epsilon > 0$ and $\epsilon_c > 0$. Sort ϵ_c in an increasing fashion, so that $\epsilon_{c_1} \leq \epsilon_{c_2} \leq \ldots \leq \epsilon_{c_{|\mathcal{C}|}}$. If $\epsilon_{c_1} \geq \epsilon$, then the lemma holds for $q_c^d = r_c^{\cdot d}/B^d U^d + \epsilon/|\mathcal{C}|$. Assume thus that $\epsilon_{c_1} < \epsilon$. Let $k = \max\{j : \sum_{i=1}^j \epsilon_{c_i} < \epsilon\}$. Then $1 \leq k < |\mathcal{C}|$, as $\sum_{c \in \mathcal{C}} \epsilon_c \overset{(8b)}{=} M - 1 + \epsilon > M - 1 > \epsilon$ for $M \geq 2$. Then, $\epsilon' = \epsilon - \sum_{i=1}^k \epsilon_{c_i} > 0$, by the definition of k. Let $q_{c_i}^d = r_c^{\cdot d}/BU + \epsilon_{c_i}$ for $i \leq k$ and $q_{c_i}^d = r_c^{\cdot d}/BU + \epsilon'/(|\mathcal{C}| - k)$ for $i > k$. Then $q_{c_i}^d = p_{c_i}^d > \lambda_c/BU$ for $i \leq k$. For $i > k$, $q_{c_i}^d > r_c^{\cdot d}/BU$ as $\epsilon' > 0$ while $\epsilon'/(|\mathcal{C}| - k) \leq \epsilon' \leq \epsilon_{c_{k+1}}$, as otherwise $\sum_{i=1}^{k+1} \epsilon_{c_i} < 1$, a contradiction. Moreover, $\epsilon_{c_{k+1}} \leq \epsilon_{c_i}$ for all $i \geq k$, so $q_{c_i}^d \leq r_{c_i}^{\cdot d}/BU + \epsilon_{c_i} \leq p_c^d$. Finally, $\sum_c q_c^d = \sum_{i=1}^k (r_{c_i}^{\cdot d}/BU + \epsilon_{c_i}) + \sum_{i=k+1}^{\mathcal{C}} r_{c_i}^{\cdot d}/BU + \epsilon' = \sum_c r_c^{\cdot d}/BU + \epsilon = 1$, and the lemma follows. $\square$

D. PROOF OF THM. 3

Every modification in the first phase of the algorithm incurs at most one cache write, and reduces the l_1 norm—*i.e.*, the imbalance—between the vectors $B\mathbf{q}$ and $B\mathbf{q}'$ by 2. As such, the first phase terminates in at most $B\alpha/2$ operations, at a total cost of at most $B\alpha/2$ writes. In the second phase, every greedy reduction reduces the l_1 distance—*i.e.*, the imbalance—between vectors $B\boldsymbol{\pi}$ and $B\boldsymbol{\pi}'$ by 2, at the cost of one write operation. In the third phase, every switch maintains the imbalance constant; moreover, there can be no more than $M - 1$ consecutive switch operations that must immediately be followed by a greedy reduction. As such, the imbalance reduces by 1 in at most M write operations. At termination of the third phase, since C_- is a has size at most $M - 1$, and each item is missing at most one replica, the imbalance is at most $2M$. Since after phase one the imbalance was $N \sum_c |\pi_c - \pi_c'| \leq B(\alpha + \beta)$, the total number of write operations in the second and third phase is at most $(M - 1)(B/2)(\alpha + \beta)$. $\square$

Tradeoffs in CDN Designs for Throughput Oriented Traffic

Minlan Yu*   Wenjie Jiang[†]   Haoyuan Li[‡]   Ion Stoica[‡]

* University of Southern California   † Princeton University   ‡ University of California Berkeley

ABSTRACT

Internet delivery infrastructures are traditionally optimized for *low-latency* traffic, such as the Web traffic. However, in recent years we are witnessing a massive growth of *throughput-oriented* applications, such as video streaming. These applications introduce new tradeoffs and design choices for content delivery networks (CDNs). In this paper, we focus on understanding two key design choices: (1) What is the impact of the number of CDN's peering points and server locations on its aggregate throughput and operating costs? (2) How much can ISP-CDNs benefit from using path selection to maximize its aggregate throughput compared to other CDNs who only have control at the edge? Answering these questions is challenging because content distribution involves a complex ecosystem consisting of many parties (clients, CDNs, ISPs) and depends on various settings which differ across places and over time. We introduce a simple model to illustrate and quantify the essential tradeoffs in CDN designs. Using extensive analysis over a variety of network topologies (with varying numbers of CDN peering points and server locations), operating cost models, and client video streaming traces, we observe that: (1) Doubling the number of peering points roughly doubles the aggregate throughput over a wide range of values and network topologies. In contrast, optimal path selection improves the CDN aggregate throughput by less than 70%, and in many cases by as little as a few percents. (2) Keeping the number of peering points constant, but reducing the number of location (data centers) at which the CDN is deployed can significantly reduce operating costs.

Categories and Subject Descriptors

C.4 [**Performance of Systems**]: Design studies; C.2.1 [**Computer-communication networks**]: Network Architecture and Design—*Distributed networks*

General Terms

Design, Performance

Keywords

content distribution networks, throughput, multipath

1. INTRODUCTION

Content delivery networks (CDNs) are serving an ever increasing number of throughput-oriented applications such as video streaming, software, games, and movie downloads. In particular, video streaming represents a significant fraction of today's Internet traffic [1, 2], as many content publishers start to deliver content through the Internet: Netflix has reached 20 million US subscribers, and YouTube streams over 2 billion of videos per day [3]. A recent Cisco report predicts that 90% of the consumer traffic will be video by 2013 [4].

The massive growth of the throughput-oriented applications introduces new design choices for CDNs. CDNs have traditionally been optimized for latency-oriented applications, such as web browsing, rather than throughput-oriented applications. It is important to revisit these CDN designs for the throughput metric. A flow can experience throughput bottleneck at the clients, the servers, or along the network paths in between. Clients have no choice other than upgrading the connection. CDNs often have strong incentives to buy more bandwidths to eliminate throughput bottlenecks. Therefore, the most challenging problem is to avoid throughput bottlenecks inside the network.

Primarily, there are two ways to improve the CDN throughput: (1) use path selection and multipath routing to avoid network bottleneck between a CDN server and a client, and (2) increase the number of peering points of the CDN. ISP-CDNs, such as AT&T and Verizon, can use both these approaches to improve the CDN aggregate throughput [5, 6, 7, 8, 9, 10], as they control both the network and the CDN peering. In contrast, traditional CDNs are left with increasing the number of peering points, as the main choice to improve their throughput. In this context, we consider the following design question: *What are the benefits of optimal path selection–beyond increasing the number of peering points– to improve the aggregate throughput of a CDN)?* In other words, we want to quantify the advantage that the ISP-CDNs may have over traditional CDNs, when it comes to maximizing the throughput.

Another design decision that a CDN faces is choosing the number of locations (data centers) at which to deploy its

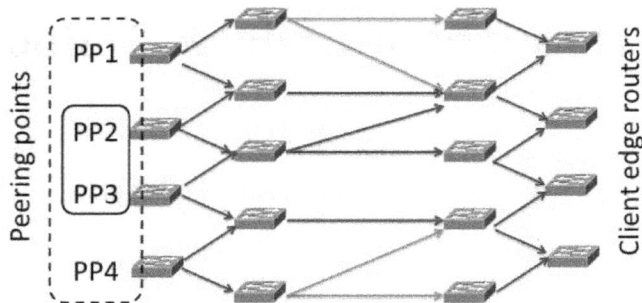

Figure 1: An example comparing the throughput from multipath and more PPs (The capacities of links going out of the PPs are 2. The capacities of all the other links are 1).

servers. For example, Akamai takes a more *distributed* approach by deploying its servers at thousands of locations across the world, while Level3 and Limelight take a more *centralized* approach by building a few data centers, each peering with many ISPs. There are at least two metrics of interest when choosing the number of locations: aggregate throughput and costs. In this paper, we consider the natural question: *How does the number of locations impact the CDN's aggregate throughput and its operating cost?*

Answering the above questions is challenging as content distribution involves a complex ecosystem consisting of many parties (e.g., clients, CDNs, and ISPs), depends on a variety of settings (e.g., topology, routing, business relationships between ISPs and CDNs, operating cost), and evolves rapidly over time. Many of these information are hard to obtain, as they are related to business contracts between different companies. These contracts are difficult to infer even by operators of a single ISP or CDN, letting alone academic researchers. Even if we were able to obtain detailed measurements for the existing CDNs, it would still be difficult to extrapolate the CDN performance for future scenarios. For example, with more peering links between CDNs and ISPs and more investment in increasing edge network capacity [11], it is no longer clear whether the throughput bottleneck will appear at the edge or inside the network.

In this paper we introduce a simple model for understanding CDN design choices on improving throughput. The model is not intended to be a complete representation of reality (e.g., which CDN is better), but instead, is intended to illustrate and quantify the essential tradeoffs in CDN designs in a way that makes it easy to evaluate various scenarios in today's and the future Internet. We focus on modeling two aspects: (1) ISP's ability of path selection inside the network and what path information they expose to CDNs; (2) CDN's choices of server locations and peering points with different operating cost. We drive the model with various settings of both synthetic and Internet network topologies [12, 13], Akamai and Limelight server locations [14], client video streaming demands from Conviva [15], and different types of operating cost. We make two observations:

1. Beyond increasing the number of peering points, optimal path selection has relatively little impact on the throughput. Although path selection and multipath

routing are effective in improving the throughout of point-to-point communication, we show that this is not always the case for throughput-oriented video traffic which typically originates at multiple server locations. This is because increasing the number of peering points essentially increases the min-cut size. In contrast, improving path selection only approximates the min-cut size. For example, in Figure 1, the min-cut size from two peering points (PP2,PP3) to four client locations is 4 (the best throughput improvement from multipath is 4/3). In contrast, by doubling the peering points (PP1-PP4), the min-cut size increases to 8. Our evaluations on various settings show that doubling the number of peering points from 10 to 20 can improve the throughput *linearly*, i.e., between 64.1%-157.1%, while optimal path selection can only improve the throughput by 0.7%-69.4% in most cases. This result indicates that CDNs can go a long way to improve their throughput by adding new peering points, while ISP-CDNs can derive relatively little benefits from their ability to optimize the routes.

2. To achieve the same throughput, the highly distributed CDNs incur higher operating cost than the more centralized CDNs We model various types of operating cost functions, such as bandwidth cost at the peering points, power and maintenance costs associated to hosting, and the cost of content replication across data centers. One of our results shows that a CDN with 150 peering points can reduce its operating costs by as much as 69% by deploying its servers at 15 instead of 80 locations. One natural question is then what is the minimum number of locations that a CDN should deploy its servers. To answer this question, we show that in today's Internet, a CDN can *directly* reach over 80% of all IP addresses by deploying its severs only at the top 54 PoP locations.[1] Thus, a CDN doesn't need to deploy its servers at hundreds or thousands of locations to directly reach the majority of clients. Based on these results, it should come as no surprise that most CDNs today choose a more centralized deployment for throughput-oriented traffic.[2]

The remaining of the paper is organized as follows: Section 2 discusses CDN's design goals of improving throughput and reducing operating cost in practice. Section 3 presents our simple model of understanding CDN design choices on path selection and peering point selection. Section 4 compares the effect of path selection and increasing the number of peering points under a variety of settings. Section 5 analyzes the performance and cost tradeoff for more centralized and more distributed CDN designs. Section 6 and 7 discuss related work and conclude the paper.

2. CDN DESIGN GOALS

In this section, we discuss two key goals of the CDN design: (1) improving throughput performance: Some CDNs can only control server and peering point selection at the edge of the network, while others (especially ISP-CDNs) can also control path selection inside the network. (2) Reducing operating cost: Some CDNs (like Akamai) use a large number of locations to improve aggregate throughput, while others (like Limelight, Level 3) take the more centralized ap-

---

[1]These are the IP addresses owned by the ISPs that peer at the top 54 PoP locations.
[2]Even Akamai is moving towards the more centralized approach for videos.[16].

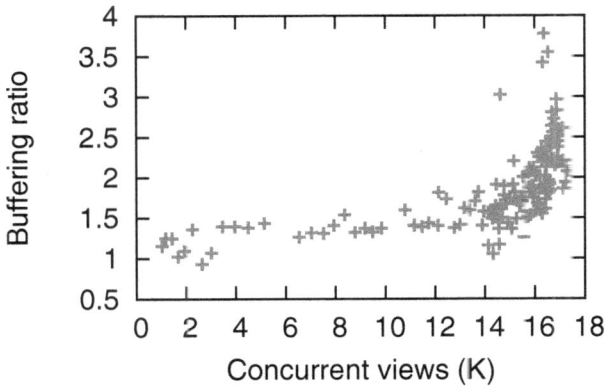

Figure 2: The congestion of a local ISP reduces video quality for viewers from all the CDNs. (The bottleneck is caused by network congestion because viewers with the same CDN server have different performance experiences.)

proach to reduce operating cost by leveraging the economy of scale.

2.1 Improving Throughput

The majority of today's Internet traffic is throughput oriented, including video streaming, software updates, and game and movie downloads. According to Sandvine's report, real-time entertainment applications (including Netflix, YouTube, games, IPTV) alone account for 60% of the Internet traffic in North America [1]. For this traffic (video in particular), throughput is often more important than delay. For example, the start-up time of a video, which is critical for user experience [17], is determined by the time it takes to fill an initial buffer, which depends on throughput. Of course, latency is still important: as most video traffic is streamed over TCP, high round-trip-time can negatively affect the throughput. However, new streaming technologies, such as HTTP chunking [18], allow clients to download multiple chunks in parallel. For these reasons, in this paper we do not consider the impact of latency on throughput.

There are three points at which a flow can experience bottleneck: at the client, at the server, or along the network path. On the client side there is little choice other than upgrading the client device or the connection. On the server side, CDNs often have strong incentives to buy more bandwidth from ISPs and to upgrade the server capacities to match clients' demands, alleviating the server-side bottlenecks.

Recently, the network has emerged as the major bottleneck for video distribution. Netflix has reported that most clients cannot sustain the highest rate (4.8 Mbps) due to ISP limited capacity [19]. Similarly, Akamai has stated that as the video traffic increases, the bottleneck "is no longer likely to be just at the origin data center. It could be at a peering point, or a network's backhaul capacity, or an ISP's upstream connectivity" [20]. Conviva [15], a company that manages video distribution, has seen significant network congestion during flash crowds. Figure 2 shows that

the buffering ratio[3] of viewers across all the CDNs inside one ISP during a popular college football game. When there are more than 14K concurrent viewers, there is a clear degradation of the delivery performance caused by network congestion. We expect the network bottleneck to worsen, as the popularity of throughput-oriented applications increases (e.g., people watching online videos for longer time, and at a higher rate). As a result, more traffic "elephants" will start to step on each other, which significantly decreases the benefits of statistical multiplexing and introduces more challenges in bandwidth provisioning.

To improve the throughput and Internet resource utilization, there has been a growing interest in providing multiple paths and better path selection solutions [5, 6, 7, 8, 9, 10]. These designs are moving closer to reality, as many Internet Service Providers (ISPs), such as AT&T and Verizon, move up the revenue chain to deliver *content* by building their own CDNs. These ISP-CDNs are in the best position to take advantage of controlling both path and server selection to improve the network throughput. In contrast, existing CDNs improve throughput by deploying servers at more locations and setting up more peering points to ISPs. Therefore, it is important to compare the impact of path selection, in addition to server and peering point selection, on improving the end-to-end throughput, and understand the tradeoffs between the ISP-CDNs and other CDN designs.

2.2 Reducing CDN operating cost

CDNs incur three types of operating cost: *(1) Management cost:* At each server location, CDNs pay for the electricity, cooling, equipment maintenance, and human resources. *(2) Content replication cost:* the cost of replicating and caching content across different locations. For the content whose popularity follows a long-tail distribution (e.g., YouTube), CDNs often replicate the most popular content at many locations. In contrast, for rare content, CDNs may only use a single server location and redirect traffic to that location. There are both the storage cost of storing extra replicas and the bandwidth cost of redirecting traffic for rarely accessed contents. *(3) Bandwidth cost:* CDNs often pay ISPs for the bandwidth they use at the peering points based on some mutually-agreed billing model (e.g., 95 percentile usage). Since the peering bandwidth cost is not publicly available, in our model, we use publicly available transit prices as an upper bound for peering cost. This is because the alternative to peering is to simply send traffic to an upstream transit provider [21, 22].

One of the main CDN Design choices is where to deploy the servers. Broadly speaking, in this context, there are two designs that are largely guided by the performance (i.e., throughput) and cost tradeoffs:

Highly distributed approach: Traditionally, Akamai has placed its servers at thousands of locations across the world, which ensures that each client can find a nearby server. Moreover, with a large number of server locations, a client has more chances to find a high-throughput path, simply because there are more choices of paths between a client and the server locations. However, these advantages do not come for free, as the management cost increases with

---

[3]The buffering ratio is the percentage of time a client spend in buffering and is a common metric to indicate video streaming throughput performance.

the number of server locations. Furthermore, the same data item may need to be replicated (cached) to a larger number of locations, increasing the content replication cost.

In terms of bandwidth cost, Akamai traditionally has hosted servers at many ISPs for "free". However, as ISPs start to provide their own CDN services, it is very hard for other CDNs to place servers for free any more. Even Akamai today can only place servers for free for a few small ISPs without many clients, but has to pay those large ISPs for placing the servers. In addition, Akamai is deploying more capacity in large data centers, and thus incurring the peering bandwidth cost as other CDNs. According to the SEC fillings [23], Akamai's bandwidth costs are higher than Limelight's (of course, Akamai carries significantly more traffic, but still it shows that Akamai doesn't get the bandwidth for free).

More centralized approach: CDNs, such as Level3 and Limelight, build large data centers at only a few key locations, and set up peering points from their data centers to a large number of ISPs to increase their reach. Since these CDNs consist of only a few data centers, the cost of data replication and synchronization across data centers is relatively small. In terms of management and bandwidth cost, CDNs with a few larger data centers can benefit from the economy of scale.

3. MODELING CDN DESIGN CHOICES

We propose a simple model to understand CDN design choices. Our model is by no means a thorough representation of the reality. Instead, we design our model to make it both tractable and yet useful in understanding the ecosystem of CDNs and ISPs, as well as quantifying the tradeoffs in CDN design. We focus on modeling two ways of improving the throughput: (1) CDN's choices of server locations and peering points; (2) ISP's ability of path selection inside the network and what path information they expose to CDNs.

3.1 CDNs: Increase peering points at the edge

To improve throughput, CDNs can increase server locations and their peering points at the edge of the network, optimize the selections across these peering points. It is challenging to model existing CDN server locations and peering points, because they depend on business relationships and thus differ across CDNs. Even a single CDN may have to optimize differently for Asia and North America locations, as there are fewer peering links available in Asia. In addition, the CDN architecture evolves rapidly as traditional CDNs peering with more ISPs and many ISP-CDNs also joining the business. Because CDN designs are driven by economic incentives and business relationships, which are difficult to infer even for operators of a single ISP or CDN, letting alone academic researchers. Historical facts also play roles in designs. For example, Akamai already has a wide spread of servers (some are free), while it is challenging for a new CDN to deploy these servers at a low cost.

Modeling peering points: Instead of modeling any specific CDN implementation, we focus on comparing two fundamental types of CDN designs—more centralized and more distributed approaches as discussed in Section 2. The two methods differ in two parameters: the number of server locations at which the CDN deploys servers (n_s), and how many peering points (PP) the CDN sets up at each location

to connect to ISPs ($n_p(s)$). First, to study the throughput of different numbers of PPs ($N_s = \sum_{n_s} n_p(s)$), we model PPs in the network independent of the number of servers n_s and their locations. Next, to compare the cost between more centralized and more distributed CDN designs, we fix the total amount of PPs (N_s) and select different number of servers (n_s). We model content replication by introducing a duplication threshold δ. We duplicate top *delta* popular contents at all the locations but place the rest at a random location. We can fully generalize the design choices of various CDNs beyond Akamai and Limelight by using this model.

Optimal peering point selection: To explore the impact of peering points on throughput, we assume CDNs can perform optimal peering point selection that maximizes the throughput of all clients. Assume a CDN has N_s peering points, N_c client locations. Let P_{sc} be the set of paths between peering point s and client c, and let x_p^{sc} be the amount of traffic traversing path $p \in P_{sc}$. We use routing matrix d_{lp} to specify whether l is on path p ($d_{lp} = 1$) or not ($d_{lp} = 0$). Since a client might download more than one content item at a time, we assume arbitrary splitting of client traffic across different server locations x_p^{sc}. We formulate peering point selection as the following optimization problem: the CDN maximizes the throughput (Eq. (1)), given the link capacity constraint (Eq. (2)). The problem can be easily extended to consider peering point selection for different contents by replacing x_p^{sc} to x_p^{scd} where d represents the specific content.

$$\max \quad \sum_{(s,c)} \sum_{p \in P_{sc}} x_p^{sc} \quad (1)$$

$$\text{s.t.} \quad \sum_{(s,c)} \sum_{p \in P_{sc}} x_p^{sc} * d_{lp} \leq Cap_l \quad (2)$$

$$\text{variables} \quad x_p^{sc} >= 0 \quad (3)$$

The problem runs in time $O(|P_{sc}| \times N_c \times N_s)$. In the AS-level Internet topology where $N_s = 1K$ and $N_c = 12K$, a single simulation on the Internet topology takes about 12 hours. Therefore, to evaluate many settings, we did most of evaluations with smaller topologies and verify the results with the Internet topology.

Client demand constraints: The throughput optimization highly depends on the distribution of client demands across client locations. We start with a simple model that does not have any constraints on client demands to understand the upper bound of the throughput we can get from the network and the CDNs. We then extend the model to understand the impact of client distribution. We set lower and upper bounds on the traffic demand as $Lower_c \leq \sum_s \sum_{p \in P_{sc}} x_p^{sc} \leq Upper_c$ for each client location c. When the network does not have enough bandwidth capacity to serve all the clients, CDNs start to reject clients. We introduce an acceptance ratio a^{sc} ($\in [0,1]$), and ensure $\sum_{p \in P_{sc}} x_p^{sc} \leq a^{sc} Upper_c$. In fact, the new constraint is the same with the original constraint without rejection, because we can use a new rate variable $\hat{x}_p^{sc}$ to replace x_p^{sc}/a^{sc}. We drive the client demand model with the Conviva traces on the number of video streaming sessions from each client location. Assume a location consist of 100 client sessions with video streaming rates ranging from 100 Kbps to 1 Mbps. In this case, the

Scenarios	CDN design	ISP design	Optimality	CDN's path changes
1. Today: no cooperation (labeled as "1path")	peering point selection	shortest path (e.g., OSPF)	not optimal	none
2. Better contracts: k shortest paths (labeled as "mpath")	pick dedicated paths + peering point selection	provide k shortest paths (e.g., setting MPLS)	sub-optimal	fast
3. ISP-CDN: Joint opt. (labeled as "mcf")	Joint traffic engineering and peering point selection		optimal	slow

Table 1: Interactions of CDNs and ISPs

lower and upper bounds at that location are 10 Mbps and 100 Mbps respectively.

3.2 ISPs: Improve path selection at the core

We model the ISP's path selection process based on how much path information the ISP exposes to the CDN, which leads to different levels of engineering overhead and throughput optimality (Table 1). Our model should capture both ISP-CDNs where both servers and clients are located within the same ISP, and those CDNs that spread servers across many ISPs. We first discuss three ways to implement server (path) selection assuming a single ISP, and then extend the model to include multiple ISPs.

CDN performs peering point selection; ISP uses shortest path. Today, there is no cooperation between CDNs and ISPs (Scenario 1). Given a client, the CDN selects a server, and then uses the shortest path provided by the ISP to deliver the content to the client. To improve the throughput, the CDN has to increase server locations at the edge and optimize peering point selection based on end-to-end performance measurements. The optimization problem for peering point selection is captured by Eq. (1)-(3) with $|P_{sc}| = 1$.

Better CDN and ISP contracts: ISPs expose multiple paths to the CDN. To further improve the throughput, the CDN may negotiate with the ISP the ability to use multiple-paths. The ISP can still make their own traffic engineering decisions, but provide *multiple shortest paths* for each pair of client locations and server peering points (e.g., using MPLS tunneling). The CDN can flexibly split traffic on these paths and pick peering points to optimize throughput (Scenario 2). The more paths the ISP provides to the CDN, the better the CDN can leverage the available bandwidth in the network. On the downside, exposing more paths increases the management overhead of ISPs. To model this setting, we set P_{sc} as k shortest paths [4], and solve the optimization problem for joint selection of peering points and paths captured by Eq. (1)-(3).

ISP-CDNs: Joint optimization of traffic engineering and server selection (Scenario 3). ISP-CDNs have full control on both CDN servers and network paths, and thus perform a joint optimization of server selection and path selection to achieve the *optimal* throughput. To understand the upper bound of the throughput that any multipath approach can achieve, we formulate the joint optimization as a *multi-commodity flow problem (mcf)* as shown in Eq. (4)-(8).

$$\max \quad \sum_{(s,c)} x_{sc} \tag{4}$$

$$\text{s.t.} \quad \sum_{(s,c)} x_{sc} * r_l^{sc} \leq Cap_l, \forall l \tag{5}$$

$$\sum_{l \in in(v)} r_l^{sc} - \sum_{l \in out(v)} r_l^{sc} = I_{v=c} \tag{6}$$

$$(\forall(s,c) \forall v \in V - \{s\}) \tag{7}$$

$$\text{variables} \quad 0 \leq r^{sc} \leq 1, \forall(s,c), \forall l \tag{8}$$

The variable in the problem is r_l^{sc}, denoting the splitting ratio of the traffic from client location c to peering point s at link l. In practice, path selection may happen at a lower frequency than server selection, because it involves route recomputing and network reconfiguration.

Similarly to the single ISP case, when a CDN connects to multiple ISPs, the CDNs may leverage existing shortest paths (the AS level paths following BGP policies) to maximize throughput (Scenario 1). The CDNs may also get multiple shortest paths from each peering point to ISPs (Scenario 2).

4. QUANTIFY THROUGHPUT BENEFITS

In this section, we compare two approaches to maximize the throughput: (1) increase the number of peering points, and (2) select multiple paths between CDN peering points and client locations to maximize the throughput. We first use max-flow min-cut theorem to illustrate the differences of the two approach. Next, through evaluations on a variety of network and server settings, we conclude that doubling the number of peering points roughly doubles the aggregate throughput over a wide range of values and network topologies. In contrast, optimal path selection improves the CDN aggregate throughput by less than 70%, and in many cases by as little as a few percents. Furthermore, we show that multipath is even less effective with client demand dynamics and long tail distribution of content accesses based on our analysis on Conviva video demands [15].

4.1 Multipath is not necessary for CDNs

Multipath increases throughput significantly for single-source, single-destination applications. However, CDNs' clients can access content from multiple servers via different peering points, which makes multipath less effective compared with increasing the number of peering points. This is illustrated by the max-flow min-cut theorem [24].

We reduce the multi-commodity flow problem formulated in Eq. (4)-(8) to the single source and single sink max flow problem. We assume perfect content replication in servers, such that all the servers and their peering points are treated equally in their abilities to serve clients. The clients are also treated equally with their different demands' lower and

---

[4]k is an upper bound and there may exist fewer than k shortest paths.

upper bounds. Therefore, we can add a new super source that is connected to all servers, as well as a new super sink. According to the max-flow min-cut theorem, the maximum flow passing from the super source to the super sink is equal to the minimum capacity over all source-sink cuts *(i.e., min-cut size)*. Therefore, the throughput that any multipath solution can achieve is always bounded by the min-cut size (i.e., the throughput from the *mcf* solution).

In contrast, increasing peering points adds new edges (from the new super source to new peering points) to the graph, which potentially grows the min-cut size. As the example shown in Figure 1, when we add two more peering points (PP1, PP4), the min cut size increases from 4 to 8. In contrast, the best throughput multipath can achieve with two peering points (PP1, PP2) is only 4.

Since the optimal multipath (*mcf*) is less effective than increasing peering points at the edge, other path selection solutions perform even worse for CDNs traffic improvement. Therefore, CDNs can go a long way to improve their throughput by just adding new peering points, while ISP-CDNs can derive relatively little benefits from their ability to optimize the routes. Furthermore, as suggested by [25], even using the static routes provided by ISPs, the CDNs can get most of the benefits of path selection by choosing the peering point from which to deliver the content.

To verify this conclusion, we quantify the throughput improvement to compare the optimal multipath solution *mcf* and increasing peering points solutions in the entire CDN design space (with different network topologies, link capacities, and client workloads).

4.2 Evaluation Setup

It is challenging to quantify the benefits of CDN designs because of the complexity of the network, clients, and servers. They may change over time, and are also highly related to business decisions. Instead of studying a point of design by measuring some existing CDNs, we perform an extensive evaluation to understand the effect of *mcf* and more peering points in a variety of settings (Table 2). For each setting, we run the simulation 100 times and take the average throughput.

Network topology and link capacity: The network topology and link capacity are two important factors for the CDN throughput. Network topologies are diverse and keep evolving. For example, the Internet is becoming flatter and peering links keeps increasing[5]. Therefore, it is important to not only study existing Internet topologies but also the other common topologies to fully understand their effect on throughput performance. We evaluate our model under many realistic and synthetic topologies: To understand ISP-CDNs, we take the router-level topologies in several ISPs (e.g., Comcast, Cox) from ITDK data set [12]. We choose the AS-level Internet topology from Cyclops [13].[6] for CDNs spreading across multiple ISPs. To understand the impact of topologies with different levels of connectivity, we use BRITE [27] to generate three types of synthetic

topologies: power-law graph, random graph, and the hierarchical graph.[7]

To the best of our knowledge, there is no good understanding of link capacity available inside the networks for CDNs, because it is hard to get precise packet timing (from iplane [28]'s experience [29]), and hard to congest a link inside the Internet and measure the link capacity before ISPs react to congestion. It is even more challenging with the Internet evolving over time (e.g., with growing investments on home access networks). Therefore, the best thing we can do is to follow the normal practice [30] and to evaluate our model under a variety of link capacity distributions. According to previous work on Internet measurement and modeling [31, 32, 28], we choose three representative link capacity distributions (power law, uniform, and pareto) within the range of 100 Mbps to 10 Gbps.[8] We also assign different link capacities inside and between ASes in the hierarchical topology [28, 31] (e.g., with "high peering cap", we increase link capacity between ASes is twice of those inside ASes.)

Peering point and client selection: We get the realistic Akamai and Limelight server IP addresses from PlanetLab measurement collected at Nov. 2010 [14] and map them to the ASes where the servers are located using Quova [33]. Akamai has 1026 ASes while Limelight has 216 ASes. To understand the entire CDN design space, we study two ways of peering point selection in synthetic topologies: First, to compare the throughput gains of increasing PPs and increasing paths (independent of different CDN designs), we pick the peering points (PPs) randomly from the network. Next, to compare the cost of more centralized and more distributed CDNs, we rank the nodes in the network based on their outgoing degrees and pick the high-degree nodes as servers and set peering points from those nodes connecting to the server nodes. Similarly, we pick low-degree nodes to model more distributed CDNs. We choose client locations randomly from a pool of low-degree nodes, because clients typically have only a few access links to their upper tiers.

Path selection: In a single ISP (router-level ISP and synthetic topologies), we can easily select single shortest paths, k shortest paths, and optimal paths. In the AS-level topology, we choose paths based on policies: *(1) Optimal case (mcf):* To understand the throughput upper bound, we view the AS graph as an undirected graph, ignoring all BGP policies. *(2) Single path case (1path):* We model the path selection based on the Gao-Rexford conditions [34] (following Valley free, local preference, shortest path, and the other tie breaking policies). *(3) k shortest paths:* To understand the best possible multipath choices that can be realized by multipath BGP protocols [7,.35], we *only* enforce the valley free policies for *k* shortest paths.

---

[5]Fixed orbit reports 144K peering links in 2012 [26].

[6]We ignore the links inside an AS to reduce the problem size. The result should not be affected because peering links between ASes are more likely to become the bottleneck than the links inside ASes.

[7]Following the guidelines in BRITE, in the random graph, we use the waxman model and set the parameters $\alpha = 0.2, \beta = 0.15$. In the hierarchical graph, we choose 10 ASes, each AS with an average of 50 nodes. Within the ASes and among the ASes, we create links based on the power law model.

[8]Note that the link capacity is the bandwidth that can be used for a content delivery application. Only the relative values of capacity among links affect our results.

Topology	#nodes	#links	$\dfrac{Thpt_{mcf}-Thpt_{1path}}{Thpt_{1path}}$ (#PP=10..250)	$\dfrac{Thpt_{20PP}-Thpt_{10PP}}{Thpt_{10PP}}$ (1path)	$\dfrac{Thpt_{100PP}-Thpt_{10PP}}{Thpt_{10PP}}$ (1path)
AS-level Internet (Akamai: 1026 ASes)	~12K	~120K	18.1%	Akamai/Limelight=205.4%	
AS-level Internet (Limelight: 216 ASes)	~12K	~120K	27.2%		
power law (uniform cap dist.)	500	997	0.7%-10.3%	96.8%	789.5%
power law dense (uniform cap dist.)	500	1990	20.2%-32.2%	64.1%	195.8%
power law (exp cap dist.)	500	997	9.2%-15.1%	157.1%	298.8%
power law (pareto cap dist.)	500	997	0.7%-15.1%	149.3%	322.1%
random (uniform cap dist.)	500	1000	2.3%-69.4%	96.4%	659.9%
hierarchy (uniform cap dist.)	500	1020	3.5%-26.4%	120.0%	745.6%
hierarchy (high peering cap)	500	1020	1.9%-31.7%	95.6%	225.7%
AS 13367 Comcast (uniform cap dist.)	382	421	1.8%-11.8%	81.2%	424.7%
AS 12064 Cox (uniform cap dist.)	326	378	110.3-584.0%	337.0%	2755.2%

Table 2: Increasing #PP (Col. 5, 6) is more effective than increasing #paths (Col. 4) in achieving throughput over various topologies.

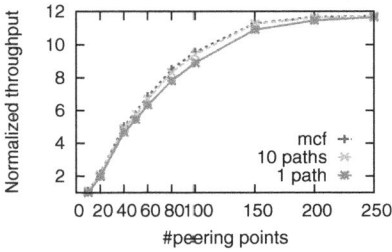

(a) Increasing #PP

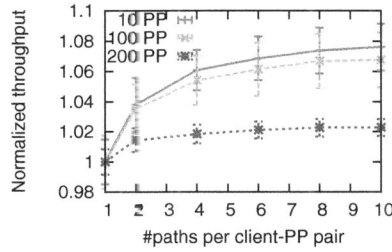

(b) Increasing #paths

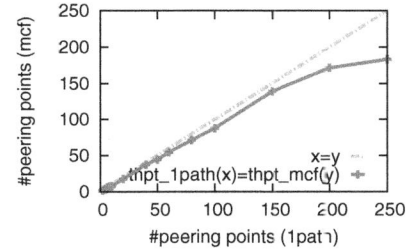

(c) #PP of 1path vs mcf for the same thpt

Figure 3: Multipath has little throughput improvement over increasing #server locations (power law graph)

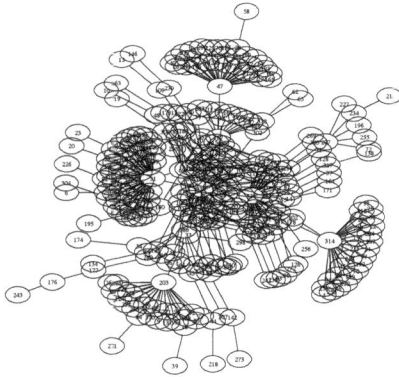

Figure 4: Cox topology

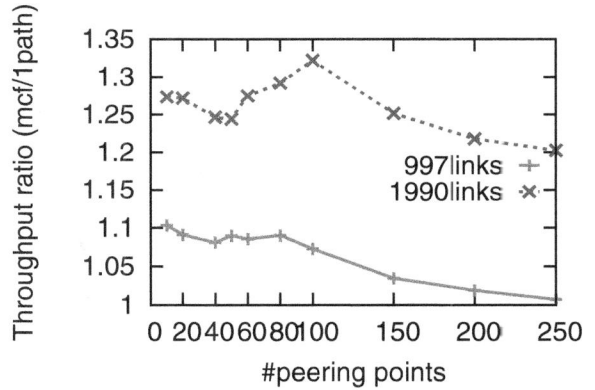

Figure 5: Effect of multipath

4.3 Quantify the throughput improvement

With evaluations on various settings, we show that doubling the number of peering points from 10 to 20 can improve the throughput linearly, i.e., between 64.1%-157.1%, while optimal path selection can only improve the throughput by 0.7%-69.4% in most cases (Table 2). One interesting example is the Cox topology, where both multipath and more PPs have better throughput improvement because there is a few internal routers with high degree.

More peering points also reduce the delay while multipath often increases the delay. Moreover, with more peering points, the throughput benefits of multipath decreases in most cases. One exception is the power law dense graph

with less than 100 PPs, the benefits of multipath increase slowly with increasing PPs.

Increasing #paths vs increasing #peering points (PPs): In the AS-level Internet topology, the optimal multiple path solution (mcf) improves the throughput over the single shortest path (1path) by 18.1% on average for Akamai and 27.2% for Limelight. In the power law topology (Figure 3(a)), the throughput increases by 96.8% from 10 to 20 PPs, and by 789.5% from 10 to 100 PPs. However, mcf can only improve the throughput by 0.7%-10.3%. As shown in Figure 3(b), with 10 PPs, 10 shortest paths improve the throughput by 7.6% compared with 1path, approximating the optimal multipath solution (mcf).

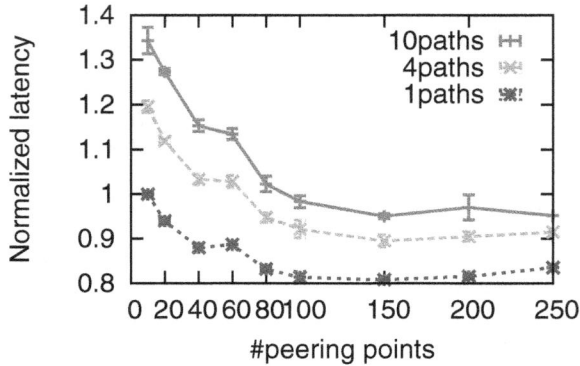

Figure 6: Effect on delay

Figure 3(c) quantifies the number of PPs with *mcf* needed to achieve the same throughput with the number of PPs with *1path*. For example, 100 PPs with *1path* can reach the same throughput with 88 PPs with *mcf*. The gap between the two curves in the figure indicates the benefits of multipath over single path. The gap is small with less than 100 PPs, indicating few benefits from multipath. Beyond 100 PPs, the gap becomes larger. This is because the network capacity is mostly explored and the throughput improvements from both more PPs and *mcf* become small (within 5%). As a result, we need a lot more PPs to match the same throughput improvement when PPs are small.

Effect of network topology: The throughput benefits of more paths and more PPs differ with different link capacities and topologies. For example, the *mcf* has more benefits in the power law dense graph, while increasing PPs works better in the power law graph with fewer links. This is because multipath has more benefits in networks with more path options and higher aggregate link capacity. One interesting topology is the Cox network with a few high-degree internal routers (Figure 4). With a uniform distribution of link capacity, the throughput from *1path* to *mcf* increases by 110.3%-584.0%, which is comparable to double PPs from 10 to 20 (337.0%). This is because even with more PPs, the traffic still have to traverse through the same set of internal routers (i.e., the min-cut size remains almost the same).

Effects of multipath with the increase of #PPs: In general, the more PPs, the less useful is multipath, as shown in Figure 5. This is because more PPs increases the network utilization, leaving less space for multipath to improve throughput. However, for the graph with more links (power law dense), when the number of PPs grows from 10 to 100, the benefits of multipath increase by about 5%. This is because with the growth of PPs, the throughput bottleneck moves from the edge to the network, where multipath can have more benefits.

Effect on delay: In practice, CDNs may also care about delay in addition to the throughput metric. With more PPs, we can improve the throughput and reduce the delay at the same time. In contrast, multipath increases the throughput at the expense of increasing the delay. In Figure 6, we assign the link latency of the realistic topologies based on the geolocation information of the routers, and the latency of synthetic topologies based on the uniform distribution with

an average of 50 ms. The propagation delay drops by 20% from 10 to 100 PPs, but remains the same beyond 100 PPs. In contrast, increasing the number of paths from 1 to 10 increases the delay by about 35%.

4.4 Understand the effect of client settings

There are three key client-side settings that may affect the throughput: (1) client location popularity (i.e., some client location has more demands than others); (2) content popularity (especially contents whose accesses follow a long-tail distribution); (3) Client demand changes over time (especially during flash crowds). Considering these settings, we show that the gap of throughput benefits between more PPs and multipath becomes even larger.

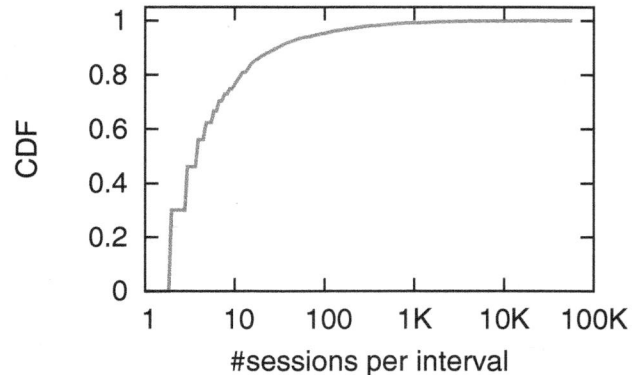

Figure 8: Client sessions distribution across ASes

We study three sets of session-level traces from Conviva collected between Dec. 2011 and April. 2012: the *normal trace*, the *long-tail trace* with a long-tail content distribution, and the *flash-crowd trace* containing flash crowds during a popular local event. We calculate the number of sessions from each AS based on the client IP addresses every five-minute interval. The clients of each trace spread over 12K ASes. Figure 8 shows the CDF of the average # sessions per interval at each AS for the normal trace. The normal trace and the long-tail trace contain an average 340K sessions per interval and remain stable across intervals. The flash crowd trace contains an average of 450K sessions and a peak of 630K sessions per interval. We set the upper and lower bounds of the sending rate per session as 300 kbps and 3 Mbps respectively. We time the rate bound with the number of sessions to get the throughput demand bounds at each location $Lower_c$ and $Upper_c$. For those synthetic topologies, we map these throughput demands randomly to client locations.

Fairness among client locations: One concern is whether the throughput gains of more PPs come from a few popular client locations. We evaluate the normal trace in the power-law topology, where client locations have diverse demands. The throughput improves by 494.9% from 10 PPs to 100 PPs, but only by 0.3% with *mcf*. This is consistent with the results in Table 2 without client constraints. We also calculate the Jain's fairness index across the throughput of all the clients in Figure 7(a). When there are more than 20 PPs, the throughput is relatively equal among clients (The

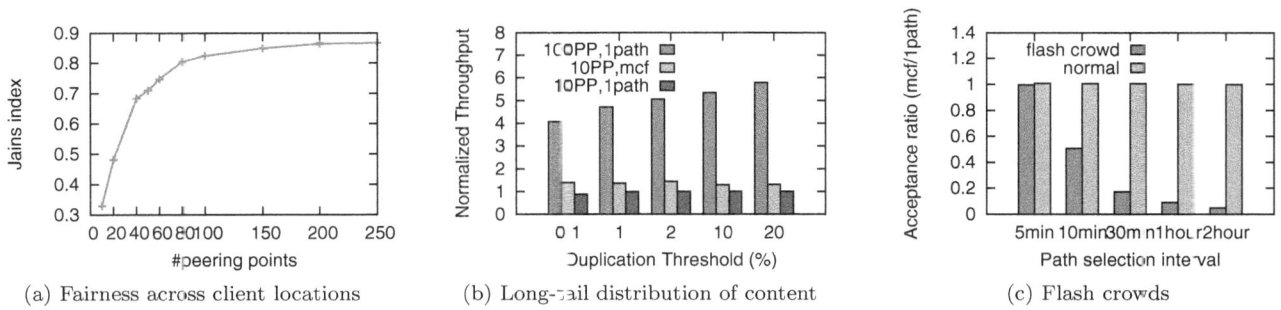

(a) Fairness across client locations   (b) Long-tail distribution of content   (c) Flash crowds

Figure 7: Effect of client-side settings

index is above 0.5). This is because there is a large amount of clients (200 out of 500 nodes) evenly distributed across the network. These clients have equal chances to use the network bandwidth, as long as their access links are not bottlenecked. The broad spread of CDN clients across the Internet is true in practice because of the growth of video streaming traffic as observed from our analysis on Conviva traces.

The long-tail distribution of contents: The throughput performance is highly related to content replication decisions, which in turn depend on content popularity. We use the long-tail trace to understand the effect of content popularity. We set a replication threshold δ based on server capacity. We replicate top δ popular contents across all the server locations, but randomly pick a single server to store the other contents. As shown in Figure 7(b), with different levels of replications (δ=0.1%-20%), more PPs always improve throughput more than mcf. When there are fewer replications (δ=0.1%), the throughput improvement of mcf increases, and the improvement of more PPs decreases. This is because without replication the content delivery is closer to the single-source traffic.

Flash crowds: It takes different time intervals to adjust peering point selection and path selection to client demand changes. We compare two cases: (1) the traditional CDNs that can only select peering points with a single path between each client-PP pair. (2) the ISP-CDNs that can perform joint server and path selection. It takes longer time to switch paths because it requires path computation, network reconfiguration, and routing propagation. Therefore, we fix the server/peering point selection interval as 5 minutes for both cases, but set the path selection intervals ranging from 5 minutes to 2 hours for ISP-CDNs. During the periods when ISP-CDNs only perform server selection, we keep the routing decisions based on the last time when a joint optimization is performed and kept unchanged throughput the entire interval.[9] We use equal splitting across k shortest paths to approximate the optimal path selection (calculated by the multi-commodity flow problem), as we observe a small gap between the two solutions with a large k (e.g., k=10) according to our previous evaluations (e.g., Figure 3 (a) and (b)). We use the normal and flash-crowd traces in the power law graph with 50 PPs.

---

[9] However, it might not able to learn the routing information sometimes, for instance, a client may not appear (i.e., zero demand) at time t, but have a large demand at time $t+1$. The routing decision for this client at time t is arbitrary and hence can be quite sub-optimal at time $t+1$.

Since the client demands change significantly during the flash crowd event, it is sometimes impossible to satisfy all the clients if the demand is very high. To understand the potential of delivering flash crowd events, we define the acceptance ratio (a^{sc} defined in Section 3) as the fraction of demands the CDN can deliver. Figure 7(c) compares the acceptance ratios with different path selection intervals with the single path case with PP selection only. As expected, when the path selection interval is the same with PP selection, mcf only has 0.7% improvement in acceptance ratio than $1path$ case. Worse still, during the flash crowd event, when the path selection interval increases, the acceptance ratio drops significantly. For example, with 10 minute interval, the ratio drops by 50% from $1path$'s ratio; with 1 hour interval, the ratio is only 8% of that of $1path$ case. This is because when the traffic changes rapidly during flash crowds but the ISP-CDN cannot adjust its path selection quickly, the routing decision at one time is far from optimal for the traffic at the following time intervals. In contrast, the CDN who takes a simpler approach of fast and optimal peering selection at the edge can achieve a much higher acceptance ratio.

5. CENTRALIZED & DISTRIBUTED CDNS

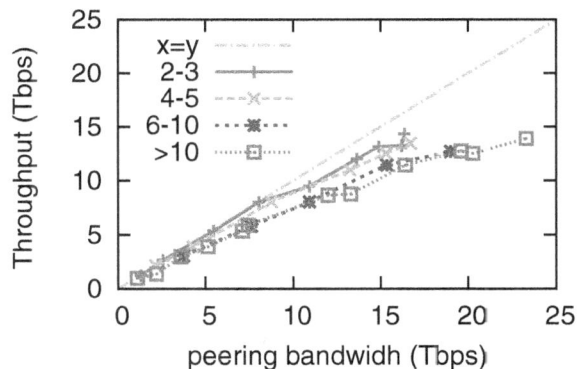

Figure 9: Comparing CDN throughput with different number of server locations (power law graph)

There are two ways to increase peering points to improve throughput: the more distributed CDNs (e.g., Akamai) increase the number of server locations to increase peering

153

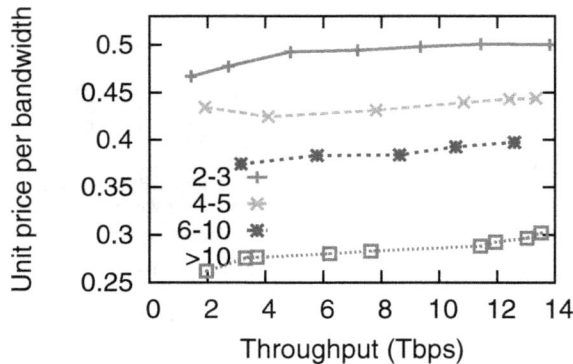

Figure 10: Comparing CDN cost (Polynomial cost) with different number of server locations (power law graph)

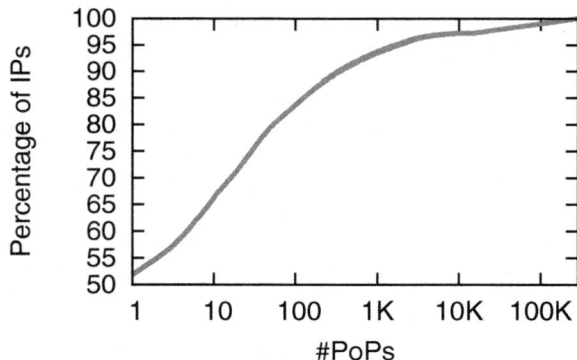

Figure 11: Percentage of IP addresses top x PoPs can reach

Cost function	Avg unit price				$\frac{P_{>10}}{P_{2-3}}$
	2-3	**4-5**	**6-10**	**>10**	
Bw: Poly. bw^{α},($\alpha = -\log 2$)	49.0	43.6	38.6	28.5	58.2%
Bw: Amazon [36]	5.4	5.1	4.3	3.1	57.4%
Bw: OC3 [37]	89.4	59.8	44.3	31.9	35.7%
Mngt: $c \cdot e^{a \cdot bw}, a < 0$	30.3	26.7	25.4	25.0	82.5%
Elec: $c \cdot \log(bw + a), c < 0$	64.5	57.4	49.6	28.5	44.2%
Linear $c \cdot bw + a, c < 0$	89.5	84.6	76.6	27.5	30.7%
Per-PP bw: $(bw/n_p)^{\alpha}$	64.6	68.6	72.3	82.4	1.3

Table 3: Cost comparison of centralized and distributed solutions. (Each cost function value is normalized into [0,100]. Power-law graph)

points; the more centralized CDNs (e.g., Limelight) only deploy servers at a few locations but set up many peering points at each location. Our evaluation of various types of cost functions shows that given a total of 150 peering points, more centralized CDNs achieve 22.5% less throughput than more distributed CDNs, but can reduce the operating cost per bit of bandwidth by as much as 69%. We also analyze the Internet topology to understand the minimum number of server locations a CDN should have in practice. Our results are consistent with the fact that most CDNs today choose a more centralized deployment for throughput-oriented traffic.

5.1 Comparing the throughput

To understand the general tradeoff of CDN design rather than looking into specific CDNs, we study different approaches of picking server locations based on the peering points (PPs) at each location. We classify the potential server locations into four categories: the locations with 2-3, 4-5, 6-10, and >10 PPs at each location. We fix the total number of peering points, and then pick more server locations with 2-3 PPs per location to model more distributed CDNs. We can also pick fewer locations >10 PPs each to model more centralized CDNs, or pick the other server locations with 4-5, 6-10 PPs to model the CDNs in between. For example, to get 150 total peering points, the more distributed CDN has 80

server locations with 2-3 PPs each, while the more centralized CDN has 15 server locations with >10 PPs each.

Given the same number of peering points with the same aggregate peering bandwidth, different types of CDNs have different throughput (Figure 9). More distributed CDNs with more locations ("2-3") can better explore the available bandwidth inside the network and thus provide better throughput than more centralized CDNs with fewer locations (">10"). For example, when there are around 150 peering points with a total of about 78 Tbps peering bandwidth, the more distributed solution ("2-3") reaches 8.0 Tbps, while the more centralized solution (">10") reaches 6.2 Tbps.

5.2 Comparing per-bandwidth cost

Although more distributed CDNs can achieve a better throughput, they often incur more operating cost. By evaluating different types of cost functions, we conclude that to achieve the same throughput, more centralized CDNs are cheaper to build than more distributed CDNs.

We model the operating cost per *unit traffic* for a server location as $f(bw)$, where bw is the traffic volume at this location. In general, $f(bw)$ is a decreasing function of the used bandwidth. We introduce a family of cost functions based on sensitivity of unit price with respect to throughput as shown in Table 3: The polynomial cost function[10], step functions (Amazon [36] and OC3[37]) to model bandwidth cost, exponential function for management cost, log function for electricity cost, and the linear cost function. The content replication cost can be modeled as one or a combination of the above functions depending on CDN designs.

More centralized CDNs incur less operating cost than more distributed CDNs: As shown in Table 3, the more centralized CDNs consistently achieve the lowest price per bit of bandwidth, across all cost types and different values of aggregate throughput. For example, in Figure 10, fixing the total number 150 PPs, the unit price of more centralized solution (15 locations with > 10 PPs each) is only 58.3% of the more distributed solution (80 locations with 2-3 PPs each). This is because with a few server locations, more centralized CDNs already achieve good throughput at each location and hence attain a low price per bit of bandwidth. In contrast, due to the low traffic volume at each location, more distributed CDNs ("2-3") the highest unit price.

The cost advantage of more distributed CDNs is independent of CDN sizes and aggregate throughput. We have

---

[10]We get the function based on the transit bandwidth cost— 1$ at 1G, 0.5$ at 10G, and 0.25$ at 100G [15].

consistent observations with different parameter choices in all the cost functions listed in Table 3, and a linear combination of these functions. The results also hold for multiple paths because multipath has limited effect on throughput.

More centralized CDNs have a higher price variation w.r.t. throughput: We also observe that the unit price for more centralized CDNs grows faster with the throughput increase than more distributed CDNs. For example, in Figure ??(b), the unit price grows by 7.1% for more distributed CDNs ("2-3") from 2 Tbps to 14 Tbps, but grows by 15.4% for more centralized CDNs (>10). With the linear cost function, the price increases by 300% from 2 Tbps to 14 Tbps for the more centralized CDNs. This is because more centralized CDNs cannot keep up with the throughput growth with more peering points (i.e., achieves less throughput with the same total PPs), and thus incur a faster unit price growth. Note that even with faster growth, when we push the throughput close to the network capacity, the unit price for more centralized CDNs is still lower than more distributed CDNs.

More distributed CDNs have a lower unit price when CDNs pay bandwidth cost for each peering point separately: At each server location, CDNs may pay for peering bandwidth purchased from different ISPs separately. We model the per-PP bandwidth cost as $f(bw/n_p) = (bw/n_p)^\alpha$, where n_p is the number of peering points a server location has. Opposite to other cost functions, here more centralized CDNs have higher unit price than more distributed CDNs (Table 3). This is because given the same number of PPs, more distributed CDNs have a higher per-PP traffic volume than more central CDNs and thus incur a better unit price.

5.3 How many server locations in practice?

Based on the tradeoffs between throughput and cost, the more centralized a CDN is, the less cost it takes to achieve a given throughput. However, in practice, we cannot just have a single server location because it is almost impossible to find a single best position to peer with all the ISPs. One natural question is then what is the minimum number of locations that a CDN should deploy its servers. We analyze the PoP-level Internet topology of about 12K ASes with 177K PoPs, and the IP addresses owned by each AS [28]. Figure 11 shows that the top 54 PoPs already have peering links to those ISPs who own over 80% of the IP addresses. This means a CDN does not need to deploy its servers at hundreds or thousands of locations to directly reach the majority of clients.

6. RELATED WORK

Understanding CDN performance from measurement: Many works take a *measurement-based* approach to understand CDN performance and the CDN-ISP relations from the *delay* perspective [38, 39, 40, 41]. Unfortunately, using measurement studies alone is not sufficient to understand CDN design choices. For example, [40, 41] uses a combination of web-browser clients, SpeedTest [42] servers located near Akamai servers, and active probing to measure the delay and throughput provided by both of Akamai and Limelight. However, despite these careful measurements, the study provides little information about the routes used to deliver content to various clients, the overall throughput, and the costs incurred by CDNs [43]. Instead of studying an existing CDN, we choose a simple model to understand

the fundamental design choices of CDNs in the design space, and simulate the model using video streaming traces and a diversity of network topologies (with varying CDN peering points and server locations).

Better ISP support for network performance: There have been many works on improving path selection and providing multiple paths to improve network performance [5, 6, 7, 8, 9, 10]. While better path selection does provide better performance and more reliability for single-source, single destination applications, our evaluations show that even optimal multipath solution has limited impact for CDNs with many peering points and massive clients.

The papers [44, 45] show the benefits of multihoming in improving delay and throughput compared to overlay routing. We reach a more general conclusion that more peering points at the edge can improve the throughput much more than multiple paths inside the network across a wide variety of network topologies and settings. We also study the right number of CDN server locations considering the throughput and cost tradeoffs.

7. CONCLUSION

It is crucial to revisit the design space for CDNs, with more throughput-oriented applications (e.g., video steaming). We provide a simple model of essential CDN designs and perform extensive evaluations on a variety of network topologies (with varying numbers of CDN peering points and server locations), operating cost models, and client video streaming traces. Our results show that adding new peering points helps CDNs improve the throughput most. On the other hand, ISP-CDNs could not benefit much from their ability to optimize the routes. In addition, CDNs should choose the more centralized CDN design with many peering points, because it requires lower operating cost than the more distributed approach to achieve the same throughput.

8. ACKNOWLEDGMENT

We thank our shepherd Timothy G. Griffin, the anonymous reviewers, John Chuang, Ali Ghodsi, Xin Jin, Srinivas Narayana, Peng Sun, and Vytautas Valancius, for their comments on earlier versions of this paper. We especially thank Dahai Xu for improving the scalability of our optimization code and David Choffnes for providing us the locations of Akamai and Limelight servers from their PlanetLab measurement.

9. REFERENCES

[1] Sandvine, "Global Internet phenomena report." Technical report, 2011.

[2] G. Maier, A. Feldmann, V. Paxson, and M. Allman, "On dominant characteristics of residential broadband Internet traffic," in *IMC*, 2009.

[3] http://youtube-global.blogspot.com/2010/05/at-five-years-two-billion-views-per-day.html.

[4] E. Schonfeld, "Cisco: By 2013 video will be 90 percent of all consumer ip traffic and 64 percent of mobile." http://tinyurl.com/nw8jxg, 2009.

[5] D. Wischik, C. Raiciu, A. Greenhalgh, and M. Handley, "Design, implementation and evaluation of congestion control for multipath TCP," in *NSDI*, 2011.

[6] D. Xu, M. Chiang, and J. Rexford, "PEFT: Link-state routing with hop-by-hop forwarding can achieve optimal traffic engineering," in *IEEE INFOCOM*, 2008.

[7] W. Xu and J. Rexford, "MIRO: Multi-path interdomain routing," in *SIGCOMM*, 2006.

[8] M. Motiwala, M. Elmore, N. Feamster, and S. Vempala, "Path splicing," in *SIGCOMM*, 2008.

[9] "Routescience." http://support.avaya.com/css/Products/P0345.

[10] "Cisco optimized edge routing (oer)." http://www.cisco.com/en/US/products/ps6628/products_ios_protocol_option_home.html, 2010.

[11] P. Gill, M. Arlitt, Z. Li, and A. Mahanti, "The flattening internet topology: Natural evolution, unsightly barnacles or contrived collapse?," in *PAM*, 2008.

[12] "The internet topology data kit, caida." http://www.caida.org/data/active/internet-topology-data-kit.

[13] Y.-J. Chi, R. Oliveira, and L. Zhang, "Cyclops: The internet as-level observatory.," in *CCR*, 2008.

[14] A. J. Su, D. R. Choffnes, A. Kuzmanovic, and F. E. Bustamante, "Drafting behind Akamai (travelocity-based detouring)," in *SIGCOMM*, 2006.

[15] www.conviva.com.

[16] "Private conversations with akamai operators.."

[17] F. Dobrian, V. Sekar, A. Awan, I. Stoica, D. Joseph, A. Ganjam, J. Zhan, and H. Zhang, "Understanding the impact of video quality on user engagement," in *SIGCOMM*, 2011.

[18] "Adobe. http dynamic streaming." http://www.adobe.com/products/httpdynamicstreaming.

[19] http://techblog.netflix.com/2011/01/netflix-performance-on-top-isp-networks.html.

[20] E. Nygren, R. K. Sitaraman, and J. Sun, "The Akamai network: A platform for high-performance internet applications," in *ACM SIGOPS Operating Systems Review*, 2010.

[21] D. Clark, W. Lehr, and S. Bauer, "Interconnection in the internet: The policy challenge," *Research Conference on Communication, Information and Internet Policy*, 2011.

[22] http://drpeering.net/AskDrPeering/blog/articles/Peering_vs_Transit___The_Business_Case_for_Peering.html.

[23] http://www.akamai.com/dl/investors/10k_2010_1.pdf.

[24] T. Leighton and S. Rao, "Multicommodity max-flow min-cut theorems and their use in designing approximation algorithms," in *Journal of the ACM*, 1999.

[25] M. Caesar, M. Casado, T. Koponen, J. Rexford, and S. Shenker, "Dynamic route computation considered harmful," in *CCR*, 2010.

[26] http://www.fixedorbit.com/stats.htm.

[27] www.cs.bu.edu/brite.

[28] H. V. Madhyastha, T. Isdal, M. Piatek, C. Dixon, T. Anderson, A. Krishnamurthy, and A. Venkataramani, "iPlane: An information plane for distributed services," in *OSDI*, 2006.

[29] "Private conversation with iplane group.."

[30] L. Qiu, Y. R. Yang, Y. Zhang, and S. Shenker, "On selfish routing in internet-like environments," in *SIGCOMM*, 2003.

[31] L. Li, D. Alderson, W. Willinger, and J. Doyle, "A first-principles approach to understanding the internet's router-level topology," in *SIGCOMM*, 2004.

[32] T. Hirayama, S. Arakawa, S. Hosoki, and M. Murata, "Models of link capacity distribution in isp's router-level topology," in *International Journal of Computer Networks and Communications (IJCNC)*, 2011.

[33] www.quova.com.

[34] L. Gao and J. Rexford, "Stable internet routing without global coordination," in *TON*, 2001.

[35] P. B. Godfrey, I. Ganichev, S. Shenker, and I. Stoica, "Pathlet routing," in *SIGCOMM*, 2009.

[36] http://aws.amazon.com/ec2/\#pricing.

[37] D. K. Goldenberg, L. Qiu, H. Xie, Y. R. Yang, and Y. Zhang, "Optimizing cost and performance for multihoming," in *SIGCOMM*, 2004.

[38] R. Krishnan, H. V. Madhyastha, S. Srinivasan, S. Jain, A. Krishnamurthy, T. Anderson, and J. Gao, "Moving beyond end-to-end path information to optimize CDN performance," in *IMC*, 2009.

[39] V. K. Adhikari, S. Jain, and Z.-L. Zhang, "YouTube traffic dynamics and its interplay with a tier-1 ISP: An ISP perspective," in *IMC*, 2010.

[40] C. Huang, Y. A. Wang, J. Li, and K. W. Ross, "Measuring and evaluating large-scale CDNs," in *Microsoft Research Technical Report MSR-TR-2008-106*, 2008.

[41] Y. A. Wang, C. Huang, J. Li, and K. W. Ross, "Estimating the performance of hypothetical cloud service deployments: A measurement-based approach," in *IEEE INFOCOM*, 2011.

[42] www.speedtest.net.

[43] "Akamai and limelight say testing methods not accurate in microsoft research paper." http://blog.streamingmedia.com/the_business_of_online_vi/2008/10/akamai-responds.html.

[44] A. Akella, B. Maggs, S. Seshan, A. Shaikh, and R. Sitaraman, "A measurement-based analysis of multihoming," in *SIGCOMM*, 2003.

[45] A. Akella, J. Pang, B. Maggs, S. Seshan, and A. Shaikh, "A comparison of overlay routing and multihoming route control," in *SIGCOMM*, 2004.

Dealer: Application-aware Request Splitting for Interactive Cloud Applications

Mohammad Hajjat[†]   Shankaranarayanan P N[†]   David Maltz[‡]

Sanjay Rao[†]   Kunwadee Sripanidkulchai[*]

[†]Purdue University, [‡]Microsoft Corporation, [*]NECTEC Thailand

ABSTRACT

Deploying interactive applications in the cloud is a challenge due to the high variability in performance of cloud services. In this paper, we present *Dealer*– a system that helps geo-distributed, interactive and multi-tier applications meet their stringent requirements on response time despite such variability. Our approach is motivated by the fact that, at any time, only a small number of application components of large multi-tier applications experience poor performance. *Dealer* abstracts application structure as a component graph, with nodes being application components and edges capturing inter-component communication patterns. *Dealer* continually monitors the performance of individual component replicas and communication latencies between replica pairs. In serving any given user request, *Dealer* seeks to minimize user response times by picking the best combination of replicas (potentially located across different data-centers). While *Dealer* does require modifications to application code, we show through integration with two multi-tier applications that the changes required are modest. Our evaluations on two multi-tier applications using real cloud deployments indicate the $90\%ile$ of application response times could be reduced by a factor of 3 under natural cloud dynamics compared to conventional data-center redirection techniques which are agnostic of application structure.

Categories and Subject Descriptors

C.4 [**Performance of systems**]: Design studies; Reliability, availability, and serviceability; Modeling techniques; C.2.3 [**Computer communication networks**]: Network operations—*Network management; Network monitoring*

Keywords

Cloud Computing, Interactive Multi-tier Applications, Request Redirection, Geo-distribution, Service Level Agreement (SLA), Performance Variability

1 Introduction

Cloud computing promises to reduce the cost of IT organizations by allowing them to purchase as much resources as needed, only when

needed, and through lower capital and operational expense stemming from the cloud's economies of scale. Further, moving to the cloud greatly facilitates the deployment of applications across multiple geographically distributed data-centers. Geo-distributing applications, in turn, facilitates service resilience and disaster recovery, and could enable better user experience by having customers directed to data-centers close to them.

While these advantages of cloud computing are triggering much interest among developers and IT managers [40, 21], a key challenge is meeting the stringent *Service Level Agreement (SLA)* requirements on availability and response times for interactive applications (e.g. customer facing web applications, enterprise applications). Application latencies directly impact business revenue [13, 9]– e.g., Amazon found every $100ms$ of latency costs 1% in sales [9]. Further, the SLAs typically require bounds on the $90th$ (and higher) percentile latencies [29, 12].

Meeting such stringent SLA requirements is a challenge given outages in cloud data-centers [1, 10], and the high variability in performance of cloud services [44, 33, 23]. This variability arises from a variety of factors such as the sharing of cloud services across a large number of tenants, and limitations in virtualization techniques [44]. For example, [33] showed that the $95\%ile$ latencies of cloud storage services such as tables and queues is 100% more than the median values for four different public cloud offerings.

In this paper, we argue that it is critically important to design applications to be intrinsically resilient to cloud performance variations. Our work, which we term *Dealer*, is set in the context of geo-distributed, multi-tier applications, where each component may have replicas in multiple data-centers. *Dealer* enables applications to meet their stringent SLA requirements on response times by finding the combination of replicas –potentially located across multiple data-centers– that should be used to serve any given request. This is motivated by the fact that only a small number of application components of large multi-tier applications experience poor performance at any time.

Multi-tier applications consist of potentially hundreds of components with complex inter-dependencies and hundreds of different transactions all involving different subsets of components [28]. Detailed knowledge of the components involved in every single type of transaction is hard to obtain. Instead, *Dealer* abstracts application structure as a component graph, with nodes being application components and edges capturing inter-component communication patterns. To predict which combination of replicas can result in the best performance, *Dealer* continually monitors the performance of individual component replicas and communication latencies between replica pairs.

Operating at a component-level granularity offers *Dealer* several advantages over conventional approaches that merely pick an ap-

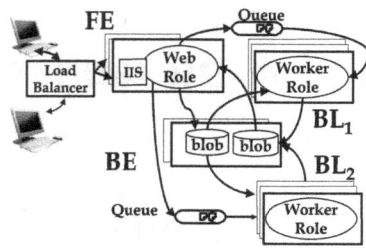

(a) Thumbnails application architecture and data-flow. The application is composed of a Front-End (FE), Back-End (BE), and two Business-Logic components BL_1 (creates thumbnail) and BL_2 (creates Grayscale, rotating images).

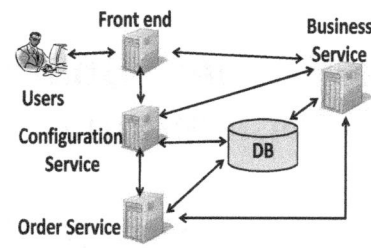

(b) *StockTrader* architecture and data-flow. Components include a front-end (FE), Business Server (BS), Order Service (OS) (handles buys/sells), Database (DB), and a Config Service (CS) that binds all components. The precise data-flow depends on transaction type.

Figure 1: Applications Testbed.

Figure 2: Box plot for total response time, and contributing processing and communication delays for Thumbnail application.

propriate data-center to serve user requests [26, 39, 45, 35]. Modern web applications consist of many components, not all of which are represent in each data-center, and the costs are extremely high to over-provision each component in every data-center to be able to handle all the traffic from another data-center. *Dealer* is able to redistribute work away from poorly performing components by utilizing the capacity of all component replicas that can usefully contribute to reducing the latency of requests.

While much of the *Dealer* design is independent of the particular application, integrating *Dealer* does require customization using application-specific logic. First, stateful applications have constraints on which component replicas can handle a given request. While *Dealer* proposes desired split ratios (or probabilities with which a request must be forwarded to different downstream component replicas), the application uses its own logic to determine which component replicas can handle a given request. Further, application developers must properly instrument their applications to collect the per-component performance data needed for *Dealer*. However, in our experience, the work required by application developers is modest.

We have evaluated *Dealer* on two stateful multi-tier applications on Azure cloud deployments. The first application is data-intensive, while the second application involves interactive transaction processing. Under natural cloud dynamics, using *Dealer* improves application performance by a factor of 3 for the 90th and higher delay percentiles, compared to DNS-based data-center-level redirection schemes which are agnostic of application structure. Overall, the results indicate the importance and feasibility of *Dealer*.

2 Performance and Workload Variability

In this section, we present observations that motivate *Dealer*'s design. In §2.1, we characterize the extent and nature of the variability in performance that may be present in cloud data-centers. Our characterization is based on our experiences running multi-tier applications on the cloud. Then, in §2.2, we characterize the variability in workloads of multi-tier applications based on analyzing web server traces of a large campus university.

2.1 Performance variability in the cloud

We measure the performance variability with two applications. The first application, *Thumbnail* [18] involves users uploading a picture to the server (FE) and getting back either a thumbnail (from BL1) or a rotated image (from BL2). The second application, *StockTrader* [3], is an enterprise web application that allows users to buy/sell stocks, view portfolio, etc. Figure 1(a) and Figure 1(b) respectively

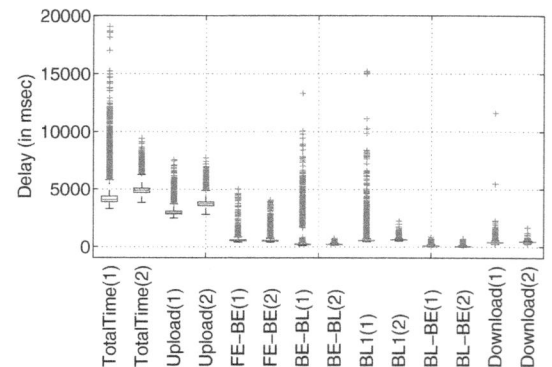

show the component architecture and data-flow for each application.

We ran each application simultaneously in two separate data-centers (DC1 and DC2), both located in the United States, and subjected them to the same workload simultaneously. More details of how we configured the deployments are presented in §5.1. We instrumented each application to measure the total response time, as well as the delays contributing to total response time. The contributing delays include processing delays encountered at individual application components, communication delay between components (internal data-center communication delays), and the upload/download delays (Internet communication delays between users and each data-center).

We now present our key findings:

Performance of component replicas in multiple data centers is not correlated: Figure 3 shows a two hour snapshot from an experiment comparing the latency of database(DB) transactions for *StockTrader* across two consecutive days. The figure shows that the DB latency for DC1 on Day1 is significantly higher than on Day2, and has more prominent variation. The figure also shows that on Day1, the DB in DC2 performed significantly better than the DB in DC1 on the same day. This illustrates that the performance of similar components across multiple data-centers is not correlated. Further investigation revealed that the performance variability was due to high load on the data-center during a 9 day period [15]. Our interaction with the cloud providers indicated that during this period, different subsets of databases were impacted at different time snapshots.

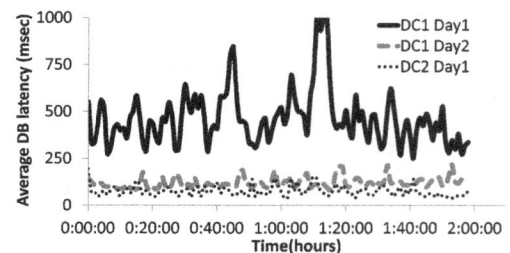

Figure 3: Comparing the latency of DB transactions in DC1 and DC2 across two consecutive days. The curve for DC2 Day2 is very similar to DC2 Day1 and is therefore omitted.

All application components show performance variability: Figure 2 considers the *Thumbnail* application and presents a box plot for the total response time (first two) and each of the individual contributing delays for each data-center. The X-axis is annotated

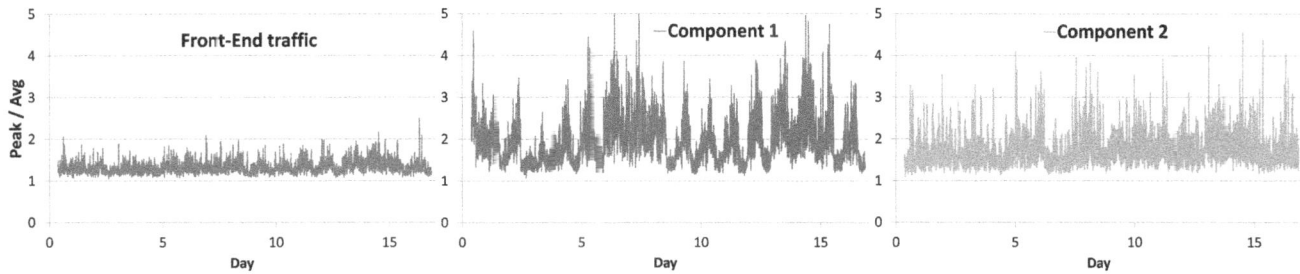

Figure 4: Short-term variability in workload for three components in a multi-tier web-service deployed in a large campus network. The peak and average rates are computed during each 10 minutes window and the *peak-to-average* ratio over each window is plotted as a function of time.

with the component or link whose delay is being measured and the number in parenthesis represents the data-center to which it belongs (DC1 or DC2). For example, BL-BE(1) represents the delay between the Business-Logic (BL) and the Back-End (BE) instances, at DC1. The bottom and top of each box represent the 25th and 75th percentiles, and the line in the middle represents the median. The vertical line (whiskers) extends to the highest datum within 3*IQR of the upper quartile, where IQR is the inter-quartile range. Points larger than this value are considered outliers and shown separately.

The figure shows several interesting observations. First, there is significant variability in all delay values. For instance, while the $75\%ile$ of total response time is under 5 seconds, the outliers are almost 20 seconds. Second, while the median delay with DC1 is smaller than DC2, DC1 shows significantly more variability. Third, while the Internet upload delays are a significant portion of total response time (since the application involves uploading large images), the processing delays at BL, and the communication delays between the BE and BL show high variability, and contribute significantly to total response times. Our experiments indicate that the performance of the application components vary significantly with time, and is not always correlated with the performance of their replicas in other data-centers.

2.2 Workload Dynamics

We now show the nature and extent of short-term variability in workload for multi-tier applications and the implications on cloud deployments.

While cloud computing allows for dynamic invocation of resources during peak periods, starting up new server instances takes several minutes (typically 10 minutes) in many commercial cloud deployments today. Further, besides the time to provision new instances, it may take even longer to warm up a booted server, e.g., by filling its cache with relevant data to meet its SLA. Therefore, applications typically maintain *margins* (i.e., pools of servers beyond the expected load [30, 20, 41]) to handle fluctuations in workload.

To examine workload variability and margin requirements for multi-tier applications, we collect and study the workload of a web-service in a large campus network. In the service, all requests enter through a front-end, which are then directed to different downstream components based on the type of request (e.g., web, mail, department1, department2, etc.). Figure 4 illustrates the variability in workload for the front-end and two downstream components. While the *peak-to-average* ratio is around 1.5 for the front-end, it is much higher for each of the other components, and can be as high as 3 or more during some time periods. The figure indicates that a significant margin may be needed even in cloud deployments to handle shorter-term workload fluctuations.

Furthermore, the figure not only illustrates the need for margins with cloud deployments, but also shows the heterogeneity in margin that may be required for different application tiers. While the

margin requirement is about 50% for the front-end, it is over 300% for the other components during some time periods. In addition, the figure also illustrates that the exact margin required even for the same component is highly variable over time.

The high degree of variability and heterogeneity in margins make it difficult to simply over-provision an application component on the cloud since it is complicated to exactly estimate the extent of over-provisioning required, and over-provisioning for the worst-case scenario could be expensive. Moreover, failures and regular data-center maintenance actions make the application work with lower margins and render the application vulnerable to even modest workload spikes.

3 *Dealer* Design Rationale

In this section, we present the motivation behind *Dealer*'s design, and argue why traditional approaches don't suffice. *Dealer* is designed to enable applications meet their SLA requirements despite performance variations of cloud services. *Dealer* is motivated by two observations: (i) in any data-center, only instances corresponding to a small number of application components see poor performance at any given time; and (ii) the latencies seen by instances of the same component located in different data-centers are often uncorrelated.

Dealer's main goal is to dynamically identify a replica of each component that can best serve a given request. *Dealer* may choose instances located in different data-centers for different components, offering a rich set of possible choices. In doing so, *Dealer* considers performance and loads of individual replicas, as well as intra- and inter-data-center communication latencies.

Dealer is distinguished from DNS-based [26, 39, 45] and server-side [35] redirection mechanisms, which are widely used to map users to appropriate data-centers. Such techniques focus on alleviating performance problems related to Internet congestion between users and data-centers, or coarse-grained load-balancing at the granularity of data-centers. *Dealer* is complementary and targets performance problems of individual cloud services inside a data-center. There are several advantages associated with the *Dealer* approach:

• *Exploit heterogeneity in margins across different components:* In large multi-tier applications with potentially hundreds of components [28], only a few services might be temporarily impacted in any given data-center. *Dealer* can reassign work related to these services to other replicas in remote data-centers if they have sufficient margins. For instance, *Dealer* could tackle performance problems with storage elements (e.g., a blob) by using a replica in a remote data-center, while leveraging compute instances locally. Complete request redirection, however, may not be feasible since instances of other components (e.g., business-logic servers) in the remote data-center may not be over-provisioned adequately over their normal load to handle the redirected requests. In fact, Figure 4 shows significant variation in workload patterns of individual

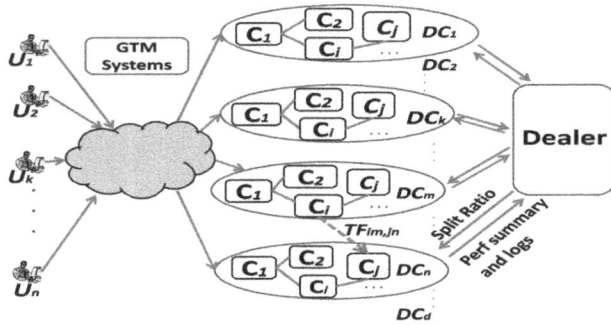

Figure 5: System overview

components of multi-tier applications, indicating the components must be provisioned in a heterogeneous fashion.

• *Utilize functional cloud services in each data-center: Dealer* enables applications to utilize cloud services that are functioning satisfactorily in all data-centers, while only avoiding services that are performing poorly. In contrast, techniques that redirect entire requests fail to utilize functional cloud services in a data-center merely due to performance problems associated with a small number of other services. Further, the application may be charged for the unutilized services (for example, they may correspond to already pre-paid reserved compute instances [2]). While *Dealer* does incur additional inter data-center communication cost, our evaluations in §5.5.4 indicate these costs are small.

• *Responsiveness:* Studies have shown that DNS-based redirection techniques may have latencies of over 2 hours and may not be well suited for applications which require quick response to link failures or performance degradations [34]. In contrast, *Dealer* targets adaptations over the time-scale of tens of seconds.

4 System Design

In this section we present the design of *Dealer*. We begin by presenting an overview of the design, and then discuss its various components.

4.1 System Overview

Consider an application with multiple components $\{C_1..C_l\}$. We consider a multi-cloud deployment where the application is deployed in d data-centers, with instances corresponding to each component located in every one of the data-centers. Note that there might be components like databases which are only present in one or a subset of data-centers. We represent all replicas of component C_i in data-center m as C_{im}.

Traffic from users is mapped to each data-center using standard mapping services used today based on metrics such as geographical proximity or latencies [39]. Let U_k denote the set of users whose traffic is mapped to data-center k. We refer to data-center k as the primary data-center for U_k, and to all other data-centers as the secondary data-centers. The excess capacity of each component replica is the additional load that can be served by that replica which is not being utilized for the primary traffic of that data-center. Traffic corresponding to U_k can use the entire available capacity of all components in data-center k, as well as the excess capacity of components in all other data-centers.

For each user group U_k, *Dealer* seeks to determine how application transactions must be split in the multi-cloud deployment. In particular, the goal is to determine $TF_{im,jn}$, that is the number of user transactions that must be directed between component i in data-center m to component j in data-center n, for every pair of <component,data-center> combinations. In doing so, the objec-

tive is to ensure the overall delay of transactions can be minimized. Further, *Dealer* periodically recomputes how application transactions must be split given dynamics in behavior of cloud services.

Complex multi-tier applications may have hundreds of different transactions all involving different subsets of application components. Detailed knowledge of the components involved in every single type of transaction is hard to obtain. Instead, *Dealer* dynamically learns a model of the application that captures component interaction patterns. In particular, *Dealer* estimates the fraction of requests that involve communication between each pair of application components, and the average size of transactions between each component pair. In addition, *Dealer* estimates the processing delays of individual components replicas, and communication delays between components, as well as the available capacity of component replicas in each data-center, (i.e., the load each replica can handle). We will discuss how all this information is estimated and dynamically updated in the later subsections.

4.2 Determining delays

There are three key components to the estimation algorithms used by *Dealer* when determining the processing delay of components and communication delays between them. These include: (i) passive monitoring of components and links over which application requests are routed; (ii) heuristics for smoothing and combining multiple estimates of delay for a link or component; and (iii) active probing of links and components which are not being utilized to estimate the delays that may be incurred if they were used. We describe each of these in turn:

Monitoring: Monitoring distributed applications is a well studied area, and a wide range of techniques have been developed by the research community and industry [22, 27, 7] that can be used for measuring application performance. Of these techniques, *X-Trace* [27] is the most suitable for our purposes, since it can track application performance at the granularity of individual requests. However, integrating the monitoring code with the application is a manual and time consuming process. To facilitate easy integration of *X-Trace* with the application, we automate a large part of the integration effort using *Aspect Oriented Programming (AOP)* techniques [5]. We write an *Aspect* to intercept each function when it is called and after it returns, which constitutes the *pointcuts*. We record the respective times inside the Aspect. The measured delay values are then reported periodically to a central monitor. A smaller reporting time ensures greater agility of *Dealer*. We use reporting times of 10 seconds in our implementation, which we believe is reasonable.

Smoothing delay estimates: It is important to trade-off the agility in responding to performance dips in components or links with potential instability that might arise if the system is overly aggressive. To handle this, we use a weighted moving average (WMA) scheme. For each link and component, the average delay seen during the last W time windows of observation is considered. The weighted average of these values is then computed according to the following formula:

$$D(t) = \frac{\sum_{i=1}^{W}(W - i + 1) * D(t-i) * N(t-i)}{\sum_{i=1}^{W}(W - i + 1) * N(t-i)} \quad (1)$$

Briefly, the weight depends on the number of samples seen during a time window, and the recency of the estimate (i.e., recent windows are given a higher weight). $D(t)$ is the delay seen by a link/component in Window t, and $N(t)$ is the number of delay samples obtained in that window (to ensure higher weight for windows with more transactions). The use of WMA ensures that *Dealer* reacts to prolonged performance episodes that last several seconds, while not aggressively reacting to extremely short-lived problems within a window. W determines the number of windows for which a link/component must perform poorly (well) for it to be avoided (reused). Our empirical experience has shown choosing W values between 3 and 5 are most effective for good performance.

Probing: *Dealer* uses active probes to estimate the performance of components and links that are not currently being used. This enables *Dealer* to decide if it should switch transactions to a replica of a component in a different data-center, and determine which replica must be chosen. Probe traffic is generated by test-clients using application workload generators (e.g., [8]). We restrict active probes to read-only requests that do not cause changes in persistent application state. While this may not accurately capture the delays for transactions involving writes, we have found the probing scheme to work well for the applications we experiment with. We also note that many applications tend to be read-heavy and it is often more critical to optimize latencies of transactions involving reads.

To bound probes' overhead, we limit the probe rate to 10% of the application traffic rate. *Dealer* biases the probes based on the quality of the path. In particular, the probability P_i that a path is probed is given as:

$$P_i = \frac{CR_i}{\sum_j CR_j} \qquad (2)$$

Here, CR_i is the compliance ratio– the fraction of requests that use a given path with a response time lower than its SLA. The intuition is that a path that has generally been good might temporarily suffer poor performance. Biasing the probing ensures that such a path is likely to be probed more frequently, which ensures *Dealer* can quickly switch back to it when its performance improves. Also, *Dealer* probes 5% of the paths at random to ensure more choices can be explored. In the initialization stage, *Dealer* probes paths in a random fashion. As an enhancement, *Dealer* can bias probing during the initialization phase based on coarse estimates of link delays. Such coarse estimates can be obtained based on the size of transactions exchanged between components (obtained through monitoring application traffic) and the bandwidth between data-centers.

While probing may add a non-negligible overhead on applications, we are investigating ways to restrict our use of active probing to only measuring inter-data-center latency and bandwidth. The key insights behind our approach are to (i) use passive user-generated traffic to update component processing delays and inter-component link latencies [1]; and (ii) limit active probes to measuring inter-data-center latency and bandwidth. These measurements can then be combined, along with passive measurements on transaction sizes observed between components, to estimate the performance of any combination. Further, rather than having each application measure the bandwidth and latency between every pair of data-centers, cloud providers could provide such services in the future, amortizing the overheads across all applications. We leave further exploration of this as future work.

4.3 Determining transaction split ratios

In this section, we discuss how *Dealer* uses the processing delays of components and communication times of links to compute the split ratio matrix **TF**. Here, $TF_{im,jn}$ is the number of user transactions that must be directed between component i in data-center m to component j in data-center n, for every <component, data-center > pair. In determining the split ratio matrix, *Dealer* considers several factors including i) the total response time; ii) stability of the overall system; and iii) capacity constraints of application components.

In our discussion, a *combination* refers to an assignment of each component to exactly one data-center. For e.g., in Figure 5, a map-

ping of C_1 to DC_1, C_2 to DC_k, C_i to DC_m and C_j to DC_m represents a combination. The algorithm iteratively assigns a fraction of transactions to each combination. The split ratio matrix is easily computed once the fraction of transactions assigned to each combination is determined. We now present the details of the assignment algorithm:

Considering total response time: *Dealer* computes the mean delay for each possible combination like in [28]. It is the weighted sum of the processing delays of nodes and communication delay of links associated with that combination. The weights are determined by the fraction of user transactions that traverse that node or link. Specifically, consider a combination where component i is assigned to data-center $d(i)$. Then, the mean delay of that combination is:

$$\sum_i \sum_j f_{ij} * D_{id(i),jd(j)} \qquad (3)$$

Here, $D_{id(i),jd(j)}$ denotes the communication delay between component i in data-center $d(i)$, and component j in data-center $d(j)$. When $i = j$, D represents the processing delay of component i. Further, f_{ij} denotes the fraction of transactions that involve an interaction between application components i and j, and f_{ii} denotes the fraction of transactions that are processed at component i. The fractions f_{ij} may be determined by monitoring the application in its past window like in § 4.2. Once the delays of combinations are determined, *Dealer* sorts the combinations in ascending order of mean delay such that the best combinations get utilized the most, thereby ensuring a better performance.

Ensuring system stability: To ensure stability of the system and prevent oscillations, *Dealer* avoids abrupt changes in the split ratio matrix in response to minor performance changes. To achieve this, *Dealer* limits the maximum fraction of transactions that may be assigned to a given combination. The limit (which we refer to as the damping ratio) is based on how well that combination has performed relative to others, and how much traffic was assigned to that combination in the recent past. In particular, the damping ratio (DR) for each combination is calculated periodically as follows:

$$DR(L_i, t) = \frac{W(L_i,t)}{\sum_k W(L_k,t)}, where$$
$$W(L_i,t) = \sum_{\ell=0}^{W-1} Rank(L_i, t-\ell) * Req(L_i, t-\ell) \qquad (4)$$

Here, $Rank(L, t)$ is the ranking of combination L at the end of time window t (the lower the value of mean delay, the higher the ranking). $Req(L, t)$ is the number of requests sent on combination L during t. The algorithm computes the weight of a combination based on its rank and the requests assigned to it in each of the last W windows. Similar to §4.2, we found that W values between 3 and 5 results in the best performance.

Honoring capacity constraints: In assigning transactions to a combination of application components, *Dealer* ensures the capacity constraints of each of the components is honored as described in Algorithm 1. *Dealer* considers the combinations in ascending order of mean delay (line 8). It then determines the maximum fraction of transactions that can be assigned to that combination without saturating any component (lines 9-11). *Dealer* assigns this fraction of transactions to the combination, or the damping ratio, whichever is lower (line 12). The available capacities of each component and the split ratio matrix are updated to reflect this assignment (lines 14-16). If the assignment of transactions is not completed at this point, the process is repeated with the next best combination (lines 17-18).

Algorithm 1 Determining transaction split ratios.

1: **procedure** COMPUTESPLITRATIO()
2:     Let $C[i, m]$ be the capacity matrix, with each cell (i, m) corresponding to capacity of component C_{im} (component i in data-center m), calculated as in §4.4
3:     Let $AC[i, m]$ be the available-capacity matrix for C_{im} Initialized as $AC[i, m] \leftarrow C[i, m]$
4:     Let $T[i, j]$ be the transaction matrix, with each cell (i, j) indicating the number of transactions per second between application components i and j
5:     Let T_i be the load on each component ($\sum_j T_{ji}$)
6:     Let FA be fraction of transactions that has been assigned to combinations. Initialized as FA $\leftarrow 0$
7:     **Goal**: Find $TF[im, jn]$: the number of transactions that must be directed between C_{im} and C_{jn}
8:     Foreach combination L, sorted by mean delay values
9:         For each C_{im} in L
10:             $f_i \leftarrow \frac{AC[i,m]}{T_i}$
11:         $min_f \leftarrow \min_{\forall i}(f_i)$
12:         $ratio = \min(min_f, DR(L, t))$
13:         Rescale damping ratios if necessary
14:         For each C_{im} in L
15:             $AC[i, m] \leftarrow AC[i, m] - ratio * T_i$
16:             $TF[id(i), jd(j)] \leftarrow TF[id(i), jd(j)] + ratio * T_{ij}, \forall i, j$
17:         $FA \leftarrow FA + ratio$
18:     *Repeat until FA = 1*
19: **end procedure**

Algorithm 2 Dynamic capacity estimation.

1: **procedure** COMPUTETHRESH(T, D)
2:     **if** $D > 1.1 * DelayAtThresh$ **then**
3:         **if** $T <= Thresh$ **then**
4:             $LowerThresh \leftarrow 0.8 * T$
5:             $ComponentCapacity \leftarrow Thresh$
6:         **else**
7:             $Thresh \leftarrow unchanged$
8:             $ComponentCapacity \leftarrow Thresh$
9:         **end if**
10:     **else if** $D <= DelayAtThresh$ **then**
11:         **if** $T >= Thresh$ **then**
12:             $Thresh \leftarrow T$
13:             $ComponentCapacity \leftarrow T + 5\% of T$
14:         **else**
15:             $Thresh \leftarrow unchanged$
16:             $ComponentCapacity \leftarrow Thresh$
17:         **end if**
18:     **end if**
19: **end procedure**

4.4 Estimating capacity of components

We now discuss how *Dealer* determines the capacity of components in terms of the load each component can handle. Typically, application delays are not impacted by an increase in load up to a point which we term as the *threshold*. Beyond this, application delays increase gradually with load, until a breakdown region is entered where vastly degraded performance is seen. Ideally, *Dealer* must operate at the threshold to ensure the component is saturated while not resulting in degraded performance. The threshold is sensitive to transaction mix changes. Hence, *Dealer* relies on algorithms for dynamically estimating the threshold, and seeks to operate just above the threshold.

Dealer starts with an initial threshold value based on a conservative stress test assuming worst-case load (i.e., transactions that are expensive for each component to process). Alternately, the threshold can be obtained systematically (e.g., using *knee* detection schemes [37]) or learnt during boot-up phase of an applica-

---

Algorithm 3 Integration with stateful applications.

Original code:
    procedure SENDREQUEST(Component cmp, Request req)
        Replica replica $\leftarrow$ cmp.Replica
        replica.Send(req)
    end procedure
With *Dealer*:
    procedure SENDREQUEST(Component cmp, Request req)
        Replica replica $\leftarrow$ metaData[req.ID][cmp]
        if replica is null **then**   ▷ *Not in meta-data.*
            replica $\leftarrow$ GetDealerReplica(cmp) ▷ *Use* Dealer *suggestion.*
            if cmp is stateful **then**   ▷ *Cmp is stateful but its information has not been propagated yet in meta-data.*
                metaData[req.ID][cmp] $\leftarrow$ replica
            end if
        end if
        replica.Send(req)
    end procedure

---

tion in the data-center, given application traffic typically ramps up slowly before production workloads are handled. Since the initial threshold can change (e.g., due to changes in transaction mix), *Dealer* dynamically updates the threshold using Algorithm 2. The parameter *DelayAtThresh* is the delay in the flat region learnt in the initialization phase, which is the desirable levels to which the component delay must be restricted. At all times, the algorithm maintains an estimate of *Thresh*, which is the largest load in recent memory where a component delay of *DelayAtThresh* was achieved. T and D represent the current transaction load on the component, and the delay experienced at the component respectively. The algorithm strives to operate at a point where D is slightly more than *DelayAtThresh*, and T slightly more than *thresh*. If *Dealer* operated exactly at *thresh,* it would not be possible to know if *thresh* has increased, and hence discover if *Dealer* is operating too conservatively.

The algorithm begins by checking if the delay is unacceptably high (line 2). In such case, if $T \leq Thresh$, (line 3) the threshold is lowered. Otherwise (line 6), the threshold remains unchanged and the component capacity is lowered to the threshold. If D is comparable to *DelayAtThresh* (line 10), it is an indication the component can take more load. If $T \geq Thresh$ (line 11), then the threshold is too conservative, and hence it gets increased. Further, *ComponentCapacity* is set to slightly higher than the threshold to experiment if the component can absorb more requests. If however $T < Thresh$, (line 14), then *ComponentCapacity* is set to *Thresh* to allow more transactions be directed to that component.

We note that the intuition behind the choice of parameters is to increase the load the component sees by only small increments (5%) but back-off more aggressively (by decreasing the load in each round by 20%) in case the delay starts increasing beyond the desired value. We believe the choice of parameters is reasonable; however, we defer testing the sensitivity of the algorithm to these parameters as a future work. Finally, while component delays were used as a mean of estimating if the component is saturated, one could also use other metrics such as CPU, memory utilization and queues sizes.

4.5 Integrating *Dealer* with applications

We integrated *Dealer* with both *Thumbnail* and *StockTrader*, and we found that the overall effort involved was small. Integrating *Dealer* with applications involves: i) adding logic to re-route requests to replicas of a downstream component across different data-centers; and ii) maintaining consistent state in stateful applications.

Re-routing requests. To use *Dealer*, application developers need to make only a small change to the *connection logic* – the code segment inside a component responsible for directing requests to downstream components. *Dealer* provides both push and pull API's for retrieving split ratios (§4.3). Instead of forwarding all requests to a single service endpoint, the connection logic now allocates requests to downstream replicas in proportion to the split ratios provided by *Dealer*.

Integration with stateful applications. While best practices emphasize that cloud applications should use stateless services whenever possible [6, 4], some applications may have stateful components. In such cases, the application needs to affinitize requests to component replicas so that each request goes to the replicas that hold the state for processing the request. Integrating *Dealer* with such applications does not change the consistency semantics of the application. *Dealer* does not try to understand the application's policy for allocating requests to components. Instead, it proposes the desired split ratios to the application, and the application uses its own logic to determine which replicas can handle a request.

In integrating *Dealer* with stateful applications, it is important to ensure that related requests get processed by the same set of stateful replicas due to data consistency constraints. For instance, the *StockTrader* application involves session state. To integrate *Dealer*, we made sure all requests belonging to the same user session use the same combination, and *Dealer*'s split-ratios only determine the combination taken by the first request of that session. *StockTrader* persists user session information (users logged in, session IDs, etc.) in a database. We modified the application so that it also stores the list of stateful replicas for each session. We also note that some web applications maintain the session state in the client side through session cookies. Such information could again be augmented to include the list of stateful replicas.

To guarantee all requests within the same session follow the same combination, the application must be modified to propagate *meta-data* (such as a unique session ID and the list of stateful replicas associated with it) along all requests between components. Many web applications (such as *StockTrader*) use SOAP and RESTful services that provide *Interceptors* which can be easily used to propagate meta-data with very minimal modifications. In the *StockTrader* application, we used *SOAP Extensions* [16] to propagate meta-data. In other cases where Interceptors cannot be used, endpoint interfaces can be changed or overloaded to propagate such data.

The propagated meta-data is used by components to guide the selection of downstream replicas. Algorithm 3 illustrates this. A component initiating a request must first check if the downstream component is stateful (by examining the meta-data) and if it is, it picks the replica specified in the meta-data. Otherwise, it picks the replica suggested by *Dealer*. If a downstream stateful component is visited for the first time, it picks the replica that *Dealer* suggests and saves this information into the meta-data which gets propagated along requests to the front-end.

While handling such state may require developer knowledge, we found this required only moderate effort from the developer in the applications we considered. As future work, we would like to integrate *Dealer* with a wider set of applications with different consistency requirements and gain more experience with the approach.

5 Experimental Evaluation

In this section, we evaluate the importance and effectiveness of *Dealer* in ensuring good performance of applications in the cloud. We begin by discussing our methodology in §5.1. We then evaluate the effectiveness of *Dealer* in responding to various events that occur naturally in a real cloud deployment (§5.2). These experiments both highlight the inherent performance variability in cloud environments, and evaluate the ability of *Dealer* to cope with them. We then evaluate *Dealer* using a series of controlled experiments which stress the system and gauge its effectiveness in coping with extreme scenarios such as sharp spikes in application load, failure of cloud components, and abrupt shifts in application transaction sizes.

5.1 Evaluation Methodology

We study and evaluate the design of *Dealer* by conducting experiments on *Thumbnail* and *StockTrader* (introduced in §2).

Cloud testbed and application workloads: All experiments were conducted on Microsoft Azure by deploying each application simultaneously in two data-centers located geographically apart in the U.S. (North and South Central). In all experiments, application traffic to one of the data-centers (referred to as DC_A) is controlled by *Dealer*, while traffic to the other one (DC_B) was run without *Dealer*. The objective was to not only study the effectiveness of *Dealer* in enhancing performance of traffic to DC_A, but also ensure that *Dealer* did not negatively impact performance of traffic to DC_B.

Application traffic to both data-centers was generated using a Poisson arrival process when the focus of an experiment is primarily to study the impact of cloud performance variability. Furthermore, to study the impact of workload dynamics, we also use real campus workload traces (described in §2.2) and conduct experiments that involve abrupt changes of the rate of the Poisson process. In *Thumbnail*, we set the transaction mix (fraction of requests to BL_1 and BL_2) according to the fraction of requests to Component1 and Component2 in the trace. Another key workload parameter that we did vary was the size of pictures uploaded by users. Requests in *Thumbnail* had an average upload size of 1.4 MB (in the form of an image) and around 3.2 (860) KB download size for BL_1 (BL_2) transactions. *StockTrader*, on the other hand, had a larger variety of transactions (buying/selling stocks, fetching quotes, etc.) with relatively smaller data size. To generate a realistic mix of transactions, we used the publicly available DaCapo benchmark [24], which contains a set of user sessions, with each session consisting of a series of requests (e.g., login, home, fetch quotes, sell stocks, and log out). A total of 66 PlanetLab users, spread across the U.S., were used to send requests to DC_A. Further, another set of users located inside a campus network were used to generate traffic to DC_B.

Application Deployments: Applications were deployed with enough instances of each component so that they could handle typical loads along with additional margins. We estimated the capacities of the components through a series of stress-tests. For instance, with an average load of $2 \frac{req}{sec}$ and 100% margin (typical of real deployments as shown in §2), we found empirically that 2/5/16 instances of $FE/BL_1/BL_2$ components were required. Likewise for *StockTrader*, handling an average load of $1 \frac{req}{sec}$ ($0.25 \frac{session}{sec}$) required 1/2/1 instances of FE/BS/OS.

In *StockTrader*, we deployed the DB in both data-centers and configured it in master-slave mode. We used SQL Azure Data Sync [14] for synchronization between the two databases. We note that *Dealer* can be integrated even if the application uses sharding or has weaker consistency requirements (§4.5) – the choice of master-slave is made for illustration purposes. While reads can occur at either DB, writes are made only at the master DB (DC_B). Therefore, transactions involving writes (e.g., buy/sell) can only occur through the BS and OS instances in DC_B. Thus, the BS component would see a higher number of requests (by $\approx 20\%$) than the FE and therefore requires higher provisioning than FE.

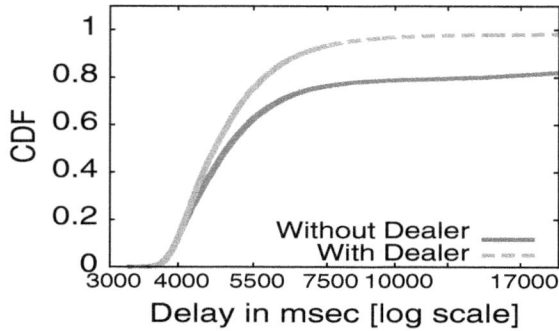

Figure 6: CDF of total response time under natural cloud dynamics.

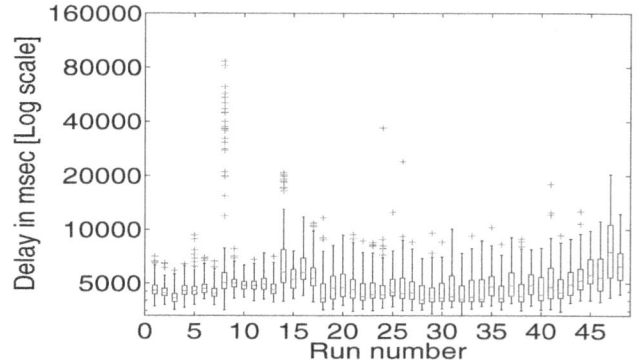

(a) With *Dealer*.

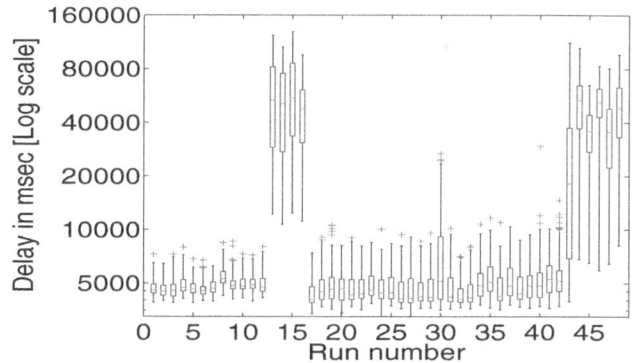

(b) Without *Dealer*.

Figure 7: Box-plots of total response time under natural cloud dynamics.

Further, each component can only connect to its local CS and DB to obtain communication credentials of other components. Finally, all requests belonging to a user session must use the same set of components given the stateful nature of the application.

Comparison with existing schemes: We evaluate *Dealer* against two prominent load-balancing and redirection techniques used today:

• *DNS-based redirection*: Azure provides *Windows Azure Traffic Manager (WATM)* [19] as its solution for DNS-based redirection. WATM provides *Failover*, *Round-Robin* and *Performance* distribution policies. Failover deals with total service failures and sends all traffic to the next available service upon failure. Round-robin routes traffic in a round-robin fashion. Finally, Performance forwards traffic to the closest data-center in terms of network latency. In our experiments, we use the Performance policy because of its relevance to *Dealer*. In WATM, requests are directed to a single URL which gets resolved through DNS to the appropriate data-center based on performance tables that measure the round trip time (RTT) of different IP addresses around the globe to each data-center. We believe WATM is a good representative of DNS-based redirection schemes for global traffic management. However, its redirection is based solely on network latency and is agnostic to application performance. We therefore compare *Dealer* with another scheme that considers overall application performance.

• *Application-level Redirection*: We implemented a per-request load-balancer, that we call *Redirection*, which re-routes each request as a single unit, served completely by a single data-center. *Redirection* re-routes requests based on the overall performance of the application, calculated as the weighted average of total response time (excluding Internet delays) across all transactions. If it finds the local response time of requests higher than that of the remote data-center, it redirects clients to the remote data-center by sending a `302 HTTP` response message upon receiving a client request. It re-routes requests as long as the remote data-center is performing better, or until capacity limits are reached remotely (limited by the capacity of lowest margin component). Similar to *Dealer*, re-routing in *Redirection* does not depend on transaction types. We use the same monitoring and probing infrastructure described in §4.2.

5.2 *Dealer* under natural cloud dynamics

In this section, we evaluate the effectiveness of *Dealer* in responding to the natural dynamics of real cloud deployments. Our goal is to explore the inherent performance variability in cloud environments and evaluate the ability of *Dealer* to cope with such variability.

We experiment with *Thumbnail* and compare its performance with and without *Dealer*. Ideally it is desirable to compare the two

schemes under identical conditions. Since this is not feasible on a real cloud, we ran a large number of experiments alternating between the two approaches. The experiment was 48 hours, with each hour split into two half-hour runs; one without activating *Dealer*, and another with it. Traffic was generated using a Poisson process with an average request rate of $2 \frac{req}{sec}$ to each data-center.

Figure 6 shows the CDF of the total response time for the whole experiment. *Dealer* performs significantly better. The 50th, 75th, 90th, and 99th percentiles with *Dealer* are 4.6, 5.4, 6.6 and 12.7 seconds respectively. The corresponding values without *Dealer* are 4.9, 6.8, 43.2 and 90.9 seconds. The reduction is more than a factor of 6.5x for the top 10 percentiles.

Figure 7 helps understand why *Dealer* performs better. The figure shows a box-plot of total response time for each run of the experiment. The X-axis shows the run number and the Y-axis shows the total response time in milliseconds. Figure 7(a) shows the runs with *Dealer* enabled, and 7(b) shows the runs with *Dealer* disabled (i.e., all traffic going to DC_A stay within the data-center). In both figures, runs with the same number indicate that the runs took place in the same hour, back to back. The figures show several interesting observations:

• First, without *Dealer*, most runs had a normal range of total response time (median ≈ 5 seconds). However, the delays were much higher in runs 13-16 and 43-48. Further investigation showed these high delays were caused by the BL instances in DC_A, which had lower capacity to absorb requests during those periods, and consequently experienced significant queuing. Such a sudden dip in capacity is an example of the kind of event that may occur in the cloud, and highlights the need for *Dealer*.

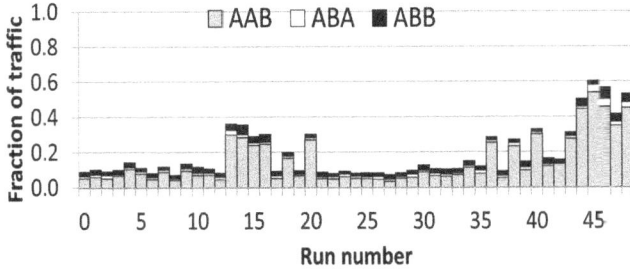

Figure 8: Fraction of *Dealer* traffic sent from DC$_A$ to DC$_B$.

• Second, *Dealer* too experienced the same performance problem with BL in DC$_A$ during runs 13-16 and 43-48. However, *Dealer* mitigated the problem by tapping into the margin available at DC$_B$. Figure 8 shows the fraction of requests directed to one or more components in DC$_B$ by *Dealer*. Each bar corresponds to a run and is split according to the combination of components chosen by *Dealer*. Combinations are written as the location of FE, BE, BL$_1$ and BL$_2$ components[2] respectively, where A refers to DC$_A$ and B to DC$_B$. For example, for run 0 around 9% of all requests handled by *Dealer* used one or more components from DC$_B$. Further for this run, 5% of requests used the combination AAB, while 1% used ABA, and 3% used ABB. Further, most requests directed to DC$_B$ during the problem take the path AAB, which indicates the BL component in DC$_B$ is used.

• Third, we compared the performance when runs 13-16 and 43-48 are not considered. While the benefits of *Dealer* are not as pronounced, it still results in a significant improvement in the tail. In particular the 90th percentile of total response time was reduced from 6.4 to 6.1 seconds, and the 99th percentile was reduced from 18.1 to 8.9 seconds. Most of these benefits come from *Dealer*'s ability to handle transient spikes in workload by directing transactions to the BL replica in DC$_B$. There were also some instances of congestion in the blob of DC$_A$ which led *Dealer* to direct transactions to the blob of DC$_B$.

• Finally, Figure 7(a) shows that the performance is not as good in run 8. Further inspection revealed that the outliers during this run were all due to the high upload delays of the requests directed to DC$_B$. This was likely due to Internet congestion between the users and DC$_B$. We note that such performance problems are not the focus of *Dealer*, and should rather be handled by schemes for Global Traffic Management such as DNS-based redirection [45, 26].

5.3 Reaction to changes in transactions size

Multi-tier applications show a lot of variability not only in request rates but also in the mix and size of transactions, as we discussed in §2. In this section, we evaluate the effectiveness of *Dealer* in adapting to changes in transactions size using the *Thumbnail* application. Using the same configuration described earlier, we change the size of images that users upload to DC$_A$ from 860 KB to 1.4 MB during time 400 to 800, and reduce it back to 860 KB after that. Figure 9 shows the total response time, comparing the performance with and without *Dealer*. The performance without *Dealer* is significantly affected even by a moderate increase in image size. Further, although the problem lasted for only 400 seconds (6.6 minutes), it

---
[2]Since all transactions in this experiment were of type BL$_1$, we drop the 4th tuple.

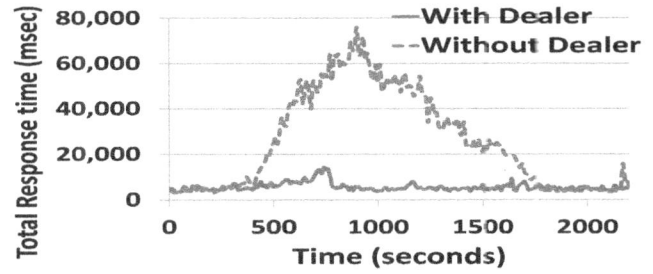

Figure 9: Performance under varying transaction size (*Thumbnail*).

took the application without *Dealer* around 960 seconds (16 minutes) to recover after transaction sizes returned to normal due to the large build-up of queues. However, the performance with *Dealer* is good as the application could dynamically direct transactions to DC$_B$.

5.4 *Dealer* vs. DNS-based redirection

Global Traffic Managers (GTM) are used to route user traffic across data-centers to get better application performance and cope with failures. We conducted an experiment with the same setup mentioned in §5.2 to compare *Dealer* against WATM (§5.1). Figure 10 shows that *Dealer* achieves a reduction of at least 3x times in total response time for the top 10 percentiles. Like before, we found the BL instances had lower capacity in some of the runs leading to a higher total response time in GTM. Since the GTM approach only takes into account the network latency and not the application performance, it was unable to react to performance problems involving the BL instances.

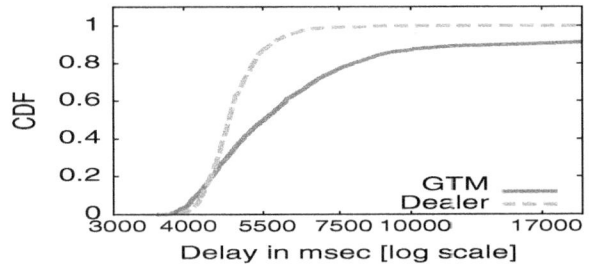

Figure 10: CDF of total response time for GTM vs. *Dealer* (*Thumbnail*).

5.5 *Dealer* vs. application-level redirection

In this section, we evaluate the effectiveness of *Dealer* in adapting to transient performance issues and compare its performance with application-level redirection described in §5.1.

5.5.1 Reaction to transient performance problems

We present our evaluation of *Dealer*'s response to performance variation in the cloud by deploying *StockTrader* at both data-centers, using the master-slave mode as described in §5.1. We emulate a performance degradation in the database (DB) at DC$_A$ using the traces we collected during the DB performance issue in §2.1 by taking a 10 minutes period with high DB latency and using the corresponding data points to induce delay at the DB.

Figure 11 shows that during the period of performance degradation at the DB (9-18th and 27-36th min), the average response time of *Dealer* is significantly better than that of *Redirection*. Figure 11(b) shows that *Dealer* takes ABB and switches requests over

165

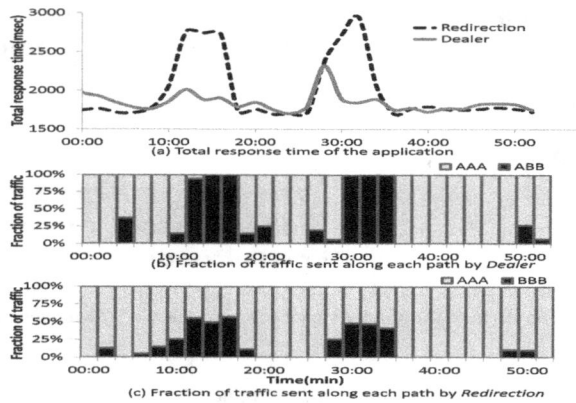

Figure 11: Performance of *Dealer* vs. *Redirection* using traces collected during the DB performance issue. A combination (FE, BS, OS) is represented using the data-center (DC$_A$ or DC$_B$) to which each component belongs. 20% of transactions perform DB writes (combination ABB), hence we exclude them for better visualization.

to the BS and OS at DC$_B$ to avoid the high latency at DB. Similarly, Figure 11(c) shows the path (BBB) taken by *Redirection* and how this scheme switches a fraction of the requests entirely to the data-center, DC$_B$. The fraction of traffic redirected to BBB in (c) is less than the fraction of traffic sent through ABB in (b). This is because *Dealer* is able to better utilize the margin available at the BS by switching a larger fraction of requests to the BS in DC$_B$. On the other hand, *Redirection* is constrained by the available capacity at the FE (DC$_B$) and hence is not able to completely utilize the margin available at the BS (DC$_B$).

5.5.2 Reaction to transient component overload

In this section, we evaluate *Thumbnail* under natural cloud settings using a real workload trace from §2. We use two intervals, each around 30 minutes long, and replay them on DC$_A$ and DC$_B$ simultaneously. The two intervals are about 4 hours away from each other, allowing us to simulate realistic load that may be seen by data-centers in different time-zones. We ran the experiment in a similar fashion to §5.2 for 5 hours alternating between *Dealer* and *Redirection*. We subjected BL$_1$ and BL$_2$ to the same request rate seen by Component1 and Component2. A total of 55 VM's were used to deploy the application in both data-centers. We picked the margin for each component as the average peak-to-average ratio during each interval. Margins ranged between 190% and 330%.

Figure 12 shows that the 90^{th}(99th) percentiles for *Dealer* were 11.9 (14.4) seconds, compared to 13.3 (19.2) seconds for *Redirection*– a reduction of over 10.5% in response times for the top 10 percentiles. Further investigation revealed that this was due to a short-term overload affecting the BL$_1$ replica in DC$_A$. *Dealer* was able to mitigate the problem by splitting requests to BL$_1$ between its replicas in both data-centers. *Redirection*, on the other hand, could not re-direct all excess traffic to DC$_B$ since BL$_2$ did not have sufficient capacity in the remote data-center to handle all the load from DC$_A$. Figure 13 shows that at times 400-500, BL$_1$ in DC$_A$ experienced a surge in request rate exceeding its available margin. At the same time, BL$_1$(BL$_2$) in DC$_B$ had a request rate that is lower(higher) than its average. These results highlight the importance and effectiveness of *Dealer*'s fine-grained component level mechanism in adapting to transient overload of individual components.

5.5.3 Reaction to failures in the cloud

Applications in the cloud may see failures which reduce their margins, making them vulnerable to even modest workload spikes.

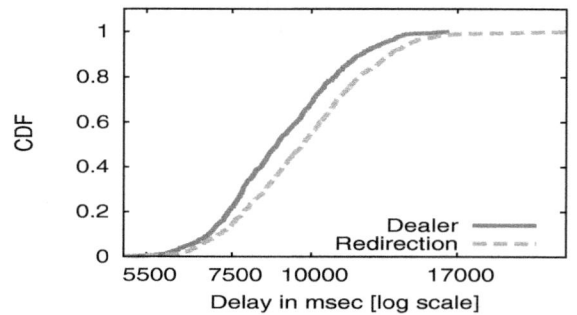

Figure 12: CDF of total response time of *Dealer* vs. *Redirection* using real workload trace under natural spikes and transaction mix changes (*Thumbnail*). Latencies with both schemes are higher than Figure 6 because transactions to BL$_2$ involve heavier processing (image rotation).

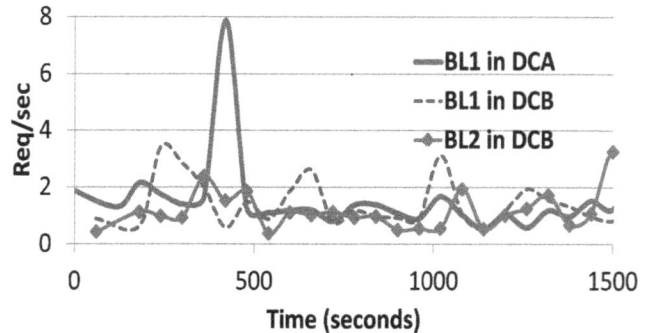

Figure 13: Request rate for each component in both data-centers. BL$_2$ in DC$_A$ not shown for better visualization.

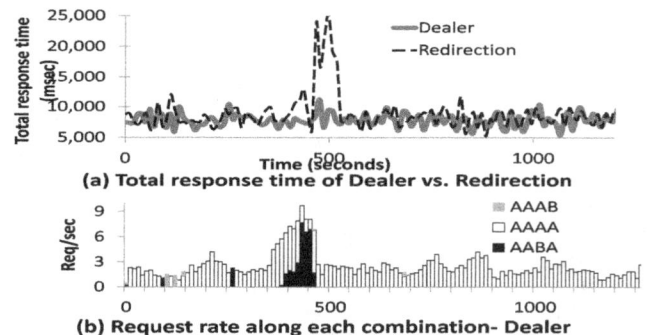

Figure 14: Performance of *Dealer* vs. *Redirection* using real workload trace with cloud failures (*Thumbnail*).

Failures can happen due to actual physical outages or due to maintenance and upgrades. For example, Windows Azure's SLA states that a component has to have 2 or more instances to get 99.95% availability [17] as instances can be taken off for maintenance and upgrades at any time.

In Figure 14, we reproduced the case of a single fault-domain failure at time 300 affecting BL$_2$ instances in DC$_B$[3]. The combination AABA represents requests which were served by FE, BE, BL$_2$ at DC$_A$ and BL$_1$ at DC$_B$. For the same reasons described in §5.5.2, *Dealer* maintained a significantly lower response time during the surge in workload (130% lower). The results show that *Dealer* is effective in handling failures in the cloud.

---

[3]This involved bringing 4 BL$_2$ VM's offline since Azure deploys each component's VMs on 2 or more fault-domains.

5.5.4 Inter data-center bandwidth costs

A potential concern arises due to wide-area traffic that *Dealer* introduces in re-routing requests across data-centers. In this section, we compute the cost percentage increase for *Thumbnail* and *Stock-Trader* based on the experiments described in §5.5.1 and §5.5.2.

We consider the bandwidth, storage and compute (small instances) costs based on Microsoft Azure tariffs in January, 2012. The bandwidth cost is based on all transactions exiting each data-center (incoming transactions do not incur bandwidth costs in Azure). The average size of each request in *Thumbnail* (*StockTrader*) is 1.5MB (2 KB). *StockTrader* uses SQL Azure DB (Web Ed.) and *Thumbnail* uses Azure blobs for storage. We calculate the storage cost for *Thumbnail* based on the number of storage transactions and storage size consumed. The cost of the DB and compute instances is normalized to the duration of the experiments.

The cost percentage increase for *Thumbnail* and *StockTrader* were found to be 1.94% and 0.06% respectively. This shows that the cost introduced due to inter data-center bandwidth is minimal, even for data-intensive applications such as *Thumbnail*. We have repeated our calculations using the Amazon EC2 pricing scheme [2], and we have found similar results. Finally, we note that in our evaluations we assume compute instances in both data-centers cost the same. However, in practice, application architects are likely to provision *reserved instances* in each data-center [2] (i.e., instances contracted over a longer period for a lower rate). Under such scenarios, *Dealer* has the potential to incur lower costs than *Redirection* by leveraging reserved instances in each data-center to the extent possible.

6 Related Work

Several researchers have pointed out the presence of performance problems with the cloud (e.g., [44, 33, 23]). In contrast, our focus is on designing systems to adapt to short-term variability in the cloud.

The cloud industry already provides mechanisms to scale up or down the number of server instances in the cloud (e.g., [36, 11]). However, it takes tens of minutes to invoke new cloud instances in commercial cloud platforms today. Recent research has shown the feasibility of starting new VMs at faster time scales [32, 43]. For instance, [32] presents a VM-fork abstraction which enables the cloning of a VM into multiple replicas on-the-fly. While such schemes are useful for handling variability in performance due to excess load on a component, they cannot handle all types of dynamics in the cloud (e.g., problems in blob storage, network congestion, etc.). Further, ensuring the servers are warmed up to serve requests after instantiation (e.g., by filling caches, running checks, copying state, etc.) demands additional time. In contrast, *Dealer* can enable faster adaptation at shorter time-scales, and is intended to complement solutions for dynamic resource invocation.

DNS-based techniques [26, 39, 45] and server-side redirection mechanisms [35] are widely used to map users to appropriate data-centers. However, such techniques focus on alleviating performance problems related to Internet congestion between users and data-centers, and load-balance user traffic coarsely at the granularity of data-centers. In contrast, *Dealer* targets performance problems of individual cloud components inside a data-center, and may choose components that span multiple data-centers to service an individual user request. This offers several advantages in large multi-tier applications (with potentially hundreds of components [28]) where possibly only a small number of components are temporarily impacted. When entire user requests are redirected to a remote data-center as in [26, 39, 45, 35], not all components in the remote data-center may be sufficiently over-provisioned to handle the redirected requests. Further, redirecting entire user requests does not

utilize functional resources in the local data-center that have already being paid for. For instance, the local data-center may have underutilized *reserved* instances [2], while the remote data-center might require the use of more expensive *on-demand* instances. The cost could be substantial over a large number of components. Finally, studies have shown that the use of DNS-based redirection techniques may lead to delays of more than 2 hours and thus may not be suitable for applications which require quick response to failures [34]. We note that [35] does mention doing the redirection at the level of the bottleneck component; however, *Dealer* is distinguished in that it makes no a priori assumption about which component is the bottleneck, and dynamically reacts to whichever component or link performs poorly at any given time.

Several works [38, 42, 46] study utility resource planning and provisioning for applications. [38] studies resource planning for compute batch tasks by building predictive models in shared computing utilities. Further, [42, 46] build analytic models for handling workload variability (changing transaction mix and load) in multi-tier applications. For example, [42] aims at handling peak workloads by provisioning resources at two levels: predictive provisioning that allocates capacity at the time-scale of hours or days, and reactive provisioning that operates at time scales of minutes. While such techniques are complementary to *Dealer*, their focus is not applications deployed in public clouds. *Dealer* not only deals with workload variability, but also handles all types of performance variability (e.g., due to service failures, network congestion, etc.) in geo-distributed multi-tier applications, deployed in commercial public clouds. *Dealer* provides ways to avoid components with poor performance and congested links via re-routing requests to replicas in other data-centers at short time scales.

Other works [31, 25] study the performance of multi-tier applications. [31] tries to control the performance of such applications by preventing overload using self-tuning proportional integral (PI) controller for admission control. Such a technique can be integrated with *Dealer* to control the load directed to each component replica. Further, [25] combines performance modeling and profiling to create analytical models to accomplish SLA decomposition. While SLA decomposition is outside the scope of *Dealer*, component profiling may be incorporated with *Dealer* to capture component's performance as a function of allocated resources (e.g., CPU) to achieve performance prediction.

7 Conclusions and Future Work

In this paper, we have shown that it is important and feasible to architect latency-sensitive applications in a manner that is robust to the high variability in performance of cloud services. We have presented *Dealer*, a system that can enable applications to meet their SLA requirements by dynamically splitting transactions for each component among its replicas in different data-centers. Under natural cloud dynamics, the $90th$ and higher percentiles of application response times were reduced by more than a factor of 3 compared to a system that used traditional DNS-based redirection. Further, *Dealer* not only ensures low latencies but also significantly outperforms application-level redirection mechanisms under a range of controlled experiments. Integrating *Dealer* with two contrasting applications only required a modest level of change to code.

As future work, we plan to explore and gain more experience integrating *Dealer* with a wider set of cloud applications with various consistency constraints. Further, we intend to study ways for reducing probing overhead by limiting active probes to measuring inter-data-center bandwidth and latency only. Finally, we will evaluate the performance of *Dealer* under scale and explore more cloud infrastructures (such as Amazon EC2 and Google App Engine).

8 Acknowledgments

This material is based upon work supported in part by the National Science Foundation (NSF) under Career Award No. 0953622 and NSF Award No. 1162333, and was supported by cloud usage credits from Microsoft Azure under NSF/Microsoft's Computing in the Cloud program. Any opinions, findings, and conclusions or recommendations expressed in this material are those of the authors and do not necessarily reflect the views of NSF or Microsoft.

Finally, we thank the reviewers and our shepherd, Prashant Shenoy, for their feedback which helped us improve the paper.

9 References

[1] Amazon cloud outage. http://aws.amazon.com/message/2329B7/.

[2] Amazon EC2 pricing. http://aws.amazon.com/ec2/pricing/.

[3] Apache, Project Stonehenge. http://wiki.apache.org/incubator/StonehengeProposal.

[4] Architecting for the Cloud: Best Practices. http://jineshvaria.s3.amazonaws.com/public/cloudbestpractices-jvaria.pdf.

[5] Aspect Oriented Programming. http://msdn.microsoft.com/en-us/library/aa288717%28v=vs.71%29.aspx.

[6] Coding in the Cloud. Use a stateless design whenever possible. http://www.rackspace.com/blog/coding-in-the-cloud-rule-3-use-a-stateless-design-whenever-possible/.

[7] Event Tracing for Windows (ETW). http://msdn.microsoft.com/en-us/library/aa363668.aspx.

[8] Grinder Load Testing Framework. http://grinder.sourceforge.net/index.html.

[9] Latency - it costs you. http://highscalability.com/latency-everywhere-and-it-costs-you-sales-how-crush-it.

[10] Microsoft Live outage due to DNS corruption. http://windowsteamblog.com/windows_live/b/windowslive/archive/2011/09/20/follow-up-on-the-sept-8-service-outage.aspx.

[11] Microsoft Windows Azure. http://www.microsoft.com/windowsazure/.

[12] Response Time Metric for SLAs. http://testnscale.com/blog/performance/response-time-metric-for-slas.

[13] Slow pages lose users. http://radar.oreilly.com/2009/06/bing-and-google-agree-slow-pag.html.

[14] SQL Azure Data Sync. http://social.technet.microsoft.com/wiki/contents/articles/sql-azure-data-sync-overview.aspx.

[15] SQL Azure Performance Issue. http://cloudfail.net/513962.

[16] Using SOAP Extensions in ASP.NET. http://msdn.microsoft.com/en-us/magazine/cc164007.aspx.

[17] Windows Azure SLA. http://www.microsoft.com/windowsazure/sla/.

[18] Windows Azure Thumbnails Sample. http://code.msdn.microsoft.com/windowsazure/Windows-Azure-Thumbnails-c001c8d7.

[19] Windows Azure Traffic Manager (WATM). http://msdn.microsoft.com/en-us/gg197529.

[20] AHMAD, F., ET AL. Joint optimization of idle and cooling power in data centers while maintaining response time. *ASPLOS 2010.*

[21] ARMBRUST, M., ET AL. Above the Clouds: A Berkeley View of Cloud Computing. Tech. rep., EECS, University of California, Berkeley, 2009.

[22] BARHAM, P., ET AL. Magpie: Online modelling and performance-aware systems. In *HOTOS 2003.*

[23] BARKER, S., AND SHENOY, P. Empirical evaluation of latency-sensitive application performance in the cloud. In *MMSys 2010.*

[24] BLACKBURN, S. M., AND ET AL. The DaCapo benchmarks: Java benchmarking development and analysis. In *OOPSLA 2006.*

[25] CHEN, Y., IYER, S., LIU, X., MILOJICIC, D., AND SAHAI, A. SLA decomposition: Translating service level objectives to system level thresholds. In *ICAC'07.*

[26] DILLEY, J., ET AL. Globally distributed content delivery. *Internet Computing, IEEE* (2002).

[27] FONSECA, R., PORTER, G., KATZ, R., SHENKER, S., AND STOICA, I. X-trace: A pervasive network tracing framework. In *NSDI 2007.*

[28] HAJJAT, M., ET AL. Cloudward bound: Planning for beneficial migration of enterprise applications to the cloud. *SIGCOMM 2010.*

[29] HASTORUN, D., ET AL. Dynamo: amazons highly available key-value store. In *In Proc. SOSP* (2007).

[30] HONG, Y.-J., ET AL. Dynamic server provisioning to minimize cost in an iaas cloud. In *ACM SIGMETRICS, 2011.*

[31] KAMRA, A., MISRA, V., AND NAHUM, E. Yaksha: A self-tuning controller for managing the performance of 3-tiered web sites. In *IWQOS 2004.*

[32] LAGAR-CAVILLA, ET AL. SnowFlock: rapid virtual machine cloning for cloud computing. In *ACM EuroSys, 2009.*

[33] LI, A., YANG, X., KANDULA, S., AND ZHANG, M. CloudCmp: comparing public cloud providers. In *IMC 2010.*

[34] PANG, J., ET AL. On the responsiveness of DNS-based network control. In *IMC 2004.*

[35] RANJAN, S., KARRER, R., AND KNIGHTLY, E. Wide area redirection of dynamic content by Internet data centers. In *INFOCOM 2004.*

[36] RIGHTSCALE INC. Cloud computing management platform. http://www.rightscale.com.

[37] SATOPAA, V., ET AL. Finding a 'Kneedle' in a Haystack: Detecting Knee Points in System Behavior. In *SIMPLEX Workshop, 2011.*

[38] SHIVAM, P., BABU, S., AND CHASE, J. Learning application models for utility resource planning. In *ICAC'06.*

[39] SU, A., ET AL. Drafting behind Akamai. *SIGCOMM 2006.*

[40] SYMANTEC. 2010 State of the Data Center Global Data. http://www.symantec.com/content/en/us/about/media/pdfs/Symantec_DataCenter10_Report_Global.pdf.

[41] URGAONKAR, B., AND SHENOY, P. Cataclysm: Handling extreme overloads in internet services. In *PODC 2004.*

[42] URGAONKAR, B., SHENOY, P., CHANDRA, A., AND GOYAL, P. Dynamic provisioning of multi-tier internet applications. In *ICAC 2005.*

[43] VRABLE, M., ET AL. Scalability, fidelity, and containment in the potemkin virtual honeyfarm. In *ACM SOSP, 2005.*

[44] WANG, G., AND NG, T. S. E. The impact of virtualization on network performance of Amazon EC2 data center. In *IEEE INFOCOM 2010.*

[45] WENDELL, P., ET AL. DONAR: decentralized server selection for cloud services. In *SIGCOMM 2010.*

[46] ZHANG, Q., CHERKASOVA, L., AND SMIRNI, E. A regression-based analytic model for dynamic resource provisioning of multi-tier applications. In *ICAC'07.*

Energy Consumption Anatomy of 802.11 Devices and its Implication on Modeling and Design

Andres Garcia-Saavedra*, Pablo Serrano*, Albert Banchs*†, Giuseppe Bianchi‡
{agsaaved,pablo,banchs}@it.uc3m.es, giuseppe.bianchi@uniroma2.it

*Universidad Carlos III de Madrid	†Institute IMDEA Networks	‡CNIT / Universita' Tor Vergata
Avda. Universidad, 30	Avda. Mar Mediterráneo, 22	Via del Politecnico, 1
28911 Leganés, Spain	28918 Leganés, Spain	00133 Roma, Italy

ABSTRACT

A thorough understanding of the power consumption behavior of *real world* wireless devices is of paramount importance to ground energy-efficient protocols and optimizations on realistic and accurate energy models. This paper provides an in-depth experimental investigation of the per-frame energy consumption components in 802.11 Wireless LAN devices. To the best of our knowledge, our measurements are the first to unveil that a *substantial* fraction of energy consumption, hereafter descriptively named *cross-factor*, may be ascribed to each individual frame while it *crosses* the protocol/implementation stack (OS, driver, NIC). Our findings, summarized in a convenient new energy consumption model, contrast traditional models which either neglect or amortize such energy cost component in a fixed baseline cost, and raise the alert that, in some cases, conclusions drawn using traditional energy models may be fallacious.

Categories and Subject Descriptors

C.2.1 [**Computer-Communication Networks**]: Network Architecture and Design—*Wireless Communication*

General Terms

Design, Experimentation, Measurement, Performance

Keywords

WLAN, 802.11, Energy consumption anatomy, Energy measurements, Cross-factor

1. INTRODUCTION

The increase in energy density of current state of the art (Lithium-Ion) batteries is far from following Moore's Law, the current challenge being "just" a twofold density increase in the next 10 years [37]. This is not a good technological premise behind the energy greediness of wireless connectivity, second only to that required to backlight displays in most handheld devices. Moreover, battery powered wireless devices are becoming ubiquitous, and are frequently part of the network infrastructure itself; even besides the obvious case of wireless sensor networks, battery powered relays or opportunistic intermediaries are widely considered in ad hoc, mesh, DTN scenarios, or emergency deployments.

It is hence not nearly a surprise that a *huge* research effort has been dedicated to find ways for reducing energy consumption in the wireless access and communication operation [24, 39]. For instance, with reference to the 802.11 WLAN (WiFi) technology [2], indeed the focus of this paper, energy efficiency improvements span very diverse aspects of the 802.11 operation, from management procedures [34], to usage of opportunistic relays [19] or infrastructure on demand [22], to PHY [31] and MAC [12] layer parameters' optimizations, and so on.

Obviously, a *quantitative* treatment of the attainable energy improvements is greatly simplified by the availability of realistic and accurate energy models, also considering that *fine-grained* per-frame experimental measurements (versus coarse aggregate power consumption statistics) may be non trivial to achieve. Most of the literature works, including but not limited to [7,9,11,12,15,17,23,30,40], ground their proposed analyses, optimizations, or algorithm/protocol designs, on the widely accepted paradigm that the energy toll may be ascribed to two components: a baseline one, plus a second one linear with (transmission/reception) air time. The specific weights are of course tailored to the interface state (transmit, receive, idle, sleep), and can be gathered by data sheets [13] or experimental measurements [1, 16].

Questioning the classical per-frame energy model

With such a widespread acceptance, questioning the above mentioned *classical* energy model seems tough. Actually, such model makes perfectly sense if we just focus on the network interface card consumption. But, in practice, processing in the host device drains energy as well. So, the question at stake is whether (and to what extent) there is some *energy toll in the device*, which is imputable to TX/RX processing, but which is *improperly accounted in such classical model*, e.g., because it can be neither considered (*i*) independent of the radio operation and thus (implicitly) accounted in the fixed baseline energy consumption component, nor (*ii*) strictly proportional to the traffic load in bytes, hence (implicitly) accounted in the linear air time energy cost component.

Our paper not only raises this question (apparently unnoticed in most prior work), but, more significantly, provides a (we believe) compelling answer, via extensive and tailored experiments[1] providing a detailed *anatomy* of the energy consumption in the protocol stack.

Two major findings appear to emerge. First, a *substantial* energy consumption occurs while a frame is delivered across the protocol stack, namely from the operating system to the driver to the NIC (and conversely for reception). Such "new" energy cost component, descriptively referred to as *cross-factor*, cannot be neglected; on the contrary, in some experiments it even accounts to *more than half* of the per-frame energy cost. Second, such cross-factor can be neither dealt with as an extra baseline component, nor (perhaps more surprisingly) as a cost proportional to the traffic load. Actually, this energy toll appears mostly *associated to the very fact that a frame is handled*, i.e., irrespective (to a very large extent) of the actual frame size in bytes.[2]

Our findings, which we wrap into a convenient and easy to exploit new energy model, have a twofold implication. First, they suggest new energy reduction strategies, such as *batching* packets while they travel across the protocol stack, or avoiding stack crossing when possible (the energy savings for both strategies are preliminary quantified via tailored experiments). Second, the fact that a substantial amount of energy is drained by the processing of packet units (i.e., independent of their size, or air time, or modulation and coding scheme) may play havoc with some specific optimizations proposed in the past. For instance, we show that energy-efficient optimizations leveraging relay nodes may yield *qualitatively different* conclusions when the cross-factor energy component is accounted for.

Our contribution

This paper makes the following original contributions.

Power consumption characterization. In contrast to previous works, our measurement methodology is (*i*) based on a convenient power measurement device rather than specialized hardware and complex measurement configurations; (*ii*) it exploits techniques to reduce measurement uncertainties due to scale limitation, and (*iii*) it characterizes the *total* device power consumption versus that consumed by just the wireless interface.

Power consumption anatomy and unveiling of the cross-factor. Targeted measurements devised to break down the energy cost in specific components, reveal (and quantify) that a substantial fraction of energy is consumed by the processing of packets throughout the protocol/implementation stack. Such *cross-factor* energy toll exhibits two notable features: (*i*) in some (common) radio settings, it may become the *dominant* source of energy consumption, and (*ii*) it is primarily associated to the *frame processing itself*, rather than to the amount of bytes handled. Interpreting such cost as proportional to the load seems thus intuitively appealing, and may work as long as the frame size is fixed, but is incorrect for the general case of variable frame sizes.

New energy model and relevant validation. We summarize our findings in a simple and convenient energy model which overcomes traditional models limited to NIC consumption [7, 9, 11, 12, 15, 17, 23, 30, 40]. We validate such new energy model with several experiments.

Practical implications. Focusing (for space reasons) on selected use-case examples, we show that some energy optimizations proposed in the past may yield fundamentally different conclusions when revisited with the awareness of our more realistic energy consumption findings. Of course, such conclusion may or may not apply on a case by case basis, but, on a more general line, our findings appear to raise the alert that there might be other cases where past conclusions should be reconsidered. Moreover, we discuss possible new means to take advantage of our findings for improved energy efficiency; we especially quantify, through software developed for measurement purposes, the savings introduced by two schemes that simplify the crossing of the protocol stack.

2. RELATED WORK

Energy consumption of devices. A number of previous works in the area analyze, like us, the consumption of the complete device, either a laptop [1, 3, 25] or a mobile phone [10, 33]. Some of these works deal with specific issues, such as quantification of the consumption of components other than wireless interfaces (e.g., CPU, screen, memory) [10], power consumption measurements via available APIs for estimating the battery discharge state [25], assessment of trade-off between CPU consumption due to data compression and wireless consumption due to data transmission [3], but do not tackle the per-frame energy consumption domain. Only [1] briefly mentions that the energy consumption associated to packet processing might be non negligible, but does not provide any measurement or evidence. [33] finds that message size can have a non-intuitive impact on the energy consumption, but their guess is either the existence of some power management threshold or a bug in the wireless firmware (indeed, energy bugs in mobile devices are a current concern [28]). We distinguish from all these works in the fact that *we perform a fine-grained per-packet energy consumption decomposition*, versus their energy consumption analyses on a much coarser scale.

Energy consumption of interfaces. Unlike the previous papers, most characterizations of the wireless interface consumption are done on a per-packet basis. The seminal work of [16] shows that transmission/reception of an 802.11 frame has a linear dependency on its length. This result is caused by the four different states a wireless NIC can be in, namely: sleep, idle, receiving and transmitting. [16] also identifies a fixed cost per frame, caused by control frames (e.g., RTS/CTS). The results are extended in [14] for different modulation and coding schemes and transmission power configurations, and a similar approach is followed in a recent work [18] for the case of 802.11n. While in these cases the 802.11 interface is treated as a whole, [32] distinguishes between the (approximately constant) Application-Specific Integrated Circuit (ASIC) consumption, and the Power Amplifier (PA) consumption occurring only outside idle periods. None of these works analyze the energy consumption of a frame as it is delivered to/from the NIC.

Energy consumption models. The (implicit or explicit) assumption of all previous energy consumption models [7, 9, 11, 12, 15, 17, 23, 30, 40] is that the PA operations dominate the consumption of the whole device, which allows to model consumption with a finite number of states, e.g., {ac-

---

[1]Primarily on a Soekris net4826-48 device, but the general findings are duly confirmed by further measurements on two other platforms, an Alix2d2 and a Linksys WRT54GL.

[2]While some previous works had already identified a per-frame energy cost, such cost was ascribed to different factors from the ones we find in this paper (like e.g. control frames).

tive, idle} [9, 11], {transmission, reception, idle} [15, 17, 40], and so on. More specifically, the common approach followed by all these papers (as well as that recently included in the NS3 network simulator [41]) is to model the NIC consumption using data sheet parameters [13], and add to this a fixed amount to account for the non-wireless power consumption of the device. In [30], the authors propose an extended model that accounts for the power conversion efficiency of the PA, but eventually the model suffers from the same limitations. As we will see in this paper, these energy consumption models *fail to capture crucial aspects of how energy is consumed in real world devices*, and therefore their use might bias conclusions.

Energy efficient mechanisms. Proposals for energy-efficient operation can be found at practically all layers of the 802.11 stack. Starting from the lowest layer, [31] pre-computes the optimal rate-power configuration for each data frame. Several works aim at reducing the energy wastage in the WLAN by adapting the contention parameters [12, 17] or extending the backoff operation [7, 23]. The use of co-operative relaying for energy efficiency is analyzed in [19]; [27] exploits idle period predictions to switch from active to sleep states. Increasing the sleep state time is the main energy saving target in the standard Power Saving Mechanism (PSM) [39], and in traffic management (and shaping) schemes such as NAPman [34], or in 'infrastructure on demand' schemes [22] devised to (de)activate Access Points based on client load. All these proposals are based either on (i) the energy consumption of the PA, which might be detailed but underestimates the consumption of the complete device, or on (ii) the coarse-grained estimated consumption of the complete device, which precludes a thorough understanding of the per-packet delivery implications.

3. METHODOLOGY TO MEASURE ENERGY

802.11 devices

For development convenience, most results have been obtained using a **Soekris net4826-48** device, equipped with an Atheros AR5414-based 802.11a/b/g Mini-PCI card, and configured to use the 802.11a PHY. The hardware comprises a 233MHz AMD Geode SC1100 CPU, 2 Mini-PCI sockets, 128 Mbyte SDRAM and 256 Mbyte compact flash circuits for data storage, extended with a 2 GB USB drive. The OS is a Gentoo 10.0 Linux (kernel 2.6.24), and the driver is MadWifi v0.9.4.

Two additional platforms, employing different WLAN PHY and bands, and different hardware architectures, have been further used to verify the most crucial findings (e.g., Fig. 1), to remove the doubt that such findings could be biased by the specifically chosen reference device or WLAN band/card/PHY. These two additional platforms are: (i) an **Alix2d2** device, equipped with a Broadcom BCM4319 802.11b/g Mini-PCI card, 500 MHz AMD Geode LX800, 256 MByte SDRAM, kernel 2.6.29, and (ii) a **Linksys WRT54GL** device, equipped with an integrated Broadcom BCM4320 802.11b/g chipset, 200Mhz BCM5352 CPU, 16 MByte RAM, kernel 2.6.32.

To generate traffic, we used the mgen tool[3] to send UDP packets. Additional devices in monitor mode have been employed to sniff all traffic to confirm that all wireless activity was caused only by our experiments. To ensure that no packets were dropped at any layer of the protocol stack, which may bias the conclusions of the results, we checked that the information logged by the system at the different layers matched the actual wireless transmissions that we observed through the external sniffer.

Power-related issues

Power consumption was measured via a low-cost PCE PA-6000 power meter,[4] which provides instantaneous values of current voltage and power factor (among other parameters), at a sample rate above 5 sample/second. This instrument can be connected in series between an AC or DC power source and the device under study, without *dismantling* it, as for instance needed with some specialized equipments, which thus may restrict experimentation to, e.g., devices using card extenders.

For what concerns powering the devices while gathering measurements, we extensively tested two alternatives: via AC supply, and via DC supply. At last (discussion omitted for space reasons), we resorted to the second configuration, to prevent periodic AC power fluctuations from the wall socket which would have affected accuracy. The PCE PA-6000 power meter was thus powered with 6 AA batteries, and we employed a Protek 3033B device[5] to power the wireless device.

3.1 Improving measurements accuracy

Power measurements were obtained by measuring the voltage v and the current i, and taking the relevant product $p = v \cdot i$. Reducing the native inaccuracies of the measurement instrument employed was a major practical challenge. Indeed, according to the vendors' specification sheet, the PA-6000 provides a resolution of $\Delta v = 0.1$ V for the voltage and $\Delta i = 0.01$ A for the current. Considering a typical baseline power measurement for the considered device, these inaccuracies yield the following relative errors:

$$v = 12.5 \pm 0.1 \ V \ = 12.5 \ V \ \pm 0.8\%$$
$$i = 0.20 \pm 0.01 \ A = 0.20 \ A \ \pm 5\%$$
$$p \approx 2.5 \pm 0.145 \ W = 2.5 \ W \ \pm 5.8\%$$

where in the last power measurement expression we have made usage of the well known fact that the relative error for the product $p = v \cdot i$ is approximated by the sum of the relative errors for v and i [38].

Reducing uncertainty

In most of our experiments, an uncertainty in the order of more than 5% is too coarse, as it would undermine our ability to quantify small, but for our purposes extremely meaningful, trends (e.g., power consumption variations for an increased frame size). The methodology that we followed in order to improve this accuracy[6] consists in using, instead of a single device, K devices in parallel *running the same experiment* (over different non-interfering wireless channels,

---

[3] http://cs.itd.nrl.navy.mil/work/mgen/

[4] http://www.industrial-needs.com/technical-data/power-analyser-PCE-PA-6000.htm

[5] http://www.protektest.com/ProdInfo.asp?prodId=3033B

[6] In our case, averaging N samples does not help to reduce uncertainty, which is determined by the "reading scale". Indeed, the average would retain the same accuracy as the original samples [38].

Table 1: Accuracy improvement with K devices.

K	v (V)		i_K (A)		p_K (W)	p_d (W)
1	12.6		0.19		2.4±6.1 %	2.4 ±6.1 %
2	12.4	±0.1	0.41	±0.01	5.1±3.2 %	2.5 ±3.2 %
3	12.2		0.63		7.7±2.4 %	2.56±2.4 %
4	12.3		0.84		10.3±2.0 %	2.58±2.0 %

Table 2: Soekris Baseline consumption profile

Config.	Description	Cons. (W)
w/o card	no NIC connected	2.29 ± 2.2%
WiFi off	NIC connected driver not loaded	2.58 ± 2.0% (+0.29)
Idle (ρ_{id})	NIC activated+associated to AP no RX/TX besides beacons	3.56 ± 1.7% (+0.98)

of course). Thus, the instrument's uncertainty on the current measurements, namely 0.01 A, now applies to the *total* current (as well as the total power, voltage being the same) drained by the K (equivalent) devices, yielding a relative error reduction of a factor K. The power consumed by a single device is finally computed as $1/K$th of the total power, with the same (reduced) relative error (division by a constant does not affect the relative error [38]).

Table 1 shows measurements taken over 30 seconds on $K = 1$ to 4 devices in parallel, for the case of devices without wireless interfaces, which is the configuration that consumes the least power and therefore has the largest relative errors. The table reports measured voltage v, total current i_K, total consumed power p_K with associated uncertainty, and per-device consumed power p_d with associated uncertainty. With $K = 4$, accuracy improves from about 6% of single device measurements to a more satisfactory 2%.[7]

In the rest of the paper we use such a *parallel device* methodology in which each experiment is conducted with K different devices of the same type (software and hardware) performing the same operations. Unless otherwise specified, we will use $K = 4$ for 802.11a and $K = 3$ for 802.11g.[8] As shown by the results of the next section, these K values provide sufficient accuracy to analyze the behavior of the different energy components of 802.11 devices.

4. ENERGY CONSUMPTION ANATOMY

In order to characterize the power consumption of the 802.11 devices, we have conducted an in-depth experimental investigation of the considered 802.11 devices. For space reasons, all the measurements presented here are for the devices operating under the infrastructure mode; however, we verified that the devices show a very similar behavior when operating under the ad-hoc and monitor modes.

A pre-requirement for characterization of 802.11 devices consists in quantifying their "baseline" power consumption, i.e., when the devices neither send nor receive traffic. Table 2 reports measurements for the Soekris platform in three "baseline" configurations. Note that plugging the wireless card ("WiFi off") increases consumption by 0.29 W (+12.6%), whereas loading the driver and associating to an AP ("Idle") further increases the consumption by 0.98 W, indeed an extra 25% increment. The power consumed in the "Idle" state, named ρ_{id}, will be used as baseline reference in what follows.

4.1 Understanding transmission costs

Results in this section aim at characterizing the energy cost of transmissions, and providing our best effort to ac-

curately explain and justify the relevant findings. For this reason, in the remainder of this section, results are obtained for unicast *unacknowledged* frames, so as to avoid biasing results with the cost of ACK reception (separately quantified later on). ACKs have been disabled by setting the `noack-policy` bit of the WMM parameters for the Access Point parameter set: this introduces an Information Element in beacon frames that prevents associated stations from replying with ACKs (confirmed by sniffed traces). Unless otherwise specified, each result is obtained by measuring the power consumption over a 20 seconds experiment.

Transmission power consumption patterns

A large number of *total* device power consumption measurements have been carried out, spanning several combinations of four quantities/parameters: (*i*) frame size L in the range 100 to 1500 bytes, (*ii*) modulation and coding schemes (MCS $\in \{6, 12, 24, 48\}$ Mbps), (*iii*) configured transmission power[9] (`txpower` $\in \{6, 9, 12, 15\}$ dBm), and (*iv*) frame generation rate λ_g, up to 2000 frames per second (fps).

It turns out that the most insightful way to represent such results is via *power/airtime plots*, shown in Fig. 1.[10] Since these results appear crucial, we repeated them for *all the three platforms* (Soekris in Fig. 1-a, Alix in Fig. 1-b, and Linksys in Fig. 1-c), adapting when needed the parameters (for instance, the very cheap Linksys device cannot sustain a load greater than about a thousand fps). Such plots report the average power consumed by the whole device, versus the percentage τ_{tx} of channel airtime, computed as

$$\tau_{tx} = \lambda_g T_L, \quad (1)$$

where λ_g is the frame generation rate, and $T_L = T_{PLCP} + (H + L)/MCS$ is the time required to transmit a frame of size L using the modulation and coding scheme MCS, duly accounting for the Physical Layer Convergence Protocol preamble T_{PLCP}, and the MAC overhead H (MAC header plus FCS). For reference purposes, the plots also report the baseline power consumption ρ_{id} when the target device is in "Idle" state.

Besides the *quantitative* differences among the considered platforms, these plots provide compelling evidence that the total device power consumption, denoted **P**, appears articulated into three main components,[11]

$$\mathbf{P} = \rho_{id} + P_{tx} + P_{xg}(\lambda_g), \quad (2)$$

---

[7]From the experiments conducted in this paper, we confirmed that the maximum difference observed between our measurements and the proposed model matches the measurement inaccuracy predicted, which validates the results of this section.

[8]The reason for using $K = 3$ in the latter case is that 802.11g only allows 3 non-interfering channels.

[9]We have selected four values within the range of allowed transmission power values, which goes from 5 to 15 dBm.

[10]The values shown in the figures are the result of applying a simple linear regression to the measurements and computing their standard asymptotic error [26].

[11]The good match between the experimental figures and equation 2 is confirmed in Fig. 1, in which the values predicted by the equation are plotted using lines.

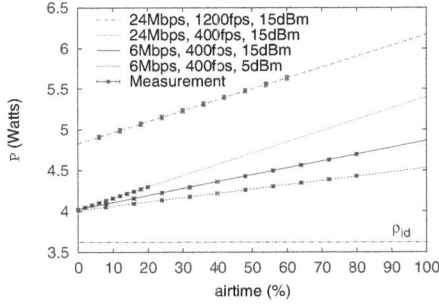

(a) Soekris

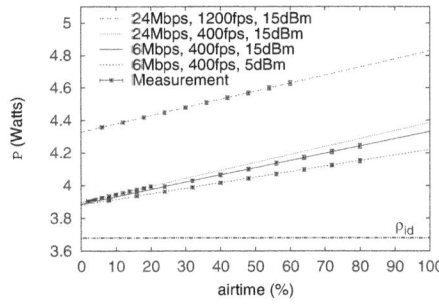

(b) Alix

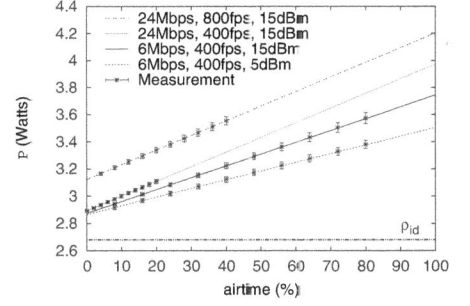

(c) Linksys

Figure 1: Total power consumed by (unacknowledged) transmissions vs. airtime percentage τ_{tx}.

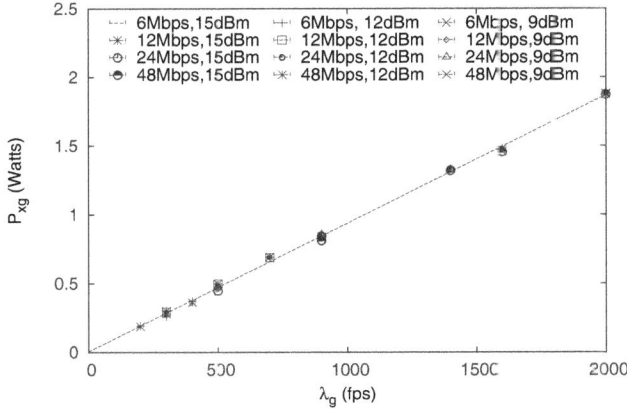

Figure 2: Relation between $P_{xg}(\lambda_g)$ and λ_g.

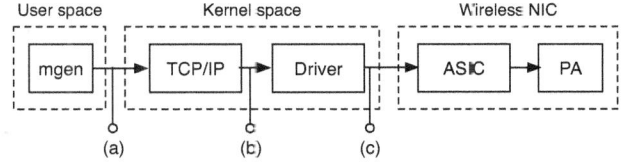

Figure 3: Interfaces and modules crossed during transmission.

where:

- The first component, ρ_{id}, is the (platform-specific) baseline power consumption;
- The second component, P_{tx}, is the classical one in traditional energy consumption models, which linearly grows with the airtime percentage τ_{tx}, i.e., $P_{tx} = \rho_{tx}\tau_{tx}$. The slope ρ_{tx} depends on the target platform and on the radio transmission parameters MCS and txpower: the greater the MCS and/or the txpower, the greater the slope;
- The third component, $P_{xg}(\lambda_g)$, accounts for the fact that the above linear trend does *not* start from the baseline power consumption level ρ_{id}, but rather *starts from a relatively large positive offset* (e.g., in the Soekris case, +12% and +35% increment over the baseline level ρ_{id} for 400 and 1200 fps, respectively); offset which is *not accounted by classical energy models* [7, 9, 11, 12, 15, 17, 23, 30, 40]. Moreover, Fig. 1 suggests that such component depends only on the frame generation rate λ_g.

Per-frame processing toll

To more closely investigate the nature of such emerging power consumption offset $P_{xg}(\lambda_g)$, Fig. 2 plots its value obtained from several measurements taken for different configuration of the NIC parameters (MCS, txpower) over the Soekris platform (results are qualitatively analogous for the

other two platforms). The plot clearly shows that $P_{xg}(\lambda_g)$ is *proportional* to the frame generation rate λ_g, whereas it is practically *independent of* the frame size or the radio settings.

Thus, if we denote with $\gamma_{xg} = P_{xg}(\lambda_g)/\lambda_g$ the proportionality constant, it appears that γ_{xg} is the *energy toll associated to the processing of each individual frame*, irrespective of its size or radio transmission parameters. Note that this energy toll is *not* associated to protocol operations such as RTS/CTS or ACKs, indeed disabled in such experiments.

Cross-factor

To grasp deeper insights on the reasons behind such a per-frame energy toll γ_{xg}, (named *cross-factor*, for reasons that will become clear throughout this section), we have engineered tailored measurements on the Soekris platform, devised to *quantify* how this energy toll splits across the frame processing chain along the protocol-implementation stack (roughly) depicted in Fig. 3.

Specifically, we have run three sets of experiments, where we discard packets at a given level of the stack and we measure the relevant power consumed up to that level:

- **App.** - packets are regularly generated by mgen, but are discarded before being delivered to the OS, i.e., at the mark (a) in Fig. 3, by sending them to the "sink device" (/dev/null);
- **TCP/IP** - packets are discarded at the bottom of the TCP/IP stack (mark (b) in Fig. 3), by deactivating the ARP lookup function, so that the device cannot retrieve the MAC destination from the ARP cache and therefore must drop the frame;
- **Driver** - packets are discarded after the MadWifi driver's processing (mark (c) in Fig. 3), by commenting the hardstart command which performs the actual delivery of the frame to the NIC.

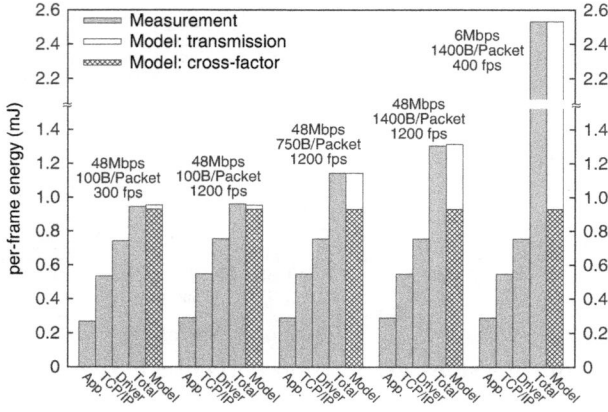

Figure 4: Per-frame energy cost in transmission.

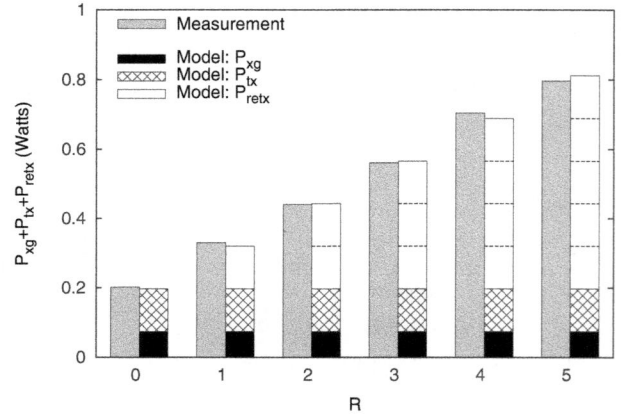

Figure 5: Impact of retransmissions on the power consumption.

Representative measurements (energy per frame) are shown in Fig. 4, along with the total energy consumption per properly transmitted frame ('Total') and the values predicted by applying equation 2 ('Model').

The figure clearly shows that the energy toll due to frame processing is practically *independent of* the frame generation rate *and* the frame size. Moreover, it shows that the energy consumed while crossing the host device stack (i.e., up to the driver included) is *substantial*, around 0.75 mJ per frame, and may become the *major* energy cost in several scenarios (e.g., short packets and/or large MCS - in essence short airtime).

Finally, even if direct measurements were not technically attainable below the driver level, Fig. 4 permits to determine that a further constant per-frame energy drain occurs at the driver-to-NIC interface level and/or below. Its quantification may be estimated by analyzing the energy consumed with very short packets and large MCS, being wireless transmission cost marginal in this case (very small airtime). Summarizing, for a Soekris device, the cross-factor coefficient amounts to about 0.93 mJ. Such per-frame processing cost appears to roughly split as follows: 24% application; 33% TCP/IP stack, 21% driver, and 22% NIC.

The above results clearly show that the energy toll is caused by the frame processing at the different layers of the protocol stack, which depends on the operating system implementation. To gain insight into the impact of the OS on the cross-factor, we evaluated the energy consumption of Soekris devices running OpenBSD. The measurements obtained confirm that the qualitative behavior with OpenBSD is the same as with Linux, and show that the cross-factor is of the same order for both operating systems (1.27 mJ for OpenBSD and 0.93 mJ for Linux).

A key result from the above is that the the energy toll is independent of the frame size. To better understand the reasons for this, we conducted some tailored experiments with applications that perform memory and CPU operations with data elements of different sizes, and observed that the resulting energy consumption is largely independent of the size of the data elements involved. This explains why the energy consumed in crossing the stack, which involves similar types of operations, is agnostic of the frame size.

Retransmissions

Intuitively, retransmissions at the MAC layer, e.g. after a failed transmission, should not be affected by the cross-factor toll. This can be verified by *provisionally assuming* that this is the case, i.e., modeling retransmission cost as purely due to the over the air transmission cost component, and then checking whether the resulting model matches experimental measurements.

Along this line, let P_{retx} be the power drained by retransmissions, and assume that

$$P_{retx} = R \cdot \rho_{tx}\tau_{tx} = R \cdot \rho_{tx}\lambda_g T_L. \tag{3}$$

where R is the number of retransmissions. Then, the *total* power consumed by packets retransmitted R times is readily obtained as the baseline component ρ_{id} plus:

$$P_{xg}(\lambda_g) + P_{tx} + P_{retx}, \tag{4}$$

where the first addendum is the per-frame processing toll (paid once), the second addendum is the power consumed by the very first transmission, and the last addendum is the extra retransmission cost as per (3). Fig. 5 compares the modeling prediction (4) with the power (additional to the baseline component ρ_{id}) consumed by a device configured to send 1400 B UDP frames generated at a rate of 80 fps to fake addresses (to prevent the reception of ACKs). The number of allotted retransmissions R (configured via the `ah_setupTxDesc` driver's descriptor) was varied from 0 to 5, and, for simplicity (i.e., to avoid the need to non trivially configure the driver so as to prevent MCS downgrade in front of persistent losses), frames were transmitted over the wireless channel using the 6 Mbps basic MCS. As shown in Fig. 5, theoretical results tightly match the experimental measurements, thus confirming that the cross-factor has (if any) negligible impact on retransmission.

4.2 Reception power consumption analysis

The analysis of the power consumption of the device while *receiving* frames is somewhat dual to that carried out in depth for the previous transmission case, hence may be dealt with much faster. We use the same configurations of MCS and `txpower` as in Section 4.1 (ACK disabled as well), with different combinations of the frame length L and frame *reception* rate λ_r. The resulting *power/airtime* plot is shown

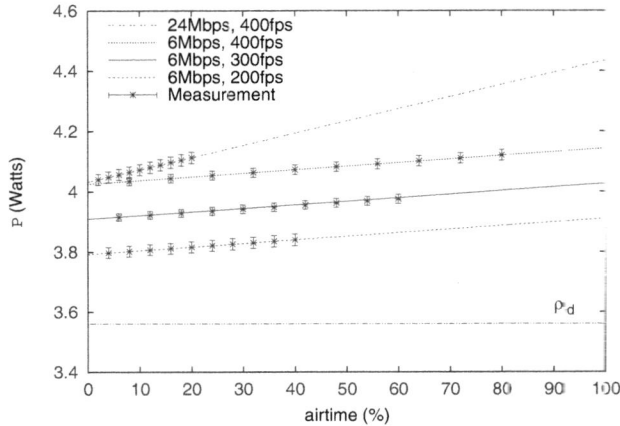

Figure 6: Power consumed by (unacknowledged) reception versus airtime.

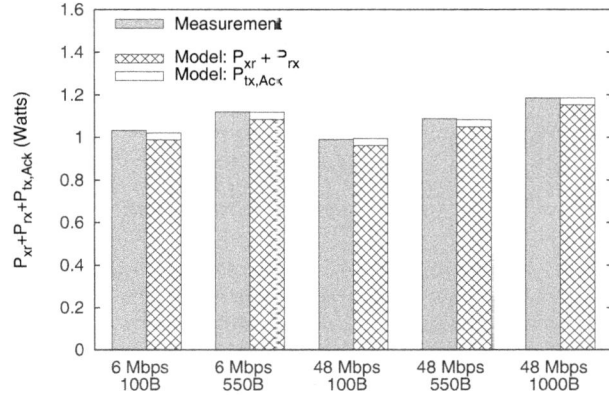

Figure 7: Impact of ACKs on reception.

in Fig. 6 (Soekris device), airtime now given by $\tau_{rx} = \lambda_r T_L$. The `txpower` parameter is not shown, as it does not affect the power consumption (as indeed well known from [14]).

Fig. 6 exhibits the same qualitative pattern found in the transmission scenario. The increment of the power consumption over ρ_{id} is composed of two components: a first one linear with the airtime and accounting for the power required to receive frames, P_{rx} (indeed in line with traditional energy models), and a second one proportional to the number of frames received and accounting for the cross-factor energy toll, $P_{xr}(\lambda_r)$. The total power consumption at the receiving side is thus:

$$\mathbf{P} = \rho_{id} + P_{rx} + P_{xr}(\lambda_r) = \rho_{id} + \rho_{rx}\tau_{rx} + \lambda_r\gamma_{xr} \quad (5)$$

where γ_{xr} is the cross-factor in reception, i.e., the per-packet processing toll to deliver the received frame across the protocol stack, and $\rho_{rx}\tau_{rx}$ is the traditional reception cost proportional to the airtime. Again, Fig. 6 confirms that results from the above equation (lines) closely match the experimental measurements (symbols).

4.3 Characterization of additional aspects

To complete our anatomy, it remains to characterize the additional power consumed for sending/receiving acknowledgments (both the previous sections have considered unacknowledged operation), and the power consumption experienced while overhearing a collision.

ACKs and other control frames

Since ACK frames, like retransmissions, do not have to cross the stack but are internally generated by the NIC, we assume that their power consumption can be characterized by just the cost of the relevant ACK transmission or reception. Under such assumption, the power consumed for replying with ACKs to received frames (arriving at rate λ_r) is trivially given by

$$P_{tx,Ack} = \rho_{tx}\lambda_r T_{Ack}, \quad (6)$$

where $T_{Ack} = T_{PLCP} + ACK/MCS_C$ is the time required to transmit an ACK frame, i.e., a PLCP preamble plus the 14B ACK frame transmitted at the modulation and coding scheme MCS_C configured for control traffic. Similarly, the

power consumed to receive an ACK is readily computed as

$$P_{rx,Ack} = \rho_{rx}\lambda_g T_{Ack}. \quad (7)$$

For space reasons, we show in Fig. 7 the experimental validation for the ACK transmission case, only. Such experimental results, obtained with $\lambda_r = 1000$ fps, confirm that the measurements match the results predicted by the model, which includes the energy consumed by the reception of frames ($P_{xr} + P_{rx}$) and the transmission of the ACKs ($P_{tx,Ack}$).

We also verified that other control frames that do not cross the stack, such the RTS and CTS frames, show the same behavior and their consumption is given by the cost of the corresponding transmission or reception only (results are not shown for space reasons).

Collisions and other transmissions

At last, we analyze the impact on the energy consumption in reception when the medium is occupied by collisions or by transmissions addressed to another device (i.e., sent to another MAC address).

To analyze the energy consumed by collisions, we configured a communication between two nodes and set up another node to act as interferer. This interferer was implemented by setting the carrier sense threshold at the highest value, which practically results in no carrier sensing, and using the lowest values for the CW, $SIFS$ and MCS parameters while deactivating the use of ACKs. In order to control the amount of time the interferer was sending data (i.e., the 'interference rate'), we used the `quiet element` option to silence the interface for a given amount of time every beacon period. Prior to our measurements, we performed extensive tests using different configurations of the `txpower` parameter and varying the relative physical location of the devices, to have a configuration in which simultaneous transmissions resulted in all frames being lost (i.e., no capture effect).

We present in Table 3 the main results from our analysis, namely, (i) power consumed in reception depends exclusively on the traffic actually received (see, e.g., when the interference rate goes from 0% to 50%), and (ii) collisions have the same impact as an idle medium (e.g., the cases with 100% interference rate coincides with ρ_{id}). Based on this, we conclude that collisions have no practical impact on the energy consumption at the receiver (for the transmitter, they have already been modeled in our analysis of retransmissions).

Table 3: Impact of collisions on reception.

Sent	Int. Rate	Received	Meas.	Model
1.2 Mbps	0%	1.2 Mbps	3.67	3.68
2.4 Mbps	50%	1.2 Mbps	3.67	3.68
2.4 Mbps	100%	0 Mbps	3.56	3.56
2.4 Mbps	0%	2.4 Mbps	3.80	3.81
4.8 Mbps	50%	2.4 Mbps	3.80	3.81
4.8 Mbps	100%	0 Mbps	3.56	3.56

To analyze the impact of the transmissions addressed to another station, we configured a communication between two nodes and measured the energy consumption at a third node that was in the transmission range of this communication. We observed that the energy consumed by this node was the same as if the medium was idle, which confirms that transmissions addressed to other stations practically do not consume energy. This is in agreement with our previous results: according to (5), the energy cost of listening to the PLCP plus headers is only 38 μJ/frame (for 6 Mbps MCS), which has practically no impact on the overall consumption.

5. ENERGY CONSUMPTION MODEL

The complete model

Based on the results obtained in the previous section, we now build the *complete model* for the power consumption of 802.11 devices. Summarizing our findings of (1)–(7), we have that the power consumed by an 802.11 device consists of the following components: (i) the idle consumption, ρ_{id}, (ii) the cross-factor for the packets generated by the application, P_{xg}, (iii) the power required to transmit them, P_{tx}, (vi) the power consumed in retransmissions, P_{retx}, (v) the power spent in receiving frames, P_{rx}, (vi) the cross-factor for the received frames, P_{xr}, and (vii) the power spent on sending and receiving ACK frames, $P_{rx,Ack}$ and $P_{tx,Ack}$:

$$\mathbf{P} = \rho_{id} + P_{tx} + P_{xg} + P_{retx} + P_{rx} + P_{xr} + P_{rx,Ack} + P_{tx,Ack}. \tag{8}$$

By substituting the expressions obtained in the previous section for all the above components and regrouping the terms, we obtain:

$$\begin{aligned} \mathbf{P} &= \rho_{id} + \rho_{tx}(\lambda_g T_L + \lambda_g T_L R + \lambda_r T_{Ack}) \\ &+ \rho_{rx}(\lambda_r T_L + \lambda_g T_{Ack}) + \gamma_{xg}\lambda_g + \gamma_{xr}\lambda_r. \end{aligned} \tag{9}$$

By taking into account that $\lambda_g T_L + \lambda_g T_l R + \lambda_r T_{Ack}$ corresponds to the transmission airtime percentage τ_{tx}, and $\lambda_r T_L + \lambda_g T_{Ack}$ to reception airtime percentage τ_{rx}, the above equation can be rewritten as:

$$\boxed{\mathbf{P} = \rho_{id} + \rho_{tx}\tau_{tx} + \rho_{rx}\tau_{rx} + \gamma_{xg}\lambda_g + \gamma_{xr}\lambda_r.} \tag{10}$$

The above expression gives the model for the power consumption of an 802.11 device that we propose in this paper. As already mentioned in the previous section, the key difference between the above model and the 'traditional' one used in many previous works [7,9,11,12,15,17,23,30,40] is that the traditional model only includes the first three components (namely ρ_{id}, $\rho_{tx}\tau_{tx}$ and $\rho_{rx}\tau_{rx}$) while our model adds to these three components two additional ones ($\gamma_{xr}\lambda_r$ and $\gamma_{xg}\lambda_g$). As shown by our measurements, these two additional components account for a very significant portion of the power consumption, which renders the traditional model highly inaccurate.

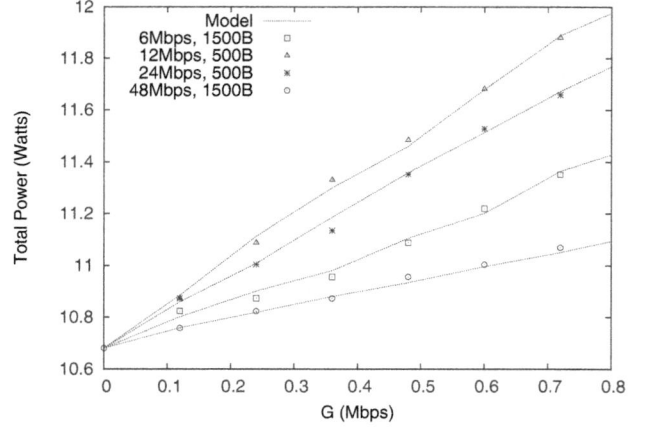

Figure 8: Model validation with multiple stations.

Out of the 9 variables in (10), 5 are constant parameters that depend on the device and the configuration of its communication parameters (ρ_{id}, ρ_{tx}, ρ_{rx}, γ_{xr} and γ_{xg}), while the other 4 parameters are variables that depend on the number of stations in the WLAN and their traffic generation behavior (τ_{tx}, τ_{rx}, λ_r and λ_g). In the following, we characterize the 5 constant parameters that determine the power consumption of the considered 802.11 devices for different values of MCS and `txpower`. To obtain these parameters, we use the expressions for the simple linear regression and the standard asymptotic error [26]. Following this, we obtain the numerical values given in Tables 4, 5 and 6 for the parameters that characterize the energy consumption of the Soekris, the Linksys and the Alix devices, respectively.

Model Validation

To validate our model in a general scenario with multiple sending and receiving stations, we consider a WLAN with one AP and three stations. Each station generates unicast traffic to the AP at a rate G, while the AP sends unicast traffic at the same rate G to each station. To apply the model of (10), we need to obtain the parameters τ_{tx}, τ_{rx}, λ_r and λ_g. These can be obtained from typical statistics recorded by the wireless driver, namely, number of generated frames (N_g), successful frames (N_{tx}), transmissions attempts (N_{at}), and received frames (N_{rx}). With these, if the experiment is run for a duration of T, λ_g and λ_r are computed as

$$\lambda_g = N_g/T, \quad \lambda_r = N_{rx}/T. \tag{11}$$

To compute τ_{tx} we account for all transmission attempts of the device plus the time spent sending the Acks, i.e.,

$$\tau_{tx} = (N_{at}T_L + N_{rx}T_{Ack})/T. \tag{12}$$

Similarly, to compute τ_{rx} we need to take into account the frames and the Acks received,

$$\tau_{rx} = (N_{rx}T_L + N_{tx}T_{ack})/T. \tag{13}$$

We compare the results given by our model against those obtained from measurements. Fig. 8 depicts these results for various combinations of L and MCS, sweeping along different traffic generation rates G in the x axis. We conclude from the figure that the proposed model is able to accurately predict the power consumption in a general scenario.

Table 4: Parametrization of the power consumption model for the Soekris device.

MCS		6 Mbps	12 Mbps	24 Mbps	48 Mbps
ρ_{rx} (W)		$0.16 \pm 8\%$	$0.27 \pm 5.6\%$	$0.6 \pm 11\%$	$1.14 \pm 3.5\%$
ρ_{tx} (W)	6 dBm	$0.52 \pm 3.1\%$	$0.55 \pm 4.6\%$	$0.81 \pm 5.3\%$	$1.2 \pm 1.6\%$
	9 dBm	$0.57 \pm 2.1\%$	$0.59 \pm 1.8\%$	$0.88 \pm 2.3\%$	$1.24 \pm 2.7\%$
	12 dBm	$0.70 \pm 1.7\%$	$0.73 \pm 2.2\%$	$1.02 \pm 2.8\%$	$1.37 \pm 3.1\%$
	15 dBm	$0.86 \pm 2.2\%$	$0.89 \pm 2.3\%$	$1.17 \pm 2.5\%$	$1.58 \pm 3.3\%$
ρ_{id} (W)	$3.56 \pm 1.7\%$	γ_{xg} (mJ)	$0.93 \pm 1.2\%$	γ_{xr} (mJ)	$0.93 \pm 2.2\%$

Table 5: Parametrization of the power consumption model for the Linksys device.

MCS		6 Mbps	12 Mbps	24 Mbps	48 Mbps
ρ_{rx} (W)		$0.19 \pm 5.3\%$	$0.29 \pm 3.4\%$	$0.53 \pm 2.3\%$	$0.74 \pm 4.4\%$
ρ_{tx} (W)	6 dBm	$0.70 \pm 1.1\%$	$0.72 \pm 2.2\%$	$0.75 \pm 2.0\%$	$0.81 \pm 3.7\%$
	9 dBm	$0.77 \pm 1.4\%$	$0.81 \pm 2.6\%$	$0.84 \pm 2.3\%$	$0.88 \pm 3.4\%$
	12 dBm	$0.84 \pm 1.2\%$	$0.85 \pm 1.5\%$	$0.92 \pm 2.4\%$	$0.99 \pm 4.0\%$
	15 dBm	$0.97 \pm 0.9\%$	$1.0 \pm 1.5\%$	$1.04 \pm 2.1\%$	$1.08 \pm 3.7\%$
ρ_{id} (W)	$2.73 \pm 0.4\%$	γ_{xg} (mJ)	$0.46 \pm 3.3\%$	γ_{xr} (mJ)	$0.43 \pm 4.2\%$

Table 6: Parametrization of the power consumption model for the Alix device.

MCS		6 Mbps	12 Mbps	24 Mbps	48 Mbps
ρ_{rx} (W)		$0.24 \pm 4.2\%$	$0.27 \pm 3.7\%$	$0.31 \pm 6.4\%$	$0.44 \pm 6.8\%$
ρ_{tx} (W)	6 dBm	$0.27 \pm 7.4\%$	$0.33 \pm 9.1\%$	$0.35 \pm 11.4\%$	$0.38 \pm 5.2\%$
	9 dBm	$0.30 \pm 6.7\%$	$0.35 \pm 8.6\%$	$0.36 \pm 11.1\%$	$0.39 \pm 5.3\%$
	12 dBm	$0.35 \pm 5.7\%$	$0.38 \pm 7.9\%$	$0.39 \pm 7.7\%$	$0.43 \pm 7.0\%$
	15 dBm	$0.4 \pm 7.5\%$	$0.44 \pm 6.8\%$	$0.45 \pm 8.9\%$	$0.46 \pm 8.7\%$
ρ_{id} (W)	$3.68 \pm 0.5\%$	γ_{xg} (mJ)	$0.11 \pm 7.6\%$	γ_{xr} (mJ)	$0.09 \pm 8.5\%$

6. IMPLICATIONS ON DESIGN

The new energy consumption insight gathered in this paper may have significant implications on the design of energy-efficient mechanisms. On the one hand, existing schemes may need to be revisited so as to properly account for the impact of the cross-factor component. Indeed, according to traditional power consumption models (i.e., only baseline component plus a toll proportional to the airtime), mechanisms yielding shorter airtimes would *surely* bring about energy gains. With the cross factor, this *might not be any-more the case*, when the power savings attained at the radio interface are paid with an increased frame handling and its associated (*non marginal*) power consumption. On the other hand, the gained knowledge that a frame crossing the stack brings about a *fixed* penalty unrelated to the frame size may be exploited to devise techniques to *avoid* or *reduce* such energy toll.

In the following, with no pretense of completeness, we present *quantitative* examples that show how our new insights may affect existing energy efficient mechanisms as well as inspire novel approaches.

6.1 Reconsidering existing schemes

Packet relaying

Packet relaying in WLANs is commonly used to improve performance [6] and energy efficiency [19]. The rationale is that the use of a relay permits shorter transmission times, which compensate the impact of the extra number of hops, introducing a net gain. However, classical energy-efficiency analyses do not balance the airtime energy saving with the energy drain introduced by the additional frame processing,

a penalty which may *fundamentally affect the relevant conclusions.*

To quantitatively support this claim, we deployed a two-hop scenario comprising three nodes (sender, relay and receiver), and compared the power consumption in two different configurations (MCS chosen as in [6]): (*i*) traffic directly sent to the receiver (1-hop, at 6 Mbps), and (*ii*) relay node used (2-hops, both at 48 Mbps). Traffic is generated at a rate of $\lambda_g = 400$ fps with different frame sizes L, and packet forwarding in the relay is performed at the routing layer. In both configurations, the relay node is always active.[12]

Three types of results are shown in Fig. 9a: (*i*) experimental measurements, (*ii*) theoretical predictions using a traditional model that neglects the impact of crossing the protocol stack ('old'), and (*iii*) predictions using the model presented in this paper ('new'), with a cross-factor of 0.8 mJ at the relay to capture the cost of forwarding a packet at the routing layer.

Not (anymore) surprisingly, results for the two models are *qualitatively* different. According to the traditional model, packet relaying always provides a gain, since the energy consumption of the 2-hops case is always smaller than that of the 1-hop case. In contrast, according to the actual measurements and our model, we only gain from using the relay when packets are sufficiently long (i.e., when the airtime cost becomes dominant over the cross-factor penalty).

Multicasting in WLAN

In order to multicast a packet stream from an AP to N stations in a WLAN, two alternatives are possible: (*i*) an application layer multicast (ALM) service [20], and (*ii*) the

---

[12]In most of the analyses on energy efficiency of relaying, the relay does not use the "sleep mode" (see e.g. [19,36]).

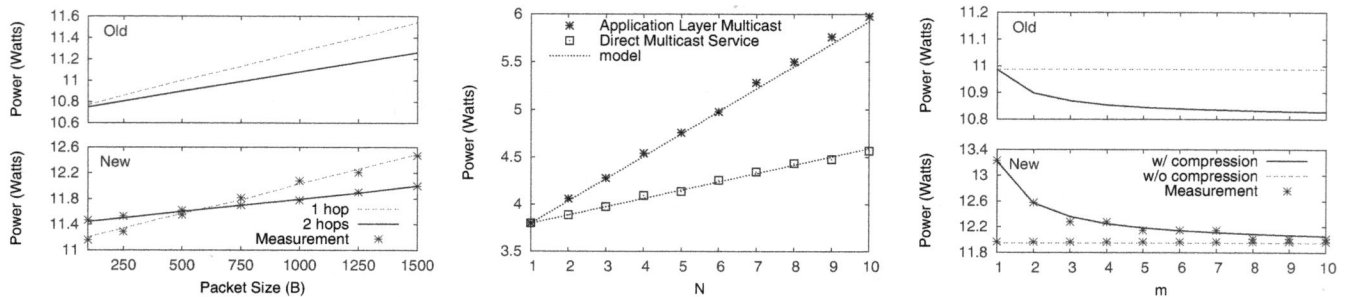

(a) Power consumption with and without relay as a function of the frame size.

(b) Power consumption as a function of the number of multicast receivers.

(c) Power consumed as a function of the compression factor.

Figure 9: Revisiting previous schemes under the new model.

Direct Multicast Service (DMS), part of the 802.11aa standard [4].[13] In the first case, the application generates each frame for each destination; in the second case, the MAC layer takes care of replicating the frame for each station subscribed to the multicast group.

Both approaches generate the same traffic over the air. Thus, according to the traditional model they should consume the same energy, whereas we expect DMS to be *significantly* more energy efficient, since less frames cross the protocol stack.

Indeed, we have experimentally verified this claim by deploying both techniques in a WLAN testbed, and by measuring the relevant power consumption of the AP. The experimental settings are: $MCS = 48$ Mbps, $L = 1000$ B, $\lambda_g = 200$ fps and a varying number of stations N. Fig. 9b shows that measurements well match the model predictions.[14] More interestingly, results show that DMS can save up to 25% (1.5 W) of the total power consumption (i.e., as much as 60% of the consumption over the baseline energy cost ρ_{id}) with respect to ALM for $N = 10$.

Data compression in multi-hop networks

In wireless multi-hop networks, data compression at intermediary nodes has been proposed to reduce the information relayed to the next hop [5,35]. According to traditional energy models, this operation *surely* saves energy, whereas our new energy consumption insights suggest that this may not be always true.

To analyze this, we used a three-node testbed consisting of a source, a sink and a relay, all using $MCS = 48$ Mbps. The source node generates 500-byte packets at 1200 fps and sends them to the relay. The relay runs an application that receives these packets, and *emulates* compression by forwarding 1 frame for every m frames received. Thus, our experiments do not capture the processing toll of the compression, and hence results reflect the best possible case for the performance of this compression scheme.

Fig. 9c shows total power consumption results (experimental ones, as well as predictions from old and new energy model), for different values of the compression ratio m, when

data is compressed (and forwarded) at the application layer. These results are compared against the case where data is not compressed at the relay node but simply forwarded towards the sink at the routing layer.

As anticipated, the old model (top curve) predicts that compression is always advantageous. However, experimental results, matched by the new model predictions (bottom curve) show that data compression does not provide any gain in terms of energy consumption, not even for compression rates as high as 10. The reason is that the energy gain resulting from the data compression is outweighted by the extra cost of handling the packets at the application layer (cross-factor of 0.93 mJ for sending and 0.93 mJ for receiving) instead of the routing layer (cross-factor of 0.8 mJ for forwarding). This example thus shows that mechanisms devised on the basis of traditional energy models may not only fail to provide the expected energy gains but may even *worsen* the actual energy consumption.

6.2 Novel ways to tackle energy efficiency

Packet Batching

As emerged in our work, energy consumption across the protocol stack relates to the handling of frame *units*, and is practically independent of the frame size. This suggests a straightforward energy saving strategy: *batch packets* into bundles at the highest suitable layer for a considered scenario, deliver the bundle across the stack, thus paying the energy price associated to a *single* unit, and then restore the original frames as late as possible down the stack. Unlike previous aggregation schemes for wireless networks, this mechanism (*i*) does not change the packets that are actually sent, but only modifies the way they are handled *within* the device [21], and (*ii*) does not save energy by reducing the cumulative *tail energy* consumed as a result of lingering in high power states after completing a transmission [8,29].

We quantified the attainable energy savings by implementing the scheme depicted in Fig. 10, which consists of (*i*) an "aggregator" at the application layer, which waits for n packets to generate a bundle and pass it to the TCP/IP stack, and (*ii*) a "de-aggregator" at the wireless driver, which splits the bundle back into the original frames. Experimental measurements are reported in Fig. 11 for 100 bytes packets, bundled up to an "aggregation factor" $n = 10$, and for various (application layer) frame generation rates λ_g. Frames are transmitted over the wireless channel at $MCS = 48$ Mbps.

---

[13]Both alternatives apply to traffic generated by a station as well as by a sender in the Internet; in the latter case, the traffic reaches the AP, which uses these techniques to multicast the traffic in the WLAN.

[14]The model accounts for a cross-factor of 0.75 mJ to reach the MAC and of 0.18 mJ from the MAC to the wireless card.

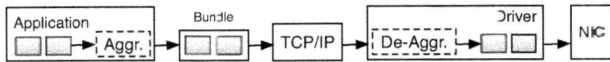

Figure 10: Packet batching with $n = 2$.

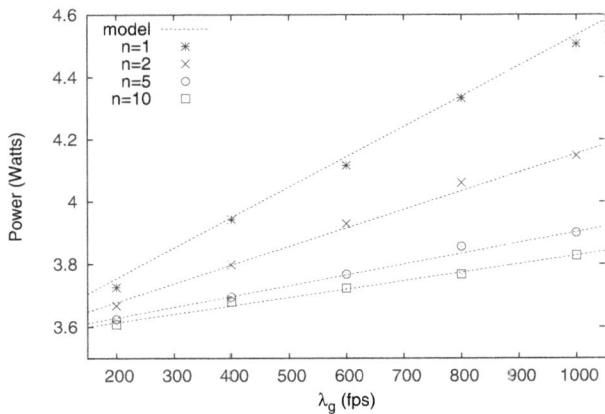

Figure 11: Energy consumption as a function of the 'aggregation factor'.

Table 7: Impact of using raw sockets.

MCS	L (B)	fps	Power (W) raw	UDP	Δ	Δ/fps
6 Mbps	1000	0.5k	4.26	4.35	0.09	0.19 mJ
12 Mbps	500	1k	4.50	4.69	0.19	0.19 mJ
24 Mbps	100	2k	5.05	5.48	0.43	0.21 mJ
48 Mbps	100	2k	5.03	5.44	0.41	0.20 mJ

7. CONCLUSIONS

In this paper, we have conducted a thorough measurement analysis of the power consumption of 802.11 devices that, in contrast to previous works, provides a detailed anatomy of the per-packet consumption and characterizes the total consumption of the device, and not only of its wireless interface. Our analysis is, to the best of our knowledge, the first one to reveal that a substantial fraction of energy is consumed when packets cross the protocols stack (the *cross-factor*). While other platforms than the ones analyzed (like e.g. mobile devices) may present quantitatively different results, our analysis shows that the cross-factor is likely to be substantial and cannot be neglected. Based on our findings, we have proposed a convenient energy consumption model that accurately predicts the power consumption of WLAN devices. We have shown that some schemes targeting energy efficiency may not provide the expected gains, and even worsen performance, when the cross-factor is taken into account. We have further shown some illustrative examples where the understanding gained with our analysis can be used to devise novel algorithms that save energy by reducing the cross factor, either by bundling packets, skipping parts of the protocol stack, or operating at the MAC layer. The lessons learned from these experiments provide some guidelines for applications developers pursuing energy-efficient operation in WLANs.

8. ACKNOWLEDGMENTS

This work has been supported by the European Community's Seventh Framework Programme under grant agreement no. 257263 (FLAVIA project) and by the Spanish Ministry of Economy and Competitiveness under grant agreement TEC2010-10440-E (DISTORSION project). We would like to thank F. Giust, M. Gramaglia and P. Salvador for their help in running remote experiments. We would also like to thank the shepherd and anonymous reviewers for their valuable feedback.

Results shown in Fig. 11 have a twofold implication. First, they provide further evidence that the cross-factor toll is practically independent of the frame size: the model matches well the measurements, and the use of an n-bundle reduces the energy toll above the driver by n. Second, energy savings are notable: with 1000 fps, an aggregation factor of 10 yields a saving of almost 0.8 W, and even the aggregation factor of just two packets may yield considerable savings (e.g., from 4.5 W to 4.15 W).

Obviously, casting the above described scheme into target applications (or even more general frameworks) is not straightforward,[15] and is out of the scope of this paper. Nevertheless, the above results suggest that such effort may be rewarded with notable energy saving.

Raw sockets

Since energy is consumed while crossing each layer of the protocol stack, another way to reduce energy consumption is to *skip layers* when they are not strictly necessary (e.g., in direct host-to-host wireless communication). To quantify the relevant gains, we have implemented an application that uses `raw` sockets, thus skipping the TCP/IP OS stack. Table 7 compares the power consumed using raw sockets ('raw') versus that consumed by using standard sockets ('UDP'), and reports the difference ('Δ'), for different configurations of L, MCS and λ_g.

Results show that the cross-factor can be reduced by approx. 0.2 mJ when skipping the TCP/IP layer, in line with the results of Fig. 4. This suggests to application developers with severe energy concerns that an extra development effort to avoid an unnecessary protocol stack is worth.

---

[15]Further technical problems must be dealt with, including the interaction with the TCP/IP protocol stack (e.g., if the target application requires data to be delivered as independent TCP/IP packets) and the application's requirements (e.g., the target application scenario must tolerate the extra batching delay introduced).

9. REFERENCES

[1] Power Consumption and Energy Efficiency Comparisons of WLAN Products. White paper, Atheros Comm., Apr. 2004.

[2] IEEE 802.11: Wireless LAN Medium Access Control (MAC) and Physical Layer (PHY) Specifications, 2007.

[3] Data Transfer over Wireless LAN Power Consumption Analysis. White paper, Intel Corp., Feb. 2009.

[4] IEEE 802.11: Amendment 2. MAC Enhancements for Robust Audio Video Streaming, 2012.

[5] S. J. Baek, G. de Veciana, and X. Su. Minimizing energy consumption in large-scale sensor networks through distributed data compression and hierarchical aggregation. *IEEE J. Selected Areas Comm.*, 22(6):1130–1140, Aug. 2004.

[6] P. Bahl et al. Opportunistic use of client repeaters to improve performance of WLANs. *IEEE/ACM Trans. on Networking*, 17(4):1160–1171, Aug. 2009.

[7] V. Baiamonte and C.-F. Chiasserini. Saving energy during channel contention in 802.11 WLANs. *Mobile Networks and Appl.*, 11(2):287–296, Apr. 2006.

[8] N. Balasubramanian, A. Balasubramanian, and A. Venkataramani. Energy consumption in mobile phones: A measurement study and implications for network applications. In *Proc. of ACM Internet Measurement Conference*, Nov. 2009.

[9] R. Bruno, M. Conti, and E. Gregori. Optimization of efficiency and energy consumption in p-persistent CSMA-based wireless LANs. *IEEE Trans. on Mobile Computing*, 1(1):10–31, Mar. 2002.

[10] A. Carroll and G. Heiser. An analysis of power consumption in a smartphone. In *Proc. of USENIX ATC*, June 2010.

[11] M. Carvalho, C. Margi, K. Obraczka, and J. Garcia-Luna-Aceves. Modeling energy consumption in single-hop IEEE 802.11 ad hoc networks. In *Proc. of ICCCN*, Oct. 2004.

[12] J.-C. Chen and K.-W. Cheng. EDCA/CA: Enhancement of IEEE 802.11e EDCA by contention adaption for energy efficiency. *IEEE Trans. on Wireless Comm.*, 7(8):2866–2870, Aug. 2008.

[13] S. Chiaravalloti, F. Idzikowski, and L. Budzisz. Power consumption of WLAN network elements. Technical report, Tech. Univ. Berlin, Aug. 2011.

[14] J.-P. Ebert, B. Burns, and A. Wolisz. A trace-based approach for determining the energy consumption of a WLAN network interface. In *Proc. of European Wireless*, Feb. 2002.

[15] M. Ergen and P. Varaiya. Decomposition of energy consumption in IEEE 802.11. In *Proc. of IEEE ICC*, June 2007.

[16] L. Feeney and M. Nilsson. Investigating the energy consumption of a wireless network interface in an ad hoc networking environment. In *Proc. of IEEE INFOCOM*, Apr. 2001.

[17] A. Garcia-Saavedra, P. Serrano, A. Banchs, and M. Hollick. Energy-efficient fair channel access for IEEE 802.11 WLANs. In *Proc. of IEEE WoWMoM*, June 2011.

[18] D. Halperin, B. Greenstein, A. Sheth, and D. Wetherall. Demystifying 802.11n power consumption. In *Proc. of HotPower*, Oct. 2010.

[19] X. He and F. Li. Throughput and energy efficiency comparison of one-hop, two-hop, virtual relay and cooperative retransmission schemes. In *Proc. of European Wireless*, Apr. 2010.

[20] M. Hosseini, D. Ahmed, S. Shirmohammadi, and N. Georganas. A survey of application-layer multicast protocols. *IEEE Comm. Surveys and Tutorials*, 9(3):58 –74, Sept. 2007.

[21] A. Jain and M. Gruteser. Benefits of packet aggregation in ad-hoc wireless network. Technical report, Univ. of Colorado at Boulder, Aug. 2003.

[22] A. P. Jardosh et al. Green WLANs: On-Demand WLAN Infrastructures. *Mobile Networks and Appl.*, 14(6):798–814, Dec. 2009.

[23] E.-S. Jung and N. H. Vaidya. An Energy Efficient MAC Protocol for Wireless LANs. In *Proc. of IEEE INFOCOM*, June 2002.

[24] G. Y. Li et al. Energy-efficient wireless communications: tutorial, survey, and open issues. *IEEE Wireless Comm.*, 18(6):28–35, Dec. 2011.

[25] E. Lochin, A. Fladenmuller, J. yves Moulin, S. Fdida, and A. Manet. Energy consumption models for ad-hoc mobile terminals. In *Proc. of Med-Hoc Net*, June 2003.

[26] J. S. Milton and J. C. Arnold. *Introduction to probability and statistics, 4th ed.* McGraw-Hill Higher Education, 2003.

[27] A. W. Min, R. Wang, J. Tsai, M. A. Ergin, and T.-Y. C. Tai. Improving energy efficiency for mobile platforms by exploiting low-power sleep states. In *Proc. of Computing Frontiers*, May 2012.

[28] A. Pathak, Y. C. Hu, and M. Zhang. Bootstrapping energy debugging on smartphones: a first look at energy bugs in mobile devices. In *Proc. of ACM HotNets*, Nov. 2011.

[29] F. Qian et al. Characterizing radio resource allocation for 3G networks. In *Proc. of ACM Internet Measurement Conference*, Nov. 2010.

[30] D. Qiao, S. Choi, A. Jain, and K. G. Shin. MiSer: an optimal low-energy transmission strategy for IEEE 802.11a/h. In *Proc. of ACM Mobicom*, Sept. 2003.

[31] D. Qiao, S. Choi, and K. Shin. Interference analysis and transmit power control in IEEE 802.11a/h wireless LANs. *IEEE/ACM Trans. on Networking*, 15(5):1007–1020, Oct. 2007.

[32] E. Rantala, A. Karppanen, S. Granlund, and P. Sarolahti. Modeling energy efficiency in wireless internet communication. In *Proc. of ACM MobiHeld*, Aug. 2009.

[33] A. Rice and S. Hay. Measuring mobile phone energy consumption for 802.11 wireless networking. *Pervasive and Mobile Computing*, 6(6):593–606, Dec. 2010.

[34] E. Rozner, V. Navda, R. Ramjee, and S. Rayanchu. NAPman: network-assisted power management for WiFi devices. In *Proc. of ACM MobiSys*, June 2010.

[35] A. B. Sharma, L. Golubchik, R. Govindan, and M. J. Neely. Dynamic data compression in multi-hop wireless networks. In *Proc. of ACM SIGMETRICS*, June 2009.

[36] C. Sun and C. Yang. Is two-way relay more energy efficient? In *Proc. of IEEE GLOBECOM*, Dec. 2011.

[37] J.-M. Tarascon. Key challenges in future Li-battery research. *Phil. Trans. of Royal Society A*, 368(1923):3227–3241, July 2010.

[38] J. R. Taylor. *An introduction to error analysis.* Oxford University Press, 1982.

[39] S.-L. Tsao and C.-H. Huang. A survey of energy efficient MAC protocols for IEEE 802.11 WLAN. *Computer Comm.*, 34(1):54–67, Jan. 2011.

[40] X. Wang, J. Yin, and D. P. Agrawal. Analysis and optimization of the energy efficiency in the 802.11 DCF. *Mobile Networks and Appl.*, 11(2):279–286, Apr. 2006.

[41] H. Wu, S. Nabar, and R. Poovendran. An energy framework for the network simulator 3 (NS-3). In *Proc. of SIMUTools*, Mar. 2011.

Traffic-Aware Techniques to Reduce 3G/LTE Wireless Energy Consumption

Shuo Deng and Hari Balakrishnan
Computer Science and Artificial Intelligence Laboratory
Massachusetts Institute of Technology
Cambridge, MA, USA
shuodeng@csail.mit.edu, hari@csail.mit.edu

ABSTRACT

The 3G/LTE wireless interface is a significant contributor to battery drain on mobile devices. A large portion of the energy is consumed by unnecessarily keeping the mobile device's radio in its "Active" mode even when there is no traffic. This paper describes the design of methods to reduce this portion of energy consumption by learning the traffic patterns and predicting when a burst of traffic will start or end. We develop a technique to determine when to change the radio's state from Active to Idle, and another to change the radio's state from Idle to Active. In evaluating the methods on real usage data from 9 users over 28 total days on four different carriers, we find that the energy savings range between 51% and 66% across the carriers for 3G, and is 67% on the Verizon LTE network. When allowing for delays of a few seconds (acceptable for background applications), the energy savings increase to between 62% and 75% for 3G, and 71% for LTE. The increased delays reduce the number of state switches to be the same as in current networks with existing inactivity timers.

CATEGORIES AND SUBJECT DESCRIPTORS

C.2.1 [**Computer-Communication Networks**]: Network Architecture and Design—*Wireless communication*; C.4 [**Performance of Systems**]: Performance attributes; Design studies

GENERAL TERMS

Design, Performance

KEYWORDS

Cellular Networks, Energy Saving

1. INTRODUCTION

Over a fifth of the 5.5 billion active mobile phones today have "broadband" data service, and this fraction is rapidly growing. Smartphones and tablets with wide-area cellular connectivity have become a significant, and in many cases, dominant, mode of network access. Improvements in the quality of such network connectivity suggest that mobile Internet access will soon overtake desktop access, especially with the continued proliferation of 3G networks and the emergence of LTE and 4G.

Wide-area cellular wireless protocols need to balance a number of conflicting goals: high throughput, low latency, low signaling overhead (signaling is caused by mobility and changes in the mobile device's state), and low battery drain. The 3GPP and 3GPP2 standards (used in 3G and LTE) provide some mechanisms for the cellular network operator and the mobile device to optimize these metrics [22, 3], but to date, deployed methods to minimize energy consumption have left a lot to be desired.

The 3G/LTE radio consumes significant amounts of energy; on the iPhone 4, for example, the stated talk time is "up to 7 hours on 3G" (i.e., when the 3G radio is on and in "typical" use) and "up to 14 hours on 2G".[1] On the Samsung Nexus S, the equivalent numbers are "up to 6 hours 40 minutes on 3G" and "up to 14 hours on 2G".[2] That the 3G/LTE interface is a battery hog is well-known to most users anecdotally and from experience, and much advice on the web and on blogs is available on how to extend the battery life of your mobile device.[3] Unfortunately, essentially all such advice says to "disable your 3G data radio" and "change your fetch data settings to reduce network usage". Such advice largely defeats the purpose of having an "always on" broadband-speed wireless device, but appears to be the best one can do in current deployments.

We show the measured values of 3G energy consumption for multiple Android applications in Figure 1.[4] This bar graph shows the percentage of energy consumed by different 3G radio states. For most of these applications (which are all background applications that can generate traffic without user input, except for Facebook), less than 30% of the energy consumed was during the actual transmission or reception of data. Previous research arrived at a similar conclusion [4]: about 60% of the energy consumed by the 3G interface is spent when the radio is not transmitting or receiving data.

In principle, one might imagine that simply turning the radio off or switching it to a low-power idle state is all it takes to reduce energy consumption. This approach does not work for three reasons. First, switching between the active and the different idle states takes a few seconds because it involves communication with the base station, so it should be done only if there is good reason to believe that making the transition is useful for a reasonable duration of time in the future. Second, switching states consumes energy, which means that if done without care, overall energy consumption will increase compared to not doing anything at all. Third, the switching incurs signaling overhead on the wireless network, which means

---

[1] http://www.apple.com/iphone/specs.html
[2] http://www.gsmarena.com/samsung_google_nexus_s-3620.php
[3] http://www.intomobile.com/2008/07/23/extend-your-iphone-3gs-battery-life/
[4] An HTC G1 phone connected to a power monitor [13], with only one application running, at one indoor location.

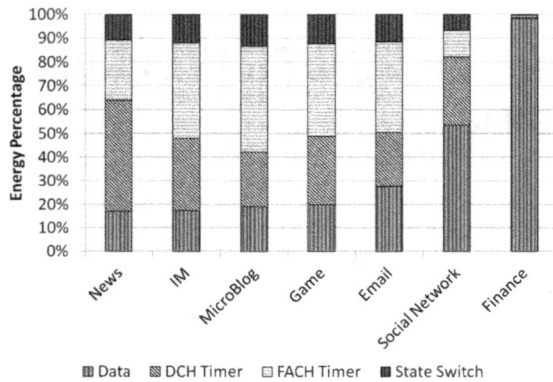

Figure 1: Energy consumed by the 3G interface. "Data" corresponds to a data transmission; "DCH Timer" and "FACH Timer" are each the energy consumed with the radio in the idle states specified by the two timers, and "State Switch" is the energy consumed in switching states. These timers and state switches are described in §2.

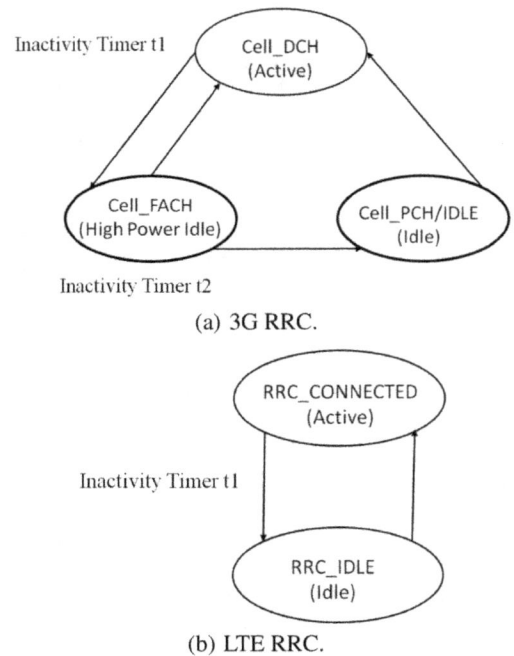

(a) 3G RRC.

(b) LTE RRC.

Figure 2: Radio Resource Control (RRC) State Machine.

that it should be done only if the benefits are substantial relative to the cost on the network.

This paper tackles these challenges and develops a solution to reduce 3G/LTE energy consumption without appreciably degrading application performance or introducing a significant amount of signaling overhead on the network. Unlike currently deployed methods that simply switch between radio states after fixed time intervals—an approach known to be rather crude and sub-optimal [21, 4, 11, 19])– our approach is to observe network traffic activity on the mobile device and switch between the different radio states by adapting to the workload.

The key idea is that by observing network traffic activity, a *control module* on the mobile device can adapt the 3G/LTE radio state transitions to the workload. We apply statistical machine learning techniques to predict network activity and make transitions that are suggested by the statistical models. This approach is well-suited to the emerging *fast dormancy* mechanism [1, 2] that allows a radio to rapidly move between the Active and Idle states and vice versa. Our goal is to reduce the energy consumed by networked background applications on mobile devices.

This paper makes the following contributions:

1. A traffic-aware design to control the state transitions of a 3G/LTE radio taking energy consumption, latency, and signaling overhead into consideration. The design incorporates two algorithms:
   (a) MakeIdle, which uses aggregate traffic activity to predict the end of an active session by building a conditional probability distribution of network activity.
   (b) MakeActive, which delays the start of a new session by a few seconds to allow multiple sessions to all become active at the same time and therefore reduce signaling overhead. This method is appropriate for non-interactive background applications that can tolerate some delay.
2. An experimental evaluation of these methods on real usage data from nine users over 28 total days on four different carriers. We find that the energy savings compared to the status quo range between 51% and 66% across the carriers for 3G, and is 67% on the Verizon LTE network. When allowing for delays of a few seconds (acceptable for background applications), the energy savings increase to between 62% and 75% for 3G, and 71% for

LTE. The increased delays reduce the number of state switches to be the same as in current networks with existing inactivity timers.

2. BACKGROUND

This section describes the 3G/LTE state machine and its energy consumption.

2.1 3G/LTE State Machine

The Radio Resource Control (RRC) protocol, which is part of the 3GPP standard, incorporates the state machine for energy management shown in Figure 2.

The base station maintains two inactivity timers, t_1 and t_2, for each mobile device. For a device maintaining a dedicated channel in the Active (Cell_DCH) state with the base station, if the base station sees no data activity to or from the device for t_1 seconds, it will switch the device from the dedicated channel to a shared low-speed channel, transitioning the device to the "High-power idle" (Cell_FACH) state. This state consumes less power than "Active", but still consumes a non-negligible amount of power. If there is no further data activity between the device and base station for another t_2 seconds, the base station will turn the device to either the Cell_PCH or IDLE state. We refer to the Cell_PCH and IDLE states together as the "Idle" state, because the device consumes essentially no power in either state. For LTE networks (Figure 2(b)), there are only two states: RRC_CONNECTED and RRC_IDLE (there are substates in RRC_CONNECTED [8], which we do not discuss here because they are not relevant), and one inactivity timer, shown as t_1.

The inactivity timers (t_1 and t_2) are useful because a state transition from "Idle" to "Active" (Cell_DCH) incurs significant delays. For example, in our measurements in the Boston area, these values are ≈ 1.4 seconds on AT&T's 3G network, ≈ 3.6 seconds on T-Mobile's 3G network, ≈ 2.0 seconds on Sprint's 3G network, ≈ 1.0 second on Sprint's LTE network, ≈ 1.2 seconds on Verizon's 3G network, and ≈ 0.6 seconds on Verizon's LTE network (these numbers may vary across different regions). Each state transition also consumes energy on the device and incurs signaling overhead for the base station to allocate a dedicated channel to the device. The inactivity timers also prevent the base station from frequently releasing and re-allocating channels to devices which causes per-packet delay for the device to be high.

The description given above captures the salient features of the 3GPP standard. Another popular 3G standard is 3GPP2 [3]. Although 3GPP2 networks use different techniques, from the perspective of energy consumption, they are essentially identical to 3GPP [21]; like 3GPP, 3GPP2 networks also have different power levels for different states on the device side, and use similar inactivity timers for state transitions. For concreteness, in this paper, we focus on 3GPP networks.

2.2 Energy Consumption

We measured the power consumption and inactivity timer values using the Monsoon Power Monitor [13]. Figure 3 shows graphs of our measurements during a radio state switches cycle on an HTC Vivid smartphone in AT&T's 3G network and on a Galaxy Nexus smartphone in Verizon's LTE network. (We show results for other carriers in Section 6.) During the High-power idle (FACH for AT&T) and part of Active (DCH for AT&T, RRC_CONNECTED for Verizon) states, there is no data transmission. The RRC state machine keeps the radio on here in case a new transmission or reception occurs in the near future. Consistent with previous work [4], we use the term *tail* to refer to this duration when the radio is on but there is no data transmission.

We measured the inactivity timer values in AT&T's 3G network in the Boston area to be $t_1 \approx 6.2$ seconds and $t_2 \approx 10.4$ seconds. The energy consumed at the end of a data transfer when the radio is in one of the two Idle states before turning off is termed the *tail energy*; this energy can be 60% or more of the total energy consumption of 3G [4].

3GPP Release 7 [1] proposed a feature called *fast dormancy*, which allows the device to actively release the channel by itself before the inactivity timer times out on the base station. One of the issues that then arises is that the base station loses control over the connection when mobile devices are able to disconnect by themselves. In 3GPP Release 8 [2], fast dormancy was changed: the mobile device first sends a fast dormancy request, and the base station will decide to release the channel or not. In Europe, Nokia Siemens Networks has applied Network Controlled Fast Dormancy based on 3GPP Release 8. Because it is not entirely clear what policy any given network carrier will use to decide whether to release the channel upon receiving a request at a base station, in our simplified model, we assume that if the base station is running 3GPP Release 8, whenever the phone sends a fast dormancy request to the base station, the base station will accept and release the channel. Our goal is to evaluate the network signaling overhead of such a strategy as a way to help inform network-carrier policy.

3. DESIGN

The key insight in our approach to reduce 3G energy consumption is that by observing and adapting to network activity, a *control module* can predict when to put the radio into its Idle state, and when to move from Idle to Active state. These state transitions take a non-trivial amount of time—between 1 and 3 seconds—and also add signaling overhead because each transition is accompanied by a few messages between the device and the base station. Hence, the intuition in our approach is to predict the occurrence of *bursts* of network activity, so that the control module can put the radio into the idle mode when it believes a burst has ended, which means there will not be any more traffic in the future for a relatively long period of time. Conversely, the idea is to put the radio in active mode when "enough" bursts of traffic accumulate.

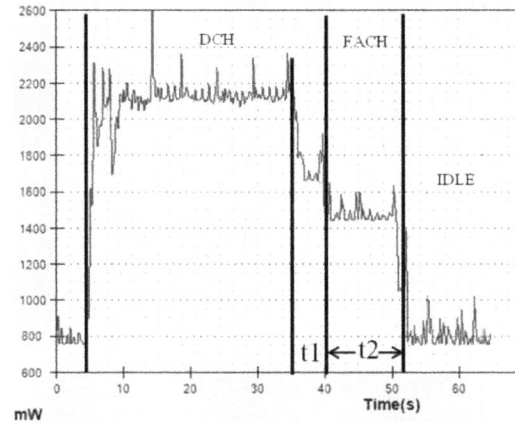

(a) HTC Vivid in AT&T 3G Network.

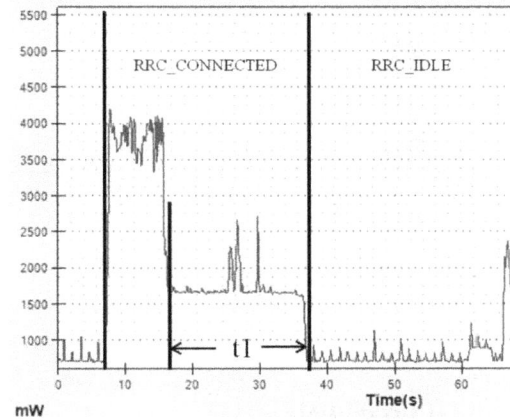

(b) Galaxy Nexus in Verizon LTE Network.

Figure 3: The measured power consumption of the different RRC states. Exact values can be found in Table 2. In these figures the power level for IDLE/RRC_IDLE is non-zero because of the CPU and LED screen power consumption.

To achieve the prediction, our approach needs to observe network activity and be able to pause data transmissions. To make our approach work with existing applications, we should not require any change to the application code. To achieve these goals, we modified the socket layer and added a control module inside the Android OS source code.

Our system has two software modules: one that modifies the library used by applications to communicate with the socket layer, and another that implements the control module, as shown in Figure 4. The first module informs the control module of all socket calls; in response, the control module configures the state of the radio. The fast dormancy interface is shown as a dashed module because our system uses it if it is available.

The control module implements two different methods. The first method, called MakeIdle, runs when the radio is in the Active state (Cell_DCH or RRC_CONNECTED) and determines when the radio should be put into the Idle (IDLE or Cell_PCH or RRC_IDLE) state. The second method, called MakeActive, runs when the radio is in the Idle state. In this state, it cannot send any packets without first moving to the Active state; MakeActive determines how long the radio should be idle before moving to active state.

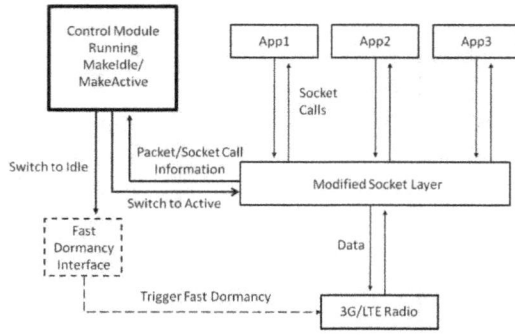

Figure 4: System design.

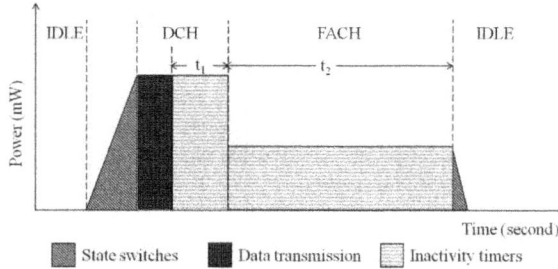

Figure 5: Simplified power model for 3G energy consumption (for an LTE model, t_2 equals to zero).

4. MAKEIDLE ALGORITHM

Instead of using a fixed inactivity timer, the MakeIdle method dynamically decides when to put the radio into Idle mode after each packet transmission or reception. We first show in §4.1 how to compute the optimal decision *given* complete knowledge of a packet trace: the result is that the radio should be turned to Idle if there is a gap of more than a certain threshold amount of time in the trace, which depends on measurable parameters. Then, in §4.2, we develop an online method to predict idle durations that will exceed this threshold by modeling the idle time using a conditional probability distribution.

4.1 Optimal Decision From Offline Trace Analysis

Suppose we are given a packet trace containing the timestamps of packets sent and received on a mobile device. Our goal is to determine offline when to turn the radio to the Idle state to minimize the energy consumed.

Figure 5 shows a simplified power model we use to calculate tail energy. If the inter-arrival time between two adjacent packets is t seconds, then $E(t)$, the energy consumed by the current RRC protocol with inactivity timer values t_1 and t_2 (see Figure 2), is

$$E(t) = \begin{cases} t \cdot P_{t_1} & 0 < t \leq t_1 \\ t_1 \cdot P_{t_1} + (t-t_1) \cdot P_{t_2} & t_1 < t \leq t_1 + t_2 \\ t_1 \cdot P_{t_1} + t_2 \cdot P_{t_2} + E_{switch} & t > t_1 + t_2 \end{cases}$$

Here, P_{t_1} and P_{t_2} are the power values for the active state and high-power idle state, respectively; the power consumed in the low-power idle state is negligible. E_{switch} is the energy consumed by switching the radio to Idle mode after the first packet transmission and then switching it back to Active for the second packet transmission. It

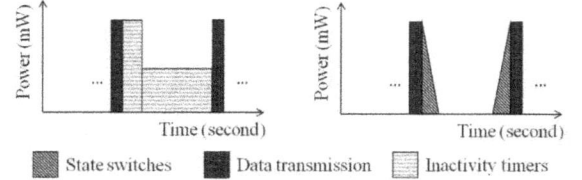

Figure 6: If the energy consumed by the picture on the right is less than the one on the left, then turning the radio to Idle soon after the first transmission will consume less energy than leaving it on. The energy is easily calculated by integrating the power profiles over time.

is a fixed value for a given type of mobile device and is easy to measure.

On the other hand, if the radio switches to Idle mode immediately after the first packet transmission finishes, the energy consumed is just E_{switch}.

To minimize the energy consumed between packets, the radio should switch to Idle mode after a packet transmission if, and only if, $E_{switch} < E(t)$. Notice that because $E(t)$ is a monotonically non-decreasing function of t, there exists a value for t, which we call $t_{threshold}$, for which $E_{switch} < E(t)$ if and only if $t > t_{threshold}$. This expression quantifies the intuitive idea that after each packet, the radio should switch to Idle mode only if we know that next packet will not arrive soon; concretely, not arrive in the following $t_{threshold}$ seconds. For example, on an HTC Vivid phone in the AT&T 3G network deployed in the Boston area, $t_{threshold}$ works out to be 1.2 seconds.

4.2 Online Prediction

To minimize energy consumption in practice, we need to predict whether the next packet will arrive (to be received or to be sent) within $t_{threshold}$ seconds. Of course, we would like to make this prediction as quickly as possible, because we would then be able to switch the radio to Idle mode promptly. We make this prediction by assuming that the packet inter-arrival distribution observed in the recent past will hold in the near future. After each packet, the method waits for a short period of time and sees whether any more packets arrive. If a packet arrives, the method resets and waits, but if not, it means a transfer may be finished and the radio should switch to Idle mode.

The strategy works as follows:

1. Without loss of generality, suppose the current time is $t = 0$. Compute the conditional probability that no packet will arrive within $t_{wait} + t_{threshold}$ seconds, *given that* no packet has arrived in t_{wait} seconds.

$$P(t_{wait}) = \mathbb{P}(\text{no packet in } t_{wait} + t_{threshold} | \text{no packet in } t_{wait})$$

This conditional distribution is easy to compute given observations of the packet arrival times of the last several packets. From the traces we collected, we observed that $P(t_{wait})$ increases as t_{wait} increases, when t_{wait} is in the range of $[0, t_{threshold}]$ (if t_{wait} is greater than $t_{threshold}$, it means the radio has been idle for too long time after the packet transmission and there is not much room for energy saving). This property implies that the longer the radio waits and sees no packet, the higher the likelihood that no packet will arrive soon.

2. Now we need to find t_{wait} in order to make the likelihood "high enough". During t_{wait}, the radio consumes energy, so to decide how much is "high enough", we should take energy consump-

tion into account. Our answer is: $P(t_{wait})$ is "*high enough*" if the expected energy consumption of waiting for t_{wait} and then switching states is less than the expected consumption of waiting for the inactivity timer to time out in the next t_{wait} seconds.

The method determines t_{wait} by *minimizing* the expected energy consumption across all possible values of t_{wait}, and taking the value that minimizes the consumption. We explain how below.

The expected energy consumption of waiting for t_{wait} and then switching states is:

$$\mathbb{E}[E_{wait\_switch}] \quad = \quad [E_{switch} + E(t_{wait})]$$

Here, $E(t_{wait})$ is the energy consumed by waiting for t_{wait} seconds and E_{switch} is the energy consumed by state switches.

The expected energy consumption of waiting for inactivity timer to time out is:

$$\mathbb{E}[E_{no\_switch}] = \int_{t=0}^{t_1+t_2} \mathbb{P}(inter\_arrival\_time = t)\frac{aE(t)}{dt}dt \quad (1)$$

The following expression now is a function of t_{wait}:

$$f(t_{wait}) = \mathbb{E}[E_{no\_switch}] - \mathbb{E}[E_{wait\_switch}]. \quad (2)$$

The best t_{wait} is the one that maximize $f(t_{wait})$, which means that the corresponding value for t_{wait} gives us highest expected gains over the current RRC protocol.

In implementing this algorithm, we take the latest n packets (we discuss how to choose n in Section 6.3) that the control module has seen, to construct the inter-arrival distribution. As new packets are seen, the "window" of the n packet slides forward, and the distribution is adjusted accordingly.

5. MAKEACTIVE ALGORITHM

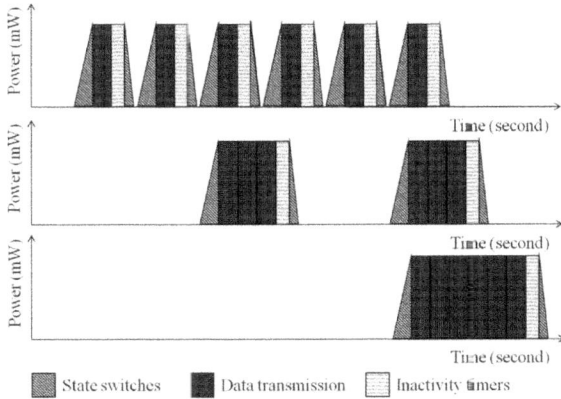

Figure 7: "Shift" traffic to reduce number of state switches.

MakeIdle reduces the 3G wireless energy consumption by switching the radio to Idle mode frequently. Figure 7 (top) shows that MakeIdle may bring more state switches from Idle to Active and from Active to Idle. These switches cause signaling overhead at the base station. One idea to reduce the signaling overhead is to "shift" the traffic bursts in order to combine several traffic bursts together [19, 4], as shown in Figure 7(middle and bottom chart). The longer earlier bursts are delayed, the more bursts we can accumulate and the fewer state switches occur.

In this section, we only consider those background applications for which one can delay the traffic for a few seconds without appreciably degrading the user's experience, not interactive applications where delaying by a few seconds is unacceptable. Our approach differs from previous work [19, 4], where the authors aim to reduce energy consumption by batching bursts of traffic together so that they can share the tail energy. By contrast, because the MakeIdle algorithm already reduces energy by turn radio to the idle mode, MakeActive focuses on reducing the number of state switches to a level comparable to the status quo. As a result, the amount of delay introduced by this method should be much smaller than in previous work.

We first consider a relatively straightforward scheme in which the start of a session (i.e., a burst of packets) can be delayed by at most a certain maximum delay bound, T_{fix_delay}. We then apply a machine learning algorithm, which induces the same number of state switches as the fixed delay bound method, but in addition reduces the delay for each traffic burst. Our contribution lies in the application of this algorithm to learn idle durations for the radio, balancing signaling overhead and increased traffic latency.

5.1 Fixed Delay Bound

A simple strawman is to set a fixed delay bound, T_{fix_delay}. When the radio is in Idle state and a socket tries to start a new session at current time t, and no other such requests are pending, the control module decides to delay turning the radio to Active mode until $t + T_{fix\_delay}$, so that other new sessions that might come between time t and $t + T_{fix\_delay}$ will all get buffered and will start together at time $t + T_{fix\_delay}$. There is a trade-off between the delay bound and the number of sessions that can be buffered. Note that once a session begins, its packets do not get further delayed, which means that TCP dynamics should not be affected by this method.

In the current RRC protocol, the inactivity timers t_1 and t_2 guarantee that after each traffic burst, any new burst comes within $t_1 + t_2$ will not introduce extra state switches between Idle and Active. So in our implementation, we make $T_{fix\_delay} = k \times (t_1 + t_2)$ where k is the average number of bursts during each of the radio's active period.

5.2 Learning Algorithm

The problem with a fixed delay bound is that it does not adapt to the traffic pattern. Every time the delay is triggered, the first transmission may incur a delay of as long as T_{fix_delay}. We show in the evaluation that a large portion of the traffic bursts get delayed by T_{fix_delay}. However, waiting as long as T_{fix_delay} may be overkill; as data accumulates (especially from different sessions), there comes a point when the radio should switch to Active and data sent before this delay elapses, which will reduce the expected session delay while still saving energy.

We apply the *bank of experts* machine learning algorithm [14, 16]. Each "expert" proposes a *fixed* value for the session delay. In each iteration (each time the radio is in Idle mode and a transmission occurs), we computed a weighted average value from the experts and update the weights according to a *loss function*. The process to update each expert's weight is a standard machine learning process, detailed in the appendix.

The loss function is a crucial component of the scheme and depends on the details of the problem to which the learning is applied. Because our goal is to reduce number of state switches by batching, in addition to the delay, the loss function should express the trade-off between the total time delayed for all the buffered sessions and the number of session buffered. The following equation captures this tradeoff:

$$L(i) = \gamma Delay(T_i) + \frac{1}{b}, \gamma > 0$$

Here, γ is a constant scaling parameter between the two parts of the loss function (we chose 0.008 in our implementation because it gave the best energy-saving results among the values we tried). $Delay(T_i)$ is the aggregate time delayed over b sessions, if we choose expert i. b is the number of sessions currently buffered, which is equivalent to the number of state switches avoided. The $1/b$ term ensures that as the number of buffered sessions increases, the value of this part of the loss function reduces, while the other term $\gamma Delay(T_i)$ may increase.

Let t_j be the arrival time of the jth session. Then,

$$Delay(T_i) = \sum_{j=1}^{b} T_i - t_j.$$

6. EVALUATION

We evaluate MakeActive and MakeIdle using trace-driven simulation. We first describe the simulation setup. Then, we evaluate the two methods using traces collected from popular applications run by a few real users. Finally, we compare these methods across different cellular networks.

6.1 Simulation Setup

Energy model. One challenge in our simulations is to accurately estimate the energy consumed given a packet trace containing packet arrival times and packet lengths. Previous work [8] showed that for 3G/LTE, the value of the energy consumed per bit changes as the size of traffic bursts changes. Because our methods may change the size of the traffic bursts, (e.g., MakeIdle may decide to switch the radio to Idle mode within a burst), we build our energy model using the energy consumed per second, which is the power for sending or receiving data.

Network	Sending Power (mW)	Receiving Power (mW)
AT&T 3G	2043	1177
Verizon LTE	2928	1737

Table 1: Average power in mW measured on Galaxy Nexus in Verizon Network. The energy consumed by CPU and screen is subtracted.

Table 1 shows the average power consumed when the phone is sending or receiving bulk data using UDP. Based on this value, we estimate the energy consumed within a traffic burst using the packet inter-arrival time and the packet direction (incoming/outgoing): for each packet reception, the energy consumed is the inter-arrival time multiplied by the average receive power, and similarly for each packet transmission.

To justify this method, we measure the smartphone's energy consumption when it is sending and receiving TCP bulk transfers of different lengths. Each experiment contains five runs. In each run, the phone sends and receives TCP bulk transfers of three lengths (10 kBytes, 100 kBytes and 1000 kBytes) one after another, with a long-enough idle period between each transfer. We find that, on average, the error in the estimated energy consumption is within 10% or less of the true measured value.

One caveat in our energy model is that because fast dormancy is not yet supported on US 3G/LTE networks, we were unable to accurately measure the delay to turn the radio from Active to Idle and the energy consumed. We believe, however, that one can

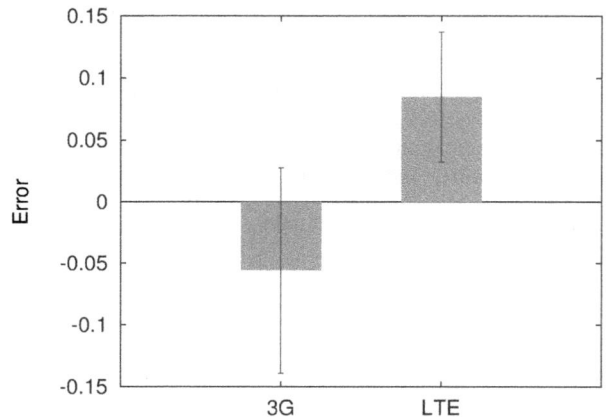

Figure 8: Simulation energy error for Verizon 3G and LTE networks.

approximate this value by measuring the delay and energy consumed in turning the data connection off on the phone. In practice, we expect the delay and energy of fast dormancy switching to be lower, so we model the turn-off energy and delay for fast dormancy to be 50% of the values measured while turning the radio off. We also evaluated our methods for reasonable fractions (10%, 20%, 40%) other than 50%, and found that the results did not change appreciably; hence, we believe that our conclusions are likely to hold if one were to implement the methods on a device that supports fast dormancy.

Trace data sets. We collected `tcpdump` traces on an HTC G1 phone running Android 2.2 for the seven different categories of applications listed below. For each category, we choose a popular application in the Android Market. Each collected trace was 2 hours long. Most of these applications have the "always on" property in that they usually send or receive data over the network whenever they run, without necessarily requiring user input.

News: A news reader that has a background process running to fetch breaking news.

Instant Message (IM): An IM application that sends heartbeat packets to the server periodically, typically every 5 to 20 seconds.

Micro-blog: A micro-blog application, which automatically fetches new tweets without user input.

Game with ad bar: A game that can run offline, but with an advertisement bar that changes the content roughly once per minute.

Email: This application is run mostly in the background, synchronizing with an email server every five minutes.

Social Network: A user using the social network application to read the news feeds, clicks to see pictures, and posts comments. When running in background, this application updates only every 30 minutes. We did not collect much background traffic from it. We use the foreground traffic trace for comparison trace.

Finance: An application for monitoring the stock market, which updates roughly once per second when running in the foreground.

We also collected real user data from six different users using Nexus S phones in T-Mobile's 3G network and from four different users using Galaxy Nexus phones in Verizon's 3G/LTE network. All the phones run `tcpdump` in the background. Across all users, we collected 28 days of data. For each user, the amount of data collected varies from two to five days.

6.2 Comparison of Energy Savings

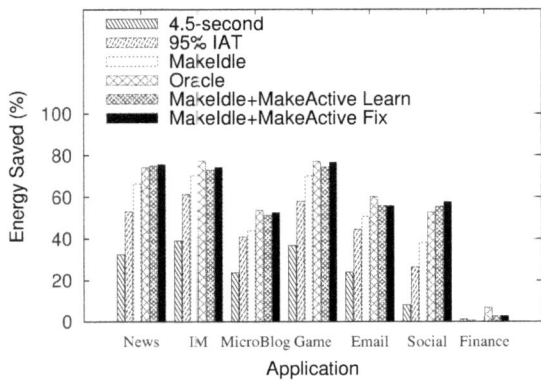

Figure 9: Energy savings for different applications. "4.5-second" sets the inactivity timer to 4.5 seconds. "95% IAT" uses the 95th percentile of packet inter-arrival time observed over the entire trace as the inactivity timer. "MakeIdle" shows the energy saved by our MakeIdle algorithm. "MakeIdle +MakeActive Learn" and "MakeIdle +MakeActive Fix" show the energy savings when running MakeIdle together with two different MakeActive algorithms: learning algorithm and fixed delay bound algorithm. Oracle shows the maximum achievable energy savings without delaying any traffic.

We compare MakeIdle against MakeIdle together with Make-Active (shown as MakeIdle+MakeActive), and against two other schemes. The first other scheme is proposed in [6], where a trace analysis found that 95% of the packet inter-arrival time values are smaller than 4.5 seconds. The proposal sets the inactivity timer to a fixed value, $t_1 + t_2 = 4.5$ seconds. We call this approach "4.5-second tail".

The second other scheme is that instead of using the value of 4.5 seconds, we draw the CDF of our traces and get the 95th percentile of packet inter-arrival time observed in each user's trace. We call this approach "95% IAT", which for the data shown in Figure 9 corresponding to one user happened to be 1.67 seconds (the value does vary across users and also across applications). In our evaluation, we are granting this scheme significant leeway because we test the scheme over the same data on which it has been trained. Despite this advantage, we find that this scheme has significant limitations.

The "Oracle" is an algorithm in which the packet inter-arrival time is known before packet comes, and the algorithm compares the inter-arrival time with the $t_{threshold}$ defined in Section 4.1. The Oracle scheme gives us an upper bound of how much energy can be saved without introducing extra delay. Our MakeIdle + MakeActive algorithm sometimes outperforms the Oracle because it can delay packets and further reduce the number of state switches.

Figure 9 shows that MakeIdle consistently achieves energy savings close to the Oracle scheme, and outperforms the "4.5-second" and "95%" IAT schemes. When both MakeIdle and MakeActive are combined, the savings are greater.

The "95% IAT" scheme gives little or negative savings for "News" and "IM", while the other schemes provide significant positive savings. This is because the 95% percentile of the inter-arrival time is highly variable and cannot guarantee savings in all situations. It is not a robust method.

Figures 10(a) and 11(a) show the estimated energy savings for each user in the Verizon 3G and Verizon LTE networks, respectively.

In these results, the different schemes are as explained above, except that the 95% IAT scheme uses per-user (but not per-application) inter-arrival time CDFs. The gains of MakeIdle and MakeActive over the other schemes are substantial in most cases. In the LTE case, the 95% IAT scheme sometimes saves the most energy (for user 2 and user 3), but sometimes performs worse than MakeIdle (for user 1); it depends on the user, again showing a lack of robustness. Perhaps more importantly, the number of state switches is enormous compared to the other schemes, making it extremely unlikely to be useful in practice.

6.3 MakeIdle Evaluation

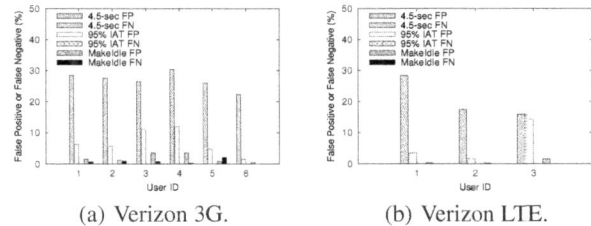

(a) Verizon 3G. (b) Verizon LTE.

Figure 12: False ("FP" short for false positive) and missed switches ("FN" short for false negative).

To understand why MakeIdle outperforms the other methods, we calculate the fraction of *false switches* and *missed switches* for each method. We use "Oracle" as ground truth and define these ratios as follows:

FalseSwitch(FalsePositive) = $N_{FS}/(N_{FS} + N_{TN})$. Here, N_{FS} is the number of cases where the algorithm switches the radio to Idle but Oracle decides to keep the radio in Active mode. N_{TN} is the number of cases where both Oracle and the algorithm decide to keep the radio Active.

MissedSwitch(FalseNegative) = $N_{MS}/(N_{MS} + N_{TP})$. Here, N_{MS} is the number of cases where the algorithm decides to keep the radio in the Active mode but Oracle switches the radio to Idle. N_{TP} is the number of cases where both Oracle and the algorithm switch the radio to Idle. A high missed switch value means the algorithm tends to keep the radio in Active mode, which may not be energy-efficient.

Figure 12 shows these two ratios for different data sets. Note that these values for MakeIdle are much smaller than for the other two algorithms.

Figure 13 shows the false positive and false negative rates (in percentage) as a function of the number of recent packets used to construct the distribution defined in Section 4.2. We find that the false negative rate is relatively constant, while the false positive rate decreases as the window size increases. For all the other results shown in §6, we use $n = 100$.

Another factor that affects battery consumption is the waiting time between a packet arrival and the time at which the algorithm actually switches the radio to Idle. For the "4.5-second tail" scheme, the waiting time is always 4.5 seconds. Similarly, the waiting time for "95% IAT" is 0.85 seconds for 3G and 0.01 seconds for LTE. In contrast, MakeIdle chooses the waiting time dynamically, achieving better gains. Figure 14 shows an example of waiting time changes in a user's trace in Verizon 3G network.

6.4 MakeActive Evaluation

Although shortening t_{wait} with the MakeIdle algorithm saves considerable amounts of energy, it may bring about more state switches between the Low-power idle and Active states. But when there are multiple applications running at the same time, or when one

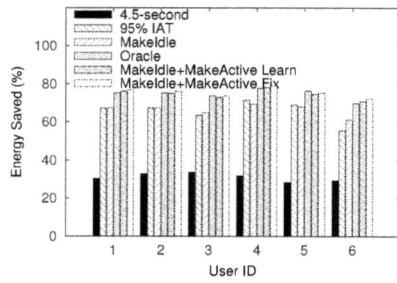

(a) Energy savings.

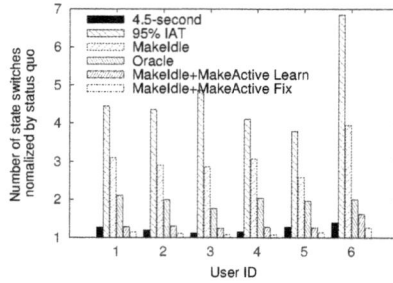

(b) Number of state switches normalized by status quo.

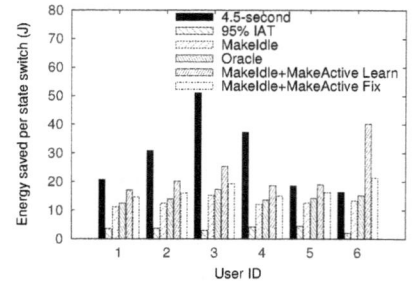

(c) Energy saved per state switch.

Figure 10: Energy savings and signaling overhead (number of state switches) across users in the Verizon 3G network.

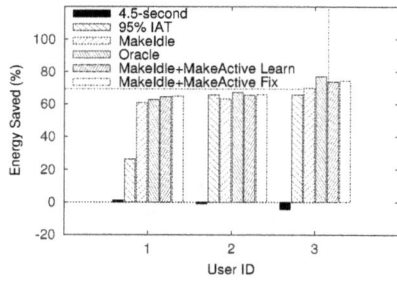

(a) Energy savings.

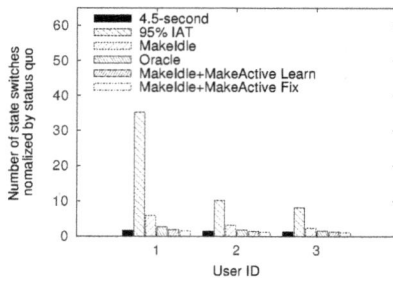

(b) Number of state switches normalized by status quo.

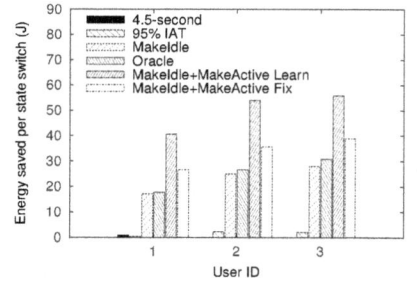

(c) Energy saved per state switch.

Figure 11: Energy savings and signaling overhead (number of state switches) across users in the Verizon LTE network.

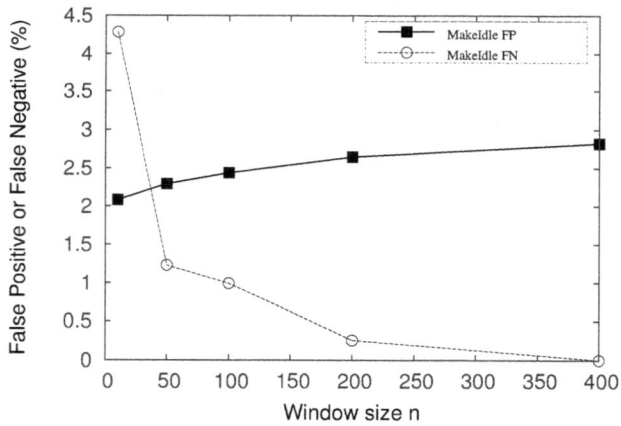

Figure 13: False ("FP") and missed switches ("FN") changes as the number of packets used to construct distribution defined in Section 4.2.

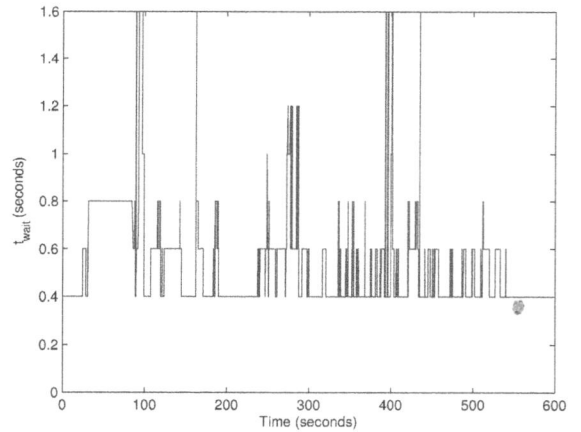

Figure 14: Waiting time changes in MakeIdle.

application starts multiple connections, we can reduce the number of state switches by delaying the connections and batching them together using MakeActive.

Figures 10(b) and 11(b) show the number of state switches using different algorithms, normalized by the number measured in the status quo. Each user has several applications running on the phone. For MakeIdle only, in the 3G/LTE network, the number of state switches is at most four to five times higher than the status quo. For

MakeIdle with MakeActive, either using the learning algorithm or the fixed-delay bound, the number of state switches is about the same as the status quo, meaning that by delaying traffic bursts, our algorithm can reduce the energy consumption without introducing any extra signaling overhead. Notice that for the "95% IAT" algorithm in the LTE network, the number of state switches is as high as $35\times$ the status quo because the corresponding timer value is only 0.01 seconds. As a result, this method will always switch the radio

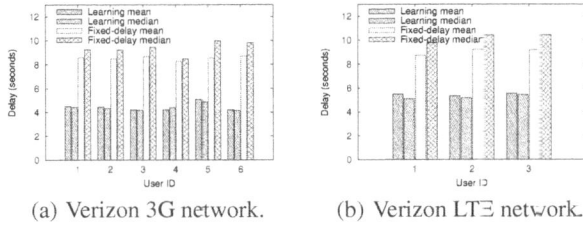

(a) Verizon 3G network. (b) Verizon LTE network.

Figure 15: Mean and median delays for traffic bursts using learning algorithm and fixed delay bound scheme.

to Idle even if there is only a small gap between packets. In a few cases, that does save energy, but at great expense.

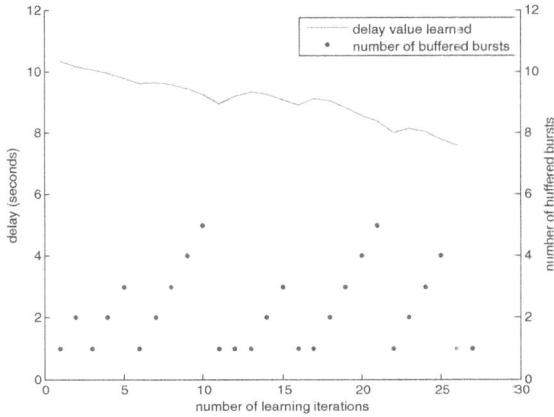

Figure 16: Delay value changes as the learning proceeds.

In Section 5, we described both the fixed-delay bound and a learning algorithm. Figure 15 shows that using the learning algorithm reduces the average delay for each traffic burst by 50% compared to the fixed-delay bound, while both methods induce a comparable number of state switches (Figure 10(b) and Figure 11(b)). The learning algorithm is able to reduce the delay because the loss function (defined in Section 5.2) balances the tradeoff between the number of buffered bursts and the total delay. Figure 16 shows that due to the loss function, the algorithm will reduce the delay bound as the number of buffered bursts increase.

6.5 Different Carriers

To gain a better understanding on how different carriers' RRC state machine configurations affect the observed improvement, in this part of the evaluation we run our trace-driven simulation on different RRC profiles measured from the four major US carriers. In Table 2 we list the measured RRC parameters. There are two cases where the inactivity timer $t_2 = 0$ (effectively), because we cannot clearly distinguish t_1 and t_2 from the energy difference.

Figure 17 shows the percentage of energy saved compared to the status quo. Figure 18 shows the corresponding signaling overhead. We find that the "MakeIdle+MakeActive" method outperforms the "4.5-second tail" method in all the carrier settings. Figure 18 shows the number of state switches (proportional to signaling overhead) of different schemes divided by the number of state switches without using any scheme.

The maximum signaling overhead for MakeIdle is less than 3.1× the baseline where no fast dormancy is triggered. For "MakeI-

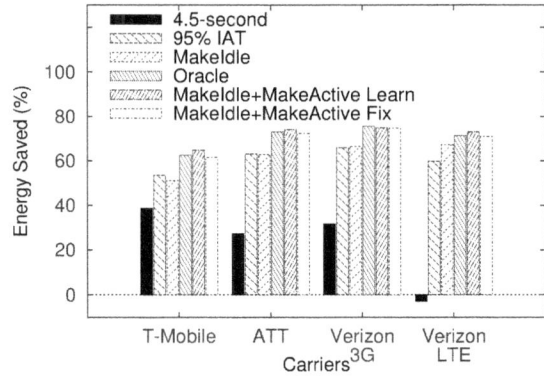

Figure 17: Energy saved for different carrier parameters using different methods. For "MakeIdle", the maximum gain is 67% in Verizon LTE netwrok. For "MakeIdle+MakeActive", the maximum gain is 75% achieved in Verizon 3G.

dle+MakeActive", the signaling overhead reduces to only 1.33× or less, a 62% reduction from the previous 3.1×, and is close to the signaling overhead of "4.5-second tail". The session delays brought by MakeActive are listed in Table 3.

In both Figure 17 and 18, the result shown as MakeIdle has no traffic batching, which corresponds to the case when all the traffic is treated as delay-sensitive, for example, web browsing. The MakeActive method is disabled in this case to make sure that the user's experience is not adversely affected. One possible method to decide when to disable MakeActive is for the control module maintain a list of delay-sensitive or interactive applications; when any of these applications is running in the foreground, the system disables MakeActive.

Even without MakeActive, the reduction in energy consumption is still significant in all the 4 carrier settings. The maximum gain is for Verizon LTE, where MakeIdle save 67% energy over status quo. With MakeIdle, the maximum gain is Verizon 3G, where the energy saving reaches 75%, and the corresponding median delay is 4.48 seconds.

6.6 Energy overhead of running algorithms

To measure the Energy overhead of running our methods, we

Network	P_{snd}	P_{rcv}	P_{t_1}	P_{t_2}	t_1	t_2
T-Mobile 3G	1202	737	445	343	3.2	16.3
AT&T HSPA+	1539	1212	916	659	6.2	10.4
Verizon 3G	2043	1177	1130	1130	9.8	0
Verizon LTE	2928	1737	1325	-	10.2	-

Table 2: Power and inactivity timer values for different networks. Power values are in mW, times are in seconds.

Network	Mean Delay	Median Delay
T-Mobile 3G	5.11	5.11
AT&T HSPA+	4.80	4.65
Verizon 3G	4.67	4.48
Verizon LTE	4.62	4.38

Table 3: The mean and median session delays brought by MakeIdle for different carriers (in seconds).

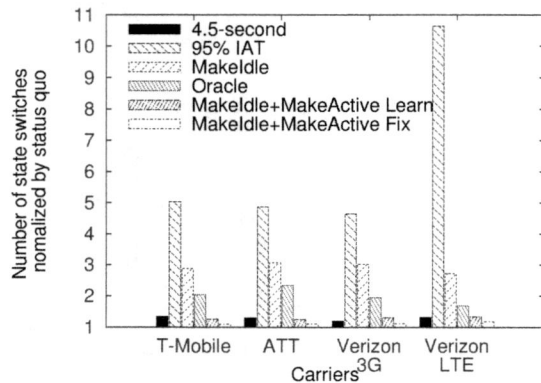

Figure 18: Number of state switches (signaling overhead) for different methods divided by number of state switches using the current inactivity timers.

implemented the algorithms on our test phones. We then generated traffic from the phone based on the user traces we collected. We ran the traffic generator with and without our methods enabled, ensuring that it generates the same traffic in all the experiments. We used the power monitor to measure the total energy consumed in both cases. The energy overhead for running our algorithm is 1.7% for AT&T HTC Vivid and 1.9% for Verizon Galaxy Nexus.

7. RELATED WORK

We divide related work into measurement studies of 3G energy consumption and approaches to reduce that energy, 3G usage profiling, and WiFi power saving methods.

3G energy mitigation strategies:

Past work aimed at eliminating the tail energy falls into three categories: inactivity timer reconfiguration, tail cutting, and tail sharing.

Inactivity timer reconfiguration. Lee et al. [11] developed analytic models for energy consumption in WCDMA and CDMA2000 and showed that the inactivity timer should be dynamically configured. Falaki et al. [6] proposed an empirical method by plotting the CDF of packet inter-arrival times for traces collected on smartphones communicating over 3G radio over long period of time (several days). They found that 95% of the packet inter-arrival time values are smaller than 4.5 seconds, and proposed setting the inactivity timer to a fixed value, $t_1 + t_2 = 4.5$ seconds. Our approach finds a dynamic inactivity timer value using traffic pattern information within a short period of time.

Tail cutting. Qian et al. [19] gave an algorithm, *TOP*, to help the device decide when to trigger fast dormancy based on the information provided by applications running on the device. Their algorithm requires the application to predict when the next packet will come and report it to the OS. This approach requires modifications to the applications, and it is not clear how each application should make these predictions. Our work requires no modification to the application code and does not require the application to predict its traffic.

Traffic batching. Balasubramanian et al. [4] propose an application-layer protocol, *TailEnder*, to coalesce separate data transfers by delaying some of them. For delay-tolerant applications such as email, TailEnder allows applications to set a deadline for the incoming transfer requests; they suggest and evaluate a relatively long delay of 10 minutes for such applications. For applications

that can benefit from prefetching, TailEnder prefetches 10 web documents for each user query. Their design need to re-implement the application and let each application propose their own delay tolerant timers, whereas our design is able to "pause" the traffic transmission at OS layer.

Liu et al. [12] proposed *TailTheft*, a traffic queuing and scheduling mechanism to batch traffic among different applications and share the tail energy among them. One idea of this work is to setup a timeout value for delay-tolerant transfers, and transfer data when timeouts or other delay-sensitive transfer have triggered the radio to Active mode. Similar to *TailEnder*, they require the application to specify how much delay is acceptable.

Another traffic batching approach is prefetching. Qian et al. [18] proposed a prefetching algorithm for YouTube, which erases the tail between transfers of video pieces.

3G resource usage profiling:

Qian et al. [17] designed an algorithm to infer RRC state machine states using packet traces. The per-application analysis shows that some of the popular mobile applications have traffic patterns that are not energy-efficient, due to low bit-rate transmission, inefficient prefetching, and aggressive refresh.

WiFi power-saving algorithms:

Much prior work has focused on WiFi power-saving algorithms [9, 10, 20]. The problem in WiFi networks is qualitatively different from 3G; in WiFi, the time and energy consumed to transition between states is negligible; what is important is to dynamically determine the best sleep duration when the WiFi radio is off. In this state, no packets can be delivered, but the access point will be able to buffer them; the problem is finding the longest sleep time that ensures that no packets are delayed (say, by a specified maximum delay). In the 3G context, changing the state of the radio consumes time, energy, and network signaling overhead, but there is no risk of receiving packets with excessive delay because the base station is able to notify a mobile device that packets are waiting for it even if the device is in Idle state. Thus, we cannot simply apply WiFi power-saving algorithms to 3G networks. Also, machine learning algorithms has been applied to the 802.11 power saving mode configuration problem [15], but the problem setup is different for the 3G energy environment because of different tradeoffs we aim to balance.

Power-saving for processors:

Though not directly related to the problem we address, previous work on processor power-saving has used a similar model to us in which the different power states and transitions between different states are abstracted as a state machine [5]. Here, the power-saving mechanisms are categorized into static methods and adaptive methods, with the adaptive methods using a nonlinear regression over previous idle/active periods and knowledge of how successful previous power-saving decisions are.

8. CONCLUSION AND FUTURE WORK

3G/LTE energy consumption is widely recognized to be a significant problem [4]. We developed a system to reduce the energy consumption using knowledge of the network workload. In evaluating the methods on real usage data from 9 users over 28 total days on four different carriers, we find that the energy savings range between 51% and 66% across the carriers for 3G, and is 67% on the Verizon LTE network. When allowing for delays of a few seconds (acceptable for background applications), the energy savings increase to between 62% and 75% for 3G, and 71% for LTE. The increased delays reduce the number of state switches to be the same as in current networks with existing inactivity timers.

The key idea in this paper is to adapt the state of the radio to network traffic. To put the 66% saving (without any delays) or 75% saving (with delay) in perspective, we note that according to the Nexus S specifications, the reduction in lifetime from using the 3G radio instead of 2G is 7.3 hours; while it is not clear what application mix produces these numbers, one might speculate that saving 66% of the energy might correspond to an increase in lifetime by about 66% of 7.3 hours, or about 4.8 hours.

There are two areas for future work. First, studying the effects of triggering fast dormancy on the base station side would be useful, considering issues such as handling multiple phones triggering the feature, and whether the base station can actively help the phone to make decisions on fast dormancy by buffering incoming traffic for the phone. Second, extending the system to include server or base station functions to coordinate with the mobile device to further reduce energy consumption.

9. ACKNOWLEDGMENTS

We thank Katrina LaCurts, Lenin Ravindranath, Keith Winstein, Jonathan Perry, and Raluca Ada Popa for useful comments on earlier versions of this paper. We also thank the reviewers and our shepherd, Srikanth Krishnamurthy, for their insightful comments. This material is based upon work supported by the National Science Foundation under Grant No. CNS-0931550.

10. REFERENCES

[1] 3GPP Release 7: UE Fast Dormancy behavior, 2007. 3GPP discussion and decision notes R2-075251.

[2] 3GPP Release 8: 3GPP TS 25.331, 2008.

[3] Data Service Options for Spread Spread Spectrum Systems: Service Options 33 and 66, May 2006.

[4] N. Balasubramanian, A. Balasubramanian, and A. Venkataramani. Energy consumption in mobile phones: A measurement study and implications for network applications. In *Internet Measurement Conference*, 2009.

[5] L. Benini, A. Bogliolo, and G. D. Micheli. A survey of design techniques for system-level dynamic power management. *Very Large Scale Integration (VLSI) Systems, IEEE Transactions on*, 8(3):299 –316, june 2000.

[6] H. Falaki, D. Lymberopoulos, R. Mahajan, S. Kandula, and D. Estrin. A First Look at Traffic on Smartphones. In *Internet Measurement Conference*, 2010.

[7] M. Herbster and M. K. Warmuth. Tracking the best expert. *Machine Learning*, 32:151–178, 1998.

[8] J. Huang, F. Qian, A. Gerber, Z. M. Mao, S. Sen, and O. Spatscheck. A close examination of performance and power characteristics of 4g lte networks. In *MobiSys*, 2012.

[9] R. Krashinsky and H. Balakrishnan. Minimizing Energy for Wireless Web Access with Bounded Slowdown. In *MobiCom*, 2002.

[10] R. Krashinsky and H. Balakrishnan. Minimizing Energy for Wireless Web Access with Bounded Slowdown *ACM Wireless Networks*, 11(1–2):135–148, Jan. 2005.

[11] C.-C. Lee, J.-H. Yeh, and J.-C. Chen. Impact of inactivity timer on energy consumption in WCDMA and CDMA2000. In *IEEE Wireless Telecomm. Symp.(WTS)*, 2004.

[12] H. Liu, Y. Zhang, and Y. Zhou. TailTheft: Leveraging the wasted time for saving energy in cellular communications. In *MobiArch*, 2011.

[13] Monsoon power monitor. http://www.msoon.com/ LabEquipment/PowerMonitor/.

[14] C. Monteleoni. Online learning of non-stationary sequences. In *AI Technical Report 2003-011, S.M. Thesis*, Artificial Intelligence Laboratory, Massachusetts Institute of Technology, May 2003.

[15] C. Monteleoni, H. Balakrishnan, N. Feamster, and T. Jaakkola. Managing the 802.11 energy/performance tradeoff with machine learning. Technical Report MIT-LCS-TR-971, MIT CSAIL, 2004.

[16] C. Monteleoni and T. Jaakkola. Online learning of non-stationary sequences. In *Neural Information Processing Systems 16*, Vancouver, Canada, December 2003.

[17] F. Qian, Z. Wang, A. Gerber, Z. Mao, S. Sen, and O. Spatscheck. Profiling resource usage for mobile applications: a cross-layer approach. In *MobiSys*, 2011.

[18] F. Qian, Z. Wang, A. Gerber, Z. M. Mao, S. Sen, and O. Spatscheck. Characterizing radio resource allocation for 3G networks. In *Internet Measurement Conference*, 2010.

[19] F. Qian, Z. Wang, A. Gerber, Z. M. Mao, S. Sen, and O. Spatscheck. TOP: Tail Optimization Protocol For Celluar Radio Resource Allocation. In *ICNP*, 2010.

[20] T. Simunic, L. Benini, P. W. Glynn, and G. D. Micheli. Dynamic power management for portable systems. In *MobiCom*, 2000.

[21] J.-H. Yeh, J.-C. Chen, and C.-C. Lee. Comparative Analysis of Energy-Saving Techniques in 3GPP and 3GPP2 Systems. *IEEE Trans. on Vehicular Technology*, 58(1):432 –448, Jan. 2009.

[22] J.-H. Yeh, C.-C. Lee, and J.-C. Chen. Performance analysis of energy consumption in 3GPP networks. In *IEEE Wireless Telecomm. Symp. (WTS)*, 2004.

APPENDIX

Here we show how *bank of experts* works. We bound the maximum delay to n seconds. Each expert "proposes" a delay value T_i:

$$T_i = i, i \in 1 \ldots n.$$

The output of the algorithm is the weighted average over all the experts:

$$T_t = \sum_{i=1}^{n} p_t(i) T_i$$

For each iteration of the updates, the algorithm calculates the probability of each possible hidden state (in our case, the identity of the expert) based on some observation y_t. Here, we can define the probability of predicting observation y_t as $P(y_t|T_i) = e^{-L(i,t)}$. The observation is the number of sessions we batched at time t, and $L(i,t)$ is the loss function. Then we can apply the following equation to get the weight $p_t(i)$:

$$p_t(i) = \frac{1}{Z_t} \sum_{j=1}^{n} p_{t-1}(j) e^{-L(j,t-1)} P(i|j, \alpha).$$

Here, Z_t is a normalization factor that makes sure $\sum_i p_t i = 1$. The $P(i|j, \alpha)$ shows the probability of switching between experts. There are different versions to solve this part. The one we chose [7] supports switching between the experts and is suitable for cases where the observation may change rapidly, which matches the bursty character of network traffic. $P(i|j, \alpha)$ is defined as:

$$P(i|j, \alpha) = \begin{cases} (1-\alpha) & i = j \\ \frac{\alpha}{n-1} & i \neq j \end{cases}$$

$0 \leq \alpha \leq 1$ is a parameter that determines how quickly the algorithm changes the best experts. α close to 1 means the network condition changes rapidly and the best expert always changes. One problem with this algorithm is that it is hard to choose a good α. In reality, α should not be a fixed value since the network traffic pattern may change rapidly or remain stationary. We use a more adaptive algorithm, Learn-α [14, 16], to dynamically choose α.

The basic idea is to first assign m α-experts and use the algorithm above to learn the proper value of α in each iteration, and then use the up-to-date α to learn T_t [14, 16]. The final equation for this "two-layer learning" is:

$$T_t = \sum_{j=1}^{m} \sum_{i=1}^{n} p_t'(j) p_{t,j}(i) T_i \tag{3}$$

Here, $p_t'(j)$ is the weight for the jth α-expert, which is given by:

$$p_t'(j) = \frac{1}{Z_t} p_{t-1}'(j) e^{-L(\alpha_j, t-1)} \tag{4}$$

This equation shows that $p_t'(j)$ is updated from the previous value $p_{t-1}'(j)$; the initial values are: $p_1'(j) = 1/m$. $-L(\alpha_j, t-1)$ is the α loss function, defined as:

$$L(\alpha_j, t) = -\log \sum_{i=1}^{n} p_{t,j}(i) e^{-L(i,t)} \tag{5}$$

Here, $L(i,t)$ is the loss function, discussed in §5.2. t is the present time; the loss function value for the current iteration is calculated from information learned at time $t-1$.

Computing While Charging: Building a Distributed Computing Infrastructure Using Smartphones

Mustafa Y. Arslan *
UC Riverside
marslan@cs.ucr.edu

Indrajeet Singh
UC Riverside
singhi@cs.ucr.edu

Shailendra Singh
UC Riverside
singhs@cs.ucr.edu

Harsha V. Madhyastha
UC Riverside
harsha@cs.ucr.edu

Karthikeyan Sundaresan
NEC Labs America, Inc.
Princeton, NJ, USA
karthiks@nec-labs.com

Srikanth V.
Krishnamurthy
UC Riverside
krish@cs.ucr.edu

ABSTRACT

Every night, a large number of idle smartphones are plugged into a power source for recharging the battery. Given the increasing computing capabilities of smartphones, these idle phones constitute a sizeable computing infrastructure. Therefore, for an enterprise which supplies its employees with smartphones, we argue that a computing infrastructure that leverages idle smartphones being charged overnight is an energy-efficient and cost-effective alternative to running tasks on traditional server infrastructure. While parallel execution and scheduling models exist for servers (e.g., MapReduce), smartphones present a unique set of technical challenges due to the heterogeneity in CPU clock speed, variability in network bandwidth, and lower availability compared to servers.

In this paper, we address many of these challenges to develop CWC—a distributed computing infrastructure using smartphones. Specifically, our contributions are: (i) we profile the charging behaviors of real phone owners to show the viability of our approach, (ii) we enable programmers to execute parallelizable tasks on smartphones with little effort, (iii) we develop a simple task migration model to resume interrupted task executions, and (iv) we implement and evaluate a prototype of CWC (with 18 Android smartphones) that employs an underlying novel scheduling algorithm to minimize the makespan of a set of tasks. Our extensive evaluations demonstrate that the performance of our approach makes our vision viable. Further, we explicitly evaluate the performance of CWC's scheduling component to demonstrate its efficacy compared to other possible approaches.

Categories and Subject Descriptors

C.2.1 [**Network Architecture and Design**]: Wireless communication

---

*Mustafa Arslan is currently a research staff member at NEC Laboratories America Inc., Princeton, NJ USA.

Keywords

Smartphone, Distributed Computing, Scheduling

1. INTRODUCTION

Today, a number of organizations supply their employees with smartphones for various reasons [1]; a survey from 2011 [2] reports that 66% of surveyed organizations do so and many of these organizations have 75–100% of their employees using smartphones. For example, Novartis [3] (with 100,000 employees in 140 countries) handed out smartphones for its employees to manage emails, calendars, as well as information about health issues; Lowe's [4] did so for its employees to have real time access to key product information and to allow managers to handle administrative tasks.

In this paper, we argue that in such settings, an enterprise can harness the aggregate computing power of such smartphones, to construct a distributed computing infrastructure. Such an infrastructure could reduce both the capital and energy costs incurred by the enterprise. First, this could reduce the number of servers to be purchased for computing purposes. For example, Novartis awarded a contract of $2 million to IBM to build a data center for their computational tasks [5]. If they could exploit the smartphones handed out to their employees to run some portion of their workload, it is conceivable that the cost of their computing infrastructure could have been reduced. Due to recent advancements in embedded processor design, now a smartphone can replace a normal desktop or a server running a dual core processor for computation. According to Nvidia, their Quad Core CPU, Tegra 3, outperforms an Intel Core 2 Duo processor in number crunching [6]; for other workloads, one can expect the performance of the two CPUs to be comparable.

Our second motivation for the smartphone-based computing infrastructure is that the enterprise could benefit from significant energy savings by shutting down its servers by offloading tasks to smartphones. The power consumed by a commercial PC CPU such as the Intel Core 2 Duo is 26.8W [7] at peak load. In contrast, a smartphone CPU can be over 20x more power efficient, e.g., the Tegra 3 has a power consumption of 1.2W [7, 8]. Since their computing abilities are similar, it is conceivable that one can harness 20 times more computational power while consuming the same energy by replacing a single server node with a plurality of smartphones. In fact, to harness the energy efficiency of embedded processors, cloud service providers are already pushing towards ARM-based data centers [9].

The construction and management of such a distributed computing infrastructure using smartphones however, has a number of associated technical challenges. We seek to articulate these challenges and build an efficient framework towards making such a platform viable. In particular, the biggest obstacles to harnessing smartphones for computing are the phone's battery-life and bandwidth. If a smartphone is used for computing during periods of use by its owner, we run the risk of draining its battery and rendering the phone unusable. Further, today data usage on 3G carriers are typically capped, and thus, shipping large volumes of data using 3G is likely to be impractical. Thus, our vision is to use these smartphones for computing when they are being charged, especially at night. During these periods, the likelihood of active use of the phone by its owner will be low. Moreover, the phone will be static and, will likely have access to WiFi in the owner's home (today, 80% of the homes in the US have WiFi connectivity [10]); this will both reduce fluctuations in network bandwidth, and allow the transfer of data to/from the smartphones at no cost.

We name our framework CWC, which stands for computing while charging. To realize CWC, we envision the use of a single server, connected to the Internet, for scheduling jobs on the smartphones and collecting the outputs from the computations. The scheduling algorithms executed on the server are lightweight, and thus, a rudimentary low cost PC will suffice. Smartphones are only utilized for computation when being charged. If an owner disconnects the phone from the power outlet, the task is suspended, and migrated to a different phone that is connected to a power outlet. Towards building CWC, our contributions are as follows:

- **Profiling charging behaviors:** While an enterprise can possibly mandate that its employees charge their smartphones when they are not being actively used, we examine the typical charging behaviors of smartphone owners. Using an Android application that we develop, we gather charging statistics on the phones of 15 volunteers. Our results demonstrate that, on average, a typical user charges his phone for up to 8 hours every night.

- **Scheduling tasks on smartphones:** As a fundamental component of CWC, we design a scheduler that minimizes the makespan of completing the jobs at hand, taking into account both the CPU and bandwidth available for each smartphone. Since the optimal allocation of jobs across phones is NP-hard, we design a greedy algorithm for the allocation, and show via experiments that it outperforms other simple conceivable heuristics.

- **Migration of tasks across phones:** CWC executes tasks on smartphones only when they are being charged. Tasks are suspended if phones are unplugged during execution. We design and implement an approach to efficiently migrate such tasks to other phones that are plugged in.

- **Automation of task executions:** The typical means of running an application on smartphones is to have the phone's owner download, install, and run the application. However, we cannot rely on such human intervention to leverage smartphones for a computing infrastructure. We demonstrate how task executions on phones can be realized in a completely automated manner. Note that, while we recognize the potential privacy implications of running automated tasks on smartphones, we simply assume here that an enterprise would not run malicious tasks on its employees' smartphones. Improving the isolation of tasks implemented in typical smartphone operating systems is beyond the scope of our work.

- **Preserving user experience:** Blindly executing tasks for extended durations on a smartphone being charged, can prolong the time taken for the phone to fully charge. We show that intensive use of a phone's CPU can delay a full charge by 35%. We design and implement a CPU throttling mechanism, which ensures that task executions do not impact the charging times.

- **Implementation and experimentation:** Finally, to demonstrate the viability of CWC, we implement a prototype and conduct extensive experiments on a testbed of 18 Android phones. Specifically, we show the efficacy of the scheduling and task migration algorithms within CWC.

2. RELATED WORK

To the best of our knowledge, no prior study shares our vision of tapping into the computing power of smartphones. However, some efforts resemble certain aspects of CWC.

Smartphone testbeds and distributed computing platforms. Publicly-available smartphone testbeds have been proposed [11, 12] to enable smartphone OS and mobile applications research. CrowdLab [13] and Seattle [14] provide resources on volunteer devices. There also exist systems where users voluntarily contribute idle time on their PCs to computational tasks (e.g., [15]). In contrast, our vision is not for the smartphone infrastructure to be used for research and testing, but to enable energy and cost savings for real enterprises. Moreover, the issues that we address have not been considered by these efforts. In addition to these systems, flavors of MapReduce for smartphones have been implemented (e.g., [16]). However, such efforts do not address the issues of detecting idle phone usage and partitioning tasks across phones with diverse capabilities. They do envision using phones to offer a distributed computing service.

The system that is closest in spirit to CWC is Condor [17]. Condor can be used to queue and schedule jobs across a distributed set of desktop machines. These machines are either dedicated to running jobs on them or are operated by regular users for routine activities. In the latter case, Condor monitors whether user machines are idle and harnesses such idle CPU power to perform the computations required by jobs. It also preempts computations on these machines once the users continue their routine use (i.e., the machine is no more idle).

While the above features of Condor may be similar to CWC, the two have the following key differences:

- CWC tries to preserve the charging profile of smartphones via its CPU throttling technique. This is a challenge not addressed by Condor since desktop machines do not exhibit such a problem.

- Desktop machines mostly differ in terms of their CPU clock speed, memory (RAM) and disk space. In a cluster, these machines are connected via Ethernet switches and this typically results in uniform bandwidth across machines. Thus, systems such as Condor do not typically consider machine bandwidth in their scheduling decisions. In contrast, smartphones have highly variable wireless bandwidths (in addition to their variable CPU clock speed and RAM). This can lead to sub-optimal scheduling decisions if bandwidth is not taken into account (details in Section 3 and Section 5).

Participatory sensing. Recent studies such as [18], advocate the collective use of the sensing, storage, and processing capabilities of smartphones. With participatory sensing [19], users collect and analyze various types of sensor readings from smartphones. Unlike these efforts, a distinguishing aspect of CWC is that the data to be processed does not originate from the phones. In addition, CWC allows the execution of a variety of tasks unlike above, where typically a fixed task (sensing) is supported. Finally, CWC seeks to leverage compute resources on smartphones, rather than tapping human brain power [20].

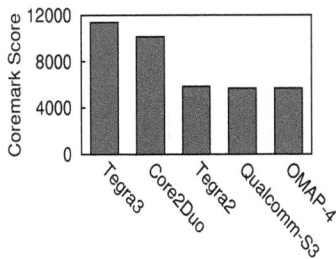

Figure 1: Benchmarking smartphone CPUs against the Intel Core 2 Duo.

Measurements of smartphones. There have been measurement studies [21, 22] to characterize typical network traffic and energy consumption on smartphones. In contrast, our focus is on developing a scalable platform for gathering measurements from the phones in CWC. Several prior studies [23, 24] have observed that phones are idle and are being charged for significant periods of time every day. We are however the first to recognize that these idle periods can be harnessed to build a distributed computing infrastructure.

Provisioning tasks on cloud services. Prior efforts have also tried to identify when the use of cloud services is appropriate (e.g., [25]), discuss the challenges involved in using them (e.g. [26]) or present solutions for provisioning applications (e.g. [27]). However, these efforts focus on traditional server-based cloud services. Prior efforts on managing resources in the cloud (e.g., [28]) do not tackle challenges associated with provisioning tasks on heterogenous resources nor deal with the variability of wireless links.

3. FEASIBILITY STUDY

In this section, we examine (a) the challenges associated with building a smartphone-based computing infrastructure and (b) the potential savings in capital and energy costs offered by such an infrastructure.

3.1 Challenges

Adequacy of computing power: The smartphone infrastructure is only attractive if it can effectively accomplish the computing tasks undertaken on today's servers. Due to rapid advances in embedded processor technologies, numerous smartphones with Quad Core CPUs are emerging [29]. Some of these CPUs offer clock speeds of up to 2.5 Ghz per core (Qualcomm snapdragon quad-core APQ8064) and their computational capabilities are *beyond that* of typically used server machines. To compare the performance of a smartphone CPU with that of typical desktop and server CPUs, we refer to the well known CoreMark benchmarks [30]. Figure 1 (borrowed from [8, 30]) shows the performance of major smartphone CPUs against a widely used desktop and server CPU—the Intel Core 2 Duo; the higher the CoreMark score, the better. We see that while the Nvidia Tegra-3 outperforms the Intel Core 2 Duo, the Core 2 Duo outperforms the other processors by more than 50%. This shows that state-of-the-art smartphones like Samsung Galaxy S-3 (running on Tegra-3 CPU) can only replace a single-core server or desktop machine. In our smartphone testbed, most of the smartphones are running on Tegra-2, Snapdragon S-3, and Ti OMAP-4 CPUs; in spite of this, we can execute a typical server job with two or three (of these older) smartphones.

Availability of idle task execution periods: Beyond the dramatic improvements in their compute capabilities, smartphones are attractive for a computing service because their resources are un-

used for long periods of time. Most users leave their phones idle overnight while the batteries are being recharged. When being recharged, a smartphone typically runs only light-weight background jobs (e.g., downloading e-mail) that require minimal computation and intermittent network access. Scheduling jobs on a phone during such periods is unlikely to impact the phone owners

To identify and utilize idle periods, we have implemented an Android application to *profile* the charging behaviors of users (Apple iOS also supports the core functionality required). The application tracks three states on every phone: (a) *plugged*: when the user is charging the phone, (b) *unplugged*: when the phone is detached from the charger, and (c) *shutdown*: when the phone is powered off. When there is a change in state (i.e., *unplugged* to *plugged*), the application logs the change to a server along with a timestamp (of the user's local timezone). In addition, it logs the total bytes transmitted and received over all wireless interfaces (cellular and WiFi) when in the *plugged* state; this statistic is reset every time the phone newly enters the *plugged* state. The server parses the log files and computes for every charging interval of a particular user: (a) the duration of the interval, and (b) the number of bytes (transmitted and received) during that interval.

We conduct a study of realistic user behavior by having 15 volunteers (real users) install our application on their phones and gathering statistics. In Fig. 2(a), we plot the distribution of charging interval lengths, with every interval assigned to day or night; if the *plugged* state occurs between 10 p.m. and 5 a.m. of a user's local time, that interval is considered to be in the night, else in the day. We observe that the median charging interval is around 30 minutes and 7 hours long, at day and night respectively. In addition, there are fewer charging intervals in the night. This suggests that users charge their phones for an uninterrupted stretch of several hours at night. During the day, charging is interrupted frequently, resulting in a large number of short intervals.

We now focus only on the charging intervals at night. Fig. 2(b) plots the CDF of data transfers over all night charging intervals. Although the user is unlikely to be actively using the phone, there is background data in the form of periodic e-mail checks, push notifications from news and social media, etc.. However, we find that the total network activity is less than ≈ 2 MB for 80% of all night charging intervals.

Using the network activity data, we identify night charging intervals that can be considered idle to be the ones in which the data transfer is less than 2 MB. Fig. 2(c) shows that the users, on average, have at least 3 hours of idle charging at night. However, the characteristics highly depend on the individuals. Users with the highest idle durations (users 3, 4, and 8) have lower variability in their behavior; this suggests that they regularly charge their phones for 8 to 9 hours at night. In addition, users very rarely turn their phones off while charging (only 3% of the logs are in the *shutdown* state). The consistent low load at night (as also reported by [31]) suggests that idle usage patterns occur in large-scale settings as well. Given this, we speculate that this will provide an overlap of long idle charging times across users, yielding several operational hours for computing, without disturbing users' routine activities.

Next, we also examine the *plugged* and *unplugged* activity of each user. Our goal is to identify periods where, the phones are most likely to be unplugged. In our setting, we consider *unplugging* as a failure since we do not execute tasks when a phone is *unplugged*. Figure 3(a) plots the CDF of *unplugged* activity (failure) for all users. It is seen that the likelihood of failure between 12 AM to 8 AM is less than 30%. In CWC, we simply migrate such failed tasks to other phones that are still plugged in (discussed later).

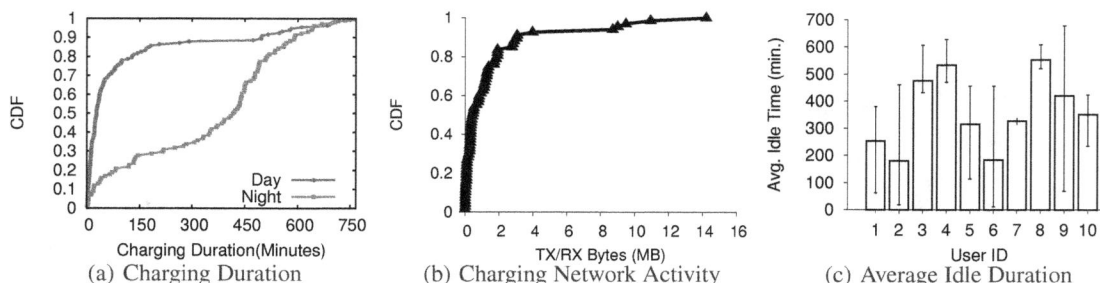

(a) Charging Duration

(b) Charging Network Activity

(c) Average Idle Duration

Figure 2: The median charging interval at night is around 7 hours and the data transfer is mostly below 2MB.

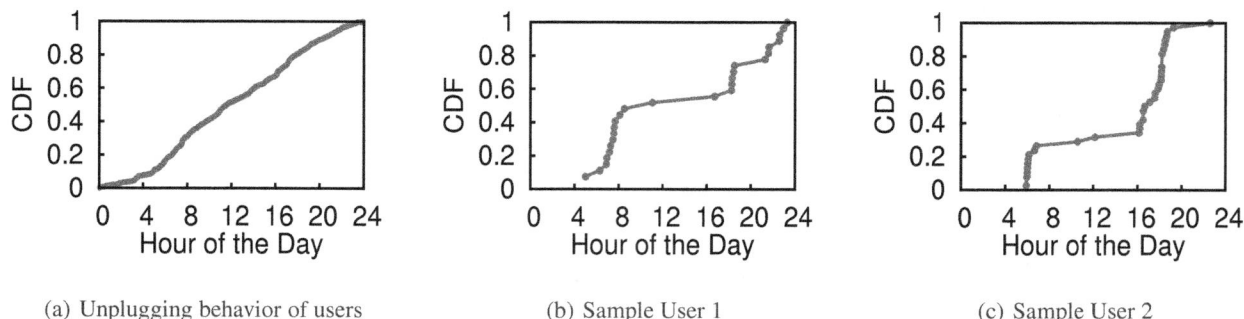

(a) Unplugging behavior of users

(b) Sample User 1

(c) Sample User 2

Figure 3: Availability of smartphones for CWC task scheduling.

Profiling an individual user's behavior can allow the prediction of device specific failures. This can help since tasks can be migrated to phones that are less likely to fail at the time of consideration. Figures 3(b) and 3(c) show the unplugging behaviors of two representative users from our study. The likelihoods of failure in both cases are very low between 12 A.M. and 6 A.M. It increases between 6 A.M. and 9 A.M. when people begin using their phones. During the day, the likelihood of *unplugged* activity is high; it decreases when phones are charged again at night.

Our study suggests that the charging behaviors of users are typically consistent at night, and offer an opportunity for harnessing the computing power of idle phones during these times.

Stability of the wireless network: To fully utilize the idle periods to execute jobs, a stable network connection is necessary. Since we only schedule jobs when a phone is on charge (typically at night), it is safe to assume that the channel qualities do not fluctuate much. The location of a device may, however, affect the bandwidth (due to fading); to account for temporally varying fading effects, a periodic (short) bandwidth measurement test is required prior to scheduling jobs on the phones. To examine the stability of these measurements over WiFi links, we conduct experiments at three different locations (within a 2 mile radius), when the phones are put on charge. Figure 4 depicts the results of such a bandwidth test for WiFi links where we run an *iperf* session from the phones to the server for 600 seconds.

We see that the variation in bandwidth for WiFi links is very low; this means that we can use infrequent (periodic) bandwidth measurements. Since we expect that communications between the smartphones and the supporting server will typically be via WiFi at users' homes, we conclude that bandwidth stability is not likely to be an issue. Cellular links can also be utilized as appropriate, but will require more frequent bandwidth measurements since they may exhibit high instability[32].

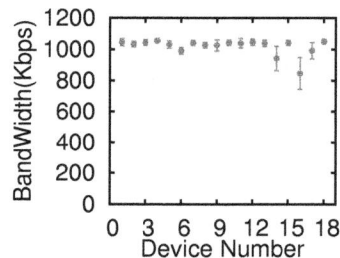

Figure 4: WiFi network stability.

Variability of bandwidth across smartphones: Although we showed that the bandwidth of a static smartphone is relatively stable, there may still be high variability in bandwidth *across* smartphones [1]. The task executable and the input data have to be shipped wirelessly to smartphones. This makes task completion times sensitive to the bandwidth variability across smartphones. To validate this in practice, we design a simple experiment where we have a central server (a regular PC) that interacts with 6 smartphones. The phones have identical CPU clock speeds but they differ in terms of their wireless bandwidths to the server. The server has 600 files to be processed by the phones (each phone finds the largest integer in the file). For each file, the typical cycle is the following. The server sends the file to one of the idle phones, which then processes the file and returns the result back to the server. If there are no idle phones (i.e., all phones are busy receiving and processing some file), the file is queued. Since all the phones are initially idle, the server can copy the first 6 files in parallel without any queue-

---

[1]Note that this is in contrast to the typical setting where desktop machines are inter-connected via Ethernet.

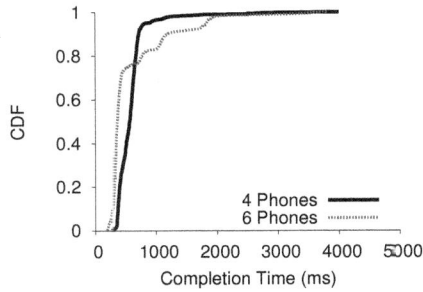

Figure 5: CDF of file processing times.

ing. The server logs the turn-around time for each file, which is computed as the difference between the time that the phone returns the result and the time that the file was queued. After this first experiment, we remove the two phones that have the "slowest" connections and schedule the 600 files on the remaining 4 phones. We observe from Fig. 5 that with 6 phones, 90% of the tasks finish in less than 1200 milliseconds. On the other hand, choosing a reduced number of phones albeit with fast wireless connections, improves the 90th percentile to 700 milliseconds (though the queueing delay increases). Our experiment reveals that simply accounting for the CPU clock speed and using all the phones results in poor task completion times. If this experiment were conducted on a cluster of 6 PCs with identical CPU clock speed, using more machines would have reduced the completion times (since the PCs would have the same bandwidth). In summary, one should also take wireless bandwidth into account when scheduling tasks across smartphones. This factor is unique to a smartphone environment and is not accounted for in systems such as Condor [17].

3.2 Benefits

Savings in infrastructure costs: Since the idle compute resources on already deployed smartphones are used, the cost borne by corporations to bootstrap the platform will be minimal in comparison to that in setting up a similar service on a server-based infrastructure. Companies have either to invest in buying hardware (e.g., servers, switches) or in outsourcing their tasks to third party cloud services. In addition, establishing computing infrastructure requires careful planning with regards to factors such as space, federal and state regulations, and the provisioning of power and cooling support. In contrast, the use of a smartphone infrastructure obviates such considerations. To leverage existing smartphones as the elements of a utility computing service, an enterprise will need no more than a central, lightweight server to identify idle resources and allocate them to computational tasks.

Savings in energy costs: A primary concern of cloud service providers is the power consumption in their data centers. A typical data center server can consume 26.8 Watts (Intel Core 2 Duo) to 248 Watts (Intel Nehalem) [33] of power, depending on the configuration. More importantly, this does not account for the power required for cooling. To calculate the total power consumption, we use an Average Power Usage Effectiveness (PUE) ratio [34] of 2.5; for every Watt consumed by a server, 2.5 watts are in addition consumed for cooling and power distribution. Extrapolating this, we can project the energy cost of a Intel Core 2 Duo server to be:

$$\frac{67}{1000} KWH \times 24 \text{ hrs} \times 365 \text{ days} \times \$0.127 = \$74.5/year$$

(using the average commercial price of 12.7c/KWH in the US in April 2011). Note that a more powerful server (like the Intel Nehalem) may cost up to $689 /year.

In comparison to a datacenter server, the power consumption of a smartphone is as low as 1.2 Watts at peak load. We estimate the cost of operating a smartphone (with a similar model) to be:

$$\frac{1.2}{1000} KWH \times 24 \text{ hrs} \times 365 \text{ days} \times \$0.127 = \$1.33/year$$

Note that the PUE ratio does not apply in case of smartphones since they do not require any cooling. The above analysis suggests that energy costs of operating the smartphone computing infrastructure are significantly lower (by an order of magnitude) than using typical datacenter servers.

Example applications: Next, we describe some example applications that are suitable for execution on CWC in a real enterprise setting. The first is an example taken from the Condor website [17]. A movie production company can render each scene in a movie, in parallel, using smartphones. A second example is where, a department store gathers the sales records from several locations. These records can be partitioned and shipped to phones to quantify what types of goods are sold the most. We believe Lowe's would be a typical example for this [4]. Lastly, the IT department in an enterprise can gather machine logs throughout the day and analyze them for certain types of failures at night.

4. DESIGN AND ARCHITECTURE

In this section, we describe the design of CWC. We first describe the parallel task (job) execution model for CWC [2], and then seek answers to the following. **(a)** How can we predict task execution times?, **(b)** How can we implement automated task execution on smartphones without requiring direct user interaction?, and **(c)** How can we preserve user experience while the tasks are being executed on the phones?

Task model: In CWC, a task is a program that performs a computation on an input file, such as counting the number of occurrences of a word in a text file. Similar to the model in MapReduce, a central server partitions a large input file into smaller pieces, transmits the input partitions (together with the executable that processes the input) to the smartphones in CWC. Upon receiving the executable and the corresponding input, the phones execute the task in parallel and return their results to the central server when they finish executing the task. The central server performs a logical aggregation of the returned results, depending on the task. For the word count example, the server can simply sum the number of occurrences reported by each phone (obtained by processing their respective input partitions) to compute the number of occurrences in the original input file. We call such tasks *breakable tasks* to reflect that in this class, a task does not exhibit dependencies across partitions of its input and hence, can be broken into an arbitrary number of concurrent pieces.

While the above model is suitable for parallel tasks in general, some tasks *cannot* be broken into smaller pieces on which computations can be performed followed by merging the results, to produce a logical outcome. We call such tasks *atomic tasks*; such a task (and its input) can only be executed on a single phone due to the dependencies in its input. An example of an atomic task is photo filtering (e.g., blurring a photo). A blur is typically obtained by computing a new pixel value based on the neighboring pixels. Since the blurred pixel value depends on its neighboring pixels a blur on a photo cannot be obtained by breaking the photo into smaller pieces, blurring the pixels in each individual piece and merging the results. Although an atomic task cannot be parallelized, there are still concurrency benefits when many such tasks are executed in batches.

---

[2]We use the terms task and job interchangeably.

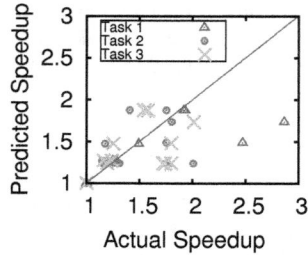

Figure 6: Predicted speedup vs. the measured speedup.

For example, if one needs to filter 1000 photos, each individual photo can be transferred to a phone and thus, multiple photos can be filtered in parallel. CWC accounts for both breakable tasks and batch atomic tasks in its scheduler (details in Section 5).

We realize that the RAM on most phones is smaller (1-2 GB) than most desktop machines (4 GB). This constraint can easily be overcome by splitting a given job input data into smaller fragments so that each data partition fits in the smartphone memory. We believe 1 GB RAM per phone is enough to run most of the MapReduce style distributed jobs. Note here that the work in [35] reports that the median job input size for such jobs is less than 14 GB. One can easily partition such jobs across 15-20 phones and still schedule them using CWC. Next, we describe how CWC predicts task execution times.

4.1 Predicting Task Execution Times

When a task is scheduled on a phone, there are two important factors that affect the completion time of that task. First, it takes time to copy the executable (i.e., binary) and the input file partition to a phone. This depends on the achievable data rate on the link between the phone and the central server that copies the data. Second, the same task takes different times to complete on different phones (depending on the computational capabilities of the phone). While "computational capabilities" is broad and can include characteristics such as the speed of reading a file from the disk (e.g., the SD card on a phone) or the size and speed of the cache, we only focus on the CPU clock speed of a phone; a phone with a fast CPU (in GHz) should execute a given task in less time as compared to a phone with a slow CPU.

Next, we introduce some basic notation that we use in the subsequent discussions. b_i is the time that it takes to copy 1 KB of data from the central server to phone i. c_{ij} is the time it takes to execute task j on 1 KB of input data using phone i. E_j is the size (in KB) of the executable for task j and L_j is the size (in KB) of input data that task j needs to process. Given this notation, the completion time of task j, when it is scheduled to run on phone i, is equal to $E_j * b_i + L_j * (b_i + c_{ij})$. The first term accounts for the time that it takes to copy the executable to the phone and the second term accounts for the copying of the input data and executing the task on it. If phone i is assigned a piece of job j's input file, we denote this by l_{ij} and one can simply replace L_j with l_{ij} in the above formula to account for executing input partitions.

The estimation of the b_i values are via direct measurements in CWC (bandwidth tests described earlier). While we focus on describing how task execution times are estimated in the following paragraphs, we emphasize that the bandwidth to a smartphone is taken into account when making scheduling decisions.

The estimation of c_{ij} for each phone task pair has to be low-cost since many such combinations may exist. To estimate c_{ij} values, we resort to a scaling technique where we first execute each task j

on 1 KB of its input using the slowest phone with a S MHz CPU speed. If the slowest phone takes T_s milliseconds to locally execute task j on a 1 KB input (excluding the associated 'executable and data' copying costs), a phone with 'A' MHz CPU speed is expected to complete the same task in $T_s * \frac{S}{A}$ milliseconds. This technique avoids the cost of profiling each phone-task pair and as we show in Figure 6, is a fairly accurate representation of actual task completion times. In plotting Figure 6, we first run a task on the slowest phone in our testbed (HTC G2 with 806 MHz CPU). We then run the same task on all the other phones (the relevant executable code and data are transferred a priori). Comparing the actual runtimes of each phone i (denoted t_i) to the run time of the slowest phone (denoted t_s), we have the measured speedup, $\frac{t_s}{t_i}$. We then compute the expected speedup based on CPU clock speeds. If a phone has a X MHz CPU, then the expected speedup with respect to the HTC G2 is equal to $\frac{X}{806}$. We do this comparison for three different tasks (described later in detail in Section 6). Figure 6 shows that the CPU scaling model captures the actual speedup for most of the points (the points are clustered around the $y = x$ line), with a few exceptions where the actual speedup is higher than what is predicted by the model (the rightmost points on the x-axis).

The above model is used by CWC's task scheduler (described in Section 5), which runs on the central server and periodically assigns partitions of tasks to a set of phones based on the predicted task completion time. The phones return their results along with the time it actually took to locally execute their last assigned task. The scheduler then updates its prediction for each phone (and task) based on the reported execution times and uses it for predicting the run time in the following scheduling period. With this, CWC accounts for the few cases that the initial prediction fails to capture with regards to task execution.

4.2 Automating Task Execution

One of the key requirements of CWC is that a task be executed without requiring user input. The typical means of "running a task" on smartphones today is running an application (i.e., "app"). When a user wants to execute a new task on her phone, she needs to download and install the app. This process typically requires human input for various reasons (e.g., Android users are presented a list of app permissions and have to manually validate the installation). Such a mechanism is clearly not apt for CWC, since the tasks are to be dynamically scheduled on smartphones.

To run tasks on the phones, we leverage a cross-platform mechanism that uses the Java Reflection API for the Android OS. With reflection, a Java executable (i.e., a .class file) can dynamically load other executables, instantiate their objects and execute their methods, at runtime. This allows CWC to ship different task executables and input files to a particular phone in an automated fashion. In addition, the reflection functionality can be implemented as an Android service [3] thus, bypassing the need for human input. Note that dynamic class loading is not specific to Android; such capabilities are also available with other smartphone OSs (e.g., iOS permits this via shared libraries).

With reflection implemented on the smartphone side, CWC does not require any additional infrastructure at the central server. In fact, developers can continue to use their traditional Java programs and have them scheduled for parallel execution by CWC. Since Android can execute Java code, we just require developers to implement their tasks in Java (no knowledge of Android API required). In Fig. 7, we depict the flow chart of a typical CWC task. The .java source files are compiled into .class files at the cen-

---

[3] Android services do not display graphical elements to users and can run in the background.

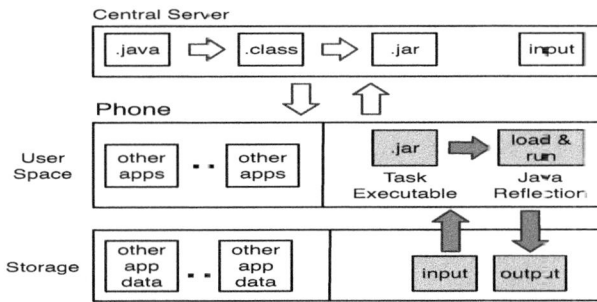

Figure 7: Flow chart of a CWC task (shown in shaded components).

```
1 public class Task {
2     public static void main (String[] args) {
3         executeTask(args[0]);
4     }
5     public static void executeTask (String filename
      ) {
6     //read and process input
7     }
8 }
```

Figure 8: Task.java to be compiled at the central server.

```
1 String path = getFilesDir().getAbsolutePath();
2 String jarFile = path + "/task.jar";
3 DexClassLoader classLoader = new DexClassLoader(
    jarFile, path, null, getClass().getClassLoader
    ());
4 Class[] types = {new String[]{}.getClass(),};
5 Class<?> myClass = classLoader.loadClass("Task");
6 Method m = myClass.getMethod("main", types);
7 Object[] passed = {new String[]{path + "/input.txt"
    }};
8 Object x = m.invoke(classLoader, passed);
```

Figure 9: Reflection functionality on the smartphone.

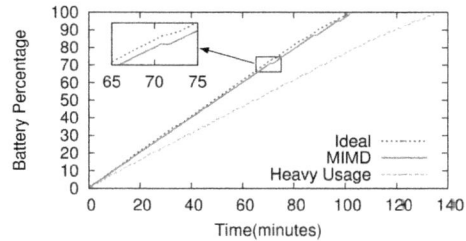

Figure 10: Charging times under different schemes for the HTC Sensation phones.

tral server, which are then packaged as .jar files using the Android tool chain (i.e., the *dx* command). The .jar file (containing the executable for the Android VM) together with the input data is copied to the phone. The phone extracts the .jar file and uses reflection to load and run the task, producing an output of results. Figure 8 shows the Java implementation of a typical CWC task. When the .java file is compiled and packaged in a .jar file, the task is executed on the phone using the code snippet in Figure 9. Thus, each phone concurrently processes the input partition *input.txt* assigned to it and this is transparent to the developers who implement their tasks (with the template in Figure 8) with a single machine in mind.

4.3 Preserving User Expectations

While predicting task execution times and automating them are important, we must note that phones are personal devices. Thus, first it is important to ensure that when a user chooses to use her phone, CWC stops the execution of the last assigned task to that phone so as not to adversely impact the end-user experience (e.g., task execution on the CPU can affect the responsiveness of the user interface). The tasks that are thus stopped, are then migrated to other phones that are still plugged in (as discussed).

Second, running tasks on phones that are are plugged in, should have a minimal impact on the charging times of the phones' batteries. We observe that a heavy utilization of a phone's CPU draws power and therefore, in some cases, prolongs the time taken to fully charge a phone's battery. Specifically, we conduct experiments where we first fully charge many types of phones (i.e., from 0% residual battery to 100%) in two settings; the first setting is without any job running on the phone, and the second setting corresponds to a case wherein a CPU intensive task is continuously run. As an example, we discuss results in the case of HTC Sensation phones, where we repeatedly run a CPU intensive task of counting the number of prime numbers in a large input file continuously during the charging period. We observe that while it takes around 100 minutes to complete full charging in the first setting, the time increases to 135 minutes in the second setting. Note that this increase could be phone-specific. In fact, we repeated the same experiment with HTC G2 phones and observed no significant effect (results are not reported due to space limitations). Our observation is that the more powerful the phone, the higher the penalty in terms of the increase in the charging period. Further note that, if the tasks are only scheduled after the phone is fully charged, there is no penalty (the phone remains fully charged); this is because the energy from the power outlet is directly applied to CPU computations. However, this would delay task processing and is thus avoided in CWC; moreover, users may not leave their phones plugged in until they are fully charged.

Our goal is to minimize the aforementioned adverse effect on a device's charging profile. If the CPU utilization can be controlled, we could achieve our goal. Prior approaches dynamically vary the voltage and/or the frequency of the CPU [36]. However, the modification of the voltage and frequency values require root privileges on the phone, and is therefore not applicable in our setting (using root privileges voids the phone warranty). Thus, our approach is to periodically pause the tasks being executed on the phones, and leave the CPU idle during such paused intervals. Next, we discuss when and for how long, we pause the execution of a task.

To begin with, our experiments demonstrate that the residual battery percentage (reported by the operating system) exhibits a predictable linear change with respect to time (as seen from Figure 10) in the case where no jobs run on the phone (referred to as the phone's charging profile). The rate of this linear change is specific to the device and the power source, but the relation remains linear across all the devices. When a task runs on the CPU of the phone, it draws power and thus, the charging profile deviates from this linear profile. We seek to minimize this deviation.

If there was no other task (e.g., background jobs not scheduled by CWC) running on the phone, we could determine the deviation due to CWC. Unfortunately, the process is complicated by the existence of such other tasks (possibly at different times) each of which with unpredictable CPU requirements and therefore power consumption patterns. Further, there could be fluctuations in the input power drawn from the supply (e.g. charging using a USB vs. a wall charger). Given this, our approach is to continuously monitor the rate at which the battery is charged, and either increase or decrease CPU utilization accordingly; the amount by which we increase the CPU utilization is called the scaling factor.

Specifically, we first measure the time it takes for the residual battery charge (δ) to increase by 1% of its preceding value, without any jobs running on the phone. This value of δ is referred to as the target charging parameter. Then, we run the task for a time period of $\delta/2$ and put the process to sleep for the next $\delta/2$ seconds. We repeat this process until the overall residual battery charge increases by 1 %. Let the time taken for this be $\beta(\geq \delta)$; this is referred to as the actual charging parameter. If $\beta = \delta$, there may be energy available to further ramp up the CPU utilization (the power from the outlet might be higher than what is required for charging). In this case, we decrease the sleep time during each δ period by a factor of 0.75, thereby inherently increasing CPU utilization; a new β is then computed based on the new settings. If $\beta > \delta$, the power drawn by the CPU is affecting the battery charging profile. Thus, we increase the sleep time by a factor of 2. Again, a new β value is computed. The process is repeated continuously. Note that the above strategy is akin a multiplicative increase/multiplicative decrease (MIMD) of the period for which the CPU is kept idle. Finally, since the phone's charging profile could change with time (as an example due to other tasks), we recompute the value of δ each time the residual battery charge changes by 5 %.

We plot the results with our adaptive MIMD based CPU scheduling in Fig. 10 for the HTC Sensation phones. The results from an ideal charging profile (no tasks) as well as a case where the CPU is heavily utilized without our approach are also shown. We see that our approach allows the phone to charge in a time that is almost the same as in the ideal case; the MIMD behavior of our approach is highlighted in the zoomed insert in the figure. Without our approach, the charging time increases by 35 %. Note here that, the use of the adaptive approach results in an increase in computation time of about 24.5 % compared to the heavily utilized scenario (due to the sleep cycles).

5. TASK SCHEDULING

In this section, we detail how tasks are scheduled in CWC. We are given a set J of jobs and a set P of smartphones. As discussed earlier, each job $j \in \mathcal{J}$ and phone $i \in \mathcal{P}$. The time it takes i to process x KB of j's input is given by

$$E_j * b_i + x * (b_i + c_{ij}) \tag{1}$$

where, E_j is the size (in KB) of job j's executable, b_i is the time (in milliseconds) that it takes phone i to receive 1 KB of data from the server, and c_{ij} is the time that it takes for phone i to execute the job j on 1 KB of input data. Our objective is to schedule the tasks across the phones such that the time it takes for the last phone to complete, T, (the *makespan*) is minimized. In the schedule, each job j's input can be split into pieces and each piece can be assigned to a phone. l_{ij} denotes the size (in KB) of job j's input partition assigned to phone i. $l_{ij} = 0$ simply indicates that phone i is not assigned any input partition of job j. u_{ij} is an indicator variable that denotes whether or not a partition of job j's input is scheduled to run on phone i. The scheduling problem (SCH) is then captured by the following quadratic integer program.

SCH: Minimize T

s.t. $\sum_j u_{ij} * (E_j * b_i + l_{ij} * (b_i + c_{ij})) \leq T, \ \forall i \in \mathcal{P}$

$\sum_i l_{ij} = L_j, \ \forall j \in \mathcal{J}$

$u_{ij} \in \{0, 1\} \quad \forall i \in \mathcal{P}, \forall j \in \mathcal{J}$

$\sum_i u_{ij} = 1 \ \forall \text{ atomic } j \in \mathcal{J}$

where we minimize the makespan, T. The first constraint requires that all phones finish executing their assigned tasks before T. The second constraint ensures that for every job, all of its input is processed. The last constraint ensures that atomic jobs are allocated to a single phone [4]. SCH reflects the general case for the minimum makespan scheduling (MMS) problem, which is known to be NP-hard. MMS is defined as: "*Given a set of jobs and a set of identical machines, assign the jobs to the machines such that the makespan is minimized*" [37]. A more general version of MMS is scheduling using unrelated machines (U-MMS), where each machine has different capabilities and thus, can execute tasks in different times. In both of these problems, only atomic jobs are considered. In other words, the goal is to assign each job to exactly one of the machines such that the makespan is minimized. SCH is a general case of U-MMS. We consider both atomic and breakable tasks and the machine capabilities are different. Since the special case of SCH (U-MMS) is NP-hard, the hardness carries over to SCH as well.

Our Solution: We address the SCH problem by solving the complementary bin packing problem (CBP), similar to the approach in [38]. In CBP, the objective is to pack items using at most $\|\mathcal{P}\|$ bins (with capacity C) such that the maximum height across bins is minimized. Here, the items correspond to the tasks and the bins correspond to the phones. The correlation between CBP and SCH can be drawn as follows. Let us assume that there is an optimal solution to CBP where the maximum height across the bins is M. If one rotates each bin 90° to the right, each bin visually appears as a phone in makespan scheduling. Items packed on top of each other in a bin correspond to input partitions assigned to a phone one after the other. Clearly, M corresponds to the maximum completion time across the set of phones in the rotated visualization. Thus, packing all items (tasks) using at most $\|\mathcal{P}\|$ bins (phones) and minimizing the maximum height across bins will minimize the makespan [5].

The pseudocode of our greedy algorithm to solve CBP is given in Algorithm 1. The idea is to first sort the tasks in decreasing order of local execution time. The first item in the sorted list is the one where $R_j * c_{sj}$ is the largest; s is the slowest CPU phone in the system and R_j is the remaining input size (in KB) of item (job) j that is yet to be assigned to some phone. Initially $R_j = L_j$.

In each iteration, we search for the first item in the list that can be packed in any of the previously opened bins (an open bin represents a phone that has previously been assigned some input partition). Note that determining whether an item can be packed in a bin depends on whether the current height of the bin plus the execution cost of that item in the particular bin is less than the bin capacity. If we can find such an item, we pack it in the bin with the minimum height at that time (i.e., the phone with the least total execution time). When packing such an item (line 6), we pack its largest input partition that can fit. If the item can fit without partitioning it, we prefer packing it as a whole.

---

[4]Although not currently addressed in the paper, CWC can handle memory constraints. One can add $l_{ij} \leq r_i$ to ensure that any job j's partition assigned to phone i is less than or equal to the phone's RAM (denoted here by r_i).

[5]The reader can refer to [38] for details.

Algorithm 1 Greedy Packing Algorithm

```
 1:  L : sorted list in decreasing order of execution time
 2:  C : bin capacity
 3:  repeat
 4:     find the first item in L that can fit in any opened bin
 5:     if such an item exists then
 6:        pack the item in the bin with min. height
 7:        if the item was packed as a whole then
 8:           remove it from L
 9:        else
10:           insert its remaining input in L
11:           re-sort L
12:        end if
13:     else
14:        if there are un-opened bins then
15:           open the best bin for the largest item in L
16:           pack the item in the opened bin
17:           if the item was packed as a whole then
18:              remove it from L
19:           else
20:              insert its remaining input in L
21:              re-sort L
22:           end if
23:        else
24:           cannot open any more bins
25:           cannot finish packing with C
26:        end if
27:     end if
28:  until all jobs are packed
```

The idea behind our design is the following. If a task is broken down to N pieces, the central server would have to aggregate N partial results, which would be an extra overhead at the server when the phones return their results. Thus, if two packings produce the same minimum bin height, we would prefer one with fewer partitions. If packing an item as a whole is not possible (simply because doing so would result in the bin height exceeding the capacity), we pack that item's largest partition that can fit without violating the bin capacity (with the purpose of keeping the number of partitions low). If no item can fit in the opened bins (line 13), we check if we can open a new bin. If not, the algorithm cannot find a feasible packing for the given capacity. If we can open a new bin, we open the bin that would accept the largest item in L, with the minimum increase in its height (line 15). Clearly, such a bin is the one that minimizes Equation 1 for the largest item in L. After opening the bin, we again try to pack the item as a whole (line 17). If not, we pack the item's largest partition subject to the bin capacity.

The above algorithm is repeated multiple times for different selections of bin capacities. Here, we adopt an approach similar to binary search. We first determine an upper bound (UB) on the bin height. Clearly, the maximum bin height occurs when all items are assigned to the bin that maximizes Equation 1 (i.e, the worst bin). For the lower bound (LB), we initially pick a loose bound where all items are packed in a single magical bin that has the aggregate processing capability and the aggregate bandwidth of all bins; there are no other bins. This magical bin represents the ideal case where the inputs are partitioned without the executable cost. After determining these initial bounds, we execute Algorithm 1 with $C = \frac{(LB+UB)}{2}$. If the algorithm succeeds packing all items with bin capacity C, we let $UB = C$. If the algorithm cannot find a feasible packing with the initial C, we let $LB = C$. The algorithm is then repeatedly executed with $C = \frac{(LB+UB)}{2}$, until the algorithm succeeds with the minimum C. Here, the binary search simply reduces the search space for the minimum bin capacity, with which the algorithm packs all the items.

When CWC determines the schedule as described above, it starts copying the relevant executables and the input partitions to each phone. This is done on a per-partition basis; the next assigned task to the phone is copied only after the phone completes executing its last assigned task. When the phones inform the central server about a task completion, they report the partial results together with the time it takes to locally execute the assigned task. As described in Section 4, CWC uses such execution reports to update its prediction on execution times of tasks. If the same task is assigned to the same phone in the future (albeit with a different input partition), CWC uses the updated prediction for scheduling.

Handling Failures: In CWC's task execution cycle, some phones may naturally fail while executing a given task. In our setting, the term failure can correspond to a variety of cases. For example, when a phone is plugged off the charger, we treat it as a failed node since continuing to execute a CPU-intensive task on it would drain the battery (a critical concern for CWC). In CWC, such failures are communicated back to the central server whenever possible (i.e., when the phone still has a network connection), and the execution can be resumed from the point where it failed (details of task state migration are in Section 6). We call these class of failures where the phone maintains a connection with the server "online failures". Other scenarios may include harder failures, in which the phone loses its connection to the server (e.g., wireless driver suddenly crashes or the network connection is dropped), and thus, cannot report its failed state back to the central server (the description of detecting such failures at the central server is again deferred to Section 6). We call this class of failures "offline failures".

Assume that at time instant A, we compute a schedule X. With X, each phone i has a set of tasks X_i that it will execute as time progresses. CWC starts copying the executable and input partitions in X_i to i one task at a time and waits for i to either report a completion or a failure. If no report is received for the last copied task, say $last_i$ (due to an offline failure), CWC marks i as failed and inserts $last_i$ and all the remaining tasks in X_i to a list F_A that contains all failed tasks after A. If i reports completion, CWC simply copies the next task in X_i and again waits for reports. If on the other hand, i reports failure for $last_i$, the report contains additional information: **(a)** how much of the input was processed by i by the failure instance, and **(b)** what was the intermediate (partial) result associated with the processing. CWC still inserts $last_i$ (and all that remains in X_i) in F_A, but now $last_i$ is inserted with only the part of the input not processed by i (and the intermediate results are saved). Now assume that we have a new schedule to be computed at time instant B. Some new tasks have entered the system at this point and are awaiting scheduling. Now, CWC computes a schedule for all such new tasks and F_A combined. The reason that we avoid immediate re-scheduling of tasks in F_A and wait until B is to account for the possibility that failed phones may re-enter the system after a short period of unavailability (e.g., the user plugs her phone to the charger after a few minutes or the connectivity is restored). Note that this is in contrast with typical MapReduce architectures, where failures may result in long periods of unavailability [39].

6. IMPLEMENTATION AND EVALUATION

Our testbed consists of 18 Android phones with varying network connectivity and CPU speeds. The network interfaces vary from WiFi (both 802.11a and 802.11g are considered) to EDGE, 3G and 4G. The CPU clock speeds vary from 806 MHz to 1.5 GHz. Each phone registers with a central server and reports its CPU clock speed. We measure b_i values (bandwidth to each smartphone i) with the *iperf* tool. The phones host the CWC software, which maintains a persistent TCP connection with the server and permits dynamic task execution as instructed by the scheduler. To maintain long-lived flows, we use the $SO\_KEEPALIVE$ option in the connection sockets as well as implement custom application layer keep-alive messages. The latter also serve as a means of detecting offline failures. If a phone fails to respond to a preset number of keep-alive requests from the server, it is marked as failed. In our implementation, the keep-alive message period is 30 seconds and the number of response failures tolerated, is 3.

Several techniques exist to migrate failed tasks and resume their state on a target machine; for example, the authors in [40] modify the Android virtual machine (VM) itself to migrate the state of execution but this requires changes to the original Android VM. To make it more user and developer friendly, we ported JavaGO – a Java program migration library [41] to the Android. JavaGO is based on a "source-code-level" transformation technique, where the JavaGo translator takes the user program as input and outputs the migratory Java code. The translated code can run on any Java interpreter and can be compiled by any Just-in-Time (JIT) compiler. JavaGo provides flexibility by allowing programmers to annotate their code using three added language constructs to the Java language, namely *go*, *undock* and *migratory*. The *go* statement specifies the IP address of the machine where the failed application will be resumed. The *undock* construct specifies the area to be migrated in the execution stack while *migratory* construct declares which methods are migratory so that only those methods are modified by the JavaGo compiler. In CWC, we translate the annotated java task files with JavaGo translator to produce the migratory `.jar` task file. In case of a failure, the state of a task is saved and transmitted to the central server (via the *go* construct). Our server records the transmitted state but does not itself resume the computation at that state. At the next scheduling instant, the server sends the recorded state of each failed task to a newly assigned phone, which then resumes the task. Details on migration can be found in [41].

The server is implemented as a multi-threaded Java NIO server. Non-blocking threads allow the server to concurrently copy data to a phone while reading the completion reports of other phones. We host the server on a small Amazon EC2 instance to show its lightweight implementation and economical viability. The small instance is the default configuration offered by EC2. It offers one virtual core with 1.7 GB of memory, which represent a machine that is far less capable than state-of-the-art workstations. Currently, Amazon charges 8 cents per hour for a small Linux instance. This clearly shows that the lightweight central server in CWC incurs very small cost for a typical enterprise (although the exact value may change over time).

Prototype Evaluation: In evaluating CWC, we use a variety of tasks. The first task involves counting the occurrences of prime numbers in an input file. The second task is to count the number of occurrences of a word in the input file and the third task is to blur the pixels in a photo. While we are able to directly use the desktop Java versions of the first two tasks, doing this was not possible for the photo blurring task. The challenge relates to the lack of compatibility between the graphics classes on the desktop Java virtual machine and the Dalvik virtual machine in Android. While the code works on JVM, the reflection class loader on Android complained about the part of the code that reads the pixels from the image file (in particular BufferedImage class does not exist in Android). To eliminate the phone's reading the pixels directly from the image, we do the following modification. We first pre-process the pictures to read the pixels (at the central server) and create text files that contain a pixel value in each of its lines. Each phone was able to process the text files as before. After this, the server re-creates each photo from the blurred pixels returned by each phone.

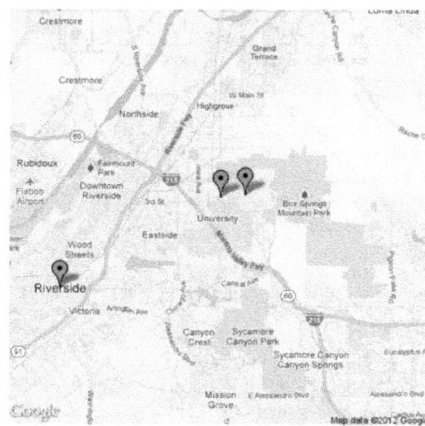

Figure 11: Map of the phone locations.

Comparison with simple practical schedulers: At the server, we also implement simpler alternatives to CWC. The first alternative splits each breakable job into $|\mathcal{P}|$ pieces without accounting for the different bandwidth and CPU speeds of phones in $\mathcal{P}$. The atomic jobs are assigned to phones in a round-robin manner (phone 1 gets atomic job 1 and so on). In the second alternative, both breakable and atomic jobs are assigned in a round-robin manner.

Setup: We distribute our 18 phones in three houses (the locations are shown in Fig. 11). In two of these houses, we have a 802.11g WiFi network and an abundance of interfering residential access points using the 2.4 GHz band. In the third house, we have a 802.11a WiFi AP without interference from neighboring APs. Of the 6 phones we place in each house (phones are plugged to power outlets), we associate 2 phones with the WiFi AP and 4 phones are configured to use varying cellular technologies (from the slowest EDGE to the fastest 4G). Before running the CWC scheduler, we initiate *iperf* sessions from each phone to the EC2 server and log the measured data rate in KBps (the inverse of this value is used as b_i). The workload comprises of the following. We have 50 instances of task 1 (counting primes) with varying input data sizes, we have 50 instances of task 2 (counting word occurrences) with varying input sizes and, 50 variable size photos to be blurred (atomic task 3).

Results: In the first experiment, we run our greedy scheduler followed by the two alternate scheduling strategies described above; we do not consider phone failures. Fig.12(a) presents the task execution timeline for a select set of phones. We do not show the plots for every phone for better visualization (the patterns are similar across the phones). The vertical black stripes in a phone's timeline correspond to the time intervals where the phone is receiving the task executable and the corresponding input partition from the server. The white regions correspond to the time intervals where the phone executes the task locally. From Fig. 12(a), we observe that while some phones (2 and 9) finish their tasks earlier than others, the load is well balanced for most of the phones (4, 12, 13, 14 complete at similar time instants). Phones 2 and 9 finished early because of a mismatch between the expected speedup and the measured speedup (recall Fig. 6 in Section 5). In particular, these phones are faster than what is indicated by their CPU clock speeds and thus, finish earlier than the scheduler's prediction. We see that the difference in the completion times between the earliest phone (2 finishes at around 900 seconds) and the last phone (12 finishes at around 1100 seconds) is $\approx 20\%$ of the makespan. In addition, our scheduler's predicted makespan of 1120 seconds was only 20 seconds more than the actual makespan of 1100 seconds. Fig.12(b) shows the CDF of the number of input partitions for each of the

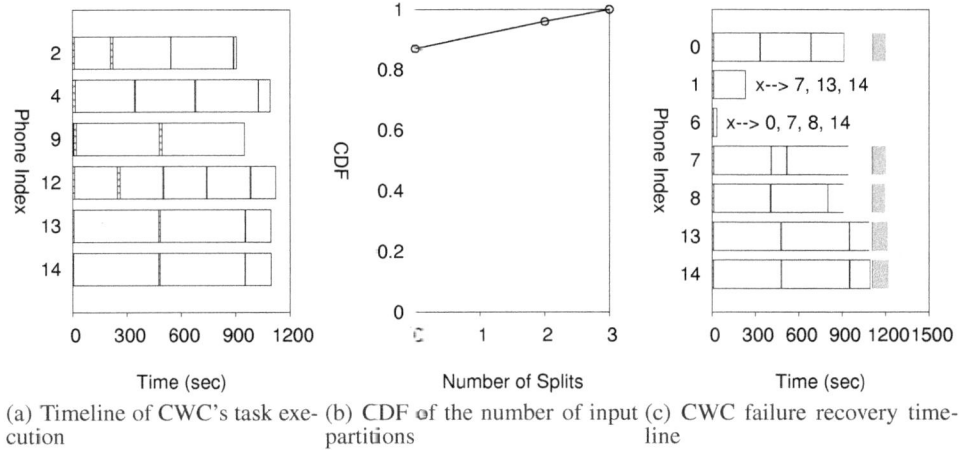

(a) Timeline of CWC's task exe- (b) CDF of the number of input (c) CWC failure recovery time-
cution   partitions   line

Figure 12: Our greedy scheduler produces very few input partitions (b) and provides support for failure recovery (c).

150 tasks considered. An input partition of 0 indicates that the task was atomically assigned to a single phone. While 33% of the tasks by definition cannot be partitioned (the photo tasks are atomic), we observe that our scheduler preserves atomicity for most of the tasks ($\approx$90%) and thus, significantly reduces the aggregation cost at the server. In contrast, we observe that the equal split strategy had a makespan of 1720 seconds, and produced a large number of input partitions since each breakable task is split into $|\mathcal{P}|$ pieces. While the round-robin strategy avoided excessive input partitions, it achieved a makespan of 1805 seconds. *In summary, our greedy scheduler is around 1.6x faster than the alternative schedulers and it achieves this while with almost negligible aggregation costs.*

In Fig. 12(c), we plot the timeline for a different run of the above experiment. Here, we introduce failures by unplugging three phones (phones 1, 6 and 17) at random instances during task execution (the plot again shows a subset of phones). As discussed in Section 5, in the next round of scheduling, our scheduler re-schedules tasks from previously failed phones across the remaining set of phones. The x marks on Fig. 12(c) indicate the assignment of the failed tasks of a phone. The shaded task executions depict the execution of re-scheduled tasks. We observe that phone 1's tasks were partitioned across phones 7, 13 and 14. On the other hand, phone 6's failed tasks were re-scheduled across phones 0, 7, 8 and 14. Since phone 6 failed at the very beginning of its schedule, it had more tasks to be re-scheduled. Our scheduler mainly chose faster phones (phones 0, 7 and 8 completed ahead of time in the original schedule) to re-schedule these failed tasks. Overall, re-scheduling failed tasks required 113 seconds after the original makespan.

Benchmarking the Scheduler: Next, we try to get a lower bound on the makespan to benchmark the performance of our algorithm. This requires optimally solving the quadratic integer program formulated in Section 5, which is NP-hard owing to the integral nature. While the integral part can be relaxed by allowing the variables u_{ij} and l_{ij} to take fractional values and hence producing a loose lower bound, we still cannot use standard LP solvers to compute the bound owing to the quadratic nature. To address this, we can re-formulate the problem by transforming the first constraint to $\sum_j u_{ij} * (E_j * b_i) + l_{ij} * (b_i + c_{ij}) \leq T$, where now u_{ij} applies only to the first term. However, to prevent the solution from allocating jobs to a phone ($l_{ij} > 0$) without accounting for the shipping cost of its executable ($u_{ij} = 0$), we add another constraint $(1 - u_{ij})l_{ij} = 0, \ \forall i, j$. The latter can now easily be relaxed

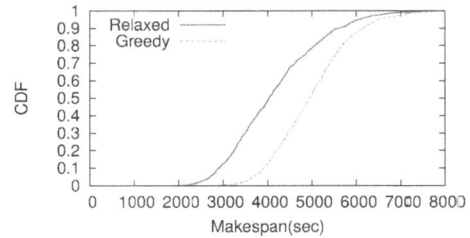

Figure 13: Comparison of the makespans of the greedy scheduler and the solution to the relaxed problem.

as $l_{ij} \leq L_j * u_{ij}$, thereby resulting in an LP relaxation, which can be solved to obtain a loose lower bound (smaller makespan than optimal due to relaxation) on the solution. Thus, we have $T_{relaxed} \leq T_{optimal} \leq T_{cwc}$, where T is the makespan produced by each of these solutions.

To understand how close we are to the optimal, we input various combinations of tasks and bandwidth profiles and solve the problem with **(a)** our greedy scheduler and **(b)** using the relaxed formulation above. We simulate the solutions by generating random b_i values between 1 and 70 milliseconds (the minimum and maximum values measured in our experiments). We consider the same set of 150 tasks and we get the c_{ij} values from the phones in our testbed. We generate 1000 random configurations and for each configuration, we first obtain the makespan for the relaxed formulation and subsequently we obtain the makespan produced by our greedy scheduler. Fig. 13 shows the CDF (over random configurations) of these makespans. It is seen that the median makespan of our greedy scheduler is approximately 18% worse than the relaxed formulation's solution.

7. CONCLUSIONS

In this paper, we envision building a distributed computing infrastructure using smartphones for the enterprise. Our vision is based on several compelling observations including (a) enterprises provide their employees with smartphones in many cases, (b) the phones are typically unused when being charged, and (c) such an infrastructure could potentially yield significant cost benefits to the enterprise. We articulate the technical challenges in building such an infrastructure. We address many of them to design CWC, a framework that supports such an infrastructure. We have a prototype implementation of CWC on a testbed of 18 Android phones. Using this implementation, we demonstrate both the viability and efficacy of various components within CWC.

Acknowledgements

We would like to thank Dr. Konstantina Papagiannaki, the anonymous reviewers and the program chairs Dr. K. K. Ramakrishnan and Dr. Patrick Thiran for their helpful suggestions towards improving the paper. This work was partially supported by the US Army Research Office MURI grant W911NF-07-1-0318.

8. REFERENCES

[1] Iphone in Business. http://bit.ly/LE4dAp.

[2] Enterprise Smartphone Usage Trends. http://bit.ly/loIqE1.

[3] Novartis: Apps for good health. http://bit.ly/KEdJbh.

[4] Lowe's : Building better customer service. http://bit.ly/MiT9bk.

[5] IBM gets US$2mn data center contract from Novartis. bit.ly/L51P8i.

[6] NVIDIA says Tegra 3 is a "PC-class CPU". http://engt.co/srvibU.

[7] S. Harizopoulos and S Papadimitriou. A Case for Micro-Cellstores: Energy-Efecient Data Management on Recycled Smartphones. In *DaMoN*, 2011.

[8] Variable SMP - A Multi-Core CPU Architecture for Low Power and High Performance. bit.ly/n65KzQ.

[9] Smart Phone Chips Calling for Data Centers. bit.ly/LdM9fS.

[10] WiFi Bandwidth Use in the U.S. Home Forecast to More Than Double in the Next Four Years. http://yhoo.it/L9Po9A.

[11] PhoneLab. http://bit.ly/NYwRhI.

[12] Almudeua Díaz Zayas and Pedro Merino Gómez. A testbed for energy profile characterization of IP services in smartphones over live networks. *Mob. Netw. Appl.*

[13] E. Cuervo, P. Gilbert, Bi Wu, and L.P. Cox. CrowdLab: An architecture for volunteer mobile testbeds. In *COMSNETS*, 2011.

[14] J. Cappos, I. Beschastnikh, A. Krishnamurthy, and T. Anderson. Seattle: A Platform for Educational Cloud Computing. In *SIGCSE*, 2009.

[15] SETI@home. http://setiathome.berkeley.edu.

[16] P. R. Elespuru, S. Shakya, and S. Mishra. MapReduce System over Heterogeneous Mobile Devices. In *SEUS*, 2009.

[17] http://research.cs.wisc.edu/condor/.

[18] Tathagata Das, Prashanth Mohan, Venkata N. Padmanabhan, Ramachandran Ramjee, and Asankhaya Sharma. PRISM: platform for remote sensing using smartphones. In *ACM MobiSys*, 2010.

[19] D. Estrin. Participatory Sensing: Applications and Architecture. In *ACM MobiSys*, 2010.

[20] N. Eagle. txteagle: Mobile Crowdsourcing. In *Internationalization, Design and Global Development*, 2009.

[21] Earl Oliver. The challenges in large-scale smartphone user studies. In *ACM HotPlanet*, 2010.

[22] Hossein Falaki, Dimitrios Lymberopoulos, Ratul Mahajan, Srikanth Kandula, and Deborah Estrin. A first look at traffic on smartphones. In *IMC*, 2010.

[23] Alex Shye, Benjamin Scholbrock, Gokhan Memik, and Peter A. Dinda. Characterizing and modeling user activity on smartphones: Summary. In *ACM SIGMETRICS*, 2010.

[24] Earl Oliver. Diversity in smartphone energy consumption. In *ACM workshop on Wireless of the students, by the students, for the students*, 2010.

[25] Mohammad Hajjat, Xin Sun, Yu-Wei, Eric Sung, David Maltz, and Sanjay Rao. Cloudward Bound: Planning for Beneficial Migration of Enterprise Applications to the Cloud. In *ACM SIGCOMM*, 2010.

[26] Timothy Wood, Emmanuel Cecchet, K.K. Ramakrishnan, Prashant Shenoy, Jacobus van der Merwe, and Arun Venkataramani. Disaster Recovery as a Cloud Service: Economic Benefits & Deployment Challenges. In *USENIX HotCloud*, 2010.

[27] Azbayar Demberel, Jeff Chase, and Shivnath Babu. Reflective control for an elastic cloud application: an automated experiment workbench. In *USENIX HotCloud*, 2009.

[28] Thomas A. Henzinger, Anmol V. Singh, Vasu Singh, Thomas Wies, and Damien Zufferey. Static Scheduling in Clouds. In *USENIX HotCloud*, 2011.

[29] Quad-core smartphones: This is their year. http://cnet.co/xvlHX5.

[30] Coremark benchmark. http://www.coremark.org/.

[31] C. Peng, S. Lee, S. Lu, H. Luo, and H. Li. Traffic-Driven Power Saving in Operational 3G Cellular Networks. In *ACM MobiCom*, 2011.

[32] Justin Manweiler, Sharad Agarwal, Ming Zhang, Romit Roy Choudhury, and Paramvir Bahl. Switchboard: a matchmaking system for multiplayer mobile games. ACM MobiSys, 2011.

[33] Andrew Krioukov, Prashanth Mohan, Sara Alspaugh, Laura Keys, David Culler, and Randy Katz. NapSAC: Design and Implementation of a Power-Proportional Web Cluster. In *Workshop on Green Networking*, 2010.

[34] Green grid data center power efficiency metrics: PUE and DCIE. bit.ly/MioRIt.

[35] Antony Rowstron, Dushyanth Narayanan, Austin Donnelly, Greg O'Shea, and Andrew Douglas. Nobody ever got Þred for using Hadoop on a cluster. In *HotCDP*, 2012.

[36] Sebastian Herbert and Diana Marculescu. Analysis of dynamic voltage/frequency scaling in chip-multiprocessors. ISLPED '07, 2007.

[37] Vijay V. Vazirani. *Approximation Algorithms*. Springer, 2004.

[38] JR. E. G. Coffman, M. R. Garey, and D. S. Johnson. An Application of Bin-Packing to Multiprocessor Scheduling. *SIAM Journal of Computing*, 7(1), Feb 1978.

[39] J. Dean and S. Ghemawat. MapReduce: Simplified Data Processing on Large Clusters. In *USENIX OSDI*, 2004.

[40] Byung-Gon Chun, Sunghwan Ihm, Petros Maniatis, Mayur Naik, and Ashwin Patti. CloneCloud: elastic execution between mobile device and cloud. ACM EuroSys, 2011.

[41] Tatsurou Sekiguchi, Hidehiko Masuhara, and Akinori Yonezawa. A Simple Extension of Java Language for Controllable Transparent Migration and Its Portable Implementation. COORDINATION, 1999.

Weeble: Enabling Low-Power Nodes to Coexist with High-Power Nodes in White Space Networks

Božidar Radunović
Microsoft Research
Cambridge
bozidar@microsoft.com

Ranveer Chandra
Microsoft Research
Redmond
ranveer@microsoft.com

Dinan Gunawardena
Microsoft Research
Cambridge
dinang@microsoft.com

ABSTRACT

One of the key distinctive requirements of white-space networks is the power asymmetry. Static nodes are allowed to transmit with 15dB-20dB higher power than mobile nodes. This poses significant coexistence problems, as high-power nodes can easily starve low-power nodes. In this paper, we propose Weeble, a novel distributed and state-less MAC protocol that solves the coexistence problem. One of the key building blocks is an adaptive preamble support, an add-on to the PHY layer that allows high-power nodes to detect a low-power transmission even when the difference in transmit power is as high as 20dB. The other key building block is a MAC protocol that exploits the adaptive preambles functionality. It implements a virtual carrier-sensing and automatically adapts the preamble size to optimize network performance. We extensively evaluate our system in a test-bed and in simulations. We show that we can prevent starvation of low-power nodes in almost all existing scenarios and improve the data rates of low-power links several-fold over existing MACs, and as a trade-off we decrease the throughput of the rest of the system by 20%-40%.

Categories and Subject Descriptors

C.2.1 [**Network Architecture and Design**]: Wireless communication

General Terms

Design

Keywords

Coexistence, White-spaces

1. INTRODUCTION

There is recent interest in using the TV white spaces (unoccupied TV channels) for unlicensed communication. The FCC issued an official approval for the US [6]; the UK [28], Canada [2], Brazil and Singapore have made significant progress towards similar decisions. The industry is moving quickly with the development of

the white space database [7] and hardware [34]. The IEEE is even developing standards for different applications over this spectrum.

This excitement stems primarily from the excellent propagation characteristics of the TV spectrum – it not only extends the reach of a transmission, it also enables faster transmissions at short distances because of higher SNR. Both these benefits lead to different applications. The former is useful in regional area networks (WRANs) as is enabled by the IEEE 802.22 standard [16]. The latter is useful for in-home media distribution applications, which have been proposed by Dell, Philips, and other companies, and will be enabled by the 802.11af standard [3]. This has led to an important question – can these low power (in-home) and high power (regional-area applications) coexist on the same spectrum?

The FCC has defined the operational parameters of the low and high power nodes. The *high power* nodes, such as base-stations or regional network back-haul nodes, can transmit with a power of up to 4W. Per the rules, these nodes have to be static and query the spectrum database [7] so that they do not create interference on the existing TV channels[1]. The *low power* nodes are limited to 40mW or 100mW of transmit power (depending whether they are adjacent to an active TV channel) and can be mobile. Note that both high and low power nodes are unregulated, except for the spectral mask and the requirements mentioned above. In principle, even consumer devices could use high-power transmissions in any available white-space channel to boost the quality of home network. However, this is unlikely to happen as it would increase the power consumption, heat dissipation, the form factor and the cost of the devices.

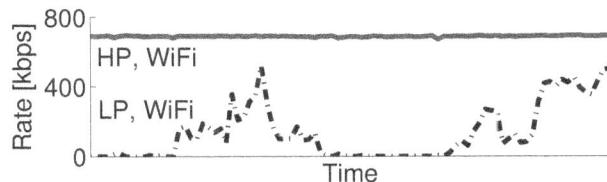

Figure 1: Starvation of a mobile low-power (LP) link in presence of high-power (HP) link.

This large power asymmetry poses a significant challenge to network design. A high-power node might not sense the transmission of a low-power node, and hence, can easily overwhelm the low-power node with interference and interrupt communication (hidden terminal). We observe the starvation in Figure 1, which shows the throughput of a low power and high power node in our white space test-bed (described in Section 5) when using the Wi-Fi MAC.

---

[1]The database is not used to allocate spectrum to (low or high power) white-space nodes, but only to prevent them from interfering with the incumbents.

The IEEE has recognized this problem as well and formed the IEEE 802.19 working group [14] that also addresses this coexistence problem.

A strawman approach to deal with the coexistence problem is to assign disjoint frequencies to high-power and low-power nodes (or frequency division multiplexing, FDM). However, determining the frequency separation is non-trivial because of varying white space availability, different population densities, and mobility of low-power nodes. Moreover, any such frequency assignment needs to be dynamic and global. This makes it extremely difficult to manage. Furthermore, as we show in Section 6, such a technique can also be very inefficient.

In this paper we present Weeble, a novel, fully distributed MAC design for coexistence among high-power and low-power nodes. The main idea behind Weeble is to repair the carrier sense mechanism in a power asymmetric setting and then build a CSMA-like distributed reservation protocol on top of it. We note that our problem is different from the problem of coexistence with legacy devices, i.e. those that cannot be modified [13, 8, 27, 12]. In this paper, our goal is to design a mechanism that can be adapted by both the high and low-power nodes.

A key component of designing Weeble is to define coexistence among low and high-power nodes. In this paper we define coexistence as avoiding starvation of low-power nodes due to high power interference and, more generally, to run the network efficiently and fairly. However, fairness and efficiency are fundamentally conflicting goals [30] and there is no commonly accepted definition of fairness in white-space networks. One can argue that high-power links (such as base-stations and back-haul links) are more important than the low-power links. Thus, our design goals are, in the following order: (a) to avoid starvation of any link, (b) avoid significant performance deterioration of high-power links and (c) increase the total throughput as much as possible.

Weeble achieves the above goals by leveraging two key innovations:

Technique for detecting transmissions at low SNR : First, we design an adaptive preamble detector that allows low power nodes to signal their presence to nodes that receive the signal at very low SNR (even lower than -15 dB). Our design uses two types of preambles to significantly decrease the false positives and it does not require any prior synchronization between the nodes (unlike [12, 9, 33]). By tunning the length of the preamble, one can control the signalling range and the preamble overhead. We build our preamble detector in FPGA as an add-on to an existing OFDM PHY design, and we also show that our implementation is much more efficient than conventional preamble detector designs.

MAC that allows low power and high power nodes to coexist: Second, we design a distributed reservation mechanism for low-power nodes that is based on adaptive preamble signalling (Section 4). In the absence of carrier sense it is not possible to detect the end of a packet transmission. Instead, our low-power reservations are of fixed duration. To make an efficient use of each reservation period, all low-power nodes are allowed to contend and transmit multiple packets when possible during the period. We balance the traffic between the high-power and low-power nodes by prioritizing the access of high-power nodes in between low-power reservation periods (Section 4.1). Finally, we propose an algorithm to adapt the preamble size to maximize the spatial reuse and limit the protocol overhead (Section 4.2).

We have implemented our system on the Lyrtech SDR platform. Using a set of micro-benchmarks we first demonstrate that our adaptive signalling works with 90% accuracy at SNRs below -15dB (Section 6.1). We then evaluate the full Weeble MAC design in a small scale test-bed on several topologies (Section 6.2). In contrast to the recent software-defined radio deployments [33, 36, 9, 8, 12] that do not implement MAC protocols but rely on offline processing of channel traces, we implement and run both PHY and MAC on the deployed nodes. We show that we avoid starvation of low-power flows and we achieve 50% median increase in rates of low-power flows over 802.11 MAC, at the expense of less than 6% median decrease of rates of high-power flows. We further evaluate Weeble on larger topologies using Qualnet simulations with PHY layer parameters as measured in the test-bed (Section 6). We observe up to 10-fold rate improvement of low-power flows over 802.11 MAC and FDM (frequency division multiplexing MAC), with an inevitable trade-off being a 20%-40% rate decrease of high-power flows.

2. WEEBLE OVERVIEW

Carrier sense is a simple and very efficient signaling primitive for sharing the medium in unlicensed wireless networks, such as Wi-Fi. Weeble attempts to provide a similar functionality in white space networks even though not all nodes are in carrier sensing range of each other, for example in networks where different nodes transmit at different transmission powers. To ensure that low power nodes get time to communicate without interference from high power nodes we enhance carrier sense with a new technique called *low-power reservations*.

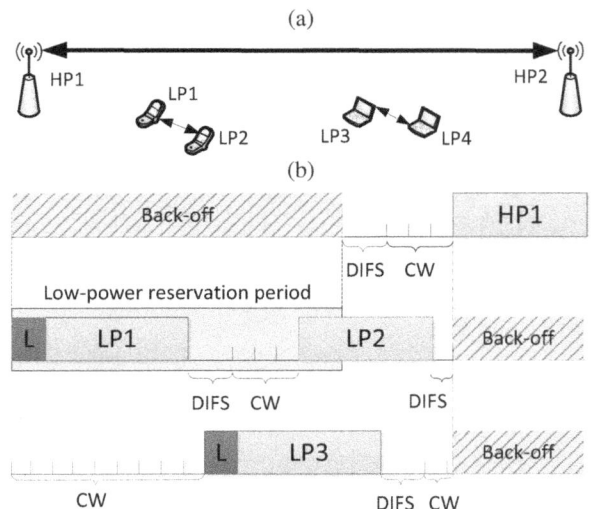

Figure 2: Illustration of the low-power reservation period (HP - high-power transmissions, LP - low-power transmissions, L - adaptive preamble): (a) network topology, (b) sample packet exchange

To signal a start of a low-power reservation to a high power node, we introduce a special preamble. Since this preamble might not always be needed (for example, when the interference does not affect packet reception), a low-power node may decide to prepend this special preamble to its packets only if it experiences interference. All nodes that detect the preamble will refrain from sending for the duration of the reservation (that will be defined later).

To ensure that low-power reservations do not block out a large region, we design a preamble of adaptive size. The longer the preamble, the lower the SNR is at which it can be detected. We choose the preamble size of a low-power link such that it can be detected only by those high-power nodes whose concurrent transmission can cause a packet loss on the respective low-power link. If the preamble is too short, this will lead to packet losses at the low-power link. If it is too long, it will hamper spatial reuse. We describe the algorithm to determine the preamble length in Section 4.2.

For simplicity, we set the duration of a low-power reservation to be a constant. To efficiently use the reservation period, it is shared by all low-power nodes in the vicinity. The low-power nodes use the conventional carrier sense among themselves and the node that initializes the reservation period (by sending an adaptive preamble) transmits the first packet. It will be followed by other low-power nodes until the reservation expires. Once the reservation has expired, the high-power nodes will resume contending for the access among themselves and the other low-power nodes.

We illustrate the functionality of Weeble MAC in Figure 2. We consider a network depicted in Figure 2 (a) with one high-power and two low-power links. We assume that LP1 and LP2 are sufficiently far from LP3 and LP4 so that they cannot hear each other. Everyone can hear HP1 and HP2 because HP1 and HP2 use much higher transmit power.

One sample execution of Weeble MAC is given in Figure 2 (b). In this example, node LP1 first sends the low-power preamble and starts the low-power reservation period. This causes HP1 and HP2 to back off for the duration of the period. LP3 is not aware of all this, but as it does not sense any transmission it keeps on counting down and eventually starts transmitting during the same low-power reservation period. As LP3 is not aware of LP1, it also includes the low-power preamble in its transmission. Since it is received during an ongoing low-power reservation period, HP1 and HP2 will ignore it. Also note that all low-power nodes are allowed to keep on transmitting once the low-power reservation period has expired, but they are not guaranteed that these transmissions will not be corrupted by a concurrent high-power transmission. We explain the Weeble MAC in more detail in Section 4.1.

3. ADAPTIVE PREAMBLES

Weeble is built upon a new preamble design that (a) allows preamble detection at SNRs below -15dB, (b) has an adaptive detection range, (c) works well, i.e. has few false positives and false negatives, in the presence of interference, and (d) is simple and cheap to implement (in terms of silicon area, and hence also power consumption). We describe our design corresponding to the first three goals in this section – using repetitive preambles for detection at low SNRs, support for adaptive preamble lengths, and a detection mechanism that works in the presence of interference. Although the design of our detector is for an OFDM PHY, which is used in most of the relevant white space standards (802.22, 802.11af), our idea can easily generalize to other PHYs.

A key challenge in the design of our preamble detector is synchronization. State-of-the art implementations of preamble detection [9, 33], are able to detect preambles of size 1 OFDM symbol at SNRs of down to -15dB, but require synchronization between the nodes [12]. Synchronization is difficult to achieve in our scenario since low-power nodes might never be able to communicate with interfering high-power nodes. We thus decided to use longer preambles, which increases the detector's complexity. We show how our design can be implemented without consuming significantly more silicon.

3.1 Detecting preambles at low SNR

We use the well-known phenomenon that the detection accuracy increases with the length of the preamble [20]. A key question then is how to design such a preamble without increasing the complexity of the detector [35].

The preamble in OFDM is used to synchronize with the start of a packet transmission. Hence the preamble sequence **P** is a pseudo-

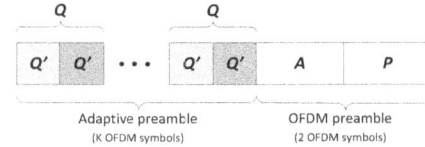

Figure 3: The structure of the PHY header, comprising an adaptive preamble and a standard OFDM preamble (A, P).

random sequence with as little auto-correlation as possible. In our application, in which the high power node only needs to detect (and not decode) low-power packet transmissions, we are *not interested in the detection with such an accurate timing*. It is sufficient to detect the packet transmission with a timing precision even as high as a few tens of micro-seconds. We leverage this lee-way to simplify the receiver design by using repetitive instead of purely pseudo-random preambles.

We use a symmetric preamble $\mathbf{Q} = (\mathbf{Q}', \mathbf{Q}')$ as the main building block where sequence $\mathbf{Q}' = (Q_0, \cdots, Q_{S/2-1})$ is a pseudo-random sequence. The size of $\mathbf{Q}$ is one OFDM symbol and S is the number of samples per OFDM symbol (typically $S = 64$ or more). Note that this is the same type of preamble used in the state-of-the-art detectors [32, 35]. The key difference in our design is that when we increase the size of the preamble, we do not increase the size of $\mathbf{Q}'$, but we repeat the same basic preamble. Our repetitive preamble $\mathbf{L} = (\mathbf{Q}, \cdots, \mathbf{Q})$ consists of K repetitions of $\mathbf{Q}$ and lasts K OFDM symbols. The preamble is illustrated in Figure 3.

Let $C_n^S = \sum_{i=0}^{S/2-1} (Q_i')^* Y_{n+i}$ be the correlation (multiplication) of the complex input base-band samples Y_n with a complex conjugate of one half preamble $\mathbf{Q}'$. We then calculate the preamble correlation C_n at time n as

$$ C_n = \left(\sum_{k=0}^{K-1} C_{n+kS}^S \right) \left(\sum_{k=0}^{K-1} C_{n+S/2+kS}^S \right)^* . \quad (1) $$

The signal is detected at time n if the correlation C_n is higher than a threshold. We give a schematic representation of our FPGA implementation of the detector in Figure 4.

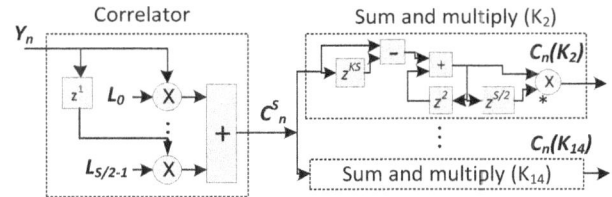

Figure 4: Adaptive detector for different preamble repetitions $K = \{2, 6, 10, 14\}$. **Symbol** z^n **denotes a delay element of** n **cycles.**

In other words, we take the first halves of each of the K repetitions of the preamble (lightly shaded squares in Figure 3), and sum them. We sum the second halves as well (darker shaded squares in Figure 3), we conjugate the sum of the second halves and multiply with the first ones. Intuitively, with (1) we have achieved two important goals: firstly, both factors in (1) grow with K, which allows us to detect the preamble at low SNR; secondly, by multiplying with the complex conjugate of the second, identical copy we get rid of the unknown phase bias, as explained in [35].

Complexity of the detector: We compare the complexity of our detector against the conventional detector [35]. To correlate a preamble of size K OFDM symbols, we do not need to run the full, sample-by-sample correlation of K OFDM symbols ($KS/2$ sam-

207

ples). Our detector needs $S/2$ complex multipliers and $S/2$ complex adders to calculate C_n^S, and we need one complex multiplier and $2K$ complex adders to calculate C_n. The conventional detector [35] (that does not use a repetitive but a long pseudo-random preamble) performs the same operation, but with $K' = 1$ (no repetitions) and $S' = KS$ (to achieve the same preamble length). For example, for $S = 64, K = 14$ our design requires 416 fewer complex multipliers (93% less) and 388 fewer complex adders (87% less). We evaluate the complexity of our implementation Section 5.

3.2 Adaptive preamble length detector

By choosing the number of the repetitions K, a transmitter can effectively control how far the preamble can be heard. For practical reasons, we limit $K \in \{2, 6, 10, 14\}$. It is the responsibility of the transmitter to choose the appropriate K (we present an adaptive algorithm for choosing K in Section 4.2), and we require that the detector at a receiver does not need to know a priori the number of repetitions K a transmitter has decided to use in the preamble. To that end, we implement four detectors (1) in parallel, for each $K \in \{2, 6, 10, 14\}$. A preamble is *detected* if any of the four detectors exceeds its corresponding threshold.

To illustrate that the detector does not need to know which value of K the transmitter has choosen, consider an example where the transmitter chooses $K = 10$ repetitions. If the correlator $K = 10$ misses the preamble, then it is very likely that the correlator $K = 14$ will also miss the preamble. This is because, in addition to 10 repetitions of the preamble $\mathbf{Q}$, correlator $K = 14$ also correlates 4 other arbitrary OFDM symbols, and the correlation level is lower then expected for a preamble of length 14. Similarly, the correlators $K = 2$ and $K = 6$ are also likely to miss the preamble if $K = 10$ misses it, because the detection accuracy increases with the preamble size. Hence, the performance of the correlation is as good as when only the correlator $K = 10$ is used.

3.3 High-power and low-power preambles

We next discuss the effect of false positives from high-power interferers, which we illustrate using a simple experiment in our test-bed (described in Section 6.1). We place two nodes close to each other, and we put a variable attenuator at the transmit antenna of the transmitting node. In one experiment, the transmitter transmits adaptive preambles $\mathbf{L}$. In the second experiment the transmitter transmits regular OFDM packets without adaptive preambles $\mathbf{L}$ (mimicking high-power nodes' packets). In the third experiment the transmitter is switched off and we only receive the background noise. In all three experiments we measure the maximum correlation value C_n observed in a fixed time interval. We plot each observed C_n against the SNR at the receiver (calculated from the corresponding attenuation values) in Figure 5[2]. False positives have more negative impact on the system performance (as they can potentially starve high-power nodes), hence we plot 90% for confidence intervals for the signal and 99% confidence intervals for the noise.

We see that the correlation against the background noise, when the transmitter is idle, is very low. It visually seems that the signal can be reliably detected versus the background noise for all measured SNRs. However, we also see that the correlation with the OFDM interference can be much higher[3]. For example, the interfering packets at 0dB (the noise level) have 5dB higher correlation than the background noise. It seems from visually inspecting Fig-

---

[2]The signal correlation stops the increase at high SNRs due to the saturation of the receiver's dynamic range

[3]This is because the background noise and the interfering packets have different statistical properties.

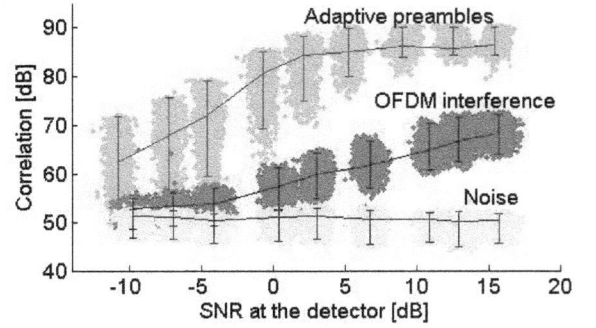

Figure 5: Correlation as a function of SNR for the loopback link and preamble length 10 OFDM symbols ($K = 10$).

ure 5 that if we set a correlation threshold of 55dB to reliably detect low-power packets at an SNR of -10dB, we will have a large number of false positives from high-power packets at 0dB and below, which we cannot otherwise detect using energy-based carrier sensing.

To address the problem of false positives, we define a unique short preamble $\mathbf{H}$ for high-power nodes, which is a repetition of $K = 2$ OFDM symbols, different from the ones in the $\mathbf{L}$ preamble. We then use the following detection algorithm

---

Adaptive detection algorithm

if for any K, $C_n^{L(K)} \geq T^{L(K)}$ and $C_n^H < T^H$
and *RSSI* < *CS threshold*
  declare *preamble detected*

---

where $C_n^{L(K)}$ is the correlation with the preamble $\mathbf{L}$ of length K OFDM symbols and C_n^H is the correlation with the preamble $\mathbf{H}$ at time n, RSSI is the received signal strength indication, and $T^{L(K)}$, T^H and *CS Threshold* are the corresponding thresholds[4].

The main intuition for this algorithm is as follows. The variance in correlation value comes from random attenuation in the system (channel, noise, etc). False positive from high-power interference is more likely at times when the random attenuation is low, hence the interfering signal is high. But at the same time, the correlation with the $\mathbf{H}$ is also likely to be high. So the idea is that, if we detect *both* preambles $\mathbf{L}$ and $\mathbf{H}$ during a short time interval, we can conclude that it is an interfering packet and ignore it. Furthermore, we also ignore correlation if energy is sensed (this implies a regular back-off instead of a low-power reservation).

4. WEEBLE MAC DESIGN

In this section we discuss the Weeble MAC design in detail.

4.1 Low-power Reservations

One of the key challenges in our design, described in Section 2, is how to determine the length of the reservation period. A simple idea would be to use another preamble to signal the end of the period. However, this is unwise for two reasons. Firstly, if the preamble for the end of the period is missed by a high-power node, this node might get starved[5]. Secondly, sending another preamble

---

[4]We set the threshold levels to the minimal values that are not exceeded when correlating with the white noise. These thresholds are similar in nature to the CS Threshold, and can be calibrated in the same way in practice.

[5]whereas if the start of the period preamble is missed, this will cause a loss of a single low-power packet.

increases the protocol overhead and the complexity (as we need to detect two different types of preambles).

Instead, we opt to use a reservation period of a fixed duration and we rely on contending low-power nodes to make an efficient use of it. Any node can signal a start of a low-power reservation period. Once a period has started, all high-power nodes that heard the preamble will refrain from transmitting for the fixed period of time. All low-power nodes may contend for the access for the fixed duration of the period using CSMA. Once the packet that initiated the reservation period has ended, other nodes may start transmitting. Also, other low-power nodes in other collision domains will likely transmit in parallel (as already observed in [5] in the context of multi-hop networks). They will not hear the L preamble that initiated the reservation period, but they will find the medium idle from high-power transmission and use the opportunity to access it. Both cases are illustrated in Figure 2 in Section 2.

Once a low-power reservation period expires, both high-power and low-power nodes contend for transmission. If a low-power node wins the contention, it sends an adaptive preamble. Then another low-power reservation period starts, and all high-power nodes back off. Otherwise, a high-power transmission will start.

Another challenge is how to prevent performance impairment and potential starvation of the high-power nodes. As illustrated in Figure 2 in Section 2, several low-power nodes that do not hear each other may enchain the reservations and starve a possible multitude of high-power nodes. To avoid this scenario, a high-power node ignores any L preambles it detects during an ongoing low-power reservation period.

Another effect, illustrated in Figure 2, gives priority to high-power nodes. If many low-power nodes contend for access, it is very likely that someone will be transmitting at the very end of the a low-power reservation period. However, at this point, high power nodes start contending again, and decreasing the back-off counter. Thus it is more likely that a high-power link will gain access right after a low-power reservation period. Note that the winning high-power transmission (HP in Figure 2) may destroy the last low-power transmission extending beyond the reservation period (the second LP in Figure 2). However, this does not affect the high-power transmission because its SNR is sufficiently high, and hence does not reflect on the efficiency of the network.

To avoid starvation of the low-power nodes, each low-power node contends separately for a low-power reservation period. A low-power period will start whenever any of the low-power nodes wins the medium and sends an adaptive preamble. Hence, the more low-power nodes there are, the more likely they are to gain the access. Clearly, the more low-power nodes there are, the lesser are the chances that a high-power node will get an access, but this is in accordance to the principle of fair medium access.

The duration of the low-power reservation should not be too large, to avoid over-booking the air if there are not too many low-power nodes. It should also not be too small, because each reservation period is preceded by an adaptive preamble, hence short periods incur high overhead. For a network with 802 11a/g PHY, we choose a standard low-power reservation duration of 600 μs. As we illustrate in Section 6.3, this is a good compromise between fairness and efficiency.

Finally, we mention the issue of the hidden terminal problem in our setting. As we have seen in the example from Figure 2, the L preamble of node LP3 is ignored by HP1 and HP2 because it was transmitted during an ongoing reservation period. However, that same preamble could have been respected by some other HP node (say HP3, not shown in Figure 2) who cannot detect LP1 and hence it missed its L preamble, but can detect LP3. Since the two reservation periods are not in sync. node LP3 cannot fully utilize the newly acquired reservation period at HP3. The key thing to observe here is that while LP3 started the reservation period, the same reservation period will be used by other LP nodes obstructed by HP3, hence the efficiency of the network should still be high. This is confirmed by our simulation results, presented in Section 6.3.

We give the pseudo-code of the MAC algorithm below, extending WiFi MAC (HP - true if the node is high-power, LP - true if the node is low-power, L - low-power preamble).

Medium access protocol

---

if L detected **and** *reservation timer* > *reservation length* **then**
  start *reservation timer*
if HP **and** *reservation timer* $\leq$ *reservation length* **then**
  freeze cw counter
if *carrier sense start* **then** freeze cw counter
if *carrier sense end* **then** count DIFS
if *DIFS count end* **then** unfreeze cw counter
if $cw = 0$ **then**
  if LP **and** *reservation timer* > *reservation length* **then**
    transmit preamble of *preamble_size*
    start *reservation timer*
  transmit packet
  if *no ACK received* **then**
    increase $CW = \min(2\,CW, CW_{max})$
  else $CW = CW_{min}$
  $cw = \text{rand}[0, CW]$

4.2 Adaptation Algorithm

Sending an adaptive preamble incurs overhead. It also prevents any high-power node that detects it from transmitting concurrently. It is thus important to carefully decide when to send adaptive preambles, and how long should they be. We want to use packet losses as a feedback whether to increase or decrease (or switch off) adaptive preambles. However, we need to be able to distinguish losses due to a high-power interferer from other types of losses.

There are three primary reasons why a low-power wireless link will lose packets. The first one is due to interference from concurrent high-power transmissions. The second reason is a MAC level contention. In DCF, as the number of nodes contending for medium access increases, so does the number of collisions that are due to two or more links starting transmitting at the exact same slot (and thus not having enough time to detect each other and avoid collision). If packets are lost due to contention, we do not want to use this as a signal to start using adaptive preambles or increase the preamble length. In fact, longer preambles can only make things worse by introducing additional overhead to an already congested medium. The third reason for wireless losses is the link loss, due to wireless channel changes. We do not want to switch on adaptive preambles or increase the preamble size due to these losses either.

We start by observing that in case of the second and third type of losses, we are not very likely to see many consecutive losses. For example, we measure that the average number of consecutive losses with 16 contending nodes is 2.5. Similarly, most modern rate adaptation algorithms are able to adapt the rate with minimal channel losses (less than 10%-15%), hence wireless losses are unlikely to occur consecutively.

On the contrary, losses due to interference are very likely to occur in a sequence. Namely, if a high-power node has data to send, and if it does not hear a low-power node, it will continuously transmit and kill several subsequent low-power transmissions. Also, consecutive packet losses are particularly bad for the link performance, as they will exponentially increase the back-off counter, and cause link starvation. If the high-power nodes interfere only sporadically, we will not activate the preamble protection, as this will not create starvation of low-power nodes.

We propose an adaptive preamble tunning algorithm based on the additive-increase, multiplicative-decrease (AIMD) principles. We use the number of consecutive packet losses as a measure of interference. We choose AIMD form of adaptation to be more conservative in blocking HP nodes. The pseudo-code of the algorithm is given below.

Preamble adaptation algorithm

Initialization:
    $consecutive \leftarrow 0$;
    $counter \leftarrow 0$;
    if consecutive loss **then** $consecutive$++;

After every packet transmission:
    if consecutive loss **then** $consecutive$++;
    else $consecutive \leftarrow 0$;
    if $consecutive = 6$ **then** $counter$++; $consecutive$++;
    else $counter \leftarrow counter \times 0.9$;
    if $counter \leq 2$ **then** $preamble\_size \leftarrow 0$;
    else $K \leftarrow (2, 6, 10, 14)$;
        $preamble\_size \leftarrow K[\lfloor counter \rfloor - 2]$;

Due to the scale of the power difference between the low-power and the high-power nodes, low-power nodes that contend among themselves are likely to see the same high-power interferers. Although each of them runs the adaptive algorithm on its own, it is very likely that they will use a similar level of protection, regardless of who started a low-power reservation period.

5. IMPLEMENTATION

We have prototyped the MAC and physical layer protocols on the Lyrtech Software Defined Radio SFF-SDR platform [25].

Adaptive preamble detector: We implement the adaptive preambles and the corresponding detection algorithm described in Section 3.2, on the top of an OFDM transceiver in FPGA (Xilinx Virtex-4 SX35). We compare the complexity of our adaptive detector with the complexity of a conventional implementation [35], as described in Section 3.1. The FPGA die consumption for the two implementations is given in Figure 6 (b).

As we can see, the conventional implementation consumes significantly more FPGA slices than the adaptive implementation. For example, the 8 OFDM symbols standard implementation consumes more die than the adaptive implementation that supports correlation across 2, 6, 10 and 14 (repeated) OFDM symbols at the same time. Moreover, we cannot fit a single standard 14 OFDM symbols correlator alone on our FPGA. As a comparison, an entire OFDM transceiver design with a conventional preamble detector fits onto a single Xilinx Virtex-4 SX35 FPGA. This means that a naive detector implementation would take more die (and most likely power as well) than the entire OFDM transceiver design.

Weeble MAC: In contrast to the recent software-defined radio deployments [33, 36, 9, 8, 12] that only use SDRs to collect channel traces and process them offline, we implement the full Weeble MAC in the Lyrtech SDR's DSP using the Colombo SDK [10] for rapid SDR MAC prototyping. This allows us to evaluate if the preambles indeed provide protection from a high-power interferer in different topologies and channel conditions, if the adap-

Detector length	#slices
Std. (1 symbol)	3,164
Std. (2 symbols)	4,834
Std. (4 symbols)	8,105
Std. (8 symbols)	14,617
Adaptive	13,850

Figure 6: (a) A picture of a HP node in the test-bed; (b) FPGA die consumption for different detectors

tive preamble algorithm correctly chooses preamble sizes to prevent starvations, as well as to assess the effectiveness of Weeble in the real world in presence of multiple high-power transmitters.

The separation of functionality between the FPGA and the DSP, imposed by the limited FPGA size, introduces an overhead. Due to long packet transfer time between the FPGA and the DSP imposed by board's architecture, the minimum MAC slot length is approximately 20 times longer than the Wi-Fi MAC slot length. Consequently, to ensure protocol correctness, we proportionally scale the intra-packet times – SIFS, DIFS and CW. Moreover, to achieve the same ratio between the packet duration and the inter-packet times as in WiFi, we scale the packet transmission times proportionally (our packet transmission lasts 4.5ms, about 20 times longer than it takes to transmit a 1.5 KB packet at 54Mbps). We compare Weeble MAC with WiFi MAC in the same implementation, hence we do not introduce any performance bias.

The only overhead that does not scale is the duration of the adaptive preamble. However, this is a relatively small overhead. It takes $224\mu s$ for a 802.11a/g PHY to transmit a 1500B packet at 54 Mbps, which is augmented by a constant MAC overhead of $181\mu s$ [26]. The longest preamble takes $56\mu s$, which is 13.8% of the total packet transmission time. These extreme preamble lengths will not be used very often in practice, as illustrated in Figure 9(c), hence the expected overhead from preambles will be even lower. Thus our test-bed results represent a close approximation of the real system's performance.

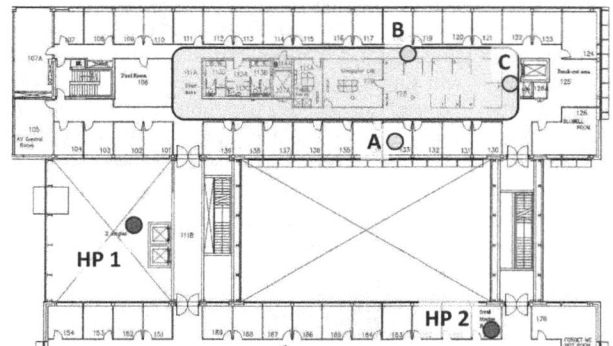

Figure 7: Floorplan of our building with the locations of measurements. Building dimensions are approximately 60m × 45m. The high power nodes HP 1 and HP 2 are located on the ground floor and second floor respectively and the nodes on the top wing are located on the first floor.

Testbed & Simulation Platform: We set the carrier frequency of the radio transmission to 580 MHz. Our channel bandwidth is 10 MHz. Our indoor test-bed spans both wings and all three floors or our buildings. Its floorplan is given in Figure 7. High-power nodes

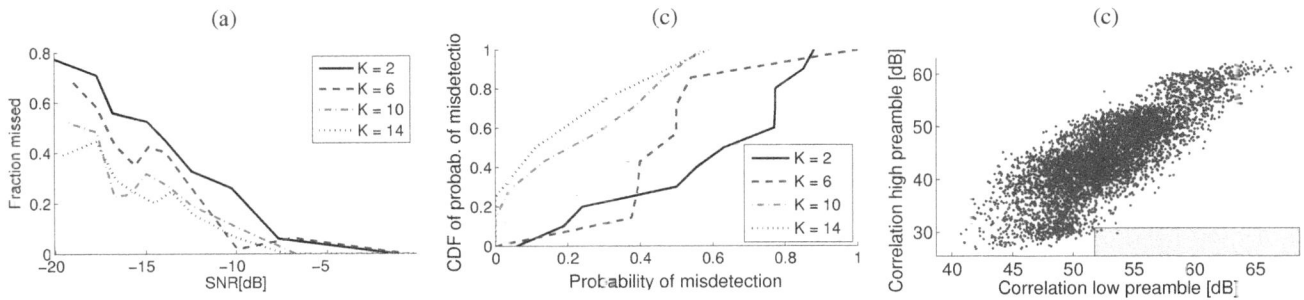

Figure 8: (a): **The average number of missed adaptive preambles as a function of SNR and the preamble length** K; (b) **CDF of probability of misdetection across different channel profiles, for SNR = -16.5 dB;** (c) **False positives with H and L preambles.**

(shown in Figure 6 (a)) have a transmit power of 4W, and low-power nodes transmit at 40mW. To test the scalability of our design in larger networks, we further implement the full Weeble PHY and MAC in QualNet. We use measurements from Section 6.1 to tune the realistic PHY model parameters in QualNet for long preamble detection.

6. PERFORMANCE EVALUATION

In this section we quantify the performance of Weeble in three stages. First, we micro-benchmark the core building block of Weeble – the adaptive preamble technique. Second, we evaluate the benefits of Weeble in our small scale testbed spanning an entire building. Finally, we study the protocol's performance in a large setting using the QualNet simulator.

6.1 Reliability of Adaptive Preambles

We micro-benchmark our adaptive preamble detector in a building-wide deployment by measuring its reliability when detecting preambles at low SNR. We set up a high-power node (HP1, Figure 7) in the atrium of the ground floor and we configure it to send packets, each with a sequence number and the expected length of the preamble to follow. We also set up a low-power node that replies with a preamble of the corresponding length. We move the low-power node, walking slowly, throughout the shaded area on the first floor.

We cannot directly measure the receive SNR at the high-power node because it is below 0dB. Instead, we log the receive (LP) SNR at the low-power node. In various measurements we observed that the channel is approximately symmetric (with only a few dBs of difference) and we record an approximate SNR as the observed LP SNR at the low-power node minus 20dB of transmit power difference.

Detection accuracy: We first evaluate the detection accuracy as a function of the SNR. We divide the range of the recorded SNR into bins, and calculate the aggregate preamble detection rates for the entire duration of the experiment for each bin, for different preamble lengths. This is plotted in Figure 8 (a). Note that the curves are not strictly decreasing in SNR because different channel profiles have different performances for the same SNR. We see that for adaptive preamble lengths $K = 10 - 14$ for SNR > -17 dB, we can have detection probability of 70-80%. Note that, if the SNR = -17dB at the high-power receiver, the interference it creates at the low-power receiver is at most 3 dB (because the power difference is $15 - 20$ dB). This is of the same order as a typical carrier sensing threshold [23], so we see that our virtual carrier sensing mechanisms can guarantee the same level of interference protection as the real carrier sense, with 70%-80% success rate even when the power difference is 20dB.

Next, we look at how the probability of detection varies across links with similar SNR values. We divide all the received packets

in batches of 20. Since the packets are sent back-to-back, we see that all packets within a batch see the same SNR. For each batch we record a single probability of detection (out of 20 packets in a batch). We then aggregate batches with the similar SNR. We plot the CDF of the probability of misdetection for the lowest SNR of interest in Figure 8 (b). Clearly, different links will take different position on these curves. However, we see that except for the 20% most unfavorable links, we can have more than 70% success detection rates with SNRs as low as -16.5 dB (meaning we are able to prevent a high-power interference on a low-power node stronger than 3.5 dB).

The remaining question is whether a high-power interference will affect the reception of low-power packets in cases when preambles are missed. We defer this discussion to the next section, where we evaluate Weeble MAC in the test-bed.

Avoiding false positives caused by HP interferers: Finally, we evaluate our detection algorithm from Section 3.3 that addresses the problem of false positives. We calculate $C^{L(K)}$ (for $K = 10$) and C^H for about 50,000 packets transmitted by the HP1 node, and received by the LP node at various locations in the shaded area in Figure 7. We present the results in Figure 8 (c). On the x axis we plot the correlation with the **L** preamble $C^{L(K)}$ and on the y axis with the **H** preamble C^H. The lower shaded box is the area of false positives - a packet that detects the low preamble but fails to detect the high preamble. The observed probability of false positive is 10^{-4}.

6.2 Performance of Weeble in a Small Testbed

We now show the performance of Weeble in our building-wide test-bed. We deploy two fixed high power nodes and two mobile low power nodes in the area depicted in Figure 7. The high power nodes do not carrier sense each other, and hence transmit simultaneously. All nodes are backlogged with UDP traffic[6].

Due to the limited size of the FPGAs (a low-end Virtex-4 SX35), we were unable to fit the entire OFDM transceiver and the adaptive detector in the same circuit. Instead, the high-power nodes comprise of a transmitter, an adaptive detector, and the full MAC implementation (where we assume that all transmissions are successfully acknowledged). Consequently, HP1 and HP2 do not need paired receivers in the experiments. Note that this does not greatly affect the experiments, as the nodes always have backlogged packets to transmit, regardless of the results of their previous transmission. Low-power nodes do not require an adaptive correlator and we implement them in full. In this section we compare Weeble's performance to the WiFi protocol (since IEEE 802.11a for white spaces [3] is WiFi-based).

---

[6] We cannot run TCP traffic as it times out due to our down-clocked MAC implementation.

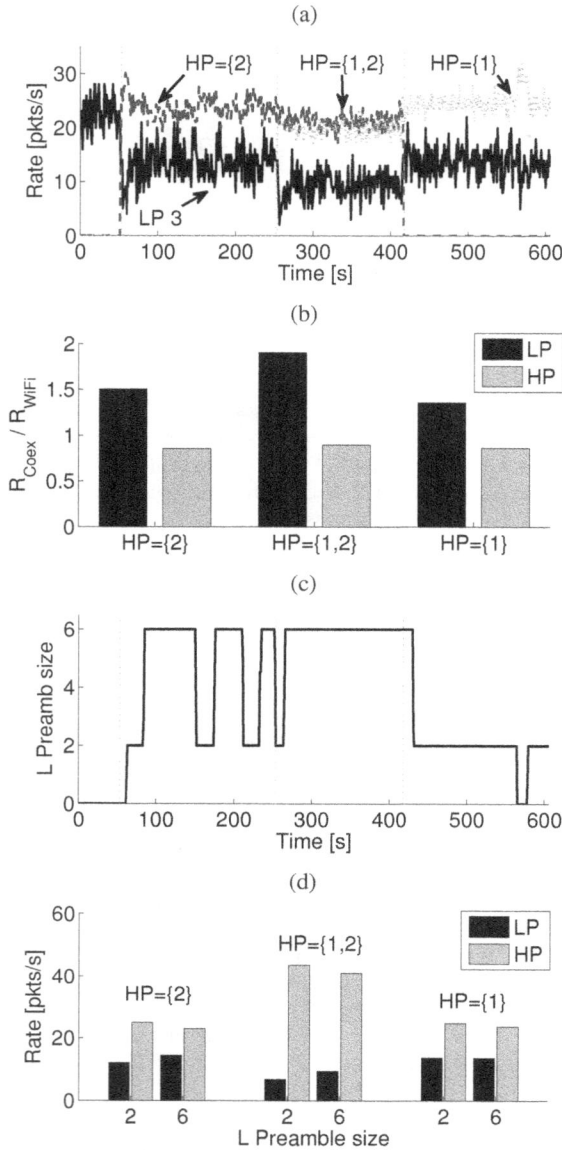

Figure 9: Example scenario with different number of high-power nodes: (a) The rates of flows in time, (b) The relative increase of flow rates when using Weeble MAC instead of WiFi, (c) The evolution of the L preamble size and (d) The average rates of LP and HP flows when using different L preamble sizes.

6.2.1 Weeble MAC in action

We first illustrate the dynamics of Weeble in a network where the two low-power nodes are placed at positions A and B in Figure 7. Figure 9 (a) depicts how the link rates change in time, as we switch on and off the interfering HP nodes.

On turning on one HP flow ($t = 50$s), the rate of the LP flow drops by about half. The sending rate of the HP flow drops by about 10%. The total throughput is higher because the medium is more efficiently utilized by two flows than by a single flow. As expected, the HP flow gets a larger share, and the LP flow is not starved.

When both HP flows are turned on ($t = 250$s), the LP flow's rate drops only slightly. This is because the two HP flows do not interfere with each other and the MAC converges to the optimal schedule: simultaneous HP1 and HP2 transmissions alternate with a single LP transmission. The adaptive preamble detection mechanism proves to be successful in presence of two non-coordinated high-power transmissions.

We compare the performance improvement over the WiFi MAC protocol in Figure 9 (b). We see that the rate of the LP flow improves by 50%-90% at the expense of a modest (10%-15%) decrease of the rates of the HP flows. Note that in this example WiFi exhibits slightly lower efficiency than Weeble MAC. This is because the low-power packets in WiFi MAC are frequently lost due to collisions.

Finally, in Figure 9 (c) we see the dynamics of the preamble adaptation algorithm (Section 4.2). HP2 can very accurately detect low-power preambles of length $K = 6$ from the LP node, which yields very low loss rates on the LP link. After a period of a low loss, the low-power link will reduce its preamble size to 2, which will in turn increase the loss and the adaptive algorithm will force the preamble size back to 6. As we see in Figure 9 (a), the adaptation process does not reflect substantially on the short-term flow rates (it does not cause any temporary starvations) because the preamble length is only decreased, and not entirely switched off.

In Figure 9 (d) we see the data rates achieved with different lengths K of low-power preambles. We see that in the first period, when LP and HP2 are active, both flows have similar flow rates for $K = 2$ and $K = 6$, hence the algorithm oscillates between the two values. In the second period, when LP, HP1 and HP2 are active, the LP flow sees a further increase in packet losses and a decrease in rate, hence its switches to using exclusively $K = 6$, and achieving a more fair rate. Finally in the third period, when LP and HP1 are active, $K = 6$ has no visible benefits on protecting LP but slightly decreases both rates due to the overhead. For that reason, the algorithm chooses $K = 2$.

We also see from Figure 9 (a) that it takes a 10s-20s for the MAC algorithm to react to an activation/deactivation of a high-power link. Given that the packet transmission times are ≈ 20x longer than in a WiFi network (see Section 5 for the discussion), an implementation of Weeble that uses WiFi data rates would observe sub-second reaction times.

6.2.2 Performance in different topologies

Setup: We place one LP node either in location B or C, and the other LP node on a trolley at many different locations, all around the shaded area in Figure 7. We record the data rates at each location pair. We repeat the same set of experiments with different parameters (running traffic from B to C, C to B or both directions, and/or having one or two interfering HP nodes), both with Weeble and WiFi MAC.

Starvation: In Figures 10 (1HP-a) and (2HP-a) we see that Weeble successfully avoids starvation of the LP flows. Using Weeble, no flow has recorded a rate below 4 pkts/s in any measured location. With WiFi, 10% of LP flows had rates of less than 4 pkts/s. Also, the median rate of the LP flows running Weeble are about 50% larger than the median rate of the LP flows running WiFi. Both findings are true when either a single or both HP flows are active.

Total throughput: Figures 10 (1HP-b) and (2HP-b) plot the CDFs of the sum of the rates of all flows in the network. We see that when a single HP node is active, the sum of the rates is almost the same for WiFi and Weeble (and occasionally Weeble achieves a higher sum of the rates, as discussed in Section 6.2.1). In the presence of 2 HP flows, the sum of the rates are slightly smaller with Weeble than with WiFi (on average by about 6%). This is because a single LP transmission competes with two concurrent HP transmissions and any extra rate allocated to the LP flow decreases the rates of both HP flows.

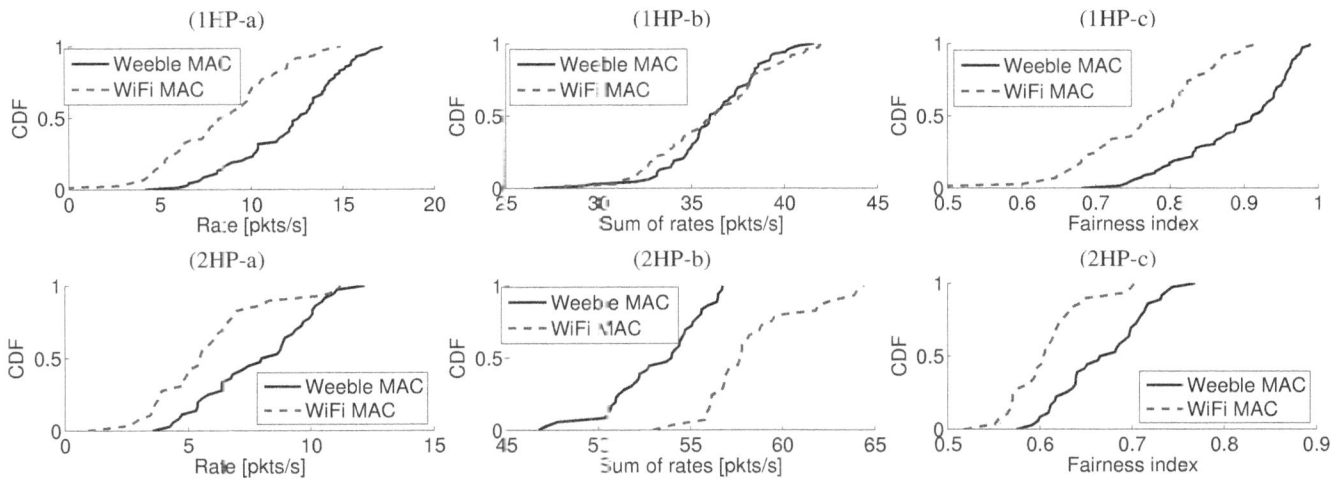

Figure 10: Cumulative distribution functions of the sum of the rates of the LP flows ((1HP-a) and (2HP-a)), the sum of rates of all flows ((1HP-b) and (2HP-b)) and the fairness indices ((1HP-c) and (2HP-c)) for Weeble MAC and WiFi for networks with one and two high-power (HP) nodes.

Fairness: Finally, in Figure 10 (1HP-c) and (2HP-c) we plot the Jain's fairness index [17]. In the design requirements we ask that HP flows get more rate than the LP flows, hence the fairness index is far from one in both cases (and it is smaller when 2 HP flows are active). However, we see that Weeble achieves a median fairness index by 10%-20% higher than WiFi.

Overall, we see that Weeble MAC improves fairness and avoids starvation of low-power flows with a minimal impact on the performance of high-power flows. These observations are consistent through a large number of topologies we evaluated and with one and two active high-power links.

6.3 Detailed Evaluation in Simulations

We now evaluate Weeble in QualNet. There are three main goals of the evaluation in simulations. Firstly, we want to verify that our approach scales to larger networks. Secondly, we want to evaluate the performance with more realistic network parameters, such as TCP traffic and variable data rates. Finally, we want to quantify the overhead of the long preambles with respect to various WiFi data rates.

Setup: We developed a performance model of the preamble detection algorithm from the measurement results obtained in our tested (Section 6.1), and plugged it into the QualNet simulator. We use autorate as the rate adaptation protocol. In Weeble we select the low-power reservation duration (Section 2) to be 600us.

We compare Weeble to two alternative approaches: WiFi and Frequency Division Multiplexing (FDM) where HP and LP links are allocated different frequencies. In our WiFi implementation, all nodes use the standard WiFi MAC, regardless of the transmit power. In our FDM implementation we divide the available channel into two sub-bands and assign one of the sub-bands to low-power and the other to high-power nodes. The key question when analyzing the FDM's performance is how to split the available bandwidth between the two sub-bands. Clearly, if one knew the exact number of nodes in each band and split the bandwidth proportionally between them, FDM would be the optimal approach. However, this is precisely the difficulty of the problem we are studying, as the network is dynamic, some geographic areas may have more high-power and others more low-power nodes, and there is no centralized coordinator available. We thus assume a topology-oblivious approach in which we assign half the bandwidth to each band. Within each sub-band, nodes compete using WiFi MAC. We

double the DCF time-slot in the FDM implementation to keep the overhead proportional to the packet size.

We note that Jain's fairness index is only meaningful for comparing fairness in systems with similar overall rates [17]. In the test-bed evaluation (Section 6.2) we observe that the sum of rates of all the flows are similar in all cases, and we use the Jain's fairness index. This is not the case in the larger networks considered in this section, so instead we use the number of starved flows as the fairness metrics[7]. We also study the rates of the LP flows as a fairness metric, and the sum of the rates of all flows as an efficiency metric.

We evaluate the performance of our MAC on a set of random topologies. We consider a 1km × 1km square area and a single channel. We randomly place 20 low-power nodes (10 low-power links) and 4 high-power nodes (2 high-power links) in the area and on the same channel. For example, this case could correspond to a real-world scenario with 200 low power links and 40 high power links uniformly spread across 10 available TV channels. High-power links transmit with 4W transmit power and low-power links transmit either with 40 mW or 100 mW (as in the White Space scenario [6]). Link lengths are selected randomly, but in such way that the achievable link rate is at least 12 Mbps. We run a single FTP flow over each link. Flows are single hop. All packet sizes are 1000B.

We select 10 random network topologies. For each topology we execute five runs and each run lasts 20s. We calculate the average rates of flows over all five runs for each topology and we plot the CDFs of different metrics over the 10 random topologies.

Starvation: In Figure 11 (a) we plot the TCP rate of the flow with the smallest rate in the network. We see that the smallest rates of the high-power flows are comparable for all three MAC designs, even in presence of a large number of low-power links. However, Weeble MAC assigns significantly better rates to the smallest low-power flows. Both WiFi and FDM MAC yielded zero throughput to at least one flow in 90% of the cases. This did not happen with Weeble MAC.

We next look at the number of starved flows, that is the number of flows that achieve TCP rate lower than 100 kbps. This is depicted in Figure 11 (b). FDM on average starves around 2 low-power flows

---

[7]Note that since our test-bed is relatively small there are no starved flows, hence the number of starved flows metric is not applicable to the test-bed evaluation.

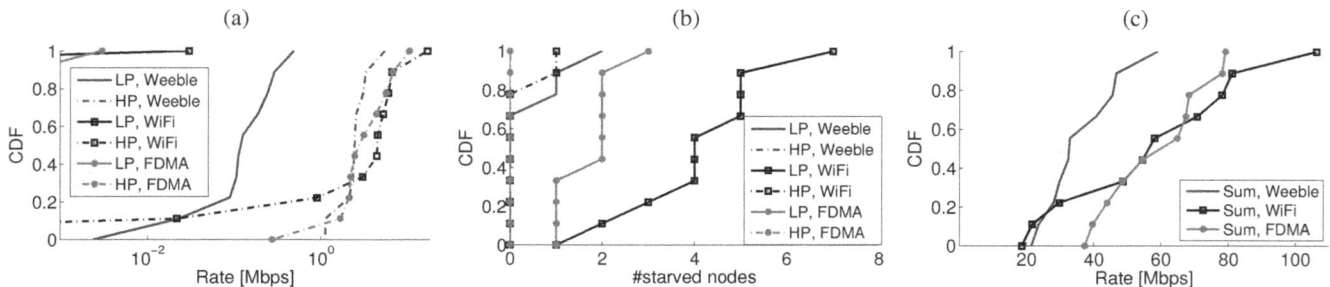

Figure 11: Performance for random scenarios: (a) TCP rate of the flow with the smallest rate; (b) number of starved flows in the network (flows with the TCP rate less than 100 kbps); (c) Sum of TCP rates of all flows in the network.

per network topology (20% of flows) and WiFi around 4 low-power flows per network topology (40% of flows). We see that Weeble starves on average 4% of flows, and in 7 out of 10 topologies it did not starve any flow. We also note that WiFi starves one of the two high-power flows in 20% of the cases. Weeble does not starve high-power flows.

WiFi is particularly bad in starving low-power links because high-power nodes cannot detect them. FDM also starves some low-power links because it reserves only half of the bandwidth for 10 low-power links formed by 20 competing nodes running TCP flows. By design, Weeble MAC is able to dynamically share the capacity among available links, regardless of how many low-power or high-power links are present.

Total throughput: Finally, we look at the total network throughput for the three MAC protocols. We see that the loss in total throughput is 0%-40% when compared to WiFi and 20%-35% when compared to FDM. This inefficiency is due to imperfect carrier sensing. Weeble has to speculatively schedule low-power reservation periods of fixed lengths (particularly bad when a TCP window doesn't have packets to send) whereas with WiFi and FDM the backlogged nodes can resume the countdown whenever the RSSI has gone down. This inevitable trade-off is due to power asymmetry that implies that any signalling between the low-power and high-power nodes comes at a cost. In contrast, WiFi ignores low-power nodes and FDM isolates them in a static sub-band. In both cases there is no signalling between the low and high power nodes. The protocols are non-adaptive, and cause starvations.

Comparison with test-bed results: We see that the effects of interference of high-power flows on low-power flows in simulations are more severe than in the test-bed results, presented in Section 6.2. This is because the simulated network has more links hence there is more contention, and also because the links use TCP, whose performance is more affected by interference. We also see that the total network throughput is more affected than in the test-bed evaluation results. This is again because the simulated network has more low-power links and more medium access time has to be reserved for them.

7. RELATED WORK

Coexistence: Most prior work on how to coexist with an incumbent (a legacy transmitter) or with a high-power node can be divided into two groups. The first group comprises of the designs in which a new technology tries to avoid being starved (avoid interference from incumbents or high-power nodes). One idea is to transmit when the incumbents/high-power node is idle (see e.g. [13]), but it fails when the incumbent is always active. Jung et al [19] propose to use high-power signaling packets to avoid starvation of low-power nodes. This is impossible in our setting due to power and regulatory constraints. Gollakota et al [8] suggest using orthog-

onal MIMO streams to avoid incumbents. This approach works well with 802.11n against legacy hardware (which mainly uses single antenna for transmission) but it is not suitable for coexistence in white-spaces. In white-spaces, MIMO may be deployed on the high-power nodes; the low-power nodes are assumed portable and MIMO is highly impractical[8]. Both requirements are incompatible with the approach from [8].

The second group are the designs where a new technology tries to avoid starving incumbents/low-power nodes. One example is IEEE 802.11h standard [15] that imposes power control to WiFi nodes to avoid interference with satellite communications. Another example is IEEE 802.22 [16], where secondary users need to sense and back-off when primaries are present. Also, UWB must detect and avoid WiMAX devices in certain regulatory domains [27]. However, in all these cases the detection of primary signals takes long time (as we discuss below) and the packet-level statistical multiplexing is not possible. SWIFT [31] addresses the coexistence problem through dynamic frequency adaptation. However, it does not apply to our asymmetric power setting.

Detection: An important part of the coexistence problem is how can a high-power node detect whether a low-power user is disturbed by its interference. One way of detecting a legacy interferer is cyclo-stationary detection (c.f. [12, 22] and references therein). However, cyclo-stationary is slow at low SNR and one is not able to use it for statistical multiplexing at a packet level. Other feature-based detection techniques, such as [38, 1, 36], also do not work at SNRs below 0dB. The other approach is to detect a known preamble, which is also used as a part of the carrier-sense mechanism [18]. Busy tone approach [11] is a special case of detecting a known preamble. Several recent papers [9, 33] show that it is possible to detect an interferer with 80% accuracy at SNR as low as -14dB, but only if all nodes are coarsely synchronized (see [12, 9, 33] for discussion). Coarse-level synchronization is not possible in our setting. Also, repetitive preambles are used in 802.11 standard for coarse-grained synchronization, but they do not work at low SNR and they are not adaptive. It is worth noting that there are other detector designs for multi-path channels with Gaussian noise, such as [29], but it is not a priori clear how they could be modified to be adaptive, simple and to scale to very low SNR.

Adaptive carrier-sensing: Several papers consider adapting the carrier sensing threshold [37, 21] to optimize the network performance. However, these techniques do not consider power-asymmetric networks and cannot be used when the SNR is below the noise floor.

Antenna design: The use of directional antennas is one approach to tackle the hidden terminal problem and increase network performance [4, 24]. This approach mitigates but it does not solve the coexistence issue, and it increases the complexity. Similarly,

---

[8]the wavelength of the white-space bands is around $1/2$m

high-gain antennas do not solve the problem as they extend both the reception and the transmission range of high-power nodes.

Existing TV white-space standard activities: IEEE 802.22 [16] is a regional network standard. It introduces a spectrum manager entity at each node, whose goal is to provide the dynamic spectrum access according to constraints obtained from different sources (geo-database, policy, sensing). The time-scale of spectrum allocation is much longer than a packet duration. Another white-space related standard activity is 802.11af [3], which focuses on in-home devices. In order to keep the network simple and leverage on the existing silicon design for 802.11, it extends 802.11 design to address the challenges of white-space networks. Coexistence between high-power and low-power nodes is currently an open problem in the 802.11af standardization process, which we aim to solve with this paper. Our work is also aligned with IEEE 802.19 [14], another ongoing standardization activity that is planning to address similar coexistence problems.

8. DISCUSSION AND FUTURE WORK

Can Weeble MAC ideas be used for different MAC designs? Weeble MAC can be seen as a set of generic signaling and reservation techniques. For example, they could also be applied in conjunction with a spectrum manager proposed in IEEE 802.22 [16] to allow for coexistence among several administrative domains, in case two non-coordinated spectrum managers belonging to two different administrative domains happen to allocate different networks to the same channel. Evaluating such a design remains as a future work.

Can Weeble be generalized to multiple power-level classes? Our protocol naturally extends to multiple power-level classes. Each power-level class i should have has its own L_i and H_i preambles. A node at power-level i should be able to detect and back-off on all preambles L_j coming from nodes at lower power-levels $j < i$. It should also be able to detect and ignore all high-power preambles H_k for all $k \geq i$. However, this generalization increases the PHY complexity as each node in the network should implement as many correlators as there are power-level classes in the network.

Can one adjust the priorities of high-power and low-power traffic? Our design goal is to avoid starvation of low-power nodes with a minimum impact on the performance of high-power nodes. However, it is easy to extend our design to achieve arbitrary prioritization of different high-power and low-power devices. For example, to guarantee an absolute priority to a low-power wireless mic, one could mandate the high-power nodes to back-off whenever an LP preamble is detected (even within an ongoing low-power reservation periods), and keeping the rest of the MAC the same. An actual implementation of a particular variant of the MAC would crucially depend on the design requirements for different devices and is out of scope of this paper.

Can Weeble MAC work with variable channel widths? Our current preamble detector design assumes that all nodes use the same channel width (e.g. one TV channel). This can be generalized to a scenario where channel bonding is allowed, similarly to the way a green-field 802.11g link can detect a legacy 802.11a/g link. We leave the further exploration for future work.

9. CONCLUSIONS

In this paper we have presented a design, implementation and evaluation of a fully decentralized Weeble MAC for coexistence between low and high-power nodes. It avoids starvation of low-power links, and it only slightly drops the efficiency of the network. The main components of our design are the adaptive preamble mecha-

nism and the low-power reservation protocol. We implement and evaluate our design in a software-designed radio test-bed and in Qualnet simulator and we show that it avoids starvation in all cases with only a slight drop in efficient, unlike the existing distributed MACs for white-spaces.

10. REFERENCES

[1] P. Bahl, R. Chandra, T. Moscibroda, R. Murty, and M. Welsh. White space networking with wi-fi like connectivity. In *Sigcomm*, 2009.

[2] I. Canada. Consultation on a policy and technical framework for the use of non-broadcasting applications in the television broadcasting bands below 698 mhz, Aug. 2011.

[3] H.-S. Chen and W. Gao. Mac and phy proposal for 802.11af, 2010.

[4] R. R. Choudhury, X. Yang, R. Ramanathan, and N. Vaidya. Using directional antennas for medium access control in ad hoc networks. In *Mobicom*, 2002.

[5] M. Durvy and P. Thiran. A packing approach to compare slotted and non-slotted medium access control. In *Infocom*, 2006.

[6] FCC. Second order, FCC 10-174. 2010.

[7] FCC. Order, FCC 11-131. 2011.

[8] S. Gollakota, F. Adib, D. Katabi, and S. Seshan. Clearing the rf smog: Making 802.11 robust to cross-technology interference. In *Sigcomm*, 2011.

[9] S. Gollakota and D. Katabi. Zigzag decoding: combating hidden terminals in wireless networks. In *Sigcomm*, 2008.

[10] D. Gunawardena and B. Radunović. Colombo SDK - simulating the innards of a wireless MAC. In *Mobicom Demo*, 2011.

[11] Z. Haas and J. Deng. Dual busy tone multiple access (DBTMA): A multiple access control scheme for ad hoc networks. *IEEE Trans. on Comm.*, 50(6):975–985, 2002.

[12] S. Hong and S. Katti. DOF: A local wireless information plane. In *Sigcomm*, 2011.

[13] J. Huang, G. Xing, G. Zhou, and R. Zhou. Beyond co-existence: Exploiting wifi white space for zigbee performance assurance. In *ICNP*, 2010.

[14] IEEE. IEEE 802.19 wireless coexistence working group.

[15] IEEE. Amendment 5: Spectrum and transmit power management extensions in the 5 ghz band in europe, 2003.

[16] IEEE. Ieee 802.22 wireless regional area networks 2010.

[17] R. Jain, D. M. Chiu, and W. Hawe. A quantitative measure of fairness and discrimination for resource allocation in shared computer systems. In *DEC TR-301*, 1984.

[18] K. Jamieson, B. Hull, A. Miu, and H. Balakrishnan. Understanding the real-world performance of carrier sense. In *EWIND*, 2005.

[19] E.-S. Jung and N. Vaidya. A Power Control MAC Protocol for Ad Hoc Networks. In *MOBICOM*, 2002.

[20] S. M. Kay. *Fundamentals of Statistical Signal Processing, Volume 2: Detection Theory*. Prentice Hall, 1998.

[21] T.-S. Kim, J. Hou, and H. Lim. Improving spatial reuse through tuning transmit power, carrier sense threshold, and data rate in multihop wireless networks. In *MOBICOM*, 2006.

[22] K. Kyouwoong, I. Akbar, K. Bae, J. Urn, C. Spooner, and J. Reed. Cyclostationary approaches to signal detection and classification in cognitive radio. In *DySpan*, 2007.

[23] LAN/MAN Standards Committee. Part 11: Wireless LAN MAC and PHY specifications, 2003.

[24] X. Liu, A. Sheth, M. Kaminsky, K. Papagiannaki, S. Seshan, and P. Steenkiste. Pushing the envelope of indoor wireless spatial reuse using directional access points and clients. In *Mobicom*, 2010.

[25] Lyrtech. Lyrtech small form factor software defined radio.

[26] E. Magistretti, K. Chintalapudi, B. Radunovic, and R. Ramjee. WiFi-Nano:reclaiming wifi efficiency through 800 ns slots. In *Mobicom*, 2011.

[27] S. M. Mishra, R. W. Brodersen, S. ten Brink, and R. Mahadevappa. Detect and avoid: An ultra-wideband/WiMAX coexistence mechanism. *IEEE Communications Magazine*, 45(6):68–75, 2007.

[28] MocoNews.net. Uk gives green light to fast wireless broadband service, free to all comers, Sept. 2011.

[29] S. Nagaraj, S. Khan, C. Schlegel, and M. Burnashev. Differential preamble detection in packet-based wireless networks. *IEEE Transactions on Wireless Communications*, 8(2):599–607, 2009.

[30] B. Radunovic and J.-Y. Le Boudec. Rate performance objectives of multi-hop wireless networks. In *Infocom*, 2004.

[31] H. Rahul, N. Kushman, D. Katabi, C. Sodini, and F. Edalat. Learning to share: Narrowband-friendly wideband networks. In *Sigcomm*, 2008.

[32] T. Schmidl and D. Cox. Robust frequency and timing synchronization for OFDM. *IEEE Trans. on Comm.*, 45(12), 1997.

[33] S. Sen, R. R. Choudhury, and S. Nelakuditi. CSMA/CN: Carrier sense multiple access with collision notification. In *Mobicom*, 2010.

[34] F. Times. Microsoft trial to use uk tv signals for wifi, June 2011.

[35] F. Tufvesson, O. Edfors, and M. Faulkner. Time and frequency synchronization for OFDM using PN-sequence preambles. In *VTC*, 1999.

[36] L. Yang, W. Hou, C. Cao, B. Zhao, and H. Zheng. Supporting demanding wireless applications with frequency-agile radios. In *USENIX NSDI*, 2010.

[37] X. Yang and N. Vaidya. On the physical carrier sense in wireless ad hoc networks. In *INFOCOM*, 2005.

[38] R. Zhou, Y. Xiong, G. Xing, L. Sun, and J. Ma. Zifi: Wireless lan discovery via zigbee interference signatures. In *MobiCom*, 2010.

WiFox: Scaling WiFi Performance for Large Audience Environments

Arpit Gupta,* Jeongki Min,* Injong Rhee
Dept. of Computer Science, North Carolina State University
{agupta13, jkmin, rhee}@ncsu.edu

ABSTRACT

WiFi-based wireless LANs (WLANs) are widely used for Internet access. They were designed such that an Access Points (AP) serves few associated clients with symmetric uplink/downlink traffic patterns. Usage of WiFi hotspots in locations such as airports and large conventions frequently experience poor performance in terms of downlink goodput and responsiveness. We study the various factors responsible for this performance degradation. We analyse and emulate a large conference network environment on our testbed with 45 nodes. We find that presence of asymmetry between the uplink/downlink traffic results in backlogged packets at WiFi Access Point's (AP's) transmission queue and subsequent packet losses. This traffic asymmetry results in maximum performance loss for such an environment along with degradation due to rate diversity, fairness and TCP behaviour. We propose our solution *WiFox*, which (1) adaptively prioritizes AP's channel access over competing STAs avoiding traffic asymmetry (2) provides a fairness framework alleviating the problem of performance loss due to rate-diversity/fairness and (3) avoids degradation due to TCP behaviour. We demonstrate that *WiFox* not only improves downlink goodput by 400-700 % but also reduces request's average response time by 30-40 %.

Categories and Subject Descriptors

C.2 [**Computer-Communication Networks**]: Local and Wide-Area Networks–Access schemes

General Terms

Design, Experimentation, Measurement, Performance

Keywords

WiFi, large audience environments, goodput, traffic asymmetry

*Authors' names in alphabetical order

1. INTRODUCTION

WLANs are the most popular means of access to the Internet. The proliferation of mobile devices equipped with WiFi interfaces, such as smart phones, laptops, and personal mobile multimedia devices, has heightened this trend. The performance of WiFi hotspots serving locations such as large conventions and busy airports has been extremely poor. In such a setting, more than one WiFi access points (APs) provide wireless access to the Internet for many user devices (STAs). The followings are the commonly cited causes of this problem.

- **Contention and collision.** When many STAs are competing for channel resources using CSMA/CA, the overhead of handling high contentions, such as carrier sensing, back-off and collisions, can be very high.

- **Rate diversity and fairness.** In an access network, different STAs may have different channel conditions. WiFi typically adopts an automatic rate adaptation scheme where poorer channel STAs use lower-rate modulation schemes which has a side effect of occupying longer channel time for transmission of the same size packets. As poorer STAs will use more channel resources, the overall throughput is reduced.

- **Random losses and TCP performance.** TCP is the most commonly used transport protocol. But it treats all packet losses as congestion related and reduces its transmission rates for each packet loss. Unfortunately, wireless channels are prone to random packet losses unrelated to congestion. TCP throughput in WiFi can be low when many losses occur due to low channel quality and collisions.

- **Traffic asymmetry.** In an access network, a single AP serves all associated clients. Moreover our analysis of network traces [27, 28] shows that downlink (AP to STAs) traffic is much greater than uplink traffic (4-10 times), attributable to commonly used client-and-server based applications (e.g., web and email). This asymmetry of data traffic combined with IEEE 802.11 DCF providing equal opportunity for channel access to both APs and STAs results in congested APs and subsequent packet losses.

There have been many proposals to fix or ameliorate these problems. However, the existing solutions do not sufficiently address the problem. Major limitations of existing solutions are as follows.

First, the existing approaches [3, 36, 31, 14] to the performance optimization of WiFi are highly atomistic, focusing only on fixing one or a subset of these problems. In general, performance optimization must take a holistic approach with careful considerations of complex interactions among various control "knobs" of optimization. Tweaking an unsuitable combination of knobs may not bring sufficient performance improvement and may even negatively impact the performance.

Second, many existing solutions are not amenable to practical deployment because nearly all cases require changes in both APs and clients and sometimes also in the MAC layer coordination that can be realized only by modifying the firmware of wireless interface cards. While deploying a new (modified) AP is relatively easy in a hotspot, deploying client solutions is difficult because of the diversity of client devices. For practical and incremental deployability, a proposed modification must be limited to AP.

Third, many existing solutions are not tested in real networks with realistic network workloads. Most of them are based on simulation or theoretical analysis [18, 17, 9]. There is a significant gap among the results predicted from real network experiments, simulation and theoretical analysis. Therefore, it is hard to predict the actual performance of these proposed solutions.

All the above factors deter the deployment of these solutions in production networks. In this paper we demonstrate that solving the problem of traffic asymmetry results in maximum performance improvements for large audience environments. We find correlation between the presence of asymmetry in network traffic and instantaneous transmission queue at the WiFi AP and develop a *mechanism* where traffic asymmetry is inferred in real time, prioritizing the AP accordingly for channel resource access over competing STAs. For large audience environments, the prioritization of AP's traffic enables efficient realization of AP-only fairness solutions. The key contribution of our work is the empirical study of the performance implications of these solutions in order to optimize the performance of busy WiFi hotspots. To add realism to our results, we implemented our solutions in an off-the-shelf commercial IEEE 802.11g AP, constructed a real network testbed of 45 WiFi nodes and tested the performance of various optimization settings in network traffic loads emulating the traffic patterns captured from real traces [27, 28].

In the ensuing sections, we start with understanding the characteristics of wireless networks in Large Audience Environments (LAE) in section 2. We discuss the attributes of a desired solution based on these observations and in section 3 discuss design and implementations of our solution. Description of testbeds and experimental procedures are provided in section 4 and experimental results are provided in section 5. Later we discuss related works in section 6 and finally conclude our contributions in section 7.

2. TRAFFIC CHARACTERISTICS

In this section, we characterize the nature of WLAN traffic patterns for large audience environments. In past Maier et al. [20] analysed the traffic characteristics for residential broadband Internet traffic while Raghavendra et al. [23] and Rodrig et al. [27] analysed the same for large conference environments. Of the two Rodrig et al. [27] analysed network traces for SIGCOMM 2004 and reported presence of

the asymmetric traffic patterns with around 80 % of total consisting of downlink traffic. To further confirm the similar trend in a relatively more contemporary data set, we analysed the SIGCOMM 2008 traces [28] which capture the WLAN traffic occurring during the event.

Figure 1a & 1b show the number of active STAs and aggregate network throughput measured each minute. Figure 1a shows the difference in the number of active clients sending uplink requests and receiving downlink responses. Figure 1b shows relatively low wireless throughput for such an environment. These two figures show that for large number of associated clients, many STAs couldn't receive any response from servers resulting in degraded throughput attributable mainly to the bottleneck for downlink traffic at the AP. We also observe that downlink throughput is significantly higher than uplink most of the time. Figure 1c shows the CDF of the ratio of the downlink traffic volume over the total traffic volume measured from all traces. More than 90% of the traces have the ratio greater than 50%. These figures clearly show the presence of high asymmetry between uplink and downlink traffic which is further quantified in Table 1.

		% of Protocol	% Out of Total
Downlink	TCP	91.2	83.4
	UDP	8.8	
Uplink	TCP	82.5	16.6
	UDP	17.5	

Table 1: Ratio of TCP and UDP of Downlink and Uplink Traffic in terms of number of bytes

Application Type	TCP (%)	UDP (%)
Web	56.54	0.00
IPSec	0.00	59.46
Email	12.99	0.00
Chat	0.59	0.00
Service Discovery	0.00	1.36
File Sharing	0.50	0.00
DNS	0.00	8.60
NetBIOS	0.72	9.44
Secure Shell	5.62	0.00
Streaming	0.69	0.00
Remote Desktop Service	0.42	0.00
Network Configuration	0.00	1.71
Others	21.93	19.43

Table 2: Types of applications in TCP and UDP traffic.

We classified the application types of the captured packets in Table 2, based on their port addresses. Among identified TCP packets, 57% of TCP traffic is Web traffic, 13% is email, and 6% is SSH. For UDP traffic, 60% is for IPSec NAT traffic, 10% is for NetBIOS, and 9% is for DNS. These data indicate that most of the TCP and UDP traffic are for client-and-server applications (Web, email, NAT, DNS, and NetBIOS) whose servers are running in the Internet.

Figure 2 shows the inter-arrival times for uplink UDP and TCP packets. They can be fit to exponential distributions using the maximum likelihood estimation. The average inter-arrival times are about 47 ms for TCP and 88

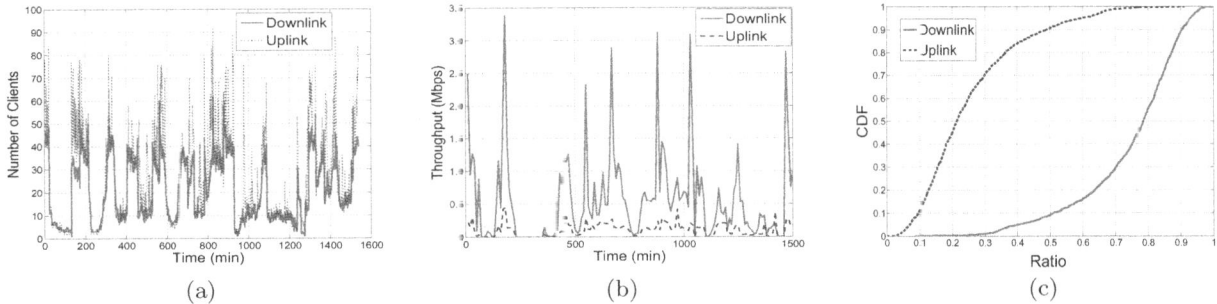

Figure 1: (a) Number of STAs sending Uplink/Downlink requests per minute (b) Downlink/Uplink throughput averaged over one minute (c) Distribution of Downlink/Uplink over total traffic volume ratio

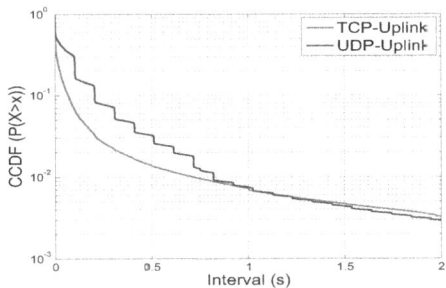

Figure 2: Distribution of Interval of TCP and UDP Uplink

ms for UDP. Note that these rates are conservative because not all STAs are associated with the measurement AP.

Rodrig et al. [27] illustrates that the ratio of STAs experiencing network failure over all STAs increases as the number of STAs increases in a wireless network. Further our analysis of traffic also validates the results obtained by Rodrig et al. [27]. We highlight two major points from our analysis.

- WLAN traffic is highly asymmetric in nature. On average, about 80% of the total traffic is downlink.

- The majority of the traffic (80 to 90%) is TCP. A majority of the TCP traffic (~70%) is from web and email, both known to generate heavy-tail traffic patterns [10, 29].

We leverage these results to design our testbed emulating such an environment. These network characteristics also guide the design choices of our solutions. It is evident from this analysis that the asymmetry in network traffic intensifies with the increase in the number of associated STAs. This results in performance bottleneck at the AP for downlink traffic and thus motivates the need for a mechanism to prioritize medium access for the AP over STAs under heavy traffic load. In next section we will discuss design and implementations of our solution.

3. DESIGN AND IMPLEMENTATION

Previously we discussed various factors that result in performance degradation for WIFi in LAE. In this section we will discuss how we tackled each of those problems. We describe our novel method for AP's adaptive priority control

(APC) which solves the problem of traffic asymmetry. We then present our implementation of AP-only fairness framework which addresses the problem of unfair resource allocations due to rate diversity. We further discuss our implementations of TCP Proxy/ECN to resolve the problems of TCP performance for LAE. Combining all these solutions in an optimal manner we propose our solution called **Wi**Fi **Fo**r Large **C**onference Environment (*WiFox*).

Class	CWmin	CWmax	AIFS	TXOPLimit
AP	1	5	1	64
STAs	5	10	N/A	N/A

Table 3: An example of parameter value setting enabling the highest priority channel access by the AP. TXOPLimit is denoted in terms of the number of 5 *us* slots. The default value of AIFS in IEEE 802.11e is 2. The settings for STAs is the default setting of IEEE 802.11g which uses DIFS instead of AIFS and does not define TXOP (so its value is set to 0). DIFS is much larger than AIFS.

3.1 Priority Control

The asymmetric nature of WLAN traffic as discussed in Section 2 causes congestion at the AP which becomes a bottleneck under heavy traffic load. The DCF-based IEEE 802.11 MAC is designed to give the AP the same opportunity to the wireless medium as the STAs in the basic service set even though the AP has the greatest amount of the traffic to transmit. Under heavy downlink load coupled with high contention from many active STAs, the AP cannot flush its traffic quickly, thus becoming a performance bottleneck and suffering a high rate of packet losses from both transmission queue overflow and collisions due to high contention. This motivates the need for a mechanism enabling a controlled preferential treatment to the overloaded AP over STAs for medium access.

We cannot give the AP high priority over STAs by default. It has an adverse effect on network performance: because the uplink traffic in the form of client requests from the STAs will be stifled, it will lead to a decreased downlink traffic which in light network load, can reduce the network goodput. Therefore a fine balance is required between uplink and downlink traffic in order to optimize network throughput.

We propose an APC scheme wherein the percentage of

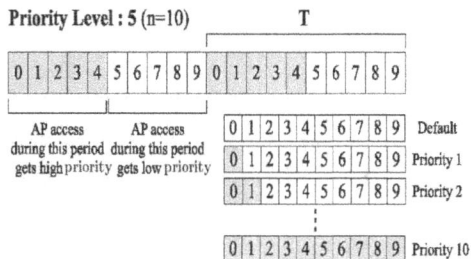

Figure 3: The illustration of the WiFox priority control model. For ease of illustration, the random k slots of high priority is chosen to be slot 0 to $k-1$ in each cycle of T.

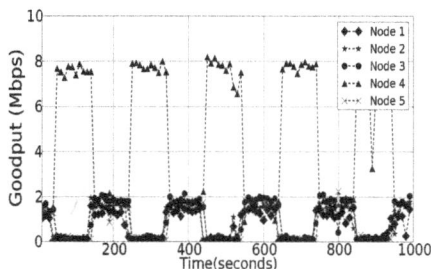

Figure 4: Effect of a priority setting on UDP Throughput. Node 4 runs with the HIGH priority setting specified in Table 3 while the other nodes run at the DEFAULT setting

downlink traffic being given priority is proportionately controlled based on the dynamic traffic load at the AP. This ensures that at low load the STAs get an equal opportunity as the AP to transmit requests and at higher loads the AP have a higher access priority proportional to the amount of downlink traffic. APC is designed in two steps. First, we deal with a priority model to define fine-grained MAC-level priority levels which are easy to control. Second, we develop an algorithm for adaptive control of priority levels that adjusts the channel access priority of the AP according to dynamic downlink traffic load.

3.1.1 Linear Scaling Priority Model

A common way to control the priority of channel access is to reduce the inter frame space (IFS) of WiFi and back-off duration values of each packet transmission so that the packet transmission starts before all other nodes start checking for the availability of the wireless medium. The following four parameters of IEEE 802.11e are commonly available from software WiFi drivers: (1) the minimum contention window size $2^{CW_{min}}$; (2) the maximum contention window size $2^{CW_{max}}$; (3) the Transmission Opportunity Limit (TX-OPLimit), defined as the maximum duration that a node can transmit without contending for the wireless channel with Short Inter Frame Space (SIFS); and (4) inter frame spaces (DIFS or AIFS, PIFS and SIFS).

Striking good balance between uplink and downlink traffic in the presence of dynamically varying traffic load requires a fine-grain control of channel access priority. This requires (a) a set of fine-grained priority levels, and (b) an estimation of the impact of each level on the probability of channel access by the AP and STAs. But these requirements are very

difficult to meet by simply adjusting the MAC parameters, especially because the impact of each particular parameter value, let alone their combinations, on the channel access probability of the AP and STAs is not well defined. For instance, given two value settings: ($CW_{min} = 2$, $CW_{max} = 6$, $TXOPLimint = 32$, $AIFS = 3$), and (3,5,0,2), which one has higher priority? If one has higher priority than the other, then how much do they differ in terms of channel access probability?

To address this problem, we take a novel approach that allows for a linear scaling of the access probability. The linear scaling permits convenient and accurate control of the channel access probability of the AP. We first define a setting of the MAC parameters that assigns the highest priority for the AP – when the AP competes for channel access with that setting, it wins the access most of the time. We call such a setting HIGH. The default value setting of these parameters is called DEFAULT. Table 3 shows one particular example of such a setting. Note that some of these parameters are defined only in IEEE 802.11e. However, this setting is compatible with STAs supporting any of IEEE 802.11 a/b/g/n. We only need the AP software to support IEEE 802.11e. The MADWIFI driver of WLAN provides the interfaces for controlling these parameters.

To get a set of fine-grained priority levels satisfying our requirements, we then divide the channel time of the AP into continuous intervals of time T. Each unit of T is further divided into n slots of duration T/n. If the AP has a priority level $k \leq n$, then k random slots out of the n slots within each T are high priority slots and the remaining slots are low priority slots. When the AP has a packet to transmit, if its current real-time indicates it is in a high priority slot, it accesses the channel with the HIGH setting; otherwise, it accesses the channel with the DEFAULT setting. Figure 3 illustrates this model. The random choice of the high priority slots with each cycle of T is intended to avoid collision among WiFox APs running in proximity. Because CW_{max} of HIGH is set to 5, even if multiple WiFox APs are competing, they have a room for random backoffs (up to 32 slots). With proper planning of LAE, a situation where many WiFox APs are competing in the same interference range can be avoided. Note that this model does not require time synchronization with STAs, nor with other APs. because it controls the access priority of the AP – the STAs simply use their default settings governed always by whatever IEEE 802.11 standard they are currently following.

This way, n fine grained priority levels can be obtained by controlling the number of slots (in each interval T) in which the AP receives very high priority. This scheme supports a nice linear scaling property where the average throughput of the high priority node increases in linear proportion to its priority level. This linear scaling makes it very convenient to design an adaptive control algorithm.

To verify that the parameter value setting in Table 3 increases the priority of packet transmissions correctly, we conducted a simple experiment consisting of 5 senders transmitting an Iperf UDP flow to one receiver. All nodes uses Netgear IEEE 802.11b/g card with Atheros chipset. We modified the MADWIFI driver in one of the senders to implement our priority model which is activated in alternating periods of 100 seconds. The other nodes always use the default IEEE 802.11 standard. We measure the throughput of each sender. Figure 4 shows the alternating periods of

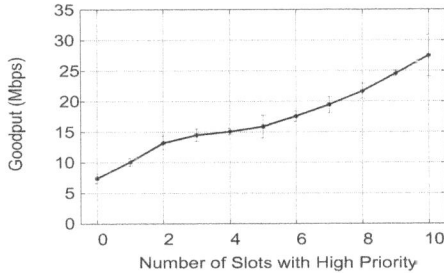

Figure 5: Linear scaling property of our priority model. The average throughput of the high priority node increases more or less linearly proportionally to its priority level

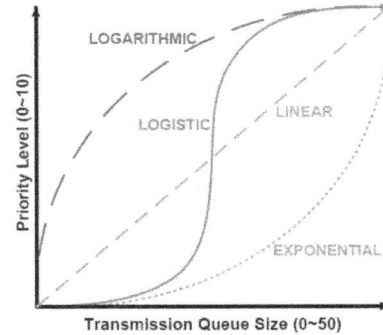

Figure 6: Four representative priority control functions.

100s where the high priority node (node 4) gets much higher throughput than the other nodes. In the remaining periods, the throughput of all nodes is comparable because all the nodes use the same default IEEE 802.11g setting.

To verify the linear scaling property of our priority model, we set n to 10 and T to 100ms, and vary the number of prioritized slots from 1 to 10 in the experiment taken in Figure 5. We measure the average throughput of node 4 for each priority level only during the intervals of prioritized accesses. Figure 5 shows the linear scaling property of our priority model being closely approximated in terms of the throughput achieved by the high priority node with various priority level settings.

3.1.2 Adaptive Priority Control

It is rational to assume that the provision of priority to the downlink traffic at the AP needs to be closely related to the dynamic traffic load at the AP. Dynamic downlink traffic load at the AP can be reliably estimated by the instantaneous transmission queue size of the AP where the maximum queue size is limited by an upper bound, Q_{max}. Therefore, we design adaptive priority control(APC) models determining the priority level depending on the transmission queue size at the AP for WiFox. Here, we map 10 priority levels into the slotted queue size whose maximum, Q_{max} is 50. We apply two intuitive criteria in designing APC models. First, APC models should have the lowest priority (e.g., no downlink) at zero queue size and the highest priority at max queue size. Second, the priority level of APC models should be monotonically increasing as the queue size increases. There may exist uncountably many models satisfying the criteria but amongst them, we choose 4 representative models which lead to totally different behaviors in the priority control and in the queue size variation. The models we choose are depicted in Fig. 6 and their characteristics are described below.

Logarithmic APC model (PC-LGA) provides a steep growth of the priority level for a small increase in the low queue size. Then, the growth speed diminishes as the queue size approaches the maximum. PC-LGA shows the most aggressive priority control among the 4 models as it maintains downlink priority unless the queue size becomes too low. PC-LGA serves more downlink traffic even under low queue size however this eventually tends to empty the queue because choking the data request in the uplink may result the lack of data arrival to the downlink queue of the AP in future.

Exponential APC model (PC-EXP) provides an exponential growth of the priority level at the high queue size. From a different point of view, it rapidly backs off the priority of the downlink when the queue size starts to reduce. It loses the chance of serving downlink traffic for low and medium queue size but this conservative back-off will bring about a large amount of data arrivals, hence the queue has a very low probability of becoming empty.

Linear APC model (PC-LIN) provides a non-special growth of the priority level. It balances the downlink and uplink proportionally. There will be no aggressiveness in serving downlink traffic nor rapid back-off.

Logistic APC model (PC-LGI) provides a combinational priority control of the exponential growth and the logarithmic reduction in the middle level of queue size. Thus, PC-LGI is aggressively serving downlink traffic at the high queue size and rapidly backs off when the queue size drops below a certain level. (e.g., half of Q_{max}) PC-LGI can be considered as a threshold policy in controlling priority since it determines only on and off according to the threshold value.

3.2 Fairness Control

WiFox integrates a fairness control with APC. It does not advocate one particular notion of fairness over another. Instead it offers a framework in which the system designer can plug in his own implementation of a control algorithm that best suits his needs.

WiFox can help realize the potential of AP-only fairness control. During the period of heavy downlink traffic, WiFox assigns a high priority level to AP, and thus, AP packets will always get high priority over uplink packets. Since the channel time will be consumed mostly by AP with its prioritized accesses, this ensures that channel time allocation asymptotically follows whatever notion of fairness the implemented control strives to accomplish.

WiFox offers a framework where the AP-only fairness algorithm is implemented as a kernel module of the AP which functions in the IP layer just above the MAC layer (where APC runs). The module contains a separate transmission queue for each active destination STA. It uses *Netfilter* architecture to capture outgoing packets using the *POST ROUTING* hook before they reach the MAC layer. If the captured packets are destined for the wireless interface, they are enqueued in their queues corresponding to their destinations. Queues are dynamically created and deleted on an as needed basis.

Figure 7 illustrates the architecture of the WiFox frame-

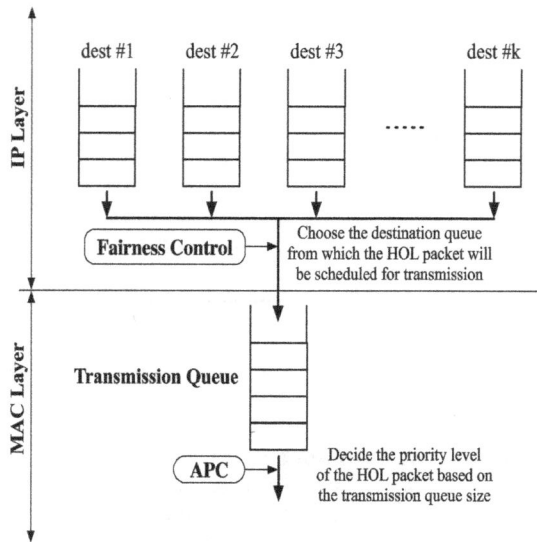

Figure 7: The architecture of the WiFox framework

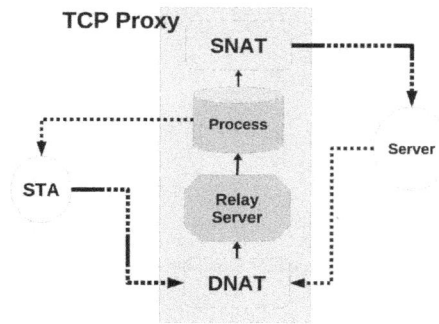

Figure 8: TCP Proxy implementation at AP

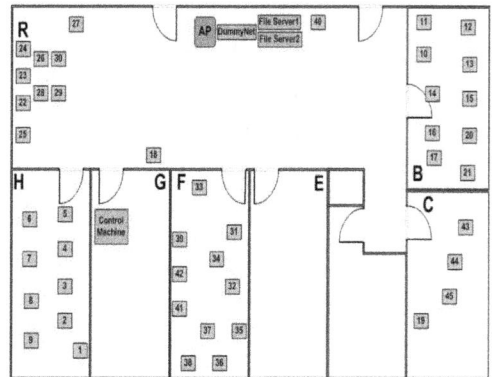

Figure 9: Placement of various nodes in our Testbed. Distance between AP and STAs ranges between 10-40 meters

work. The system designer can plug in his own fairness control algorithm here. For instance, time fairness can be implemented as follows. The kernel module maintains a channel occupancy time table of which entries maintain exponentially weighted moving averages of channel occupancy time for all destination queues it current holds. The module periodically monitors the instantaneous transmission queue size in the MAC layer. If space is available, the scheduler picks a non-empty queue with the minimum channel occupancy time and sends a packet from that queue to the MAC layer for transmission. If two or more queues have the same minimum channel occupancy time, it selects one in a round robin manner. The channel occupancy time of a transmitted packet is computed based on its size and the estimate of the current data rate. The channel occupancy times of all the queues are periodically updated by taking a moving average with the total channel occupancy time that their packets transmitted since the last update. It should be noted that our post-routing netfilter hooks filter out TCP data packets and queue them in appropriate destination queues and all other packets traverse directly to the AP's TxQ. This ensures that WiFox does not interferes with the network stack traversal of other packets and can easily support functionalities like pure link layer forwarding etc.

3.3 TCP Proxy/ECN

Apart from prioritization and fairness solutions, we will discuss briefly how we dealt with performance degradation due to *Random Losses and TCP Performance* under our design constraints. In the past, the problem of random losses interpreted as packet loss due to congestion has been solved using *Explicit Congestion Notifications (ECN)* [25]. To enable ECN, we modified AP's MAC driver and TCP stack to send congestion notification to the server with STA's acknowledgements when its instantaneous transmission queue (TxQ) exceeds a predetermined threshold. *TCP proxy* can further avoid performance degradation by bringing the server closer to the STA virtually and enabling faster reactions to its fluctuating network conditions [19]. TCP Proxy (Fig 8) is

implemented at AP using IPtables and NAT and it receives all requests from the clients as a virtual server and transmits new requests as a virtual client to real Internet servers. In next section we will discuss the experimental set-up under which we tested the performances of these proposed solutions.

4. EXPERIMENTAL SETUP

In this section we present our detailed experimental methodology for evaluating WiFox on our testbed. We will discuss how we built our testbed, emulated the traffic patterns similar to those of SIGCOMM 2008 traces [28] and conducted experiments to quantify performance gains of our solutions.

4.1 Testbed

Our experimental set-up consists of a testbed with multiple APs and 45 STAs deployed at our research lab (about 2600 sqft area). The architecture and layout of the testbed are shown in Figures 10 and 9 respectively. Scaling the layout from Figure 9, we can see that distance between STAs and AP ranges between 10-40 meters. The testbed consists of 24 STAs and 2 File Servers (FSs) of Type A and 21 STAs and an AP of Type B. Type A machines have an AMD Dual Core processor with 2 GB RAM, 160 GB Hard Disk, Netgear IEEE 802.11b/g wireless card with Atheros chipset and Debian OS with kernel version 2.6.27.12-1. Type B machines have a VIA processor with 1 GB RAM, 60 GB Hard Disk and the rest of the configuration is the same as Type A. It should be noted that machines we used as APs are not

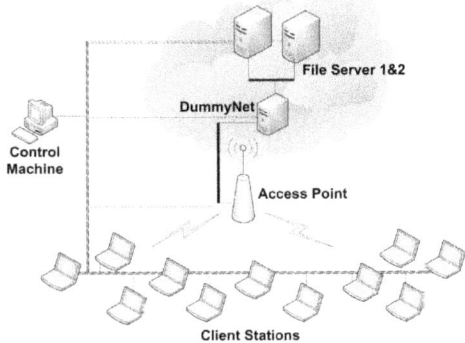

Figure 10: Test Bed Architecture

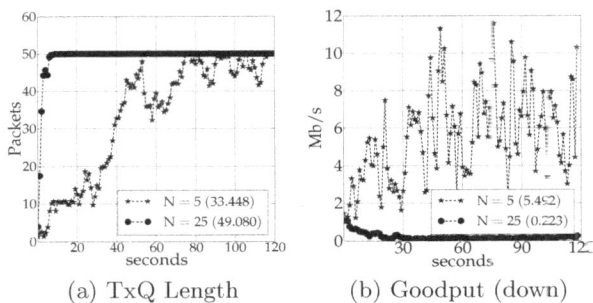

(a) TxQ Length (b) Goodput (down)

Figure 11: (a) We observe that traffic asymmetry is correlated with TxQ length (b) Downlink goodput for entire network drops significantly when number of associated clients increase from 5 to 25

computation intensive ones and are comparable to ones commercially used for such network environments Also usage of netfilter hooks should not limit the scalability of our solution as they can be efficiently embedded with basic routing module itself for the APs.

The wireless interface card uses the MADWIFI [2] Linux Device Driver, an open source project under GPL. We have two File Servers (FSs) which act like remote servers over the Internet. All STAs can access these FSs through an AP. To give more realistic network delay between all STAs and FSs, we place a DummyNet [1] using FreeBSD DummyNet assigns different delays per tcp traffic flow. We configure the DummyNet to give flow delay values between 5-200 ms.

4.2 Traffic Modeling

We use SURGE [7], a web traffic generator, and *Iperf*, for traffic generation. To reflect more contemporary web traffic patterns consisting of large file sizes, we adopt a modified form of SURGE [12] which makes available a number of parameters for tuning the traffic patterns. In our setup, SURGE generates web requests and the file servers generate replies by sending random sized files. The inter-arrival time of requests in SURGE follows an exponential distribution and can be controlled using the SURGE *rate* parameter. By default, we set the average inter-arrival time of TCP requests to 2 seconds, with which 5-45 active STAs each running between 5-25 threads, gives the aggregate inter-arrival time

of about 40-200 ms which is close to what we observed for the uplink rate of TCP measured from the SIGCOMM 2008 traces [28]. By varying the number of active STAs, we can evaluate WiFox under various work loads.

From the traffic analysis [28], we can see that UDP traffic from STAs or APs is constantly generated. This UDP packet transmission in uplink traffic affects the downlink TCP traffic from APs. To emulate this phenomenon, we generate uplink UDP traffic from each STA in our experiments. So, we also use UDP traffic as well as the TCP requests for the uplink traffic. By doing so, we also expect that the UDP traffic could play a role of other interferences which prevents APs' packet transmission [9], thus we refer this UDP traffic as *Background Traffic*. Most of the experiments we performed are tested for background traffic in the range 0-30 Kbps per STA. However, even with the different UDP traffic rate, overall pattern for most of our results remains unchanged and thus until specified otherwise we present results with 25 Kbps only.

4.3 Experimental Procedure

Most experiments in this paper involve one AP and a set of STAs associated with it. All machines are connected to a server from which we can control all testbed components. We use *tcpdump* to gather every trace file at the file servers and STAs and uses *tshark* to extract the relevant data from the tcpdump files. UDP data is analysed with our own tool. We have several kernel modules of the modified MADWIFI driver at the AP for our implementations of various schemes which are dynamically loaded according to testing requirements. Each data point has been obtained by averaging the results from experiments repeated for 5-30 rounds with the duration of each round in the range of 120-240 secs.

We implement various different fairness control algorithms for WiFox like throughput maximization (TM), time fairness (TF) and round robin (RR) etc. Among them we chose time-fairness (TF) for our evaluation. We used 10 prioritization levels as it was a good number to implement our dynamic adaptation scheme. We tried various other quantization levels but there were no benefits in terms of network performance. We evaluate the following protocols for comparison.

- NPC: the default IEEE 802.11g with no priority control.

- WANG: the protocol proposed in [36]. The only existing work on solving traffic asymmetry in WiFi networks that does not require change in STAs.

- NPC-{TF}: NPC is combined with TF.

- PC-{LIN,EXP,LOG,LIG}: APC with one of the linear, exponential, logarithmic, and logistic priority control functions.

To corroborate our understanding of traffic asymmetry problem in real LAE, we run an experiment with default NPC module on our emulated LAE testbed. Figure 11a, shows variation of TxQ length for the duration of experiment. For lesser number of associated STAs, problem of TxQ saturation and subsequent packet losses is not significant, but as associated STAs increase we observe immediate TxQ saturation. Figure 11b shows severe goodput degradation as AP saturates, which conforms with our observation for LAE from SIGCOMM 2008 traces [28].

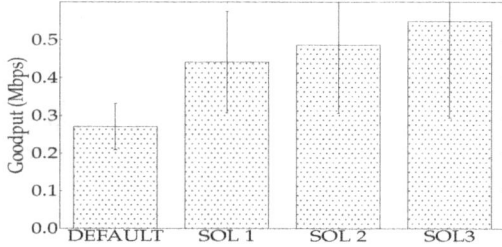

Figure 12: Here default is NPC, TCP Proxy/ECN is solution 1, AP-only TF realization is solution 2 and their combination is solution 3. Clearly these solutions result in 70-100 % improvement in downlink goodput for 25 associated clients

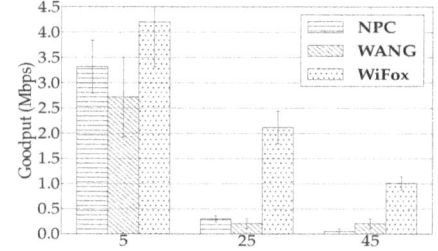

Figure 14: Network downlink goodput benefits significantly with prioritization and performance gains upto 700 % are achievable

5. EVALUATION

In this section we present a detailed analysis and results of the experiments carried to test the performance of WiFox. We summarize the major results as follows.

- AP only TF, TCP ECN & Proxy solutions result in improvements of around 70-100 % for downlink goodput.

- Among all the performance degradation factors, traffic asymmetry results in maximum performance loss for LAE. WiFox adaptively prioritizes AP's channel access and results in 400-700 % goodput improvement for downlink traffic and 50-150 % total goodput improvement.

- WiFox enhances user experiences with a faster requests serve rate. It results in the reduction of response time by 40-60 %.

- All variants of APC perform significantly better than existing solutions.

5.1 Non-APC Solutions

Since we strive to ensure that our solution will be easily deployable, we limit our evaluation to existing solutions that require modifications only to APs and require no further changes in STAs or 802.11 MAC protocol. Figure 12 shows the performance comparison for TCP/ECN and AP-only fairness realizations for 25 associated clients. We observe that downlink goodput performance improves by 70-100% when these solutions are applied. Clearly solution 2 does not uses TCP Proxy/ECN and yet shows performance improvements as compared to NPC, thus we should expect performance improvements for solutions without TCP Proxy (NAT boxes) also. All the solutions presented here are practical realizations of existing works [33, 25, 19] focusing on one particular performance degradation factor. We expect even better performance gains by solving the problem of traffic asymmetry.

5.2 WiFox

WiFox combines implementations of TCP Proxy/ECN and AP-only fairness with adaptive AP priority control (APC). We will now analyze the performance of WiFox with other existing schemes.

5.2.1 Performance

We compare the performance of WiFox with default NPC and WANG. For brevity of discussion we chose PC-LGA from among many APC variants for comparison in this section. Later we will compare the performance of all APC variants in Section 5.2.3. Figure 13a shows that dynamically prioritizing AP over STAs avoids queue saturation and packet losses due to buffer overflow and increased contention. Average TxQ length for 45 clients is slightly less than that for 25 clients which is attributable to the logarithmic nature of the mapping function. In Figure 13b, we observe that for WiFox TCP retransmission rate is not affected by the increased number of associated clients as it results in reduced contention by prioritizing AP traffic. Figure 13c strongly demonstrates significant goodput performance gains achieved through priority control. As the amount of traffic load increases with the number of associated clients we observe a slight decrease in uplink traffic which is compensated with significant improvement for downlink goodput (Figure 14) for *WiFox*.

Figure 15 shows that downlink goodput improvements are not achieved at the cost of fairness. We compared time fairness performance of various schemes using Proportional Fairness Index (PFIndex), which is defined as $PF = \frac{\sum_{i=1}^{N} X_i \log X_i}{N}$ where X_i is the goodput of node $i \in [1, N]$ and N is the number of clients. We also observe that fairness performance for WiFox is marginally better than NPC-TF because AP gets more airtime for WiFox enabling effective realization of fairness schemes [33]. To improve our understanding of whether prioritizing AP impacts link rate adaptation, we observed the corresponding average link rates for each station. Figure 16 shows that no such correlation exists and we have similar average link rate with or without priority control.

5.2.2 User Experience

So far we have discussed performance in terms of network goodput and fairness. WiFox results in significant goodput performance improvement, but that does not always correlate with better user experience. Reduced response time for a request is considered as more critical than improved goodput for activities such as web browsing [8]. In this section we probed whether WiFox results in reduced response time. We developed an experiment *Fixed and Inflated*, where each client sends a fixed number of requests (25), and observation duration is inflated from two to four minutes. Sending fixed number of requests for a longer duration ensures reception of all sent requests by the server. Figure 17, shows the cu-

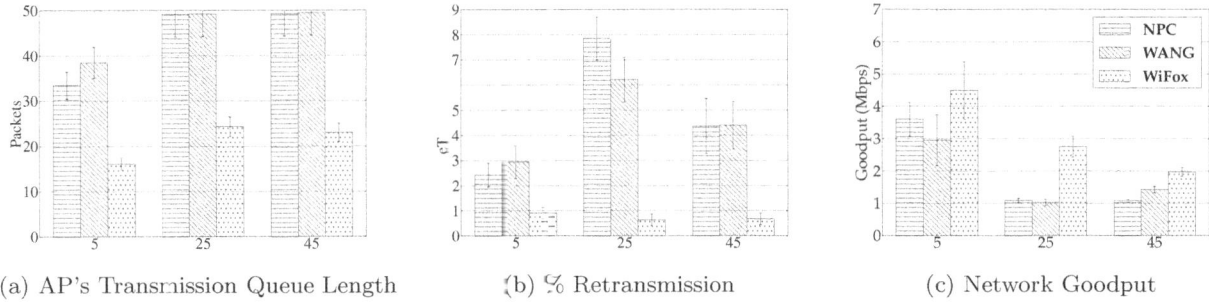

(a) AP's Transmission Queue Length   (b) % Retransmission   (c) Network Goodput

Figure 13: All three graphs use the same legend. (a) Dynamically prioritizing AP traffic reduces TxQ length by 40-50 % (b) Number of retransmissions are reduced by 70-80 % (c) thus consequently resulting in aggregate goodput improvements by 75-125 %

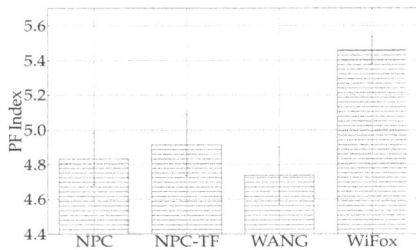

Figure 15: Proportional Fairness Index for 25 clients shows marginal improvement of 10-20 % in fairness among contending STAs

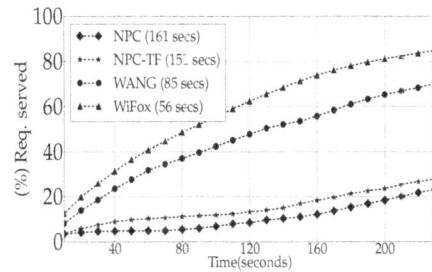

Figure 17: WiFox requests serve rate is 4 times faster than NPC and it reduces response time by 40-60 %. Values in parenthesis give the average response time for each scheme

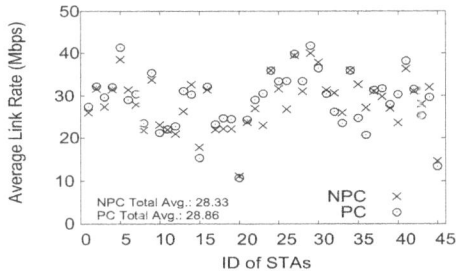

Figure 16: Prioritization does not affects the link rates

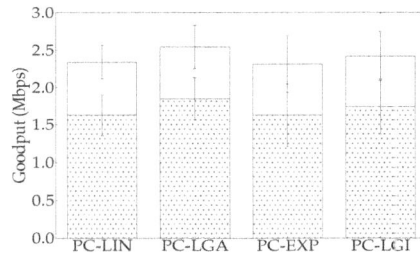

Figure 18: Goodput for APC variants with 25 associated clients

mulative distribution of completed requests with respect to time. Here a steeper slope ensures faster requests serve rate. We observe that WiFox results in reduced response time, as backlogged packets in TxQ are promptly served. As WiFox ensures higher channel access priority to APs, thus delay at its TxQ for response packets is lesser as compared to other schemes. 70-80 % of sent requests are not served within the observation interval for AP's without priority control. Shorter response time for WiFox not only improves the user experience, but with the philosophy of "race to sleep" will save energy for smart devices [24].

5.2.3 APC Variants

So far we have discussed results with PC-LGA scheme for brevity. In this section we will compare performance differences among all the APC variants. We carried out an

experiment with all variants on similar lines as explained in section 4.3. Figure 18 shows their goodput performance for 25 associated clients. In terms of goodput, there is little difference, though PC-LGA performs slightly better than the others. We observed earlier that for 25 or more associated clients, the queue saturates instantly to the maximum value. PC-LGA is aggressive in assigning higher priority to downlink traffic, but under a heavy load as emulated from real LAE, it outperforms other APC variants. Aggressive priority assignment of PC-LGA is evident in Figure 19 as it has the smallest TxQ length of all the variants. As PC-EXP is the least aggressive its TxQ has more packets backlogged at any given time, similarly, as expected PC-LGI is bounded by exponential and logarithmic mappings. Figure 20 shows the

225

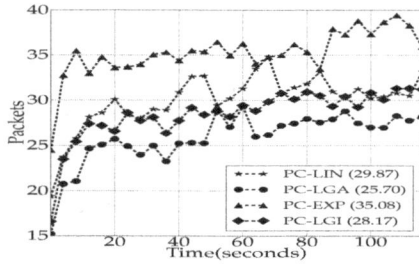

Figure 19: TxQ length for AP with 25 clients for APC variants. Values in parenthesis gives the average TxQ length for each scheme

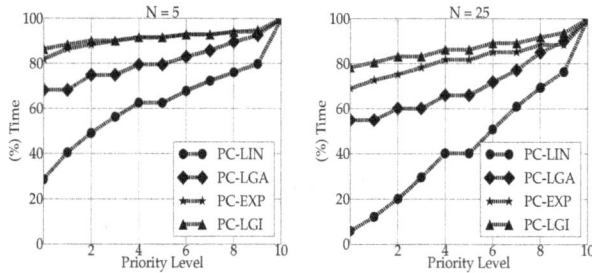

Figure 22: Goodput for varying UDP background trafic with respect to zero background goodput of each

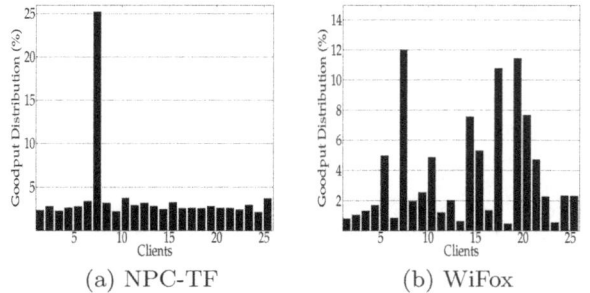

Figure 20: Distribution of Priority Level for APC Variants for 5 and 25 associated clients respectively

cumulative distribution of time spent at each priority level by APC variants for two disparate traffic loads. PC-LIN is uniformly distributed for all priority levels, with a steeper slope for 25 clients. With fewer associated clients PC-LGI follows PC-EXP, contending with default priority for most of the time and swiftly moves towards PC-LGA as the traffic load increases.

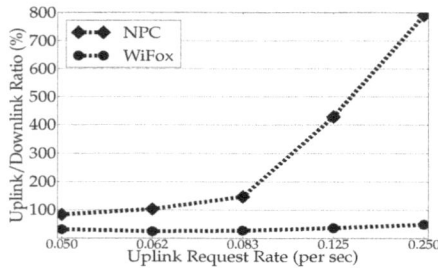

Figure 21: Performance with varying Uplink TCP Traffic for 25 STAs. For entire experiment downlink request rate for each client was 0.50 per second

5.3 Test for Robustness

To evaluate the performance of our scheme for robustness, we tested WiFox for following scenarios.

5.3.1 Impact of varying Uplink Traffic

In all our previous experiments tcp uplink traffic is generated by requests sent by STAs to web servers. To account for TCP uplink traffic generated by activities like photo up-

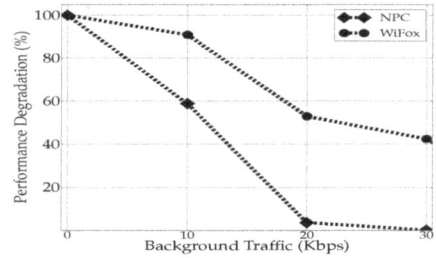

(a) NPC-TF	(b) WiFox

Figure 23: Normalized distribution of downlink goodput for each STA. STA_{mischv} (STA 7) requests files of large size and impacts the performance of other clients for NPC-TF scheme

loads, cloud synchronization etc, we test WiFox for varying uplink traffic. Wireless stations respond to the requests generated by the web server at different rates. Figure 21 shows the performance of WiFox compared to NPC for varying additional uplink traffic. For default NPC, we observe significant improvement in uplink goodput at the cost of downlink traffic. Conversely for WiFox we observe a slight increase in uplink/downlink goodput ratio. WiFox prioritizes downlink traffic and ensures service of downlink requests is not affected with increasing uplink traffic. Such a behaviour is highly desirable for a large audience environment, where excess uplink activities of a few clients can impact the downlink performance of an entire network.

5.3.2 Impact of Background UDP Traffic

In this experiment, all associated clients generate TCP traffic using SURGE as usual, but they vary the amount of uplink UDP traffic from 0 to 30 Kbps. As previously discussed, increase in background traffic, results in intensified channel contentions for AP. Also more UDP uplink requests imply fewer TCP requests sent to the server and thus results in reduced TCP downlink traffic. In figure 22, we show downlink goodput degradation for varying UDP traffic with respect to the goodput without any UDP traffic for both the schemes. We observe widening of the performance degradation gap with increasing background traffic. For background traffic of 30 Kbps per STA, we observe TCP downlink traffic for other schemes is nearly zero, whereas WiFox still manages to serve TCP requests.

5.3.3 *Impact of bulky downloads*

So far we considered all users requesting short transfers when using the web. In this experiment we want to test what happens if a client downloads large files. All the other 24 STAs send TCP requests as usual, except for one STA (STA_{mischv}) which requests large sized files (150 Mb) In order to ensure that TxQ has maximum packets for STA_{mischv}, we start its transfer two seconds before the others. Figure 23 shows the distribution of downlink goodput achieved by each node for NPC-TF and WiFox. It is evident that STA_{mischv} dominates the TxQ at the AP and achieves maximum goodput without prioritization. Whereas WiFox ensures that downlink airtime is fairly shared among all STAs avoiding unfairness due to bulk download. With prioritization, AP has maximum access to channel resources and ensures effective realization of AP-only fairness schemes. It should be noted that Figure 23 shows normalized downlink goodput distribution for each associated STAs and thus the two figures are not directly comparable to each other in terms of actual downlink goodput observed.

5.3.4 *Impact of Multiple APs*

The application domain for WiFox are LAEs which implies presence of multiple APs. This necessitates the analysis of WiFox's behaviour in presence of multiple APs. At the macro level we discussed in section 3.1 that high priority slots are assigned randomly. This ensures that multiple APs operating in proximity of each other are not much affected by their neighbour's priority assignment. At micro level, WiFox requires that all APs operating in proximity of each other should use same set of 802.11e parameters. This ensures that even when two APs are concurrently assigned high priority they can compete with each other for channel access as usual. Clearly for such an event the APs downlink performance improvement will be lesser but since prioritization works as usual thus we can ensure better performance than NPC APs for similar network environment. Moreover random priority assignment ensures that such events do not have much impact over longer run.

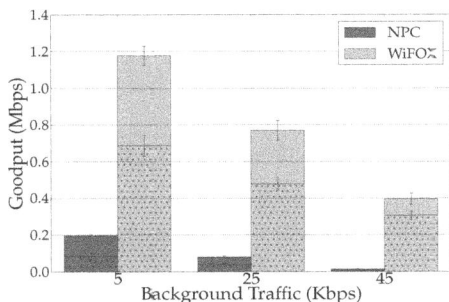

Figure 24: For Multi AP scenario, aggregate downlink goodput for WiFox APs is significantly better than NPC ones. Downlink network goodput for AP2 is stacked over AP1's to enable aggregate goodput comparison

To corroborate our understanding for multiple AP scenario we conducted an experiment with two APs on our testbed. Each AP is associated with 20 STAs and operate in close proximity of each other. The placements of APs and nodes are similar to our original configuration and STAs are randomly selected to connect to either of the two APs. Figure 24, shows the downlink goodput performance of each AP for WiFox and NPC. We observe that APs with NPC suffer significantly as compared to those with WiFox. We observe around 10 times improvement in overall network goodput for 25 Kbps background traffic. Clearly the performance improvements are more than single AP scenario as we discussed earlier which supports our understanding that NPC APs suffer more in multiple AP scenario as compared to WiFox.

6. RELATED WORK

WLAN performance enhancement has received a considerable amount of attention in the research community. Research in the area explores centralized solutions for appropriate channel assignments [21, 26], evaluating capacity for each AP [35, 13], or concurrent connections with multiple APs [16, 32] etc. to improve the overall network performance. These solutions can be orthogonally combined with our proposed solution to improve the performance of a large scale WiFi network.

There have been many proposals to resolve the problems associated with the asymmetric access patterns of WiFi to improve the overall network throughput (e.g., [3, 36]). Most of these proposals either require modifications in both APs and STAs [18, 22, 17], require all nodes to support 802.11e [17], or focus on equalizing the downlink and uplink traffic volume [22, 36]. Since downlink traffic is 4 to 10 times greater than uplink traffic in LAE, these solutions are not effective and even detrimental to the overall performance. Though Bruno et al. [9] makes modification only at APs but requires knowledge of optimal collision probability. Estimating this optimal value for diverse network traffic is non-trivial and limits the robustness of the solution.

Some of the related work on performance enhancement of wireless LANs [15, 33, 6, 30], focuses on the issue of the existence of rate diversity. They propose different methods of providing fairness amongst the STAs as a measure to alleviate overall network performance. Tan et al. [33] proposed a *Time Based Fairness* algorithm (TBR) to achieve a significant gain in the throughput as compared to the *Throughput Based Fairness* provided by IEEE 802.11 DCF in multi-rate WLANs. This paper proposes an AP-only scheme for allocation of equal channel occupancy time to all STAs to improve the aggregate throughput in infrastructure networks. Banchs et al. [6] also propose to solve the *performance anomaly* [11] problem in IEEE 802.11 DCF by the use of proportional fairness for throughput allocation. Aziz et al. [4], attempts to solve the problem of jointly providing efficiency and fairness in wireless networks in general as a utility maximization problem. Our approach of prioritizing AP for channel access enables efficient realization of these fairness schemes([30, 33, 11, 4, 34, 5]).

7. CONCLUSION

In this paper we have examined the factors responsible for poor performance of WiFi for large audiences. We have emulated a large conference like network environment on our testbed with 45 nodes. We have give the reasoning how presence of traffic asymmetry is one of the major factor for performance degradation for such an environment and proposed *WiFox* which solves the problem of traffic asymmetry along with performance degradation due to rate-diversity/fairness and TCP behaviour. On our testbed we have demonstrated that it improves downlink goodput by 400-700 % and enhances user experience by reducing average response time for a request by 30-40 %. We have tested *WiFox* for robustness and have demonstrated that under various test conditions it outperforms the existing WiFi implementations. WiFox requires modifications to AP's software only and is adaptive to various traffic loads, making it a suitable candidate for wide scale deployments.

There are few open problems related to design of WiFox: exploring relationship between different traffic patterns and appropriate APC variants, characterizing performance of WiFox for MIMO based 802.11n APs and developing a priority aware scheduler enabling QoS support. WiFox improves the overall network goodput achieved thus we expect it to improve the performance for real time applications also for LAEs. We believe that it should be possible to ensure QoS and support real time applications with appropriate tuning of prioritization parameters and we intend to pursue this direction in future. Our testbed currently supports evaluation for 802.11g only and we plan to further extend our analysis for 802.11n also.

8. ACKNOWLEDGEMENTS

We would like to thank the following people. Our shepherd, Bhaskar Raman, for his helpful feedback, as well as Suman Banerjee, Venkata N. Padmanabhan, Kyunghan Lee for their valuable comments. We would also like to thanks Marhn Fullmer for his help in setting up the testbed. This work is supported in part by NSF awards CNS-1016216 and IIS-0910868. Any opinions, findings and conclusions expressed in this work are those of the authors and do not necessarily reflect the views of NSF.

9. REFERENCES

[1] DummyNet: http://info.iet.unipi.it/ luigi/dummynet/.
[2] MADWIFI Project: http://madwifi-project.org/.
[3] E. Aguilera, J. Casademont, J. Cotrina, and A. Rojas. Perf. enhancement of wlan IEEE 802.11 for asymmetric traffic. In *IEEE PIMRC*, 2005.
[4] A. Aziz, J. Herzen, R. Merz, S. Shneer, and P. Thiran. Enhance &; explore: an adaptive algorithm to maximize the utility of wireless networks. In *International Conference on Mobile computing and networking*, MobiCom '11. ACM, 2011.
[5] A. Babu, L. Jacob, and V. Brijith. A novel scheme for achieving time based in IEEE 802.11 multirate wireless LANs. In *IEEE ICON, 2005*.
[6] A. Banchs, P. Serrano, and H. Oliver. Proportional fair throughput allocation in multirate IEEE 802.11 e wireless LANs. *Wireless Networks*, 2007.
[7] P. Barford and M. Crovella. Generating representative Web workloads for network and server performance evaluation. In *ACM SIGMETRICS Perform. Eval. Rev.*, 1998.
[8] M. Belshe. More bandwidth doesn't matter (much),
[9] R. Bruno, M. Conti, and E. Gregori. Design of an enhanced AP to optimize TCP perf. in Wi-Fi hotspot networks. *Wirel. Netw.*, 2007.
[10] M. Crovella and A. Bestavros. Self-Similarity in www Traffic: Evidence and Possible Causes. *IEEE/ACM ToN*, 5, 1997.
[11] M. H. Franck, F. Rousseau, G. Berger-sabbatel, and A. Duda. Performance Anomaly of 802.11b. In *IEEE INFOCOM*, 2003.

[12] S. Ha, L. Le, I. Rhee, and L. Xu. Impact of background traffic on performance of high-speed TCP variant protocols. *Computer Networks*, 2007.
[13] N. Hegde, A. Proutiere, and J. Roberts. Evaluating the voice capacity of 802.11 wlan under distributed control. In *Local and Metropolitan Area Networks, 2005. LANMAN 2005. The 14th IEEE Workshop on*, pages 6–pp. IEEE, 2005.
[14] J. Jeong, S. Choi, and C. Kim. Achieving weighted fairness bw uplink and downlink in IEEE 802.11 DCF-based WLANs. In *QShine*, 2005.
[15] L. B. Jiang and S. C. Liew. Proportional fairness in wireless LANs and ad hoc networks. In *IEEE WCNC*, 2005.
[16] B. T. Kandula S., Lin K. and K. D. FatVAP: Aggregating AP Backhaul Capacity to Maximize Throughput. In *USENIX NSDI*, 2008.
[17] F. Keceli, I. Inan, and E. Ayanoglu. Weighted Fair Uplink/Downlink Access Provisioning in IEEE 802.11 e WLANs. In *IEEE ICC*, 2008.
[18] S. W. Kim, B. Kim, and Y. Fang. Downlink and uplink resource alloc. in IEEE 802.11 wlans. *IEEE TVT*, 2005.
[19] S. Kopparty, S. Krishnamurthy, M. Faloutsos, and S. Tripathi. Split tcp for mobile ad hoc networks. In *GLOBECOM*, 2002.
[20] G. Maier, A. Feldmann, V. Paxson, and M. Allman. On dominant characteristics of residential broadband internet traffic. In *Internet Measurement Conference*. ACM, 2009.
[21] R. Murty, J. Padhye, R. Chandra, A. Wolman, and B. Zill. Designing high perf. enterprise wi-fi networks. In *NSDI*, 2008.
[22] N. Nandiraju, H. Gossain, D. Cavalcanti, K. Chowdhury, and D. Agrawal. Achieving Fairness in Wireless LANs by Enhanced IEEE 802.11 DCF. In *IEEE WiMob*, 2006.
[23] R. Raghavendra, E. Belding, K. Papagiannaki, and K. Almeroth. Unwanted link layer traffic in large ieee 802.11 wireless networks. *Mobile Computing, IEEE Transactions on*, 9(9):1212 –1225, sept. 2010.
[24] C. Raiciu, D. Niculescu, M. Bagnulo, and M. Handley. Opp. mobility with mptcp. In *MobiArch*, 2011.
[25] K. K. Ramakrishnan, S. Floyd, and D. Black. The Addition of Explicit Congestion Notification (ECN) to IP, 2001.
[26] S. Rayanchu, V. Shrivastava, S. Banerjee, and R. Chandra. Fluid: improving throughputs in enterprise wlans through flexible channelization. MobiCom '11, 2011.
[27] M. Rodrig, C. Reis, R. Mahajan, D. Wetherall, and J. Zahorjan. Measr. based char. of 802.11 in a hotspot setting. In *ACM E-WIND*, 2005.
[28] A. Schulman, D. Levin, and N. Spring. On the fidelity of 802.11 packet traces. In *PAM*, 2008.
[29] S. Shah and B. Noble. A study of e-mail patterns. *Software, Practice & Practice*, May 2007.
[30] J. Shin, H. Roh, D. Lee, and S. Kim. Generalized proportional fair rate allocation schemes for IEEE 802.11e wireless LANs. In *APCC*, 2008.
[31] S. Shin and H. Schulzrinne. Balancing uplink and downlink delay of VoIP traffic in WLANs using Adaptive Priority Control (APC). In *ACM QShine*, 2006.
[32] H. Soroush, P. Gilbert, N. Banerjee, B. Levine, M. Corner, and L. Cox. Concurrent wi-fi for mobile users: analysis and measurements. In *ACM CoNEXT 2011*.
[33] G. Tan and J. Guttag. Time-based fairness improves performance in multi-rate WLANs. In *USENIX ATC*, 2004.
[34] I. Tinnirello and S. Choi. Temporal Fairness Provisioning in Multi-Rate Contention-Based 802.11e WLANs. In *IEEE WoWMoM*, 2005.
[35] H. Velayos, I. Mas, and G. Karlsson. Overload protection for ieee 802.11 cells. In *Quality of Service, 2006. IWQoS 2006. 14th IEEE International Workshop on*, 2006.
[36] X. Wang and S. A. Mujtaba. Perf. enhancement of 802.11 wlan for asymm. traffic using an adaptive MAC layer protocol. In *IEEE VTC*, 2002.

MAClets: Active MAC Protocols over Hard-Coded Devices

Giuseppe Bianchi
CNIT
Universitá degli Studi
di Roma Tor Vergata
Italy
giuseppe.bianchi@uniroma2.it

Pierluigi Gallo
CNIT / Universitá degli Studi
di Palermo - Italy
pierluigi.gallo@unipa.it

Domenico Garlisi
CNIT / Universitá degli Studi
di Palermo - Italy
domenico.garlisi@unipa.it

Fabrizio Giuliano
CNIT / Universitá degli Studi
di Palermo - Italy
fabrizio.giuliano@unipa.it

Francesco Gringoli
CNIT / Universitá degli Studi
di Brescia - Italy
francesco.gringoli@unibs.it

Ilenia Tinnirello
CNIT / Universitá degli Studi
di Palermo - Italy
ilenia.tinnirello@unipa.it

ABSTRACT

We introduce MAClets, software programs uploaded and executed on-demand over wireless cards, and devised to change the card's real-time medium access control operation. MAClets permit seamless reconfiguration of the MAC stack, so as to adapt it to mutated context and spectrum conditions and perform tailored performance optimizations hardly accountable by an once-for-all protocol stack design. Following traditional active networking principles, MAClets can be directly conveyed within data packets and executed on hard-coded devices acting as virtual MAC machines. Indeed, rather than executing a pre-defined protocol, we envision a new architecture for wireless cards based on a protocol interpreter (enabling code portability) and a powerful API. Experiments involving the distribution of MAClets within data packets, and their execution over commodity WLAN cards, show the flexibility and viability of the proposed concept.

Categories and Subject Descriptors

C.2.1 [**Computer-Communication Networks**]: Network Architecture and Design—*Network communications, Wireless communication*

General Terms

Design, Experimentation, Management

Keywords

programmable MAC; WLAN 802.11, reconfigurability; cognitive radio

1. INTRODUCTION

It was the end of the last century since cognitive [1] and active [2] wireless networks were considered near to come. The promise was that wireless networks would have soon become capable of being dynamically reprogrammed so as to best fit unpredictable and dynamically mutating context situations; adapt to user preferences, usage patterns, or service demand variations; smartly exploit temporarily unused radio spectrum, etc.

The aftermath is that such a vision is still fighting with the limited flexibility of *commercial* wireless products and standards. Whereas, in the last decade, the scientific community emerged with open-source, fully programmable DSP, FPGA, or SDR platforms, most wireless manufacturers have consistently pursued a closed products' design strategy, which reduces programmability to the tuning of some pre-defined device parameters. On the other side, although many standards include different configurable operation modes, they are designed to be comprehensive, *one-size-fits-all* and may fail to be effective in specific niche contexts or particular network situations.

With specific reference to the Medium Access Control functionalities, on which this paper is focused, flexibility has been so far accomplished by standardizing a set of configurable parameters, as well as the means to dynamically signal, control, and enforce the relevant settings. Even the 802.22 MAC layer, specifically defined for cognitive networks, is based on *pre-defined* transport modes (combining polling, contention and unsolicited bandwidth grants mechanisms) that can be selected according to the service requirements [3]. Another example is the case of the 802.11 QoS (EDCA) extensions, originally standardized in the 802.11e amendment, which permits dynamic configuration, via beacons, of the key parameters characterizing each traffic category, namely contention windows, transmission opportunities, and arbitration inter frame spaces. Such parameters can then be exploited to optimize performance for dynamically varying context conditions such as number of competing stations [4, 5].

The current solutions prevent to extend configuration facilities to new MAC parameters or functions, unless a relevant standard amendment is first approved and then adopted by manufacturers. With this paper, we aim to show that a radically different approach allowing wireless devices to dynamically download and install *on-the-fly* a full protocol logic (rather than a set of parameter settings), customized for specific contexts and conditions, is technically feasible even in a multi-vendor scenario. As a basic use-case, imagine a terminal associating to an Access Point in a specific context, for instance an home or an airport. The network provider has programmed a number of custom MAC protocols, each optimized for the specific context and for a different operation or traffic/service condition. Upon association (or upon changes in conditions), the terminal downloads a new MAC protocol from the AP, and starts using it. This network management approach (which makes concrete, at least for what concerns the MAC protocol stack, the futuristic vision described in [6]) is not anymore hindered by the reliance on standards; it suffices that all terminals support i) a "default" protocol operation, for instance WiFi, for first communicating with the AP, and ii) an architecture which permits the real time programming of the MAC protocol, and which runs a same software on different hardware platforms, *say something as Java for wireless MAC protocols* (adapting a quote from [6] - indeed this justifies the name "MAClet" we use throughput this paper). Note that in a single vendor scenario (or in an idealistic scenario where all clients are open source devices), this would trivially reduce to load a new firmware in the wireless cards. Rather, the challenging real world hurdle to overcome is how to re-program, or, even better, dynamically reconfigure in real time the MAC protocol operation, under the constraint that such reconfiguration is done in a way that does *not require* vendors to open their platforms.

Our contribution

In order to program MAC protocols on closed devices, suitable Programming Interfaces are mandated. This problem has recently received crucial attention, and the identification of a MAC programming interface appears to emerge (explicitly or implicitly) from a number of recent works [7, 8, 9, 10], where a number of common primitives (core functions in [7], modules in [8], components in [9], actions/event/conditions in [10]) have been proposed for assembling different MAC schemes in an high-level programming language.

This paper leverages, as starting point, our prior findings described in [10], where we proposed to formally describe a MAC protocol through extended finite state machines, executed by a *Wireless MAC Processor* (WMP) architecture running inside the wireless card. The further steps taken in the present work involve both technical and application aspects. From the technical side, several extensions to the framework described in [10] were necessary to support real-time code switching (and MAC multi-threading) with negligible (sub microseconds) delay. On top of the extended WMP architecture, we developed a control framework for supporting MAClet code mobility, i.e. for moving, loading and activating MAC software programs embedded into ordinary data packets (akin to traditional active networks' *capsules*) along with relevant meta-data such as initial state and startup conditions. From the application side, this paper takes a completely different perspective with respect to [10]:

from the *node-level* ability to run different MAC protocols, to the *network-level* perspective of managing and dynamically reconfiguring, in real-time, the network, well beyond the parameter-based reconfiguration of today WLAN deployments [11, 12]. The network-level reconfiguration capabilities of the framework have been validated in two interesting use-cases examples (including dynamic spectrum access and support of virtual operators using different MAC protocols over a same, time-shared, infrastructure).

Our contribution focuses on the actual MAC stack reconfiguration via dynamically delivered MAClets. We *do not* claim any contribution on i) the strategies for disseminating mobile code, being many already available in the literature, and on ii) the measurement gathering, learning and decision processes by which a reconfiguration is triggered, being these tasks mostly orthogonal to the "act phase" perspective (using cognitive networking terminology) we tackle in this paper.

2. WIRELESS MAC PROCESSORS

In what follows we briefly review the WMP main concepts [10] and anticipate some discussion on extensions for supporting code switching. Indeed, a pre-requirement of *any* wireless active MAC framework is the ability to support customized MAC operation on general-purpose wireless devices, and the possibility to switch to a desired MAC protocol logic described through suitably formal languages and application programming interfaces.

Concept

The Wireless MAC Processor architecture somewhat mimics the organization of ordinary computing systems, where programmability is accomplished by specifying i) an adequate *instruction set* which permit to perform elementary tasks on a machine; ii) a *programming language* which conveys multiple instructions (suitably assembled to implement a desired behavior or algorithm) to the machine, and iii) a Central Processing Unit (CPU), which executes such program inside the machine, by fetching and invoking instructions, updating relevant registers, and so on.

Instruction set: Actions, Events, Conditions

A breakdown analysis of MAC protocols reveals that they are well described in terms of three types of elementary building blocks: *actions*, *events* and *conditions*.

Actions are commands acting on the radio hardware. In addition to ordinary arithmetic, logic, and memory related operations, dedicated actions implement atomic MAC functions such as transmit a frame, set a timer, build an header field, switch to a different frequency channel, etc. Actions are *not* meant to be programmable. As the instruction set of an ordinary CPU, they are provided by the hardware vendor. The set of actions may be extended at will by the device vendor, and complex actions may be considered, so as actions not necessarily restricting to MAC primitives (e.g. perform a PHY encoding/decoding).

Events include hardware interrupts such as channel up/down signals, indication of reception of specific frame types, expiration of timers, signals conveyed from the higher layers such as a queued packet, and so on. As in the case of actions, also the list of supported events is a-priori provided by the hardware design.

Conditions are boolean expressions evaluated on internal *configuration registers*. These registers are either explicitly updated by actions, or implicitly updated by events. Some registers are dedicated to store general MAC layer information (such as channel used, power level, queue length), frame related information (source or destination address, frame size, etc), or more specific MAC parameters (contention window, backoff parameters, etc - used to achieve a more compact protocol description in case of specific MAC designs such as CSMA-based ones).

Actions, events, and registers on which conditions may be set, form the application programming interface exposed to third party programmers. This API is implemented (in principle) once-for-all. meaning that programs may *use* such building blocks to compose a desired operation, but have no mean to modify them. In [10] we proposed an API able of supporting several MAC behaviors, including a TDMA-like and a multi-channel medium access control. However, this API was not envisioned for supporting code mobility. For instance, we could not enforce conditions to control the switching between a previously running MAC code and a newly uploaded one. Thus, we needed to extend the WMP *internals* to implement an extended API accounting for new actions, events and registers, tailored to dynamic code management.

Programs: Extended Finite State Machines

MAC protocols are well suited to be described in terms of Finite State Machines. Indeed, they are used in the formal appendices of the 802.11 (and many other) standard. We chose to rely on the more powerful and expressive model of eXtended Finite State Machines (XFSM). XFSMs are a generalization of the finite state machine model and permit to conveniently control the *actions* performed by the MAC protocol as a consequence of the occurrence of *events* and *conditions* on configuration registers.

An XFSM is formally specified through an abstract 7-tuple (S, I, O, D, F, U, T): the meaning of such symbolic states and the correspondence with the MAC terminology above introduced is summarized in Table 1 (configuration commands being a special case of *actions*, devised to update registry status).

A *MAC program* is simply a table listing all possible state transition relations. Note that the number and meaning of the set of *protocol states* is specified by the programmer. By formally describing, per each protocol state, which events and conditions do trigger a state transition, and by associating actions and configuration commands to each state transition, the programmer may access the available hardware primitives, and enforce a desired MAC behavior within the radio hardware. Since the configuration memory is not explicitly represented in the state space, XFSMs allow to model complex protocols with relatively simple transitions and limited state space. For an example, the table *programming* the legacy 802.11 Distributed Coordination Function MAC protocol is coded in less than 600 bytes, and hence *can be transmitted in just a single packet.*

XFSM formal notation		meaning
S	symbolic states	MAC protocol states
I	input symbols	Events
O	output symbols	MAC actions
D	n-dimensional linear space $D_1 \times \cdots \times D_n$	all possible settings of n configuration registers
F	set of enabling functions $f_i : D \to \{0,1\}$	Conditions to be verified on the configuration registers
U	set of update functions $u_i : D \to D$	Configuration commands, update registers' content
T	transition relation $T : S \times F \times I \to S \times U \times O$	Target state, actions and configuration commands associated to each transition

Table 1: MAC programs expressed as Extended Finite State Machines

CPU: MAC engine

The ability to *timely* react to events is a crucial property of lower-MAC protocols (e.g. for triggering a transmission right at the end of a timer expiration). In the Wireless MAC Processor architecture, this is accomplished by implementing an XFSM execution engine, called MAC engine, directly on the radio hardware. The MAC program, namely the table containing all the possible state transitions, is loaded in a memory space deployed on the hardware. Starting from an initial (default) state, the MAC engine fetches the table entry corresponding to the state, and loops until a triggering event associated to that state occurs. It then evaluates the associated conditions on the configuration registers, and if this is the case, it triggers the associated action and register status updates (if any), executes the state transition, and fetches the new table entry for such destination state.

Multi-thread extensions

The MAC engine work-flow allows to easily support *code switching*: in analogy to usual multi-threading, this entails the time-shared execution of *different MAC programs* simultaneously uploaded on the device. Indeed, the MAC engine does not need to know to which MAC program a new fetched state belongs, so that a code switching is basically achieved by moving to a state in a different transition table and by updating the platform configuration registers (e.g. the operating channel, the transmission power, etc.) when needed. The definition of code switching transitions are logically independent of the MAC program definition. Therefore, rather than adding them to the MAC program, we chose to program the switching transitions into a second-level state machine (*meta state machine*), whose states represent the MAC program under execution.

To simplify the management of error conditions due to the dynamic loading of multiple transition tables, we assumed that each table can be loaded starting from a pre-defined memory position, called memory slot. For each memory slot, a dedicated register describes the state of the slot as empty, available for re-writing, ready to be executed, or under execu-

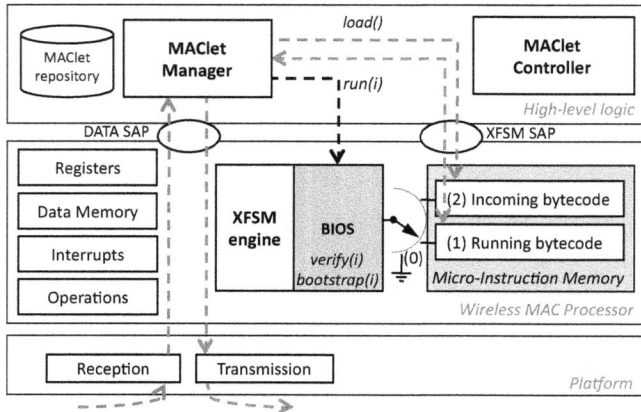

Figure 1: Architecture for MAClet support: extended WMP and external MAClet Control.

WMP Control Interface	
load i	load a MAC program on memory slot i
run i, e	activate MAC program on slot i (asynch. or at the event e)
verify i	recognize trusted code by means of an hard-coded signature computation
switch $i, j, t, a/r$	add or remove a switching transition t from the slot i to j

Table 2: WMP Commands to be locally or remotely invoked

tion. Although the number of these slots can be in principle arbitrary, we consider the simplest case of two slots only [1].

Summarizing, the time needed to *change* a MAC program (i.e. the MAC stack reconfiguration delay) consists in the time needed to fetch a new state plus the time needed to update the WMP configuration registers (i.e. a series of memory accesses). All this accounts for a marginal, sub-microseconds, time (a few MAC engine clock cycles, the exact time depending on the platform's clock frequency and on the number of registers to be updated).

3. MACLET CONTROL ARCHITECTURE

In this section we describe how low-level MAC functionalities can be *encapsulated* in a MAClet and transferred from a node to another of the network by exploiting the WMP API and a MAClet distribution protocol.

Figure 1 shows the envisioned system: the control architecture is a *pure* software architecture, running at the application level, that interacts with the enriched WMP by means of an open control API. This approach has several advantages. First, the selection of the MAC protocol can be based not only on low-level performance parameters (such as the link quality, the interference conditions, etc.), but also on high-level context estimates, including the application requirements, the network topology, the user preferences, and so on. Second, the code distribution model (handshaking mechanisms, peer-to-peer code sharing, server-client uploading, etc.) is completely independent on the underlying programmable interface, thus allowing full flexibility and a wide range of applications for the same platform. Moreover, the communication delays between the host and the card have a minimum impact on the MAClet Control, since the dynamics of the networks (which require MAC protocol customizations)

---

[1]Such a choice has been also confirmed by the analysis of different use cases requiring prompt adaptations of the MAC operations. We never found an actual need to switch between more than two protocols at a frequency so high to require the simultaneous loading of multiple transition tables on the device.

are reasonably much slower than the processing delay due to an application-level decision module.

More into details, the architecture is based on four main components: the WMP control interface, the MAClet manager, the MAClet Controller and the MAClet repository. The WMP control interface is the interface to the hard-coded device, through which new MAC state machines and switching conditions are loaded on the card, as summarized in table 2. The MAClet manager is responsible of receiving/transmitting MAClets and MAClet protocol messages, enabling the loading on the card, and programming MAC reconfigurations. The MAClet Controller is the intelligent part of the system, dealing with the network-level configuration decisions in a centralized way (e.g. at the Access Point only, as assumed in this paper), or in a distributed way (e.g. by involving multiple cooperating controllers, sharing both the monitored data and the available MAClet tables). Finally, the MAC program repository contains the MAClets available to the network operator, including either standard as well as customized (context-specific) MAC protocols.

3.1 MAClets

A key component of our architecture is the code transport unit, i.e. the MAClet. A MAClet is a *coded state machine* with an *initial state description* to be fed on the wireless device.

Being n_s the number of symbolic protocol states and n_e the number of events revealed by the device, a common approach for coding XFSMs is using a $n_s \times n_e$ table, where at each location (i, j) is stored the state transition when event j is received at state i. A transition is defined by a triplet (a, c, s), specifying the action label a, the enabling condition label c and the target state label s. As each state generally reacts to a number of input events much lower than the total input number, the state machine coding can be optimized by skipping null-transitions. The initial state (from which the state machine has to be run) includes the protocol logic state and the platform configuration registers. For example, according to the API defined in [10], these registers (of equal size) specify the settings of the physical channel, the slot size, the contention window values, the current backoff, the transmission power, the retry limit, generic protocol timers and MAC addresses to be filtered. Optionally, the initial state descriptor can be extended with a signed digest of the MAClet code to be used for verifying trusted code sources[2].

---

[2]Although most of the security issues can be demanded to the MAClet Control, this function can be used by manufac-

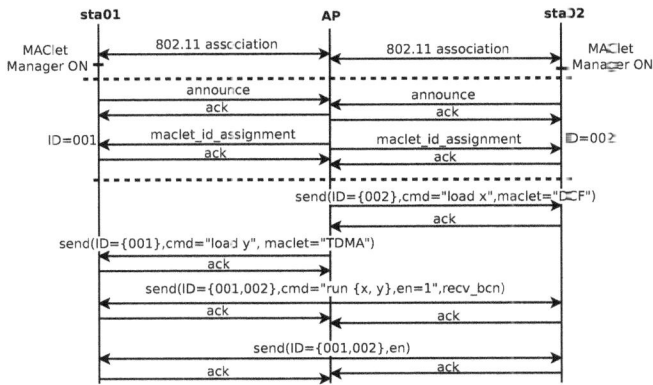

Figure 2: Messages of the MAClet Distribution Protocol: an example.

As detailed in what follows, MAClets are transmitted with a special message of the MAClet Distribution Protocol, called MAClet action message.

3.2 MAClet Distribution Protocol

MAClets can be propagated in the network by means of a *physical transport network*. This means that nodes can negotiate the activation of a new MAC protocol only if they belong to the same network (on a given channel) and employ a compatible MAC protocol. Standard MAC protocols can assume the role of default *common* protocols to be executed (eventually, on a pre-defined *common* channel) for supporting dynamic reconfigurations. We assume that the default protocol and configuration parameters are pre-loaded in each WMP as a *bios* state machine (e.g. in our implementation, the bios machine is a legacy DCF working on channel 1).

The MAClet Control process runs as a normal distributed application, whose messages are defined by a protocol called MAClet Distribution Protocol. This protocol is responsible of: i) collecting information for estimating the network context; ii) negotiating the network reconfiguration decisions iii) transporting the MAClets and the relative activation signals; iv) verifying the network consistency after a reconfiguration. Although the general definition of the MAClet distribution protocols is out of the scope of the present work, we defined some core messages to be used in case of centralized decision processes. Specifically, in the following we always assume that the reconfiguration decisions are taken in a centralized way (as in [13, 14]) at the AP side, thus significantly simplifying the negotiation phase (which is basically limited to the transport of station measurements to the AP) and the verification of consistency.

The protocol includes two types of messages: MAClet *management messages* for associating each MAClet manager to a MAClet Controller running the distribution logic and confirming control operations, and MAClet *action messages* for transporting MAClets and remotely invoking the desired WMP control functions. When a new station activates, it tries to associate to an AP (acting as a MAClet Controller) by using

turers for controlling the MAC program origins and limiting or avoiding third-party reconfigurations.

the bios state machine. In case of success, the MAClet manager is activated for enabling the reception of AP messages. An announcement message is sent to the AP for notifying the activation of the new MAClet Manager and receiving an identifier. According to its decision logic, the AP is then able to send a specific MAClet action messages to each associated station, to a group of stations or to all the network stations (see figure 2).

The MAClet action message comprises the following fields: the list of destination addresses of the relevant MAClet managers, a command to be executed on the addressed WMPs, the MAClet bytecode, the MAClet configuration parameters, and the MAClet activation data. Not all fields are always included in the action messages: for example, it is possible to specify a new set of parameters for a MAClet already loaded on the station without carrying the relevant bytecode.

3.3 MAClet Synchronization

Achieving a network-level reconfiguration is obviously much more complicated than working on a single node, because it is necessary introducing some forms of coordination. In particular, the activation of a new MAClet on different nodes could require a common reference signal for avoiding critical inconsistencies (such a temporary use of different transmitting channels) leading to disassociations or other network errors.

The MAClet Control Architecture provides the primitives for programming the desired synchronization and error recovery operations, but the specific solutions are left to the MAClet Decision Logic (synchronization) and MAC program (management of error conditions) defined by the network operator. For example, in section 5 we describe two different use cases requiring network-level reconfigurations, for which two different synchronization solutions have been envisioned. The synchronization signals can be based on the events and conditions available in the WMP and are specified in the MAClet activation data.

In order to activate a new MAClet on a group of stations, the AP sends a "run" action message to the stations list. If the command does not include an activation data field, each station can starts the program asynchronously, i.e. without a common reference signal. If present, the activation data specifies the triggering event that is usually a control frame sent by the AP or the expiration of a (relative or absolute) timer. While the relative timer is in turns expressed as a function of a network synchronization event (e.g. the next channel busy time), for using an absolute time reference the MAClet Control Process has to rely on a time synchronization function. In our infrastructure scenario, such a synchronization is easily provided by the beacon timestamps, while in general scenarios it has to be explicitly supported by the MAClet Distribution Protocol.

Different activation solutions based on a 3-way handshake mechanism can also be defined in the distribution protocol. After the reception of the run message, each station involved in the network reconfiguration sends a confirmation message. When the AP receives all the confirmation messages, it sends an enabling message. Only after the reception of this message, the stations switch to the new MAC program at the

Initial State Descriptor

```
0x0BC0:  0100 FFFF 0B00 0014 A5FF 6ADA 0014 A5FF
0x0BD0:  6ADA 6C00 80A4 FF00 FF00 3600 80EE FF00
0x0BE0:  FF00 0000 80BB FF00 FF00 0600 2C01 0600
0x0BF0:  0000 0000 0000 0000 0000 0000 0000 0000

          00   01   02   03        Coded state machine
0x0C00:  0100 0100 0100 0401 0108 0508 1C01 010B
0x0C10:  010B 3001 010D 0200 FFFF 5101 010E 030D
0x0C20:  0000 0100 010F C100 0102 0602 E100 0106
0x0C30:  0106 0401 0108 0508 1C01 010B 030B FFFF
0x0C40:  CD00 0104 0E0C 0000 0100 0D00 FFFF 0E01
0x0C50:  0109 0909 1C01 010B 0D0B FFFF C700 0103
0x0C60:  0C03 E100 0106 0106 FFFF 6601 0110 1600
0x0C70:  0000 0100 0000 FFFF 0000 0109 0109 1C01
0x0C80:  010B 010B FFFF 5F01 010F 0A00 0000 0100
0x0C90:  0D00 FFFF C100 0102 0A02 C700 0103 0B03
0x0CA0:  E100 0106 0D06 FFFF D300 0105 0D05 E100
0x0CB0:  0106 0D06 FFFF D300 0105 0705 B100 0106
0x0CC0:  0106 FFFF 6D01 0111 1800 0000 0100 0100
0x0CD0:  0000 0100 0D10 7401 0112 1512 0000 0100
0x0CE0:  1111 9601 0113 0513 0000 0100 0500 0000
0x0CF0:  0100 0304 E100 0106 1206 0401 0108 0508
0x0D00:  1C01 010B 120B FFFF A901 0115 0100 B401
0x0D10:  0117 1200 0000 0100 0100 0000 0100 1214
0x0D20:  B901 0118 0310 0000 0100 0300 0401 0108
0x0D30:  1708 1501 010A 1C01 010B 010D C501
0x0D40:  0119 0800 0000 0100 0500 3001 010D 0200
0x0D50:  0401 0108 0508 1C01 010B 180B CB01 011A
0x0D60:  0200 0000 0100 0100 0000 0000 0000 0000
0x0D70:  0000 0000 0000 0000 0000 0000 0000 0000
0x0D80:  0000 0000 0000 0000 0000 0000 0000 0000

          00   01
0x0D90:  00F0 03FE 0DF2 13FE 20FE 27FE 2BFE 35FE
0x0DA0:  3CFE 43FE 4AFE 54FE 5BFE 62F2 68F0 6BF2
0x0DB0:  71F2 77F0 7AFE 84F4 8DF0 90F2 96F4 9FF2
0x0DC0:  A5F4 AEF2 0000 0000 0000 0000 0000 0000
0x0DD0:  0000 0000 0000 0000 0000 0000 0000 0000
```

Outgoing transitions for state 01
```
0401 0108 0508 = trans. 1
1C01 010B 010B = trans. 2
3001 010D 0200 = trans. 3
FFFF          = delimiter
```

Transition 1
```
0401 = event pointer
01   = event parameter
08   = event index
05   = target state
08   = action
```

State 01
```
03 = transitions offset (9 bits)
E  = FFFF delimiter
```

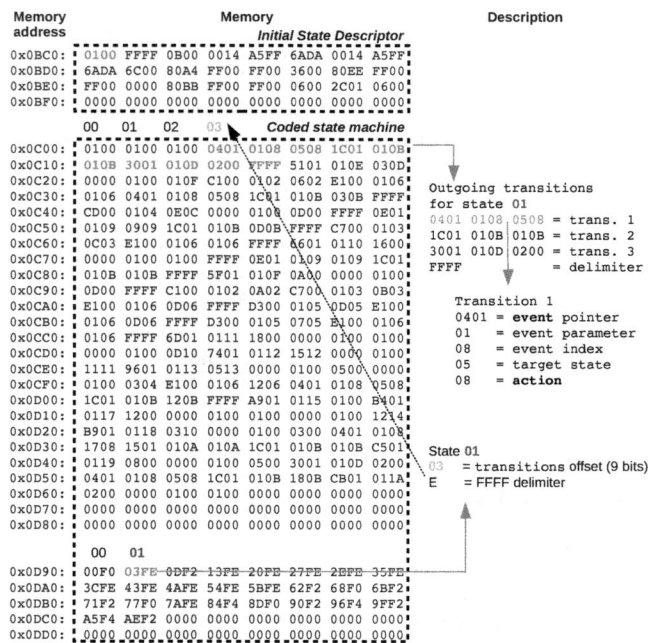

Figure 3: MAClet binary implementation, as stored in the micro-instruction memory

occurrence of the next triggering event. Figure 2 shows an example of messages exchanged between the AP and two stations for loading two different MAClets (a legacy DCF on station 2 and a TDMA protocol on station 1), whose activation is triggered by the first beacon received after the enabling message.

4. NODE-LEVEL VALIDATION

To prove te viability of the MAClet distribution framework, we worked into two different directions: on one side, we modified the MAC Engine and the actions implemented *within* our previous WMP implementation on the Broadcom card (i.e. at the firmware level), by also adding some new condition registers; on the other side, we developed a simple MAClet Control process (including the MAClet manager, repository and controller) at the application level (*outside* the card). For supporting the upper-MAC operations and interacting with the other protocol layers, we used the *b43* soft-MAC driver (without any modifications). Finally, we also extended the WMP machine language (i.e. the labels of actions, events and conditions) in order to code the new API.

4.1 Implementation

The implementation of the MAClet Control Architecture has been based on the development of a new firmware and an application-level software. Regarding the firmware, we developed and pre-installed the micro-code procedures corresponding to the WMP Control API (i.e. the *load*, *bootstrap*, *run*, and *switch* primitives - the *verify* command has not been currently implemented) and added new registers indicating the state of the program slots and the program under execution. We also worked on the MAC Engine work-flow,

MAClet Management Messages	
announce	sent by stations to request a MAClet ID
id_assign	sent by AP to assign unique MAClet ID
poll	sent by AP to check if a station is attached
en	enable command (requires activation message)
ack	message acknowledgment
MAClet Action Message Fields	
ID_set	MAClet_IDs addressed by the message
maclet	MAClet program or BYTECODE
params	set of MAClet parameters
cmd	MAClet command (load, run, en flag, dump, set timer)
activation	MAClet triggering event

Table 3: MAClet management and action messages.

for allowing the execution of the meta machines. Specifically, the new engine pre-fetches the switching transitions (defined in the meta-machine) of the program under execution and adds such a list to the transition list of the program state. In case of events triggering a transition to a new program, the transition action executed by the engine is the bootstrap of the new program. Finally, the WMP machine language has been revised for coding the new API and for trying to guarantee a compact representation of the MAClet bytecode.

Figure 3 shows an *actual* example of MAClet bytecode for the legacy DCF, where we can recognize the initial state descriptor (for configuring the platform registers) and the transition table. The table is coded by: i) a list of transition lists, and ii) a list of states represented by the pointer to the relative transition list. For example, the state in the second position of the list (whose symbolic label 01 corresponds to the position index) points to the transition list coded from the third byte of the table and ends at the occurrence of the first $FFFF$ delimiter. As evident from the figure, the code is very compact (only 544 bytes).

The application-level software has been developed according to a simple client-server paradigm, since we considered a centralized decision logic implemented at the Access Point. The key component of the application is the MAClet manager that implements the MAC Distribution Protocols summarized in table 3 (for loading and executing MAClets on different network nodes). In our implementation, MAClet management messages are unicast, while MAClet action messages are broadcasted to all stations and filtered at the application level according to the "ID_set". The MAClet distribution logic, that is the block responsible of network configuration decisions, has a very simplified structure. Basically, rather than implementing a context estimation module and a programming interface for the operators, we pre-scheduled some decisions at the Access Point and pre-set the other nodes to accept MAClets and switching commands sent by the AP.

4.2 MAClet Switching

We run some simple experiments of MAClet switching in order to test the MAClet *intra-node* functionalities and measure the switching latency of our implementation. A more complete validation also involving multi-node coordination is described in the next section. In our tests, we used a USRP

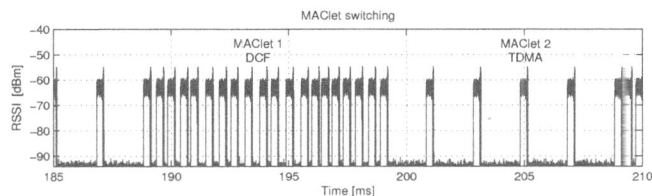

Figure 4: An experimental trace of medium occupancy times under MAClets switching (DCF and TDM) performed at regular time intervals (10 ms).

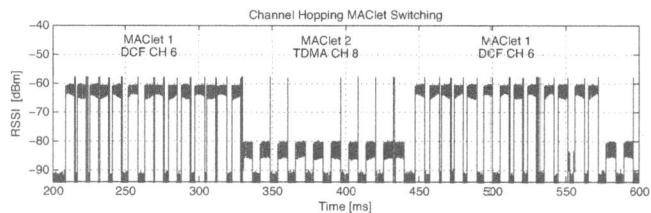

Figure 5: An experimental trace of MAClet switchings involving a channel switching operation.

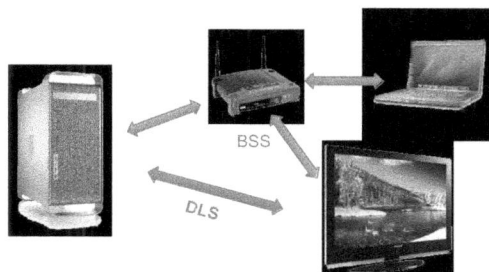

Figure 6: Use case 1: a streaming server (left) delivers HD video to an Internet enabled TV; a laptop (right) is connected to the internet via the AP.

board for acquiring the channel activity trace of the card performing the MAClet switching. The trace is processed by MATLAB for deriving the time-varying RSSI values corresponding to channel idle and busy states. In order to clearly visualize the change of the MAC protocol under execution we considered the switching between the random-access of standard DCF and the deterministic-access of a TDMA protocol. The two corresponding state machines have been loaded on the two different program slots of the card. A synchronization transition has been programmed by specifying a switching event corresponding to the expiration of a 10ms timer.

Figure 4 shows a channel activity trace of 15 ms, captured by the USRP board when the card is fed with a saturated traffic (generated by the *iperf* tool, with a packet payload of 1470 bytes) transported over UDP. The MAClet initial state descriptor specifies that the card is set to operate on channel 6 and with a modulation rate of 24 Mbps, while the protocol initial state is set to an idle state for both the MAClets. When the switching to the TDMA protocol expires during a frame transmission, the first packet transmission is skipped, in order to avoid deferrals of subsequent packet schedules. The figure allows to easily identify frame transmissions (characterized by an RSSI value of about -60 dBm), acknowledgments (with an RRSI value of about -55dBm), and idle times (with an RSSI value of about -92 dBm). Thanks to the different inter-frame spaces (2ms under TDMA, random under DCF), we can clearly distinguish the protocol under execution at a generic time instant. Moreover, the MAClet switching time is practically negligible and not quantifiable from the figure. Even considering a much longer trace, we practically observed that the channel accesses performed under the TDMA protocol are always scheduled at regular intervals of 2 ms as in the case of a permanent TDMA execution (i.e. cumulative switching delays are not observable in a temporal trace of 5 minutes). In fact, the switching time is practically given by the execution of the bootstrap action, which in turns require to set the configuration registers (12 registers in our implementation), jump to the transition list of the new protocol state and load the new list of events. The execution of these operations requires on average 20 clock cycles, which correspond to about 0.2μs (being the clock frequency of the card at 88MHz).

Figure 5 shows an experiment similar to the previous one, where we also include a different configuration of the PHY layer in the descriptor of the MAClet initial states. Specifically, we set the DCF MAClet to operate on channel 6 and the TDMA MAClet to operate on channel 8, while the physical transmission rate is set to 1 Mbps for both the MAClets. We set the most robust modulation scheme since we verified that, at this rate, the receiver station on channel 6 is able to correctly demodulate the frame transmitted on channel 8, without performing the channel hopping (which would have requested to implement a synchronized MAClet switching also at the receiver side). Similarly, although the USRP receiver is set on channel 6, the board is able to detect part of the power transmitted on channel 8. The switching time is set to 200ms. In the figure, we can recognize the transmissions performed on channel 6 (whose RSSI values are about -60 dBm) from the transmissions performed on the out-of-band channel 8 (whose RSSI values are about -80 dBm). From the figure, it is evident that the radio does not exhibit any remarkable latency for hopping between the two channels.

5. NETWORK-LEVEL VALIDATION

We consider a generic infrastructure network, with an Access Point and a given number of associated stations in radio visibility. Despite of the scenario simplicity, we show two different use cases in which network reconfigurations can be really beneficial. The solutions proposed are on purpose *not general*: they are meant to be just examples (which can be further technically improved) devised to highlight our framework's flexibility and test the MAClet transport, loading, and switching functionalities. In particular, we focus on two important features of the proposed architecture: the ability to coordinate the execution of different MAC schemes at two different stations (*multi-thread*), and the ability to support heterogeneous node configurations performed by two different operators (*virtualization*) and permit their coexistence on a same shared channel.

235

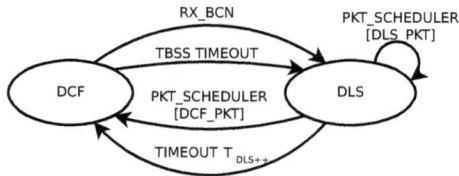

Figure 7: DLS++ protocol definition as a meta machine between two different threads.

5.1 Use case 1: Multi-Thread

Scenario Description

The considered scenario is summarized in Figure 6. A WiFi ADLS domestic router connects three stations to the Internet. This usually works well if traffic to the stations comes from the outside. However, when the kids are at home and start downloading a high definition video from a streaming server (on the left) to the Internet-enabled TVset (in the middle), it is likely that who is trying to work on the laptop will get impaired performance, as the legacy DCF protocol requires traffic to be first routed from the server to the AP and then again to the TVset, thus duplicating the bandwidth used on the wireless channel.

This problem is obviously not nearly new, and indeed was specifically addressed by the 802.11e task group with the introduction of the Direct Link Setup (DLS), further extended in the 802.11z-2010 amendment. However, a direct link setup is not automatic (i.e. the kids should take care of changing the settings of the TVset during the streaming!). Moreover, the direct link uses the same wireless channel, thus, although to a lower extent, the station connected to the Internet still suffers of a bandwidth reduction.

Using the MAClet Control Architecture, the stations in the networks are not expected to implement any specific DLS amendment. By default, their Wireless MAC processor card runs a MAC program implementing just the legacy 802.11 DCF operation. As soon as the AP detects that two associated stations are involved in a greedy data session, it delivers a MAClet to just the two involved stations. Stations are configured to accept and install MAClets coming from the home AP. The AP further signals the (same) time instant at which the two stations will start the installed MAClet. From that time on, the two stations will implement a *custom* MAC protocol.

The custom MAC protocol may be designed to be strictly tailored to the considered context. For instance, the owner of the network *knows* that at most one direct link connection will be deployed, and that this direct link will always involve the two same radio interfaces (the server and the TVset ones). Moreover, the network owner wants to push bandwidth optimization further, by setting the direct link on a *separate frequency channel*, but of course avoiding that the stations will lose the association to the AP.

MAC Customization: Enhanced Direct Link

We have designed a protocol, hereafter referred to as Enhanced Direct Link (DLS++), for coping with the above sce-

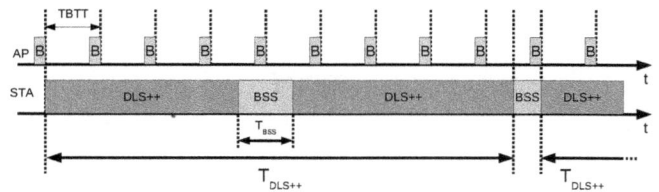

Figure 8: DLS++ timing

nario. The Enhanced Direct Link (DLS++) is meant to be a simple variant of DLS able to simultaneously work on two different channels. The primary channel is that of the AP network; the station has to periodically access such channel for receiving beacons and retaining association. The secondary channel is ad-hoc set up and independently managed by the peer stations. Under DLS++, the channel selection and the associated channel access mode is performed frame by frame. If the head of line frame is directed to the peer station, the frame is sent on the secondary channel as it was sent by the AP (i.e. with the from DS bit set to 1, and with the sender address of the AP)[3]. In absence of collisions, the random backoff on the secondary channel is suspended (by using a backoff counter permanently equal to 0) for optimizing the capacity of the streaming. If the head of line frame is a probe request frame or another frame directed to the AP, the station switches back to the primary channel and to the DCF protocol. It then returns to the secondary channel after a short T_{BSS} time interval. For simplicity of development, the described operation is not yet optimized to prevent packet losses; especially, buffering at the AP side should be performed when a DLS++ station is set on the secondary channel (this extension can be developed by mimicking the standard mechanisms used for power savings).

Multi-threading and Synchronization

The above scheme requires that the peer stations use standard DCF rules on the primary channel and direct-link access rules on the secondary one. This behavior can be programmed by defining a DLS++ meta machine switching from DCF to DLS and vice versa. The DLS machine is derived from the DCF one by changing the addressing operations for both data frames and acknowledgments. Moreover, it can be configured with independent contention window values, thus allowing to support more aggressive access operations. Figures 7 and 8 shows the envisioned meta machine and the relevant timings. The direct link operations are executed after the reception of an AP beacon. At regular time intervals T_{DLS++} (slightly lower than a multiple N of TBTT beacon intervals), the station suspends DLS transmissions in order to receive an AP beacon on the primary channel. This operation is necessary for keeping the synchronization to the AP clock and for receiving other MAClets[4]. A transitions to

---

[3]Without changing the driver, it is not possible to support simultaneously the ad-hoc and infrastructure addressing modes. Therefore, we chose to provisionally employ a kind of address spoofing for confining the updates in the MAC state machine.

[4]*Clock synchronization* of all the nodes belonging to the same network is a requirement for DCF (clock skews may toughen

236

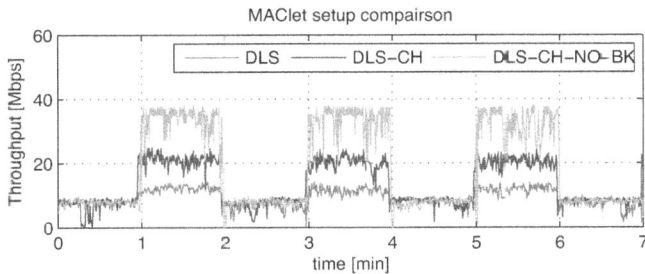

Figure 9: Throughput comparison under legacy DCF, DLS, and two versions of DLS++.

DCF can also occur when the head of line frame is a probe request or another frame directed to the AP. At the expiration of another timer T_{BSS}, the station switches back to DLS.

In order to minimize the frame losses due to the use of the two channels, the peer stations should activate the DLS++ protocol simultaneously. To this purpose, we used a synchronization mechanism based on the specification of an absolute time (after which, the switching are managed by the multi-thread meta-machine). The activation time is computed by adding the desired time offset to the current Access Point time-stamp, to which all the stations are continuously aligned.

Performance evaluation

We setup a testbed in our laboratory with two client stations (the ones with the peer-to-peer traffic) and the AP equipped with our MAClet Control framework. A third client was statically set to the primary channel with a legacy DCF protocol. We repeated the MAClet loading and activation test periodically, by programming the AP to alternatively send (to the two programmable clients) the DLS++ MAClet and the legacy DCF MAClet at regular intervals of 1 minute. The DLS++ MAClet is built by programming the meta machine described above, while the legacy DCF MAClet is activated by sending a run command for the bios program. The DLS++ protocol has been configured by setting T_{DLS++} to 890 ms, T_{DCF} to 6 ms, and N ito 9 TBTT. For the other protocol parameters, we used three different configurations: both the primary channel and secondary channels set to channel 6; the primary channel set to channel 6 and the secondary channel set to channel 11; the primary channel set to channel 6, the secondary channel set to channel 11, and the secondary channel contention window set to 0.

Figure 9 shows the throughput results of the client station sending saturated UDP traffic to the second client under the three settings (labeled, respectively, as DLS, DLS-CH, DLS-CH-NO-BK). The experiments were carried out during the hours of the day (i.e. in presence of background traffic due to students and researchers working in our department). Starting from legacy DCF, the clients switch to the different DLS++ configurations at 1, 3, and 5 minutes, and come back to standard DCF at 2, 4 and 6 minutes. From the figure it is evident that the customized direct-link access may bring dramatic improvements, especially when it is managed on a

---

frame acknowledgement). Therefore, we always assume that the bios machine provides a clock synchronization function.

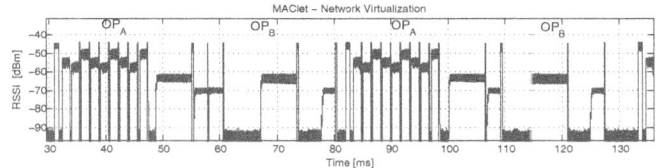

Figure 10: An experimental trace of network virtualization: operator A and operator B use the channel in different time intervals with independent access schemes (TDM and DCF).

secondary channel without backoff (from about 12 Mbps of the normal DLS case to about 38 Mbps under the DLS++ without backoff).

5.2 Use case 2: Virtualization

Scenario Description

In this second use case we assume that the same Access Point (belonging to a public network) is shared between two different WiFi operators. The scenario is obviously not new, and indeed it has been specifically addressed by many manufacturers that allow to define Virtual APs, each advertising a distinct SSID and capability set. Virtual APs allow operators to share the same physical infrastructure, while offering access to distinct networks, but they typically suffer of a scarce level of *isolation*, since the resources allocated to each one cannot be really partitioned when stations employ random access schemes and suffer of unpredictable interference.

Suppose that the two operators want to implement a different service model: the first operator (operator A) advertises "FIXED" SSID, offering access to the Internet with a fixed (guaranteed) bandwidth, while the second one (operator B) advertises "BEST" SSID, offering a traditional best effort access. Although the standard includes PCF and HCCA for managing the medium access by means of polling, the lack of support in commercial products prevents an easy solution. Using MAClets, the resource partition between the two operators can be addressed in a very effective and flexible manner. If all the stations employ a MAClet Control architecture, each operator can send a MAClet to the associated stations for enabling the medium access at regular time intervals (for example, in a fraction of the beacon interval reserved to the specific operator) and preventing it in the rest of the time. Moreover, the time reserved to each operator can be dynamically tuned (by updating the MAClet configuration parameters) according to the traffic conditions and to the agreements between operators.

MAC Virtualization and Synchronization

Different solutions are possible for addressing the beaconing and the MAC pausing in the above scenario. We chose to transmit two SSID Information Elements within each beacon, thus leaving the beacon interval unchanged. The MAC pausing has been programmed in a meta machine between the operator-dependent MAC program and a simple state machine with a waiting state only. At the expiration of the pausing time, each station enters the waiting state until a new activation event is revealed. In the waiting state, the stations continue to receive beacons from the AP for keeping the synchronization to the time interval of their operator.

According to the SSID specified in the association request, each station receives a different MAClet: a legacy DCF program for the stations associated "BEST" SSID, and a TDMA program for the stations associated to the "FIXED" SSID. The DCF MAClet is a legacy DCF protocol that is suspended at the reception of a new beacon. The reactivation is triggered at the expiration of a parametric timer set before the suspension. The opposite activation and deactivation actions are performed for the TDMA MAClet. This mechanism guarantees a perfect coexistence and isolation between the two networks, since stations accessing the medium during the same time interval employ uniform channel rules, and no station associated to a given operator can interfere with the other operator network. Isolation is not obviously guaranteed with other external interfering networks.

The configuration parameters of the DCF MAClet are the DCF contention parameters that are uniformly set to all the stations (although some forms of user prioritization could be easily supported by differentiating these parameters in the MAClet directed to each station). Conversely, the MAClet transmitted to a new station associated to the "FIXED" SSID specifies a different program parameter indicating the slot numbers allocated to the station (multiple slots can be allocated to the same station). In each TDMA slot, frame transmissions still follow a 2-way handshake mechanism. When the MAClets are loaded on a new arriving station, the reception of the first beacon frame activates the execution of the program. Subsequent beacons are used as synchronization events for pausing the DCF programs and resuming the TDMA ones, as well as for activating the DCF suspension timer and computing the beginning of the TDMA slots. Although beacon frames are scheduled at regular time intervals, they can be delayed because of ongoing frame transmissions. These transmissions can be due to external interference, but also to stations associated to the "BEST" SSID starting a frame transmission right before the expiration of the operator time (no control is indeed implemented on the residual time before starting a transmission). In case of delay, to guarantee the fixed rate of TDMA stations, the time allocated to the "BEST" SSID operator can be reduced in the subsequent beacon interval. The possibility to dynamically tune the DCF activation time can also be exploited for performing a dynamic repartition of the resources allocated to each operator.

Figure 10 shows an example of resource repartitions between operators A and B in two consecutive beacon intervals. The figure plots the channel activity trace captured by the USRP: for better distinguishing the two virtual networks, the TDMA stations transmit at 11 Mbps while the best effort stations transmit at lower data rates (5.5 Mbps and 2 Mbps). Note that in the first TDMA slot the channel is busy (i.e. a transmission has been originated in that slot), but no acknowledgment is received because of channel errors.

Performance Evaluation

We setup a testbed with a fixed number of stations associated to the "FIXED" SSID and a time-varying number of stations

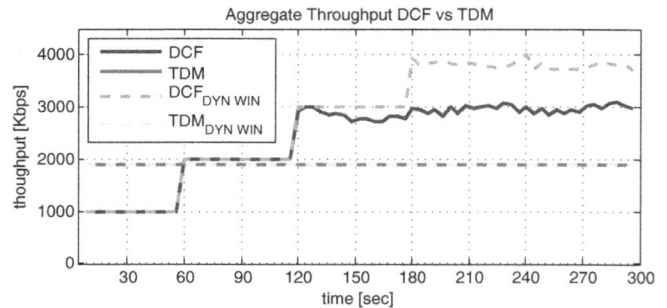

Figure 11: Resource repartition between two different operators using different access rules (TDM and DCF).

associated to the "BEST" SSID. Specifically, three stations access the channel by using TDMA, while five stations join sequentially the best-effort network at regular intervals of one minute. The TDMA frame is organized in nine allocated slots, uniformly assigned to all the stations (three slots each). The beacon interval is set to 50ms, while the slot size is set to 1.7ms (enough to accommodate the transmission of a payload equal to 1470 byte at 11 Mbps). All the stations transmit at 11 Mbps.

We repeated two different virtualization tests: in the first one, each operator receives an equal share of the available bandwidth (i.e. the activation time is one half of the beacon interval), while in the second one, the TDMA operator agrees to release the available bandwidth to the other operator. TDMA stations have a traffic rate of 630 kbps (smaller than the maximum guaranteed bandwidth, namely $3 \cdot 1470 \cdot 8/50ms = 705.6kbps$), in order to have a non-null probability to have some slots empty. DCF stations work with a traffic rate of 1 Mbps.

Figure 11 shows the per-operator throughput results obtained in both the experiments. In case of equal share of the bandwidth, after the third station joins the network the throughput of the best-effort operator (blue curve) saturates to about 3 Mbps (i.e. one half of the total network capacity at 11 Mbps). TDMA network is obviously under utilized because it consumes only 1.89 Mbps (being 3 Mbps the available capacity). By adjusting the time allocated to the best-effort operator, the third station can join the network without causing any throughput degradation. The aggregated network throughput (green line) for the best-effort network is now about 4 Mbps, while TDMA stations performance are not affected by increased DCF traffic.

6. RELATED WORK

Programmable wireless platforms

The advent of WLAN soft-MAC [15] designs, endorsed by several brand-name vendors (including Intel, Ralink, Realtek, Atheros, Broadcom), has transferred non time-critical MAC layer functionalities from the WLAN card to the host, thus permitting their modifications by reprogramming relevant open-source drivers. Moreover, several low level MAC/PHY parameters (contention windows, TX power, TX/RX antenna settings, etc) can now be accessed through configuration interfaces. However, this level of flexibility is not enough to bring into real world several optimizations solutions which require small changes into the low-level MAC operations. For example, in [16] the experimental validation of receiver-initiated MAC protocols, which have been shown to improve the overall network capacity, could not rely on commercial 802.11 cards, since these cards do not allow to define new frame handshakes spaced of a SIFS time. Other promising solutions, such as the dynamic scheduling proposed in [17], require advanced monitoring operations not supported by current cards and drivers. To overcome this hurdle the research community has developed *custom* programmable wireless platforms, typically revolving around an FPGA or DSP core and software radio. For example, WARP [18] or Airblue [8] are stand-alone software defined radio boards equipped with fast and large FPGAs, hence not constrained anymore (unlike, e.g., GNURadio [19]) by an host back-end PC running part of the needed processing. Similar performance are obtained by SORA [20] by exploiting parallel computing. By (re)implementing all the wireless protocol stack, from the level of signals to that of frame payloads, these solutions support full MAC layer customization and cross-layer designs. More recently, custom MAC programmability was made possible also on commodity card, thanks to the disclosure of a (simplified) open source firmware [21] for a brand name card.

Clearly, the ability to access and modify the source code of a wireless card or wireless custom boards permits *in principle* any modification. In practice, extreme expertise is needed with the device internals and the low level programming languages (e.g. VHDL or assembler, at best C), as well as with the understanding of how software modules do interact with each other. An alternative solution which is currently emerging in other networking domains (such as flow switching technologies [22]) is the shift from open source code modifications to device reprogramming via open and suitably identified *Application Programming Interfaces*. This approach may perhaps restrict generality, but comes along with huge advantages: much simpler and faster programmability, code portability across different vendors' platforms, no need for manufacturers to disclose their internal architecture. A first step in this direction was taken by the *split functionality* approach proposed in [7]. The architecture proposed in this work comprises a radio hardware, which implements (part of) the core MAC functionalities, and a host PC which runs a control software implementing the MAC protocol control logic. The identification of how to most conveniently decompose a MAC protocol into core functions is a further major contribution (a similar analysis is carried out also in [9, 10]).

TRUMP [9] makes the further step of designing an *integrated* platform which permits to compose a MAC protocol operation using elementary modules. The core of this platform is a *Wiring Engine* which connects the core functions according to a programmable control flow, described through a newly introduced language syntax for PHY/MAC protocol description, and an associated compiler. The extended *Wireless MAC Processor* that we propose in this paper promotes a more versatile description and dissemination of MAC protocols in terms of extended finite state machines that can be encapsulated into common data packets. Central, in such approach, is the design of the *MAC Engine*, namely a generic finite state machine executor devised to play the role of MAC program interpreter.

Active Networks and Code Mobility

Despite the hype in the midst of the nineties [23], the application of active networking principles to the wireless domain has lagged behind. In the vision of [2], adaptations, envisioned in terms of selection of PHY functionalities (spectrum access, modulation, and coding) were expected to leverage software radio technologies. But proposed wireless active networking frameworks [24] have mainly addressed issues at layers *higher than low-MAC/PHY* (e.g., QoS, network topology adaptation, mobility, ad hoc network formation, etc).

The interest for code mobility, also embedded in in-band data packets (*capsules*, as per [25]), has more recently emerged in the wireless sensor networks arena. Indeed, in large sensor networks, code mobility may be the only possibility for upgrading the sensors' behavior, given that physical access to the nodes may not be viable. But, again, programmability has been restricted to higher layers, and for tasks such as changes in the monitoring functionalities or in the application operation [26].

Especially in the sensor network field, several issues concerning code distribution protocols [27, 28] and architectures [29] have been considered. Obviously, the programmability requirements for wireless local networks have some differences from the sensor network ones. Sensor nodes deployed in the same network are usually homogeneous, with the same Tiny OS and hardware. A binary code image can be moved from a node to another in active messages (natively supported by TinyOS). Albeit not strictly necessary, bytecode interpreters [30] may significantly improve efficiency of code distribution, i.e. for giving an high-level virtual code representations which significantly reduces the code length and/or facilitate incremental updates. All the above referred solutions limit programmability to network, transport and application protocols, and assume that the lower stack dealing with medium access and single-hop communications is not modifiable [30].

7. WMP DEVELOPMENT PLATFORM

The WMP implementation for the AirForce54G card (by Broadcom) has been released to the research community together with a detailed documentation of the available API (i.e. the list of events, actions and conditions supported by the card) and developing tools [31]. By replacing the original card firmware with the WMP one, the card can work as a generic state machine executor able to run a MAC bytecode. The developing tools include: i) a graphical tool, working as an editor for composing a MAC program in terms of a graphical representation of state transitions and state labels; ii) compiling tool, able to map the graphical representation into a textual transition table and in a bytecode; iii) a MAClet manager, able to load and run the bytecode in the card. The combination of the MAC Engine, graphical editor, compiler, MAClet manager and driver is a complete and cheap toolchain that allows developing and testing a new MAC scheme in a very simple, robust and quick way over an ultra-cheap platform. The current WMP implementation supports both the infrastructure and the ad-hoc mode, it is compatible (in terms of protocol timings, frame fields, etc.) with legacy DCF stations in b and g mode, and it provides throughput performance comparable with the proprietary card firmware when executing the DCF state machine[5].

8. CONCLUSIONS

This paper proposes a wireless active network framework devised to permit seamless and dynamic MAC stack reconfiguration via MAClets, namely MAC programs conveyed into data packets. This is accomplished by extending our formerly proposed Wireless MAC Protocol architecture with primitives to dynamically handle code inside the radio hardware, by developing an overlay software control framework for moving and launching MAClets, and by experimentally assessing the flexibility and performance of the system operation over commodity WLAN cards.

Besides the specific technical contributions, we believe that a further significance of our proposed approach is that protocol reconfiguration is accomplished via application programming interfaces, rather than via binary images or access to open source devices, thus perhaps permitting its possible future endorsement also in the real commercial world.

Acknowledgement

This work has been carried out in the frame of the EU FP7-FLAVIA project, contract number 257263. We thank the reviewers and our shepherd Ruben Merz for the insightful and constructive feedback that helped us in revising the paper.

9. REFERENCES

[1] J. Mitola III, G. Q. Maguire, "Cognitive radio: Making software radios more personal", IEEE Personal Communications, vol. 6, no. 4, pp. 13–18, August 1999.

[2] V. Bose, D. Wetherall, J. Guttag, "Next century challenges: RadioActive networks", ACM/IEEE MobiCom '99, Seattle, USA, pp. 242–248.

[3] C. R. Stevenson, Z. Lei, W. Hu, S.J. Shellhammer, W. Caldwell, "IEEE 802.22: The First Cognitive Radio Wireless Regional Area Network Standard", IEEE Communication Magazine, January 2009, pp. 130-138

[4] A. Banchs, P. Serrano and H. Oliver, "Proportional fair throughput allocation in multirate IEEE 802.11e wireless LANs," Wireless Networks, 2007, vol. 13, pp. 649-662.

[5] L. Scalia, I. Tinnirello, J.W. Tantra, C.H. Foh, "Dynamic MAC Parameters Configuration for Performance Optimization in 802.11e Networks," IEEE Globecom 2006

[6] C. Partridge, "Realizing the future of wireless data communications," Commun. ACM, Sep. 2011, Vol. 54, issue 9, pp. 62-68

[7] G. Nychis, T. Hottelier, Z. Yang, S. Seshan, P. Steenkiste, "Enabling MAC Protocol Implementations on Software-defined Radios", NSDI'09, 2009.

[8] M. C. Ng, K. E. Fleming, M. Vutukuru, S. Gross, Arvind, H. Balakrishnan, "Airblue: A System for Cross-Layer Wireless Protocol Development", ACM/IEEE ANCS 2010.

[9] X. Zhang, J. Ansari, G. Yang and P. Mahonen "TRUMP: Supporting Efficient Realization of Protocols for Cognitive Radio Networks", IEEE DySPAN 2011

[5]The implementation has been tested on 4311 and 4318 chipset revisions, under the driver b43 and with kernel 3.1.4 (for more information see the specific documentation).

[10] I. Tinnirello, G. Bianchi, P. Gallo, D. Garlisi, F. Giuliano, F. Gringoli, "Wireless MAC Processors: Programming MAC Protocols on Commodity Hardware" IEEE INFOCOM, March 2012.

[11] Wireless Management Suite. Data sheet, Enterasys Networks, Inc., March 2009.

[12] AirWave Management Platform. Data Sheet DS AWMP US 081117, Aruba Networks, Inc., Nov. 2008

[13] Li-Hsing Yen and Tse-Tsung Yeh. SNMP-Based Approach to Load Distribution in IEEE 802.11 Networks. In IEEE 63rd VTC'06-Spring, vol. 3, pp. 1196-1200, May 2006

[14] B-S. Jeon, E-J. Ko, and G-H. Lee. Network Management System for Wireless LAN Service. In 10th International Conference on Telecommunications, 2003. ICT 2003, volume 2, pages 948-953, March 2003.

[15] M. Neufeld, J. Fifield, C. Doerr, A. Sheth, D. Grunwald, "SoftMAC - Flexible Wireless Research Platform" HotNets, Nov. 2005.

[16] T. S. Bonfim and M. M. Carvalho, Reversing the IEEE 802.11 Backoff Algorithm for Receiver-Initiated MAC Protocols, IEEE IWCMC 2012, Cyprus, 2012.

[17] M. Fang, D. Malone, K. R. Duffy and D. J. Leith, Decentralised learning MACs for collision-free access in WLANs, Wireless Networks. To Appear.

[18] Wireless Open Access Research Platform, http://warp.rice.edu/trac.

[19] The GNURadio Software Radio, http://gnuradio.org/trac

[20] K. Tan, J. Zhang, J. Fang, H. Liu, Y. Ye, S. Wang, Y. Zhang, H. Wu, W. Wang, G. M. Voelker, "Sora: High Performance Software Radio Using General Purpose Multi-core Processors", NSDI 2009.

[21] Open firmware for WiFi networks, http://www.ing.unibs.it/openfwwf/

[22] N. McKeown, T. Anderson, H. Balakrishnan, G. Parulkar, L. Peterson, J. Rexford, S. Shenker, J. Turner, "OpenFlow: enabling innovation in campus networks", ACM SIGCOMM Comp. Commun. Review archive, Vol. 38(2), April 2008

[23] D. Tennenhouse, J. Smith, D. Sincoskie, D. Wetherall, G. Minden, "A Survey of Active Network Research", IEEE Communications Magazine, January 1997.

[24] A. Campbell, H. De Meer, M. Kounavis, K. Miki, J. Vicente, D. Villela, "A survey of programmable networks", ACM SIGCOMM 1999, pp. 7 – 23.

[25] D. Wetherall, J. Guttag, D. Tennenhouse, "ANTS: A Toolkit for Building and Dynamically Deploying Network Protocols", IEEE Open Architectures and Network Programming, April 1998, pp. 117-129.

[26] R. K. Panta, I. Khalil, S. Bagchi, "Stream: Low Overhead Wireless Reprogramming for Sensor Networks", IEEE INFOCOM 2007, May 2007, Anchorage, pp. 928-936.

[27] M. Krasniewski, R. Panta, S. Bagchi, C.L. Yang, W. Chappell, "Energy-efficient on-demand reprogramming of large-scale sensor networks", ACM Trans. on Sensor Networks, February 2008, Vol. 2, pp. 1-38.

[28] P. Levis, N. Patel, S. Shenker, and D. Culler, "Trickle: A Self-Regulating Algorithm for Code Propogation and maintenance in Wireless Sensor Network," NSDI 2004.

[29] S. R. Madden, M. J. Franklin, J. M. Hellerstein, and W. Hong, "TinyDB: an acquisitional query processing system for sensor networks," ACM Trans. on Database Systems., vol. 30, no. 1, pp. 122-173, 2005.

[30] P. Levis and D. Culler, "Mate: a tiny virtual machine for sensor networks," 10th int. conf. on Arch. support for programming languages and operating systems, 2002, pp. 85-95.

[31] WMP Project, http://wmp.tti.unipa.it/.

Automatic Test Packet Generation

Hongyi Zeng[†*], Peyman Kazemian[†*], George Varghese[§], Nick McKeown[†]
[†]Stanford University, [§]UCSD & Microsoft Research
{hyzeng,kazemian,nickm}@stanford.edu, varghese@cs.ucsd.edu
*These authors contributed equally to this work.

ABSTRACT

Networks are getting larger and more complex; yet administrators rely on rudimentary tools such as `ping` and `traceroute` to debug problems. We propose an automated and systematic approach for testing and debugging networks called "Automatic Test Packet Generation" (ATPG). ATPG reads router configurations and generates a device-independent model. The model is used to generate a minimum set of test packets to (minimally) exercise every link in the network or (maximally) exercise every rule in the network. Test packets are sent periodically, and detected failures trigger a separate mechanism to localize the fault. ATPG can detect both functional (e.g., incorrect firewall rule) and performance problems (e.g., congested queue). ATPG complements but goes beyond earlier work in static checking (which cannot detect liveness or performance faults) or fault localization (which only localize faults given liveness results).

We describe our prototype ATPG implementation and results on two real-world data sets: Stanford University's backbone network and Internet2. We find that a small number of test packets suffices to test all rules in these networks: For example 4000 packets can cover all rules in Stanford backbone network while 54 is enough to cover all links. Sending 4000 test packets 10 times per second consumes less than 1% of link capacity. ATPG code and the data sets are publicly available[1] [1].

Categories and Subject Descriptors

C.2.3 [**Computer-Communication Networks**]: Network Operation—*Network monitoring*; D.2.5 [**Software Engineering**]: Testing and Debugging—*Testing tools*

General Terms

Algorithm, Reliability

---

[1]Each figure/table in Section 7 (electronic version) is clickable, linking to instructions on reproducing results.

Keywords

Test Packet Generation, Data Plane Analysis, Network Troubleshooting

1. INTRODUCTION

> "Only strong trees stand the test of a storm." —
> *Chinese idiom*

It is notoriously hard to debug networks. Every day network engineers wrestle with router misconfigurations, fiber cuts, faulty interfaces, mis-labeled cables, software bugs, intermittent links and a myriad other reasons that cause networks to misbehave, or fail completely. Network engineers hunt down bugs using the most rudimentary tools (*e.g.* `ping`, `traceroute`, SNMP, and `tcpdump`), and track down root causes using a combination of accrued wisdom and intuition. Debugging networks is only becoming harder as networks are getting *bigger* (modern data centers may contain 10,000 switches, a campus network may serve 50,000 users, a 100Gb/s long haul link may carry 100,000 flows), and are getting *more complicated* (with over 6,000 RFCs, router software is based on millions of lines of source code, and network chips often contain billions of gates). Small wonder that network engineers have been labeled "masters of complexity" [30]. Consider two examples:

Example 1. Suppose a router with a faulty line card starts dropping packets silently. Alice, who administers 100 routers, receives a ticket from several unhappy users complaining about connectivity. First, Alice examines each router to see if the configuration was changed recently, and concludes that the configuration was untouched. Next, Alice uses her knowledge of the topology to triangulate the faulty device with `ping` and `traceroute`. Finally, she calls a colleague to replace the line card.

Example 2. Suppose that video traffic is mapped to a specific queue in a router, but packets are dropped because the token bucket rate is too low. It is not at all clear how Alice can track down such a *performance fault* using `ping` and `traceroute`.

Troubleshooting a network is difficult for three reasons. First, the forwarding state is distributed across multiple routers and firewalls and is defined by their forwarding tables, filter rules and other configuration parameters. Second, the forwarding state is hard to observe, because it typically requires manually logging into every box in the network. Third, there are many different programs, protocols and humans updating the forwarding state simultaneously. When

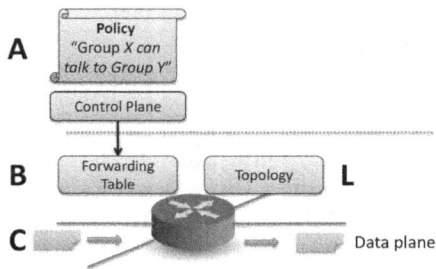

Figure 1: Static versus Dynamic Checking: A policy is compiled to forwarding state, which is then executed by the forwarding plane. Static checking (*e.g.* [14]) confirms that $A = B$. Dynamic checking (e.g. ATPG in this paper) confirms that the topology is meeting liveness properties (L) *and* that $B = C$.

Alice uses `ping` and `traceroute`, she is using a crude lens to examine the current forwarding state for clues to track down the failure.

Figure 1 is a simplified view of network state. At the bottom of the figure is the forwarding state used to forward each packet, consisting of the L2 and L3 forwarding information base (FIB), access control lists, *etc*. The forwarding state is written by the control plane (that can be local or remote as in the SDN model [30]), and should correctly implement the network administrator's policy. Examples of the policy include: "Security group X is isolated from security Group Y", "Use OSPF for routing", and "Video traffic should receive at least 1Mb/s".

We can think of the controller compiling the policy (A) into device-specific *configuration* files (B), which in turn determine the forwarding behavior of each packet (C). To ensure the network behaves as designed, all three steps should remain consistent at all times, *i.e.* $A = B = C$. In addition, the topology, shown to the bottom right in the figure, should also satisfy a set of liveness properties L. Minimally, L requires that sufficient links and nodes are working; if the control plane specifies that a laptop can access a server, the desired outcome can fail if links fail. L can also specify performance guarantees that detect flaky links.

Recently, researchers have proposed tools to check that $A = B$, enforcing consistency between *policy* and the *configuration* [5, 14, 23, 29]. While these approaches can find (or prevent) software logic errors in the control plane, they are *not* designed to identify liveness failures caused by failed links and routers, bugs caused by faulty router hardware or software, or performance problems caused by network congestion. Such failures require checking for L and whether $B = C$. Alice's first problem was with L (link not working) and her second problem was with $B = C$ (low level token bucket state not reflecting policy for video bandwidth).

In fact, we learned from a survey of 61 network operators (see Table 1 in Section 2) that the two most common causes of network failure are hardware failures and software bugs, and that problems manifest themselves *both* as reachability failures and throughput/latency degradation. Our goal is to automatically detect these types of failures.

The main contribution of this paper is what we call an Automatic Test Packet Generation (ATPG) framework that *automatically* generates a minimal set of packets to test the liveness of the underlying topology *and* the congruence between data plane state and configuration specifications. The tool can also automatically generate packets to test *performance* assertions such as packet latency. In Example 1 instead of Alice manually deciding which `ping` packets to send, the tool does so periodically on her behalf. In Example 2, the tool determines that it must send packets with certain headers to "exercise" the video queue, and then determines that these packets are being dropped.

ATPG detects and diagnoses errors by independently and exhaustively *testing* all forwarding entries, firewall rules, and any packet processing rules in the network. In ATPG, test packets are generated algorithmically from the device configuration files and FIBs, with the minimum number of packets required for complete coverage. Test packets are fed into the network so that every rule is exercised directly from the data plane. Since ATPG treats links just like normal forwarding rules, its full coverage guarantees testing of every link in the network. It can also be specialized to generate a minimal set of packets that merely test every link for network liveness. At least in this basic form, we feel that ATPG or some similar technique is fundamental to networks: Instead of *reacting* to failures, many network operators such as Internet2 [12] *proactively* check the health of their network using pings between all pairs of sources. However all-pairs `ping` does not guarantee testing of all links, and has been found to be unscalable for large networks such as PlanetLab [28].

Organizations can customize ATPG to meet their needs; for example, they can choose to merely check for network liveness (link cover) or check every rule (rule cover) to ensure security policy. ATPG can be customized to check only for reachability or for performance as well. ATPG can adapt to constraints such as requiring test packets from only a few places in the network, or using special routers to generate test packets from every port. ATPG can also be tuned to allocate more test packets to exercise more critical rules. For example, a health care network may dedicate more test packets to Firewall rules to ensure HIPPA compliance.

We tested our method on two real world data sets - the backbone networks of Stanford University and Internet2, representing an enterprise network and a nationwide ISP. The results are encouraging: thanks to the structure of real world rulesets, the number of test packets needed is surprisingly small. For the Stanford network with over 757,000 rules and more than 100 VLANs, we only need 4,000 packets to exercise all forwarding rules and ACLs. On Internet2, 35,000 packets suffice to exercise all IPv4 forwarding rules. Put another way, we can check every rule in every router on the Stanford backbone ten times every second, by sending test packets that consume less than 1% of network bandwidth. The link cover for Stanford is even smaller, around 50 packets which allows proactive liveness testing every millisecond using 1% of network bandwidth.

The contributions of this paper are: (1) A survey of network operators revealing common failures and root causes (Section 2), (2) A test packet generation algorithm (Section 4.1), (3) A fault localization algorithm to isolate faulty devices and rules (Section 4.2), (4) ATPG use cases for functional and performance testing (Section 5), (5) Evaluation of a prototype ATPG system using rulesets collected from the Stanford and Internet2 backbones (Section 6 and Section 7).

2. CURRENT PRACTICE

To understand the problems network engineers encounter,

Category	Avg	% of ≥ 4
Reachability Failure	3.67	56 90%
Throughput/Latency	3.39	52 54%
Intermittent Connectivity	3.38	53 45%
Router CPU High Utilization	2.87	31 67%
Congestion	2.65	28 07%
Security Policy Violation	2.33	17 54%
Forwarding Loop	1.89	10 71%
Broadcast/Multicast Storm	1.83	9 62%

(a) Symptoms of network failure.

Category	Avg	% of ≥ 4
Switch/Router Software Bug	3.12	40 35%
Hardware Failure	3.07	41 07%
External	3.06	42 37%
Attack	2.67	29 82%
ACL Misconfig.	2.44	20 00%
Software Upgrade	2.35	18 52%
Protocol Misconfiguration	2.29	23 64%
Unknown	2.25	17 65%
Host Network Stack Bug	1.98	16 00%
QoS/TE Misconfig.	1.70	7 41%

(b) Causes of network failure.

Table 1: Ranking of symptoms and causes reported by administrators (5=most often, 1=least often). The right column shows the percentage who reported ≥ 4.

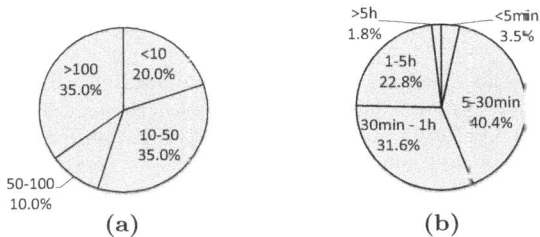

(a)   (b)

Figure 2: Reported number of network related tickets generated per month (a) and time to resolve a ticket (b).

and how they currently troubleshoot them, we invited subscribers to the NANOG[2] mailing list to complete a survey in May-June 2012. Of the 61 who responded, 12 administer small networks (<1k hosts), 23 medium networks (1k-10k hosts), 11 large networks (10k-100k hosts) and 12 very large networks (>100k hosts). All responses (anonymized) are reported in [31], and are summarized in Table 1. The most relevant findings are:

Symptoms: Of the six most common symptoms, four cannot be detected by static checks of the type $A = B$ (throughput/latency, intermittent connectivity, router CPU utilization, congestion) and require ATPG-like dynamic testing. Even the remaining two failures (reachability failure and security Policy Violation) may require dynamic testing to detect forwarding plane failures.

Causes: The two most common symptoms (switch and router software bugs and hardware failure) are best found by dynamic testing.

Cost of troubleshooting: Two metrics capture the cost of network debugging - the number of network-related tickets per month and the average time consumed to resolve a ticket (Figure 2). 35% of networks generate more than 100 tickets

---

[2]North American Network Operators' Group.

Category	Avg	% of ≥ 4
ping	4.50	86.67%
traceroute	4.18	80.00%
SNMP	3.83	60.10%
Configuration Version Control	2.96	37.50%
netperf/iperf	2.35	17.31%
sFlow/NetFlow	2.60	26.92%

Table 2: Tools used by network administrators (5=most often, 1=least often).

per month. 40.4% of respondents estimate it takes under 30 minutes to resolve a ticket. But 24.6% report that it takes over an hour on average.

Tools: Table 2 shows that ping, traceroute and SNMP are by far the most popular tools. When asked what the ideal tool for network debugging would be, 70.7% reported a desire for automatic test generation to check performance and correctness. Some added a desire for "long running tests to detect jitter or intermittent issues", "real-time link capacity monitoring", and "monitoring tools for network state".

In summary, while our survey is small, it supports the hypothesis that network administrators face complicated symptoms and causes; the cost of debugging is nontrivial, due to the frequency of problems and the time to solve these problems; classical tools such as ping and traceroute are still heavily used, but administrators desire more sophisticated tools.

3. NETWORK MODEL

ATPG uses the *header space* framework — a geometric model of how packets are processed we described in [14] (and used in [29]). In header space, protocol-specific meanings associated with headers are ignored: a header is viewed as a flat sequence of ones and zeros. A header is a point (and a flow is a region) in the $\{0,1\}^L$ space, where L is an upper bound on header length. By using the header space framework, we obtain a unified, vendor-independent and protocol-agnostic model of the network[3] that simplifies the packet generation process significantly.

3.1 Definitions

Figure 3 summarizes the definitions in our model.

Packets: A packet is defined by a $(port, header)$ tuple, where the *port* denotes a packet's position in the network at any time instant; each physical port in the network is assigned a unique number.

Switches: A *switch transfer function*, T, models a network device, such as a switch or router. Each network device contains a set of forwarding rules (e.g., the forwarding table) that determine how packets are processed. An arriving packet is associated with exactly one rule by matching it against each rule in descending order of priority, and is dropped if no rule matches.

Rules: A *rule* generates a list of one or more output packets, corresponding to the output port(s) the packet is sent to; and defines how packet fields are modified. The rule abstraction models all real-world rules we know including IP forwarding (modifies port, checksum and TTL, but not IP address); VLAN tagging (adds VLAN IDs to the header);

---

[3]We have written vendor and protocol-specific parsers to translate configuration files into header space representations.

Bit	$b = 0 \mid 1 \mid \mathtt{x}$
Header	$h = [b_0, b_1, \ldots, b_L]$
Port	$p = 1 \mid 2 \mid \ldots \mid N \mid \mathtt{drop}$
Packet	$pk = (p, h)$
Rule	$r : pk \to pk$ or $[pk]$
Match	$r.matchset : [pk]$
Transfer Function	$T : pk \to pk$ or $[pk]$
Topo Function	$\Gamma : (p_{src}, h) \to (p_{dst}, h)$

```
function T_i(pk)
    #Iterate according to priority in switch i
    for r ∈ ruleset_i do
        if pk ∈ r.matchset then
            pk.history ← pk.history ⋃{r}
            return r(pk)
    return [(drop, pk.h)]
```

Figure 3: The network model - basic types (left) and the switch transfer function (right)

and ACLs (block a header, or map to a queue). Essentially, a rule defines how a region of header space at the ingress (the set of packets matching the rule) is transformed into regions of header space at the egress [14].

Rule History: At any point, each packet has a *rule history*: an ordered list of rules $[r_0, r_1, \ldots]$ the packet matched so far as it traversed the network. Rule histories are fundamental to ATPG, as they provide the basic raw material from which ATPG constructs tests.

Topology: The *topology transfer function*, Γ, models the network topology by specifying which pairs of ports (p_{src}, p_{dst}) are connected by links. Links are rules that forward packets from p_{src} to p_{dst} without modification. If no topology rules matches an input port, the port is an edge port, and the packet has reached its destination.

3.2 Life of a packet

The life of a packet can be viewed as applying the switch and topology *transfer functions* repeatedly (Figure 4). When a packet pk arrives at a network port p, the switch function T that contains the input port $pk.p$ is applied to pk, producing a list of new packets $[pk_1, pk_2, \ldots]$. If the packet reaches its destination, it is recorded. Otherwise, the topology function Γ is used to invoke the switch function containing the new port. The process repeats until packets reach their destinations (or are dropped).

```
function network(packets, switches, Γ)
    for pk_0 ∈ packets do
        T ←find_switch(pk_0.p, switches)
        for pk_1 ∈ T(pk_0) do
            if pk_1.p ∈ EdgePorts then
                #Reached edge
                record(pk_1)
            else
                #Find next hop
                network(Γ(pk_1), switches, Γ)
```

Figure 4: Life of a packet: repeating T and Γ until the packet reaches its destination or is dropped

4. ATPG SYSTEM

Based on the network model, ATPG generates the minimal number of test packets so that every forwarding rule in the network is exercised and covered by at least one test packet. When an error is detected, ATPG uses a fault localization algorithm to determine the failing rules or links.

Figure 5 is a block diagram of the ATPG system. The system first collects all the forwarding state from the network (step 1). This usually involves reading the FIBs, ACLs and config files, as well as obtaining the topology. ATPG uses

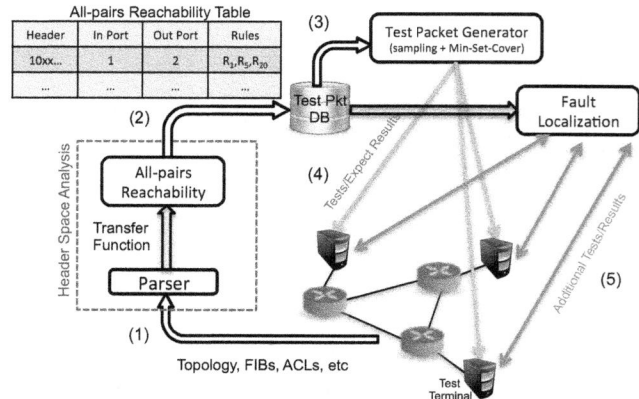

Figure 5: ATPG system block diagram.

Header Space Analysis [14] to compute reachability between all the test terminals (step 2). The result is then used by the test packet selection algorithm to compute a minimal set of test packets that can test all rules (step 3). These packets will be sent periodically by the test terminals (step 4). If an error is detected, the fault localization algorithm is invoked to narrow down the cause of the error (step 5). While steps 1 and 2 are described in [14], steps 3 through 5 are new.

4.1 Test Packet Generation

4.1.1 Algorithm

We assume a set of *test terminals* in the network can send and receive test packets. Our goal is to generate a set of test packets to exercise *every* rule in *every* switch function, so that *any* fault will be observed by at least one test packet. This is analogous to software test suites that try to test every possible branch in a program. The broader goal can be limited to testing every link or every queue.

When generating test packets, ATPG must respect two key constraints: (1) *Port:* ATPG must only use test terminals that are available; (2) *Header:* ATPG must only use headers that each test terminal is permitted to send. For example, the network administrator may only allow using a specific set of VLANs. Formally:

PROBLEM 1 (TEST PACKET SELECTION). *For a network with the switch functions, $\{T_1, \ldots, T_n\}$, and topology function, Γ, determine the minimum set of test packets to exercise all reachable rules, subject to the port and header constraints.*

ATPG chooses test packets using an algorithm we call *Test Packet Selection (TPS)*. TPS first finds all *equivalent classes* between each pair of available ports. An equivalent

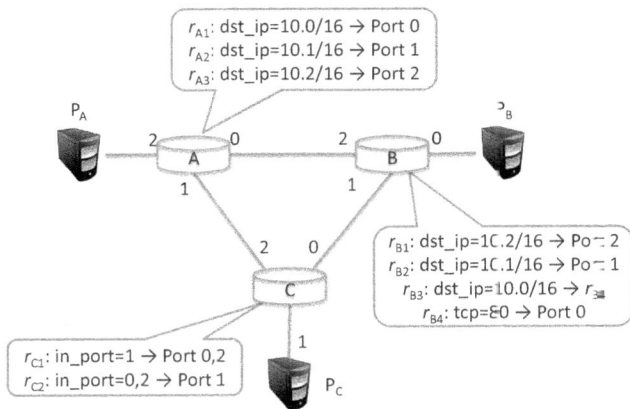

Figure 6: Example topology with three switches.

class is a set of packets that exercises the same combination of rules. It then *samples* each class to choose test packets, and finally *compresses* the resulting set of test packets to find the minimum covering set.

Step 1: Generate all-pairs reachability table. ATPG starts by computing the complete set of packet headers that can be sent from each test terminal to every other test terminal. For each such header, ATPG finds the complete set of rules it exercises along the path. To do so, ATPG applies the all-pairs reachability algorithm described in [14]: on every terminal port, an all-x header (a header which has all wild-carded bits) is applied to the transfer function of the first switch connected to each test terminal. Header constraints are applied here. For example, if traffic can only be sent on VLAN A, then instead of starting with an all-x header, the VLAN tag bits are set to A. As each packet pk traverses the network using the network function, the set of rules that match pk are recorded in $pk.history$. Doing this for all pairs of terminal ports generates an *all-pairs reachability table* as shown in Table 3. For each row, the header column is a wild-card expression representing the equivalent class of packets that can reach an egress terminal from an ingress test terminal. All packets matching this class of headers will encounter the set of switch rules shown in the Rule History column.

Header	Ingress Port	Egress Port	Rule History
h_1	p_{11}	p_{12}	$[r_{11}, r_{12}, \ldots]$
h_2	p_{21}	p_{22}	$[r_{21}, r_{22}, \ldots]$
...	...	...	...
h_n	p_{n1}	p_{n2}	$[r_{n1}, r_{n2}, \ldots]$

Table 3: All-pairs reachability table: all possible headers from every terminal to every other terminal, along with the rules they exercise.

Figure 6 shows a simple example network and Table 4 is the corresponding all-pairs reachability table. For example, an all-x test packet injected at P_A will pass through switch A. A forwards packets with $dst\_ip = 10.0/16$ to B and those with $dst\_ip = 10.1/16$ to C. B then forwards $dst\_ip = 10.0/16, tcp = 80$ to P_B, and switch C forwards $dst\_ip = 10.1/16$ to P_C. These are reflected in the first two rows of Table 4.

Step 2: Sampling. Next, ATPG picks at least one test packet in an equivalence class to exercise every (reachable) rule. The simplest scheme is to randomly pick one packet per

class. This scheme only detects faults for which all packets covered by the same rule experience the same fault (*e.g.* a link failure). At the other extreme, if we wish to detect faults specific to a header, then we need to select every header in every class. We discuss these issues and our fault model in Section 4.2.

Step 3: Compression. Several of the test packets picked in Step 2 exercise the same rule. ATPG therefore selects a minimum subset of the packets chosen in Step 2 such that the union of their rule histories cover all rules. The cover can be chosen to cover all links (for liveness only) or all router queues (for performance only). This is the classical Min-Set-Cover problem. While NP-Complete, a greedy $O(N^2)$ algorithm provides a good approximation, where N is the number of test packets. We call the resulting (approximately) minimum set of packets, the *regular test packets*. The remaining test packets not picked for the minimum set are called the *reserved test packets*. In Table 4, $\{p_1, p_2, p_3, p_4, p_5\}$ are regular test packets and $\{p_6\}$ is a reserved test packet. Reserved test packets are useful for fault localization (Section 4.2).

4.1.2 Properties

The TPS algorithm has the following useful properties:

PROPERTY 1 (COVERAGE). *The set of test packets exercise all reachable rules and respect all port and header constraints.*

Proof Sketch: Define a rule to be *reachable* if it can be exercised by at least one packet satisfying the header constraint, and can be received by at least one test terminal. A reachable rule must be in the all-pairs reachability table; thus set cover will pick at least one packet that exercises this rule. Some rules are not reachable: for example, an IP prefix may be made unreachable by a set of more specific prefixes either deliberately (to provide backup) or accidentally (due to misconfiguration).

PROPERTY 2 (NEAR-OPTIMALITY). *The set of test packets selected by TPS is optimal within logarithmic factors among all tests giving complete coverage.*

Proof Sketch: This follows from the logarithmic (in the size of the set) approximation factor inherent in Greedy Set Cover.

PROPERTY 3 (POLYNOMIAL RUNTIME). *The complexity of finding test packets is $O(TDR^2)$ where T is the number of test terminals, D is the network diameter, and R is the average number of rules in each switch.*

Proof Sketch: The complexity of computing reachability from one input port is $O(DR^2)$ [14], and this computation is repeated for each test terminal.

4.2 Fault Localization

ATPG periodically sends a set of test packets. If test packets fail, ATPG pinpoints the fault(s) that caused the problem.

4.2.1 Fault model

A rule fails if its observed behavior differs from its expected behavior. ATPG keeps track of where rules fail using a *result function* R. For a rule r, the result function is defined as

245

	Header	Ingress Port	Egress Port	Rule History
p_1	dst_ip=10.0/16, tcp=80	P_A	P_B	r_{A1}, r_{B3}, r_{B4}, link AB
p_2	dst_ip=10.1/16	P_A	P_C	r_{A2}, r_{C2}, link AC
p_3	dst_ip=10.2/16	P_B	P_A	r_{B2}, r_{A3}, link AB
p_4	dst_ip=10.1/16	P_B	P_C	r_{B2}, r_{C2}, link BC
p_5	dst_ip=10.2/16	P_C	P_A	r_{C1}, r_{A3}, link BC
(p_6)	dst_ip=10.2/16, tcp=80	P_C	P_B	r_{C1}, r_{B3}, r_{B4}, link BC

Table 4: Test packets for the example network depicted in Figure 6. p_6 is stored as a reserved packet.

$$R(r, pk) = \begin{cases} 0 & \text{if } pk \text{ fails at rule } r \\ 1 & \text{if } pk \text{ succeeds at rule } r \end{cases}$$

"Success" and "failure" depend on the nature of the rule: a forwarding rule fails if a test packet is not delivered to the intended output port, whereas a drop rule behaves correctly when packets are dropped. Similarly, a link failure is a failure of a forwarding rule in the topology function. On the other hand, if an output link is congested, failure is captured by the latency of a test packet going above a threshold.

We divide faults into two categories: *action faults* and *match faults*. An action fault occurs when *every* packet matching the rule is processed incorrectly. Examples of action faults include unexpected packet loss, a missing rule, congestion, and mis-wiring. On the other hand, match faults are harder to detect because they only affect *some* packets matching the rule: for example, when a rule matches a header it should not, or when a rule misses a header it should match. Match faults can only be detected by more exhaustive sampling such that at least one test packet exercises each faulty region. For example, if a TCAM bit is supposed to be x, but is "stuck at 1", then all packets with a 0 in the corresponding position will not match correctly. Detecting this error requires at least two packets to exercise the rule: one with a 1 in this position, and the other with a 0.

We will only consider action faults, because they cover most likely failure conditions, and can be detected using only one test packet per rule. We leave match faults for future work.

We can typically only observe a packet at the edge of the network after it has been processed by every matching rule. Therefore, we define an end-to-end version of the result function

$$R(pk) = \begin{cases} 0 & \text{if } pk \text{ fails} \\ 1 & \text{if } pk \text{ succeeds} \end{cases}$$

4.2.2 Algorithm

Our algorithm for pinpointing faulty rules assumes that a test packet will succeed only if it succeeds at every hop. For intuition, a `ping` succeeds only when all the forwarding rules along the path behave correctly. Similarly, if a queue is congested, any packets that travel through it will incur higher latency and may fail an end-to-end test. Formally:

ASSUMPTION 1 (FAULT PROPAGATION). $R(pk) = 1$ *if and only if* $\forall r \in pk.history, R(r, pk) = 1$

ATPG pinpoints a faulty rule, by first computing the minimal set of potentially faulty rules. Formally:

PROBLEM 2 (FAULT LOCALIZATION). *Given a list of $(pk_0, R(pk_0)), (pk_1, R(pk_1)), \ldots$ tuples, find all r that satisfies $\exists pk_i, R(pk_i, r) = 0$.*

We solve this problem opportunistically and in steps.

Step 1: Consider the results from sending the regular test packets. For every passing test, place all rules they exercise into a set of passing rules, P. Similarly, for every failing test, place all rules they exercise into a set of potentially failing rules F. By our assumption, one or more of the rules in F are in error. Therefore $F - P$ is a set of *suspect rules*.

Step 2: ATPG next trims the set of suspect rules by weeding out correctly working rules. ATPG does this using the *reserved packets* (the packets eliminated by Min-Set-Cover). ATPG selects reserved packets whose rule histories contain *exactly one* rule from the suspect set, and sends these packets. Suppose a reserved packet p exercises only rule r in the suspect set. If the sending of p fails, ATPG infers that rule r is in error; if p passes, r is removed from the suspect set. ATPG repeats this process for each reserved packet chosen in Step 2.

Step 3: In most cases, the suspect set is small enough after Step 2, that ATPG can terminate and report the suspect set. If needed, ATPG can narrow down the suspect set further by sending test packets that exercise two or more of the rules in the suspect set using the same technique underlying Step 2. If these test packets pass, ATPG infers that none of the exercised rules are in error and removes these rules from the suspect set. If our Fault Propagation assumption holds, the method will not miss any faults, and therefore will have no *false negatives*.

False positives: Note that the localization method may introduce *false positives*, rules left in the suspect set at the end of Step 3. Specifically, one or more rules in the suspect set may in fact behave correctly.

False positives are unavoidable in some cases. When two rules are in series and there is no path to exercise only one of them, we say the rules are *indistinguishable*; any packet that exercises one rule will also exercise the other. Hence if only one rule fails, we cannot tell which one. For example, if an ACL rule is followed immediately by a forwarding rule that matches the same header, the two rules are indistinguishable. Observe that if we have test terminals before and after each rule (impractical in many cases), with sufficient test packets, we can distinguish every rule. Thus, the deployment of test terminals not only affects test coverage, but also localization accuracy.

5. USE CASES

We can use ATPG for both functional and performance testing, as the following use cases demonstrate.

5.1 Functional testing

We can test the functional correctness of a network by testing that every reachable forwarding and drop rule in the network is behaving correctly:

Forwarding rule: A forwarding rule is behaving cor-

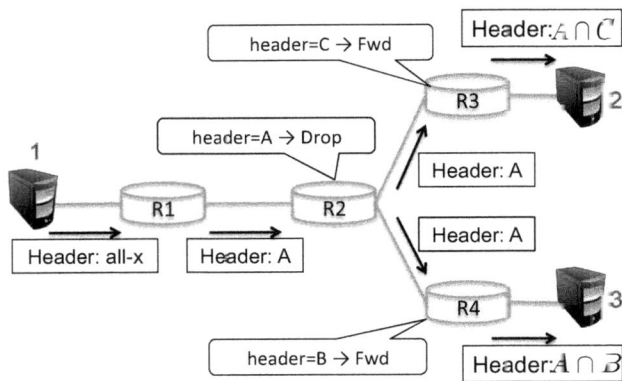

Figure 7: Generate packets to test drop rules: "flip" the rule to a broadcast rule in the analysis.

rectly if a test packet exercises the rule, and leaves on the correct port with the correct header.

Link rule: A link rule is a special case of a forwarding rule. It can be tested by making sure a test packet passes correctly over the link without header modifications.

Drop rule: Testing drop rules is harder because we must verify the *absence* of received test packets. We need to know which test packets might reach an egress test terminal if a drop rule was to fail. To find these packets, in the all-pairs reachability analysis we conceptually "flip" each *drop* rule to a *broadcast* rule in the transfer functions. We do not actually change rules in the switches - we simply emulate the drop rule failure in order to identify all the ways a packet could reach the egress test terminals.

As an example, consider Figure 7. To test the drop rule in $R2$, we inject the all-x test packet at Terminal 1. If the drop rule was instead a broadcast rule it would forward the packet to all of its output ports, and the test packets would reach Terminals 2 and 3. Now we sample the resulting equivalent classes as usual: we pick one sample test packet from $A \cap B$ and one from $A \cap C$. Note that we have to test *both* $A \cap B$ and $A \cap C$ because the drop rule may have failed at $R2$, resulting in an unexpected packet to be received at either test terminal 2 ($A \cap C$) or test terminal 3 ($A \cap B$). Finally, we send and expect the two test packets *not* to appear, since their arrival would indicate a failure of $R2$'s drop rule.

5.2 Performance testing

We can also use ATPG to monitor the performance of links, queues and QoS classes in the network, and even monitor SLAs.

Congestion: If a queue is congested, packets will experience longer queuing delays. This can be considered as a (performance) fault. ATPG lets us generate one way congestion tests to measure the latency between every pair of test terminals; once the latency passed a threshold, fault localization will pinpoint the congested queue, as with regular faults. With appropriate headers, we can test links or queues as in Alice's second problem.

Available bandwidth: Similarly, we can measure the available bandwidth of a link, or for a particular service class. ATPG will generate the test packet headers needed to test every link, or every queue, or every service class; a stream of packets with these headers can then be used to measure bandwidth. One can use destructive tests, like `iperf/netperf`, or more gentle approaches like packet pairs

and packet trains [17]. Suppose a manager specifies that the available bandwidth of a particular service class should not fall below a certain threshold; if it does happen ATPG's fault localization algorithm can be used to triangulate and pinpoint the problematic switch/queue.

Strict priorities: Likewise, ATPG can be used to determine if two queues, or service classes, are in different strict priority classes. If they are, then packets sent using the lower priority class should never affect the available bandwidth or latency of packets in the higher priority class. We can verify the relative priority by generating packet headers to congest the lower class, and verifying that the latency and available bandwidth of the higher class is unaffected. If it is, fault localization can be used to pinpoint the problem.

6. IMPLEMENTATION

We implemented a prototype system to automatically parse router configurations and generate a set of test packets for the network. The code is publicly available [1].

6.1 Test packet generator

The test packet generator, written in Python, contains a Cisco IOS configuration parser and a Juniper Junos parser. The data plane information, including router configurations, FIBs, MAC learning tables, and network topologies, is collected and parsed through the command line interface (Cisco IOS) or XML files (Junos). The generator then uses the Hassel [11] header space analysis library to construct switch and topology functions.

All-pairs reachability is computed using the `multiprocess` parallel-processing module shipped with Python. Each process considers a subset of the test ports, and finds all the reachable ports from each one. After reachability tests are complete, results are collected and the master process executes the Min-Set-Cover algorithm. Test packets and the set of tested rules are stored in a SQLite database.

6.2 Network monitor

The network monitor assumes there are special test agents in the network that are able to send/receive test packets. The network monitor reads the database and constructs test packets, and instructs each agent to send the appropriate packets. Currently, test agents separate test packets by IP Proto field and TCP/UDP port number, but other fields, such as IP option, can also be used. If some of the tests fail, the monitor selects additional test packets from reserved packets to pinpoint the problem. The process repeats until the fault has been identified. The monitor uses JSON to communicate with the test agents, and uses SQLite's string matching to lookup test packets efficiently.

6.3 Alternate implementations

Our prototype was designed to be minimally invasive, requiring no changes to the network except to add terminals at the edge. In networks requiring faster diagnosis, the following extensions are possible:

Cooperative routers: A new feature could be added to switches/routers, so that a central ATPG system can instruct a router to send/receive test packets. In fact, for manufacturing testing purposes, it is likely that almost every commercial switch/router can already do this; we just need an open interface to control them.

SDN-based testing: In a software defined network (SDN) such as OpenFlow [25], the controller could directly instruct the switch to send test packets, and to detect and forward received test packets to the control plane. For performance testing, test packets need to be time-stamped at the routers.

7. EVALUATION

7.1 Data Sets: Stanford and Internet2

We evaluated our prototype system on two sets of network configurations: the Stanford University backbone and the Internet2 backbone, representing a mid-size enterprise network and a nationwide backbone network respectively.

Stanford Backbone: With a population of over 15,000 students, 2,000 faculty, and five /16 IPv4 subnets, Stanford represents a large enterprise network. There are 14 operational zone (OZ) Cisco routers connected via 10 Ethernet switches to 2 backbone Cisco routers that in turn connect Stanford to the outside world. Overall, the network has more than 757,000 forwarding entries and 1,500 ACL rules. Data plane configurations are collected through command line interfaces. Stanford has made the entire configuration rule set public [1].

Internet2: Internet2 is a nationwide backbone network with 9 Juniper T1600 routers and 100 Gb/s interfaces, supporting over 66,000 institutions in United States. There are about 100,000 IPv4 forwarding rules. All Internet2 configurations and FIBs of the core routers are publicly available [12], with the exception of ACL rules, which are removed for security concerns. Although IPv6 and MPLS entries are also available, we only use IPv4 rules in this paper.

7.2 Test Packet Generation

We ran ATPG on a quad core Intel Core i7 CPU 3.2GHz and 6GB memory using 8 threads. For a given number of test terminals, we generated the minimum set of test packets needed to test all the reachable rules in the Stanford and Internet2 backbones. Table 5 shows the number of test packets needed. For example, the first column tells us that if we attach test terminals to 10% of the ports, then all of the reachable Stanford rules (22.2% of the total) can be tested by sending 725 test packets. If every edge port can act as a test terminal, 100% of the Stanford rules can be tested by sending just 3,871 test packets. The "Time" row indicates how long it took ATPG to run; the worst case took about an hour, the bulk of which was devoted to calculating all-pairs reachability.

To put these results into perspective, each test for the Stanford backbone requires sending about 907 packets per port in the worst case. If these packets were sent over a single 1 Gb/s link, the entire network could be tested in less than 1 ms, assuming each test packet is 100 bytes and not considering the propagation delay. Put another way, testing the entire set of forwarding rules ten times every second would use less than 1% of the link bandwidth!

Similarly, all the forwarding rules in Internet2 can be tested using 4,557 test packets per port in the worst case. Even if the test packets were sent over 10 Gb/s links, all the forwarding rules could be tested in less than 0.5 ms, or ten times every second using less than 1% of the link bandwidth.

We also found that 100% *link* coverage (instead of *rule* coverage) only needed 54 packets for Stanford and 20 for

Internet2. The table also shows the large benefit gained by compressing the number of test packets — in most cases, the total number of test packets is reduced by a factor of 20-100 using the minimum set cover algorithm. This compression may make proactive link testing (that was considered infeasible earlier [28]) feasible for large networks.

Coverage is the ratio of the number of rules exercised to the total number of reachable rules. Our results shows that the coverage grows linearly with the number of test terminals available. While it is theoretically possible to optimize the placement of test terminals to achieve higher coverage, we find that the benefit is marginal for real data sets.

Rule structure: The reason we need so few test packets is because of the structure of the rules and the routing policy. Most rules are part of an end-to-end route, and so multiple routers contain the same rule. Similarly, multiple devices contain the same ACL or QoS configuration because they are part of a network wide policy. Therefore, the number of distinct regions of header space grow linearly, not exponentially, with the diameter of the network.

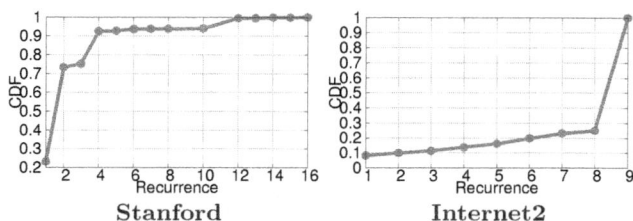

Figure 8: The cumulative distribution function of rule repetition, ignoring different action fields.

We can verify this structure by clustering rules in Stanford and Internet2 that match the same header patterns. Figure 8 shows the distribution of rule repetition in Stanford and Internet2. In both networks, 60%-70% of matching patterns appear in more than one router. We also find that this repetition is correlated to the network topology. In the Stanford backbone, which has a two-level hierarchy, matching patterns commonly appear in 2 (50.3%) or 4 (17.3%) routers, which represents the length of edge-to-Internet and edge-to-edge routes. In Internet2, 75.1% of all distinct rules are replicated 9 times, which is the number of routers in the topology.

7.3 Testing in an Emulated Network

To evaluate the network monitor and test agents, we replicated the Stanford backbone network in Mininet [18], a container-based network emulator. We used Open vSwitch (OVS) [27] to emulate the routers, using the real port configuration information, and connected them according to the real topology. We then translated the forwarding entries in the Stanford backbone network into equivalent OpenFlow [25] rules and installed them in the OVS switches with Beacon [3]. We used emulated hosts to send and receive test packets generated by ATPG. Figure 9 shows the part of network that is used for experiments in this section. We now present different test scenarios and the corresponding results:

Forwarding Error: To emulate a functional error, we deliberately created a fault by replacing the action of an IP *forwarding* rule in *boza* that matched $dst\_ip = 172.20.10.32/27$ with a *drop* action (we called this rule R_1^{boza}). As a result of this fault, test packets from *boza* to *coza* with $dst\_ip =$

Stanford (298 ports)	10%	40%	70%	100%	Edge (81%)
Total Packets	10,042	104,236	413,158	621,402	438,686
Regular Packets	725	2,613	3,627	3,871	3,319
Packets/Port (Avg)	25.00	18.98	17.43	12.99	18.02
Packets/Port (Max)	206	579	874	907	792
Time to send (Max)	0.165ms	0.463ms	0.699ms	0.726ms	0.634ms
Coverage	22.2%	57.7%	81.4%	100%	78.5%
Computation Time	152.53s	603.02s	2,363.67s	3,524.62s	2,807.01s
Internet2 (345 ports)	10%	40%	70%	100%	Edge (92%)
Total Packets	30,387	485,592	1,407,895	3,037,335	3,036,948
Regular Packets	5,930	17,800	32,352	35,462	35,416
Packets/Port (Avg)	159.0	129.0	134.2	102.8	102.7
Packets/Port (Max)	2,550	3,421	2,445	4,557	3,492
Time to send (Max)	0.204ms	0.274ms	0.196ms	0.365ms	0.279ms
Coverage	16.9%	51.4%	80.3%	100%	100%
Computation Time	129.14s	582.28s	1,197.07s	2,173.79s	1,992.52s

Table 5: Test packet generation results for Stanford backbone (top) and Internet2 (bottom), against the number of ports selected for deploying test terminals. "Time to send" packets is calculated on a per port basis, assuming 100B per test packet, 1Gbps link for Stanford and 10Gbps for Internet2.

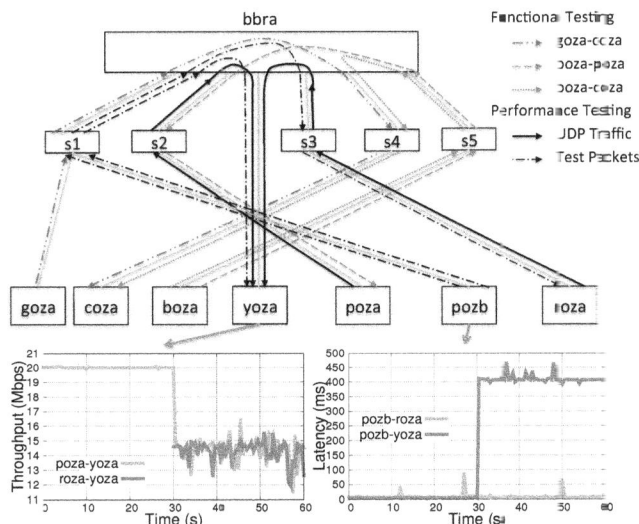

Figure 9: A portion of the Stanford backbone network showing the test packets used for functional and performance testing examples in Section 7.3.

172.20.10.33 failed and were not received at *coza*. Table 6 shows two other test packets we used to localize and pinpoint the fault. These test packets shown in Figure 9 in $goza - coza$ and $boza - poza$ are received correctly at the end terminals. From the *rule history* of the passing and failing packets in Table 3, we deduce that only rule $R_1^{b \approx a}$ could possibly have caused the problem, as all the other rules appear in the rule history of a received test packet.

Congestion: We detect congestion by measuring the one-way latency of test packets. In our emulation environment, all terminals are synchronized to the host's clock so the latency can be calculated with a single time-stamp and one-way communication[4].

To create congestion, we rate-limited all the links in the emulated Stanford network to 30 Mb/s, and created two 20 Mb/s UDP flows: *poza* to *yoza* at $t = 0$ and *roza* to *yoza* at $t = 30s$, which will congest the link $bbra - yoza$ starting at $t = 30s$. The bottom left graph next to *yoza* in Figure 9 shows the two UDP flows. The queue inside the routers will build up and test packets will experience longer queuing delay. The bottom right graph next to *pozb* shows the latency experienced by two test packets, one from *pozb* to *roza* and the other one from *pozb* to *yoza*. At $t = 30s$, the $bozb - yoza$ test packet experiences much higher latency, correctly signaling congestion. Since these two test packets share the $bozb - s_1$ and $s_1 - bbra$ links, ATPG concludes that the congestion is not happening in these two links; hence ATPG correctly infers that $bbra - yoza$ is the congested link.

Available Bandwidth: ATPG can also be used to monitor available bandwidth. For this experiment, we used Pathload [13], a bandwidth probing tool based on packet pairs/packet trains. We repeated the previous experiment, but decreased the two UDP flows to 10 Mb/s, so that the bottleneck available bandwidth was 10 Mb/s. Pathload reports that $bozb - yoza$ has an available bandwidth[5] of 11.715 Mb/s, $bozb - roza$ has an available bandwidth of 19.935 Mb/s, while the other (idle) terminals report 30.60 Mb/s. Using the same argument as before, ATPG can conclude that $bbra - yoza$ link is the bottleneck link with around 10 Mb/s of available bandwidth.

Priority: We created priority queues in OVS using Linux's `htb` scheduler and `tc` utilities. We replicated the previously "failed" test case $pozb - yoza$ for high and low priority queues respectively.[6] Figure 10 shows the result.

We first repeated the congestion experiment. When the low priority queue is congested (*i.e.* both UDP flows mapped to low priority queues), only low priority test packets are affected. However, when the high priority slice is congested, low and high priority test packets experience the congestion and are delayed. Similarly, when repeating the available bandwidth experiment, high priority flows receive the same available bandwidth whether we use high or low priority

---

[4]To measure latency in a real network, two-way communication is usually necessary. However, relative change of latency is sufficient to uncover congestion.

[5]All numbers are the average of 10 repeated measurements.
[6]The Stanford data set does not include the priority settings.

Header	Ingress	Egress	Rule History	Result
$dst\_ip = 172.20.10.33$	goza	coza	$[R_1^{goza}, L_{goza}^{S_1}, S_1, L_{S_1}^{bbra}, R_1^{bbra}, L_{bbra}^{S_4}, S_4, R_1^{coza}]$	Pass
$dst\_ip = 172.20.10.33$	boza	coza	$[R_1^{boza}, L_{boza}^{S_5}, S_5, L_{S_5}^{bbra}, R_1^{bbra}, L_{bbra}^{S_4}, S_4, R_1^{coza}]$	Fail
$dst\_ip = 171.67.222.65$	boza	poza	$[R_2^{boza}, L_{boza}^{S_5}, S_5, L_{S_5}^{bbra}, R_2^{bbra}, L_{bbra}^{S_2}, S_2, R_2^{poza}]$	Pass

Table 6: Test packets used in the functional testing example. In the rule history column, R is the IP forwarding rule, L is a link rule and S is the broadcast rule of switches. R_1 is the IP forwarding rule matching on 172.20.10.32/27 and R_2 matches on 171.67.222.64/27. L_b^e in the link rule from node b to node e. The table highlights the common rules between the passed test packets and the failed one. It is obvious from the results that rule R_1^{boza} is in error.

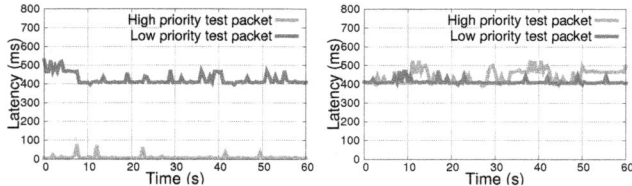

(a) Low   (b) High

Congested Slice	Terminal	Result/Mbps
High	High	11.95
	Low	11.66
Low	High	23.22
	Low	11.78

(c) Available bandwidth

Figure 10: Priority testing: Latency measured by test agents when low (a) or high (b) priority slice is congested; available bandwidth measurements when the bottleneck is in low/high priority slices (c).

test packets. But for low priority flows, the high priority test packets correctly receive the full link bandwidth.

7.4 Testing in a Production Network

We deployed an experimental ATPG system in 3 buildings in Stanford University that host the Computer Science and Electrical Engineering departments. The production network consists of over 30 Ethernet switches and a Cisco router connecting to the campus backbone. For test terminals, we utilized the 53 WiFi access points (running Linux) that were already installed throughout the buildings. This allowed us to achieve high coverage on switches and links. However, we could only run ATPG on essentially a Layer 2 (bridged) Network.

On October 1-10, 2012, the ATPG system was used for a 10-day `ping` experiment. Since the network configurations remained static during this period, instead of reading the configuration from the switches dynamically, we derived the network model based on the topology. In other words, for a Layer 2 bridged network, it is easy to infer the forwarding entry in each switch for each MAC address without getting access to the forwarding tables in all 30 switches. We only used `ping` to generate test packets. Pings suffice because in the subnetwork we tested there are no Layer 3 rules or ACLs. Each test agent downloads a list of `ping` targets from a central web server every 10 minutes, and conducts `ping` tests every 10 seconds. Test results were logged locally as files and collected daily for analysis.

During the experiment, a major network outage occurred on October 2. Figure 11 shows the number of failed test cases during that period. While both all-pairs `ping` and ATPG's selected test suite correctly captured the outage, ATPG uses significantly less test packets. In fact, ATPG

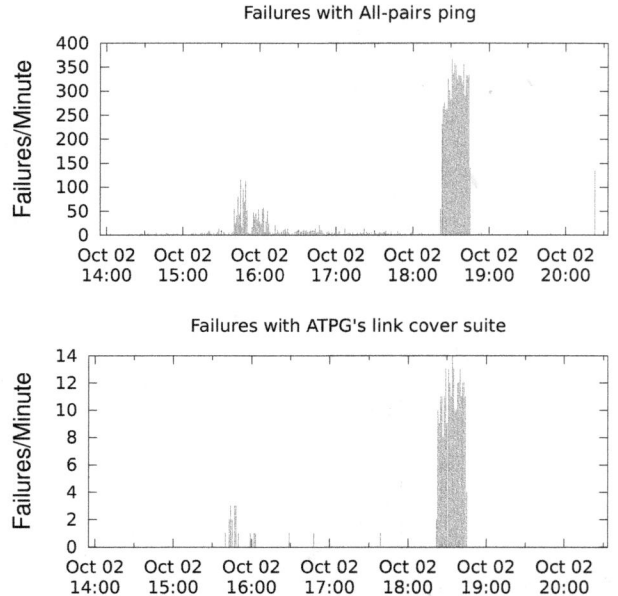

Figure 11: The Oct 2, 2012 production network outages captured by the ATPG system as seen from the lens of an inefficient cover (all-pairs, top picture) and an efficient minimum cover (bottom picture). Two outages occured at 4PM and 6:30PM respectively.

uses only 28 test packets per round compared with 2756 packets in all-pairs `ping`, a 100x reduction. It is easy to see that the reduction is from quadratic overhead (for all-pairs testing between 53 terminals) to linear overhead (for a set cover of the 30 links between switches). We note that while the set cover in this experiment is so simple that it could be computed by hand, other networks will have Layer 3 rules and more complex topologies requiring the ATPG minimum set cover algorithm.

The network managers confirmed that the later outage was caused by a loop that was accidentally created during switch testing. This caused several links to fail and hence more than 300 pings failed per minute. The managers were unable to determine why the first failure occured. Despite this lack of understanding of the root cause, we emphasize that the ATPG system correctly detected the outage in both cases and pinpointed the affected links and switches.

8. DISCUSSION

8.1 Overhead and Performance

The principal sources of overhead for ATPG are polling

the network periodically for forwarding state and performing all-pairs reachability. While one can reduce overhead by running the offline ATPG calculation less frequently, this runs the risk of using out-of-date forwarding information. Instead, we reduce overhead in two ways. First, we have recently sped up the all-pairs reachability calculation using a fast multithreaded/multi-machine header space library. Second, instead of extracting the complete network state every time ATPG is triggered, an *incremental* state updater can significantly reduce both the retrieval time and the time to calculate reachability. We are working on a real-time version of ATPG that incorporates both techniques.

Test agents within terminals incur negligible overhead because they merely demultiplex test packets addressed to their IP address at a modest rate (e.g. 1 per millisecond) compared to the link speeds (> 1 Gbps) most modern CPUs are capable of receiving.

8.2 Limitations

As with all testing methodologies, ATPG has limitations:
1) Dynamic boxes: ATPG cannot model boxes whose internal state can be changed by test packets. For example, a NAT that dynamically assigns TCP ports to outgoing packets can confuse the online monitor as the same test packet can give different results. **2) Non-deterministic boxes**: Boxes can load-balance packets based on a hash function of packet fields, usually combined with a random seed; this is common in multipath routing such as ECMP. When the hash algorithm and parameters are unknown, ATPG cannot properly model such rules. However, if there are known packet patterns that can iterate through all possible outputs, ATPG can generate packets to traverse every output. **3) Invisible rules**: A failed rule can make a backup rule active, and as a result no changes may be observed by the test packets. This can happen when, despite a failure, a test packet is routed to the expected destination by other rules. In addition, an error in a backup rule cannot be detected in normal operation. Another example is when two drop rules appear in a row: the failure of one rule is undetectable since the effect will be masked by the other rule **4) Transient network states**: ATPG cannot uncover errors whose lifetime is shorter than the time between each round of tests. For example, congestion may disappear before an available bandwidth probing test concludes. Finer-grained test agents are needed to capture abnormalities of short duration. **5) Sampling**: ATPG uses sampling when generating test packets. As a result, ATPG can miss match faults since the error is not uniform across all matching headers. In the worst case (when only one header is in error), exhaustive testing is needed.

9. RELATED WORK

We are unaware of earlier techniques that automatically generate test packets from configurations. The closest related work we know of are offline tools that check invariants in networks. In the control plane, NICE [5] attempts to exhaustively cover the code paths symbolically in controller applications with the help of simplified switch/host models. In the data plane, Anteater [23] models invariants as boolean satisfiability problems and checks them against configurations with a SAT solver. Header Space Analysis [14] uses a geometric model to check reachability, detect loops, and verify slicing. Recently, SOFT [16] was proposed to verify consistency between different OpenFlow agent implementations that are responsible for bridging control and data planes in the SDN context. ATPG complements these checkers by directly *testing* the data plane and covering a significant set of dynamic or performance errors that cannot otherwise be captured.

End-to-end probes have long been used in network fault diagnosis in work such as [6–8, 15, 21, 22, 24]. Recently, mining low-quality, unstructured data, such as router configurations and network tickets has attracted interest [10, 19, 32]. By contrast, the primary contribution of ATPG is not fault localization, but determining a compact set of end-to-end measurements that can cover every link or every rule. Further, ATPG is not limited to liveness testing but can be applied to checking higher level properties such as performance.

There are many proposals to develop a measurement-friendly architecture for networks [9, 20, 26, 33]. Our approach is complementary to these proposals: by incorporating input and port constraints, ATPG can generate test packets and injection points using existing deployment of measurement devices.

Our work is closely related to work in programming languages and symbolic debugging. We made a preliminary attempt to use KLEE [4] and found it to be 10 times slower than even the unoptimized header space framework. We speculate that this is fundamentally because in our framework we directly *simulate* the forward path of a packet instead of *solving constraints* using an SMT solver. However, more work is required to understand the differences and potential opportunities.

10. CONCLUSION

Testing liveness of a network is a fundamental problem for ISPs and large data center operators. Sending probes between every pair of edge ports is neither exhaustive nor scalable [28]. It suffices to find a minimal set of end-to-end packets that traverse each link. But doing this requires a way of abstracting across device specific configuration files (e.g., header space), generating headers and the links they reach (e.g., all-pairs reachability), and finally determining a minimum set of test packets (Min-Set-Cover). Even the fundamental problem of automatically generating test packets for efficient liveness testing requires techniques akin to ATPG.

ATPG, however, goes much further than liveness testing with the same framework. ATPG can test for reachability policy (by testing all rules including drop rules) and performance health (by associating performance measures such as latency and loss with test packets). Our implementation also augments testing with a simple fault localization scheme also constructed using the header space framework. As in software testing, the formal model helps maximize test coverage while minimizing test packets. Our results show that all forwarding rules in Stanford backbone or Internet2 can be exercised by a surprisingly small number of test packets (<4,000 for Stanford, and <40,000 for Internet2)

Network managers today use primitive tools such as `ping` and `traceroute`. Our survey results indicate that they are eager for more sophisticated tools. Other fields of engineering indicate that these desires are not unreasonable: for example, both the ASIC and software design industries are buttressed by billion dollar tool businesses that supply techniques for both static (e.g., design rule) and dynamic (e.g., timing) verification. In fact, many months after we built and named our system, we discovered to our surprise that ATPG was a well-known acronym in hardware chip testing, where it stands for Automatic Test *Pattern* Generation [2]. We hope network ATPG will be equally useful for automated dynamic testing of production networks.

11. ACKNOWLEDGEMENT

We would like to thank our shepherd, Dejan Kostic, and the anonymous reviewers for their valuable comments. We thank Johan van Reijendam, Charles M. Orgish, Joe Little (Stanford University) and Thomas C. Knoeller, Matthew P. Davy (Internet2) for providing router configuration sets and sharing their operation experience. This research was funded by NSF grants CNS-0832820, CNS-0855268, CNS-1040593, and Stanford Graduate Fellowship.

12. REFERENCES

[1] ATPG code repository. http://eastzone.github.com/atpg/.

[2] Automatic Test Pattern Generation. http://en.wikipedia.org/wiki/Automatic_test_pattern_generation.

[3] Beacon. http://www.beaconcontroller.net/.

[4] C. Cadar, D. Dunbar, and D. Engler. Klee: unassisted and automatic generation of high-coverage tests for complex systems programs. In *Proceedings of OSDI'08*, pages 209–224, Berkeley, CA, USA, 2008. USENIX Association.

[5] M. Canini, D. Venzano, P. Peresini, D. Kostic, and J. Rexford. A NICE way to test openflow applications. *Proceedings of NSDI'12*, 2012.

[6] A. Dhamdhere, R. Teixeira, C. Dovrolis, and C. Diot. Netdiagnoser: troubleshooting network unreachabilities using end-to-end probes and routing data. In *Proceedings of the 2007 ACM CoNEXT conference*, pages 18:1–18:12, New York, NY, USA, 2007. ACM.

[7] N. Duffield. Network tomography of binary network performance characteristics. *IEEE Transactions on Information Theory*, 52(12):5373–5388, dec. 2006.

[8] N. Duffield, F. Lo Presti, V. Paxson, and D. Towsley. Inferring link loss using striped unicast probes. In *Proceedings IEEE INFOCOM 2001*, volume 2, pages 915–923 vol.2, 2001.

[9] N. G. Duffield and M. Grossglauser. Trajectory sampling for direct traffic observation. *IEEE/ACM Trans. Netw.*, 9(3):280–292, June 2001.

[10] P. Gill, N. Jain, and N. Nagappan. Understanding network failures in data centers: measurement, analysis, and implications. In *Proceedings of the ACM SIGCOMM 2011 conference*, pages 350–361, New York, NY, USA, 2011. ACM.

[11] Hassel, the header space library. https://bitbucket.org/peymank/hassel-public/.

[12] The Internet2 Observatory Data Collections. http://www.internet2.edu/observatory/archive/data-collections.html.

[13] M. Jain and C. Dovrolis. End-to-end available bandwidth: measurement methodology, dynamics, and relation with tcp throughput. *IEEE/ACM Trans. Netw.*, 11(4):537–549, Aug. 2003.

[14] P. Kazemian, G. Varghese, and N. McKeown. Header Space Analysis: static checking for networks. *Proceedings of NSDI'12*, 2012.

[15] R. R. Kompella, J. Yates, A. Greenberg, and A. C. Snoeren. Ip fault localization via risk modeling. In *Proceedings of NSDI'05 - Volume 2*, pages 57–70, Berkeley, CA, USA, 2005. USENIX Association.

[16] M. Kuzniar, P. Peresini, M. Canini, D. Venzano, and D. Kostic. A SOFT way for openflow switch interoperability testing. In *Proceedings of the 2012 ACM CoNEXT Conference*, 2012.

[17] K. Lai and M. Baker. Nettimer: a tool for measuring bottleneck link, bandwidth. In *Proceedings of USITS'01 - Volume 3*, pages 11–11, Berkeley, CA, USA, 2001. USENIX Association.

[18] B. Lantz, B. Heller, and N. McKeown. A network in a laptop: rapid prototyping for software-defined networks. In *Proceedings of Hotnets '10*, pages 19:1–19:6, New York, NY, USA, 2010. ACM.

[19] F. Le, S. Lee, T. Wong, H. S. Kim, and D. Newcomb. Detecting network-wide and router-specific misconfigurations through data mining. *IEEE/ACM Trans. Netw.*, 17(1):66–79, Feb. 2009.

[20] H. V. Madhyastha, T. Isdal, M. Piatek, C. Dixon, T. Anderson, A. Krishnamurthy, and A. Venkataramani. iplane: an information plane for distributed services. In *Proceedings of OSDI'06*, pages 367–380, Berkeley, CA, USA, 2006. USENIX Association.

[21] A. Mahimkar, Z. Ge, J. Wang, J. Yates, Y. Zhang, J. Emmons, B. Huntley, and M. Stockert. Rapid detection of maintenance induced changes in service performance. In *Proceedings of the 2011 ACM CoNEXT Conference*, pages 13:1–13:12, New York, NY, USA, 2011. ACM.

[22] A. Mahimkar, J. Yates, Y. Zhang, A. Shaikh, J. Wang, Z. Ge, and C. T. Ee. Troubleshooting chronic conditions in large ip networks. In *Proceedings of the 2008 ACM CoNEXT Conference*, pages 2:1–2:12, New York, NY, USA, 2008. ACM.

[23] H. Mai, A. Khurshid, R. Agarwal, M. Caesar, P. B. Godfrey, and S. T. King. Debugging the data plane with anteater. *SIGCOMM Comput. Commun. Rev.*, 41(4):290–301, Aug. 2011.

[24] A. Markopoulou, G. Iannaccone, S. Bhattacharyya, C.-N. Chuah, Y. Ganjali, and C. Diot. Characterization of failures in an operational ip backbone network. *IEEE/ACM Trans. Netw.*, 16(4):749–762, Aug. 2008.

[25] N. McKeown, T. Anderson, H. Balakrishnan, G. Parulkar, L. Peterson, J. Rexford, S. Shenker, and J. Turner. OpenFlow: enabling innovation in campus networks. *SIGCOMM Comput. Commun. Rev.*, 38:69–74, March 2008.

[26] OnTimeMeasure. http://ontime.oar.net/.

[27] Open vSwitch. http://openvswitch.org/.

[28] All-pairs ping service for PlanetLab ceased. http://lists.planet-lab.org/pipermail/users/2005-July/001518.html.

[29] M. Reitblatt, N. Foster, J. Rexford, C. Schlesinger, and D. Walker. Abstractions for network update. In *Proceedings of the ACM SIGCOMM 2012 conference*. ACM, 2012.

[30] S. Shenker. The future of networking, and the past of protocols. http://opennetsummit.org/talks/shenker-tue.pdf.

[31] Troubleshooting the Network Survey. http://eastzone.github.com/atpg/docs/NetDebugSurvey.pdf.

[32] D. Turner, K. Levchenko, A. C. Snoeren, and S. Savage. California fault lines: understanding the causes and impact of network failures. *SIGCOMM Comput. Commun. Rev.*, 41(4):–, Aug. 2010.

[33] P. Yalagandula, P. Sharma, S. Banerjee, S. Basu, and S.-J. Lee. S3: a scalable sensing service for monitoring large networked systems. In *Proceedings of INM '06*, pages 71–76, New York, NY, USA, 2006. ACM.

Reproducible Network Experiments
Using Container-Based Emulation

Nikhil Handigol⋆†, Brandon Heller⋆†, Vimalkumar Jeyakumar⋆†, Bob Lantz◇†, Nick McKeown⋆
[nikhilh,brandonh,jvimal,rlantz,nickm]@[◇cs.]stanford.edu
⋆ Stanford University, Palo Alto, CA USA   ◇ Open Networking Laboratory, Palo Alto, CA USA
† These authors contributed equally to this work

ABSTRACT

In an ideal world, all research papers would be *runnable*: simply click to replicate all results, using the same setup as the authors. One approach to enable runnable *network systems* papers is Container-Based Emulation (CBE), where an environment of virtual hosts, switches, and links runs on a modern multicore server, using real application and kernel code with software-emulated network elements. CBE combines many of the best features of software simulators and hardware testbeds, but its performance fidelity is unproven.

In this paper, we put CBE to the test, using our prototype, Mininet-HiFi, to reproduce key results from published network experiments such as DCTCP, Hedera, and router buffer sizing. We report lessons learned from a graduate networking class at Stanford, where 37 students used our platform to replicate 16 published results of their own choosing. Our experiences suggest that CBE makes research results easier to reproduce and build upon.

Categories and Subject Descriptors

C.2.1 [**Computer Systems Organization**]: Computer - Communication Networks—*Network Communications*; D.4.8 [**Operating Systems**]: Performance—*Simulation*

Keywords

Reproducible research, container-based emulation

1. INTRODUCTION

The scientific method dictates that experiments must be reproduced before they are considered valid; in physics and medicine, reproduction is a part of the culture. In computer science, reproduction requires open access to all code, scripts, and data used to produce the results.

As Donoho noted,

"... a scientific publication is not the scholarship itself, it is merely advertising of the scholarship. The actual scholarship is the complete software development environment and the complete set of instructions which generated the figures."

Reproducible, runnable papers do not appear to be standard practice in network systems research,¹ so calls from Knuth [1], Claerbout [2], Donoho [3] and Vandewalle [4] for reproducible experiments and results still resonate.

This paper advocates reproducible networking experiments using *Container-Based Emulation*, which runs real code on an emulated network using lightweight, OS-level virtualization techniques combined with careful resource isolation and monitoring. The approach provides the topology flexibility, low cost, and repeatability of simulation with the functional realism of testbeds. The performance fidelity of network emulation is largely unproven, so we focus on exploring the ability of CBE to reproduce experiments by comparing performance results from our prototype, *Mininet-HiFi*, with results published at top-tier networking conferences.

Our specific contributions include the following:

- Implementation of a Container-Based Emulator, Mininet Hi-Fi,² which enables reproducible network experiments using resource isolation, provisioning, and monitoring mechanisms (§3).

- Reproduced experiments from published networking research papers, including DCTCP, Hedera, and Sizing Router Buffers (§5).

- Practical lessons learned from unleashing 37 budding researchers in Stanford's *CS244: Advanced Topics in Networking* course upon 13 other published papers (§6).

To demonstrate that network systems research can indeed be made repeatable, each result described in this paper can be repeated by running a single script on an Amazon EC2 [5] instance or on a physical server. Following Claerbout's model, clicking on each figure in the PDF (when viewed electronically) links to instructions to replicate the experiment that generated the figure. We encourage you to put this paper to the test and replicate its results for yourself.

---

¹(or indeed Computer Science at large)
²Available at `https://github.com/mininet`.

	Simulators	Testbeds		Emulators
		Shared	Custom	
Functional Realism		✓	✓	✓
Timing Realism	✓	✓	✓	???
Traffic Realism		✓	✓	✓
Topology Flexibility	✓	(limited)		✓
Easy Replication	✓	✓		✓
Low cost	✓			✓

Table 1: Platform characteristics for reproducible network experiments.

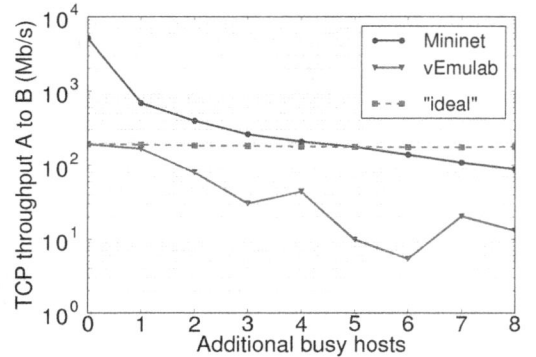

Figure 1: Emulator realism suffers without adequate performance isolation.

2. GOALS

If we are to create *realistic* and *reproducible* networking experiments, then we need a platform with the following characteristics:

Functional realism. The system must have the same functionality as real hardware in a real deployment, and should execute exactly the same code.

Timing realism. The timing behavior of the system must be close to (or indistinguishable from) the behavior of deployed hardware. The system should detect when timing realism is violated.

Traffic realism. The system should be capable of generating and receiving real, interactive network traffic to and from the Internet, or from users or systems on a local network.

In addition to providing realism, the system must make it easy to reproduce results, enabling an entire network experiment workflow – from input data to final results – to be easily created, duplicated, and run by other researchers:

Topology flexibility. It should be easy to create an experiment with any topology.

Easy replication. It should be easy to duplicate an experimental setup and run an experiment.

Low cost. It should be inexpensive to duplicate an experiment, e.g. for students in a course.

Commonly used platforms in networking systems research include *simulators*, *testbeds*, and *emulators*. Table 1 compares how well each platform supports our goals for realism and reproducibility.

Simulators for networking advance virtual time as a result of simulated events [6, 7, 8]. Their experiments are convenient and reproducible, but models for hardware, protocols, and traffic generation may raise fidelity concerns.

Testbeds for networking can be shared among many researchers [9, 10, 11, 12] or specific to one project [13, 14, 15]. Though realistic, they cost money to build and keep running, have practical resource limits (especially before paper deadlines), and may lack the flexibility to support experiments with custom topologies or custom forwarding behavior.

Emulators for networking meet nearly all of our crite-

ria. Like testbeds, emulators run real code (e.g. OS kernel, network applications) with interactive network traffic. Like simulators, they support arbitrary topologies, their virtual "hardware" costs very little, and they can be "shrink-wrapped" with all of their code, configuration and data into disk images to run on commodity virtual or physical machines. *Full-System Emulation*, e.g. DieCast [16] or VMs coupled using Open vSwitch [17], uses one virtual machine per host. *Container-Based Emulation* (CBE), e.g. virtual Emulab (*vEmulab* in this paper) [18], NetKit [19], Trellis [20], CORE [21], Mininet [22] and many others, employs lighter-weight OS-level containers that share a single kernel to achieve better scalability than VM-based systems on a single system [23, 22].

However, emulators, regardless of their type, may not provide adequate performance isolation for experiments. Figure 1 plots the TCP bandwidth for a simple benchmark where two virtual hosts communicate at full speed over a 200Mb/s link. In the background, we vary the load on a number of other (non-communicating) virtual hosts. On Mininet, the TCP flow exceeds the desired performance at first, then degrades gradually as the background load increases. Though vEmulab correctly rate-limits the links, that alone is not sufficient: increasing background load affects the network performance of other virtual hosts, leading to unrealistic results. Ideally, the TCP flow would see a constant throughput of 200Mb/s irrespective of the background load on the other virtual hosts.

For experiments that are limited by network resource constraints (such as bandwidth or latency, as is usually the case for networking research experiments), we conjecture that one can accurately emulate and reproduce experiments on a network of hosts, switches, and links by *carefully allocating and limiting* CPU and link bandwidth, then *monitoring* the experiment to ensure that the emulator is operating "within its limits" and yielding realistic results.

The next section describes the architecture, performance isolation features, and monitoring mechanisms of our Container-Based Emulator, Mininet-HiFi.

3. MININET-HIFI ARCHITECTURE

Mininet-HiFi is a Container-Based Emulator that we have developed to enable repeatable, realistic network experiments. Mininet-HiFi extends the original Mininet architecture [22] by adding mechanisms for performance isolation, resource provisioning, and monitoring for performance fidelity.

3.1 Design Overview

The original Mininet system [22] follows the approach of systems such as Imunes [24] and vEmulab [18] which use lightweight, OS-level virtualization to emulate hosts, switches, and network links. The Linux *container* mechanism (used by Mininet) follows the design of *jails* in BSD and *zones* in Solaris by allowing groups of processes to have independent views of (or *namespaces* for) system resources such as process IDs, user names, file systems and network interfaces, while still running on the same kernel. Containers trade the ability to run multiple OS kernels for lower overhead and better scalability than full-system virtualization

For each virtual host, Mininet creates a container attached to a *network namespace*. Each network namespace holds a virtual network interface, along with its associated data, including ARP caches and routing tables. Virtual interfaces connect to software switches (e.g Open vSwitch [17]) via virtual Ethernet (`veth`) links. The design resembles a Virtual Machine server where each VM has been replaced by processes in a container attached to a network namespace.

3.2 Performance Isolation

Mininet, as originally implemented, does not provide any assurance of *performance fidelity*, because it does not isolate the resources used by virtual hosts and switches. vEmulab provides a way to limit link bandwidth, but not CPU bandwidth. As we saw earlier, this is insufficient: a realistic emulator requires both CPU and network bandwidth limiting at minimum. In Mininet Hi-Fi, we have implemented these limits using the following OS-level features in Linux:

Control Groups or *cgroups* allow a group of processes (belonging to a container/virtual host) to be treated as a single entity for (hierarchical) scheduling and resource management [25].[3]

CPU Bandwidth Limits enforce a maximum time quota for a `cgroup` within a given period of time [26]. The period is configurable and typically is between 10 and 100 ms. CPU time is fairly shared among all `cgroups` which have not used up their quota (slice) for the given period.

Traffic Control using `tc` configures link properties such as bandwidth, delay, and packet loss.

Figure 2 shows the components of a simple hardware net-

---

[3]Resources optionally include CPU, memory, and I/O. CPU caches and Translation Lookaside Buffers (TLBs) cannot currently be managed.

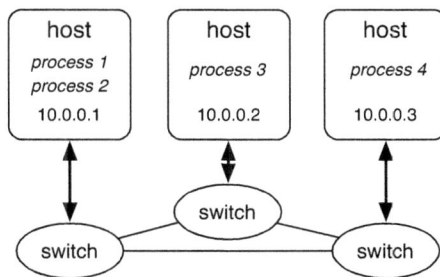

Figure 2: A simple hardware network in a △ topology.

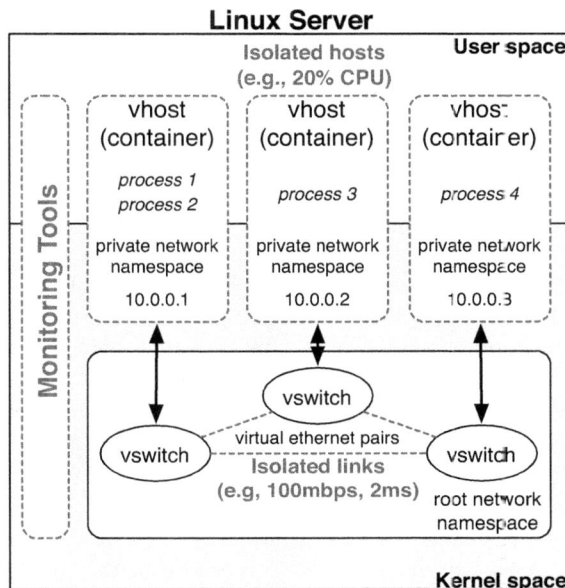

Figure 3: Equivalent Mininet-HiFi network. Dashed lines indicate performance isolation and monitoring features.

work, and Figure 3 shows its corresponding realization in Mininet-HiFi using the above features.

Adopting these mechanisms in Mininet-HiFi solves the performance isolation problem shown in Figure 1: the "ideal" line is in fact the measured behavior of Mininet-HiFi.

3.3 Resource provisioning

Each isolation mechanism must be configured appropriately for the system and the experiment. Fortunately, careful provisioning — by splitting the CPU among containers and leaving some margin to handle packet forwarding, based on offline profiling — can yield a result that matches hardware. We report benchmarks comparing Mininet-HiFi with a hardware setup for multiple traffic types (UDP and TCP) and topologies (single link, stars, and trees) in [27].

However, the exact CPU usage for packet forwarding varies with path length, lookup complexity, and link load. It is hard to know in advance whether a particular configuration will provide enough cycles for forwarding. Moreover, it may be desirable to overbook the CPU to support a larger

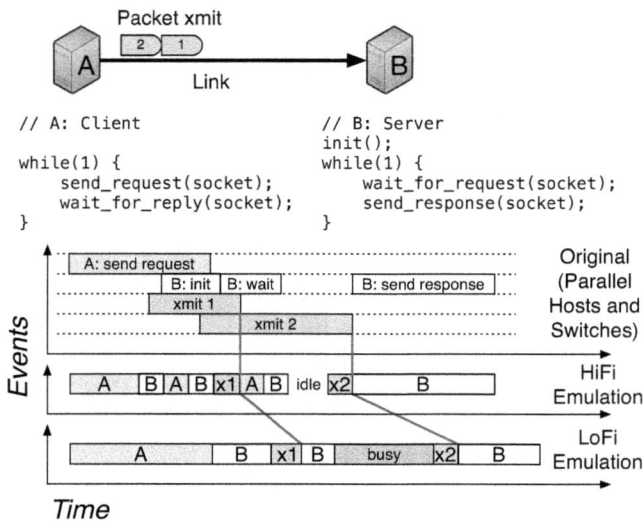

Figure 4: Time multiplexing may cause delayed packet transmissions and host scheduling.

experiment if some links are partially loaded. Mininet-HiFi lets the experimenter allocate link speeds, topologies, and CPU fractions based on their estimated demand, and can also monitor performance fidelity to help verify that an experiment is operating realistically.

3.4 Monitoring Performance Fidelity

Any Container-Based Emulator must contend with infidelity that arises when multiple processes execute serially on the available cores, rather than in parallel on physical hosts and switches. Unlike a simulator running in virtual time, Mininet-HiFi runs in real time and does not pause a host's clock to wait for events. As a result, events such as transmitting a packet or finishing a computation can be delayed due to serialization, contention, and background system load.

Figure 4 compares the timing of a hardware network with two hosts, A and B, sending two packets as part of one request over one link, against emulated versions on a single processor. The bottom part of the figure shows an accurate "HiFi" emulation, along with an inaccurate "LoFi" emulation that has a coarser scheduler granularity and an interfering background process. The slanted lines show that packets in the LoFi version have been delayed and their relative timing has changed, possibly compromising full link throughput and performance fidelity.

To provide assurance that an experiment ran with sufficient fidelity, we want to track when conditions like these occur. Specifically, if the micro-scale scheduling and queueing behavior closely matches hardware, as seen in the HiFi trace, we expect the macro-scale system-level behavior to also match hardware. More precisely, if Mininet-HiFi can (a) start and complete the execution of virtual hosts on time (i.e. within a small delay bound of the corresponding hardware execution times), and (b) dequeue packets on time (i.e.

within a small delay bound of the corresponding switch dequeue times), then we can expect high-fidelity results. These are necessary conditions. Since Mininet-HiFi runs inside a single clock domain, it can track the delays accurately.

Link and switch fidelity. We monitor network accuracy by measuring the inter-dequeue times of packets. Since links run at a fixed rate, packets should depart at predictable times whenever the queue is non-empty. For each experiment described in Section 5, we record these samples to determine link and switch fidelity.

Host fidelity. Although CPU bandwidth limiting ensures that no virtual host receives *excessive* CPU time, we also need to determine whether each virtual host is receiving *sufficient* time to execute its workload. We do so by monitoring the fraction of time the CPU is idle. Empirically, we have found the presence of idle time to be a good indicator of fidelity, as it implies that a virtual host is not starved for CPU resources. In contrast, the absence of idle time indicates that the CPU limit has been reached, and we conservatively assume that the emulator has fallen behind, fidelity has been lost, and the experiment should be reconfigured.

Mininet-HiFi uses hooks in the Linux Tracing Toolkit [28] to log these process and packet scheduler events to memory. We next describe the space of experiments suitable for Mininet-HiFi, before testing whether it can actually replicate experiments with high fidelity in §5.

4. EXPERIMENTAL SCOPE

In its current form, Mininet-HiFi targets experiments that (1) are *network-limited* and (2) have aggregate resource requirements that fit within a single modern multi-core server.

Network-limited refers to experiments that are limited by network properties such as bandwidth, latency, and queueing, rather than other system properties such as disk bandwidth or memory latency; in other words, experiments whose results would not change on a larger, faster server. For example, testing how a new version of TCP performs in a specific topology on 100 Mb/s links would be an excellent use of Mininet-HiFi, since the performance is likely to be dependent on link bandwidth and latency. In contrast, testing a modified Hadoop would be a poor fit, since MapReduce frameworks tend to stress memory and disk bandwidth along with the network.

Generally, Mininet-HiFi experiments use less than 100 hosts and links. Experiment size will usually be determined by available CPU cycles, virtual network bandwidth, and memory. For example, on a server with 3 GHz of CPU and 3 GB RAM that can provide 3 Gb/s of internal packet bandwidth, one can create a network of 30 hosts with 100 MHz CPU and 100 MB memory each, connected by 100 Mb/s links. Unsurprisingly, this configuration works poorly for experiments that depend on several 1 Gbps links.

Overall, Mininet-HiFi is a good fit for experiments that benefit from flexible routing and topology configuration and have modest resource requirements, where a scaled-down version can still demonstrate the main idea, even with imperfect fidelity. Compared with hardware-only testbeds [9, 10, 11, 12], Mininet-HiFi makes it easier to reconfigure the network to have specific characteristics, and doesn't suffer from limited availability before a conference deadline. Also, if the goal is to scale out and run hundreds of experiments at once, for example when conducting a massive online course or tutorial, using Mininet-HiFi on a public cloud such as Amazon EC2 or on the laptops of individual participants solves the problem of limited hardware resources.

If an experiment requires extremely precise network switching behavior, reconfigurable hardware (e.g. NetFP-GAs) may be a better fit; if it requires "big iron" at large scale, then a simulator or testbed is a better choice. However, the Container-Based Emulation approach is not fundamentally limited to medium-scale, network-limited experiments. The current limitations could be addressed by (1) expanding to multiple machines, (2) slowing down time [29], and (3) isolating more resources using Linux Containers [30].

The next sections (§5 and §6) show the range of network-limited network experiments that Mininet-HiFi appears to support well. All are sensitive to bandwidth, queues, or latency, and, to generate enough traffic to saturate links, are necessarily sensitive to raw CPU.

5. EXPERIMENTAL EVALUATION

To evaluate and demonstrate Mininet-HiFi, this section details several reproducible experiments based on published networking research. The first goal is to see whether results measured on Mininet-HiFi can qualitatively match the results generated on hardware for a range of network-limited network experiments. The second goal is to see whether the monitoring mechanisms in Mininet-HiFi can indicate the fidelity of an experiment.

Each published result originally used a custom testbed, because there was no shared testbed available with the desired characteristics; either the experiment required custom packet marking and queue monitoring (§5.1), a custom topology with custom forwarding rules (§5.2), or long latencies and control over queue sizes (§5.3). Each Mininet-HiFi result uses an Intel Core i7 server with four 3.2 GHz cores and 12 GB of RAM. If the corresponding results from the testbed and server match, then perhaps the testbed was unnecessary.

For each experiment, we link to a "runnable" version; clicking on each figure in the PDF (when viewed electronically) links to instructions to replicate the experiment.

5.1 DCTCP

Data-Center TCP was proposed in SIGCOMM 2010 as a modification to TCP's congestion control algorithm [14] with the goal of simultaneously achieving high throughput and low latency. DCTCP leverages the Explicit Congestion Notification [31] feature in commodity switches to detect and

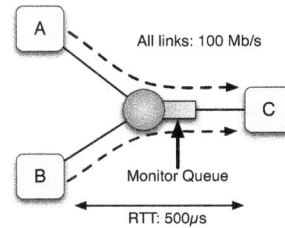

Figure 5: Topology for TCP and DCTCP experiments.

react not only to the presence of network congestion but also to its *extent*, measured through the sequence of ECN marks stamped by the switch.

To test the ability of Mininet-HiFi to precisely emulate queues, we attempt to replicate an experiment in the DCTCP paper showing how DCTCP can maintain high throughput with very small buffers. We use the same publicly available Linux DCTCP patch [32]. In both Mininet-HiFi and on real hardware in our lab,[4] we created a simple topology of three hosts A, B and C connected to a single 100 Mb/s switch, as shown in Figure 5. In Mininet-HiFi, we configured ECN through Linux Traffic Control's RED queuing discipline and set a marking threshold of 20 packets.[5] Hosts A and B each start one long-lived TCP flow to host C. We monitor the instantaneous output queue occupancy of the switch interface connected to host C. Figure 6 shows the queue behavior in Mininet-HiFi running DCTCP and from an equivalently configured hardware setup. Both TCP and DCTCP show similar queue occupancies in Mininet-HiFi and hardware, with a bit more variation in Mininet-HiFi. The main takeaway is that this experiment could be emulated using Mininet-HiFi.

Verifying fidelity: DCTCP's dynamics depend on queue occupancy at the switch, so the experiment relies on accurate link emulation. As described earlier, Mininet-HiFi verifies the link emulation accuracy by monitoring the dequeue times on every link. An ideal 100 Mb/s link would take 121.1 μs to transmit a 1514 byte packet, while a 1 Gb/s link would take 12.11 μs. We compute the percentage deviation of inter-dequeue times from the ideal (121.1 μs for 100 Mb/s). That is, if x_i is a sample, the percentage deviation is $100 \times |x_i - 121.1|/121.1$. Figure 7 shows the complementary CDF when we emulate links at 100 Mb/s and 1 Gb/s.

The htb link scheduler emulates 100 Mb/s well: the inter-dequeue times are within 10% of an ideal link for 99% of packets observed in a 2 s time window, and within 1% for ~ 90% of packets. The scheduler falls behind for 1 Gb/s links. The inter-dequeue time deviations are far from ideal for over 10% of packets in the same 2 s time window. Though not shown, the average bottleneck link utilization (over a period of 1 s) drops to ~ 80% of the what was observed on hardware, and the CPU shows no idle time. This tells the

---

[4]We used the same Broadcom switch as the authors.
[5]As per [14], 20 packets exceeds the theoretical minimum buffer size to maintain 100% throughput at 100 Mb/s.

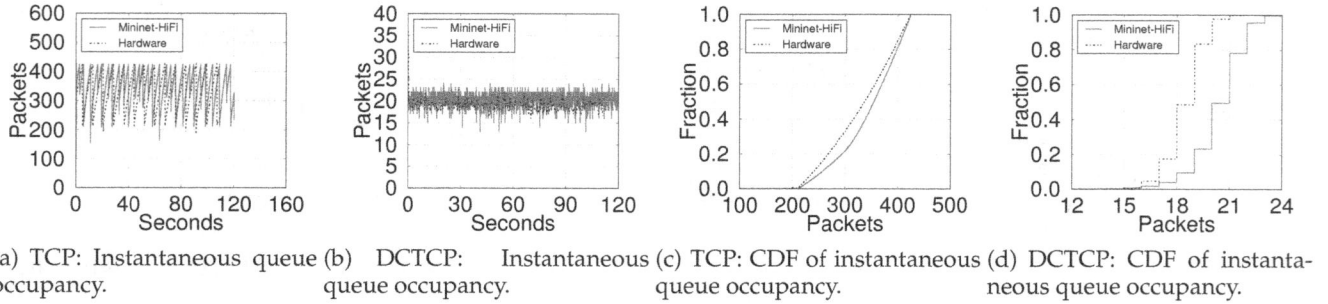

(a) TCP: Instantaneous queue occupancy. (b) DCTCP: Instantaneous queue occupancy. (c) TCP: CDF of instantaneous queue occupancy. (d) DCTCP: CDF of instantaneous queue occupancy.

Figure 6: Reproduced results for DCTCP [14] with Mininet-HiFi and a identically configured hardware setup. Figure 6(b) shows that the queue occupancy with Mininet-HiFi stays within 2 packets of hardware.

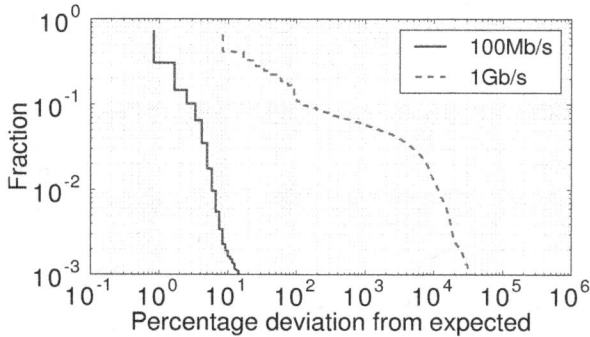

Figure 7: Complementary CDF of inter-dequeue time deviations from ideal; high fidelity at 100 Mb/s, low fidelity at 1 Gb/s.

experimenter that, for this experiment, Mininet-HiFi can emulate the links accurately at 100 Mb/s, but not at 1 Gb/s.

Scaling the experiment: The DCTCP paper showed experimental results for 1 Gb/s and 10 Gb/s bottleneck links, but Mininet-HiFi could only emulate up to a 100 Mb/s link. We expect 1 Gb/s would be attainable with some effort, but 10 Gb/s seems unlikely in the near term. A 10 Gb/s link dequeues packets every 1.2 μs, which stretches the limits of today's hardware timers. In particular, we found that the best timer resolution offered by Linux's High Resolution Timer (`hrtimer`) subsystem was about 1.8 μs, whose limits depend on the frequency of the hardware clock, and its interrupt and programming overheads.

5.2 Hedera

In our second example we use Mininet-HiFi to reproduce results that were originally measured on a real hardware testbed in *Hedera* [13], a dynamic flow scheduler for data center networks, presented at NSDI 2010. With Equal-Cost Multi-Path (ECMP) routing, flows take a randomly picked path through the network based on a hash of the packet header. ECMP hashing prevents packet reordering by ensuring all packets belonging to a flow take the same path [33]. Hedera shows that this simple approach leads to random

hash collisions between "elephant flows" – flows that are a large fraction of the link rate – causing the aggregate throughput to plummet. With this result as the motivation, Hedera proposes a solution to intelligently re-route flows to avoid collisions, and thus, exploit all the available bandwidth.

More specifically, as part of the evaluation, the authors compare the throughput achieved by ECMP with that of an ideal "non-blocking" network (the maximum achievable) for 20 different traffic patterns (Figure 9 in the original paper [13]). The authors performed their evaluation on a hardware testbed with a $k = 4$ Fat Tree topology with 1 Gb/s links. The main metric of interest is the aggregate throughput relative to the full bisection bandwidth of the network.

To test the ability of Mininet-HiFi to emulate a complex topology with many links, switches, and hosts, we replicate the ECMP experiment from the paper. We use the same $k = 4$ Fat Tree topology and the same traffic generation program provided by the Hedera authors to generate the same traffic patterns. To route flows, we use RipL-POX [34], a Python-based OpenFlow controller. We set the link bandwidths to 10 Mb/s and allocate 25% of a CPU core on our eight core machine to each of 16 hosts (i.e. a total of 50% load on the CPU). We set the buffer size of each switch to 50 packets per port, our best estimate for the switches used in the hardware testbed.

Figure 8 shows the normalized throughput achieved by the two routing strategies – ECMP and non-blocking – with Mininet-HiFi, alongside results from the Hedera paper for different traffic patterns. The Mininet-HiFi results are averaged over three runs. The traffic patterns in Figure 8(a) are all bijective; they should all achieve maximum throughput for a full bisection bandwidth network. This is indeed the case for the results with the "non-blocking" switch. The throughput is lower for ECMP because hash collisions decrease the overall throughput. We can expect more collisions if a flow traverses more links. All experiments show the same behavior, as seen in the `stride` traffic patterns. With increasing stride values (1, 2, 4 and 8), flows traverse more layers, decreasing throughput.

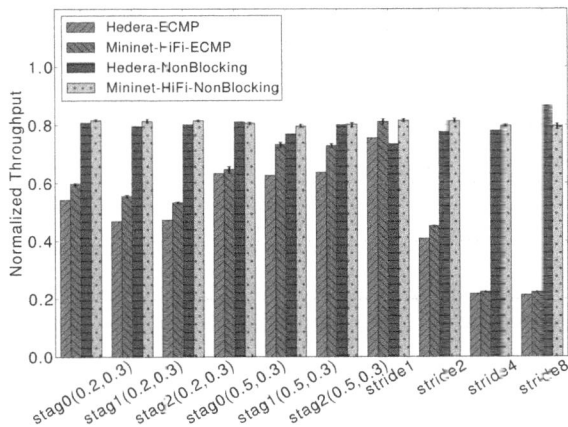

(a) Benchmark tests from Hedera paper (Part 1).

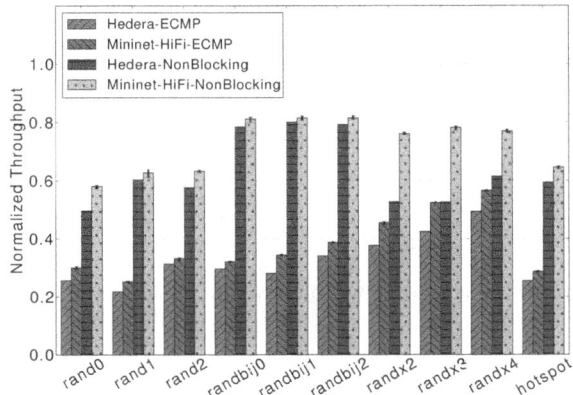

(b) Benchmark tests from Hedera paper (Part 2).

Figure 8: Effective throughput with ECMP routing on a $k = 4$ Fat Tree vs. an equivalent non-blocking switch. Links are set to 10 Mb/s in Mininet-HiFi and 1 Gb/s in the hardware testbed [13].

Remark: The ECMP results obtained on the Hedera testbed and Mininet-HiFi differed significantly for the `stride-1, 2, 4` and `8` traffic patterns shown in Figure 8(a). At higher stride levels that force all traffic through core switches, the aggregate throughput with ECMP should reduce. However, we found the extent of reduction reported for the Hedera testbed to be exactly consistent with spanning-tree routing results from Mininet-HiFi. We postulate that a misconfigured or low-entropy hash function may have unintentionally caused this style of routing. After several helpful discussions with the authors, we were unable to explain a drop in the ECMP performance reported in [13]. Therefore, we use spanning tree routing for Mininet-HiFi Hedera results for *ail* traffic patterns. For consistency with the original figures, we continue to use the "ECMP" label.

The Mininet-HiFi results closely match those from the hardware testbed; in 16 of the 20 traffic patterns they are nearly identical. In the remaining four traffic patterns (`randx2,3,4` and `stride8`) the results in the paper have lower throughput because – as the authors explain – the commercial switch in their testbed is built from two switching chips, so the total buffering depends on the traffic pattern. To validate these results, we would need to know the mapping of hosts to switch ports, which is unavailable.

The main takeaway from this experiment is that Mininet-HiFi reproduces the *performance* results for this set of datacenter networking experiments. It appears possible to collect meaningful results in advance of (or possibly without) setting up a hardware testbed. If a testbed is built, the code and test scripts used in Mininet-HiFi can be reused without change.

Verifying fidelity: Unlike DCTCP, the Hedera experiment depends on coarse-grained metrics such as aggregate throughput over a period of time. To ensure that no virtual

host starved and that the system had enough capacity to sustain the network demand, we measured idle time during the experiment (as described in §3.4). In all runs, the system had at least 35% idle CPU time every second. This measurement indicates that the OS was able to schedule all virtual hosts and packet transmissions without falling behind an ideal execution schedule on hardware.

Scaling the experiment: In the Hedera testbed, machines were equipped with 1 Gb/s network interfaces. We were unable to use Mininet-HiFi to replicate Hedera's results even with 100 Mb/s network links, as the virtual hosts did not have enough CPU capacity to saturate their network links. While Hedera's results do not qualitatively change when links are scaled down, it is a challenge to reproduce results that depend on the absolute value of link/CPU bandwidth.

5.3 Sizing Router Buffers

In our third example we reproduce results that were measured on a real hardware testbed to determine the number of packet buffers needed by a router. The original research paper on *buffer sizing* was presented at SIGCOMM 2004 [35]. All Internet routers contain buffers to hold packets during times of congestion. The size of the buffers is dictated by the dynamics of TCP's congestion control algorithm: the goal is to make sure that when a link is congested, it is busy 100% of the time, which is equivalent to making sure the buffer never goes empty. Prior to the paper, the common assumption was that each link needs a buffer of size $B = RTT \times C$, where RTT is the average round-trip time of a flow passing across the link and C is the data-rate of the bottleneck link. The authors showed that a link with n flows requires no more than $B = \frac{RTT \times C}{\sqrt{n}}$. The original paper included results from simulation and measurements from a real router, but not for a real network. Later, at SIGCOMM 2008, this result was demon-

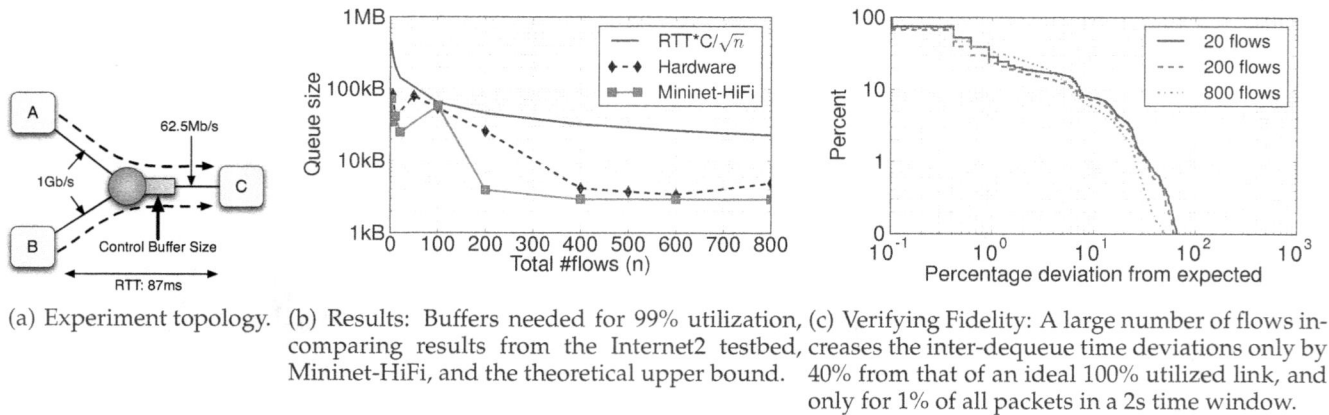

(a) Experiment topology. (b) Results: Buffers needed for 99% utilization, (c) Verifying Fidelity: A large number of flows increases the inter-dequeue time deviations only by comparing results from the Internet2 testbed, from Mininet-HiFi, and the theoretical upper bound. 40% from that of an ideal 100% utilized link, and only for 1% of all packets in a 2s time window.

Figure 9: Buffer sizing experiment.

strated on a hardware testbed running on the Internet2 backbone.[6]

To test the ability of Mininet-HiFi to emulate hundreds of simultaneous, interacting flows, we attempt to replicate this hardware experiment. We contacted the researchers and obtained results measured on their hardware testbed, then compared them with results from Mininet-HiFi; the Mininet-HiFi topology is shown in Figure 9(a). In the hardware experiments, a number of TCP flows go from a server at Stanford University (California) to at a server at Rice University (Houston, Texas) via a NetFPGA [36] IPv4 router in the Internet2 POP in Los Angeles. The link from LA to Houston is constrained to 62.5 Mb/s to create a bottleneck, and the end-to-end RTT was measured to be 87 ms. Once the flows are established, a script runs a binary search to find the buffer size needed for 99% utilization on the bottleneck link. Figure 9(b) shows results from theory, hardware, and Mininet-HiFi. Both Mininet-HiFi and hardware results are averaged over three runs; on Mininet-HiFi, the average CPU utilization did not exceed 5%.

Both results are bounded by the theoretical limit and confirm the new rule of thumb for sizing router buffers. Mininet-HiFi results show similar trends to the hardware results, with some points being nearly identical. If Mininet-HiFi had been available for this experiment, the researchers could have gained additional confidence that the testbed results would match the theory.

Verifying fidelity: Like the DCTCP experiment, the buffer sizing experiment relies on accurate link emulation at the bottleneck. However, the large number of TCP flows increases the total CPU load. We visualize the effect of system load on the distribution of deviation of inter-dequeue times from that of an ideal link. Figure 9(c) plots the CDF of deviations (in percentage) for varying numbers of flows. Even for 800 flows, more than 90% of all packets in a 2 s time interval were dequeued within 10% of the ideal dequeue time (of 193.8 μs for full-sized 1514 byte packets). Even though inter-dequeue times were off by 40% for 1% of all packets, results on Mininet-HiFi qualitatively matched that of hardware.

Scaling the experiment: The experiment described in the original paper used multiple hosts to generate a large number of TCP flows. To our surprise, we found that a single machine was capable of generating the same number (400–800) of flows and emulating the network with high fidelity. While results on Mininet-HiFi qualitatively matched hardware, we found that the exact values depended on the version of the kernel (and TCP stack).

6. PRACTICAL EXPERIENCES

After successfully replicating several experiments with Mininet-HiFi, the next step was to attempt to reproduce as broad a range of networking research results as possible, to learn the limits of the approach as well as how best to reproduce others' results. For this task we enlisted students in CS244, a masters-level course on Advanced Topics in Networking in Spring quarter 2012 at Stanford, and made reproducing research the theme of the final project. In this section, we describe the individual project outcomes along with lessons we learned from the assignment.

6.1 Project Assignment

The class included masters students, undergraduate seniors, and remote professionals, with systems programming experience ranging from a few class projects all the way to years of Linux kernel development. We divided the class of 37 students into 18 teams (17 pairs and one triple).

For their final project, students were given a simple, open-ended request: choose a published networking research paper and try to replicate its primary result using Mininet-HiFi on an Amazon EC2 instance. Teams had four weeks: one week to choose a paper, and three weeks to replicate it. Amazon kindly donated each student $100 of credit for use on

---

[6]Video of demonstration at http://www.youtube.com/watch?v=ykga6N_x27w.

Project	Image	Result to Replicate	Outcome
CoDel [37]		The Controlled Delay algorithm (CoDel) improves on RED and tail-drop queueing by keeping delays low in routers, adapting to bandwidth changes, and yielding full link throughput with configuration tweaking.	replicated + extra results
HULL [38]		By sacrificing a small amount of bandwidth, HULL can reduce average and tail latencies in data center networks.	replicated
MPTCP [39]		Multipath TCP increases performance over multiple wireless interfaces versus TCP and can perform seamless wireless handoffs.	replicated
		Over 3G and WiFi, optimized Multipath TCP with at least 600 KB of receive buffer can fully utilize both links.	replicated, w/differences
Outcast [40]		When TCP flows arrive at two input ports on a tail-drop switch and compete for the same output port, the port with fewer flows will see vastly degraded throughput.	replicated
		The problem described for Outcast [40] occurs in a topology made to show the problem, as well as in a Fat Tree topology, and routing style does not necessarily alleviate the issue.	replicated + extra results
Jellyfish [41]		Jellyfish, a randomly constructed network topology, can achieve good fairness using k-shortest paths routing, comparable to a Fat Tree using ECMP routing, by using MPTCP.	replicated + extra results
		Jellyfish, a randomly constructed network topology, can achieve similar and often superior average throughput to a Fat Tree.	replicated
DCTCP [14]		Data Center TCP obtains full throughput with lower queue size variability than TCP-RED, as long as the ECN marking threshold K is set above a reasonable threshold.	replicated
Hedera [13]		The Hedera data center network flow scheduler improves on ECMP throughput in a $k = 4$ Fat Tree, and as the number of flows per host increase, the performance gain of Hedera decreases.	replicated
Init CWND [42]		Increasing TCP's initial congestion window can significantly improve the completion times of typical TCP flows on the Web.	replicated
		Increasing TCP's initial congestion window tends to improve performance, but under lossy network conditions an overly large initial congestion window can hurt performance.	replicated
Incast [43]		Barrier-synchronized TCP workloads in datacenter Ethernets can cause significant reductions in application throughput.	unable to reproduce
DCell [44]		DCell, a recursively-defined data center network topology, provides higher bandwidth under heavy load than a tree topology.	replicated + extra results
		The routing algorithm used for DCell can adapt to failures.	replicated
FCT [45]		The relationship between Flow Completion Time (FCT) and flow size is not ideal for TCP; small flows take disproportionately long.	replicated
TCP Daytona [46]		A misbehaving TCP receiver can cause the TCP sender to deliver data to it at a much higher rate than its peers.	replicated
RED [47]		Random Early Detection (RED) gateways keep average queue size low while allowing occasional bursts of packets.	unable to reproduce

Table 2: Student projects for CS244 Spring 2012, in reverse chronological order. Each project was reproduced on Mininet-HiFi on an EC2 instance. The image for each project links to a full description, as well as instructions to replicate the full results, on the class blog: http://reproducingnetworkresearch.wordpress.com.

EC2. Each team created a blog post describing the project, focusing on a single question with a single result, with enough figures, data, and explanation to convince a reader that the team had actually reproduced the result – or discovered a limitation of the chosen paper, EC2, or Mininet-HiFi. As an added wrinkle, each team was assigned the task of running another team's project to reproduce their results, given only the blog post.

6.2 Project Outcomes

Table 2 lists the teams' project choices, the key results they tried to replicate, and the project outcomes. If you are viewing this paper electronically, clicking on each experiment image in the table will take you to the blog entry with instructions to reproduce the results. Students chose a wide range of projects, covering transport protocols, data center topologies, and queueing: MPTCP [48, 39], DCTCP [14], Incast [43], Outcast [40], RED [47], Flow Completion Time [45], Hedera [13], HULL [38], Jellyfish [41], DCell [44], CoDel [37], TCP Initial Congestion Window [42], and Misbehaving TCP Receivers [46]. In eight of the eighteen projects, the results were so new that they were only published after the class started in April 2012 (MPTCP Wireless, Jellyfish, HULL, TCP Outcast, and CoDel).

After three weeks, 16 of the 18 teams successfully reproduced at least one result from their chosen paper; only two teams could not reproduce the original result.[7] Four teams added new results, such as understanding the sensitivity of the result to a parameter not in the original paper. By "reproduced a result", we mean that the experiment may run at a slower link speed, but otherwise produces qualitatively equivalent results when compared to the results in the papers from hardware, simulation, or another emulated system. For some papers, the exact parameters were not described in sufficient detail to exactly replicate, so teams tried to match them as closely as possible.

All the project reports with the source code and instructions to replicate the results are available at `reproducingnetworkresearch.wordpress.com`, and we encourage the reader to view them online.

6.3 Lessons Learned

The most important thing we learned from the class is that paper replication with Mininet-HiFi on EC2 is reasonably *easy*; students with limited experience and limited time were able to complete a project in four weeks. Every team successfully validated another team's project, which we credit to the ability to quickly start a virtual machine in EC2 and to share a disk image publicly. All experiments could be repeated by another team in less than a day, and most could be repeated in less than an hour.

---

[7]The inability to replicate RED could be due to bugs in network emulation, a parameter misconfiguration, or changes to TCP in the last 20 years; for Incast, we suspect configuration errors, code errors, or student inexperience.

The second takeaway was the breadth of replicated projects; Table 2 shows that the scope of research questions for which Mininet HiFi is useful extends from high-level topology designs all the way down to low-level queueing behavior. With all projects publicly available and reproducible on EC2, the hurdle for extending, or even understanding these papers, is lower than before.

When was it easy? Projects went smoothly if they primarily required configuration. One example is TCP Outcast. In an earlier assignment to learn basic TCP behavior, students created a parking-lot topology with a row of switches, each with an attached host, and with all but one host sending to a single receiver. Students could measure the TCP sawtooth and test TCP's ability to share a link fairly. With many senders, the closest sender to the receiver saw lower throughput. In this case, simply configuring a few `iperf` senders and monitoring bandwidths was enough to demonstrate the TCP outcast problem, and every student did this inadvertently.

Projects in data center networking such as Jellyfish, Fat Tree, and DCell also went smoothly, as they could be built atop open-source routing software [49, 34]. Teams found it useful to debug experiments interactively by logging into their virtual hosts and generating traffic. A side benefit of writing control scripts for emulated (rather than simulated) hosts is that when the experiment moves to the real world, with physical switches and servers, the students' scripts can run without change [22].

When was it hard? When kernel patches were unavailable or unstable, teams hit brick walls. XCP and TCP Fast Open kernel patches were not available, requiring teams to choose different papers; another team wrestled with an unstable patch for setting microsecond-level TCP RTO values. In contrast, projects with functioning up-to-date patches (e.g. DCTCP, MPTCP, and CoDel) worked quickly. Kernel code was not strictly necessary – the Misbehaving TCP Receivers team modified a user-space TCP stack – but kernel code leads to higher-speed experiments.

Some teams reported difficulties scaling down link speeds to fit on Mininet-HiFi if the result depended on parameters whose dependence on link speed was not clear. For example, the Incast paper reports results for one hardware queue size and link rate, but it was not clear when to expect the same effect with slower links, or how to set the queue size [43]. In contrast, the DCTCP papers provided guidelines to set the key parameter K (the switch marking threshold) as a function of the link speed.

7. RELATED WORK

Techniques and platforms for network *emulation* have a rich history, and expanded greatly in the early 2000s. Testbeds such as PlanetLab [10] and Emulab [12] make available large numbers of machines and network links for researchers to programmatically instantiate experiments. These platforms use tools such as NIST Net [50], Dummynet [51], and `netem` [52], which each configure network link properties such as delays, drops and reordering. Emulators built on full-system virtualization [53], like DieCast [16] (which superseded ModelNet [54]) and several other projects [55], use virtual machines to realistically emulate end hosts. However, VM size and overhead may limit scalability, and variability introduced by hypervisor scheduling can reduce performance fidelity [56].

To address these issues, DieCast uses *time dilation* [29], a technique where a hypervisor slows down a VM's perceived passage of time to yield effectively faster link rates and better scalability. SliceTime [56] takes an alternate *synchronized virtual time* approach – a hybrid of emulation and simulation that trades off real-time operation to achieve scalability and timing accuracy. SliceTime runs hosts in VMs and synchronizes time between VMs and simulation, combining code fidelity with simulation control and visibility. FPGA-based simulators have demonstrated the ability to replicate data center results, including TCP Incast [43], using simpler processor cores [57].

The technique of *container-based virtualization* [23] has become increasingly popular due to its efficiency and scalability advantages over full-system virtualization. Mininet [22], Trellis [20], IMUNES [24], vEmulab [18], and Crossbow [58] exploit lightweight virtualization features built for their respective OSes. For example, Mininet uses Linux containers [30, 25], vEmulab uses FreeBSD jails, and IMUNES uses OpenSolaris zones.

Mininet-HiFi also exploits lightweight virtualization, but adds resource isolation and monitoring to verify that an experiment has run with high fidelity. In this paper, we have demonstrated not only the feasibility of a fidelity-tracking Container-Based Emulator on a single system, but also have shown that these techniques can be used to replicate previously published results.

8. DISCUSSION

We envision a world where every published research work is easily reproducible.[8] The sheer number and scope of the experiments covered in this paper – 19 successfully reproduced – suggest that this future direction for the network systems research community is possible with Container-Based Emulation. CBE, as demonstrated by Mininet-HiFi, meets the goals defined in Section 2 for a reproducible research platform, including functional realism, timing realism, topology flexibility, and easy replication at low cost.

Sometimes, however, CBE can replicate the *result*, but not the exact *experiment*, due to resource constraints. A single server running in real time will inevitably support limited aggregate bandwidth, single-link bandwidth, and numbers of processes. When scaling down an experiment, the right parameters may not be clear, e.g. queue sizes or algorithm

---

[8]Technical societies such as the ACM and IEEE can facilitate reproducible research by providing persistent online repositories for runnable papers.

tunables. A different result from the scaled-down version may indicate either a configuration error or a not-so-robust result, and the truth may not reveal itself easily.

We intend to build on the work of others to overcome these limits to experiment scale. In the space dimension, Model-Net [54] and DieCast [16] scale emulation to multiple servers. There are research challenges with using this approach in the cloud, such as measuring and ensuring bandwidth between machines with time-varying and placement-dependent network performance. In the time dimension, Time Dilation [29] and SliceTime [56] show methods to slow down the time perceived by applications to run an experiment with effectively larger resources. Perhaps our fidelity measurement techniques could enable a time-dilating CBE to adapt automatically and run any experiment at the minimum slowdown that yields the required level of fidelity.

As a community we seek high-quality results, but our results are rarely reproduced. It is our hope that this paper will spur such a change, by convincing authors to make their next paper a runnable one, built on a CBE, with public results, code, and instructions posted online. If enough authors meet this challenge, the default permissions for network systems papers will change from "read only" to "read, write and execute" – enabling "runnable conference proceedings" where every paper can be independently validated and easily built upon.

9. ACKNOWLEDGMENTS

This runnable and largely "crowd-sourced" paper would not have been possible without the dedicated efforts of the students who developed the 18 reproducible experiments in Table 2: Rishita Anubhai, Carl Case, Vaibhav Chidrewar, Christophe Chong, Harshit Chopra, Elliot Conte, Justin Costa-Roberts, MacKenzie Cumings, Jack Dubie, Diego Giovanni Franco, Drew Haven, Benjamin Helsley, John Hiesey, Camille Lamy, Frank Li. Maxine Lim, Joseph Marrama, Omid Mashayekhi, Tom McLaughlin, Eric Muthuri Mibuari, Gary Miguel, Chanh Nguyen, Jitendra Nath Pandey, Anusha Ramesh, David Schneider, Ben Shapero, Angad Singh, Daniel Sommermann, Raman Subramanian, Emin Topalovic, Josh Valdez, Amogh Vasekar, RJ Walsh, Phumchanit Watanaprakornkul, James Whitbeck, Timothy Wong, and Kun Yi.

We are grateful to the anonymous reviewers and our shepherd Sonia Fahmy for their valuable comments and feedback, which helped to improve the final version. We thank the Hedera, Buffer Sizing, and DCTCP authors for sharing their experiment code. This work was partly funded by NSF FIA award CNS-1040190 (NEBULA), the Stanford University Clean Slate Program, and a Hewlett-Packard Fellowship.

References

[1] D. E. Knuth. Literate Programming. *The Computer Journal [Online]*, 27:97–111, 1984.

[2] J. Claerbout. Electronic documents give reproducible research a new

meaning. *Proc. 62nd Ann. Int. Meeting of the Soc. of Exploration Geophysics*, pages 601–604, 1992.

[3] J. B. Buckheit and D. L. Donoho. Wavelab and reproducible research. *Time*, 474:55–81, 1995.

[4] P. Vandewalle, J. Kovacevic, and M. Vetterli. Reproducible research. *Computing in Science Engineering*, pages 5–7, 2008.

[5] Amazon Elastic Compute Cloud. http://aws.amazon.com.

[6] The network simulator - ns-2. http://nsnam.isi.edu/nsnam/.

[7] The ns-3 network simulator. http://www.nsnam.org/.

[8] OPNET modeler.
http://www.opnet.com/solutions/network_rd/modeler.html.

[9] Global Environment for Network Innovations. http://www.geni.net/.

[10] B. Chun, D. Culler, T. Roscoe, A. Bavier, L. Peterson, M. Wawrzoniak, and M. Bowman. Planetlab: an overlay testbed for broad-coverage services. *SIGCOMM Computer Communication Review*, 33(3):3–12, 2003.

[11] J. DeHart, F. Kuhns, J. Parwatikar, J. Turner, C. Wiseman, and K. Wong. The open network laboratory. In *SIGCSE '06 Technical Symposium on Computer Science Education*, pages 107–111. ACM, 2006.

[12] Emulab - network emulation testbed. http://emulab.net/.

[13] M. Al-Fares, S. Radhakrishnan, B. Raghavan, N. Huang, and A. Vahdat. Hedera: Dynamic flow scheduling for data center networks. In *NSDI '10*. USENIX, 2010.

[14] M. Alizadeh, A. Greenberg, D. A. Maltz, J. Padhye, P. Patel, B. Prabhakar, S. Sengupta, and M. Sridharan. Data Center TCP (DCTCP). In *SIGCOMM '10*, pages 63–74. ACM, 2010.

[15] N. Beheshti, Y. Ganjali, R. Rajaduray, D. Blumenthal, and N. McKeown. Buffer sizing in all-optical packet switches. In *Optical Fiber Communication Conference*. Optical Society of America, 2006.

[16] D. Gupta, K. V. Vishwanath, and A. Vahdat. DieCast: Testing distributed systems with an accurate scale model. In *NSDI '08*, pages 407–421. USENIX, 2008.

[17] Open vSwitch: An open virtual switch. http://openvswitch.org/.

[18] M. Hibler, R. Ricci, L. Stoller, J. Duerig, S. Guruprasad, T. Stack, K. Webb, and J. Lepreau. Large-scale virtualization in the Emulab network testbed. In *USENIX '08 Annual Technical Conference*, pages 113–128, Berkeley, CA, USA, 2008. USENIX.

[19] M. Pizzonia and M. Rimondini. Netkit: easy emulation of complex networks on inexpensive hardware. In *International Conference on Testbeds and research infrastructures for the development of networks & communities*, TridentCom '08, pages 7:1–7:10, Brussels, Belgium, 2008. ICST.

[20] S. Bhatia, M. Motiwala, W. Muhlbauer, Y. Mundada, V. Valancius, A. Bavier, N. Feamster, L. Peterson, and J. Rexford. Trellis: a platform for building flexible, fast virtual networks on commodity hardware. In *CoNEXT '08*, pages 72:1–72:6. ACM, 2008.

[21] J. Ahrenholz, C. Danilov, T. Henderson, and J. Kim. CORE: A real-time network emulator. In *Military Communications Conference, MILCOM '08*, pages 1–7. IEEE, 2008.

[22] B. Lantz, B. Heller, and N. McKeown. A network in a laptop: rapid prototyping for software-defined networks. In *HotNets '10*, pages 19:1–19:6. ACM, 2010.

[23] S. Soltesz, H. Pötzl, M. Fiuczynski, A. Bavier, and L. Peterson. Container-based operating system virtualization: a scalable, high-performance alternative to hypervisors. *ACM SIGOPS Operating Systems Review*, 41(3):275–287, 2007.

[24] M. Zec and M. Mikuc. Operating system support for integrated network emulation in IMUNES. In *Workshop on Operating System and Architectural Support for the on demand IT InfraStructure (OASIS)*, 2004.

[25] cgroups.
http://www.kernel.org/doc/Documentation/cgroups/cgroups.txt.

[26] P. Turner, B. B. Rao, and N. Rao. CPU bandwidth control for CFS. In *Linux Symposium '10*, pages 245–254, 2010.

[27] Handigol, N., Heller, B., Jeyakumar, V., Lantz, B., and McKeown, N. CSTR 2012-02 Mininet performance fidelity benchmarks.
http://hci.stanford.edu/cstr/reports/2012-02.pdf.

[28] Linux Trace Toolkit - next generation. http://lttng.org/.

[29] D. Gupta, K. Yocum, M. McNett, A. Snoeren, A. Vahdat, and G. Voelker. To infinity and beyond: time warped network emulation. In *SOSP '05*, pages 1–2. ACM, 2005.

[30] lxc linux containers. http://lxc.sf.net.

[31] K. Ramakrishnan and S. Floyd. A proposal to add explicit congestion notification (ECN) to IP. Technical report, RFC 2481, January 1999.

[32] DCTCP patches.
http://www.stanford.edu/~alizade/Site/DCTCP.html.

[33] D. Thaler and C. Hopps. Multipath issues in unicast and multicast next-hop selection. Technical report, RFC 2991, November 2000.

[34] Ripcord-Lite for POX: A simple network controller for OpenFlow-based data centers. https://github.com/brandonheller/riplpox.

[35] G. Appenzeller, I. Keslassy, and N. McKeown. Sizing router buffers. In *SIGCOMM '04*, pages 281–292. ACM, 2004.

[36] J. Lockwood, N. McKeown, G. Watson, G. Gibb, P. Hartke, J. Naous, R. Raghuraman, and J. Luo. NetFPGA – an open platform for gigabit-rate network switching and routing. In *Microelectronic Systems Education, MSE '07*, pages 160–161. IEEE, 2007.

[37] K. Nichols and V. Jacobson. Controlling queue delay. *Communications of the ACM*, 55(7):42–50, 2012.

[38] M. Alizadeh, A. Kabbani, T. Edsall, B. Prabhakar, A. Vahdat, and M. Yasuda. Less is more: Trading a little bandwidth for ultra-low latency in the data center. In *NSDI '12*. USENIX, 2012.

[39] C. Raiciu, C. Paasch, S. Barre, A. Ford, M. Honda, F. Duchene, O. Bonaventure, and M. Handley. How hard can it be? designing and implementing a deployable multipath TCP. In *NSDI '12*, pages 29–29. USENIX, 2012.

[40] P. Prakash, A. Dixit, Y. Hu, and R. Kompella. The TCP outcast problem: Exposing unfairness in data center networks. In *NSDI '12*. USENIX, 2012.

[41] A. Singla, C.-Y. Hong, L. Popa, and P. B. Godfrey. Jellyfish: Networking data centers randomly. In *NSDI '12*. USENIX, 2012.

[42] N. Dukkipati, T. Refice, Y. Cheng, J. Chu, T. Herbert, A. Agarwal, A. Jain, and N. Sutin. An argument for increasing TCP's initial congestion window. *SIGCOMM Computer Communication Review*, 40(3):27–33, 2010.

[43] V. Vasudevan, A. Phanishayee, H. Shah, E. Krevat, D. Andersen, G. Ganger, G. Gibson, and B. Mueller. Safe and effective fine-grained TCP retransmissions for datacenter communication. *SIGCOMM Computer Communication Review*, 39(4):303–314, 2009.

[44] C. Guo, H. Wu, K. Tan, L. Shi, Y. Zhang, and S. Lu. DCell: a scalable and fault-tolerant network structure for data centers. In *SIGCOMM '08*. ACM, 2008.

[45] N. Dukkipati and N. McKeown. Why flow-completion time is the right metric for congestion control. *SIGCOMM Computer Communication Review*, 36(1):59–62, 2006.

[46] S. Savage, N. Cardwell, D. Wetherall, and T. Anderson. TCP congestion control with a misbehaving receiver. *SIGCOMM Computer Communication Review*, 29(5):71–78, 1999.

[47] S. Floyd and V. Jacobson. Random Early Detection gateways for congestion avoidance. *IEEE/ACM Transactions on Networking*, 1(4):397–413, 1993.

[48] C. Raiciu, S. Barre, C. Pluntke, A. Greenhalgh, D. Wischik, and M. Handley. Improving datacenter performance and robustness with multipath TCP. In *SIGCOMM Computer Communication Review*. ACM, 2011.

[49] The OpenFlow switch. http://www.openflow.org.

[50] M. Carson and D. Santay. NIST Net – a Linux-based network emulation tool. *SIGCOMM Computer Communication Review*, 33(3):111–126, 2003.

[51] M. Carbone and L. Rizzo. Dummynet revisited. *SIGCOMM Computer Communication Review*, 40(2):12–20, 2010.

[52] Linux network emulation module. http://www.linuxfoundation.org/collaborate/workgroups/networking/netem.

[53] P. Barham, B. Dragovic, K. Fraser, S. Hand, T. Harris, A. Ho, R. Neugebauer, I. Pratt, and A. Warfield. Xen and the art of virtualization. In *SOSP '03*, pages 164–177. ACM, 2003.

[54] A. Vahdat, K. Yocum, K. Walsh, P. Mahadevan, D. Kostić, J. Chase, and D. Becker. Scalability and accuracy in a large-scale network emulator. In *OSDI '02*, pages 271–284. USENIX, 2002.

[55] OpenFlow Virtual Machine Simulation.
http://www.openflow.org/wk/index.php/OpenFlowVMS.

[56] E. Weingärtner, F. Schmidt, H. Vom Lehn, T. Heer, and K. Wehrle. Slicetime: A platform for scalable and accurate network emulation. In *NSDI '11*, volume 3. ACM, 2011.

[57] Z. Tan, K. Asanovic, and D. Patterson. An FPGA-based simulator for datacenter networks. In *Exascale Evaluation and Research Techniques Workshop (EXERT '10), at ASPLOS '10*. ACM, 2010.

[58] S. Tripathi, N. Droux, K. Belgaied, and S. Khare. Crossbow virtual wire: network in a box. In *LISA '09*, pages 4–4. USENIX, 2009.

A SOFT Way for OpenFlow Switch Interoperability Testing

Maciej Kuźniar[†]   Peter Perešíni[†]   Marco Canini[‡*]   Daniele Venzano[†]   Dejan Kostić[•*]

[†]EPFL, Switzerland   [‡]TU Berlin / T-Labs, Germany   [•]Institute IMDEA Networks, Spain

[†]{name.surname}@epfl.ch   [‡]m.canini@tu-berlin.de   [•]dkostic@imdea.org

ABSTRACT

The increasing adoption of Software Defined Networking, and OpenFlow in particular, brings great hope for increasing extensibility and lowering costs of deploying new network functionality. A key component in these networks is the OpenFlow agent, a piece of software that a switch runs to enable remote programmatic access to its forwarding tables. While testing high-level network functionality, the correct behavior and interoperability of any OpenFlow agent are taken for granted. However, existing tools for testing agents are not exhaustive nor systematic, and only check that the agent's basic functionality works. In addition, the rapidly changing and sometimes vague OpenFlow specifications can result in multiple implementations that behave differently.

This paper presents SOFT, an approach for testing the interoperability of OpenFlow switches. Our key insight is in automatically identifying the testing inputs that cause different OpenFlow agent implementations to behave inconsistently. To this end, we first symbolically execute each agent under test in isolation to derive which set of inputs causes which behavior. We then crosscheck all distinct behaviors across different agent implementations and evaluate whether a common input subset causes inconsistent behaviors. Our evaluation shows that our tool identified several inconsistencies between the publicly available Reference OpenFlow switch and Open vSwitch implementations.

Categories and Subject Descriptors

C.2.6 [**Computer-Communication Networks**]: Internetworking—*Routers*; C.4 [**Performance of Systems**]: Reliability, availability, and serviceability; D.2.5 [**Software Engineering**]: Testing and Debugging—*Symbolic execution*

Keywords

Switches, Bugs, Reliability, OpenFlow, Symbolic execution

---

[*]Work done when the author was with EPFL.

1. INTRODUCTION

Software defined networking (SDN) holds the promise to lower the barrier for deploying and managing new functionality in networks. For example, Google recently outlined how it uses SDN to solve the problem of scheduling bursty traffic among its datacenters [1]. The main thrust in SDN is currently OpenFlow [21]. In OpenFlow, the software running at a logically centralized controller manages a collection of switches hosting programmable forwarding tables.

It is crucial to have reliable networks, and this requirement does not change with SDN. Unfortunately, with the introduction of greater programmability, the chances of software faults (or bugs) are also on the rise. Debugging application software that runs at the controller has recently started receiving attention. For example, NICE [11] subjects the controller software to a wide range of packet streams to uncover race conditions and other bugs.

However, an aspect that is mostly going unnoticed is that OpenFlow switches also run software, which must behave correctly. This software takes the name of *OpenFlow agent*, and its role is to expose a standardized programmatic interface to the switch forwarding tables and to handle the communication with the controller. However, while testing high-level network functionality, the interoperability and correct behavior of any OpenFlow agent are taken for granted. In practice, a real OpenFlow deployment likely has switches from multiple vendors managed by one or more controllers. To ensure correct network operation, *all* switches must work properly. In other words, it may take just one buggy switch to cause problems in the form of lost connectivity, unauthorized accesses, traffic overload, and so on. If failures start occurring in OpenFlow deployments, *the hard-earned ability to innovate in the networking space will be severely hampered by mistrust*. In addition, hardware switches run OpenFlow agents in the form of embedded firmware. Firmware is difficult to upgrade due to the impact of downtime, has longer debug cycles than ordinary software, and is notoriously challenging to troubleshoot in the wild [23]. These issues only raise the importance of trying to ensure that the firmware is right during its development stage.

Several issues make it difficult to produce error-free switch software. Consider that just the rule installation command (`Flow Mod`) in the OpenFlow specifications [5] is two and a half pages long. Moreover, the specifications are in rapid flux (going through three revisions in slightly over one year). Further, even given specifications have interpretation ambiguities or gives explicit implementation freedom. In some cases, vendors do not even follow the specifications [22].

Despite advances in writing provably correct software, testing remains the prime technique for ensuring dependability. We observe that local testing and debugging (*e.g.*, by using OFTest [2]) can get the basic functionality working. Beyond this, the only way of gaining confidence in the behavior of multiple different switches currently is interoperability testing. One way of doing this involves placing personnel and switches at a third-party location for several days, and running OFTest and similar test suites [3]. Besides being expensive, this task is complex, in part because the number of new OpenFlow switch implementations is quickly growing. Of course, any new version of the specifications require a new round of interoperability testing.

Moreover, since local test suites are unlikely to be exhaustive, the above interoperability testing will not be exhaustive either. For instance, vendors typically test control plane software using manually-composed test cases, refined over time. Evidence shows that critical interoperability bugs survive this process. For example, in two recent episodes, 100% protocol-compliant BGP messages caused significant connectivity problems [6, 7]. These examples strongly confirm that local test cases are incomplete even for well-established router software.

Towards achieving exhaustive testing, we propose an approach to interoperability testing that leverages the multiple, existing OpenFlow implementations and herein identifies potential interoperability problems by crosschecking their behaviors. Exploring code behaviors in a systematic way is key to observe behavioral inconsistencies. Researchers recently applied symbolic execution [18], a systematic program code analysis technique, to test systems software with considerable success [8, 9, 12]. Symbolic execution effectively asks the code itself to provide the test inputs that are needed to traverse all code paths at least once. The reasoning here is that it is sufficient to test each code path once to exercise all behaviors. Doing this is relatively simple for single-machine code, while trying to find memory-related bugs.

While appealing, the use of symbolic execution is generally met with the scalability challenges of exhaustive path coverage, which we must face. In addition, it would not be practical to assume that a tool for interoperability testing would have access to the source code of commercial OpenFlow implementations from all vendors.[1] It is then our goal to make symbolic execution scale to crosscheck different OpenFlow implementations and find interoperability issues *without having simultaneous access to all source codes*.

In this paper, we introduce SOFT (Systematic OpenFlow Testing), a tool that automates interoperability testing of OpenFlow switches. Operating in two phases, SOFT uses symbolic execution and constraint solving. In the first testing phase, symbolic execution runs locally on each vendor's source code. Then, using the outputs of symbolic execution (not the source codes), SOFT determines the input ranges (*e.g.*, fields in OpenFlow messages) that cause two OpenFlow agent implementations to exhibit different behaviors.

Unlike normal execution, symbolic execution runs a program with symbolic variables as inputs. A symbolic vari-

able initially has no constraints on its actual value. As the execution progresses, the possible values of symbolic variables become constrained based on how the program uses these variables (*e.g.*, in conditional expressions). At every code branch based on a symbolic variable, symbolic execution logically forks and follows both branches, on each path maintaining a set of constraints, called the path condition, which must hold for the execution of that path.

Using symbolic execution as a base for interoperability testing is conceptually similar to checking functional equivalence on a per-path basis. Assume we have two functions that take a single argument and implement the same algorithm in different ways. We can check functional equivalence by simply feeding them the same symbolic argument and verifying they return the same value. In practice, when applying symbolic execution to OpenFlow agent testing, we must address several challenges. First, the input space is theoretically infinite as an OpenFlow agent is a non-terminating program. Simply limiting the input space (*i.e.*, OpenFlow messages and data packets) to N symbolic bytes is not effective, given that it means feeding completely unstructured inputs. Intuitively, with such inputs, the symbolic execution engine would quickly run into the path explosion problem (number of paths grows exponentially with the number of branches on symbolic inputs). Second, there is no immediate or a standard way to compare the behaviors of different agents. Demanding modifications to the agents' source code for inspecting the state is clearly undesirable. Third, the straightforward equivalence check outlined above requires simultaneous access to both OpenFlow agents' source codes, which is likely to be impossible for commercial implementations.

The contributions of this paper are as follows:

1. We use symbolic execution to systematically identify and collate code paths in OpenFlow agents to determine input subspaces that result in the same outputs. To achieve this, we address the difficult problems of managing the combination of symbolic and concrete inputs, as well as determining internal agent state by observing external actions. This step overcomes the first challenge in applying symbolic execution to interoperability testing.

2. We demonstrate a novel use of a constraint solver to compute an intersection of input subspaces belonging to different agent implementations. By doing so, we quickly determine inputs that cause different behavior in multiple agents (inconsistencies). In addition, we do so without an *a priori* definition of correct behavior and overcome the second challenge (crosschecking implementation behaviors). This phase is separate from symbolic execution and does not require access to source code. By this virtue, it addresses the third aforementioned challenge.

3. We demonstrate the effectiveness of our approach by applying it to the Reference Switch (55K LoC) and Open vSwitch (80K LoC), the two publicly available OpenFlow agent implementations. SOFT quickly finds several inconsistencies between the two. Further, we demonstrate SOFT's effectiveness in finding manually injected differences.

The remainder of this paper is organized as follows. We provide an overview of our approach in Section 2, and follow it with the detailed description in Section 3. Section 4 contains the details of our prototype, and we proceed to evaluate it in Section 5. We place our work in the context of related work in Section 6 and conclude in Section 7.

---

[1]Although modern symbolic execution engines only require access to the binary code, this still needs to be produced with a particular compiler or be interpreted at runtime, which may incur impractical overhead. Also, it may not be possible to simply use the binary form since the execution environment is generally not known a priori.

2. OVERVIEW

In this section, we first give a brief introduction to symbolic execution, the technique our approach is built on. Next, we describe the kind of implementation inconsistencies we target. We then use an example to guide an overview of our approach and discuss the intended usage of SOFT.

2.1 Symbolic execution

Our approach is inspired by the successful use of symbolic execution [18] in automated testing of systems software [8–10, 12, 15]. The idea behind symbolic execution is to exercise all possible paths in a given program. Therefore, unlike normal execution which runs the program with concrete values, symbolic execution runs program code on symbolic input variables, which are initially allowed to take any value. During symbolic execution, code is executed normally until it reaches a branch instruction where the conditional expression *expr* depends (either directly or indirectly) on a symbolic value. At this point, program execution is logically forked into two executions—one path where the variables involved in *expr* must be constrained to make *expr* true; another path where *expr* must be false. Internally, the symbolic execution engine invokes a constraint solver to verify the feasibility of each path. Then, program execution resumes and continues down all feasible paths. On each path, the symbolic execution engine maintains a set of constraints, called the path condition, which must hold for the execution of that path. For every explored path, symbolic execution passes the path condition to a constraint solver to create a test case with the respective input values that led execution on that path. Since program state is (logically) copied at each branch, the symbolic execution engine can explore multiple paths simultaneously or independently.

Like others [19], we observe that, to deal with loops, symbolic execution would potentially need to explore an unbounded number of paths. As described in Section 3.2, we effectively side-step this problem by exploiting knowledge of the OpenFlow message grammar to construct inputs that ensure we explore a bounded number of paths.

Therefore, symbolic execution is a powerful program analysis technique—rather than having a linear execution where concrete values are used, symbolic execution covers a tree of executions where symbolic values are used. However, the usefulness of symbolic execution is limited by its scalability because the number of paths through a program generally grows exponentially in the number of branches on symbolic inputs. This problem is commonly known as the "path explosion" problem. The path explosion is exacerbated by the fact that the program under test interacts with its environment, e.g., by invoking OS system calls and calls to various library functions. External functions present an additional problem if the symbolic execution engine does not have visibility into their source code. A typical solution to this problem is to abstract away the complexity of the underlying execution environment using models. These models are typically a simplified implementation of a certain subsystem such as file system, network communication, etc.. Besides using environment models to "scale" symbolic execution, it is possible and often sufficiently practical to selectively mark as symbolic only the inputs that are relevant for the current analysis. As we show later in Section 3, carefully mixing symbolic and concrete inputs is key to being able to symbolically execute OpenFlow agents.

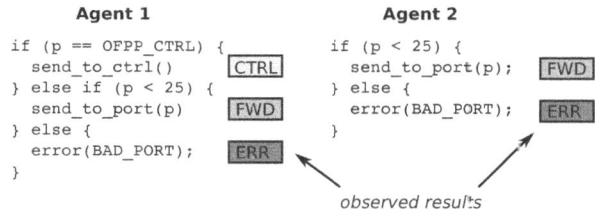

Figure 1: Example OpenFlow agents having different PACKET_OUT message implementations.

2.2 Defining inconsistencies

Switches that are capable of supporting the OpenFlow Switch Specification [5] do so by running an OpenFlow agent. This agent is a piece of software primarily responsible for state management. It receives and processes control messages sent by OpenFlow controllers (*e.g.*, Flow Mod, Packet Out, *etc.*), and configures the switch forwarding tables accordingly to the given commands. In addition, the OpenFlow agent may take part in packet forwarding itself—in a hardware switch, for packets that are forwarded to the controller; in a pure software implementation, for every packet.

As such, the execution of the OpenFlow agent is mainly driven by external events (*e.g.*, rule installation requests). *We call inputs the data reaching the agent as part of either OpenFlow control messages or packets.*

Intuitively, an *inconsistency* occurs when two (or more) OpenFlow agents which are presented with the same input sequence produce different results. Here, results refer to both externally observable consequences when processing an input (*e.g.*, replying to a request for flow table statistics), and internal state changes (*e.g.*, updating the flow table with a new entry).

To be able to identify inconsistencies, we assume the agents support the OpenFlow interface and we check for inconsistencies in operations at the interface level. To crosscheck behaviors, we rely either on externally observable results or, when necessary, on probe packets to infer the internal state.

Note that, in the case of hardware switches, we are not interested to verify the underlying switching hardware correctness. In fact, such verification is typically already part of the ASIC design process. However, we assume that there is a way to execute the OpenFlow agent without the switching hardware, *e.g.*, through an emulation layer that is commonly readily available for development and testing purposes.

2.3 Example

Our approach to automatically finding inconsistencies among OpenFlow agent implementations is most easily introduced through an example.

Consider an input sequence that only includes one control message of type Packet Out. This message instructs the OpenFlow agent to send out a packet on port p, where p is a 16-bit unsigned integer that identifies a specific port or is equal to one of several preset constants (*e.g.*, flood the packet or send to controller). For the sake of presentation, we assume that only p is symbolic (*i.e.*, p is the only part of this input that varies) and we omit the case $p = 0$ (for which an error message would be produced).

We first symbolically execute an OpenFlow agent implementation while feeding it with this input sequence. When executing symbolically, we automatically partition the in-

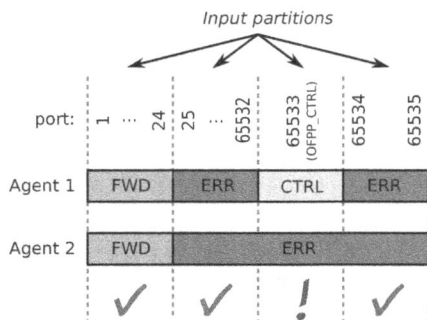

Figure 2: Input space partitions & inconsistency check.

put space of p into several subspaces. Each subspace is an equivalence class of inputs that, in this case, describes which values of p follow the same code path. To make the point more tangible, consider Agent 1 in Figure 1: if $p \in [1, 24]$ the program executes the code path that sends the packet on port p; if $p =$ OFPP_CTRL (the predefined controller port) the program executes a different code path that encapsulates the packet in a **Packet In** message and sends it to the controller; and so on. Besides determining the input space partition, we log the output results produced when executing each code path (*e.g.*, we log what packet comes out from which port). Therefore, for each input subspace there exists a corresponding output trace.

Next, we symbolically execute a different OpenFlow agent implementation (Agent 2 in Figure 1) and determine the partitions of input space of p. However, assume that this second OpenFlow agent does not support the special port number OFPP_CTRL. Instead, the program sends an error message to the controller when it encounters this case. Likewise, we log the output results produced when executing each code path.

At this point, we have two input space partitions (one for each OpenFlow agent implementation), as depicted in Figure 2. Within each partition, we then group the subspaces by output result (illustrated with different colors in Figure 2). That is, we merge together two subspaces (two code paths), if they produce the same outputs. Such grouping results in two coarse-grained input space partitions–one for each agent. Next, we consider the cross product of the coarse-grained partitions (*i.e.*, all pair-wise combinations of subspaces between the two partitions). From the cross product, we exclude pairs of subspaces that correspond to identical output results. Finally, we intersect the two subspaces in every remaining pair. A *non-empty intersection* defines a subspace of inputs that give different results for different OpenFlow agents: this is an inconsistency. For each inconsistency we discover, we construct a concrete test case that reproduces the observed results. Relative to our current example, we identify that one inconsistency exists and, to reproduce it, we construct the example with input $p =$ OFPP_CTRL as illustrated in Figure 2.

2.4 Usage

OpenFlow switch vendors can use SOFT for interoperability testing in two phases. In the first phase, each vendor independently runs SOFT on its OpenFlow agent implementation to produce a set of intermediate results that contain the input space partitions and the relative output results.

One benefit of this approach is that a vendor does not require access to the code of other vendors.

In the second phase, SOFT collects and crosschecks these intermediate results to identify inconsistencies. This phase can take place as a part of an inter-vendor agreement (*e.g.*, under an NDA), or during wider interoperability events [3]. Alternatively, a third-party organization such as Open Networking Foundation (ONF) may conduct the tests.

While we focus the presentation of SOFT on interoperability testing, we want to clarify that there exist other applications. For example, SOFT can automate performing regression testing. In addition, it can be used to compare against a well-known set of path conditions that are bootstrapped from unit tests.

We observe that an OpenFlow agent is potentially a software component of a hardware device. As such, some operations can install state directly in the switching hardware (*e.g.*, forwarding rules), seemingly outside of SOFT's reach. We note, however, that vendors typically have a way of running their firmware inside a hardware emulator for testing purposes. We only require that the hardware emulator is integrated with the symbolic execution engine. Previous work (*e.g.*, [12]) demonstrates that it is indeed possible to run complex software systems live, including closed-source device drivers.

3. SYSTEMATIC OPENFLOW TESTING

Our goal is to enable systematic exploration of inconsistencies across multiple OpenFlow agent implementations. In other words, we want to find whether there exists any sequence of inputs under which one OpenFlow agent behaves differently than another agent. To do this, we require a way of (*i*) constructing sequences of test inputs that cover all possible executions for each OpenFlow agent, and (*ii*) comparing the output results that each input produces to identify inconsistencies.

We accomplish the subgoal of finding test inputs by using symbolic execution. The outcome of symbolic execution is twofold: (*i*) a list of path conditions, each of which summarizes the input constraints that must hold during the execution of a given path, and (*ii*) a log of the observed output results for each path executed.

We then identify inconsistencies by grouping the path conditions that share the same output results on a per-agent basis and finding the input subspaces that satisfy the conjunction of the path conditions. Figure 3 provides an illustration of the operation of SOFT as described above. In the remainder of this section, we discuss our approach in detail. After a brief description of a strawman approach for utilizing symbolic execution in functional equivalence testing, we analyze improvements required to apply it to complex software such as OpenFlow agents. Finally, we discuss how we solve the second problem, namely collecting and comparing relevant outputs.

3.1 Automating equivalence testing

Our form of interoperability testing can be viewed as checking the functional equivalence of different OpenFlow agents at the interface level (*i.e.*, the OpenFlow API). To understand how we can use symbolic execution for this purpose, let us first consider a simpler problem.

A strawman approach. Assume we have two functions that implement the same algorithm differently and we want

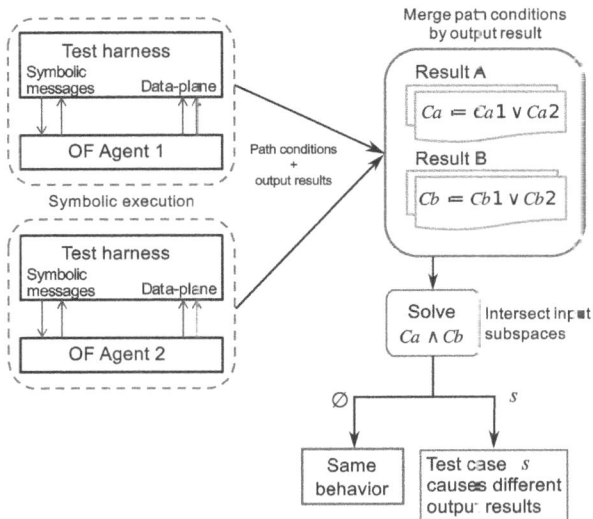

Figure 3: SOFT overview.

to test if they are indeed functionally equivalent. To do this, it is sufficient to symbolically execute both functions by passing identical symbolic inputs to both of them and checking whether they return the same value. If the results differ, the symbolic execution engine can construct a test case to exercise the problematic code path. In essence, symbolic execution enables us to crosscheck the two functions' results through all possible execution paths. This simple approach is sound, *i.e.*, it identifies all cases where results differ, provided that symbolic execution can solve all constraints it encounters. It is also relatively straightforward to extend this approach to crosscheck console utility programs by running with the same symbolic environment and comparing the data printed to `stdout`, as shown in [9].

Challenges and approach. Scaling up this approach to our target system is not an easy task. An OpenFlow agent is a non-terminating, event-driven program that interacts intensely with its environment. In this case, the environment consists of the network data plane, other switch components (*e.g.*, FIB) and the controller.

The first challenge this raises is that the input space is inherently infinite, thus making the problem of comparing OpenFlow agents over unbounded inputs intractable. Instead, to make our problem tractable, we must limit the length of any input sequence used for testing.

Secondly, crosschecking the results of different OpenFlow agents is challenging because there exists no notion such as "switch return value". Furthermore, there does not exist a universal `stdout` format that enables textual comparison unlike console utilities. Instead, we must collect a trace of switch *output results* that enables comparison using detailed information from both the OpenFlow and the data plane interfaces. In other words, we must for example capture packets and OpenFlow messages emitted by the switch, and maintain a non-ambiguous representation of these events.

Third, the approach above works by feeding both functions with the same symbolic input. In turn this requires that both agents be locally available. However, we cannot assume that SOFT will operate on different OpenFlow agents at the same time. Instead, we make a conscious de-sign choice to decouple the symbolic execution phase from the crosschecking phase.

3.2 Creating symbolic inputs

An OpenFlow agent reacts to OpenFlow messages and data plane packets it receives. Therefore, sequences of such messages can be considered inputs to the agent. In this subsection, we only consider the control channel inputs (the messages sent by the controller) because our goal is to test a switch at the OpenFlow interface (and not the data plane interface).

3.2.1 Structuring inputs

Feeding unstructured inputs is ineffective. As the input space containing sequences of arbitrary numbers of arbitrary messages is infinite, we need to enforce the maximum length of the sequence. A straightforward way to limit the input size would be to use N-byte symbolic inputs, with N bounded. Unfortunately, this approach quickly hits the scalability limits of exhaustive path exploration because these inputs do not contain any information that is of either syntactic or semantic value. As a result, symbolic execution must consider all possible ways in which these symbolic inputs can be interpreted (most of which represent invalid inputs anyway) to exhaust all paths. As an example, consider feeding an agent with the mentioned sequence of N symbolic bytes. Since there exist different types of control messages, some of which have variable lengths, this stream of N bytes can be parsed (depending on its content) as: one message of N bytes, or as any combination of two messages whose lengths add up to N, or as combinations of three messages, *etc.*

Moreover, two messages, `Flow Mod` and `Packet Out`, are variable in length. This is because they both contain the actions field which is a container type for possible combinations of forwarding actions. The major issue arises as each individual action is itself variable in length. As such, we are again in the situation where symbolic execution is left to explore all possible combinations in which it can interpret N symbolic bytes as multiple action items. Although individual lengths must be multiple of 8 bytes to be valid, the combinatorial growth quickly becomes impractical.

Structuring the inputs improves scalability. We overcome the aforementioned problems by using a finite number of finite-size inputs. Most importantly, we construct inputs that adhere to valid format boundaries of OpenFlow control messages rather than leaving symbolic execution to guess the correct sizes. This means that we feed the agent with one symbolic control message at a time and pass the actual message length as a concrete value in the appropriate header field. In practice, we must also make the message type concrete before establishing a valid message length, as the latter is essentially determined by the former. This is not an issue, since every message must be identified by a valid code (at present about 20 codes exist, all described in the protocol specifications [5]). In a similar fashion, for messages that have variable length actions, we predetermine the number of action items and the relative lengths as concrete values.

3.2.2 Choosing the size of inputs

As we choose to limit the size of inputs, the immediate question we face is up to what input size is it practical to symbolically execute an OpenFlow agent, given today's technology? Indeed, it is known that the scalability of symbolic execution is limited by the path explosion problem: *i.e.*, the number of feasible paths can grow exponentially with the size of the inputs and number of branches. On the other hand, to make testing meaningful, the chosen inputs need to provide satisfactory coverage of agent's code and functionality. In practice, we seek answers through empirical observations. The input size varies along two dimensions: (*i*) number of symbolic control messages, and (*ii*) number of symbolic bytes in each message.

Covering the input space of each message is generally feasible. We first explore to what extent the number of symbolic bytes in each message represents a hurdle to our approach. As we discuss below, we find that the overhead to exhaustively cover the input space of each message is generally acceptable, given the current protocol specifications. We already mentioned that the message length depends in the first place on the message type. It should also be clear that the processing code and especially the processing complexity varies across message types. For example, it is trivial to symbolically execute a message of type `Hello`, which contains no message body. On the other hand, the `Flow Mod` message, which drives modifications to the flow table, carries tens of data fields that need validation and ultimately determine what actions the switch will perform. Indeed, we observe through experimentation that the number of feasible paths varies significantly between different message types (two orders of magnitude between `Flow Mod` and `Packet Out` messages). Most importantly, symbolic execution runs to completion in all cases when testing with the reference OpenFlow implementation.[2]

Achieving good coverage requires just two symbolic messages. However, the question remains about how many symbolic control messages we should inject in practice. Again, the answer depends on what type of messages one considers. We find that for complex messages we can at most use a sequence of three messages. This number may seem small, but it is worth noting that we do not need long message sequences for the type of testing we target. In fact, one symbolic message is already sufficient to cover all feasible code paths involved in message processing. With the subsequent message, we augment the coverage to include additional paths that depend on parts of switch state that are rendered symbolic as a result of running with the first symbolic message. Effectively, the second message enables us to explore the cross-interactions of message pairs. In addition, such interactions exist only for a small fraction of possible message type combinations. For example, two `Flow Mod` messages may affect the same part of the switch state; that is not true for `Echo Request` followed by `Flow Mod`. As such, the increase in instruction coverage due to the second message is a fraction of what the first message covers. A third message does not significantly improve coverage further as shown in Figure 4. Thus, careful consideration of inputs is key to successfully achieving our goals through symbolic execution.

3.2.3 Defining relevant input sequences.

Exploiting domain specific knowledge is essential to construct input sequences that target interesting uses of OpenFlow messages to further reduce the testing overhead. First, although the protocol specifications define about 20 mes-

---
[2]Our experimental setup is introduced in Section 5.

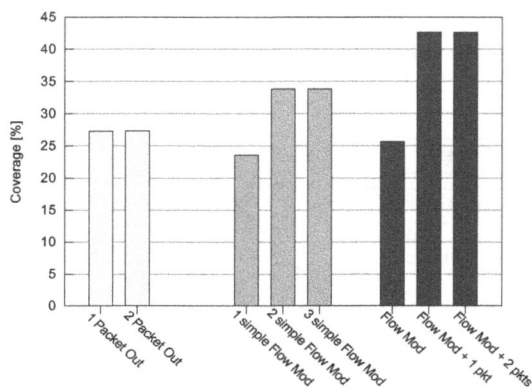

Figure 4: Reference switch code coverage as a function of the number of symbolic messages.

sages, some of these are clearly more important than others. For example, the `Hello` and `Echo` messages are simple connection establishment and keep-alive messages, respectively. We focus on complex messages such as `Flow Mod`, `Packet Out`, `Set Config` that require validation and modify the state of an agent. We also note that because these messages are meant to affect different functional aspects of the agent, we find it unnecessarily time-consuming to check all pair-wise combinations of these messages. Section 5 details the actual sequences of messages we use for testing.

3.3 Collecting output results

So far we have shown how our approach uses exhaustive path exploration to obtain the input space partitions (or equivalence classes of inputs). However, we still need to know what end result each partition produces because only the results enable the comparison across different OpenFlow agents.

As we feed a symbolic message to an OpenFlow agent, its state might be updated. Additionally, there are two possible outcomes: (*i*) the agent outputs some data (*i.e.*, messages back to the controller or data plane packets), or (*ii*) the agent does not produce externally observable data. In this work we treat only data explicitly returned by an agent (OpenFlow messages and data plane packets) as an output. Instead of directly fetching the internal state, we use additional packets and messages to infer the impact of the state on agent's behavior.

Capturing output data. To collect the outputs, we make use of the OpenFlow and data plane interfaces to capture data. Specifically, we log all OpenFlow messages and packets emitted by the agent. Note that the entire analysis runs in software (the output data may even contain symbolic inputs); therefore, with data plane interface we simply mean the socket API (or equivalent) that the agent uses to send packets.

Using concrete packets for probing state. Regardless of whether the agent does or does not output data, we cannot immediately determine if the symbolic message caused any internal state change (*e.g.*, the `Flow Mod` message installs a new rule in the flow table). Differences in internal state not necessarily result in differences in observed behavior. Moreover, we want to avoid directly fetching an agent's internal state as this would require a dependency on the specific implementation. As a solution, following any poten-

270

tially state changing symbolic message, we inject a concrete packet through the data plane interface as a simple state probe. The effect of this probe is that it enables symbolic execution to exercise the code that matches incoming packets and the code that applies the forwarding actions. The probe packet is then either forwarded (to a port or controller), in which case we log it, or it is dropped, in which case we log an empty probe response.

Normalizing results. Rather than saving the logs verbatim, we normalize the output results to remove certain data from the results for which spurious differences are expected. For example, the buffer identifiers used by different agents may differ and such a difference should not be considered an inconsistency.

3.4 Finding inconsistencies

In this phase, we seek to find inconsistencies between two OpenFlow agents denoted A and B.

With respect to agent A, we denote with PC_A the set of path conditions (outcome of symbolic execution). For each $pc \in PC_A$, let $res_A(pc)$ be the normalized output result when executing the path represented by pc. We denote the set of distinct output results as RES_A.

Grouping paths by output results. Our first step is to group all different path conditions that produce the same output result. Formally, $\forall r \in RES_A$ we set $C_A(r) = \bigvee \{pc \mid pc \in PC_A; res_A(pc) = r\}$ to be the disjunction of all path conditions that share the same output result PC_B, RES_B, and C_B are similarly defined.

Intersecting input subspaces. In our second and last step, for each pair of different outputs of agents A and B, we check if there exists at least one common input that leads to these inconsistent outputs. For each pair (i, j) of results $i \in RES_A$, $j \in RES_B$ s.t. $i \neq j$, we query a satisfiability solver (STP [14]) to obtain an example test case that satisfies the condition $C_A(i) \wedge C_B(j)$. If the solver can satisfy this conjunction, then we have an inconsistency.

Discussion. It is easy to note that an upper bound of the number of queries to the solver for our approach is $|RES_A| \cdot |RES_B|$. In addition, note that our approach produces only one inconsistency example per pair of different output results. In other words, we do not provide one example for each path that produces the inconsistency. If this is desired, one can omit grouping all paths that share the same output. However, doing so has an inherent overhead cost because it increases the number of STP queries. Instead, our approach amortizes the start-up costs of a multitude of solver invocations by using fewer larger queries and enables the solver to apply built-in optimizations to handle such larger queries.

As with any bug finding tool, it is important to know whether our approach incurs in false positives/negatives. We observe that SOFT does not produce false positives: each identified inconsistency is evidence of divergent behavior. Note this does not necessarily mean that one agent does something in violation to the specifications. According to our previous definition, an inconsistency is reported if the tested agents perform different actions when exposed to the same input. However, the tool might have false negatives for two reasons. The first is that our path coverage may not be complete. For instance, symbolic execution might not cover all feasible paths due to path explosion. The second

is that all agent implementations under test might contain the same bug, and therefore produce the same output.

4. SOFT PROTOTYPE

We built our SOFT prototype on top of the Cloud9 [8] symbolic execution engine. SOFT consists of three major components: (i) a test harness, which drives the testing of OpenFlow agents, (ii) a grouping tool to group path conditions that share output results, and (iii) a tool for finding inconsistencies.

4.1 Test harness and Cloud9

To provide the necessary execution environment for the OpenFlow agent, we build a test harness that emulates both a remote controller and the underlying network. The emulated controller is capable of injecting symbolic inputs.

As a symbolic execution engine, Cloud9 can symbolically execute only a single binary. We therefore create a test "driver" by linking the OpenFlow agent and our test harness controller together. Upon startup, the test driver forks into two processes, one of which runs the OpenFlow agent while the second runs the test harness itself. The two processes are connected via standard UNIX sockets. Upon startup, the OpenFlow agent connects to the test harness. After the connection setup and exchange of the initial `Hello` messages, the test harness injects a sequence of several symbolic OpenFlow messages and/or probes, one at a time (we discuss the input sequences in more details in Section 5). Upon confirming that the switch processed all messages and probes, we kill the execution.

To use Cloud9 for our goal, we had to improve its environment model. Cloud9 provides a symbolic model of the POSIX environment. Such a model, most importantly, allows us to efficiently use the socket API without accessing the entire networking stack. As a result, all symbolic variables remain symbolic after being transferred as data in a packet. However, such a model needs to provide all functions used by the tested application. Notably, we needed to implement the RAW socket API which was missing in Cloud9 but is used by the OpenFlow agents in our tests. Moreover, we replace or simplify some library functions as described next.

We assume that the agents correctly use network versus host byte ordering, and we change functions `ntoh` and `hton` to simply return their argument unchanged. This simplifies constraints by removing double-shuffling (first when the test harness creates a message, second when the OpenFlow agent parses the message). We also simplify checksum and hash functions to return constants or identities, because they cannot be reversed or it is computationally very expensive to do so (this is a well-known issue in using a constraint solver). The aforementioned modifications reduce complexity and improve symbolic execution efficiency.

Finally, the symbolic execution engine may use several search strategies that prioritize different goals while exploring the program. We choose to use the default Cloud9 strategy that is an interleaving of a random path choice and a strategy that aims to improve coverage. However, the choice of the search strategy has small impact on our tool. By controlling the inputs we tend to exhaustively cover all possible execution paths, which in turn diminishes the impact of choosing a particular search strategy. Moreover, SOFT is capable of working with traces that are only partially covering agents' code.

4.2 Tools

Apart from the test harness, we provide two tools for manipulating Cloud9 results. Both of these tools are written in C++ and heavily reuse existing Cloud9 code for reading, writing and manipulating path conditions. The tools contain less than 200 lines of new code in total.

The group tool reads multiple files (results of Cloud9 execution), identifies different output results and groups the path conditions by result. To improve performance of further constraint parsing, we group path conditions by building a balanced binary tree minimizing the depth of nested expressions. The inconsistency finder tool expects two directories holding grouped results as its arguments. The tool iterates over all combinations of different results and queries the STP solver to check for inconsistencies. If there is an inconsistency (the condition is satisfiable), the STP solver provides an example set of variables that satisfy the condition. This is a test case that can be used to understand and trace the root cause of the inconsistency and verify if a behavior is erroneous.

5. EVALUATION

We evaluate SOFT using two publicly available OpenFlow agents compatible with the specifications in version 1.0. The first one is a reference OpenFlow switch implementation written in C released with version 1.0 of the specifications. Its main purpose is to clarify the specifications and present available features. Although the reference implementation is not designed for high performance, it is expected to be correct as others will build upon and test against it. We are referring to this version as Reference Switch (55K LoC). The second is Open vSwitch 1.0.0 [4] (80K LoC). It is a production quality virtual switch written in C and used in several commercial switches.[3] OpenFlow is just one the supported protocols. We also created a third OpenFlow agent by modifying the Reference Switch and introducing different corner case behaviors (Modified Switch). This way we can tell how efficiently SOFT finds the injected differences and which of them remain unnoticed.

To evaluate SOFT we use the set of tests summarized in Table 1. We run our experiments using a machine with Linux 3.2.0 x86_64 that has 128 GB of RAM and a clock speed of 2.4 GHz. Our implementation does not use multiple cores for a single experiment.

5.1 Can SOFT identify inconsistencies?

In this section, we report and analyze the inconsistencies SOFT detects. We apply a set of tests to all three OpenFlow agents and compare Reference Switch with both Modified Switch and Open vSwitch.

5.1.1 Modified Switch vs. Reference Switch

First, we look for differences between Reference Switch and Modified Switch. Two team members who did not take part in the tool's implementation and test preparation were designated to introduce a few modifications to the Reference Switch. The modifications were meant to affect the externally visible behavior of the OpenFlow agent. Having

---

[3]For example, in Pica8 products: http://www.pica8.org/.

Test	Description
Packet Out	A single Packet Out message containing a symbolic action and a symbolic output action.
Stats Request	A single symbolic Stats Req. It covers all possible statistics requests.
Set Config	A symbolic Set Config message followed by a probing TCP packet.
FlowMod	A symbolic Flow Mod with 1 symbolic action and a symbolic output action followed by a probing TCP packet.
Eth FlowMod	Symbolic Flow Mod with 1 symbolic action and a symbolic output action. Fields not related to Ethernet are concretized. The message is followed by a probing Ethernet packet.
CS FlowMods	2 Flow Mod. The fist one is concrete, the second is symbolic.
Concrete	4 concrete 8-byte messages. These are the messages that do not have variable fields.
Short Symb	A 10-byte symbolic message. Only the OpenFlow version field is concrete.

Table 1: Tests used in the evaluation.

purposefully injected changes, we set out to check how many can be detected by SOFT.

SOFT is able to correctly pinpoint 5 out of 7 injected modifications. We further investigate the cases in which SOFT failed to flag the effect of the differences. It turns out that one of them concerns the Hello message received while establishing a connection to the controller. SOFT does not recognize this problem because it establishes a correct connection first and then performs the tests. The second missed modification manifests itself only when a rule is deleted because of a timeout. This occurs because the symbolic execution engine is not able to trigger timers. As part of our future work, we plan to extend our approach to deal with time, e.g., similarly to MODIST [24].

5.1.2 Open vSwitch vs. Reference Switch

Knowing that SOFT is capable of finding inconsistencies, we compare the Reference Switch with Open vSwitch to verify how useful SOFT is when applied to a production quality OpenFlow agent. The list of differences between the two major software agents contains a few significant ones. In the following, we present the observed inconsistencies and analyze their root causes.

Packet dropped when action is invalid. This case describes a Packet Out message containing a packet that is silently dropped by Open vSwitch while the Reference Switch forwards it. The inconsistency appears when the Packet Out control message satisfies the following conditions: (i) it contains the packet that the agent should forward and (ii) one of the actions is setting the value of VLAN or IP Type of Service field. Further investigation leads us to the conclusion that Open vSwitch validates whether a new VLAN value set by the action fits in 12 bits and similarly whether the last two bits of the TOS value are equal to 0. When an action specified in the message does not pass this strict validation, Open vSwitch silently ignores the whole message. Additional tests with Flow Mod messages reveal a similar issue. These tests also show that the vlan_pcp field undergoes additional validation in Open vSwitch. Reference Switch does not validate values of the aforementioned fields, but it automatically modifies them to fit the expected format.

The specifications do not state that the OpenFlow agent should perform such a precise validation of any of the men-

272

Test	Message count	Reference Switch				Modified Switch				Open vSwitch			
		CPU time	Path count	Constraints		CPU time	Path count	Constraints		CPU time	Path count	Constraints	
				avg size	max size			avg size	max size			avg size	max size
Packet Out	1	14s	49	71.57	93	24s	117	74.09	91	44s	241	63.48	79
Stats Request	1	44s	218	53.10	65	46s	218	53.10	65	186s	136	52.63	67
Set Config	2	446s	207	76.89	112	451s	207	76.89	112	569s	207	80.97	116
Eth FlowMod	2	40m	7680	101.12	132	83m	14280	106.62	136	198m	27682	98.56	127
FlowMod	2	373m	87828	109.77	164	>140h	>356753	123.09	164	60h	181620	123.28	159
CS FlowMods	2	69m	29179	96.63	133	121m	51419	99.74	139	36h	462488	115.22	173
Concrete	4	6s	1	0	0	6s	1	0	0	8s	1	0	0
Short Symb	1	50s	31	27.9	69	50s	31	27.9	69	12s	14	27.5	50

Table 2: Symbolic execution statistics for selected tests for all 3 OpenFlow agents. We report time, number of explored paths (input equivalence classes) and constraint size (average and maximum size).

tioned fields. Therefore, both implementations might be considered correct. However, such a difference in behavior might cause unexpected packet drops if the controller developers test their applications with switches that are different from those deployed in the network.

Forwarding a packet to an invalid port. Here we describe a case in which the tested OpenFlow agents return error messages concerning incorrect output ports in an inconsistent fashion. According to the specifications, the agent has to return an error message if the output port will never be valid. However, if the port may become valid in the future, the message might either be rejected with an error, or the agent may drop packets intended for this port while it is not valid. The differences in interpretation when the port will be invalid forever lead to a few differences between OpenFlow agents. First, when the ingress port in the match is equal to the output port, the Reference Switch returns an error, as no packets will ever be forwarded to this port.[4] Open vSwitch accepts such a rule and drops all matching packets. On the other hand, Open vSwitch immediately returns an error when the action defines an output port greater than a configurable maximum value. Reference Switch does not validate ports this way.

Thus, if the controller application relies on error messages received, it may misbehave when deployed with a different agent than it was tested with. If the agent used in testing considered a port valid but the other agent did not, the controller would fail to install rules it was designed to install. The opposite situation is equally unsafe. The rule installation that used to return an error succeeds, but all matching packets get dropped. As a result, some packets will not to be sent to the controller, although they were expected to be.

Lack of error messages. We have already presented a few cases when one of the agents silently drops the incorrect message without returning an error. SOFT detects another instance of such a problem in the Reference Switch while testing with `Packet Out` and `Flow Mod` messages. When the `buffer_id` field refers to a non-existent buffer, the Reference Switch handles the message but does not apply actions to any packet and does not report any error. Open vSwitch replies with an error message, but installs the flow as well. We analyzed the Reference Switch source code and discovered that although the error is returned by the message handler, it is not propagated further as an OpenFlow message.

OpenFlow agent terminates with an error. There are three independent cases when the Reference Switch crashes.

First, when the OpenFlow agent receives a `Packet Out` message with output port set to `OFPP_CTRL`. This may be a rare case (e.g., when the developer demands such behavior) but it is not forbidden by the specifications. Second, when the agent executes an action setting the `vlan` field in a `Packet Out` message the same error appears and the agent crashes. Finally, when the agent receives a queue configuration request for port number 0, it encounters a memory error. All the aforementioned problems are not only inconsistencies, but also major reliability problems in the OpenFlow agent.

Different order of message validation. In this case, the order in which message fields should be validated is not made explicit in the specifications. This vagueness results in externally visible differences in agents' behavior. The same incorrect message may induce two different error messages, or an error message and a lack of response in case of the mentioned problem. We encountered such a situation for a `Packet Out` message with an incorrect buffer id and output port.

Statistics requests silently ignored. The Reference Switch silently ignores requests for statistics to which it is not able to respond. This behavior is a specific case of the "Lack of error messages" problem. Even though the handler returns an error it is not converted to an OpenFlow message. The problem was detected because Open vSwitch sends an error in response to an invalid or unknown request.

Missing features. SOFT is able to detect features that are missing in one OpenFlow agent, but are present in the other. We were able to automatically infer that Open vSwitch does not support emergency flow entries that are defined in the specifications. Secondly, Reference Switch being purely an OpenFlow switch, does not support the traditional forwarding paths (`OFPP_NORMAL`).

5.2 What is the overhead of using SOFT?

In this section, we present the performance evaluation of the two key stages of SOFT's execution.

Symbolic execution. In the first stage, the OpenFlow agent is symbolically executed with an input sequence and SOFT gathers path constraints and corresponding outputs. For all three OpenFlow agents we report the running time, as well as the number and size (number of boolean operations in a path condition) of paths (equivalence classes of inputs) in Table 2. These metrics are strongly variable and depend not only on the input length but also on the message type. Moreover, adding a second message or a probe packet significantly increases complexity by orders of magnitude. Additionally, Open vSwitch–the most complex of the tested agents–is noticeably more challenging for symbolic execu-

---

[4] A special `OFPP_IN_PORT` port must be explicitly used to forward packets back to the port they came from [5].

Test	Grouping results				Inconsist. checking	
	Reference Switch		Open vSwitch			
	time	#res	time	#res	time	#
Packet Out	0.038s	6	0.090s	10	26s	14
Stats Request	0.116s	8	0.061s	9	10s	7
Set Config	0.141s	69	0.43s	69	236s	0
Eth FlowMod	8s	12	23s	31	23m	58
CS FlowMods	79s	4	344m	6	>28h	≥8
Short Symb	0.039s	9	0.01s	7	6s	4

Table 3: Time needed to find overlapping input subspaces and number of created test cases. Each test case represents one intersection of overlapping input subspaces. Additionally, time needed to group constraints by the output and a number of distinct outputs for Reference Switch and Open vSwitch.

Test	Reference Switch		Open vSwitch	
	Inst.(%)	Branch(%)	Inst.(%)	Branch(%)
No Message	12.21	8.27	19.03	13.34
Packet Out	26.23	19.31	25.68	17.28
Stats Request	30.27	24.15	24.31	16.75
Set Config	26.23	19.31	23.98	16.16
Eth FlowMod	41.74	34.65	38.15	25.49
FlowMod	42.65	34.25	38.24	26.27
Concrete	17.13	11.42	20.16	13.62
Short Symb	19.92	13.39	21.60	14.34

Table 4: Instruction and branch coverage for selected tests for Reference Switch and Open vSwitch.

Test	Time	Paths	Coverage
Fully Symbolic	31h	226224	42.93%
Concrete Match	12m	2634	40.60%
Concrete Action	193m	30396	37.32%
Concrete Probe	48m	9216	41.6%
Symbolic Probe	172m	33168	43.9%

Table 5: Effects of concretizing on execution time, generated paths and instruction coverage.

tion (we note that it is possible to use even partial results of symbolic execution to look for inconsistencies). As a result of multiple additional validations, the test input space for Open vSwitch is partitioned into 3-15 times more subspaces than for the Reference Switch.

Subspaces intersections. We distinguish between two sub-stages of the second stage: (i) grouping input subspaces by the same output, (ii) intersecting subspaces corresponding to potential inconsistencies.

For the first sub-stage we report the time required to group and the number of distinct outputs. As presented in Table 3, this part requires orders of magnitude less time than symbolic execution. Grouping constraints dramatically reduces the number of expressions that need to be checked for satisfiability, as there are only up to 30 distinct outputs (a 1-5 orders of magnitude reduction compared to the initial number of equivalence classes).

The search for overlapping subspaces depends on the complexity of constraints and usually finishes within a couple of minutes. There is one exceptional case in which the STP solver is unable to solve the merged constraints in one day. In the future we plan to investigate grouping constraints into smaller groups for such cases.

The achieved results in finding inconsistencies confirm our expectations. Usually one difference manifests itself multiple times and affects many subspaces of inputs. In the extreme example, although there are 58 reported inconsistencies, manual analysis reveals only 6 distinct root causes of differences.

5.3 How relevant is input sequence selection?

To quantify the relevance of chosen tests, we measure the instruction and branch coverage provided by Cloud9. The instruction/branch reached at least once in the execution is considered covered, regardless of its arguments. We consider only the sections of OpenFlow agent's code relevant to OpenFlow processing. The initialization that is repeated for each test covers 12% of instructions and 8% of branches. The test specific results, shown in Table 4, are spread between 20 and 40%. To verify that the low reported coverage is a result of the fact that each test targets a few specific message handlers, we manually analyze cumulative coverage of all tests. We observe that SOFT covers approximately 75% of the code and that the remaining instructions belong mostly to code that is not accessible in standard execution (e.g., command line configuration, dead code, cleanup functions, logging functions).

The importance of concretizing inputs. Due to time

and memory constraints it is often convenient to concretize selected fields in the message. We evaluate the benefits and drawbacks of using the domain knowledge to reduce the input space. As a baseline, we choose a test where a single symbolic Flow Mod message containing 2 symbolic actions and 2 symbolic output actions is followed by a TCP probe packet. We then compare the results of: (i) the baseline, (ii) a version of the baseline with a concrete match (wildcard), and (iii) a version of the baseline with a single concrete action instead of 4 symbolic ones. All values are summarized in the upper part of Table 5. While the drop in the coverage percentage is only 2-5% in comparison to the baseline test, the difference in time and path count is noticeable. Specifically, the tests finish 10 to 50 times quicker, while generating 1 to 2 orders of magnitude less paths.

To verify how much coverage we lose by not using symbolic probes, we create a separate test. This test first installs a partially symbolic Flow Mod that applies actions to Ethernet packets. It then sends a short probe packet that is concrete or symbolic depending on the test version. Results in the lower part of Table 5 show that a symbolic probe adds just 2% to the coverage. The cost is 3.5 times longer running time and 3.5 times more paths.

To summarize, concretizing parts of the inputs significantly reduces the time needed to conduct the test at the cost of leaving small portion of additional instructions uncovered. Therefore, it is possible to use the concretized inputs to conduct regular tests more often. When combined with careful choice of concrete fields, the coverage is marginally affected. The fully symbolic messages can be used just for the final checks before a major release when the best coverage possible is required, and testing time is less of an issue.

6. RELATED WORK

We present in the following generic techniques that can be applied to testing OpenFlow switches, as well controller applications and networks in general.

6.1 Testing OpenFlow switches

There are multiple testing approaches applicable to OpenFlow switches. The approaches differ in terms of the scope and type of problems they aim for, as well as the process in which the test cases are created. As an exhaustive review is beyond the scope of this paper, we briefly describe a few relevant to our discussion.

System testing. System-level testing is concerned with an integrated system such as an OpenFlow switch. This approach treats the device under test as a black box. To ensure that the tested device does not depend on external factors, the interactions with the controller and other network elements are commonly emulated by the testing framework. This approach typically requires a large number of test cases to achieve high coverage. Each test case is carefully designed to target a specific feature and checks the correctness of simple functionalities. A developer, using tools such as OFTest [2] or the default OpenFlow Perl testing framework, has to manually provide a step by step execution scenario containing the inputs and expected outputs. This process is time-consuming and additionally makes designing non-trivial and complex test cases complicated.

Symbolic and concolic execution. Others have successfully applied symbolic execution [9] and selective symbolic execution [12] to testing of systems code. As we already mentioned, blindly applying symbolic execution results in an exponential explosion of code paths. It also requires excessive human effort to specify correct behavior. SOFT effectively overcomes these issues. With these issues resolved, one could use symbolic execution for crosschecking switch behaviors, but it results in excessive, time-consuming overhead. SOFT goes one step further in that eliminates this step by coalescing constraints that result in the same output, and using the constraint solver to identify inconsistent behaviors.

Others have considered the problem of manipulating inputs to conform to an input grammar, in the form of white-box "fuzz" testing [16]. By doing so, the symbolic execution engine can quickly pass over the validation checks to try to reach deeper in the code. The problem that SOFT addresses is even harder, as we need to be careful about the number and type of messages, as well as the nature of individual fields. In addition, we address the problem of observing internal state.

Canini *et al.* [10] use a variant of symbolic execution called concolic execution to identify faults in federated, heterogeneous distributed systems. Their system, called DiCE, tests the impact of feeding various inputs to participating nodes (*e.g.*, BGP routers) in isolation. DiCE and SOFT differ in several ways. DiCE is an online technique, whereas SOFT is used for interoperability testing prior to deployment. Moreover, SOFT's goal is crosschecking of different implementations. Finally, SOFT does not require the definition of correct behavior to be specified. Complementary to SOFT, Kothari *et al.* [19] use symbolic execution to identify protocol manipulation attacks. The goal here is for a node to try to determine harmful behavior induced upon itself by received messages from other participants. In contrast, SOFT systematically determines and compares the input subspaces of multiple implementations to find inconsistencies, without prior knowledge of correct behavior.

Performance testing. Performance tests are a subset of system tests used to determine device's capability under high load. Not only is this type of tests able to detect performance problems such as slow packet forwarding or control plane communication, but can also be successfully applied to find correctness problems that may not appear in other scenarios. As shown in OFLOPS [22], a continuous packet stream may be used to check the consistency between data plane and control plane in case of the OpenFlow barrier commands. Moreover, this method is able to discover timing issues that require multiple events occurring with a specific time correlation. On the other hand, it may potentially miss functional errors and classify them as correct behavior in some circumstances. Finally, performance testing requires that, while under test, the system works under realistic conditions. Packets, for example, need to be injected to the device at the rate and times defined in the scenario. Consequently, in addition to the usual setup time, the tests need to be run in real time and cannot be sped up.

6.2 Testing OpenFlow controllers

NICE [11] is a tool for testing unmodified OpenFlow controller applications. It combines model checking and concolic execution in order to systematically explore the behavior of the network under a variety of possible event orderings. The tool starts with the network topology model containing the controller, switches and end hosts, and exercises sequences of state transitions on these network elements. NICE and SOFT target fundamentally different parts of the network: controller vs. switches. In NICE, only the controller is running the unmodified application, while other elements (switches, end hosts) are replaced with simplified models. In contrast, SOFT finds inconsistencies among the implementations of OpenFlow agents that run in the switches.

Further, SOFT does not require the specification of correct behavior for the tested software, while NICE uses correctness properties provided by developers or testers.

6.3 Trace-based debugging of a network

OFRewind [23] is a tool that enables temporary consistent network event trace recording in a running system, as well as replaying it later. Despite available mechanisms allowing operators to filter recorded events, the debugging process is still manual. Neither problem detection, nor its root cause localization and analysis is automatic and needs supervision. The operator has to first realize that there is an issue in the network, and then find the root cause by replaying subsets of the recorded trace. Although the tool is directed toward debugging, it should be possible to use a similar technique to create test inputs based on previously recorded traces. The efficiency of using pre-recorded traces for future network testing is limited, as the traces explore only one specific execution path (set of network events) and might miss important corner cases.

6.4 Other approaches

Approaches exist for statically analyzing network configurations. For example, RCC [13] identifies misconfigurations in intradomain BGP routers. Anteater [20] uncovers problems in the data plane due to forwarding misconfigurations. Header Space Analysis (HSA) [17] checks the network configurations to identify network configuration problems. Automatic Test Packet Generation (ATPG) [25] is a solution based on HSA that creates a minimum set of test packets required to cover all links or rules in the network. Then, ATPG uses these packets to detect and localize failures. We consider these approaches orthogonal to ours as they focus on testing the network from the data plane perspective whereas we test switch behaviors as driven by the OpenFlow interface.

7. CONCLUSIONS

Software Defined Networking, and its OpenFlow incarnation in particular, stands a real chance of enabling cheap and easy extensibility in networks. OpenFlow owes its increasing adoption to the relatively simple changes that enable control over the way packets are forwarded by the OpenFlow switches. With little attention on ensuring reliability of OpenFlow switches, danger exists that failures in production networks could erode trust in this new technology. In particular, the OpenFlow specification changes rapidly, and allows for different interpretations. As a result, switches from multiple vendors can behave differently and cause an inconsistency in the network.

In this paper, we have described a tool that automates the task of identifying such deviations in behavior among different switches. We demonstrate the effectiveness of our tool by using it to identify several inconsistencies involving the Reference OpenFlow switch and the Open vSwitch. While the work centered around the specific details of OpenFlow, we posit our approach could find more general application with other router software and heterogeneous networked systems.

8. ACKNOWLEDGMENTS

We thank our shepherd Christos Gkantsidis and the anonymous reviewers who provided excellent feedback. We are grateful to Stefan Bucur for supporting us with using Cloud9 and Jennifer Rexford for useful discussions and comments on earlier drafts of this work. The research leading to these results has received funding from the European Research Council under the European Union's Seventh Framework Programme (FP7/2007-2013) / ERC grant agreement 259110.

9. REFERENCES

[1] Going With the Flow: Google's Secret Switch to the Next Wave of Networking. http://www.wired.com/wiredenterprise/2012/04/going-with-the-flow-google/all/1.

[2] OFTest. http://oftest.openflowhub.org.

[3] ONF Holds Its First Test Event. https://www.opennetworking.org/?p=249&option=com_wordpress&Itemid=72.

[4] Open vSwitch: An Open Virtual Switch. http://openvswitch.org.

[5] OpenFlow Switch Specification. http://www.openflow.org/documents/openflow-spec-v1.0.0.pdf.

[6] Research experiment disrupts Internet, for some. http://www.computerworld.com/s/article/9182558/Research_experiment_disrupts_Internet_for_some.

[7] Staring Into The Gorge: Router Exploits. http://www.renesys.com/blog/2009/08/staring-into-the-gorge.shtml.

[8] S. Bucur, V. Ureche, C. Zamfir, and G. Candea. Parallel Symbolic Execution for Automated Real-World Software Testing. In EuroSys, 2011.

[9] C. Cadar, D. Dunbar, and D. R. Engler. KLEE: Unassisted and Automatic Generation of High-Coverage Tests for Complex Systems Programs. In OSDI, 2008.

[10] M. Canini, V. Jovanović, D. Venzano, B. Spasojević, O. Crameri, and D. Kostić. Toward Online Testing of Federated and Heterogeneous Distributed Systems. In USENIX Annual Technical Conference, 2011.

[11] M. Canini, D. Venzano, P. Perešíni, D. Kostić, and J. Rexford. A NICE Way to Test OpenFlow Applications. In NSDI, 2012.

[12] V. Chipounov, V. Kuznetsov, and G. Candea. The S2E Platform: Design, Implementation, and Applications. ACM Transactions on Computer Systems, 30(1):1–49, 2012.

[13] N. Feamster and H. Balakrishnan. Detecting BGP Configuration Faults with Static Analysis. In NSDI, 2005.

[14] V. Ganesh and D. L. Dill. A Decision Procedure for Bit-Vectors and Arrays. In CAV, 2007.

[15] P. Godefroid, N. Klarlund, and K. Sen. DART: Directed Automated Random Testing. In PLDI, 2005.

[16] P. Godefroid, M. Y. Levin, and D. A. Molnar. Automated Whitebox Fuzz Testing. In NDSS, 2008.

[17] P. Kazemian, G. Varghese, and N. McKeown. Header Space Analysis: Static Checking for Networks. In NSDI, 2012.

[18] J. C. King. A new approach to program testing. In Proceedings of the international conference on Reliable software, 1975.

[19] N. Kothari, R. Mahajan, T. Millstein, R. Govindan, and M. Musuvathi. Finding Protocol Manipulation Attacks. In SIGCOMM, 2011.

[20] H. Mai, A. Khurshid, R. Agarwal, M. Caesar, P. B. Godfrey, and S. T. King. Debugging the Data Plane with Anteater. In SIGCOMM, 2011.

[21] N. McKeown, T. Anderson, H. Balakrishnan, G. Parulkar, L. Peterson, J. Rexford, S. Shenker, and J. Turner. OpenFlow: Enabling Innovation in Campus Networks. SIGCOMM Comput. Commun. Rev., 38:69–74, March 2008.

[22] C. Rotsos, N. Sarrar, S. Uhlig, R. Sherwood, and A. W. Moore. Oflops: An open framework for openflow switch evaluation. In PAM, 2012.

[23] A. Wundsam, D. Levin, S. Seetharaman, and A. Feldmann. OFRewind: Enabling Record and Replay Troubleshooting for Networks. In USENIX ATC, 2011.

[24] J. Yang, T. Chen, M. Wu, Z. Xu, X. Liu, H. Lin, M. Yang, F. Long, L. Zhang, and L. Zhou. MODIST: Transparent Model Checking of Unmodified Distributed Systems. In NSDI, 2009.

[25] H. Zeng, P. Kazemian, G. Varghese, and N. McKeown. Automatic Test Packet Generation. In CoNEXT, 2012.

FindAll: A Local Search Engine for Mobile Phones

Aruna Balasubramanian
University of Washington
arunab@cs.washington.edu

Niranjan Balasubramanian
University of Washington
niranjan@cs.washington.edu

Samuel J. Huston
UMass Amherst
sjh@cs.umass.edu

Donald Metzler
USC
metzler@isi.edu

David J. Wetherall
University of Washington
djw@cs.washington.edu

ABSTRACT

We present the design and evaluation of *FindAll*, a local search engine that lets users search and retrieve web pages, even in the absence of connectivity. Our user study with 23 users show that mobile users often search for web pages that they have previously visited, known as re-finding. This re-finding behavior makes the case for a local solution. *FindAll* goes beyond caching and using keyword search, and instead, implements a full blown search engine. The key challenge in *FindAll* is in designing a search engine, which is both memory- and energy-intensive, on the constrained phone environment. To this end, *FindAll* balances the cost of running the search engine with the expected benefits of serving a web page locally. *FindAll* estimates the benefits of local search, by learning the re-finding behavior of users. We implement *FindAll* on Android by adapting a publicly available search engine. Our evaluations, based on the traces collected from our user study, shows that *FindAll* reduces search latency by two-folds for users who re-find often, and reduces 3G data usage by up to 100 MB a month.

Categories and Subject Descriptors

C.2 [**Computer Communication Network**]: Network Architecture and Design— *Wireless Communication*

General Terms

Algorithms, Design, Performance

Keywords

Web search, Latency, Energy savings, Local search, Refinding, Measurement, User study

1. INTRODUCTION

Many popular smartphone apps, including web search, maps, yelp, and others, solely rely on the cloud for its operations. The apps fail completely during periods of no connectivity and perform poorly during periods of bad connectivity. This reliance on the

cloud can severely degrade user experience, especially on cellular networks—cellular networks have high round trip delays [14], offer poor connectivity [27], and are often unavailable [7]. Even with good cellular connectivity, a web search session is an order of magnitude slower on mobile phones than on desktops [15, 25]. 3G data is also becoming increasingly expensive, and as cellular providers introduce tiered data plans [21], users are becoming more aware of their 3G data usage.

Improving the local availability of content can help mitigate these issues. Mobile storage is advancing at a rapid pace, and technology trends suggest that storage capacity will continue to rise and will remain cheap [15]. Thus, trading local storage for connectivity is an attractive alternative to *always* relying on the cloud.

In this work, we focus on using local storage to improve the performance of *web search*. To this end, we leverage the *re-finding* behavior of web search users; users often search for web pages that they have previously visited [23]. Re-finding queries constitute nearly 80% of the total queries issued by more than half the population of mobile users [18] . If users can effectively search through their local caches, a significantly large fraction of searches queries can be answered locally.

Imagine that a mobile user Alice is browsing some product web pages on her laptop or her phone. She wants to re-find a specific product page on her phone when she goes to a store, but the connectivity to 3G is poor. How should her smartphone support local search? Manually browsing through the browser history is cumbersome [4]. Web caches require that Alice has access to the URL link, which is usually long, not easy to remember, and is rarely used for re-finding [10]. Search engines such as Google [20] and Bing [19] store user history in the cloud. However, using the search engine's cloud-history feature requires network connectivity, and further, storing the user history in the cloud raises privacy concerns.

We present *FindAll*, a system that collects all web pages that the user visits on all of her devices, caches them locally, and indexes [1] them. *FindAll* then implements a full scale search engine over this local index to allow users to effectively search over their local history.

A local search engine will allow Alice to re-find desired web pages quickly, privately, and without depending on network connectivity. The key challenge in *FindAll* is the high resource cost of running a conventional search engine on the phone. Building search engine indexes is both a memory- and an energy-intensive operation.

The *FindAll* design is motivated by a user study in which we logged the mobile search and browsing patterns of 23 participants

---

[1] An index is a data structure used by search engines for fast and efficient retrieval.

for 30 days. We also logged the corresponding desktop search patterns for a subset of the users. We find that, similar to other mobile studies, re-finding was common in our dataset with 52% of the queries being re-finding queries. We leverage two key findings from our study to design *FindAll*. First, almost 45% of the re-finding queries were submitted within 50 minutes of the original request. This suggests that we need to locally index web pages near when they are browsed, rather than indexing pages in the cloud and periodically downloading them. Second, there is a large diversity in re-finding behavior across users, but each user tends to be relatively consistent in their level of re-finding. This suggests that *FindAll* should adapt to the user's re-finding patterns, so that the index computation, an energy intensive operation, is performed only when it is beneficial to the user.

FindAll seeks to balance two goals: maximizing the local availability of web pages, while ensuring that the energy consumption for *FindAll* operations is no more than that of default search. The central question in the *FindAll* design is: When should *FindAll* index web pages? If web pages are indexed frequently they are more available in the local cache, but the energy to index the web pages increases. If the web pages are indexed less frequently, they will not be available locally when the user tries to re-find the web page.

The *FindAll* algorithm indexes web pages when the energy to index is lower than the expected cost of not indexing. By not indexing a web page locally, *FindAll* incurs a cost, because the web page will have to be downloaded from the Internet. However, *FindAll* incurs this cost *only if* the user searches for the web page. *FindAll* estimates the probability that a user will search for a web page by learning user behavior; it uses this probability estimate to compute the benefits of indexing. As a result, *FindAll* aggressively indexes when users are expected to re-find often, and indexes more conservatively when users are not expected to re-find.

We implement *FindAll* in Android by adapting Galago [2], a publicly available search engine, to mobile phones. We evaluate our implementation using traces from real mobile users. We find that *FindAll* significantly improves web search performance by increasing local availability of web pages by 40%. By improving availability, *FindAll* reduces search latency by a factor of two for the users who re-find often. By reducing Internet downloads, *FindAll* reduces 3G data usage by up to 100 MB a month for users who re-find often.

Importantly, these improvements do not come at an energy cost: *FindAll* reduces the overall energy consumption by 30% for users who re-find often, and does not increase the overall energy consumption for users who do not re-find often. Adapting to the re-finding behavior of users provides significant benefits. Non-adaptive strategies do not change their indexing policies according to users re-finding patterns; as a result, they index more often than needed for users who do not re-find, resulting in up to 50% increase in energy consumption compared to default web search. On the other hand, they index less often than needed for users who do re-find often, resulting in 39% lower availability compared to *FindAll*.

We make three key contributions in this work. First, our measurement study presents the day-to-day browsing and re-finding behavior of real mobile users and highlights implications for mobile search. Second, we develop a local search engine that is suitable for constrained phone environments: *FindAll* indexes web pages within the memory constraints of phones and according to the energy implications of indexing. Third, we show using an extensive evaluation, that *FindAll* improves both latency and availability of mobile search.

2. BACKGROUND

2.1 The Re-finding problem

Re-finding is a well-studied topic in web search, where users issue search queries for web pages that they have previously seen. Studies have shown that 40% to 60% of all search queries from desktops are re-finding queries [22, 10]. Even on mobile phones, 50% of mobile users issue more than 80% re-finding queries [15]. In our own user study, 52% of search queries were re-finding queries (§3).

Because of the dynamic nature of Internet content, re-finding is not always easy– search results change constantly [5, 22], users often do not remember the exact query they typed originally [6], and the target web page may not be among the top web pages returned by the search engine even when the same query is issued repeatedly [24].

Poor cellular connectivity further exacerbates the re-finding problem. Users need to first download the search results page, search for the link to the specific web page, and then re-download the web page. High latency in cellular networks can make this experience tedious [15]. Even if web pages are cached locally, searching through the history is cumbersome [4], and users seldom look through their search history for re-finding [10].

A database lookup, consisting of a <query,webpage> map, could make searching through the local history easier [15]. A database requires that the original search query and the re-finding query be the same, since the query is used as the lookup key. However, the re-finding query is often different from the original query [23]. In our study, the query used to re-find a web page was different from the original query for 24% of the cases (§3). As a result, *FindAll* was 27% more effective in searching web pages, compared to a database lookup (§7).

Further, a database solution can only help retrieve web pages that are found through search; if a user visits a web pages through other sources such as social media and email, these web pages will not be stored in the database.

2.2 Search engines

FindAll uses a state-of-the-art information retrieval system to efficiently and effectively search through locally stored content.

Given locally stored content, a simple alternative to using a search engine is to use keyword matching; i.e., every web page that contains the keyword is retrieved, but results are not ordered in any manner. Keyword matching is not effective for search. Imagine that the user has tens of web pages about hotels in Anchorage, but the user is looking for a particular hotel called *Anchorage Hotel*. A keyword search on *Anchorage Hotel* will return all the web pages, in no particular order. Finding the relevant web page from this unordered list is cumbersome, especially in small form-factor phones that display 3-4 search results per page.

Instead, search engines and most modern information retrieval systems go beyond simple boolean search and *rank* web pages in response to a user query. Search engines leverage several types of features such as the frequency of the query words within the document, the proximity of the query words, and their distribution in various sections of the document (URL, title, body etc). Our evaluations (§7) show that the *FindAll* is 33% more effective in returning the relevant web page as one of the top results, compared to keyword matching.

To retrieve and rank web pages efficiently, search engines first index all of the web pages. The index comprises of a mapping between words and the list of web pages in which they occur, and allows fast retrieval. The core of any indexing algorithm is to sort the <word, web page> tuple. Sorting is usually implemented as an external-merge sort because the entire list of tuples is too large be held in main memory [26]. However, this task is both memory- and energy-intensive.

Finally, with the growing variety of mobile apps, re-finding is likely to become a common phenomenon across other apps, such as news readers, social media, maps, etc. As the number of re-found content scales, a search engine solution is likely to become essential. As a first step, we focus on re-finding *web pages*. This is because the need for re-finding is well-established for web search, and browsing remains a frequent activity for many mobile users; traces of mobile browsing activity give us a basis for evaluating our system

3. USER STUDY

To measure day to day browsing and re-finding patterns of real mobile users, we conduct a user study. We built a logging application that records anonymized user browsing history. We use the data that we record during the study to drive the evaluation of *FindAll*.

3.1 Re-finding Defined

A re-finding query is the set of keywords entered by a user, used to retrieve a previously viewed web page. We call the corresponding web page that is visited through the query as the re-finding or the re-found web page.

Knowing if a query is a re-finding query is a hard problem since it depends on user intent. In the past, researchers have focused on *re-finding URLs*. In contrast, in *FindAll*, we are interested in knowing if the web page itself (i.e., the *content* of the URL) is re-found. Given this goal, we define *re-finding* to be revisiting a previously visited web page when:

- The web page is revisited via a search query.
- The content of the web page remains unchanged from the previous visit.

Refinding example

URL:http://conferences.sigcomm.org/co-next/2012/   ...   **Search query:** 'conext 2012"   **URL:** http://conferences.sigcomm.org/co-next/2012/   ...   **Search query:** "networking conference nice france"   **URL:** http://conferences.sigcomm.org/co-next/2012/

Non-Refinding example

Search query: "weather"   **URL:** www.weather.com   ...   **Search query:** "weather"   **URL:** www.weather.com   ...
URL: http://wikipedia.org/wiki/J._K._Rowling   ...   **URL:** http://wikipedia.org/wiki/J._K._Rowling

Figure 7: Refinding and Non-refinding examples

Figure 7 shows examples of re-finding and non re-finding behavior. For example, the CoNext 2012 web page is re-found twice. Note that the search query is different for each re-find request. On the other hand, the web-page for the URL "www.weather.com" is visited twice but is not marked as re-finding even though it was

found via a search query. This is because the webpage is likely to have changed since the previous visit. Finally, the wikipedia entry for J. K. Rowling is not marked re-find because the web page is not visited via a search query.

3.2 Measurement methodology

3.2.1 Logging software

The *FindAll* logger application records the user's browsing activity on their phones and personal computers. To encourage user participation, the logger anonymizes the browsing logs of the user. URLs of web pages are hashed using a user-specific key[2], such that two identical URLs are hashed to the same value. Similarly, search queries are also hashed using a user-specific key.

On the phone, the application logs the following items: (i) Time (ii) URL hash (iii) Hash of the search queries (iv) Size of the web page (iv) Connection status (3G/WiFi). The logger uses the Android bookmark database to log browser activity. We ensure that the logs do not contain spurious URLs due to client-side redirections or due to the user pressing the "back" button.

On the computer, the application logs the following items: (i) Time (ii) URL hash (iii) Hash of the search queries. The logger periodically polls the browser's sqlite database to obtain browser information. The same hash key is used to hash the content of the user's phone and user's computer.

3.2.2 Data collection

We logged mobile browsing history from 23 users for 1 month. In addition, we collected the computer browsing history from 7 of the 23 users for a month to give us cross-device browsing history. Table 1 shows the user characteristics. All except two of the participants were undergraduate or graduate students from two different universities.

We note that 9 of the 23 users either had limited 3G plan or did not have 3G plan at all on their phones. A system such as *FindAll* is especially useful for such users.

	Users		Users
Undergraduate	13	Graduate students	8
Computer science majors	12	Other majors	9
No 3G plan	4	Limited 3G plan	5

Table 1: Characteristics of user study participants.

During post-processing of the collected logs, we mark a query and the corresponding web page visited through the query as re-finding, if it satisfies the definition (§3.1). Note that we can identify repeated requests to the same web page since the URLs are hashed to the same value. However, we cannot access the content of the web page because of anonymization; therefore, we cannot identify web pages whose content has changed since the last visit. This is a difficult problem.

However, to alleviate this problem, we created a list of URLs whose content change frequently. We obtained the top 500 most popular web pages from Alexa [1]. We then identify the web pages that are "not cacheable", as marked in their HTTP headers. The *FindAll* logger software marks all web pages in the top 500 popular pages that are "not cacheable", and these web pages are automatically marked original (or non re-find).

---

[2]We employ one way hashing which does not allow original data to be recovered even with the user-specific key.

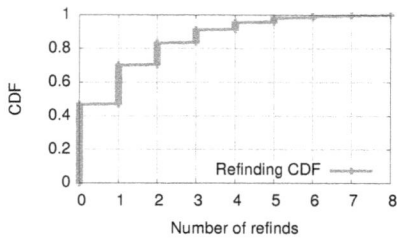

Figure 1: CDF of re-finding pages for all 23 users. Over 52% of the web pages are re-found.

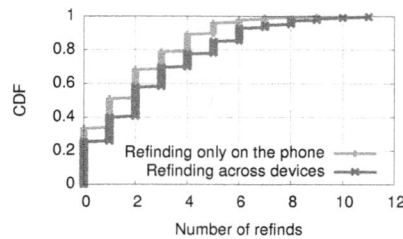

Figure 2: Re-finding when cross-device indexes are used, for the 7 users from whom we collect cross-device indexes.

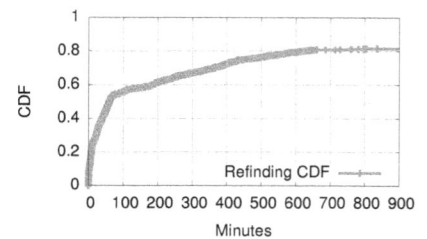

Figure 3: CDF of the time between when a web page is re-found and the first time the page is visited.

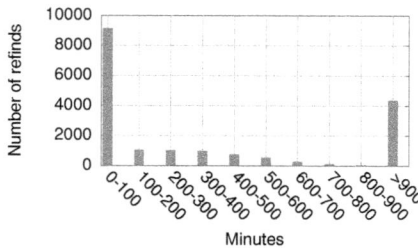

Figure 4: PDF of the time between when a web page is re-found and the first time the page is visited.

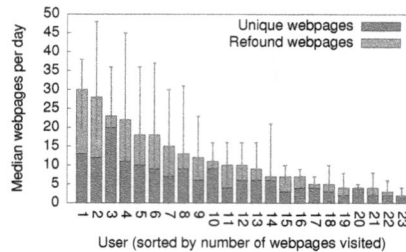

Figure 5: Browsing and re-finding statistics per user. The percentile bar shows the 25th and 75th percentile.

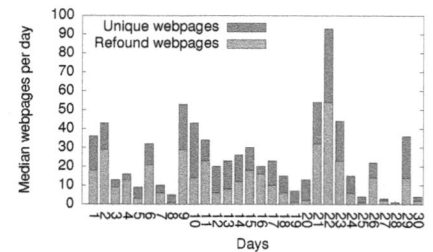

Figure 6: Browsing and re-finding statistics of one user across all the days of the experiment.

3.3 User Study Results

3.3.1 Re-finding across users

More than half of all visited web pages are re-found at least once. Figure 1 shows the CDF of the number of times web pages are re-found by the user; 0 indicates that the page is not re-found, 1 indicates that the page is re-found once, and so on. The figure shows that 52% of the web pages are re-found at least once, and 25% of the web pages are re-found two or more times. This finding is consistent with previous studies that showed re-finding is wide-spread among web search users [23, 15].

Re-finding increases when considering cross-device browsing history. In Figure 2, we compare the cross-device re-finding characteristics. For measuring cross-device re-finding, a web page visited on the phone is marked as re-found if it satisfies the re-finding definition, and is previously viewed either on the user's computer or the user's phone. For the subset of 7 users with cross-device history, the percentage of re-found web pages on the phone increases from 58% to 72%, when the web pages visited on the computer are also included in estimating re-finding. This suggests that leveraging cross-device history can provide substantial benefits for *FindAll*.

Most re-find occur either within the first 50 minutes or after 10 hours. Figure 3, shows the time difference between the first visit to a web page and subsequent visits to the same web page. About 45% of the time, re-finding occurs within the next 50 minutes; a further 20% of the time, web pages are accessed no sooner than 900 minutes after the web page was first visited. (Note that the figure is cropped at 900 minutes.) Figure 4 shows the probability density function of the same data. Taken together, the figures show that web pages need to be indexed relatively soon after a user visits them, to improve availability.

3.3.2 Diversity in browsing and re-finding

Next, we focus on the re-finding behavior of individual users. Figure 5 shows the browsing and re-finding characteristics for each

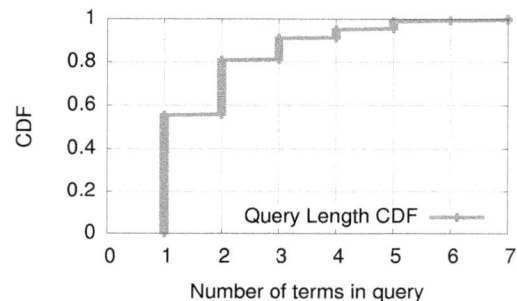

Figure 8: The CDF of the number of terms in a user query.

of the 23 users. The figure shows the median number of web pages browsed by the user.

Three important characteristics emerge from this graph: 1) Users have varied browsing characteristics. While 33% of the users browse more than 15 web pages a day, 30% of the users browse less than 3 web pages per day. 2) The re-finding characteristics vary for different users. For 8 of the 23 users, nearly half of the web pages are re-found web pages, but for 6 of the 23 users, less than 10% of the web page visits are re-finding visits. 3) Even for a given user, browsing behavior varies across different days. The percentile bars shown in Figure 5 are the 25th and the 75th percentile of browsing behavior for a user, and their difference shows that there is significant variability.

3.3.3 Per user browsing and re-finding patterns

Re-finding percentage is consistent for a given user, despite daily variability in browsing patterns. Figure 6 shows the browsing and re-finding behavior across the 30 days for a single, example user. While there is a large variability in browsing patterns for a single user, the re-finding percentage does not vary greatly across days. For the user in Figure 6, the average re-finding over the 30 days is 47% with a standard deviation of only 9%. Analyzing our data we find that the re-finding percentage is fairly consistent across days for most users.

3.3.4 Query characteristics

Figure 8 shows a CDF of the number of terms in each user query. 40% of the queries contain more than 2 terms, with a maximum of 7 terms in a query.

More interestingly, we find that for 24% of the re-find queries, the original query and the re-find query were different (not shown in figure); two queries are different if at least one term in the query do not match. Two queries with the same terms but in different order are considered to be the same.

This finding is consistent with previous studies on the search characteristics of desktop users, which also showed that the original query and re-find query are often different [23].

3.4 Summary

We find two key characteristics of mobile re-finding behavior that have implications for the design of *FindAll*:

1. *Nearly 45% of web pages are re-found in the first 50 minutes*. This motivates the need for a local search engine solution that indexes web pages as soon as they arrive, to improve availability.

2. *Users have diverse but consistent re-finding patterns*. Since some users may seldom re-find web pages, *FindAll* learns the re-finding pattern of users, so that the energy-intensive indexing operation is performed only if there is associated benefit.

We note that the aggregate findings from our user study are consistent with findings of a much larger re-finding study using 8000 Bing mobile users [18]. The Bing study also shows that: (1) mobile users exhibit high re-finding behavior, and (2) users have diverse re-finding characteristics. In addition, our study characterizes non-aggregate day-to-day behavior of mobile search users. For example, we learn that user's show consistent re-finding behavior across days, that a large fraction of re-finding occurs soon after the original search, and that user's often re-find across devices. We also characterize the query term distribution of mobile search queries.

4. FINDALL

FindAll is a local search engine designed specifically for mobile phones.

4.1 Goals

The two main goals of *FindAll* are: (i) to increase local availability of web pages, and (ii) to operate within the memory and battery constraints of phones.

We say that a web page is available locally, if the web page has been indexed locally and can be retrieved from the local cache when the user issues a re-find request. Increasing local availability provides multiple benefits: (1) It enables users to re-find more web pages easily by searching through a smaller collection of locally available web pages. (2) It reduces search latency and reduces the use of expensive 3G data, by avoiding repeated downloads of web pages from the Internet.

In terms of resource constraints, memory and energy are the two most limited resources on mobile phones. We design *FindAll* such that it consumes no more energy than default; the default in our case is Internet-based web search. With respect to memory, we design the *FindAll* indexing algorithm to write to disk frequently, to avoid overflowing available memory.

Next, we discuss the *FindAll* architecture and challenges.

4.2 Architecture

Figure 9 shows the FindAll architecture. *FindAll* stores web pages as a user downloads them, and then indexes them in blocks. *FindAll* stores both the index and the cached web pages on its external memory card.

When a query is submitted to *FindAll*, it runs the retrieval algorithm on the index. The algorithm returns a results page with a set of links, similar to search engines such as Google or Bing. When the user clicks on one of the links, the corresponding web page is fetched from the local cache. If the results page does not contain any link or if none of the links are relevant to the user, the user switches to Internet-based search.

FindAll also indexes web pages on all other devices that the user browses, such as their laptop and desktop computers. When the phone is being charged, *FindAll* downloads the cross-device indexes on to the phone and merges them with the existing index. *FindAll* also downloads the corresponding web page cache to the phone.

4.2.1 Partial indexes

Traditionally, search engines use static indexing, which are designed to index large collections of documents in one-go. However, static indexing approaches cannot effectively handle the frequent updates necessary for maintaining high-availability in *FindAll*'s local search engine.

Therefore, we implement a dynamic indexer that is designed for handling frequent updates [17]. Our implementation builds partial indexes of smaller blocks of web pages in main memory. Partial indexes allow for web pages to be indexed as they arrive, increasing the local availability of a web page. The partial indexes are then merged periodically.

Maintaining the partial index in memory is more energy efficient, as merging partial indexes that are in-memory requires less energy and compute resources. However, because of the severe memory constraints in phones, *FindAll* writes the partial indexes to disk as soon as they are created. To illustrate the memory constraint in phones, consider the following example. The HTC thunderbolt phone, released in 2011, has around 800 MB RAM. However, only 240 MB is available for applications. In our experiments, indexing 50 web pages and maintaining the index in-memory resulted in the phone running out of memory. In this instance, no other application was using the memory. In the presence of multiple background applications, the number of web page indexes that can be maintained in memory becomes even less.

As a consequence of not maintaing in-memory partial indexes, *FindAll* incurs higher energy costs due to merging. We note that it is essential that the partial indexes be merged; as the number of partial indexes grow, the retrieval latency increases, because the retrieval algorithm needs to search through each partial index. Our experiments show that, as the number of partial indexes grow, the retrieval latency becomes higher than the latency of downloading from the Internet, thus reducing the benefits of a local search engine.

4.2.2 When to index?

FindAll buffers downloaded web pages and indexes them as a block. The central question in *FindAll*'s architecture is in deciding when to index the buffered web pages.

On the one hand, indexing in smaller block sizes improves local availability and consumes less energy by reducing number of Internet downloads. On the other hand, indexing in smaller block sizes consumes more energy during indexing due to the need for frequent merging of the partial indexes.

To understand the trade-off between indexing small block sizes vs indexing large block sizes, we conduct a simple experiment.

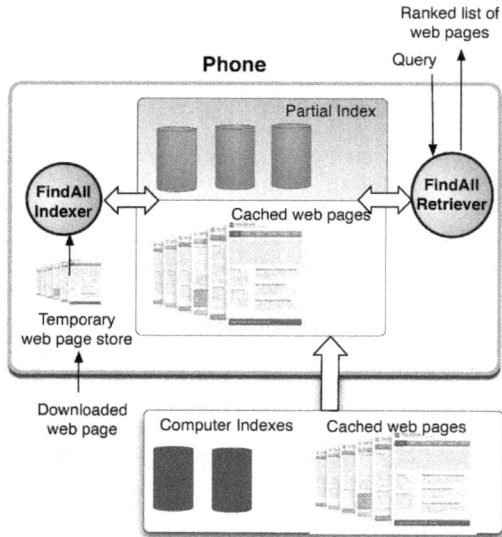

Figure 9: *FindAll* **local search engine**

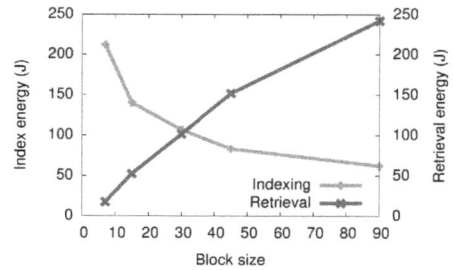

Figure 10: Experiment that shows the trade-off between avail-ability and indexing energy.

We index 90 web pages obtained from the Microsoft Search logs, with a total size of 12.3MB. We adapt a publicly available search engine called Galago [2] to index the web pages. We conduct all our energy measurement using the Monsoon Power Monitor [3] using a Motorola Droid phone. All network activities are conducted on the 3G interface.

Figure 10 shows the trade-off between the index energy and availability. The x axis shows the block size; a block size of 15 implies that indexes are created when 15 web pages are downloaded. The left y axis shows the energy required to index the web pages; indexing all the 90 web pages together consumes only 52 Joules, while indexing in block sizes of 15 web pages require 140 Joules, a nearly 3-fold increase. This is because of the additional energy cost incurred due to merging.

We then assume that 20% of the search queries are re-finding queries, uniformly; note that this is a conservative estimate. The right y axis shows the energy cost of not indexing (i.e., the cost to download the search result from the Internet) for different block sizes. For example, if we wait for all 90 web pages to be downloaded before indexing, 18 re-found web pages will need to be downloaded from the Internet because they are not available locally. Clearly, there is an optimal block size that balances the two opposing goals.

In the next section, we describe how *FindAll* estimates when to index a block of web pages, to balance its twin goals of availability and energy.

5. FINDALL INDEXING ALGORITHM

The *FindAll* indexing algorithm decides when to index a set of buffered web pages. The goal of the indexing decision is to maximize local availability, while ensuring that *FindAll* consumes no more energy than default search.

Figure 11 shows the *FindAll* indexing algorithm. *FindAll* makes indexing decisions by comparing the expected energy cost of index-ing web pages ($E[I]$) and the expected cost of not indexing web pages ($E[\neg I]$).

- The cost of indexing web pages ($E[I]$) includes the cost of indexing the current block of web pages, as well as a penalty

based on expected cost of indexing future web pages. The penalty is designed to penalize indexing of small block sizes.

- The cost of not indexing web pages ($E[\neg I]$) is simply the energy required to search and download each web page from the Internet; in other words it is the energy required for default web search.

FindAll will decide to index a block of web pages, if the cost of indexing ($E[I]$) is lower than the cost of using default web search ($E[\neg I]$). Next, we describe the estimation of $E[I]$ and $E[\neg I]$.

5.1 Expected cost of indexing ($E[I]$)

We estimate indexing cost as the sum of the current indexing cost and a penalty. The penalty is the estimated impact of the current indexing decision on future indexing operations.

The penalty is designed to discourage indexing small blocks, which can lead to more merge operations in the future. Specifically, if *FindAll* decides to index a block of B web pages, it estimates the cost of indexing future web pages, as if all future pages are also indexed in blocks of size B. The penalty is then computed as the energy to index future web pages normalized over the total number of blocks. Our evaluations (§7.4) show that this simple heuristic for penalty estimation provides a good balance between availability and energy, compared to alternate indexing strategies that do not penalize indexing in small blocks.

5.1.1 Energy for indexing and merging

The energy spent in indexing a block of B web pages is the sum of the energy to index the block and then merge the partial index with the existing index. Let the number of bytes in the block of B web pages be denoted by $|B|$ and number of bytes in the existing index be denoted by $|P|$. The value of $|P|$ is known. Then,

$$\text{Expected energy to index/merge } B \text{ web pages} =$$
$$\text{Energy to index } |B| \text{ bytes}$$
$$+\text{Energy to merge indexes of sum size } |B| + |P| \text{ bytes} \quad (1)$$

We use a simple linear model to estimate the energy to index and merge web pages of a certain size. To this end, we index web pages of various sizes (without merging) from 0 to 5MB in 200K intervals, and fit a linear model to the data. This allows us to compute the energy to index web pages for a given number of bytes. Similarly, we build a linear model to estimate the energy to merge two indexes of a given sum size.

5.1.2 Penalty

To penalize energy decisions that index in small blocks, we assume that the remaining web pages for the day will also be indexed using a block size of B.

Suppose that there are W additional pages that the user will download during the day [3]. Then the penalty for indexing the remaining W web pages in blocks of B is given by:

$$\text{Penalty} = \frac{B}{W} \times \{ \frac{W}{B} \times \text{Energy to index } |B| \text{ bytes } +$$
$$\text{Energy to merge } \frac{W}{B} \text{ partial indexes} \} \quad (2)$$

We note that $\frac{B}{W}$ is the normalization/amortization factor.
The expected cost of indexing a block of B web pages is then given by:

$$E[I] = \text{Expected energy to index/merge } B \text{ web pages} + \text{Penalty} \quad (3)$$

5.2 Expected cost of not indexing ($E[\neg I]$)

To estimate the cost of not indexing a block of web pages *FindAll* first estimates the probability that a web page will be re-found. We first describe how *FindAll* estimates this probability, and then describe the estimation of $E[\neg I]$.

5.2.1 Predicting re-finding probability

FindAll uses the re-finding patterns of users to estimate the probability that a web page will be re-found. To this end, we built an *online* classifier, which when given a web page and the time of evaluation, estimates the probability that the web page will be re-found in the next T time units. The variable T is the same time interval used by the *FindAll* indexing algorithm (Figure 11).

Features:.

We use three features to train our classifier:,

- Base re-find probability – The fraction of user requests that are re-find requests. This feature encodes the intuition that if the user re-finds often in the past, then she is likely to re-find often in the future. Recall that the user's refinding patterns remain consistent across different days (§3.3.3), and is therefore a consistent signal for re-finding. This feature takes fraction values between 0 and 1.

- Session features – Is the user currently in a browsing session? The intuition for this feature is that, if the user is not currently in a browsing session, then it is unlikely that the user will be browsing, and in turn, it is unlikely that the user will re-find webpages. The session feature takes a binary value of 0 or 1, depending on whether the user is in a browsing session or not.

- Download history of the page – Has the web page been re-found recently? The intuition is that if the user recently re-found a web page, then it is likely that the user will re-find the web page again [23]. The download history feature takes a binary value of 0 or 1, depending on whether the web page has been re-found recently or not.

Classifier training:.

To train the classifier, we use half of the data we collect from each user in our user study. Starting from the beginning of the trace, we gather all web pages that were downloaded in each T time unit. We assign labels to each web page in this set: *re-find* if the web page was indeed re-found in the next T time units; *not-refind* otherwise.

---

[3] *FindAll* keeps track of the average web pages browsed per day to estimate W.

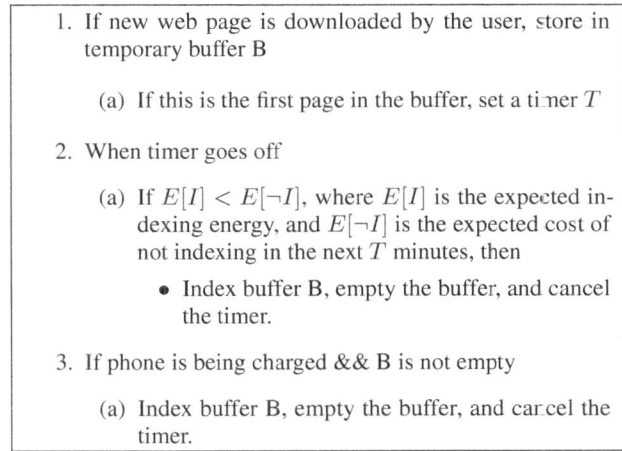

---

1. If new web page is downloaded by the user, store in temporary buffer B

    (a) If this is the first page in the buffer, set a timer T

2. When timer goes off

    (a) If $E[I] < E[\neg I]$, where $E[I]$ is the expected indexing energy, and $E[\neg I]$ is the expected cost of not indexing in the next T minutes, then

        - Index buffer B, empty the buffer, and cancel the timer.

3. If phone is being charged && B is not empty

    (a) Index buffer B, empty the buffer, and cancel the timer.

Figure 11: *FindAll* indexing.

The process is repeated for each T interval to obtain a set of labeled instances. Each of these labeled instances are represented using the the three features described above.

We learn a logistic regression classifier; the goal of the classifier is to minimize classification errors on this training data. On its completion, the learning algorithm outputs a set of weights corresponding to each feature. At each time instance, the re-finding probability of a web page is computed as the weighted sum of each feature value at that time instance. As previously noted, the weights for the weighted sum computation are obtained from the learning algorithm.

The classifier only needs to be trained once a day during periods of inactivity or when the phone is being charged. Since the prediction only involves computing a weighted sum of feature values, there is little energy consumption for the prediction.

Our prediction algorithm used only three simple sets of features; our evaluations show that *FindAll* is able to use the predictions to avoid indexing web pages for low re-find users (§7.4). Due to the privacy preserving nature of the data collection, we did not use any text based features in our prediction algorithm. An actual implementation of the system, however, will have access to the queries, the URLs and the text of the web pages. Such a system can use several textual features, further improving the prediction.

5.2.2 Estimating cost of not indexing

Given our estimates of the re-finding probability, we first make a simplifying assumption that the re-finding probabilities of each web page is independent. Then, given a block of B web pages, the cost of not indexing each web page $w \in B$ is the energy to search and download web page w, if w were re-found. Therefore,

$$E[\neg I] = \sum_{w \in B} \text{Energy to search and download } w \times$$
$$\text{Probability(w will be re-found)} \quad (4)$$

To estimate the energy to search and download w, we build a simple model, similar to the one described in [11]. We download web pages of varying sizes over 3G, and measure the power consumption using the Power Monitor [3]. We use the measurements to build a linear model of energy consumed to download a web page or a search result page of a given size. Similarly, we model the energy consumption over WiFi links. *FindAll* determines the energy consumption to download the search results page and the web page, based on the network in which it is currently operating

6. IMPLEMENTATION

We implement *FindAll* on the Android operating system. The search engine is adapted from the publicly available Galago search engine [2]. We implement dynamic indexing in Galago to allow blocks of web pages to be indexed into partial indexes. We use the machine learning tool Weka [13] to perform our classifications.

Although we implement *FindAll* over Galago, the indexing strategy is agnostic to the search engine. *FindAll* provides a strategy for creating partial indexes of <word, web page> tuples and merging the indexes in a constrained environment. Any dynamic indexer will need to perform similar indexing and merging activities.

The *FindAll* indexer is implemented as a service on Android, and it periodically indexes web pages, according to the algorithm in Figure 11. We set the time interval T to 5 minutes; i.e., *FindAll* makes indexing decisions every 5 minutes. This ensures that web pages frequently get a chance to be indexed.

Both the cached web pages and the indexes are stored in the memory card. When the user issues a query to *FindAll*, it searches over its local index and returns a search result page with links. When a user clicks on the link, the locally cached web page is retrieved. If the web page is not indexed, *FindAll* falls back to default search, and retrieves the search results from the Internet.

FindAll also indexes web pages on the user's computers. When the phone is being charged, the *FindAll* software on the phone downloads the computer indexes (and the corresponding cached web pages) on to the phone.

In the current version of our implementation, we assume that the user specifies if the query is a re-find query. If it is a re-find query, then the *FindAll* system retrieves the web pages locally; else the web pages are retrieved from the Internet. A mechanism for automatically determining if a query is a re-find request will further enhance the usability of *FindAll*.

We conduct all our evaluations using this *FindAll* implementation using a Motorola DroidX phone. The phone has both a WiFi and a 3G interface, and uses Verizon as the cellular provider.

7. EVALUATION

Our evaluations aim to show that

- *FindAll* improves local availability of web pages and as a result, decreases search latency and 3G data usage.
- *FindAll*'s local availability benefits do not come at an energy cost.
- Compared to alternate indexing strategies that either always index or use the cloud for indexing, *FindAll*'s indexing strategy is more energy efficient and improves availability.
- *FindAll*'s index-based search significantly improves search effectiveness compared to keyword matching or using a database lookup.

7.1 Evaluation methodology

We use the browser logs collected during the user study to evaluate *FindAll*. Our user study collects the time when the user issues a query or requests a web page, the hash values of the query/web page, and the size of the subsequent download. Recall (§3.2.1) that we perform an offline analysis to mark each query/web page as *re-find* or *not re-find*. For our experiments, we assume that this marking represents the user specifying whether a query is a re-find query or a first-time query. All direct web page visits, that are not reached through a search query, are always marked *non re-find*.

Since the traces only contain hashes of the search queries and visited web pages, we map these hashes to real queries and web pages. For each <query hash, web page hash> pair in our logs,

we pick an appropriate <real query, real web page> pair from the Microsoft search query logs obtained from Microsoft Live Labs [4]. To perform the mapping, we keep track of the different re-find queries used to search the same web page, both in our traces and in the Microsoft search logs. This allows us to map different variations of queries in our log to different variation of the real queries; recall that 24% of the re-find queries in our logs were different from the original query. Clearly, the same query/web page hash in our logs are mapped to the same query/web page in the Microsoft logs.

To emulate the search session, we replay the log traces. For web pages in the trace that are not reached through a search request, we directly download the web page from the Internet. For other requests, we do the following:

Default search: For each search query, we submit the query to Google, download the search results page, and subsequently download the web page(s) visited by the user through the search query.

FindAll: For each search query marked *re-find*, we submit the search query to *FindAll*. *FindAll* searches the local cache and returns a search results page. If the *FindAll* search is successful, then the results page will contain links to the web pages subsequently visited by the user. These are then fetched from the local cache. If *FindAll* is unsuccessful, either because the page is not indexed/cached yet or if the search algorithm could not retrieve the relevant web page, then we fall back to default search. If the search query is marked *non re-find*, we use default search to retrieve the web pages.

As the search session is played, *FindAll* indexes web pages according to the implementation (§6). The first half of the user's log is used for training *FindAll*'s prediction algorithm. We conduct our experiments using the second half of the logs. We assume that the users use the 3G network for all their interactions. Unless specified, we do not use the cross-device indexes and only use the mobile indexes for search.

7.2 FindAll benefits

FindAll trades storage for Internet connectivity to improve local availability. Figure 12 shows that *FindAll* often retrieves web pages from the local cache, without requiring Internet connectivity: For 6 of the 23 users, *FindAll* retrieves over 40% of the web pages locally. We call these users high re-find users. *FindAll* improves local availability by an average of 20% for the remaining users.

Improving local availability reduces the need for downloading web pages from the Internet, resulting in two key benefits: (1) reduced search latency, and (2) reduced 3G data usage.

FindAll reduces search latency by 2-folds for high re-find users. Figure 13 shows that at its best, *FindAll* reduces per request retrieval latency from 3.35 seconds to 1.65 seconds. As can be expected, *FindAll* does not provide uniform improvements for all users; *FindAll* provides less than 10% latency improvement for 5 of the 23 users, due to the low re-finding behavior of these users.

FindAll reduces search latency by over 3-folds when using cross-device indexes. Figure 14 shows that when browsing logs from all of the user's devices are cached and indexed, the local availability increases even further, reducing the search latency by over 3-folds compared to default search, for certain users.

FindAll reduces 3G data usage by up to 100 MB a month for high re-find users. Figure 15 shows the savings in 3G data usage compared to default web search. On an average, *FindAll* saves 80 MB of 3G data a month for the 6 high re-find users. For one user, the 3G savings is 100 MB a month. If the user has a 500 MB limit on their 3G data plan, a 100 MB savings translates to 20% of the

---

[4] The search logs are available to research labs, but are not available online.

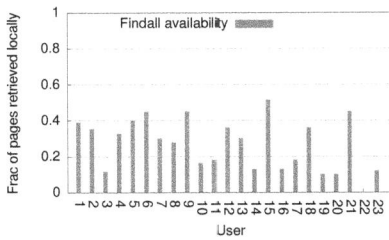

Figure 12: Benefits: *FindAll* increases availability by retrieving web pages from the local cache for over 30% of search queries for 10 of the 23 users.

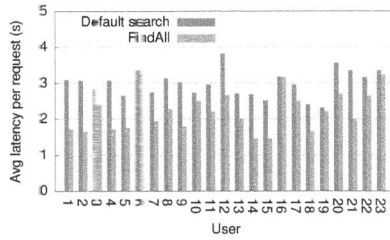

Figure 13: Benefits: Increasing availability results in lower search latency compared to default search. At its best case, *FindAll* reduces latency from 3.35 to 1.65 seconds.

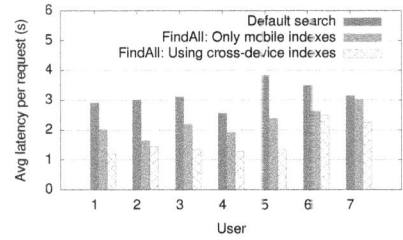

Figure 14: Benefits: Using cross-device indexes that combines browser history from all devices of a given user, further reduces search latency by up to 3-folds compared to default search.

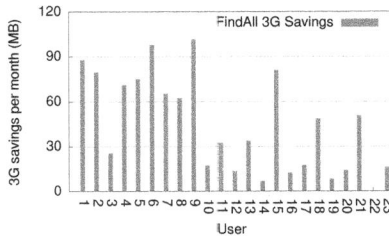

Figure 15: Benefits: Improving local availability results in considerable savings in 3G data usage, that is especially important given tiered data plans.

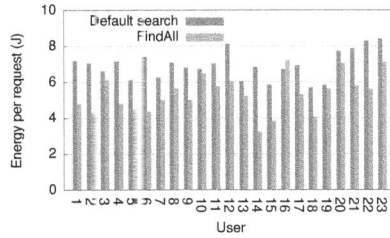

Figure 16: Cost: *FindAll*'s latency and 3G savings does not come at an energy cost. In fact, *FindAll* reduces energy consumption by 30% for high re-find users.

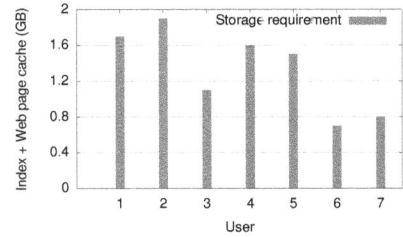

Figure 17: Cost: *FindAll*'s storage requirements, even when indexing across all of the user's devices, is considerably lower than current memory card capacities.

user's 3G limit. As carriers impose stricter 3G caps and introduce tiered payment plans [21], 3G savings using a local search engine will become more and more attractive to users.

7.3 FindAll costs

FindAll's benefit with respect to availability, latency, and 3G data usage, does not come at an energy cost. To perform the energy experiment, we run the user trace on the phone for both default search and *FindAll*, as before, and measure the power consumption using the Monsoon Power Monitor [3]. The power monitor provides accurate energy measurements by sampling the current drawn from the battery with a frequency of 5000 Hz.

FindAll reduces the energy consumption by 30% for high re-find users. We first note that our goal in *FindAll*'s design is to ensure that the energy consumption of *FindAll* is no more than that of default search. Figure 16 shows that *FindAll* in fact saves energy by retrieving web pages locally. For the 6 high re-find users, *FindAll* reduces the energy consumption by over 30%. More importantly, even for users who do not re-find often, *FindAll* does not increase overall energy consumption.

FindAll's energy benefits are primarily due to its indexing algorithm; *FindAll* takes into account the re-finding patterns of each user before making an indexing decision. We show in §7.4 that, instead, if web pages were indexed as soon as they arrive, a local search engine will consume significantly more energy compared to default search.

FindAll's storage requirements are modest. Figure 17 presents the storage requirement for *FindAll*'s indexes and cached web pages for 30 days. We present the storage requirement for the 7 users for whom we store cross-device indexes; these users have the largest storage requirement (the remaining users had a storage requirement

of less than 0.3 GB per month). At its maximum, the storage requirement for *FindAll* is less than 1.9 GB; most phones have external memory cards that have a capacity of 64 GB or more. Thus, a 1-month index occupies only a small fraction of the available storage.

7.4 Comparing with alternate indexing strategies

FindAll balances availability and energy cost using its indexing algorithm. At its core, *FindAll* determines when to index a block of web pages by predicting the users re-finding behavior. Below, we compare *FindAll*'s indexing strategy with 4 alternate strategies.

- *Always-Index*: Indexes every web page as soon as it is downloaded (i.e., the block size is always 1).
- *Cloud-Index*: Indexes web pages in the cloud and periodically uploads the incremental indexes to the mobile.
- *Fixed-Block-Index*: Indexes web pages in fixed-sized blocks.
- *Never-Index*: No indexing; default search.

For clarity, we present the results of our experiments for a subset of 6 users, two users in each of the three categories: *High re-find users*, for whom 40% or more web pages are retrieved locally, *Medium re-find users*, for whom 15% to 25% of web pages are retrieved locally, and *Low re-find users*, for whom less than 10% of the web pages are retrieved locally. We also repeated the experiments for the remaining users and found the results to be qualitatively similar (not shown here).

When using the Cloud-Index strategy, we upload data from the cloud every 30 minutes; when using Fixed-Block-Index strategy, we index documents in block sizes of 5 web pages. We evaluated

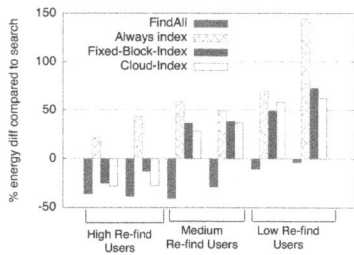

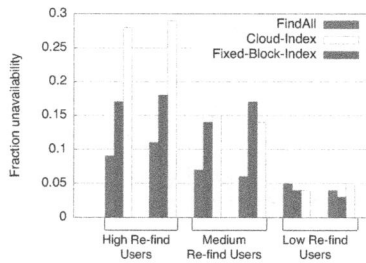

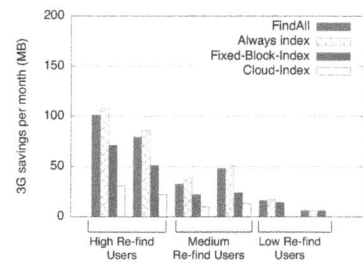

Figure 18: Comparing energy cost: The Always-Index strategy consumes considerably more energy compared to default, for all users. The Cloud-Index and Fixed-Block-Index strategies consume more energy compared to default search for low re-find users.

Figure 19: Comparing unavailability: The Cloud-Index strategy is up to 67% more unavailable, and Fixed-Block-Index strategy is up to 39% more unavailable compared to *FindAll* for high re-find users. High unavailability will result in lower latency and 3G saving benefits.

Figure 20: Comparing 3G saving benefits: The 3G savings of the Always-Index strategy is only 5% better than *FindAll*, even though it has 0 unavailability. *FindAll* provides more 3G savings than Cloud-Index and Fixed-Block-Index strategies by improving availability.

other upload periods and block sizes, and chose these values as they provided the best energy and availability trade-off.

All alternate indexing strategies consume significantly more energy compared to default search.. Figure 18 compares the increase/decrease in the percentage energy consumption compared to default search. The Always-Index strategy has the worst energy characteristics, and at its worst, incurs a 140% increase in energy consumption compared to default search. For low re-find users, all three alternate indexing strategies perform worse than default search with respect to energy. This is because, the alternate strategies do not adapt to the user's re-finding patterns, and instead index web pages even if the user is unlikely to re-find. For low re-find users, indexing web pages do not provide any energy benefit, resulting in a net energy wastage. In contrast, *FindAll* does not index often for low re-find users, reducing its energy consumption.

At its peak, the absolute energy difference between the Always-Index strategy and default search is 140 Joules (not shown in figure). Going beyond web search, this difference will become even more significant as local indexes are used to retrieve content for other apps. For example, we repeated the above experiment using the desktop search history from our logs; users download considerably more web pages on their desktops than on their mobile phones. The absolute energy difference between Always-Index and default search when using desktop logs increased to 960 Joules.

FindAll improves local availability compared to Cloud-Index and Fixed-Block-Index strategies. Figure 19 compares the unavailability across the different indexing strategies. We define *unavailability* as the fraction of time user issues a re-find query, but the corresponding web page is not available in the index. For high re-find users, the indexing frequency of Cloud-Index and Fixed-Block-Index strategies are too low; as a result, several re-find queries are not satisfied locally. The unavailability of the Always-Index strategy is 0, since the web pages are indexed immediately. Although the Always-Index strategy has lowest unavailability, we see next that its benefits are only slightly better than that of *FindAll*.

FindAll saves significantly more 3G data compared to both Fixed-Block-Index and Cloud-Index strategy. Recall that one of *FindAll*'s benefits is that it reduces 3G data usage compared to default web search by retrieving web pages locally. Figure 20 shows that by reducing unavailability, *FindAll* substantially improves 3G savings compared to the Cloud-Index and Fixed-Block-Index strategies. The Cloud-Index strategy performs especially poorly with respect to 3G data usage because it uploads indexes periodically through the cloud.

For low re-find users, we omit the 3G savings using the Cloud-Index strategy, because the Cloud-Index strategy uses more 3G data than default web search. More importantly, even though the Always-Index strategy has 0 unavailability, it only saves 3G data usage by an additional 5% over *FindAll*.

7.5 FindAll vs Keyword matching vs Database lookup

Next, we compare *FindAll* with two alternate search techniques: (i) Keyword matching: Returns all web pages that contain the query terms in no particular order, and (ii) Database lookup: Stores already seen web pages in a database, as <query, web page> pairs. Web pages are retrieved by using the query as the key.

7.5.1 Search effectiveness

The effectiveness of a search engine depends on whether the search results contain the relevant web page that the user is searching for. This is especially true in mobile phones where only 3-4 search results can be presented on the screen. If the relevant web page is returned as, say, the 20th search result, the user has to scroll through multiple screens before finding the relevant page.

In Figure 21 we ran the three alternate strategies, and counted the number of times the relevant web page was within the top 3 search results. The relevant web page is the page the user eventually clicks on, and we obtain this information from our logs. *FindAll returns the relevant web page 96% of the time within the top 3 search results, compared to 64% when using keyword matching, and 71% when using database lookup.*

The database lookup fails to return the relevant web page if the original query and the re-find query are different. Recall (§3) that the re-find query and the original query are different for 24% of the queries in our log. For a small percentage of cases (8%), the database lookup failed to return the relevant web page because the original web page was not retrieved through a search query. This can happen, for example, if the user visits a web page originally via social media but wants to re-find the web page later through search. Keyword matching is not effective in searching for a specific web page, since it returns every web page that contains the query terms.

7.5.2 Performance under no connectivity

To understand the importance of search effectiveness, we conduct experiments in a simulated *no connectivity* environment. One of the

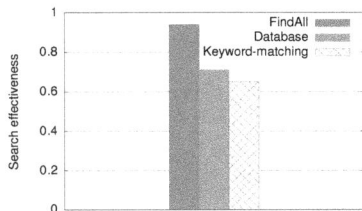

Figure 21: *FindAll* returns the relevant web page 96% of the time within the top 3 search results, compared to 64% when using keyword matching and 71% when using database lookups.

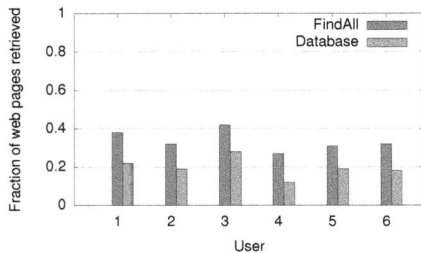

Figure 22: *FindAll* doubles the number of web pages that are retrieved even in the absence of connectivity, compared to using a database lookup.

main advantages of a local search engine is that web pages can be retrieved even when there is no connectivity.

Figure 22 shows the percentage of web pages retrieved if we assume that there is no connectivity for 50% of the trace for each user. We randomly choose the periods of no connectivity and repeat the experiment 5 times with different seed values. We present the average. Note that this scenario is not far fetched; 4 of the 23 users in our user study did not have a 3G data plan. Such users may not be connected to the Internet for large parts of their day.

We present the results for the 6 high re-find users. *FindAll* retrieves the relevant web page for 35–40% of the search queries even when there is no connectivity. In contrast, search using a database lookup only returns the relevant web page for 20% of the search queries. This is a direct consequence of the poorer search effectiveness of a database lookup.

8. RELATED WORK

Our work is inspired by several related research efforts. Below we contrast our work from existing work.

8.1 Local database

The Pocket Cloudlets [15] work explores storage architectures that allow mobile phones to trade-off connectivity for local storage. The goals of *FindAll* align well with the goals of Pocket Cloudlets. The core idea in Pocket Cloudlets is to store the *search results page* in a local database and use the query as the key to the lookup database. The search results are retrieved in response to a query using the database lookup; however, the web page itself is not stored locally. The web page needs to be re-downloaded from the Internet. The goal of PocketCloudlets is to only eliminate the latency in retrieving the search results page, and not the web page itself.

The database lookup cannot retrieve the web page if the re-find query is different from the original query. *FindAll* uses a full blown search engine; as a result, *FindAll* works even if the re-find query

terms are different from the original query terms (§7.5). In addition, *FindAll* stores the web pages in the phone, so that they can be retrieved locally, unlike PocketCloudlets. This results in additional benefits with respect to latency and 3G data savings.

PocketWeb [18], a system built on top of the PocketCloudlets system, dynamically updates web pages stored in the mobile cache, by learning the browsing behavior of users. The goals of PocketWeb is complimentary to the goals of *FindAll*. In the current implementation of *FindAll*, the web pages stored in the cache are not refreshed. Periodically refreshing the local web pages using a PocketWeb-like system can further increase the utility of *FindAll*.

Finally, the authors of PocketWeb [18] and PocketCloudlets [15] conduct a mobile user study using Bing search logs. In an earlier section (§3), we detail the similarities and differences between these studies and the *FindAll* study.

8.2 Cloud solutions

Several commercial solutions allow users to search through their history, or sync the browser history across devices. For example, search engines such as Bing and Google provide a history feature that allows (logged-in) users to search through their search history. The search engines store the history in the cloud. The Chrome Sync feature on the chrome browser allows users to sync all the URLs they visit, across their devices. The Chrome Sync feature augments search, but the user still needs to connect to the Internet to retrieve the web page.

The search engine and the chrome browser solutions require that the user have good Internet connectivity, whereas *FindAll* operates even when connectivity to the Internet is poor or unavailable. Further, *FindAll* allows users to store their search history under their own control, alleviating some of the privacy concerns of letting a search provider store the history.

8.3 Cache-based approaches

Browser history and bookmarks store a link to a web page previously downloaded by the user. To re-find a web page, the user has to manually browse through the history, which is tedious on mobile phones.

Similarly, Web caching solutions [9, 8, 12, 28] store a copy of the web page locally, to reduce latency and improve performance of web browsing. However, web caching can be leveraged for re-finding only if the user has a link to the URL; usually users do not remember the URL. Some browsers such as Opera and Safari cache URLs and match new URL requests character by character to cached ones, to provide hints to users. However, even these solutions require that the users remember partial URLs. Further, previous research has shown that users rarely look through their history or their cache to re-find web pages [10].

8.4 Cross-device synchronization

The Dessy system [16] is a mobile desktop search system. Dessy indexes files across multiple devices and uses the mobile phone to search through the index. The authors build the search engine indexes in the cloud and upload the index to the mobile phone. Instead, *FindAll* implements a search engine locally on the phone, and we show that the local index performs better than a cloud-based index.

Finally, *FindAll* goes beyond search–*FindAll* indexes all web pages that the user downloads; not just those found through a search engine. Today, a large proportion of browsing activity originates from social networking apps and emails. Say, Bob reads an article that he finds through facebook, and wishes to re-find this article. The search engine or a database lookup will not have stored this

287

article because it was not found through search. However, *FindAll* indexes all web pages, and therefore can retrieve the article for Bob. The search interface in *FindAll* can also potentially leverage the re-finding characteristics of other apps, including social networking apps, maps, and movie databases.

Similarly, *FindAll* is useful not only to re-find previously viewed web pages, but also to search within previously viewed web pages. For example, a user searching for hotels in Alaska may want to look for "Valet Parking" within the hotels that she previously viewed. By building an index, *FindAll* allows users to issue new queries to their local cache.

9. CONCLUSIONS AND FUTURE WORK

In this work, we developed *FindAll*, a local search engine that supports re-finding on mobile phones. To aid with its design and to better understand mobile re-finding, we conducted a user study with 23 users over 30 days. The study showed that users have diverse browsing and re-finding habits, and 45% of the URLs are re-found within 50 minutes. Therefore, the key design goal in *FindAll* is to design a search engine that indexes web pages locally and soon after the URL is first visited, to improve availability. The challenge is in designing a search engine for a resource-constrained mobile environment, while adapting to the user's re-finding behavior. To this end, *FindAll* indexes web pages only when the expected energy benefit of indexing outweigh the indexing cost. *FindAll* estimates the benefits of indexing by learning the re-finding patterns of each user and predicting the re-finding probability. We implemented *FindAll* over Android by adapting a publicly available search engine called Galago. Our evaluations show that *FindAll* reduces search latency by two-folds for users who re-find often. *FindAll* also reduces 3G data usage by up to 100 MB a month by serving over 40% of the web pages locally.

10. ACKNOWLEDGEMENTS

We thank our shepherd, Y. Charlie Hu, and all anonymous reviewers. Their reviews and comments greatly helped improve the presentation of this paper. We thank all the participants of our user study who helped us collect data. This work was supported in part by an NSF Computing Innovation Fellowship and NSF grant CNS-1217644.

11. REFERENCES

[1] Alexa top 500 websites.: http://www.alexa.com/topsites.
[2] Galago search engine: http://www.galagosearch.org/.
[3] Monsoon power monitor.: http://www.msoon.com/.
[4] D. Abrams, R. Baecker, and M. Chignell. Information archiving with bookmarks: personal web space construction and organization. In *Proceedings of the SIGCHI conference on Human factors in computing systems*, pages 41–48, 1998.
[5] E. Adar, J. Teevan, and S. T. Dumais. Resonance on the web: web dynamics and revisitation patterns. In *Proceedings of the 27th international conference on Human factors in computing systems*, pages 1381–1390, 2009.
[6] A. Aula, N. Jhaveri, and M. Käki. Information search and re-access strategies of experienced web users. In *Proceedings of the 14th international conference on World Wide Web*, WWW '05, pages 583–592, New York, NY, USA, 2005. ACM.
[7] A. Balasubramanian, R. Mahajan, and A. Venkataramani. Augmenting mobile 3g using wifi. In *MobiSys '10: Proceedings of the 8th international conference on Mobile systems, applications, and services*, pages 209–222, New York, NY, USA, 2010. ACM.
[8] G. Barish and K. Obraczka. World wide web caching: Trends and techniques. *IEEE Communications Magazine*, 38:178–184, 2000.
[9] E. Benson, A. Marcus, D. Karger, and S. Madden. Sync kit: a persistent client-side database caching toolkit for data intensive

[10] websites. In *Proceedings of the 19th international conference on World wide web*, WWW '10, pages 121–130, New York, NY, USA, 2010. ACM.
[10] A. Cockburn, S. Greenberg, S. Jones, B. Mckenzie, and M. Moyle. Improving web page revisitation: analysis, design and evaluation. *IT & Society*, 1:159–183, 2003.
[11] E. Cuervo, A. Balasubramanian, D.-k. Cho, A. Wolman, S. Saroiu, R. Chandra, and P. Bahl. Maui: making smartphones last longer with code offload. In *MobiSys '10: Proceedings of the 8th international conference on Mobile systems, applications, and services*, pages 49–62, New York, NY, USA, 2010. ACM.
[12] T. Fagni, R. Perego, F. Silvestri, and S. Orlando. Boosting the performance of web search engines: Caching and prefetching query results by exploiting historical usage data. *ACM Trans. Inf. Syst.*, 24:51–78, January 2006.
[13] M. Hall, E. Frank, G. Holmes, B. Pfahringer, P. Reutemann, and I. Witten. The weka data mining software: an update. *ACM SIGKDD Explorations Newsletter*, 11(1):10–18, 2009.
[14] J. Huang, Q. Xu, B. Tiwana, Z. M. Mao, M. Zhang, and P. Bahl. Anatomizing application performance differences on smartphones. In *Proceedings of the 8th international conference on Mobile systems, applications, and services*, MobiSys '10, pages 165–178, New York, NY, USA, 2010. ACM.
[15] E. Koukoumidis, D. Lymperopoulos, K. Strauss, J. Liu, and D. Burger. Pocket cloudlets. In *Proceedings of the sixteenth international conference on Architectural support for programming languages and operating systems*, ASPLOS '11, pages 171–184, New York, NY, USA, 2011. ACM.
[16] E. Lagerspetz, T. Lindholm, and S. Tarkoma. Dessy: Towards flexible mobile desktop search. In *Proceedings of the DIALM-POMC International Workshop on Foundations of Mobile Computing, Portland, Oregon, August 16, 2007, CD-ROM*. ACM, 2007.
[17] N. Lester, A. Moffat, and J. Zobel. Efficient online index construction for text databases. *ACM Trans. Database Syst.*, 33:19:1–19:33, September 2008.
[18] D. Lymperopoulos, O. Riva, K. Strauss, A. Mittal, and A. Ntoulas. Pocketweb: instant web browsing for mobile devices. *SIGARCH Comput. Archit. News*, 40(1):1–12, Mar. 2012.
[19] Microsoft. See your search history: http://onlinehelp.microsoft.com/en-us/bing/ff808483.aspx.
[20] P. Shodjai. Your slice of the web: http://tinyurl.com/24vhmw, 2007.
[21] Sprint Capping Unlimited 3G Data Service at 5GB. http://gizmodo.com/391887/oh-no-sprint-capping-unlimited-3g-data-service-at- 2008.
[22] J. Teevan, E. Adar, R. Jones, and M. A. S. Potts. Information re-retrieval: repeat queries in yahoo's logs. In *Proceedings of the 30th annual international ACM SIGIR conference on Research and development in information retrieval*, pages 151–158, 2007.
[23] S. K. Tyler and J. Teevan. Large scale query log analysis of re-finding. In *Proceedings of the third ACM international conference on Web search and data mining*, pages 191–200, 2010.
[24] S. K. Tyler, J. Wang, and Y. Zhang. Utilizing re-finding for personalized information retrieval. In *Proceedings of the 19th ACM international conference on Information and knowledge management*, pages 1469–1472, 2010.
[25] Z. Wang, F. X. Lin, L. Zhong, and M. Chishtie. How effective is mobile browser cache? In *Proceedings of the 3rd ACM workshop on Wireless of the students, by the students, for the students*, S3 '11, pages 17–20, New York, NY, USA, 2011. ACM.
[26] I. Witten, A. Moffat, and T. Bell. *Managing gigabytes: compressing and indexing documents and images*. Morgan Kaufmann, 1999.
[27] J. Wortham. Customers Angered as iPhones Overload 3G. http://www.nytimes.com/2009/09/03/technology/companies/03att.html?_r=2&partner=MYWAY&ei=5065/, 2009.
[28] Y. Xie and D. R. O'Hallaron. Locality in Search Engine Queries and Its Implications for Caching. In *Proc. IEEE Infocom*, pages 1238–1247, June 2002.

VMTorrent: Scalable P2P Virtual Machine Streaming

Joshua Reich
CS Dept., Princeton University
Princeton, NJ, USA
jreich@cs.princeton.edu

Oren Laadan
CS Dept., Columbia University
New York, NY, USA
orenl@cs.columbia.edu

Eli Brosh
Vidyo
Hackensack, NJ, USA
eli@vidyo.com

Alex Sherman
Google
New York, NY, USA
asherman@google.com

Vishal Misra, Jason Nieh, and Dan Rubenstein
CS Dept., Columbia University
New York, NY, USA
{misra,nieh,danr}@cs.columbia.edu

ABSTRACT

Clouds commonly store *Virtual Machine* (VM) images on networked storage. This poses a serious potential scalability bottleneck as launching a single fresh VM instance requires, at minimum, several hundred MB of network reads. As this bottleneck occurs most severely during read-intensive launching of new VMs, we focus on scalably minimizing time to boot a VM and load its critical applications.

While effective scalable P2P streaming techniques for Video on Demand (VOD) scenarios where blocks arrive in-order and at constant rate are available, no techniques address scalable large-executable streaming. VM execution is non-deterministic, divergent, variable rate, and cannot miss blocks. VMTORRENT introduces a novel combination of block prioritization, profile-based execution prefetch, on-demand fetch, and decoupling of VM image presentation from underlying data-stream. VMTORRENT provides the first complete and effective solution to this growing scalability problem that is based on making better use of existing capacity, instead of throwing more hardware at it.

Supported by analytic modeling, we present comprehensive experimental evaluation of VMTORRENT on real systems at scale, demonstrating the effectiveness of VMTORRENT. We find that VMTORRENT supports comparable execution time to that achieved using local disk. VMTORRENT maintains this performance while scaling to 100 instances, providing up to *11x* speedup over current state-of-the-art and *30x* over traditional network storage.

Categories and Subject Descriptors

C.2.4 [**Computer-Communication Networks**]:
Distributed Systems—*Distributed applications*

Keywords

BitTorrent, Cloud Computing, File Systems, On-Demand, P2P, Swarming, Virtual Appliances, Virtual Machines

1. INTRODUCTION

Traditionally, *virtual machine monitors (VMMs)*[1] have run *virtual machines (VMs)* off locally stored VM images. By combining host-level virtualization with modern networking and data center facilities, the *cloud computing* paradigm has enabled a wide range of new applications for VM technology. Both virtualized public (*e.g.,* Amazon EC2, Microsoft Hyper-V cloud) and private (*e.g.,* Cisco UCS, IBM Cloudburst, Oracle Exalogic Elastic Cloud) *Infrastructure as a Service (IaaS)* clouds have enabled businesses to move their operations from applications (*e.g.,* compute node, webserver, user desktop) running on dedicated hardware to shared infrastructure on which *virtual servers, virtual appliances,* and *virtual desktops* run. Doing so enables more efficient hardware utilization, easier management, and quicker failure recovery.

However, to realize these benefits, VMs may often need to be launched on machines that have not been pre-loaded with a copy of the corresponding VM image. By far the most common cloud setup stores VM images remotely on either *storage area network (SAN)* or *network-attached storage (NAS)*, as either *primary* or *secondary* storage Systems utilizing the network for primary storage employ a remote file system abstraction to stream VM images directly from network storage (*e.g.,* Amazon EC2/EBS). Systems utilizing the network as secondary storage, must first download a VM's complete virtual disk image (*e.g.,* OpenStack Glance, Amazon EC2/S3) to local primary storage before the VM can run. In either case, attempts to launch large numbers of fresh VM instances run straight into a network bottleneck.

1.1 The Network Bottleneck

Depending on the VM, and whether network storage is primary or secondary, hundreds of MB to several GB of VM image reads must pass over the network to launch even a single fresh VM instance. In the private cloud, this problem has proven sufficiently common to earn the moniker "boot storm". Likewise, users of OpenStack, open source software for building private and public clouds, have reported that "scale limits are due to simultaneous loading rather than total number of nodes" [16]. In response, at least one recent developer proposal has been made to replace or supplement VM launch architecture for greater scalability [14]. Moreover, with the advent of spot-pricing schemes that encourage the unpredictable launch of large temporary VM deploy-

---

[1] Also known as *hypervisors.*

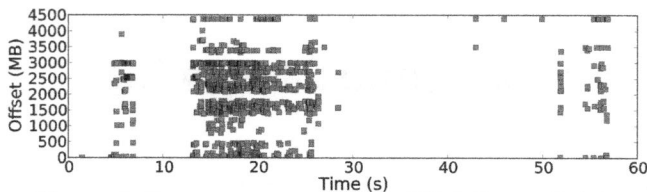

Figure 1: Image access pattern. Win7/PowerPoint.

ments and cross-cloud VM ensemble migration, this issue will likely become more significant for the public clouds[2].

Commercial solutions have addressed this network bottleneck to storage by throwing hardware at it: over-provisioning SAN/NAS, adding flash based storage [2], solid state drives [1], and other in-network hardware caches. However, often this approach becomes prohibitively expensive at current scales, and cloud sizes look to only increase in the future.

1.2 VMTorrent

VMTORRENT aims to *scalably minimize time needed for cloud-based VMs to boot and load critical applications*. Realizing this goal will improve both virtual desktop user experience and virtual server/appliance deployment.

VMTORRENT addresses this challenge by recognizing its similarity to that of data distribution. The networking community has developed highly effective scalable peer-to-peer (P2P) techniques for both bulk data download (*e.g.*, BitTorrent) and streaming strictly-ordered data (*e.g.*, Video on Demand). However, the space in between these two extremes has been left open. No techniques exist for scalably streaming partially structured data such as that shown in Figure 1, which plots the clustering of disk accesses in both space (*y*-axis) and time (*x*-axis) for a representative run of a PowerPoint application on a Windows 7 VM. This is, perhaps, because up until recently, there has been little application for such generalization. Cloud-based virtual machine image execution provides that motivation.

We provide the first P2P approach to the general problem of streaming large files whose access patterns are not strictly structured like video. VMTORRENT leverages the structure of individual VM images[3] in a straightforward way to radically increase the number of VMs which may be efficiently launched on a given hardware configuration. VMTORRENT applies to both IaaS public and private clouds, Virtual Desktop Infrastructure (VDI), and is VMM agnostic.

1.3 Contributions

In this paper, we make the following contributions:

1. Decouple P2P-delivery from stream presentation: Instead of requiring applications purpose-written for P2P data streams, VMTORRENT makes the P2P data stream transparent to applications by using the same file system abstraction as traditional remote file systems - allowing almost any application to easily use P2P-streamed data (Section 2.1).

2. Profile-based image streaming: We introduce novel

---

[2]Regrettably, we cannot currently quantify the size and scope of this problem, as cloud providers are reluctant to provide access to their data due to its commercial value.

[3]VMTORRENT naturally handles VM images comprising guest OS and applications. However, our techniques require modification for persistent VM images that diverge over time. While many, if not most, VMs are either non-persistent or non-divergent, we provide discussion of how divergent images may be handled in Section 2.3.

mechansims enabling effective VM image streaming by prefetching pieces based on *VM image profiling* and utilization of *piece selection* policies that balance cache misses against swarm efficiency (Section 2.2).

3. Model profile-based P2P image streaming: We express the expected playback pattern of a given VM image in terms of a small set of parameters - including network speed, image size, and number of instances launched - providing a concrete foundation for discussing design choices and extrapolating performance (Section 3).

4. VMTORRENT prototype: Implemented and deployed on two different hardware testbeds. We measure performance on a variety of VM/workload combinations, using up to 100 physical client peers. We find VMTORRENT delivers up to an **11x speedup** over a standard P2P approach that does not incorporate profiling and a **30x speedup** over traditional remote file system approaches. VMTORRENT provides equivalent performance to that of local disk execution for all workload sizes (Section 4).

2. SYSTEM DESIGN

VMTORRENT's design incorporates two novel features:

1. It decouples the P2P-delivery from data stream presentation mechanism - allowing hypervisors to access this data stream as if it were stored locally.

2. It introduces novel profile-based prefetch - allowing VM images to be scalably streamed with a P2P swarm

To decouple the delivery from the data stream, VMTORRENT utilizes a *custom file system server (FS)* that effectively virtualizes the VM image. Through a user-level file system front-end, FS provides the appearance of a completely local VM image, while servicing VMM reads and writes by connecting to a network backend (Section 2.1).

This decoupling allows us to make that network backend one which utilizes P2P techniques for scalable download. However, current P2P techniques, such as bulk download and Video on Demand (VOD), are not well suited to VM image streaming. Thus our *custom P2P manager (P2PM)* incorporates novel piece selection policies, based on VM image access *profiling*, in order to serve the FS (Section 2.2).

Figure 2 illustrates the operation of the system. As the VM starts to execute, (1) the VMM tries to access the disk image in response to the guest's virtual disk accesses. If a block is not yet present (a cache miss), then (2) FS requests that block from P2PM. Meanwhile, (3) based on incoming FS requests, P2PM fetches and, based on VM image *profiles*, prefetches image pieces. (4) Concurrently, P2PM uploads local pieces to other swarm members in response to their requests. P2PM stores each piece locally and (5) passes the file blocks comprising this piece to the file server as they are requested by the VMM (6). The file server handles incoming write requests using *copy-on-write* to local storage or memory, while P2PM retains the unmodified original block to share with peers.

VMTORRENT instances are intended to run as close to the VMM as possible, replacing the primary data store. To integrate with a cloud orchestration platform, the hypervisor must be redirected from the former VM image location mounted on primary storage to the FS mount which connects both to network storage (via a dedicated VMTORRENT seed instance deployed on/near the network storage) and other peers. The only requirement for applications using

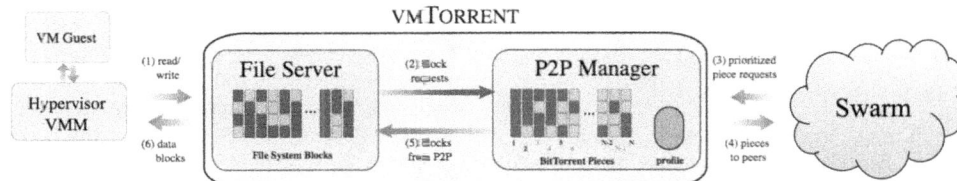

Figure 2: vmTorrent architecture

vmTorrent is that they tolerate occasional high-latency operations on files - currently non-uncommon for accesses through traditional remote file systems.

2.1 File Server

The vmTorrent FS is responsible for providing read and write access to the guest VM's disk image. FS operates similarly to traditional remote file systems: the FS root directory is mounted in a designated location, making its files visible to the system. All disk accesses performed to the sub-tree under that mount point are intercepted by the operating system and delegated to FS. In this way FS enables a standard file system view that is indistinguishable from that of other common remote file systems such as NFS and CIFS, and with similar latency properties - making vmTorrent both fully transparent to the VMM and inter-operable with the SAN/NAS compatible hypervisors used in today's clouds.

When a new guest VM is launched, FS creates a placeholder file for that VM's disk image, which from the VMM's view of the file system is indistinguishable from a complete local copy of the image. However, initially this file is empty; its content is gradually streamed in from the P2P network. As soon as the local placeholder is present FS can begin to serve requests to access the data - even if no data is yet present. For requested blocks that have been prefetched (cache hits), the server will respond immediately. However, if the VMM suffers a cache miss, attempting to access blocks that are not yet present, FS will issue *demand requests* for these blocks to P2PM which will stall until the needed blocks have been received from the swarm.

2.2 P2P Manager

To support smooth VM execution, P2PM needs to provide low-latency delivery of requested pieces to FS. This requires both proportionally many cache hits and minimally delayed network delivery on cache misses.

2.2.1 Applicability of P2P VOD

P2P VOD streaming [18] addresses the first of these two (proportionally many cache hits) by dividing its bandwidth between pieces needed urgently and random pieces from elsewhere in the video. Since pieces of a video are almost always accessed sequentially, it is trivial to determine the active *playback window* (those pieces needed immediately to ensure smooth playback) when the video is encoded with a constant bit rate (CBR).

However, this sequentiality proves a double-edged sword. Should requests be restricted to only pieces in the playback window, all VOD peers starting at the same time will request the exact same small set of pieces from the seed(s). In such a case, there will be little *piece diversity* amongst peers, meaning that they have little to share with one another. Hence, *swarming efficiency* (the effective upload rate offered by the swarm) - and thereby scalability - drops dramatically. To avoid this and ensure sufficient piece diversity,

VOD techniques add random piece requests. There is relatively little downside to devoting a fraction of bandwidth to random prefetches, as all pieces in the video stream will eventually be used.

2.2.2 The Challenge of VM Image Streaming

P2PM pursues a similar strategy. However, VM image streaming faces issues CBR video streaming does not.

- **Sparsity**: the large majority of a VM image may never be accessed in a complete execution cycle (see Table 2). Thus, randomly downloaded pieces will likely never be of use, the bandwidth used to obtain them being entirely wasted.

- **Stochasticity**: VM image playback varies dynamically and sometimes unpredictably as different workloads execute. We have found that the set of blocks accessed and the order of access varies from run to run - even when executing the same workload on the same machine. This makes predicting the VM's "playback window" challenging.

- **Rate variability**: VM image access rates vary drastically during the course of execution. Sequences for boot, login, and application startup consist of one or more highly-intense spikes in read request rates, interspersed by periods of almost no image I/O activity. This is as, if not more, challenging than optimizing P2P variable bit rate (VBR) video delivery - a problem that is currently not well understood.

- **Execution sensitivity**: P2P VOD can tolerate piece delivery failure of individual blocks and still continue correct playback. However, correct VM image execution requires every requested piece be obtained and thus must stall on even a single cache miss.

These factors combine with one another to pose a much greater challenge that that of CBR video streaming. Sparsity and stochasticity together imply that a successful VM image streaming system must predict future accesses and do so well - as false positive mispredictions will most likely never be used. Stochasticity combined with execution sensitivity makes cache misses likely and expensive (compared to the unlikely and individually un-impactful VOD missed deadlines). Rate variability requires the development of new analytic models and, combined with execution sensitivity, forces the optimal P2P piece selection policy to vary dependent on the expected upcoming access rate from the current playback point.

Perhaps counter-intuitively, if the expected upcoming access rates will exceed that of the network, then it may be better for a peer to randomize its requests - since it will have to stall anyway - and increase the swarm capacity. Conversely, when upcoming access rates are slightly lower than that of the network, the optimal strategy may be to exploit the swarm to obtain pieces within the upcoming playback window instead - since potentially costly stalls may be avoided.

We begin addressing this wide set of challenges by first introducing simple *profiling* techniques for playback window prediction (Section 2.2.3) and playback window randomized piece selection policies to balance swarm efficiency against cache misses (Section 2.2.4).

2.2.3 Profiling

The first goal of profiling is to mitigate image sparsity by identifying which pieces are highly unlikely ever to be accessed and blacklist them from ever being prefetched. Since the majority of pieces are never accessed, only those that have been seen in at least one profiled run will be entered into the profile. The second goal of profiling is support calculation of the VM playback window, a pre-requisite for effective prefetching.

In this work, we took a straightforward approach to building a profile. Each profile built was specific to both a VM image and a workload. For each image/workload pair, we ran the workload one or more times from boot through shutdown. Through FS, in each run we tracked which image pieces were accessed and when. For each piece that showed up in at least one run, we averaged the times at which it appeared and ordered the pieces accordingly from earliest to latest. The profile produced comprised this ordered list of rows, each row containing average appearance time, piece index, and proportion of runs in which that piece appeared.

The advantages of this approach are several.

- These profiles are inexpensive/quick to construct. A single-run profile can be created in the time it takes to execute the workload once and can support reasonably accurate playback window prediction. Multi-run profiles help further.

- Such profiles are compact. Both single and multi-run profiles created this way are of negligible size ($<$512KB before compression), especially when compared to that of the corresponding VM images. This compactness facilitates either pre-loading or distributing many profiles on the fly.

- They can produce very low overhead playback window predictions. Utilizing a single profile, the playback window will simply be the list of pieces highest in the profile that have not yet been either used or cached.

- They can be used as building blocks for more sophisticated prediction. The playback window prediction component may track which of several profiles best matches the current execution pattern and uses the current best match, or some weighted combination of the top several matches.

- Finally, they are conceptually simple - both facilitating manual inspection and serving as a baseline for future work.

This approach does have clear limitations. The playback window predictions we produce are not optimal. Moreover, potentially significant information is lost in the averaging process. Future work might be able to preserve more of this information without increasing the profile size too dramatically. Finally, these profiles are specific to each image/workload combination. More general profiling techniques may analyze common access sequences across workloads, or utilize guest file system level information to generalize across similar VM images.

2.2.4 Piece Selection

The goal of the VMTORRENT piece selection policy is to balance the need to (1) *minimize cache misses* and (2) *maximize swarm efficiency*.

In this work, motivated by execution sensitivity, we have chosen to give cache misses absolute priority over prefetches (although prefetches already in-progress will not be pre-

empted). To provide some piece diversity, we utilize a *window-randomized* selection policy that picks one of the first k pieces in the predicted playback window to request. This window size k is a tunable parameter that attempts to balance the urgency of pieces against the need for sufficient peer diversity. If a large k is chosen, pieces fail to be prefetched in the order of predicted use, resulting in expensive cache misses. On the other hand, the choice of an overly small k will damage swarm efficiency, leading to scalability problems since too little piece diversity will be achieved. Consequently, as the number of peers decreases or the workload diversity increases, the optimal k will tend to be lower (since the pressure on centralized servers is lower and the relative piece diversity in the network greater) and vice-versa.

2.3 VMTorrent's Place in the Cloud

VMTORRENT targets a very specific problem - getting those parts of the VM image needed by VMMs to those VMMs with minimal delay. VMTORRENT handles writes through copy-on-write to a local cache residing within the FS front-end. These changes disappear unless copied back across the network by some other mechanism. VMTORRENT's design focuses on scenarios in which a single unchanging (or infrequently changed) image needs to be rapidly scaled up and down. Examples of such images include standardized software development environments, front-end servers for traditional tiered web applications, pre-configured compute nodes, or standardized user desktop environments in which transactional user data and customizations are stored in a traditional network file system which the guest VM is pre-configured to access [10].

However, this choice by no means restricts VMTORRENT's applicability to only such scenarios. By tracking those blocks that have been modified and saving these along with other image metadata to the SAN/NAS, we can support data write-back within the VM while still preserving P2P fetch for those majority of unchanged blocks in the VM image (particularly those encoding the boot sequence and applications). We can further extend our technique using mechanisms such as Content-Based Block Caching [21], along the lines described in [31].

3. MODEL

The primary goal of this section is to capture the essential dynamics of P2P VM image streaming. We aim to thereby explain our design and experimental results, extrapolate VMTORRENT's performance outside of our experimental setting for sensitivity testing, provide performance bounds, and rigorously define our objective function.

A VM image streaming system's designer has (at least) two critical choices - that of *piece selection policy ψ* and *distribution model ϕ*. The selection policy specifies the order and timing of piece requests originating from a given peer - clearly critical in determining whether playback will progress or stall at any given moment. The distribution model determines which nodes provide upload capacity. One centralized source will run out of upload capacity as the number of peers grows, while the raw upload capacity of P2P distribution scales with the number of peers. Of particular interest is that the selection policy may effect the comparative performance of different distribution models. Section 3.1 presents two simplified policy models, while Section 3.2 considers fully centralized and fully decentralized distributions.

These policy and distribution model choices combine with parameters drawn from the cloud setting and particular VM image to form a complete description of the VM image streaming scenario. These parameters are: the *service wait time* between peer request and receipt of first download bit (W), network speed (r_{net}), piece size (S), and the ideal VM image playback function $M(t)$ (in bytes accessed by time t) modeling the total image size accessed by hypervisor executing on a fully memory-cached image[4]. Given these, our goal is to express the *average playback process* $P(t)$ of a VMTORRENT instance (*peer*).

With P, we can now rigorously define the objective specified in Section 1 as

$$\min_{\psi} \left\{ P_{\psi}^{-1}(A) - M^{-1}(A) \right\} \qquad (1)$$

where A is the total number of bytes accessed from root through workload completion.

3.1 Policy Model

For the sake of simplicity, we consider only strict demand fetching and in-order profile based prefetching in this section. These scenarios are covered, respectively, by Sections 3.1.1 and 3.1.2 which express $P(t)$ in terms of the quantities defined above and one additional term, the *effective peer download rate* r. r describes a peer's effective download as a function of r_{net}, W, S, and n.

3.1.1 Demand

We begin by considering the policy ψ_{demand} where peers only fetch blocks as they are needed. The playback that occurs in a very short time-span will either be the number of bytes a fully-memory cached version would achieve from the current playback point y_t, or, if the effective peer rate was insufficient to sustain this, the amount that could be streamed in this time

$$P(t + dt) - P(t) = \min(M(y_t + dt) - M(y_t), r\,dt). \qquad (2)$$

The current playback point itself is determined by first calculating the number of bytes played back, which is simply $P(t)$. We then compute the corresponding time y_t that a fully-memory cached version would have accessed that same number of bytes by inverting M

$$y_t = M^{-1}(P(t)).$$

Equation (2) can be easily manipulated to express $P(t)$ in differential form (playback rate)

$$\Rightarrow \frac{P(t + dt) - P(t)}{dt} = \min(\frac{r\,dt}{dt}, \frac{M(y_t + dt) - M(y_t)}{dt}) \qquad (3)$$

$$\Rightarrow \frac{dP}{dt}(t) = \min(r, \frac{dM}{dt}(y_t)). \qquad (4)$$

3.1.2 In-Order Profile Prefetch

To incorporate the impact of prefetching, we add a buffer to our model. In any period during which the access rate is lower than the effective rate, content will be buffered. In periods where the access rate is higher than the effective rate, buffered accesses can make up (some) of the difference.

Denoting the buffer as $E(t)$, we can express the buffer's evolution as a continuous-time Lindley process

$$B(t + dt) = [(B(t) + r\,dt) - (M(y_t + dt) - M(y_t))]^+. \qquad (5)$$

We then adapt the demand model shown in equation (4) to include the extra content added from the buffer $B(t)$ to that available from the network

$$\Rightarrow \frac{dP}{dt}(t) = \min(r + \frac{B(t)}{dt}, \frac{dM}{dt}(y_t)). \qquad (6)$$

Since dt is infinitesimal and the buffer size cannot be negative, we may re-write Equation 6 as the more intuitive

$$\frac{dP}{dt}(t) = \begin{cases} \frac{dM}{dt}(y_t) & \text{if } B(t) > 0 \\ \min(r, \frac{dM}{dt}(y_t)) & \text{if } B(t) = 0. \end{cases} \qquad (7)$$

The reader will note that this model describes a simplified situation in which (a) demand fetches always take precedence over prefetches, (b) prefetched pieces are always immediately utilizable (*i.e.*, perfect prediction). Assumption (a) accurately reflects our choice (Section 2.2.4) to deterministically prioritize demand over prefetch. We make assumption (b) as modeling the dynamics of prefetched pieces that cannot be immediately utilized becomes quite complicated. Consequently, the playback function produced by this model will provide an upper bound on actual performance.

3.2 Distribution Model

Sections 3.2.1 and 3.2.2 provide approximations for r as for the centralized and P2P scenarios, respectively.

3.2.1 Centralized

We begin by assuming the server splits available bandwidth r_{net} evenly among the n peers. For a server, the service wait time W combines two potential factors: network round-trip time (RTT) and the time until the serving peer has a piece ready. This latter component represents server congestion and grows very slowly in its first phase after which it spikes sharply [39]. Accordingly, the time needed for a single peer to obtain a single piece is simply the service wait time plus the time for the download to complete

$$t_{piece} = W_{cs}(n) + S/\frac{r_{net}}{n}. \qquad (8)$$

Assuming that the hypervisor will not issue new read and write requests while it blocks on those previously issued[5], the effective peer download rate r is

$$\frac{S}{r} = t_{piece} = W_{cs}(n) - \frac{S}{\frac{r_{net}}{n}} \Rightarrow r = \frac{r_{net}S}{n(\frac{r_{net}}{n}W_{cs}(n) + S)}. \qquad (9)$$

3.2.2 P2P

Assuming that the network provides full bi-sectional bandwidth allowing any pair of peers to exchange data at r_{net}, by the pigeonhole principle each peer should be able to download at rate r_{net}. Additionally, peers each maintain a fixed number of connections with other peers which does not grow with n. Consequently, unlike in the server case, the wait

---

[4]It is trivial to obtain M during profiling so long as the profiled hardware matches the streaming hardware, although, as for profiling, a new M must be produced for each VM/workload pair.

[5]In practice, the hypervisor may issue several read requests simultaneously. However, these requests are for consecutive byte ranges (thus falling within the same one or two pieces) the vast majority of the time in our experience.

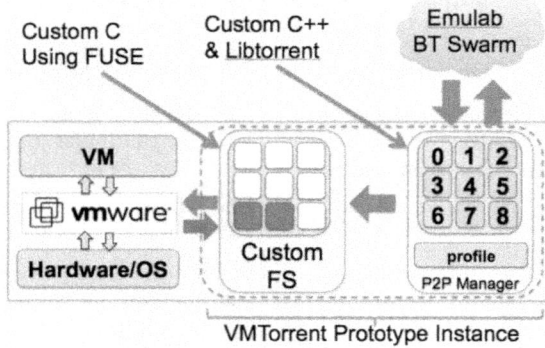

Figure 3: vmTorrent prototype.

time W will not depend directly on n. Here W is an inverse function of piece diversity d: the higher d, the shorter the wait until one of the fixed number of peers has that piece available. However, d itself is a function of n, t and the fetch/prefetch policy ψ. As in modeling VOD, as the number of peers increases, the time needed to achieve high piece diversity under a given fetch/prefetch scheme ψ will become increasingly significant [29]. Thus the time to download one piece from the swarm is

$$t_{piece} = W_{p2p}(d(\psi, n, t)) + \frac{S}{r_{net}} \qquad (10)$$

giving the effective swarm rate

$$r_{swarm} = \frac{r_{net}S}{r_{net}W_{p2p}(d(\psi, n, t)) + S}. \qquad (11)$$

However, our architecture does utilize a dedicated network storage seed. Consequently, the rate a vmTorrent peer in swarming mode should expect is the swarm rate plus the rate given in Equation (9)

$$r = \frac{r_{net}S}{r_{net}W_{p2p}(d(\psi, n, t)) + S} + \frac{r_{net}S}{n(\frac{r_{net}}{n}W_{cs}(n) + S)}.^6 \quad (12)$$

This equation provides an analytic basis for our decision to utilize a window-randomized piece selection policy (which decreases W_{p2p}) instead of an in-order piece selection policy.

4. EXPERIMENTAL EVALUATION

We implement a prototype version of vmTorrent for Linux hosts and conduct extensive experimental evaluation. Our foremost aim is to determine vmTorrent's efficacy in providing quick and scalable VM distribution and execution. Our primary assessment metric is *completion time* $P^{-1}(A)$: the time that it takes to execute a VM/workload.

4.1 Experimental Setup

Our prototype, shown in Figure 3, comprises a user-space file server tightly integrated with a P2P client. This implementation is capable of transparent operation with any VMM/guest VM combination, and without requiring any changes to the VMM or guest VMs.

Our file server builds on *bindfs* [3], a FUSE [35]-based file system for directory mirroring. The server provides a virtual file system that stores a locally modifiable copy of the guest VM image. While a user-level file server potentially

---

[6] Note that for $n = 1$, $d = 0$ (since there are no other peers) implying $W_{p2p} = \infty$, $r_{swarm} = 0$, and $r = \frac{r_{net}S}{r_{net}W_{cs}(1)+S}$.

introduces performance penalties over that of a kernel-based implementation, we show this overhead is sufficiently low for our purposes (Section 4.3).

Our prototype's P2P component is built on top of the *libtorrent* 0.15.5 [25] library. Like most BitTorrent clients, libtorrent optimizes its piece selection policy to maximize file download throughput. Since our goal is to minimize the delay for downloading particular pieces needed for the VM execution, we modify libtorrent's default rarest-first piece selection policy to support the low-latency prioritized piece download vmTorrent requires (Section 2.2.4).

The majority of our results come from deployment of vmTorrent on the University of Utah's Emulab network testbed [40]. Each experiment consists of multiple hosts and an initial server which stays in the system for the duration of the experiment. The hosts are selected from a pool of 160 "d710" machines at the University of Utah's Emulab installation. Each host was equipped with a 64-bit 2.4 GHz Quad-Core Intel Xeon X5530 CPU, 12 GB RAM, and a Barracuda ES.2 SATA 3.0- Gbps/7200-RPM/250- GB local disk. The hosts run 64-bit Ubuntu 10.04.1 LTS with a modified 2.6.32-24 Linux kernel provided by Emulab. The hosts use VMware Workstation 7.1.0 build-261024 as the VMM. All experiment control and logging are conducted on a separate control network interface.

As this testbed only provides for 100 Mbps LAN connectivity, slow for today's production environments, we supplement these results with ongoing experiments from Princeton's recently deployed VICCI (1 Gbps) testbed [32]. The VICCI testbed consists of 70 Dell R410 PowerEdge servers, each with 2 Intel Xeon X5650 CPUs and 48GB RAM. However, unlike Emulab, VICCI does not provide bare-metal access. Instead vmTorrent instances run in virtual containers and have access to only a fraction of the overall system resources. Likewise network capacity is shared communally among the simultaneous experiments of multiple investigators and there is no separate control network.

4.2 Methodology

To study the system's scalability, we vary the number n of concurrent physical machines hosting vmTorrent instances (peers) from 2 to 100. For each set of parameters, we present the results averaged over several trials.

We consider the performance of the four scenarios produced by combining piece selection policies {demand, profile-based prefetch} and distribution models {centralized, P2P}, plus that of image access from local spinning disk.

1. `cs_d`: centralized distribution, demand policy.

2. `cs_p`: centralized distribution, profile policy.

3. `p2p_d`: P2P distribution, demand policy.

4. `p2p_p`: P2P distribution, window-randomized profile policy (window size $k = 300$).

5. `local`: Pre-distributed on local spinning disk.

Comparing `p2p_p` against `local` is helpful in providing insight as to whether and how well a given cloud setup can support virtualized execution. However, our main comparison is `p2p_p` against `cs_d`, and `p2p_d`, which represent, respectively, the standard and current state-of-the-art solutions in this domain *vis-a-viz* scalability (Section 5).

Running trials at scale for centralized distribution took the lion's share of our hardware time. Since our model pre-

Workload	OS Type	Description
Boot-Shutdown	All	Boot, login, and shutdown.
Latex	Linux	Compile 30-page Latex document, view result in PDF viewer.
DocEdit	Linux	Create new OpenOffice document, save, reopen, edit, spell-check.
PowerPoint	Windows	View PowerPoint slide-show.
Multimedia	Windows	Play 30 second music file.

Table 1: Workloads.

VM	Size	A (access to complete workload)	%
Fedora	4.2 GB	320 MB- 360 MB	8-9%
Ubuntu	3.9 GB	235 MB- 400 MB	6-10%
Win7	4.3 GB	295 MB- 350 MB	7-8%

Table 2: Virtual machines.

dicts that `cs_d` and `cs_p` converge as n increases - an intuitive result as opportunity for prefetch becomes negligible when server bandwidth is saturated, we chose to run only `cs_d` for all scaling experiments, as it is by far more widely-deployed than `cs_p`.

We use two profiles for our experiments per VM/workload combination: a small profile and a large profile. The small profile uses just one sample run. It simply lists the order in which blocks are accessed for the first time in the sample run. The large profile is built using 1000 runs. As both the small and large profiles are of negligible size (<512K), we pre-distribute them.

For simplicity, our evaluation focuses on non-persistent VM sets, but this by no means restricts vmTorrent's applicability. Section 2.3 provides further discussion. For the same reason, we run identical workloads on each peer as we wished to focus on scalability, not playback-window prediction. That said, our results indicate that the greater piece diversity produced by running mixed workload sets, might well offset the increased cache-miss rates of using a less accurate profile (see Sections 4.4 and 4.5).

Unless otherwise noted, we normalize our results with respect to M the fully memory-cached playback function M provides a theoretical best-case scenario as neither network nor disk I/O is incurred (Section 3).

4.2.1 VMs and Workloads

For our experiments we used a set of workload scenarios designed to simulate common short VDI user workloads. Table 1 lists the usage scenarios for our experiments. These scenarios represent different user activities on desktop virtual appliances. Each benchmark consists of first booting the guest VM, then executing a script that performs a desired workload by mimicking user actions and finally shutdown the guest VM. To automate the execution of these benchmarks, we configured guest VMs to auto-login once booted, and then execute a script that selects the appropriate workload to run.

While the set of workloads we could explore in this work were necessarily limited, we believe the results produced apply to both longer VDI workloads, as well as those run on virtual servers and virtual appliances. For each of these, as we will shortly see, the boot and login sequence poses the greatest challenge in both latency and volume of image access. Consequently, shorter workloads provide the most challenging test with respect to our objective function. vmTorrent's performance on longer workloads should only exceed that of shorter ones. Moreover, the workloads we examine (*e.g.*, Latex compile, playing a music file) possess the same essential characteristics of those involved in launching

virtual servers and appliances: boot and load critical applications. Likewise, the VDI workload set contains both I/O-intensive interactive and CPU/RAM-intensive batch workloads, corresponding to those seen by virtual servers and appliances (*e.g.*, interactive webserver workload, batch processing workload).

In Table 2, we list VM size, the range of A (the total number of bytes accessed from boot through workload completion) across the workloads considered, and percentage of A in total image size.

4.3 Baseline Performance

We begin our investigation by exploring the performance that can be expected for a single peer, $n = 1$. Our goals in this section are to (1) check our model predictions using quantitative evaluation on actual experimental parameters and (2) provide intuition as to how 100 Mbps and 1 Gbps network rates are likely to affect baseline performance by examining the bounds produced by our model.

For $n = 1$, there is no distinction between distribution method (as there are no peers to share with). Indeed in this case both our centralized and P2P distribution models predict the same effective rate

$$r = \frac{r_{net}S}{r_{net}W_{cs}(1) + S} \quad (13)$$

(refer to Equations (9), (12) and Footnote 5).

Accordingly in this sub-section, the only design variable is selection policy. We examine the policies **demand** and in-order **profile**. We utilize in-order, instead of window-randomized, prefetching here as we are concerned with bounding performance and in-order provides the our best prediction mechanism.

4.3.1 Experimental Parameters

As mentioned above, $n = 1$ and $r_{net} = \{100\,Gbps, 1\,Mbps\}$. M and A were collected during profiling for each combination of VM and workload. The piece size S used for all experiments was 16 KB, which leaves only $W_{cs}(1)$ undefined.

As discussed in Section 3.2.1, W_{cs} has two components, a network-delay term and a server congestion term. Since there are no other peers and the server is dedicated, this second term is a small constant Q representing the base time needed for the server to processes a request

$$W_{cs}(1) = RTT_{net} + Q. \quad (14)$$

Our implementation provided Q in the range of 5×10^{-4} s. The measured network RTT at 100 Mbps averaged roughly 5×10^{-4} s as well. For 1 Gbps networks, bit rates should be 10x larger than at 100 Mbps, yielding $RTT_{1\,Gops} = 5 \times 10^{-5}$ s. Substituting into Equation (14) fully defines r for both 100 Mbps and 1 Gbps.

4.3.2 Model Correspondence

With r defined, we can utilize M and A to quantitatively evaluate Equations (3) and (7), respectively, to predict P for policies **demand** and **profile** at 100 Mbps and 1 Gbps.

Figure 4 plots the *cumulative delay* - difference in actual playback and memory-cached playback ($P(t) - M(t)$) - (y-axis) against time (x-axis), for one sample VM/workload combination: an Ubuntu VM running the latex compile and view workload (a mix of batch and interactive operations). **demand** plots are identified with triangle markers,

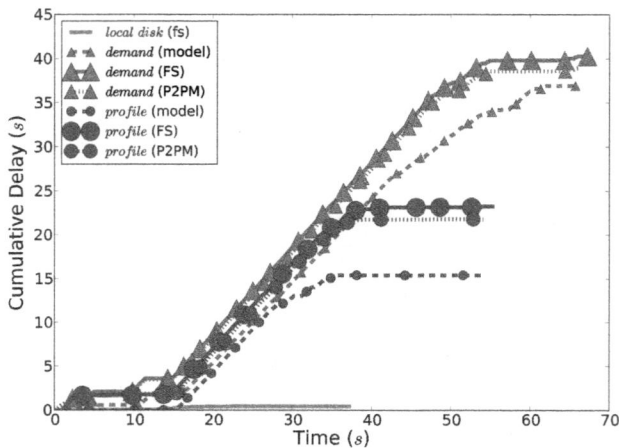

Figure 4: Cumulative delay vs. time: Ubuntu/Latex.

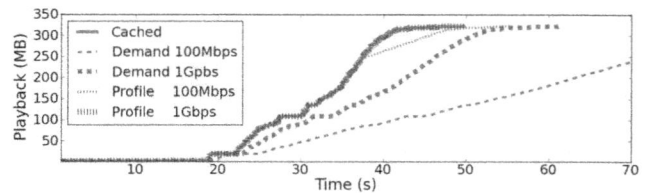

Figure 5: Fedora Playback, 100 Mbps,1 Gbps.

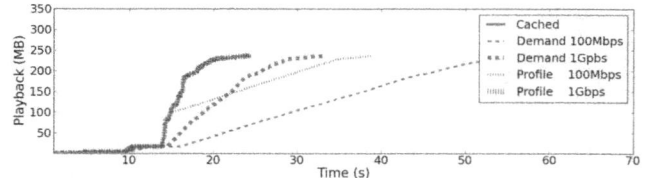

Figure 6: Ubuntu Playback, 100 Mbps,1 Gbps.

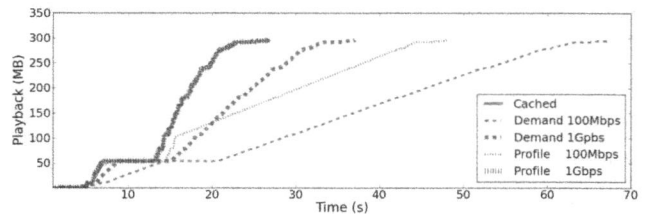

Figure 7: Win7 Playback, 100 Mbps,1 Gbps.

while `profile` plots are identified with circle markers. The model-predicted curves are those with the smallest respective marker size.

The first item to note is that the model appears to more tightly bound `demand` than `profile`. The second is that while the both predicated curves under-estimate the delay seen experimentally (largest marker curves) by several seconds, the curve shapes themselves match quite closely.

This first observation can be easily explained by recalling that `profile` cannot predict the playback window perfectly. As Equation (7) assumes perfect prediction, it is no surprise that `profile`'s actual performance is further from that indicated by the model, than that of `demand` for which no such discrepancy exists.

With respect to the second observation, the difference between measurements and model predictions could have originated from additional delays introduced either on the client-side, in the network, or on the server. To provide some visibility, we instrumented vMTORRENT to track both the delays seen by the FS and P2PM components respectively. If delay was being introduced by vMTORRENT itself (as opposed to delays introduced due to CPU/RAM sharing between vMTORRENT and the hypervisor), this is where it would appear.

The medium and large marker symbols denote delays respectively seen by FS and P2PM in Figure 4. Examining these, it is immediately apparent that overhead induced inside of the vMTORRENT implementation can be seen in the small gap between these curves by the end of execution, but also, that this overhead is relatively modest for a research prototype (∼2 s). For `demand`, the unexplained difference between model and P2PM is roughly another 3 s, which we find more than tolerable for a 66 s run (being ∼5% error).

4.3.3 Access Patterns and Performance Bounds

Having validated our model's single peer predictions against experimental results, we now use that model to provide insight into the differing performance produced from 100 Mbps and 1 Gbps networks. Figures 5-7 plot model-predicted VM playback (execution) progress (y-axis) over time (x-axis). Along with the memory-cached playback M, we plot both `demand` and `profile` policies for both network rates. We produce one plot for each VM, all of which run the same Boot-Shutdown workload.

Several features in these plots are noteworthy. Without profiling, even a 1 Gbps network provides insufficient bandwidth for `demand` to stay close to local caching. However, with profiling a 1 Gbps download rate can enable `profile` to achieve essentially ideal performance (despite misprediction). Finally and most interestingly, the relative performance of `demand` at 1 Gbps and `profile` at 100 Mbps depends on M. When M spikes sharply early-on and then flattens, as it does in the boot section of both the Ubuntu and Win7 VM images, there is relatively little opportunity for prefetching to fill the buffer before the spike, after which it just plays catch up on cache misses. Thus the dominant performance factor becomes the rate at which cache misses can be filled, giving `demand` at 1 Gbps a distinct advantage. Conversely, when M increases more gradually and at a latter time - as it does for the Fedora VM - a large playback buffer can be prefetched, and if prefetch is reasonably accurate it trumps the 10x difference in network speed.

4.4 Scalability

We now proceed to our primary concern, scalability. We show the results of running: `p2p_p`, `p2p_d`, `cs_d` and `local` where a number of clients attempt to execute a VM workload. We find that `p2p_p` both performs with roughly the same efficiency as `local` and that it scales far better than the respective current standard and state-of-the art solutions `p2p_d` and `cs_d`.

All experiments consist of a dedicated seed with a complete copy of disk image cached in memory and a set of peers running vMTORRENT instances.

4.4.1 100 Mbps

We begin by exploring performance on a 100 Mbps network. Figure 8 plots mean normalized run time $P^{-1}(A)/M^{-1}(A)$ (y-axis) against the number of peers (swarm size) (x-axis) `p2p_p` with a large profile (large circle marker), p2p_p with a small profile (small circle), p2p_d (square), cs_d (triangle) and local (dashed line). Additionally, model curves are plotted with decreasing width bands for cs_d, p2p_p, and p2p_d. Each sub-figure corresponds to a combination of VM and workload[7] described in Section 2.2.3.

Examining the cs_d plot lines, clear scalability issues have already arisen by $n = 4$ at 100 Mbps and appear to grow linearly with the swarm size, resulting in run times 40-70x greater than the ideal memory-cached playback time (A) by $n = 100$. Contrastingly, p2p_p run times for $n = 100$ are only two to three times A.

The effect of utilizing randomized prefetch in combination with P2P swarming is likewise undeniable. Naive use of P2P by p2p_d scales significantly better than cs_d, but far worse than p2p_p, which benefits from far greater piece diversity. The performance advantage of p2p_p is best measured in orders of magnitude: **4-11**x better than p2p_d and **16-30**x better than cs_d.

Profile size (and implicitly prediction accuracy) appears to be a secondary factor in determining scalability. Both small and large profiles perform essentially the same with respect to scaling, indicating that as n grows large, ensuring piece diversity is the key to scalability, not perfect playback window prediction. This result is also encouraging in that it demonstrates a small amount of profiling can go a long way.

We observe the small gap between p2p_p and local on both the Ubuntu and Win7 VMs across all workloads. On the Fedora VM this is even more pronounced with VM-TORRENT significantly outperforming execution from local. This occurs for the same reason noted in Section 4.3.3: Fedora's boot-and-login access pattern is very prefetch-friendly, giving p2p_p a leg up on local. Moreover, here the effect is multiplied since p2p_p peers have long period in which to prefetch. While prefetching p2p_p randomizes piece requests which increases effective bandwidth, and thereby scalability, as predicted by Equation 12. However, when p2p_p hits the catch-up phase, only demand requests are made (due to our design decision to give cache misses absolute priority over prefetches), reducing the piece diversity on which P2P scalability relies. With its relatively long and gradual access curve, the Fedora VM maximizes p2p_p's scalability compared to both p2p_d and cs_d (Note the large gap in Figure 8(a) between p2p_p and p2p_d/cs_d).

Finally, we turn to our model predictions. All model parameters needed for the model curves have been defined in Section 4.3.1, save one - W. For cs_d, we note that even 100 nodes should be well below the server congestion threshold. Thus we set

$$W_{cs}(n) = RTT_{net} + Q.$$

For p2p_d, our intuition suggests that piece diversity will decline proportionally to the increase in swarm size

$$W_{p2p}(\texttt{demand}, n) = RTT_{net} + Qn$$

while for p2p_p, this decline should be less than proportional, but higher than logarithmic (since randomized prefetch

---

[7]We ran into problems automating large scale experiments on Windows 7 for both cs_d and p2p_d. The reason for this is that Windows 7 contains an undocumented auto-login timeout that we could not disable. Consequently, when delay exceeded a certain threshold (roughly 3x memory cached), auto-login would fail causing the need for manual intervention, which was not feasible on large test populations and skewed results for p2p_d at $n = \{4, 8\}$.

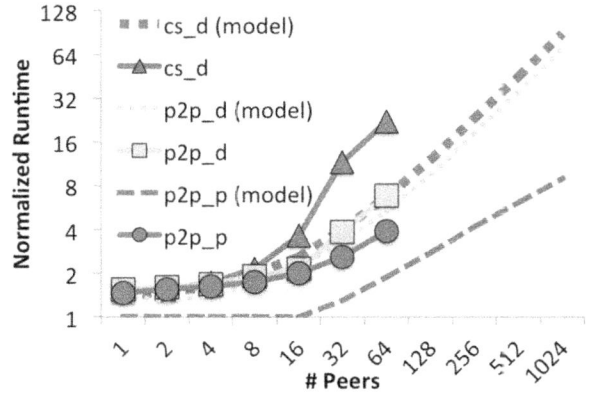

Figure 9: Normalized runtime vs. swarm-size (1 Gbps).

is strictly superseded by cache misses, limiting opportunity to generate piece diversity)

$$W_{p2p}(\texttt{profile}, n) = RTT_{net} + Q\sqrt{n}. \qquad (15)$$

we can see that these simple functions capture the scalability dynamics reasonably well, although for $1 < n < 16$ piece diversity is clearly over-estimated by Equation (15) - as seen by the discrepancy in p2p_p model and observed across all three graphs.

4.4.2 1 Gbps

We ran 1 Gbps experiments on the VICCI testbed. Figure 9 plots normalized playback ($P^{-1}(A)/M^{-1}(A)$) against peer size for the Ubuntu VM/Boot-Shutdown workload. Examining the cs_d plot lines, scalability issues become apparent by $n = 16$ at 1 Gbps (4x the number of peers for which scalability became an issue at 100 Mbps).

Here we see that while the model curves capture the rough shape of scalability, there are significant discrepancies. The first major discrepancy is that p2p_p's actual performance is roughly 1.5x slower than predicted by the model (although here constraint $P(t) \leq M(t)$ decreases the impact of Equation (15)'s early over-estimation of piece diversity). Secondly, cs_d plots sharply higher than expected.

A study of the logs suggests this is caused by several peculiarities of VICCI not possessed by Emulab. Recall from Section 4.1 that VICCI utilizes virtual containers that share both hardware and network resources among multiple investigators. Apparently, VICCI also suffers from irregularities in its CPU assignment algorithm, lowering performance and exacerbating already variable testbed behavior.

Consequently, given that we do see a correspondence here in shape and scaling, we conclude that our model curves provide a reasonable indicator of 1 Gbps performance. Based on this, we provide extrapolations for up to 1024 nodes and find that p2p_p again provides significantly more scalability than current approaches. However, at $8A$ this performance leaves significant room for improvement. Thus a main challenge for future work is to develop new policies that support better swarming efficiency - likely by relaxing our restriction that cache-misses take absolute priority over prefetches.

4.5 Swarming Efficiency

We now study the swarming efficiency on the Ubuntu VM running the Boot-Shutdown workload at 100 Mbps. We measure swarming efficiency for p2p_p directly by plotting

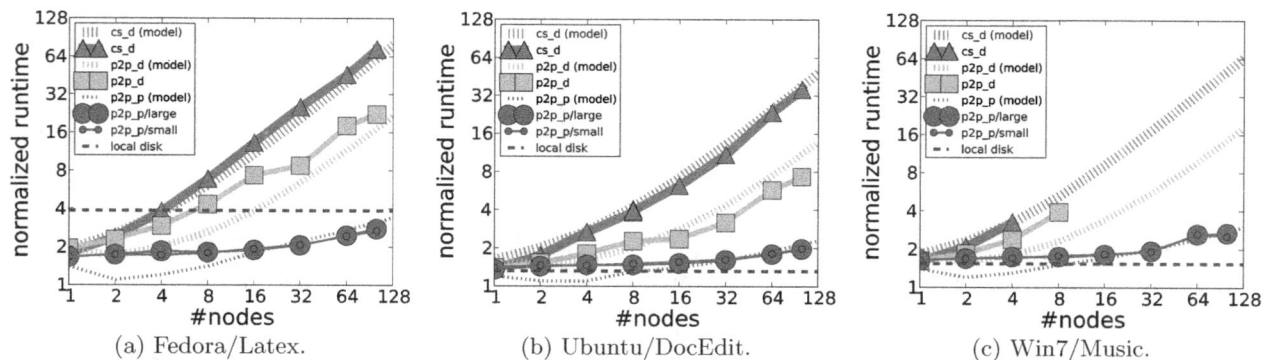

(a) Fedora/Latex. (b) Ubuntu/DocEdit. (c) Win7/Music.

Figure 8: Normalized run time vs. swarm-size (100 Mbps).

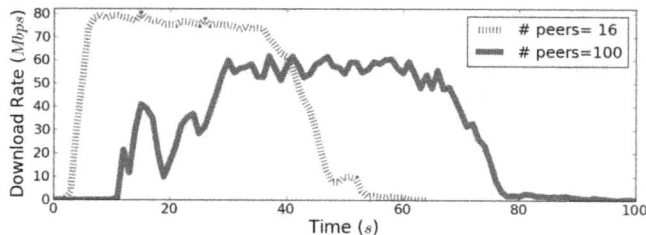

Figure 10: Swarming efficiency.

peer download rate r over time for swarm sizes $n = 16, 100$ in Figure 10.

Examining Figure 10, we see the average peer download rate hit a peak of roughly 80 Mbps after 6 s and remain relatively stable thereafter (until a drop-off when the profile is exhausted and VMTORRENT transitions to `demand`). Contrastingly, the behavior shown for 100 peers differs greatly. Firstly, the peak rate drops to 60 Mbps - a 25% drop from 16 peers. Secondly, the startup period required to attain the peak rate takes almost 6x longer than for the 16 peer swarm. Finally, the rate fluctuates significantly more in the startup phase.

These observations provide additional evidence that the non-optimal scaling behavior stems from our decision to give cache-misses absolute priority over prefetches. With 16 peers, the server still has more than enough capacity to fill all demand requests while still servicing prefetch requests. However, by 100 peers, it appears that the server must often starve prefetch requests in order to keep up with demand requests - leading to a slower, choppier buildup of the piece diversity needed to enable peak efficiency, and ultimately achieves a lower peak rate than that of 16 peers.

5. RELATED WORK

There are only a few studies of efficient on-demand deployment of virtual appliances or machines in the *local area network (LAN)*. The first set of related work presented focuses on efficiently *migrating* - transferring and executing individual VM images, while the second set is predominantly concerned with *reduplication* - scalably distributing copies of VM images.

5.1 Migration

Internet Suspend/Resume (ISR) [23] focuses on the related problem of *VM migration* - suspending a VM on one hardware platform, transferring that VM over the WAN, and resuming its execution at another location. While migration faces none of the scalability concerns posed by our problem of replicated deployment, latency until execution can proceed is of critical importance in both their domain and ours. Their *pure demand-fetch* inspired the on-demand components of both [7] and our own work. Like our own work, ISR also leverages over-the-network pre-fetch, warming the cache by transferring the migrating VM's *working set*. However, this *working set* is a reactive mechanism, simply being composed of those blocks recently accessed in the particular execution being migrated. It provides no help in warming the cache *for tasks a user has yet to do*, since those blocks lie outside of the *working set*. Clark *et al.* [8] extends this working set concept to that of a *write-able working set* in order to reduce the time needed to *stop-and-copy* the migrating VM image. Contrastingly, the Collective [6], a server-based system delivery of managed appliances to personal computer (PC) users, takes a proactive approach to pre-fetching VMs in order to reduce startup and execution delays. The Collective pre-fetches and fills its cache with the most frequently accessed blocks, taken over all appliances. Our technique takes this approach a step further, *predicting* future block accesses based on profiles of block access patterns. These profiles are built by observing previous executions of tasks similar to that being executed by the VM.

Post-copy migration [15] provides another interesting point of comparison. Instead of pre-copying a VM's in-memory working set in multiple rounds, post-copy migration immediately begins the VM running on the target machine and retrieves cache misses across the network (the image itself is stored on the network and thus does not need to be transferred). With a good prediction algorithm, post-copy could proactively prefetch those portions of the working set which were most likely to be needed, reducing execution delay. Our FS and profiling components mirror this strategy, but instead of prefetching pages from a working set, we prefetch pieces from an image file.

More generally, we note that prefetching is not a novel idea. Prefetching has been used to improve storage and file systems for many years. Known techniques rely on leveraging past accesses [5], application hints [30], or training prefetching parameters using sample traces [22], to predict future accesses. However, previous work in this space focus on finding the right trade-off between prediction accuracy and low (CPU and memory) overhead and exploiting domain-specific characteristics, *e.g.*, parallelism in storage systems. Contrastingly, our scenario is far less constrained by memory and focused on specific VM workloads, allowing us to build more comprehensive and targeted access profiles. Further, our work focuses on not just prefetching, but the combined problem of prefetching and data distribution across peers to maximize performance - making precication accuracy of lesser importance.

5.2 Reduplication

The most straightforward approach to optimizing VM deployment without use of additional hardware is to sequentially copy VM images to the target nodes, instead of downloading them in parallel. This approach is common in data centers, which employ provisioning servers to distribute and execute pre-customized images on-demand [26, 34]. However, sequential distribution can lead to long distribution times and network hotspots when VM demand is high.

The work on the Collective evolved into the commercial solution MokaFive [27]. While the internal details of MokaFive are not available, based on publicly available materials, we suspect scalability is achieved with this approach using a combination of hardware over-provisioning and modifying VM image and hypervisor - both of which are proprietary.

The Snowflock implementation [24] of the VM fork abstraction provides for highly efficient and scalable cloning of VMs by building a custom application-level multicast library (*mcdist*) into a modified Xen hypervisor. To obtain such performance, their approach also calls for use of modified VM images, guest OSes, and applications. Finally, the *mcdist* library runs on top of IP-multicast, although they note that to the best of their knowledge cloud providers do not currently enable IP-multicast. Contrastingly, our approach is minimally invasive, requiring no changes to network, hypervisor, VM image, guest, or applications.

IP multicast [19, 20] provides a truly scalable solution for VM image delivery [33] - but also has several drawbacks. Multicast is not geared towards on-demand image distribution since different peers will need only partially overlapping sets of data (and or different schedules), and is not well suited to delivering data to geographically distributed networks, *e.g.*, multi-region data centers or corporations. Even in a single network, multicast has significant setup overhead and is not used by many organizations as a result [12, 17]. More recently, when Etsy attempted to utilize IP multicast functionality to distribute large files within their network via rsync "multicast traffic saturated the CPU on [Etsy] core switches causing all of Etsy to be unreachable", which led them to utilize a P2P solution instead [13].

P2P provides an alternative to IP multicast that sidesteps synchronization and setup issues. We are not the first to apply P2P techniques to VM delivery. However, we have taken a more nuanced approach in the application of P2P, for which performance delays are best measured in seconds, instead of minutes or hours.

Zhang *et al.* [41] proposes a play-on-demand solution for desktop applications. The basic idea is to store user's data at a USB device, and at run time, download desktop applications using P2P (specifically, via unmodified BitTorrent [9]). These applications are then run in a lightweight virtualization environment. The downloaded images here are not standalone VMs, making this approach of more limited applicability. These images are orders of magnitude smaller than those of VMs, consequently a naive application of P2P provides adequate performance and scalability. However, when this same approach is used to distribute VMs to stu-

dent machines in a training environment [28] both performance and scalability suffer - distribution taking 1-4 hours for a 22 machine deployment on a 100 Mbps network. Chen *et al.* [7] adds on-demand download to naive P2P which improves performance by an order of magnitude on a somewhat larger number of machines. Yet in even fairly small deployments, the wait until a VM can even begin execution takes more than 20 minutes - still not nearly good enough for deployments where time-to-use is critical. The *lxcloud* project at CERN used a customized BitTorrent client to deploy almost 500 10GB VM images in 23 minutes, without on-demand download [38]. However, their base network of 1 Gbps was $10x$ faster than those used by [28, 7]. A general purpose P2P distributed file system such as Shark [4] or CFS [11] could be expected to provide similar performance in provisioning VM images.

Contrastingly, VMTORRENT focuses on streaming performance, instead of full-download. By incorporating profile-based prefetch, VMTORRENT can fully execute VM tasks in a fraction of the time required by even the best of previous P2P approaches, and do so at scale. However, doing so is not trivial. To obtain efficient piece exchange, VMTORRENT seeks to balance the immediate download requirement of the VMM with maintaining a high level of piece diversity in the system. This approach to creating diversity is inspired by P2P video streaming systems which use a sliding window to download pieces needed for immediate playback, while still acquiring non urgent pieces for diversity [37, 42].

In a complementary approach [31] examines the distribution of VMs within several small-to-medium IBM datacenters, finding a high level of similarity in VM content. Their VDN system hashes blocks and then caches them according to hash value, enabling multiple related VM-images to share the same content block. More efficient utilization of the cache fronting their image store, provides for significant performance improvement. Also related is Twitter's Murder system [36] which dramatically cuts down the distribution time for software binaries by optimizing BitTorrent for the data-center. Again, their techniques are complementary to our own and could be used to improve the performance of our BitTorrent backend which is based on the WAN-optimized libtorrent library.

6. CONCLUSIONS

We have presented the design, implementation and evaluation of VMTORRENT. VMTORRENT decouples P2P-delivery from stream presentation - allowing applications to easily use P2P-streamed data. Doing so enables scalable VM image streaming - based on a combination of novel *profile-based* prefetching and *piece selection* policies that balance cache misses against swarm efficiency. Both our analytic models and experimental evaluation show VMTORRENT outperforms current techniques by orders of magnitudes

7. ACKNOWLEDGMENTS

This work was supported in part by NSF grants CNS-1018355, CNS-0905246, CNS-1162021, CNS-1162447, CNS-1017934, and CCF-0964497.

8. REFERENCES

[1] IOMEGA Solid State Drive to Address Boot Storm Issues. Retrieved from `http://iomega.com/about/prreleases/2011/20110526_vdi_bootstorm.html`, May 2011.

[2] Fusion-io VDI Overview. Retrieved from `http://www.fusionio.com/overviews/fusion-io-virtual-desktop-infrastructure-vdi-overview/`, 2012.

[3] Bindfs: Mount a Directory to Another Location and Alter Permission Bits. Retrieved from `http://code.google.com/p/bindfs`, n.d.

[4] S. Annapureddy et al. Shark: Scaling File Servers via Cooperative Caching. In *USENIX NSDI*, May 2005.

[5] S. H. Baek and K. H. Park. Prefetching with Adaptive Cache Culling for Striped Disk Arrays. In *USENIX ATC*, June 2008.

[6] R. Chandra et al. The Collective: A Cache-Based System Management Architecture. In *USENIX NSDI*, May 2005.

[7] Z. Chen et al. Rapid Provisioning of Cloud Infrastructure Leveraging Peer-to-Peer Networks. In *IEEE ICDCS Workshops*, June 2009.

[8] C. Clark et al. Live Migration of Virtual Machines. In *USENIX NSDI*, May 2005.

[9] B. Cohen. Incentives Build Robustness in BitTorrent. In *P2PECON*, June 2003.

[10] L. P. Cox et al. Pastiche: Making Backup Cheap and Easy. In *USENIX OSDI*, December 2002.

[11] F. Dabek et al. Wide-Area Cooperative Storage with CFS. *ACM SOSP*, October 2001.

[12] A. El-Sayed et al. A Survey of Proposals for an Alternative Group Communication Service. *IEEE Network*, Vol. 17, January/February 2003.

[13] Etsy. Turbocharging Solr Index Replication with BitTorrent. Retrieved from `http://codeascraft.etsy.com/2012/01/23/solr-bittorrent-index-replication`, January 2012.

[14] R. Harris. OpenStack Proposal Blueprint: Download Images using BitTorrent (in XenServer). Retrieved from `https://blueprints.launchpad.net/nova/+spec/xenserver-bittorrent-images`, June 2012.

[15] M. R. Hines and K. Gopalan. Post-Copy Based Live Virtual Machine Migration Using Adaptive Pre-Paging and Dynamic Self-Ballooning. In *ACM VEE*, March 2009.

[16] R. Hirschfeld. OpenStack Deployments Abound at Austin Meetup. Retrieved from `http://www.openstack.org/blog/2011/12/openstack-deployments-abound-at-austin-meetup-129/`, December 2011.

[17] M. Hosseini et al. A Survey of Application-Layer Multicast Protocols. *IEEE Communications Surveys & Tutorials*, Vol. 9, Third Quarter 2007.

[18] Y. Huang et al. Challenges, Design and Analysis of a Large-scale P2P-VoD System. In *ACM SIGCOMM*, August 2008.

[19] IANA. RFC 3171, 2001.

[20] IANA. RFC 4291, 2006.

[21] C. B. M. III and D. Grunwald. Content-Based Block Caching. In *IEEE MSST*, May 2006.

[22] T. Kimbrel et al. A Trace-Driven Comparison of Algorithms for Parallel Prefetching and Caching. In *USENIX OSDI*, October 1996.

[23] M. Kozuch and M. Satyanarayanan. Internet Suspend/Resume. In *IEEE Hotmobile*, February 2002.

[24] H. A. Lagar-Cavilla et al. SnowFlock: Virtual Machine Cloning as a First-Class Cloud Primitive. *ACM TOCS*, February 2011.

[25] libtorrent. libtorrent: C++ Bittorrent Library. Retrieved from `http://www.rasterbar.com/products/libtorrent/index.html`, n.d.

[26] R. Mietzner and F. Leymann. Towards Provisioning the Cloud: On the Usage of Multi-Granularity Flows and Services to Realize a Unified Provisioning Infrastructure for SaaS Applications. In *IEEE SERVICES*, July 2008.

[27] MokaFive. Retrieved from `http://www.mokafive.com/products/components.php`, n.d.

[28] C. M. O'Donnell. Using BitTorrent to Distribute Virtual Machine Images for Classes. In *ACM SIGUCCS*, October 2008.

[29] N. Parvez et al. Analysis of BitTorrent-Like Protocols for On-Demand Stored Media Streaming. In *ACM SIGMETRICS*, June 2008.

[30] R. H. Patterson et al. Informed Prefetching and Caching. In *ACM SOSP*, December 1995.

[31] C. Peng et al. VDN: Virtual Machine Image Distribution Network for Cloud Data Centers. In *IEEE INFOCOM*, July 2012.

[32] L. Peterson et al. VICCI: A Programmable Cloud-Computing Research Testbed. Technical report, Princeton University, 2011.

[33] M. Schmidt et al. Efficient Distribution of Virtual Machines for Cloud Computing. *Euromicro PDP*, February 2010.

[34] L. Shi et al. Iceberg: An Image Streamer for Space and Time Efficient Provisioning of Virtual Machines. In *IEEE ICPP Workshops*, September 2008.

[35] M. Szeredi. FUSE: File System in Userspace. Retrieved from `http://fuse.sourceforge.net/`, n.d.

[36] Twitter. Twitter's Murder Project at Github. Retrieved from `https://github.com/lg/murder`, n.d.

[37] A. Vlavianos et al. BiToS: Enhancing BitTorrent for Supporting Streaming Applications. In *IEEE Global Internet Symposium*, April 2006.

[38] R. Wartel et al. Image Distribution Mechanisms in Large Scale Cloud Providers. *IEEE CloudCom*, November 2010.

[39] M. Welsh, D. Culler, and E. Brewer. SEDA: An Architecture for Well-Conditioned, Scalable Internet Services. In *ACM SOSP*, October 2001.

[40] B. White et al. An Integrated Experimental Environment for Distributed Systems and Networks. In *USENIX OSDI*, December 2002.

[41] Y. Zhang et al. Portable Desktop Applications Based on P2P Transportation and Virtualization. In *USENIX LISA*, November 2008.

[42] Y. Zhou et al. A Simple Model for Analyzing P2P Streaming Protocols. *IEEE ICNP*, October 2007.

Cloud-based Social Application Deployment using Local Processing and Global Distribution

Zhi Wang[*], Baochur Li[†], Lifeng Sun[*], and Shiqiang Yang[*]

[*]Beijing Key Laboratory of Networked Multimedia
Department of Computer Science and Technology, Tsinghua University
[†]Department of Electrical and Computer Engineering, University of Toronto
{wangzhi04@mails., sunlf@, yangshq@}tsinghua.edu.cn, bli@eecg.toronto.edu

ABSTRACT

Social applications represent a paradigm shift on how the Internet is to be used, and have already changed the way we work, live, and play. When it comes to deploying social applications, cloud computing platforms are used to meet the Internet-scale, self-propagating, and fast-growing demands from these applications. Yet, to deploy social media applications in the most effective and economic fashion, we need to strategically design and follow a set of theoretical and practical principles. In this paper, we seek to design a set of new principles to guide social application deployment. Learning from large-scale measurement-based observations using a real-world social application, the gist of our principles is to detach the typically integrated "collection → processing → distribution" workflows in social applications into separate *local processing* and *global distribution* procedures, which can be effectively deployed using different cloud services. Moreover, based on a predictive model of regional propagation, we formulate the resource allocation problems in the processes of collecting/processing and distributing content as two optimization problems, which can be solved by efficient algorithms. Finally, based on our theoretical design, we have implemented an example social application on Amazon EC2 and Google AppEngine, where IaaS-based computation instances perform content collection and processing, and the PaaS-based platform is employed to distribute the contents that are widely propagating. Our PlanetLab-based trace-driven experiments have further confirmed the superiority of our design.

Categories and Subject Descriptors

C.2.4 [**Distributed System**]: Distributed Applications H.4 [**Information Retrieval**]: Social Network

General Terms

Measurement, Design

Keywords

Social application deployment, online social network, cloud computing

1. INTRODUCTION

Applications deployed in online social networks [18] have emerged as one of the most popular means for users to access multimedia contents in today's Internet [14]. This is due to a new development scheme in online social networks: by simply becoming *developers*[1] of large social networks like Facebook, social media companies can use user profiles and social relationships via Open APIs[2], and are able to develop applications for millions of potential users, without building a new social network. At the end of March 2012, over 9 million apps integrated with Facebook are using such a development paradigm[3].

In this paper, we focus on the problem faced by social media companies after new applications have been developed: how do we effectively and economically deploy these applications? The deployment of a social application is challenging due to a number of unique evolution characteristics: (1) It is potentially Internet-scale from the beginning, since a social application depends on an online social network to directly attract its global users, making the number of users grow much faster than traditional multimedia applications; (2) it is self-propagating, since the application can be recommended to users by their friends when they are using the social application; and (3) it is fast-growing, since the number of users can increase rapidly due to propagation caused by the social effects. As an example, the social application *WeChat* depends on Tencent Inc.'s social network services, and has hit a record of 200 million users in less than 14 months[4].

Since highly scalable and elastic network resources are required to deploy new social applications, it is promising to deploy social applications in the cloud for a number of reasons: (1) Small social application companies, which develop

---

[1]http://developers.facebook.com/
[2]http://en.wikipedia.org/wiki/Open_API
[3]http://newsroom.fb.com/content/default.aspx?NewsAreaId =137
[4]http://www.wechatapp.com

social applications for large social networks, can build their own global service by simply becoming customers of cloud providers; (2) the system can easily scale when the number of its users and the volume of its contents increase; and (3) social applications can be easily implemented in the cloud due to complete control of servers based on virtualization (*e.g.*, virtual machines (VMs) running different operating systems).

Cloud computing has been widely used to handle various traditional multimedia contents [15, 22], *e.g.*, Netflix has been delivering its movies to users based on the Amazon cloud infrastructure since 2010 [3]. Due to its unique propagation patterns, efforts have been devoted in the deployment of social media. Wang *et al.* [30] observed that information in an online social network can be used to predict content access in a standalone content sharing system, which can guide content deployment. Cheng *et al.* [9] have studied the partitioning schemes for social contents to achieve a balanced load at the servers and preserve social relationship. Wu *et al.* [31] have studied cost-effective video distribution in a social network by migrating videos in geo-distributed clouds. However, existing studies only solve the *content distribution* problem in social media; in this paper, we study the *deployment* of social *application*, which includes content collection, processing and distribution.

In a typical social application, user-generated contents (UGCs) are the dominant form of contents, *i.e.*, they are first generated by users, then collected and processed by the system, and finally distributed to other users through the social relationships. To deploy a social application, we take the characteristics of social media into account as follows: (1) Users are the sources of contents in social media. Instead of central content providers, users are the ones who generate contents for social media [11]; (2) social media is dynamically processed and aggregated, *i.e.*, contents generated by users are uploaded to the social media system, which performs various *processing* to these contents and distributes the processed contents to users [19]; and (3) the distribution of social media is severely affected by social propagation [29]. Propagation with social media is no longer random — it is determined by the social network topology and user sharing [8][27].

According to the properties of content collection, processing and distribution, we allocate computation, storage and network resources from the cloud to deploy a new social application as follows. (1) *Local processing* — contents are initially collected and processed by cloud servers that are geographically close to the user generating them. Since *content processing* varies from one application to another, we deploy the processing part using IaaS (Infrastructure as a Service)-based instances, *e.g.*, VM instances provided by Amazon EC2 (Elastic Compute Cloud) [1], where the application can be implemented in various programming languages. However, it is costly and difficult to build a highly scalable and global distribution platform to serve users over the world based on IaaS only. (2) *Global distribution* — processed contents are finally distributed by servers that are geographically close to users who receive such contents. Fortunately, cloud computing provides another resource allocation scheme, PaaS (Platform as a Service), *e.g.*, Google AppEngine [2], where resource is provided to users in an auto-scaled manner. In our design, we build the distribution

platform using PaaS to distribute the contents processed by IaaS-based computation instances.

In our cloud-based social application deployment, we are presented with the following challenges: (1) How should we allocate IaaS-based computation instances to process contents generated by users located within different *regions*? (2) How should we choose contents to be replicated to a PaaS-based distribution platform to serve global users? and (3) How should we design efficient protocols to connect local content processing and global content distribution?

In this paper, we answer these questions by connecting the characteristics in social media propagation with its deployment design. Our contributions can be summarized as follows: (1) We conduct extensive measurements to study the propagation characteristics in social media and motivate our design; (2) We provide theoretical guidelines for social application deployment using local processing and global distribution; and (3) We implement an example social application to evaluate the effectiveness and efficiency of our design based on Amazon EC2, Google AppEngine and PlanetLab.

The remainder of this paper is organized as follows. We review related work in Sec. 2. We conduct large-scale measurements to study the characteristics of social media in Sec. 3. We present our detailed design and analysis in Sec. 4. We discuss our implementations in Sec. 5. We evaluate the performance of our design in Sec. 6. Finally, we conclude the paper in Sec. 7.

2. RELATED WORK

In this section, We discuss our work in light of the existing literature on social media deployment and cloud computing, respectively.

Online social applications. In a social media system, contents spread among users by users sharing them. A number of research efforts have been devoted to studying content propagation in social media applications. Kwak *et al.* [20] investigated the impact of users' retweets on information diffusion in Twitter. Social applications have greatly changed our assumptions in traditional content service deployment, *e.g.*, content distribution is shifted from a central-edge manner to an edge-edge manner, resulting in the massive volume of user-generated contents and a dynamically skewed popularity distribution [7]. In this paper, we not only focus on the distribution of contents already in an online social network, but also the collection and processing and contents generated by users in a social application. In particular, we explore the deployment of social applications based on cloud computing.

Social application deployment based on cloud computing. Cloud computing is a new computing paradigm in which both hardware and software are provided to users over the Internet as services, in the form of virtualized resources [12]. Different cloud providers provide different types of services [26], including IaaS, PaaS, SaaS (Software as a Service), *etc.*, based on different pricing schemes [6], *e.g.*, by actual CPU cycles in Google AppEngine [2] or by the number of VM instances in Amazon EC2. Due to its elasticity, cloud computing has also been widely used by startup companies whose demands of resources grow over time [15]. Traditional systems, such as the Web [22] and video streaming [3], have been being successfully deployed in the cloud. Among multiple cloud providers, Li *et al.* [21] have proposed a service comparison methodology to compare the performance with different cloud providers. Rehman *et al.* [25] have proposed a multi-criteria cloud service selection strategy, to determine the service that best matches the users' requirements from amongst numerous available services. Chohan *et al.* [10] have studied the extension of PaaS to facilitate the distributed execution of applications over virtualized cluster resources.

In the context of social applications, cloud computing has been explored for the social media distribution. Pujol *et al.* [24] have investigated the difficulties of scaling online social network, and designed a social partitioning and replication middleware in which users' friends can be co-located in the same server. Tran *et al.* [28] have studied the partition of contents in the online social network by taking social relationships into consideration. Cheng *et al.* [9] have studied the partitioning schemes for social contents to achieve a balanced load at the servers and preserve the social relationships. Wu *et al.* [31] have studied the problem of cost-effective video distribution in a social network by migrating videos in geo-distributed clouds.

Different from related works, in this paper, we study how content processing and distribution are jointly performed by the cloud. Particularly, we design deployment strategies for social applications by taking the characteristics in social media into account, based on measurement studies of real-world online social networks.

3. BACKGROUND AND MEASUREMENT STUDY

In this section, we explore the design principles of social application deployment and present the benefit of the cloud-based design using real-world measurements. We first show an example that has the general features of social applications. Then, based on an extensive measurement study of real-world online social networks and cloud systems, we show that contents in a social application can be processed locally and distributed globally.

3.1 Framework of a General Social Application

Though different social applications are designed to provide users with different contents and experiences, they share many common features: (1) Users contribute contents to the applications; (2) contents are aggregated by various approaches and provided to different users; and (3) contents propagate through social connections of the online social network.

To study the cloud-based deployment of social applications with these features, we use an example social application in our measurements and our system design. We design our example application to be as general as possible to capture most of the features in social applications. Our example social application is called *SICS*, a social and interest-based content sharing system. In SICS, besides contents shared by a user's friends as in Twitter-like systems, other contents are also recommended to the user, which is based on content processing, where computation resources are required to parse the contents and execute the processing algorithms. After content processing, SICS provides the user a set of enriched contents with the recommended ones. Fig. 1 illustrates the paradigm of SICS. a and b are the original contents generated by user A and user B; while a'

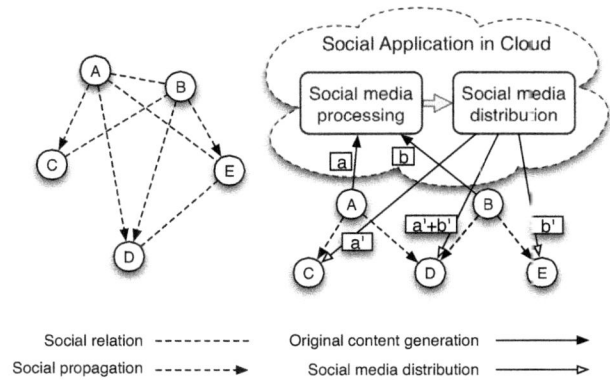

Figure 1: Content generation, propagation and distribution in a social application.

and b' are the enriched contents after content processing, *i.e.*, $a' = \{a, a_1, a_2, \ldots\}$, where a_k is a recommended content based on the original content a, and $b' = \{b, b_1, b_2, \ldots\}$, where b_k is a recommended content based on content b. a' and b' are then provided to users C, D and E according to social propagation. As an example social application, SICS contains the general content generation, processing and distribution procedures. We observe that a general social application framework is similar to a microblogging system, *e.g.*, users have social relationships between them, contents are generated by users and processed by the system, and then distributed to other users who are socially connected. We next study how the social application can be effectively deployed, using a measurement-driven approach based on the traces from Tencent Weibo.

3.2 Regional Analysis for Social Application Deployment

Our measurement study is based on traces collected from the operation team of Tencent Weibo [4], which is a microblogging website, where users can broadcast a message including at most 140 characters to their friends. Tencent Weibo features several social activities in the system, *e.g.*, online chatting with friends who mutually follow each other. We obtained Weibo traces from the technical team of Tencent, containing valuable runtime data of the system in 20 days (October 9 – October 29) in 2011. Each entry in the traces corresponds to one microblog published (which will be regarded as an item of user-generated content), including the ID of the microblog, the IP address and geographic region of the publisher, the timestamp when the microblog was posted, the IDs of the parent and root microbloggers if it is a re-post, and contents of the microblog.

Since we are focused on how multimedia contents should be handled in a social application, in our measurement study, we have targeted at video contents which are imported from external websites. In particular, we have collected more than 300,000 links from 5 popular video sharing sites. We then retrieve the microblogs which are related to these links, *i.e.*, the microblogs either include the links to these videos in the contents or they are re-shares of the ones that include the links. These links cover about 2 million microblogs in the time span, which are posted or re-shared by over 1 million users, from more than 100 regions in the propagation

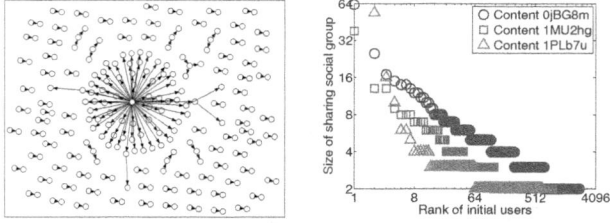

(a) Social groups sharing the same content.

(b) Size of social group versus the rank of user initiating the sharing.

Figure 2: Social groups sharing the same content initialized by different users.

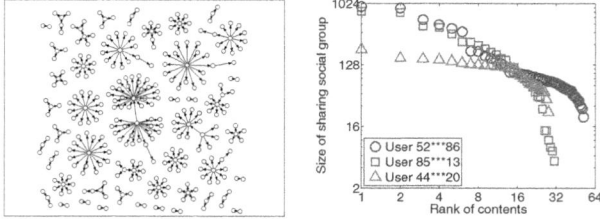

(a) Social groups initiated by the same user.

(b) Size of the social group versus the rank of contents.

Figure 3: Social groups initialized by the same user sharing different contents.

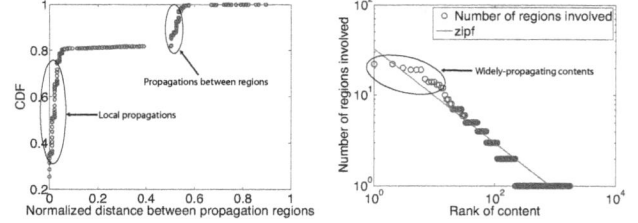

Figure 4: Normalized distances between the propagation region pairs.

Figure 5: The number of regions involved in the distribution of a specific content.

(each region is defined by Tencent as a city-level geographical area). In addition, we have also retrieved the social connections of these users. In our study, how contents are used by Weibo users will guide our design of social application deployment.

3.2.1 Dynamics of Users

The most important characteristic of a social application is that contents are propagated between users through their social connections. As a result, user influence is critical in social media application deployment. In Fig. 2(a), a circle represents a user, a directed edge represents the propagation between two users, and the connected components (trees) are social groups initiated by different users sharing the same content. We observe that while some users can attract a large number of friends to join the group, many others have much little influence. Particularly, in Fig. 2(b), each sample represents the size of the sharing group versus the rank of the user initiating the group. We observe that when the same content is shared by different users, the size of the sharing groups varies significantly.

3.2.2 Dynamics of Contents

Further, we also observe that social media sharing is highly affected by the contents themselves. In Fig. 3(a), the trees are social groups initialized by the same user sharing different contents. We observe that different contents can attract quite different numbers of friends. In particular, in Fig. 3(b), each sample represents the size of the sharing group versus the rank of the content shared in the group. We have observed that when different contents are initially shared by the same user, the size of the sharing groups varies significantly as well.

The propagation of contents in social applications can be

dynamically affected by both users and contents. To effectively allocate cloud resources for deployment, in our study, we analyze propagation within a regional level, in which propagation statistics can be highly stable and predictable. Next, we will present the efficiency of local processing and global distribution, both of which are carried out using a regional analysis approach.

3.3 Efficiency of Local Processing

3.3.1 Locality of Content Propagation

First, we show the propagation locality between content generation and distribution. We define a normalized geographic distance to measure two regions in our study as $\frac{d_{ij}}{\max\{d_{ij}\}}$, where d_{ij} is the real great-circle distance between region i and region j. Fig. 4 illustrates the normalized geographic distances between the region where new content is generated and the regions where the content is distributed to according to the social connections. We observe that the normalized geographic distances for most of the media content propagations are very small, e.g., more than 80% of the propagations are within a normalized distance of 0.1. The reason is that a dominant portion of the contents generated by users within a region will be served to the users mainly from the same region, according to social connections that determine how information flows in an online social network [8].

Furthermore, we also observe the locality in content distribution. We define a region involved in the content's generation (distribution) as a region where the content is generated from (to be distributed to). Fig. 5 illustrates the number of regions involved in the distribution of a specific content in one day. Contents are ranked in a descending order with respect to the number of regions involved in their distribution. Each sample represents the number of regions involved in the distribution versus the rank of the content. We observe that for most of the contents, only a few regions are involved in their distributions. The reason is that most of the contents are distributed locally, i.e., many users are located within the same region. The observations indicate that in social application deployment, computation instances could be allocated at multiple regions so as to collect, process and distribute the contents locally, reducing inter-region traffic to deliver the contents across regions.

3.3.2 Stability of Regions Involved Over Time

Due to the locality of propagation, the social application system will allocate computation instances within different regions to process the contents locally. However, how many and which regions should be selected to deploy the computation instances is still a question. To answer this question, we next study which regions are involved in content propagation.

Fig. 6(a) illustrates the number of contents generated by users from all the regions over time. Each sample represents the number of contents generated by users in a time slot (hour) versus the time. We observe obvious daily pattern — much more contents are generated during the peak hours (about 7000 per hour) than during the off-peak hours (about 500 per hour). We then study the regions involved in content generation.

Comparing to the number of generated contents, no evident daily pattern is observed in the number of regions involved in the generation, as illustrated in Fig. 6(b). Each sample in Fig. 6(b) represents the number of regions involved in content generation versus the time. We observe that the number of regions involved in content generation remains at a relatively high level over time (with the largest number 37 and the smallest number 33 per hour). Similar results are also observed in content distribution. Fig. 6(c) illustrates the number of regions involved in content distribution over time. We observe that the number of regions involved in content distribution also stays at a stable level.

These observations indicate that contents are always generated from and to be distributed to almost all the regions (the total number of regions is 41 in our traces).

3.3.3 Predictability of Regional Propagation

According to the observations above, we need to allocate computation instances at almost all the regions available to collect and process the contents locally. We next investigate how much network and computation resources within each region we should allocate, by studying the number of contents generated by users at each region.

Let the *content generation rate* of a region denote the number of contents generated by users within the region in a given time slot. In Fig. 7, regions are ranked according to their content generation rates. Each sample in this figure represents the content generation rate of a region versus the rank of the region. The popularity distribution of regions is not even — some regions can generate much more contents than other regions. Fig. 8 illustrates the distribution of the content generation rates at 4 different regions randomly selected (in Fig. 8, the content generation rates at level x are in $[40x, 40(x+1))$). We observe that the distributions of content generation rates at different regions are also quite different. However, in Fig. 9 which illustrates content generation rate of each region over time, we observe strong evidences of daily patterns for all regions. This observation indicates that the content generation rate of a region is highly predicable.

Based on the observations, we are able to design a predictive model to estimate the *regional* content generation rate, which will be utilized in local content processing. We will discuss our detailed design in Sec. 4.

3.4 Efficiency of Global Distribution

To handle the social contents generated at different regions locally, we allocate computation instances at different regions to collect, process and distribute the contents locally. In social media, some contents can be very popular

with many requesting users. Such contents are referred to as *widely-propagating contents*, which can attract users from a large number of regions, as illustrated in Fig. 5. In the distribution of a widely-propagating content, a large fraction of users will experience low download performance if they all download the content from the computation instance where the content is originally collected and processed, since these users can be located at other regions far away from the original region, resulting in a low download bandwidth. To address this problem, a global distribution platform which can effectively distribute widely-propagating contents to users within many regions is needed. Due to dynamic social propagation, it is not always easy to predict the popularity of social media contents, which is affected by not only the social network topology but also the influence and preference of users.

In our measurements, we will show that contents processed by computation instances can be effectively replicated to a global distribution platform, which is able to significantly improve the distribution performance. We implement the computation instances in C++ on Amazon EC2 micro nodes and the distribution platform in Python on Google AppEngine. We choose the following different sizes for contents that can be generated by users: 1.1 MB, 160 KB and 50 KB. We allocate computation instances in the 7 regions provided by EC2: Virginia (US East), Oregon (US West), California (US West), Ireland (EU West), Singapore (Asia Pacific), Tokyo (Asia Pacific) and Sao Paulo (South America). Meanwhile, 57 PlanetLab nodes are implemented to upload and download contents as well, simulating the social application users. The detailed implementation is to be discussed in Sec. 6.

3.4.1 Connectivity Between Local Processing and Global Distribution

When using the distribution platform to deliver the widely-propagating contents, these contents have to be first replicated from the computation instances (EC2) to the distribution platform (GAE). We measure the overhead for such replication. As illustrated in Fig. 11, we compare the times computation instances at different regions spend on uploading the contents to the distribution platform, with the average time that the instances spend on directly uploading them to the PlanetLab nodes at different locations, in the case that the distribution platform is not employed.

We observe that the time computation instances spend on uploading the processed contents to the distribution platform is much smaller than the average time computation instances spend on uploading the contents to the users directly. This observation indicates that the replication overhead is small, compared to the time the instances spend on uploading the contents to the users directly.

3.4.2 Benefits of a Global Distribution Platform

Next, we show that the GAE-based distribution platform outperforms the EC2-based computation instances in distributing widely-propagating contents to users at multiple regions. Fig. 12 compares the download times achieved by the computation instances and by the distribution platform. In this figure, each sample represents the average time that a PlanetLab node takes to download the content from the computation instance or the distribution platform. We observe that for most of the PlanetLab nodes, their download

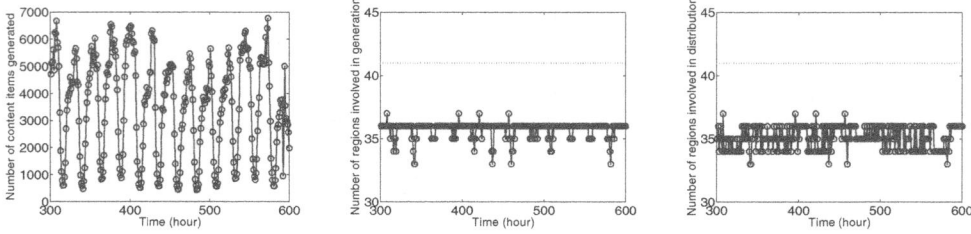

(a) The number of contents uploaded by users over time.

(b) The number of regions involved in content generation over time.

(c) The number of regions involved in content distribution over time.

Figure 6: Social media generation and distribution.

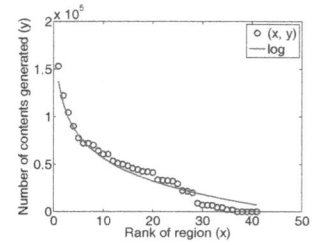

Figure 7: The number of contents generated within a region versus the rank of the region.

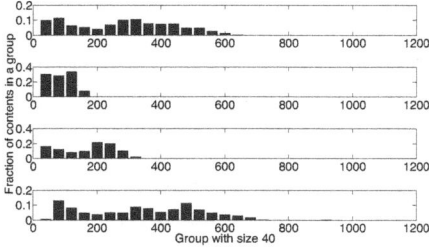

Figure 8: Distribution of content generation rate at four regions.

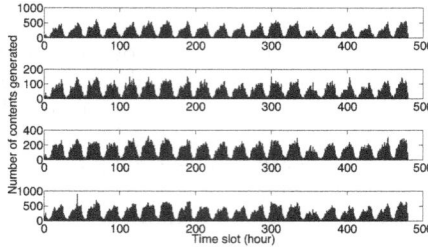

Figure 9: The content generation rate over time at four regions.

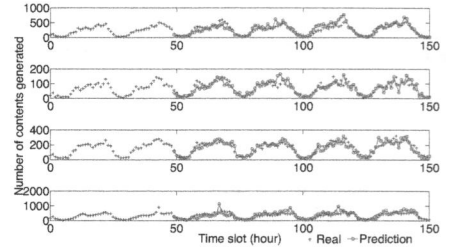

Figure 10: Prediction of content generation rates.

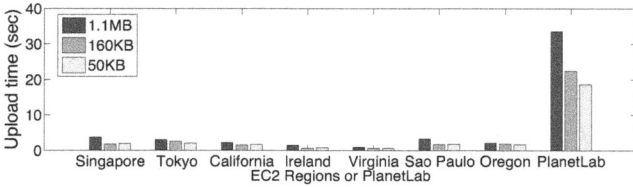

Figure 11: Delivery time comparison between the computation instances to the distribution platform and the computation instances to users.

times at EC2 are much larger than that at GAE. The reason is that GAE has already automatically replicated the contents to different locations, so that users can be redirected to servers that can best serve them. Though it is not the focus of this paper, interested readers are referred to the related works devoted to the distribution of social media contents [29][31]. The observation indicates that in social media distribution, a global distribution platform is needed when new content is supposed to attract users from many different locations. Motivated by this observation, we design a hybrid replication strategy to distribute the contents based on both local computation instances and the global distribution platform, where contents attracting more users from multiple regions will be replicated to the distribution platform.

4. DETAILED DESIGN OF THE SOCIAL APPLICATION DEPLOYMENT IN CLOUD

In our measurement study, we show that a social application can be effectively deployed based on local processing instances and a global distribution platform. In this section,

we first present a new framework for social application deployment, and then describe our detailed design on how to collect contents generated by users, process them and distribute the processed contents to the users.

4.1 Framework

In a social application, though users are globally distributed within different regions when they generate contents for and download the contents from the system, content propagation is highly localized. To effectively handle the contents in a social application, we design a new framework as illustrated in Fig. 13: (1) IaaS-based computation instances are allocated to collect the contents generated by users within different regions and perform the content processing locally; and (2) a PaaS-based distribution platform is allocated to assist the distribution of widely-propagating contents. We next demonstrate the advantages of our new framework.

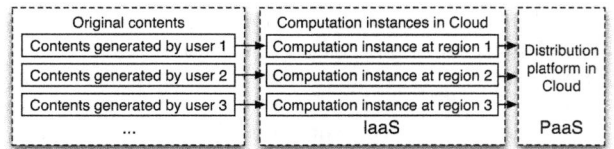

Figure 13: Framework of the social application deployment.

Local collection and processing. In content processing, allocating computation instances at multiple regions has the following advantages: (1) Allocating computation instances close to users can improve the performance for them to upload and download the contents; (2) we observe that the propagation is highly localized in our measurements, *i.e.*,

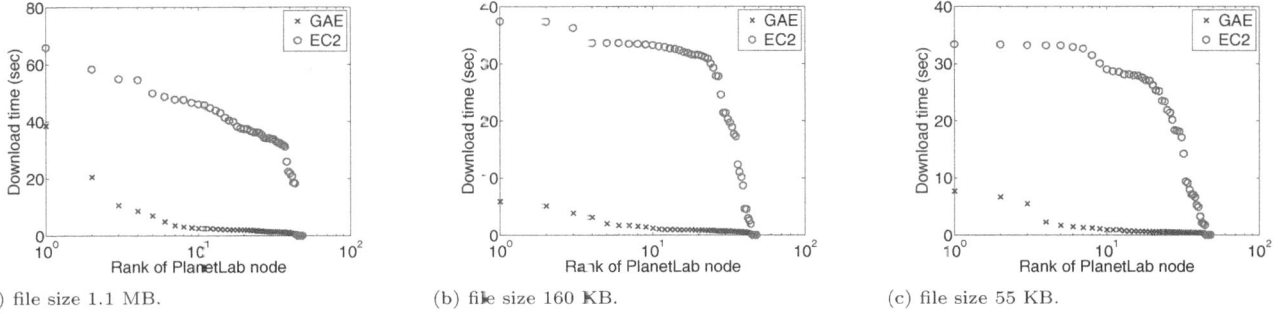

(a) file size 1.1 MB. (b) file size 160 KB. (c) file size 55 KB.

Figure 12: Comparison of download times users experience when downloading contents from the computation instances and the distribution platform.

contents generated within one region are likely to be requested by users within the same region. Deploying computation instances close to users can reduce the inter-region transmission cost [17]; and (3) the prices for computation instances at different locations can be different [6] — it is intriguing to investigate how to allocate cloud resource from different locations so that the generated contents can be efficiently processed with minimum costs.

Global distribution. After being processed by computation instances, users can directly download these contents from the instances. In our measurements, we observe that the PaaS-based distribution platform can achieve much smaller download times for users to obtain some popular contents, which are requested by the users at many regions. In our deployment design, we strategically select a set of such widely-propagating contents over time, and replicate these contents from the local computation instances to the global distribution platform. The social application system can dramatically improve the distribution performance when the distribution platform upload to users that are far away from the original computation instances. Due to the large number of contents generated and the limited budget for distribution, we need to strategically determine which contents should be replicated to the distribution platform and which ones are only served by the local computation instances. Table 1 summarizes important notations for ease of reference.

4.2 Computation Instance Allocation for Local Processing

Given that computation instances allocated in multiple regions can benefit social application deployment, the problem is to determine the allocation strategy, *i.e.*, the capacities of computation instances at different regions.

4.2.1 Allocation Scheme and Cost

A social media company has to perform instance allocation according to its budgetary constraints. In IaaS, the general pricing rules are as follows: (1) The more instances the social application allocates, the more the cloud provider will charge; (2) The prices vary with different regions, *e.g.*, the unit price of a VM instance in US West is higher than the price in US East in May 2012; and (3) The prices also vary over time.

The cost is determined by instance allocation. In our design, we let vector $\vec{\mu} = \{\mu_1, \mu_2, \ldots\}$ denote the cloud instance allocation scheme. Each entry $\mu_j, j \in \mathcal{R}^C$ in $\vec{\mu}$ determines the aggregate *content processing rate* of the cloud

Table 1: Important notations

$\mathcal{R}^C$	Set of regions having computation instances
$\mathcal{R}^U$	Set of regions where users are located in
P^H	Unit price for content processing rate of computation instance
P^U	Unit price for upload capacity of distribution platform
P^S	Unit price for storage of distribution platform
λ_i	Content generation rate from region i
λ_{ij}	Content generation rate redirected from region i to j
Λ_j	Content generation rate redirected to region j
μ_j	Content processing rate allocated at region j
$M_c(\vec{\mu})$	Processing cost under allocation scheme $\vec{\mu}$
$\mathcal{D}^{(T)}$	Set of candidate contents for replication
$\mathcal{S}^{(T)}$	Set of processed contents served by the global distribution platform
$M_d(\mathcal{S})$	Distribution cost for the contents in $\mathcal{S}$

instances allocated at region j, and $\mathcal{R}^C$ denotes the set of regions where the computation instances can be allocated, *i.e.*, the cloud provider has deployed servers in data centers within these regions. Larger μ_j indicates that more contents can be processed in region j per time unit, resulting in a higher cost. In our design, the cost of an allocation scheme $\vec{\mu}$ can be estimated as follows:

$$M_c(\vec{\mu}) = \sum_{j \in \mathcal{R}^C} P_j^H \mu_j,$$

where P_j^H is the unit price of processing rate at region j. Note that we assume proportional upload and download bandwidths are also allocated at region j according to μ_j, so that the generated contents can be collected and distributed by the computation instances. The prices for bandwidths are included in P_j^H.

4.2.2 Prediction of the Content Generation Rate in Each Region

To efficiently allocate the computation instances within a region, *i.e.*, to determine the content processing rate, we can refer to the content generation rate in that region. The rationale is that it would be a waste if the content processing rate is much larger than the content generation rate;

while it takes too long for content to be processed when the content processing rate is much smaller than the content generation rate. The efficient content processing rates depend on the actual content generation rates. According to our measurements, the regional content generation rate is highly predictable.

Let $\lambda_i^{(T)}, i \in \mathcal{R}^U$ denote the content generation rate at region i in time slot T, where $\mathcal{R}^U$ is the set of all regions that users are located at (generally, $\mathcal{R}^C \neq \mathcal{R}^U$). In Sec. 3, we observe that the content generation rate at each region shows strong evidence of the daily pattern. It indicates that the content generation rates can be predicted using autoregressive models [5].

In our design, we predict $\lambda_i^{(T)}$ based on the historical content generation rates $\{\lambda_i^{(T-1)}, \lambda_i^{(T-2)}, \ldots, \lambda_i^{(T-M)}\}$, where M is the number of previous generation rates to refer to in the prediction. An ARIMA (AutoRegressive Integrated Moving Average) [23] model is used, i.e.,

$$(1 - \sum_{k=1}^{p} \Phi_k L_k) Y^{(T)} = (1 + \sum_{k=1}^{q} \Theta_k L_k) \varepsilon^{(T)},$$

where p is the order of autoregressive and q is the order of moving average. Φ_k and Θ_k are the parameters of the autoregressive and moving average parts, respectively. $\varepsilon^{(T)}$ is the white noise for the stationary distribution. $Y^{(T)}$ is defined as follows,

$$Y^{(T)} = (1 - L)^d \lambda_i^{(T)},$$

where L is the lag operation, i.e., $L^d \lambda_i^{(T)} = \lambda_i^{(T-d)}$. In our design, the content generation rate at each region ($\lambda_i^{(T)}$) is recorded hourly. To capture the daily pattern, we choose the period of $d = 24$ hours, so that $Y^{(T)}$ can be regarded as wide-sense stationary. In our experiments, 48 hours of historical records are utilized to predict $\lambda_i^{(T)}$, by training the predictive parameters using a maximum likelihood estimation. Based on the implementation of ARIMA in R with parameters $p = 48$ and $q = 0$, we present the prediction results of the four randomly chosen regions used in our measurement in Fig. 10. We observe that the predictive model only needs a small learning window to give an relatively accurate estimate of the content generation rate.

4.2.3 Computation Instance Allocation

In the computation instance allocation, we regard each content generated from a region in $\mathcal{R}^U$ as a task for the computation instances to process. After a content is uploaded by a user to a computation instance, it is queued to be processed at the computation instance. A content will be available to users only after it has been processed. Our objective is to allocate computation instances strategically to minimize the average time for a content to be available to users. Fig. 14 illustrates the procedure of the computation instance allocation: (1) Historical content generation rates at different regions in $\mathcal{R}^U$ are collected; (2) The current content generation rates are estimated using the predictive model; (3) The predicted content generation rates are scheduled to different computation instances within regions in $\mathcal{R}^C$; and (4) According to the scheduled content generation rates, content processing rates are allocated. We will provide more details next.

Prediction and schedule of generated contents. For sim-

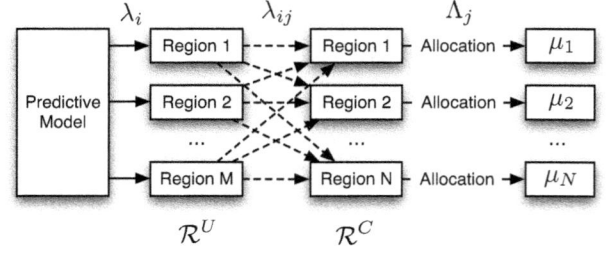

Figure 14: The allocation of computation instances.

plicity, we use λ_i to denote the predicted content generation rate from region i in time slot T, and λ_{ij} to denote the rate of contents generated at region i to be scheduled to the computation instances at region j in time slot T. The schedule is as follows:

$$\lambda_{ij} = \begin{cases} \lambda_i, & j = \arg\min_k d_{ik}, \\ 0, & j \neq \arg\min_k d_{ik}, \end{cases} \quad i \in \mathcal{R}^U, j \in \mathcal{R}^C.$$

The rationale is that we assign a user to the region that is closest to him, so that he can spend the minimum amount of time on uploading the generated contents to the system. Let Λ_j denote the rate of contents from all regions to be uploaded to instances allocated at region j, i.e., $\Lambda_j = \sum_{i \in \mathcal{R}^U} \lambda_{ij}, j \in \mathcal{R}^C$.

Allocation of processing rates. Let $W_c(\vec{\mu})$ denote the average waiting time for the original contents to be processed using the allocation scheme $\vec{\mu}$. According to the queuing model [13], we have the average waiting time for a content to be processed by the social application system as follows:

$$W_c(\vec{\mu}) = \frac{\sum_{j \in \mathcal{R}^C} \frac{\Lambda_j}{(\mu_j - \Lambda_j)}}{\sum_{j \in \mathcal{R}^C} \Lambda_j}.$$

To make the processed contents available to users as soon as possible, $\vec{\mu}$ is regarded as an optimization variable to minimize $W_c(\vec{\mu})$. We model the computation instance allocation as the following optimization problem:

$$\min_{\vec{\mu}} W_c(\vec{\mu}), \quad (1)$$

subject to:

$$\mu_j \geq \Lambda_j, j \in \mathcal{R}^C,$$

$$M_c(\vec{\mu}) \leq B^C,$$

where B^C is the budget for the allocation. We let $\mu_j \geq \Lambda_j, j \in \mathcal{R}^C$ so that the waiting time for a content to be processed is limited. $\mu_j \geq \Lambda_j, j \in \mathcal{R}^C$ indicates that we always allocate enough instances for the estimated volumes of contents generated by users, i.e., $M_c(\{\Lambda_1, \Lambda_2, \ldots\}) \leq B^C$. The optimization is a convex programming, which can be efficiently solved by a general water-filling like algorithm: we iteratively allocate a small amount of resources to the computation instances within region k with the largest marginal time deduction, as follows:

$$k = \arg\min_{j \in \mathcal{R}^C} \frac{\partial W_c}{\partial \mu_j} = \arg\min_{j \in \mathcal{R}^C} \frac{-\Lambda_j}{\sum_{j \in \mathcal{R}^C} \Lambda_j (\mu_j - \Lambda_j)^2},$$

until the budget is used up. In Sec. 5, we will present how the algorithms are implemented to allocate computation instances dynamically.

4.3 Replication for Global Distribution

In the PaaS-based distribution platform, since both storage and upload capacity are charged according to the usage, our design is to determine which contents to be replicated to the distribution platform. When choosing processed contents to be replicated to the distribution platform, we select the widely-propagating contents that will be requested by users from many external regions, and let the computation instances serve other contents that are mostly requested by local users. The selection is based on not only the popularities of the contents, but also the social connections of the users generating these contents.

Let $\mathcal{S}^{(T)} = \{c_1, c_2, \ldots, c_S\}$ denote the set of processed contents served by the distribution platform in the time slot T, i.e., users can download contents in $\mathcal{S}^{(T)}$ in time slot T. The distribution replication is then to determine the contents in $\mathcal{S}^{(T)}$.

In the content replication, there is also a budget B^D for the allocation of the distribution platform. Let $M_d(\mathcal{S}^{(T)})$ denote the cost when contents in $\mathcal{S}^{(T)}$ are served by the distribution platform. The cost includes both the storage and upload bandwidths, which can be formulated as follows:

$$M_d(\mathcal{S}^{(T)}) = P^S \sum_{c \in \mathcal{S}^{(T)}} A(c) + P^U \sum_{c \in \mathcal{S}^{(T)}} N(c)$$

where P^S is the unit storage price, P^U is the unit upload price, $A(c)$ is the size of the content c, and $N(c)$ is the amount of bytes to be uploaded to the users that are downloading the content from the distribution platform. $N(c)$ can be estimated as follows:

$$N(c) = v_c \sum_{i \in \mathcal{R}^U - \{R(c)\}} |\mathcal{F}_{u_c, i}|,$$

where u_c is the user who generate content c, $\mathcal{F}_{u_c, i}$ is the set of user u_c's friends that are located at region i, $R(c)$ is the region where content c is originally processed and served, and v_c is the average number of bytes served for the content. v_c can be estimated by an empirical value $\alpha A(c)$, where α is the average fraction of a video that users usually download [16]. The rationale of $N(c)$ is that the distribution platform will be in charge of uploading the content to u_c's friends that are located at external regions to reduce the download times.

The cloud distribution platform automatically replicates contents in $\mathcal{S}^{(T)}$ to different locations so that users can be better served. We design a content replication index $r(c)$ as follows:

$$r(c) = \sum_{i \in \mathcal{R}^U - \{R(c)\}} |\mathcal{F}_{u_c, i}| d_{i, R(c)},$$

where $d_{i, R(c)}$ is the geographic distance between region i and region $R(c)$. Larger $r(c)$ indicates that content c will be requested by more users from more external regions, and c should be replicated to the distribution platform for these users to download.

In our distribution platform allocation, we determine which contents to be replicated to the distribution platform by solving the following problem:

$$\max_{\mathcal{S}^{(T)}} \sum_{c \in \mathcal{S}^{(T)}} r(c), \qquad (2)$$

subject to:

$$M_d(\mathcal{S}^{(T)}) \leq B^D,$$

$$\mathcal{S}^{(T)} \subset \mathcal{D}^{(T)},$$

where $\mathcal{D}^{(T)}$ is the set of candidate contents that can be downloaded by users in the future. In a social application, since users mainly request the contents recently generated by users, $\mathcal{D}^{(T)}$ can be formed from the contents recently processed by the computation instances.

The rationale of Eq. (2) is that we select the contents that can attract more users from more external regions. Such contents cannot be well served by only local computation instances. By replicating these contents to the distribution platform, which automatically replicates them to servers close to users, better download performance can be achieved for users that are not located closely to the original computation instances. The optimization can be heuristically solved by a dynamic programming algorithm in Sec. 5.

Next, we will discuss the implementation of the cloud-based social application deployment.

5. DISCUSSION OF SYSTEM IMPLEMENTATION

In this section, we discuss the details of our implementation. Our implementation is based on Amazon EC2 and Google AppEngine.

5.1 Computation Instance Allocation

We allocate the computation instances on Amazon EC2. The computation instance allocation algorithm is illustrated in Algorithm 1. Due to the limited number of regions where the computation instances can be allocated, the algorithm is carried out in a centralized manner periodically.

First, we collect the recent content generation rates from all the regions in $\mathcal{R}^U$, which are used to predict the current content generation rates $\lambda_i, i \in \mathcal{R}^U$. We assume the unit prices $P_j^H, j \in \mathcal{R}^C$ are also provided by the cloud provider. By solving the convex optimization problem in Eq. (1), we have the content processing rates $\mu_j, j \in \mathcal{R}^C$. According to the content processing rates, we allocate instances from EC2 — the processing rates determine the number and the model of the computation instances.

Second, the computation instances will receive and process the contents generated by users. At each region, a priority queue is utilized to store the contents uploaded by users. The contents are prioritized to be processed by the computation instances as follows: (1) Contents posted in the same region with the computation instance will be prioritized, and (2) contents are processed according to the timestamps they are uploaded.

5.2 Content Replication

According to our design illustrated in Sec. 4.3, the optimization can be solved using the dynamic programming algorithm, assuming that both the distribution price and budget can be regarded as positive integers. The replication procedure is illustrated in Algorithm 2. Contents in set $\mathcal{D}^{(T)}$ are the recently processed ones collected from all the computation instances, $M_d(\cdot)$ is the price function, and $r(\cdot)$ is the replication index function. We assume contents in $\mathcal{D}^{(T)}$ can be indexed from 1 to $|\mathcal{D}^{(T)}|$. Let $r(i, j)$ denote

---

Algorithm 1 Allocation of computation instances.

1: **procedure** ALLOCATION($\lambda_i^{(t)}, i \in \mathcal{R}^U, t = T - 1, T - 2, \ldots, T - M, P_j^H, j \in \mathcal{R}^C$)
2:    predict $\lambda_i, i \in \mathcal{R}^U$ using the predictive model
3:    $\mu_j \leftarrow \Lambda_j, j \in \mathcal{R}^C$
4:    **while** $M_c(\vec{\mu}) \leq B^C$ **do**
5:       $k \leftarrow \arg\min_{j \in \mathcal{R}^C} \frac{\partial W_c}{\partial \mu_j}$
6:       $\mu_k \leftarrow \mu_k + \Delta$
7:    **end while**
8:    allocate instances according to processing rates $\mu_j, j \in \mathcal{R}^C$
9: **end procedure**

Algorithm 2 Replication of processed contents.

1: **procedure** REPLICATION($\mathcal{D}^{(T)}, M_d(\cdot), r(\cdot)$)
2:    **for** d **from** 0 **to** B^D **do**
3:       $\mathcal{S}(0, d) \leftarrow \Phi$
4:       $r(0, d) \leftarrow 0$
5:    **end for**
6:    **for** i **from** 1 **to** $|\mathcal{D}^{(T)}|$ **do**
7:       **for** j **from** 0 **to** B^D **do**
8:          **if** $j \geq M_d(\{c_i\})$ **and** $r(i-1, j) < r(i-1, j - M_d(\{c_i\}))$ **then**
9:             $\mathcal{S}(i, j) \leftarrow \mathcal{S}(i-1, j) \bigcup \{c_i\}$
10:            $r(i, j) \leftarrow r(i-1, j - M_d(\{c_i\})) + r(c_i)$
11:          **else**
12:            $\mathcal{S}(i, j) \leftarrow \mathcal{S}(i-1, j)$
13:            $r(i, j) \leftarrow r(i-1, j)$
14:          **end if**
15:       **end for**
16:    **end for**
17:    $\mathcal{S}^{(T)} = \mathcal{S}(|\mathcal{D}^{(T)}|, B^D)$
18: **end procedure**

---

the optimized replication gain of deploying the candidate contents indexed 1 to i under the budget j, $\mathcal{S}(i, j)$ denote the contents selected for replication. Using the dynamical programming algorithm, $\mathcal{S}(i, j)$ and $r(i, j)$ are iteratively updated, and the solution to our replication problem in (2) is then $\mathcal{S}^{(T)} = \mathcal{S}(|\mathcal{D}^{(T)}|, B^D)$.

After replication, for a content in $\mathcal{S}^{(T)}$, users are able to download it from either the computation instance where it is processed, or the distribution platform, to achieve the best download rate. Stale contents in the distribution platform are removed to make room for new ones in an LFU manner. After a content is removed from the distribution platform, users can still download it from the computation instance.

6. EXPERIMENTAL RESULTS

In this section, we evaluate the performance of our design based on a prototype of the example social application implemented on Amazon EC2 and Google AppEngine.

6.1 Experiment Setup

Social application system. Amazon EC2 provides computation instances at 7 regions given in Sec. 3. We have launched one micro VM instance[5] at each region, where we implement the content collection and processing mod-

---

[5]http://aws.amazon.com/ec2/instance-types/

ules using C++. Since we are using the free-tier micro VM nodes which have low computation capacities, to evaluate different content processing rates in Algorithm 1, the content processing in the prototype is simplified so that the number of processed contents is directly determined by the processing rates without actual computing load. The implementation can be easily replaced by other content processing algorithms for different social applications. The prices for Amazon EC2 micro instances are following the latest prices provided on the website[6]. For the content distribution, we implemented a Python-based distribution platform on Google AppEngine with 5GB storage capacity and 1GB outbound bandwidth per hour. In our experiments, the distribution budget B^D is determined by the storage and bandwidth limitations, *i.e.*, we replicate contents to the distribution platform under the storage and bandwidth capacities. The distribution uses the data storage APIs provided by Google AppEngine to accept contents uploaded from the computation instances and serve users.

Users. We employ 57 PlanetLab nodes to upload and download contents according the traces from Tencent Weibo as follows: (1) In each round of the experiments, a set of 41 PlanetLab nodes are randomly selected and mapped to the 41 regions in $\mathcal{R}^U$; (2) The content generation rate of each PlanetLab node is determined by the traces, as used in our measurement in Sec. 3.3.3; and (3) After the contents are processed by the social application system, the nodes simulate to download the processed contents: followers of the users who have generated the contents will download the processed contents. The rationale is that it is highly possible for these followers to download the contents, and we use them to estimate the actual downloaders, though the number of total followers can be larger than the number of users who actually download the contents in real systems (*e.g.*, some users are never online to receive the contents).

Protocols. We present the practical protocols used to connect the users and the social application system. Contents are transferred as follows. (1) A user can upload a content to one of his local computation instances over TCP using private protocol; (2) If a processed content should be served by the distribution platform, the computation instance requests an uploading URL from the distribution platform, which is generated by the data storage API provided by Google AppEngine; (3) Using the upload URL, the content instance can upload the processed content by posting it to the given URL over HTTP; and (4) When downloading contents, a user is first provided with a XML file indicating where the contents can be downloaded, *i.e.*, either from a computation instance or the distribution platform. The user then downloads these contents from the computation instances or the distribution platform.

Records. In our experiments, we simulate two different content sizes for users to upload and download: 1.1 MB and 160 KB. Each PlanetLab node will record the time spent on uploading and downloading the contents. At each Amazon EC2 instance, we also implement the instance to record the time spent on processing each content. Based on these records, we evaluate the performance of content collection, processing and distribution in terms of the time spent on each task.

---

[6]May, 2012: http://aws.amazon.com/ec2/pricing/. California 0.025, Virginia 0.02, Oregon 0.02, Singapore 0.025, Ireland 0.025, Tokyo 0.027 and Sao Paulo 0.027 (USD per hour)

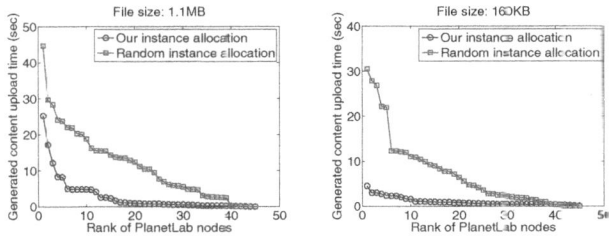

(a) file size 1.1 MB.

(b) file size 160 KB

Figure 15: Comparison of upload time in content collection.

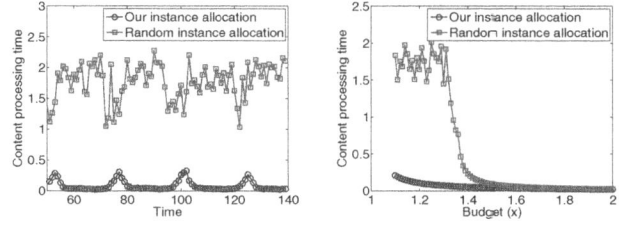

(a) Processing time over time.

(b) Processing time versus budget.

Figure 16: Comparison of processing time in content processing.

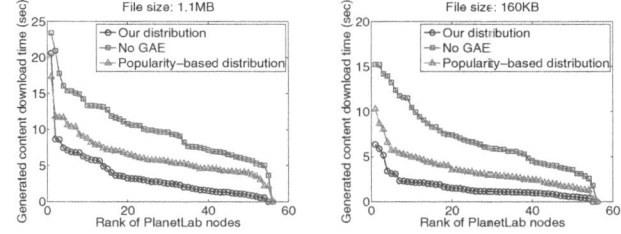

(a) file size 1.1 MB.

(b) file size 160 KB.

Figure 17: Comparison of download time in content distribution.

6.2 Performance Evaluation

Content collection. First, we evaluate the performance for users to upload the generated contents to the social application system. We compare our instance allocation with a random instance allocation scheme, where processing rates at the instances are allocated randomly. The budget for both strategies is the same, $1.2 \sum_{j \in \mathcal{R}^C} P_j^H \Lambda_j$. The rationale is that the social media company spends 20% more than the estimated demand on the allocation. We collect the average time each PlanetLab node spends on uploading the contents to the computation instances. Fig. 15 compares the upload times in the two allocation schemes. Each sample represents the average upload time at a node versus the rank of the node. We observe that it is much faster for users to upload contents in our design than in the random scheme — in our design, about 2/3 of the nodes can upload the contents with size 1 MB in less than 1 second, while most of the nodes have to spend more than 5 seconds to upload the same contents in the random scheme. The reason is that by taking the regional content generation rates into consideration, bandwidths can be allocated efficiently at the computation instances to satisfy users' uploading requests.

Content processing. Next, we evaluate the performance of content processing, in terms of the average processing time, which is defined as the average delay for a content to be available to users after it has been uploaded to the system. Fig. 16(a) compares our instance allocation with the random scheme over time, under the same budget of $1.2 \sum_{j \in \mathcal{R}^C} P_j^H \Lambda_j$. The contents to be processed at a computation instance are the contents uploaded by users. We observe that the processing time in the random scheme is about 10 times larger than that in our design. The reason is that many contents have to wait a long time to be processed when being queued at a computation instance with a small processing rate in the random scheme. We also observe that in our design, the processing time is correlated with the content generation rate, *i.e.*, it takes longer for a content to be processed during the peak hours; while in the random scheme, the processing times are randomly distributed.

We next investigate the content processing performance under different budgets. Fig. 16(b) illustrates the processing time versus the budget $x \sum_{j \in \mathcal{R}^C} P_j^H \Lambda_j$. We observe that the processing time decreases when the budget is increased in both algorithms, since more computation resource is allocated for the generated contents; however, the processing time is much smaller in our design than in the random scheme when the budget is small (*e.g.*, $x < 1.5$), indicating that our design can benefit the social media companies when they have a limited budget. Both algorithms can achieve

a small processing time when enough resource is allocated (*e.g.*, $x > 1.8$).

Content distribution. We also evaluate the performance for the distribution of the processed contents. Similarly, the PlanetLab nodes record the times spent on downloading the contents from both the computation instances and the distribution platform. We compare our design with two simple schemes: (1) No GAE strategy in which users only download the contents from the original computation instances; and (2) Popularity-based distribution where contents in $\mathcal{D}^{(T)}$ are replicated from the computation instances to the distribution platform according to only the popularities of the users who generate the contents, *i.e.*, a content is more likely to be replicated to the distribution platform if the user has more friends. Fig. 17 illustrates the download time versus the rank of the PlanetLab node. Again, we observe that our distribution replication achieves the lowest download times for almost all the PlanetLab nodes. We also observe that popularity-based replication achieves better distribution performance than the no-GAE scheme.

The experimental results indicate that by only allocating limited storage and outbound bandwidth (*e.g.*, the free-tier GAE platform in our experiments) at the distribution platform, widely-propagating social contents can be well served to global users.

7. CONCLUDING REMARKS

Large online social networks are providing Open APIs for developers to implement different social applications. It is promising for small social media companies to obtain user relationships and social actions without building a new social network. In this paper, we explore an efficient and economical cloud-based social application deployment after a social media company has developed their application. With measurement studies, we show that even if the social application is attracting users globally, the propagation can be quite localized; and even if the propagation is highly dynamical for users and contents, the regional propagation patterns can be highly predictable. A local processing and global distribution design principle can be effectively used in cloud-based social application deployment. We developed a theoretical framework to design our algorithms for computation instance allocation and content replication, which are implemented in our prototype of an example social application on Amazon EC2 and Google AppEngine. The superiority of our design is confirmed by trace-driven experiments.

Acknowledgment

This work has been partially supported by the National Basic Research Program of China (973) under Grant No. 2011CB302206, the National Natural Science Foundation of China under Grant No. 60933013/61272231, the National Significant Science and Technology Projects of China under Grant No. 2012ZX01039001-003, and the research fund of Tsinghua-Tencent Joint Laboratory for Internet Innovation Technology.

8. REFERENCES

[1] http://aws.amazon.com/ec2/.
[2] http://code.google.com/appengine/.
[3] http://techblog.netflix.com/2012/01/auto-scaling-in-amazon-cloud.html.
[4] http://t.qq.com/.
[5] H. Akaike. Fitting Autoregressive Models for Prediction. *Annals of the Institute of Statistical Mathematics*, 21(1):243–247, 1969.
[6] M. Armbrust, A. Fox, R. Griffith, A. Joseph, R. Katz, A. Konwinski, G. Lee, D. Patterson, A. Rabkin, I. Stoica, et al. A View of Cloud Computing. *Communications of the ACM*, 53(4):50–58, 2010.
[7] F. Benevenuto, T. Rodrigues, M. Cha, and V. Almeida. Characterizing User Behavior in Online Social Networks. In *Proc. of ACM IMC*, 2009.
[8] M. Cha, A. Mislove, and K. Gummadi. A measurement-driven analysis of information propagation in the flickr social network. In *Proc. of ACM WWW*, 2009.
[9] X. Cheng and J. Liu. Load-Balanced Migration of Social Media to Content Clouds. In *Proc. of NOSSDAV*, 2011.
[10] N. Chohan, C. Bunch, S. Pang, C. Krintz, N. Mostafa, S. Soman, and R. Wolski. AppScale: Scalable and Open AppEngine Application Development and Deployment. *Cloud Computing*, 34(2):57–70, 2010.
[11] N. Ellison et al. Social Network Sites: Definition, History, and Scholarship. *Journal of Computer-Mediated Communication*, 13(1):210–230, 2007.
[12] B. Furht and A. Escalante. *Handbook of Cloud Computing*. Springer-Verlag New York Inc, 2010.
[13] B. B. V. Gnedenko and I. Kovalenko. *Introduction to Queueing Theory*. Birkhauser, 1989.
[14] L. Guo, E. Tan, S. Chen, X. Zhang, and Y. Zhao. Analyzing Patterns of User Content Generation in Online Social Networks. In *Proc. of ACM SIGKDD*, 2009.
[15] P. Hofmann and D. Woods. Cloud Computing: the Limits of Public Clouds for Business Applications. *Internet Computing*, 14(6):90–93, 2010.
[16] Y. Huang, T. Fu, D. Chiu, J. Lui, and C. Huang. Challenges, Design and Analysis of a Large-Scale P2P-VoD System. In *Proc. of ACM SIGCOMM*, 2008.
[17] B. Huffaker, M. Fomenkov, D. Plummer, D. Moore, and K. Claffy. Distance Metrics in the Internet. In *Proc. of IEEE International Telecommunications Symposium (ITS)*, 2002.
[18] A. Kaplan and M. Haenlein. Users of the World, Unite! the Challenges and Opportunities of Social Media. *Business horizons*, 53(1):59–68, 2010.
[19] I. Konstas, V. Stathopoulos, and J. Jose. On Social Networks and Collaborative Recommendation. In *Proc. of ACM SIGIR*, 2009.
[20] H. Kwak, C. Lee, H. Park, and S. Moon. What Is Twitter, a Social Network or a News Media? In *Proc. of ACM WWW*, 2010.
[21] A. Li, X. Yang, S. Kandula, and M. Zhang. CloudCmp: Comparing Public Cloud Providers. In *Proc. of ACM IMC*, 2010.
[22] M. Miller. *Cloud Computing: Web-Based Applications That Change the Way You Work and Collaborate Online*. Que, 2008.
[23] T. Mills. *Time Series Techniques for Economists*. Cambridge Univ Pr, 1991.
[24] J. Pujol, V. Erramilli, G. Siganos, X. Yang, N. Laoutaris, P. Chhabra, and P. Rodriguez. The Little Engine(s) That Could: Scaling Online Social Networks. *ACM SIGCOMM Computer Communication Review*, 40(4):375–386, 2010.
[25] Z. Rehman, F. Hussain, and O. Hussain. Towards Multi-Criteria Cloud Service Selection. In *Proc. of IEEE International Conference on Innovative Mobile and Internet Services in Ubiquitous Computing*, 2011.
[26] B. Rimal, E. Choi, and I. Lumb. A Taxonomy and Survey of Cloud Computing Systems. In *IEEE International Joint Conference on INC, IMS and IDC*, 2009.
[27] S. Scellato, C. Mascolo, M. Musolesi, and J. Crowcroft. Track Globally, Deliver Locally: Improving Content Delivery Networks by Tracking Geographic Social Cascades. In *Proc. of ACM WWW*, 2011.
[28] D. A. Tran, K. Nguyen, and C. Pham. S-CLONE: Socially-Aware Data Replication for Social Networks. *Computer Networks*, 56(7):2001 – 2013, 2012.
[29] Z. Wang, L. Sun, X. Chen, W. Zhu, J. Liu, M. Chen, and S. Yang. Propagation-based Social-aware Replication for Social Video Contents. In *Proc. of ACM Multimedia*, 2012.
[30] Z. Wang, L. Sun, C. Wu, and S. Yang. Guiding Internet-Scale Video Service Deployment Using Microblog-Based Prediction. In *Proc. of IEEE INFOCOM Mini-Conference*, 2012.
[31] Y. Wu, C. Wu, B. Li, L. Zhang, Z. Li, and F. C. Lau. Scaling Social Media Applications Into Geo-Distributed Clouds. In *Proc. of IEEE INFOCOM*, 2012.

FRAppE: Detecting Malicious Facebook Applications

Md Sazzadur Rahman, Ting-Kai Huang, Harsha V. Madhyastha, and Michalis Faloutsos
Dept. of Computer Science, University of California, Riverside
Riverside, CA 92507
rahmanm, huangt, harsha, michalis@cs.ucr.edu

ABSTRACT

With 20 million installs a day [1], third-party apps are a major reason for the popularity and addictiveness of Facebook. Unfortunately, hackers have realized the potential of using apps for spreading malware and spam. The problem is already significant, as we find that at least 13% of apps in our dataset are malicious. So far, the research community has focused on detecting malicious posts and campaigns.

In this paper, we ask the question: given a Facebook application, can we determine if it is malicious? Our key contribution is in developing FRAppE—Facebook's Rigorous Application Evaluator—arguably the first tool focused on detecting malicious apps on Facebook. To develop FRAppE, we use information gathered by observing the posting behavior of 111K Facebook apps seen across 2.2 million users on Facebook. First, we identify a set of features that help us distinguish malicious apps from benign ones. For example, we find that malicious apps often share names with other apps, and they typically request fewer permissions than benign apps. Second, leveraging these distinguishing features we show that FRAppE can detect malicious apps with 99.5% accuracy, with no false positives and a low false negative rate (4.1%). Finally, we explore the ecosystem of malicious Facebook apps and identify mechanisms that these apps use to propagate. Interestingly, we find that many apps collude and support each other; in our dataset, we find 1,584 apps enabling the viral propagation of 3 723 other apps through their posts. Long-term, we see FRAppE as a step towards creating an independent watchdog for app assessment and ranking, so as to warn Facebook users before installing apps.

Categories and Subject Descriptors

D.4.6 [**OPERATING SYSTEMS**]: Security and Protection—*Access controls; Verification*

General Terms

Measurement, Security, Verification

Keywords

Facebook Apps, Malicious Apps, Profiling Apps, Online Social Networks

1. INTRODUCTION

Online social networks (OSN) enable and encourage third party applications (apps) to enhance the user experience on these platforms. Such enhancements include interesting or entertaining ways of communicating among online friends, and diverse activities such as playing games or listening to songs. For example, Facebook provides developers an API [10] that facilitates app integration into the Facebook user-experience. There are 500K apps available on Facebook [25], and on average, 20M apps are installed every day [1]. Furthermore, many apps have acquired and maintain a large userbase. For instance, FarmVille and CityVille apps have 26.5M and 42.8M users to date.

Recently, hackers have started taking advantage of the popularity of this third-party apps platform and deploying malicious applications [17, 21, 24]. Malicious apps can provide a lucrative business for hackers, given the popularity of OSNs, with Facebook leading the way with 900M active users [12]. There are many ways that hackers can benefit from a malicious app: (a) the app can reach large numbers of users and their friends to spread spam, (b) the app can obtain users' personal information such as email address, home town, and gender, and (c) the app can "re-produce" by making other malicious apps popular. To make matters worse, the deployment of malicious apps is simplified by ready-to-use toolkits starting at $25 [13]. In other words, there is motive and opportunity, and as a result, there are many malicious apps spreading on Facebook every day [20].

Despite the above worrisome trends, today, a user has very limited information at the time of installing an app on Facebook. In other words, the problem is: given an app's identity number (the unique identifier assigned to the app by Facebook), can we detect if the app is malicious? Currently, there is no commercial service, publicly-available information, or research-based tool to advise a user about the risks of an app. As we show in Sec. 3, malicious apps are widespread and they easily spread, as an infected user jeopardizes the safety of all its friends.

So far, the research community has paid little attention to OSN apps specifically. Most research related to spam and malware on Facebook has focused on detecting malicious posts and social spam campaigns [31, 32, 41]. A recent work studies how app permissions and community ratings correlate to privacy risks of Facebook apps [29]. Finally, there are some community-based feedback-driven efforts to rank applications, such as Whatapp [23]; though these could be very powerful in the future, so far they have received little adoption. We discuss previous work in more detail in Sec. 8.

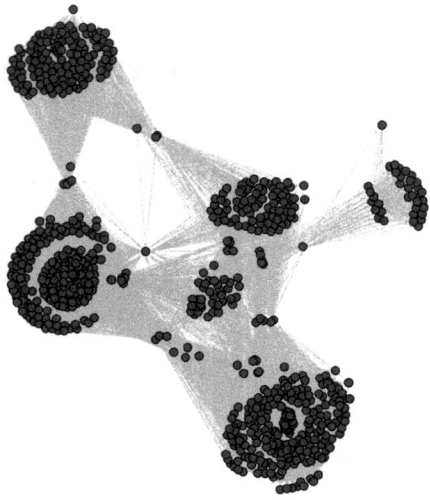

Figure 1: The emergence of AppNets on Facebook. Real snapshot of 770 highly collaborating apps: an edge between two apps means that one app helped the other propagate. Average degree (no. of collaborations) is 195!

In this work, we develop FRAppE, a suite of efficient classification techniques for identifying whether an app is malicious or not. To build FRAppE, we use data from MyPageKeeper, a security app in Facebook [14] that monitors the Facebook profiles of 2.2 million users. We analyze 111K apps that made 91 million posts over nine months. This is arguably the first comprehensive study focusing on malicious Facebook apps that focuses on quantifying, profiling, and understanding malicious apps, and synthesizes this information into an effective detection approach.

Our work makes the following key contributions:

- **13% of the observed apps are malicious.** We show that malicious apps are prevalent in Facebook and reach a large number of users. We find that 13% of apps in our dataset of 111K distinct apps are malicious. Also, 60% of malicious apps endanger more than 100K users each by convincing them to follow the links on the posts made by these apps, and 40% of malicious apps have over 1,000 monthly active users each.

- **Malicious and benign app profiles significantly differ.** We systematically profile apps and show that malicious app profiles are significantly different than those of benign apps. A striking observation is the "laziness" of hackers; many malicious apps have the same name, as 8% of unique names of malicious apps are each used by more than 10 different apps (as defined by their app IDs). Overall, we profile apps based on two classes of features: (a) those that can be obtained on-demand given an application's identifier (e.g., the permissions required by the app and the posts in the application's profile page), and (b) others that require a cross-user view to aggregate information across time and across apps (e.g., the posting behavior of the app and the similarity of its name to other apps).

- **The emergence of AppNets: apps collude at massive scale.** We conduct a forensics investigation on the malicious app ecosystem to identify and quantify the techniques used to promote malicious apps. The most interesting result is that apps collude and collaborate at a massive scale. Apps promote other apps via posts that point to the "promoted" apps. If we describe the collusion relationship of promoting-promoted apps as a graph, we find 1,584 promoter apps that promote 3,723 other apps. Furthermore, these apps form large and highly-dense connected components, as shown in Fig. 1.

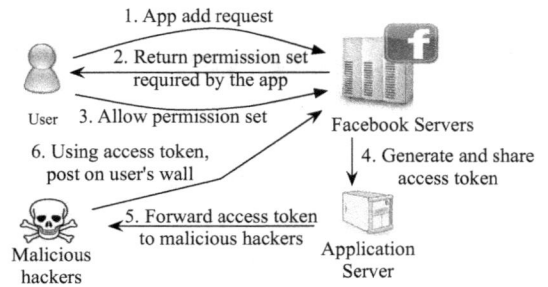

Figure 2: Steps involved in hackers using malicious applications to get access tokens to post malicious content on victims' walls.

Furthermore, hackers use fast-changing indirection: applications posts have URLs that point to a website, and the website dynamically redirects to many different apps; we find 103 such URLs that point to 4,676 different malicious apps over the course of a month. These observed behaviors indicate well-organized crime: one hacker controls many malicious apps, which we will call an AppNet, since they seem a parallel concept to botnets.

- **Malicious hackers impersonate applications.** We were surprised to find popular good apps, such as 'FarmVille' and 'Facebook for iPhone', posting malicious posts. On further investigation, we found a lax authentication rule in Facebook that enabled hackers to make malicious posts appear as though they came from these apps.

- **FRAppE can detect malicious apps with 99% accuracy.** We develop FRAppE (Facebook's Rigorous Application Evaluator) to identify malicious apps either using only features that can be obtained on-demand or using both on-demand and aggregation-based app information. FRAppE Lite, which only uses information available on-demand, can identify malicious apps with 99.0% accuracy, with low false positives (0.1%) and false negatives (4.4%). By adding aggregation-based information, FRAppE can detect malicious apps with 99.5% accuracy, with no false positives and lower false negatives (4.1%).

Our recommendations to Facebook. The most important message of the work is that there seems to be a parasitic eco-system of malicious apps within Facebook that needs to be understood and stopped. However, even this initial work leads to the following recommendations for Facebook that could potentially also be useful to other social platforms:

a. Breaking the cycle of app propagation. We recommend that apps should not be allowed to promote other apps. This is the reason that malicious apps seem to gain strength by self-propagation.

b. Enforcing stricter app authentication before posting. We recommend a stronger authentication of the identity of an app before a post by that app is accepted. As we saw, hackers fake the true identify of an app in order to evade detection and appear more credible to the end user.

2. BACKGROUND

In this section, we discuss how applications work on Facebook, provide an overview of MyPageKeeper (our primary data source), and outline the datasets that we use in this paper.

2.1 Facebook Apps

Facebook enables third-party developers to offer services to its users by means of Facebook applications. Unlike typical desktop and smartphone applications, installation of a Facebook applica-

Dataset Name	# of apps	
	Benign	Malicious
D-Total	111,167	
D-Sample	6,273	6,273
D-Summary	6,067	2,528
D-Inst	2,257	491
D-ProfileFeed	3,227	6,063
D-Complete	2,255	487

Table 1: Summary of the dataset collected by MyPageKeeper from June 2011 to March 2012.

App ID	App name	Post count
235597333185870	What Does Your Name Mean?	1006
159474410806928	Free Phone Calls	793
233344430035859	The App	564
296128667112382	WhosStalking?	434
142293182524011	FarmVile	210

Table 2: Top malicious apps in D-Sample dataset.

tion by a user does not involve the user downloading and executing an application binary. Instead, when a user adds a Facebook application to her profile, the user grants the application server: (a) permission to access a subset of the information listed on the user's Facebook profile (e.g., the user's email address), and (b) permission to perform certain actions on behalf of the user (e.g., the ability to post on the user's wall). Facebook grants these permissions to any application by handing an OAuth 2.0 [4] token to the application server for each user who installs the application. Thereafter, the application can access the data and perform the explicitly-permitted actions on behalf of the user. Fig. 2 depicts the steps involved in the installation and operation of a Facebook application.

Operation of malicious applications. Malicious Facebook applications typically operate as follows.

- Step 1: Hackers convince users to install the app, usually with some fake promise (e.g., free iPads).
- Step 2: Once a user installs the app, it redirects the user to a web page where the user is requested to perform tasks, such as completing a survey, again with the lure of fake rewards
- Step 3: The app thereafter accesses personal information (e.g., birth date) from the user's profile, which the hackers can potentially use to profit.
- Step 4: The app makes malicious posts on behalf of the user to lure the user's friends to install the same app (or some other malicious app, as we will see later).

This way the cycle continues with the app or colluding apps reaching more and more users. Personal information or surveys can be "sold" to third parties [2] to eventually profit the hackers.

2.2 MyPageKeeper

MyPageKeeper [14] is a Facebook app designed for detecting malicious posts on Facebook. Once a Facebook user installs MyPageKeeper, it periodically crawls posts from the user's wall and news feed. MyPageKeeper then applies URL blacklists as well as custom classification techniques to identify malicious posts. Our previous work [41] shows that MyPageKeeper detects malicious posts with high accuracy—97% of posts flagged by it indeed point to malicious websites and it incorrectly flags only 0.005% of benign posts.

The key thing to note here is that MyPageKeeper identifies social malware at the granularity of individual posts, without grouping together posts made by any given application. In other words, for every post that it crawls from the wall or news feed of a subscribed user, MyPageKeeper's determination of whether to flag that

post does not take into account the application responsible for the post. Indeed, a large fraction of posts (37%) monitored by MyPageKeeper are not posted by any application; many posts are made manually by a user or posted via a social plugin (e.g., by a user clicking 'Like' or 'Share' on an external website). Even among malicious posts identified by MyPageKeeper, 27% do not have an associated application.

MyPageKeeper's classification primarily relies on a Support Vector Machine (SVM) based classifier that evaluates every URL by combining information obtained from all posts containing that URL. Examples of features used in MyPageKeeper's classifier include a) the presence of spam keywords such as 'FREE', 'Deal', and 'Hurry' (malicious posts are more likely to include such keywords than normal posts), b) the similarity of text messages (posts in a spam campaign tend to have similar text messages across posts containing the same URL), and c) the number of 'Like's and comments (malicious posts receive fewer 'Like's and comments). Once a URL is identified as malicious, MyPageKeeper marks all posts containing the URL as malicious.

2.3 Our Datasets

In the absence of a central directory of Facebook apps [1], the basis of our study is a dataset obtained from 2.2M Facebook users, who are monitored by MyPageKeeper [14].

Our dataset contains 91 million posts from 2.2 million walls monitored by MyPageKeeper over nine months from June 2011 to March 2012. These 91 million posts were made by 111K apps, which forms our initial dataset D-Total, as shown in Table 1. Note that, out of the 144M posts monitored by MyPageKeeper during this period, here we consider only those posts that included a non-empty "application" field in the metadata that Facebook associates with every post.

The D-Sample dataset: Finding malicious applications. To identify malicious Facebook applications in our dataset, we start with a simple heuristic: if any post made by an application was flagged as malicious by MyPageKeeper, we mark the application as malicious; as we explain later in Section 5, we find this to be an effective technique for identifying malicious apps. By applying this heuristic, we identified 6,350 malicious apps. Interestingly, we find that several popular applications such as 'Facebook for Android' were also marked as malicious in this process. This is in fact the result of hackers exploiting Facebook weaknesses as we describe later in Section 6.2. To avoid such mis-classifications, we verify applications using a whitelist that is created by considering the most popular apps and significant manual effort. After whitelisting, we are left with 6,273 malicious applications (D-Sample dataset in Table 1). Table 2 shows the top five malicious applications, in terms of number of posts per application.

The D-Sample dataset: Including benign applications. To select an equal number of benign apps from the initial D-Total dataset, we use two criteria: (a) none of their posts were identified as malicious by MyPageKeeper, and (b) they are "vetted" by Social Bakers [19], which monitors the "social marketing success" of apps. This process yields 5,750 applications, 90% of which have a user rating of at least 3 out of 5 on Social Bakers. To match the number of malicious apps, we add the top 523 applications in D-Total (in terms of number of posts) and obtain a set of 6,273 benign applications. The D-Sample dataset (Table 1) is the union of these 6,273 benign applications with the 6,273 malicious applications ob-

[1]Note that Facebook has deprecated the app directory in 2011, therefore there is no central directory available for the entire list of Facebook apps [9].

315

tained earlier. The most popular benign apps are FarmVille, Facebook for iPhone, Mobile, Facebook for Android, and Zoo World.

For profiling apps, we collect the information for apps that is readily available through Facebook. We use a crawler based on the Firefox browser instrumented with Selenium [18]. From March to May 2012, we crawl information for every application in our D-Sample dataset once every week. We collected app summaries and their permissions, which requires two different crawls as discussed below.

The D-Summary dataset: Apps with app summary. We collect app summaries through the Facebook Open graph API, which is made available by Facebook at a URL of the form `https://graph.facebook.com/App_ID`; Facebook has a unique identifier for each application. An app summary includes several pieces of information such as *application name*, *description*, *company name*, *profile link*, and *monthly active users*. If any application has been removed from Facebook, the query results in an error. We were able to gather the summary for 6,067 benign and 2,528 malicious apps (D-Summary dataset in Table 1). It is easy to understand why malicious apps were more often removed from Facebook.

The D-Inst dataset: App permissions. We also want to study the permissions that apps request at the time of installation. For every application *App_ID*, we crawl `https://www.facebook.com/apps/application.php?id=App_ID`, which usually redirects to the application's installation URL. We were able to get the permission set for 487 malicious and 2,255 benign applications in our dataset. Automatically crawling the permissions for all apps is not trivial [29], as different apps have different redirection processes, which are intended for humans and not for crawlers. As expected, the queries for apps that are removed from Facebook fail here as well.

The D-ProfileFeed: Posts on the app profile. Users can make posts on the profile page of an app, which we can call *the profile feed* of the app. We collect these posts using the Open graph API from Facebook. The API returns posts appearing on the application's page, with several attributes for each post, such as *message*, *link*, and *create time*. Of the apps in the D-Sample dataset, we were able to get the posts for 6,063 benign and 3,227 malicious apps. We construct the D-Complete dataset by taking the intersection of D-Summary, D-Inst, and D-ProfileFeed datasets.

Coverage: While the focus of our study is to highlight the differences between malicious and benign apps and to develop a sound methodology to detect malicious apps, we cannot aim to detect all malicious apps present on Facebook. This is because MyPageKeeper has a limited view of Facebook data—the view provided by its subscribed users—and therefore it cannot see all the malicious apps present on Facebook. However, during the nine month period considered in our study, MyPageKeeper observed posts from 111K apps, which constitutes a sizable fraction (over 20%) of the approximately 500K apps present on Facebook [25]. Moreover, since MyPageKeeper monitors posts from 2.4 million walls on Facebook, any malicious app that affected a large fraction of Facebook users is likely to be present in our dataset. Therefore, we speculate that malicious apps missing from our dataset are likely to be those that affected only a small fraction of users.

Data privacy: Our primary source of data in this work is our MyPageKeeper Facebook application, which has been approved by UCR's IRB process. In keeping with Facebook's policy and IRB requirements, data collected by MyPageKeeper is kept private, since it crawls posts from the walls and news feeds of users who have explicitly given it permission to do so at the time of MyPageKeeper installation. In addition, we also use data obtained via Facebook's open graph API, which is publicly accessible to anyone.

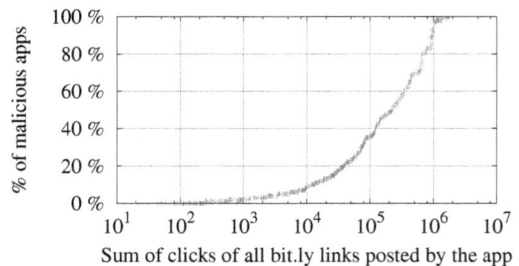

Figure 3: Clicks received by `bit.ly` links posted by malicious apps.

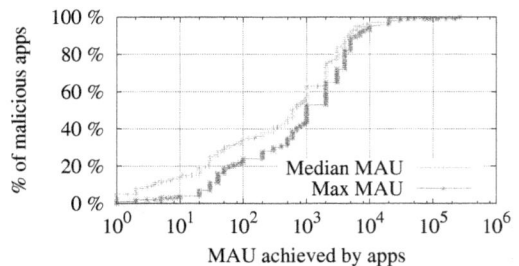

Figure 4: Median and maximum MAU achieved by malicious apps.

3. PREVALENCE OF MALICIOUS APPS

The driving motivation for detecting malicious apps stems from the suspicion that a significant fraction of malicious posts on Facebook are posted by apps. We find that 53% of malicious posts flagged by MyPageKeeper were posted by malicious apps. We further quantify the prevalence of malicious apps in two different ways.

60% of malicious apps get at least a hundred thousand clicks on the URLs they post. We quantify the reach of malicious apps by determining the number of clicks on the the links included in malicious posts. For each malicious app in our D-Sample dataset, we identify all `bit.ly` URLs in posts made by that application. We focus on `bit.ly` URLs since `bit.ly` offers an API [6] for querying the number of clicks received by every `bit.ly` link; thus our estimate of the number of clicks received by every application is strictly a lower bound. On the other hand, each `bit.ly` link that we consider here could potentially also have received clicks from other sources on web (i.e., outside Facebook); thus, for every `bit.ly` URL, the total number of clicks it received is an upper bound on the number clicks received via Facebook.

Across the posts made by the 6,273 malicious apps in the D-Sample dataset, we found that 3,805 of these apps had posted 5,700 `bit.ly` URLs in total. We queried `bit.ly` for the click count of each URL. Fig. 3 shows the distribution across malicious apps of the total number of clicks received by `bit.ly` links that they had posted. We see that 60% of malicious apps were able to accumulate over 100K clicks each, with 20% receiving more than 1M clicks each. The application with the highest number of `bit.ly` clicks in this experiment—the 'What is the sexiest thing about you?' app—received 1,742,359 clicks.

40% of malicious apps have a median of at least 1000 monthly active users. We examine the reach of malicious apps by inspecting the number of users that these applications had. To study this, we use the Monthly Active Users (MAU) metric provided by Facebook for every application. The number of Monthly Active Users is a measure of how many unique users are engaged with the appli-

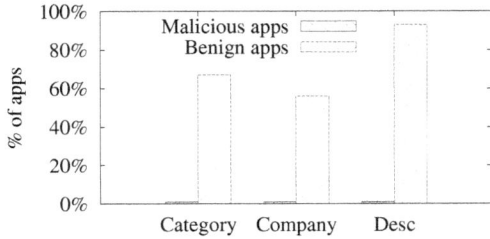

Figure 5: Comparison of apps whether they provide category, company name or description of the app.

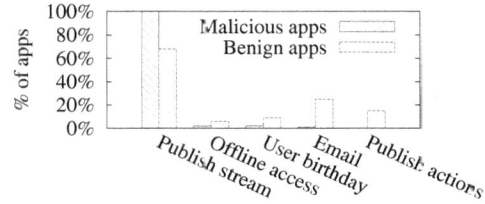

Figure 6: Top 5 permissions required by benign and malicious apps.

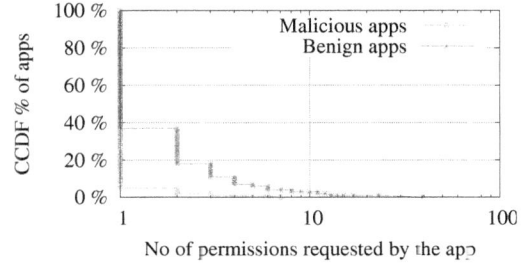

Figure 7: Number of permissions requested by every app.

cation over the last 30 days in activities such as installing, posting, and liking the app. Fig. 4 plots the distribution of Monthly Active Users of the malicious apps in our D-Summary dataset. For each app, the median and maximum MAU values over the three months are shown. We see that 40% of malicious applications had a median MAU of at least 1000 users, while 60% of malicious applications achieved at least 1000 during the three month observation period. The top malicious app here—'Future Teller'—had a maximum MAU of 260,000 and median of 20,000.

4. PROFILING APPLICATIONS

Given the significant impact that malicious apps have on Facebook, we next seek to develop a tool that can identify malicious applications. Towards developing an understanding of how to build such a tool, in this section, we compare malicious and benign apps with respect to various features.

As discussed previously in Section 2.3, we crawled Facebook and obtained several features for every application in our dataset. We divide these features into two subsets: on-demand features and aggregation-based features. We find that malicious applications significantly differ from benign applications with respect to both classes of features.

4.1 On-demand features

The on-demand features associated with an application refer to the features that one can obtain on-demand given the application's ID. Such metrics include app name, description, category, company, and required permission set.

4.1.1 Application summary

Malicious apps typically have incomplete application summaries. First, we compare malicious and benign apps with respect to attributes present in the application's summary—*app description*, *company name*, and *category*. Description and company are free-text attributes, either of which can be at most 140 characters. On the other hand, category can be selected from a predefined (by Facebook) list such as 'Games', 'News', etc. that matches the app functionality best. Application developers can also specify the company name at the time of app creation. For example, the 'Mafia Wars' app is configured with description as 'Mafia Wars: Leave a legacy behind', company as 'Zynga', and category as 'Games'. Fig. 5 shows the fraction of malicious and benign apps in the D-Summary dataset for which these three fields are non-empty. We see that, while most benign apps specify such information, very rarely malicious apps do so. For example, only 1.4% of malicious apps have a non-empty description, whereas 93% of benign apps configure their summary with a description. We find that the benign

apps that do not configure the description parameter are typically less popular (as seen from their monthly active users).

4.1.2 Required permission set

97% of malicious apps require only one permission from users. Every Facebook application requires authorization by a user before the user can use the app. At the time of installation, every app requests the user to grant it a set of permissions that it requires. These permissions are chosen from a pool of 64 permissions pre-defined by Facebook [16]. Example permissions include access to information in the user's profile such as gender, email, birthday, and friend list, and permission to post on the user's wall.

We see how malicious and benign apps compare based on the permission set that they require from users. Fig. 6 shows the top five permissions required by both benign and malicious apps. Most malicious apps in our D-Inst dataset require only the 'publish stream' permission (ability to post on the user's wall). This permission is sufficient for making spam posts on behalf of users. In addition, Fig. 7 shows that 97% of malicious apps require only one permission, whereas the same fraction for benign apps is 62%. We believe that this is because users tend not to install apps that require larger set of permissions; Facebook suggests that application developers do not ask for more permissions than necessary since there is a strong correlation between the number of permissions required by an app and the number of users who install it [8]. Therefore, to maximize the number of victims, malicious apps seem to follow this hypothesis and require a small set of permissions.

4.1.3 Redirect URI

Malicious apps redirect users to domains with poor reputation. In an application's installation URL, the 'redirect URI' parameter refers to the URL where the user is redirected to once she installs the app. We extracted the redirect URI parameter from the installation URL for apps in the D-Inst dataset and queried the trust reputation scores for these URIs from WOT [22]. Fig 8 shows the corresponding score for both benign and malicious apps. WOT assigns a score between 0 and 100 for every URI, and we assign a

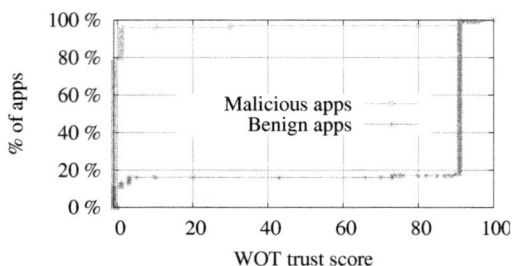

Figure 8: WOT trust score of the domain that apps redirect to upon installation.

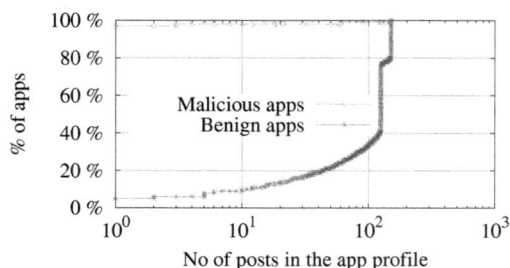

Figure 9: Number of posts in app profile page.

Domains	Hosting # of malicious apps
thenamemeans3.com	34
fastfreeupdates.com	53
wikiworldmedia.com	82
technicalyard.com	96
thenamemeans2.com	138

Table 3: Top five domains hosting malicious apps in D-Inst dataset.

score of -1 to the domains for which the WOT score is not available. We see that 80% of malicious apps point to domains for which WOT does not have any reputation score, and in addition, 95% of malicious apps have a score less than 5. In contrast, we find that 80% of benign apps have redirect URIs pointing to the apps.facebook.com domain and therefore have higher WOT scores. We speculate that malicious apps redirect users to web pages hosted outside of Facebook so that the same spam/malicious content, e.g., survey scams, can also be propagated by other means such as email and Twitter spam.

Furthermore, we found several instances where a single domain hosts the URLs to which multiple malicious apps redirect upon installation. For example, thenamemeans2.com hosts the redirect URI for 138 different malicious apps in our D-Inst dataset. Table 3 shows the top five such domains; these five domains host the content for 83% of the 491 malicious apps in the D-Inst dataset.

4.1.4 Client ID in app installation URL

78% of malicious apps trick users into installing other apps by using a different client ID in their app installation URL. For a Facebook application with ID A, the application installation URL is https://www.facebook.com/apps/application.php?id=A. When any user visits this URL, Facebook queries the application server registered for app A to fetch several parameters, such as the set of permissions required by the app. Facebook then redirects the user to a URL which encodes these parameters in the URL. One of the parameters in this URL is the 'client ID' parameter. If the user accepts to install the application, the ID of the application which she will end up installing is the value of the client ID parameter. Ideally, as described in the Facebook app developer tutorial [8], this client ID should be identical to the app ID A, whose installation URL the user originally visited. However, in our D-Inst dataset, we find that 78% of malicious apps use a client ID that differs from the ID of the original app, whereas only 1% of benign apps do so. A possible reason for this is to increase the survivability of apps. As we show later in Sec. 6, hackers create large sets of malicious apps with similar names, and when a user visits the installation URL for one of these apps, the user is randomly redirected to install any one of these apps. This ensures that, even if one app from the set gets blacklisted, others can still survive and propagate on Facebook.

4.1.5 Posts in app profile

97% of malicious apps do not have posts in their profiles. An application's profile page presents a forum for users to communicate with the app's developers (e.g., to post comments or questions about the app) or vice-versa (e.g., for the app's developers to post updates about the application). Typically, an app's profile page thus accumulates posts over time. We examine the number of such posts on the profile pages of applications in our dataset. As discussed earlier in Sec. 2.3, we were able to crawl the app profile pages for 3,227 malicious apps and 6,063 benign apps.

From Fig. 9, which shows the distribution of the number of posts found in the profile pages for benign and malicious apps, we find that 97% of malicious apps do not have any posts in their profiles. For the remaining 3%, we see that their profile pages include posts that advertise URLs pointing to phishing scams or other malicious apps. For example, one of the malicious apps has 150 posts in its profile page and all of those posts publish URLs pointing to different phishing pages with URLs such as http://2000forfree.blogspot.com and http://free-offers-sites.blogspot.com/. Thus, the profile pages of malicious apps either have no posts or are used to advertise malicious URLs, to which any visitors of the page are exposed.

4.2 Aggregation-based features

Next, we analyze applications with respect to aggregation-based features. Unlike the features we considered so far, aggregation-based features for an app cannot be obtained on-demand. Instead, we envision that aggregation-based features are gathered by entities that monitor the posting behavior of several applications across users and across time. Entities that can do so include Facebook security applications installed by a large population of users, such as MyPageKeeper, or Facebook itself. Here, we consider two aggregation-based features: similarity of app names, and the URLs posted by an application over time. We compare these features across malicious and benign apps.

4.2.1 App name

87% of malicious apps have an app name identical to that of at least one other malicious app. An application's name is configured by the app's developer at the time of the app's creation on Facebook. Since the app ID is the unique identifier for every application on Facebook, Facebook does not impose any restrictions on app names. Therefore, although Facebook does warn app developers not to violate the trademark or other rights of third-parties during app configuration, it is possible to create multiple apps with the same app name.

We examine the similarity of names across applications. To measure the similarity between two app names, we compute the Damerau-Levenshtein edit distance [30] between the two names

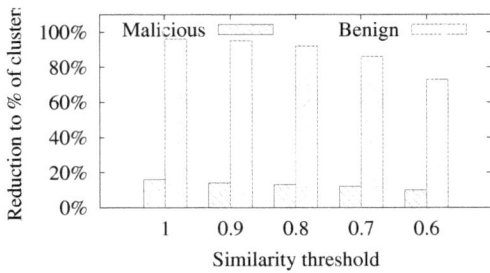

Figure 10: Clustering of apps based on similarity in names.

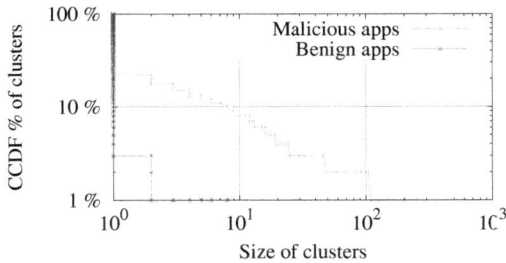

Figure 11: Size of app clusters with identical names.

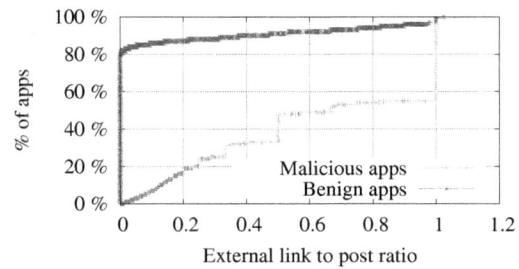

Figure 12: Distribution of external links to post ratio across apps.

and normalize this distance with the maximum of the lengths of the two names. We then apply different thresholds on the similarity scores to cluster apps in the D-Sample dataset based on their name; we perform this clustering separately among malicious and benign apps.

Fig. 10 shows the ratio of the number of clusters to the number of apps, for various thresholds of similarity; a similarity threshold of 1 clusters applications that have identical app names. We see that malicious apps tend to cluster to a significantly larger extent than benign apps. For example, even when only clustering apps with identical names (similarity threshold = 1), the number of clusters for malicious apps is less than one-fifth that of the number of malicious apps, i.e., on average, 5 malicious apps have the same name. Fig. 11 shows that close to 10% of clusters based on identical names have over 10 malicious apps in each cluster. For example, 627 different malicious apps have the same name 'The App'. On the contrary, even with a similarity threshold of 0.7, the number of clusters for benign apps is only 20% lesser than the number of apps. As a result, as seen in Fig. 11, most benign apps have unique names.

Moreover, while most of the clustering of app names for malicious apps occurs even with a similarity threshold of 1, there is some reduction in the number of clusters with lower thresholds. This is due to hackers attempting to "typo-squat" on the names of popular benign applications. For example, the malicious application 'FarmVile' attempts to take advantage of the popular 'FarmVille' app name, whereas the 'Fortune Cookie' malicious application exactly copies the popular 'Fortune Cookie' app name. However, we find that a large majority of malicious apps in our D-Sample dataset show very little similarity with the 100 most popular benign apps in our dataset. Our data therefore seems to indicate that hackers creating several apps with the same name to conduct a campaign is more common than malicious apps typo-squatting on the names of popular apps.

4.2.2 External link to post ratio

Malicious apps often post links pointing to domains outside Facebook, whereas benign apps rarely do so. Any post on Face-

book can optionally include an URL. Here, we analyze the URLs included in posts made by malicious and benign apps. For every app in our D-Sample dataset, we aggregate the posts seen by MyPageKeeper over our nine month data gathering period and the URLs seen across these posts. We consider every URL pointing to a domain outside of `facebook.com` as an external link. We then define a 'external link to post ratio' measure for every app as the ratio of the number of external links posted by the app to the total number of posts made by it.

Fig. 12 shows that the external link to post ratios for malicious apps are significantly higher than those for benign apps. We see that 80% of benign apps do not post any external links, whereas 40% of malicious apps have one external link on average per post. This shows that malicious apps often attempt to lead users to web pages hosted outside Facebook, whereas the links posted by benign apps are almost always restricted to URLs in the `facebook.com` domain.

Note that malicious apps could post shortened URLs that point back to Facebook, thus potentially making our external link counts over-estimates. However, we find that malicious apps rarely do so. In our D-Sample dataset, we find 5700 *bit.ly* URLs (which constitute 92% of all shortened URLs) were posted by malicious apps. *bit.ly*'s API allowed us to determine the full URL corresponding to 5197 of these 5700 URLs, and only 386 of these URLs ($<$ 10%) pointed back to Facebook.

5. DETECTING MALICIOUS APPS

Having analyzed the differentiating characteristics of malicious and benign apps, we next use these features to develop efficient classification techniques to identify malicious Facebook applications. We present two variants of our malicious app classifier—FRAppE Lite and FRAppE. It is important to note that MyPageKeeper, our source of "ground truth" data, cannot detect malicious apps; it only detects malicious posts on Facebook. Though malicious apps are the dominant source of malicious posts, MyPageKeeper is agnostic about the source of the posts that it classifies. In contrast, FRAppE Lite and FRAppE are designed to detect malicious apps. Therefore, given an app ID, MyPageKeeper cannot say whether it is malicious or not, whereas FRAppE Lite and FRAppE can do so.

5.1 FRAppE Lite

FRAppE Lite is a lightweight version which makes use of only the application features available on-demand. Given a specific app ID, FRAppE Lite crawls the on-demand features for that application and evaluates the application based on these features in real-time. We envision that FRAppE Lite can be incorporated, for example, into a browser extension that can evaluate any Facebook application at the time when a user is considering installing it to her profile.

Features	Source
Is category specified?	`http://graph.facebook.com/appID`
Is company name specified?	`http://graph.facebook.com/appID`
Is description specified?	`http://graph.facebook.com/appID`
Any posts in app profile page?	`https://graph.facebook.com/AppID/feed?access_token=`
Number of permissions required	`https://www.facebook.com/apps/application.php?id=AppID`
Is client ID different from app ID?	`https://www.facebook.com/apps/application.php?id=AppID`
Domain reputation of redirect URI	`https://www.facebook.com/apps/application.php?id=AppID and WOT`

Table 4: List of features used in FRAppE Lite.

Training Ratio	Accuracy	FP	FN
1:1	98.5%	0.6%	2.5%
4:1	99.0%	0.1%	4.7%
7:1	99.0%	0.1%	4.4%
10:1	99.5%	0.1%	5.5%

Table 5: Cross validation with FRAppE Lite.

Feature	Accuracy	FP	FN
Category specified?	76.5%	45.8%	1.2%
Company specified?	72.1%	55.0%	0.8%
Description specified?	97.8%	3.3%	1.0%
Posts in profile?	96.9%	4.3%	1.9%
Client ID is same?	88.5%	1.0%	22.0%
WOT trust score	91.9%	13.4%	2.9%
Permission count	73.3%	49.3%	4.1%

Table 6: Classification accuracy with individual features.

Feature	Description
App name similarity	Is app's name identical to a known malicious app?
External link to post ratio	Fraction of app's posts that contain links to domains outside Facebook

Table 7: Additional features used in FRAppE.

Table 4 lists the features used as input to FRAppE Lite and the source of each feature. All of these features can be collected on-demand at the time of classification and do not require prior knowledge about the app being evaluated.

We use the Support Vector Machine (SVM) [28] classifier for classifying malicious apps. SVM is widely used for binary classification in security and other disciplines [35,39]. The effectiveness of SVM depends on the selection of kernel, the kernel's parameters, and soft margin parameter C. We used the default parameter values in libsvm [28] such as radial basis function as kernel with degree 3, $coef_0 = 0$ and $C = 1$ [28]. We use the D-Complete dataset for training and testing the classifier. As shown earlier in Table 1, the D-Complete dataset consists of 487 malicious apps and 2,255 benign apps.

We use 5-fold cross validation on the D-Complete dataset for training and testing FRAppE Lite's classifier. In 5-fold cross validation, the dataset is randomly divided into five segments, and we test on each segment independently using the other four segments for training. We use accuracy, false positive (FP) rate, and false negative (FN) rate as the three metrics to measure the classifier's performance. Accuracy is defined as the ratio of correctly identified apps (i.e., a benign/malicious app is appropriately identified as benign/malicious) to the total number of apps. False positive (negative) rate is the fraction of benign (malicious) apps incorrectly classified as malicious (benign).

We conduct four separate experiments with the ratio of benign to malicious apps varied as 1:1, 4:1, 7:1, and 10:1. In each case, we sample apps at random from the D-Complete dataset and run a 5-fold cross validation. Table 5 shows that, irrespective of the ratio of benign to malicious apps, the accuracy is above 98.5%. The higher the ratio of benign to malicious apps, the classifier gets trained to minimize false positives, rather than false negatives, in order to maximize accuracy. However, we note that the false positive and negative rates are below 0.6% and 5.5% in all cases. The ratio of benign to malicious apps in our dataset is equal to 7:1; of the 111K apps seen in MyPageKeeper's data, 6,273 apps were identified as malicious based on MyPageKeeper's classification of posts and an additional 8,051 apps are found to be malicious, as we show later. Therefore, we can expect FRAppE Lite to offer roughly 99.0% accuracy with 0.1% false positives and 4.4% false negatives in practice.

To understand the contribution of each of FRAppE Lite's features towards its accuracy, we next perform 5-fold cross validation on the D-Complete dataset with only a single feature at a time. Table 6 shows that each of the features by themselves too result in reasonably high accuracy. The 'Description' feature yields the

highest accuracy (97.8%) with low false positives (3.3%) and false negatives (1.0%). On the flip side, classification based solely on any one of the 'Category', 'Company', or 'Permission count' features results in a large number of false positives, whereas relying solely on client IDs yields a high false negative rate.

5.2 FRAppE

Next, we consider FRAppE—a malicious app detector that utilizes our aggregation-based features in addition to the on-demand features. Table 7 shows the two features that FRAppE uses in addition to those used in FRAppE Lite. Since the aggregation-based features for an app require a cross-user and cross-app view over time, in contrast to FRAppE Lite, we envision that FRAppE can be used by Facebook or by third-party security applications that protect a large population of users.

Here, we again conduct a 5-fold cross validation with the D-Complete dataset for various ratios of benign to malicious apps. In this case, we find that, with a ratio of 7:1 in benign to malicious apps, FRAppE's additional features improve the accuracy to 99.5%, as compared to 99.0% with FRAppE Lite. Furthermore, the false negative rate decreases from 4.4% to 4.1%, and we do not have a single false positive.

5.3 Identifying new malicious apps

We next train FRAppE's classifier on the entire D-Sample dataset (for which we have all the features and the ground truth classification) and use this classifier to identify new malicious apps. To do so, we apply FRAppE to all the apps in our D-Total dataset that are not in the D-Sample dataset; for these apps, we lack information as to whether they are malicious or benign. Of the 98,609 apps that we test in this experiment, 8,144 apps were flagged as malicious by FRAppE.

Validation. Since we lack ground truth information for these apps flagged as malicious, we apply a host of complementary techniques to validate FRAppE's classification. We next describe these validation techniques; as shown in Table 8, we were able to validate 98.5% of the apps flagged by FRAppE.

Criteria	# of apps validated	Cumulative
Deleted from Facebook graph	6,591(81%)	6,591(81%)
App name similarity	6,055(74%)	7,869(97%)
Post similarity	1,664 (20%)	7,907(97%)
Typosquatting of popular apps	5(0.1%)	7,912(97%)
Manual validation	147 (1.8%)	8051(98.5%)
Total validated	-	8051(98.5%)
Unknown	-	93 (1.5%)

Table 8: Validation of apps flagged by FRAppE.

Deleted from Facebook graph: Facebook itself monitors its platform for malicious activities, and it disables and deletes from the Facebook graph malicious apps that it identifies. If the Facebook API (https://graph.facebook.com/appID) returns false for a particular app ID, this indicates that the app no longer exists on Facebook; we consider this to be indicative of blacklisting by Facebook. This technique validates 81% of the malicious apps identified by FRAppE. Note that Facebook's measures for detecting malicious apps are however not sufficient; of the 1 464 malicious apps identified by FRAppE (that were validated by other techniques below) but are still active on Facebook, 35% have been active on Facebook since over four months with 10% dating back to over eight months.

App name similarity: If an application's name exactly matches that of multiple malicious apps in the D-Sample dataset, that app too is likely to be part of the same campaign and therefore malicious. On the other hand, we found several malicious apps using version numbers in their name (e.g., 'Profile Watchers v4.32', 'How long have you spent logged in? v8'). Therefore, in addition, if an app name contains a version number at the end and the rest of its name is identical to multiple known malicious apps that similarly use version numbers, this too is indicative of the app likely being malicious.

Posted link similarity: If an URL posted by an app matches the URL posted by a previously known malicious app, then these apps are likely part of the same spam campaign, thus validating the former as malicious.

Typosquatting of popular app: If an app's name is "typosquatting" that of a popular app, we consider it malicious. For example, we found five apps named 'FarmVile', which are seeking to leverage the popularity of 'FarmVille'.

Manual verification: Lastly, for the remaining 232 apps unverified by the above techniques, we first cluster them based on name similarity among themselves and verify one app from each cluster with cluster size greater than 4. For example, we find 83 apps named 'Past Life'. This enabled us to validate an additional 147 apps marked as malicious by FRAppE.

Validation of ground truth. Note that some of the above-mentioned techniques also enable us to validate the heuristic we used to identify malicious apps in all of our datasets: if any post made by an application was flagged as malicious by MyPage-Keeper, we marked the application as malicious. As of October 2012, we find that, out of the 6273 malicious apps in our D-Sample dataset, 5440 apps have been deleted from the Facebook graph. An additional 667 apps have an identical name to one of the 5440 deleted apps. Therefore, we believe that the false positive rate in the data that we use to train FRAppE Lite and FRAppE is at most 2.6%.

6. THE MALICIOUS APPS ECOSYSTEM

Equipped with an accurate classifier for detecting malicious apps, we next analyze how malicious Facebook apps support each other. Some of our analysis in Sec. 4 is already indicative of the

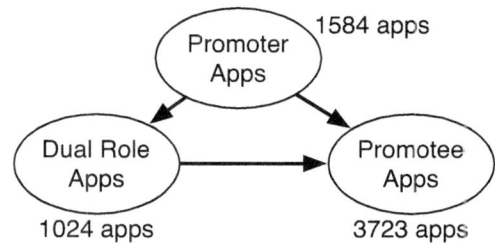

Figure 13: Relationship between collaborating applications

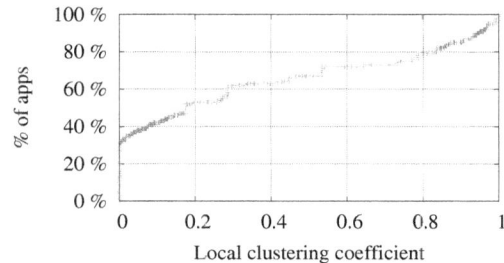

Figure 14: Local clustering coefficient of apps in the Collaboration graph.

fact that malicious apps do not operate in isolation—many malicious apps share the same name, several of them redirect to the same domain upon installation, etc. Upon deeper investigation, we identify a worrisome and, at the same time, fascinating trend: malicious apps work collaboratively in promoting each other. Namely, apps make posts that contain links to the installation pages of other apps. We use the term AppNets do describe these colluding groups; we claim that they are for the social world what botnets are for the world of physical devices.

6.1 The emergence of AppNets

We identify 6,331 malicious apps in our dataset that engage in collaborative promotion. Among them, 25% are *promoters*, 58.8% are *promotees*, and the remaining 16.2% play both roles. Here, when *app*1 posts a link pointing to *app*2, we refer to *app*1 as the promoter and *app*2 as the promotee. Fig. 13 shows this relationship between malicious apps. Intrigued, we study this group of applications further.

AppNets form large and densely connected groups. Let us consider the graph that is created by having an edge between any two apps that collude, i.e., an edge from *app*1 to *app*2 if the former promotes the latter. We call this graph the *Collaboration graph*. In this graph, we identify 44 connected components among the 6,331 malicious apps. The top 5 connected components have large sizes: 3484, 770, 589, 296, and 247.

Upon further analysis of these components, we find

- *High connectivity:* 70% of the apps collude with more than 10 other apps. The maximum number of collusions that an app is involved in is 417.

- *High local density:* 25% of the apps have a local clustering coefficient [2] larger than 0.74 as shown in Fig. 14.

---

[2]Local clustering coefficient for a node is the number of edges among the neighbors of a node over the maximum possible number of edges among those nodes. Thus, a clique neighborhood has a coefficient of value 1, while a disconnected neighborhood (the neighbors of the center of a star graph) has a value of 0.

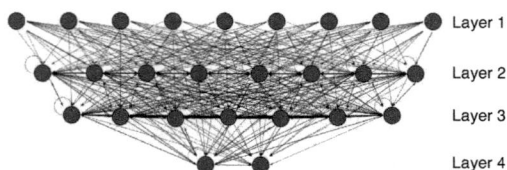

Figure 15: Example of collusion graph between applications.

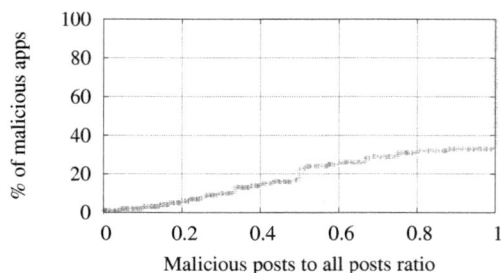

Figure 16: Distribution across apps of the fraction of an app's posts that are malicious.

As an example, in Fig. 15, we show the local neighborhood of the "Death Predictor" app, which has 26 neighbors and has a local clustering coefficient of 0.87. Interestingly, 22 of the node's neighbors share the same name.

App collusion happens in two different ways. The promoting app can post a link that points directly to another app, or it can post a link that points to a *redirection URL*, which points dynamically to multiple different apps.

a. Posting direct links to other apps. We find 692 promoter apps in our D-Sample dataset which promoted 1,806 different apps using direct links. This activity was intense: 15% of the promoters promoted at least 5 promotee apps. For example, 'The App' was promoting 24 other apps with names 'The App' or 'La App'.

b. Indirect app promotion. Alternatively, hackers use websites outside Facebook to have more control and protection in promoting apps. Specifically, a post made by a malicious app includes a shortened URL and that URL, once resolved, points to a website outside Facebook. This external website forwards users to several different app installation pages over time.

The use of the indirection mechanism is quite widespread, as it provides a layer of protection to the apps involved. We identify 103 indirection websites in our dataset of colluding apps. To identify all the landing websites, for one and a half months from mid-March to end of April 2012, we follow each indirection website 100 times a day using an instrumented Firefox browser.

Apps with the same name often are part of the same AppNet. These 103 indirection website were used by 1,936 promoter apps which had only 206 unique app names. The promotees were 4,676 apps with 273 unique app names. Clearly, there is a very high reuse of both names and these indirection websites. For example, one indirection website distributed in posts by the app '*whats my name means*' points to the installation page of the apps '*What ur name implies!!!*', '*Name meaning finder*', and '*Name meaning*'. Furthermore, 35% of these websites promoted more than 100 different applications each. Following the discussion in Sec. 4.2.1, it appears that every hacker reuses the same names for his applications. Since all apps underlying a campaign have the same name, if any app in the pool gets black listed, others can still survive and carry on the campaign without being noticed by users.

Amazon hosts a third of these indirection websites. We investigate the hosting infrastructure that enables these redirection websites. First, we find that most of the links in the posts were shortened URLs and 80% of them were using the `bit.ly` shortening service. We consider all the `bit.ly` URLs among our dataset of indirection links (84 out of 103) and resolve them to the full URL. We find that one-third of these URLs are hosted on `amazonaws.com`.

6.2 App piggybacking

From our dataset, we also discover that hackers have found ways to make malicious posts appear as if they had been posted by popular apps. To do so, they exploit weaknesses in Facebook's API. We call this phenomenon **app piggybacking**. One of the ways in which hackers achieve this is by luring users to

'Share' a malicious post to get promised gifts. When the victim tries to share the malicious post, hackers invoke the Facebook API call `http://www.facebook.com/connect/prompt_feed.php?api_key=POP_APPID`, which results in the shared post being made on behalf of the popular app POP_APPID. The vulnerability here is that any one can perform this API call, and Facebook does not authenticate that the post is indeed being made by the application whose ID is included in the request. We illustrate the app piggybacking mechanism with a real example here: [3].

We find instances of app piggybacking in our dataset as follows. For every app that had at least one post marked as malicious by MyPageKeeper, we compute the fraction of that app's posts that were flagged by MyPageKeeper. We look for apps where this ratio is low. In Fig. 16, we see that 5% of apps have a *malicious posts to all posts ratio* of less than 0.2. For these apps, we manually examine the malicious posts flagged by MyPageKeeper. Table 9 shows the top five most popular apps that we find among this set.

7. DISCUSSION

In this section, we discuss potential measures that hackers can take to evade detection by FRAppE. We also present recommendations to Facebook about changes that they can make to their API to reduce abuse by hackers.

Robustness of features. Among the various features that we use in our classification, some can easily be obfuscated by malicious hackers to evade FRAppE in the future. For example, we showed that, currently, malicious apps often do not include a category, company, or description in their app summary. However, hackers can easily fill in this information into the summary of applications that they create from here on. Similarly, FRAppE leveraged the fact that profile pages of malicious apps typically have no posts. Hackers can begin making dummy posts in the profile pages of their applications to obfuscate this feature and avoid detection. Therefore, some of FRAppE's features may no longer prove to be useful in the future while others may require tweaking, e.g., FRAppE may need to analyze the posts seen in an application's profile page to test their validity. In any case, the fear of detection by FRAppE will increase the onus on hackers while creating and maintaining malicious applications.

On the other hand, we argue that several features used by FRAppE, such as the reputation of redirect URIs, the number of required permissions, and the use of different client IDs in app installation URLs, are robust to the evolution of hackers. For example, to evade detection, if malicious app developers were to increase the number of permissions required, they risk losing potential victims; the number of users that install an app has been observed to be inversely proportional to the number of permissions required by

App name	# of posts	Post msg	Link in post
FarmVille	9,621,909	WOW I just got 5000 Facebook Credits for Free	http://offers5000credit.blogspot.com
Links	7,650,858	Get your FREE 450 FACEBOOK CREDITS	http://free450offer.blogspot.com/
Facebook for iPhone	5,551,422	NFL Playoffs Are Coming! Show Your Team Support!	http://SportsJerseyFever.com/NFL
Mobile	4,208,703	WOW! I Just Got a Recharge of Rs 500.	http://ffreerechargeindia.blogspot.com/
Facebook for Android	3,912,955	Get Your Free Facebook Sim Card	http://j.mp/oRzBNU

Table 9: Top five popular apps being abused by app piggybacking.

the app. Similarly, not using different client IDs in app installation URLs would limit the ability of hackers to instrument their applications to propagate each other. We find that a version of FRAppE that only uses such robust features still yields an accuracy of 98.2%, with false positive and false negative rates of 0.4% and 3.2% on a 5-fold cross validation.

Recommendations to Facebook. Our investigations of malicious apps on Facebook identified two key loopholes in Facebook's API which hackers take advantage of. First, as discussed in Sec. 4.1.4, malicious apps use a different client ID value in the app installation URL, thus enabling the propagation and promotion of other malicious apps. Therefore, we believe that Facebook must enforce that when the installation URL for an app is accessed, the client ID field in the URL to which the user is redirected must be identical to the app ID of the original app. We are not aware of any valid uses of having the client ID differ from the original app ID. Second, Facebook should restrict users from using arbitrary app IDs in their prompt feed API: http://www.facebook.com/connect/prompt_feed.php?api_key=APPID. As discussed in Sec. 6.2, hackers use this API to piggyback on popular apps and spread spam without being detected.

8. RELATED WORK

Detecting spam on OSNs. Gao et al. [32] analyzed posts on the walls of 3.5 million Facebook users and showed that 10% of links posted on Facebook walls are spam. They also presented techniques to identify compromised accounts and spam campaigns. In other work, Gao et al. [31] and Rahman et al. [41] develop efficient techniques for online spam filtering on OSNs such as Facebook. While Gao et al. [31] rely on having the whole social graph as input, and so, is usable only by the OSN provider, Rahman et al. [41] develop a third-party application for spam detection on Facebook. Others [37,44] present mechanisms for detection of spam URLs on Twitter. In contrast to all of these efforts, rather than classifying individual URLs or posts as spam, we focus on identifying malicious applications that are the main source of spam on Facebook.

Detecting spam accounts. Yang et al. [46] and Benevenuto et al. [26] developed techniques to identify accounts of spammers on Twitter. Others have proposed a honey-pot based approach [36,43] to detect spam accounts on OSNs. Yardi et al. [47] analyzed behavioral patterns among spam accounts in Twitter. Instead of focusing on accounts created by spammers, our work enables detection of malicious apps that propagate spam and malware by luring normal users to install them.

App permission exploitation. Chia et al. [29] investigated the privacy intrusiveness of Facebook apps and concluded that currently available signals such as community ratings, popularity, and external ratings such as Web of Trust (WOT) as well as signals from app developers are not reliable indicators of the privacy risks associated with an app. Also, in keeping with our observation, they found that popular Facebook apps tend to request more permissions. They also found that 'Lookalike' applications that have names similar to popular applications request more permissions than is typical. Based on a measurement study across 200 Face-

book users, Liu et al. [38] showed that privacy settings in Facebook rarely match users' expectations.

To address the privacy risks associated with the use of Facebook apps, some studies [27, 45] propose a new application policy and authentication dialog. Makridakis et al. [40] use a real application named 'Photo of the Day' to demonstrate how malicious apps on Facebook can launch DDoS attacks using the Facebook platform. King et al. [34] conducted a survey to understand users' interaction with Facebook apps. Similarly, Gjoka et al. [33] study the user reach of popular Facebook applications. On the contrary, we quantify the prevalence of malicious apps, and develop tools to identify malicious apps that use several features beyond the required permission set.

App rating efforts. Stein et al. [42] describe Facebook's Immune System (FIS), a scalable real-time adversarial learning system deployed in Facebook to protect users from malicious activities. However, Stein et al. provide only a high-level overview about threats to the Facebook graph and do not provide any analysis of the system. Furthermore, in an attempt to balance accuracy of detection with low false positives, it appears that Facebook has recently softened their controls for handling spam apps [11]. Other Facebook applications [5,7,15] that defend users against spam and malware do not provide ratings for apps on Facebook. Whatapp [23] collects community reviews about apps for security, privacy and openness. However, it has not attracted much reviews (47 reviews available) to date. To the best of our knowledge, we are the first to provide a classification of Facebook apps into malicious and benign categories.

9. CONCLUSIONS AND FUTURE WORK

Applications present a convenient means for hackers to spread malicious content on Facebook. However, little is understood about the characteristics of malicious apps and how they operate. In this work, using a large corpus of malicious Facebook apps observed over a nine month period, we showed that malicious apps differ significantly from benign apps with respect to several features. For example, malicious apps are much more likely to share names with other apps, and they typically request fewer permissions than benign apps. Leveraging our observations, we developed FRAppE, an accurate classifier for detecting malicious Facebook applications. Most interestingly, we highlighted the emergence of AppNets—large groups of tightly connected applications that promote each other. We will continue to dig deeper into this ecosystem of malicious apps on Facebook, and we hope that Facebook will benefit from our recommendations for reducing the menace of hackers on their platform.

10. REFERENCES

[1] 100 social media statistics for 2012. http://thesocialskinny.com/100-social-media-statistics-for-2012/.

[2] 11 Million Bulk email addresses for sale - Sale Price $90. http://www.allhomebased.com/BulkEmailAddresses.htm.

[3] App piggybacking example.
    `https://apps.facebook.com/mypagekeeper/?status=scam_report_fb_survey_scam_Converse_shoes_2012_05_17_boQ`.

[4] Application authentication flow using oauth 2.0.
    `http://developers.facebook.com/docs/authentication/`.

[5] Bitdefender Safego. `http://www.facebook.com/bitdefender.safego`.

[6] bit.ly API. `http://code.google.com/p/bitly-api/wiki/ApiDocumentation`.

[7] Defensio Social Web Security. `http://www.facebook.com/apps/application.php?id=177000755670`.

[8] Facebook developers.
    `https://developers.facebook.com/docs/appsonfacebook/tutorial/`.

[9] Facebook kills App Directory, wants users to search for apps. `http://zd.net/MkBY9k`.

[10] Facebook Opengraph API. `http://developers.facebook.com/docs/reference/api/`.

[11] Facebook softens its app spam controls, introduces better tools for developers. `http://bit.ly/LLmZpM`.

[12] Facebook tops 900 million users.
    `http://money.cnn.com/2012/04/23/technology/facebook-q1/index.htm`.

[13] Hackers selling $25 toolkit to create malicious Facebook apps. `http://zd.net/g28HxI`.

[14] MyPageKeeper. `https://www.facebook.com/apps/application.php?id=167087893342260`.

[15] Norton Safe Web. `http://www.facebook.com/apps/application.php?id=310877173418`.

[16] Permissions Reference.
    `https://developers.facebook.com/docs/authentication/permissions/`.

[17] Pr0file stalker: rogue Facebook application.
    `https://apps.facebook.com/mypagekeeper/?status=scam_report_fb_survey_scam_pr0file_viewer_2012_4_4`.

[18] Selenium - Web Browser Automation.
    `http://seleniumhq.org/`.

[19] SocialBakers: The receipe for social marketing success.
    `http://www.socialbakers.com/`.

[20] Stay Away From Malicious Facebook Apps.
    `http://bit.ly/b6gWn5`.

[21] The Pink Facebook - rogue application and survey scam.
    `http://nakedsecurity.sophos.com/2012/02/27/pink-facebook-survey-scam/`.

[22] Web-of-trust. `http://www.mywot.com/`.

[23] Whatapp (beta) - A Stanford Center for Internet and Society website with support from the Rose Foundation.
    `https://whatapp.org/facebook/`.

[24] Which cartoon character are you - rogue Facebook application. `https://apps.facebook.com/mypagekeeper/?status=scam_report_fb_survey_scam_whiich_cartoon_character_are_you_2012_03_30`.

[25] Wiki: Facebook Platform. `http://en.wikipedia.org/wiki/Facebook_Platform`.

[26] F. Benevenuto, G. Magno, T. Rodrigues, and V. Almeida. Detecting spammers on Twitter. In *CEAS*, 2010.

[27] A. Besmer, H. R. Lipford, M. Shehab, and G. Cheek. Social applications: exploring a more secure framework. In *SOUPS*, 2009.

[28] C.-C. Chang and C.-J. Lin. LIBSVM: A library for support vector machines. *ACM Transactions on Intelligent Systems and Technology*, 2, 2011.

[29] P. Chia, Y. Yamamoto, and N. Asokan. Is this app safe? a large scale study on application permissions and risk signals. In *WWW*, 2012.

[30] F. J. Damerau. A technique for computer detection and correction of spelling errors. *Commun. ACM*, 7(3), Mar. 1964.

[31] H. Gao, Y. Chen, K. Lee, D. Palsetia, and A. Choudhary. Towards online spam filtering in social networks. In *NDSS*, 2012.

[32] H. Gao, J. Hu, C. Wilson, Z. Li, Y. Chen, and B. Y. Zhao. Detecting and characterizing social spam campaigns. In *IMC*, 2010.

[33] M. Gjoka, M. Sirivianos, A. Markopoulou, and X. Yang. Poking facebook: characterization of osn applications. In *Proceedings of the first workshop on Online social networks*, WOSN, 2008.

[34] J. King, A. Lampinen, and A. Smolen. Privacy: Is there an app for that? In *SOUPS*, 2011.

[35] A. Le, A. Markopoulou, and M. Faloutsos. Phishdef: Url names say it all. In *Infocom*, 2010.

[36] K. Lee, J. Caverlee, and S. Webb. Uncovering social spammers: social honeypots + machine learning. In *SIGIR*, 2010.

[37] S. Lee and J. Kim. Warningbird: Detecting suspicious urls in twitter stream. In *NDSS*, 2012.

[38] Y. Liu, K. P. Gummadi, B. Krishnamurthy, and A. Mislove. Analyzing facebook privacy settings: user expectations vs. reality. In *IMC*, 2011.

[39] J. Ma, L. K. Saul, S. Savage, and G. M. Voelker. Beyond blacklists: learning to detect malicious web sites from suspicious urls. In *KDD*, 2009.

[40] A. Makridakis, E. Athanasopoulos, S. Antonatos, D. Antoniades, S. Ioannidis, and E. P. Markatos. Understanding the behavior of malicious applications in social networks. *Netwrk. Mag. of Global Internetwkg.*, 2010.

[41] M. S. Rahman, T.-K. Huang, H. V. Madhyastha, and M. Faloutsos. Efficient and Scalable Socware Detection in Online Social Networks. In *USENIX Security*, 2012.

[42] T. Stein, E. Chen, and K. Mangla. Facebook immune system. In *Proceedings of the 4th Workshop on Social Network Systems*, 2011.

[43] G. Stringhini, C. Kruegel, and G. Vigna. Detecting spammers on social networks. In *ACSAC*, 2010.

[44] K. Thomas, C. Grier, J. Ma, V. Paxson, and D. Song. Design and Evaluation of a Real-Time URL Spam Filtering Service. In *Proceedings of the IEEE Symposium on Security and Privacy*, 2011.

[45] N. Wang, H. Xu, and J. Grosshlags. Third-party apps on facebook: privacy and the illusion of control. In *CHIMIT*, 2011.

[46] C. Yang, R. Harkreader, and G. Gu. Die free or live hard? empirical evaluation and new design for fighting evolving twitter spammers. In *RAID*, 2011.

[47] S. Yardi, D. Romero, G. Schoenebeck, et al. Detecting spam in a twitter network. *First Monday*, 2009.

Defending Against Large-scale Crawls in Online Social Networks

Mainack Mondal, Bimal Viswanath, Allen Clement,
Peter Druschel, Krishna P. Gummadi, Alan Mislove†, Ansley Post

MPI-SWS
{mainack, bviswana, aclement, druschel
gummadi, abpost}@mpi-sws.org

†Northeastern University
amislove@ccs.neu.edu

ABSTRACT

Thwarting large-scale crawls of user profiles in online social networks (OSNs) like Facebook and Renren is in the interest of both the users and the operators of these sites. OSN users wish to maintain control over their personal information, and OSN operators wish to protect their business assets and reputation. Existing rate-limiting techniques are ineffective against crawlers with many accounts, be they fake accounts (also known as Sybils) or compromised accounts of real users obtained on the black market.

We propose Genie, a system that can be deployed by OSN operators to defend against crawlers in large-scale OSNs. Genie exploits the fact that the browsing patterns of honest users and crawlers are very different: even a crawler with access to many accounts needs to make many more profile views per account than an honest user, and view profiles of users that are more distant in the social network. Experiments using real-world data gathered from a popular OSN show that Genie frustrates large-scale crawling while rarely impacting honest users; the few honest users who are affected can recover easily by adding a few friend links.

Categories and Subject Descriptors

C.2.0 [**Computer-Communication Networks**]: General—*Security and protection*

General Terms

Security, Design, Algorithms

Keywords

Sybil attacks, social networks, network-based Sybil defense

1. INTRODUCTION

Online social networking sites (OSNs) like Facebook, MySpace, and Orkut have the personal data of hundreds of millions of users. OSNs allow users to browse the (public) profiles of other users in the network, making it easy for users to connect, communicate, and share content. Unfortunately, this functionality can be exploited by third-parties to aggregate and extract data about millions of OSN users. Once collected, the data can be re-published [20], monetized, and mined in ways that may violate users' privacy. For instance, it has been shown that private user attributes like sexual orientation can be inferred from a user's set of friends and their profile attributes [20, 29]; a third party with access to aggregated user data could easily apply these techniques.

These third-party aggregators, which we refer to as *crawlers*, represent a significant problem for OSN site operators as well. User data provides OSN operators with a revenue stream (e.g., via targeted advertisements); stopping crawlers is therefore in the OSN operators' business interests. Additionally, OSN operators cannot ensure that data collected by a third party is used according to the operator's privacy policy. Yet, OSN operators are likely to be held responsible if crawled data is used in ways that violate the policy, at least in the court of public opinion. For example, Facebook was widely blamed in the popular press [12] when a single crawler gathered public profiles of over 100 million users [20]. Thus, OSN operators need effective mechanisms to thwart large-scale crawling of OSN sites [40][1].

Today, OSN operators typically limit the rate at which a single user account or IP address can view user profiles [41], in order to discourage large-scale data collection. Unfortunately, crawlers can circumvent these schemes by creating a large number of fake user accounts [3], by employing botnets [21] or cloud services [8] to gain access to many IP addresses, or by using the compromised accounts of a large number of real users [1].

In this paper, we propose Genie, a system that OSN operators can deploy to limit large-scale crawlers. Genie leverages the differences in the browsing patterns of honest users and crawlers to effectively thwart large-scale crawls of user profiles. Genie's design is based on the insight that honest users tend to view the profiles of others who are well connected and close in the social network. A crawler, on the other hand, is limited in his ability to form or control enough links to be close to all users whose profiles he wishes to view. Genie exploits this fact by enforcing rate limits in

---

[1]Not all large-scale crawls are for nefarious purposes. Researchers, for instance, already tend to obtain the consent of the OSN operator before doing their crawls for research purposes (e.g., [9, 22]): such authorized crawlers can be whitelisted even if a defense is in place.

a way that is sensitive to the distance and degree of connectivity between viewer and viewee.

Using profile view data from RenRen, a Facebook-like OSN that is popular in China [39], we observe that average social network distance between honest users and the profiles they view tends to be low (1.62 social network hops). We demonstrate that a crawler, on the other hand, would require a very large number of well-distributed accounts (e.g., controlling 3% of all existing accounts in OSN) to be able to view the profiles of all users while maintaining the same low average distance.

Genie works by deriving a credit network [10, 14, 15] from the social network. In brief, credit is associated with links in the social network, and a viewer must "pay" credits to the viewee, along a path in the social network, when viewing a profile. Compared to conventional per-account or per-IP address rate-limiting, credit networks offers two key advantages. First, in a credit network, the rate limits are associated with social network links rather than user accounts or addresses. As a result, a crawler gains little by creating many Sybil accounts or using many IP addresses [22]. Second, the greater the distance between viewer and viewee in the social network, the stricter the rate limit is imposed by the credit network on profile views. Consequently, even crawlers with access to a relatively large number of compromised user accounts are unable to crawl the network quickly.

The contributions of this work are as follows:

- We analyze profile viewing data from the Renren social network and show that the average distance in the social network between a honest viewer and a viewee is significantly smaller than that of a crawler. Moreover, a crawler interested in crawling the entire social network is fundamentally unable to blend in with honest viewers unless he controls a very large proportion of strategically positioned user accounts.

- We present the design of Genie, which leverages credit networks derived from the already-existing social network to block large-scale crawling activity, while allowing honest users' browsing unhindered.

- We demonstrate the feasibility of deploying Genie with an evaluation using large partial social network graphs obtained from Renren, Facebook, YouTube, and Flickr, and a mix of real and synthetically generated profile viewing traces. We demonstrate that Genie effectively blocks crawlers while the impact on honest users is minimal.

- We show that Genie can scale to networks having millions of nodes by scaling up credit network operations. Thus, Genie is practical on the large OSNs of today.

2. RELATED WORK

In this section, we describe relevant prior work on limiting large-scale crawls of OSNs and leveraging social networks to defend against Sybil attacks.

Limiting large-scale crawlers There exist a number of techniques that aim to prevent crawls of web services. Two techniques commonly used in practice are robots.txt [4], and IP-address- or account-based rate limiting [18, 38, 46].

robots.txt is a file stored at the web server that indicates a set of pages that should not be crawled. Compliance with this policy is voluntary; robots.txt consequently provides little defense against malicious crawlers.

Large websites like Yahoo! often rely on a simple per-IP-address rate limit to control access to their web services [38]. Each IP address is allocated a maximum number of requests, which are replenished in 24 hour intervals. Once a user exceeds this limit, the operator either stops serving the user or may require that the user solve a CAPTCHA [5]. This approach limits the number of views a crawler can perform from an individual IP address, but is not effective against botnets that control many IPs. Additionally, dedicated crawlers can bypass defenses like CAPTCHA using available CAPTCHA-solving service providers [32], and other schemes exist that can bypass IP-address-based rate-limiting approaches [8, 16].

Online social networks like Facebook, Google Plus or Twitter [18, 41, 46] often use account-based rate limits on requests to view profile pages. Similar to IP-based rate limits, this approach works well if crawlers control at most a small number of accounts; in the face of Sybils or compromised accounts, it is not effective.

Wilson et al. proposed SpikeStrip [52], a system designed to discourage OSN crawlers. SpikeStrip uses cryptography to make information aggregation from OSN websites inefficient. SpikeStrip rate limits the number of profile views allowed per browsing session and prevents different browsing sessions from sharing data. Thus, crawlers cannot aggregate or correlate data gathered by different sessions.

Despite its elegant design, SpikeStrip restricts the functionality of the OSN. For example, SpikeStrip does not allow two OSN users to share website links of a common friend. Moreover, SpikeStrip would require OSNs like Facebook to change the way they use content distribution networks like Akamai to serve users' content. Unlike SpikeStrip, Genie does not affect the OSN functionality or content distribution. As we will show later, Genie can be deployed with minimal disruption to the browsing activities of honest users.

Social network-based Sybil defenses Recently there have been proposals to leverage social networks to defend against Sybil attacks [11, 28, 35, 37, 44, 45, 53, 54].

Sybil defense proposals such as SybilLimit [53] or SybilInfer [11] try to detect Sybils in the network and then block them from the service. However these Sybil detection mechanisms are not designed to address compromised accounts. Additionally, recent work has shown that these Sybil detection schemes suffer from limitations due to assumptions they make concerning the structure of the social network [30, 50].

The design of Genie borrows credit network [10, 14, 15] techniques from Sybil-tolerant [48] systems like Ostra [28] and Bazaar [35], and uses Canal [49] to manage credit network operations. In contrast to Sybil detection schemes, Sybil tolerant systems do not aim to detect Sybil users; instead they minimize the impact of Sybils on honest users.

Genie differs from existing Sybil tolerant systems in two fundamental ways: First, Genie considers crawlers that have access to both Sybil and compromised accounts; previous work considered only Sybil attacks. Second, unlike Ostra and Bazaar (which rely on users to provide feedback on whether a communication is spam or whether a transaction is fraudulent), Genie infers whether or not activity is malicious by exploiting differences in the browsing patterns of crawlers and honest users.

3. SYSTEM AND ATTACK MODEL

3.1 System model

OSN sites such as Facebook, Renren [39], Google+, and Orkut share a common system model: Users create accounts, establish friend links with other users, and post content (often of a personal nature). Users have a "home page" on the OSN that links to all of the user's content; we refer to this as the user's *profile*. The graph formed by the entire set of friend links forms a social network. In the OSNs of interest to us, forming a friend link requires the consent of both users.

Users can typically choose to make their data *private* (i.e., visible only to the user and the site operator), *public* (i.e., visible to every user of the social network), or *semi-public* (i.e., visible to subsets of the user's friends or to friends of user's friends). In practice, many users choose to make their profile information public [24], despite the private nature of some of the information posted. Contributing to this choice may be that sites encourage public sharing [43], that the default privacy setting is "public" [36], that other privacy choices are not always intuitive [42], and that many users are not fully aware of the privacy risks [24]. It is these public profiles (that typically represent a large fraction of all user profiles [23]) that Genie is concerned with protecting.

3.2 Attack model

Today, social networking sites tend to impose a rate limit on the profile views a single user can request in order to slow down crawlers. However, there are two ways in which a crawler can overcome these limits.

A crawler can conduct a *Sybil attack* by creating multiple user accounts, thereby overcoming the per-user rate limit. It is important to note that while the crawler can create an arbitrary number of links between Sybil accounts he controls, we assume that his ability to form links between his Sybil accounts and honest users is limited by his ability to convince honest users to accept a friend link, regardless of how many user accounts he controls. The significance of this point will become clear in the following section, where we describe how Genie leverages social links to limit crawling activity.

A crawler can also conduct a *compromised account attack* by taking control (e.g., by obtaining the password) of existing accounts in the system. The crawler can gain access to such accounts via phishing attacks, by guessing the user's password, or by purchasing the credentials of already compromised accounts on the black market. A compromised account attack is more powerful than a Sybil attack, because every additional compromised account increases the number of links to honest users that the crawler has access to. Again, the significance of having access to such links will become clear in the following section.

We assume that a crawler with access to compromised accounts cannot compromise the accounts of strategically positioned users of his choosing. Defending against a crawler who can access any account of his choosing would require preventing social engineering attacks, which are outside Genie's attack model. Instead, we assume that compromised accounts are randomly distributed throughout the network. Additionally, we assume that the crawler does not actively form new links involving compromised accounts, as such ac-

tivity would likely alert the actual owner of the account that their account has been compromised.

We are concerned about attacks where the crawler greedily attempts to gather as many distinct user profiles as possible. We assume that the crawler is agnostic to *which* users he crawls. Our crawler model captures both third-party crawlers [2] as well as research-oriented crawlers (e.g., used in studies of Facebook [22], Flickr [27], and Twitter [9]). However, our model excludes some crawlers that may be interested in repeatedly crawling the accounts of a small subset of users over an extended period of time, perhaps to gather their changing profile information. We make no assumptions about the crawler's strategy, i.e., whether the crawler employs random walks or BFS or DFS to fetch user profiles. Consequently, we simulate attacks employing the strategy that optimizes for the crawler's goal of fetching as many distinct user profiles as possible.

4. WORKLOAD ANALYSIS

In this section, we compare profile viewing workloads of honest users and crawlers. In later sections, we show how Genie can exploit the differences in the browsing behavior of honest users and crawlers to rate-limit crawlers, while rarely affecting honest users.

4.1 Honest users' profile viewing workload

We obtained anonymized user profile browsing data [22] from the RenRen social network [39], a Facebook-like social network that is popular in China. The data covers users in RenRen's Peking University (RR-PKU) network, and includes the links between PKU users and all other RenRen users. We pre-processed the social network and browsing trace to only include the subgraph of the PKU users, and then extracted the largest connected component (LCC) from the social network. Similar to prior work [28,49], our analysis only examines users in the LCC (representing 91.2% of the users and 94.3% of the links from the pre-processed network). The LCC of the RR-PKU network has 33,294 users and 705,248 undirected links.

The data set also includes a trace of all profiles (both friends and non-friends) that each user browsed during a two-week period during September, 2009. Unfortunately, the RenRen trace does not provide timestamps or an ordering for profile views. Therefore, in experiments where we need the profile views to be ordered, we generate a time series by assigning each profile view a timestamp chosen uniform randomly within the two-week period covered by the trace. This time series was used in all analyses conducted in the paper. We highlight our key findings below.

1. Most users make (receive) few profile views, but a small number of users make (receive) a large number of views. Figure 1 shows the distribution of profile views made and received by individual users in the RR-PKU network. The plots show a considerable skew in the distributions: Most (> 90%) users make or receive fewer than 10 views, while a handful of users (< 0.4%) view 50 or more profiles. In particular, there are three users who viewed 1,827, 612 and 272 profiles (respectively) over a period of two weeks. These users show significant crawler-like behavior, and we return to discuss these users in Section 6.4. Thus, most users in the social network tend to make

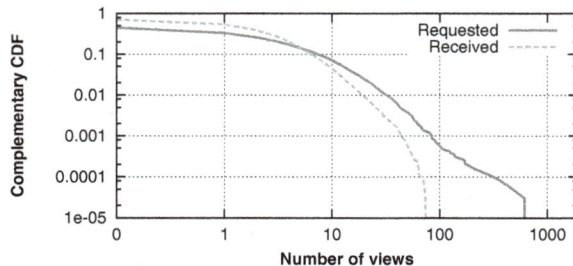

Figure 1: Complementary cumulative distribution of the number of profile view requests made and received by RR-PKU users during a two-week period.

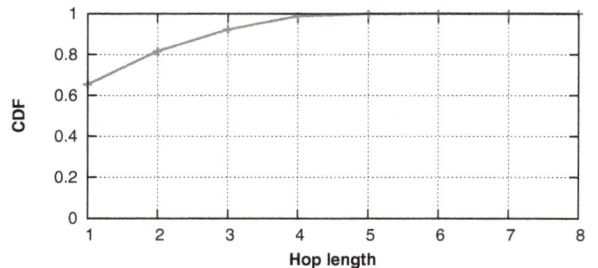

Figure 2: Cumulative distribution of hop distance separating viewers and viewees in RR-PKU network. The profile viewing activities are highly local.

or receive views from a small number of other users in the network.

2. The number of profile views made (received) by users is significantly correlated with their degree. The Pearson correlation coefficients between the rankings of users ordered based on the number of views they make (receive) and their degree is 0.67 (0.5). The high correlation coefficient affirms the intuitive hypothesis that users who are more active in the social network would also have more friends in the network. This finding is consistent with the profile browsing behavior previously studied in Facebook [6] and Orkut [7].

This observation suggests that the *imbalance* in user activity (defined to be the difference between the number of profile views made and received by a user, divided by their degree) would be tightly bounded. We find this to be true: over 99.9% of users have an imbalance lower than 10, with a median value of 0.05.

3. Not all profiles views are unique; a small but non-trivial number of views are repeated. Users tend to repeatedly visit the profiles of others to track updates. In our two-week trace, we found 17,307 (17.8%) of the profile views to be such repeat views. Our estimate of the fraction that repeat views represent is likely to be conservative, as we are restricted to a two-week trace. (One would expect the percent of repeat views to increase with the length of the workload trace.) However, the implication of the presence of repeat views is that repeat views decrease the number of distinct profiles viewed by users. For crawlers, repeat views represent sub-optimal use of resources, as their goal is to view the profiles of as many distinct users as possible.

4. Users tend to make (receive) profile views of others who are within their immediate (1 or 2-hop) network neighborhood. Figure 2 shows the distribution of network distance, measured in terms of hops, between the

viewers and viewees in our RR-PKU trace. We observe that over 80% of all profile views are between users who are separated by no more than two hops. This observation is consistent with prior studies of the Orkut social network [7], as well as studies of friendship formation in the Flickr social network [26].

Our analysis considers only a single network, due to the difficulty in obtaining detailed profile viewing data. However, we note that many of our findings are consistent with prior studies of other social networks [6,7,26,51], suggesting that our RenRen data is likely to be representative of other social networks.

4.2 Crawlers' profile viewing workload

We now turn to examining the workload that a crawler would generate when run on the RenRen network from the previous section and three others: the Facebook New Orleans regional network [47], YouTube [27], and Flickr [26]. Table 1 provides more details on the number of users, links, and average degree in these networks.

We simulate crawlers of varying strength by allowing crawlers to "compromise" 1, 10, 100, and 1,000 randomly chosen users within the network. Table 2 shows the number of links that connect user accounts under the crawlers' control to honest users in the different graphs. Note that while a crawler with 1,000 compromised accounts might not seem particularly strong, it is important to consider the size of the networks. For example, the crawler controlling 1,000 accounts controls around 0.1% of all users in the YouTube network. As a point of reference, this would be equivalent to controlling 1,000,000 compromised accounts in the real-world Facebook network.

To generate the crawling workload, we implement the fol-

Network	Users	Links	Average degree
RR-PKU [22]	33,294	705,262	21.2
Facebook [47]	63,392	816,886	25.7
Youtube [27]	1,134,889	2,987,624	5.2
Flickr [26]	1,624,991	15,476,835	19.0

Table 1: Number of users, links, and average user degree in the large-scale social networks used to evaluate Genie.

Network	Number of compromised accounts			
	1	10	100	1000
RR-PKU [22]	26	415	3,638	14,938
Facebook [47]	13	237	2,123	15,970
Youtube [27]	6	26	592	4,129
Flickr [26]	5	613	2,242	16,015

Table 2: Strength of crawlers in different social graphs. Each column corresponds to specific number of random compromised accounts, and the corresponding number of attack links in different graphs.

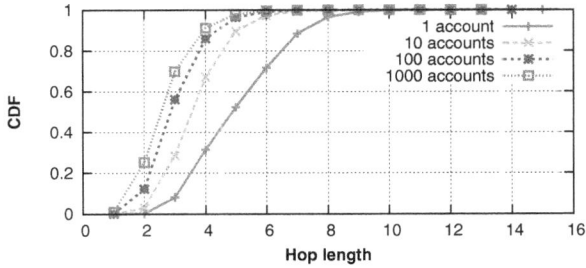

Figure 3: Cumulative distribution of the distance of crawler profile views in Flickr with different numbers of compromised accounts. To fully mimic the high locality in honest user views the crawlers have to control more than 1,000 compromised honest user accounts.

lowing strategy for the crawler: We assume that all crawler's accounts collude to view profiles of all honest users in the network. Each honest user is viewed only once, and the crawler's account nearest to an honest user will be assigned the task of viewing that user's profile. This strategy maximizes locality in profile views, making the crawler's workload look as "close" to the honest users' workload as possible.

We now compare the resulting crawler workload with that of honest users, noting two important differences.

1. In contrast to honest users' workload, profile views by crawlers are highly non-local. Figure 3 and Figure 4 shows the locality in profile visits by crawlers with different attacking capacities for the Flickr and Facebook graphs (the other graphs show similar behavior and are removed for brevity). For large network graphs like the Flickr and YouTube samples, we observe that even a powerful crawler with 1,000 accounts has only a small fraction (less than 30%) of requested profiles within the 2-hop neighborhood of the users under his control. For small network graphs like the Facebook and RenRen samples, the crawler does have a majority of users (around 80-90%) within a 2-hop neighborhood. However, in these networks, 1,000 compromised accounts represent 3% of all users; considering that controlling 3% would require controlling 29 million user accounts in the current complete Facebook network, this is a very powerful attack indeed.

Overall, the results indicate that to mimic the high locality in profile views for honest users, crawlers would fundamentally have to control a very large fraction of all accounts.

2. In contrast to honest users, crawlers request many more profile views than they receive. We observe that the median imbalance per link in profile views is 8.3 for a crawler with 100 user accounts, compared to honest users' median imbalance of 0.05. Such an imbalance is necessary, as even with 100 accounts, the crawler makes significantly more profile views that an honest user. In the next section, we present a system design that exploits these differences in browsing patterns of honest users and crawlers.

5. GENIE DESIGN

In this section, we present the design of Genie, analyze its security properties, and discuss how Genie can be used to maliciously deny service to honest users.

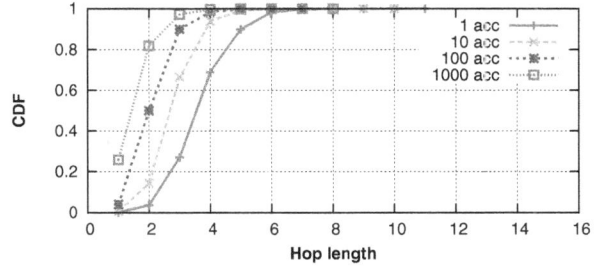

Figure 4: Cumulative distribution of the distance of crawler profile views in Facebook with different numbers of compromised accounts.

5.1 Strawman

To motivate the need for Genie's more elaborate approach, we briefly consider a simple distance-based rate-limiting technique as a strawman design, and show that it is ineffective against Sybil crawlers. We know from Section 4.1 that honest users rarely view profiles outside their neighborhood social graph, whereas the crawlers have to view distant profiles. Our strawman uses distance based rate limiting to leverage this finding.

In the strawman design each user account is allowed to view user profiles at a maximal rate r, where viewing a profile K hops away counts as viewing $K - 1$ profiles. (Thus, viewing a friend's profile is not subject to rate-limiting.) The scheme discriminates heavily against crawlers, who tend to view distant profiles. However, just like the existing rate-limiting schemes discussed in Section 2, this design is vulnerable to Sybil attacks. A crawler can simply create more Sybil accounts to overcome the per-account rate limit. The same would be true for any per-account or per-IP-address rate-limiting approach, no matter how much it discriminates against workloads typical of crawlers.

To summarize, if the profile viewing privileges are assigned based only on the viewing user, then a crawler can view more profiles simply by creating additional Sybils. Instead, Genie attaches the profile viewing privileges to *paths* in the network, rather than users, as we describe in the following section.

5.2 Genie design overview

Now, we present the design of Genie. Genie relies on a credit network [14, 15] to make sure Genie's rate limits cannot be circumvented by using more Sybil accounts. Moreover, Genie uses the credit network to impose rate limits that discriminate against a crawlers' workload, in order to slow down powerful crawlers that use many compromised user accounts.

A credit network is a directed graph $G = (V, E)$, where each edge $(u, v) \in E$ is labeled with a scalar credit value $c_{uv} \geq 0$. Each node in Genie's credit network corresponds to an OSN user and there is a pair of directed edges $(u, v), (v, u)$ in the credit network iff the users u, v are friends in the OSN. Genie allows user s to view user t's profile information iff the max-flow between s and t in the credit network is at least $f(d_{st})$, where f is a non-decreasing cost function, and d_{st} is the length of the shortest path between s and t in the social network.

Thus Genie computes the *amount of credit charged* for

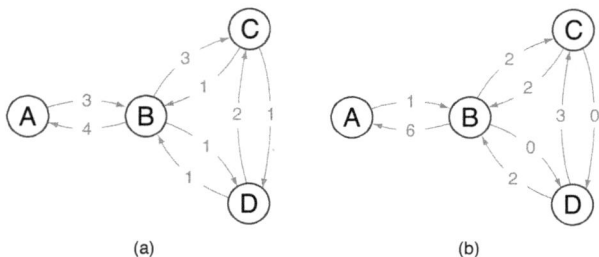

Figure 5: Example of Genie on a small credit network. (a) User A wishes to view D's profile; let us assume this costs two credits. No single path has two credits available, so both $A \to B \to C \to D$ and $A \to B \to D$ are debited 1 credit. (b) The state of the credit network afterwards; note that intermediate nodes B and C maintain the same total credit available, as debiting from one link automatically adds credit to the opposite link.

a profile view based on the shortest path length between the viewer and viewee. However, the credits can actually be exchanged over any set of paths between the viewer and viewee. For example, Figure 5 (a) shows an example of Genie in a small network, where user A wishes to view D's profile. A is charged based on the shortest-path distance (two hops) to D, but the credits may be exchanged over a set of longer, different paths.

If the view is allowed, then the credit value on each link (u, v) on each path p_i that comprises the flow is reduced by c_{p_i}; the credit on each link (v, u) is correspondingly increased by c_{p_i}, where $c_{p_i} \leq f(d_{st})$. An example of this credit adjustment is presented in Figure 5 (b). It is worth noting that Genie rejecting a profile view request does not necessarily mean the operator must block the user making the request; Genie merely flags individual views as suspicious. How the provider responds is a matter of policy—normally, the OSN operator provider would deny or delay the view, effectively slowing down the suspected crawler's activity, but not block the user permanently.

The net effect of this transaction should be that the viewer has $f(d_{st})$ fewer credits available while the viewee has $f(d_{st})$ more credits available for future activity. If j is an intermediate user on one of the paths p_i then the total number of credits available to intermediate user j is unchanged, though the distribution of credit among links adjacent to j is different. As long as user j is well connected and can reach other users through any adjacent link, the change in credit distribution is unlikely to impact the user [10]; if j is not well connected, then attempted views may be flagged due to a lack of *liquidity*.[2]

Social networks exhibit a very high degree of connectivity, ensuring good liquidity in the credit network for most users. New users, inactive users, or small fringe communities that have not (yet) established strong connections to the rest of the network may have issues with liquidity. We will consider this issue in more detail in Section 6.

Genie leverages three key characteristics of honest user activity identified in Section 4 to thwart large-scale crawlers.

---

[2]Liquidity in the context of credit networks is defined as the capacity to route credit payments [10].

Leveraging unbalanced view ratios We observed in Section 4 that honest users have a balanced ratio of views requested to views received, while crawlers issue many more views than they receive. Genie allows a user to use credits obtained by being viewed to perform views in the future. This ensures liquidity amongst honest users with balanced activity ratios while draining credits from crawlers.

Because honest users do not have a perfect balance of views, even honest users run the risk of eventually exhausting all of their credit. To address this concern, Genie rebalances the credits on a pair of links $(u, v), (v, u)$ at a fixed rate r_b. For example, this can be implemented by dividing time into intervals, and at the beginning of each interval

$$c_{uv} \leftarrow c_{uv} - \frac{r_b}{2}(c_{uv} - c_{vu})$$
$$c_{vu} \leftarrow c_{vu} + \frac{r_b}{2}(c_{uv} - c_{vu})$$

where $0 < r_b \leq 1$.

Leveraging different path lengths Honest users tend to view profiles of other users that are nearby in the social network; crawling a significant fraction of the social network requires crawlers to view users who are disproportionately far from the crawler in the social network. Genie discriminates against crawlers by charging more credits to view distant users. The cost, in credits, to view a user that is distance d_{st} away in the social network is defined by the simple cost function $f(d_{st}) = d_{st} - 1$.

Leveraging repeated views Honest users repeatedly view the same subset of profiles in the network; crawlers eschew repeat views unless they are re-crawling the network to track changes. Genie does not charge for repeat views that occur within a given time period. If user s views the profile of user t within T days of when s was last charged for viewing t then s is not charged for the profile view; if more than T days have elapsed then s is charged as normal. A typical value of T would be on the order of months.

5.3 Security properties

We now describe the security properties provided by Genie.

Let $C \in V$ be the set of user accounts controlled by the crawler and $H = V \setminus C$ be the set of user accounts not controlled by the crawler (i.e., the honest users). The crawler's goal is to view the profiles of all users in H as quickly as possible. (He can trivially obtain the profiles of users in C.)

We call a link (c, h) in the social network an *attack link* if $c \in C$ and $h \in H$. The cut separating C and H (i.e., the set of attack links) is called the *attack cut*.

To determine the rate r_c at which a crawler can view profiles in H, we need only consider the attack cut, because all of the crawler's views have to cross this cut. Profile views within H or within C are irrelevant, because they must cross the attack cut an even number of times, and do not change the credit available along the cut.

The rate r_c is determined by the following factors:

- A, the size of the attack cut (number of attack links): a powerful crawler has a large attack cut.
- d_h, the average OSN distance for honest profile views.
- d_c, the average OSN distance between users in H and the corresponding closest user in C.
- r_c, the expected rate of profile views received by users in C from users in H: per our threat model, the crawler has little control over this rate, and we can conserva-

tively assume that it is the same as the expected rate of views received by a user in H.

- r_b, the rebalancing rate.
- f, the view cost function.

Using $f(d) = d - 1$, the maximal steady-state crawling rate

$$r_c = A \frac{r_b + r_c(d_h - 1)}{d_c - 1}$$

The numerator is the crawler's "income", the rate at which he can acquire credits. The denominator is the crawler's "cost", in credits, per profile view. As we can see, the maximal crawling rate increases linearly with the number of attack links, at a slope defined by the second term. A larger r_b, r_c or d_h increases, a larger d_c decreases the slope.

The credit network effectively makes the power of a corrupted account attack proportional to the number of acquired attack links.

A crawler can increase the crawling rate by obtaining additional attack links, which are difficult to obtain in large quantities. Obtaining an attack link requires forming a social link with a user not already controlled by the crawler, or compromising a user account that has social links with users not already controlled by the crawler. Creating more user accounts by itself is ineffective, because it does not yield new attack links. As a result, the credit network renders Sybil attacks as such ineffective. Additionally, purchasing many compromised accounts is unlikely to provide the attacker with much additionally crawling ability: many accounts available in underground marketplaces have been observed to not be well connected users, but rather poorly connected users on the fringes of the OSN [33].

5.4 Potential for denial-of-service attacks

Credit exhaustion is a key concern for any credit network-based system where a crawler can consume credits to prevent honest user activity. In the context of Genie we consider two distinct resource exhaustion attacks: First, can a crawler prevent honest users' profile views from taking place? Second, can a crawler target weakly-connected honest users from viewing other profiles or from being viewed? Due to space constraints, we can only summarize the results of our analysis; details can be found in a technical report [31].

A crawler would have to be quite powerful to be able to have a noticeable effect on cuts through the core of the network, which would be necessary for the crawler to impact large numbers of users. However, a modestly strong crawler can impair users in small fringe communities. However, such users can respond by forming additional links to the core of the network.[3] We will further explore the impact of crawlers on honest users empirically in Section 6.

6. EVALUATION

In this section, we evaluate the performance of Genie over several different social networks. When evaluating Genie's performance, we focus on the two primary metrics of interest: (1) the time required for a crawler to crawl a Genie-

---

[3]Recall our assumption that a crawler cannot compromise the accounts of specific users of his choosing. If a crawler were able to do this, he could target weakly connected users or small communities very effectively.

Network	Users	Profile views
RR-PKU [22]	33,294	77,501
Facebook [47]	63,392	98,960
Youtube [27]	1,134,889	984,425
Flickr [26]	1,624,991	1,703,831

Table 3: Statistics of synthetic profile view workloads generated for different networks.

protected network and (2) the amount of honest users' activity flagged by Genie.

6.1 Datasets used

To evaluate the performance of Genie, we need four datasets: (i) a social network graph, (ii) a time-stamped trace of honest users' profile views in the form of (X, Y, t) where user X views user Y's profile at time t, (iii) a crawler's topology (i.e., how the user accounts controlled by the crawler are embedded in the network), and (iv) the crawler's profile crawling trace.

Social network graphs We evaluate the performance of Genie on social network graphs taken from four different online social networks: RenRen [22] (RR-PKU), Facebook [47], YouTube [27] and Flickr [26]), which were introduced in Section 4.2. Table 1 shows their high-level characteristics.

Gathering and generating workload traces Gathering profile viewing traces for large social networks is rather difficult, as it requires explicit cooperation from social network site operators. Unfortunately, many OSN operators are reluctant to share such traces due to competitive and privacy concerns [34]. Thus, we were able to obtain a profile viewing trace for the RR-PKU [22] network only.

As a result, we design a workload generator that reproduces the key features of the original RR-PKU profile viewing trace that we observed in Section 4. We focus on two features that capture the correlation between profile view request/receiver user degree and the number of views per user, and the locality of profile views.

It is difficult to preserve the correlation between both requester and receiver user degrees and number of interactions while ensuring the locality of interactions because of varying degree distribution and path length distribution across different networks. Instead, we generated two synthetic traces: a *receiver trace* that preserves the correlation between the receiver user degree and number of received views while ensuring the locality of interaction, and a *requester trace* that preserves the correlation corresponding to requester user degree and number of requests made while ensuring locality of interaction. Due to space constraints, we only present results for the *receiver trace*. Results for requester traces are similar and are shown in our extended technical report [31]. The high level statistics of the receiver trace workloads are shown in Table 3.

One concern with our trace generation is that if the social networks are sparse and have very high average path length, the generated trace may not ensure locality of interaction while preserving the correlation between user degree and number of interactions. We cross check whether our traces preserve the intended key features. We do this by testing whether the newly generated traces preserve the two key features we aim to reproduce: (i) locality of interactions and

(ii) the correlation between user degree and number of profile views received. Both of these two features for the synthetic traces match quite closely (results not shown) with the original RR-PKU trace indicating that the synthetic workload generator retains the key properties of the original workload. We used 5 synthetic traces generated using different random seeds for each of the Facebook, Youtube and Flickr networks.

Crawler's attack topology We model crawlers by simulating that the crawler has compromised the accounts of random users in the social network. We simulate 1, 10, 100 and 1,000 corrupted user accounts in the RR-PKU, Facebook, YouTube and Flickr networks. As the crawler obtains access to more corrupted accounts in the network, he also acquires many more attack links to honest users. The varying strength of crawlers on different networks was discussed in Section 4.2 and Table 2.

Crawler's profile crawling trace To generate the crawler crawling workload, we follow the same crawler model discussed in Section 4.2. This models a crawler that achieves the lowest average path distance to the crawled profiles, and is the optimal attacker strategy.

Unless otherwise noted, all results are the average across 25 different runs of our simulator (5 synthetic honest user profile viewing traces, each paired with 5 synthetic crawler traces).

6.2 Trace-driven simulation methodology

To evaluate the performance of Genie, first we built a max-flow path based trace driven simulator. We use the social graph connecting the users to simulate a credit network. For each profile view in the workload trace, our simulator checks if there exists a set of paths in the credit network that allow $p - 1$ units of credits to flow between the viewer and the viewee, where p denotes the shortest path length separating the viewer and the viewee. To this end, our simulator computes the max-flow paths [35] between the viewer and the viewee. If the max-flow is larger than $p - 1$, then the profile view is allowed and if it is not, then the view is flagged. If the profile view is allowed, the credits along the links of the max-flow paths are updated as described in Section 5.

A key input to our simulator is the credit refreshment rate, which denotes the rate at which exhausted credits on the links are replenished. We set the credit refreshment rate in our simulator by tuning the following two parameters described in Section 5.2: (i) the initial credit value, i, assigned to each link in the network at the beginning of the simulation, and (ii) the credit rebalance rate, r_b, which restores some of the exhausted credits on the links after each time step, say of duration t. We set the parameter r_b to 1, which has the effect of restoring the credit values on all links to i after every refresh time period (2 weeks in our experiments). So $\frac{i}{t}$ represents the effective credit refreshment rate, which determines the number of profile views accepted both for crawlers and honest users. As the value of credit refreshment rate increases, more profile views will be accepted from both crawlers and honest users. Thus, the key evaluation challenge that we address using our simulator is: *Does there exist a credit replenishment rate that significantly slows down crawlers, while flagging few views by honest users?*

For a real-life deployment the OSN operator can estimate initial credits by using past browsing activity of users. The

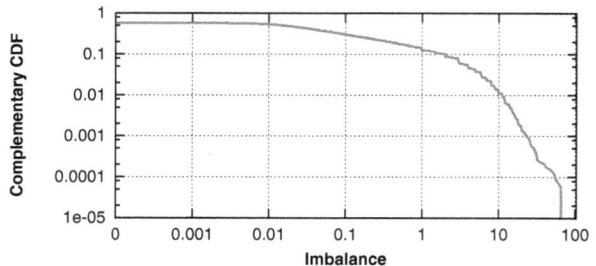

Figure 6: Complementary cumulative distribution of the imbalance of RR-PKU users (views are weighted by cost function mentioned in Section 5). Only 226 (0.7%) users have an imbalance greater than 12.

operator can build a distribution of user activity based on the imbalance between average number of profile views requested and received (weighted by the cost function mentioned in Section 5) made per outgoing link per user. Then the operator can pick an initial credit value/link from this distribution so that most (e.g. 99.9%) users' activity is allowed, but a few profile views are flagged (probably from super active users or crawlers). We check this methodology with our current RR-PKU dataset. Our implicit assumption here is that honest user behavior shows constant trends over time. We show the weighted imbalance distribution in Figure 6. From this figure we can estimate the number of users affected at a given credit value. For example with a credit value of 12, our estimate shows that views from 33,068 (99.3%) users will be allowed and 226 users will have some views flagged. We will show in section 6.4 that our estimate is quite good and indeed 275 users are flagged with this particular credit setting.

Scaling simulations to large graphs While we were able to run our max-flow path based simulator over the smaller RR-PKU network with 33,000 users, we found it computationally expensive to scale our simulations to the much larger YouTube and Flickr social networks with millions of users, links, and profile views. The computational complexity arises for three reasons: (i) even a single max-flow computation over a large graph is expensive, the most efficient algorithms for the maximum flow problem run in $O(V^3)$ [17] or $O(V^2 \log(E))$ [13] time; (ii) we have to perform millions of such computations, one for each profile view in the trace, and (iii) even worse, the computations cannot be parallelized and have to be performed online and in sequence, as the max-flow computation for a profile view has to account for credit changes on links in the network due to all prior profile views in the workload trace.

To allow Genie to be deployed on much larger networks, we leverage the recently proposed *Canal* [49] framework. Canal speeds up computations over credit networks and enables credit operations on very large-scale credit networks (on the order of millions of users) with low latency (on the order of a few milliseconds or less). Canal uses a novel landmark routing based technique to pre-compute paths with available credit (between different users in the network) continuously in the background as new credit operations are processed. Canal trades off accuracy for speed to achieve

Network	Avg. time (ms)	95th percentile time (ms)
RR-PKU [22]	0.16	0.78
Facebook [47]	0.21	0.86
Youtube [27]	0.46	1.45
Flickr [26]	0.65	1.41

Table 4: Average and 95th percentile time taken by Canal implementation to process one view request.

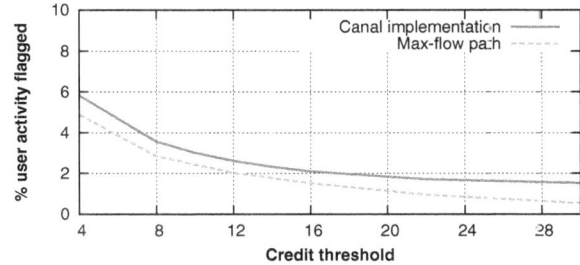

Figure 7: Variation of the fraction of user activities flagged with different credit values in RR-PKU in the presence of a crawler with 10 compromised accounts. We compare the results obtained using Canal implementation (red solid line) with those obtained using the max-flow based technique (green dotted line). The red solid line provides a close upper bound for the green line.

this goal. It explores only a subset of all possible paths between two users to complete a credit network operation between them. Thus, Canal may not always find sufficient paths with available credit between two users, even if such a path exists. However, Canal can achieve over 94% accuracy on various large-scale social networks [49]. Using Canal we were able to use Genie on data from online social networks including YouTube and Flickr that contain millions of users and links. We show the latency for processing one profile view with the Canal implementation of Genie in Table 4. Our current Canal implementation runs on a single machine. Results in [49] shows that, using a single machine with 48 GB RAM and 24 CPU cores, Canal can support operations on graphs with over 220 million links. Canal could likely be scaled to networks with a billion links using multiple machines and graph parallel processing frameworks [19,25].

Simulating Genie with Canal We implemented Genie using the Canal library. While processing a profile view, Genie asks Canal for the shortest path length between the viewer and viewee. It should be noted that Canal can only provide an approximate shortest path length because it uses a subset of all possible paths between two users. Genie uses this path length as the basis of charging for the view and then queries Canal again for a set of paths from viewer to viewee with sufficient credit values. If Canal returns a set of paths then the view is allowed and Genie deducts credit along the returned set of paths. Otherwise the view is flagged. Canal requires two parameter settings to configure the amount of path data to be pre-computed. We use the same settings[4] used in the original Canal paper [49]. (These settings provided over 94% accuracy when applied to the Bazaar [35] system.)

As Canal may fail to find sufficient credit when it exists, but will not find credit that does not actually exist deploying Genie with Canal provides an upper bound for the number of flagged profile views. We now examine how close the Canal estimates are to the true level of flagged user activity.

To understand the effect of approximation error introduced by Canal in terms of flagged honest user activities, we compare the Canal implementation output with the output from the max-flow path based technique. We use the RR-PKU network for this part of the evaluation as the relatively smaller size of RR-PKU enabled us to use the max-flow path based technique. Figure 7 shows the percentage of flagged honest user activity for the two techniques in the presence of a crawler with 10 compromised accounts. As the amount of credit available per refresh period increases, the percentage of flagged activity decreases for both techniques. On average, the absolute difference in flagged activities between the two techniques is only 0.7% of all user activities,

suggesting that Canal provides good accuracy. In the rest of our evaluation we will present results using our Canal implementation.

6.3 Limiting crawlers vs. flagging activity

We now switch our attention to the core tradeoff that is being made as we select the appropriate credit refreshment rate: namely, the amount of time it takes the crawler to crawl the entire graph and the fraction of honest users' activity that is flagged. We have already observed that to slow down crawlers effectively we need to replenish credits at a slow rate. However, a limited rate of credit replenishment opens up the possibility of honest users' views getting flagged. In this section, we explore the extent to which honest users' activity is flagged by Genie as it tries to limit crawlers.

We ran our Canal implementation for various different values of available credit per refresh period. For each replenishment rate, we compute two metrics: (i) the time it would take for a crawler to finish its crawl and (ii) the percentage of honest users' activity that is flagged. We compare these two metrics looking for a good tradeoff where crawlers are effectively slowed down, while good user activity is rarely flagged. We present the basic tradeoff for our different social networks in Figure 8.

For each social network, we show the results for crawlers of different strengths. On YouTube and Flickr graphs with more than 1 million users, we considered a crawler controlling up to 1,000 user accounts, while for RR-PKU with only 30,000 user accounts, we limited the crawler strength to 10 users. While the absolute number of compromised accounts controlled by the crawler might seem small, it is worth noting that the percentage of compromised users in these networks is still substantial as discussed earlier in section 4.2.

The plots show that it is possible to slow down crawls sufficiently to force a crawler to spend several months to tens of months to complete a single crawl. At the same time, the percentage of flagged user activity can be held to less than 5%. In many instances, the flagged activity can be held lower than 1%. Thus, there are two important take-aways from these results: first, with Genie, a certain amount of honest users' activity will unavoidably be flagged. Second,

---

[4]20 level-3 landmark universes

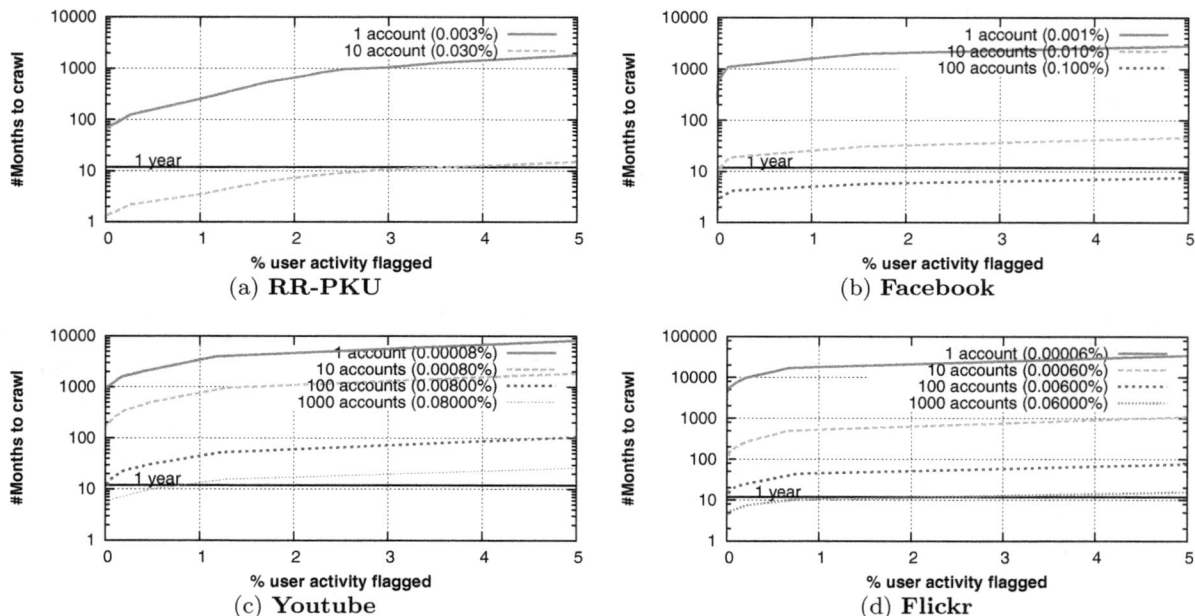

Figure 8: Trade-off between fraction of user activity flagged and time taken to finish a complete crawl with crawlers of varying strengths over different social network graphs. We measure crawler strength by the total number as well as the percentage (shown in parentheses) of compromised accounts in the network under control of the crawler. We conservatively allowed crawlers to exhaust the credits on links before allowing any honest users' activity.

unless the crawler is powerful and possesses over 0.1% of the accounts, the impact of the crawler on honest users is small.

6.4 Alternate strategies for flagged users

We observed in the previous section that a certain amount of blockage of honest users' activity is unavoidable. In section 5.2, we discussed that the OSN operator can make a choice based on some policy, once the profile view is flagged (or blocked) by Genie. Normally, the OSN operator would deny or delay the view to slow down the crawler's activity.

We now pose a simple question: can users do anything to minimize the amount of their flagged activity? To answer this question, we first investigate the flagged views in more detail. We then propose some recourse available to users with flagged activity.

We analyze the set of flagged activities in our extensive RR-PKU simulation, where we compute max-flow paths to verify if a profile view has to be allowed. We intentionally focused on max-flow based simulations because of the certainty that profile views flagged during such simulations are flagged due to lack of credit in the network.

For the analysis in this section, we focus on one particular simulation experiment with credit value 12, where 2.6% (or 2,574 activities) of the user activities are flagged and the crawler controlling 10 compromised accounts needs 8 months to complete the crawl.

A profile view can be flagged for one of three reasons: (i) the profile viewer runs out of credit on all links connected to itself (i.e., source blocked), (ii) the credit on links connecting the profile viewee is exhausted (i.e., destination blocked), or (iii) the view is flagged due to credit exhaustion somewhere

in the middle of the network. Strikingly, only 190 out of 2,574 (7%) flagged views (i.e., 0.18% of all views) are flagged due to lack of credit on links in the middle of the network. The remaining 2,384 (out of which 1,961 views were blocked at the source) views which includes 93% of the flagged activities is due to credit exhaustion on links directly next to the viewers or the viewees. On examining the degrees of these viewers and viewees who are flagged, we find that 96% of them have degree 1 and 99% of them have degree of 5 or less. That is, most activities flagged near the source or destination is due to source or destination users having too few friends and lying on the fringes of the network graph. These results support our observation in Section 5 that social network graphs are sufficiently well connected in their core that most flagged activity (and credit exhaustion) occurs close to the fringes.

Next, we investigated the amount of flagged activities for individual users. We found that a small number of users are bearing the brunt of the flagged activities. 1,808 of the 2,574 (or 70%) of the flagged profile views are made by 3 users in the network. These are the same super-active users mentioned in Section 4.1. Interestingly, all 3 users issue two orders of magnitude more views than an average RR-PKU user and they are all flagged near the source. Further investigation suggests that these three users exhibit crawler-like characteristics with more than 60% of viewed profiles lying beyond their 2-hop neighborhood. Ignoring these three users (who bear strong resemblance to crawlers), the percentage of total flagged activity falls to less than third of its original value, which is already a low percentage (2.6%) of all activity.

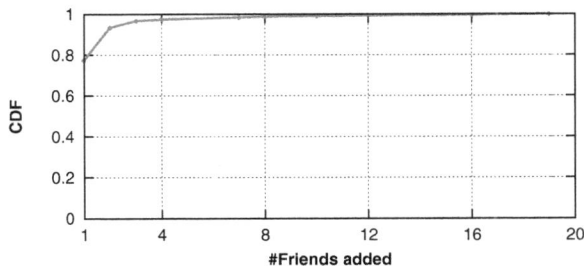

Figure 9: Cumulative distribution of how many extra links flagged RR-PKU users needed for completing their activities. Evidently majority of them needed just a few more links.

For the remaining users who contribute to only 30% of flagged views, we have already observed that most (99%) of the users have degree less than five. These are users who got flagged because their low number of friend links are insufficient to support the reasonable number (on average 6 views) of views they issued. However, we argue that there is a simple and natural recourse available to them: they can simply form more links in the online social network.

In order to test this hypothesis, we perform a simple experiment. We re-run the Genie simulation where each flagged user (i.e., 275 users falling in the low degree category), establishes a friend link to the destination of the flagged view (i.e requester sends a link request and the receiver approves it). This immediately leads to the acceptance of that view. At the end of the simulation, we look at the number of friend links established by each flagged user so that all the earlier flagged views could now be accepted.

Figure 9 shows the distribution of number of friend links established versus the ranked set of users. A significant majority (269 out of 275 or 97%) of the flagged users can get their views accepted by only establishing very few links (less than 4). Thus, most of the honest user activity flagged by Genie would be accepted if the users of the flagged views spent a minimal effort to establish a small number of friends. In fact, if Genie were to be deployed, it would naturally incentivize users to form a few more friend links. Given that many OSN sites already explicitly encourage their users to form more friend links, we believe that the overhead from Genie would be acceptable for a majority of users.

7. CONCLUSION

In this paper, we address the problem of preventing large-scale crawls in online social networks, and present Genie, a system that can be deployed by OSN operators to thwart crawlers. Based on trace data from the RenRen OSN, we show that the browsing patterns of honest users and crawlers are very different. While most honest users view the profiles of a modest number of users who tend to be nearby in the social network, even a strong, strategic crawler must view profiles of users who are further away. Genie exploits this fact by limiting the rate of profile views based on the connectivity and social network distance between a profile viewer and viewee. An experimental evaluation on multiple OSNs shows that Genie frustrates large-scale crawling while rarely impacting browsing of honest users; the few honest

users who are affected can recover easily by adding a few additional friend links.

Acknowledgements

We thank our shepherd Athina Markopoulou and the anonymous reviewers for their helpful comments. We also thank Ben Zhao and Christo Wilson for their assistance with the RR-PKU trace. This research was supported by the Max Planck Society and NSF grants IIS-0964465 and CNS-1054233.

8. REFERENCES

[1] 45,000 Facebook accounts compromised: What to know. http://bit.ly/TUY3i8.
[2] Crawl packages for social networks. http://80legs.com/crawl-packages-social-networks.html.
[3] 83 million Facebook accounts are fakes and dupes. http://bit.ly/Np3seb.
[4] A standard for robot exclusion. http://www.robotstxt.org/orig.html, 1994.
[5] L. V. Ahn, M. Blum, N. J. Hopper, and J. Langford. Captcha: Using hard AI problems for security. In *Proceedings of the 22nd Annual International Conference on the Theory and Applications of Cryptographic Techniques (EUROCRYPT'03)*, 2003.
[6] L. Backstrom, E. Bakshy, J. M. Kleinberg, T. M. Lento, and I. Rosenn. Center of attention: How Facebook users allocate attention across friends. In *Proceedings of the 5th International AAAI Conference on Weblogs and Social Media (ICWSM'11)*, 2011.
[7] F. Benevenuto, T. Rodrigues, M. Cha, and V. Almeida. Characterizing user behavior in online social networks. In *Proceedings of the 9th ACM/USENIX Internet Measurement Conference (IMC'09)*, 2009.
[8] C. Canali, M. Colajanni, and R. Lancellotti Data acquisition in social networks: Issues and proposals. In *Proceedings of the International Workshop on Services and Open Sources (SOS'11)*, 2011.
[9] M. Cha, H. Haddadi, F. Benevenuto, and K. P. Gummadi. Measuring user influence in twitter:The million follower fallacy. In *Proceedings of the 4TH International AAAI Conference on Weblogs and Social Media(ICWSM'10)*, 2010.
[10] P. Dandekar, A. Goel, R. Govindan, and I. Post. Liquidity in credit networks: A little trust goes a long way. In *Proceedings of the 12th ACM Conference on Electronic Commerce (EC'11)*, 2011.
[11] G. Danezis and P. Mittal. SybilInfer: Detecting Sybil nodes using social networks. In *Proceedings of the 16th Network and Distributed System Security Symposium (NDSS'09)*, 2009.
[12] Details of 100 million Facebook users published online. http://on.msnbc.com/qvLkX2.
[13] E. A. Dinic. An algorithm for the solution of the max-flow problem with the polynomial estimation. *Doklady Akademii Nauk SSSR*, 1970.
[14] D. do B. DeFigueiredo and E. T. Barr. Trustdavis: A non-exploitable online reputation system. In *Proceedings of the 7th IEEE International Conference on E-Commerce Technology (IEEE E-Commerce'05)*, 2005.
[15] A. Ghosh, M. Mahdian, D. M. Reeves, D. M. Pennock, and R. Fugger. Mechanism design on trust networks. In *Proceedings of the 3rd International Workshop on Internet and Network Economics (WINE'07)*, 2007.
[16] M. Gjoka, M. Kurant, C. Butts, and A. Markopoulou. Practical recommendations on crawling online social networks. In *Selected Areas in Communications, IEEE Journal on Measurement of Internet Topologies*, 2011.

[17] A. V. Goldberg and R. E. Tarjan. A new approach to the maximum flow problem. In *Proceedings of the 18th annual ACM Symposium on Theory of Computing (STOC'86)*, 1986.

[18] Google Plus rate limiting. https://developers.google.com/console/help/#cappingusage.

[19] D. Gregor and A. Lumsdaine. The parallel BGL: A generic library for distributed graph computations. In *Proceedings of the Parallel Object-Oriented Scientific Computing (POOSC)*, 2005.

[20] Hacker proves Facebook's public data Is public. http://tcrn.ch/9JvvmU.

[21] Inside a Facebook botnet. http://bit.ly/JSeRYs.

[22] J. Jiang, C. Wilson, X. Wang, P. Huang, W. Sha, Y. Dai, and B. Y. Zhao. Understanding latent interactions in online social networks. In *Proceedings of the 10th ACM/USENIX Internet Measurement Conference (IMC'10)*, 2010.

[23] E. A. Kolek and D. Saunders. Online disclosure: An empirical examination of undergraduate Facebook profiles. *Journal of Student Affairs Research and Practice*, 2008.

[24] Y. Liu, K. P. Gummadi, B. Krishnamurthy, and A. Mislove. Analyzing Facebook privacy settings: User expectations vs. reality. In *Proceedings of the 11th ACM/USENIX Internet Measurement Conference (IMC'11)*, 2011.

[25] G. Malewicz, M. H. Austern, A. J. Bik, J. C. Dehnert, I. Horn, N. Leiser, and G. Czajkowski. Pregel: A system for large-scale graph processing. In *Proceedings of the International Conference on Management of Data (SIGMOD'10)*, 2010.

[26] A. Mislove, H. S. Koppula, K. P. Gummadi, P. Druschel, and B. Bhattacharjee. Growth of the Flickr social network. In *Proceedings of the 1st ACM SIGCOMM Workshop on Social Networks (WOSN'08)*, 2008.

[27] A. Mislove, M. Marcon, K. P. Gummadi, P. Druschel, and B. Bhattacharjee. Measurement and analysis of online social networks. In *Proceedings of the 7th ACM/USENIX Internet Measurement Conference (IMC'07)*, 2007.

[28] A. Mislove, A. Post, K. P. Gummadi, and P. Druschel. Ostra: Leveraging trust to thwart unwanted communication. In *Proceedings of the 5th Symposium on Networked Systems Design and Implementation (NSDI'08)*, 2008.

[29] A. Mislove, B. Viswanath, K. P. Gummadi, and P. Druschel. You are who you know: Inferring user profiles in online social networks. In *Proceedings of the 3rd ACM International Conference of Web Search and Data Mining (WSDM'10)*, 2010.

[30] A. Mohaisen, A. Yun, and Y. Kim. Measuring the mixing time of social graphs. In *Proceedings of the 10th ACM/USENIX Internet Measurement Conference (IMC'10)*, 2010.

[31] M. Mondal, B. Viswanath, A. Clement, P. Druschel, K. P. Gummadi, A. Mislove, and A. Post. Defending against large-scale crawls in online social networks. Technical Report 2011-006, MPI-SWS, November 2011. http://www.mpi-sws.org/tr/2011-006.pdf.

[32] M. Motoyama, K. Levchenko, C. Kanich, D. McCoy, G. M. Voelker, and S. Savage. Re: Captchas: Understanding CAPTCHA-solving services in an economic context. In *Proceedings of the 19th USENIX conference on Security (SEC'10)*, 2010.

[33] M. Motoyama, D. McCoy, K. Levchenko, S. Savage, and G. M. Voelker. Dirty jobs: The role of freelance labor in web service abuse. In *Proceedings of the 20th USENIX conference on Security (SEC'11)*, 2011.

[34] Netflix-AOL data leak. http://cnet.co/6JiHr8.

[35] A. Post, V. Shah, and A. Mislove. Bazaar: Strengthening user reputations in online marketplaces. In *Proceedings of the 8th Symposium on Networked Systems Design and Implementation (NSDI'11)*, 2011.

[36] Public posting now the default on Facebook. http://bit.ly/RkoIWR.

[37] D. Quercia and S. Hailes. Sybil attacks against mobile users: Friends and foes to the rescue. In *Proceedings of the 29th Conference on Information Communications (INFOCOM'10)*, 2010.

[38] Rate limiting for yahoo! search web services. http://developer.yahoo.com/search/rate.html.

[39] Renren. http://www.renren.com.

[40] Spokeo privacy and safety concerns. http://en.wikipedia.org/wiki/Spokeo#Privacy_and_safety_concerns.

[41] T. Stein, E. Chen, and K. Mangla. Facebook immune system. In *Proceedings of the 4th Workshop on Social Network Systems (SNS'11)*, 2011.

[42] K. Strater and H. R. Lipford. Strategies and struggles with privacy in an online social networking community. In *Proceedings of the 22nd British HCI Group Annual Conference on People and Computers: Culture, Creativity (BCS-HCI'08)*, 2008.

[43] The day has come: Facebook pushes people to Go public. http://rww.to/7Zhc6N.

[44] N. Tran, J. Li, L. Subramanian, and S. S. Chow. Optimal Sybil-resilient node admission control. In *Proceedings of the 30th Conference on Information Communications (INFOCOM'11)*, 2011.

[45] N. Tran, B. Min, J. Li, and L. Subramanian. Sybil-resilient online content voting. In *Proceedings of the 6th Symposium on Networked Systems Design and Implementation (NSDI'09)*, 2009.

[46] Twitter rate limiting. https://dev.twitter.com/docs/rate-limiting-faq#measurement.

[47] B. Viswanath, A. Mislove, M. Cha, and K. P. Gummadi. On the evolution of user interaction in Facebook. In *Proceedings of the 2nd ACM SIGCOMM Workshop on Social Networks (WOSN'09)*, 2009.

[48] B. Viswanath, M. Mondal, A. Clement, P. Druschel, K. P. Gummadi, A. Mislove, and A. Post. Exploring the design space of social network-based Sybil defense. In *Proceedings of the 4th International Conference on Communication Systems and Network (COMSNETS'12)*, 2012.

[49] B. Viswanath, M. Mondal, K. P. Gummadi, A. Mislove, and A. Post. Canal: Scaling social network-based Sybil tolerance schemes. In *Proceedings of the 7th European Conference on Computer Systems (EuroSys'12)*, 2012.

[50] B. Viswanath, A. Post, K. P. Gummadi, and A. Mislove. An analysis of social network-based Sybil defenses. In *Proceedings of the Annual Conference of the ACM Special Interest Group on Data Communication (SIGCOMM'10)*, 2010.

[51] C. Wilson, B. Boe, A. Sala, K. P. N. Puttaswamy, and B. Y. Zhao. User interactions in social networks and their implications. In *Proceedings of the 4th European Conference on Computer Systems (EuroSys'09)*, 2009.

[52] C. Wilson, A. Sala, J. Bonneau, R. Zablit, and B. Y. Zhao. Don't tread on me: Moderating access to osn data with spikestrip. In *Proceedings of the 3rd ACM SIGCOMM Workshop on Social Networks (WOSN'10)*, 2010.

[53] H. Yu, P. B. Gibbons, M. Kaminsky, and F. Xiao. SybilLimit: A near-optimal social network defense against Sybil attacks. In *Proceedings of the IEEE Symposium on Security and Privacy (IEEE S&P'08)*, 2008.

[54] H. Yu, M. Kaminsky, P. B. Gibbons, and A. Flaxman. SybilGuard: Defending against Sybil attacks via social networks. In *Proceedings of the Annual Conference of the ACM Special Interest Group on Data Communication (SIGCOMM'06)*, 2006.

Cachet: A Decentralized Architecture for Privacy Preserving Social Networking with Caching

Shirin Nilizadeh
Indiana University
Bloomington
shirnili@indiana.edu

Sonia Jahid
University of Illinois at
Urbana-Champaign
sjahid2@illinois.edu

Prateek Mittal
University of California,
Berkeley
pmittal@eecs.berkeley.edu

Nikita Borisov
University of Illinois at
Urbana-Champaign
nikita@illinois.edu

Apu Kapadia
Indiana University
Bloomington
kapadia@indiana.edu

ABSTRACT

Online social networks (OSNs) such as Facebook and Google+ have transformed the way our society communicates. However, this success has come at the cost of user privacy; in today's OSNs, users are not in control of their own data, and depend on OSN operators to enforce access control policies. A multitude of privacy breaches has spurred research into privacy-preserving alternatives for social networking, exploring a number of techniques for storing, disseminating, and controlling access to data in a decentralized fashion. In this paper, we argue that a combination of techniques is necessary to efficiently support the complex functionality requirements of OSNs.

We propose Cachet, an architecture that provides strong security and privacy guarantees while preserving the main functionality of online social networks. In particular, Cachet protects the confidentiality, integrity and availability of user content, as well as the privacy of user relationships. Cachet uses a distributed pool of nodes to store user data and ensure availability. Storage nodes in Cachet are untrusted; we leverage cryptographic techniques such as attribute-based encryption to protect the confidentiality of data. For efficient dissemination and retrieval of data, Cachet uses a hybrid structured-unstructured overlay paradigm in which a conventional distributed hash table is augmented with social links between users. Social contacts in our system act as caches to store recent updates in the social network and help reduce the cryptographic as well as the communication overhead in the network.

We built a prototype implementation of Cachet in the FreePastry simulator. To demonstrate the functionality of existing OSNs we implemented the 'newsfeed' application. Our evaluation demonstrates that (a) decentralized architectures for privacy preserving social networking are feasible,

and (b) use of social contacts for object caching results in significant performance improvements.

Categories and Subject Descriptors

C.2.4 [**Computer-Communication Networks**]: Distributed Systems—Distributed Applications; K.6.m [**Management of Computing and Information Systems**]: Miscellaneous—Security

General Terms

Algorithms, Security

Keywords

privacy, peer-to-peer systems, social networking, caching

1. INTRODUCTION

In the last decade, online social networks (OSNs) such as Facebook, Google+, and Twitter have revolutionized the way our society communicates and have become the de facto mechanism for information sharing between users. Their user bases exceed hundreds of millions of users and their adoption is still growing at a rapid pace.[1]

However, the success of OSNs has come at the cost of user privacy. Users are not in control of their data and depend on the OSN operator to protect their sensitive information. Users' expectations of privacy are often at odds with the operator's business incentives, and, in fact, several providers have been caught selling user data [53]. Moreover, the privacy policies of OSNs are often hard to understand, and constant changes therein further magnify this problem [48]. Additionally, existing centralized architectures present a single point of failure in the system. Any vulnerability in these systems (or even accidental leaks) can be exploited by a malicious adversary to obtain unencrypted sensitive user data.

This lack of user privacy in deployed OSNs has spurred research into the design of mechanisms for privacy-preserving social networking. Some work has focused on using cryptography to protect the contents stored by a centralized OSN provider [7, 17, 30]; our view, however, is that this does not sufficiently protect users' privacy as it allows the provider to learn user relationships and patterns of interactions by

---

[1] http://newsroom.fb.com/

means of traffic analysis. Decentralized architectures can address this issue, yet present a new series of challenges, as in addition to confidentiality and integrity protection that cryptography can provide, it is necessary to ensure the availability of and efficient access to data that is necessary to support common OSN functionality, such as a 'newsfeed'.

Previous work on decentralized OSNs [3, 7, 13, 18, 22, 40] has explored several design decisions: how nodes are organized (in a structured distributed hash table (DHT) or with links between social contacts), where content is stored (by the owner, social contacts, or in a DHT), how it is disseminated (push or pull), and how access control is enforced (cryptographically or with online authentication). We argue that to efficiently support the complex functionality of an OSN, a combination of methods must be used. For example, replicating data at random DHT nodes ensures its availability even when users are offline; however, assembling a newsfeed requires thousands of DHT lookups and, as we saw in our preliminary work [32], can take hundreds of seconds to generate. Likewise, encrypting stored content can provide strong confidentiality guarantees, yet we found that we need online authentication of updates and annotations to ensure the availability of data. Furthermore, attribute-based encryption schemes that provide highly flexible policies are computationally expensive and contribute significantly to the above performance overhead.

In our preliminary design [32], we showed how the confidentiality and integrity of data can be protected by a cryptographic mechanism so that they can be stored in untrusted nodes of a DHT. However, the design suffers from performance issues that arise due to the fetching and decryption of hundreds of small objects belonging to friends, which is required for viewing their walls or for viewing one's own newsfeed. We therefore propose Cachet, a decentralized architecture for social networks that provides strong security and privacy guarantees while efficiently supporting the central functionality of OSNs. Central to Cachet is a hybrid structured-unstructured overlay in which a conventional distributed hash table is augmented with social links between users. We use the distributed hash table as a base storage layer, but add a gossip-based social caching algorithm that dramatically increases performance. New updates are immediately propagated to online social contacts. When an offline user comes back online a presence protocol is used to locate online contacts and query them directly for updates. Additionally, these contacts are used to retrieve cached updates from mutual contacts who are offline as well as speed the discovery of other online contacts. The DHT is then used to retrieve updates that may not be cached, ensuring high availability of data. As mentioned earlier, while several works have been proposed for privacy-enhanced OSNs, Cachet is the first that offers a comprehensive design for OSNs that combines decentralization, attribute-based encryption, and the use of caches to provide high availability, low latencies, and flexible policies for protecting data.

Data in Cachet are stored in container objects that include content, such as status updates and photos, as well as references to other containers; authorized contacts can add comments or other annotations to containers. A container is protected by a cryptographic structure that ensures confidentiality and integrity while supporting multi-principal interactions without revealing policies or user relationships to the storage nodes. The structure includes two components:

cryptographic capabilities used by the storage nodes to authenticate update requests and attribute-based encryption used to provide flexible and fine-grained access policies. To reduce computational overhead cached containers are stored in decrypted form and are shared with other contacts upon verifying that they satisfy the corresponding access policy; as such, containers must be decrypted only when fetched directly from the DHT. Storage nodes are trusted only to provide availability of the data with replication used to defend against node failures or intentional misbehavior.

We develop a prototype implementation of Cachet in the FreePastry simulator [51]. To demonstrate the functionality of existing OSNs, we also build and evaluate the newsfeed application. Our results show the importance of using social caching, which reduces the latency of displaying a newsfeed from hundreds of seconds in the base architecture to less than 10. Our architecture thus demonstrates how a careful combination of several distributed systems and cryptographic techniques can be used to provide a compelling privacy-preserving alternative to centralized OSNs.

2. REQUIREMENTS AND PROPERTIES

Functional Model. At a high level OSN functionality consists primarily of users sharing some form of content with their contacts, who then view, comment on, and annotate it. To support this generic functionality, we define a *container object* that consists of a main content object and a list of annotations. The main content can take many types, such as a status, a web URL, a photo, or a collection of container objects (e.g., a photo album, or a 'wall'). Annotations take the form of references to other container objects. A key application common in OSNs is a 'newsfeed', which aggregates and displays recent updates from a user's social contacts; implementing such a newsfeed efficiently is a key challenge in a decentralized OSN.

The container also becomes the unit of access control, with a potentially different set of permissions associated with a container, internally referenced objects, and each individual annotation. Access policies can be defined over social contacts and their attributes, as well as social network distance (e.g., 'friend-of-friend'). Usable access controls in OSNs remain an area of active research [19, 26, 38], so a highly flexible and fine-grained permissions architecture is necessary to support future developments in this field.

Security Requirements. The primary security requirements are confidentiality and integrity of user data, stored in distributed and untrusted storage nodes, and availability of the correct and latest version of the data. Users should be able to have complete control over the permissions to content they create and no user should be able to access content unless explicitly authorized by the owner. Finally, user relationships should remain hidden from third parties, such as the storage nodes.

Threat Model. We assume that the participants in the decentralized OSN may be malicious (or compromised), Byzantine, and capable of launching both active and passive attacks. Distributed systems are vulnerable to the problem of Sybil attacks [24]. However, existing mechanisms are available to defend against them [15, 37]. We consider that up to 25% of the nodes in the system can be malicious, since, beyond that, existing mechanisms [15] are not able to securely route in distributed hash tables, which is a necessary prerequisite to provide both integrity and availability guarantees. We also assume the existence of mechanisms to defend against denial-of-service (DoS) attacks [25, 49].

3. BASE ARCHITECTURE

Our efficient newsfeed algorithm builds on our preliminary work, which describes a basic storage architecture for decentralized social networks [32].

In our base architecture, privacy is provided through a combination of design features including a DHT for decentralization, cryptography to enforce attribute-based policies, and data representation in terms of objects. Users can define relationships of various types asymmetrically. The basic prototype supports user profile and wall features including status updates, wall posts from social contacts, commenting on posts, and a basic newsfeed algorithm. Existing OSNs such as Facebook, Google+, and Twitter feature such functionality as a major use case.

3.1 Policies

Policies are described through user identities or attributes, as required. Identity-based policies define user-specific access, whereas attribute-based (AB) policies define access for a group of social contacts sharing some common features. AB policies represent formulas over attributes, using operators such as $\wedge$, $\vee$, and k-of-n. Examples of AB policy are: $(friend \wedge coworker) \vee family$, and $2\ of\ \{friend, family, coworker\}$.

Each object is protected with three policies: 1) *Read Policy*, defined through user attributes, describes who can view an object; 2) *Write Policy*, generally set to the object owner's identity, describes who can delete or overwrite the object; and 3) *Append Policy*, an attribute-based policy, defines who can append to an object—in other words, who can comment on an object.

These policies are defined by the owner at the time of object creation and stored in the object metadata. The Read Policy is enforced through the use of cryptography. The Write and Append Policies are enforced through a combination of cryptography and authorization by DHT nodes. The authorization does not reveal a user's identity, hence the storage node is not aware of the identities of users storing or retrieving data from it, and therefore a user's social graph is hidden from the storage nodes. DHT nodes also implement a special append operation that adds a new annotation to the object while leaving existing content unmodified.

3.2 Cryptography

Access policies are enforced cryptographically through a hybrid scheme of traditional public key and attribute-based encryption (ABE) [11, 31]. In ABE an object is encrypted with an AB policy; for example, $P = friend \wedge family$. Each of the intended parties is issued a unique secret key by a key authority defining what attributes apply to that person. For example, a person *Alice* may receive a key with the attributes *"friend"*, *"colleague"*. A person can decrypt an object if and only if her secret key satisfies the policy used to encrypt it (the object). In the hybrid mode, the message is encrypted with a randomly chosen symmetric encryption key, which is in turn encrypted with ABE. In the previous example, Alice cannot decrypt a ciphertext that was encrypted with P since her key does not satisfy the policy P.

We place the Read Policy in the object reference rather than the object itself to protect policy privacy from the storage nodes. The main motivation for this choice is that the version of ABE we are using lacks policy privacy and this approach keeps the policy hidden from untrusted storage nodes. The reference is a part of the parent object and is encrypted with its symmetric key. As a result, the reference cannot reveal the policy. Therefore, confidentiality is ensured through a hybrid approach where the object is encrypted with a symmetric key, and the symmetric key, placed as a part of the reference, is encrypted with ABE. The ABE scheme that we use is an extended version of EASiER, which supports efficient revocation for Ciphertext Policy Attribute-based Encryption [11] with the help of a minimally trusted proxy. Please refer to this extended scheme [31] for further details on the cryptographic scheme.

Integrity of objects is guaranteed through digital signatures. Object owners sign the content of the object. The Write and Append policies are enforced by controlling access to the corresponding signature keys. The Write Policy key is generally encrypted to the object owner, and the Append Policy key is encrypted with an attribute-based policy. The public part of the Write Policy key is also made available as a part of the object reference to ensure its authenticity and prevent vandalism from the storage node. Comment references are signed by commenters using Append Policy keys, thus ensuring the integrity of the comment. Note that when someone comments on an object, status, for example, both the commenter and the status owner's policies are enforced since each of the objects is encrypted using the policies defined by its owner.

An object reference is constructed as follows:

$$objRef \stackrel{\text{def}}{=} (objID, \text{ABE}(K, P), WPK)$$

where *objID* is a random object identifier used to locate it in the DHT, K is the symmetric key used to encrypt the referenced object, P is the read policy, and WPK is the Write-Policy signature public key. $ABE(K, P)$ represents ABEncryption of K with the policy P.

3.3 Data Storage

In the base architecture, users form a DHT, such as Pastry [51] or Kademlia [41]. Data is stored as an object in the DHT using *objID* as the DHT key. In addition to the standard *get* and *put* operations, the DHT also supports an *append* operation. Additionally, the storage nodes verify the Write Policy on objects.

Several security and privacy issues are taken care of through existing mechanisms: lookups can be secured against attacks [5, 15, 33, 46]; availability is ensured through replication; and malicious data overwrites are prevented through write-policy verification. The write policy prevents malicious users from creating modifications that will be accepted by the readers, as they cannot produce a correct signature, but they may overwrite and destroy legitimate data. To address this, the write-policy public key is stored unencrypted as part of the object metadata. The storage node will refuse to overwrite the stored object unless the new data is properly signed by the write-policy key; deletions must likewise be authenticated with a signature. The write policy public key is random and unique for each object to prevent linking an object to its owner.

3.4 Newsfeed

A user's newsfeed is a collection of the latest *status update objects* from each of her social contacts. To provide users with their newsfeed, we designed a basic newsfeed algorithm in our base architecture. However, the algorithm in the base architecture is inefficient — the latest status update objects are fetched sequentially, and each of them is decrypted individually, which makes viewing the newsfeed non-practical. This means that if a user has hundreds of social contacts, then she has to wait until all of her contacts' latest status update objects are fetched and decrypted. In addition, users have to decrypt the wall objects of all of their social contacts and decrypt the most recent reference on the wall. In Cachet though, the update object contains a link to the most recent update and the user does not need to decrypt the potentially large wall object. Additionally, since the ABE format contains the policy necessary for decryption, users can infer whether they will be able to decrypt the object or not and do not need to spend time decrypting the object if they are not authorized to read it.

Decryption is time-consuming. Besides, we do not perform any type of caching or utilize social links to expedite the loading of a user's newsfeed in the base architecture. Furthermore, in practice a user may not be interested in viewing all of her contacts' latest statuses, but subscribe to a few selected ones instead. In Section 4 we will present our enhanced design in which social contacts are employed to cache update objects and a social caching algorithm is used to provide faster access to the objects.

3.5 Example

User Alice joins Cachet by generating several keys, creating profile information and a wall, and saving this information as root and wall objects (respectively) in the DHT. To establish the relationship *friend, co-worker* with Bob, Alice generates an ABE secret key for Bob with the attributes *friend, co-worker*. Bob may establish a different type of relationship with Alice. The necessary keys are exchanged out-of-band.

Figure 1 shows an example object structure. To post a status update to her wall, Alice creates a status object, complete with version number, contents, and public and secret keys for the Write and Append policies (WPK_1, WSK_1, APK_1, ASK_1). She generates a signature over the Write-policy signature key (WSK_1). She then picks a random symmetric encryption key K_1 and encrypts the object (except for WPK_1 and APK_1) and the signature. She also chooses a random ID ID_1 and uses this to insert the object into the DHT. Finally, she creates a reference to the status update, including ID_1, K_1, and her Write-Policy public key (WPK_1) and adds it to her wall.

When Bob wants to read Alice's update, he finds the reference on Alice's wall and decrypts K_1 with his attribute-based secret key that he got from Alice. He then retrieves the object from the DHT with the key ID_1 and decrypts the encrypted fields using K_1. Finally, he verifies the signature to ensure the integrity of the object. To comment, Bob first creates a comment object following a process similar to Alice's creation of her update. He then uses the *append* operation to insert a reference to the new object into Alice's update. Assuming he satisfies the A-policy AP_1, Bob decrypts ASK_1 and uses it to generate a signature on the reference.

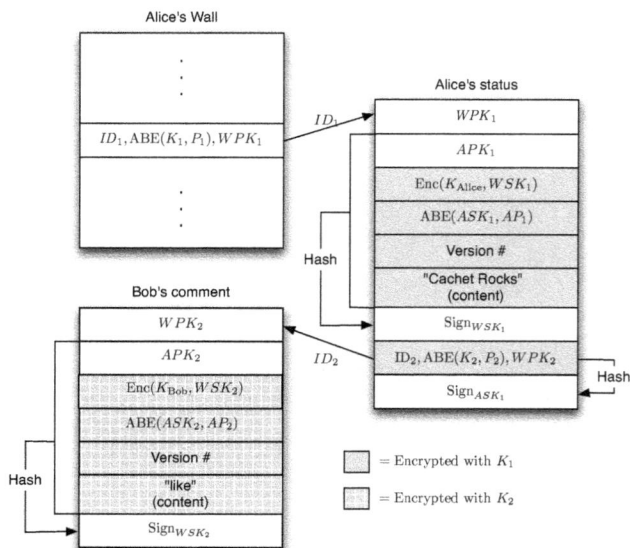

Figure 1: Example objects

Please refer to our prior workshop paper for further details [32].

4. SOCIAL CACHING

Given the use of decentralization and cryptography in our base architecture, downloading and reconstructing a social contact's wall or an aggregated newsfeed is a lengthy process requiring the following steps: 1) decrypting update objects, which are ABEncrypted, to yield metadata such as an update's DHT key and symmetric decryption key; 2) accessing multiple small objects located in different storage nodes using DHT keys provided in the previous step; and 3) decrypting the retrieved update objects with their corresponding symmetric keys. Our preliminary analysis [32] indicates that these operations can take hundreds of seconds, and thus the design needs to be improved for practical deployments.

We propose a gossip-based social caching algorithm that, in combination with an underlying DHT, leverages social trust relationships for dramatically increased performance and reliability. Nodes maintain continuous secure (SSL) connections with online contacts to receive updates directly as soon as they are produced. We describe a presence protocol, which itself uses social caching for finding online contacts. Since ABDecryption of objects is a time-consuming bottleneck, online social contacts who satisfy the ABE policy are leveraged to provide cached, decrypted objects to other contacts who also satisfy the policy for objects related to offline contacts. We emphasize that a data object is not cached by a social contact unless he/she satisfies the ABE policy. Thus, the original ABE policies provided by our base architecture are also preserved by Cachet. The basic object structure in Cachet is extended to include a list of users' IDs that are authorized to decrypt and read the object. Therefore, an object can be forwarded to/cached by the intersection set of one's social contacts and the users in the attached list, and the ABE policies are honored as before.

Our algorithm also seeks to minimize the number of such decryptions (corresponding to DHT lookups for the objects) by dynamically learning which peers yield the most cached objects. Yet, this approach provides reliability by treating the DHT as a persistent store for objects that may not be cached. Moreover, social caching improves data locality because the social contacts of a user are usually geographically co-located, which minimizes the needed bandwidth for downloading an object.

Gossip-based protocols are reliable and robust tools for data dissemination especially when used in P2P and wireless networks [9, 10, 20, 29, 42]. However, relying purely on gossip protocols for disseminating updates through the social network has some drawbacks: 1) redundant information is passed around and stored in the network, even at nodes that do not desire this information; and 2) social circles have correlated patterns of online presence, making it challenging to ensure availability when large parts of a circle are offline.

4.1 Presence Protocol

Usually a centralized server keeps track of users' presence information (e.g., their current IP address) in P2P networks [3, 52]. In Cachet a distributed approach is applied where every peer stores a presence object in the DHT so that social contacts can obtain a peer's presence information at any time. The presence object has the same structure as other objects, and is ABEncrypted so that the storage node cannot learn the contents of the presence object.[2] It contains the peer's current IP address, and port. With this IP address, peers can connect to their social contacts directly and maintain live connections. The object is signed so that the storage node only allows the owner to update or rewrite it. Whenever a peer joins or leaves the Cachet network, it updates its presence information.

Note that retrieving and decrypting presence objects for all of one's social contacts will have overhead similar to constructing a newsfeed directly from the DHT. To speed up this process presence objects are cached using gossip-based social caching along with content updates. As such, once a few social contacts have been located, discovery of other contacts can proceed at an accelerated pace. Once links to online contacts have been established, subsequent updates are pushed to online contacts directly using the caching protocol described next.

4.2 Gossip-based Social Caching

When a node comes online and joins the Cachet network, it does not have the presence or newsfeed information for any of its social contacts. We now describe the caching algorithm used to progressively retrieve cached, unencrypted versions of these objects to greatly speed up the process of loading the newsfeed. The basic idea of the caching algorithm is for the user to perform a few DHT lookups to get presence objects of some social contacts. Then, she identifies those who are online and contacts them to 1) inform them that she is online, and 2) pull both the cached presence objects and the cached recent updates of their mutual social contacts. The user then uses the new unencrypted presence objects to recursively repeat the two steps above until no new contacts are obtained. At this point another DHT lookup is made for a social contact whose status is unknown and the process is repeated until the presence and status objects of all contacts have been obtained. If a user is contacted by a social contact Q who was offline before,

she pushes her all cached objects that Q is authorized to read. This algorithm is thus a pull-push based gossiping algorithm because it involves both operations; a joining node pulls information from online nodes, and a node generating an update pushes them to other online nodes.

Algorithms 1 and 2 are employed by a user P when she joins the social network and the algorithm includes the following steps:

1. *Creating the Presence Table*: User P maintains a presence table that lists all social contacts along with their presence statuses. The social contacts are listed in descending order based on the number of mutual social contacts in common with P — a social contact who has the most mutual social contacts in common with P appears at top of the list. Listing social contacts in descending order of mutual contacts is a greedy approach that attempts to minimize the number of DHT lookups and communications that are needed to retrieve data objects. Thus, by contacting the social contacts on top of the table, more data objects can be potentially obtained. Initially, the presence status for all contacts is *undefined*.

2. *Selecting a Contact*: P chooses an unvisited contact Q from the presence list as follows. P chooses the first contact in the presence table whose status is known to be online. If none exist, then it chooses the top contact with an undefined status. If all contacts are visited or known to be offline, P proceeds to step 7;

3. *DHT Lookup and Connection*: If the presence status of Q is undefined, then P retrieves Q's presence object from the DHT and decrypts it. If Q is offline, then it returns to step 2 to select another contact;

4. *Pulling Information*: Since Q is online, P marks Q as visited and creates a secure connection to Q. P uses this connection to pull presence and update objects for mutual social contacts that P and Q have in common;

5. *Caching Information*: P caches the pulled objects (in unencrypted form). We assume that the object cache is unlimited and can store all social contacts' updates during a session. As argued by Mega et al. [42] most of the objects such as status, posts, comments, links, and pictures are small enough; large objects such as videos can be retrieved from the DHT or online services (e.g., YouTube) on demand only;

6. *Updating Presence Table*: P updates the presence table with the online status of social contacts based on information learned from Q. Then it returns to Step 2 to locate the next social contact to connect to;

7. *Performing DHT Lookups for Offline social contacts with No Mutual Social Contacts*: If the recent updates of some social contacts are missing, then this shows that they do not have any online mutual social contacts with P, and P must obtain these objects from the DHT. Thus, to retrieve the newsfeed, P needs to 1) derive the key for their updates by ABDecryption of their reference embedded in the parent/containing object; 2) perform DHT lookups for them; and 3) decrypt the updates by their corresponding symmetric key.

---

[2]It could be a separate object or simply embedded in the profile or root object.

By exchanging presence status and recent updates between online social contacts, the presence table and the cache are always up-to-date. Thus, for viewing the newsfeed, peer P just retrieves recent updates from the cache.

4.3 Identifying Mutual Contacts and Authorized Users

Many of the benefits of social caching come from being able to identify mutual social contacts. Although relationships between users are privacy sensitive, in practice many users are comfortable sharing this information with at least their immediate social circle. For further privacy protection it is possible to use a social contact discovery protocol that reveals only mutual social contact relationships and nothing else [21].

Since cached content is stored unencrypted, it is also important to verify that a contact satisfies the access policy associated with the object. It should be possible to extend the private contact discovery protocol to learn the attributes shared by P and Q and thus make an authorization decision based on that.[3] For simplicity, however, in our current implementation we instead include an explicit list of authorized users in each container that can be used to mediate sharing.

We note that users who wish to conceal their social relationships, or reveal only a selected subset, may do so, trading off privacy for the efficiency of social caching.

Algorithm 1: User P joins the network

```
1
2   //User P joins the network
3   generatePresenceTable(table);
4   socialCachingAlg(table, cache);
5   for(social contact Q : table.keySet()){
6     if(!cache.contains(Q.update)){
7       getDHTKeyFor(Q.update);
8       encUpdate = dhtLookUp(Q, Q.updateObj);
9       update = decrypt(encUpdate);
10      cache.put(Q, update);
11    }
12  }
```

Algorithm 2: Social caching algorithm

```
1
2   void socialCachingAlg(presenceTable table,
3     Cache cache){
4     for(SocialContact Q : table.keySet()){
5       Q.visited = TRUE;
6       dhtLookUp(Q, Q.presenceObj);
7       if(Q.presence.status){
8         sendTo(Q, Q.presenceObj);
9         receiveMessageFrom(Q, bufr);
10        if(bufr.contains(presenceObj))
11          updateTable(table, bufr);
12        if(bufr.contains(UpdateObj))
13          selectUpdatesToKeep(cache, bufr);
14      }
15      SocialContact R = selectSocialContact(&table);
16      socialCachingAlg(R, table);
17  }
```

4.4 Deletion and Revocation

When a user deletes an object or modifies the access policy to an object (including changes to a social contact's at-

tributes) these changes are reflected immediately for data that are ABEncrypted and fetched from the DHT. Affected data in the caches must be updated or invalidated. While we do not specify the protocol here, in short: users can send *object invalidation requests* to remove deleted objects from caches, and *revocation requests* to update the access policies for cached objects, i.e., the list of names to be removed from the access lists for various objects. We leave the evaluation of such deletion and revocation to future work.

5. EVALUATION

In this section, we evaluate the performance of our presence and social-caching algorithms. We do not compare Cachet's performance with other caching mechanisms [12, 36, 42, 56, 59] since they are not specifically designed for providing security and privacy as in our setting.

5.1 Implementation and Simulation Setup

We built a simulator for Cachet based on the FreePastry simulator [51], which implements the underlying DHT. We simulate the cryptographic operations for EASiER [31] with 1 attribute policy and 100 revocations run on a standard machine with 2.40GHz Intel Core 2 Duo, 4GB memory, and running Ubuntu 10.04. With this setting, the ABDecryption takes 422ms. The symmetric key decryption (openssl aes-128-enc) takes 0.04ms on a file of size 2500 bytes, the average size of a status update object. We simulated the communication overhead between peers by setting the average communication latency to be 180 ms.[4] To simulate the social graph in Cachet, we used the Facebook friendship graph from the New Orleans regional network [54]. This data set contains a list of all of the user-to-user links from the Facebook New Orleans network and consists of 63,732 nodes and 1.54 million edges. This data set has been used for simulating social graphs in other published work [43,47,55].

We evaluated the performance of Cachet by averaging results over the following unit experiment: we used FreePastry to setup a DHT amongst all nodes in the social network, except a particular random user P. We then generate updates for the entire social circle of node P, and simulate Cachet's algorithms. Although our system could be used to cache comments on objects as well, for evaluation we considered a model where newsfeeds include status updates only; we assume a usage model where users click on a particular item to fetch specific comments for that item.

Next we introduce churn in the network, and consider different percentages of nodes amongst P's social contacts and FoFs that remain online — 10%, 30% and 50%. We focus on an online/offline model where different percentages of online friends will affect the caching performance. We note that we are not attempting to evaluate the impact of churn at the DHT layer. In this work we are assessing the effect of nodes joining/leaving and impacting the performance at the caching layer based on how many social, trusted contacts are available. Due to the lack of pertinent data about online/offline patterns in OSNs, we picked various percentages. The 10–30% range is perhaps more pertinent because, for example, Skype has about 45M concurrent users online and 200M active users per month.[5]

---

[3]Briefly, instead of a contact certificate as in [21] one would use a (contact,attribute) certificate for each attribute.

[4]http://pdos.csail.mit.edu/p2psim/kingdata/

[5]Skype Reaches A 45M Concurrent User Peak, And What

We then simulate the node join process for node P, and measure the performance of the newsfeed application.

Performance metrics. We measure performance using the following metrics.

- *Hit Rate*: the percentage of the newsfeed or the presence objects that has been provided by social contacts. To measure worst-case performance, we assume that the number of updates on a user's newsfeed is equal to the number of her social contacts.

  Let e_m be a single unit experiment for a user u with m social contacts. Let d be the number of DHT lookups (involving ABDecryptions) that have been performed for obtaining either u's newsfeed or u's social contacts' presence objects, then:

  $$hitRate(e_m) = \frac{m-d}{m}$$

  This metric measures what fraction of objects were found in the cache.

- *Progressive Hit Rate*: the percentage of the newsfeed or the presence status objects that have been obtained after d DHT lookups and pulling social contacts' cached objects. Let e_m be a single unit experiment for a user, u, who should retrieved presence information of m social contacts and let $\sigma(d)$ be the number of obtained social contacts' presence or status objects after d DHT lookups, then:

  $$hitRate(e_m) = \frac{\sigma(d)}{m}$$

  This metric gives an indication of what percentage of the total objects have been obtained after some number of lookups.

5.2   Results

- *Social caching provides most of the update objects for viewing the newsfeed*

  Figure 2(a) depicts the average *Newsfeed Hit Rate* as a function of number of updates (equal to the number of social contacts of a person) and the fraction of online social contacts. As it is expected, the Newsfeed Hit Rate increases with a larger percentage of online social contacts. However, interestingly, retrieving a larger newsfeed where each of its objects corresponds to a social contact does not decrease the Newsfeed Hit Rate, because more online social contacts are available to push the cached data to the user.

  We repeated a slightly different experiment where online FoFs are also be contacted by a user to get cached objects belong to their mutual offline social contacts by adding them to the presence table. Although Figure 2(b) shows that leveraging FoFs increases the hit rate slightly, the difference is not very high. Thus, we decided to not include FoFs in our algorithm given the additional overhead of caching FoF objects.

  These figures are dependent on the social network graph, and they show what fraction of updates can be provided by social contacts using the social caching algorithm. The results indicate that by using social caching one can rely on her social network to provide most of her newsfeed objects. However, social caching alone is insufficient to

  Looks Like A New Stage Of Momentum, TechCrunch, Oct. 14, 2012.

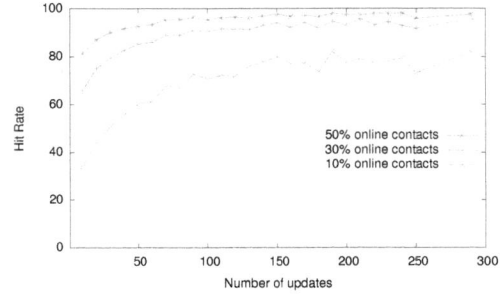

(a) Only social contacts are contacted

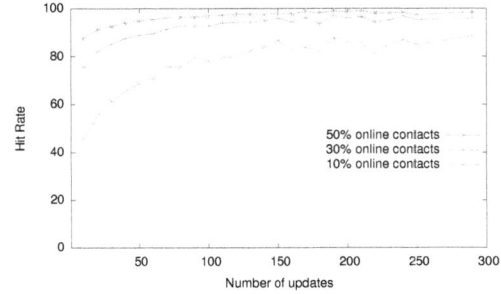

(b) Social Contacts and if needed FoFs are contacted

Figure 2: These figures depict the average *Newsfeed Hit Rate* as a function of the number of updates and the fraction of online social contacts. It can be seen that social caching provides most of the update objects needed for viewing the newsfeed. By comparing the two figures it can be seen that leveraging FoFs increases the hit rate slightly, but the difference is not great.

ensure availability of the complete newsfeed, necessitating the DHT storage layer.

- *Social caching decreases the latency for retrieving the newsfeed*

  The results illustrated in Figure 2 imply that with social caching, the latency for viewing the newsfeed would be much lower than loading all objects from the DHT and decrypting them. To investigate, we examined the latency for retrieving the newsfeed in Cachet both with and without social caching enabled.

  To calculate the latency, in each single experiment, we considered the simulation time for 1) the communication latency between peers, 2) ABDecrypting the references to both presence and update objects that are not provided by social contacts, 3) performing DHT lookups for retrieving these objects, and 4) decrypting the objects.

  Figure 3 shows that using just the base architecture, the latency for obtaining newsfeed is very high and is also highly dependent on the number of updates; it is also dominated by the ABDecryption latency time. In contrast, applying social caching, the latency decreases by up to an order of magnitude. The time needed to view a newsfeed decreases as the number of online social contacts grows, but even with only 10% of social contacts online,

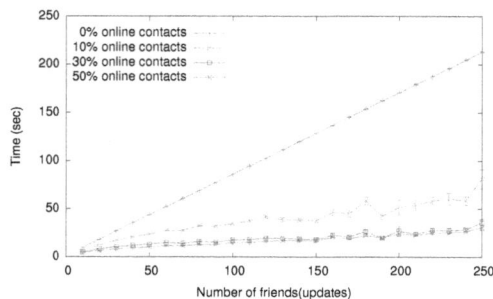

Figure 3: This Figure shows the latency for retrieving the newsfeed in Cachet both with and without social caching enabled. It can be seen that even with only 10% of social contacts online, social caching provides a dramatic performance improvement.

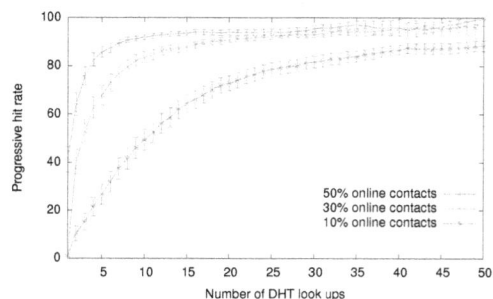

Figure 4: This Figure shows the *Average Progressive Hit Rate* for users who have 100 to 200 social contacts. It can be seen that after a few DHT lookups, users learn about online/offline status of most of thier social contacts. Similarly, most of newsfeed updates can be retrieved after performing a few DHT lookups and contacting the identified online social contacts.

social caching provides a dramatic performance improvement.

- *Most of the presence objects would be available after a few DHT lookups and decryptions*

We measured the number of presence (or newsfeed update) objects that is provided by online social contacts after contacting them. Figure 4 plots the *Average Progressive Hit Rate* after d DHT lookups and ABDecryptions. For this experiment, we plotted the *Average Progressive Hit Rate* for users with $100 \leq m \leq 200$ where m is one's number of social contacts. As it can be seen, having 50%, 30%, and 10% online social contacts, one can receive about 70% of all presence objects by performing about 2, 5, and 18 DHT lookups (and ABDecryptions) respectively.

This figure shows that users do not need to wait until all presence (or update) objects are retrieved. Furthermore, they can identify most online social contacts (and their updates) by looking up only a few presence (or update) objects and contacting the social contacts who are identified to be online. Thus, user perceived latency can be reduced by rendering the newsfeed when a threshold number of objects are retrieved, and then the feed is updated as more objects are fetched. For example, with 30% online social contacts, 70% of the newsfeed can be loaded after only a tenth of the total lookups, corresponding to load times of the majority of the newsfeed in under a second.

6. RELATED WORK

6.1 Access Control in Decentralized OSNs

Researchers have designed and proposed several decentralized OSNs such as Diaspora [22], PeerSon [13], Safebook [18], LotusNet [3], SCOPE [40], and Persona [7]. These works do not focus on caching or leveraging social links for fast and efficient data retrieval, but address privacy either through cryptography, architectural modifications, or decentralization of the provider. We have shown that in the absence of social caching, the performance overhead due to cryptography and decentralization is high.

Diaspora is a social network that users install on their own personal web servers without support for encryption. We note that Diaspora is a deployed system with several hundreds of thousands of users [58] and demonstrates the fea-

sibility of large scale decentralized approaches to social networking. Backes et al. [6] present a core API for social networking, which can also constitute a plug-in for distributed OSNs. Their primary focus is on an API that supports anonymous data access in a distributed OSN. However, they assume that the server is trusted with the data for access control. PeerSon, LotusNet, Safebook, and SCOPE benefit from DHTs in their architecture. PeerSon and Safebook suggest access control through encryption, but they fall short in providing fine-grained policies compared to ABE-based access control in Cachet. Moreover, in all of these schemes, the overhead of key revocation affects performance whereas revocation in Cachet is efficient through the use of a semi-trusted proxy (please refer to the base architecture [32]).

In LotusNet, which is based on Likir [4], the authors consider the distributed storage to be trusted and do not perform encryption. Likir uses signed grants to specify permissions and provide access control. Safebook is based on a peer-to-peer overlay network named "Matryoshka". The end-to-end privacy in Matryoshka is provided by leveraging existing hop-by-hop trust of the links. In contrast to using hop-by-hop trust for data lookup and privacy, we leverage trust relationships to improve performance and ensure privacy using cryptographic techniques.

SCOPE is a distributed data management system for specialized P2P social networks. Clients connect to and store data on a group of super-nodes with higher computation and storage capacity. However, clients do not participate in the DHT; only the super-nodes run the DHT code. Clients connect to super-nodes and rely on them for sharing and access control on their data.

Persona [7] combines ABE with a decentralized OSN architecture to ensure data confidentiality. However, Persona does not support fine-grained policies and lacks suitable revocation mechanisms [11]. Persona is not built upon a DHT; users and applications use a storage service hosted on a dedicated storage server or a user's own storage server. The storage service authenticates write operations through the requester's public key and hence can learn the user's social contacts.

We note that some techniques leverage a centralized

provider for maintaining the overall functionality of an OSN but encrypt messages to keep them confidential from the provider [8, 27, 39]. These approaches, however, allow the OSN provider to monitor the interactions of users, censor or remove content by users, and even regulate who can be part of the network. Cachet and the other decentralized solutions attempt to democratize such systems by getting rid of such a powerful centralized provider.

6.2 Information Dissemination in OSNs

One approach for disseminating information in a network is based on gossiping techniques. Mostly, this approach has been applied for disseminating information through wireless networks [9, 28, 29, 44] and P2P networks [34, 35, 60]. However, very few have done research on dissemination of information through decentralized social networks.

Datta and Sharma propose GoDisco [20], a gossip-based decentralized mechanism in which information can be disseminated by using social links and exploiting semantic context. This mechanism is targeted at probabilistic publish/-subscribe systems where a vector of interest categories is attached to each message, and information is broadcast to receivers who may be interested in the message. This mechanism is thus orthogonal to our work — while GoDisco disseminates *public* information to *interested* parties, Cachet focuses on disseminating *private* information to *authorized* parties.

Abbas et al. [1] propose a basic gossip-based protocol for establishing friendship links in a distributed social network considering network dynamics. However, many requirements of social networks, such as dissemination of updates, availability of data, and privacy were not in the scope of their work.

Mega et al. [42] show that applying gossiping algorithms for disseminating users' updates through a P2P social network is feasible. They focus their analysis on the coverage of disseminated updates to the social network, average latency for an update to reach a destination, and the average load in terms of messages sent and received. They do not consider privacy or access control in their design and updates are pushed to all friends and FoFs. In addition, their system relies purely on gossiping protocols for disseminating updates through the social network, which has several drawbacks; for example, there is no guarantee that all updates will be available over time, and a large amount of redundant information is passed around and stored in the network. In Cachet though, updates are stored in the DHT so available over time and friends cache updates for a short time.

Carrasco et al. [14] address the problem of loading newsfeeds efficiently in *centralized* social networks, where data is stored in distributed databases (e.g., at a data center). They propose partitioning the social network based on users activities over time so that data belonging to users in a partition can be stored in a way that improves locality. The proposed solution implicitly assumes that a centralized management system keeps track of all users over time to facilitate on data partitioning, but such information is not available in decentralized social networks. Nevertheless, distributed algorithms to improve locality of information in the context of decentralized social networks could improve newsfeed performance, and we leave such an exploration to future work.

7. DISCUSSION

Searching social contacts. To enable users to search for their social contacts, we propose leveraging a centralized directory service that maintains the mapping between user names and their root objects (profile page). To prevent the directory service from inferring user relationships, users can either (a) use anonymous communication channels such as Tor [23] to query the server, or (b) leverage private information retrieval protocols [16] to hide the user name mapping that is being retrieved from the server.

Privacy issues. While we believe that Cachet's privacy guarantees surpass existing systems, there is still room for further improvement. First, users that do not satisfy the access control policy of a particular object will be aware that they are being excluded from accessing the object, as opposed to being oblivious to its existence (as in current OSNs). Second, our social caching algorithm leaks information about the identities of users who satisfy a particular policy to all of those identities. Finally, our newsfeed algorithm also reveals information about when a user comes online or offline. However, we emphasize that "online" does not necessarily mean that users are logged in and available. It could be that the person's laptop/desktop is connected to the Internet and participating in the DHT and caching protocol, although the person is not at the computer. In future work we will investigate techniques to limit such sources of information leakage.

Deployment challenges. In contrast to the deployment model of today's popular OSNs, users in Cachet face the burden of (a) spending additional computational resources, and (b) volunteering data storage and bandwidth. However, we note that our social gossiping and caching algorithms make the computational overhead of decrypting ABEncrypted objects practical. Furthermore, online social networks are mostly used to store small objects such as status posts and comments, minimizing the burden for users to volunteer excessive storage and bandwidth.

The decentralized architecture of Cachet brings with it several challenges from a networking viewpoint. First, resilience against node churn becomes an important consideration. The underlying DHT should have enough replication to handle temporary instabilities. We note that data objects are also available through our caching mechanism to alleviate instability issues due to churn. In future work we will study the use of less structured overlay topologies, e.g., the use of more stable 'super peers' [2, 40, 50, 57] to further improve stability. Second, users behind NAT make it difficult to realize peer-to-peer connections with other users. Our architecture requires NAT hole-punching mechanisms, such as that of Evans et al. [45].

Social and economic challenges. Existing OSNs such as Facebook and Google+ already have several hundred million users. Thus a significant challenge for new social network architectures is to be able to attract enough users to achieve a critical mass. We believe that enhanced privacy properties of decentralized architectures such as Cachet would give an incentive to users to switch. Furthermore, government regulations or standards encouraging inter-operable OSN architectures can also help to offset the economic challenges for deployment.

Scalability issues. DHTs are designed to be scalable, but as the network becomes very large, e.g., with one billion nodes, scalability concerns are valid — nodes will be involved in more overhead for maintaining the DHT structure, and the amount of cached objects may be larger. We leave such evaluations to future work but comment that our caching algorithm scales with the number of friends, and thus we do not expect the large network size to overly affect the performance of our caching algorithm.

8. CONCLUSION

We have presented Cachet, a decentralized architecture for social networks that provides strong security and privacy guarantees while efficiently supporting the central functionality of OSNs. Cachet uses an object-oriented design for flexible data management, attribute-based cryptography for access control, and a hybrid combination of distributed hash table and social contacts for information retrieval. The use of social contacts is the key to making the architecture practical; social contacts in Cachet not only provide information about their own updates, but also about updates from other mutual contacts. Our experimental evaluation using the FreePastry simulator shows that the average time to reconstruct an aggregate newsfeed is less than 10 seconds, as compared with hundreds of seconds without the use of social caching. Our architecture thus demonstrates that a decentralized approach to privacy-preserving social networking is practical.

9. ACKNOWLEDGMENTS

This material is based upon work supported by the National Science Foundation under Awards CNS–0953655 and CNS–1115693, by the Boeing Trusted Software Center at the University of Illinois and by the National Security Agency. We thank John McCurley for his editorial help, and also anonymous reviewers for their useful comments. We also thank our shepherd Cristina Nita-Rotaru.

10. REFERENCES

[1] S. M. A. Abbas, J. A. Pouwelse, D. H. J. Epema, and H. J. Sips. A gossip-based distributed social networking system. In *Proceedings of the 2009 18th IEEE International Workshops on Enabling Technologies: Infrastructures for Collaborative Enterprises*, WETICE '09, pages 93–98, Washington, DC, USA, 2009.

[2] D. Adami, C. Callegari, S. Giordano, M. Pagano, and T. Pepe. A real-time algorithm for skype traffic detection and classification. In S. Balandin, D. Moltchanov, and Y. Koucheryavy, editors, *Smart Spaces and Next Generation Wired/Wireless Networking*, volume 5764 of *Lecture Notes in Computer Science*. Springer Berlin / Heidelberg, 2009.

[3] L. Aiello and G. Ruffo. LotusNet: tunable privacy for distributed online social network services. *Computer Communications*, 35(1):75–88, 2012.

[4] L. M. Aiello, M. Milanesio, G. Ruffo, and R. Schifanella. Tempering Kademlia with a robust identity based system. In *P2P*, 2008.

[5] M. S. Artigas, P. G. Lopez, J. P. Ahullo, and A. F. G. Skarmeta. Cyclone: A novel design schema for hierarchical DHTs. In *P2P*, pages 49–56, Washington, DC, USA, 2005. IEEE Computer Society.

[6] M. Backes, M. Maffei, and K. Pecina. A security API for distributed social networks. In *NDSS*, 2011.

[7] R. Baden, A. Bender, N. Spring, B. Bhattacharjee, and D. Starin. Persona: an online social network with user-defined privacy. In *ACM SIGCOMM*, 2009.

[8] F. Beato, M. Kohlweiss, and K. Wouters. Scramble! your social network data. In *Proceedings of the 11th international conference on Privacy enhancing technologies*, PETS'11, pages 211–225, Berlin, Heidelberg, 2011. Springer-Verlag.

[9] S. Ben Mokhtar, A. Pace, and V. Quema. FireSpam: Spam Resilient Gossiping in the BAR Model. In *29th IEEE Symposium on Reliable Distributed Systems (SRDS 2010)*, Nov. 2010.

[10] M. Bertier, D. Frey, R. Guerraoui, A.-M. Kermarrec, and V. Leroy. The GOSSPLE anonymous social network. In *Proceedings of the ACM/IFIP/USENIX 11th International Conference on Middleware*, Middleware '10, pages 191–211. Springer-Verlag, 2010.

[11] J. Bethencourt, A. Sahai, and B. Waters. Ciphertext-policy attribute-based encryption. In *IEEE Security & Privacy*, 2007.

[12] S. Borst, V. Gupta, and A. Walid. Distributed caching algorithms for content distribution networks. In *Proceedings of the 29th conference on Information communications*, INFOCOM'10. IEEE Press, 2010.

[13] S. Buchegger, D. Schiöberg, L. H. Vu, and A. Datta. PeerSoN: P2P social networking — early experiences and insights. In *SNS*, 2009.

[14] B. Carrasco, Y. Lu, and J. M. F. da Trindade. Partitioning social networks for time-dependent queries. In *Proceedings of the 4th Workshop on Social Network Systems*, SNS '11. ACM, 2011.

[15] M. Castro, P. Druschel, A. Ganesh, A. Rowstron, and D. Wallach. Secure routing for structured peer-to-peer overlay networks. In *OSDI*, 2002.

[16] B. Chor, E. Kushilevitz, O. Goldreich, and M. Sudan. Private information retrieval. *J. ACM*, 45(6), 1998.

[17] E. D. Cristofaro, C. Soriente, G. Tsudik, and A. Williams. Hummingbird: Privacy at the time of Twitter. *IACR Cryptology ePrint Archive*, 2011:640, 2011.

[18] L. A. Cutillo, R. Molva, and T. Strufe. Safebook: Feasibility of transitive cooperation for privacy on a decentralized social network. In *WOWMOM*, 2009.

[19] G. Danezis. Inferring privacy policies for social networking services. In *Proceedings of the 2nd ACM workshop on Security and artificial intelligence*, AISec '09, pages 5–10, New York, NY, USA, 2009. ACM.

[20] A. Datta and R. Sharma. GoDisco: Selective gossip based dissemination of information in social community based overlays. In *ICDCN'11*, pages 227–238, 2011.

[21] E. De Cristofaro, M. Manulis, and B. Poettering. Private discovery of common social contacts. In *9th International Conference on Applied Cryptography and Network Security (ACNS)*, volume 6715 of *LNCS*, pages 147–165. Springer, 2011.

[22] Diaspora*. https://joindiaspora.com/.

[23] R. Dingledine, N. Mathewson, and P. F. Syverson. Tor: The second-generation onion router. In *USENIX Security Symposium*, 2004.

[24] J. Douceur. The Sybil Attack. In P. Druschel, F. Kaashoek, and A. Rowstron, editors, *International Workshop on Peer-to-Peer Systems (IPTPS)*, volume 2429 of *Lecture Notes in Computer Science*, pages 251–260. Springer, Mar. 2002.

[25] D. Dumitriu, E. Knightly, A. Kuzmanovic, I. Stoica, and W. Zwaenepoel. Denial-of-service resilience in peer-to-peer file sharing systems. In *ACM SIGMETRICS*, 2005.

[26] L. Fang and K. LeFevre. Privacy wizards for social networking sites. In *Proceedings of the 19th international conference on World wide web*, WWW '10, pages 351–360, New York, NY, USA, 2010. ACM.

[27] A. J. Feldman, A. Blankstein, M. J. Freedman, and E. W. Felten. Social networking with Frientegrity: privacy and integrity with an untrusted provider. In *Proceedings of the 21st USENIX conference on Security symposium*, Security'12, Berkeley, CA, USA, 2012. USENIX Association.

[28] D. Gavidia. A gossip-based distributed news service for wireless mesh networks. In *In Proc. 3rd IEEE Conf. on Wireless On demand Network Syst. and Services (WONS '06*, pages 59–67. IEEE Computer Society, 2006.

[29] D. Gavidia, G. P. Jesi, C. Gamage, and M. van Steen. Canning spam in gossip wireless networks. In *Procedings of the 4th IEEE Conference on Wireless On demand Network Systems and Services (WONS)*, Jan. 2007.

[30] S. Guha, K. Tang, and P. Francis. NOYB: privacy in online social networks. In *Proceedings of the first workshop on Online social networks*, WOSN '08, pages 49–54. ACM, 2008.

[31] S. Jahid, P. Mittal, and N. Borisov. EASiER: Encryption-based access control in social networks with efficient revocation. In *ASIACCS*, 2011.

[32] S. Jahid, S. Nilizadeh, P. Mittal, N. Borisov, and A. Kapadia. DECENT: A decentralized architecture for enforcing privacy in online social networks. In *SESOC*, 2012.

[33] A. Kapadia and N. Triandopoulos. Halo: High-Assurance Locate for Distributed Hash Tables. In *NDSS*, 2008.

[34] D. Kempe, A. Dobra, and J. Gehrke. Gossip-based computation of aggregate information. In *Proceedings of the 44th Annual IEEE Symposium on Foundations of Computer Science*, FOCS '03. IEEE Computer Society, 2003.

[35] A.-M. Kermarrec and M. van Steen. Gossiping in distributed systems. *SIGOPS Oper. Syst. Rev.*, 41(5):2–7, Oct. 2007.

[36] B. Klein and H. Hlavacs. A socially aware caching mechanism for encounter networks. *Telecommunication Systems*, 2011.

[37] C. Lesniewski-Laas and M. F. Kaashoek. Whanau: a Sybil-proof distributed hash table. In *NSDI*, 2010.

[38] Y. Liu, K. P. Gummadi, B. Krishnamurthy, and A. Mislove. Analyzing Facebook privacy settings: user expectations vs. reality. In *Proceedings of the 2011 ACM SIGCOMM conference on Internet measurement conference*, IMC '11, pages 61–70, New York, NY, USA, 2011. ACM.

[39] M. M. Lucas and N. Borisov. FlyByNight: mitigating the privacy risks of social networking. In *Proceedings of the 7th ACM workshop on Privacy in the electronic society*, WPES '08, New York, NY, USA, 2008. ACM.

[40] M. Mani, A.-M. Nguyen, and N. Crespi. SCOPE: A prototype for spontaneous P2P social networking. In *PerCom Workshops*, 2010.

[41] P. Maymounkov and D. Mazières. Kademlia: A peer-to-peer information system based on the XOR metric. In *IPTPS*, 2002.

[42] G. Mega, A. Montresor, and G. P. Picco. Efficient dissemination in decentralized social networks. In *Peer-to-Peer Computing*, pages 338–347, 2011.

[43] P. Mittal, M. Caesar, and N. Borisov. X-Vine: Secure and pseudonymous routing using social networks. In *NDSS*, 2012.

[44] E. Modiano, D. Shah, and G. Zussman. Maximizing throughput in wireless networks via gossiping. In *Proceedings of the joint international conference on Measurement and modeling of computer systems*, SIGMETRICS '06/Performance '06. ACM, 2006.

[45] A. Müller, N. Evans, C. Grothoff, and S. Kamkar. Autonomous nat traversal. In *10th IEEE International Conference on Peer-to-Peer Computing (IEEE P2P 2010)*, pages 61–64. IEEE, 2010.

[46] A. Nambiar and M. Wright. Salsa: a structured approach to large-scale anonymity. In *ACM CCS*, 2006.

[47] S. Nilizadeh, N. Alam, N. Husted, and A. Kapadia. Pythia: a privacy aware, peer-to-peer network for social search. In *Proceedings of the 10th annual ACM workshop on Privacy in the electronic society*, WPES '11, pages 43–48, New York, NY, USA, 2011. ACM.

[48] K. Opsahl. Facebook's eroding privacy policy: A timeline. https://www.eff.org/deeplinks/2010/04/facebook-timeline.

[49] I. Osipkov, P. Wang, and N. Hopper. Robust accounting in decentralized P2P storage systems. In *ICDCS*, 2006.

[50] J. A. Pouwelse, P. Garbacki, J. Wang, A. Bakker, J. Yang, A. Iosup, D. H. J. Epema, M. Reinders, M. R. van Steen, and H. J. Sips. TRIBLER: a social-based peer-to-peer system: Research articles. *Concurr. Comput. : Pract. Exper.*, 20(2):127–138, 2008.

[51] A. Rowstron and P. Druschel. Pastry: Scalable distributed object location and routing for large-scale peer-to-peer systems. In *Middleware*, 2001.

[52] Skype. http://www.skype.com/.

[53] E. Steel and J. E. Vascellaro. Facebook, MySpace confront privacy loophole. The Wall Street Journal, May 2010.

[54] B. Viswanath, A. Mislove, M. Cha, and K. P. Gummadi. On the evolution of user interaction in Facebook. In *Proceedings of the 2nd ACM SIGCOMM Workshop on Social Networks (WOSN'09)*, August 2009.

[55] B. Viswanath, A. Post, K. P. Gummadi, and A. Mislove. An analysis of social network-based sybil defenses. In *Proceedings of the ACM SIGCOMM 2010 conference*, SIGCOMM '10, pages 363–374, New York, NY, USA, 2010. ACM.

[56] C. Wang, L. Xiao, Y. Liu, and P. Zheng. Distributed

caching and adaptive search in multilayer P2P networks. In *Proceedings of the 24th International Conference on Distributed Computing Systems (ICDCS'04)*, ICDCS '04. IEEE Computer Society, 2004.

[57] Z. Xu and Y. Hu. SBARC: A supernode based peer-to-peer file sharing system. In *Computers and Communication, 2003.(ISCC 2003). Proceedings. Eighth IEEE International Symposium on*, pages 1053–1058. IEEE, 2003.

[58] H. Zhang and S. Vasudevan. Design and analysis of a choking strategy for coalitions in data swarming systems. In *INFOCOM*, 2012.

[59] J. Zhao, P. Zhang, and G. Cao. On cooperative caching in wireless P2P networks. In *Proceedings of the 2008 The 28th International Conference on Distributed Computing Systems*, ICDCS '08. IEEE Computer Society, 2008.

[60] R. Zhou and K. Hwang. Gossip-based reputation aggregation for unstructured peer-to-peer networks. *Parallel and Distributed Processing Symposium, International*, 0, 2007.

BotFinder: Finding Bots in Network Traffic Without Deep Packet Inspection

Florian Tegeler
University of Göttingen
tegeler@cs.uni-goettingen.de

Xiaoming Fu
University of Göttingen
fu@cs.uni-goettingen.de

Giovanni Vigna
UC Santa Barbara
vigna@cs.ucsb.edu

Christopher Kruegel
UC Santa Barbara
chris@cs.ucsb.edu

ABSTRACT

Bots are the root cause of many security problems on the Internet, as they send spam, steal information from infected machines, and perform distributed denial-of-service attacks. Many approaches to bot detection have been proposed, but they either rely on end-host installations, or, if they operate on network traffic, require deep packet inspection for signature matching.

In this paper, we present BOTFINDER, a novel system that detects infected hosts in a network using only high-level properties of the bot's network traffic. BOTFINDER does not rely on content analysis. Instead, it uses machine learning to identify the key features of command-and-control communication, based on observing traffic that bots produce in a controlled environment. Using these features, BOTFINDER creates models that can be deployed at network egress points to identify infected hosts. We trained our system on a number of representative bot families, and we evaluated BOTFINDER on real-world traffic datasets – most notably the Net-Flow information of a large ISP that contains more than 25 billion flows. Our results show that BOTFINDER is able to detect bots in network traffic without the need of deep packet inspection, while still achieving high detection rates with very few false positives.

Categories and Subject Descriptors

C.2.0 [General]: Security and Protection

Keywords

Malware Detection, Security, NetFlow Analysis

1. INTRODUCTION

Many security problems on today's Internet such as spam, distributed denial-of-service (DDoS) attacks, data theft, and click fraud are caused by malicious software running undetected on end-user machines. The most efficient, and arguably, most relevant kind of such malware are *bots*. The malicious software components are co-

ordinated over a *command and control (C&C)* channel by a single entity – called the *botmaster* – and form a *botnet* [5,13,29] to carry out a number of different criminal activities. Consequently, defenses against malware infections are a high priority, and the identification of infected machines is the first step to purge the Internet of bots.

Acknowledging the limitations of traditional host-based malware detection, such as anti-virus scanners, network-based bot detection approaches are increasingly deployed for complementary protection. Network devices provide a number of advantages, such as the possibility to inspect a large number of hosts without the need for any end-point software installation.

Recently, a trend toward smaller botnets [6] and a shift [11] in malware development from a for-fun activity to a for-profit business was observed. This introduces very stealthy bots with encrypted *C&C* communication and we derive three core design goals for network based solutions to capture such bots: (a) The system should be able to detect individual bot infections. (b) The system should rely only on network-flow information to be resilient to encrypted traffic, and (c) should work for stealthy bots that do not send spam or carry out DoS attacks but steal sensitive data (e.g., credit cards or login credentials).

In this paper, we present BOTFINDER, a system that detects individual, bot-infected machines by monitoring their network traffic. BOTFINDER leverages the observation that *C&C* connections associated with a particular bot family follow certain regular patterns. That is, bots of a certain family send similar traffic to their *C&C* server to request commands, and they upload information about infected hosts in a specific format. Also, repeated connections to the command and control infrastructure often follow certain timing patterns.

BOTFINDER works by automatically building multi-faceted models for *C&C* traffic of different malware families. To this end, we execute bot instances that belong to a single family in a controlled environment and record their traffic. In the next step, our system extracts features related to this traffic and uses them to build a detection model. The detection model can then be applied to unknown network traffic. When traffic is found that matches the model, we flag the host responsible for this traffic as infected.

Due to its design, BOTFINDER offers a combination of salient properties that sets it apart from previous work and fulfills the aforementioned design goals. Our solution is able to detect individual bot infections and does not correlate activity among multiple hosts during the detection phase as, for example, BotSniffer [18], Bot-Miner [16], or TAMD [37]. Moreover, such systems rely on noisy activity, such as spamming and DoS activity (for example called A-

Plane in BotMiner) which prevents the detection of stealthy bots. Yet, many existing systems [15, 17, 36] allow the detection of individual infections, but they use deep packet inspection. In contrast, BOTFINDER requires only high-level (NetFlow-like [5]) information about network connections; it does not inspect payloads. Thus, it is resilient to the presence of encrypted bot communication, and it can process network-level information (e.g., NetFlow) that is typically easier to obtain than full-packet dumps (because of the privacy concerns of network operators).

We evaluated our approach by generating detection models for a number of botnet families. These families are currently active in the wild, and make use of a mix of different infection and *C&C* strategies. Our results show that BOTFINDER is able to detect malicious traffic from these bots with high accuracy. We also applied our detection models to traffic collected both on an academic computer laboratory network and a large ISP network (with tens of billions of flows), demonstrating that our system produces promising results with few false positives.

In summary, this paper makes the following contributions:

- We observe that *C&C* traffic of different bot families exhibits regularities (both in terms of traffic properties and timing) that can be leveraged for network-based detection of bot-infected hosts. Being independent of packet payloads, our detection approach can handle encrypted or obfuscated traffic.

- We present BOTFINDER, a learning-based approach that automatically generates bot detection models. To this end, we run bot binaries in a controlled environment and record their traffic. Using this data, we build models of characteristic network traffic features.

- We develop a prototype of BOTFINDER, and we show that the system is able to operate on high-performance networks with hundreds of thousands of active hosts and Gigabit throughput in real time. We apply BOTFINDER to real traffic traces and demonstrate its high detection rate and low false positive rate. Additionally, we show that BOTFINDER outperforms existing bot detection systems and discuss how BOTFINDER handles certain evasion strategies by adaptive attackers.

2. SYSTEM OVERVIEW

BOTFINDER detects malware infections in network traffic by comparing statistical features of the traffic to previously-observed bot activity. Therefore, BOTFINDER operates in two phases: a *training* phase and a *detection* phase. During the training phase, our system learns the statistical properties that are characteristic of the command and control traffic of different bot families. Then, BOTFINDER uses these statistical properties to create models that can identify similar traffic. In the detection phase, the models are applied to the traffic under investigation. This allows BOTFINDER to identify potential bot infections in the network, even when the bots use encrypted *C&C* communication.

Figure 1 depicts the various steps involved in both phases: First, we need to obtain input for our system. In the training phase, this input is generated by executing malware samples in a controlled environment (such as Anubis [2], BitBlaze [30], CWSandbox [35], or Ether [8]) and capturing the traffic that these samples produce. In the second step, we reassemble the flows[1] in the captured traffic; a step that can be omitted when NetFlow data is used instead of full packet captures. In the third step, we aggregate the flows in traces – chronologically-ordered sequences of connections between two

---

[1]We will use the words *flow* and *connection* interchangeably in this paper.

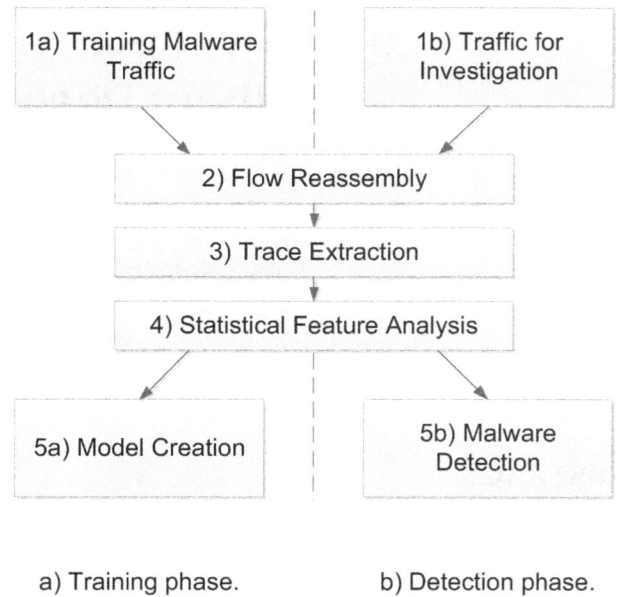

Figure 1: General architecture of BOTFINDER.

IP addresses on a given destination port. BOTFINDER then extracts five statistical features for each trace in the forth step. These statistical features are the average *time* between the start times of two subsequent flows in the trace, the average *duration* of a connection, the *number of bytes* on average transferred to the source, the number of bytes on average transferred to the destination, and a *Fourier Transformation over the flow start times* in the trace. The latter allows us to identify underlying frequencies of communication that might not be captured by using simple averages. Finally, in the fifth step, BOTFINDER leverages the aforementioned features to build models. During model creation, BOTFINDER clusters the observed feature values. Each feature is treated separately to reflect the fact that we did not always observe correlations between features: For example, a malware family might exhibit similar periodicity between their *C&C* communications, but each connection transmits a very different number of bytes. The combination of multiple clusters for each of a bot's features produces the final malware family model.

When BOTFINDER works in the detection phase, it operates on network traffic and uses the previously-created models for malware detection.

It is important to note that we do not rely on any payload information of the traffic for the whole process, but we work on the statistical properties exhibited by the command and control communication only.

3. SYSTEM DETAILS

This section provides more details on how BOTFINDER and the previously-mentioned five steps work.

3.1 Input Data Processing

The input for BOTFINDER is either a traffic capture or NetFlow data. During the training phase, malware samples are executed in a controlled environment, and all network traffic is recorded. In this step, it is important to correctly classify the malware samples

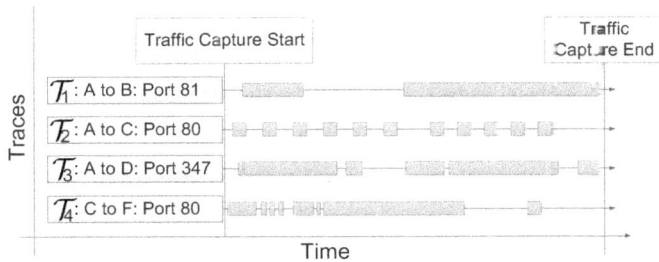

Figure 2: Traces with different statistical behaviors.

so that different samples of the same malware family are analyzed together. Our classification is based on the output of various antivirus scanners executed via VirusTotal[2] and on the results of behavioral similarity analysis in Anubis [1]. Of course, incorrectly classified samples are possible. This might affect the quality of the produced models. However, as explained later, BOTFINDER tolerates a certain amount of noise in the training data.

3.2 Flow Reassembly

If NetFlow data is available, BOTFINDER directly imports it, otherwise, we reassemble flows from captured packet data. For each connection, properties such as start and end times, the number of bytes transferred in total, and the number of packets is extracted. As a final result of this reassembly step, our system yields aggregated data similar to NetFlow, which is the industry standard for traffic monitoring and IP traffic collection. For all further processing steps, BOTFINDER only operates on these aggregated, content-agnostic data.

3.3 Trace Extraction

Traces are an important concept in BOTFINDER: A trace $\mathcal{T}$ is a sequence of chronologically-ordered flows between two network endpoints. Figure 2 illustrates different shapes of traces showing start times and durations of flows. For example, the trace $\mathcal{T}_2$ from A to C on port 80 shows a highly regular behavior. The regularity in $\mathcal{T}_2$ allows BOTFINDER to extract the recurrence and statistical features over all flows of $\mathcal{T}_2$. Here, the roughly constant distance between two flows and the similar duration of communication allows for an accurate description of the whole trace, using the average time distance between flows and their average duration.

To obtain meaningful statistical data, we require at least a minimal number of connections $|\mathcal{T}|_{min}$ (typically between 10 and 50) in a trace $\mathcal{T}$. This minimal length requirement is consistent with the fact that command-and-control traffic consists of multiple connections between the infected host and the $C\&C$ server.

A challenge in performing fully-automated analysis of malware samples is to distinguish between traces that correspond to actual command and control interactions and traces that are just additional "noise." Many bots connect to legitimate sites, for various different reasons, such as checking for network connectivity, checking for the current time, or for sending spams. Some bot variants even deliberately create noisy benign traffic to legitimate websites to cloak their own $C\&C$ communication [9,10,26] and to counter automatic signature generation systems. We use two ways to filter the traffic and identify the relevant traffic traces: First, we easily whitelist common Internet services such as Microsoft Update and Google. In addition, if available, we leverage third-party knowledge and com-

pare our training traffic (whenever un-encrypted) to known signatures or special communication patterns. Moreover, we compare the destination IP addresses to a list of known $C\&C$ servers. Another, more advanced and automated technique that allows identification of previously unknown $C\&C$ servers is JACKSTRAWS [21], an approach that leverages additional system call information from the bot sample execution. Distinguishing between $C\&C$ traffic and unrelated traces allows models to capture only characteristic bot traffic. Interestingly, when traffic that is not related to $C\&C$ connections is included into the model generation process, the resulting models are typically of low confidence (as shown later). As a result, they have little impact on the detection results.

3.4 Feature Extraction

After trace generation, BOTFINDER processes each trace to extract relevant statistical features for subsequent trace classification. We focus on the following five features:

- The average **time interval** between the start times of two subsequent flows in the trace. The botmaster has to ensure that all bots under his control receive new commands and updates frequently. Often, communication from the $C\&C$ server to the bots, following a push model, is impossible. The reason is that many infected hosts in private networks are behind NAT boxes or not registered with the $C\&C$ server yet. We assume that most bots use a constant time interval between $C\&C$ connections (or a random value within a certain, specific time interval). This leads to detectable periodicity in the communication. For the communication pattern, the botmaster has to balance the scalability and agility of his botnet with the increasing risk of detection associated with an increasing number of $C\&C$ server connections. As mentioned before, some bot variants already open random, benign connections [9, 10, 26] to distract signature generation and malware detection systems. Other approaches, such as "connect each day at time X" also suffer from issues like the requirement of synchronization between the bots' host clocks. Nevertheless, malware authors might craft their bots explicitly to not show periodic behavior. As we discuss in more detail in Section 6, mimicking random, benign traffic is hard and often detectable. Based on our observations working with different malware families, we found that a significant fraction of current malware follows our assumption and exhibit loosely periodic $C\&C$ communication.

- The average **duration** of connections. As bots often do not receive new commands, most of the communication consists of a simple handshake: The bot requests new commands and the $C\&C$ server responds that no new commands have been issued. Thus, we expect that the durations for most flows in a $C\&C$ trace are similar.

- The average number of **source bytes** and **destination bytes** per flow. By splitting up the two directions of communication using source and destination bytes, we are able to separate the request channel from the command transmission. That is, the request for an updated spam address list might always be of identical size, while the data transferred from the $C\&C$ server, containing the actual list, varies. As a result, a $C\&C$ trace might contain many flows with the same number of source bytes. Similar considerations apply to the destination bytes – for example, when the response from the $C\&C$ server has a fixed format.

- The **Fast Fourier Transformation** (FFT) over a binary sampling of the $C\&C$ communication with the goal to detect underlying communication regularities. In this step, we sample our trace like a binary signal by assigning it to be 1 at each connection start, and 0 in-between connections. To calculate a high-quality FFT, we

[2]http://www.virustotal.com

used a sampling interval of 1/4th of the smallest time interval in the trace, which ensures that we do not undersample. However, if the distance between two flows is extremely small and large gaps occur between other flows of the trace, this sampling method can lead to a significant amount of data points. In such cases, we limit the length of our FFT trace to $2^{16} = 65,536$ datapoints and accept minor undersampling. We chose this value as the FFT is fastest for a length of power of two, and, with this value, only a few datapoints in our experiments were (under)sampled as a single one. More precisely, for the observed $C\&C$ traces, 18% showed undersampling, which resulted in a median of only 1% of the start times that were sampled together.

In the next step, we compute the Power Spectral Density (PSD) of the Fast Fourier Transformation over our sampled trace and extract the most significant frequency. The FFT peaks are correlated with time periodicities and resistant against irregular large gaps in the trace (as we will show in Section 6). We observed the introduction of gaps in the wild for bots in which communication with the $C\&C$ server is periodic and then pauses for a while. When malware authors randomly vary the $C\&C$ connection frequency within a certain window, the random variation lowers the FFT peak. However, the peak remains detectable and at the same frequency, enabling the detection of the malware communication.

3.5 Model Creation (Training)

We create models via clustering of the five features: average time, average duration, average source bytes, average destination bytes, and the FFT. We process the dataset for each feature separately, as we observed malware behavior with non-correlated features. As an example of such behavior, two versions of a bot might connect to different versions of $C\&C$ servers C_1 and C_2 and transfer different amounts of bytes, depending of their version. Nevertheless, these two bot versions might still follow the same communication periodicity pattern.

After clustering, we typically observe a number of rather large clusters that contain the –suspected – actual malware-specific behavior. In addition, there are often some smaller clusters with more diverse data (lower clustering quality) and even individual traces present. These small clusters are typically related to non-$C\&C$ traffic, and our analysis drops them. A final model for a malware family contains five sets of clusters, one set for each feature. A set of clusters for a feature characterizes the expected values for this feature. In human terms, a model can be understood as:

> *An average interval between connections of 850 or 2,100 seconds, a transfer of 51kB to the source, 140 bytes to the destination, a flow duration of 0.2 or 10 seconds, and a communication frequency of around 0.0012Hz or 0.04Hz indicate a Dedler infection.*

To cluster the trace-features for a bot family, we use the CLUES (CLUstEring based on local Shrinking) algorithm [34], which allows non-parametric clustering without having to select an initial number of clusters. In short, CLUES iteratively applies gravitational clustering [23] and selects a number of clusters that complies best to a cluster strength measure such as the Silhouette index by Kaufman and Rousseuw [22].

To confirm the applicability of CLUES for BOTFINDER, we applied CLUES to our datasets and compared its clustering results with the results obtained by running the well-known k-means algorithm [20]. For our datasets, the fully automated, non-supervised CLUES algorithm typically showed the same results as manually-supervised k-means clustering. In some cases, we even found bet-

ter cluster formation than with k-means. This demonstrates that CLUES is a good candidate for our clustering scenario.

After calculating cluster centers and members, we judge the quality of each individual cluster using a quality rating function. As we tend to trust large clusters with highly similar values over smaller, more diverse clusters, we relate the standard deviation sd of the cluster with its mean c and calculate the fraction sd/c. This fraction is then used as part of an exponentially decreasing quality rating function $q_{cluster} = \exp(-\beta \cdot \frac{sd}{c})$ with a control factor β, empirically set to 2.5.

The average $q_{cluster}$ over all clusters is a measure of the overall input trace similarity. A high average cluster quality indicates that many binary samples generated highly similar traces that yield similar extracted features. If the traces are more diverse, more clusters of lower quality exists, which is, however, not necessarily a bad sign: Imagine a malware family that has a fixed interval in its periodic $C\&C$ communication but tries to evade detection by adding artificial, random traffic. As described in Section 3.3, we are trying to extract the relevant $C\&C$ communication from the traffic generated by the malware sample, yet this process is error prone. Throughout the clustering process, the fixed interval $C\&C$ communication emitted by most samples is clustered in a high quality cluster whereas the random traffic clusters very bad and generates very loose clusters with high standard deviation. Such clusters have a low quality and reduce the average cluster quality, however the cluster that captured the actual $C\&C$ communication is still of high quality and expresses the relevant malware behavior well.

3.6 Model Matching (Detection)

To check whether a trace $\mathcal{T}$ matches a given model M, we compare each statistical feature of this trace with the model's clusters that were generated in the previous steps. If, for example, the trace's average time property lies in one of M's clusters for this feature, we count this as a "hit" and increase a score γ_M. The amount by which the score γ_M is increased depends on the quality of the cluster and the quality of the (feature of the) trace. These "qualities" reflect the uncertainties inherited by trace collection and feature extraction during the previous steps. Additionally, we consider how "tight" the feature of a trace (for example, the average time) is regarding its periodicity. In general, for higher cluster qualities and tighter traces, γ_M is increased more. More precisely, we add $q_{cluster} \cdot \exp\{-\beta \frac{sd_{trace}}{avg_{trace}}\}$, with β again set to 2.5, to γ_M for all values that hit a cluster by matching its cluster center $\pm$ two times the cluster's standard deviation. The limitation to this range is primarily motivated to optimize processing speed. Mathematically the described exponential scoring function decreases very quickly, therefore comparison of any value with the cluster center would contribute nearly 0 to γ_M for values off more than twice the standard deviation.

To allow hits in multiple models M_1 and M_2 for different bot families, we maintain a γ_M for each model. Note that clusters of low quality, which are often introduced as artifacts of the training data (from traffic unrelated to $C\&C$ communication), only lead to a small increase of γ_M. In this fashion, the system implicitly compensates for some noise in the training data.

Finally, the highest γ is compared to a global pre-specified acceptance threshold a, which has to be set by the BOTFINDER administrator. If $\gamma > a$, the model is considered to have matched, and BOTFINDER raises an alarm. To reduce false positives and not rely on a single feature alone, we allow the user to specify a minimal number of feature hits h. That is, in addition to the requirement $\gamma > a$, the trace has to have matches for at least h features. This rule avoids accidental matches solely based on a single feature. For

Table 1: Malware families used for training. A high cluster quality indicates a low standard deviation within the clusters.

Family	Samples	Total Traces	Cluster Quality [0,1]
Banbra	29	29	0.99
Bifrose	33	31	0.52
Blackenergy	34	67	0.57
Dedler	23	46	0.75
Pushdo	55	106	0.49
Sasfis	14	14	0.83
Average	32	49	0.70

example, consider a trace with features "average time" and "FFT" that match the model clusters very well (so that the condition $\gamma > a$ is satisfied). By setting $h = 3$, BOTFINDER requires that an additional feature, such as the "average duration" or one of the byte transmission features, hits its respective model to actually raise an alarm.

4. TRAINING

We trained BOTFINDER on six different malware families that are a representative mix of families currently active and observed in the wild. More precisely, we picked active malware samples that we observed in Anubis within a window of 30 days in June 2011. Anubis receives and analyzes tens of thousands of samples every day. This selection process ensures that our system operates on malware that is active and relevant.

For each family, we executed on average 32 samples in a Windows XP VM in our controlled, Virtualbox[3]-based environment for one to two days and captured all network traffic. The virtual machine runs a real OS, is connected to the Internet, and contains realistic user data. Of course, we restricted SPAM and DoS attempts. The malware families used for training are:

- **Banbra**: A Trojan horse/spyware program that downloads and installs further malware components.

- **Bifrose** (also represented in Trojan variants called *Bifrost*): A family of more than 10 variants of backdoor Trojans that establish a connection to a remote host on port 81 and allow a malicious user to access the infected machine. It periodically sends the hosts status information and requests new commands.

- **Blackenergy**: A DDoS bot that communicates through HTTP requests. Blackenergy's current version 2 increased detection countermeasures, such as strong encryption and polymorphism.

- **Dedler**: A classical spambot that evolved through different versions from a simple worm that spreads through open fileshares to an advanced Trojan/spambot system. Whereas initial versions appeared already in 2004, recent versions are still prevalent and active and in the traffic traces analyzed, massive spam output was observed.

- **Pushdo** (also known as *Pandex* or *Cutwail*): An advanced DDoS and spamming botnet that is active and continuously evolving in the wild since January 2007.

- **Sasfis**: A Trojan horse that spreads via spam and allows the remote control of compromised machines. Following typical bot behavior, the C&C channel is used to transfer new commands or download additional malware to the computer.

Table 1 shows the detailed distribution of malware samples and associated malware traces. The "Cluster Quality" column reflects

the quality rating function's results. A high value implies close clusters (low standard deviation) and indicates that our core assumption holds: Different binaries of the same malware family produce similar C&C traffic, and this traffic can be effectively described using clustering techniques. However, as aforementioned, a low average cluster quality does not necessarily reflect ineffective capture of a malware's behavior. For example, the largest clusters for each feature in the Pushdo model have a high quality > 0.9. However, many small clusters with low qualities reduce the overall cluster quality. Still the large, high quality clusters give a good representation of the Pushdo behavior. For Bifrose, the clusters are in general more diverse due to higher variances in the traces generated by the malware binaries and the model has to be considered weaker than for the other bot families. For the clustering we used the default values as described in Chang et al. [4] and obtained on average 3.14 (median 3) clusters per feature for each family.

5. EVALUATION

To evaluate BOTFINDER, we performed a number of experiments on two real-world datasets (see Table 2 for a summary): The first dataset, *LabCapture*, is a full packet capture of 2.5 months of traffic of a security lab with approximately 80 lab machines. According to the lab policy, no malware-related experiments should have been executed in this environment, and the *LabCapture* should consist of only benign traffic. As we have the full traffic capture, we are also able to manually verify reported infections. The second dataset, *ISPNetFlow*, covers 37 days of NetFlow data collected from a large network. The captured data reflects around 540 Terabytes of data or 170 Megabytes per second of traffic. We are aware that we do not have ground truth for the second network dataset, as we lack the underlying, full traffic capture that would be required for full content inspection. Nevertheless, we can compare our identified hits to known malware IP blacklists, identify clusters of infected machines, and judge the usability of our approach for the daily operation of large networks.

After developing a prototype implementation, we performed the following experiments (for a detailed description please refer to the respective subsections):

- A cross-validation experiment based on our ground truth training data and the *LabCapture* dataset: In short, the training data is split into a training set and a detection set. The latter is then mixed with all traces from the *LabCapture* data that should not contain bot traces. After BOTFINDER has learned the bots' behavior on the training set, we analyzed the detection ratio and false positives in the dataset that contained both the remaining known malicious traces and the *LabCapture* data. [**Section 5.2**]

- Comparison to related work: In our case, the most relevant related work is the well-known, packet-inspection-based system *BotHunter* [17]. We performed all experiments on a set of a fraction of ground truth C&C traces mixed with the *LabCapture* dataset. [**Section 5.3**]

- *ISPNetFlow* analysis: We trained BOTFINDER on all training traces and ran it on the *ISPNetFlow* dataset in daily slices. We investigated the identified malicious traces and compared it to blacklisted malicious C&C server IPs. [**Section 5.4**]

5.1 Implementation and Performance

We implemented BOTFINDER in Python. For flow reassembly from full packet data captures, we utilized the intrusion detection system Bro [25]. Our implementation also operates on FlowTools[4]-

---

[3] http://www.virtualbox.org

[4] http://www.splintered.net/sw/flow-tools/.

Table 2: Evaluation Datasets

Name	Traffic	Internal Hosts	Concurrently Active	Start Time	Length	Connections	Long Traces
LabCapture	≈ 3.6 TB	≈ 80	≈ 60	2011-05-04	84 days	$\approx 64.3 \cdot 10^{6}$	≈ 39k
ISPNetFlow	≈ 540 TB	≈ 1M	≈ 250k	2011-05-28	37 days	$\approx 2.5 \cdot 10^{10}$	≈ 30M

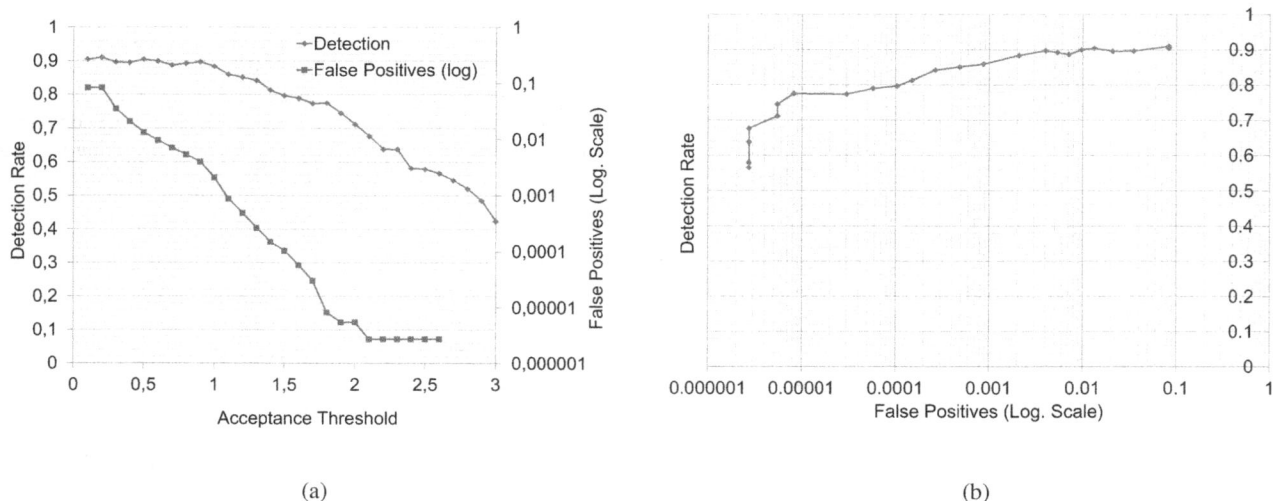

(a)   (b)

Figure 3: Detection rate and false positives of BOTFINDER in cross validation experiments.

compressed NetFlow data. BOTFINDER is able to process network information, even for high-speed Gigabit networks, in real time. In our setup, we used a lab machine equipped with an Intel Core i7 CPU with eight cores and 12GB of RAM. Using this setup, we were able to process half a billion NetFlow records or ≈ 33 GB of stored NetFlows, which reflected approximately one day of traffic in the *ISPNetFlow* dataset network, in about three hours.

As the feature extraction for a given trace $\mathcal{T}_A$ does not depend on any features of another trace $\mathcal{T}_B$, we were able to distribute the computational load of statistical analysis. Our implementation supports remote machines that receive traces to analyze, and reply with the aggregated features for these traces. On the worker site, these thin clients use Python's multiprocessing library to fully utilize all cores, especially for the FFT sampling and calculations, which we performed in the statistical computing environment R [28]. During our analysis of the large *ISPNetFlow* dataset, we used eight remote workers from our cluster (48 cores in total) for data processing and the aforementioned lab machine for data reading and analysis.

As our system allows an arbitrary number of worker CPUs, the primary bottleneck is reading and writing back to disk. Roughly, BOTFINDER requires 1.2 seconds to read $100,000$ lines of Flow-Tools compressed NetFlow and 0.8 seconds to read $100,000$ lines of Bro IP flow output. Each line represents a connection dataset. If a full packet traffic capture is analyzed, it is necessary to add the processing time for Bro to pre-process the output and create the IP flow file. Please note that all data handling and most of the processing is performed directly in Python; a native fast programming language can be expected to boost the processing performance significantly.

We used pyflowtools `http://code.google.com/p/pyflowtools/` for handling FlowTools files in Python.

5.2 Cross-Validation

To determine the detection capabilities of BOTFINDER we performed a cross-validation experiment based on our labeled ground truth training data and the *LabCapture* dataset. Both datasets were collected in the same network environment to ensure similarly capable connectivity settings. For each varying acceptance threshold a, we performed 50 independent cross-validation runs as follows:

1: We split our ground truth malware dataset (from Table 1) into a training set $\mathcal{W}$ (70% of the traces) and a detection set $\mathcal{D}$ (the remaining 30%).

2: We mixed $\mathcal{D}$ with the traces from the *LabCapture* dataset and assumed the *LabCapture* dataset to be completely infection-free, and therefore a reasonable dataset to derive the false positive ratio of BOTFINDER.

3: Further, we trained BOTFINDER and created models on the bot behavior exhibited in the traces in $\mathcal{W}$.

4: Finally, we applied these models to the mixed set combined from $\mathcal{D}$ and the *LabCapture* dataset.

The analysis is performed on a per-sample level, as we have the information of which malware binary generated a specific trace. More precisely, if one trace of a sample is correctly identified by a trace match, we count the entire sample as correctly identified; if a trace of a given malware is classified as a different malware, we consider this match as a false positive.

Figure 3 shows the detection rates for $a \in [0, 3]$ and $h = 3$. Very low acceptance thresholds yield high detection rates of above 90%, but with high false positives. For example, the false positive rate was greater than 1% for $a \leq 0.6$. As can be seen in Figure 3(a), the false positive rate decreases exponentially (near linear in

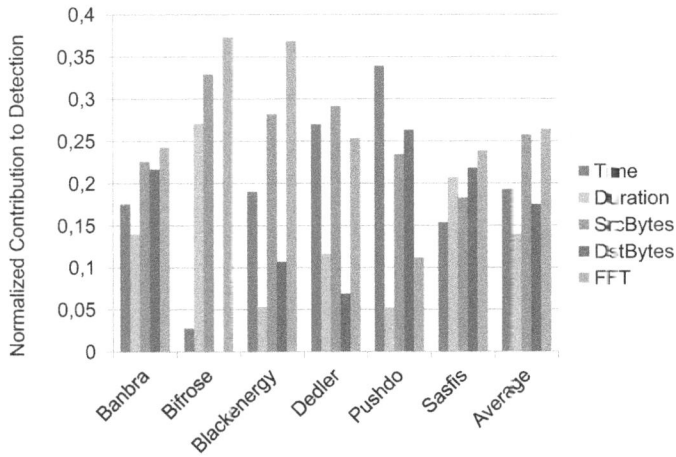

Figure 4: Normalized contribution of the different features toward a successful detection.

Table 3: Detection rate and false positive results of BOTFINDER (acceptance threshold a=1.8) in the cross-validation experiment and compared to *BotHunter*.

Malware Family	BOTFINDER Detection	BOTFINDER False Positives	*BotHunter* Detection
Banbra	100%	0	24%
Bifrose	49%	0	0%
Blackenergy	85%	2	21%
Dedler	63%	0	n/a
Pushdo	81%	0	11%
Sasfis	87%	1	0%

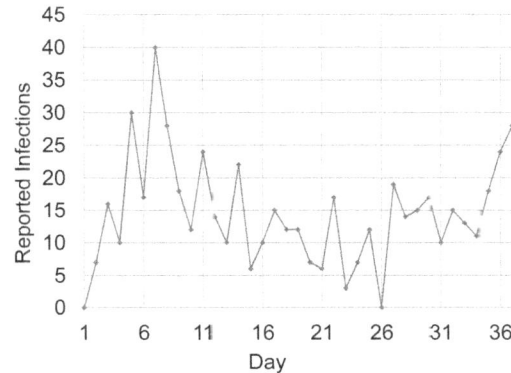

Figure 5: On average, BOTFINDER reported 15 infections per day.

logarithmic scaling) whereas the detection rate decreases roughly linearly. This yields to a good threshold of $a \in [1.7, 2.0]$ — compare the lower left corner of Figure 3(b) – with good detection rates and reasonably low false positives. For an acceptance threshold of $a = 1.8$ we achieve 77% detection rate with $5 \cdot 10^{-6}$ false positives. For this parameter, Table 3 shows the detection rates of the individual malware families, averaged over the 50 cross-validation runs. Here, all Banbra samples and $\approx 85\%$ of the Blackenergy, Pushdo and Sasfis samples were detected. The only false positives were raised by Blackenergy (2) and Sasfis (1).

As one can see, detection rates vary highly for different bot families. For example, the Banbra samples all show highly periodic behavior and are very similar, which allows for good clustering quality, and, as a consequence, 100% detection rate. Blackenergy has relatively weak clusters (high standard deviation) but is still producing a roughly similar behavior. Unfortunately, the "broader" clusters lead to a higher false positive rate. Bifrose has the lowest detection rate among the malware families analyzed, which is a result of highly diverse – and therefore low quality – clusters as described in Section 4. Additionally, the quality of the Bifrose traces themselves is lower than for other bot families due to some strong, non-periodic behavior.

Another interesting experiment is the more realistic analysis of the *LabCapture* dataset in daily intervals, similar to a system administrator checking the network daily. More precisely, the traffic captures are split into separate files spanning one day each and analyzed in slices via BOTFINDER. Overall, 14 false positives – 12 Blackenergy and 2 Pushdo – were observed over the whole 2.5 month time span.

5.2.1 Contribution of Features toward Detection

To asses the quality of BOTFINDER's detection algorithm and the weighting of the different features toward a successful detection, we extracted the normalized contribution of each feature to γ_m. Figure 4 shows the averaged contribution of each feature to successful trace-to-malware identification.

Interestingly, we found fundamentally different distributions for the bots under investigation: Whereas the bot families of Banbra and Sasfis are equally periodic – and thereby well detectable – in

each dimension, the remaining bots show significant discrepancies between the features. For Pushdo, the duration and the FFT is of lower significance for detection, which is primarily based on the average time interval and the number of bytes transmitted on average. The feature of destination bytes is of low importance for the remaining three bot families Bifrose, Blackenergy and Dedler, whereby Bifrose does not benefit from the feature at all. However, the source byte destination – the request toward the *C&C* server – highly contributes toward detection.

Of special interest is the impact of the Fast Fourier Transform, especially considering that the FFT accounts for the vast majority of the overall computational complexity of BOTFINDER. For all malware families except Dedler and Pushdo, the FFT is the most significant feature to detect a malware infection in the network traffic. Hereby, Bifrose is of special interest, as the average time feature contributes only minimally toward detection whereas the FFT contributes most. This indicates a much better quality and periodicity of underlying frequencies compared to the simple averaging – an indication that is verified under inspection of the underlying models which cluster significantly better for the FFT frequencies.

For the averaged contribution over all malware families (the rightmost bars in Figure 4), a relatively balanced contribution is observed. Still, the FFT and the source bytes dimension contribute slightly more toward successful detection than, e.g., the average duration or the destination bytes. Considering the mode of operation of typical bots, this outcome fits the concept of bots sending similar requests to the *C&C* and receive answers of changing size. Additionally, the superiority of underlying FFT frequencies over simple averages for the flow interval times can be seen.

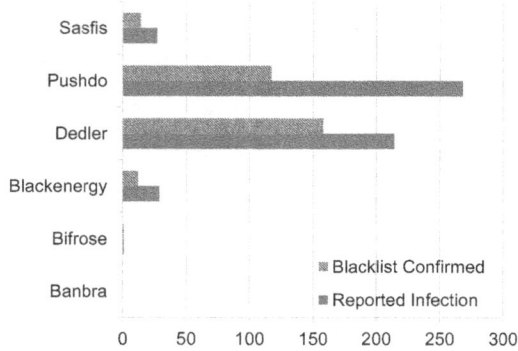

Figure 6: Reported infections by malware family. 56% of the reported malware traces had a destination IP to a know malicious, blacklisted host.

5.3 Comparison with BotHunter

Although BOTFINDER is content-agnostic, we compare our system to the well-known packet inspecting bot detection system *BotHunter* since – to the best of our knowledge – no other system allows individual bot detection in a content-agnostic manner. *BotHunter* [17] is a sophisticated bot detection system that relies on a substantially-modified Snort[5] intrusion detection system for flow identification combined with anomaly detection. It leverages detection mechanisms on the whole infection and malware execution lifecycle: Port scanning activities and dangerous binary transfers (e.g., encoded or encrypted HTTP POSTs or shell code) are used to detect the first step of the infection process. Malware downloads ("egg downloads") and, eventually, structural information regarding the command and control server plus IP blacklisting of multiple list providers are used to identify infected hosts. The later released *BotMiner* [16] adds horizontal correlation between multiple hosts, which is not in scope of this paper. Furthermore, *BotHunter* is made publicly available[6] by the authors.

We ran version 1.6.0 of *BotHunter* on full traffic dumps of our training samples and the *LabCapture* dataset. We installed the system strictly following the User Guide[7] and configured it for batch processing. We chose this *BotHunter* version as its release time fits the time of execution of our *LabCapture* traffic capture and approximates the execution time of our malware samples. As can be seen in Table 3, very few alarms were raised by *BotHunter* for the training samples. The detection rate varies between 0 and 24 percent for the different families, and we observed a high dependency on IP blacklisting for successful detection. Note that *BotHunter* had access to the full payload for the experiments, while BOTFINDER only operates on flows.

The low detection rates of *BotHunter* are – to the best of our understanding – a result of the different detection approaches and the weighting that *BotHunter* assigns to its various detection steps. *BotHunter* uses an algorithm that classifies network communication events as potential dialog steps in a malware infection process. It then correlates the observed network dialog events and compares the result to an abstract malware infection lifecycle model. Hereby, *BotHunter* works on a large number of dialog classes such as scanning, inbound attacks like web hijack attempts, DNS lookups of

the client to known *C&C* sites, egg downloads, connections to a monitored Russian Business Network site, outbound attacks and scans, P2P coordination, and outbound connections to known malware sites. As we injected the malware communication into the *LabCapture* dataset, our experimental setup does not reproduce the complete malware infection lifecycle. In particular, the victim host infection and the binary download was not observable by *BotHunter*. However, these steps seem to significantly contribute to raise the score above *BotHunter*'s predefined alarm threshold (and, since they are missing, cause *BotHunter* to miss the malicious traffic). This finding is consistent with the following analysis on the mixed dataset.

Regarding the test with *BotHunter* on the malware traces mixed with the *LabCapture* dataset, we received alarms for 41 distinct IP addresses. For four IP addresses with a significant peak of alarms, we could actually confirm a bot infection, as researchers executed malware in a bridged VM. As BOTFINDER was not trained for the specific bot family that the researcher was working on, it is not surprising that BOTFINDER missed this infection. For most IP addresses (37), we were unable to confirm an actual infection. Often, the connections were made to IRC servers (BitCoin trades) or raised because of the high NXDOMAIN activity of the University's core router. In another instance, *BotHunter* identified the download of an Ubuntu Natty ISO as an exploit (Windows Packed Executable and egg download). This shows that the number of false positives is significantly higher than those raised by our system on the same traffic.

5.4 ISPNetFlow Analysis

The *ISPNetFlow* dataset is the most challenging dataset to analyze, as we do not have much information about the associated network. We trained BOTFINDER with all available training malware traces and applied BOTFINDER to the dataset.

Overall, BOTFINDER labeled 542 traces as evidence of bot infections, which corresponds to an average of 14.6 alerts per day. This number of events can be easily handled by a system administrator, manually during daily operations or by triggering an automated user notification about potential problems. Figure 5 shows the evolution of infections over the analysis time frame, which varies from days with no infections at all to days with a maximum of 40 reported infections. Figure 6 illustrates the total number of reported incidents per bot. Pushdo and Dedler are dominating the detected infections with 268 and 214 reports, respectively, followed by Sasfis with 14 and Blackenergy with 12. Bifrose was found only once in the traffic.

We investigated the IP addresses involved in suspicious connections to judge the detection quality of BOTFINDER. We received the internal IP ranges from the *ISPNetFlow* system administrators and were able to split the set of all involved IPs into internal and external IP addresses. Only two out of the 542 traces had their source and destination IP addresses both inside the network. This indicates that our system is not generating many – most probably false – indications of internal infections where both the bot and the *C&C* server are inside the observed network. We compared the remaining 540 external IP addresses to a number of publicly available blacklists[8] and *had a positive match for 302 IPs or 56%*. This result strongly supports our hypothesis that BOTFINDER is able to identify real malware infections with a relatively low number of false positives.

Whereas the 302 blacklist-confirmed IP addresses do not strongly

---

[5]http://www.snort.org
[6]http://www.bothunter.org/
[7]http://www.bothunter.net/OnlinePDF.html

[8]The **RBLS** http://rbls.org/ service allows to analyze a large number of blacklists using a single query. We ignored "RFC-ignorant" listings.

Table 4: Top-5 aggregated clusters of non-blacklisted destination IP addresses in the *ISPNetFlow* dataset.

Size	Service or Organization
46	Apple Inc.
21	A company that offers web services and dedicated servers
7	A Russian BitTorrent tracker
6	A company that offers dedicated servers
5	NTT / Akamai

cluster to specific networks, the 238 non-confirmed IP addresses show multiple large clusters and in total, 85 IPs contribute to the Top-5 destination networks. Table 4 lists the companies or services offered by the Top-5 found in the list of not blacklisted destination IP addresses. Overall, we found 46 destination IP addresses to point to servers of the Apple Incorporation, which can be considered a false positive. Two services offer a variety of web services and advertise dedicated web servers for rent. Although only speculation, a possible cause might be malware authors that rent dedicated servers. Paying by maliciously obtained payment information allows botmasters access to *C&C* servers while hiding their trails and evading law enforcement. However, this assumption is unable to be verified in the scope of this paper. A company located in the Seychelles offers a Russian BitTorrent tracker. No information is available on the service offered at the final 5 destination IPs which point to NTT / Akamai.

If we add Apple Inc. to the whitelist, effectively a rate of 61% (302 of 496 destination IP addresses) matching blacklist-entries is observed. Considering that various not blacklisted destination IP addresses belong to rented dedicated servers or other web providers, it is a reasonable assumption that a significant fraction of the 194 not blacklisted IP addresses actually belong to malicious servers.

5.5 Summary

In our evaluation we showed that BOTFINDER

- has a detection rate around 80% for a parameter setting with low false positives,
- outperforms the content-inspection-based IDS *BotHunter*,
- is able to operate on large datasets,
- and identifies likely true positive connections to *C&C* hosts in the *ISPNetFlow* dataset.

Overall, BOTFINDER proved that the malware families under investigation exhibit a behavior regular enough to allow high detection rates using network-statistics only.

6. BOT EVOLUTION

By detecting malware without relying on deep packet (content) inspection – which is an inherently difficult task – BOTFINDER raises the bar for malware authors and might trigger a new round of bot evolution. In the following, we will introduce potential evasion techniques that malware authors might try to thwart BOTFINDER, and we discuss how we can handle these techniques.

6.1 Adding Randomness

We assume regularity in the communication between bots and their *C&C* servers and showed that this assumption holds for the bots under investigation. Nevertheless, malware authors might intentionally modify the communication patterns of their bots to evade detection, as suggested, for example, by Stinson et al. [31]. More specifically, botnet authors could randomize the time between connections from the bot to the *C&C* server or the number of bytes

that are exchanged. For the botmaster, this comes at the price of loss of network agility and degraded information propagation within the botnet. However, by using randomization techniques, the malware author effectively decreases the quality of the trace for BOTFINDER, which lowers the detection quality. Interestingly, BOTFINDER already operates on highly fluctuating traces and is, as our detection results show, robust against significant randomization around the average. To further illustrate BOTFINDER's resilience against randomization, we analyzed the *C&C* trace detection rate with (artificially) increasing randomization. A randomization of 50% means that we subtract or add up to 50% of the mean value. For example, for an interval of 100 seconds and a randomization rate of 20%, we obtain a new interval between 80 and 120 seconds. Figure 7(a) shows the effect on the detection rate of BOTFINDER with randomization on the time (impacting the "average time" and the "FFT" feature), randomization of time and "duration," and with randomized "source bytes", "destination bytes," and "duration". As can be seen, BOTFINDER's detection rate drops slightly but remains stable above 60% even when the randomization reaches 100%.

6.2 Introducing Larger Gaps

Malware authors might try to evade detection by adding longer intervals of inactivity between *C&C* connections. In this case, the Fast Fourier Transformation significantly increases BOTFINDER's detection capabilities: Due to its ability to separate different *C&C* communication periodicities, the introduction of large gaps into the trace (which impacts the average) does not significantly reduce the FFT detection rate. For a randomization between 0 and 100 percent of the base frequency, Figure 7(b) shows the fraction of FFTs that detected the correct, underlying communication frequency. As can be seen, the introduction of large, randomly distributed long gaps does not significantly reduce the detection quality of the FFT-based models.

6.3 High Fluctuation of C&C Servers

Malware programs might try to exploit the fact that BOTFINDER requires collection of a certain, minimal amount of data for analysis. Now, if the *C&C* server IP addresses are changed very frequently, BOTFINDER cannot build traces of minimal length $|\mathcal{T}|_{min} = 50$. *Currently, we do not observe such high C&C server fluctuations (IP flux) in our collected malware data.* Even a highly domain-fluxing malware, such as Torpig (as analyzed in [32]) uses two main communication intervals of 20 minutes (for upload of stolen data) and 2 hours for updating server information. Still, Torpig changes the *C&C* server domain in weekly intervals. Nevertheless, we already introduce a countermeasure (that might also help with P2P botnets) by using elements of horizontal correlation. This is an additional pre-processing step that operates before the full feature extraction (Step 4 in Figure 1). The step constructs longer traces from shorter traces (e.g, of length 20 to 49) that exhibit similar statistical features. Hereby, we again utilize the observation that *C&C* communication exhibits higher regularity than other frequent communication.

To decide whether to merge two sub-traces $\mathcal{T}_A$ and $\mathcal{T}_B$, we use two factors:

- We require that the standard deviation of the combined $\mathcal{T}_{AB}$ is lower than the standard deviation of at least one of the individual traces. Thereby, traces around a significantly different average – even with relatively low fluctuations – do not match and are automatically excluded.
- We use a quality rating function analog to the model-matching algorithm to rate each individual feature. If the sum over all

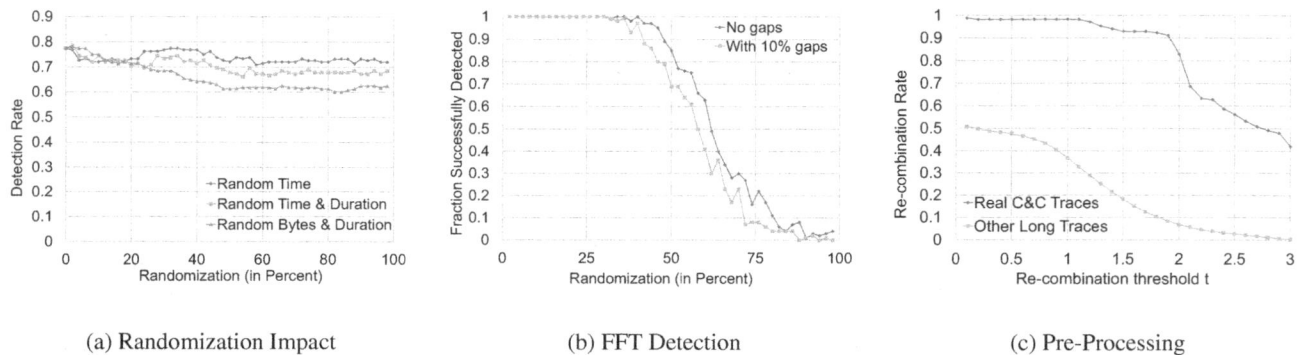

(a) Randomization Impact   (b) FFT Detection   (c) Pre-Processing

Figure 7: (a) depicts BOTFINDER's detection rate with increasing randomization, (b) summarizes the degrading of the FFT periodicity detection capability, and (c) depicts the re-combination ratio during the pre-processing step of real *C&C* and other, long traces.

feature-qualities of the combined trace $\mathcal{T}_{AB}$ is above a threshold t, we accept the trace recombination.

The lower the value of t is, the more sub-trace combinations we accept and the higher the additional workload for BOTFINDER is. We applied the presented pre-processing step on real-world data and investigated:

- The ability to re-assemble real *C&C* traces.
- The re-assembly difference between real *C&C* and other, long traces.
- The amount of additional traces that need to be analyzed by BOT-FINDER and the implied additional workload.
- The false positive ratio of the newly generated traces.

The impact of the higher periodicity of *C&C* traffic can be clearly seen in Figure 7(c), which illustrates the re-assembly rates of bisected real *C&C* traces and of long non-*C&C* traces for different acceptance thresholds t. For $t = 1.9$, BOTFINDER *re-assembled 91% of the real C&C traces* and combined only 8% of non-*C&C* long traces.

Further, when running on the 2.5 months of *LabCapture* data, we (incorrectly) re-assembled only 3.4 million new traces. Using the same detection threshold as in our evaluation ($a = 1.8$), this does not introduce any new false positives. As we would typically run pre-processing over shorter time frames – as it is a countermeasure against fast flux – even fewer new traces will be generated. For example, in a ten day NetFlow traffic set, only 0.6% of the IP addresses with more than one sub-trace generated additional traces. Computing these traces increased the workload for BOTFINDER by 85% compared to normal operation. That is, with a modest increase in overhead, BOTFINDER also covers cases where bots frequently switch IP addresses.

6.4 P2P Bots

BOTFINDER might be able to detect P2P networks by concatenating the communication to different peers in one trace. Nevertheless, complementing BOTFINDER with elements from different existing different approaches might be beneficial: BOTFINDER could be expanded by a component that creates structural behavior graphs, as proposed by Gu et al. [16, 17], or be complemented by P2P net analysis techniques similar to BotTrack [12] or BotGrep [24], which try to reveal members of a bot network by surveillance of a single member of the network. Still, completely changing to a P2P-based botnet also imposes significant challenges for the

botmaster. These include the ease of enumeration of all participating bots by every member in the botnet (for example, a honeypot-caught bot under control of a security researcher as performed by BotGrep, and the time to disseminate commands. Hence, most botnets today use a centralized infrastructure.

6.5 Bot-like Benign Traffic

Although unlikely, benign communication might accidentally exhibit a similar traffic pattern as a bot family. For example, a POP3 mail server might get queried in the same interval as a bot communicates with its *C&C* server, and the traffic sizes might accidentally match. If these services operate on a static IP, a system administrator can easily exclude these false positives by whitelisting this IP address. A local BOTFINDER installation should be configured to ignore communication between hosts under the same local authority. For popular web services with similar features, a generic whitelisting is possible.

6.6 Discussion

BOTFINDER is able to learn new communication patterns during training and is robust against the addition of randomized traffic or large gaps. Furthermore, given the pre-processing step, even changing the *C&C* server frequently is highly likely to be detected. Nevertheless, BOTFINDER is completely reliant on statistical data and regularities. If the attacker is willing to:

- significantly randomize the bot's communication pattern,
- drastically increase the communication intervals to force BOT-FINDER to capture traces over longer periods of time,
- introduce overhead traffic for source and destination byte variation,
- change the *C&C* server extremely frequently, e.g., after each tenth communication,
- use completely different traffic patterns after each *C&C* server change, then

BOTFINDER's detection fails as minimal or no statistical consistency can be found anymore. On the contrary, a malware author who implements such evasion techniques, has to trade the botnets performance in order to evade BOTFINDER: Using randomization and additional traffic increases the overhead and reduces synchronization and the network-agility of the botnet. In particular, especially the frequent change of *C&C* servers is costly and requires an increased amount of work and cost by the botmaster: Domains

358

need to be pre-registered and paid and new globally routeable IP addresses must be obtained. Hereby, the bots need to know to which $C\&C$ server to connect, so the new domains must either follow a pre-defined and malware-hardcoded pattern – which allows take-over attacks by security researchers such as in Stone-Gross et al. [32] (with a weekly changing domain) – or lists of new $C\&C$ servers need to be distributed to the members of the botnet. Both ways increase the botnet operator's costs and reduce stability and performance of the malware network.

7. RELATED WORK

Research in network based bot detection can be classified into two main directions: In *vertical correlation* the network traffic is inspected for evidence of bot infections, such as scanning, spamming or command and control communication. *BotHunter* [17], for instance, applies a combination of signature and anomaly-based intrusion detection components to detect a typical infection lifecycle, whereas Rishi [15] and Binkley et al. [3] examine and model IRC-based network traffic for nickname patterns that are frequently used by bots. Unfortunately, some of these techniques are tailored to a specific botnet structure [3, 15], or rely on the presence of a specific bot-infection lifecycle [17]. Moreover, most techniques rely on the presence of noisy behavior such as scans, spam, or DoS attack traffic. Wurzinger et al. [36] and Perdisci et al. [27] automatically generate signatures that represent the behavior of an infected host. The key point in these strategies is that bots receive commands from the bot master and then respond in specific ways that allow signature generation.

Although these approaches are shown to achieve a very high detection rate and a limited false positives ratio, they require inspecting packet content and can thus be circumvented by encrypting the $C\&C$ communication. Giroire et al. [14] presented an approach which is similar to BOTFINDER in this aspect as both focus on temporal relationships. However, our system differs fundamentally in the way malware detection is performed. In particular, Giroire's work is based on the concept of destination atoms and persistence. Destination atoms group together communication toward a common service or web-address, whereas the persistence is a multi-granular measure of destination atoms' temporal regularity. The main idea is to observe the per-host initiated connections for a certain (training) period and group them into destination atoms. Subsequently, very persistent destination atoms form a host's whitelist, which will be compared against the very persistent destination atoms found once the training session ends. Thus, very persistent destination atoms will be flagged as anomalous and potentially identify a $C\&C$ host.

The second direction is the *horizontal correlation* of network events from two or more hosts, which are involved in similar, malicious communication. Interesting approaches are represented by BotSniffer [18], BotMiner [16], TAMD [37], and the work by Strayer et al. [33]. Except the latter, which works on IRC analysis, the main strength of these systems is their independence of the underlying botnet structure, and thus, they have shown to be effective in detecting pull-, push-, and P2P-based botnets. By contrast, correlating actions performed by different hosts requires that at least two hosts in the monitored network are infected by the same bot. As a consequence, these techniques cannot detect single bot-infected hosts. In addition, the detection mechanisms require that some noisy behavior is observed [16]. Unfortunately, low-pace, non-noisy, and profit-driven behavior [11, 19] is increasing in bots as witnessed in the past few years [32].

Another way to detect P2P botnets is shown by BotGrep [24], BotTrack [12], and Coskun et al. [7] "Friends of An Enemy" (FoE),

which leverage the underlying communication infrastructure in the P2P overlay. Whereas BotGrep uses specifics of the DHT interactions, BotTrack operates on NetFlows only and is comparable to BOTFINDER in this aspect. For FoE [7], mutual communication graphs are calculated based on mutual communication without packet content inspection. However, all systems need to be bootstrapped with the botnet under investigation, typically by utilizing a participating active malware sample in a honeypot. Connections of this bot under surveillance reveal other members of the network. This requirement of an active source in the honeypot is a significant drawback. Nevertheless, concepts from these solutions might complement BOTFINDER to allow detection of P2P based bots during NetFlow analysis as well.

8. FUTURE WORK

BOTFINDER can be seen as a bot detection framework that allows improvement on multiple layers. Potential future optimizations, for example, cover:

1: The sandboxed training environment can be improved to better circumvent malware authors to probe for virtual machine settings and react by stopping all activity.

2: A separate problem – of the general anti malware research community – is the classification of malware to families. Currently we rely on Anubis signatures and VirusTotal labels which yield sufficiently good results – especially because we drop small clusters in the model building process and thereby rely only on more persistent features among multiple binary malware samples. However, more accurate classifiers will definitely benefit our system.

3: We would also like to experiment with unsupervised learning approaches in the training phase. Hereby, a machine learning algorithm might be able to select the ideal features that describe a given malware family best and weight the features correspondingly for the detection phase.

4: The malware detection might be improved by more sophisticated features that do not exploit periodicity alone but periodicity of communication sequences learned in the training phase, such as recurring three times a 20 minutes interval followed by a longer gap of 2 hours.

A substantial advantage is the fact that many improvements can be performed on the training side alone, which makes changes to any deployed BOTFINDER scanning installation unnecessary.

9. CONCLUSION

We presented BOTFINDER, a novel malware detection system that is based on statistical network flow analysis. After a fully-automated, non-supervised training phase on known bot families, BOTFINDER creates models based on the clustered statistical features of command and control communication. We showed that the general assumption of $C\&C$ communication being periodic holds and that BOTFINDER is able to detect malware infections with high detection rates of nearly 80% via traffic pattern analysis. A significant novelty is BOTFINDER's ability to detect malware without the need of IP blacklisting or deep packet inspection. BOTFINDER is therefore able to operate on fully-encrypted traffic, raising the bar for malware authors.

10. ACKNOWLEDGEMENTS

We gracefully acknowledge the help of Bryce Boe throughout the project. This work was supported by the Office of Naval Research (ONR) under Grant N000140911042, the Army Research Office (ARO) under grant W911NF0910553, and the National Science Foundation (NSF) under grants CNS-0845559 and CNS-0905537.

11. REFERENCES

[1] U. Bayer, P. M. Comparetti, C. Hlauschek, C. Kruegel, and E. Kirda. Scalable, Behavior-Based Malware Clustering. In *NDSS*, 2009.

[2] U. Bayer, C. Kruegel, and E. Kirda. Anubis: Analyzing Unknown Binaries. In *http://anubis.iseclab.org/*, 2008.

[3] J. R. Binkley. An algorithm for anomaly-based botnet detection. In *SRUTI*, 2006.

[4] F. Chang, W. Qiu, R. H. Zamar, R. Lazarus, and X. Wang. clues: An R Package for Nonparametric Clustering Based on Local Shrinking. *Journal of Statistical Software*, 33(4):1–16, 2 2010.

[5] B. Claise. Cisco systems netflow services export version 9. RFC 3954, IETF, Oct. 2004.

[6] E. Cooke, F. Jahanian, and D. McPherson. The Zombie roundup: understanding, detecting, and disrupting botnets. In *SRUTI*, 2005.

[7] B. Coskun, S. Dietrich, and N. Memon. Friends of An Enemy: Identifying Local Members of Peer-to-Peer Botnets Using Mutual Contacts. In *ACSAC*, 2010.

[8] A. Dinaburg, P. Royal, M. Sharif, and W. Lee. Ether: malware analysis via hardware virtualization extensions. In *ACM CCS*, 2008.

[9] P. Fogla and W. Lee. Evading network anomaly detection systems: formal reasoning and practical techniques. In *ACM CCS*, 2006.

[10] P. Fogla, M. Sharif, R. Perdisci, O. Kolesnikov, and W. Lee. Polymorphic blending attacks. In *USENIX Security*, 2006.

[11] J. Franklin, V. Paxson, A. Perrig, and S. Savage. An Inquiry into the Nature and Causes of the Wealth of Internet Miscreants. In *ACM CCS*, 2007.

[12] J. Franï£¡ois, S. Wang, R. State, and T. Engel. Bottrack: Tracking botnets using netflow and pagerank. In *IFIP Networking*. 2011.

[13] F. Freiling, T. Holz, and G. Wicherski. Botnet tracking: Exploring a root-cause methodology to prevent distributed denial-of-service attacks. In *ESORICS*, 2005.

[14] F. Giroire, J. Chandrashekar, N. Taft, E. M. Schooler, and D. Papagiannaki. Exploiting Temporal Persistence to Detect Covert Botnet Channels. In *RAID*, 2009.

[15] J. Goebel and T. Holz. Rishi: Identify Bot Contaminated Hosts by IRC Nickname Evaluation. In *USENIX HotBots*, 2007.

[16] G. Gu, R. Perdisci, J. Zhang, and W. Lee. BotMiner: Clustering Analysis of Network Traffic for Protocol- and Structure-Independent Botnet Detection. In *USENIX Security*, 2008.

[17] G. Gu, P. Porras, V. Yegneswaran, M. Fong, and W. Lee. BotHunter: Detecting Malware Infection Through IDS-Driven Dialog Correlation. In *USENIX Security*, 2007.

[18] G. Gu, J. Zhang, and W. Lee. BotSniffer: Detecting Botnet Command and Control Channels in Network Traffic. In *NDSS*, 2008.

[19] P. Gutmann. The Commercial Malware Industry. In *Proceedings of the DEFCON conference*, 2007.

[20] J. A. Hartigan and M. A. Wong. A k-means clustering algorithm. *JSTOR: Applied Statistics*, 28(1), 1979.

[21] G. Jacob, R. Hund, C. Kruegel, and T. Holz. Jackstraws: Picking Command and Control Connections from Bot Traffic. *USENIX Security*, 2011.

[22] L. Kaufman and P. Rousseeuw. *Finding Groups in Data An Introduction to Cluster Analysis*. Wiley Interscience, New York, 1990.

[23] S. Kundu. Gravitational clustering: a new approach based on the spatial distribution of the points. *Pattern Recognition*, 32(7):1149 – 1160, 1999.

[24] S. Nagaraja, P. Mittal, C.-Y. Hong, M. Caesar, and N. Borisov. Botgrep: finding p2p bots with structured graph analysis. In *USENIX Security*, 2010.

[25] V. Paxson. Bro: a System for Detecting Network Intruders in Real-Time. *Computer Networks*, 31(23-24):2435–2463, 1999.

[26] R. Perdisci, D. Dagon, P. Fogla, and M. Sharif. Misleading worm signature generators using deliberate noise injection. In *IEEE S&P*, 2006.

[27] R. Perdisci, W. Lee, and N. Feamster. Behavioral clustering of http-based malware and signature generation using malicious network traces. In *USENIX NSDI*, 2010.

[28] R Development Core Team. *R: A Language and Environment for Statistical Computing*. R Foundation for Statistical Computing, Vienna, Austria, 2010.

[29] M. A. Rajab, J. Zarfoss, F. Monrose, and A. Terzis. A Multifaceted Approach to Understanding the Botnet Phenomenon. In *ACM IMC*, 2006.

[30] D. Song, D. Brumley, H. Yin, J. Caballero, I. Jager, M. Kang, Z. Liang, J. Newsome, P. Poosankam, and P. Saxena. BitBlaze: A New Approach to Computer Security via Binary Analysis. In *ICISS*. 2008.

[31] E. Stinson and J. C. Mitchell. Towards systematic evaluation of the evadability of bot/botnet detection methods. In *USENIX WOOT*, 2008.

[32] B. Stone-Gross, M. Cova, L. Cavallaro, B. Gilbert, M. Szydlowski, R. Kemmerer, C. Kruegel, and G. Vigna. Your Botnet is My Botnet: Analysis of a Botnet Takeover. In *ACM CCS*, 2009.

[33] W. T. Strayer, R. Walsh, C. Livadas, and D. Lapsley. Detecting botnets with tight command and control. In *Proceedings of the 31st IEEE Conference on Local Computer Networks*, pages 195–202, 2006.

[34] X. Wang, W. Qiu, and R. H. Zamar. Clues: A non-parametric clustering method based on local shrinking. *Computational Statistics and Data Analysis*, 52(1):286 – 298, 2007.

[35] C. Willems, T. Holz, and F. Freiling. Toward Automated Dynamic Malware Analysis Using CWSandbox. *IEEE S&P*, 2007.

[36] P. Wurzinger, L. Bilge, T. Holz, J. Goebel, C. Kruegel, and E. Kirda. Automatically Generating Models for Botnet Detection. In *ESORICS*, 2009.

[37] T.-F. Yen and M. K. Reiter. Traffic Aggregation for Malware Detection. In *DIMVA*, 2008.

New Opportunities for Load Balancing in Network-Wide Intrusion Detection Systems

Victor Heorhiadi
UNC Chapel Hill
victor@cs.unc.edu

Michael K. Reiter
UNC Chapel Hill
reiter@cs.unc.edu

Vyas Sekar
Stony Brook University
vyas@cs.stonybrook.edu

ABSTRACT

As traffic volumes and the types of analysis grow, network intrusion detection systems (NIDS) face a continuous scaling challenge. Management realities, however, limit NIDS hardware upgrades to occur typically once every 3-5 years. Given that traffic patterns can change dramatically, this leaves a significant scaling challenge in the interim. This motivates the need for practical solutions that can help administrators better utilize and augment their existing NIDS infrastructure. To this end, we design a general architecture for network-wide NIDS deployment that leverages three scaling opportunities: *on-path* distribution to split responsibilities, *replicating* traffic to NIDS clusters, and *aggregating* intermediate results to split expensive NIDS processing. The challenge here is to balance both the compute load across the network and the total communication cost incurred via replication and aggregation. We implement a backwards-compatible mechanism to enable existing NIDS infrastructure to leverage these benefits. Using emulated and trace-driven evaluations on several real-world network topologies, we show that our proposal can substantially reduce the maximum computation load, provide better resilience under traffic variability, and offer improved detection coverage.

Categories and Subject Descriptors

C.2.3 [**Computer-Communication Networks**]: Network Operations—*network monitoring, network management*; C.2.0 [**Computer-Communication Networks**]: General—*Security and protection*

General Terms

Algorithms, Management, Security

Keywords

Intrusion Detection, Network Management

1. INTRODUCTION

Network intrusion detection systems play a critical role in keeping network infrastructures safe from attacks. The driving forces

for increased deployment include regulatory and policy requirements, new application traffic patterns (e.g., cloud, mobile devices), and the growing complexity of attacks [22,41]. In conjunction with these forces, the rapid growth in traffic volumes means that NIDS deployments face a continuous scaling challenge to keep up with the increasing complexity of processing and volume of traffic.

The traditional response in the NIDS community to address this scaling challenge has been along three dimensions: better algorithms (e.g., [33]); specialized hardware capabilities such as TCAMs (e.g., [42]), FPGAs (e.g., [17]), and graphics processors (e.g., [38]); and parallelism through the use of multi-core or cluster-based solutions (e.g., [37, 39]). These have been invaluable in advancing the state-of-the-art in NIDS system design. However, there is a significant delay before these advances are incorporated into production systems. Furthermore, budget constraints and management challenges mean that network administrators upgrade their NIDS infrastructure over a 3-5 year cycle [32]. Even though administrators try to provision the hardware to account for projected growth, disruptive and unforeseen patterns can increase traffic volumes. Thus, it is critical to complement the existing research in building better NIDS systems with more immediately deployable solutions.

Past work has shown that distributing responsibilities across intrusion detection systems on an end-to-end path can offer significant benefits for monitoring applications [6, 29]. This provides a way for administrators to handle higher traffic loads with their *existing* NIDS deployment without requiring a forklift upgrade to deploy new NIDS hardware. Our premise is that these past proposals for distributing monitoring functions do not push the envelope far enough. Consequently, this not only restricts the scaling opportunities, but also constrains the detection capabilities that a network-wide deployment can provide on three key dimensions:

- First, these focus on strictly *on-path* distribution. While such on-path processing is viable (e.g., [7]), there is an equally compelling trend toward consolidating computing resources using datacenter deployments within and outside enterprise networks. These offer natural management and multiplexing benefits that are ideally suited to the compute-intensive and dynamic nature of NIDS workloads. Other, concurrent work in research and in industry is motivated by similar benefits of consolidated cloud deployments for NIDS-like processing, as well [1,2,11,32].

- Second, this past work assumes that the NIDS analysis occurring at a network node is *self-contained*. That is, the NIDS nodes act as standalone entities and provide equivalent monitoring capabilities without needing to interact with other nodes. This restriction leads to certain types of aggregated analysis being topologically constrained. For example, in the case of scan detection, all traffic needs to be processed at the ingress gateway for each host [29].

- Third, prior work implicitly assumes that each NIDS node can always provide processing capabilities that are *semantically equivalent* to running the analysis at manually created chokepoints. Unfortunately, practical networking realities (e.g., asymmetric routing) may often violate such requirements; i.e., the forward and reverse flows in an end-to-end session may not always be observed at the same location for stateful NIDS processing.

Our vision is a *general* NIDS architecture that goes beyond on-path distribution to allow new scaling opportunities via traffic *replication* and analysis *aggregation*. *Replication* enables us to offload processing to lightly loaded nodes that might be off-path and accommodate trends for building consolidated compute clusters. Furthermore, replication enables new detection functionality that would have been previously infeasible. For example, our framework enables stateful NIDS analysis even when the two flows in a session do not traverse a common node. *Aggregation* allows us to split an expensive NIDS task into smaller subtasks that can then be combined to provide equivalent analysis capabilities. This enables more fine-grained scaling opportunities for NIDS analyses that would otherwise be topologically constrained (e.g., scan detection).

A key constraint here is to enable these opportunities with minimal communication costs. Thus, our goal is to assign processing responsibilities to balance the tradeoff between the communication cost imposed by replication and aggregation vs. the reduction in computation load. Our specific focus in this paper is on passive monitoring devices such as NIDS and as such replication or aggregation do not affect the latency perceived by end user applications. We envision a network-wide management module that assigns processing, aggregation, and replication responsibilities across the network [12, 19]. To systematically capture these tradeoffs, we design formal linear programming (LP) based optimization frameworks. In order to execute these management decisions without requiring modifications to existing NIDS implementations, we interpose a lightweight *shim* layer that runs on each NIDS node (or at an upstream router to which the NIDS is attached).

We evaluate our architecture and implementation using a combination of "live" emulation on Emulab [40] and trace-driven simulations on a range of real-world topologies. Our results show that a replication-enabled NIDS architecture can reduce the maximum computation load by up to $10\times$; is significantly more robust to variability in traffic patterns by reducing the peak load more than $20\times$; and can lower the detection miss rate from 90% to zero in some scenarios where routes may not be symmetric. These benefits are achieved with little overhead: computing the analysis and replication responsibilities takes < 1.6 seconds with off-the-shelf LP solvers, and our shim layer imposes very low overhead.

Contributions and Roadmap: Our contributions are:

- Identifying new replication and aggregation opportunities for NIDS scaling (Section 2).
- Formal models for balancing compute-communication tradeoffs in a general NIDS architecture that subsumes existing on-path distribution models (Section 4, Section 5, Section 6).
- A backwards-compatible architecture (Section 3) and implementation (Section 7) to realize these benefits.
- Extensive evaluation of the potential benefits over a range of real-world network topologies (Section 8).

We discuss outstanding issues in Section 9 and related work in Section 10, before concluding in Section 11.

2. MOTIVATION

In this section, we begin by describing the prior work for *on-path* distribution [29]. Then, we discuss three motivating scenarios that

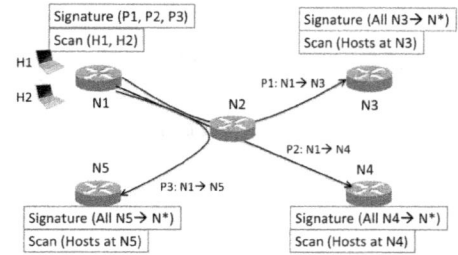

Figure 1: NIDS deployments today are single-vantage-point solutions where the ingress gateway is responsible for monitoring all traffic.

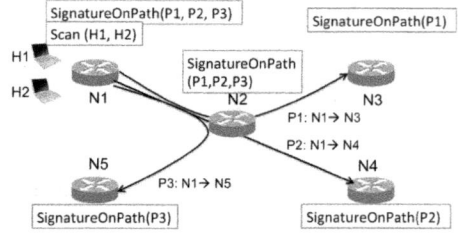

Figure 2: NIDS with on-path distribution [29]: Any node on the path can run `Signature` detection; `Scan` detection cannot be distributed.

argue for a general NIDS architecture that can incorporate traffic *replication* and analysis *aggregation*.

2.1 On-path distribution

Suppose there are two types of NIDS analysis: `Signature` for detecting malicious payloads and `Scan` for flagging hosts that contact many destination addresses. Figure 1 shows how today's NIDS deployments operate, wherein all types of analysis occur only at the gateway node. That is, node N1 runs `Scan` and `Signature` detection for all traffic to/from hosts H1–H2 on paths P1–P3; the other nodes run the corresponding analysis for the hosts for which they are the gateway nodes. A natural limitation with this architecture is that if the load exceeds the provisioned capacity on a node, then that node has to either drop some functionality (e.g., disable expensive modules) or drop packets.

A natural solution to this problem is to exploit spare resources elsewhere in the network. For example, nodes N2–N5 may have some spare compute capacity when N1 is overloaded. Prior work shows an architecture in which any node on the end-to-end path of a session can run the analysis if it can perform the analysis in a self-contained fashion without needing any post-processing [29]. Many NIDS analysis such as `Signature` detection occur at a per-session granularity. Thus, the signature detection responsibilities can be split across the nodes on each end-to-end path by dividing the sessions across the path as shown in Figure 2. This can reduce the load on node N1 by leveraging spare compute resources on N2–N5. Note, however, that the `Scan` module cannot be distributed. `Scan` detection involves counting the number of unique destinations a source contacts, which requires a complete view of all traffic to/from a given host. Thus, the ingress node alone is capable of running the analysis in a self-contained manner.

2.2 New Opportunities

Relaxing the on-path requirement: Now, the traffic on P1 might

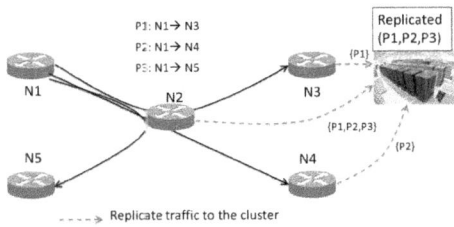

Figure 3: Replicating traffic to a compute cluster. With on-path alone, the cluster at N3 cannot be used to handle traffic on P2 and P3.

overload all nodes N1–N3 on the path. In this case, it is necessary to look for spare resources that are *off-path*. For example, nodes could locally offload some analysis to one-hop neighbors. Additionally, administrators may want to exploit compute clusters elsewhere in the network. Such consolidated clusters or datacenters are appealing because they amortize deployment and management costs.

Consider the scenario in Figure 3. The network has a compute cluster located at node N3. When the processing load on the paths P2 and P3 exceed the provisioned capacity of their on-path nodes, we can potentially replicate traffic from node N2 to node N3 and run the analysis at the cluster. This assumes that: (1) there is sufficient network bandwidth to replicate this traffic and (2) the logic to do such replication has low overhead. For (1), we note that the primary bottleneck for many NIDS deployments is typically the number of active connections and the complexity of analysis, and not volume of traffic in bytes [8]. As we will show in Section 7, we can implement a lightweight shim layer to implement (2).

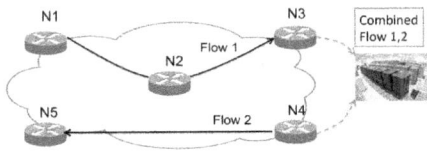

Figure 4: The analysis needs to combine Flow 1 and Flow 2 (e.g., two directions of a session or two connections in a stepping stone), but they traverse non-intersecting paths. In this case, replication is necessary to avoid detection misses.

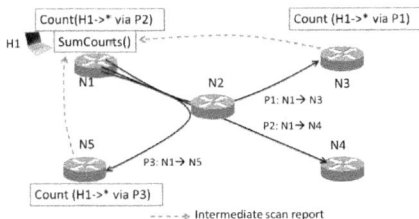

Figure 5: Aggregating intermediate results lets us distribute analyses that might be topologically constrained.

Network-wide views: Certain kinds of scenarios and analysis may need to combine traffic from different nodes. For example, "hot-potato" like effects may result in non-intersecting routing paths for the forward and reverse flows within a bidirectional session [36]. Thus, stateful NIDS analysis that needs to observe both sides of a

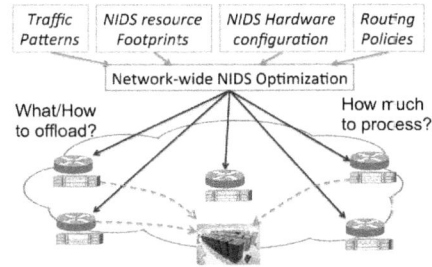

Figure 6: Network-wide framework for assigning NIDS processing and replicating responsibilities.

session is impossible. A similar scenario occurs for stepping stone detection [43], if the two stages in the stepping stone do not encounter a common NIDS node. In Figure 4, traffic flows Flow 1 and Flow 2 need to be combined, but no single node can observe both flows. Thus, we need to replicate this traffic to a common location to analyze this traffic. Similarly, certain types of anomaly detection [3, 16] require a network-wide view that no single node can provide.

Aggregation for fine-grained splitting: As we saw earlier, prior work requires each type of NIDS analysis to be self-contained. Consequently, analyses such as `Scan` detection are topologically constrained. Allowing the NIDS to communicate intermediate results provides further opportunities for distributing the load. Consider the setup in Figure 5. Each node on the path runs a subset of the `Scan` analysis. The nodes send their intermediate results to an aggregation node that eventually generates alerts. (In this example, the aggregation happens at the ingress, but that is not strictly necessary.) A natural constraint here is to ensure that the result generated after aggregation is semantically equivalent to a centralized analysis. We defer to Section 6 on how we achieve this in practice.

The above scenarios highlight the need to look beyond pure on-path opportunities for distributing NIDS responsibilities in a network. In the next section, we begin with a high-level system overview before delving into the specific formulations for incorporating replication and aggregation opportunities in subsequent sections.

3. SYSTEM OVERVIEW

Our goal is to optimally assign processing, aggregation, and replication responsibilities across the network. Optimality here involves a tradeoff between the compute load on the NIDS elements and the communication costs incurred. Next, we give an overview of the key entities and parameters involved in our framework (Figure 6).

In the spirit of many recent efforts, we assume a logically centralized management module that configures the NIDS elements (e.g., [12]). This module periodically collects information about the current traffic patterns and routing policies. Such data feeds are routinely collected for other network management tasks [9]. Based on these inputs, the module runs the optimization procedures (described later) to assign NIDS responsibilities. The optimization is run periodically (e.g., every 5 minutes) or triggered by routing or traffic changes to adapt to network dynamics. Note that the network administrators only need to specify high-level policy objectives (e.g., how much link capacity to allow for replication) and set up the optimization module to receive the relevant data feeds. Afterwards, the configuration is completely automated.

We briefly describe the high-level inputs that this network-wide NIDS controller needs:

1. *Traffic and routing patterns:* This categorizes the traffic into

different logical *classes*. Each such class may be identified by a source and destination prefix-pair and some application level ports (e.g., HTTP, IRC). Let $\mathcal{T}_c$ denote the set of end-to-end sessions of the traffic class c and let $|\mathcal{T}_c|$ denote the volume of traffic in terms of the number of sessions. We initially assume that each class has a unique symmetric routing path P_c (P for *Path*),[1] and then subsequently relax this assumption. We use the notation $N_j \in P_c$ to denote that NIDS node N_j is *on the routing path*. Note that some nodes (e.g., a dedicated cluster) could be completely off-path; i.e., it does not observe traffic on any end-to-end routing path unless some other node explicitly forwards traffic to it.

2. *Resource footprints:* Each class c may be subject to different types of NIDS analyses. For example, HTTP sessions may be analyzed by a payload signature engine and through application-specific rules, while all traffic (itself a class) might be subject to Scan analysis. We model the cost of running the NIDS for each class on a specific *resource* r (e.g., CPU cycles, resident memory) in terms of the expected per-session resource footprint F_c^r, in units suitable for that resource (F^r for *Footprint* on r). We expect these values to be relatively stable and can be obtained either via NIDS vendors' datasheets or estimated using offline benchmarks [8]. Our approach can provide significant benefits even with approximate estimates of these F_c^r values.

3. *NIDS hardware:* Each NIDS hardware device N_j is characterized by its resource capacity Cap_j^r in units suitable for the resource r. In the general case, we assume that hardware capabilities may be different across the network, e.g., because of upgraded hardware running alongside legacy equipment. $\mathcal{N}$ denotes the set of all NIDS nodes.

Communication Costs: We model communication costs in one of two ways. First, in the case of replication, we want to bound the additional *link load* imposed by the inter-NIDS communication. This addresses the concern that network administrators may have with the additional traffic introduced by replication; this ensures that we do not overload network links (and thus avoid unnecessary packet losses). Similar to the notion of a router being on the path, we use the notation $Link_l \in P_c$ to denote that the network link l is on the path P_c. Second, for aggregation, we count the total *network footprint* imposed by the inter-NIDS communication, measured in *byte-hops*. For example, if NIDS N_1 needs to send a 10KB report to NIDS N_2 four hops away, then the total footprint is $10 \times 4 = 40$ *KB-hops*.

Given this setup, we describe the formal optimization frameworks in the following sections.

4. NIDS WITH REPLICATION

As we saw in Figure 3, we can reduce the NIDS load by replicating the traffic to nodes that are off-path if they have spare resources. In this section, we provide a general framework for combining on-path distribution with off-path replication. For the discussion, we assume that the NIDS analyses run at a *session-level* granularity. This is typical of most common types of NIDS analyses in use today [24,34]. We also assume that each class has a single symmetric routing path. (We relax this in Section 5.) Figure 7 shows the LP formulation for our framework, to which we refer throughout this section.

---

[1]Different classes may share the same routing path; e.g., the classes corresponding to HTTP and IRC between the same pair of source and destination prefixes are distinct logical classes but still traverse the same path.

Minimize *LoadCost* subject to

$$LoadCost = \max_{r,j}\{Load_j^r\} \qquad (1)$$

$$\forall c: \sum_{j:N_j \in P_c} \left(p_{c,j} + \sum_{\substack{j':N_{j'} \in M_j \\ N_{j'} \notin P_c}} o_{c,j,j'}\right) = 1 \qquad (2)$$

$$\forall r,j: \ Load_j^r = \sum_{\substack{c: \\ N_j \in P_c}} \frac{F_c^r \times |\mathcal{T}_c| \times p_{c,j}}{Cap_j^r} \ + $$

$$\sum_{\substack{j',c: \\ N_j \in M_{j'}; N_j \notin P_c}} \frac{F_c^r \times |\mathcal{T}_c| \times o_{c,j',j}}{Cap_j^r} \qquad (3)$$

$$\forall l: \ LinkLoad_l = BG_l \ + $$

$$\sum_{\substack{c,j,j': \\ Link_l \in P_{j,j'}; N_{j'} \in M_j}} \frac{|\mathcal{T}_c| \times o_{c,j,j'} \times Size_c}{LinkCap_l} \qquad (4)$$

$$\forall l: \ LinkLoad_l \leq \max\{MaxLinkLoad, BG_l\} \qquad (5)$$

$$\forall c,j: \ 0 \leq p_{c,j} \leq 1 \qquad (6)$$

$$\forall c,j,j': \ 0 \leq o_{c,j,j'} \leq 1 \qquad (7)$$

Figure 7: LP formulation for replication

For each NIDS node, N_j, we introduce the notion of a *mirror set* $M_j \subseteq \mathcal{N}$ (M for *Mirror*) that represents a candidate set of nodes to which N_j can offload some processing. This allows us to flexibly capture different replication strategies. In the most general case all nodes are candidates, i.e., $\forall j: M_j = \mathcal{N} \setminus \{N_j\}$. In case of a single datacenter, we set $\forall j: M_j = \{N_{DC}\}$ where N_{DC} is the datacenter. We can also consider local offload policies where M_j is the set of N_j's one- or two-hop neighbors. Let $P_{j,j'}$ denote the routing path between N_j and the mirror node $N_{j'}$.

At a high-level, we need to decide if a given NIDS node is going to *process* a given session or *replicate* that traffic to one of its candidate mirror nodes (or neither). We capture these determinations with two control variables. First, $p_{c,j}$ (p for *process*) specifies the fraction of traffic on the path P_c of class c that the node N_j *processes* itself. To capture offloading via replication, we have an additional control variable: $o_{c,j,j'}$ (o for *offload*) which represents the fraction of traffic on the path P_c that N_j *offloads* to its mirror node $N_{j'}$. Note that there is no need to replicate traffic to elements that are already on-path; if $N_{j'} \in P_c$ then the variables $o_{c,j,j'}$ will not appear in the formulation. The bounds in Eq (6) and (7) ensure that these variables can only take fractional values between zero and one.

Recall that our goal is to assign processing and offloading responsibilities across the network to balance the tradeoff between the *computation load* and the *communication cost*. Here, we focus on the communication cost as a given constraint on the maximum allowed link load *MaxLinkLoad* imposed by the replicated traffic. For example, network administrators typically want to keep links at around 30–50% utilization in order to absorb sudden bursts of traffic [10].

Our main constraint is a *coverage requirement*; we want to ensure that for each class, the traffic is processed by some node either on- or off-path. Eq (2) models this by considering the sum of the locally processed fractions $p_{c,j}$ and the offloaded fractions $o_{c,j,j'}$ and setting it to 1 for full coverage.

Eq (3) captures the stress on each resource for each node. There are two sources of load on each node: the traffic it needs to process locally from on-path responsibilities (as captured by $p_{c,j}$ values) and the total traffic it processes as a consequence of other nodes offloading traffic (as captured by $o_{c,j',j}$ values) to it. The inversion in the indices for the o contribution is because the load on N_j is a function of what other $N_{j'}$'s offload to it.

Then, Eq (4) models the link load on the link l imposed by the traffic between every pair of N_j and its mirror nodes. Because $|\mathcal{T}_c|$ only captures the number of sessions, we introduce an extra multiplicative factor $Size_c$ to capture the average size (in bytes) of each session of class c. We also have an additive term EG_l to capture the current load on the link due to the normal traffic traversing it before replication (BG for *BackGround*). These additive terms can be directly computed given the traffic patterns and routing policy, and as such we treat them as constant inputs in the formulation.

As discussed earlier, we bound the communication cost in terms of the maximum link load in Eq (5). The max is needed because the background load may itself exceed the given constraint $MaxLinkLoad$; in this case, Eq (5) ensures that no new traffic is induced on such overloaded links.

Here, we focus on a specific load balancing objective to minimize the maximum load across all node-resource pairs. Surveys show that overload is a common cause of appliance failure especially for NIDS and is a key cause of concern for network operators [32]. Our min-max objective will improve the robustness of the system, allowing for sudden bursts of traffic to be handled if necessary with little or no penalty. We use standard LP solvers to obtain the optimal $p_{c,j}$ and $o_{c,j,j'}$ settings which we convert into per-node processing configurations (see Section 7).

Extensions: Our framework can accommodate more general policies for capturing the stress on the links and NIDS locations. Instead of an upper bound on each $LinkLoad_l$ as the max of the two terms as shown, we can model the aggregate link utilization cost incurred across all links in terms of a piece-wise linear cost function that penalizes higher values of the incurred link load [10]. This provides a more graceful tradeoff rather than a tight upperbound of $MaxLinkLoad$ on the link load costs. Similarly, instead of capturing $LoadCost$ as the max over all $Load_j^r$, we can model it as a cost function that penalizes higher values of load or as weighted combinations of the $Load_j^r$ values.

5. SPLIT TRAFFIC ANALYSIS

Next, we focus on the scenario from Figure 4 in which we need to replicate traffic because the forward and reverse paths are asymmetric. For simplicity, we focus on the case where there is one datacenter node, rather than generalized mirror sets. Thus, we use $o_{c,j}$ instead of $o_{c,j,j'}$ implicitly fixing a single mirror node N_{DC} for all N_j.

To model this scenario, we modify how the routing paths for each class $\mathcal{T}_c$ are specified. In the previous section, we assumed that the forward and reverse paths are symmetric and thus each $\mathcal{T}_c$ has a unique path P_c. In the case where these paths are asymmetric or non-overlapping, instead of defining a single set of eligible NIDS nodes P_c, we define three types of nodes:

1. P_c^{fwd} that can observe the "forward" direction;[2]
2. P_c^{rev} that can observe the "reverse" direction; and
3. $P_c^{common} = P_c^{fwd} \cap P_c^{rev}$, which may be empty.

We assume here that these types of nodes can be identified from the network's routing policy [31]. Having identified these common, forward, and reverse nodes, we split the coverage constraint in Eq (2) into two separate equations:

$$\forall c : cov_c^{fwd} = \sum_{j:N_j \in P_c^{common}} p_{c,j} + \sum_{j:N_j \in P_c^{fwd}} o_{c,j}^{fwd} \qquad (8)$$

$$\forall c : cov_c^{rev} = \sum_{j:N_j \in P_c^{common}} p_{c,j} + \sum_{j:N_j \in P_c^{rev}} o_{c,j}^{rev} \qquad (9)$$

Now, for stateful analysis, the notion of coverage is meaningful only if both sides of the session have been monitored. Thus, we model the effective coverage as the minimum of the forward and reverse coverage values:

$$\forall c : cov_c = \min\{cov_c^{fwd}, cov_c^{rev}, 1\} \qquad (10)$$

We make three observations here. First, the locally processed fraction $p_{c,j}$ only applies for nodes in P_c^{common}. Second, we separately specify the coverage guarantee for the forward and reverse directions for each $\mathcal{T}_c$ and cap the effective coverage at 1. Third, we also allow the nodes in P_c^{common} to offload processing to the datacenter. (Because the nodes in P_c^{common} also appear on P_c^{fwd} and P_c^{rev}, they have corresponding $o_{c,j}^{fwd}$ and $o_{c,j}^{rev}$ variables.)

Now, it may not always be possible to ensure complete coverage for some deployment scenarios. That is, for a particular combination of forward-reverse paths, and a given constraint on the maximum allowable link load, we may not have a feasible solution to ensure that each $cov_c = 1$.[3] In this case, we want to minimize detection misses and thus, we introduce a new term in the minimization objective to model the fraction of traffic that suffers detection misses because we cannot monitor both sides of the connection. That is,

$$MissRate = \frac{\sum_c (1 - cov_c) \times |\mathcal{T}_c|}{\sum_c |\mathcal{T}_c|} \qquad (11)$$

Given the $MissRate$, we update the objective to be:

$$\text{Minimize: } LoadCost + \gamma MissRate$$

with γ set to a large value to have a very low miss rate.

In summary, the formulation to handle such split traffic is as follows. We retain the same structure for the compute load and link load equations as in Eq (3) and Eq (4) respectively. (There are small changes to incorporate the notion of o_{cj}^{fwd} and $o_{c,j}^{rev}$. We do not show these for brevity.) We replace the single coverage equation in Eq (2) with the new coverage models in Eqs (8), (9), and (10). Rather than force each coverage value to be 1, which could be infeasible to achieve, we focus instead on minimizing the effective miss rate by changing the objective function.

One subtle issue here is that we need to ensure that the nodes on the forward and reverse path act in a consistent manner. For example, we cannot have the forward direction of a session being processed locally at N_j and the reverse direction offloaded. We achieve this consistency by using bidirectional semantics when mapping the decision variables into actual per-flow actions executed by each node as described in Section 7.

Extensions: We can extend the model to quantify $MissRate$ in terms of the class c with the largest fraction of detection misses (i.e., $MissRate = \max_c\{1 - cov_c\}$), or consider a general weighted combination of these coverage values to indicate higher priority for some traffic.

---

[2]We assume a well-defined notion of forward and reverse directions, say based on the values of the IP addresses.

[3]Note that this is in contrast to the formulation from Section 4, where there is always a feasible solution to get full coverage by simply running the analyses locally, but potentially incurring a higher $LoadCost$.

6. NIDS WITH AGGREGATION

Next, we discuss scaling via aggregation. The high-level idea is to split a NIDS task into multiple sub-tasks that can be distributed across different locations. Each NIDS node generates *intermediate reports* that are sent to an aggregation point to generate the final analysis result. As a concrete example, we focus on the `Scan` detection module that counts the number of distinct destination IP addresses to which a given source has initiated a connection in the previous measurement epoch. The high-level approach described here can also be extended to other types of analysis amenable to such aggregation (e.g., DoS or flood detection).

For clarity, we focus on using aggregation without replication and assume a single symmetric path for each class. This means that we just need to assign the local processing responsibilities captured by the $p_{c,j}$ variables.[4]

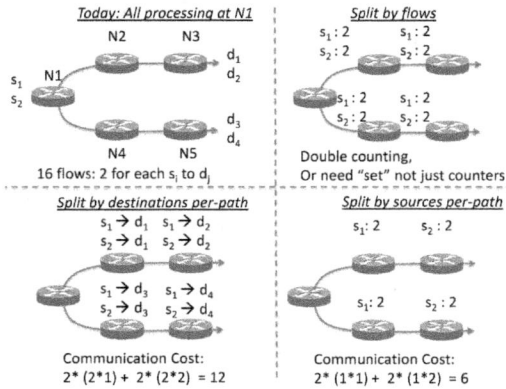

Figure 8: Different options for splitting the `Scan` detection responsibilities

Because the choice of intermediate reports and aggregation points may vary across different detection tasks, we use a general notion of *network distance* between node N_j and the location to which these reports are sent. This is captured by $D_{c,j}$ (D for *Distance*); the indices indicate that the location may depend on the specific class c. For example, in `Scan` detection, we may choose to send the reports back to the ingress for the host because it is in the best position to decide if an alert should be raised, e.g., based on past behavior observed for the hosts.

We do, however, need to be careful in choosing the granularity at which we distribute the work across nodes. Consider the example in Figure 8 where our goal is to count the number of destinations that each source contacts. Suppose there are two sources s_1, s_2 contacting four destinations d_{1-4} as shown and there are two flows for every src-dst pair. Here, each NIDS runs a per-src `Scan` counting module on its assigned subset of the traffic. Then, each node sends these local per-src counters to the aggregation point, which outputs the final result of suspicious sources. Now, we could choose three different strategies to split the monitoring responsibilities:

1. *Flow-level:* The nodes on a path split the traffic traversing that path on a per-flow basis, run a local `Scan` detection module on the set of observed flows and send intermediate reports back to the ingress.

---

[4]We retain the c subscript for notational consistency; for `Scan` detection the classes simply correspond to end-to-end paths rather than application-level classes.

$$\text{Minimize } LoadCost + \beta \times CommCost \text{ subject to}$$

$$LoadCost = \max_{r,j}\{Load_j^r\} \tag{12}$$

$$CommCost = \sum_{c,j}(|\mathcal{T}_c| \times p_{c,j}) \times Rec_c \times D_{c,j} \tag{13}$$

$$\forall c : \sum_{j:N_j \in P_c} p_{c,j} = 1 \tag{14}$$

$$\forall r,j : Load_j^r = \sum_{\substack{c: \\ N_j \in P_c}} \frac{F_c^r \times |\mathcal{T}_c| \times p_{c,j}}{Cap_j^r} \tag{15}$$

$$\forall c,j : 0 \leq p_{c,j} \leq 1 \tag{16}$$

Figure 9: LP formulation for aggregation

2. *Destination-level:* We do a split based on destinations for each path. In the example, node N2 checks if each source contacted d_1, node N3 for d_2, and so on.

3. *Source-level:* Each node focuses on a subset of the sources on each path; e.g., N2 and N3 monitor s_1 and s_2, respectively.

Notice that with a flow-based split, if we only report per-src counters, then we could end up overestimating the number of destinations if a particular source-destination pair has multiple flows. In this case, each node must report the full set of $\langle src, dst \rangle$ tuples, thus incurring a larger communication cost. The aggregator then has to compute the logical union of the sets of destinations reported for each source. With a destination-based split, we do not have this double counting problem. The aggregator simply adds up the number of destinations reported from each node on each path. In the worst case, however, the number of entries each node reports will be equal to the number of sources. Thus, the total communication cost could be 12 units, assuming aggregation is done at N1: each node sends a 2-row report (one row per src), the report from N2, N4 traverses one hop and those from N3, N5 take two hops. The third option of splitting based on the sources provides both a correct result without over-counting and also a lower communication cost of 6 units. Each node sends a report consisting of the number of destinations each source contacts and the aggregator can simply add up the number of destinations reported across the different paths for each source.[5] Thus, we choose the source-level split strategy since it offers both correct and communication-minimal operation in the common case. In general, we envision our NIDS controller specifying this reporting schema to a shim layer running on each node as we discuss in the next section.

In practice, there are a few natural cases that cover most common NIDS modules that can benefit from such aggregation (e.g., per-src, per-destination). Having chosen a suitable granularity of intermediate reports, we need as input the *per-report size Rec_c* (in bytes) for class c.[6]

As in the previous section, we want to balance the tradeoff between the computation cost and the communication cost. Because the size of the reports (at most a few MB) is unlikely to impact the link load adversely, we drop the *MaxLinkLoad* constraints in Eqs (4), (5). Instead, we introduce a new *communication cost* term *CommCost* in the objective, with a weight factor β, which is scaled appropriately to ensure that the load and communication cost terms are comparable. We have the familiar coverage constraint in

---

[5]Assuming that there is a unique and fixed path for a specific source-destination during this measurement epoch.

[6]This also depends on how these reports are encoded, e.g., key-value pairs for a source-split.

Eq (14), and the resource load model in Eq (15). (Because there is no traffic replication, the "offload" o variables do not appear in this formulation.) The additional equation required here is to model the total communication cost $CommCost$ in Eq (13). For each entry, this is simply the product of the volume of traffic, the per-unit record size, and the network distance as shown.

7. IMPLEMENTATION

We start by describing how the management engine translates the output of the LP optimizations into device configurations. Then, we describe how we implement these management decisions using a *shim* layer that allows us to run off-the-shelf NIDS software.

7.1 Optimization and configurations

We solve the LP formulations described in the previous sections using off-the-shelf LP solvers such as CPLEX. Given the solution to the optimization, we run a simple procedure to convert the solution into a configuration for each shim instance. The main idea is to map the decision variables—$p_{c,j}$ and $o_{c,j,j'}$ values—into non-overlapping *hash ranges*. For each c, we first run a loop over the $p_{c,j}$ values, mapping each to a hash-range, and extending the range as we move to the next j. We then run a similar loop for the $o_{c,j,j'}$. (The specific order of the NIDS indices does not matter; we only require some order to ensure the ranges are non-overlapping.) Because the optimization frameworks ensure that these $p_{c,j}$ and $o_{c,j,j'}$ add up to 1 for each c, we are guaranteed that the union of these hash ranges covers the entire range.

7.2 Shim layer

To allow network operators to run their existing NIDS software without needing significant changes, we interpose a lightweight *shim* between the network and the NIDS. We implement this using the Click modular software router [15] with a combination of default modules and a custom module (255 lines of C++ code). The shim maintains persistent tunnels with its mirror node(s) to replicate the traffic and uses a virtual TUN/TAP interface to the local NIDS process. This requires a minor change to the way the NIDS process is launched so that it reads from the virtual interface rather than a physical interface. We tested two popular NIDS: Bro [24] and Snort [34]; both had no difficulties running unmodified on top of the shim layer.

As a packet arrives, the shim computes a lightweight hash [5] of the IP 5-tuple (protocol, src/dst IPs and ports). It looks up the corresponding class (e.g., based on the port numbers and src/dst IPs) to infer the assigned hash range (from the above configuration) and decides whether to send this packet to the local NIDS process, replicate it to a mirror node, or neither. One subtle issue here is that we need to ensure that this hash is bidirectional to ensure that both directions are consistently "pinned" or offloaded to the same node. For example, we can achieve this by converting the IP 5-tuple into a canonical form such that the source IP is always less than the destination IP before computing the hash [37]. For aggregation, the hash is over the appropriate field used for splitting the task. i.e., per-source or per-destination depending on the analysis.

7.3 Aggregation

Aggregation requires two components: (1) a new shim module at each NIDS node that periodically sends reports; and (2) an aggregator to post-process these reports. As discussed earlier, the choice of reporting schema and where the aggregation runs may vary across different NIDS tasks. In the specific case of Scan detection, we want to report sources that contact $> k$ destinations and send these reports to the gateway nodes for each host. Now, the measured

value at an individual NIDS may not exceed k, but the aggregate might. Thus, we apply the threshold k only at the aggregator and configure each individual NIDS to have a reporting threshold of $k = 0$, to retain the same detection semantics as running the scan detector at the gateway node for each host.

8. EVALUATION

We use real network topologies from educational backbones (Internet2, Geant), inferred PoP-level topologies from Rocketfuel [35], and a multi-site Enterprise topology [30]. For each topology, we construct a traffic matrix for every pair of ingress-egress PoPs using a gravity model based on city populations [27], with shortest-path routing based on hop counts. For brevity, we consider a single aggregate traffic class and do not partition traffic based on application port numbers.

8.1 System evaluation

Computation time: Table 1 shows the time to compute the optimal solution for different PoP-level topologies using an off-the-shelf LP solver (CPLEX). This result shows that the time to recompute optimal solutions is well within the timescales of network reconfigurations (typically on the order of few minutes).

Topology	# PoPs	Time (s)	
		Replication	Aggregation
Internet2	11	0.05	0.02
Geant	22	0.10	0.02
Enterprise	23	0.10	0.01
TiNet (AS3257)	41	0.29	0.02
Telstra (AS1221)	44	0.40	0.03
Sprint (AS1239)	52	1.30	0.05
Level3 (AS3356)	63	1.19	0.04
NTT (AS2914)	70	1.59	0.11

Table 1: Time to compute the optimal solution for the replication and aggregation formulations.

Shim overhead: The hash computations and lookups impose little overhead over the processing and packet capture that a NIDS has to run natively. In our microbenchmarks, the shim implementation does not introduce any (additional) packet drops up to an offered load of 1 Gbps for a single-threaded Bro or Snort process running on a Intel Core i5 2.5GHz machine.

Live emulation in Emulab: To investigate the benefits of off-path replication, we evaluate our system with an emulated Internet2 topology with 11 nodes using Emulab [40]. We implemented an offline traffic generator using Scapy [28] that takes as input the topology, traffic matrix, and template traces, and that generates a traffic trace according to these. We used real full-payload packet traces as the "seed" templates [18]. To faithfully emulate the ordering of packets within a logical session, we introduced a stateful "supernode" that is logically connected to every network ingress. This supernode injects packets within each session in order and at the appropriate ingress using the BitTwist tool [4]. Each NIDS node runs on a Pentium III 850 Mhz node with 512 MB of RAM[7] running Snort (version 2.9.1) using the default configuration of rules and signatures.

Figure 10 shows the total number of CPU instructions used by the Snort process, measured using the PAPI performance instru-

---

[7]The choice of low-end nodes was to ensure repeatability as it is hard to obtain a large number of high-end nodes for extended periods of time on Emulab.

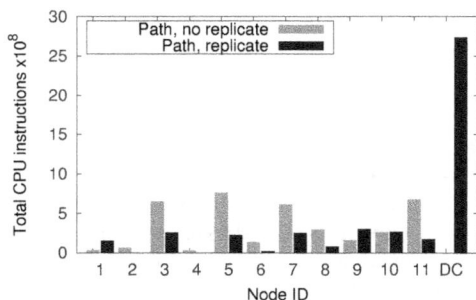

Figure 10: Maximum absolute CPU usage of each NIDS node in our Emulab experiment

mentation library [23]), on each NIDS node for the emulated Internet2 topology with 11 nodes. The result shows the configurations for two NIDS architectures: *Path, No replicate* [29] and *Path, Replicate* which represents our framework from Section 4. For our setup, we ran the formulation with a single data center (DC) with 8× the capacity of the other NIDS nodes and assuming $MaxLinkLoad = 0.4$. (We did not explicitly instantiate a 8× capacity.) Figure 10 confirms that replication provides 2× reduction in resource usage on the maximally loaded node (excepting the DC). This result is identical to that obtained using trace-driven simulations, as will be shown in Figure 13, allowing us to conclude that sensitivity analysis performed in Section 8.2 is representative of live performance.

8.2 Replication: Sensitivity analysis

Due to the difficulty of scaling our Emulab setup for larger topologies and further sensitivity analysis, we use trace-driven analysis for these evaluations.

Setup: To model the total traffic volume, we start with a baseline of 8 million sessions for the Internet2 network with 11 PoPs, and then scale the total volume for other topologies linearly proportional to the number of PoPs. We model the link capacities $LinkCap_l$ as follows. We compute the traffic volume traversing the maximum congested link (assuming the above shortest path routes). Then, we set the link capacity of each to be 3× this traffic load on the most congested link. As such, $\max_l\{BG_l\} = 0.3$; this reflects typical link utilization levels in networks today [10]. To model the node capacities Cap_j^r, we simulate the Ingress-only deployment and find the maximum resource requirement across the network, and provision each node with this inferred capacity. Thus, by construction the Ingress deployment has a maximum compute load of one. We model a single data center with $\alpha\times$ the capacity of the other NIDS nodes.

In this discussion, we examine the effects of varying the location and capacity of the data center node (Cap_{DC}^r), the maximum allowed link load with replication ($MaxLinkLoad$), alternative local replication architectures, and the impact of traffic variability.

Choice of datacenter location: The first parameter of interest is the placement of the datacenter. Here, we fix the datacenter capacity to be 10× the single NIDS capacity, but choose different locations based on four natural strategies: (1) the PoP from which most traffic originates, (2) the PoP that observes the most traffic, including traffic for which this is a transit PoP, (3) the PoP which lies on the most end-to-end shortest paths, and (4) the PoP which has the smallest average distance to every other PoP (the medoid).

We find that for most topologies the gap between the different placement strategies is very small and that placing the datacenter at the PoP that observes the most traffic works best across all topologies. (Not shown; please see our extended report [13].) Thus for the rest of the evaluation, we choose this placement strategy.

Effect of increasing allowed link load: Next, we fix the placement of the datacenter as described above and its capacity to 10×, and study the impact of increasing $MaxLinkLoad$ in Figure 11. For most topologies, we see diminishing returns beyond $MaxLinkLoad = 0.4$, since at that value, the compute load on the datacenter is close to the load on the maximum NIDS node as well. This result suggests that network administrators need not be concerned about the additional load induced by the replication traffic since we can achieve near-optimal benefits at 40% link utilization.

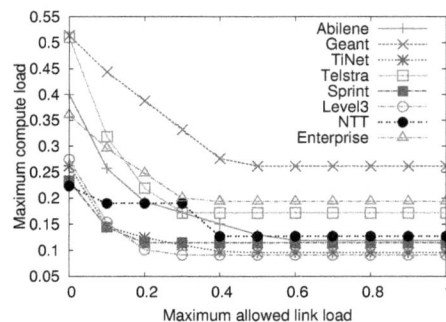

Figure 11: Varying $MaxLinkLoad$ with datacenter capacity = 10×.

Increasing the data center capacity: A natural question then is how much to provision the datacenter. To address this, we studied the impact of varying the datacenter capacity. Most topologies show a natural diminishing property as we increase the capacity, with the "knee" of the curve occurring earlier with lower link load. This is expected; with lower $MaxLinkLoad$, there are fewer opportunities for replicating traffic to the datacenter and thus increasing the datacenter capacity beyond 8–10× does not really help (not shown).

Visualizing maximum loads: To better understand the previous effects, we visualize a high-level summary of how the optimization allocates the compute and offload responsibilities throughout the network. We consider four configurations here: $MaxLinkLoad \in \{0.1, 0.4\}$ and a datacenter capacity Cap_{DC}^r of 2× and 10×. Figure 12 shows the difference between the compute load on the datacenter node (*DCLoad*) and the maximum compute load on non-datacenter NIDS nodes (*MaxNIDSLoad*) for the different topologies. We see that at low link load and high data center capacity ($MaxLinkLoad = 0.1$ and Cap_{DC}^r of 10×), the datacenter is underutilized. With larger link loads or lower link capacity, we find that the load stress on the datacenter is the same as the maximum load across the network (i.e., the gap is zero).

Comparison to alternatives: Using the previous results as guidelines, we pick a configuration with the datacenter capacity fixed at 10× the single NIDS capacity and with $MaxLinkLoad = 0.4$. Figure 13 compares this configuration (labeled *Path, Replicate*) against two alternatives: (1) today's *Ingress*-only deployment where NIDS functions run at the ingress of a path; and (2) *Path, No Replicate*, strict on-path NIDS distribution [29]. One concern is that our datacenter setup has more aggregate capacity. Thus, we also consider a *Path, Augmented* approach where each of the $|\mathcal{N}|$ NIDS

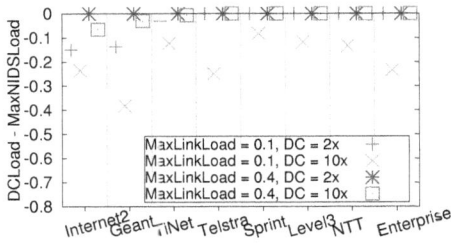

Figure 12: Comparing the compute load on the datacenter vs. maximum load on interior NIDS nodes.

nodes gets a $\frac{1}{|\mathcal{N}|}$ share of the $10\times$ additional resources. The fact that we can consider these alternative designs within our framework further confirms the *generality* of our approach.

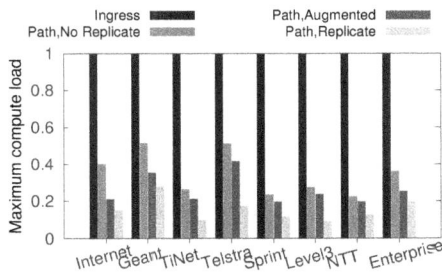

Figure 13: Maximum compute load across topologies with different NIDS architectures.

Recall that the current deployments of *Ingress*-only have a maximum compute load of one by construction. The result shows that *Path, Replicate* has the best overall performance; it can reduce the maximum compute load by $10\times$ compared to today's deployments and up to $3\times$ compared to the proposed on-path distribution schemes.

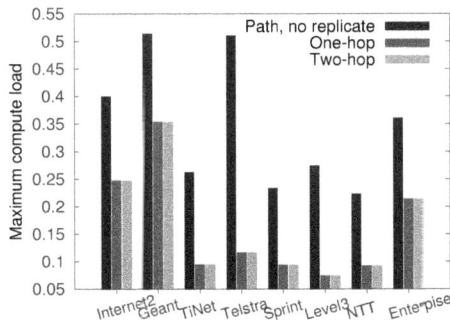

Figure 14: Local one- and two-hop replication.

Local offload: The above results consider a setup where the network administrator has added a new datacenter. Alternatively, they can use the existing NIDS infrastructure with *local* replication strategies. Specifically, we consider the mirror sets (M_js) consisting of 1-hop or 2-hop neighbors in addition to the existing on-path distribution. Figure 14 compares the maximum compute load vs. a pure on-path distribution again setting $MaxLinkLoad = 0.4$. Across all

topologies, allowing replication within a one-hop radius provides up to $5\times$ reduction in the maximum load. We also see that going to two hops does not add significant value beyond one-hop offload. This suggests a replication-enhanced NIDS architecture can offer significant benefits even without needing to augment the network with additional compute resources.

Performance under traffic variability: The results so far consider a static traffic matrix. Next, we evaluate the effect of traffic variability. To obtain realistic temporal variability patterns, we use traffic matrices for Internet2 [14]. From this, we compute empirical CDFs of how each element in a traffic matrix varies (e.g., probability that the volume is between $0.6\times$ and $0.8\times$ the mean). Then, using these empirical distributions we generate 100 time-varying traffic matrices using the gravity model for the mean volume.

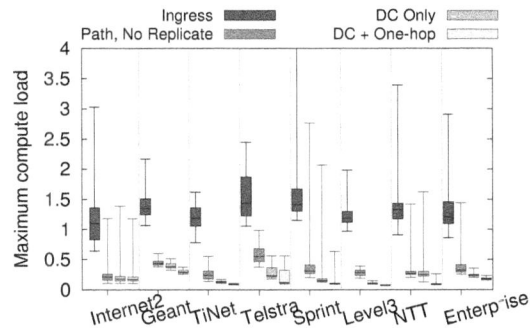

Figure 15: Comparison between NIDS architectures in the presence of traffic variability.

Figure 15 summarizes the distribution of the peak load across these 100 runs using a box-and-whiskers plot showing the minimum, 25th %ile, median, 75th %ile, and the maximum observed load. We consider four NIDS architectures: *Ingress*; *Path, No replicate*; *Path, replicate* with a datacenter node $10\times$ capacity (labeled DC Only); and *Path, replicate* with the flexibility to offload responsibilities to either a datacenter and within a 1-hop radius (labeled DC + One-hop). We find that the replication-enabled NIDS architectures outperform the non-replication strategies significantly, with the median values roughly mirroring our earlier results. The worst-case performance of the no-replication architectures can be quite poor, e.g., much larger than 1. (Ideally, we want the maximum compute load to be less than 1.) We also analyzed how the augmentation strategy from Figure 13 performs; the worst-case load with the *Path, Augmented* case is $4\times$ more than the replication enabled architecture (not shown).

8.3 Replication with routing asymmetry

In this section, we evaluate how replication is effective for scenarios where the forward and reverse flows may not traverse the same route as we saw in Section 2.

We emulate routing asymmetry as follows. For each ingress-egress pair, we assume the forward traffic traverses the expected shortest path from the ingress to the egress; i.e., F_c^{fwd} is the shortest-path route. However, we set the reverse path P_c^{rev} such that the expected *overlap* (over all ingress-egress pairs) between the forward and reverse paths reaches a target overlap ratio θ. Here, we measure the overlap between two paths P_1 and P_2 in terms of the Jaccard similarity index: $\frac{P_1 \cap P_2}{P_1 \cup P_2}$, which is maximum ($= 1$) when they are identical and lowest (= 0) if there is no overlap. For each end-to-end path, we precompute its overlap metric with every other path. Then, given a value of θ' (drawn from a Gaussian distribution with mean = θ and standard deviation = $\frac{\theta}{5}$), we find a path from this precomputed set that is *closest* to this target value.[8] For each target θ, we generate 50 random configurations. For each configuration, we run the extended formulation from Section 5 for the *Ingress*-only architecture, the *Path, no replicate* architecture, and our proposed framework with a datacenter. We report the *median* across the 50 runs for two metrics: the detection *miss rate* — the total fraction of traffic that could not be analyzed effectively by any NIDS node — and the compute load as in the previous evaluations.

Figure 16 shows the median miss rate as a function of the overlap factor for the different configurations. We see that the miss rate with an *Ingress*-only setup is greater than 85% even for high values of the overlap metric. The *MaxLoad* curve in Figure 17 is interesting because *Ingress* is lower than the other configurations. The reason is that there is little useful work being done here — It ignores more than 90% of the traffic! Another curious feature is that *MaxLoad* for the replication architecture first increases and then decreases. In this setup with low overlap, the datacenter is the most loaded node. At low θ, however, the *MaxLinkLoad* constraint limits the amount of traffic that can be offloaded and thus the datacenter load is low.

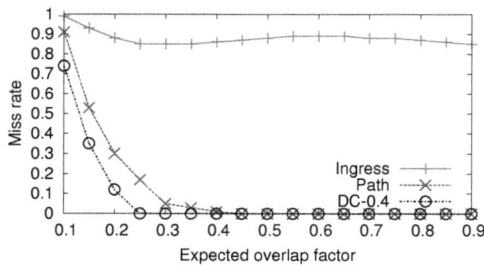

Figure 16: Detection miss rate vs. degree of overlap

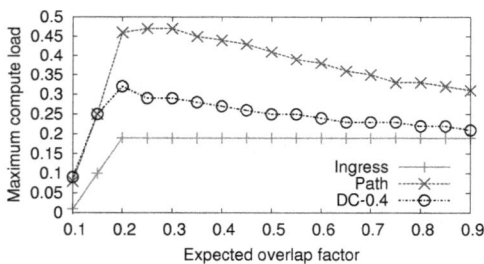

Figure 17: Maximum load vs. degree of overlap

8.4 NIDS with aggregation

In this section, we highlight the benefits of aggregation using the framework from Section 6. As discussed earlier, we focus on `Scan` detection.

[8] The exact details of how these paths are chosen or the distribution of the θ values are not the key focus of this evaluation. We just need some mechanism to generate paths with a target overlap ratio.

Figure 18 shows how varying β trades off the communication cost (*CommCost*) and compute cost (*LoadCost*) in the resulting solution, for the different topologies. Because different topologies differ in size and structure, we normalize the x- and y-axes using the maximum observed *LoadCost* and *CommCost* respectively over the range of β for each topology. As such, the point closest to the origin can be viewed as the best choice of β for the corresponding topology. This figure shows that for many topologies, there are choices of β that yield relatively low *CommCost* and *LoadCost* simultaneously, e.g., both being less than 40% of their maximums.

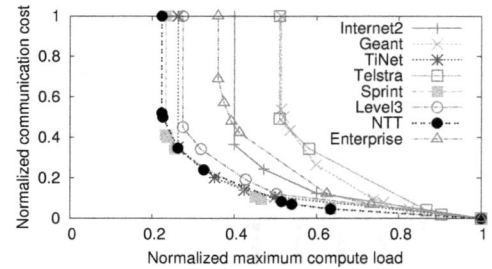

Figure 18: Tradeoff between the compute load and communication cost with aggregation as we vary β

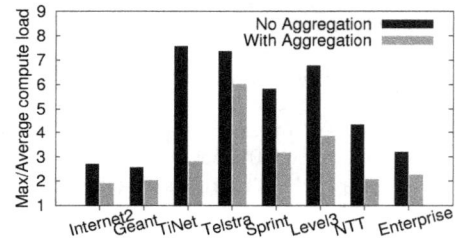

Figure 19: Ratio between maximum and average compute load with and without aggregation.

To illustrate the load balancing benefits of aggregation, Figure 19 shows the ratio of the compute load of the most loaded node to the average compute load. Here, for each topology, we pick the value of β that yields the point closest to the origin in Figure 18. A higher number represents a larger variance or imbalance in the load. Figure 19 compares this ratio to the same ratio when no aggregation is used. As we can see, aggregation reduces the load imbalance substantially (up to $2.7\times$) for many topologies.

8.5 Summary of key results

Our main results are:

- The optimization step and shim impose low overhead.
- Administrators need not worry about optimal choice of data center location, capacity, or the maximum link load. Our approach provides benefits over a range of practical and intuitive choices.
- Replication reduced the maximum compute load by up to $10\times$ when we add a NIDS cluster or up to $5\times$ with one-hop offload.

- In the presence of traffic dynamics, replication provided up to an order of magnitude reduction in maximum load.
- Replication reduced the detection miss rate from 90% to zero in the presence of partially overlapping routes.
- Aggregation reduced the load imbalance by up to $2.7\times$.

9. DISCUSSION

Consistent configurations: One concern with distribution is ensuring consistency when configurations are recomputed. We could use standard techniques from the distributed systems literature (e.g., two-phase commit [21]). We can also use simpler domain-specific solutions; e.g., whenever new configurations are pushed out, the NIDS nodes continue to honor both the previous and new configurations during the transient period. This may potentially duplicate some work, but ensures correctness of operation.

Shim for higher line-rates: Our current shim implementation imposes close to zero overhead for a single-threaded NIDS running on a single core machine for traffic up to 1 Gbps. We plan to extend our implementation using recent advances in packet capture [25, 26]

Robustness to dynamics: A sudden, significant shift in traffic patterns (adversarial or otherwise) could render the current distribution strategies ineffective. One approach to counter this is to allow for some "slack" (e.g., using the 80-th percentile values instead of the mean) in the input traffic matrices to tolerate such sudden bursts.

Extending to NIPS and active monitoring: Our approach can be generally applied to any *passive* traffic monitoring system without affecting the forwarding paths or latency of traffic. Our framework can also be extended to the case of intrusion prevention systems (NIPS), though unlike NIDS, NIPS are on the critical forwarding path which raises two additional issues that we need to handle. These arise from the fact that we are not actually replicating traffic in this case; rather, we are *rerouting* it. First, we can no longer treat the BG_l as a constant in the formulation. Second, we need to ensure that the latency penalty for legitimate traffic due to rerouting is low.

Combining aggregation and replication: As future work we plan to explore if a unified formulation that combines both opportunities offers further improvements. For example, we might be able to use replication to reduce the communication cost of aggregation. One challenge is that the analyses benefiting from aggregation may need to split the traffic at a different granularity (e.g., per source) vs. those exploiting replication (e.g., stateful signature matching on a per-session basis). Thus, we need a more careful shim design to avoid duplicating the effort in packet capture across different nodes in order to combine these ideas.

10. RELATED WORK

Scaling NIDS hardware: NIDS involve computationally intensive tasks (e.g., string and regular-expression matching). There are many proposals for better algorithms for such tasks (e.g., [33]), using specialized hardware such as TCAMs (e.g., [20, 42]) FPGAs (e.g., [17]), or GPUs (e.g., [38]). The dependence on specialized hardware increases deployment costs. To address this cost challenge, there are ongoing efforts to build scalable NIDS on commodity hardware to exploit data-level parallelism in NIDS workloads (e.g., [37,39]). These efforts focus on scaling *single-vantage-point* implementations and are thus complementary to our work. Our framework allows administrators to optimally use their existing hardware or selectively add NIDS clusters.

NIDS management: Our use of centralized optimization to assign NIDS responsibilities follows in the spirit of our prior work [29]. The approach we propose here extends our prior work in three key ways. First, we generalize on-path distribution to include replication and aggregation. Second, this previous framework cannot handle the types of split-traffic analysis with asymmetric routes as we showed in Figure 16. Third, on a practical note, this past approach requires source-level changes to the NIDS software. In contrast, our implementation allows administrators to run off-the-shelf NIDS software.

Offloading NIDS: A recent proposal makes a case for outsourcing all network processing functionality including NIDS to cloud providers [32]. While this may work for small businesses and enterprises, larger enterprises and ISPs would likely retain in-house infrastructure due to security and policy considerations. Furthermore, this proposal does not focus on computation-communication tradeoffs. Our approach can also incorporate a cloud datacenter and can offer ways to augment existing infrastructure instead of getting rid of it altogether.

Distributed NIDS: Prior work makes the case for network-wide visibility and distributed views in detecting anomalous behaviors (e.g., [16]). These focus primarily on algorithms for combining observations from multiple vantage points. Furthermore, specific attacks (e.g., DDoS attacks, stepping stones) and network scenarios (e.g., asymmetric routing as in Section 2) inherently require an aggregate view. Our focus is not on the algorithms for combining observations; rather, we build a framework for enabling such aggregated analysis.

11. CONCLUSIONS

While there are many advances in building better NIDS hardware, there is a substantial window before networks can benefit from these in practice. Our work complements existing research in scaling NIDS hardware with techniques to better utilize and augment existing NIDS deployments. To this end, we proposed a general NIDS architecture to leverage three opportunities: offloading processing to other nodes on a packet's routing path, traffic replication to off-path nodes (e.g., to NIDS clusters), and aggregation to split expensive NIDS tasks. We implemented a lightweight shim that allows networks to realize these benefits with little to no modification to existing NIDS software. Our results on many real-world topologies show that this architecture reduces the maximum compute load significantly, provides better resilience under traffic variability, and offers improved detection coverage for scenarios needing network-wide views.

Acknowledgements

We are grateful to Geoff Voelker for commenting on drafts of this paper and to Chad Spensky for initial discussions on this research. This work was supported in part by NSF grants 0831245 and 1040626, and by grant number N00014-10-1-0155 from the Office of Naval Research.

12. REFERENCES

[1] Powering virtual network services. http://embrane.com.
[2] ZScaler Cloud Security. http://www.zscaler.com.
[3] Allman, M., Kreibich, C., Paxson, V., Sommer, R., and Weaver, N. Principles for developing comprehensive network visibility. *In Proc. HOTSEC'08*, 2008.
[4] Bittwist. http://bittwist.sourceforge.net.
[5] Bob hash. http://burtleburtle.net/bob/hash/doobs.html.

[6] Cantieni, G. R., Iannaccone, G., Barakat, C., Diot, C., and Thiran, P. Reformulating the monitor placement problem: optimal network-wide sampling. *In Proc. CoNEXT '06*, 2006.

[7] Cisco blade servers. http://www.cisco.com/en/US/products/ps10280/index.html.

[8] Dreger, H., Feldmann, A., Paxson, V., and Sommer, R. Predicting the resource consumption of network intrusion detection systems. *In Proc. SIGMETRICS '08*, 2008.

[9] Feldmann, A., Greenberg, A., Lund, C., Reingold, N., Rexford, J., and True, F. Deriving traffic demands for operational IP networks: methodology and experience. *IEEE/ACM Trans. Netw.*, 9(3):265–280, June 2001.

[10] Fortz, B., Rexford, J., and Thorup, M. Traffic engineering with traditional IP routing protocols. *Communications Magazine, IEEE*, 40(10):118 – 124, Oct 2002.

[11] Gibb, G., Zeng, H., and McKeown, N. Outsourcing network functionality. In *Proc. HotSDN*, 2012.

[12] Greenberg, A., Hjalmtysson, G., Maltz, D. A., Myers, A., Rexford, J., Xie, G., Yan, H., Zhan, J., and Zhang, H. A clean slate 4D approach to network control and management. *SIGCOMM Comput. Commun. Rev.*, 35(5):41–54, Oct. 2005.

[13] Heorhiadi, V., Reiter, M. K., and Sekar, V. Balancing computation-communication tradeoffs in scaling network-wide intrusion detection systems. Technical Report TR12-001, UNC Chapel Hill, 2012.

[14] Internet2 trafficx matrices. http://www.cs.utexas.edu/~yzhang/research/AbileneTM.

[15] Kohler, E., Morris, R., Chen, B., Jannotti, J., and Kaashoek, M. F. The click modular router. *ACM Trans. Comput. Syst.*, 18(3):263–297, Aug. 2000.

[16] Lakhina, A., Crovella, M., and Diot, C. Diagnosing network-wide traffic anomalies. *In Proc. SIGCOMM '04*, 2004.

[17] Lee, J., Hwang, S. H., Park, N., Lee, S.-W., Jun, S., and Kim, Y. S. A high performance NIDS using FPGA-based regular expression matching. *In Proc. SAC '07*, 2007.

[18] M57 packet traces. https://domex.nps.edu/corp/scenarios/2009-m57/net/.

[19] McKeown, N., Anderson, T., Balakrishnan, H., Parulkar, G., Peterson, L., Rexford, J., Shenker, S., and Turner, J. OpenFlow: enabling innovation in campus networks. *SIGCOMM Comput. Commun. Rev.*, 38(2):69–74, Mar. 2008.

[20] Meiners, C. R., Patel, J., Norige, E., Torng, E., and Liu, A. X. Fast regular expression matching using small TCAMs for network intrusion detection and prevention systems. *In Proc. USENIX Security'10*, 2010.

[21] Mohan, C. and Lindsay, B. Efficient commit protocols for the tree of processes model of distributed transactions. *SIGOPS Oper. Syst. Rev.*, 19(2):40–52, Apr. 1985.

[22] Network security spending to soar in the next 5 year. http://www.v3.co.uk/v3-uk/news/1998293/network-security-spending-soar.

[23] PAPI: Performance application programming interface. http://icl.cs.utk.edu/papi/.

[24] Paxson, V. Bro: a system for detecting network intruders in real-time. *In Proc. Usenix Security'98*, 1998.

[25] Pfq homepage. http://netserv.iet.unipi.it/software/pfq/.

[26] Pf_ring. http://www.ntop.org/products/pf_ring/.

[27] Roughan, M. Simplifying the synthesis of internet traffic matrices. *SIGCOMM Comput. Commun. Rev.*, 35(5):93–96, Oct. 2005.

[28] Scapy packet manipulation toolkit. http://www.secdev.org/projects/scapy/.

[29] Sekar, V., Krishnaswamy, R., Gupta, A., and Reiter, M. K. Network-wide deployment of intrusion detection and prevention systems. *In Proc. CoNEXT '10*, 2010.

[30] Sekar, V., Ratnasamy, S., Reiter, M. K., Egi, N., and Shi, G. The middlebox manifesto: enabling innovation in middlebox deployment. *In Proc. HotNets '11*, 2011.

[31] Shaikh, A. and Greenberg, A. Ospf monitoring: architecture, design and deployment experience. *In Proc. NSDI'04*, 2004.

[32] Sherry, J., Hasan, S., Scott, C., Krishnamurthy, A., Ratnasamy, S., and Sekar, V. Making middleboxes someone else's problem: Network processing as a cloud service. *In Proc. SIGCOMM*, 2012.

[33] Smith, R., Estan, C., and Jha, S. XFA: Faster signature matching with extended automata. *In Proc. IEEE S&P'08*, 2008.

[34] Snort. http://www.snort.org.

[35] Spring, N., Mahajan, R., Wetherall, D., and Anderson, T. Measuring isp topologies with rocketfuel. *IEEE/ACM Trans. Netw.*, 12(1):2–16, Feb. 2004.

[36] Teixeira, R., Shaikh, A., Griffin, T., and Rexford, J. Dynamics of hot-potato routing in IP networks. *In Proc. SIGMETRICS '04/Performance '04*, 2004.

[37] Vallentin, M., Sommer, R., Lee, J., Leres, C., Paxson, V., and Tierney, B. The NIDS cluster: scalable, stateful network intrusion detection on commodity hardware. *In Proc. RAID'07*, 2007.

[38] Vasiliadis, G., Polychronakis, M., Antonatos, S., Markatos, E. P., and Ioannidis, S. Regular expression matching on graphics hardware for intrusion detection. *In Proc. RAID '09*, 2009.

[39] Vasiliadis, G., Polychronakis, M., and Ioannidis, S. MIDeA: a multi-parallel intrusion detection architecture. *In Proc. CCS '11*, 2011.

[40] White, B., Lepreau, J., Stoller, L., Ricci, R., Guruprasad, S., Newbold, M., Hibler, M., Barb, C., and Joglekar, A. An integrated experimental environment for distributed systems and networks. *SIGOPS Oper. Syst. Rev.*, 36(SI):255–270, Dec. 2002.

[41] World intrusion detection and prevention markets. http://www-935.ibm.com/services/us/iss/pdf/esr_intrusion-detection-and-prevention-systems-markets.pdf.

[42] Yu, F., Lakshman, T. V., Motoyama, M. A., and Katz, R. H. SSA: a power and memory efficient scheme to multi-match packet classification. *In Proc. ANCS '05*, 2005.

[43] Zhang, Y. and Paxson, V. Detecting stepping stones. *In Proc. Usenix Security'00*, 2000.

Author Index

www.ingramcontent.com/pod-product-compliance
Lightning Source LLC
Chambersburg PA
CBHW080710220326
41598CB00033B/5371